Conflict of Laws

ASPEN CASEBOOK SERIES

Conflict of Laws
Cases and Materials

Eighth Edition

Lea Brilmayer

**Howard M. Holtzmann Professor
of International Law
Yale University**

Jack Goldsmith

**Henry L. Shattuck Professor of Law
Harvard University**

Erin O'Hara O'Connor

**Dean and McKenzie Professor
Florida State University
College of Law**

Carlos M. Vázquez

**Scott K. Ginsburg Professor of Law
Georgetown University Law Center**

Wolters Kluwer

Published by Wolters Kluwer in New York.

Wolters Kluwer Legal & Regulatory U.S. serves customers worldwide with CCH, Aspen Publishers, and Kluwer Law International products. (www.WKLegaledu.com)

To contact Customer Service, e-mail customer.service@wolterskluwer.com, call 1-800-234-1660, fax 1-800-901-9075, or mail correspondence to:

Wolters Kluwer
Attn: Order Department
PO Box 990
Frederick, MD 21705

Printed in the United States of America.

1 2 3 4 5 6 7 8 9 0

ISBN 978-1-4548-9956-3

Library of Congress Cataloging-in-Publication Data

Names: Brilmayer, Lea, author. | Goldsmith, Jack L., author. | O'Connor, Erin O'Hara, 1965- author. | Vázquez, Carlos M., author.
Title: Conflict of laws : cases and materials / Lea Brilmayer, Howard M. Holtzmann Professor of International Law, Yale University; Jack Goldsmith, Henry L. Shattuck Professor of Law, Harvard University; Erin O'Hara O'Connor, Dean and McKenzie Professor, Florida State University College of Law; Carlos M. Vázquez, Professor of Law, Georgetown University Law Center.
Description: Eighth edition. | New York : Wolters Kluwer, [2020] | Series: Aspen casebook series | Includes bibliographical references and index. | Summary: "Casebook on conflict of laws for law students studying conflict of laws" — Provided by publisher.
Identifiers: LCCN 2019027445 (print) | LCCN 2019027446 (ebook) | ISBN 9781454899563 (hardcover) | ISBN 9781543815078 (ebook)
Subjects: LCSH: Conflict of laws — United States. | LCGFT: Casebooks (Law)
Classification: LCC KF410 .M37 2020 (print) | LCC KF410 (ebook) | DDC 342.73/042 — dc23
LC record available at https://lccn.loc.gov/2019027445
LC ebook record available at https://lccn.loc.gov/2019027446

About Wolters Kluwer Legal & Regulatory U.S.

Wolters Kluwer Legal & Regulatory U.S. delivers expert content and solutions in the areas of law, corporate compliance, health compliance, reimbursement, and legal education. Its practical solutions help customers successfully navigate the demands of a changing environment to drive their daily activities, enhance decision quality and inspire confident outcomes.

Serving customers worldwide, its legal and regulatory portfolio includes products under the Aspen Publishers, CCH Incorporated, Kluwer Law International, ftwilliam.com and MediRegs names. They are regarded as exceptional and trusted resources for general legal and practice-specific knowledge, compliance and risk management, dynamic workflow solutions, and expert commentary.

To Our Teachers and Students

Summary of Contents

Contents   xi
Preface to the Eighth Edition   xix
Acknowledgments   xxi
Introduction   xxiii

Chapter 1.   Conflict of Laws: An Overview   1
Chapter 2.   Traditional Approaches to Choice of Law   15
Chapter 3.   Modern Approaches to Choice of Law   171
Chapter 4.   Constitutional Limitations on Choice of Law   281
Chapter 5.   The Jurisdiction of Courts over Persons and Property   363
Chapter 6.   Conflict of Laws in the Federal System   465
Chapter 7.   Recognition of Judgments   501
Chapter 8.   Extraterritoriality of Federal Law   575
Chapter 9.   Choosing Legal Regimes   647
Chapter 10. Choice of Law in Complex Litigation   737

Table of Cases   805
Table of Secondary Authorities   817
Table of Restatement Sections   829
Index   833

Contents

Preface to the Eighth Edition   xix
Acknowledgments   xxi
Introduction   xxiii

Chapter 1.   Conflict of Laws: An Overview   1

Problem 1: Prenuptial Agreements and Spousal Support   2
    Questions and Comments   4
Problem 2: The Long Arm of the Law   4
    LICRA and UEJF v. Yahoo! Inc.   5
    Questions and Comments   7
Problem 3: Whose Artwork?   9
    Questions and Comments   12

Chapter 2.   Traditional Approaches to Choice of Law   15

A. Torts   15
  1. Nonintentional Torts   15
    Alabama Great Southern Railroad v. Carroll   15
    Questions and Comments   20
    Selections from the First Restatement of Conflicts, on Wrongs   25
  2. Intentional Torts   28
    Bullard v. MRA Holding, LLC   29
    Questions and Comments   31
B. Contracts   33
    Selections from the First Restatement of Conflicts,
      on Contracts   33
    Poole v. Perkins   38
    Linn v. Employers Reinsurance Corp.   42
    Questions and Comments   44
    An Exercise   47
C. Domicile   48

Selections from the First Restatement of Conflicts,
on Domicile 48
White v. Tennant 51
Rodriguez Diaz v. Sierra Martinez 53
Questions and Comments 61

D. Marriage 63

Selections from the First Restatement of Conflicts, on
Marriage and Legitimacy 63
Ghassemi v. Ghassemi 65
Questions and Comments 74
People v. Ezeonu 76
Questions and Comments 78

E. Property 79

Selections from the First Restatement of Conflicts, on Real
Property 79
Burr v. Beckler 82
Thomson v. Kyle 83
Questions and Comments 86
Selections from the First Restatement of Conflicts, on
Personal Property 87
Blackwell v. Lurie 89
Morson v. Second National Bank of Boston 93
Questions and Comments 94

F. Corporations 97

Selections from the First Restatement of Conflicts, on
Corporations 97
McDermott Inc. v. Lewis 99
Irving Trust Co. v. Maryland Casualty Co. 103
Questions and Comments 105

G. Wrinkles in the Theory 108
1. Characterization 108
Haumschild v. Continental Casualty Co. 109
Questions and Comments 112
2. Renvoi 114
In re Estate of Damato 114
University of Chicago v. Dater 117
Questions and Comments 121
3. Substance vs. Procedure 122
Selections from the First Restatement of Conflicts,
on Procedure 122
Sampson v. Channell 124
O'Leary v. Illinois Terminal Railroad 129
Questions and Comments 131
Grant v. McAuliffe 132
Questions and Comments 135
4. Statutes of Limitations 136

Selections from the First Restatement of Conflicts, on
    Statutes of Limitations 136
    Duke v. Housen 136
    Questions and Comments 145
  5. Public Policy 146
    Selection from the First Restatement of Conflicts, on
      Public Policy 146
    Laboratory Corp. of America v. Hood 146
    Holzer v. Deutsche Reichsbahn-Gesellschaft 151
    Questions and Comments 153
  6. Penal Laws 156
    Selections from the First Restatement of Conflicts, on Penal
      Laws and Tax Claims 156
    Paper Products Co. v. Doggrell 157
    Questions and Comments 161
H. Proof of Foreign Law 163
    Tidewater Oil Co. v. Waller 163
    Questions and Comments 165

Chapter 3. Modern Approaches to Choice of Law   **171**

A. Introduction 171
  1. The "Choice-of-Law Revolution": Critical Foundations 171
  2. The Choice-of-Law Revolution in the Courts: The New York
    Experience 172
B. Interest Analysis: In Theory and in Practice 184
  1. Theoretical Foundations of Interest Analysis 184
    Currie, Notes on Methods and Objectives in the
      Conflict of Laws 184
  2. Judicial Applications 187
    a. True Conflicts 187
      Lilienthal v. Kaufman 187
    b. True Conflicts vs. Apparent Conflicts 191
      Bernkrant v. Fowler 191
      Questions and Comments 193
    c. Unprovided-for Cases 195
      Hurtado v. Superior Court 195
      Questions and Comments 198
  3. Theoretical Criticisms of Interest Analysis 199
  4. A Short Note on Interest Analysis in Other Nations 202
C. Comparative Impairment 203
    Bernhard v. Harrah's Club 204
    Questions and Comments 210
    Kearney v. Salomon Smith Barney, Inc. 211
    Questions and Comments 214
D. The "Better Rule" 218

	Leflar, Conflicts Law: More on Choice-Influencing Considerations	218
	Milkovich v. Saari	220
	Questions and Comments	224
E.	The Restatement Second and the Most Significant Relationship	227
	Phillips v. General Motors Corp.	229
	Questions and Comments	241
	America Online, Inc. v. National Health Care Discount, Inc.	243
	Questions and Comments	245
F.	Wrinkles in the Theory	249
	1. Domicile	249
	Reich v. Purcell	249
	Questions and Comments	250
	2. Renvoi	254
	Pfau v. Trent Aluminum Co.	254
	Questions and Comments	255
	Richards v. United States	256
	Questions and Comments	258
	3. Substance and Procedure	260
	4. Statutes of Limitations	261
	Ledesma v. Jack Stewart Produce, Inc.	261
	Global Financial Corp. v. Triarc Corp.	264
	Questions and Comments	266
	5. Public Policy	268
	6. Postscript	269
	Paul v. National Life	269
	Questions and Comments	273
G.	Statutory Resolution of Choice-of-Law Problems	274
	Salavarria v. National Car Rental System, Inc.	274
	Questions and Comments	278

Chapter 4.   Constitutional Limitations on Choice of Law   281

A.	Constitutional Limitations on Choice of Law	282
	Home Insurance Co. v. Dick	282
	Questions and Comments	286
	Pacific Employers Insurance Co. v. Industrial Accident Commission	288
	Questions and Comments	291
	Watson v. Employers Liability Assurance Corp.	292
	Clay v. Sun Insurance Office, Ltd.	294
	Questions and Comments	296
	Allstate Insurance Co. v. Hague	297
	Questions and Comments	308
	Phillips Petroleum Co. v. Shutts	310
	Questions and Comments	315

		Sun Oil Co. v. Wortman	316
		Questions and Comments	325
B.	The Obligation and the Right to Provide a Forum		326
		Hughes v. Fetter	327
		Wells v. Simonds Abrasive Co.	330
		Questions and Comments	332
		Note on the Full Faith and Credit Clause in State-Court Suits Against Sister State Instrumentalities	334
C.	Constitutional Limitations on Interstate Discrimination		339
		Austin v. New Hampshire	340
		Questions and Comments	345
		G. D. Searle & Co. v. Cohn	347
		Questions and Comments	351
D.	"Extraterritorial" and "Inconsistent" Regulations		352
		Brown-Forman Distillers Corp. v. New York State Liquor Auth.	353
		Questions and Comments	356

Chapter 5.   The Jurisdiction of Courts over Persons and Property   363

A.	Consent and Waiver		364
	1.	Consent	364
		Phillips Petroleum Co. v. Shutts	364
		Questions and Comments	368
	2.	Waiver	369
		Insurance Corp. of Ireland v. Compagnie des Bauxites de Guinee	369
		Questions and Comments	373
B.	Activities as a Basis for Jurisdiction		374
	1.	General and Specific Jurisdiction	375
		Helicopteros Nacionales de Colombia, S.A. v. Hall	375
		Questions and Comments	381
		Burnham v. Superior Court of California	383
		Questions and Comments	391
		Bristol-Myers Squibb v. Superior Court	392
		BNSF Railway Co. v. Tyrrell	400
	2.	Purposeful Availment and Foreseeability	403
		World-Wide Volkswagen Corp. v. Woodson	403
		Questions and Comments	411
		Kulko v. Superior Court	413
		Questions and Comments	416
		Walden v. Fiore et al.	417
		Questions and Comments	423
		Note on Activities-Based Personal Jurisdiction for Internet Disputes	425
		Goodyear Dunlop Tires Operations, S.A. v. Brown	427
		Questions and Comments	431

	Daimler AG v. Bauman	432
	Questions and Comments	440
	Note on Personal Jurisdiction and Corporate Registration Statutes	442
	Genuine Parts Co. v. Cepec	442
C.	Jurisdiction Based on Property	445
	Shaffer v. Heitner	446
	Sternberg v. O'Neil	455
	Questions and Comments	459

Chapter 6.   Conflict of Laws in the Federal System   465

A.	The *Erie* Doctrine	465
	Erie Railroad v. Tompkins	465
	Questions and Comments	470
	Note: *Erie* and Substance vs. Procedure	471
	Questions and Comments	473
1.	*Erie* and Choice of Law	475
	Klaxon Co. v. Stentor Electric Manufacturing Co.	475
	Questions and Comments	477
	Ferens v. John Deere Co.	478
	Questions and Comments	488
	Note: *Erie* and Choice of Forum	490
2.	*Erie* and Judgments	493
	Semtek Int'l Inc. v. Lockheed Martin Corp.	493
	Questions and Comments	498

Chapter 7.   Recognition of Judgments   501

A.	Jurisdictional Requirements	504
	Durfee v. Duke	504
	Fall v. Eastin	508
	Questions and Comments	510
	Kalb v. Feuerstein	512
	Questions and Comments	514
B.	Substantive Interests of the Enforcing State	516
	Fauntleroy v. Lum	516
	Questions and Comments	519
	Thomas v. Washington Gas Light Co.	520
	Questions and Comments	532
	Baker v. General Motors Corp.	533
	Questions and Comments	541
	Note: Foreign Judgments	545
C.	The Enforcing State's Law of Judgments	547
	Union National Bank v. Lamb	547
	Watkins v. Conway	549
	Questions and Comments	550

		Treinies v. Sunshine Mining Co.	553
		Questions and Comments	555
D.		Domestic Relations: A Special Problem of Judgments	558
	1.	Ex Parte "Divisible Divorce"	558
		Estin v. Estin	558
		May v. Anderson	562
		Questions and Comments	564
		Note: Full Faith and Credit and Bilateral Divorce	565
	2.	Modifications: Child Custody and Support	567
		Yarborough v. Yarborough	567
		Questions and Comments	571

Chapter 8.   Extraterritoriality of Federal Law   575

A.		The Extraterritorial Scope of the Antitrust Laws	576
	1.	Unilateral Approaches	576
		a. The Place of the Conduct	576
		American Banana Co. v. United Fruit Co.	576
		Questions and Comments	578
		b. The Effects Test	579
		U.S. v. Aluminum Co. of America	579
		Questions and Comments	580
	2.	Multilateral Approaches	581
		Timberlane Lumber Co. v. Bank of America, N.T. and S.A.	581
		Questions and Comments	588
		Hartford Fire Ins. Co. v. California	590
		Questions and Comments	600
		Hoffman-La Roche Ltd. v. Empagran S.A.	601
		Questions and Comments	604
B.		The Court's Current Approach: The Presumption Against Extraterritoriality	606
		EEOC v. Arabian American Oil Co.	606
		Questions and Comments	613
		Morrison v. National Australia Bank Ltd.	615
		Questions and Comments	625
		RJR Nabisco, Inc. v. European Community	627
		Questions and Comments	643

Chapter 9.   Choosing Legal Regimes   647

A.		Contractual Choice of Law	648
		Nedlloyd Lines B.V. v. Superior Court of San Mateo County Seawinds Ltd.	649
		Questions and Comments	656
		Banek, Inc. v. Yogurt Ventures U.S.A., Inc.	658

	Questions and Comments	662
	Cook Sign Co. v. Combs	664
	Questions and Comments	668
	Hall v. Sprint Spectrum L.P.	669
	Questions and Comments	674
B.	Choice-of-Court Clauses	677
	The Bremen v. Zapata Off-Shore Co.	677
	Carnival Cruise Lines, Inc. v. Shute	681
	Questions and Comments	687
	America Online, Inc. v. Superior Court of Alameda County	691
	Questions and Comments	695
	Wong v. PartyGaming Ltd.	696
	Questions and Comments	704
C.	Arbitration Clauses	707
	1. The Federal Arbitration Act and Arbitrability	707
	Note: Arbitrability	710
	2. Policing the Clauses	713
	AT&T Mobility LLC v. Concepcion	714
	Brewer v. Missouri Title Loans	724
	Questions and Comments	732

Chapter 10. Choice of Law in Complex Litigation **737**

A.	Introduction	737
B.	Approaches to Choice of Law	741
	1. No Choice Necessary	741
	Ferrell v. Allstate Insurance Co.	741
	Questions and Comments	753
	2. Single Governing Law	757
	Ysbrand v. DaimlerChrysler Corp.	757
	Questions and Comments	763
	Note on General Consensus Law	767
	3. Multiple Governing Laws	773
	Schnall v. AT&T Wireless Services, Inc.	773
	In re Telectronics Pacing Systems, Inc.	785
	Questions and Comments	797

Table of Cases	805
Table of Secondary Authorities	817
Table of Restatement Sections	829
Index	833

Preface to the Eighth Edition

The teacher of Conflict of Laws already knows that it is a fascinating course. The student is about to find out. It is, moreover, one of those courses in which to be "theoretical" is to be "practical"; the supposed war between those two qualities is not even a skirmish in Conflicts law, where changes have come (and will no doubt continue to come) so quickly that the only preparation is understanding, not memorization.

This book is organized to present the heart of Conflict of Laws first: choice-of-law problems. After providing a general overview of the subject, the "traditional" approach to choice of law is exposed; in the second chapter, we turn to the struggle of the courts and the commentators to come up with a more responsive (but not unduly complicated) approach. The remaining broad topics—constitutional limitations on choice of law, personal jurisdiction, recognition of judgments, extra-territoriality of federal law, choosing legal regimes, and choice of law in complex litigation—are considered in light of the wisdom derived from consideration of the basic choice-of-law problems. We have attempted to make the materials short enough so that they really can be covered in a three- or four-credit course, but we have all experienced the temptation to slow down and inspect in detail some of the particularly intriguing questions that are raised in conflicts. We recognize that in most law schools, the students will have already covered personal jurisdiction and (to some extent) judgments enforcement in their first year civil procedure course. Our chapters on these subjects would probably be more detailed and theoretically probing if that were not the case.

Questions and comments at the end of cases or case groupings tend to be brief, concentrating on the problems raised by the principal cases, rather than adding notes about other cases. Cases have been significantly edited to eliminate citations. Thus, they do not read like real case reports, but they do read somewhat more smoothly. Citations are retained on some occasions when they refer to other important cases, when they refer to writings of important conflicts scholars, when they cite the editors of this casebook, or otherwise seem worthy of retention. Footnotes in cases and other quoted material have generally been eliminated without the use of ellipses. Those that have survived editing retain their original numbers, while the editor's footnotes employ asterisks and daggers.

A word is needed about where this book fits in the general debate over the foundations of choice-of-law theory. Readers of this Preface probably already know—indeed, probably know much more than they care to—about the contentious nature of the academic literature. The name of one of the authors of this book has become virtually synonymous with the counter-revolution in choice of law theory that has attacked the so-called "modern school." But hers is almost certainly a minority position nowadays and she is well aware of this. All of the authors of this edition are committed to open dialog and open minds; we have tried (to the degree humanly possible) to make our arguments on the merits, to take the other side's arguments seriously and honestly, and to let the reader be the judge. Occasionally the opinion of an editor may show through in questions and comments, but many questions that may seem to present a point of view are asked in the spirit of the devil's advocate. If you think that we are deluded about our own abilities to be objective, please don't give up on us—just write us angry letters!

Lea Brilmayer

July 2019, New Haven Connecticut

Acknowledgments

Numerous people deserve thanks for their contributions to the publication of the eighth edition of this casebook. Erin O'Hara O'Connor would like to thank Jeffrey Grosholz, Florida State University College of Law class of 2019, for substantial assistance in the revisions of chapters 1, 2, 9 and 10. Jack Goldsmith would like to thank Harry Graver, Harvard Law Class of 2019, for his research and related assistance. Carlos Vázquez thanks Lawton Salley, Georgetown University Law Center class of 2019, and Heather Casey of the E.B. Williams Law Library for invaluable help in revising chapters 4, 7 and 8. Lea Brilmayer thanks Sara Turk and Ruel Jerry, Yale Law School Class of 2020, who made the revision of chapters 3 and 5 go so easily and pleasantly for their grateful boss. May casebook authors always have such competent and energetic assistants!

We also thank the copyright holders whose materials we have either excerpted or adapted, including:

American Law Institute, selections from Restatement, Conflict of Laws. Copyright 1934 by The American Law Institute. All rights reserved. Reprinted with the permission of The American Law Institute.

____, selections from Restatement (Second), Conflict of Laws. Copyright 1971 by The American Law Institute. All rights reserved. Reprinted with the permission of The American Law Institute.

Currie, Comments on *Babcock vs. Jackson*. Copyright © 1963 by the Directors for the Columbia Law Review Association, Inc. All rights reserved. This article originally appeared at 63 Colum. L. Rev. 1233 (1963). Reprinted by permission of the Columbia Law Review.

Lapres, translation of Licra and UEJF v. Yahoo! Inc. (Tribunal de Grande Instance de Paris, May 22, 2000), available at *www.lapres.net/yaheb.html*. Reprinted with permission of the translator.

Leflar, Conflicts Law: More on Choice-Influencing Considerations, 54 Cal. L. Rev. 1584 (1966). Copyright © 1966, California Law Review, Inc. Reprinted by permission of the California Law Review.

Introduction

A (Very) Brief History of the Subject

Conflict of Laws encompasses several related areas of law: choice of law, constitutional limitations on choice of law, jurisdiction of courts, recognition of sister-state and foreign judgments, and *Erie* problems.

Of these topics, choice of law is at the heart of the course. A choice-of-law problem arises in the selection of the governing law for a case with connections to two or more jurisdictions. Choice-of-law questions have arisen wherever people have been subject to the authority of more than one state, nation, or tribal law. The late Professor Yntema said that a choice-of-law rule was found on the wrappings of a crocodile mummy in Egypt. Yntema, The Historic Bases of Private International Law, 2 Am. J. Comp. L. 297, 300 (1953). The Corpus Juris of the Roman Empire tended to eliminate such problems by the direct method of eliminating all laws but one (namely, Roman law). Choice-of-law problems arose again in the Middle Ages, however, especially in Italy, which was divided into many commercially active city-states. The "statutists" of medieval Italy approached conflicts problems by dividing statutes into the "real" and "personal" category—the former applied only within the jurisdiction that promulgated it; the latter followed the person wherever he went. Unfortunately, the statutes were not labeled, and the crunch came in trying to determine which statutes were which. Overriding the Italian efforts in the area was the notion of what is now sometimes termed a "superlaw," which was based in part on natural law and which was viewed as having more authority than the local laws in conflict.

In the 1600s, Holland became influential in choice-of-law theory. The greatest of the Dutch scholars was Ulric Huber, who took the position that states defer to the law of other states in appropriate cases not because some superlaw requires them to do so, but rather because of "comity"—a kind of golden rule among sovereigns. His book, *De Conflictu Legum Diversarum in Diversis Imperiis* [On The Conflict of Diverse Laws of Different States], translated in Ernest G. Lorenzen, Selected Articles on the Conflict of Laws 136 (1947), set forth three postulates from which he derived his solutions to conflicts problems:

> (1) The laws of each state have force within the limits of that government and bind all subjects to it, but not beyond.
> (2) All persons within the limits of a government, whether they live there permanently or temporarily, are deemed to be subjects thereof.

(3) Sovereigns will so act by way of comity that rights acquired within the limits of a government retain their force everywhere so far as they do not cause prejudice to the power or rights of such government or of its subjects.

Lorenzen, *supra*, at 163.

Huber's work had a strong influence on Joseph Story, a Justice of the United States Supreme Court who was considered the foremost conflicts scholar in the English-speaking world in the nineteenth century. Story's approach was similar to Huber's and helped entrench the "comity" rather than "superlaw" orientation in the United States. Story's *Commentaries on the Conflict of Laws* (1834) was the most influential work in the field until A. V. Dicey, in England, produced his vested-rights theory at the turn of the century. In the United States, Professor Joseph Beale of the Harvard Law School took up Dicey's vested-rights theory, with strong doses of territorialism. The theory was enshrined in the American Law Institute's *Restatement of Conflict of Laws* (1934) and appeared for a time to be headed for apotheosis by the United States Supreme Court as a branch of the law of due process. Beale's system tended to select a governing law on the basis of where various critical acts occurred, such as where a contract was signed or where a tort was committed.

Beale's approach was heavily criticized by three outstanding scholars—Cook, Lorenzen, and Cavers. But these criticisms had little influence in the courts for many years. In the 1950s, Professor Brainerd Currie attacked the First Restatement approach and suggested in its place a system of Conflict of Laws known as "interest analysis." Currie's work influenced courts and provided a basis for others to build on. In 1971, the American Law Institute published the *Restatement (Second) of Conflict of Laws*, which tried to accommodate the policy-based insights of Currie and others. Today choice of law in the United States is something of a hodge-podge. In the context of torts and contracts, most states have rejected the traditional approach and have adopted one of a variety of policy-based approaches. But the traditional approach fares better in other contexts, such as marriage, corporate internal affairs, and real property.

About the Terminology

The late Professor Prosser once said, in an oft-quoted comment, that "[t]he realm of the conflict of laws is a dismal swamp, filled with quaking quagmires, and inhabited by learned but eccentric professors who theorize about mysterious matters in a strange and incomprehensible jargon. The ordinary court, or lawyer, is quite lost when engulfed and entangled in it." Prosser, Interstate Publication, 51 Mich. L. Rev. 959, 971 (1953). A small amount of introduction to the terminology may then be in order. *Comity,* a term already used above, indicates the nonmandatory acceptance by one jurisdiction of the law of another. *Vested rights* is a term with meaning very similar to its meaning in constitutional law and is used in connection with theories that indicate, for example, that the victim of a tort would acquire a vested right to recovery under the law of the place where the tort occurs, a right that thereafter accompanies the person and may be used as the basis for a lawsuit, even in a jurisdiction that would not impose liability if the same events had taken place within its own borders. Closely connected with vested rights is the phrase *lex loci* and its children, *lex loci contractus* and *lex loci delicti*. *Lex loci* is simply "the law of the place," with *contractus* adding "of the contract" and *delicti* adding "of the tort." Another term important to your reading of the cases is *domicile,* which refers to the political jurisdiction (state, country, etc.) in which a person makes his or her permanent home. We will see many cases elaborating that sketchy definition.

Finally, you will probably already have noted that several terms are used interchangeably for the topic under discussion. "Conflict of Laws," "choice of law," and "private international law" are common labels for what you are about to study, although "choice of law" is often restricted to choice-of-law questions, excluding such other questions as jurisdiction and recognition of judgments.

Conflict of Laws

1

Conflict of Laws: An Overview

Conflict of Laws is a course about the allocation of sovereign authority. In most substantive law courses, discussions assume that a legal rule promulgated by "the State" binds its subjects. This course lifts that assumption to consider governing laws in a world where multiple states make laws, where people, assets, and events are located in multiple jurisdictions, and where each of these three things can be movable. When a dispute involves interstate activities, multiple states' laws potentially can govern it. It is also possible, at least in theory, that no law governs the dispute. Complicating the situation is the fact that often disputes can be resolved in multiple courts, allowing for strategic selection of the judicial forum. Moreover, if plaintiff is issued a favorable monetary judgment in State A, but all of defendant's assets are located in States B and C, plaintiff might need the cooperation of these other states in order to obtain judgment enforcement. Ideally, conflicts principles smoothly and sensibly define sovereign boundaries and aid selection of the appropriate law to be applied. In reality, conflicts principles often have failed to craft solutions that are either smooth or sensible. Those principles, including the conceptual similarities and differences found across states and nations, will be the subject of study in this course.

Which sovereigns have authority to assert jurisdiction over the people involved in the dispute? Which jurisdiction's law should govern the parties' rights and responsibilities? And to what extent can issues and claims resolved in one jurisdiction be reopened for reconsideration by another sovereign? To what extent are these issues resolved according to state law? Federal law? International treaties? To what extent might the answers to questions of sovereign authority change when parties attempt to choose their own courts and law through contract or otherwise?

1

Do the answers change when claims are aggregated into complex forms of litigation? These and other questions will be explored throughout the book.

The problem of the allocation of sovereign authority is both old and ubiquitous. *See generally* Scoles, Hay, Borchers & Symeonides, *Conflict of Laws* §§2.2-2.6 (3d ed. 2000). Moreover, conflict-of-laws problems arise in virtually every substantive field of law. Cases in the book explore the problem as it arises in contracts, torts, property, corporate law, securities law, antitrust law, trusts and estates law, family law, admiralty law, and others. Of course, the focus of attention in this course is not the substantive principles of law in those various fields; rather, the multiple fields of law illustrate both the ubiquity of conflicts problems and the difficulty of solving conflicts problems according to a single set of conflicts law. Finally, numerous conflicts approaches have been utilized over time to resolve these issues. The multiplicity of approaches continues today, even within the United States, where choices of state law typically are left to determination by the states themselves.

Conflict-of-laws issues play an increasingly large role in dispute resolution. With the fall of trade barriers, advances in communication technology, and cheaper and easier travel, people and businesses interact across borders on a daily basis. E-mail, telephone conversations, online shopping, vacations, commuting, and job and plant relocations are just a few of today's common activities that cross state or national borders and open questions regarding governing laws and courts. Any well-trained lawyer engaged in twenty-first-century litigation or transactional work should know the basic principles used to allocate sovereign authority. This knowledge can enable a skilled attorney to provide her clients with the strategic advantage of having their conduct and rights evaluated in the courts and according to the laws most favorable to them.

The specifics of conflicts principles are explored in the remaining chapters of this book. This chapter presents three problems based on actual cases to illustrate the conceptual breadth of the subject matter of Conflict of Laws and to introduce students to some of the tensions underlying the legal doctrines. The questions following the problems are designed to both help signify the scope of the problem of conflict of laws and begin to identify the types of questions that a conflicts analysis entails. Consider returning to these problems at the end of the course as a tool for reviewing the materials. At that point you will be equipped to provide more sophisticated and nuanced responses.

Problem 1: Prenuptial Agreements and Spousal Support

George Smith and Angie Linford met in 2006 and married in August 2008. Three children were born to the marriage; at the time of the divorce petition, the children were ages eleven, ten, and eight. George graduated from the University of South Florida. His work history has been sporadic. After graduating, George worked at a pizza restaurant and at a department store. In 2002, he obtained his real estate license in Florida and worked as a realtor from 2002 to 2008.

Angie earned a degree in math from the University of Wyoming and her medical degree from the University of Mississippi. She subsequently completed a fellowship in breast surgical oncology in 2011. When the parties met in 2006, Angie was employed as a general surgeon and had her medical practice in Nashville. George was winding down his real estate career in Florida, where he resided at that time. In February 2007, George moved to Nashville and resided at Angie's home. George did not work during this time. After Angie became pregnant with their first child, Angie closed her medical practice in Tennessee, and the parties moved to Florida, where the child was born.

In February 2008, Angie accepted a position in New Mexico, and the parties moved there. George stayed at home with the baby and worked at day trading. Prior to the parties' marriage, George had earned approximately $30,000 as a day trader. Angie's new position was somewhat demanding, but her mother would frequently come to stay with the family to help care for the baby.

In the summer of 2008, the parties decided to marry. Prior to marrying, Angie insisted that she would not marry George without a prenuptial agreement. Angie wanted to protect real property she owned for the benefit of her parents, and she wanted to be protected against a lawsuit that was pending against George in Pennsylvania. George downloaded a prenuptial agreement from the Internet, and the parties executed the document. George and Angie married in Colorado in August 2008.

In May 2009, Angie started a fellowship in breast cancer oncology in Pennsylvania, and the parties moved there. Angie was pregnant with the couple's second child. Initially, Angie worked part time but later started a full-time schedule. George did not obtain employment outside the home.

At the end of September 2011, the family moved to Ohio, where Angie was employed as a surgical oncologist. In Ohio, Angie worked regular business hours five days a week. George stayed home with the children, who were four, two, and an infant. The family lived in Ohio for approximately one year. In October 2012, Angie returned to practice in Nashville, and the family moved back to Tennessee. Angie's annual income in her Nashville practice has averaged $325,000 per year.

After the family returned to Tennessee, the older children enrolled in elementary and preschool, and George stayed home to care for their youngest daughter. On June 21, 2013, Angie and George purchased an operating bed and breakfast, and George took over as its manager. At this time, the couple's youngest child had started preschool, and George was able to work. All members of the family continued to live in Nashville, Tennessee, until after the couple separated.

On April 8, 2018, Angie filed a complaint for divorce in Tennessee trial court. The trial court granted the divorce and awarded the marital home to Angie and the bed and breakfast to George. Custody of the couple's three children was awarded to Angie with periodic visitation rights granted to George. Under Tennessee law, George was ordered to pay $350 each month to Angie for child support. George recently returned to live in New Mexico, and he has filed a motion in a New Mexico court for spousal support, claiming a right to support because he devoted several years to raising the children rather than earning income in the workforce. Angie has opposed the motion, citing the prenuptial agreement, under which each party "waive[d] and relinquishe[d] any claim for alimony, spousal support or maintenance." George has attacked the validity of the prenuptial agreement. By law in some states, including New Mexico and Colorado, waiver of support clauses in prenuptial agreements are unenforceable. However, these waivers are enforceable under the laws of other states, including Tennessee and Ohio.

Questions and Comments

(1) Although this motion has been filed in a New Mexico court, that court need not apply its own law if it deems it appropriate to apply another state's law instead. Indeed, as will be examined in Chapter 4, under some circumstances, states are not constitutionally permitted to apply forum law but must instead apply the law of another sovereign to resolve the case. Whose law should apply to determine the validity of the prenuptial agreement? The state where George resides? Where the divorce was granted? Where Angie and George were married? Where they signed the prenuptial agreement? Where George stayed home to care for the children? Somewhere else?

(2) More generally, when should a court defer to another state's law? Does it matter here that New Mexico may have a strong public policy against allowing parties to sign away their future rights to spousal support?

(3) Of what significance is the fact that a Tennessee court has already granted the divorce and made determinations about child custody, child support, and the division of marital assets? Should that preclude a New Mexico court from deciding the spousal support issue? As discussed in Chapter 4, the full faith and credit clause of the U.S. Constitution, Art. IV, §1, requires each U.S. state to give respect to the acts, records, and judicial proceedings of the other states. Much more respect is owed to the judgments of other states than to their acts and records, but even in the context of judgments, states' obligations are not absolute. Should it matter that the Tennessee court made no explicit determination about spousal support? Is there value to having one court make all decisions about this family and its assets?

(4) What would a Tennessee court conclude about George's right to spousal support in these circumstances? Should choice-of-law policies ensure that the same law be applied regardless of where the legal issue is resolved? If consistency is important, what about stability? Given that the couple moved multiple times during their relationship and that George moved afterward, does it make any sense for George's support rights or Angie's support obligations to change with residence? Can choice-of-law rules or the law of judgment recognition help stabilize the legal treatment of such issues? Could a federal law solve the problem? If so, what form should that law take?

Problem 2: The Long Arm of the Law

The opinion reproduced below was rendered by a French court. Plaintiffs from that litigation have asked a court in Sunnyvale, California, the location of defendant Yahoo! Inc.'s corporate headquarters, to order Yahoo! Inc. to comply with the judgment. They also seek the recovery of fines described in the French court's order.

LICRA and UEJF v. Yahoo! Inc.

Tribunal de Grande Instance de Paris (May 22, 2000)

(available at *http://www.lapres.net/yahen.html* (Daniel Lapres, trans.))

GOMEZ, First Deputy Chief Justice.

[Yahoo! Inc. ("Yahoo!"), a U.S. corporation and one of the world's leading web portals, has an Internet auction site that offered for sale Nazi memorabilia such as flags, stamps, and military souvenirs. Persons at computers in France could access this site through links on the French-language portal of Yahoo!'s French subsidiary, Yahoo! France, or by accessing Yahoo!'s portal directly from France by typing *www.yahoo.com* into a computer browser. The International League Against Racism and Anti-Semitism (LICRA) and the Union of French Jewish Students (UEJF) sued Yahoo! and Yahoo! France, alleging violations of Article R. 645-2 of the French penal code, a World War II–era law criminalizing the exhibition or sale of racist materials. The plaintiffs asked the Court to force Yahoo! to block French users' access to Nazi objects for sale on Yahoo!'s U.S. auction site.]

Yahoo! Inc. has argued that our court is not territorially competent over the matter, because the alleged fault is committed on the territory of the United States. [It further argues for rejection of plaintiffs' claims on the ground that] the duties of vigilance and prior censure which the petitioners would seek to impose upon it are impossible obligations, first in terms of the law and the American constitution, in particular the First Amendment of the Constitution which institutes the liberty of expression and then in view of the technical impossibility of identifying surfers who visit the auction service, while recalling that in its charter it warns all surfers against using the service for purposes worthy of reprobation for whatsoever motive (incitement to hatred, racial or ethnic discrimination …).

Whereas it is not challenged that surfers who call up Yahoo.com from French territory may, directly or via the link offered by Yahoo.fr, see on their screens the pages, services and sites to which Yahoo.com gives access, in particular the auction service (Auctions) lodged by Geocities.com, the lodging service of Yahoo! Inc., in particular in its declension relating to Nazi objects;

Whereas the exposition for the purpose of sale of Nazi objects constitutes a violation of French law (article R.645-2 of the Criminal Code) as well as an offence against the collective memory of a country profoundly wounded by the atrocities committed by and in the name of the Nazi criminal enterprise against its citizens and most importantly against its citizens of the Jewish religion;

Whereas while permitting the visualization in France of these objects and eventual participation of a surfer established in France in such an exposition/sale, Yahoo! Inc. thus has committed a wrong on the territory of France, a wrong, the unintentional nature of which is apparent, but which is the cause of harm to the LICRA as well as the UEJF which both have the mission of pursuing in France any and all forms of banalization of Nazism, regardless of the fact that the litigious activity is marginal in relation with the entire business of the auction sales service offered on its … Yahoo.com site;

Whereas Yahoo! Inc. claims that it is technically impossible to control access to its auction service or any other service, and that therefore it cannot prohibit any surfer from France from visualizing same on his screen;

Whereas it wishes nevertheless to emphasize that it warns all visitors against any uses of its services for purposes that are "worthy of reprobation for whatsoever reason," such as for purposes of racial or ethnic discrimination (*cf*. its user's charter);

But whereas Yahoo! Inc. is in a position to identify the geographical origin of the site which is visited, based on the IP address of the caller, which should therefore enable it to prohibit surfers from France, by whatever means are appropriate, from accessing the services and sites the visualization of which on a screen set up in France, and in some cases teledischarging and reproduction of the contents, or of any other initiative justified by the nature of the site consulted, would be likely to be qualified in France as a crime and/or constitute a manifestly illegal nuisance within the meaning of articles 808 and 809 of New Code of Civil Procedure, which is manifestly the case of the exhibition of uniforms, insignia, emblems reminiscent of those worn or exhibited by the Nazis;

Whereas as regards surfers who navigate through sites which guarantee them anonymity, Yahoo! Inc. has fewer means of control except for example through refusing systematically access to such sites to all visitors who do not disclose their geographical origin;

Whereas the real difficulties encountered by Yahoo do not constitute insurmountable obstacles;

That [Yahoo!] will therefore be ordered to take any and all measures of such kind as to dissuade and make impossible any consultations by surfers calling from France to its sites and services in dispute the title and/or contents of which infringe upon the internal public order of France, especially the site selling Nazi objects;

That Yahoo will be given two months to enable it to formulate proposals of technical measures likely to lead to a settlement of this dispute;

Whereas, as regards Yahoo France, it bears mentioning that its site Yahoo.fr does not itself offer surfers calling from France access to the sites or series the title and/or the contents of which constitute infractions of French law; that therefore, it does not provide access to the site or services for auction sales of Nazi objects;

But whereas it offers surfers a link to Yahoo.com entitled "further research on Yahoo.com," without any particular warning;

Or whereas, knowing what are the contents of the services offered by Yahoo.com, and in this case the service of auction sales including in one of its declensions the sale of Nazi objects, it behooves it to warn surfers, by a banner, prior to the surfer's entry into the Yahoo.com site, that should the result of his search on Yahoo.com ... point toward sites, pages or forums the title and or contents of which constitute a violation of French law, such as is the case of sites which, whether directly or indirectly, intentionally or unintentionally, make the apology of Nazism, it must interrupt the consultation of the site in question lest it incur the sanctions stipulated by French law or answer to legal actions which might be initiated against it;

NOW THEREFORE

At a public audience and rendering its judgment in first instance, after having heard all the parties, the Court: ...

Orders Yahoo! Inc. to take such measures as will dissuade and render impossible any and all consultation on Yahoo.com of the auction service for Nazi objects as well as any other site or service which makes apologies of Nazism or questions of the existence of Nazi crimes;

Orders [a subsequent hearing] during which Yahoo! Inc. shall submit the measures which it intends to implement to end the harm and the nuisance suffered by the plaintiffs and to prevent any new incidents of nuisance;

Finds Yahoo! Inc. liable to pay to the LICRA an amount of 10,000 Francs [approximately $133 when the case was decided] on the basis of article 700 of the New Code of Civil Procedure;

[Following this ruling, the Paris court convened a panel of Internet experts who prepared a report about the feasibility of Yahoo! blocking access in France to its U.S. auction site. The report concluded that Yahoo! could block French users from accessing its U.S. auction site with a 90 percent success rate through a combined process of (a) tracing the computer user's Internet Protocol address to its geographical source, and (b) conditioning access to the auction site on a declaration of nationality. The court embraced this conclusion, and also noted that Yahoo! had already been identifying French users to some degree because French users visiting the Yahoo! auction site were greeted with French-language advertisements. On the basis of these findings, the Court affirmed its previous ruling, gave Yahoo! three months to comply, and ordered a fine of 100,000 francs (about $13,300) per day for noncompliance after that time. *See* LICRA et UEJF v. Yahoo! Inc., Tribunal de Grande Instance de Paris (November 20, 2000), available at *www.lapres.net/yahen11.html* (translation by Daniel Lapres). Shortly after concluding the case in the French court, Yahoo! Inc. banned all Nazi paraphernalia from its U.S. auction sites but claimed that the move was not in response to the French decision. *See* Guernsey, *Yahoo to Try Harder to Rid Postings of Hateful Material*, N.Y. Times, Jan. 3, 2001, sec. 5, p. 2.]

Questions and Comments

(1) What should the California court do in response to plaintiffs' requests? Unlike the strong constitutional and federal law obligation of federal and state courts to recognize and enforce judgments from other federal and state courts, there is no corresponding federal obligation for federal or state courts to recognize and enforce judgments from other nations. What factors should a court take into account when determining the appropriate treatment of such judgments? Should a court consider whether it agrees with the policy rationale underlying the foreign judgment?

(2) The French court relied on an expert feasibility report's assessment that Yahoo! could identify the geographic locations of its users with a 90 percent probability, and ruled that any obstacles that might exist are not "insurmountable." However, compliance could be "not insurmountable" and yet be excessively costly. What would be a sufficiently intelligible principle to determine the point at which Yahoo! should be able to defend noncompliance due to excessive cost?

(3) This ruling, which states that Internet users can be feasibly and reliably traced back to their geographical location, was issued in 2000. Although the ruling may have been correct at the time, it quickly became highly disputable because tools that made it significantly harder to trace a user's Internet Protocol (IP) address to its geographical location proliferated and became much easier to use. Trimble, *The Future of Cybertravel: Legal Implications of the Evasion of Geolocation,*

22 Fordham Intell. Prop. Media & Ent. L.J. 567, 568 (2012). One example of such a tool is the proxy IP address: By connecting to the Internet through a proxy server physically placed in France, a Connecticut user would display to the rest of the Internet a French IP address. *See id.* at 602. How should a court take into account the availability of these technologies when deciding which jurisdiction's law should apply, or when requiring companies like Yahoo! to identify the geographical locations of their users?

(4) How far should the governmental authority of a nation extend on the Internet? Following the *Yahoo* decision, companies like Yahoo! and Google—based in the United States but also doing business in foreign countries—have become increasingly compliant with local censorship laws for fear of becoming unable to do business there. Stevenson, *Breaching the Great Firewall: China's Internet Censorship and the Quest for Freedom of Expression in a Connected World*, 30 B.C. Intl. & Comp. L. Rev. 531, 537-539 (2007). This means that, when a Chinese court issues an injunction to censor something on a Web site run by Google that can be accessed both from the United States and China, it need not look to U.S. courts to enforce that injunction. *Id.* at 545, 547. From the perspective of the United States, one could claim that these companies' First Amendment rights are being violated. In the *Yahoo* case, a French court attempted to reach a U.S. company through its long-arm statute. Should a court in the United States, exercising jurisdiction under a long-arm statute, be able to protect U.S. companies from censorship in countries such as China by enforcing the First Amendment?

(5) The problem of allocating governmental authority over actions on the Internet has arisen in a number of contexts. Although legitimate governmental authority typically is thought to operate territorially, the Internet does not operate according to geographic boundaries. For a debate over whether Internet disputes can be adequately treated via traditional, territorial-based approaches to choice of law, *see* Johnson & Post, *Law and Borders—The Rise of Law in Cyberspace*, 48 Stan. L. Rev. 1367 (1996) (arguing that they cannot); Goldsmith, *Against Cyberanarchy*, 65 U. Chi. L. Rev. 1199 (1998) (arguing that new technologies make geographic designations increasingly feasible).

(6) Consider also People v. World Interactive Gaming Corp., 714 N.Y.S.2d 844 (N.Y. Sup. Ct. 1999), a case in which the Attorney General of the State of New York brought criminal proceedings against the defendant company in an effort to obtain a court injunction against the company providing Internet gambling services to New York residents. World Interactive was a Delaware corporation with corporate offices in New York. Internet gambling operations were not conducted by World Interactive, but one of its wholly owned subsidiaries operated an Internet gambling operation from its location in Antigua, where gambling is legal. Customers were required to open accounts prior to gambling, and they were required to provide a permanent address as part of the account application. Any person who entered a New York State permanent address was denied access to the gambling services, but customers who provided fake addresses were permitted to gamble. The New York court found it appropriate for New York's gambling prohibition to extend to the subsidiary's activity, and it found it appropriate to hold the parent company responsible for the actions of the subsidiary. This assertion of governmental authority was deemed necessary in order to effectuate the state's "deep-rooted policy" against unauthorized gambling. The court issued the state's requested injunction and approved awards for restitution, penalties, and costs.

Is New York's assertion of governmental authority appropriate? Is this case conceptually distinguishable from *Yahoo*?

(7) Unlike Problem 1, the *Yahoo* case involves a conflict between the laws of two nations rather than a conflict between the laws of two U.S. states. Should the international character of a dispute change a court's analysis, or are sovereign conflicts the same regardless of the sovereigns involved? If the international character of the dispute might be relevant to the conflict's analysis, how does/should it differ from conflicts confined to U.S. sovereigns? This topic is considered more fully in Chapter 8 and will be raised at numerous points in the course materials.

(8) Judgment enforcement difficulties can provide natural constraints on the extraterritorial application of a nation's laws:

> The real problem is turning a judgment supported by jurisdiction into meaningful economic relief.... If an old lady in Richmond, Virginia is the victim of fraud perpetuated through the Internet by someone located in Belgium, she has a reasonable chance of convincing a Virginia circuit court that it has jurisdiction over the Belgian actor. Unless the fraud is enormous, the Belgian actor is unlikely to appear and she is likely to get a default judgment. But what can she do with her default judgment? Even if the Belgian legal system, through its equivalent of the comity doctrine, will enforce the judgment, it is improbable that she will spend the money to get a Belgian lawyer to enforce the judgment in Belgium. The transaction costs dwarf the value of the claim.

Perritt, *Will the Judgment-Proof Own Cyberspace?*, 32 Intl. Law. 1121, 1123 (1998). New York can enforce the judgment against World Interactive because the company is located in the United States and partially located in New York. What if the Antiguan company were not a subsidiary of a U.S. corporation? Would New York be able to enforce a judgment against it? Note that Congress passed the Unlawful Internet Gambling Enforcement Act of 2006, 31 U.S.C.A. §5361 et seq., which authorized federal regulations requiring financial institutions and other intermediaries to identify and block the processing of charges related to online gambling. That is one way around the problem of regulating outsiders in order to protect the welfare of residents. Are there problems with taking this route?

(9) Consider also the more recent example of the Clarifying Lawful Overseas Use of Data Act (CLOUD Act), 18 U.S.C. §2703 (Mar. 23, 2018), which obligates e-mail service providers to preserve and disclose certain information stored outside the United States when presented with a court order.

Problem 3: Whose Artwork?

Peter Plaintiff, resident of New Orleans, Louisiana, filed a declaratory judgment action in a Louisiana federal district court against Durel Defendant, a resident of the Czech Republic, seeking to quiet title to "Man in a Bottle," a painting created by Franz Artiste, which is currently in Peter's possession in New Orleans. Durel had previously sent a demand letter to Peter, claiming that the painting rightfully belonged to him as the sole heir to Aaron Birnbaum, a wealthy Austrian merchant of the Jewish faith. Birnbaum owned and possessed the painting until 1941, when he was imprisoned by the Nazis and tortured until he signed a document relinquishing all of his artwork, including "Man in a Bottle," to a Nazi art dealer who operated a gallery and auction house in Switzerland. Birnbaum died in prison shortly thereafter. In 1956, the painting was sold in Switzerland to a New York gallery. In 1963, Peter purchased the painting. Since then, the painting has been on display in his home and occasionally loaned out for exhibits around the country. Peter argues that even though the painting was effectively stolen by the Nazis who tortured Birnbaum, he was a purchaser in good faith (without knowledge of the painting's tainted ownership), and therefore he holds good title to it. Durel argues that because the painting was effectively stolen from Birnbaum, no subsequent possessor can obtain good title. Research on laws potentially relevant to resolving this dispute has uncovered the following:

Swiss Law

Under Article 934 of the Swiss Civil Code, a buyer acting in good faith will acquire valid title to stolen property after a period of five years. After the five-year period, a previous owner of a stolen object is no longer entitled to request its return from a good-faith purchaser. One is considered a good-faith purchaser if she paid reasonable consideration for the property without knowledge or reason to believe that the property was stolen. Swiss law also presumes that a purchaser acts in good faith, and a plaintiff seeking to reclaim stolen property has the burden of establishing that a purchaser did not act in good faith. That presumption has been applied to art works with a potential relationship to Germany during World War II (i.e., emanating from a German collection or created by artists deemed "degenerate" by the Nazis). In the 1950s, some other European nations rejected this presumption and determined that a dealer accepting such art works would automatically be subject to a heightened standard of diligence in order to obtain good title. In 1987, the Swiss Federal Supreme Court removed the good-faith presumption and imposed a due diligence standard on sales transactions involving second-hand luxury automobiles. Shortly thereafter it also removed the presumption as applied to the antiquities business because "in these businesses stolen property is known to be frequent; therefore a heightened alertness may be expected from buyers in these sectors." Although some Swiss legal commentators are of the opinion that the art market should also fall into this category of known frequent confiscation and theft, the Swiss Federal Supreme Court has not extended the due diligence standards to transactions with works of art.

New York Law

Under New York law, a thief cannot pass good title. "[A]bsent other considerations an artwork stolen during World War II still belongs to the original owner, even if there have been several subsequent buyers and even if each of those buyers was completely unaware that she was buying stolen goods." Turner, *The Innocent Buyer of Art Looted During World War II*, 32 Vand. J. Transnatl. L. 1511, 1534 (1999) (citing Menzel v. List, 49 Misc. 2d 300, 305 (1966), *modified as to damages*, 28 A.D.2d 516 (1st Dept. 1967), *rev'd as to modification*, 24 N.Y.2d 91 (1969)). As a result, the burden of proving that the painting was not stolen properly rests with the possessor. The manner in which the New York rule is applied reflects an overarching concern that New York not become a marketplace for stolen goods and, in particular, for stolen artwork.

In addition, a cause of action for replevin against the good-faith purchaser of stolen property accrues when the true owner makes demand for return of the chattel and the person in possession of the chattel refuses to return it. Until demand is made and refused, possession of the stolen property by the good-faith purchaser for value is not considered wrongful, and the statute of limitations does not begin to run. New York has not adopted an alternative discovery rule under which the statute of limitations runs from the time that the owner discovered or reasonably should have discovered the whereabouts of the work of art that had been stolen. Specifically, a bill proposing that a museum would be immune from future claims once it "gave required public notice of acquisition and a three-year statute of limitations period had passed" was vetoed by then Governor Mario Cuomo, who stated that he had been advised by the State Department that the bill, if law, would have caused New York to become "a haven for cultural property stolen abroad since such objects would be immune from recovery under the limited time periods established by the bill."

Louisiana Law

In general, Louisiana law provides strong protections for property owners. Under Louisiana Civil Code, ownership can never be lost by the failure to exercise it—only by the acquisition of ownership by another through possession sufficient to acquire it through "acquisitive prescription." However, pursuant to article 3491 of the Louisiana Civil Code, "one who has possessed movable property as owner for ten years acquires ownership by prescription. Neither title nor good faith is required for this prescription." The burden of proof of establishing the facts of acquisitive prescription rests on the party who makes the plea. However, the possessor is aided in this burden by a presumption that she/he possessed as owner. Louisiana Civil Code article 3488 provides: "[A]s to the fact itself of possession, a person is presumed to have possessed as master and owner, unless it appears that the possession began in the name of and for another." Possession is defined under Louisiana law as the open and continuous detention or enjoyment of a corporeal thing, movable or immovable, that one holds or exercises by himself or by another who keeps or exercises it in his name. No exceptions to these rules apply in the case of stolen artwork.

U.S. Federal Law—The Holocaust Victims Redress Act

The Holocaust Victims Redress Act provides in pertinent part:

> It is the sense of Congress that ... all governments should undertake good faith efforts to facilitate the return of the private and public property, such as works of art, to the rightful owners in cases where assets were confiscated from the claimant during the period of Nazi rule and there is reasonable proof that the claimant is the rightful owner.

Act §202, 112 Stat. at 17-18. According to the Ninth Circuit Federal Court of Appeals, the Holocaust Victims Redress Act was not intended to give individuals a private cause of action. Orkin v. Taylor, 487 F.3d 734, 739 (9th Cir. 2007). No other court has considered the question.

Transnational Law: The Terezin Declaration

The Terezin Declaration is a "legally non-binding" document promulgated on June 30, 2009, at the Prague Holocaust Era Assets Conference organized by the Czech Republic, and is intended to impose "moral responsibilities" on its signatories. Forty-six states, including the United States, Switzerland, and Austria, approved of the document. The Terezin Declaration addresses a number of continuing problems related to the treatment of Holocaust victims and their families during and after World War II. It provides, in relevant part:

Nazi-Confiscated and Looted Art

Recognizing that art and cultural property of victims of the Holocaust (Shoah) and other victims of Nazi persecution was confiscated, sequestered and spoliated, by the Nazis, the Fascists and their collaborators through various means including theft, coercion and confiscation, and on grounds of relinquishment as well as forced sales and sales under duress, during the Holocaust era between 1933 and 1945 and as an immediate consequence....

2. In particular, recognizing that restitution cannot be accomplished without knowledge of potentially looted art and cultural property, we stress the importance for all stakeholders to continue and support intensified systematic provenance research, with due regard to legislation, in both public and private archives, and where relevant to make the results of this research, including ongoing updates, available via the internet, with due regard to privacy rules and regulations. Where it has not already been done, we also recommend the establishment of mechanisms to assist claimants and others in their efforts.

3. ... [W]e urge all stakeholders to ensure that their legal systems or alternative processes, while taking into account the different legal traditions, facilitate just and fair solutions with regard to Nazi-confiscated and looted art, and to make certain that claims to recover such art are resolved expeditiously and based on the facts and merits of the claims and all the relevant documents submitted by all parties. Governments should consider all relevant issues when applying various legal provisions that may impede the restitution of art and cultural property, in order to achieve just and fair solutions, as well as alternative dispute resolution, where appropriate under law.

Questions and Comments

(1) Consider this case from Durel's perspective. What arguments might Durel wish to make to avoid a potentially adverse determination by the district court? First, presumably Peter filed this declaratory judgment action in his home state in order to avoid having to litigate elsewhere, but Durel might object to having to litigate in Louisiana. Could Durel argue that the court lacks jurisdiction to resolve the matter? Would it serve his interests if he succeeded? Is he likely to succeed? This last question might be easier to answer after reading Chapter 5 on the Jurisdiction

of Courts over Persons and Property. For now, note that because Conflict of Laws is in some respects a course on advanced procedure, some of the topics explored in your Civil Procedure course will be relevant to the study of this course.

(2) Peter filed this action in a Louisiana federal court, but the choice of forum does not necessarily dictate the law to be applied. If at root this is a property law claim, property law is controlled by state law in the United States, so the federal court would be exercising its diversity jurisdiction over the claim. When it sits in diversity, the federal court must apply state substantive law rather than federal substantive law. Erie Railroad Co. v. Tompkins, 304 U.S. 64 (1938). Even if this is a state law claim, the court could decide that Swiss (or Austrian) law rather than the law of any U.S. state should be applied to resolve the claim. Each U.S. state has developed a set of principles that are applied in its courts to determine which law applies to resolve a claim that involves people, property, and/or activities located elsewhere. When a federal court sits in diversity, the court must apply the choice-of-law principles of the state in which the court is located. Klaxon Co. v. Stentor Electric Manufacturing Co., 313 U.S. 487 (1941). (The application of *Erie* to conflict-of-laws issues is discussed in Chapter 6.) If this were a property claim, then the federal court in Louisiana would apply Louisiana choice-of-law principles to determine whether the property law of New York, Louisiana, Switzerland, or elsewhere should apply.

(3) Assuming that the court asserts jurisdiction over the case, should the merits of the case be determined according to state, federal, or transnational principles? Given that the Terezin Declaration is legally nonbinding, what relevance might it have to the resolution of the dispute? *See* Cassirer v. Thyssen-Bornesmisza Collection Found., 153 F. Supp. 3d 1148 (C.D. Cal. 2015), *rev'd on other grounds*, 862 F.3d 951 (9th Cir. 2017), *cert. denied*, 138 S. Ct. 1992 (2018) (declining to rely on the declaration as a source of law but exhorting the defendant to "pause, reflect, and consider whether it would be appropriate to work towards a mutually-agreeable resolution of this action, in light of Spain's acceptance of . . . the Terezin Declaration, and, specifically, its commitment to achieve 'just and fair solutions' for victims of Nazi persecution"). Would the court have applied the Terezin Declaration as a source of law if it had been a binding treaty? Is it significant that all three of the countries where the painting has "resided" since Nazi rule approved the Declaration? What about the federal statute? Should the Louisiana court decide that the Holocaust Victims Redress Act creates a federal private right of action? Note that if it does, the district court would be exercising federal question jurisdiction over the case. With federal question (as opposed to diversity) jurisdiction, the district court need not apply the choice-of-law principles of Louisiana. If the federal statute does not create a right of action, is it at all significant to the resolution of the dispute?

(4) Should a court consider the merits of a case when choosing law? What if it believes that Peter paid a lot of money for the painting and should be entitled to keep it? What if it believes that Durel's family was subject to so much horror that by rights it should at least get its painting returned? Are these considerations relevant? If so, why?

(5) Should a court consider the merits of competing laws when choosing law? What if the court believes that the "open and continuous" rule of Louisiana law is archaic in that it reflects a time where everyone lived in the same village so that

the victim had notice of adverse possession when another displayed his property openly? *See* Symeonides, *A Choice-of-Law Rule for Conflicts Involving Stolen Cultural Property*, 38 Vand. J. Transnatl. L. 1177 (2005).

(6) Several cases involving artwork formerly possessed by Holocaust victims have been litigated in U.S. courts with mixed results, both as to the applicable law and as to the outcome of the case. Problem 3 was based on a factual mixture of several cases. Three court opinions came to three different conclusions regarding the law that should apply to resolve the claims. *See* Dunbar v. Seger-Thomschitz, 615 F.3d 574 (5th Cir. 2010) (applying Louisiana law because the artwork was most recently possessed openly and continuously in that state); Bakalar v. Vavra, 2008 WL 4067335 (S.D.N.Y. Sept. 2, 2008) (document signed by original owner simply gave right of sale, not title, to dealer; because first sale occurred in Switzerland, validity of transfer of title should be located according to the law of that place); Bakalar v. Vavra, 619 F.3d 136 (2d Cir. 2010) (law of state with the greatest interest in this case should apply; New York and Austria have greatest interests; Austrian interests furthered by application of New York law). For a case with similar facts, *see* Cassirer v. Thyssen Bornemisza Foundation Collection, *supra*.

2

Traditional Approaches to Choice of Law

The cases and rules in this chapter represent the traditional approaches to choice of law that prevailed in the United States in the nineteenth century and first half of the twentieth century. Since then, new theories (discussed in Chapter 3) have emerged, and relatively few scholars defend the "old rules" as originally conceived. Nonetheless, ten or so states adhere to the traditional rules in the torts and contracts contexts, and many more states follow traditional approaches in other areas of law. Even in states that have abandoned traditional rules, these rules form the backdrop that makes the present state of the law more comprehensible.

A. Torts

1. Nonintentional Torts

Alabama Great Southern Railroad v. Carroll

97 Ala. 126, 11 So. 803 (1892)

MCCLELLAN, J.

The plaintiff W. D. Carroll is, and was at the time of entering into the service of the defendant, the Alabama Great Southern Railroad Company, and at the

15

time of being injured in that service, a citizen of Alabama. The defendant is an Alabama corporation operating a railroad extending from Chattanooga in the State of Tennessee through Alabama to Meridian in the State of Mississippi. At the time of the casualty complained of, plaintiff was in the service of the defendant in the capacity of brakeman on freight trains running from Birmingham, Alabama, to Meridian, Mississippi, under a contract which was made in the State of Alabama. The injury was caused by the breaking of a link between two cars in a freight train which was proceeding from Birmingham to Meridian. The point at which the link broke and the injury was suffered was in the State of Mississippi. The evidence tended to show that the link which broke was a defective link and that it was in a defective condition when the train left Birmingham. . . . The evidence went also to show that the defect in this link consisted in or resulted from its having been bent while cold, that this tended to weaken the iron and in this instance had cracked the link somewhat on the outer curve of the bend, and that the link broke at the point of this crack. It was shown to be the duty of certain employees of defendant stationed along its line to inspect the links attached to cars to be put in trains or forming the couplings between cars in trains at Chattanooga, Birmingham, and some points between Birmingham and the place where this link broke, and also that it was the duty of the conductor of freight trains and the other trainmen to maintain such inspection as occasion afforded throughout the runs or trips of such trains; and the evidence affords ground for inference that there was a negligent omission on the part of such employees to perform this duty, or if performed, the failure to discover the defect in and to remove this link was the result of negligence. . . .

The only negligence, in other words and in short, which finds support by direction or inference in any tendency of the evidence, is that of persons whose duty it was to inspect the links of the train, and remove such as were defective and replace them with others which were not defective. This was the negligence not of the master, the defendant, but of fellow-servants of the plaintiff, for which at common-law the defendant is not liable. . . .

This being the common-law applicable to the premises as understood and declared in Alabama, it will be presumed in our courts as thus declared to be the common-law of Mississippi, unless the evidence shows a different rule to have been announced by the Supreme Court of the State as being the common-law thereof. The evidence adduced here fails to show any such thing; but to the contrary it is made to appear from the testimony of Judge Arnold and by the decisions of the Supreme Court of Mississippi which were introduced on the trial below that that court is in full accord with this one in this respect. Indeed, if anything, those decisions go further than this court has ever gone in applying the doctrine of fellow-servants to the exemption of railway companies from liability to one servant for injuries resulting from the negligence of another. . . .

It is, however, further contended that the plaintiff, if his evidence be believed, has made out a case for the recovery sought under the Employer's Liability Act of Alabama, it being clearly shown that there is no such, or similar law of force in the State of Mississippi. Considering this position in the abstract, that is dissociated from the facts of this particular case which are supposed to exert an important influence upon it, there cannot be two opinions as to its being unsound and untenable. So looked at, we do not understand appellee's counsel even to deny either the proposition or its application to this case, that there can be no recovery in one State for injuries to the person sustained in another unless the infliction of the injuries is actionable under the law of the State in which they were received. Certainly this is the well established rule of law subject in some jurisdictions to the qualification that the infliction of the injuries would also support an action in the State where the suit is brought, had they been received within that State. . . .

But it is claimed that the facts of this case take it out of the general rule which the authorities cited above abundantly support, and authorize the courts of Alabama to subject the defendant to the payment of damages under section 2590 of the Code, although the injuries counted on were sustained in Mississippi under circumstances which involved no liability on the defendant by the laws of that State.

This insistence is in the first instance based on that aspect of the evidence which goes to show that the negligence which produced the casualty transpired in Alabama, and the theory that wherever the consequence of that negligence manifested itself, a recovery can be had in Alabama. We are referred to no authority in support of this proposition, and exhaustive investigation on our part has failed to disclose any. . . .

The position [that the occurrence of the negligence in Alabama would not justify applying Alabama law] appears to us to be eminently sound in principle and upon logic. It is admitted, or at least cannot be denied, that negligence of duty unproductive of damnifying results will not authorize or support a recovery. Up to the time this train passed out of Alabama no injury had resulted. For all that occurred in Alabama, therefore, no cause of action whatever arose. The fact which created the right to sue, the injury without which confessedly no action would lie anywhere, transpired in the State of Mississippi. It was in that State, therefore, necessarily that the cause of action, if any, arose; and whether a cause of action arose and existed at all or not must in all reason be determined by the law which obtained at the time and place when and where the fact which is relied on to justify a recovery transpired. Section 2590 of the Code of Alabama had no efficacy beyond the lines of Alabama. It cannot be allowed to operate upon facts occurring in another State so as to evolve out of them rights and liabilities which do not exist under the law of the State which is of course paramount in the premises. Where the facts occur in Alabama and a liability becomes fixed in Alabama, it may be enforced in another State having like enactments, or whose policy is not opposed to the spirit of such enactments, but this is quite a different matter. This is but enforcing the statute upon facts to which it is applicable all of which occur within the territory for the government of which it was enacted. Section 2590 of the Code, in other words is to be interpreted in the light of universally recognized principles of private international or interstate law, as if its operation had been expressly limited to this State and as if its first line read as follows: "When a personal injury is *received in Alabama* by a servant or employee," &c., &c. The negligent infliction of an injury here under statutory circumstances creates a right of action here, which, being transitory, may be enforced in any other State or country the comity of which admits of it; but for an injury inflicted elsewhere than in Alabama our statute gives no right of recovery, and the aggrieved party must look to the local law to ascertain what his rights are. Under that law this plaintiff had no cause of action, as we have seen, and hence he has no rights which our courts can enforce, unless it be upon a consideration to be presently adverted to. We have not been inattentive to the suggestions of counsel in the connection, which are based upon that rule of the statutory and common criminal law under which a murderer is punishable where the fatal blow is delivered, regardless of the place where death ensues. This principle is patently without application here. There would be some analogy if the plaintiff had been stricken in Alabama and suffered in Mississippi, which is not the fact. There is, however, an analogy which is afforded by the criminal law, but which points away from the conclusion appellee's counsel desire us to reach. This is found in that well established doctrine of criminal law, that where the unlawful act is committed in one jurisdiction or State and takes effect—produces the result which it is the purpose of the law to prevent, or, it having ensued, punish for—in another jurisdiction or State, the crime is deemed to have been committed and is punished in that jurisdiction or State in which the result is manifested, and not where the act was committed.

Another consideration—that referred to above—it is insisted, entitles this plaintiff to recover here under the Employer's Liability Act for an injury inflicted beyond the territorial operation of that act. This is claimed upon the fact that at the time plaintiff was injured he was in the discharge of duties which rested on him by the terms of a contract between him and defendant which had been entered into in Alabama, and, hence, was an Alabama contract, in connection with the facts that plaintiff was and is a citizen of this State, and the defendant is an Alabama corporation. These latter facts—of citizenship and domicile respectively of plaintiff and defendant—are of no importance in this connection, it seems to us, further than this: they may tend to show that the contract was made here, which is not controverted, and if the plaintiff has a cause of action at all, he, by reason of them, may prosecute it in our courts. They have no bearing on the primary question of existence of a cause of action, and as that is the question before us, we need not further advert to the fact of plaintiff's citizenship or defendant's domicile.

The contract was that plaintiff should serve the defendant in the capacity of a brakeman on its freight train between Birmingham, Alabama, and Meridian, Mississippi, and should receive as compensation a stipulated sum for each trip from Birmingham to Meridian and return. The theory is that the Employer's Liability Act became a part of this contract; that the duties and liabilities which it prescribes became contractual duties and liabilities, or duties and liabilities springing out of the contract, and that these duties attended upon the execution whenever its performance was required—in Mississippi as well as in Alabama—and that the liability prescribed for a failure to perform any of such duties attached upon such failure and consequent injury wherever it occurred, and was enforceable here because imposed by an Alabama contract notwithstanding the remission of duty and the resulting injury occurred in Mississippi, under whose laws no liability was incurred by such remission. The argument is that a contract for service is a condition precedent to the application of the statute, and that "as soon as the contract is made the rights and obligations of the parties, under the Employer's Act, became vested and fixed," so that "no subsequent repeal of the law could deprive the injured party of his rights nor discharge the master from his liabilities," &c., &c. If this argument is sound, and it is sound if the duties and liabilities prescribed by the act can be said to be contractual duties and obligations at all, it would lead to conclusions the possibility of which has not hitherto been suggested by any court or law writer, and which, to say the least, would be astounding to the profession. For instance: If the act of 1885 becomes a part of every contract of service entered into since its passage, just "as if such law were in so many words expressly included in the contract as a part thereof," as counsel insist it did, so as to make the liability of the master to pay damages from injuries to a fellow-servant of his negligent employee, a contractual obligation, no reason can be conceived why the law existing in this regard prior to the passage of that act did not become in like manner a part of every contract of service then entered into, so that every such contract would be deemed to contain stipulations for the non-liability of the master for injuries flowing from the negligence of a fellow-servant, and confining the injured servant's right to damage to a claim against his negligent fellow-servant— the former, in other words, agreeing to look alone to the latter. There were many thousands of such contracts existing in this country and England at the time when statutes similar to section 2590 of our Code were enacted, there were indeed many thousands of such contracts existing in Alabama when that section became the law of this State. Each of these contracts, if the position of plaintiff as to our statute being embodied into the terms of his contract so that its duties were contractual duties, and its liabilities contractual obligations to pay money can be maintained, involved the assurances of organic provisions, State and Federal, of the continued non-liability of the master for the negligence of his servants, notwithstanding the passage of such statutes. Yet these statutes were passed, and they have been applied to servants under pre-existing contracts as fully as to servants under subsequent contracts, and there has never been a suggestion even in any part of the common-law world that they were not rightly so applied. If plaintiff's contention is well taken, many a judgment has gone on the rolls in this State, and throughout the country, and has been satisfied, which palpably overrode vested rights without the least suspicion on the part of court or counsel that one of the most familiar ordinances of the fundamental law was being violated. Nay more, another result not heretofore at all contemplated would ensue. Contracts for service partly in Alabama might be now entered into in adjoining States where the common-law rule still obtains, as in Mississippi, for instance, where the servant has no right to recover for the negligence of his fellow, and the assumption of this risk under the law becoming, according to the argument of counsel, a contractual obligation to bear it, such contracts would be good in Alabama and as to servants entering into them, our statute would have no operation even upon negligence and resulting injury within its terms occurring wholly in Alabama. And on the other hand, if this defendant is under a contractual obligation to pay the plaintiff the damages sustained by him because of the injury inflicted in Mississippi, the contract could be of course enforced in Mississippi and damages there awarded by its courts, notwithstanding the law of that State provides that there can be no recovery under any circumstances whatever by one servant for the negligence of his fellow employee. We do not suppose that such a proposition ever has been or ever will be made in the courts of Mississippi. Yet that it should be made and sustained is the natural and necessary sequence of the position advanced in this case.

These considerations demonstrate the infirmity of plaintiff's position in this connection, and serve to show the necessity and propriety of the conclusion we propose to announce on this part of the case. That conclusion is, that the duties and liabilities incident to the relation between the plaintiff and the defendant which are involved in this case, are not imposed by and do not rest in or spring from the contract between the parties. The only office of the contract, under section 2590 of the Code, is the establishment of a relation between them, that of master and servant; and it is upon that relation, that incident or consequence of the contract, and not upon the rights of the parties under the contract, that our statute operates. The law is not concerned with the contractual stipulations, except insofar as to determine from them that the relation upon which it is to operate exists. Finding this relation the statute imposes certain duties and liabilities on the parties to it wholly regardless of the stipulations of the contract as to the rights of the parties under it, and, it may be, in the teeth of such stipulations. It is the purpose of the statute and must be the limit of its operation to govern persons standing in the relation of master and servants to each other in respect of their conduct in certain particulars within the State of Alabama. Mississippi has the same right to establish governmental rules for such persons within her borders as Alabama; and she has established rules which are different from those of our law. And the conduct of such persons toward each other is, when its legality is brought in question, to be adjudged by the rules of the one or the other States as it falls territorially within the one or the other. The doctrine is like that which prevails in respect of other relations, as that of man and wife. Marriage is a contract. The entering into this contract raises up certain duties and imposes certain liabilities in all civilized countries. What these duties and liabilities are at the place of the contract are determinable by the law of that place; but when the parties go into other jurisdictions, the relation created by the contract under the laws of the place of its execution will be recognized, but the personal duties, obligations and liabilities incident to the relation are such as exist under the law of the jurisdiction in which an act is done or omitted as to the legality, effect or consequence of which the question arises. . . .

The only true doctrine is that each sovereignty, state or nation, has the exclusive power to finally determine and declare what acts or omission in the conduct of one to another, whether they be strangers or sustain relations to each other which the law recognizes, as parent and child, husband and wife, master and servant, and the like, shall impose a liability in damages for the consequent injury, and the courts of no other sovereignty can impute a damnifying quality to an act or omission which afforded no cause of action where it transpired.

Questions and Comments

(1) Why should Alabama pay any attention at all to the law of Mississippi? Why should it ever apply any state's law but its own? Doesn't a court have an obligation to achieve a "just" result? And if Alabama's law (including its conflicts rules) tells it to apply the law of Mississippi to a case, doesn't it follow either that (a) Alabama has erred, because it should apply its own law, which is more just; or (b) Mississippi law is more just, and Alabama should change its own law?

Justice Cardozo answered these questions in the course of a famous articulation of the same vested rights theory employed in *Carroll*. In a case in which the question was whether a New York court should apply Massachusetts or New York wrongful death law to an accident that occurred in Massachusetts, Cardozo explained why Massachusetts law would normally govern:

A foreign statute is not law in this state, but it gives rise to an obligation, which, if transitory, follows the person and may be enforced wherever the person may be found. . . . [I]t is a principle of every civilized law that vested rights shall be protected. The plaintiff owns something, and we help him to get it. . . . Our own scheme of legislation may be different. We may even have no legislation on the subject. That is not enough to show that public policy forbids us to enforce the foreign right. A right of action is property. If a foreign statute gives the right, the mere fact that we do not give a like right is no reason for refusing to help the plaintiff in getting what belongs to him. We are not so provincial as to say that every solution of a problem is wrong because we deal with it otherwise at home.

Loucks v. Standard Oil Co., 224 N.Y. 99, 120 N.E. 198 (N.Y. 1918); *see also* Slater v. Mexican Natl. R.R., 194 U.S. 120, 126 (1904) (Holmes, J.) ("The theory of the foreign suit is that although the act complained of was subject to no law having force in the forum, it gave rise to an obligation, an *obligatio*, which like other obligations follows that person, and may be enforced wherever the person may be found.").

Are these convincing arguments? By assuming that the right has vested in another state, does Cardozo beg the question of what law creates the right? What benefit, if any, does the forum get from enforcing a foreign-vested right? Why is it important to the vested rights theory to insist that courts apply foreign vested rights but not foreign law? For the classic theoretical defense of the vested rights theory in the United States, *see* Beale, 1 *Conflict of Laws* 1-86 (1935). For classic criticisms of Beale's vested rights theory, *see* Cook, *The Logical and Legal Bases of the Conflict of Laws* (1942); Currie, *Selected Essays on the Conflict of Laws* (1963); Lorenzen, *Selected Articles on the Conflict of Laws* (1947).

(2) What should be the goals of a body of conflicts law? The traditional answer is, for the most part, uniformity. "The purpose of a conflict-of-laws doctrine is to assure that a case will be treated in the same way under the appropriate law regardless of the fortuitous circumstances which often determine the forum." Lauritzen v. Larsen, 345 U.S. 571, 591 (1952). Such uniformity has been equated with "fairness to the parties." Goodrich & Scoles, *Handbook of the Conflict of Laws* 5 (1964). But the answer of uniformity, though facile and traditional, is dubious: "After all, if the only purpose of choice-of-law rules is to make the result independent of forum choice, not only must there be choice-of-law rules, but also those rules must be uniform in each possible forum." Weintraub, *Commentary on the Conflict of Laws* 3 (2d ed. 1980).

The late Professor Currie suggested "[i]n all solemnity" that in certain cases the law of the state first in alphabetical order be applied. (In order to avoid discrimination and burdening the judges of the state lowest in order by making them determine foreign law all the time, he suggested that the inverse alphabetical order be used for transactions occurring in odd-numbered years.) Currie, *Selected Essays on the Conflict of Laws* 609 (1963).

It is clear, isn't it, that Currie's suggestion would achieve almost complete uniformity of result? (This is assuming, of course, that it will be non-controversial which states have enough contact that their laws should be on the list for consideration.) Moreover, predictability, the avoidance of forum-shopping, and ease of administration, three other goals sometimes mentioned, would be greatly enhanced.

What's so good about uniformity? If Missouri (or any other state) comes to a conclusion in a conflicts case that it thinks is the right and just result, what role should the desire for uniformity play? If uniformity is achieved by reaching the Missouri result, uniformity is merely superfluous. On the other hand, if Missouri is out of step with the results reached by other states, even after giving due deference to their reasoning, should it give up what is perceived as the just result in order to fall into line with the others? Wouldn't there have to be powerful arguments for uniformity in order to justify reaching what is seen as an unjust result?

It would seem, then, that there must be unarticulated goals of the conflicts system other than uniformity and its related concepts. Can we be any more specific about what those goals might be, other than to say that the court should reach a result that is "correct" or "just"? *See generally* Hay, *Flexibility Versus Predictability and Uniformity in Choice of Law*, 226 Recueil des Cours d'Academie de Droit International 285 (1991).

(3) A principle that may or may not be categorized as an ultimate goal of the conflicts system, but which pervades early conflicts cases, is that of territoriality: Generally speaking, a state has the right to control people and things located within its own borders.

A closely related—and less universally acknowledged—proposition is that states have the right to control the *effects* of people's behavior within their borders. For example, if *X* hits *Y* over the head with a baseball bat while in Missouri, it is reasonably clear that *X* may be subject to the criminal law of Missouri for that act. In many cases the law of Missouri will also be the only relevant law with respect to the civil effects of the act—but not always. Assume that *X* and *Y* are both citizens of Illinois, traveling into St. Louis only for shopping purposes. We might not be surprised to find that an Illinois court later considering the issue might apply Illinois law, rather than Missouri law, to the question whether one who kills a testator may take under the testator's will—especially if all the property to pass under the will is located in Illinois. Would Missouri even want its law to apply in such a case? Would the answer to such a question depend on whether it was Illinois or Missouri law that allowed a killer to profit from his own act? Should it matter whether or not Missouri would want its own law applied?

(4) The section of the Alabama Code analyzed in *Carroll* provided:

> When a personal injury is received by a servant or employee in the service or business of the master or employer, the master or employer is liable to answer in damages to such servant or employee, as if he were a stranger, and not engaged in such service or employment, . . . [w]hen such injury is caused by reason of the negligence of *any person in the service or employment of the master or employer*, who has the charge or control of any signal, points, locomotive, engine, switch, car, or train upon a railway, or of any part of the track of a railway.

Ala. Civ. Code §2590(5) (1886) (emphasis added). On its face, doesn't this provision apply to the facts of *Carroll*? After all, it extends the master's liability to torts caused by "any" fellow servant, and it contains no geographical limitation. Why did the court read the statute's first sentence as if it included the words "personal injury is received *in Alabama*"? Was this a fair reading of the Alabama legislature's intent? Did the Alabama legislature have the territorial "principles of private international or interstate law" in mind when it enacted the statute?

(Note that if the courts do not read some limiting principle into the statute, the statute would also apply to torts in Mississippi involving only Mississippi parties.) Or would the legislature have likely wanted the law to apply to people like Carroll—a citizen of Alabama, working for an Alabama railroad, entering a contract to do so in Alabama, and performing a good deal of the contract in Alabama? Do you think the legislature gave the choice-of-law question any thought at all? How should courts determine the geographical scope of a statute in the face of legislative silence?

(5) "The fact which created the right to sue, the injury . . . transpired in the State of Mississippi. It was in that State, *therefore*, necessarily that the cause of action, if any, arose. . . . " Why the "therefore"? Didn't the negligence equally create the right to sue, since an injury without negligence would not have been tortious? Which would you rather give up, your lungs or your heart? The "last act" may determine, of course, *when* the tort takes place (although not always) for such things as statute-of-limitations purposes.

If the court's reasoning is inadequate, how should you determine where a tort "occurs"? Can this question be answered without knowing why the place of occurrence supplies the governing law?

(6) What are the merits of the plaintiff's arguments that his contract with the defendant incorporated the Alabama statute? What is the court's answer to those arguments? "It is commonly said that existing laws at the time and place of the making of a contract enter into and form a part of the contract as fully as if expressly incorporated therein." *Williston on Contracts* §615 (3d ed. 1961). If the rule is applicable here, its effect may turn on two possible constructions of law: (a) The parties are in fact presumed to have intended the controlling law to be made part of their contract; or (b) regardless of their intentions, their contract will be interpreted to incorporate the law existing at the time of formation. If the first interpretation is correct, does it help Carroll? If the law of Alabama was to be incorporated into the contract, isn't it first necessary to interpret the law of Alabama—which the court decided did not apply to Mississippi accidents? On the other hand, if the second interpretation is correct and the incorporation rule is merely a fiction, imposed on the parties regardless of their true intent, should it be imposed regardless of where the accident occurred? Don't we need to know *why* the law was incorporated, despite the parties' intent, to know whether the rule would be applicable in a conflicts case?

Conceding, for a moment, that the contract may incorporate existing statutory law for conflicts purposes, why should the rule be, as Williston puts it, that the relevant laws are those "existing . . . at the time *and place* of the making of a contract"? If two Michiganders, both conducting business in Michigan, conclude a deal and sign a contract during a weekend at an Ontario hunting lodge, should the law of Ontario be presumed to be incorporated? Isn't it clear that the fiction of incorporation was designed without the subject of conflicts in mind and should not be mentioned further in this book?

But such is not to be. Consider the treatment given by another court to the question of what effect a statute should have on the interpretation of a contract. In Levy v. Daniels' U-Drive Auto Renting Co., 108 Conn. 333, 143 A. 163 (1928), the defendant had rented an auto in Connecticut, which by statute imposed vicarious liability on persons leasing cars for damages caused to others by the lessee. The lessee in *Levy* caused an accident in Massachusetts, which imposed no such liability on the lessor. The question was whether the law of Massachusetts, the place of the accident, or the law of Connecticut, the place of the rental, would apply. In deciding that the lessor was contractually obligated to the other party to the accident, the court said:

> If the liability of this defendant under this statute is contractual, no question can arise as to the plaintiff's right to enforce this contract. . . . The law inserted in the contract this provision. The statute did not create the liability; it imposed it in case the defendant voluntarily rented the automobile. Whether the defendant entered into this contract of hiring was his own voluntary act; if he did he must accept the condition upon which the law permitted the making of the contract.

108 Conn. at 333, 143 A. at 165.

So far we have talked about the contract theory as a means of avoiding the place-of-injury conflicts rule for torts. Assuming that the question is one of contracts, is it clear that Alabama law should control the contract, at least with respect to an accident occurring in Mississippi? The issue can probably be avoided by assuming that *if* it were clear that the contract was intended to incorporate the Alabama statute and make it applicable to Mississippi accidents, the contract law of Mississippi would probably recognize the cause of action.

(7) Note that when the place of the accident applies to the issue of rental car liability, companies renting cars in states that do not impose vicarious liability can suddenly find themselves subject to liability depending on the state where a lessee might happen to enter. Would that be a more satisfactory solution to the problem? Apparently Congress didn't think so. In 2005, it enacted the Graves Amendment, 49 U.S.C. §30106, which preempts state statutes like the one at issue in Connecticut. Under the Graves Amendment, car rental entities can no longer be held vicariously liable for lessee accidents. Federal statutes preempting state laws can eliminate choice-of-law problems within the United States but at the cost of preventing state experimentation with diverse legal solutions. As you read through the materials in the next few chapters, consider whether the benefits to federalism are worth the choice-of-law costs in each context.

(8) In the final paragraph of the court's opinion, a rather absolute rule is laid down with respect to whose law is to apply in cases like *Carroll*. Does the rule have an intuitive appeal? If so, what kinds of qualifications, if any, should be put on the rule? Should the *procedural* law of the place of injury apply? Including the size of the paper on which pleadings are typed? If the plaintiff in a tort case is a corporation and the forum state has a rule forbidding unregistered foreign corporations that do business in the state from using its courts (a common rule), should the more permissive rule of the state of injury apply to that issue?

Is there any way to characterize issues for which the law of the place of injury seems more appropriate, as opposed to those for which the law of the forum is more appealing?

(9) *Carroll* rules that Mississippi law applies because "[t]he fact which created the right to sue, the injury without which confessedly no action would lie . . . transpired in the State of Mississippi." 97 Ala. at 134, 11 So. at 806. The rule that the

applicable law in non-intentional torts is the law of the place where the injury occurred continues to be applied to similar circumstances. In Tolman v. Stryker Corp., 926 F. Supp. 2d 1255 (D. Wyo. 2013), the plaintiff broke his hip in an accident in Wyoming. He went to a hospital in Montana, where a doctor inserted a nail into his femur as part of the treatment. The nail broke when the plaintiff was in Wyoming, and he sued in Wyoming. The defendant (the manufacturer of the nail) claimed that Montana law should apply, under which the claim is time-barred. According to *Carroll*'s reasoning, which law should apply?

––––––––––––––––––––

Below (and throughout this chapter) are excerpts from the American Law Institute's Restatement of Conflict of Laws (1934). The Restatement's reporter and principal author, Harvard Law School professor Joseph Beale, was a proponent of the "vested rights" theory of which *Carroll* is an exemplar. While the Restatement gives a flavor of the traditional approach to choice of law in the American states, not all American jurisdictions embraced its principles in every respect.

Selections from the First Restatement of Conflicts, on Wrongs
§§377-379, 382, 384-387, 390-391, 398-399, 412, 421 (1934)

§377. The Place of Wrong

The place of wrong is in the state where the last event necessary to make an actor liable for an alleged tort takes place. . . .

NOTE: SUMMARY OF RULES IN IMPORTANT SITUATIONS DETERMINING WHERE A TORT IS COMMITTED

1. Except in the case of harm from poison, when a person sustains bodily harm, the place of wrong is the place where the harmful force takes effect upon the body. . . .
2. When a person causes another voluntarily to take a deleterious substance which takes effect within the body, the place of wrong is where the deleterious substance takes effect and not where it is administered. [Why?] . . .
3. When harm is caused to land or chattels, the place of wrong is the place where the force takes effect on the thing. . . .
4. When a person sustains loss by fraud, the place of wrong is where the loss is sustained, not where fraudulent representations are made. . .
5. Where harm is done to the reputation of a person, the place of wrong is where the defamatory statement is communicated. . . .

§378. Law Governing Plaintiff's Injury

The law of the place of wrong determines whether a person has sustained a legal injury. . . .

§379. Law Governing Liability-Creating Conduct

Except as stated in §382, the law of the place of wrong determines
(a) whether a person is responsible for harm he has caused only if he intended it, (b) whether a person is responsible for unintended harm he has caused only if he was negligent, (c) whether a person is responsible for harm he has caused irrespective of his intention or the care which he has exercised. . . .

§382. Duty or Privilege to Act

(1) A person who is required by law to act or not to act in one state in a certain manner will not be held liable for the results of such action or failure to act which occur in another state.

(2) A person who acts pursuant to a privilege conferred by the law of the place of acting will not be held liable for the results of his act in another state. . . .

ILLUSTRATIONS . . .

5. By the law of X, an attacked party may lawfully stand his ground and defend himself by killing if necessary; by the law of Y, he should retire without killing if it is safe to do so. A, in X, is attacked by B who apparently intends to kill A. A reasonably believes that the only way he can save his life without retiring is to shoot B. He stands his ground, shoots at B, misses him and hits C in state Y. If he shoots at B with reasonable care to avoid hitting third persons, he is not liable to C. . . .

COMMENT ON SUBSECTION (2) . . .

c. *Significance of privilege as basis for immunity*. The word "privilege" denotes the fact that conduct which, under ordinary circumstances, would subject an actor to liability, under particular circumstances does not subject him thereto (*see* Restatement of Torts, §10). It is necessary to distinguish between a situation in which an actor is not liable because of a privilege, and situations in which he is not liable because the policy of the law is not to impose liability for harm caused by a certain general type of conduct. Thus, one who intentionally shoots another is, unless privileged, liable for the harm caused. If the actor in such a case is privileged, he is not liable, but this is because of some particular circumstances which make the case exceptional. On the other hand, if a person while driving his car with due care strikes a pedestrian and injures him, he is not liable; but in this situation, the actor is immune from liability, not because of some particular circumstances which make the case an exception to the general rule, but because the general rule is that liability is imposed in such cases only when the actor has been at fault. This distinction is important in the Conflict of Laws because, as stated in §379, the general question of the liability-creating character of the actor's conduct is determined by the law of the place of wrong, while under the statement in Subsection (2) of this Section, the question of privilege is determined by the law of the place where the actor acts. . . .

[Question: Why is it any more significant that a state gives someone a "privilege" than it is that the policy of its law is not to impose liability for a certain type of conduct?]

§384. Recognition of Foreign Cause of Action

(1) If a cause of action in tort is created at the place of wrong, a cause of action will be recognized in other states.

(2) If no cause of action is created at the place of wrong, no recovery in tort can be had in any other state. . . .

§385. Contributory Negligence

Whether contributory negligence of the plaintiff precludes recovery in whole or in part in an action for negligent injury is determined by the law of the place of wrong.

§386. Liability to Servant for Tort of Fellow Servant

The law of the place of wrong determines whether a master is liable in tort to a servant for a wrong caused by a fellow servant. . . .

§387. Vicarious Liability

When a person authorizes another to act for him in any state and the other does so act, whether he is liable for the tort of the other is determined by the law of the place of wrong. . . .

§390. Survival of Actions

Whether a claim for damages for a tort survives the death of the tortfeasor or of the injured person is determined by the law of the place of wrong. . . .

§391. Right of Action for Death

The law of the place of wrong governs the right of action for death. . . .

COMMENT

. . .

b: It is the law of the place of the wrong (see §377) and not that of the place where the defendant's conduct occurs or the place of death, which governs the right.

[Question: Why is death not the "last event necessary to make the actor liable" for wrongful death?]

§398. Compensation Under Act of State of Employment

A workman who enters into a contract of employment in a state in which a Workmen's Compensation Act is in force can recover compensation under the Act in that state for bodily harm arising out of and in the course of the employment, although the harm was suffered in another state, unless the Act provides in specific words or is so interpreted as to apply only to bodily harm occurring within the state. . . .

[Question: Does this provision boil down to anything more than that the person can recover unless he can't? If not, what is the meaning of the words, "unless the Act . . . is so interpreted as to apply only to bodily harm occurring within the state"? *Cf.* the treatment of this issue in the *Carroll* case above.]

§399. Compensation Under Act of State of Harm

Except as stated in §401, a workman may recover in a state in which he sustains harm under the Workmen's Compensation Act of that state although the contract of employment was made in another state, unless the Act provides in specific words or is so interpreted as to apply only when the contract of employment is made within the state. . . .

§412. Measure of Damages for Tort

The measure of damages for a tort is determined by the law of the place of wrong. . . .

§421. Exemplary Damages

The right to exemplary damages is determined by the law of the place of wrong. . . .

2. Intentional Torts

Carroll involved an unintentional tort. Should the rules be different when the defendant's wrongful behavior is intentional? That question is considered in Bullard v. MRA Holding.

Bullard v. MRA Holding, LLC

292 Ga. 748, 740 S.E.2d 622, 41 Media L. Rep. 2708, 13 FCDR 876 (2013)

[Plaintiff, a 14-year-old from Georgia, exposed her breasts to two men who filmed her while on spring break in Florida. Defendants subsequently bought and used this image in a pornographic video without plaintiff's consent. Defendants claimed that Florida law applies because the video was shot in Florida. The court ruled that Georgia law applies because "the place of the wrong" is where the injury was sustained.]

MELTON, J.

This case is before us based upon questions certified to this Court by the United States District Court for the Northern District of Georgia regarding the availability and scope of an appropriation of likeness claim under Georgia law. [Plaintiff had initially brought this claim to the U.S. District Court. Although the District Court ruled that Georgia law controls, it certified this case to the Georgia Supreme Court because, among other reasons, it could not determine whether plaintiff's claim was viable under Georgia state law.] Because we conclude that such a claim is available to the plaintiff under the facts presented here, and because we conclude that such a claim is controlled by Georgia law even where, as here, some of the activities that ultimately gave rise to the claim took place in Florida, we outline the parameters of the claim below.

The alleged facts of this case as reported by the District Court indicate the following: In the spring of 2000, fourteen-year-old Lindsay Bullard exposed her breasts to two unknown men in a parking lot in Panama City, Florida. [Bullard, a middle school student from Georgia, was in Florida for spring break.] Bullard was aware that the men were videotaping her at the time and expressed no objection to being videotaped. The two men and Bullard had no discussion about what future use the men might make of the videotape. MRA Holding LLC, (hereinafter "MRA"), obtained the recording and included it in its *College Girls Gone Wild* video series. MRA also used a still photo of Bullard that was taken from the video clip and placed it in a prominent position on the cover of the video box for the *College Girls Gone Wild* video that it later marketed and sold nationwide. On that image, MRA blocked out Bullard's breasts and superimposed an inscription, "Get Educated!" in that block. The inscription arguably gave the appearance that Bullard was making this statement. MRA did not obtain Bullard's permission to use the video footage of her in the *College Girls Gone Wild* video or to use her photo on the video box cover. Television and internet advertisements were aired that incorporated Bullard's image. Bullard's image had no commercial value before appearing on the cover of the *College Girls Gone Wild* video. Bullard suffered humiliation and injury to her feelings and reputation as a result of the aforementioned use of her image.

Bullard sued MRA in the United States District Court for the Northern District of Georgia for, among other things, appropriation of her likeness. MRA moved for summary judgment, and, in order for the District Court to decide the motion with respect to Bullard's claim for appropriation of likeness, it certified the following questions to this Court:

Does Georgia law govern Bullard's appropriation of likeness claim when:

A. Bullard, whose domicile is in Georgia, has been videotaped in Florida;
B. when her clip has been included in a video including images of other such girls, and her image has been placed prominently on the cover of the marketing materials, with a statement arguably attributed to Bullard that she did not make;
C. when that video, along with Bullard's image and statement on the cover of the video, has been advertised nationally, including in Georgia, and when the video has been marketed and sold nationwide, including in Georgia; and
D. when the emotional injury to Bullard, such as humiliation, ridicule, and other negative consequences, has occurred in Georgia?
E. If Georgia law does not control, which state's law does govern the dispute in this case?

. . .

1. *Does Georgia law govern Bullard's appropriation of likeness claim?*

Yes. As an initial matter, because Bullard filed her lawsuit in a Georgia District Court, the Georgia federal court is to apply Georgia's conflict of laws rules. Klaxon Co. v. Stentor Elec. Mfg. Co., 313 U.S. 487 (1941) ("The conflict of laws rules to be applied by the federal court in [the forum state] must conform to those prevailing in [that] state['s] courts."). In this connection, for over 100 years, the state of Georgia has followed the doctrine of lex loci delicti in tort cases, pursuant to which "a tort action is governed by the substantive law of the state where the tort was committed." Dowis v. Mud Slingers, Inc., 279 Ga. 808, 809 (2005). See also id. at 811 ("The doctrine of lex loci delicti has served the resolution of conflict of laws issues in tort actions in [Georgia] for nearly 100 years"). The place where the tort was committed, or, "the locus delicti, is the place where the injury sustained was suffered rather than the place where the act was committed, or, as it is sometimes more generally put, it is the place where the last event necessary to make an actor liable for an alleged tort takes place." Risdon Enter., Inc. v. Colemill Enter., Inc., 172 Ga. App. 902, 903(1) (1984) (citation and punctuation omitted).

Applying the doctrine to this multi-state commercial appropriation of likeness claim, we conclude that the substantive law of Georgia governs MRA's potential liability. Although the initial video of Bullard was shot in Florida, MRA distributed Bullard's image throughout the United States, including in Georgia. Bullard lived and attended school in Georgia, where she would have sustained any injury that resulted from the distribution of her image. Since Georgia is the state "where the injury sustained was suffered," Georgia law controls here. See also Martin Luther King, Jr., Ctr. For Soc. Change, Inc. v. Am. Heritage Prods., Inc., 250 Ga. 135 (1982) (where plaintiff was domiciled in Georgia, Court applied Georgia law to claims arising from defendant marketing and selling plastic busts bearing Dr. Martin Luther King's likeness across the country).

[The court then ruled that the plaintiff has a cause of action based on Georgia law for appropriation of her image, that she may recover damages should a jury rule for her, and that she did not consent to distributing her images for commercial purposes.]

Certified questions answered.

All the Justices concur.

Questions and Comments

(1) The Georgia Supreme Court emphasizes that "for over 100 years, the state of Georgia has followed the doctrine of lex loci delicti in tort cases." 292 Ga. at 749. As of 2018, only nine states continue to adhere to the First Restatement approach to choice of law for tort cases. *See* Symeonides, *Choice of Law in the American Courts in 2018: Thirty-Second Annual Survey*, 67 Am. J. Comp. L. (forthcoming 2019). Articulate modern decisions justifying this approach include Spinozzi v. ITT Sheraton Corp., 174 F.3d 842 (7th Cir. 1999) (Posner, J.); Paul v. National Life, 352 S.E.2d 550 (W. Va. 1986), *infra* page 269; Fitts v. Minnesota Mining & Mfg. Co., 581 So. 2d 819 (Ala. 1991); and Winters v. Maxey, 481 S.W.2d 755 (Tenn. 1972).

(2) A defense from a different quarter may be found in Cavers, *The Choice-of-Law Process* (1965), based on a series of lectures at the University of Michigan. Cavers presents five imaginary cases and the opinions of various "judges," all prominent conflicts scholars. Each of the opinions was shown to the real-life professorial counterpart of the fictional judge and was revised to meet his reactions. In reaction, Professor Griswold's defense of the traditional system more or less boils down to three points:

(a) If the applicable law is not independent of the forum in which the action is brought, lawyers will not be able to advise their clients as to what course to pursue.

(b) It might be advantageous to plaintiffs to forum-shop or file multiple lawsuits.

(c) The notion of "law" is unitary, and a system that allows results to differ on the basis of forum is therefore not law.

Do these criticisms stand up to close inspection? Take the first defense. Presumably it is important for parties to know as much as possible about their prospects in court before they get to court. This allows planning and probably encourages out-of-court settlement. But how often will the plaintiff be able to obtain jurisdiction over the defendant in more than one or two states? And how often will the potential for differing results be realized—that is, won't courts from different states very often have the same opinion as to the just result, even if they abandon *lex loci*? And finally, if it is assumed that the plaintiff will choose the forum whose conflicts principles are most favorable to the plaintiff's position, isn't the only uncertainty remaining that of predicting what that particular forum will do? After a state has settled on the conflicts principles it prefers, is the uncertainty likely to be any greater than in any other kind of case?

(3) What's wrong with forum-shopping? We are all taught during our first year in law school that it is evil and that Erie Railroad v. Tompkins conquered it. But there are obvious differences, aren't there, between the kind of forum-shopping that *Erie* prevents (federal versus state court) and the kind that Professor Griswold would like to do away with? For one, *Erie* rested in part on the absence of lawmaking authority in the federal courts—that is, by applying a federal common law to cases without federal issues in them, the federal courts were making law,

even though the Constitution did not give the federal government power to make law in these areas (or, if it did, allocated that power to the Congress). But when the question is that of forum-shopping among states that have some connection with the underlying dispute, is there any question about the lawmaking authority of both states?

None of the above, of course, demonstrates that forum-shopping is good; rather a mere distinction is made between two types of forum-shopping. What are the arguments against interstate forum-shopping? It may be felt that the plaintiff has an unfair advantage by being able to choose the forum with the favorable law. But doesn't the very fact that one forum's law favors the plaintiff legitimate the plaintiff's position? Assume plaintiff chooses State *A*, with favorable law. Presumably State *A* adheres to its law because it thinks that law is best. Assume further that State *B* is another possible forum for the plaintiff, and that forum *B* has law that is unfavorable to the plaintiff. Should State *A* deliberately choose what it sees as the wrong result in order to discourage the plaintiff from suing there?

Perhaps the arguments above, however, are wide of the mark. On a statistical basis, across the United States, forum-shopping by plaintiffs to obtain more favorable controlling law should increase the number of times plaintiffs recover, without increasing the intrinsic merits of their cases. Thus, while State *A* in the argument above might view State *B*'s choice-of-law rule as wrong, but essentially a problem for State *B*, a nationwide viewpoint might see things in terms of systemic prejudices in favor of plaintiffs or defendants. Is there any way to choose between these two viewpoints?

Doesn't Professor Griswold's anxiety about the unitary nature of law arise not from our conflicts doctrines but from the fact that we have different political units that create law? Is this a fact to bemoan or to applaud?

(4) For very different but somewhat sympathetic accounts of a "rights-based" approach to choice of law, *see* Brilmayer, *Rights, Fairness, and Choice of Law*, 99 Yale L.J. 1277 (1989); Dane, *Vested Rights, Vestedness and Choice of Law*, 96 Yale L.J. 1191 (1987).

(5) Section 377 of the First Restatement of Conflict of Laws defines "the place of wrong" as "the state where the last event necessary to make an actor liable for an alleged tort takes place." The Georgia Supreme Court interprets the rule to mean that the place of wrong is "where the injury was sustained." 292 Ga. at 751. Is this an appropriate interpretation? Under the plaintiff's chosen cause of action (appropriation of likeness), didn't the "last event necessary" for the tort (the filming) occur in Florida? The court's interpretation could also incentivize plaintiffs to forum-shop by arguing that "the place where the injury is suffered" is "where the plaintiff files suit," because the injury is felt where the plaintiff is. For a decision interpreting *lex loci delicti* as the law of the place of the wrongful conduct instead of the place where the injury is sustained, *see* Marra v. Bushee, 317 F. Supp. 972 (D. Vt. 1970), *rev'd on other grounds*, 447 F.2d 1282 (2d Cir. 1971).

B. Contracts

Selections from the First Restatement of Conflicts, on Contracts

§§311-312, 314-315, 323, 325-326, 332-336, 340, 355, 358, 360-361 (1934)

§311. Place of Contracting

The law of the forum decides as a preliminary question by the law of which state questions arising concerning the formation of a contract are to be determined, and this state is, in the Restatement of this Subject, called the "place of contracting." . . .

COMMENT . . .

d. *Determination of "place of contracting."* Under its Conflict of Laws rules, in determining the place of contracting, the forum ascertains the place in which, under the general law of Contracts, the principal event necessary to make a contract occurs. The forum at this stage of the investigation does not seek to ascertain whether there is a contract. It examines the facts of the transaction in question only so far as is necessary to determine the place of the principal event, if any, which, under the general law of Contracts, would result in a contract. Then, and not until then, does the forum refer to the law of such state to ascertain if, under that law, there is a contract, although of course there normally will be a contract unless the local law of Contracts of the state to which reference is thus made differs from the general law of Contracts as understood at the forum. . . .

[Question: Why does the forum use the general law of contracts rather than its own law or the law of some other jurisdiction? Is the general law of contracts superlaw? What is the general law of contracts? Would it matter if the states involved include Saudi Arabia or the People's Republic of China?]

§312. Formal Contract

Except as stated in §313, when a formal contract becomes effective on delivery, the place of contracting is where the delivery is made.

COMMENT

a. Formal contracts are contracts under seal, recognizances and negotiable instruments (*see* Restatement of Contracts, §7), and other contracts which are given by statute the character of formal contracts. . . .

§314. Formal Contract Completed by Mail or Carriage

When a document embodying a formal contract is to be delivered by mail or by a common carrier, the place of contracting is where the document is posted or is received by the carrier.

§315. Formal Contract Delivered by Agent

When a document embodying a formal contract is delivered through an agent of the promisor, the place of contracting is where the agent delivers it.
[Question: Why this distinction between methods of delivery?]

§323. Informal Unilateral Contract

In the case of an informal unilateral contract, the place of contracting is where the event takes place which makes the promise binding.

ILLUSTRATIONS

1. An offer of reward for the arrest of a felon is published in state X. The felon is arrested in response to the offer, in state Y. The contract for reward is made in Y.
2. A father in state X promises his son $10,000 if he marries M. The son marries M in state Y. The contract for payment of the money is made in Y. . . .

§325. Informal Bilateral Contract

In the case of an informal bilateral contract, the place of contracting is where the second promise is made in consideration of the first promise.

ILLUSTRATION

1. A and B being in state X, A offers to buy B's horse for one hundred dollars, the offer to remain open for ten days. Five days later A meets B in state Y and B there accepts A's offer. The contract for the sale of the horse is made in Y.

§326. Acceptance Sent from One State to Another

When an offer for a bilateral contract is made in one state and an acceptance is sent from another state to the first state in an authorized manner the place of contracting is as follows:

(a) If the acceptance is sent by an agent of the acceptor, the place of contracting is the state where the agent delivers it;
(b) if the acceptance is sent by any other means, the place of contracting is the state from which the acceptance is sent. . . .

ILLUSTRATION

1. *A* in state *X* offers by mail to pay *B* in state *Y* $100 for a certain horse if *B* will agree to sell the horse. *B* mails a letter of acceptance in state *Z*. The letter is carried through the mails and delivered by a postman to *A* in *X*. The place of contracting for the sale of the horse is *Z*.

COMMENT . . .

b. *Acceptance by telegraph.* When an acceptance is authorized to be sent by telegraph, the place of contracting is where the message of acceptance is received by the telegraph company for transmission.

c. *Acceptance by telephone.* When an acceptance is to be given by telephone, the place of contracting is where the acceptor speaks his acceptance. . . .

§332. Law Governing Validity of Contract

The law of the place of contracting determines the validity and effect of a promise with respect to
    (a) capacity to make the contract;
    (b) the necessary form, if any, in which the promise must be made;
    (c) the mutual assent or consideration, if any, required to make a promise binding;
    (d) any other requirements for making a promise binding;
    (e) fraud, illegality, or any other circumstances which make a promise void or voidable;
    (f) except as stated in §358, the nature and extent of the duty for the performance of which a party becomes bound;
    (g) the time when and the place where the promise is by its terms to be performed;
    (h) the absolute or conditional character of the promise. . . .

§333. Capacity to Contract

The law of the place of contracting determines the capacity to enter into a contract.

COMMENT

a. *Distinction between capacity to make contract and capacity to transfer property.* There is a distinction between capacity to make a contract and capacity to transfer property. The capacity to transfer land is governed by the law of the state where the land is (*see* §216), but capacity to make a contract for the transfer of land is governed by the law of the place of contracting. So too, capacity to transfer a chattel is governed by the law of the state where the chattel is at the time of the conveyance (*see* §255), but capacity to make a contract for the transfer of a chattel is governed by the law of the place of contracting.

ILLUSTRATIONS

1. *A*, a married woman, contracts in state *X* to transfer to *B* land in state *Y*. By the law of *X*, a married woman has capacity to make such a contract; by the law of *Y*, she has no capacity to make such a contract, but she can transfer her land. The contract will be specifically enforced in a court of *Y*.

2. *A*, a married woman, contracts in state *X* to sell to *B* a horse then in state *Y*. By the law of *Y*, title to a chattel passes as the result of a valid contract to sell. By the law of *X*, a married woman has capacity to contract for the sale of a chattel; by the law of *Y*, she has not. Title to the horse passes to *B* who is obligated to pay for it according to the law of *X*.

§334. Formalities for Contracting

The law of the place of contracting determines the formalities required for making a contract.

COMMENT ...

b. *Statutes of frauds*. The requirements of writing may be a requirement of procedure or a requirement of validity, or both. If, for instance, the statute of frauds of the place of contracting is interpreted as meaning that no evidence of an oral contract will be received by the court, it is a procedural statute, and inapplicable in the courts of any other state (*see* §598). If, however, the statute of frauds of the place of contracting is interpreted as making satisfaction of the statute essential to the binding character of the promise, no action can be maintained on an oral promise there made in that or any state; and if the statute of frauds of the place of contracting makes an oral promise voidable, and the promisor avoids such a promise, the same result follows. If the statute of frauds of the place of contracting is procedural only and that of the forum goes to substance only, an oral contract will be enforced though it does not conform to either statute.

§335. Sealed Instruments

The law of the place of contracting determines whether an instrument alleged to be a contract under seal is effectively sealed; whether it is duly executed and delivered; whether it is valid without consideration, and if not whether consideration has been given.

§336. Negotiable Instruments

The law of the place of contracting determines whether a mercantile instrument is negotiable, whether it is duly executed and delivered, whether it is valid without consideration, and if not, whether consideration has been given. . . .

§340. Contracts to Transfer or to Convey Land

The law of the place of contracting determines the validity of a promise to transfer or to convey land. . . .

§355. Place of Performance

The place of performance is the state where, either by specific provision or by interpretation of the language of the promise, the promise is to be performed.

COMMENT

a. The place of performance is often fixed by the contract. If the place of performance is not stated in specific words in the contract, it must be determined by construction and interpretation. A contract may be made up of several promises, each of which has its own place of performance which is different from that of the other promises. . . .

§358. Law Governing Performance

The duty for the performance of which a party to a contract is bound will be discharged by compliance with the law of the place of performance of the promise with respect to:
    (a) the manner of performance;
    (b) the time and locality of performance;
    (c) the person or persons by whom or to whom performance shall be made or rendered;
    (d) the sufficiency of performance;
    (e) excuse for non-performance.

COMMENT

b. *Practical line separating question of obligation from question of performance.* While the law of the place of performance is applicable to determine the manner and sufficiency and conditions under which performance is to be made, it is not applicable to the point where the substantial obligation of the parties is materially altered. As stated in §332, Comment c, there is no logical line which separates questions of the obligation of the contract, which is determined by the law of the place of contracting, from questions of performance, determined by the law of the place of performance. There is, however, a practical line which is drawn in every case by the particular circumstances thereof. When the application of law of the place of contracting would extend to the determination of minute details of the manner, method, time and sufficiency of performance so that it would be an unreasonable regulation of acts in the place of performance, the law of the place of contracting will cease to control and the law of the place of performance will be applied. On the other hand, when the application of the law of the place of performance would extend to a regulation of the substance of the obligation to which the parties purported to bind themselves so that it would unreasonably determine the effect of an agreement made in the place of contracting, the law of the place of performance will give way to the law of the place of contracting. . . .

§360. Illegality of Performance

(1) If performance of a contract is illegal by the law of the place of performance at the time for performance, there is no obligation to perform so long as the illegality continues.

(2) If the legality of performance is temporary and the obligation of the contract still continues, whether the contract must be performed within a reasonable time after its performance becomes legal depends upon the law of the place of performance. . . .

§361. What Amounts to Performance

The law of the place of performance determines the details of the manner of performing the duty imposed by the contract.

ILLUSTRATIONS

1. *A* agrees to sell and *B* to buy goods to be inspected in state *X*. The law of *X* determines the method of inspection. . . .

Poole v. Perkins
126 Va. 331, 101 S.E. 240 (1919)

KELLY, J., delivered the opinion of the court.

On January 1, 1912, W. T. Poole and his wife F. D. Poole executed a joint promissory negotiable note to the order of Marvin Perkins. Poole and wife and Perkins at that time resided and were domiciled in the city of Bristol, Tennessee. More than a year after the execution of the note, but prior to the institution of this suit, all of the parties, makers and payee, became and since remained residents of and domiciled in Virginia. The note was dated, signed and delivered in Tennessee, but upon its face was payable at a bank in the city of Bristol, Virginia.

According to the laws of the State of Tennessee in force at the time of the execution and delivery of the note, and for some time thereafter, the contracts of a married woman were voidable and could not be enforced against her where there was a plea of coverture, but at the time of the institution of this suit the disability of coverture had been removed by statute in Tennessee so far as concerns the contracts of married women subsequent to the passage of the statute. This is a proceeding by notice of motion brought by Perkins against Mrs. F. D. Poole in the Circuit Court of Wythe county to recover judgment on the note. All matters of law and fact having been submitted to the court without the intervention of a jury, a judgment was rendered against her, and she thereupon obtained this writ of error.

There were other issues in the lower court, but the sole question before us is whether Mrs. Poole's common law disability of coverture at the time of the execution of the note can be successfully relied upon by her as a defense.

If the note had been made payable in Tennessee, it is clear that her plea of coverture would have been good. The reason and authority for this proposition are perfectly familiar and require no elaboration or citation. If the obligation can be enforced against her at all, it is because the note was payable in Virginia. Does the fact that it was so payable enable us to apply the law of this State in determining her capacity to make the contract? If so, it is conceded that she was liable, and that the judgment complained of is right.

It would be idle to say that the question is free from difficulty. There are substantial reasons for a difference of legal opinion and the authorities upon the subject are by no means in harmony. The exact question has never been decided in this State. It would be impossible in an opinion of reasonable length to review all of the authorities bearing upon the subject, and it would perhaps be unprofitable to do so if such a thing were feasible.

In the case of Freeman's Bank v. Ruckman, Judge Moncure announced the following general rule upon which there is practically no conflict of opinion:

> It is a general rule that every contract as to its validity, nature, interpretation and effect, or, as they may be called, the right, in contradistinction to the remedy, is governed by the law of the place where it is made, unless it is to be performed in another place, and then it is governed by the law of the place where it is to be performed.

This familiar and well settled rule, however, cannot be said to be conclusive of the instant case because as the same was applied by Judge Moncure, and as most commonly illustrated by decided cases, it does not relate specifically to the capacity of the parties to make a contract, but to the validity and effect of a contract made by concededly competent parties.

Prof. Raleigh C. Minor, in his excellent "Conflict of Laws," says at page 410:

> The only law that can operate to create a contract is the law of the place where the contract is entered into (lex celebrationis). If the parties enter into an agreement in a particular State the law of that State alone can determine whether a contract has been made. If by the law of that State no contract has been made, there is no contract. Hence, if by the lex celebrationis the parties are incapable

of making a binding contract there is no contract upon which the law of any other State can operate. It is void ab initio.

And the author in support of the text quotes from the opinion in Campbell v. Crampton, 2 Fed. 417, 423, as follows:

> Upon principle, no reason can be alleged why a contract, void for want of capacity of the party at the place where it is made, should be held good because it provides that it shall be performed elsewhere, and nothing can be found in any adjudication or text book to support such a conclusion. It is a solecism to speak of that transaction as a contract which cannot be a contract because of the inability of the persons to make it such.

Strong support for the opinion thus advanced is also found in [several cases].

In opposition to the above view is the following pronouncement by one of the most eminent of Virginia law writers, Prof. John B. Minor:

> The law which is to govern in relation to the capacity of parties to enter into a contract is much disputed by the *continental* jurists of Europe. In general, however, they hold that *the law of the party's domicile* ought to govern. But the doctrine of the common law is well established both in England and America that the capacity of parties to contract is with some few exceptions determined by the lex loci contractus—that is, the law of the place *with reference to which the contract is made*, which is usually the place where *it is made*, unless it is to be performed *in another place or country*, and then the law of that country.

We are disposed to accept the latter as the rule applicable to the instant case, for reasons which we shall now point out.

It is to be observed, in the outset, that with practical unanimity the authorities, even those relied upon by the plaintiff in error, hold that the disability of coverture arising from the law of the married woman's domicile does not follow her into other States, and that if she goes into another State than that of her domicile and makes a contract *valid by and to be performed in accordance with the* laws of such other State, she will be bound thereby, even though she would not have been competent to make the contract according to the laws of her own State. In such a case the law of the place where the contract is made will be enforced wherever the suit is brought, even in the State of her domicile, subject only to the exception that if the suit is brought in a jurisdiction whose law imposes upon married women a total incapacity to bind themselves by any contract whatever, then perhaps for reasons of public policy the contract will not be enforced. It follows, therefore, beyond question, that if Mrs. Poole had merely stepped across the State line between Bristol, Tenn., and Bristol, Virginia, and signed the note in the latter State, she would be held liable thereon in a suit brought in any State where a married woman can contract, including now the State of Tennessee.

It will be found, too, from an examination of the authorities last above cited, to which many others of like tenor and effect might be added, that most of them concede that the actual bodily presence of the contracting party is not necessary to make the contract valid according to the laws of some other State than that of the domicile. If, for example, in the instant case Mrs. Poole had delivered the note to Perkins by mailing or sending it to him in Virginia, then by the clear weight of authority she would have bound herself in accordance with the laws of the State of Virginia as fully as if she had actually crossed the State line and signed and delivered the note in that jurisdiction. This is unmistakably implied even in the New York case of Union National Bank v. Chapman, *supra*, so strongly relied upon by the plaintiff in error.

We are brought, therefore, to this question: If Mrs. Poole had actually come into Virginia and signed the note, or had sent it here for delivery and acceptance, would there have been any substantial legal difference between the case as thus supposed and the case as it actually exists? We think not. It may be stated as settled law that when parties make contracts which upon their face are to be discharged in a State other than that in which they are executed, they are presumed, in the absence of anything to the contrary, to have intended the law of the State of performance, the *lex loci solutionis*, to control, and thus, if intention can do so, to have voluntarily constituted the law of that State the law of the contract, or, as often otherwise expressed, the proper law or the governing law. So unanimous are the authorities on this proposition that those advocating the actual situs of the parties as the test of contractual capacity concede that if the intent in such cases is effective then they are in error and the *lex loci solutionis* must be regarded as the governing law.

The adoption of the intention of the parties to the contract as the true criterion is consistent with the reason which Prof. Minor assigns for his opinion that *the proper law* is the law of the place where the contract is actually signed. He says:

> It may be regarded as certain that if the party enters into a contract in the State of his domicile, though the contract is to be performed elsewhere, the proper law governing his capacity to enter into the contract is the lex domicilii no matter where the suit may be brought. But if the contract is entered into in a State other than the party's domicile, he has not the same right to claim the protection of his domiciliary law. He has voluntarily entered into another State and has there made an agreement with persons who are relying upon the law under which he is acting. To that law he has submitted himself when he makes the contract there, and a just comity will ordinarily demand that the sovereignty of that State over all acts done there should be respected in other States.

(Conflict of Laws, p. 145.) If the parties, by the mere act of signing in a State other than their domicile can give validity to a contract which would not be valid in their own State, and if the reason for this is that they are presumed to contract with reference to the law of such other State, it would seem to follow that the actual situs of the parties is only important as a factor in determining the law with reference to which they intended to contract. In this view, all that is needed to divest a married woman of her domiciliary incapacity is an intention sufficiently evidenced or expressed to contract with reference to the laws of a State in which the contract is valid, and, as we have just seen, where the contract, like the one involved in the instant case, provides upon its face for performance in a State whose laws will uphold it, such provision is alone sufficient to evidence an intention to bring the contract within the influence of the laws of the latter State [citing cases]. These cases did not involve the question of contractual capacity, but granting that the intention of the parties determines the proper law, the decisions here cited are conclusive of the proposition that the note in litigation, by providing for payment in Virginia, sufficiently expressed such intention. Citations to the same effect might be multiplied indefinitely. . . .

We conclude, therefore, that the note sued on in this case must be construed as having been executed with reference to the laws of the State of Virginia; that it became to all legal intents and purposes, so far as its validity is concerned, as truly a Virginia note as if it had been signed and delivered here; that by the laws of this State, Mrs. Poole could have legally executed the same; and that, therefore, the lower court was right in holding her liable.

The judgment is accordingly affirmed.

Linn v. Employers Reinsurance Corp.

392 Pa. 58, 139 A.2d 638 (1958)

Opinion by COHEN, J.

Plaintiff insurance brokers brought this action in law to require the defendant insurance company to account and pay to them commissions on insurance premiums received since 1953 from a New Jersey company. At the close of plaintiff's evidence, the trial judge entered a nonsuit which the court en banc refused to remove, and this appeal followed.

From the undisputed evidence it appears that in 1926 the plaintiffs were engaged in the insurance brokerage business in Philadelphia. In that year plaintiffs offered to place risks undertaken by the Selected Risks Insurance Company of New Jersey for a consideration of five per cent of all premiums collected by the defendant on such policies. Plaintiff Linn went to New York City to negotiate an agreement with one William Ehmann, an agent of the defendant. Ehmann stated that he would first have to obtain authority to accept the offer from the defendant's home office in Kansas City. He promised that he would communicate with the plaintiff "as soon as he could get word from Kansas City." Linn then returned to Philadelphia, and subsequently received a telephone call from Ehmann accepting the offer.

The defendant entered into the required treaty with the New Jersey company which, as modified and renewed, continues in effect. From 1926 until 1953 the defendant paid the plaintiffs the agreed upon commissions. But in 1953, the defendant notified the plaintiffs that it did not consider itself obligated further under the contract and that it would discontinue accounting to the plaintiffs for the premiums received from the New Jersey company.

On this evidence the trial judge found that the contract was made in New York, and applying the New York Statute of Frauds, held that the agreement was unenforceable thereunder because it was not to be performed within one year from the date it was entered into. Wherefore, the court concluded that the defendant was under no duty to account.

We recognize that the formal validity of a contract is determined by the law of the state in which the contract was made. Since the provisions of the Statute of Frauds relate to formal validity, it is to the statute of the place of contracting that we must refer.[3] It is therefore necessary for us to determine in which state the contract was made.

---

3. The rules embodied in the Pennsylvania Statute of Frauds are matters of substance, not procedure, and apply only to contracts made in Pennsylvania.

When a principal authorizes an agent to accept an offer made by a third party, as the defendant authorized Ehmann in the present case, the place of contracting is where the agent accepts the offer. In the case of acceptance by mail or telegraph, the act of acceptance is held to be effective where the acceptance was posted, or received by the telegraph company for transmission.

This court has not heretofore been required to determine the place where an acceptance spoken over the telephone is effective.

Professor Williston and the Restatement of Contracts take the position that a contract made over the telephone is no different from a contract made where the parties orally address one another in each other's presence. In the latter case the offeror does not have the risk of hearing an acceptance addressed to him, and a contract is formed only if the acceptance is heard. Consequently, the place of contracting is where the acceptance is heard and not where the acceptance is spoken. While we agree that this analysis represents a sound theoretical view, the reported cases which consider this issue are uniform in holding that by analogy to the situations in which acceptance is mailed or telegraphed, an acceptance by telephone is effective, and a contract is created at the place where the acceptor speaks. Restatement, Conflict of Laws, *supra*, §326, comment *c*. In fact, where the federal courts are charged with the duty of applying Pennsylvania law they have reached this conclusion.

We believe that in this day of multistate commercial transactions it is particularly desirable that the determination of the place of contracting be the same regardless of the state in which suit is brought. The absence of uniformity makes the rights and liabilities of parties to a contract dependent upon the choice of the state in which suit is instituted and thus encourages "forum-shopping." For this reason we choose to follow the established pattern of decisions and hold that acceptance by telephone of an offer takes place where the words are spoken.

Applying this principle to the facts before us, we conclude that the state where the contract was made is the state from which Ehmann telephoned the defendant's acceptance to Linn. However, contrary to the trial court's determination, there is no evidence in the record to indicate from which state Ehmann spoke. It is likely that he telephoned from his New York office, but it is also possible that he called from Kansas City or even Philadelphia; we cannot substitute speculation for evidence. The record of this case, therefore, must be remitted to the court below for determination of this question.

Judgment reversed and record remanded for further proceedings in accordance with this opinion. Costs to abide the event.

[Upon remand the case was tried, and on a second appeal, 153 A.2d 638 (1958), the court went over some of the same ground and added the following discussion of the determination of where the contract was made.] The court below submitted the issue of where the contract was made to the jury:

> The question is simply this: Was this contract completed and made in New York? Was the acceptance made in New York? Whether that acceptance be by the spoken word over the telephone to Mr. Linn or whether it was by an act of Mr. Ehmann which was in the nature of an acceptance, could only be construed as an acceptance.
>
> If the acceptance was not in New York but was at any other place, your verdict should be for the plaintiffs. If, however, it was in New York, your verdict must be for the defendant.

The jury returned a verdict for the plaintiffs upon which the court entered an order for the accounting.

. . . At least the jury, by its verdict, has determined that defendant's contention as to the applicability of New York law has not been sustained by the evidence. Testimony was presented to them adequate to support their finding that a telephone call of acceptance was made and that the said telephone call was not made in the State of New York. While it is true that plaintiffs have the ultimate burden of proof in convincing the jury that a valid contract was entered into, the burden of producing evidence to show that this contract was made in New York was alleged and necessarily assumed by defendant.* This burden was not met. Since it was not established that the laws of New York are applicable, the laws of the forum, Pennsylvania, are presumed to apply. Unlike the New York Statute of Frauds the various provisions in the Pennsylvania statute do not require that an agreement of this sort be in writing even if it is not to be performed within a year. It has been said that the Statute of Frauds, where applicable, is not a mere rule of evidence, but rather, is a limitation of judicial authority to afford a remedy. Our statutes do not so limit the authority of this court to grant a remedy in this case. . . .

In the light of the disposition we make of this case it is unnecessary for us to consider plaintiff's contention that even if the New York Statute of Frauds does apply its effect was waived by the admission of defendant's counsel that an oral agreement had been entered into.

Judgment affirmed.

Questions and Comments

(1) The *Poole* court's position seems to boil down to allowing the parties' intent to control resolution of the choice-of-law question. Why should intent control? What was the purpose of the common-law rule relied on by F. D. Poole as a defense against the obligation of her note? *Compare* Milliken v. Pratt, 125 Mass. 374, 382 (1878) (stating that "continental jurists" maintain that "laws limiting the capacity of infants or of married women are intended for their protection, and cannot therefore be dispensed with by their agreement; that all civilized states recognize the incapacity of infants and married women"). Is it likely that a law that voided a married woman's efforts to obligate herself on a promissory note was meant to be applicable, or not, depending on her intent? Wasn't the law intended to frustrate her intent? Note, however, that not all (or even most) state contract laws are "mandatory" in the sense of placing limits on party intent. To the contrary, many contract issues are governed by state laws viewed as "defaults" that apply unless the parties vary them in the contract. Is the distinction between default and mandatory rules of contract law relevant to intent-based theories of choice of law for contract? How? What are the advantages and disadvantages of allowing party intent to control contractual choice-of-law issues?

Assuming that intent is the appropriate criterion, how should courts determine which state's law the parties intended to choose? If the contract contains a

---

* What is the nature of the presumption the defendant must defeat?—Eds.

choice-of-law clause that recites that the contract is to be governed by the law of State *X*, the matter is not too difficult. But what if the contract contains no choice-of-law clause? Is it likely that the parties in *Poole* specifically intended Virginia law to operate by virtue of their choice of a Virginia bank as the place of payment? If the intent of the parties is to govern with respect to capacity, why not pick the state whose law upholds the contract? That is, in fact, the rule chosen by some jurisdictions, sometimes referred to as the *lex validitatis*. *See, e.g.*, Pritchard v. Norton, 106 U.S. 124 (1882).

(2) *Poole*'s intent-based approach for questions of contractual capacity is at odds with the First Restatement, which nowhere mentions the intent theory, but instead asserts that the "law of the place of contracting determines the capacity to enter into a contract." *See* Restatement §333 (reproduced *supra* pages 35-36). *Poole* thus makes clear that there were many different, and sometimes incompatible, strands to the traditional approach to choice of law for contracts. Beale, the author of the First Restatement, believed that party intent was impossible to discern with certainty. More fundamentally, he thought that party intent (including party intent as embodied in a choice-of-law clause) could not control because it would amount to "the power to do a legislative act"—a power that Beale believed private persons necessarily lacked. *See* 2 Beale, *A Treatise on the Conflict of Laws* §332.2 (1935). Do you agree with Beale? Is an intent-based rule inconsistent with a vested rights approach? Do you see why one committed to the "law of the place of the wrong" for torts might insist that the "law of the place of contract" governs contractual capacity issues? For an argument that the Restatement's approach to contracts is inconsistent with then-prevailing case law and theoretically unattractive, *see* Nussbaum, *Conflict Theories of Contracts: Cases Versus Restatement*, 51 Yale L.J. 893 (1942).

(3) Does *Poole*'s focus on intent suggest an important difference between choice of law for contract and for tort? How, if at all, should these differences translate into differences in the content of choice-of-law rules?

(4) A promissory note is said by the court to be "performed" at the place of payment. Although the opinion does not say so, presumably the Poole note was signed in return for the loan of money. Wasn't that lending by the lender the lender's performance? Why doesn't the court ask where the lender's performance took place? If Perkins lent the Pooles the money in Tennessee, should Tennessee law govern Perkins's obligations while Virginia law governs the Pooles' obligations?

(5) The *Poole* court cites another case at one point for the proposition that "every contract as to its validity . . . is governed by the law of the place where it is made, unless it is to be performed in another place, and then it is governed by the law of the place where it is to be performed." Wouldn't it be a trifle simpler to say, "[E]very contract as to its validity . . . is governed by the law of the place where it is to be performed"? Isn't that observation so obvious that it makes you a little suspicious of the court's confidence in a rule it won't state simply?

(6) If some ambiguity exists as to where performance occurred, or whose performance is critical, or whether the law of the place of contracting or performance is the applicable law, is the resulting uncertainty necessarily bad? Consider the fact that the court adjudicating F. D. Poole's obligation was a Virginia court and Virginia had no coverture rule; F. D. Poole was trying to get out of an obligation that she had once (presumably) voluntarily undertaken; and the law of Tennessee

had changed in the meanwhile. In Milliken v. Pratt, *supra*, the court hinted broadly that its decision was influenced by the fact that the law of Massachusetts, relied on there by a married woman to void her guaranty of her husband's debt, had been altered in the meanwhile by the legislature. Is a certain amount of flexibility in conflicts desirable in order to allow the court to reach the "right" result? If so, why not abandon the rules that need the oil of flexibility and use as rules (or method) the considerations that lead us to conclude that a particular result is "right"?

(7) In the *Poole* case the court said that it was clear that if Poole had signed the note in Virginia she would have been bound by Virginia law. It concluded that if she was going to be allowed to achieve that result by changing location, there was little reason to deny such an effect by having the parties determine the place of performance. If the court is speaking in practical terms, is its conclusion correct? How many parties far from the state line would actually make a trip elsewhere to settle a choice-of-law issue in signing their contracts?

(8) What was the purpose of the New York statute of frauds relied on by the defendant in the *Linn* case? Would its purpose vary with where the telephone call in question was made?

(9) Isn't it silly to make the entire result of an important business transaction like that in the *Linn* case turn on where the defendant's agent called from? Moreover, there are other possible problems arising from the *Linn* court's approach. Suppose that we had two scenarios of that telephone call, and suppose that the defendant's agent had in fact called from New York.

Scenario I

Linn: Bill, you ol' son of a gun, is that you?
Ehmann: None other, Walt.
Linn: What have you heard from K.C.?
Ehmann: It's in the bag—they said OK to your offer.
Linn: Hey, baby, that's great.

Scenario II

Linn: Good morning, Mr. Ehmann. How are you?
Ehmann: What's the matter, Walt? You aren't losing interest in the deal, are you?
Linn: Well . . .
Ehmann: Hey, come on, Walt. K.C. thinks it's a good idea. I could even offer you a free desk calendar every year.
Linn: How could I turn down a deal like that? Sold!
Ehmann: Hey, baby, that's great.

(Adapted from Cramton, Currie & Kay, *Conflict of Laws* 25 (3d ed. 1981).) Where was the contract in Scenario I formed? In Scenario II? How well will the participants remember which of these two possible 1926 conversations took place when they go to court in 1953? Does it make sense to ignore how the parties dealt with each other for 27 years and determine their dispute by the *form* of a 1926 telephone conversation? Or is it unfair to judge a rule that works well in many cases on the basis of a possibly unusual fact situation?

(10) Note that it is the place of contract formation, and not the place of performance, that the court says determines the statute of frauds issue. Why should that be?

(11) Recall that the "last act" doctrine for torts is that the governing law is that of the state where the last act necessary for a *cause of action* occurs, while the last-act approach for contracts zeroes in on the law of the state where the last act necessary for the formation of the contract occurs. Why not use the law of the place of breach in contracts cases, since that is the act necessary to give rise to a cause of action? It isn't necessary to do much violence to the language of the *Carroll* case to adopt a place-of-breach position for contracts that is "eminently sound in principle and upon logic":

> It is admitted, or at least cannot be denied, that [a contract without a breach] will not authorize or support a recovery. Up to the time [the breach occurred] no injury had resulted. For all that occurred in Alabama, therefore, no cause of action whatever arose. The fact which created the right to sue, the [breach] without which confessedly no action would lie anywhere, transpired in the State of Mississippi. It was in that State, therefore, necessarily that the cause of action, if any, arose; and whether a cause of action arose and existed at all or not must in all reason be determined by the law which obtained at the time and place when and where the fact which is relied on to justify a recovery transpired.

Fair?

An Exercise

On February 16, 1975, the *New York Times* carried an illustrated story on a case of food poisoning occurring on an international jet airliner. The following is the outline of events in the story:

(1) On February 1, a cook in Alaska handled ham to be served aboard the flight. The cook had blisters infected with staphylococcus. The ham was kept at room temperature for six hours during preparation.

(2) In Tokyo, 343 passengers boarded the flight. While the plane was flying toward Anchorage for refueling, the food trays were stored at 50° overnight. Staphylococcus multiplies at temperatures above 40° and produces a toxin that commonly causes food poisoning.

(3) The trays were loaded at Anchorage, and the plane took off for Copenhagen, its next stop.

(4) The trays were heated in a 300° oven for 15 minutes, a treatment that will not destroy the toxin, and the passengers were served. Those who ate the contaminated food began to experience the symptoms of food poisoning as the plane approached Copenhagen.

(5) In Copenhagen, 144 passengers disembarked ill. The rest flew on to Paris. Another 51 of these later became ill.

If Smith (a) arranged a tour of Japan by telephone from Michigan through American Express in New York and left from Detroit Metropolitan Airport for Japan, (b) arranged while she was in Tokyo, through the American Express office there, to take a different flight and include Europe in her travels, (c) boarded in Tokyo, (d) ate the contaminated food, which was loaded in Anchorage, while flying over Canada, (e) landed in Copenhagen, where she began to feel ill but refused medical attention, and (f) continued on to Paris, where she became violently ill and died:

(1) Whose law would determine whether an action for wrongful death would be available?

(2) Whose law would determine whether negligence was a necessary part of the cause of action or whether strict liability would apply?

(3) Whose law would apply to determine whether Smith's refusal of medical assistance in Copenhagen constituted contributory negligence? Whose law would determine whether contributory negligence was a valid defense?

(4) If an action is brought by Smith's estate for violation of an implied provision of her contract of passage that she would be transported safely, whose law would apply to determine whether the airline's behavior constituted proper performance of its contract?

(5) Whose law would determine, in a contract action, whether Smith's refusal of medical assistance constituted a failure to mitigate damages, limiting her estate's recovery?

(6) Whose law should determine whether the proper action is one in tort or in contract? If both are permitted, what should be done if the applicable tort law disallows recovery, while the applicable contract law (of a different jurisdiction) allows recovery?

C.   Domicile

Selections from the First Restatement of Conflicts, on Domicile
§§9-16, 18-21, 23, 25, 27, 41 (1934)

§9. Domicil

Domicil is the place with which a person has a settled connection for certain legal purposes, either because his home is there, or because that place is assigned to him by the law.

§10. Domicil by What Law Determined

(1) A question of domicil as between the state of the forum and another state is determined by the law of the forum.

(2) A question of domicil as between one or another of several states other than the forum, the law of each which differs from that of the other and from that of the forum, is determined by the law of the forum.

§11. One and Only One Domicil

Every person has at all times one domicil, and no person has more than one domicil at a time.

§12. Relation Between Domicil and Home

Except as stated in §§17 and 26 to 40, relating to domicil in a vehicle and to domicil by operation of law, when a person has one home and only one home, his domicil is the place where his home is.

§13. Home Defined

A home is a dwelling place of a person, distinguished from other dwelling places of that person by the intimacy of the relation between the person and the place.

§14. Domicil of Origin

(1) The domicil of origin is the domicil assigned to every child at its birth.

(2) Subject to the rule stated in §32 pertaining to divorce or separation of the parents, if the child is the legitimate child of its father, the domicil of the father at the time of its birth is assigned to it; if the child is not the legitimate child of its father, or is posthumous, the domicil assigned is that of its mother at the time of birth.

(3) Upon failure of proof of the domicil of the parent at the time of the child's birth, a court may accept as the domicil of origin the place to which a person can earliest be traced.

§15. Domicil of Choice

(1) A domicil of choice is a domicil acquired, through the exercise of his own will, by a person who is legally capable of changing his domicil.

(2) To acquire a domicil of choice, a person must establish a dwelling-place with the intention of making it his home.

(3) The fact of physical presence at a dwelling-place and the intention to make it a home must concur; if they do so, even for a moment, the change of domicil takes place.

(4) A person can acquire a domicil of choice only in one of three ways:

   (a) having no home, he acquires a home in a place other than his former domicil;

   (b) having a home in one place, he gives it up as such and acquires a new home in another place;

   (c) having two homes, he comes to regard the one of them not previously his domicil as his principal home.

§16. Requisite of Physical Presence

To acquire a domicil of choice in a place, a person must be physically present there; but a home in a particular building is not necessary for the acquisition of a domicil.

§18. Requisite of Intention

A person cannot change his domicil by removal to a new dwelling-place without an intention to make the new dwelling place his home.

§19. Nature of Intention Required

The intention required for the acquisition of a domicil of choice is an intention to make a home in fact, and not an intention to acquire a domicil.

§20. Present Intention

For the acquisition of a domicil of choice the intention to make a home must be an intention to make a home at the moment, not to make a home in the future.

§21. Presence Under Compulsion

A person cannot acquire a domicil of choice by any act done under legal or physical compulsion.

§23. Continuing Quality of Domicil

A domicil once established continues until it is superseded by a new domicil.

§25. Domicil in Dwelling-House Cut by Boundary Line

Where a person has his home in a dwelling-house which is situated upon a dividing line between political divisions of territory, his domicil is within that territorial division in which the preponderant part of his dwelling-house is situated; if there is no preponderance, the domicil is in the territorial division in which the principal entrance to the house is situated.

§27. Domicil of Married Woman

Except as stated in §28, a wife has the same domicil as that of her husband.

§41. Domicil of Corporation

A corporation is domiciled in the state where it was incorporated, and cannot acquire a domicil outside that state.

White v. Tennant

31 W. Va. 790, 8 S.E. 596 (1888)

SNYDER, J.

This is a suit brought December, 1886, in the Circuit Court of Monongalia county by William L. White and others against Emrod Tennant, administrator of Michael White deceased and Lucinda White, the widow of said Michael White, to set aside the settlement and distribution made by the administrator of the personal estate of said decedent, and to have the same settled and distributed according to the laws of the State of Pennsylvania, which State it is claimed was the domicile of said decedent, who died in this State intestate. On October 28, 1887, the court entered a decree dismissing the plaintiff's bill, and they have appealed.

The sole question presented for our determination is, whether the said Michael White at the time of his death, in May, 1885, had his legal domicile in this State or in the State of Pennsylvania. It is admitted to be the settled law, that the law of the State, in which the decedent had his domicile at the time of his death, will control the succession and distribution of his personal estate. Before referring to the facts proved in this cause, we shall endeavor to determine what in law is meant by "domicile."

Dr. Wharton says: "'Domicile' is a residence acquired as a final abode. To constitute it there must be (1) residence, actual or inchoate; (2) the nonexistence of any intention to make a domicile elsewhere." Whart. Confl. Law §21. . . . Two things must concur to establish domicile—the fact of residence, and the intention of remaining. These two must exist, or must have existed, in combination. There must have been an actual residence. The character of the residence is of no importance; and, if domicile has once existed, mere temporary absence will not destroy it, however long continued. The original domicile continues until it is fairly changed for another. It is a legal maxim that every person must have a domicile somewhere; and he can have but one at a time for the same purpose. From this it follows that one can not be lost or extinguished until another is acquired. When one domicile is definitely abandoned and a new one selected and entered upon, length of time is not important; one day will be sufficient, provided the *animus* exists. Even when the point of destination is not reached, domicile may shift *in itinere*, if the abandonment of the old domicile and the setting out for the new are plainly shown. . . . A change of domicile does not depend so much upon the intention to remain in the new place for a definite or indefinite period as upon its being without an intention to return. . . . A domicile once acquired remains until a new one is acquired elsewhere, *facto et animo*. Story Confl. Law, §47.

The material facts in the case at bar are as follows: [In 1885, Michael White, a lifelong West Virginia domiciliary, sold his farm in West Virginia. Michael had made arrangements with his family to move to a house on a 40-acre tract in Pennsylvania that was part of a larger family estate the main part of which, including the family mansion, was in West Virginia. On April 2, 1885, Michael, along with his wife Lucinda and their personal possessions, left the West Virginia home "with the declared intent and purpose of making the Pennsylvania house his home that evening." They arrived at the Pennsylvania house by sundown and unloaded their goods and stock. But because the house was cold and damp, and because Lucinda was feeling unwell, the couple returned to the mansion in West Virginia to spend the evening. When Lucinda White's illness turned out to be typhoid fever, Michael stayed at the West Virginia mansion to care for her, returning daily to the Pennsylvania home to look after it and care for the stock. Within two weeks Michael himself contracted typhoid fever and died intestate in the West Virginia mansion. Lucinda recovered, and the defendant, Emrod Tennant, Lucinda's father, administered Michael's estate in West Virginia and distributed the estate in accordance with West Virginia law, under which a widow received the decedent's entire personal estate. If the estate had been distributed under Pennsylvania law, the wife would receive only one-half of the estate, and Michael's brothers and sisters—the plaintiffs—would have received the other half.]

As the law of the State, in which the decedent had his domicile at the time of his death, must govern the distribution of his estate, the important question is, where, according to the foregoing facts, was the domicile of Michael at the time of his death? It is unquestionable, that prior to the 2d day of April, 1885, his domicile was and had been in the State of West Virginia. Did he on that day or at any subsequent day change his domicile to the State of Pennsylvania?

The facts in this case conclusively prove, that Michael White, the decedent, abandoned his residence in West Virginia with the intention and purpose not only of not returning to it, but for the expressed purpose of making a fixed place in the State of Pennsylvania his home for an indefinite time.

This fact is shown by all the circumstances as well as by his declarations and acts. He had sold his residence in West Virginia and surrendered its possession to the purchaser, and thereby made it impossible for him to return to it and make it his home. He rented a dwelling in Pennsylvania, for which he had no use except to live in and make it his home. In addition to all this, he had moved a part of his household goods into this house, and then, on the 2d of April, 1885, he with his family and the remainder of his goods and stock finally left his former home and the State of West Virginia, and moved into the State of Pennsylvania to his house in that State, and there put his goods in the house, and turned his stock loose on the premises. At the time he left his former home on that morning, and while he was on the way to his new home, his declared purpose and intention were to make that his home from that very day, and to occupy it that night. He arrived in Pennsylvania and at his new home with that intention; and it was only after he arrived there and for reasons not before known, which had no effect to change his purpose of making that his future home, that he failed to remain there from that time. There was no change in his purpose, except that after he arrived at his new home and unloaded and left his property there, he concluded on account of the condition of the house and the illness of his wife, that it would be better to go with his wife to remain one night with his relatives and return the next morning.

When he left his former home without any intention of returning and in pursuance of that intention did in fact move with his family and effects to his new home with the intention of making it his residence for an indefinite time, it is my opinion, that, when he and his wife arrived at his new home, it became *eo instanti* his domicile, and that his leaving there under the circumstances with the intention of returning the next day did not change the fact. The concurrence of his intention to make the Pennsylvania house his permanent residence with the fact, that he had actually abandoned his former residence and moved to and put his goods in the new one, made the latter his domicile. According to the authorities hereinbefore referred to he must of necessity have had a domicile somewhere. If he did not have one in Pennsylvania, where did he have one? The fact, that he left the Pennsylvania house, after he had moved to it with his family and goods, to spend the night, did not revive his domicile at his former residence on Day's run, because he had sold that, and left it without any purpose of returning there. By going from his new home to the house of his relatives to spend the night he certainly did not make the house thus visited his domicile; therefore, unless the Pennsylvania house was on the evening of April 2, 1885, his domicile, he was in the anomalous position of being without a domicile anywhere, which, as we have seen, is a legal impossibility; and, that house having become his domicile, there is nothing in this case to show, that he ever did in fact change or intend to change it or to establish a domicile elsewhere.

It follows, therefore, that that house remained his domicile up to and at the time of his death; and, that house being in the State of Pennsylvania, the laws of that State must control the distribution of his personal estate notwithstanding the fact, that he died in State of West Virginia. For these reasons the decree of the Circuit Court must be reversed, and the cause must be remanded to that court to be there further proceeded in according to the principles announced in this opinion and the rules of courts of equity.

Rodriguez Diaz v. Sierra Martinez

853 F.2d 1027 (1st Cir. 1988)

LEVIN H. CAMPBELL, C.J.

Plaintiff Wilfredo Rodriguez Diaz (Rodriguez Diaz) appeals from an order of the United States District Court for the District of Puerto Rico dismissing his complaint for negligence and medical malpractice for lack of diversity jurisdiction. Rodriguez Diaz brought this action in the district court following a motor vehicle accident in Puerto Rico when he was 17 years of age. All the defendants reside in Puerto Rico. However, between the time of the accident and the commencement of this action, Rodriguez Diaz moved from his family's home in Puerto Rico to New York, and attained his 18th birthday. He then sued in the United States District Court for the District of Puerto Rico, on his own behalf and through his parents as next friends, alleging that he is a citizen of New York and that there is diversity of citizenship under 28 U.S.C. §1332 (1982).

I

The facts relevant to the jurisdictional issue are these: On November 21, 1984, Rodriguez Diaz, while operating a motorcycle in Caguas, Puerto Rico, was in a collision with an automobile driven by Marcelo Sierra Martinez. Rodriguez Diaz suffered bodily injuries. He was immediately taken to the Hospital Regional de Caguas, from where he was transferred to the Centro Medico for emergency treatment. Rodriguez Diaz alleges in the present complaint that the treatment he received at the Centro Medico caused him to suffer a massive bone infection and aggravation of a leg injury. From Centro Medico he was transferred to Hospital General San Carlos where he alleges he also received improper treatment. Sometime later, Rodriguez Diaz was transferred to a hospital in New York City. He alleges he was living in New York at the time he brought this action in the United States District Court for the District of Puerto Rico. He further alleges in his complaint that he intends to remain in New York and make it his permanent home, and that he is now domiciled there. Rodriquez Diaz had turned 18 by the time he brought this action.[1] His parents were and still are residents and domiciliaries of Puerto Rico, where the age of majority is 21. P.R. Laws Ann. tit. 31, §971 (1967).

The defendants in the action brought by Rodriguez Diaz were the driver of the automobile, Sierra Martinez, and two Puerto Rico hospitals, all of whom are residents and domiciliaries of Puerto Rico. The defendants moved in the United States District Court for the District of Puerto Rico where the action was brought to dismiss the complaint for lack of diversity jurisdiction. The district court concluded that, under Puerto Rico law, Rodriguez Diaz is a minor, and therefore, his domicile is that of his parents. Ruling that as a matter of law Rodriguez Diaz's domicile at the time of the filing of this action was Puerto Rico, the court dismissed the complaint for lack of diversity. This appeal followed.

In its decision, the district court observed that, for purposes of diversity jurisdiction under 28 U.S.C. §1332(a)(1), state citizenship and domicile are equivalents. The court also noted that in a diversity case the capacity of a person to sue or be sued is determined by the law of the state of the litigant's domicile. Fed R. Civ. P. 17(b). The court then made certain observations crucial to its analysis. These were that the citizenship of a minor was the citizenship of his parents, and that the latter's domicile determined whether the minor had become emancipated so that he could establish a domicile of choice elsewhere. On the basis of the foregoing, the district court concluded that the law of Puerto Rico—the home of Rodriguez Diaz's parents—controlled the issue of Rodriguez Diaz's present domicile. As under Puerto Rico law plaintiff was still a minor, being under 21 at the time of suit, and as he was unemancipated under Puerto Rico law, he could not establish a domicile of choice outside Puerto Rico. It followed that he was still a domiciliary of Puerto Rico, and that, therefore, there was no diversity of citizenship.

II

While the case is close, we disagree with the district court's conclusion that the domicile of Rodriguez Diaz's parents—Puerto Rico—is the jurisdiction whose law must necessarily determine his capacity to acquire a domicile of choice.

---

1. The age of majority in New York is 18. N.Y. Civ. Prac. L. & R. 105(j) (Supp. 1988).

We begin with certain generally accepted principles: As the lower court correctly noted, state citizenship[2] for diversity purposes is ordinarily equated with domicile. A person's domicile "is the place where he has his true, fixed home and principal establishment, and to which, whenever he is absent, he has the intention of returning." Domicile generally requires two elements: 1) physical presence in a state, and 2) the intent to make such a state a home. It is the domicile at the time the suit is filed which controls, and the fact that the plaintiff has changed his domicile with the purpose of bringing a diversity action in federal court is irrelevant. Thus, except for the possible effect of his being a minor under Puerto Rico law, plaintiff's settling in New York with the requisite domiciliary intent would make him a citizen of New York and entitle him to pursue this action.

The district court ruled that since plaintiff was under 21, the age of majority in Puerto Rico, he was a minor as a matter of law, and as such he could have only one domicile, that of his parents, which in this case is Puerto Rico. It so ruled even though the age of majority in New York is 18, so that, in the eyes of New York, plaintiff could acquire a personal domicile of his own there. We shall assume for purposes of resolving the legal issue raised in this appeal that New York is plaintiff's "true, fixed home."[3] . . . The question before us is whether this is enough for plaintiff to have acquired a New York domicile for diversity jurisdiction purposes.

The parties and the district court have framed the issue as one of choice of law: which law is applicable, Puerto Rico law or New York law. It is a general principle of common law, recognized also in Puerto Rico, that the domicile of an unemancipated minor is ordinarily that of his parents. The age of majority in Puerto Rico is 21, while in New York it is 18. Plaintiff was 18 when he filed this action in the United States District Court for the District of Puerto Rico. Depending on which law is applied, the argument goes, Rodriguez Diaz will be treated as an adult or as a minor, with the capacity or lack of capacity to establish his own independent domicile. Plaintiff argues that we have to apply New York law, because that was his "domicile" at the time the action was filed. Not surprisingly, defendants argued, and the district court agreed, that whether Rodriguez

---

2. Section 1332(a)(1) provides,

The district courts shall have original jurisdiction of all civil actions where the matter in controversy exceeds the sum or value of $10,000, exclusive of interest and costs, and is between—(1) citizens of different States; . . .

Section 1332(d) provides,

The word "States" as used in this section includes the Territories, the District of Columbia, and the Commonwealth of Puerto Rico.

3. We emphasize, however, that the district court did not make a finding that Rodriguez Diaz (assuming he had the legal capacity to obtain a New York domicile) actually met the elements necessary to acquire a domicile there. To the extent there may be a genuine issue of fact as to plaintiff's "true, fixed home" and actual intention, our present assumption, arguendo, that his presence in New York meets these requirements, should not be taken as a final resolution of that issue. The only issue the district court addressed, and the only issue now before us, is whether, for diversity purposes, Rodriguez Diaz could have a domicile separate from that of his parents. We leave open the factual issue of whether plaintiff actually met the elements necessary to acquire a domicile of choice in New York.

Diaz was an adult with capacity to establish his domicile of choice is governed by Puerto Rico law.

As we see it, resolution of the issue before us does not and should not turn solely upon a conflicts of laws analysis. Although federal courts have to apply the choice of law rules of the forum to determine the substantive law in diversity cases, the "determination of litigant's state citizenship for purposes of section 1332(a)(1) is controlled by federal common law, not by the law of any state." The issue of what substantive law applies in a diversity case "is surely a different problem from that of whether a litigant should have access to federal court, and it does not conduce to clarity of analysis to suppose that the same answers will suffice for different questions." . . . That does not mean that state law and state conflicts rules regarding domicile should be ignored. At very least, they are "useful in providing basic working definitions." Stifel v. Hopkins, 477 F.2d 1116, 1120 (6th Cir. 1973). However, as the Sixth Circuit pointed out in *Stifel*, the considerations undergirding state choice-of-law rules have often been "developed in such diverse contexts as probate jurisdiction, taxation of incomes or intangibles, or divorce laws." *Id*. Choice-of-law formulae, therefore, cannot be the sole guideposts when determining, for federal diversity purposes, whether a party is domiciled in one or another state. *Id*. at 1126. The ultimate decision must be such as will best serve the aims of the federal diversity statute and the perspectives of a nationwide judicial system.

III

In the case at bar, the district court noted that in a suit brought by the next friend, the minor's domicile was controlling for diversity purposes. The court went on to state,

> Under the common law, the citizenship of a minor is the citizenship of his parents, and to determine whether the minor has become emancipated so that he may establish a domicile of choice, we look to the law of the state of the citizenship of his parents.

After noting the dilemma caused by the fact Rodriguez Diaz had achieved majority status in New York, his present home, at age 18, while remaining a minor under Puerto Rico law, the court rejected plaintiff's argument that he had the capacity to acquire a domicile of choice in New York. The court stated, "We have already concluded that the law of Puerto Rico controls the issue of Wilfredo's [Rodriguez Diaz's] domicile."

The district court went on to show that, by Puerto Rico's standards, plaintiff was unemancipated, given Puerto Rico's strict civil law requirement that emancipation occur by formal notarized document.

The difficulty with this rationale, as we see it, lies in the court's basic premise that the law of Puerto Rico controls. If Rodriguez Diaz were clearly a minor (under, say, both New York and Puerto Rico law), the court's analysis would be hard to fault. The domicile of a minor is commonly regarded as that of his parents; as Rodriguez Diaz's parents were domiciled in Puerto Rico, the law of Puerto

Rico would ordinarily be controlling as to the means whereby, being a minor, he could be emancipated and so become free to acquire a domicile of choice.[4]

The problem here, however, is that the question is not whether, as a minor, plaintiff was emancipated, but whether *he is a minor*. That, in turn, depends upon a determination of where he is domiciled, the ultimate question. We do not, therefore, find the district court's analysis persuasive.

This is not to say that Puerto Rico may not properly believe that the interest it has in its own citizens includes a legitimate concern as to the age at which a minor child reaches majority. Whether and when a person has legal capacity to, among other things, sue in Puerto Rico's own courts, make contracts, dispose of property, and sustain himself without parental support or reciprocal duty owed to his parents, are all matters properly within the state's province. However, local interests of this character are not in issue here. Rodriguez Diaz's right of access to a federal court is "one uniquely of federal cognizance." Ziady v. Curley, 396 F.2d [873 (4th Cir. 1968)] at 874; and since Rodriguez Diaz is now physically present in New York, which regards him, at 18, as having the capacity to be its domiciliary, we must weigh a ruling that would extend Puerto Rico's less favorable policy towards 18 year olds against one that would accord to plaintiff the mature status he enjoys under the law of the state in which he now resides.

In any event, the court below erred in assuming at the very outset of its inquiry that Rodriguez Diaz was a minor and, on that basis, invoking the law of his parents' domicile in preference to that of his present physical residence, which does not view him as a minor.

A similar logical difficulty occurs when we turn to the alternative approaches urged by appellees. For example, appellees point to Section 9 of the Puerto Rico Civil Code providing that,

> The laws relating to family rights and obligations or to the status, condition and *legal capacity* of persons, shall be binding upon the citizens of Puerto Rico, although they reside in a foreign country.

P.R. Laws Ann. tit. 31, §9 (1967) (emphasis supplied). Appellees argue that this article provides that the issue of plaintiff's legal capacity is governed by Puerto

---

4. We agree that, ordinarily, if a person is under 18, federal courts should follow the common law principle that he is incapable of choosing his own domicile. There is a general understanding that a person under 18 lacks the full capacity to conduct his life as he will. The years between 18 and 21, however, are currently a twilight zone. The majority of the states have adopted 18 as the age of majority. . . . A person 18 or older has the constitutional right to vote in federal and state elections. U.S. Const. amendment XXVI. Nonetheless, some states, like Puerto Rico, still consider a person under 21, but 18 or older, to be incapable (unless formally emancipated) of conducting his personal life. Although this policy is entitled to respect in federal courts for substantive law purposes, we see no necessary reason to give it special deference for diversity jurisdictional purposes when it conflicts with another state's policy judgment that an 18 year old living within its borders is of legal age and fully capable of choosing the place he regards as home. Puerto Rico, in fact, recognizes that a child may be emancipated with parental consent and, thereafter, although under age, will be capable of choosing a domicile of his own. It is generally recognized that even persons lacking the capacity to enter into contracts and other legal arrangements may have sufficient capacity to select a domicile of choice. Weintraub, *Commentary on the Conflicts of Laws* §2.4, at 18 (1980).

Rico law. The problem is, however, that the term "citizens of Puerto Rico" has been defined by the Supreme Court of Puerto Rico as equivalent to domicile. Therefore, whether Section 247 of the Civil Code, P.R. Laws Ann. tit. 31, §971—which provides that the majority age in Puerto Rico is 21—applies to Rodriguez Diaz will depend on where he is domiciled. Since this is the ultimate issue in contention, the approach does nothing to assist our resolution of the dispute.

The fact is, there is no purely logical way out of the dilemma. We cannot decide whether plaintiff is a minor under Puerto Rico law or an adult pursuant to New York law, without first determining where he is domiciled. On the other hand, we cannot make a determination whether he has the capacity to establish his own domicile without first knowing if he has reached the age of majority. We have, therefore, come full circle. To know if he has the legal capacity to establish his domicile of choice we need to know if he is an adult. But to determine whether he is an adult or a minor we first have to know where he is domiciled.

There is, to be sure, a possible way out of this circle under formal conflict of laws principles. We could apply forum law to determine Rodriguez Diaz's legal capacity. Restatement of the Law, Conflicts of Law (Second), §§13 and 15(a). (1971).[5] This might be a proper resolution had the question of plaintiff's domicile arisen in a Commonwealth of Puerto Rico court, where the question of domicile is likely to implicate local matters over which Puerto Rico has the final say. But we do not think the lex forum provides a satisfactory resolution where the overriding and ultimate question is plaintiff's *citizenship* for purposes of federal diversity jurisdiction. 28 U.S.C. §1332(a). Federal district courts sit throughout the nation. While it is unlikely a tort action like this, based on an accident in Puerto Rico, with all defendants residing there, could be pursued elsewhere than in the District of Puerto Rico, plaintiff could be involved in other federal diversity cases in other federal district courts, including the district courts located in New York. Were we to apply the rule of lex forum, Rodriguez Diaz could be viewed at one and the same time, and within the same judicial system, as both a citizen of New York and a citizen of Puerto Rico. That this is even theoretically possible suggests the unsatisfactoriness of determining state citizenship here, *for federal diversity purposes*, on the basis of lex forum. Rodriguez Diaz, we think, must be a "citizen" of one or the other state—not of both simultaneously.

We do not, moreover, see any compelling reasons of policy for adopting the law of the forum here. As pointed out already, while Puerto Rico doubtless has legitimate reasons for regulating persons such as plaintiff in respect to the making of contracts, property dispositions, support, and the like in Puerto Rico, it has little if any interest, based simply on the continuing presence of his parents in Puerto Rico, in denying to Rodriguez Diaz, while physically residing in New York, the right to sue under the diversity jurisdiction in a federal district court whether in Puerto Rico or elsewhere. While not crucial to our result, we also note that even plaintiff's parents have joined him in bringing this action: thus the parents'

---

5. "[A] person cannot acquire a domicil of choice unless he has legal capacity to do so. Whether such legal capacity exists will be determined by the law of the forum." Restatement of the Law, Conflicts of Law (Second) §13, comment d.

separate interests provide no reason to deny him the right to sue in a federal court.[6] In brief, a mechanical recourse to the lex forum does not strike us as a thoughtful solution to the current dilemma.

IV

Since neither pure logic nor conflict rules provide a meaningful solution, we feel free to make the choice we think fits best with the aims of the diversity statute and the national character of the federal judicial system. We hold that Rodriguez Diaz is a domiciliary of the State of New York—or, rather, that, if he can satisfy the district court that he meets the requisite factors of physical presence and intent, he is entitled to be a New York domiciliary for diversity purposes notwithstanding his minority status under Puerto Rico law. In reaching this result, we focus upon the physical and mental aspects of plaintiff's own situation, rather than imposing upon him a disability foreign to the law of the state where he now resides and having little meaning in this situation even to the place—Puerto Rico—whose law calls for it. To hold that one who meets all the domiciliary requirements (including capacity) of the state where he currently resides is a citizen of that state, seems clearly the most reasonable result here.

Our approach is consistent with that of other federal courts. . . . While in the ordinary case, relevant rules of state law provide the basis for the applicable federal common law, federal courts will deviate if necessary in order to achieve the purposes of the diversity statute[7] and, sometimes, simply to achieve a more equitable and coherent result.[8] Not surprisingly, a number of cases have arisen from the tension, as here, between technical presumptions as to the domicile of a minor and the realities of the minor's actual situation.

In the present case, there are perhaps no urgent reasons of federal diversity policy comparable to those found [in other cases]. Since Rodriguez Diaz is recently from Puerto Rico, and his parents reside there, it is unlikely he would encounter prejudice were he forced to sue in Puerto Rico's own courts. The more realistic comparison, however, may be between the relative unfairness of denying a federal forum to Rodriguez Diaz while granting it to another young Puerto Rican of similar age whose parents moved to New York with him. Federal diversity jurisdiction

---

6. There would, of course, be no diversity jurisdiction as to any claim of the parents, who reside in Puerto Rico. The parents sue here solely as next friends; their domicile is irrelevant in such circumstances.

7. See, *e.g.*, Ziady v. Curley, 396 F.2d 873 (4th Cir. 1968) (in deciding infant plaintiff's domicile, the court took into account a major purpose of diversity jurisdiction, which is to protect a citizen of one state from parochialism if forced to litigate in another state).

8. Bjornquist v. Boston & A. R. Co., 250 F. 929 (1st Cir.), *cert. denied*, 248 U.S. 573 (1918). In this case, this circuit refused to follow the common-law rule that a minor could not establish his own domicile for diversity purposes: the minor's parents were dead, and plaintiff's domicile was technically that of his deceased father. Nonetheless, we found that he had acquired a Maine domicile when he moved there when 19 for a relatively brief sojourn with an aunt. *See also* Stifel v. Hopkins, 477 F.2d 1116 (6th Cir. 1973) (a prisoner may show a change of domicile to a state to which he was moved by his jailers notwithstanding old rule that the pre-incarceration domicile of a prisoner must continue during his imprisonment).

exists as a matter of right for those who meet the statutory criteria, whether or not the plaintiff would actually encounter prejudice in the courts of another state. Federal courts should not, therefore, deny the right on the basis of pointless technicalities. In this case, if Rodriguez Diaz, being physically present in New York, qualifies under regular domiciliary rules as a domiciliary of New York, we do not think the difference in law between his former domicile, Puerto Rico, and New York concerning the age of majority should deny him right to sue as a citizen of New York in federal court.

Vacated and remanded for further proceedings not inconsistent herewith.

TORRUELLA, J. (dissenting).

With due respect I believe the majority has reached the wrong result, and that, by a circuitous route. Its conclusion is inevitable because its reasoning commences by "assum[ing] for purposes of resolving the legal issues raised in this appeal that New York is plaintiff's 'true, fixed home.'" I believe this is a fallacious assumption because it improperly shifts the focus of analysis.

Since the only undisputed fact in this case is that plaintiff was domiciled in Puerto Rico to begin with, it seems to me that the logical starting point is determining how plaintiff could change his domicile from Puerto Rico to New York. The answer to that question, in the context of this case, raises an issue of *capacity*, not one of intention. Since there is no case in which a change in domicile has taken place without, at the very least, a physical departure from the place of original domicile, and it is legally impossible to acquire a new domicile without first losing the old one, we must determine the legal significance of such action in that jurisdiction; *i.e.*, Puerto Rico. The issue thus is what, if any, is the legal significance, for change of domicile purposes, of an 18 year old resident of Puerto Rico leaving that jurisdiction.

The answer under Puerto Rican law is clear: none. An 18 year old is considered a minor in Puerto Rico. The domicile of an unemancipated minor is that of his parents, or in appropriate cases, his guardian. A minor can be emancipated, thus allowing him to acquire a separate domicile from his parents or guardian, only by either parent (or both if they jointly exercise the patria potestas) appearing before a civil law notary in the presence of two witness, and, with the minor's consent, signing an emancipation deed. Unless this formal proceeding is effectuated *beforehand*, a Puerto Rico-domiciled minor *lacks legal capacity* to change his domicile from that of his parents, or in the appropriate case, his guardian. His moving away from his legal domicile (*i.e.*, that of his parents or guardian), be that to a different location down the street, or to another place in Puerto Rico, or to another jurisdiction, is legally irrelevant because he cannot gain a new domicile until one has licitly lost the old one.

That a state has a paramount interest in protecting, regulating and controlling its minor citizens is beyond cavil.

. . . This paramount interest of a state in regulating the conduct of its minors is not, of course, limited to Puerto Rico, and protective legislation may be found throughout the United States varying its content in a manner reflective of local interests and attitudes.

Because this is, as it should be, an area highly reflective of local attitudes, values and mores, it is particularly unsuited to federalized tinkering. Thus, the majority is mistaken in placing emphasis on the "right of access to a federal court" as the central issue raised by this appeal. . . .

The majority, however, finds all of this authority unpersuasive. Instead, it directs a district court sitting in Puerto Rico and adjudicating a case controlled by Puerto Rico law, concerning an incident occurring in Puerto Rico, and involving an individual who is unemancipated and still a minor under Puerto Rico law, to apply New York law to determine that the youth is no longer a minor (*i.e.*, emancipated) and thus able to invoke diversity jurisdiction in Puerto Rico. . . .

Perhaps most troubling about the decision of the majority is that it is presented without reliance on any rule of law. Is the majority saying that henceforth in this circuit the age of eighteen is the age of emancipation for choosing one's own domicile for purposes of diversity jurisdiction? If so, why is eighteen chosen instead of twenty-one or any other age? Or is the rule now that we will use the law of the jurisdiction to which the youth has moved, such that if a New York nineteen-year-old leaves his parents and moves to Puerto Rico his domicile will remain in New York? Or is it that we use the law of the jurisdiction which has the youngest age of emancipation? Perhaps the rule is simply that we use the law of the jurisdiction which will create diversity jurisdiction.

Whatever the new rule is, I simply cannot see *why* it has been adopted at the expense of valid local interests—interests completely ignored by the majority. For instance, Puerto Rico may have a very legitimate interest in allowing parents to control the lawsuits of its citizens under the age of twenty-one. It may want parents deciding whether and in what court a suit is prosecuted, the Commonwealth allows parents better to control the expense and scope of litigation. In some situations, parents may decide that local court *is* the better alternative. Furthermore, Puerto Rico may have an interest in not encouraging a young person to leave home to establish domicile elsewhere so as to bring a suit in federal court contrary to the wishes of those ultimately responsible under its law for that youth. . . .

I dissent.

Questions and Comments

(1) Holmes stated: "[W]hat the law means by domicile is the one technically pre-eminent headquarters, which as a result of either fact or fiction every person is compelled to have in order that by aid of it certain rights and duties which have been attached to it by the law may be determined." Bergner & Engel Brewing Co. v. Dreyfus, 172 Mass. 154, 157 (1898).

(2) The domicile concept serves many purposes. As *White* shows, domicile provides the controlling law for questions of succession to personal property. Domicile was also the traditional choice-of-law criterion in contexts "related to personal status, such as marriage and divorce, legitimacy and adoption." 1 Beale, *The Conflict of Laws* §9.3, p. 91 (1935). As we shall see in Chapter 3, domicile is even more important for modern approaches to choice of law. Domicile also has uses beyond pure choice-of-law questions. As *Rodriguez Diaz* shows, domicile is typically equated with a natural person's citizenship for purposes of federal diversity jurisdiction. The domicile of at least one party provides the basis for divorce jurisdiction. Domicile also provides the basis for in personam jurisdiction and for determination of numerous taxation questions. There are many other functions

of the domicile concept as well. Is it likely that all of these different purposes will be served by a unitary concept? *Compare* Toll v. Moreno, 284 Md. 425 (1979) ("in Maryland, as in the majority of jurisdictions, the meaning and basic principles for determining domicile do not vary depending on the context").

(3) Is the use of domicile for choice-of-law purposes in tension with the First Restatement's emphasis on the place where events occur? Is domicile simply a different form of territorialism, focusing on where someone is from rather than where certain events occur? *See* Dane, *Conflict of Laws*, in *A Companion to the Philosophy of Law and Legal Theory* 209 (Patterson ed., 1996) (distinguishing between "act-territorial" and "person-territorial" choice-of-law rules). Why do some traditional choice-of-law rules focus on act-territorialism while others focus on person-territorialism?

(4) What does *White* suggest about the relative priority of the "intent" and "presence" prongs of domicile? What would the court have done if Mr. White died in Pennsylvania before he ever entered the house? What if he died just before he crossed the border from West Virginia into Pennsylvania?

(5) The military poses a special problem precisely because it puts in question the intent of the putative domiciliary. Can an intent to make a place one's home really be formed if one is present because of orders and subject to being moved at any time because of further orders? The same question arose in Stifel v. Hopkins, 477 F.2d 116 (6th Cir. 1973), cited by the *Rodriguez Diaz* court, in which a prisoner in a federal prison in Pennsylvania sought to sue his attorney and parents, all residents of Ohio, in federal court. Jurisdiction was based on diversity. The lower court dismissed on the grounds that the plaintiff could not by law acquire a Pennsylvania domicile while in prison. The court of appeals reversed, indicating that a per se rule is inappropriate. On remand, the lower court was ordered to

> consider factors such as the possibility of parole for appellant, the manner in which appellant has ordered his personal and business transactions, and any other factors that are relevant to corroboration of appellant's statements. These factors must be weighed along with the policies and purposes underlying federal diversity jurisdiction to determine whether appellant has overcome the presumption that he has maintained his former domicile.

477 F.2d at 1127. If you were the district judge, what kind of questions would you like to hear answered before making a new finding that won't get reversed by the court of appeals? *Compare* Restatement (Second) of Conflict of Laws §17 (1986 Revision) (stating that a person "usually" does not acquire a domicile of choice by presence under physical or legal compulsion).

(6) An unusual domicile case is Blaine v. Murphy, 265 F. 324 (D. Mass. 1920), which was brought in federal court by virtue of federal diversity jurisdiction. The plaintiff was a citizen of New York and alleged that the defendants were citizens of Massachusetts. The defendants pleaded in abatement that they were also citizens of New York. Defendants ran a hotel called the State Line Hotel, through which ran the Massachusetts-New York line, as indicated by an old marker. A later survey sponsored by the two states, however, had shown that the marker was some 50 feet east of the true line. Thus, almost all of the hotel (where the defendants lived as well as worked) lay in Massachusetts. In particular, those portions of the

building in which they ate and slept were in Massachusetts. The court did note that the outdoor toilets were in New York. Nonetheless, the court invoked the rule, "The place where a person habitually eats, sleeps, and makes his home is his domicile." It was held not to be relevant that the parties had believed their domicile (as shown by numerous documents) to be New York for at least 40 years.

(7) According to an article in *Nature* discussing the appointment of Mr. Michael Sohlman as director of the Nobel Foundation, the Sohlman family connection with Alfred Nobel dated back to the start of the twentieth century, when as Nobel's employee, Mr. Sohlman's grandfather was assigned the responsibility of moving all of the late inventor's personal assets from Paris to Sweden, where the estate was being administered. The reasoning behind locating administration of the estate in Sweden was that French law then in force deemed a person's domicile to be the place where he kept his horses. *Following Ancestral Footsteps*, 360 Nature 514 (1992).

D. Marriage

Selections from the First Restatement of Conflicts, on Marriage and Legitimacy

§§121-123, 128-130, 132-134, 136-141 (1934)

§121. Law Governing Validity of Marriage

Except as stated in §§131 and 132, a marriage is valid everywhere if the requirements of the marriage law of the state where the contract of marriage takes place are complied with.

§122. Requirements of State of Celebration

A marriage is invalid everywhere if any mandatory requirement of the marriage law of the state in which the marriage is celebrated is not complied with.

§123. "Common Law" Marriage

A marriage without any formal ceremony is valid everywhere if the acts alleged to have created it took place in a state in which such a marriage is valid.

§128. Marriage in a Nomadic Tribe

If one or both of the parties to a marriage is a member of a tribe governed by tribal law, and the marriage takes place where the tribe is at the time located, and in accordance with the tribal law, the marriage is valid everywhere.

COMMENT ...

c. *Gipsy, North American Indian, African and Esquimaux tribes.* Tribal law means the law of a tribe which by the law of the state in which it is located has its own law. The term would not be used, for instance, of the usages of a gipsy tribe not recognized by the state in which it is as having a right to a separate law. Tribal law is recognized as existing law in the case of Indian tribes in North America, of native African tribes, and of Esquimaux tribes.

§129. Evasion of Requirement of Domicil

If the requirements of the law of the state of celebration are complied with, the marriage is valid everywhere, except under the circumstances stated in §§131 and 132, although the parties of the marriage went to that state in order to evade the requirements of the law of their domicil.

§130. Remarriage After One Party to Divorce Forbidden to Remarry

If, by a decree of divorce validly granted in one state, one party is forbidden for a certain time or during his life to marry again, and he goes into another state and marries in accordance with the law of that state, the marriage, unless invalid for other reasons, is valid everywhere, even in the state in which the divorce was granted.

§132. Marriage Declared Void by Law of Domicil

A marriage which is against the law of the state of domicil of either party, though the requirements of the law of the state of celebration have been complied with, will be invalid everywhere in the following cases:

(a) polygamous marriage,
(b) incestuous marriage between persons so closely related that their marriage is contrary to a strong public policy of the domicil,
(c) marriage between persons of different races where such marriages are at the domicil regarded as odious,
(d) marriage of a domiciliary which a statute at the domicil makes void even though celebrated in another state.

§133. Effect of Foreign Marriage

Except as stated in §134, a state will give the same effect to a marriage created by the law of another state that it gives to a marriage created by its own law.

§134. Marriage Contrary to Public Policy

If any effect of a marriage created by the law of one state is deemed by the courts of another state sufficiently offensive to the policy of the latter state, the latter state will refuse to give that effect to the marriage.

§136. Law Governing Nullity

The law governing the right to a decree of nullity is the law which determined the validity of the marriage with respect to the matter on account of which the marriage is alleged to be null.

§137. Law Governing Legitimacy

The status of legitimacy is created by the law of the domicil of the parent whose relationship to the child is in question.

§138. Legitimacy at Birth

The legitimate kinship of a child to either parent from the time of the child's birth is determined by the law of the state of domicil of that parent at that time.

§139. Legitimacy from Birth

An act or event after the birth of a child who was born illegitimate may make it the legitimate child of either parent from birth if the law of the state of domicil of that parent at the time of the child's birth and the law of the parent's domicil at the time of the legitimating act so provide.

§140. Legitimation After Birth

An act done after the birth of an illegitimate child will legitimize the child as to a parent from the time of the act if the law of the state of domicil of that parent at that time so provides.

§141. Effect of Legitimacy Created by Foreign Law

The status of legitimacy, created by the law of a state having jurisdiction so to do, will be given the same effect in another state as is given by the latter state to the status when created by its own law.

Ghassemi v. Ghassemi
998 So. 2d 731 (La. Ct. App. 2008)

KUHN, J.

Plaintiff appeals a judgment declining to recognize any Iranian marriage of the parties. For the detailed reasons that follow, we reverse the judgment and remand the matter for further proceedings consistent with the opinions expressed herein. . . .

Factual and Procedural History

Plaintiff, Tahereh Ghassemi, filed suit in the East Baton Rouge Parish Family Court (family court) seeking a divorce, spousal support, and a partition of community property. In her petition, she alleged that she and the defendant, Hamid Ghassemi, were married in Bam, Iran in 1976, at which time both parties were citizens of Iran. She further alleged that a son, Hamed, was born of their union in 1977. Ms. Ghassemi contends that in that same year, Mr. Ghassemi entered the United States (U.S.) on a student visa. Ms. Ghassemi avers that when Mr. Ghassemi left Iran in 1977, it was with the understanding that he would return to Iran after he completed his studies or that he would arrange for her and Hamed to join him and establish a residence in the U.S. Unbeknownst to Ms. Ghassemi, after entering the U.S., Mr. Ghassemi contracted a "marriage" with an American woman, allegedly to enhance his legal status in this country. However, this purported "marriage" ultimately ended in "divorce."

The petition further states that, in 1995, Mr. Ghassemi made the necessary applications that allowed Hamed to enter the U.S. as his "son." However, no efforts were made on behalf of Ms. Ghassemi for her to enter the U.S. Subsequently, in 2002, Mr. Ghassemi "married" yet another woman in Baton Rouge, Louisiana, where he had become domiciled. In 2005, through the efforts of her son, Hamed, Ms. Ghassemi finally entered the U.S. as a permanent resident and also settled in Baton Rouge. On May 22, 2006, she filed the present suit.

Mr. Ghassemi responded by filing a peremptory exception pleading the objection of no cause of action. He argued that the purported marriage to Ms. Ghassemi was invalid. . . . In his pleadings, Mr. Ghassemi posited several arguments in support of his contention that the marriage was invalid, the principal one being that he and Ms. Ghassemi are first cousins. . . .

. . . The family court . . . held a "trial" on Mr. Ghassemi's request for declaratory relief. Therein, Mr. Ghassemi argued that a marriage between first cousins was a violation of a strong public policy of Louisiana and, further, that Louisiana had no obligation, under the doctrine of comity, to recognize Iranian law or to give legal effect to a marriage certificate issued by Iran.

At the conclusion of the trial, the family court stated:

> This court exercising its powers vested from the state, this court will not recognize any document, decree, judgments[,] statutes or contracts, and will not give comity . . . and no validity whatsoever from the country of Iran [s]ince that country has been declared by itself, and by its leader, to be an enemy of the United States. The United States has had no diplomatic relations with that country for 28 years, and they are not a signatory to the Hague Convention with respect to marriages. And even if the court recognizes the marriage, it will violate public policy of this state; and therefore the declaratory judgment is granted. . . .

Significantly, the judgment did not expressly state that the marriage was a violation of a strong public policy of this state. . . .

Discussion

I. Final Judgment

. . . The sole issue before us is the same as that presented to the family court: whether an Iranian marriage between first cousins will be recognized in Louisiana.

A. Applicable Law

It is axiomatic that our analysis begins with an examination of the pertinent provisions governing the conflict of laws. . . .

Specifically, Article 3520 provides:

A. A marriage that is valid in the state where contracted, or in the state where the parties were first domiciled as husband and wife, shall be treated as a valid marriage unless to do so would violate a strong public policy of the state whose law is applicable to the particular issue under Article 3519. . . .*

Comment (b) to Article 3520 explains our state's longstanding policy of "favor matrimonii." Specifically, it provides, in part, as follows:

Based on the universally espoused policy of favoring the validity of marriages if there is any reasonable basis for doing so (favor matrimonii), this Article authorizes the validation of marriages that are valid either in the state where contracted or in the state where the spouses were first domiciled as husband and wife. . . . This ancient policy of favor matrimonii and favor validatis is well entrenched in the substantive law of every state of the United States. This policy is equally important at the multistate level, where it is reinforced by the policy of avoiding "limping marriages." This Article enunciates this policy of validation and defines its limits. These limits are co-extensive with the "strong public policy of the state whose law is applicable to the particular issue under Article 3519." In order to rebut the presumptive rule of validation established by Article 3520, the party who asserts the invalidity of the marriage must prove that: (1) under Article 3519, the law of a state other than the one where the marriage was contracted or where the parties were first domiciled as husband

---

* Article 3519 provides:

The status of a natural person and the incidents and effects of that status are governed by the law of the state whose policies would be most seriously impaired if its law were not applied to the particular issue.

    That state is determined by evaluating the strength and pertinence of the relevant policies of the involved states in the light of: (1) the relationship of each state, at any pertinent time, to the dispute, the parties, and the person whose status is at issue; (2) the policies referred to in Article 3515; and (3) the policies of sustaining the validity of obligations voluntarily undertaken, of protecting children, minors, and others in need of protection, and of preserving family values and stability.

—Eds.

and wife would be applicable to the particular issue; and (2) that law would invalidate the marriage for reasons of "a strong public policy."

Thus, it is the public policy of Louisiana that every effort be made to uphold the validity of marriages. Moreover, if a foreign marriage is valid in the state where it was contracted, the marriage is accorded a presumption of validity.

In seeking declaratory relief, Mr. Ghassemi did not argue that a marriage between first cousins is invalid in Iran, where the marriage herein was purportedly contracted. Moreover, we conclude that such a marriage is not prohibited by the Iranian Civil Code. . . . Accordingly, LSA-C.C. art. 3520 is controlling herein, and such a marriage is presumed to be valid. To defeat this presumption, Mr. Ghassemi must prove that the law of another state is applicable and that state's law would invalidate the marriage for reasons of "a strong public policy." . . .

However, the majority of Mr. Ghassemi's argument in the underlying proceedings was premised on his assertion that the family court had no obligation under the doctrine of comity either to recognize (1) a marriage certificate issued by Iran or (2) the laws of Iran where the purported marriage was contracted. In so doing, Mr. Ghassemi argued, in essence, that the family court could not or should not consider whether the marriage was valid under Iranian law. Based upon its judgment, the family court clearly credited this argument and, relying on the doctrine of comity, essentially based its decision not to recognize the purported marriage in light of the state of diplomatic relations between Iran and the U.S.

However, as the parties now agree, the family court's discussion of comity and the U.S.'s diplomatic relations with Iran, or lack thereof, is irrelevant to the matter at hand. Clearly, the positive law set forth in LSA-C.C. art. 3520 is controlling herein and provides the correct standard for a court to utilize in determining the validity of this foreign marriage. Thus, we find that the family court failed to enunciate the appropriate legal standard and further failed to analyze the precise issue before it within the parameters of that standard. The proper legal standard simply requires a two-part inquiry:

(1) Was the marriage valid in the state (Iran) where it was purportedly contracted?

(2) If so, would recognition of the validity of the marriage violate "a strong public policy" of the state whose law would be applicable under LSA-C.C. art. 3519 (Louisiana)?

B. VALID IN THE STATE WHERE CONTRACTED?

In his brief to this court, Mr. Ghassemi concedes, for the sake of argument, that a marriage between first cousins is valid under Iranian law. Nevertheless, the family court, relying on the doctrine of comity, refused to consider whether such a marriage was valid in Iran. Or, to be more precise, the family court essentially refused to acknowledge the existence of **any** marriage contracted in Iran.

Specifically, the family court ruled that it would not give effect to the laws of Iran and/or a marriage document issued by Iran under the doctrine of comity. However, this is not a matter of enforcing Iranian law in Louisiana or giving automatic legal effect to an Iranian marriage certificate. To the contrary, this matter is squarely controlled by Louisiana law. Our legislature has expressly provided that a marriage valid where contracted will be recognized as valid in Louisiana absent a violation of strong public policy. Given its judgment, it is clear that the family court failed to recognize that determining whether a foreign marriage is valid where contracted—as required by Louisiana law—does not equate to enforcing a foreign law here. The family court likewise failed to appreciate the distinction between acknowledging that a foreign document is what it purports to be and blindly enforcing or giving legal effect to that document. . . . While such a document is not entitled to be given legal effect, it is certainly relevant in determining whether a marriage occurred, where it occurred, and whether it was valid where it was confected. . . .

Because a marriage between first cousins is valid in Iran, it is accorded the presumption of validity. Accordingly, it was error for the family court not to recognize the validity of first-cousin marriages under Iranian law when rendering its judgment.

C. VIOLATION OF A STRONG PUBLIC POLICY?

. . . Clearly, in determining whether Louisiana has "a strong public policy" against recognizing the validity of a foreign marriage between first cousins, it is appropriate to examine our laws governing marriages that are contracted **in this state.** Louisiana Civil Code article 90, which addresses the impediments of relationships, provides as follows:

> A. The following persons may not contract marriage with each other:
> (1) Ascendants and descendants.
> (2) Collaterals within the fourth degree, whether of the whole or of the half blood.
> B. The impediment exists whether the persons are related by consanguinity or by adoption. Nevertheless, persons related by adoption, though not by blood, in the collateral line within the fourth degree may marry each other if they obtain judicial authorization in writing to do so.

The phrase "collaterals within the fourth degree" includes aunt and nephew, uncle and niece, siblings, **and first cousins.** LSA-C.C. art. 90, comment (b); *see also* LSA-C.C. art. 901. Pursuant to LSA-C.C. art. 94, a marriage is absolutely null when contracted in this state (1) without a marriage ceremony, (2) by procuration, or (3) in violation of an impediment.

However, the mere fact that a marriage is absolutely null when contracted in Louisiana does not mean that such a marriage validly performed elsewhere is automatically invalid as violative of a strong public policy. For example, comment (b) to LSA-C.C. art. 3520 expressly states, in part: "The word 'contracted' as opposed to the word 'celebrated' is used [in this article] so as not to exclude common-law marriage from the scope of this Article." A common-law marriage is one that is performed without a ceremony. [citations omitted] Based on the language in comment (b), LSA-C.C. art. 3520 was clearly intended to encompass foreign common-law marriages, *i.e.*, marriages contracted without a ceremony, even though such a marriage contracted in Louisiana is absolutely null.

Indeed, the jurisprudence is replete with decisions recognizing that if a common-law marriage is contracted in a state whose law sanctions such a marriage, the marriage will be recognized as a valid marriage in Louisiana, even though a common-law marriage cannot be contracted in this state. [citations omitted]

Similarly, this state has recognized a foreign marriage contracted by procuration, even though such a marriage would be absolutely null if contracted here. In U.S. ex rel. Modianos v. Tuttle, 12 F.2d 927 (E.D. La. 1925), the court held that the statute prohibiting marriage by procuration only applied to marriages contracted within Louisiana and that the marriage of a citizen celebrated by proxy in Turkey was valid where it was valid under the laws of that country.

There is no Louisiana jurisprudence addressing the recognition of a foreign marriage between first cousins; however, based on the law of this state, presently and historically, we find that such a marriage, if valid where contracted, is valid in Louisiana and is not a violation of a **strong** public policy. In finding no violation, we make a clear distinction between the marriage of first cousins and marriages contracted by more closely-related collaterals, *i.e.*, uncle and niece, aunt and nephew, and siblings.

Contrary to assertions made by defense counsel to the family court, marriage between first cousins has not always been prohibited in Louisiana. It was permitted under the Civil Codes of 1804, 1808, and 1825. It was also permitted under the Civil Code of 1870 until its amendment in 1902.

Prior to its amendment in 1902, Article 95 of the Civil Code of 1870 (the source of present LSA-C.C. art. 90) provided, as follows:

> Among collateral relations, marriage is prohibited between brother and sister, whether of the whole or of the half blood, whether legitimate or illegitimate, and also between the uncle and the niece, the aunt and the nephew. . . .

Thus, prior to 1902, there was absolutely no bar to marriages between first cousins in this state.

Even so, notwithstanding the prohibitions set forth in former Article 95 (as amended in 1902), the Louisiana Legislature thereafter repeatedly ratified marriages between collaterals in the fourth degree that had been contracted in violation of the prohibition. *See* 1972 La. Acts, No. 230, and 1981 La. Acts, No. 647. Effective September 11, 1981, former Article 95 was amended by 1981 La. Acts, No. 647, to [add the following language]:

> **All such marriages heretofore made in contravention of the above provisions shall be considered as legal.** (Emphasis added.)

Hence, the Louisiana Legislature legalized all marriages between collaterals within the fourth degree that were contracted by citizens of this state before September 11, 1981.

In a similar vein, Article 113 of the Civil Code of 1870 was amended by 1904 La. Acts, No. 129:

> Every marriage contracted under the other incapacities or nullities enumerated in the second chapter of this title, may be impeached either by the married

persons themselves, or any person interested, or by the Attorney General; however, first, that marriages heretofore contracted between persons, related within the prohibited degrees either or both of whom were then and afterward domiciled in this State and were prohibited from intermarrying here, shall nevertheless be deemed valid in this State, where such marriages were celebrated in other States or countries under the laws of which they were not prohibited; second, that marriages hereinafter contracted between persons, either or both of whom are domiciled in this State and are forbidden to intermarry, shall not be deemed valid in this State, because contracted in another State or country where such marriages are not prohibited, if the parties, after such marriage, return to reside permanently in this State.

Obviously, the amendment was intended to ratify prior "fugitive marriages" but to henceforth prevent Louisiana domiciliaries from thwarting the law of this state by contracting such marriages. However, despite the express intention to prevent future fugitive marriages, the Louisiana Legislature thereafter periodically amended and reenacted former Article 113, employing essentially the same language utilized in 1904 La. Acts, No. 129. *See* 1912 La. Acts, No. 54; 1938 La. Acts, No. 426; and 1950 La. Acts, No. 242. Thus, fugitive marriages contracted by collaterals were periodically ratified.

In continually ratifying marriages between collaterals within the fourth degree, notwithstanding our law's express prohibition of such marriages, the legislature voluntarily chose to legalize marriages by Louisiana domiciliaries who had chosen either to ignore Louisiana law or flout it.

The general practice of retroactively validating prohibited marriages between collaterals only ended when 1987 La. Acts, No. 886, was enacted to revise the Civil Code articles relative to marriage. In addition to redesignating former Articles 95 and 113 as present Articles 90 and 94 respectively, that Act expressly protects those collaterals whose marriages previously had been declared legal pursuant to 1981 La. Acts, No. 647, but further evidences an intention not to continue the practice of retroactively validating such marriages. . . .

[A]s a result of the amendments and reenactments set forth in 1987 La. Acts, No. 886, LSA-C.C. art. 94, comment (d) now reads as follows:

> The retrospective provision of Article 113 of the Civil Code of 1870 concerning "fugitive marriages" has been suppressed in this revision. However, in order to protect the interests of persons who have relied on the most recent such exception, a section of the act embodying this revision . . . retroactively validates all marriages between collateral relations contracted prior to September 11, 1981, the effective date of Acts 1981, No. 647 (which similarly amended Article 95 of the Civil Code of 1870).
>
> The prospective fugitive marriage provision of Civil Code Article 113 (1870) has also been suppressed because it is unnecessary. The only situation it addressed is that in which Louisiana domiciliaries who lack capacity to marry in this state contract marriage in another state or country and then return here to live, intending to remain here. In that case the second paragraph of Civil Code Article 10 (1870) (redesignated [and] subsequently revised; see, now, C.C. art. 3520) applies, and is dispositive.
>
> There is no reason to apply a different rule to a fugitive marriage performed in another state, rather than a foreign country. . . .

Thus, a marriage contracted in another country or state now must be analyzed without making any distinction as to the parties' domiciliary status at the time the marriage is contracted. . . .

Although no "general" ratifications have occurred since 1981, in 1993, the legislature enacted LSA-R.S. 9:211, which **currently** provides:

Notwithstanding the provisions of Civil Code Article 90, marriages between collaterals within the fourth degree, fifty-five years of age or older, which were entered into on or before December 31, 1992, shall be considered legal and the enactment hereof shall in no way impair vested property rights.

In light of all of the foregoing, and for reasons more fully explained below, we are compelled to conclude that Louisiana does not have a **strong** public policy against recognizing **a marriage between first cousins** performed in a state or country where such marriages are valid.

Clearly, if Louisiana law were applied to the marriage at issue herein, it would be valid, since all marriages contracted by collaterals within the fourth degree before September 11, 1981, are legal. Thus, assuming the purported marriage herein was not valid under Iranian law, and that LSA-C.C. art. 3519 mandated the application of Louisiana law, the 1976 marriage would be valid. There is no reason a different result should obtain under LSA-C.C. art. 3520 simply because the marriage was valid in Iran.

Nevertheless, in an effort to discount the history of legislative ratifications and argue that a strong public policy in Louisiana absolutely prohibits a marriage between first cousins, Mr. Ghassemi argues that the ratification of all marriages between collaterals contracted prior to September 11, 1981, was merely intended to benefit those collaterals who were Louisiana domiciliaries when the marriage occurred and was not meant to benefit those who married before making Louisiana their domicile. We find this argument to be contrary to logic and justice. If the Louisiana legislature recognized marriages between collaterals within the fourth degree who were Louisiana domiciliaries and who had intentionally ignored or thwarted Louisiana law in order to contract their marriages, then, *a fortiori*, it would certainly recognize marriages **legally** contracted by collaterals who, before becoming domiciled here, were domiciled and married in a state or country that permitted such marriages. Moreover, all marriages contracted outside of Louisiana now are analyzed pursuant to either LSA-C.C. art. 3519 or 3520, regardless of whether the parties were domiciliaries of Louisiana or another jurisdiction at the time the marriage occurred. Hence, his attempt to urge the application of a distinction based on domiciliary status fails on this basis as well. . . .

However, we emphasize that the instant case involves the marriage of first cousins. Although the previously noted laws, both past and present, applied generally to all collaterals within the fourth degree, **we reiterate that in finding no violation of a strong public policy, we make a clear distinction between the marriage of first cousins and marriages contracted between more closely-related collaterals.** While the former is commonly accepted, the latter is greatly condemned.

"The marriage of first cousins has historically been regarded as in a different category from that of persons more closely related." 52 Am. Jur. 2d, *Marriage* §51. A marriage between first cousins neither violates natural law nor is it included in the wider list of prohibited relationships set forth in Chapter 18 of the Bible's Book of Leviticus, the font of Western incest laws. P.H. Vartanian, Annotation, *Recognition of Foreign Marriage as Affected by Policy in Respect of Incestuous Marriages*, 117 A.L.R. 186, 190 (1938). Thus, while "incestuous" marriages have traditionally constituted an exception to the general rule that a marriage valid where contracted is valid everywhere, that historical exception excludes marriages contracted between first cousins.

Our recognition of this distinction is further buttressed by the fact that relations between first cousins are not encompassed by our criminal incest statute, LSA-R.S. 14:78, which provides, in pertinent part:

> A. Incest is the marriage to, or sexual intercourse with, any ascendant or descendant, brother or sister, uncle or niece, aunt or nephew, with knowledge of their relationship.

Some U.S. states that prohibit first-cousin marriages, including states that consider such marriages void if contracted within the state, have nonetheless recognized such marriages when validly celebrated elsewhere by relying largely on the fact that their respective legislatures had not seen fit to criminalize relations between first cousins, despite prohibiting them from marrying within the state. [citations omitted] Based upon the law of Louisiana, first cousins may legally cohabitate, have intimate relations, and even produce children; however, they are merely prohibited from regularizing their union by marriage. This disparity would tend to negate any contention that Louisiana has a **strong** public policy against marriages between first cousins, since it is in conflict with this state's policy to legally solidify such unions for the good of society at large and for the benefit of any potential posterity.

Furthermore, we note that marriages between first cousins are widely permitted within the western world. "Such marriages were not forbidden at common law." 52 Am. Jur. 2d, Marriage §51. Additionally, no European country prohibits marriages between first cousins. *See* Martin Oppenheimer, Forbidden Relatives: The American Myth of Cousin Marriage, 90 (1996); Ann Laquer Estin, *Embracing Tradition: Pluralism in American Family Law*, 63 Md. L. Rev. 540, 564 (2004). Marriages between first cousins are also legal in Mexico and Canada, in addition to many other countries.

Actually, the U.S. is unique among western countries in restricting first cousin marriages. Even so, such marriages may be legally contracted in Alabama, Alaska, California, Colorado, Connecticut, Florida, Georgia, Hawaii, Maryland, Massachusetts, New Jersey, New Mexico, New York, North Carolina, Rhode Island, South Carolina, Tennessee, Vermont, Virginia, and the District of Columbia. An additional six states, Arizona, Illinois, Indiana, Maine, Utah, and Wisconsin, also allow first cousin marriages subject to certain restrictions.

Accordingly, Louisiana is one of only 25 U.S. states that flatly prohibits such marriages. However, even other states that prohibit marriages between first cousins, have nonetheless found that such marriages do not violate public policy and thus recognize such marriages as valid, if they are valid in the state or country where they were contracted. [citations omitted] Like the foregoing courts, we too find that although Louisiana law expressly prohibits the marriages of first cousins, such marriages are not so "odious" as to violate a **strong** public policy of this state. Accordingly, a marriage between first cousins, if valid in the state or country where it was contracted, will be recognized as valid pursuant to LSA-C.C. art. 3520. . . .

Questions and Comments

(1) The *Ghassemi* court's decision was significantly aided by extensive Louisiana legislation over time regarding the validity of marriages between cousins. What should a court do when the legislation at issue is a single, perhaps decades-long statute that merely provides a legislative prohibition without addressing the conflict-of-laws issue? How does the First Restatement direct courts in this circumstance? Are theories of statutory interpretation helpful?

(2) Why are the parties in *Ghassemi* disputing the validity of their marriage? It appears that neither party wished to be married to the other going forward. Yet, in order to establish rights to Mr. Ghassemi's future income and present property, Ms. Ghassemi needed to establish that she was his spouse. Thus, the dispute is really more about things than about the sanctity or policy in favor of marriage. In fact, few cases will arise where the dispute is about the validity of a marriage as a future status. The rare case is typically a criminal action. *See, e.g.*, State v. Bell, 66 Tenn. 9 (1872), and People v. Ezeonu, *infra*.

In *Ghassemi*, the putative spouse claimed the benefit of certain financial rights that apply to spouses. In other cases, statutory rights provided to spouses are often at issue, including rights to inherit, to administer estates, to collect Social Security, and/or to claim immigration status. Statutes giving special rights to surviving spouses may be indicative of the legislature's assumptions about the intent of the deceased, but are more likely to express a moral view about the surviving spouse's right to benefits. This is particularly clear in the case of statutes that give a surviving spouse a forced share of the decedent's estate, even if there is a will to the contrary. But even if such statutes are supposed to operate independently of the testator's intent, is it clear that the validity of the marriage per se is at issue? After two people have lived together for many years, might the legislature determine that the survivor is entitled to as much consideration whether the marriage was valid or not? Are the same considerations at play in the context of federal immigration or Social Security rights? Should differing considerations lead to differing results regarding the validity of marriage?

(3) Consider also the line of cases (*see, e.g.*, Metropolitan Life Insurance Co. v. Holding, 293 F. Supp. 854 (E.D. Va. 1968)) in which the question is whether the person now claiming insurance proceeds was the "wife" or "husband" of the decedent as the term was used in the insurance contract. Is it likely that a decedent who thought that a marriage was valid and who bought insurance naming "my wife" or "my husband" as beneficiary would intend to benefit someone other than his or her cohabitant, whether or not the marriage was valid?

(4) Are the considerations behind conflicts rules for marriage different from those for torts and contracts? Even an enemy of overemphasis on the desirability of uniformity would have to concede that uniformity is an attractive goal when the question is the validity of a marriage. Few people or states would wish to see marriages valid in some states while invalid in others, with cohabitants never sure

of their status with respect to the criminal law, the legitimacy of their children, or their right to obtain a divorce with property settlement, etc.

In fact, the usual tendency is not merely to aim toward a uniform result but to aim for uniformity in favor of the marriage. *Ghassemi* is a good example, because the Louisiana legislature repeatedly acted to validate void marriages despite their public policy concerns with marriages of closely related individuals. Consider also the *Holding* case, *supra*, where the court, applying Virginia conflicts law, searched for a state in which the parties' common-law marriage was valid, stating: "The public policy of Virginia is to uphold the validity of a marriage if at all possible." But if that is true, why does Virginia deny validity to its own domestic common-law marriages?

(5) Is section 132 of the Restatement (*supra* page 64) an exception that swallows much of section 121's "place of celebration" rule (see *supra* page 63)? Consider:

> The First Restatement . . . does not merely contemplate that the domicile has a potential veto over a well-defined subset of issues. It recognizes in the domicile an absolute power, exercisable by statute or otherwise, to control for any reason the validity of its people's marriages celebrated anywhere. Put another way, if a marriage of a domiciliary conducted outside the domicile is valid, it is only by the permission of the domicile. This reading, in turn, requires a new look at section 121. . . . At first, section 121 had looked like a typical First Restatement rule—a second-order, territorially based, allocation of prescriptive jurisdiction. In truth, however, section 121 does not recognize in the place of celebration any independent power to validate marriages. Rather, it reflects the first-order substantive decision of domicile states to recognize, by their own law, most marriages performed in accordance with the law of the place of celebration.

Dane, *Whereof One Cannot Speak: Legal Diversity and the Limits of a Restatement of Conflict of Laws*, 75 Ind. L.J. 511, 514 (2000). Do you agree with this interpretation? What explains the elevation of domicile over the place of celebration? Why would the state of domicile ever defer to marriages performed elsewhere? Why does the First Restatement appear to give the state of domicile more say over marriage than over tort and contract? Is uniformity more important in the marriage context? Why or why not?

(6) The *Ghassemi* court was careful to separate marriages between cousins from marriages between individuals more closely related. For a case involving marriage between an uncle and a niece, *see* In re May's Estate, 305 N.Y. 486, 114 N.E.2d 4 (1953). In *May's Estate*, the court upheld a marriage that would have been invalid in New York only because it was legally celebrated in another jurisdiction (Rhode Island). At the time of the marriage and for decades following, the putative spouses resided in New York, where they gave birth to six children. What difference should it make to the state of New York *where* related persons are married, when the dangers arise from the cohabitation itself or reproduction resulting from the marriage?

(7) When residents of State *A* step across the state line into State *B* and marry, does State *B* have any desire at all to see its law applied to the marriage? If so, why?

People v. Ezeonu
155 Misc. 2d 344, 588 N.Y.S.2d 116 (1992)

[Defendant, a Nigerian who was married under Nigerian and New York law, was prosecuted for statutory rape of a 13-year-old girl. Defendant claimed that, at the time of said rape, the complainant was his second wife offered to him by her parents. In 1992, Nigerian law allegedly recognized polygamy and New York law did not recognize rape between married persons.]

FISCH, J.

Defendant stands indicted for the crimes of rape in the first degree and rape in the second degree. The People contend the complainant was 13 years old at the time of the alleged crimes. Defendant, a Nigerian national, seeks to raise as a defense to the charge of rape in the second degree that at the time of the alleged crimes the complainant was his "second" or "junior" wife, given to him by her parents in Nigeria pursuant to the laws and tribal customs of that country. Defendant acknowledges that he already was legally married under both New York and Nigerian law at the time he entered into the purported second marriage, but asserts that the laws and tribal customs of Nigeria allow one man to have multiple wives. The following question *in limine* was stipulated between the People and defendant for the court's determination: "If defendant, a Nigerian national, were legally married under both Nigerian and New York law, and if defendant then were to contract a second marriage legal in Nigeria while still married to his first wife and bring the said second wife to New York, what is the status of the second marriage and second wife in New York; specifically, as regards the second wife, is defendant considered 'married' pursuant to Penal Law §130.30?"

Penal Law §130.30 provides that:

> "A person is guilty of rape in the second degree when, being eighteen years old or more, he or she engages in sexual intercourse with another person *to whom the actor is not married* less than fourteen years old." (Emphasis added.)

If the court finds such Nigerian marriage legally recognized in this jurisdiction, defendant may assert its existence as a factual defense to the charge of rape in the second degree. As a matter of law, the court holds that under the stipulated facts the defendant is not "married" to the complainant and therefore cannot raise marriage as a defense at trial to the charge of rape in the second degree.

Findings of Fact

The parties by stipulation, *supra*, agree that the defendant was lawfully married to a then-living wife under the laws of New York and Nigeria at the time of his purported second "marriage" to the complainant in Nigeria.

Conclusions of Law

Under the stipulation submitted for determination *in limine*, even were defendant's "marriage" to the complainant conducted in accordance with Nigerian law and custom, the marriage is null and void in New York. Therefore, as a matter of law, he is not married to her for purposes of the charge of rape in the second degree (Penal Law §130.30) and such purported marriage may not be raised at trial as a defense.

Generally, a marriage is recognized in New York if it is valid where consummated. Van Voorhis v. Brintnall, 86 N.Y. 18, 25 (1881). However, it is well established that this general rule does not apply where recognition of a marriage is repugnant to public policy. Clearly, recognition of a polygamous marriage is repugnant to public policy as evidenced by section 6 of the Domestic Relations Law which provides that:

> "A marriage is absolutely void if contracted by a person whose husband or wife by a former marriage is living, unless either:
> "1. "Such former marriage has been annulled or has been dissolved for a cause other than the adultery . . .
> "2. *[Repealed.]*
> "3. Such former marriage has been dissolved pursuant [to Domestic Relations Law]."

It is significant to note that under said statute a bigamous marriage is not "voidable" but "absolutely void." Moreover, bigamy is a crime in the State of New York. (Penal Law §255.15.)

Hence, "[i]t has been held that when this State is called upon to recognize either an incestuous or bigamous marriage, it will assert its strong public policy of condemnation thereof and refuse recognition even if that marriage was valid where consummated." (Matter of Bronislawa K. v. Tadeusz K., 90 Misc. 2d 183, 185 (1977), *citing* Matter of May, 305 N.Y. 486 (1953).) Consequently, a polygamous marriage legally consummated in a foreign country will be held invalid in New York. (Earle v. Earle, 141 A.D. 611 (1910); Cruikshank v. Cruikshank, 193 Misc. 366 (1948); Matter of Incuria v. Incuria, 155 Misc. 755, 759 (1935) ["If a citizen of a foreign State, in which State polygamy is legal, would bring his half dozen or so legal wives to our country, the marriage of the six spouses to the one spouse would not be considered legal or valid by us," citing Van Voorhis v. Brintnall, *supra*]; Rubman v. Rubman, 140 Misc. 658, 670 (1931) ["The statutory provision that a marriage is void if contracted by a person whose husband or wife by a former marriage is living, is declarative of public policy"]; see Simmons v. Simmons, 208 A.D. 195 (1924).

Recently, the Supreme Court, New York County, reached the same conclusion in a civil matter. (Uboh-Abiola v. Abiola, NYLJ, June 12, 1992, at 22, col 1 [Sup Ct, NY County].) There, the plaintiff alleged that she was married to the defendant in Nigeria and was one of defendant's 25 wives. The court refused to recognize the alleged marriage, holding that "[b]igamous or polygamous marriages even if legal where contracted are not considered valid as a matter of law and public policy." (Id., citing Application of Sood, 208 Misc. 819 (1955), *aff'd* 1 A.D.2d 939 (1956).)

Research by this court reveals that this is the first case in New York State in which a defendant asserted the validity of an admittedly bigamous marriage as a defense to a criminal charge.

For purposes of this *in limine* ruling, the parties have stipulated that defendant Dr. Ezeonu was already legally married in New York and Nigeria at the time when he purportedly married complainant. Dr. Ezeonu has advised the court that he seeks to bring from Nigeria for trial both eyewitnesses to the purported solemnization of the "marriage" and expert witnesses concerning the laws and customs applicable to such marriage in that country. While Nigerian law and custom may permit a "junior wife," New York does not recognize such status. Since at the time of his "marriage" to complainant, Dr. Ezeonu was married to his living wife, his "marriage" to her is absolutely void even were it legally consummated in Nigeria. Consequently, this court holds, as a matter of law, Dr. Ezeonu is not married to Chiweta for purposes of criminal liability for rape in the second degree, pursuant to Penal Law §130.30.

Accordingly, he cannot raise the purported marriage as a defense to that crime.

Questions and Comments

(1) The Supreme Court has upheld laws criminalizing polygamy as early as 1878. In Reynolds v. United States, 98 U.S. 145, 166 (1878), the Supreme Court appears to base its decision at least partially on its observation that "[p]olygamy has always been odious among the northern and western nations of Europe, and . . . was almost exclusively a feature of the life of Asiatic and of African people." In our contemporary age, which places great value upon respecting foreign cultures, should courts allow cultural defenses for criminal defendants? If so, how could courts prevent defendants like Ezeonu from abusing it to justify crimes like rape? Cultural defenses in criminal law have been a topic of enduring scholarly controversy. *See, e.g.,* Note, *The Cultural Defense in the Criminal Law*, 99 Harv. L. Rev. 1293 (1986) (contemplating the circumstances under which cultural defenses could be allowed); Martin, *All Men Are (or Should Be) Created Equal: An Argument Against the Use of the Cultural Defense in a Post-Booker World*, 15 Wm. & Mary Bill Rts. J. 1305 (2007) (arguing that the cultural defense should not be allowed in federal sentencing); Cohan, *Honor Killings and the Cultural Defense*, 40 Cal. W. Intl. L.J. 177 (2010) (evaluating arguments in favor of and against allowing a cultural defense for honor killings).

(2) Judge Fisch cites in support of his ruling Uboh-Abiola v. Abiola, 207 (113) NYLJ (6-12-92) 22, col. 1B, *reprinted in* 56 New York Law Journal Digest Annotator 1992, 404:700.2. In *Abiola*, the plaintiff sought child custody, divorce, and equal distribution against a Nigerian tribal chief with more than 20 wives and billions of dollars in assets. The New York Supreme Court, New York County, dismissed the case for divorce and equitable distribution because it could not recognize as valid any polygamous marriage even if the marriage was legal where it was made, but granted child custody. The plaintiff argued that she did not know that the defendant had other wives until they were married. Nadine Brozan, *Chronicle*, N.Y. Times, Oct. 17, 1991, *http://www.nytimes.com/1991/10/17/style/chronicle-662591.html*. Should the court have made an exception and recognized the marriage in the interest of justice on the grounds that the plaintiff did not know that she was entering into a polygamous marriage? Why or why not?

(3) What specific role does the legal treatment of other jurisdictions play in court reasoning about the recognition of marriage? What role should it play? Compare the comparative reasoning in *Ezeonu* with that used in *Ghassemi*.

E. Property

Selections from the First Restatement of Conflicts, on Real Property

§§211, 214, 216-223, 225-227, 237-238, 244-246, 248-251 (1934)

§211. Property in Tangible Thing: Where Created

The original creation of property in a tangible thing is governed by the law of the state where the thing is at the time of the events which create the interests.

§214. Legal Effect and Interpretation of Words Used in an Instrument of Conveyance

(1) Words used in an instrument of conveyance of an interest in land which, by the law of the state where the land is, have a given operative effect irrespective of the intent of the conveyor, will be accorded such effect in any state.

(2) Words used in an instrument of conveyance of an interest in land which, by the law of the state where the land is, have a given operative effect unless a contrary intent is shown by admissible evidence, will be accorded such effect in any state.

(3) The meaning of words used in an instrument of conveyance of an interest in land which, by the law of the state where the land is, are accorded neither of the effects described in Subsections (1) and (2), is in the absence of controlling circumstances to the contrary, determined in accordance with usage at the domicile of the conveyor at the time of the conveyance.

§216. Capacity to Convey Interest in Land

Capacity to make a valid conveyance of an interest in land is determined by the law of the state where the land is.

§217. Formalities of Conveyance of Interest in Land

The formalities necessary for the validity of a conveyance of an interest in land are determined by the law of the state where the land is.

§218. Substantial Validity of Conveyance of Interest in Land

Whether a conveyance of an interest in land, which is in due form and is made by a party who has capacity to convey it, is in other respects valid, is determined by the law of the state where the land is.

§219. Capacity of Grantee to Take or Hold Land

Whether the grantee in a conveyance of an interest in land is capable of taking or holding the interest is determined by the law of the state where the land is.

§220. Effect of Conveyance of Interest in Land

The effect upon interests in land of a conveyance is determined by the law of the state where the land is.

§221. Nature of Interest Created by Conveyance of Land

The nature of the interest in land created by a conveyance is determined by the law of the state where the land is.

§222. Non-Possessory Interests in Land

The creation, transfer and termination of non-possessory interests in land are determined by the law of the state where the land is.

§223. Transfer of Interest in Land by Operation of Law

An interest in land can be transferred by operation of law only by the law of the state where the land is.

§225. Mortgage on Land; By What Law Determined

The validity and effect of a mortgage on land is determined by the law of the state where the land is. [*But* refer back to pages 35-36 *supra*, and read again comment (*a*) to §333 concerning contracts.]

§226. Assignment of Mortgage on Land

The validity and effect of an assignment of a mortgage on land are determined by the law of the state where the land is.

§227. Foreclosure of Mortgage on Land

The method and effect of the foreclosure of a mortgage on land are determined by the law of the state where the land is.

§237. Effect of Marriage on Existing Interests in Land

The effect of marriage upon interests in land owned by a spouse at the time of marriage is determined by the law of the state where the land is.

§238. Effect of Marriage on an Interest in Land Later Acquired

The effect of marriage upon an interest in land acquired by either or both of the spouses during coverture is determined by the law of the state where the land is.

§244. Equitable Conversion of Trust Property

Whether the interest of the beneficiary of a trust of land is real estate or whether, because of a direction to sell the land, it is personal property, is determined by the law of the state where the land is.

§245. Inheritance of Land

The law of the state where the land is determines its devolution upon the death of the owner intestate.

§246. Legitimacy of Claimant by Descent

A person who is heir by the law of the state where the land is, only if legitimate, is heir if, but only if, he is born legitimate as stated in §138 or has been legitimized as stated in §139 and §140.

§248. Share of Spouse in Land upon Termination of Marriage

(1) The existence and extent of a common law or statutory interest of a surviving spouse in the land of a deceased spouse are determined by the law of the state where the land is.

(2) The effect of divorce upon the interest of one spouse in the land of another is determined by the law of the state where the land is.

§249. Will of Land

The validity and effect of a will of an interest in land are determined by the law of the state where the land is.

§250. Revocation of Will of Land

The effectiveness of an intended revocation of a will of an interest in land is determined by the law of the state where the land is.

§251. Interpretation, Construction and Effect of Will of Land

(1) Words used in a devise of an interest in land which, by the law of the state where the land is, have a given operative effect irrespective of the intent of the testator, will be accorded such effect in any state.

(2) Words used in a devise of an interest in land which, by the law of the state where the land is, have a given operative effect unless a contrary intent is shown by admissible evidence, will be accorded such effect in any state.

(3) The meaning of words used in a devise of an interest in land which, by the law of the state where the land is, are accorded neither of the effects described in Subsections (1) and (2), is, in the absence of controlling circumstances to the contrary, determined in accordance with usage at the domicile of the testator at the time when the will was made.

Burr v. Beckler

264 Ill. 230, 106 N.E. 206 (1914)

Cartwright, C.J.

The appellee, Shelton C. Burr, filed his bill in the circuit court of Cook county against Ednah J. Tobey (now Ednah J. Beckler), Charles H. Tobey, and William E. Church, trustee, to foreclose a trust deed dated March 11, 1905, made by Ednah J. Tobey and Charles H. Tobey, who was then her husband, conveying certain real estate in Chicago to secure a note of that date made by Ednah J. Tobey, payable to her own order five years after date, with interest, and endorsed by her. Ednah J. Tobey answered, alleging that she was induced to execute the note and trust deed by the false and fraudulent representation of her said husband, Charles H. Tobey; that Shelton C. Burr had notice of the fraud and was not a bona fide assignee of the note; and that the note and trust deed were void for the reason that they were executed in the state of Florida while she was a feme covert and incapable by the laws of Florida of executing the same. . . . The [intermediate appellate] court also concluded that the note and trust deed were not invalid because made in Florida while the maker was temporarily in that state, and because the note was dated at Chicago, Ill., and secured by real estate in this state, and the trust deed recited the residence of the grantors at Chicago. . . .

[I]f the note was void because executed in the state of Florida, the decree of the chancellor was in accordance with the law regardless of all other questions.

The validity, construction, force, and effect of instruments affecting the title to land depend upon the law of the state where the land lies. . . . But, if the note was void, the trust deed, which was incidental and intended to secure a performance of the obligation created by the note, could not be enforced. It is a universal rule that the validity of a contract is to be determined by the law of the place where it is made, and if it is not valid there it will not be enforced in another state in which it would have been valid if made there. . . .

A note takes effect from the time of its delivery and not from its date. Until the maker of a note parts with the possession and control of the instrument he may cancel it or dispose of it as he pleases, and a note is not executed until delivered. The note in this case was made in Florida, and the trust deed was signed at the same time and acknowledged before a notary public of the county of Dade, in that state. Charles H. Tobey had designated the United States mail as the means of transmission of the note and trust deed to him, and Ednah J. Tobey, in compliance with his request, deposited them in the mail in the state of Florida. When the note and trust deed were so deposited, Ednah J. Tobey, the maker, parted with the possession of and lost all control over the papers and all right to retake or reclaim them. Under such circumstances, the delivery was complete in Florida when the note and trust deed were placed in the mail, directed by Charles H. Tobey, trustee of the Ludington estate. . . . The fact that the domicile of Ednah J. Tobey was in Illinois did not enable her to execute a note in the state of Florida contrary to the laws of that state, under which she was not competent to enter into a contract. In Forsyth v. Barnes, *supra*, a man and his wife domiciled in the state of Illinois, made in Ohio a note and warrant of attorney authorizing the confession of a judgment. Judgment was taken in Ohio and an action of debt brought on the judgment in Illinois. It was held that the judgment entered on the warrant of attorney was void as against the wife, and subject to attack either directly or collaterally, because she was a feme covert, incapable at common law of executing the warrant, and in the absence of proof it would be presumed that the common law was in force in Ohio. The note was payable in Ohio, but that is not a ground of distinction, because the place where the contract is made determines its validity and the place of performance affects only the time, mode, and extent of the remedy. The law of the state of performance will govern in determining the rights of the parties and the effect of the contract, but if a party is not competent to make a contract, the contract is not valid and will not be enforced anywhere. The application of the rules of law in this case leads to the conclusion that the note was void.

The judgment of the Appellate Court is reversed, and the decree of the circuit court affirmed.

Thomson v. Kyle

39 Fla. 582, 23 So. 12 (1897)

. . . The appellee (complainant below), on November 14, 1891, filed a bill in equity in the circuit court of Alachua county, praying foreclosure of a mortgage on certain real estate situated in that county. The mortgage debt was evidenced by a note executed by the appellants (defendants below) to complainant, under date January 18, 1890, for $2,932, due April 10, 1890, and payable in the city of Birmingham, Alabama. The mortgage given to secure this note was executed on the same day by the defendants. The defendant, Della K. Thomson, filed her plea on January 4, 1892, whereby she alleged that prior and subsequent to, and at the time of, the execution of the note and mortgage, she was a married woman, the wife of her codefendant, and seised and possessed of a statutory separate estate in her own individual right and control, part of which was embraced in the mortgage; that the note and mortgage were executed in the state of Alabama, and that all transactions out of which the mortgage debt arose occurred in said state; that the mortgage debt was the debt of her husband exclusively, and she executed the note and mortgage as security only, and upon no other consideration; that by the laws of Alabama the obligation of a married woman executed for her husband's debt was null and void, and incapable of enforcement, and that the note and mortgage, being void as to her in the state of Alabama, were likewise void in the state of Florida. This plea was, upon argument, overruled. . . .

CARTER, J. (after stating the facts).

I

The question presented by the plea of Della K. Thomson is an interesting one, and one upon which the authorities are not in entire accord. It is not denied by appellants that, had the mortgage sought to be foreclosed in this case been executed in this state, it would have been valid, and enforceable under our laws. Indeed, it has been held by this court, on more than one occasion, that a mortgage properly executed by a married woman and her husband, conveying the wife's separate statutory real estate as security for her husband's debt, is valid. . . . It is insisted, however, that under the laws of Alabama, a married woman is without capacity to bind herself or her property as security for the debt of her husband, and, as the mortgage sought to be enforced in this case was executed, and the debt secured thereby was payable, in that state, and all the parties were there domiciled, that those laws necessarily entered into and became a part of the contract, rendering it void in that state; and that, being void in Alabama, it is, by virtue of interstate law, void in Florida. It may be admitted that this argument has strong application to the note executed by Mrs. Thomson with her husband, which the mortgage was given to secure, for, the note being a general personal obligation, if void by the laws of the state in which it was executed and made payable, it ought likewise to be void in every other state where it is sought to be enforced. But it does not follow that because Mrs. Thomson is not bound by the note it is for that reason totally void. It still remains a valid obligation of her husband, which she can, in this state, secure by a mortgage of her separate statutory property. We do not understand that any principle of interstate law requires us to test the validity or sufficiency of conveyances of or liens upon real estate in this state by the laws of other states or nations, even though such contracts may have been executed, or given to secure the performance of some act, within their jurisdiction. The reasons why we should not are obvious. The subject-matter, with reference to the title of which the conveyance or lien is executed, being at the time of such execution an immovable thing, not only located beyond the control of that sovereignty within whose jurisdiction the contract is executed, and forever so to remain, but then within the exclusive jurisdiction of another independent sovereignty, and forever so to remain, the parties to such conveyance are presumed to have contracted, at least so far as the immovable thing is concerned, with reference to the laws of that jurisdiction within whose borders the thing is situated. And no sovereign state, without express legislative sanction, is presumed to surrender to owners of immovable property within its limits the power to incumber or charge the title thereto in any other manner than that pointed out by its laws. It is, therefore, almost universally held that so far as real estate or immovable property is concerned, we must look to the laws of the state where it is situated for the rules which govern its descent, alienation, and transfer, and for the construction, validity, and effect of conveyances thereof . . . ; and it is to the same law that we must look for the rules governing the capacity of the parties to such contracts or conveyances, and their rights under the same. . . . It would seem, therefore, that upon principle the mortgage in this case should be subjected to the laws of this state, in order to ascertain its validity, construction, and the capacity of the parties to execute it, rather than to the laws of the state of Alabama, within whose borders the real estate is not situated, and as to which her laws can have no extraterritorial effect. While a contrary opinion was entertained in Ohio, . . . it has been held in several well-considered cases that, although by the laws of the state of a married woman's domicile she has no capacity to execute a mortgage upon her separate estate as security for the debt of her husband, yet if she, in that state, executes a mortgage of that character upon real estate situated in another state, whose laws permit a married woman to mortgage her property to secure such a debt, the mortgage will, in the latter state, be held valid, and enforceable in its courts by appropriate proceedings. . . . We hold that, notwithstanding Mrs. Thomson's incapacity by the laws of Alabama to execute the mortgage sought to be foreclosed here, she was capable, under our laws, of executing in Alabama a mortgage upon her separate statutory real property in this state to secure her husband's debt, and that her plea was properly overruled. This conclusion also disposes of those portions of the cross bill and answer of the defendant John M. Thomson which cover the same matters as this plea.

The answer and cross bill of the defendant John M. Thomson alleged that there was included in the obligation evidencing the mortgage debt the sum of $300, which, under the laws of the state of Alabama, was usurious interest, and that under the laws of that state usury forfeited all interest upon the principal debt as to which unlawful interest was charged. As this obligation was a personal one, and it was executed and to be performed in the state of Alabama, having no reference to immovable property in this state, we think its validity and interpretation are governed by the laws of the former state. Perry vs. Lewis, 6 Fla. 555. Therefore, although in this state there were no laws against usury at the time of the execution of this obligation, yet, if it is tainted with usury by the laws of Alabama, where it was executed and made payable, and where all the parties resided at the time of its execution, we think the infirmity follows it to this state, even when secured by a mortgage on lands in this state. The authorities are not entirely unanimous on this point, but we think the weight of them, supported by principle, sustains the proposition that a note executed and payable in one state, though secured by a mortgage on lands in another, will be governed, as to the rate of interest it shall bear, by the laws of the former; and if, by such laws, all interest is forfeited for usury, the same result will follow, upon foreclosure of the mortgage securing it, in the state where the mortgaged lands are situated. . . .

Questions and Comments

(1) Do the *Burr* and *Thomson* cases reach inconsistent results? Would it have made a difference in *Burr* if Charles had joined Ednah in making the note for which foreclosure on the mortgage was sought?

(2) Was the purpose of the Florida common-law rule of coverture served by invalidating a note made by Ednah Tobey, an Illinois resident? Was the purpose of the Alabama coverture rule fulfilled in the *Thomson* case by allowing her to mortgage her Florida land? What purpose of Florida law might have been served by the ruling in the *Thomson* case?

(3) If Alabama, with its coverture rule, followed the same conflicts approach as Florida in the *Thomson* case, what would happen in an Alabama case in which a Florida woman had executed a guaranty of her husband's note in Florida, to be paid in Florida and secured by a mortgage of land in Alabama? Wouldn't the note be enforceable under the *Thomson* approach, while the mortgage would not be? But if the note was enforceable, could the resulting judgment be satisfied by execution against the Alabama land? If so, has striking down the mortgage been limited in effect to depriving the mortgage holder of priorities that it would have had over other creditors? Has it failed in its essential purpose of protecting the married woman from her husband's overreaching? If so, what good (to Alabama) would the *Thomson* rule be? Even if Alabama used such reasoning to reject the *Thomson* approach, couldn't the plaintiff in this hypothetical get a judgment in Florida, which would apply its own law to the note, and demand enforcement of the judgment against the land in Alabama under the full faith and credit clause of the Constitution? If so, is there any way for Alabama to protect its married women, or are the conflicts rules stacked against the Alabama policy in this situation?

(4) Why all of the emphasis on the situs of real property, especially when—as we shall see—no similar obsession is present with personal property? The situs rule is frequently criticized by proponents of modern approaches to choice of law. *See, e.g.,* Weintraub, *Obstacles to Sensible Choice of Law for Determining Marital Property Rights on Divorce or in Probate: Hanau and the Situs Rule,* 25 Hous. L. Rev. 1113 (1988); Leflar, *American Conflicts Law* 410-411 (1968). Professor Leflar defends the rule on the grounds that our title recording systems are set up territorially, and a would-be purchaser needs to be able to rely on the applicability of situs law in performing a title search.

Other reasons that have been given include the fact that (a) only the state in which land is located has physical power over it (and, as we shall see in the chapter on full faith and credit to judgments, the principle is carried so far that a judgment of State *A*, purporting to directly affect title to land in State *B*, is ineffective even if State *A* possesses jurisdiction over all the concerned parties); (b) real property is of greatest concern to the state in which it is located (though one may ask, for example, whether that has anything to do with whether an out-of-state wife can guaranty the debts of her husband); and (c) it is rare that there is any uncertainty as to the location of land. *See* Introductory Note to §214 of the Restatement of

Conflict of Laws Second (Tentative Draft No. 5, April 24, 1959) (not contained in the final draft as promulgated).

For an unusual case in which the location of land itself was in question, *see* Durfee v. Duke, 375 U.S. 106 (1963), page 504 *infra*, in which title was disputed because the Missouri River, forming the border between Nebraska and Missouri, had changed course.

Selections from the First Restatement of Conflicts, on Personal Property

§§255-258, 260-261, 289-291, 300-302, 306-307 (1934)

§255. Capacity to Convey Chattel

Capacity to make a valid conveyance of an interest in a chattel is determined by the law of the state where the chattel is at the time of the conveyance.

§256. Formalities of Conveyance of Chattel

The formal validity of a conveyance of an interest in a chattel is determined by the law of the state where the chattel is at the time of conveyance.

§257. Substantial Validity of Conveyance of Chattel

Whether a conveyance of a chattel which is in due form and is made by a party who has capacity to convey it is in other respects valid, is determined by the law of the state where the chattel is at the time of conveyance.

§258. Nature of Interest Created by Conveyance of Chattel

The nature and characteristics of an interest created by a conveyance of an interest in a chattel is determined by the law of the place where the chattel is at the time of the conveyance.

§260. Moving Chattels into Another State; Effect on Title

An interest in a chattel acquired in accordance with the law of the state in which the chattel is at the time when the interest is acquired will be recognized in a state into which the chattel is subsequently taken.

§261. Chattel Embodied in a Document

(1) Whether the title to a chattel is embodied in a document is determined by the law of the place where the chattel is at the time when the document is issued.

(2) The validity of a conveyance of a chattel, title to which is embodied in a document, depends upon the validity of the conveyance of the document.

(3) The validity of a conveyance of a document in which title to a chattel is embodied as stated in Subsection (1), is determined by the law of the place where the document is at the time of the conveyance.

§289. Effect of Marriage on Title to Existing Movables

At marriage the husband and wife respectively acquire such rights or other interests in movables then belonging to the other as are given by the law of the domicil of the husband at the time of marriage.

§290. Movables Acquired During Marriage

Interests of one spouse in movables acquired by the other during the marriage are determined by the law of the domicil of the parties when the movables are acquired.

§291. Removal of Movables of Spouses to Another State

Interests in movables acquired by either or both of the spouses in one state continue after the movables have been brought into another state until the interests are affected by some new dealings with the movables in the second state.

§300. Devolution of Chattels on Death of Owner

At the death of the owner of chattels the title to the chattels passes to the executor or administrator appointed by the court of the state in which the chattels are habitually kept.

§301. Right of Widow or Child Outside Will

The right or other interest of a widow, child, or other person to a share of the movables of a decedent in preference to legatees is determined by the law of the state in which the decedent died domiciled.

§302. Enforcement of Widow's Allowance in Another State

If a widow's allowance has been granted by a court in the state of domicile of her deceased husband, it constitutes a valid claim against movable assets in another state.

§306. Will of Movables

The validity and effect of a will of movables is determined by the law of the state in which the deceased died domiciled.

§307. Revocation of Will of Movables

Whether an act claimed to be a revocation of a will is effective to revoke it as a will of movables is determined by the law of the state in which the deceased was domiciled at the time of his death.

Blackwell v. Lurie

71 P.3d 509 (N.M. Ct. App. 2003)

WECHSLER, C.J.

Robert Blackwell, liquidating trustee in bankruptcy (the Liquidating Trustee), appeals from an order of the district court quashing his petition for writ of execution. Pursuant to our conflict of laws rule, we conclude that Missouri law governs the characterization of the property at issue and that Ronald and Nancy Lurie (the Luries) hold the property as tenants by the entirety. In addition, we conclude that because the deficiency judgment is the separate debt of Ronald Lurie, the district court properly quashed the petition for writ of execution. We therefore affirm.

Background

Ronald Lurie was a general partner in the Missouri law firm of Popkin & Stern. In the early 1990s, Popkin & Stern went into bankruptcy . . . [under] Chapter 11, and the Liquidating Trustee was appointed. Pursuant to Section 723 of the Bankruptcy Code, the Liquidating Trustee obtained a deficiency judgment against Ronald Lurie in the amount of $1,121,743.

The Luries purchased a valuable sketch by Frederic Remington entitled "Scenes of Navajo Life" in Missouri in 1978. In 1993, while still domiciled in Missouri, the Luries placed the sketch on consignment at the Fenn Gallery in Santa Fe, New Mexico, where it remains. Thereafter, the Luries relocated to Montana, their present domicile. . . .

In 1995, the Missouri bankruptcy court overseeing the Popkin & Stern proceedings entered an order by which all parties were stayed from "transferring, selling, or otherwise disposing of" certain assets, including the sketch. The court lifted the order in March 2001, and the Liquidating Trustee was expressly authorized to execute on the sketch, as well as any other non-exempt assets. Accordingly, the Liquidating Trustee served the Luries with notice and filed a petition for writ of execution in [district court]. The Luries separately moved to quash the petition, arguing that the sketch is owned by them as tenants by the entirety, such that it is exempt from execution in satisfaction of the deficiency judgment. The district court conducted a hearing and quashed the Liquidating Trustee's petition for writ of execution.

The Choice of Law Issue

The legal issues presented on appeal arise out of a general rule, observed in many states including Missouri, by which tenancy by the entirety property is deemed inaccessible to all creditors except those to whom husband and wife are jointly indebted. In view of this rule, we are required to determine the nature of the Luries' interests in the sketch, as well as the status of the deficiency judgment as either a joint or a separate debt. The resolution of these subissues, in turn, depends largely upon [whether Missouri or New Mexico law applies.]

Below, the Luries . . . [convinced] the district court that both the nature of their ownership interests in the sketch and the status of the debt should be governed by the laws of the state of Missouri. By contrast, the Liquidating Trustee has relied on New Mexico's laws to support his assertion that the sketch is not tenancy by the entirety property and is therefore subject to execution in satisfaction of the deficiency judgment. . . .

Characterizing the Property Interests at Issue

We first decide which state's laws should apply for the purpose of characterizing the Luries' interests in the sketch. In New Mexico, we generally follow the conflict of laws rule by which an interest in property takes its character at the time and in the manner of its acquisition. *See* English v. Sanchez, 110 N.M. 343, 345 (1990). In this case, the Luries acquired the sketch jointly, as husband and wife, in Missouri in 1978. Under these circumstances, the Luries became joint owners of the sketch as tenants by the entirety. *See* Merrill Lynch, Pierce, Fenner & Smith, Inc. v. Shackelford, 591 S.W.2d 210, 213 (Mo. Ct. App. 1979). Accordingly, applying the time-and-manner-of-acquisition rule, the sketch would continue to be regarded as tenancy by the entirety property. . . .

Alternatively, the Liquidating Trustee argues that the Community Property Act of 1973, NMSA 1978, §§40-3-6 to -17 (the Act), has superceded the time-and-manner-of-acquisition rule, and contends that the sketch should be classified as community property in accordance with Section 40-3-8. However, the New Mexico Supreme Court has previously considered and rejected this argument. *See* Stephens v. Stephens, 93 N.M. 1, 2-3, 1197-98 (1979) (declining to conclude that New Mexico's statutory provisions defining community and separate property should apply to all property acquired during coverture, regardless of the situs of acquisition).

Although the Liquidating Trustee asserts that subsequent amendments to the Act have effectively overruled *Stephens*, we do not agree. The only pertinent modifications to the Act since *Stephens* involve the addition of the quasi-community property provisions. While these provisions broaden the scope of New Mexico's property laws, they are not broad enough to encompass the matter under consideration. A designation as quasi-community property is only significant "[f]or purposes of division of property incident to a dissolution of marriage or a legal separation," in which case the property in question is treated as community property "if both parties are domiciliaries of New Mexico at the time of the dissolution or legal separation proceeding." Section 40-3-8(D). This case does not involve a dissolution of marriage or a legal separation. Furthermore, the Luries are not domiciliaries of this state. As a result, the Act does not govern the nature of the Luries' interests in the sketch.

Finally, the Liquidating Trustee urges that we depart from the time-and-manner-of-acquisition rule in this case on the ground that the outcome is incompatible with the laws of this state. Although the "public policy exception" provides a mechanism by which the application of out-of-state law may be avoided if such laws are offensive to the public policy of this state, this exception may only be invoked in extremely limited circumstances. . . . Although tenancies by the entirety may be anachronistic, . . . [w]e . . . conclude that the public policy exception does not warrant our declining to apply Missouri law in this case.

Characterizing the Deficiency Judgment

Having determined that the sketch is properly characterized as tenancy by the entirety property, we must now consider the nature of the debt that is represented by the deficiency judgment. We again must determine whether to apply the laws of this state or that of another.

The Liquidating Trustee asserts that the laws of New Mexico, rather than the laws of Missouri, should be applied for the purpose of classifying the deficiency judgment, and contends that under the laws of this state, the debt is properly regarded as joint or community in nature. The Liquidating Trustee relies heavily on *Sproul*, 116 N.M. at 256-61, as authority for this position.

In *Sproul*, our Supreme Court held that when a foreign judgment is domesticated in New Mexico, New Mexico law must be applied in order to characterize the debt represented by the judgment. *Sproul* involved a debt that was created in New Mexico by a New Mexico resident. The real property that was subject to execution in satisfaction of the domesticated judgment was located in New Mexico and characterized as community property. Following a lengthy analysis, the Court ultimately concluded that, under New Mexico law, the debt was attributable to the community. Based upon these community property and community debt designations, the Court recognized and applied the statutory requirement that community debts be paid first from community assets.

Under New Mexico law, the debt represented by the deficiency judgment in this case might be characterized as a community debt because it appears to have been contracted or incurred during marriage. *See* §40-3-9(B). On the other hand, the debt might also be characterized as the separate debt of Ronald Lurie pursuant to §40-3-9(A)(3) (defining a "separate debt" as a debt so designated by a judgment or decree of any court having jurisdiction). Although our Supreme Court stated in *Sproul* that §40-3-9(A)(3) only applies when the foreign court's judgment or decree contains an express statement indicating that the debt is separate, the Court also noted that the character of the debt was not actually addressed by the foreign court that issued the judgment in that case. By contrast, the bankruptcy court that issued the judgment against Ronald Lurie had multiple opportunities to consider the character of the debt represented by the deficiency judgment and, at all times, treated the debt as the separate debt of Ronald Lurie. *See* In re Popkin & Stern, 289 F.3d 554, 555 (8th Cir. 2002) (implicitly characterizing the deficiency judgment at issue as the separate debt of Ronald Lurie and observing that the Liquidating Trustee was only entitled to execute against assets jointly held by the Luries up to the amount of a judgment separately obtained against Nancy Lurie); In re Popkin & Stern, 266 B.R. 146, 149 (B.A.P. 8th Cir. 2001) (same).

However, we need not resolve the issue of the character of the debt represented by the deficiency judgment because application of New Mexico law does not lead to a resolution of the issue. *Sproul* indicates that we apply the New Mexico statutory provisions pertaining to satisfaction of the debt if the debt is characterized under New Mexico law. *See* §§40-3-10, -11. However, the Luries own the sketch as tenants by the entirety. As we have noted, New Mexico has abrogated tenancies by the entirety, and the statutory provisions governing the satisfaction of debts make no mention of tenancies by the entirety. *Id*. Unlike *Sproul* in which the property could be defined under New Mexico law, this case cannot be resolved by applying existing New Mexico law. We therefore cannot afford *Sproul* the broad interpretation advanced by the Liquidating Trustee. Because New Mexico law cannot be applied for the purpose of characterizing the debt, we necessarily apply the law of Missouri, the state in which all the other pertinent activity took place.

Under Missouri law, the amenability of the sketch to execution in satisfaction of the deficiency judgment depends upon the status of the debt as joint. *See* In re Garner, 952 F.2d at 233-35 (applying Missouri law for the proposition that tenancy by the entirety property is only available to creditors if joint debts are at issue); In re Brown, 234 B.R. at 912-13 (same). Although in a usual case it would be necessary to analyze Missouri's debt and creditor law in order to arrive at a conclusion, we are aided in this case by prior rulings in parallel proceedings. The bankruptcy court presiding over the Popkin & Stern proceedings has already classified the deficiency judgment as the separate debt of Ronald Lurie, in accordance with the laws of the state of Missouri. Based upon this classification of the debt, the district court properly concluded that the sketch was not amenable to execution in satisfaction of the deficiency judgment.

Conclusion

Based on the time-and-manner-of-acquisition rule, we conclude that the sketch is held by the Luries as tenants by the entirety. Because we apply Missouri law in order to determine the character of the debt, we conclude that the deficiency judgment represents the separate debt of Ronald Lurie. Accordingly, in conformity with the general rule by which tenancy by the entirety property is deemed exempt from all but joint creditors, the sketch is not subject to the claims of the Liquidating Trustee. . . .

Morson v. Second National Bank of Boston

306 Mass. 588, 29 N.E.2d 19 (1940)

QUA, J.

This is a bill in equity by the administrator of the estate of Herbert B. Turner, late of Gloucester, alleging, in substance, that a certificate for one hundred and fifty shares of the stock of the defendant Massachusetts Mohair Plush Company, a Massachusetts corporation, had been originally issued to Herbert B. Turner, but had been delivered to the defendant bank as "transfer agent" of the plush company by the defendant Mildred Turner Copperman for transfer to her on the ground that Herbert B. Turner in his lifetime had made her a gift of the stock. The prayers are for injunctions against the transfer of the stock and for recovery of the certificate.

The judge carefully found all the materials facts in detail, upon which he ruled that there had been no completed gift of the stock for the plaintiff. The issue is whether the facts found show a valid gift of the stock, which should now be recognized by a transfer on the books of the corporation and the issuance of a new certificate to Mildred Turner Copperman. We think that they do.

Among the facts found are these: About September 20, 1937, while Turner and Mildred Turner Copperman were travelling together in Italy, Turner handed to Mildred Turner Copperman a sealed envelope previously marked by him "Property of Mildred Turner Copperman." As he did so he said, "These are yours." The certificate in his name, dated October 6, 1933, was in the envelope. He also said that he would have to sign the back of the certificate. Two days later a notary and two witnesses came to the hotel where the parties were staying. Mildred Turner Copperman produced the certificate, and "Turner signed his name on the back . . . and then he filled in the name of Miss Copperman and her address" and delivered the certificate to Mildred Turner Copperman, who "accepted it." Turner's intention at that time was "to make an absolute gift to Mildred Copperman to take effect at once."

It is provided by [Uniform Stock Transfer Act §1], that title "to a certificate and to the shares represented thereby shall be transferred only—(a) By delivery of the certificate endorsed either in blank or to a specified person by the person appearing by the certificate to be the owner of the shares represented thereby; or (b) By delivery of the certificate and a separate document containing a written assignment of the certificate or a power of attorney to sell, assign or transfer the same or the shares represented thereby, signed by the person appearing by the certificate to be the owner of the shares represented thereby. Such assignment or power of attorney may be either in blank or to a specified person." [Uniform Stock Transfer Act §22] defines "certificate" as "a certificate of stock in a corporation organized under the laws of this commonwealth or of another state whose laws are consistent with said sections." Plainly that which was done in Italy would have been sufficient, if it had been done in Massachusetts, to effect a transfer legal title to the shares.

But it is argued that the validity of the transfer is to be judged by the law of Italy, and that certain formalities required by that law for making of gifts in general were not observed. Doubtless it is true that whether or not there is a completed gift of an ordinary tangible chattel is to be determined by the law of the situs of the chattel. American Law Inst., Restatement, Conflict of Laws §§256, 257, 258. Shares of stock, however, are not ordinary tangible chattels. A distinction has been taken between the shares and the certificate, regarded as a piece of paper which can be seen and felt, the former being said to be subject to the jurisdiction of the state of incorporation and the latter subject to the jurisdiction of the state in which it is located. American Law Inst., Restatement, Conflict of Laws, §53. The shares are part of the structure of the corporation, all of which was erected and stands by virtue of the law of the state of incorporation. The law of that state determines the nature and attributes of the shares. If by the law of that state the shares devolve upon one who obtains ownership of the certificate, it may be that the law of the state of a purported transfer of the certificate will indirectly determine share ownership. But at least when the state of incorporation has seen fit in creating the shares to insert in them the intrinsic attribute or quality of being assignable in a particular manner it would seem that that state, and other states as well, should recognize assignments made in the specified manner wherever they are made, even though that manner involves dealing in some way with the certificate. Or the shares may be regarded for this purpose as remaining at home with the corporation, wherever the certificate may be—much as real estate remains at home when the deeds are taken abroad. Thus the American Law Institute in its Restatement of Conflict Laws, §53, comment *d*, says that shares created in a State which has adopted the Uniform Stock Transfer Act with its provision that title to a share can be transferred only by delivery of the certificate "may be transferred by delivery of the certificate as provided by the Act even though such delivery takes place in another state where such Act is not in force." This rule is precisely applicable to the present case. This rule has, in our opinion, the decided advantage of promoting convenience, certainty, and uniformity in the transfer of stock. We prefer to follow it.

Questions and Comments

(1) Does it make sense to peg ownership of movable property at the time and place of its conveyance? If the Luries had traveled to Russia to purchase the sketch, would their respective interests in the sketch be determined by Russian law? Assuming the soundness of a situs rule focused on the point of transfer, would it make more sense to peg the transfer of ownership of the sketch to Russian law but peg the specific nature of the spouses' interests to the law of Missouri, where they were domiciled at the time?

(2) If spouses choose a new domicile, as the Luries did, should the nature of the property owned be redefined according to the law of their new domicile? What reasons might justify defining the nature of their joint ownership by reference to the law of the current marital domicile?

(3) Why should situs matter so much? The Restatement provisions quoted above point chiefly to the locus of the tangible item to determine questions about transfers. Exceptions are made with respect to testamentary dispositions and transfers between spouses. Are the reasons discussed previously for applying the law of the situs to questions involving real property as compelling for questions of personal property?

(4) What law should determine ownership in shares of stock? Did it make sense for the *Morson* court (and the Restatement) to distinguish between certificates and shares? Suppose that Herbert had given the signed, notarized, and witnessed certificates to Mildred while sitting at the kitchen table in their home. If the couple was domiciled in Massachusetts and the stock at issue represented shares in a Panamanian corporation, whose law should apply then to determine whether the gift was effective?

(5) A particularly troublesome aspect of chattels is that they can be moved. When that fact is added to the fact that valuable chattels are often the collateral for security interests, the opportunity for a great deal of mischief arises. The Uniform Commercial Code has spelled out a set of fairly specific rules for dealing with the perfection of security interests in movable goods and in intangibles. Provisions are made for accounts, "ordinary goods," "mobile goods," goods subject to certificate-of-title legislation, and several other categories of collateral. *In general*, ordinary goods are governed by the law of their location. Accounts and mobile goods, having no handily identifiable location, are governed by the law of the debtor's location— usually its place of business. Goods subject to a certificate of title are generally subject to the law of the state that issues the certificate of title. For each category, there are rules concerning the relocation of the collateral or debtor.

For the most part, the single most important choice-of-law question concerning goods under Article 9 is where to file a financing statement in order to perfect a security interest, and in the 1972 version of the UCC, the rules of §9-103 are limited to rules on where to file. Note that this is an area in which certainty is not only the most important consideration but nearly the only consideration. UCC §1-105 governs other conflicts issues. (*See* Chapter 3 *infra*.)

(6) Consider also the problem of choice of law as applied to movable property held in trust. What law should apply when the creator ("settlor") of a trust is domiciled in State *A*, the property held in trust is located in State *B*, the trustee designated to administer the estate is located in State *C*, and the beneficiaries of the trust are domiciled in State *D*? The First Restatement, §§294-298, provided that the validity of a trust of chattels created via inter vivos transaction is determined by the law of the state where the chattel is located when the trust is created. The validity of a trust of choses in action created inter vivos is determined by the law of the place where the transaction takes place. And the validity of a trust created by will is determined by the law of the testator's domicile at the time of her death. The trust instrument is interpreted according to usage at the domicile of the settlor at the time the trust was created. And the law applied to the administration of the trust is that of the place where the trust instrument locates its administration. Does it make sense to have so many different laws applied to trusts?

Is this a situation where the settlor should be permitted to choose the law governing the trust, either by express choice-of-law clause or by choosing the location where the trust is established? Consider the following:

> In all the affairs of life there has been a vast increase of mobility. Residence is growing less and less the focal point of existence, and its practical effect is steadily diminishing. Men living in one jurisdiction often conduct their affairs in other jurisdictions, and keep their securities there. Trusts are created in business and financial centers by settlors residing elsewhere. A settlor, regardless of residence, cannot establish a trust to be administered here which offends our

public policy. If we hold that a nonresident settlor may also not establish a trust of personal property here which offends the public policy of his domicile, we shackle both the nonresident settlor and the resident trustee.

Our courts have sought whenever possible to sustain the validity even of testamentary trusts to be administered in a jurisdiction other than the domicile of the testator. . . . In regard to other conveyances or alienations of personal property situated here, they have steadfastly applied the law of the jurisdiction where the personal property is situated. The maxim that movable personal property follows its owner is restricted to the field within which the state, where that property is found, chooses to apply other laws than its own, and modern conditions have caused a limitation of the field to narrow bounds. That is true in other jurisdictions as well as here. Where a nonresident settlor establishes here a trust of personal property intending that the trust should be governed by the law of this jurisdiction, there is little reason why the courts should defeat his intention by applying the law of another jurisdiction. . . .

Hutchison v. Ross, 262 N.Y. 381 (1933) (upholding inter vivos trust created by a husband in Montreal intended to benefit his wife, also of Montreal, even though the trust was invalid under the laws of Quebec). Consider also the following statements made in Wilmington Trust Co. v. Wilmington Trust Co., 26 Del. Ch. 397 (1942), a case in which a trust was upheld under the law of the state to which the seat of the trust was relocated even though the testator's appointment violated the Rule Against Perpetuities of the state of the testator's domicile:

The diversity of judicial opinion with respect to the discovery of the jurisdiction under whose law the validity of a trust inter vivos of intangible personal property is to be determined is such that no useful purpose will be served by an attempted analysis of the decisions. Courts have variously looked to the domicile of the donor, the place of execution of the trust instrument, the situs of the trust property, the place of administration of the trust, the domicile of the trustee, the domicile of the beneficiaries, and to the intent or desire of the donor, or to a combination of some of these denominators, in deciding the troublesome question of conflict of law. In the case of a testamentary trust of personalty it is very generally held that the law of the testator's domicile is the governing law. In some jurisdictions the same rule is applied in the case of a living trust of personal property. Modern methods of transportation with a resulting change of business economy have tended, however, to obliterate state lines and to depreciate the importance of particular localities. The place of one's residence no longer is a sure indication of one's place of business; nor is ownership of property closely tied to residence. The domicile of the donor is, of course, a circumstance to be considered in the ascertainment of the seat of the trust; but courts, today, are not so much inclined to the uncompromising pursuit of abstract doctrine. They are disposed to take a more realistic and practical view of the problem; and the donor's domicile is no longer regarded as the decisive factor. The place of execution of the trust instrument and the domicile of the trustee and the place of administration of the trust—quite generally the same place—are important factors; and the intent of the donor, if that can be ascertained, has been increasingly emphasized. . . .

Contracting parties, within definite limits, have some right of choice in the selection of the jurisdiction under whose law their contract is to be governed. And where the donor in a trust agreement has expressed his desire, or if it pleases, his intent to have his trust controlled by the law of a certain state, there seems to be no good reason why his intent should not be respected by the courts, if the selected jurisdiction has a material connection with the transaction. More frequently, perhaps, the trust instrument contains no expression of choice of jurisdiction; but, again, there is no sufficient reason why the donor's choice should be disregarded if his intention in this respect can be ascertained from an examination of attendant facts and circumstances, provided that the same substantial connection between the transaction and the intended jurisdiction shall be found to exist. . . .

Are there any potential problems with allowing settlors to place their assets in trust in states where those trusts are valid even though the same trust would be invalid in the state of the settlor's domicile? What if the settlor is seeking to shield his assets from potential creditors by placing his assets in offshore trusts? *See* LoPucki, *The Essential Structure of Judgment Proofing*, 51 Stan. L. Rev. 147 (1998); Sterk, *Asset Protection Trusts: Trust Law's Race to the Bottom?*, 85 Cornell L. Rev. 1035 (2000); Hirsch, *Fear Not the Asset Protection Trust*, 27 Cardozo L. Rev. 2685 (2006). Does the substantial connection requirement indicated by the *Wilmington Trust* court solve this potential problem?

F. Corporations

Selections from the First Restatement of Conflicts, on Corporations

§§154-155, 165-166, 182-183, 187-188, 190-192, 205 (1934)

§154. Recognition of Foreign Corporation

The fact of incorporation by one state will be recognized in every other state.

§155. Questions of Incorporation

(1) Whether an association has been incorporated is determined by the law of the state in which an attempt to incorporate has been made.

(2) The effects of an unsuccessful attempt to incorporate are governed by the law of the state in which the attempt was made.

(3) Defects in the process of incorporation which may give the incorporating state a power to dissolve the corporation are governed by the law of such state.

§165. Powers of Foreign Corporation

A foreign corporation can legally perform any act within its corporate powers under the law of the state of incorporation unless the act is prohibited by the law of the state where it is to be performed.

§166. Law Governing Act of Foreign Corporation

The effect of an act directed to be done by a foreign corporation is governed by the law of the state where it is done.

§182. Law Governing Title to Share

Whether a person is a shareholder or other member of a corporation is determined by the law of the state of incorporation.

§183. Participation in Management and Profits

The right of a shareholder to participate in the administration of the affairs of the corporation, in the division of profits and in the distribution of assets on dissolution and his rights on the issuance of new shares are determined by the law of the state of incorporation.

§187. Director's or Shareholder's Liability

Except as stated in §188, the existence and extent of the liability of shareholders, officers or directors of a corporation to a creditor of the corporation for a violation of law by them, is determined by the law of the state of incorporation.

§188. Liability Imposed by State Where Corporation Acts

So far as the directors or agents are participants in acts done within the state, a state can impose liability upon the directors or agents of a foreign corporation doing business in the state for acts done within the state or for failure to do acts required by the law of the state as a condition of doing business within the state.

§190. Direct Liability of Shareholder Imposed by State of Incorporation

The state of incorporation can impose liability on a shareholder running directly to creditors, for debts of the corporation incurred in another state and this liability will be enforced in any state which has judicial jurisdiction over the shareholder.

§191. Direct Liability of Shareholder Imposed by Foreign State

Liability for an act caused by a foreign corporation to be done by its agent can be imposed on a shareholder by the law of the state where the act is done only if the shareholder

(a) is domiciled in the state, or

(b) has personally taken part in doing the act or causing it to be done, or

(c) has notice that the corporation was formed to do business there. This liability will be enforced in any state having judicial jurisdiction over the shareholder.

§192. Action Concerning Shares

Except as stated in §193 and subject to the considerations stated in the Scope Note to this Topic, a court will usually not entertain a suit brought against a foreign corporation to obtain a decree against it requiring or enjoining the issuance, transfer, or cancellation of shares.

§205. Creation of Shares by Reincorporated Association

When an association already incorporated by one state is incorporated by another, the creation of shares is governed by the law of the state which first incorporates the association.

McDermott Inc. v. Lewis

531 A.2d 206 (Del. 1987)

Before CHRISTIE, C.J., HORSEY and MOORE, JJ.

MOORE, J.:

We confront an important issue of first impression—whether a Delaware subsidiary of a Panamanian corporation may vote the share it holds in its parent company under circumstances which are prohibited by Delaware law, but not the law of Panama. Necessarily, this involves questions of foreign law, and applicability of the internal affairs doctrine under Delaware law.

Plaintiffs, Harry Lewis and Nina Altman, filed these consolidated suits in the Court of Chancery in December, 1982 seeking to enjoin or rescind the 1982 Reorganization under which McDermott Incorporated, a Delaware corporation ("McDermott Delaware"), became a 92%-owned subsidiary of McDermott International, Inc., a Panamanian corporation ("International"). Lewis and Altman are stockholders of McDermott Delaware, which emerged from the Reorganization owning approximately 10% of International's common stock. Plaintiffs challenged this aspect of the Reorganization, and the Court of Chancery granted partial summary judgment in their favor, holding that McDermott Delaware could not vote its stock in International.

We conclude that the trial court erred in refusing to apply the law of Panama to the internal affairs of International. There was no nexus between International and the State of Delaware. Moreover, plaintiffs concede that the issues here do not involve the internal affairs of McDermott Delaware. Thus, we decline to follow Norlin Corp. v. Rooney, Pace Inc., 744 F.2d 255 (2d Cir. 1984), which prohibited a similar device involving a Panamanian subsidiary seeking to vote the share it held in its Panamanian parent. Accordingly, we reverse. In so doing, we reaffirm the principle that the internal affairs doctrine is a major tenet of Delaware corporation law having important federal constitutional underpinnings.

I

International was incorporated in Panama on August 11, 1959, and is principally engaged in providing worldwide marine construction services to the oil and gas industry. Its executive offices are in New Orleans, Louisiana, and there are no operations in Delaware. International does not maintain offices in Delaware, hold meetings or conduct business here, have agents or employees in Delaware, or have any assets here.

McDermott Delaware and its subsidiaries operate throughout the United States in three principal industry segments: marine construction services, power generation systems and equipment, and engineered materials. McDermott Delaware's principal offices are in New Orleans.

Following the 1982 Reorganization, McDermott Delaware became a 92%-owned subsidiary of International. The public stockholders of International hold approximately 90% of the voting power of International, while McDermott Delaware holds about 10%.

The stated "principal purpose" of the reorganization, according to International's prospectus, was to enable the McDermott Group to retain, reinvest and redeploy earnings from operations outside the United States without subjecting such earnings to United States income tax. The prospectus also admitted that the 10% voting interest given to McDermott Delaware would be voted by International, "and such voting power could be used to oppose an attempt by a third party to acquire control of International if the management of International believes such use of the voting power would be in the best interests of the stockholders of International." An exchange offer, and thus the Reorganization, was supported by 89.59% of McDermott Delaware stockholders.

The applicable Panamanian law is set forth in the record by affidavits and opinion letters of Ricardo A. Durling, Esquire, and the deans of two Panamanian law schools, to support the claim that McDermott Delaware's retention of a 10% interest in International, and its right to vote those shares, is permitted by the laws of Panama. Significantly, the plaintiffs have not offered any contrary evidence....

II

We note at the outset that if International were incorporated either in Delaware or Louisiana, its stock could not be voted by a majority-owned subsidiary. No United States jurisdiction of which we are aware permits that practice.

Relying on Norlin Corp. v. Rooney, Pace Inc., 744 F.2d 255 (2d Cir. 1984), the Court of Chancery concluded that Panama in effect would refrain from applying its laws under the facts of this case. On that basis, the trial court then concluded that since both Delaware and Louisiana law prohibit a majority-owned subsidiary from voting its parent's stock, the device was improper. We consider this an erroneous application of both Delaware and Panamanian law.

Our analysis requires a two-step inquiry. First, we must determine if Panamanian law, in the factual context addressed by the Court of Chancery, permits International to vote its own shares through the device of McDermott Delaware's ownership. If it does not, then the inquiry ends. However, if Panamanian law permits the practice, we must consider the multifaceted issues inherent in the application of the internal affairs doctrine.

A

It is apparent that under limited circumstances the laws of Panama permit a subsidiary to vote the shares of its parent. Article 35 of Panamanian Cabinet Decree No. 247 of July 16, 1970, which is part of the General Corporation Law of Panama, restricts the exercise of voting rights on shares of certain Panamanian corporations, but Article 37 limits the scope of Article 35 to "corporations registered in the National Securities Commission [of Panama] and those whose shares are sold on the [Panamanian] market. . . . " Opinion of Ricardo A. Durling, *supra* p. 5. Based on the facts before the Court of Chancery, it is undisputed that International was not required to register, nor had it registered, with the National Securities Commission. Further, International's shares were not "sold on the market," as that term is defined by the Attorney General of Panama. Reading Articles 35 and 37 together, it is apparent that Article 35's prohibition did not apply to International.

B

Given the uncontroverted evidence of Panamanian law, establishing that a Panamanian corporation may place voting shares in a majority-owned subsidiary under the limited circumstances provided by Article 37, we turn to the fundamental issues presented by application of the internal affairs doctrine.

III

Internal corporate affairs involve those matters which are peculiar to the relationships among or between the corporation and its current officers, directors, and shareholders. It is essential to distinguish between acts which can be performed by both corporations and individuals, and those activities which are peculiar to the corporate entity.

Corporations and individuals alike enter into contracts, commit torts, and deal in personal and real property. Choice of law decisions relating to such corporate activities are usually determined after consideration of the facts of each transaction. *See* Reese & Kaufman, *The Law Governing Corporate Affairs: Choice of Law and the Impact of Full Faith and Credit*, 58 Colum. L. Rev. 1118, 1121 (1958) (hereinafter "Reese and Kaufman"). In such cases, the choice of law determination often turns on whether the corporation had sufficient contacts with the forum state, in relation to the act or transaction in question, to satisfy the constitutional requirements of due process. The internal affairs doctrine has no applicability in these situations. Rather, this doctrine governs the choice of law determinations involving matters *peculiar* to corporations, that is, those activities concerning the relationships inter se of the corporation, its directors, officers and shareholders.

The internal affairs doctrine requires that the law of the state of incorporation should determine issues relating to internal corporate affairs. Under Delaware conflict of laws principles and the United States Constitution, there are appropriate circumstances which mandate application of this doctrine.

A

Delaware's well established conflict of laws principles require that the laws of the jurisdiction of incorporation—here the Republic of Panama—govern this dispute involving McDermott International's voting rights.

The traditional conflicts rule developed by courts has been that internal corporate relationships are governed by the laws of the forum of incorporation. *See* Macey & Miller, *Toward an Interest-Group Theory of Delaware Corporate Law*, 65 Tex. L. Rev. 469, 495 (1987). As early as 1933, the Supreme Court of the United States noted:

> It has long been settled doctrine that a court—state or federal—sitting in one state will, as a general rule, decline to interfere with, or control by injunction or otherwise, the management of the internal affairs of a corporation organized under the laws of another state but will leave controversies as to such matters to the courts of the state of the domicile. . . .

Rogers v. Guaranty Trust Co. of New York, 288 U.S. 123, 130 (1933) (citations omitted).

However, in Western Air Lines, Inc. v. Sobieski, Cal. App., 191 Cal. App. 2d 399 (1961), a California court upheld an order of the California Commissioner of Corporations directing a Delaware corporation having major contacts with California to follow the cumulative voting requirements imposed by California law. After the *Western Air* decision, commentators noted that the case signaled the alleged start of a "conflicts revolution." *See* Kozyris, *Corporate Wars and Choice of Law*, 1985 Duke L.J. 1; Kaplan, *Foreign Corporations and Local Corporate Policy*, 21 Vand. L. Rev. 433 (1968). . . .

A review of cases over the last twenty-six years, however, finds that in all but a few, the law of the state of incorporation was applied without any discussion. Kozyris, *supra*, at 17-18. In fact, twenty-six years after *Western Air* the following statement remains apt:

> The umbilical tie of the foreign corporation to the state of its charter is usually still religiously regarded as conclusive in determining the law to be applied in intracorporate disputes. The fundamental reexamination of the nature of

conflict of laws over the past few years has virtually left foreign corporation matters remaining as a pocket of the past in a subject area which has otherwise been characterized by free inquiry, change and flux.

Kaplan, *supra* at 464.

The policy underlying the internal affairs doctrine is an important one, and we decline to erode the principle:

> Under the prevailing conflicts practice, neither courts nor legislatures have maximized the imposition of local corporate policy on foreign corporations but have consistently applied the law of the state of incorporation to the entire gamut of internal corporate affairs. In many cases, this is a wise, practical, and equitable choice. It serves the vital need for a single, constant and equal law to avoid the fragmentation of continuing, interdependent internal relationships. The lex incorporationis, unlike the lex loci delicti, is not a rule based merely on the priori concept of territoriality and on the desirability of avoiding forum-shopping. It validates the autonomy of the parties in a subject where the under-lying policy of the law is enabling. It facilitates planning and enhances predict-ability. In fields like torts, where the typical dispute involves two persons and a single or simple one-shot issue and where the common substantive policy is to spread the loss through compensation and insurance, the preference for forum law and the emphasis on the state interest in forum residents which are the common denominators of the new conflicts methodologies do not necessarily lead to unacceptable choices. By contrast, applying local internal affairs law to a foreign corporation just because it is amenable to process in the forum or because it has some local shareholders or some other local contact is apt to pro-duce inequalities, intolerable confusion, and uncertainty, and intrude into the domain of other states that have a superior claim to regulate the same subject matter. . . .

Kozyris, *supra* at 98. . . . In conclusion, the trial court erred as a matter of law in ignoring the uncontroverted Panamanian law, and in applying Delaware and/or Louisiana law to the internal affairs of International contrary to established Delaware law and important constitutional principles. Accordingly the judgment of the Court of Chancery is reversed.

Irving Trust Co. v. Maryland Casualty Co.

83 F.2d 168 (2d Cir. 1936)

L. HAND, J.

This is an appeal from a decree, dismissing a bill in equity for lack of equity, filed by a trustee in bankruptcy against grantees and transferees of the bankrupt. The bankrupt is a Delaware company, doing business in New York under license of the Secretary of State; an involuntary petition was filed against it on the 13th of October, 1932; it was adjudicated, and the plaintiff was appointed its trustee in the following December. On January 6, 1932, it was indebted to four surety com-panies, with which on that day it entered into two contracts on separate dates by which it promised to transfer to the companies or their nominees in payment of its debts to them certain personal property, and to procure the transfer by three of its subsidiaries of certain other real and personal property. Most of the real property was within the state of New York, but one parcel with chattels upon it was in Missouri, one was in Florida, and two were in New Jersey. The chattels consisted of the supplies, furniture, and the like; the other personalty was made up of mortgages, mortgage bonds secured by real property, insurance policies, assignments of rent, accounts receivable, and cash. The bill alleged that at the time of the contracts the bankrupt was insolvent, or in imminent danger of insolvency; that the transfers were intended to prefer the surety companies, as they well knew or had cause to know; and that in performance of the contracts the subsidiaries conveyed the real property and chattels thereon to nominees of the surety companies, and the bankrupt transferred the bonds, mortgages, accounts, etc., to the companies themselves. The suit was against the companies and the nominees, and was based upon section 114 of the Stock Corporation Law (Consol. Laws N.Y. c.59) quoted in the margin.* . . . The judge decided that section 114 applied only to the liability of officers, directors, and stockholders of foreign companies and did not make unlawful the transfers themselves; for this reason he dismissed the bill. The plaintiff appealed.

Section 114 was confessedly passed to fill the gap left in section 15 [which provided that no corporation shall make transfers or assignments in contemplation of its insolvency, and all such assignments shall be declared void,] when Vanderpoel v. Gorman construed that section as limited to domestic companies.** The result was to put domestic companies at a disadvantage as compared with foreign companies licensed by the state to do business within its borders; and in 1897 the Legislature made up its mind to end the handicap. The report of the committee then appointed particularly mentioned among other things the desirability of subjecting foreign companies to the same limitations in favor of their creditors which applied to domestic; section 114, then section 60, was the result of their efforts. . . .

A more troublesome question concerns the property outside New York. Although the bill does not say where the transfers were made, the contracts required them to be delivered in that state, and we are to assume that the parties

---

* "Liabilities of Officers, Directors and Stockholders. Except as otherwise provided in this chapter, the officers, directors and stockholders of a foreign stock corporation transacting business in this state, except a moneyed or a railroad corporation, shall be liable under the provisions of this chapter, in the same manner and to the same extent as the officers, directors and stockholders of a domestic corporation, for the making of:

1. Unauthorized dividends;
2. Unlawful loans to stockholders;
3. False certificates, reports or public notices;
4. Illegal transfers of the stock and property of such corporation, when it is insolvent or its insolvency is threatened.

Such liabilities may be enforced in the courts of this state, in the same manner as similar liabilities imposed by law upon the officers, directors and stockholders of domestic corporations."

** Vanderpoel v. Gorman, 140 N.Y. 563 (1894), involved an assignment of assets made by an insolvent corporation incorporated in New Jersey but doing business in New York. The assignment was then permitted under New Jersey but not New York law. The New York Court of Appeals interpreted New York's prohibition to apply to domestic corporations only. The court's rationale turned on the fact that states have special authority to regulate domestic corporations but comity requires deference to domicile states regarding companies incorporated elsewhere—EDS.

performed as stipulated. The receipt of the deeds by the defendants was therefore a wrong, and any liabilities imposed as a remedy would be recognized and enforced elsewhere, for the law of the place where acts occur normally fixes their jural character. Restatement of Conflict of Laws, §384. The question here is whether it makes a difference that the wrong consisted in the conveyance of property in another state, under whose laws the conveyance might perhaps have been valid. . . . The doctrine is of course well settled, certainly as to real property, and, as we shall assume arguendo, equally at the present time as to personal, that the law of the situs absolutely determines the validity of conveyances wherever made. No title will pass and no interest will arise, save as that law prescribes. We have no doubt therefore that title passed by the deeds delivered in New York to property situated in those of the three states whose laws did not forbid such transfers; yet the law of New York might still make receipt of the deed a wrong and impose a liability upon the grantee though he got a good title. That would not trench upon the sovereignty of the state of the situs whose power over the res would remain wholly unimpaired. Nobody would question this so far as concerned the grantee's liability in damages; it would be but reasonable that he should become liable to the grantor's creditors just because his title was unimpeachable. In the case of contracts for the sale of land the lex loci contractus certainly controls.

. . . Some of the relief asked by the bill cannot therefore be granted; the court cannot adjudge the transfers void as to land and chattels outside the state, except as the lex rei sitae is the same as section 114. But under his general prayer the plaintiff, if he proves his case, may have a decree as to any of the property transferred directing the defendants to reconvey it, and this he can enforce in personam. Of course he may also recover damages as a substitute if he so elects.

Decree reversed; defendants to answer over.

Questions and Comments

(1) The *McDermott* court also decided, in an omitted portion of its opinion, that its ruling was constitutionally compelled. For a discussion of the constitutional issues raised by the "internal affairs" doctrine requiring application of the law of the state of incorporation, *see* pages 363-366 *infra*. More recently, the Supreme Court of Delaware reaffirmed its claim that the internal affairs doctrine has constitutional status. VantagePoint Venture Partners 1996 v. Examen, Inc., 871 A.2d 1108 (Del. 2005).

(2) In Vanderpoel v. Gorman, 35 N.E. 932 (N.Y. 1894), a case mentioned in *Irving Trust*, the New York Court of Appeals provided the following justification for a strict application of the internal affairs doctrine:

> As to domestic corporations, we assume certain responsibilities arising out of the very liberty given by the state for their creation or formation. We provide for their birth, for their regulation and government during life, and for their death. Upon their dissolution, which no other power than the state itself, acting through its legislature or its courts, can pronounce, the whole power of the corporation ceases, and the property which the corporation leaves passes under the dominion of the sovereignty which created it. Responsible for its creation, for its government, and for its death, the state has assumed, in such cases, complete

and full jurisdiction over the corporation and its property; and accordingly the state has, in a series of statutory provisions, made certain that the corporate property shall be distributed in accordance with its own ideas of justice. On the other hand, in the case of a foreign corporation, the same kind of responsibility does not obtain. Our courts cannot dissolve it, nor can we, by virtue of our laws, in any way affect its property situated outside of the state, nor call it to any account therefore. . . .

Does this rationale provide a compelling argument for applicable rules regarding asset transfers in contemplation of bankruptcy?

(3) Although most states continue to follow the internal affairs doctrine, some states have departed from the doctrine through statutory provision. California has been the most aggressive in subjecting the internal affairs of foreign-incorporated firms to portions of its corporate code. For example, if a foreign corporation does half its business in California and if half of its voting securities are held by California residents, California law governs issues such as director elections, inspection of books and records, distribution policy, and cumulative voting. *See* Cal. Corp. Code §2115 (2001). California courts have upheld this provision against numerous legal challenges. *See* Valtz v. Penta Inv. Corp., 139 Cal. App. 3d 803 (Cal. Ct. App. 1983) (upholding California's shareholders' right to inspect laws against a Delaware corporation); Wilson v. Louisiana-Pacific Resources, Inc., 138 Cal. App. 3d 216 (Cal. Ct. App. 1982) (upholding California's cumulative voting requirements as applied to a Utah corporation). New York also applies provisions of its corporate code to foreign corporations that do business in the state. *See* N.Y. Bus. Corp. §§1317, 1318, 1319 (2001); Norlin Corp. v. Rooney, Pace Inc., 744 F.2d 255 (2d Cir. 1984) (applying New York law forbidding subsidiaries from voting shares of the parent's stock to Panamanian corporation, and observing that "principles compelling a forum state to apply foreign law come into play only when a legitimate and substantial interest of another state would thereby be served").

(4) States have also applied local law on occasion to "pseudo-foreign" or "tramp" corporations that do all their business in one state while being formally incorporated in another. *See, e.g.*, Mansfield Hardwood Lumber Co. v. Johnson, 268 F.2d 317 (5th Cir. 1959). In Weede v. Iowa Southern Utilities Co. of Delaware, 231 Iowa 784, 2 N.W.2d 372, *opinion modified*, 4 N.W.2d 869 (1942), the Supreme Court of Iowa applied forum law designed to prevent "stock watering" to a foreign corporation operating a local utility plant. The corporation had argued that Iowa was without power to interfere with the corporation's internal affairs.

In passing upon these propositions, it must be kept in mind that while the appellee is a corporation organized under the laws of Delaware, it is what the authorities or decisions speak of as a "tramp" or "migratory" corporation. "While this practice of taking out a charter in one state to do business solely in another is probably too general and too long recognized to be questioned, the courts of a state in which such business is to be done are ordinarily reluctant to adopt a construction of the local laws which would enable corporators, by resorting to such practice, to receive, by reason of foreign incorporation, more favorable treatment than similar domestic corporations." 23 Am. Jur. Section 123, p.127. Its promotors went from Iowa to Maine and first organized under the laws of the latter state. Later they reorganized under the laws of Delaware.

They had no apparent intention of operating their utility plant, or of doing any other business in Maine or Delaware. Its officers, its plant and operating property, its assets, except a bank account or two, its business, almost all of its officers, its books and records, in fact, all of its physical manifestations, have always been, and are now in Iowa, within the jurisdiction of the courts of Iowa. . . . Its creation in Delaware was purely one of convenience, or other hoped for advantage. It was not for the purpose of becoming an actual, as well as a legal, resident of Delaware. While it was, and is, in law a legal resident of Delaware, and has its technical domicile there, its "commercial" or "economic" domicile is in Iowa. It was conceived in Iowa, born in Delaware, and has lived its entire life in Iowa. The foreignness of such a corporation has been spoken of as but a "meta-physical concept." Its existence in Delaware is an illusory mirage, more atmospheric, than real. Under the circumstances it is, in actuality, more domestic than foreign. The courts of this state have full jurisdiction of the parties and the subject matter with authority to grant all of the relief prayed for, and the power at hand to fully enforce such decree.

Is forum-shopping in this context good or bad? Does the answer turn on whether the rights of third parties (i.e., persons who were in no way involved in the choice of where to incorporate) are at stake? Aren't shareholders and managers in a different position than tort victims?

(5) Problems arise in defining the contours of "internal affairs." Is piercing the corporate veil a matter of internal affairs? *See, e.g.,* Jefferson Pilot Broadcasting Co. v. Hilary & Hogan, Inc., 617 F. 2d 133 (5th Cir. 1980) (law of place of incorporation governs decision whether to disregard corporate entity). What about enforcement requests to view the corporate books? *See, e.g.,* Jefferson Industrial Bank v. First Golden Bancorporation, 762 P.2d 768 (Colo. Ct. App. 1988) (Colorado law giving shareholders access to corporate records applies to Delaware corporation conducting substantial business within the state); Sadler v. NCR Corp., 928 F.2d 48 (4th Cir. 1991) (access to stockholder list is recognized exception to internal affairs doctrine). What about officer and director duties owed to the corporation not to engage in insider trading? Friese v. Superior Court, 134 Cal. App. 4th 693 (Cal. Ct. App. 2006) (securities laws not governed by internal affairs doctrine). Note that, unlike choice of law for other subject matter, courts do not usually apply a public policy exception to the internal affairs doctrine. Does that suggest a narrower scope for the applicability of the doctrine? *See* Ribstein & O'Hara, *Corporations and the Market for Law*, 2008 U. Ill. L. Rev. 661.

(6) As *Irving Trust* suggests, there is a substantial possibility of collision between the rules of corporate capacity and those tort, property, or contract rules specifying the law of some place other than the place of incorporation. If the *ABC* Corp. injures someone in State *X*, is this a tort case governed by *X* law even if the plaintiff seeks to pierce the corporate veil and reach the assets of individual shareholders? In Pinney v. Nelson, 183 U.S. 144 (1901), the Supreme Court upheld application of forum law imposing personal liability on shareholders by citing a contract rationale. By forming a corporation to do business in the forum, the shareholders had formed their "contract" of corporation with reference to forum law. Is this convincing?

It has been suggested that the doctrine of limited liability for corporate shareholders be abandoned. Hansmann & Kraakman, *Toward Unlimited Shareholder*

Liability for Corporate Torts, 100 Yale L.J. 1879 (1991); Leebron, *Limited Liability, Tort Victims, and Creditors*, 91 Colum. L. Rev. 1565 (1991). But as has been pointed out, the feasibility of any one state abolishing the doctrine depends on whether it has a right to impose its laws on foreign corporations and shareholders, who may have little connection with the state. Alexander, *Unlimited Shareholder Liability Through a Procedural Lens*, 106 Harv. L. Rev. 387 (1992). Alexander argues that the issue would be treated as a question of "internal affairs" and would therefore be governed by the law of the state of incorporation; Hansmann and Kraakman, in a response, disagree. Hansmann & Kraakman, *A Procedural Focus on Unlimited Shareholder Liability*, 106 Harv. L. Rev. 446 (1992). Which side does *Pinney* support?

(7) Note that federal law sometimes preempts state laws that might otherwise apply. For example, federal bankruptcy laws can affect the relationship between the insolvent corporation and its shareholders and creditors. And the Sarbanes-Oxley Act, officially known as Public Company Accounting Reform and Investor Protection Act, Pub. L. No. 107-204 (2002), influences corporate board composition and internal corporate decision processes. The Dodd-Frank Act also regulates board decision making as well as director elections. Dodd-Frank Wall Street Reform and Consumer Protection Act, Pub. L. No. 111-203 (2010). These federal laws preempt state corporate law and raise their own choice-of-law questions regarding their applicability to companies incorporated outside the United States.

(8) The European Union is moving toward an internal affairs doctrine in that corporations chartered in one member country are permitted to conduct their affairs throughout the European Union, and other member nations are limited in their ability to impose local regulations on firms incorporated elsewhere. *See* Case C-212/97, Centros Ltd. v. Erhvervs-og Selskabsstyrelsen, 1999 E.C.R. I-1459, I-1490; Case C-208/00, Überseering BV v. Nordic Constr. Co. Baumanagement GmbH (NCC), 2002 E.C.R. I-9919, paras. 1-2; Case C-167/01, Kamer van Koophandel en Fabrieken voor Amsterdam v. Inspire Art Ltd., 2003 E.C.R. I-10,155, I-10, 223 to 38. Prior to these decisions by the European Court of Justice, corporate affairs in Europe were governed by the law of the "real seat" of the corporation, which often meant the location of its administrative affairs offices.

G.   Wrinkles in the Theory

1.   Characterization

In the *Carroll* case, *supra* page 15, the plaintiff attempted to avoid the application of Mississippi's fellow-servant doctrine by arguing that the issue in the case was contractual (and governed by the law of Alabama where the contract was formed), rather than tortious (and governed by the law of the place where the tort occurred). The plaintiff was unsuccessful in that attempt, but the plaintiff in Levy v. Daniel's U-Drive Auto Renting Co., note (6), *supra* pages 23-24, succeeded with a similar argument. Likewise, in Burr v. Beckler, *supra* page 82, the court had to choose between characterizing the case as one involving real property, to be governed by the law of the situs of the property, or involving the validity of a note, to be governed by the law of the place where the note was made. These cases and several others illustrate the general problem of *characterization*: Before the rules of the First Restatement may be applied, one must know whether the case is a tort case, a contract case, etc. The First Restatement says remarkably little about characterization. It does comment about determining whether a contract issue is one of obligation or performance (*see* comment *b* to §358, *supra* pages 37-38) and has a few words on the difference between the capacity to make a contract to transfer property and the capacity to transfer property (*see* comment *a* to §333, *supra* pages 35-36), but in general it offers little help.

Haumschild v. Continental Casualty Co.

7 Wis. 2d 130, 95 N.W.2d 814 (1959)

CURRIE, Justice.

[Mrs. Haumschild sued her husband for personal injuries she suffered in an automobile accident in California as a result of his negligence. Both parties were Wisconsin domiciliaries. The Wisconsin trial court dismissed the case under California's law prohibiting a wife from suing her husband in tort.]

This appeal presents a conflict of laws problem with respect to inter-spousal liability for tort growing out of an automobile accident. Which law controls, that of the state of the forum, the state of the place of wrong, or the state of domicile? Wisconsin is both the state of the forum and of the domicile while California is the state where the alleged wrong was committed. Under Wisconsin law a wife may sue her husband in tort. Under California law she cannot.

This court was first faced with this question in Buckeye v. Buckeye, 1931, 203 Wis. 248. In that case Wisconsin was the state of the forum and domicile, while Illinois was the state of the place of wrong. It was there held that the law governing the creation and extent of tort liability is that of the place where the tort was committed. From this premise it was further held that interspousal immunity from tort liability necessarily is governed by the law of the place of injury.

The principle enunciated in the *Buckeye* case and followed in subsequent Wisconsin cases, that the law of the place of wrong controls as to whether one spouse is immune from suit in tort by the other, is the prevailing view in the majority of jurisdictions in this country. It is also the rule adopted in Restatement, Conflict of Laws, §§378 and 384(2). However, criticism of the rule of the *Buckeye* case . . . , and recent decisions by the courts of California, New Jersey, and Pennsylvania, have caused us to re-examine the question afresh.

The first case to break the ice and flatly hold that the law of domicile should be applied in determining whether there existed an immunity from suit for tort based upon family relationship is Emery v. Emery, 1955, 45 Cal. 2d 421. In that case two unemancipated minor sisters sued their unemancipated minor brother and their father to recover for injuries sustained in an automobile accident that occurred in the state of Idaho, the complaint alleging wilful misconduct in order to come within the provisions of the Idaho "guest" statute. All parties were domiciled in California. The opinion by Mr. Justice Traynor recognized that the California court, in passing on the question of whether an unemancipated minor child may sue the parent or an unemancipated brother, had a choice to apply the law of the place of wrong, of the forum, or of the domicile. It was held that the immunity issue was not a question of tort but one of capacity to sue and be sued, and rejected the law of the place of injury as "both fortuitous and irrelevant." In deciding whether to apply the law of the forum, or the law of the domicile, the opinion stated this conclusion:

> Although tort actions between members of the same family will ordinarily be brought in the state of the family domicile, the courts of another state will in some cases be a more convenient forum, and thus the question arises whether the choice of law rule should be expressed in terms of the law of the forum or that of the domicile. We think that disabilities to sue and immunities from suit because of a family relationship are more properly determined by reference to the law of the state of the family domicile. That state has the primary responsibility for establishing and regulating the incidents of the family relationship and it is the only state in which the parties can, by participation in the legislative processes, effect a change in those incidents. Moreover, it is undesirable that the rights, duties, disabilities, and immunities conferred or imposed by the family relationship should constantly change as members of the family cross state boundaries during temporary absences from their home.

The two reasons most often advanced for the common law rule, that one spouse may not sue the other, are the ancient concept that husband and wife constitute in law but one person, and that to permit such suits will be to foment family discord and strife. The Married Women's Acts of the various states have effectively destroyed the "one person" concept thereby leaving as the other remaining reason for the immunity the objective of preventing family discord. This is also the justification usually advanced for denying an unemancipated child the capacity to sue a parent, brother or sister. Clearly this policy reason for denying the capacity to sue more properly lies within the sphere of family law, where domicile usually controls the law to be applied, than it does tort law, where the place of injury generally determines the substantive law which will govern.

We are convinced that, from both the standpoint of public policy and logic, the proper solution of the conflict of laws problem, in cases similar to the instant action, is to hold that the law of the domicile is the one that ought to be applied in determining any issue of incapacity to sue based upon family relationship.

After most careful deliberation, it is our considered judgment that this court should adopt the rule that, whenever the courts of this state are confronted with a conflict of laws problem as to which law governs the capacity of one spouse to sue the other in tort, the law to be applied is that of the state of domicile. We, therefore, expressly overrule [*Buckeye*].

Perhaps a word of caution should be sounded to the effect that the instant decision should not be interpreted as a rejection by this court of the general rule that ordinarily the substantive rights of parties to an action in tort are to be determined in the light of the law of the place of wrong. This decision merely holds that incapacity to sue because of marital status presents a question of family law rather than tort law.

The concurring opinion by Mr. Justice Fairchild protests that we should not adopt the conflict of laws rule, that interspousal immunity to suit in tort should be determined by the law of the domicile, because this was not urged in the briefs or arguments of counsel. . . . While the appellant's counsel did not request that we overrule *Buckeye* and the subsequent Wisconsin case dealing with this particular conflict of laws problem, he did specifically seek to have this court apply California's conflict of laws principle, that the law of the domicile is determinative of interspousal capacity to sue, to this particular case. However, to do so would violate the well recognized principle of conflict of laws that, where the substantive law of another state is applied, there necessarily must be excluded such foreign state's law of conflict of laws.

The reason why the authorities on conflict of laws almost universally reject the renvoi doctrine (permitting a court of the forum state to apply the conflict of laws principle of a foreign state) is that it is likely to result in the court pursuing a course equivalent to a never ending circle. For example, in the instant case, if the *Buckeye* line of Wisconsin cases is to be followed, the Wisconsin court first looks to the law of California to see whether a wife can sue her husband in tort. California substantive law holds that she cannot. However, California has adopted a conflict of laws principle that holds that the law of the domicile determines such question. Applying such principle the court is referred back to Wisconsin law because Wisconsin is the state of domicile. Again the court applies Wisconsin law and, under the prior holdings of the *Buckeye* line of authorities, would have to again refer to California law because such line of cases does not recognize that the law of domicile has anything to do with interspousal immunity, but holds that the law of the state of injury controls.

Wisconsin certainly should not adopt the much criticized renvoi principle in order not to overrule the *Buckeye* line of cases, and still permit the plaintiff to recover. Such a result we believe would contribute far more to produce chaos in the field of conflict of laws than to overrule the *Buckeye* line of cases and adopt a principle the soundness of which has been commended by so many reputable authorities.

Judgment reversed and cause remanded for further proceedings not inconsistent with this opinion.

FAIRCHILD, J. (concurring):

I concur in the reversal of the judgment, but do not find it necessary to re-examine settled Wisconsin law in order to do so. A fundamental change in the law of Wisconsin such as the one announced by the majority in this case, which will importantly affect many people, should be made, if at all, in a case where the question is necessarily presented. Both parties assumed that their case would be decided under the principle which is being overturned by the majority, and accordingly, we have not had the benefit of brief or argument upon the validity of the principle.

1. *Solution of this case without overruling previous decisions.* . . . It has been the rule in Wisconsin that the existence or non-existence of immunity because of family relationship is substantive and not merely procedural, and is to be determined by the law of the locus state. The law of California is that the existence or non-existence of immunity is a substantive matter, but that it is an element of the law of status, not of tort. The tort law of California is no more concerned with immunity than is Wisconsin's. Thus it makes no difference under the facts

of this case whether we look directly to the law of Wisconsin to determine that immunity is not available as a defense or look to the law of Wisconsin only because California, having no general tort principle as to immunity, classifies immunity as a matter of status.

2. *Policy questions requiring full consideration.* Under the principle announced by the majority that the existence or nonexistence of immunity is a matter of status our courts must henceforth recognize immunity as a defense where the alleged tort occurred in Wisconsin, but the parties are married and are domiciled in an immunity state. This would mean that such an act is or is not a remedial wrong depending upon the state where the parties happen to be domiciled.

The determination of domicil is not always easy, yet the courts will henceforth be required to determine it in many cases where it has heretofore been considered immaterial. A good many married couples who may have domicil in other states are in Wisconsin for extended periods. Some for example, are students at colleges and universities, some stationed here for military duty, some temporarily assigned here by employers, and some vacationing. Under the rule abandoned by the majority, a tortious act done in Wisconsin by a nonresident and injuring his spouse gave rise to the same civil liability as if done by a permanent resident.

The problem involved apparently has its principal impact because of injuries sustained in automobile accidents where members of a family travel together across state lines. Under the new rule Wisconsin courts will not countenance the defense of immunity for a Wisconsin husband when sued by his wife for an injury occurring in an immunity state. I concede there is some merit to the logic relied upon and that there may be some practical benefit to Wisconsin people. It is to be remembered, however, that under the law of many states a wife will have no cause of action for simple negligence of her husband because she will be a gratuitous guest. The fact that she and her husband are domiciled in Wisconsin and that they are on a family trip which began in Wisconsin will not exempt her from that principle of tort law. Thus the purely practical benefit to Wisconsin people which might appear at first blush to arise from the new rule will be limited.

Questions and Comments

(1) The rigidity of the First Restatement's rules, combined with its silence on the characterization issue, provides an opportunity for manipulation of characterization to achieve results that courts think are fair or desirable. For this reason, characterization is sometimes known as an "escape device." But is *this* characterization fair? After all, if there are no rules for characterization, how can characterization be used to "escape" an otherwise mandated result?

(2) Are you convinced by *Haumschild*'s reasons for concluding that "incapacity to sue because of marital status presents a question of family law rather than tort law"? How should a court resolve the characterization problem? What law should it apply in making this decision? Is *Haumschild*'s inquiry into the purposes of the interspousal immunity rule a fruitful approach? How did the *Carroll* court decide that the case involved a tort rather than a contract?

(3) Doesn't the characterization problem make it harder for the First Restatement to achieve its desired choice-of-law uniformity? Unless courts in

different states would characterize the same case in the same way, uniformity will likely be defeated.

(4) Note that in *Haumschild*, the court appeared to commit itself to applying California law on tort issues such as negligence even though it applied Wisconsin's law rejecting interspousal immunity. The process of dividing a case up into various issues governed by potentially different laws is known as *dépeçage*. Is such characterization at the level of issue rather than case appropriate? Is it consistent with the provisions of the First Restatement that you have read? Whether it is or not, does it make sense?

In Simon v. United States, 805 N.E.2d 798 (Ind. 2004), the Supreme Court of Indiana rejected the plaintiff's argument that Indiana should engage in *dépeçage* when determining what tort rules should apply in the aftermath of a plane crash. In response to a question certified by the United States Court of Appeals for the Third Circuit, the Indiana court rejected *dépeçage*, both because *dépeçage* is inconsistent with the First Restatement principles, and because *dépeçage* seemed conceptually objectionable:

> On the simple merits of *dépeçage* as a judicial technique, we find ourselves unimpressed. By making separate determinations for each issue within a claim, the process amalgamates the laws of different states, producing a hybrid that may not exist in any state. This is a problem for several reasons. First, legislatures "may enact a given law only because of its expected interaction with a complementary law." Erin A. O'Hara & Larry E. Ribstein, *From Politics to Efficiency in Choice of Law*, 67 U. Chi. L. Rev. 1151, 1193 (2000). For example, a legislature may allow recovery for certain injuries or impose a low standard of proof for liability but place a cap on the damages that might be recovered or adopt immunities for certain potential defendants. Id. Consequently, applying the law outside the context of the other laws in the jurisdiction may contravene legislative intent. In addition, applying a law in isolation increases the likelihood that its purposes and importance will be misconstrued, thereby thwarting state policy. William H. Allen & Erin A. O'Hara, *Second Generation Law and Economics of Conflict of Laws: Baxter's Comparative Impairment and Beyond*, 51 Stan. L. Rev. 1011, 1033 (1999). Ultimately, by applying *dépeçage* a court may hinder the policy of one or more states without furthering the considered policy of any state.
>
> *Dépeçage* may also produce unfair results because the hybrid law may be more favorable to one party than to another, allowing a result that could not be reached if the laws of any one state were applied. As Branierd Currie said, a party "should not be allowed to put 'together half a donkey and half a camel, and then ride to victory on the synthetic hybrid.'" Christopher G. Stevenson, *Depecage: Embracing Complexity to Solve Choice-of-Law Issues*, Note, 37 Ind. L. Rev. 303, 320 (2003) (quoting Frederick K. Juenger, *How Do You Rate a Century?* 37 Willamette L. Rev. 89, 106 (2001) (quoting Branierd Currie)). Moreover, *dépeçage* compounds the advantage of parties with greater access to legal resources because it requires a separate analysis of each issue for each state involved.

Simon, 805 N.E.2d at 802-803. Do you agree? Surely it makes sense to separate components of a legal claim sometimes. Is there a principled way to know where to draw the line?

(5) What happens when a court characterizes a claim and looks to foreign law, only to find that the foreign state characterizes the claim differently? In Colonial Life & Accident Insurance Co. v. Hartford Fire Insurance Co., 358 F.3d 1306 (11th Cir. 2004), an insurance company defending an action against its policyholder brought cross-claims and third-party claims against its liability insurers asserting, among other things, that the insurers breached their duty of good faith owed to it. The U.S. District Court for the Middle District of Alabama, applying Alabama's First Restatement choice-of-law principles, noted that Alabama characterizes a breach of the duty of good-faith claim as a contract claim and looked to South Carolina, the place of contracting, to determine its substantive contract law on the issue. As it turns out, however, South Carolina contract law did not include recognition of claims for this breach, and the District Court therefore dismissed the claim. The Eleventh Circuit reversed. South Carolina did recognize a cause of action for breach of the duty of good faith (i.e., bad faith), but under South Carolina law this claim sounded in tort rather than contract. According to the Eleventh Circuit, South Carolina law on the breach of good-faith obligations would apply to this case, regardless of how South Carolina characterized the claim.

2. Renvoi

First Restatement choice-of-law rules pick out *the law* of the place of the wrong, the contract, the property, etc. But when the chosen law is the law of another state, does the chosen "law" include the foreign state's choice-of-law rules? This is the sticky problem of renvoi. As the majority opinion in *Haumschild* suggests, the inclusion of choice-of-law rules within the law chosen by a choice-of-law rule can lead to intractable problems, and for that reason is usually—but not always—avoided. The First Restatement generally rejected the renvoi doctrine except in cases involving title to land or the validity of a decree of divorce. *See* First Restatement, §§7-8. Consider whether these exceptions make sense as you read the cases below.

In re Estate of Damato
86 N.J. Super. 107, 206 A.2d 171 (1965)

LABRECQUE, J.A.D.

This is an appeal from a judgment of the Probate Division awarding the balance in two out-of-state bank accounts to decedent's son Philip Damato.

The facts are not in dispute. Decedent died on November 6, 1960, a resident of Paterson, New Jersey. Although he had been engaged in the waste-paper business in the Paterson area for many years, he also had business interests in Florida, including the operation of a small stable of race horses. His will was admitted to probate by the Surrogate of Passaic County, his son James Damato qualifying as the executor thereof. On July 26, 1962, the executor filed a verified complaint praying, inter alia, for instructions as to the disposition of the balances remaining in two savings accounts in the Bank of Hollywood, Hollywood, Florida, which are the subject of the present controversy. . . .

Both Philip and James Damato were sons of the decedent. Philip worked for his father in the Paterson business and never knew of the accounts until after the death of his father. The passbooks for both accounts remained in decedent's possession and were found among his papers in Florida.

In awarding the balance in each account to Philip, the trial judge held that the transactions were governed by the law of Florida, their situs, and since Florida had adopted the rule of In re Totten, they were effective to pass the balance in each account to Philip upon the death of the decedent. . . .

The law is well settled that the creation of an inter vivos trust in money or securities, as distinguished from a testamentary trust, is governed by the law of the situs of the money or securities. The validity of an inter vivos trust of choses in action is determined by the law of the place where the transaction takes place.

The savings bank trust doctrine which the trial judge found to be dispositive of the issue before him was set forth in its present form in In re Totten, *supra*, to the effect that:

> A deposit by one person of his own money in his own name and as trustee for another, standing alone, does not establish an irrevocable trust during the lifetime of the depositor. It is a tentative trust merely, revocable at will, until the depositor dies or completes the gift in his lifetime by some unequivocal act or declaration, such as delivery of the passbook or notice to the beneficiary. In case the depositor dies before the beneficiary without revocation, or some decisive act or declaration of disaffirmance, the presumption arises that an absolute trust is created as to the balance on hand at the death of the depositor.

In Cutts v. Najdrowski the court held that where a New Jersey resident opened an account in a New York savings bank in his name in trust for another, since the transaction was effective there, it was effective here to pass title to the balance in the account at the depositor's death, to the other person named, under the *Totten* trust doctrine. It was so held notwithstanding that such a transaction, had it been consummated here by a New Jersey resident, would have been invalid to *pass title* as violative of our statute of wills or as an ineffective gift inter vivos. Since then, however, N.J.S.A. 17:9A-216 has been held effective to pass valid title to the balance, at death, in such an account, to the beneficiary named. . . . *Cutts* was followed in Conry v. Maloney, where a New York savings account was again involved and, through application of the law of situs, it was held that the cestui, a niece, took the balance in an account opened by the decedent "in trust for" her, to the exclusion of the decedent's widow.

The trial judge, following *Cutts* and *Conry*, held that the law of Florida applied. Concluding that the *Totten* trust doctrine had been adopted in Florida, he found that title to the bank balances passed to respondent. In so doing, he applied the substantive law of Florida as found in Seymour v. Seymour. . . .

Appellant urges that in thus applying Florida substantive law, instead of Florida conflict of laws, the trial judge fell into error. Specifically, it is argued that in *Seymour* the court was passing upon the validity, as a trust, of an account established by a domiciliary of Florida in a Florida bank, whereas we are here concerned with an account opened in Florida by a domiciliary of New Jersey. Under Florida conflicts law, the argument continues, the doctrine of mobilia sequuntur personam would be applied. Hanson v. Denckla, 100 So. 2d 378 (Fla. Sup. Ct.

1956), *reversed on grounds of lack of jurisdiction* in Hanson v. Denckla, 357 U.S. 235 (1958). Turning, then, to the law of decedent's domicile, New Jersey, appellant invokes Swetland v. Swetland as holding the transaction to be ineffective as a trust of the accounts in question. Appellant thus seeks to invoke the doctrine of renvoi to defeat respondent's claim. . . .

However, we find it unnecessary to determine the Florida conflicts rule which would be applicable in view of the conclusions which follow.

We are satisfied that the trial judge correctly ruled that the substantive law of Florida should be applied to the transaction in question. In neither *Cutts* nor *Conry* did our courts proceed any further than to apply the internal law of the place where the transaction took place. The transaction rule was also followed in Hooton v. Needl, *supra*. In the Restatement, Conflict of Laws, §7, p.11 (1934), the rule as to conflicts is set forth as follows:

> Except as stated in §8 [concerning matters involving title to land and the validity of divorce decrees], when there is a difference in the Conflict of Laws of two states whose laws are involved in a problem, the rule of Conflict of Laws of the forum is applied: (a) in all cases where as a preliminary to determining the choice of law it is necessary to determine the quality and character of legal ideas, these are determined by the forum according to its law; (b) where in making the choice of law to govern a certain situation the law of another state is to be applied, since the only Conflict of Laws used in the determination of the case is the Conflict of Laws of the forum, the foreign law to be applied is the law applicable to the matter in hand and not the Conflict of Laws of the foreign state.

In comment (d) to subsection (b) the learned authors note that, under the rule stated, the court of the forum, in a matter involving a contract, applies only the contract law of the other state, and this "may result in a decision contrary to that which would be reached by a court in that state, the law of which is being applied, by reason of the fact that a different Conflict of Laws rule prevails in the latter state."

The rule set forth in the Restatement seems grounded in reason for, if appellant's views were to be upheld, the courts would be faced with a possible unending circuity. Thus, if the Florida conflicts rule would refer the matter back to New Jersey, New Jersey, applying its full body of law, including its conflict rules, would again refer to the law of Florida because of the holdings in *Cutts, Conry* and *Hooton*. The circular process would then begin anew and continue ad infinitum. Such was the problem posed In re Tallmadge, 181 N.Y.S. 336 (Surr. Ct. 1919), where application of the renvoi doctrine was denied on account of its inconsistency with common law theory of the conflict of laws, its fundamental unsoundness and the chaos which would result from its application to conflicts arising between the laws of the several states.

Accordingly, we hold that where, in a proceeding in this State, the validity of a transaction in a foreign state—except one involving title to land or the validity of a divorce, as to which we make no determination—is, by virtue of our conflict of laws principles, made to depend upon the laws of such state, the foreign law to be applied is the law applicable to the matter in hand not the conflict of laws of the foreign state. . . .

University of Chicago v. Dater
277 Mich. 653, 270 N.W. 175 (1936)

[The facts are taken from the dissenting opinion of Justice Sharpe.] In November, 1928, negotiations were commenced to secure a loan in the sum of $75,000 on a piece of property in Chicago. The property was owned by George R. Dater and John R. Price of Benton Harbor, Mich., and they appointed H. S. Gray, an attorney of Benton Harbor, as their agent in the matter. Plaintiff agreed to make the loan if it could be assured that the title was good. A trust deed and certain promissory notes were drawn up with George R. Dater and Nellie E. Dater, his wife, and John R. Price and Clara A. Price, his wife, as parties of the first part, and the Chicago Title & Trust Company, as trustee, and as party of the second part. The notes were payable in the city of Chicago and at such place as the legal holder might appoint. The trust mortgage and notes were sent by mail to the Benton Harbor State Bank for the signature of the parties involved. The papers were signed in Benton Harbor, Mich., about December 8, 1928, and mailed to plaintiff's agent in the city of Chicago where the trust deed was placed on record, then it was found that there were some objections to certain delinquent taxes of 1927. Further negotiations followed, and finally on January 3, 1929, and after the tax objections were cleared in the title, the loan was actually made and the money paid over by check made payable to Mr. and Mrs. Dater and Mr. and Mrs. Price and cashed in Chicago, Ill.

January 29, 1929, John R. Price died, and it is conceded that Mrs. Price became the actual and record owner of at least one-half of the property after the death of her husband. Subsequent to December 1, 1933, foreclosure proceedings were commenced on the property and the property purchased at chancery sale. Suit was filed in Michigan before the foreclosure suit was completed in Chicago. The cause was heard November 7, 1934, and on June 18, 1935, judgment was rendered in favor of plaintiff against George R. Dater in the amount of $15,536.32 and from which no appeal has been taken. On the same date judgment was entered in favor of Clara Price of no cause for action, from which judgment plaintiff appeals.

WIEST, J.

The obligation in suit was executed in this state by defendant Clara A. Price, a married woman, and bore no relation to her separate estate, and, without more, carried no personal liability when sued upon in this jurisdiction. But, it is claimed, that the obligation was accepted in the state of Illinois, and was there payable and, by the law of the state, Mrs. Price is not saved from liability by reason of want of capacity under the Michigan law of coverture.

As pointed out later in this opinion, personal liability of Mrs. Price could not be enforced in Illinois under the theory of an Illinois contract.

In the case at bar negotiations for the loan, to be secured by mortgage, had reached the state where the lender prepared the note and mortgage in Illinois and sent the same to an agent in Michigan, with direction as to execution by defendants in this state, and, when executed, to be returned by such agent to the mortgagee in Illinois. Mrs. Price, at the request of the agent, executed the instruments and the agent mailed the same to the mortgagee.

The instant case does not involve conflict of laws relative to the construction, force, and effect of the instruments, signed or executed in one state to be performed in another, but that of capacity of Mrs. Price to enter into such an obligation in this state.

It is well said in a note, 26 L.R.A. (N.S.) 773:

> While there are almost numberless cases which state, with slight variations, Story's general proposition that, where the contract is either expressly or tacitly to be performed in some place other than that where it is made, the general rule is, in conformity to the presumed intention of the parties, that the contract, as to its validity, nature, obligation, and interpretation, is to be governed by the law of the place of performance, none of them can be regarded as express authority for the application of that rule to the question of the capacity of a married woman to contract. Few of them can be relied upon for the application of that rule to any question relating to the existence of a contract as distinguished from its interpretation or obligation or essential validity.

It must be agreed that this case is governed by the law of Michigan or of Illinois. If by the law of Michigan, it is clear, and is not disputed, that defendant has no personal liability on the note, recoverable from her separate estate.

Assuming, however, that by the Michigan law of the forum that case is governed by the law of Illinois, it presents the unique situation in the realm of conflict of laws that by the law of Illinois, Burr v. Beckler [page 82 *supra*] the case is governed by the law of Michigan.

In Burr v. Beckler, the wife, a resident of Illinois, was sojourning temporarily in Florida. Her husband owed a concern in Illinois, of which he was treasurer, on an overdraft. He informed his wife that he could borrow the necessary money to pay the overdraft from an estate of which he was trustee. The wife executed a note and trust deed in Florida and mailed them to her husband, as trustee, at Chicago, Ill., as he had directed her to do. The husband also signed the trust deed, but the opinion does not state when. The court held that delivery of the note and trust deed by the wife was complete in Florida, the law of that state governed her capacity to contract, and, because she was not competent to enter into a contract under the law of Florida, her note and trust deed were void.

The question is not whether the decision is in harmony with the law of Michigan, but whether it governs this case. Here, manual delivery was as complete as in the *Burr* Case because it was made to a bank which had been designated by the mortgagee for that purpose.

In neither case had there been a binding engagement by the mortgagee to make the loan prior to delivery. In neither case had the money been paid in advance of the delivery or contemporaneously therewith. There is nothing in the *Burr* Case to indicate that the mortgagee could not have refused to make the loan or that the mortgagors could not have refused to take the money or could not have abandoned the matter after the wife deposited the papers in the mail. The *Burr* opinion indicated no circumstance fixing the effect of the manual delivery which is not present here. The *Burr* Case is directly applicable, and, consequently, under the law of Illinois, it must be held that the capacity of defendant Clara A. Price is governed by the law of Michigan. Under the law of Michigan, a married woman cannot bind her separate estate through personal engagement for the benefit of others. Defendant Price is not liable.

Affirmed, with costs to defendant Price.

NORTH, C.J., and FEAD and TOY, JJ., concurred with WIEST, J.

SHARPE, J. (dissenting).

It is conceded that under the law of Illinois a married woman is as free to contract as a man, while in Michigan a married woman has not the legal capacity to bind herself or her separate estate by signing these notes. . . .

The plaintiff contends that the contract was an Illinois contract; that the signing of the notes in Michigan was not the final act in the making of the contract, but rather a preliminary step, the delivery of the note being conditional upon defendant's producing a satisfactory title, the approval of the title in Illinois was the last act necessary to make a legal delivery.

The general rule is well stated in John A. Tolman Co. v. Reed, where the court said:

> The law is well settled that contracts must be construed and their validity determined by the law of the country where they were made, unless the contracting parties clearly appear to have had some other law in view.
>
> The general rule is that the law of the place where the instrument was executed and delivered so as to become binding as a contract . . . governs the rights and liabilities of the parties thereto, except in so far as they are controlled by the law of the place where the instrument is payable. . . .

8 C.J. 87, §145.

> There is good authority for the broad proposition, however, that when a note is executed by a married woman in the state of her domicile but made payable in another state, if under the law of the former state she could not have entered into the contract but could have done so under the law of the latter state, it will be presumed that it was the intention of the parties that the note should be governed by the law of the latter state and being valid under such law should be enforced against her even in the state of her domicile. . . .
>
> It is a general rule that every contract as to its validity, nature, interpretation and effect, or, as they may be called, the right, in contradistinction to the remedy, is governed by the law of the place where it is made, unless it is to be performed in another place; and then it is governed by the law of the place where it is to be performed.

Poole v. Perkins [*supra* page 38].

The next question that presents itself in the case at bar is the place where the contract was made.

> A contract is deemed to have been made in the state where the last act necessary to make it a binding agreement takes place.

Goodrich, Conflict of Laws, 218.

> When the contract is made in one jurisdiction to be performed in another the case presents a more complicated question, the rule being that if the parties to a contract are in different jurisdictions, the place where the last act is done which is necessary to the validity of the contract is the place where the contract is entered into.

5 R.C.L. 935.

In the case at bar all of the negotiations for the loan occurred in Chicago, the property upon which the mortgage was placed was located in Chicago, and no money was to be paid by plaintiff until such time as the defendants could show good title to the property. We think the mailing of the papers to Chicago was for the purpose of enabling the plaintiff to ascertain if the title to the real estate was satisfactory and was but a preliminary step in the whole transaction. The final act in the making of the loan was the payment of the money in Chicago. This concluded the negotiations and made it an Illinois contract.

BUSHNELL, J., concurred with SHARPE, J.

BUTZEL, J. (dissenting).

I concur in the result reached by Justice Sharpe. The place of contracting controls the question of capacity of the parties to contract. Palmer National Bank v. Van Doren, 260 Mich. 310, 244 N.W. 485; American Law Institute Restatement of the Conflict of Laws, §333. The notes were dated and payable at Chicago and secured by Chicago real estate. The loan was made in Chicago 25 days after the notes had been signed and not until an actual cloud on the title to the realty had been removed. These circumstances leave no doubt that the notes in question constituted Illinois contracts. . . . The facts are entirely different from those in Re Estate of Lucas . . . in which the loan was solicited by residents of Michigan, the moneys were first received in Michigan by the borrowers, and subsequently the note was dated and signed in Michigan and was payable in Michigan. The place of contracting is where the note is first delivered for value. In Beale on Conflict of Laws, page 1047, it is said:

> Delivery, however, is not the only requisite to the creation of a contract on a negotiable instrument. Value must be given, and until, therefore, there has been a delivery for value, the instrument cannot be said to have had any inception. . . .
>
> It follows that the place of contracting of a contract on a negotiable instrument, be it the obligation of the maker, the drawer or the endorser, is the place where, after the signature of the party in question, the instrument is first delivered for value.

It is true that the physical act of signing the note in the instant case took place in Michigan and the notes were mailed to plaintiff in Chicago, but there was no absolute delivery until the plaintiff had satisfied itself of the status of the title to the mortgaged property and until an actual cloud had been removed. Until that time the transaction was conditional and the notes of no binding force and effect.

The rule is stated in Beale on Conflicts of Laws, p. 1045, as follows: "The phrase 'place of contracting' and its equivalents, the place of making or the place where the contract is made, properly mean the place in which the final act was done which made the promise or promises binding." . . .

We do not believe that the case of Burr v. Beckler . . . should in any way be controlling on this court in determining the lex loci contractus. The problem in the instant case is termed by the authorities as one of "qualifications." The prevailing view in answer to the problem is that the law of the forum should control on the question of lex loci contractus. An excellent treatment of the entire subject may be found in an article entitled, "The Theory of Qualifications and Conflict of Laws," by Professor Lorenzen in 20 Columbia Law Review, p. 247.

Were we not to be controlled by our own law and obliged each time to ascertain what a foreign state would have held under similar circumstances, our decisions would be in hopeless confusion, and it would be necessary each time to examine the decisions of other states in determining the lex loci contractus. The question, however, is foreclosed in this state, as we held in the case of Ohio v. Purse, *supra*, that the law of the place of contracting is to be determined in accordance with the law of the forum.

The judgment should be reversed, with costs to plaintiff.

BUSHNELL, J., concurred with BUTZEL, J.

Questions and Comments

(1) Terminology: *whole law* = conflicts rules + internal law.

(2) In the *Damato* case, why does New Jersey's conflicts rule refer to the law of the situs of the trust money? If the answer is that the situs state has the right to control the disposition of trust funds, doesn't the decision in the case deny that right by reaching a result that the courts of the situs would not have reached? On the other hand, of course, one could ask the same question about why Florida conflicts law defers to the state of the settlor's domicile. If it is because that state has the right to control the disposition of the money (in Florida's view), then we are in trouble, with neither state claiming the right.

(3) Wouldn't the simple answer to such a non-conflict be to say that where neither state is particularly interested, the intent of the parties ought to control, or lacking any obvious intent, the forum ought to apply its own law by default? Isn't it a bit strange that under the court's approach, New Jersey ends up applying the law of Florida, which it presumably thinks is inferior (since it has not adopted the *Totten* trust doctrine—a matter that has traditionally been a function for the courts rather than for the legislatures), while Florida would end up applying the law of New Jersey, which it thinks is inferior? Isn't this the least satisfactory solution?

(4) Why is the doctrine of renvoi accepted in American law for real property and marriage questions but not generally for other matters? With respect to the real property half of the question, some of the traditional justifications are thin. For example, the courts of State *A* will not (for jurisdictional reasons) determine matters directly affecting title to land in State *B*. Thus, our traditional concern for the poor title searcher need not concern us in a renvoi case. If the reason for renvoi with respect to real property is deference to the situs state's political control over its own land, isn't that reason weakened by the fact that in a renvoi case, by hypothesis, the situs state has already relinquished political control over its own land by applying the law of another state, rather than its own, to that land?

(5) A renvoi situation can come about in several different ways. First, the two states may have choice-of-law rules that agree but may characterize the case differently (e.g., one calling it a tort case, the other a contract case). Second, the two states may simply have two different choice-of-law rules (e.g., place of execution vs. place of performance). Third, the two states may use the same concept but define it differently (e.g., domicile). Should it make any difference to the renvoi analysis which of these situations is responsible for the problem?

(6) The court in the *Dater* case seems at one point (though it is not clear) to be saying either (a) the law of Michigan applies, or (b) the law of Illinois applies and it makes the law of Michigan apply. But if one mixes one's *a*s and *b*s, one could

say either (a) the law of Illinois applies, or (b) the law of Michigan applies and it makes the law of Illinois apply.

Isn't the basic flaw of the court's reasoning in *Dater* the fact that it fails to note the shift in meaning of "law" between the two halves of its dichotomy? That is, when it says that the law of Michigan may apply, it means the internal law, while it means the whole law of Illinois when it says that the law of Illinois may apply. Granted these different meanings of "law," the court's reasoning is correct, but its assumptions contain its conclusion—that is, the decision to refer to Illinois whole law rather than Illinois internal law is the central issue of the case, isn't it?

As *Dater* illustrates, courts often engage in renvoi without realizing it. Was the Court's conclusion in McDermott Inc. v. Lewis, *supra* page 99, that Panamanian law permitted International to vote its shares in its parent corporation an example of renvoi?

3. Substance vs. Procedure

There are certain rules and principles of conflicts that cut across various substantive areas like torts or contracts. For example, the question whether a particular issue is substantive or procedural can arise in a tort, contract, or any other kind of case.

That procedure should be governed by the law of the forum is, at least in the most basic cases, obvious. It would be strange to conclude that the size of paper required in the courts of the state whose substantive law controls would be the size required in another state adjudicating the case. But as soon as we leave the precinct of such safely "procedural" topics, the question becomes more obscure. As you read the following Restatement selections and cases, keep in mind the question why the law of the forum should apply to procedural issues as a yardstick for determining whether a particular issue should be called "procedural."

Selections from the First Restatement of Conflicts, on Procedure

§§584-585, 588, 591, 594-597, 599-601, 606 (1934)

§584. Determination of Whether Question Is One of Procedure

The court at the forum determines according to its own Conflict of Laws rule whether a given question is one of substance or procedure.

§585. What Law Governs Procedure

All matters of procedure are governed by the law of the forum.

§588. Parties

The law of the forum determines who may and who must sue and be sued.

§591. Commencement of Action

The law of the forum determines at what moment action is begun.

§594. Mode of Trial

The law of the forum determines whether an issue of fact shall be tried by the court or by a jury.

§595. Proof of Facts

(1) The law of the forum governs the proof in court of a fact alleged.
(2) The law of the forum governs presumptions and inferences to be drawn from evidence.

§596. Witnesses

The law of the forum determines the competency and the credibility of witnesses.

§597. Evidence

The law of the forum determines the admissibility of a particular piece of evidence.

§599. Integrated Contracts

When a contract is integrated in a writing by the law of the place of contracting, no variation of the writing can be shown in another state which could not be shown in a court in the place of contracting under the law of that state, whatever the law of the other state as to integrated contracts.

§600. Execution of Judgment

The law of the forum determines matters pertaining to the execution of a judgment, and what property of a judgment defendant within the state is exempt from execution and on what property within the state execution can be levied, and the priorities among competing execution creditors.

§601. Freedom from Fault

If the law of the forum makes it a condition of maintaining an action that the party bringing the action show himself free from fault, the condition must be fulfilled though there is no such requirement in the state where the cause of action arose.

§606. Limitation of Amount Recoverable

If a statute of the forum limits the amount which in any action of a certain class may be recovered in its courts, no greater amount can be recovered though under the law of the state which created the cause of action, a greater recovery would be justified or required.

Sampson v. Channell

110 F.2d 754 (1st Cir.), *cert. denied*, 310 U.S. 650 (1940)

MAGRUDER, J.

On this appeal the question presented may be stated simply, but the answer is not free from difficulty. A car driven by defendant's testator collided in Maine with a car driven by the plaintiff, injuring both the plaintiff and his wife, who was a passenger. The wife sued and recovered judgment. We affirm that judgment. . . . In this, the husband's action, the jury found specially that the plaintiff's injury was caused by the negligence of defendant's testator, but brought in a general verdict for the defendant on the issue of contributory negligence. Judgment was entered for the defendant.

The action was brought in the federal district court for Massachusetts, there being the requisite diversity of citizenship. On the issue of contributory negligence the plaintiff requested the court to charge the jury, in accordance with the local Massachusetts rule, that "the burden of proving lack of care on the part of the plaintiff is on the defendant." This the court declined to do, but upon the contrary charged, in accordance with the Maine law, that the burden was upon the plaintiff to show affirmatively that no want of ordinary care on his part contributed to cause his injuries. The sole question raised is as to the correctness of this charge, and refusal to charge as requested.

Inquiry must first be directed to whether a federal court, in a diversity of citizenship case, must follow the applicable state rule as to incidence of burden of proof. If the answer is in the affirmative, the further point to be considered is whether the applicable state rule here is that of Massachusetts, where the action was brought, or Maine, where the accident occurred.

It would be an over-simplification to say that the case turns on whether burden of proof is a matter of substance or procedure. These are not clean-cut categories. During the reign of Swift v. Tyson the federal courts in diversity of citizenship cases consistently held that the defendant had the burden of proving the plaintiff's contributory negligence, even though the suit arose in a state whose local rule was the contrary. They avoided having to apply the local rule under the Conformity Act by saying that burden of proof was not a mere matter of procedure but concerned substantive rights, as to which the federal courts on a matter of "general law" were free to take their own view. . . . The question of classification also arose where suit was brought in one state on an alleged tort committed in another state.

But here it was generally held, in the state courts at least, that burden of proof as to contributory negligence was a matter of procedure; hence the rule of the forum would be applied despite a contrary rule of the locus delicti. In these two groups of cases the courts were talking about the same thing and labelling it differently, but in each instance the result was the same; the court was choosing the appropriate classification to enable it to apply its own familiar rule.

In another and quite different setting the question of classification has frequently arisen, namely, in cases involving the constitutionality of statutes shifting from the plaintiff to the defendant the burden of proof on the issue of contributory negligence, as applied retroactively to alleged torts committed before the date of the enactment. Here the courts, federal as well as state, have upheld the statutes as so applied. . . . The courts say that such statutes introduce no change of the substantive law rule that contributory negligence is a complete bar to liability, but pertain only to the procedure by which the fact as to contributory negligence is to be established. In Easterling Lumber Co. v. Pierce, a state statute, applicable to railroads, provided that from the proof of the happening of an accident there should arise a prima facie presumption of negligence. Referring to this statute, the U.S. Supreme Court said,

> The objection to the . . . statute is that it was wanting in due process because retroactively applied to the case since the statute was enacted after the accident occurred. But the court below held that the statute cut off no substantive defense but simply provided a rule of evidence controlling the burden of proof. That as thus construed it does not violate the Fourteenth Amendment to the Constitution of the United States is also so conclusively settled as to again require nothing but a reference to the decided cases.

It is apparent, then, that burden of proof does not fall within either category of "substance" or "procedure" by virtue of any intrinsic compulsion, but the matter has been made to turn upon the purpose at hand to be served by the classification. Therefore, inasmuch as the older decisions in the federal courts, applying in diversity cases the federal rule as to burden of proof as a matter of "general law," are founded upon an assumption no longer valid since Erie Railroad Co. v. Tompkins, their classification of burden of proof as a matter of substance should be re-examined in the light of the objective and policy disclosed in the *Tompkins* case.

The opinion in that case sets forth as a moving consideration of policy that it is unfair and unseemly to have the outcome of litigation substantially affected by the fortuitous existence of diversity of citizenship. Hence, the greater likelihood there is that litigation would come out one way in the federal court and another way in the state court if the federal court failed to apply a particular local rule, the stronger the urge would be to classify the rule as not a mere matter of procedure but one of substantive law falling within the mandate of the *Tompkins* case. There will be, inescapably, a twilight zone between the two categories where a rational classification could be made either way, and where Congress directly, or the Supreme Court under authority of the Act of June 19, 1934 . . . , would have power to prescribe a so-called rule of procedure for the federal courts. Thus, if Rule 8(c) of the Federal Rules of Civil Procedure, 28 U.S.C.A. following section

723c, could be construed as imposing upon the defendant the burden of proof of contributory negligence, it seems that this would be valid and conclusive of the case at bar, despite the contrary intimation in Francis v. Humphrey. Rule 8(c) speaks of contributory negligence as an "affirmative defense," a phrase implying that the burden of proof is on the defendant. Yet the only rule laid down is one of *pleading;* the defendant must affirmatively plead contributory negligence. It is not inconsistent to require the defendant to plead contributory negligence if he wants to raise the issue, and yet to put the burden of proof on the plaintiff if the issue is raised. Since Rule 8(c) contains no prescription as to burden of proof, we must look elsewhere for the answer.

It seems to be said in Francis v. Humphrey and was suggested by counsel in the case at bar, that the question whether in diversity of citizenship cases burden of proof is to be classified as a matter of procedure or substantive law is to be determined by following the classification made by the courts of the state. No doubt we should look to those courts to tell us what their rule is and how it operates in local litigation. But once that is determined, the rule is the same whether it is labeled substantive law or procedure. Furthermore, as already pointed out, such a classification by the state court for one purpose does not mean that the classification is valid for another purpose. Surely the question whether a particular subject-matter falls within the power of the Supreme Court to prescribe rules of procedure under the Act of 1934, or is a matter of substantive law governed by the doctrine of the *Tompkins* case, cannot be foreclosed by the label given to the subject-matter by the state courts.

The inquiry then must be: considering the policy underlying Erie Railroad Co. v. Tompkins, *supra,* would that policy best be served by classifying burden of proof as to contributory negligence as a matter of procedure or substantive law? The incidence of burden of proof may determine the outcome of the case. This is true where the evidence is conflicting and the jury is not convinced either way. It is more pointedly true where, as sometimes happens, the injured person dies and no evidence is available on the issue of contributory negligence. If, in such a case, the burden of proof is on the defendant, the plaintiff wins, assuming the other elements of the cause of action are established. . . . If the burden is on the plaintiff, however, the defendant wins. . . . Assuming the state rule to be one way and the federal rule the other, then the accident of citizenship becomes decisive of the litigation. The situation seems to call for the application of the rule in the *Tompkins* case. There is no important counterconsideration here, for the state rule can be easily ascertained and applied by the federal court without any administrative inconvenience. In thus concluding that for this purpose the incidence of the burden of proof as to contributory negligence is to be classified as a matter of substantive law, we are in harmony with the spirit of the *Tompkins* case, and at the same time are adhering to the classification maintained in an unbroken line of federal court decisions under Swift v. Tyson, *supra.* Federal courts in other circuits have held, since the *Tompkins* decision, that the state rule as to burden of proof must now be applied in diversity of citizenship cases. . . .

Thus far, the case has been discussed as though suit had been brought in the federal court sitting in the state where the alleged tort occurred. But there is the complicating factor that the accident occurred in Maine and suit was brought in Massachusetts. This makes it necessary to consider three further points:

First, if the plaintiff had sued in a Massachusetts state court, would the Massachusetts Supreme Judicial Court have allowed the application of the Maine rule as to burden of proof? The answer is, no. The court would have said that burden of proof is a matter of procedure only, and would have applied the Massachusetts rule that the burden is on the defendant to establish the plaintiff's contributory negligence. Such was the holding in Levy v. Steiger and Smith v. Brown.

Second, would such a decision by the Supreme Judicial Court of Massachusetts be subject to reversal by the Supreme Court of the United States? Presumably we are permitted under the *Tompkins* case thus to attack the decision of a state court collaterally, so to speak, for the Supreme Court would hardly require the federal courts to follow a local decision which, had it been appealed, would have been reversed by the Supreme Court on constitutional grounds. . . .

Whatever the eventual development of this line of cases may be, we know of no decision indicating that the Supreme Court at the present time would reverse a decision of a state court in a case like *Levy*, applying the lex fori rather than the lex loci delicti in the matter of burden of proof. Numerous decisions to this effect have been rendered by state courts, and it has never seemed to occur to anyone that a federal question was involved. Furthermore, in *Levy*, the Massachusetts court was applying not its common law (which put the burden of proof on the plaintiff), but a statute providing that "In all actions, civil or criminal, to recover damages for injuries to the person or property or for causing the death of a person, the person injured or killed shall be presumed to have been in the exercise of due care, and contributory negligence on his part shall be an affirmative defense to be set up in the answer and proved by the defendant."

. . . To hold that this statute is unconstitutional, as applied in *Levy*, to a foreign tort, one would have to find somewhere in the Constitution an implied prohibition to the effect that no state shall pass any law altering an assumed nationally applicable body of doctrine concerning the conflict of laws, the final interpreter of which is the Supreme Court of the United States.

It follows, therefore, that the unimpeachable law of Massachusetts in the case at bar is that in a suit brought in Massachusetts the burden of proof as to contributory negligence is on the defendant, despite the contrary rule applicable in Maine where the accident occurred.

Third, this being Massachusetts law, there remains the inquiry, what law must be applied in the federal court in Massachusetts when jurisdiction is invoked on the ground of diversity of citizenship? Under *Tompkins*, is it the Massachusetts or the Maine rule? We know of no considered decision by the Supreme Court on this point. In the *Tompkins* case, suit was brought in the federal court in New York on a tort alleged to have been committed in Pennsylvania. The question was whether the railroad owed a duty of care to an undiscovered pedestrian walking on a much-used path along the right of way near the tracks. The Supreme Court held that the lower court was in error in treating this question as a matter of "general law," and sent the case back for determination in accordance with the common law of Pennsylvania as declared by its highest court. There is no doubt that in this situation the state courts of New York would have applied the same rule of conflict of laws, and would have looked to the lex loci delicti. The decision in the *Tompkins* case manifestly tended to produce a uniformity in result in that particular situation, whether action on the Pennsylvania tort were brought in a New York state court or New York federal court. . . .

Until the point is finally ruled upon by the Supreme Court, lower courts must piece out as best they can the implications of the *Tompkins* case. The theory is that the federal court in Massachusetts sits as a court coordinate with the Massachusetts state courts to apply the Massachusetts law in diversity of citizenship cases. . . . The powerful argument by Holmes, J., dissenting, in Black & White Taxi Co. v. Brown & Yellow Taxi Co., cited with approval by the majority opinion in the *Tompkins* case, seems to be applicable to that portion of the Massachusetts common law relating to conflict of laws quite as much as to the common law of contracts or torts. Except in the limited range of cases, already alluded to above, where state court decisions on points of conflict of law are subject to reversal by the United States Supreme Court under the federal constitution, the rules applicable to conflict of laws are not "a transcendental body of law outside of any particular state but obligatory within it." If the federal court in Massachusetts on points of conflict of laws may disregard the law of Massachusetts as formulated by the Supreme Judicial Court and take its own view as a matter of "general law," then the ghost of Swift v. Tyson, *supra*, still walks abroad, somewhat shrunken in size, yet capable of much mischief. In the case at bar, it is difficult to see that any gain in the direction of uniformity would be achieved by creating a discrepancy between the rules of law applicable in the Massachusetts state and federal courts, respectively, in order to bring the law of the Massachusetts federal court in harmony with the law that would be applied in the state courts of Maine.

Our conclusion is that the court below was bound to apply the law as to burden of proof as it would have been applied by the state courts in Massachusetts.

This result may seem to present a surface incongruity, viz., the deference owing to the substantive law of Massachusetts as pronounced by its court requires the federal court in that state to apply a Massachusetts rule as to burden of proof which the highest state court insists is procedural only. The explanation is that reasons of policy, set forth in the *Tompkins* case, make it desirable for the federal court in diversity of citizenship cases to apply the state rule, because the incidence of burden of proof is likely to have a decisive influence on the outcome of litigation; and this is true regardless of whether the state court characterizes the rule as one of procedure or substantive law. Certainly the federal court in Massachusetts cannot treat burden of proof as a matter of procedure in order to disregard the Massachusetts rule, and then treat it as substantive law in order to apply the Maine rule. Under the conclusion we have reached, if suit were brought in Massachusetts, the state and federal courts there would be in harmony as to burden of proof; and if suit were brought in Maine, the state and federal courts there would likewise be in harmony on this important matter. It is true that the rule applied in the Maine courts would not be the same as the rule applied in the Massachusetts courts. But this is a disparity that existed prior to *Tompkins*, and cannot be corrected by the doctrine of that case. It is a disparity that exists because Massachusetts may constitutionally maintain a rule of conflict of laws to the effect that the incidence of burden of proof is a matter of "procedure" to be governed by the law of the forum. *Levy.*

For error in the instructions given to the jury on the burden of proof, the judgment must be reversed and the cause remanded for further proceedings not inconsistent with this opinion.

O'Leary v. Illinois Terminal Railroad

299 S.W.2d 873 (Mo. 1957)

HOLLINGSWORTH, J.

Plaintiff recovered judgment against defendant in the Circuit Court of the City of St. Louis for the sum of $7,000 for personal injuries sustained when an automobile in which she was a passenger was struck by defendant's electric railway train in Granite City, Illinois. Upon appeal by defendant to the St. Louis Court of Appeals, the several assignments of error there asserted were decided adversely to defendant and the judgment of the trial court was affirmed. . . . Among the assignments considered by the Court of Appeals was defendant's contention that the trial court erred in giving plaintiff's Instruction No. 10, which casts upon defendant the burden of proving its affirmatively pleaded defense for contributory negligence on the part of plaintiff in bar of any right of recovery she otherwise might have.

In determining that question, the Court of Appeals took judicial notice that the law of Illinois made it incumbent upon plaintiff to allege and prove that she was in the exercise of ordinary care for her own safety at the time of the collision. . . . It then undertook to determine "whether the Illinois requirement that the plaintiff allege and prove that she was in the exercise of due care was a substantive and essential element of her right to recover or was merely a procedural matter to be determined by the law of Missouri." At that point, the court was confronted with a situation which it aptly described as "difficult and delicate." . . .

. . . The Court of Appeals of its own motion, transferred the case here to the end "that the law on the subject should be re-examined." . . . The parties have briefed the question anew. The importance of the question impels us to give it first consideration before discussion of the other assignments of error asserted by defendant in this court.

Plaintiff insists that the overwhelming weight of authority is that the burden of proof is a rule of evidence and as such is procedural, not substantive [citing] cases from several states, and several Missouri cases which the *Redick* case had purported to overrule and to which reference will be hereinafter made. Plaintiff has also invoked the rule of stare decisis and insists that "under this time-honored rule this court should refrain from disturbing the existing law until an authoritative court of Illinois should declare that the burden of proof as to contributory negligence is substantive and not procedural, and thereby demonstrate that the present law is 'clearly erroneous or manifestly wrong.'" . . .

We have carefully considered the cases and authorities cited by both of the parties in the instant case and the cases and authorities upon which the *Redick* case was decided. Unquestionably, there is a conflict of authority upon this subject. Oftentimes, however, a careful analysis of the precise question presented in these cases reveals that the conflict is more seeming than real. The rule applied in the more closely reasoned cases is thus stated in 11 Am. Jur., Conflict of Laws, §203, p. 523:

> Even in those jurisdictions which recognize that ordinarily matters concerning presumptions of evidence and burden of proof relate to the remedy, where the remedy prescribed by that rule of the lex loci, which attaches the burden of proof to one of the parties, is so inseparably connected with, and incorporated

in, the substantive rule creating the right that to ignore that remedy and substitute therefor the rule of the forum would destroy, prejudice, or render ineffective the right to which it is attached, substituting a local cause of action for the one arising in another state, the lex loci in its entirety will be given effect in preference to the contrary rule of the lex fori. It is sometimes stated that the burden of proof is not determinable by the lex fori if it is made a substantial part of the right of action by the laws of the jurisdiction under which it arose.

No purpose will be served by further discussion. We are convinced that the authorities upon which the decision in the *Redick* case was reached are sound. Hence we affirm that portion of the *Redick* case . . . reading:

> Is the Illinois requirement that plaintiff prove he was in the exercise of due care substantive or merely procedural? In Barker v. St. Louis County, . . . we quoted with approval from Jones v. Erie R. Co., . . . as follows: "The distinction between substantive law and procedural law is that substantive law relates to rights and duties which give rise 'to a cause of action,' while procedural law 'is the machinery for carrying on the suit.'"

We think that the Illinois requirement is substantive, just as much as is the requirement that plaintiff plead and prove the negligence of defendant. No one would argue that the latter was not substantive. Both are essential elements of plaintiff's *right to recover* under the law of Illinois. Plaintiff suggests, however, that our courts are not obligated to involuntarily have the laws of another state engrafted into our jurisprudence, . . . and that it will be Missouri rules of law that determine whether a given question is substance or procedure. . . . But certainly we should not determine the matter by mere whim or fiat. "In administering the substantive laws of a sister state we administer *them*, not our own; and we should not administer them either more or less blandly than do our sister's courts." . . .

The Restatement, Conflict of Laws, Sec. 595, ch. 12, states that:

> if a requirement concerning proof of freedom from fault exists in the law of the place of injury and if such condition is there interpreted as a condition of the cause of action itself, . . . the court at the forum will apply the rule of the foreign state. . . . In such a case, the remedial and substantive portions of the foreign law are so bound together that the application of the usual procedural rule of the forum would seriously alter the effect of the operative facts under the law of the appropriate foreign state.

The illustration following the comment is:

> *A*, in state *X*, is injured by the alleged negligence of *B*. *A* sues *B* in state *Y*. By the law of *X*, a plaintiff has no cause of action until he has shown that his own negligence did not contribute to his injury. By the law of *Y*, contributory negligence is an affirmative defense to be pleaded and proved by the defendant. *A* must show his freedom from contributory negligence.

The *Redick* case continues . . . :

> We are convinced that, to the extent the *Menard* case holds that the Illinois rule is remedial and not substantive and to the extent it holds that Missouri courts

will adhere to their rule of placing the burden of proving contributory negligence upon the defendant in a case arising in another state wherein the law of that state is as it is in Illinois, it should no longer be followed. The distinction is that the Missouri law makes a plaintiff's contributory negligence a matter of defense only, the proof of which will defeat an existing claim. But in Illinois, the plaintiff's due care, or his freedom from contributory negligence, is not a matter of defense, defeating a claim, but an essential element which must exist before there is a cause of action in the first instance.

For the reasons stated, the rule announced in the *Menard* and subsequent cases was clearly erroneous and manifestly wrong. The rule of stare decisis is never applied to prevent the repudiation of decisions that are patently wrong and destructive of substantive rights. . . .

The judgment is reversed and the cause remanded. All concur.

Questions and Comments

(1) Why does a court apply its own procedural rules even though it may be applying the substantive law of another jurisdiction? Presumably the answer lies in the desire of the forum not to complicate its task unduly. If domestic procedure can be applied without affecting the foreign rights asserted by way of foreign law, there seems little reason to borrow foreign procedure as well. On the other hand, if a matter is one that will clearly affect the outcome of the case, the tendency is to call it substantive and apply the foreign rule. Two considerations muddy the waters, however: First, it isn't always clear whether a particular rule will affect the outcome of the case (for example, the burden of proof when the question comes up on appeal by way of an attack on jury instructions); second, the forum may wish to apply its own "procedural" rule even though the outcome of a case will be affected in one respect or another because the adoption of the foreign procedure is too burdensome. This second point is particularly strong when the first factor is also operating—the adoption of troublesome foreign procedure when its effect on the outcome is doubtful is not always attractive to the forum.

Outcome determination and ease of application are not always the sole considerations, however. If the issue is the right to a jury trial, for example, the forum may have rejected trial by jury for a particular cause of action because it feels that the judge is a more reliable finder of fact for the particular kind of action in question. Thus, although there might be no difficulty in empaneling a jury in the action in question (since the forum uses juries in other types of actions), the forum might nonetheless refuse to do so on the grounds that the foreign cause of action is *better* served by forum procedure than by foreign procedure. Similarly, forum rules concerning the scope of cross-examination, competency of witnesses and documents, etc., may appeal to the forum as superior and unrelated to its obligation to apply foreign law, even though they may affect the outcome of the case. Evidentiary privileges may further complicate matters since the privilege asserted (doctor-patient privilege, for example) may have little to do either with the forum or the state whose substantive law is applicable if the communication took place in a third state.

Finally, might there be sound analytical reasons, especially in the traditional choice-of-law framework, for distinguishing between primary rights that attach normative judgments to out-of-court behavior, and adjective rights that regulate how primary rights get adjudicated? On this latter distinction, *see* Dane, *Vested Rights, Vestedness and Choice of Law*, 96 Yale L.J. 1191 (1987). And for an intelligent general discussion of the substance/procedure distinction, *see* Risinger, *"Substance" and "Procedure" Revisited*, 30 UCLA L. Rev. 189 (1982).

(2) Some of the common issues that provoke controversy as to proper categorization are:

(a) Statutes of fraud. These statutes have frequently been categorized as substantive or procedural depending on their precise wording, the search being for words that forbid *enforcement* of the obligation (procedural) as against words that forbid *creation* of the obligation (substantive). When they analyze the matter, cases taking the former view concentrate on preventing perjury in the forum's courts, while cases taking the latter view concentrate on the rights of the parties.

(b) Statutes of limitations. These are considered in the following subsection.

(c) Burdens of proof, privilege, and other evidentiary questions, including the parol evidence rule.

(d) Joinder, counterclaim, setoff, impleader, right to jury trial, and other matters usually thought of as "procedural" without regard to the conflicts controversy.

(e) Survival or revival of a cause of action.

(f) The availability of equitable relief, installment judgments, etc., and other "remedy" questions such as measure of damages.

(3) *Sampson* was cited with apparent approval by the Supreme Court in Klaxon Co. v. Stentor Manufacturing Co., 313 U.S. 487 (1941). Does the *Sampson* opinion do a convincing job of arguing that the issue there is substantive for *Erie* purposes and procedural as a matter of state law? What if two states were involved instead of a state and a federal court? That is, assume that State *A* is the forum and State *B* is the place of injury. If State *A* decides that a particular matter is substantive and that the law of State *B*, the locus delicti, therefore ought to apply to the issue, what should be done if the law of State *B* characterizes the issue as procedural?

(4) Assuming that a state places the burden of proof with respect to contributory negligence on the plaintiff because of a suspicion of negligence actions, is it likely that this extra bit of help for the defendant is important enough, in a case that actually gets to the jury, that reversal is merited when the wrong conflicts principle is applied and the plaintiff gets the extra help instead? In other words, how often does the burden of proof affect the "normal" case? Should reversals be limited to cases in which evidence is lacking and the burden issue is therefore determinative of the outcome?

Grant v. McAuliffe
41 Cal. 2d 859, 264 P.2d 944 (1953)

TRAYNOR, J.

On December 17, 1949, plaintiffs W. R. Grant and R. M. Manchester were riding west on U.S. Highway 66 in an automobile owned and driven by plaintiff

D. O. Jensen. Defendant's decedent, W. W. Pullen, was driving his automobile east on the same highway. The two automobiles collided at a point approximately 15 miles east of Flagstaff, Arizona. Jensen's automobile was badly damaged and Jensen, Grant, and Manchester suffered personal injuries. Nineteen days later, on January 5, 1950, Pullen died as a result of injuries received in the collision. Defendant McAuliffe was appointed administrator of his estate and letters testamentary were issued by the Superior Court of Plumas County. All three plaintiffs, as well as Pullen, were residents of California at the time of the collision. . . .

The basic question is whether plaintiffs' causes of action against Pullen survived his death and are maintainable against his estate. The statutes of this state provide that causes of action for negligent torts survive the death of the tortfeasor and can be maintained against the administrator or executor of his estate. Defendant contends, however, that the survival of a cause of action is a matter of substantive law, and that the courts of this state must apply the law of Arizona governing survival of causes of action. There is no provision for survival of causes of action in the statutes of Arizona, although there is a provision that in the event of the death of a party to a pending proceeding his personal representative can be substituted as a party to the action . . . if the cause of action survives. The Supreme Court of Arizona has held that if a tort action has not been commenced before the death of the tortfeasor a plea in abatement must be sustained.

Thus, the answer to the question whether the causes of action against Pullen survived and are maintainable against his estate depends on whether Arizona or California law applies. In actions on torts occurring abroad, the courts of this state determine the substantive matters inherent in the cause of action by adopting as their own the law of the place where the tortious acts occurred, unless it is contrary to the public policy of this state. "[N]o court can enforce any law but that of its own sovereign, and, when a suitor comes to a jurisdiction foreign to the place of the tort, he can only invoke an obligation of its own as nearly homologous as possible to that arising in the place where the tort occurs." Learned Hand, J., in Guinness v. Miller. But the forum does not adopt as its own the procedural law of the place where the tortious acts occur. It must, therefore, be determined whether survival of causes of action is procedural or substantive for conflict of laws purposes.

This question is one of first impression in this state. The precedents in other jurisdictions are conflicting. In many cases it has been held that the survival of a cause of action is a matter of substance and that the law of the place where the tortious acts occurred must be applied to determine the question. The Restatement of the Conflict of Laws, section 390, is in accord. It should be noted, however, that the majority of the foregoing cases were decided after drafts of the Restatement were first circulated in 1929. Before that time, it appears that the weight of authority was that survival of causes of action is procedural and governed by the domestic law of the forum. Many of the cases, decided both before and after the Restatement, holding that survival is substantive and must be determined by the law of the place where the tortious acts occurred, confused the problems involved in survival of causes of action with those in causes of action for wrongful death. The problems are not analogous. *See* Schumacher, *Rights of Action Under Death and Survival Statutes*, 23 Mich. L. Rev. 114, 116-117, 124-125. A cause of action for wrongful death is statutory. It is a new cause of action vested in the widow or next of kin, and arises on the death of the injured person. Before his death, the injured person himself has a separate and distinct cause of action and, if it survives, the same cause of action can be enforced by the personal representative of the deceased against the tortfeasor. The survival statutes do not create a new cause of action, as do the wrongful death statutes. The English courts have reached the same result in construing similar statutes. They merely prevent the abatement of the cause of action of the injured person, and provide for its enforcement by or against the personal representative of the deceased. They are analogous to statutes of limitation, which are procedural for conflict of laws purposes and are governed by the domestic law of the forum. Thus, a cause of action arising in another state, by the laws of which an action cannot be maintained thereon because of lapse of time, can be enforced in California by a citizen of this state, if he has held the cause of action from the time it accrued.

Defendant contends, however, that the characterization of survival of causes of action as substantive or procedural is foreclosed by Cort v. Steen, where it was held that the California survival statutes were substantive and therefore did not apply retroactively. The problem in the present proceeding, however, is not whether the survival statutes apply retroactively, but whether they are substantive or procedural for purposes of conflict of laws. "'Substance' and 'procedure,' . . . are not legal concepts of invariant content." [A] statute or other rule of law will be characterized as substantive or procedural according to the nature of the problem for which a characterization must be made.

Defendant also contends that a distinction must be drawn between survival of causes of action and revival of actions, and that the former are substantive but the latter procedural. On the basis of this distinction, defendant concludes that many of the cases cited above as holding that survival is procedural and is governed by the domestic law of the forum do not support this position, since they involved problems of "revival" rather than "survival." The distinction urged by defendant is not a valid one. Most of the statutes involved in the cases cited provided for the "revival" of a pending proceeding by or against the personal representative of a party thereto should he die while the action is still pending. But in most "revival" statutes, substitution of a personal representative in place of a deceased party is expressly conditioned on the survival of the cause of action itself. If the cause of action dies with the tortfeasor, a pending proceeding must be abated. A personal representative cannot be substituted in the place of a deceased party unless the cause of action is still subsisting. In cases where this substitution has occurred, the courts have looked to the domestic law of the forum to determine whether the cause of action survives as well as to determine whether the personal representative can be substituted as a party to the action. Defendant's contention would require the courts to look to their local statutes to determine "revival" and to the law of the place where the tort occurred to determine "survival," but we have found no case in which this procedure was followed.

Since we find no compelling weight of authority for either alternative, we are free to make a choice on the merits. We have concluded that survival of causes of action should be governed by the law of the forum. Survival is not an essential part of the cause of action itself but relates to the procedures available for the enforcement of the legal claim for damages. Basically the question is one of administration of decedent's estates, which is a purely local proceeding. The problem here is whether the causes of action that these plaintiffs had against Pullen before his death survive as liabilities of his estate. . . . Decedent's estate is located in this state, and letters of administration were issued to defendant by the courts of this state. The responsibilities of defendant, as administrator of Pullen's estate, for injuries inflicted by Pullen before his death are governed by the laws of this state. This approach has been followed in a number of well-reasoned cases. It retains control of the administration of estates by the local legislature, and avoids the problems involved in determining the administrator's amenability to suit under the laws of other states. The common law doctrine *actio personalis moritur cum persona* had its origin in a penal concept of tort liability. *See* Prosser, *Law of Torts* 950-951. Today, tort liabilities of the sort involved in these actions are regarded as compensatory. When, as in the present case, all of the parties were residents of this state, and the estate of the deceased tortfeasor is being administered in this state, plaintiff's right to prosecute their causes of action is governed by the laws of this state relating to administration of estates.

[A dissenting opinion is omitted.]

Questions and Comments

(1) Can calling the survival issue of this case "procedural" be justified on the basis of ease of administrability of the forum? Wouldn't dismissal on the basis of the Arizona nonsurvival rule be much easier?

(2) Why did Arizona allow abatement of the action against a dead tortfeasor? The *Grant* court cites the ancient origin of the tort law and its original penal purpose: Presumably the decedent is not significantly punished by a judgment against his estate. Professor Brainerd Currie, in writing about this case, concluded that the most probable reason for the Arizona rule was inertia in moving away from its common-law origins, but he also proposed another possible rationale for the rule: "that the living should not be mulcted for the wrongs of the dead: that the interests represented in the estate of the tort-feasor—his heirs, next of kin, devisees, legatees, creditors—should not suffer because of what he did." Currie, *Selected Essays on the Conflict of Laws* 143, 144 (1963).

Do these considerations make the rule look procedural?

(3) In the same article Professor Currie speculated as to what "really" went on in the decision of the *Grant* case:

> The judges fed the data into the machine in the usual way, but, when the machine's answer came out, they couldn't swallow it. They rebelled against the machine. They *adjudicated* the case. . . . Doubtless they felt a bit uncomfortable. . . . So they went back to the machine and fed the same data into it again, this time using a somewhat different procedure. After pressing the button marked "Procedure is governed by the law of the forum, substance by the law of the place of the wrong," they pressed the button marked "Procedural" instead of the one marked "Substantive." This time the machine came up with the answer that the court had arrived at independently.

Id. at 138-139.

(4) "We have concluded that survival of the causes of action should be governed by the law of the forum." "Decedent's estate is located in this state, and

letters of administration were issued to the defendant by the courts of this state. The responsibilities of defendant, as administrator of Pullen's estate, for injuries inflicted by Pullen before his death are governed by the laws of this state."

Question: What happens when the forum is other than the state of administration of the decedent's estate—because, for example, the decedent had property elsewhere that serves as the basis for jurisdiction? Which rule governs—that of the forum, or that of the state of administration?

(5) Justice Traynor later commented on the decision in this case: "I do not regard it as ideally articulated, developed as it had to be against the brooding background of a petrified forest. Yet I would make no more apology for it than that in reaching a rational result it was less deft than it might have been to quit itself of the familiar speech of choice of law." Traynor, *Is This Conflict Really Necessary?*, 37 Tex. L. Rev. 657, 670 n.35 (1959).

What are the reasons that led Justice Traynor to believe that he had reached a "rational" result?

4.   Statutes of Limitations

Selections from the First Restatement of Conflicts, on Statutes of Limitations

§§603-605 (1934)

§603. Statute of Limitations of Forum

If action is barred by the statute of limitations of the forum, no action can be maintained though action is not barred in the state where the cause of action arose.

§604. Foreign Statute of Limitations

If action is not barred by the statute of limitations of the forum, an action can be maintained, though action is barred in the state where the cause of action arose.

§605. Time Limitations on Cause of Action

If by the law of the state which has created a right of action, it is made a condition of the right that it shall expire after a certain period of limitation has elapsed, no action begun after the period has elapsed can be maintained in any state.

Duke v. Housen

589 P.2d 334 (Wyo.), *cert. denied*, 444 U.S. 863 (1979)

In the appeal now before the court, appellant-defendant challenges the jury verdict and district court judgment entered against him awarding the appellee-plaintiff, based upon defendant's alleged grossly negligent infection of plaintiff with venereal disease, compensatory and punitive damages in the sum of $1,300,000. . . . For the reasons stated in detail herein, we shall reverse on the ground that the action is barred by the statute of limitations. . . .

In early April, 1970, plaintiff was living, working, and going to college part-time in the Washington, D.C. area. On April 4 of that year she was introduced by her brother to defendant; and on the same night and early morning of April 5, following dinner and dancing plus moderate drinking, engaged in sexual intercourse with defendant in the front seat of his pickup truck. On April 8th, at least partially in response to defendant's sudden and convincing professions of love and desire to marry, plaintiff met defendant at the La-Guardia airport in New York and subsequently traveled by truck with him from New York to Denver, Colorado, engaging on and off in acts of sexual intercourse with defendant along the way. Upon reaching Denver, defendant, having lost interest in plaintiff, lodged her in a local hotel and left for his home in Meeteetse, Wyoming. Plaintiff, after contacting her brother and waiting for him to arrive, subsequently traveled to Meeteetse and confronted defendant concerning his behavior. As a result, it was agreed that defendant would accompany plaintiff and her brother back to Washington, D.C. and apologize to the family; yet after arriving in Washington and discussing the situation with her family, plaintiff for some reason which is neither totally clear nor probably capable of elucidation, accompanied the defendant to New York, there occupying a hotel room together and engaged once more in sexual intercourse with him. Finally, on the next morning of April 21, 1970, defendant broke off his relationship with the plaintiff and informed her for the first time that he had venereal disease, gonorrhea, and that now she probably had it too.

At trial, through the presentation of voluminous testimony by both parties, it was established that at some time prior to March 22, 1970, defendant had become aware that he was probably infected with venereal disease for on that day he visited a doctor in Dallas, Texas, complaining of pain and a urethral discharge. In response, the examining physician took a sample of the discharge for testing and administered a large dosage of fast-acting penicillin, telling defendant to return the next day for the test results. When defendant returned on March 23, 1970, the test results for gonorrhea having been found positive, a larger dose of a longer-acting penicillin was administered and defendant was advised to see his own doctor for further treatment. Defendant then left by plane for New York, arriving the same day, March 23, where immediately upon arrival he contacted his own physician, who after an external examination, stated that he could find no "clinical evidence of gonorrhea"—defendant had no current urethral discharge. On the basis of the previous treatment and this current information, defendant asserted at trial that it was his belief that as of his first sexual contact with the plaintiff on the night of April 4-5, 1970, his infection with gonorrhea had been cured.

Plaintiff, after being told by defendant on April 21, 1970, that she had probably contracted gonorrhea from him and should see a doctor, left New York for Washington, D.C. and the following day, April 22, 1970, visited her personal physician who through a smear test confirmed that gonorrhea was present. In response to medication, plaintiff's infection with what her physician described as a "classic case of asymptomatic gonorrhea" was arrested by May 14, 1970, but more serious problems were to develop. Beginning in January, 1973, plaintiff noticed a pain in her lower right side which by March, 1973, had become so severe and constant as to require medical attention. After various external medical tests provided negative results and antibiotic medication proved ineffective, major exploratory surgery was performed in July, 1973. As a result, plaintiff's physician found that because of the gonorrhea infection, and possibly other related secondary infections as well, scar tissue adhesions had formed within a number of areas of appellee's lower abdomen. He testified that although he had lysed (loosed or detached by surgical procedures) the adhesions, thus somewhat relieving temporarily the severe pain, because of the nature of the scar tissue involved, new adhesions would eventually form and the pain would very probably return again and continue in this cyclical manner for the remainder of plaintiff's life. He further advised that because of the scarring involved, plaintiff's ability to bear children had been greatly reduced. . . .

Plaintiff filed this new action on April 19, 1974, seeking hospital expenses, doctor's expenses, wage loss, future medical expense, as well as damages for pain and suffering, present and future. In addition, based on an allegation that defendant was guilty of gross negligence when he infected her with gonorrhea, plaintiff requested $1 million in exemplary damages. By interrogatory, the jury found that defendant had been infected with gonorrhea at the time of his relations with plaintiff between April 4 and April 21, 1970; and by verdict awarded plaintiff $300,000.00 in compensatory damages, and $1,000,000.00 in exemplary or punitive damages. Following denial of various posttrial motions, the appeal herein was filed.

By way of both the answer filed in response to plaintiff's complaint as well as by motions prior, during and after trial, defendant alleged and strongly argued that based upon applicable statutes and case law, plaintiff's cause of action had been barred by the passage of time and her complaint should therefore be dismissed. Rule 8(c), W.R.C.P. requires that the statute of limitations be specifically set forth as an affirmative defense. In response, the trial judge ruled that inasmuch as plaintiff's scar adhesions had not been discovered until a date much later than when the infection itself had occurred, the applicable time period for limitation of action purposes was to be computed only from discovery of the adhesions; and defendant's assertion was thus denied.

Statutes of limitation have long been a part of the jurisprudence of the United States, all its states and the State of Wyoming. They are pragmatic devices to save courts from stale claim litigation and spare citizens from having to defend when memories have faded, witnesses are unavailable by death or disappearance and evidence is lost. Statutes of limitation are arbitrary by their very nature and do not discriminate between the just and unjust claim. They are not judicially made but represent legislative and public policy controlling the right to litigate. The statutes operate against even the most meritorious of claims and courts have no right to deny their application. When considering the statute of limitations, the nature of injury, its extent, the amount of money damages involved, social considerations, and the emotional appeal the facts may have must pass to the background. The circumstances are only significant in the bearing they may have on where the cause of action arose, when it arose and when the time expired for pursuing the applicable judicial remedy.

[W]hile the basic claim raised by plaintiff, albeit an unusual one, sounds in tort, the circumstance of its pursuance in Wyoming is somewhat unique. Since, as the evidence points up, there was no sexual contact between plaintiff and defendant in Wyoming, nor any tortious injury in this state, simple logic reveals that there could be no tortious conduct, no negligent exposure of plaintiff's body to disease by defendant in this, the forum state. There can be no question that plaintiff's cause of action could only be found as having arisen elsewhere.

. . . The heavy weight of authority in interstate tort cases such as here with elements in different jurisdictions, is that the law of the place where the plaintiff sustains injury to her person controls. Restatement of Conflict of Laws, §377; 2 Harper and James, §30.4, p.1961.

At common law, the limitation period of the forum jurisdiction, the lex fori, generally controlled the time within which causes of action had to be pursued, regardless of the fact that the cause itself in all its elements may have accrued outside the forum jurisdiction. Only when the limitation of action statute of the foreign jurisdiction in which the cause arose could be deemed substantive law rather than procedural would the foreign statute be applied by the forum court. Ehrenzweig, *Conflict of Laws* §161 (1962); Vernon, *Statutes of Limitation in the Conflict of Laws; Borrowing Statutes*, 32 Rocky Mtn. L. Rev. 287 (1960). In order to avoid the confusion and problems associated with attempting to determine when a foreign limitation of action statute was substantive or procedural, a majority of states, including Wyoming, enacted what are referred to as "borrowing" statutes. Section 1-3-117, W.S. 1977, which we find to be controlling in this regard, is simple and clear:

> If by the laws of the state or country where the cause of action arose the action is barred, it is also barred in this state.

The plaintiff takes an unusual position that since the case is tried in Wyoming, it must be tried under Wyoming law as a whole, including §1-3-105, W.S. 1977, prescribing a period of limitation of four years "after the cause of action accrues," pertaining to causes of action arising in Wyoming. She then asserts that under the statutory section, since she discovered she was infected with gonorrhea "around April 22, 1970," her action was timely brought within the Wyoming four year period by filing her complaint on April 19, 1974. She elects to ignore the borrowing statute, §1-3-117, *supra*. She then relies upon [two cases] to support a 51 Am. Jur. 2d, Limitation of Actions, §66, p.645 statement as follows:

> . . . the statutes of limitation of the place where the action is brought and the remedy is sought to be enforced, and not those of the place where the contract was made, the right in tort arose, or the plaintiff resides, or of the domicil of one or the other of the persons affected by the litigation, control in the event of a conflict of laws. . . .

We have no argument with that rule in the case before us but we have no conflict of laws to make it applicable. Any conflict has been erased by the legislature by enactment of the "borrowing" statute fixing the statute of limitations of this state to be the same as that of the jurisdiction in which the cause of the action arose. That is explained in the next section (67) of the Am. Jur. 2d, *supra*, quote. The limitations law of the jurisdiction in which a cause of action arises is the law of this state and has been ever since territorial days, even though a defendant is properly before a Wyoming court, the place where he may be personally served with process and a remedy found. . . .

. . . Cope v. Anderson, 331 U.S. 461 (1947), points out that the bottom line purpose of a state's borrowing statute is to require its courts to bar suits if the right to sue had already expired in another jurisdiction where the crucial combination of circumstances giving the right to sue had taken place, the existence of which affords a party a right to judicial interference in his behalf.

Plaintiff also argues, and the trial judge so held, that the statute of limitations did not commence to run until October, 1973, when adhesions resulting from the infection were discovered because it is the injury therefrom for which the damages are sought. That position is not the accepted rule. . . .

The jury found as a fact that the defendant was the bearer of gonorrhea during the period April 4, 1970 to April 21, 1970. The plaintiff's testimony, admitted by the defendant, is that sexual intercourse between the plaintiff and defendant took place on the dates and in other state jurisdictions in accordance with an itinerary as follows:

April 4-5, 1970.	State of Virginia.
April 9-10, 1970.	State of Iowa.
April 7-8, 1970.	Tuxedo, New York.
April 10-11, 1970.	Ogallala, Nebraska.
April 8-9, 1970.	Erie, Pennsylvania.
April 20-21, 1970.	New York City, New York.

There is no evidence of sexual intercourse taking place in the State of Wyoming. We must therefore look elsewhere for a jurisdiction in which the cause arose. While it is perhaps unusual that the defendant perpetrated his negligent acts and caused injury to plaintiff's body in several different states and which may give an appearance of complexity, an application of settled rules of tort law in the jurisdictions involved clears away any suggestion of obscurity.

The limitation of action statute of the foreign jurisdiction in which the cause in question arose is applied by the forum court irregardless [*sic*] of whether or not the foreign limitation could be characterized as substantive or procedural. Thus, in almost all instances, if a plaintiff's cause of action is time-barred in the jurisdiction in which the cause of action arose, it would be barred by the passage of time in the forum court as well. Such a rule not only clears up any substantive procedural conflict problem, but eliminates as well the possibility of the plaintiff shopping for a favorable forum in which to revive a dead claim. It thus becomes of acute importance in the situation at bar to specifically determine, for limitation of action purposes, where and when plaintiff's cause of action arose. In making such a determination based upon a borrowed limitational period, in all jurisdictions having a borrowing statute, with the exception of Ohio, not only is the specific prescriptive period utilized, but all of its accouterments as well whether in the form of additional statutory provisions or interpretive judicial decisions. As the court in Devine v. Rook has very aptly stated:

But when such [limitational] statute is so borrowed, it is not wrenched bodily out of its own setting, but taken along with it are the court decisions of its own state which interpret and apply it, and the comparison statutes which limit and restrict its operation. This we think is the general law.

Thus, in applying a "borrowed" statute, we must consider not only the borrowed limitation of action statute itself, but also any applicable tolling or other statutes as well as pertinent court cases. In effect, plaintiff's cause must be viewed as if filed in the state where under the laws of that state a cause of action accrued.[7]

We find and hold that a cause of action arose in the state of New York on April 8, 1970 and April 21, 1970. New York City, New York was the place where the defendant committed his second and last acts of negligence in communicating disease to the plaintiff. In New York it has long been the rule that in classic actions of negligence, damage is the gist and essence of a plaintiff's cause, Schwartz v. Heyden Newport Chemical Corporation, and the statute of limitations commences to run at the time of injury is produced (in personal injury cases) and there is damage to the structure of the body. *Schwartz* holds that the cause of action is complete when the invasion of the body by injury takes place "independently of any actual pecuniary damage." The injury is considered a trespass upon the person of the injured plaintiff. . . .

The *Schmidt* doctrine as applied to this case means that a cause of action arose in New York when the defendant had sexual intercourse with the plaintiff at the Motel in the Mountains in Tuxedo, New York on the morning of April 8, 1970. At that time he introduced into the body of the plaintiff infectious pus producing bacteria known as gonococci, which causes the disease of gonorrhea. There is no question but that under the law of New York the defendant was guilty of a tortious act of negligence and the plaintiff was injured by the placement in her body of deleterious matter. Then on the morning of April 21, 1970, the defendant once again at a hotel in New York City, New York repeated the tortious act and once again in the same fashion introduced into the body of plaintiff the bacteria of gonococci. . . .

Having concluded a cause of action accrued in the State of New York, the "borrowing" statute of Wyoming controls the determination of whether or not plaintiff's action has been barred. Under New York law, an action to recover damages for personal injury, unless involving certain specific causes of action not relevant here, must be commenced within three years.

Plaintiff's cause of action accrued in New York at the latest on April 21, 1970, the date of last sexual contact between the parties. Disregarding for the moment any other possibly applicable statute, plaintiff's action not having been filed until April 19, 1974, it appears to be barred, and defendant has so asserted. In response,

---

7. During the remaining course of this opinion, we shall be citing and quoting from the statutes of other states. As allowed by the law of the State of Wyoming, we shall take judicial notice of those considered.

Section 1-12-303, W.S. 1977: "Every court of this state shall take judicial notice of the common law and statutes of every state, territory and other jurisdiction of the United States."

Section 1-12-303, W.S. 1977: "The court may inform itself of foreign laws in such manner as it deems proper, and the court may call upon counsel to aid it in obtaining such information."

Counsel for defendant informed the trial judge of his reliance on the statutes of limitation of other states. The statutes we set out are those applicable at the time of the occurrence herein and are found in the Wyoming State Law Library, Cheyenne.

plaintiff has urged that because of defendant's absence from New York following his tortious conduct, the applicable limitation period has by statute been tolled. N.Y. CPLR §207. We, as did the New York Supreme Court in a recent case, must disagree with the plaintiff. Burwell v. Whitmoyer, 1977, 392 N.Y.S.2d 512, 513:

> We now pass to plaintiff's contention that the statute of limitations was tolled pursuant to CPLR 207. While that section does provide for the tolling of the statute where a defendant is out of the state for more than four months after the action has accrued, subdivision 3 provides for an exception where the jurisdiction over the person can be obtained without personal delivery of the summons to him within the state. . . .

Under the provisions of N.Y. CPLR §302, the defendant, although a nondomiciliary of the state of New York, was still subject to the personal jurisdiction of the courts of that state based upon his commission of a tortious act within the confines of the state itself.

Once found subject to the court's jurisdiction, service of process could have been made upon defendant notwithstanding his absence from the state. . . . It would thus seem clear that had plaintiff brought this action against defendant in New York, the situs of its accrual, by the statutes and authorities of that state, her cause of action would be barred. The limitational period having run in New York, it has run in this, the forum state, as well. §1-3-117, W.S. 1977, *supra.*

In other jurisdictions in which defendant committed his acts of negligence, the cause of action is likewise either barred by a statute of limitations or no cause of action there arose. The defendant's first installment of negligence, April 4-5, 1970, was in the State of Virginia. Arguably, under the law of that state, the cause of action could have arisen there; if indeed it did, it is likewise barred by the state's limitations. In Virginia, the appropriate limitational period for personal injuries of the kind sustained herein is two years, and even though the defendant did not then and does not now reside in Virginia, he was still subject to the personal jurisdiction of its courts through its long arm statutes because of his allegedly tortious conduct within the state.

. . . On the other hand, if we follow the holding of the Virginia court's *Street* case, that the statute begins to run upon the date of last exposure, then the cause of action arose in New York City, New York, on April 22, 1970 where the last act of sexual intercourse took place. In the first instance, the plaintiff is barred in Virginia by its two year statute of limitations. In the other no cause of action arose in Virginia.

Even if it could be considered that a cause of action arose in Pennsylvania, its statute of limitations bars any action there. The Pennsylvania statute of limitations, 12 P.S. §34, provides that a personal injury action "must be brought within two years from the time when the injury was done and not afterwards." The tolling statute of Pennsylvania, 12 P.S. §40, applies only to residents. . . . The presence of plaintiff and defendant in Pennsylvania was only transient.

We must also conclude that no cause of action arose in Iowa. Iowa follows the Restatement, Conflict of Laws, §377 rule that: "The place of wrong is in the state where the last event necessary to make an actor liable for an alleged tort takes place." Since Iowa follows the discovery rule, as noted, it would appear that it was in Washington, D.C. that the cause of action accrued as far as that state is concerned because it was in the District of Columbia that plaintiff discovered that she had in fact suffered injury by virtue of the negligent conduct of the defendant.

[The court rejected application of the Nebraska statute for reasons discussed in connection with the statutes of other states.]

We foreclose Washington, D.C. as the place where a cause of action arose because no tortious act was committed there, nor was that a place where the plaintiff was injured by the implanting of infection by the defendant. It is true that Washington, D.C. was the place where plaintiff incurred medical expense for diagnosis and treatment of the injury inflicted upon her but has no controlling force as to where the cause arose. While she had money damages in the District of Columbia, her physical injury of contracting gonorrhea took place elsewhere. . . .

We therefore must conclude after extensive research that by virtue of Wyoming's borrowing statute, the filing of plaintiff's complaint on April 19, 1974 was untimely.

Reversed with directions to vacate the judgment for plaintiff and enter judgment for the defendant.

THOMAS, J., concurring.

I concur in the result in this case that was reached by the majority of the Court. I would, however, reach that result in a different manner. In my view this action was barred by the three-year statute of limitations of the District of Columbia, which is the place where the cause of action arose and to which we are directed by §1-3-117, W.S. 1977. The District of Columbia, like our state, follows a discovery rule with respect to the accrual of an action in tort. . . .

I am impressed with the reference in the majority opinion and the dissenting opinion to A.L.I. Restatement, Conflict of Laws, §377 (1934), which sets forth the rule as follows:

> §377. *The Place of Wrong.* The place of wrong is in the state where the last event necessary to make an actor liable for an alleged tort takes place.

As I understand the thrust of the majority opinion that place is determined to be the state of New York. Included within §377 is a section entitled "Summary of Rules in Important Situations Determining Where a Tort is Committed," and included within that section is a rule set forth as follows:

> 2. When a person causes another voluntarily to take a deleterious substance which takes effect within the body, the place of wrong is where the deleterious substance takes effect and not where it is administered.
>
> *Illustration:*
>
> 2. *A*, in state *X*, mails to *B* in state *Y* a package containing poisoned candy. *B* eats the candy in state *Y* and gets on a train to go to state *W*. After the train has passed into state *Z*, he becomes ill as a result of the poison and eventually dies from the poison in state *W*. The place of wrong is state *Z*.

This illustration seems peculiarly applicable to the factual situation herein in which the infection could have been transmitted in any one of a number of states. The plaintiff did not manifest any symptoms of the disease, and the illness was identified in Washington, D.C., upon physical examination. I have no quarrel with the general discussion of the law relative to statutes of limitations set forth in the majority opinion, but those concepts are designed to reach a degree of certainty in the law, albeit arbitrarily. Their application in this instance identifies the District of Columbia as the place of wrong. . . .

McCLINTOCK, J., dissenting.

In brief outline of the basis of my dissent, I agree with the majority that under the common law, limitations of actions are governed by the law of the forum. Section 1-3-117, W.S. 1977, the so-called borrowing statute, changes that rule only to the extent that we are required to apply the limitation of another state if it is determined that the "cause of action arose" in that other state. The majority recognize that both a wrongful act and a resulting injury are necessary to effect an actionable tort, and that the "law of the place where the plaintiff sustains injury to her person controls." The record does not disclose and neither the jury nor this court could find the specific state where either the wrongful act took place or the plaintiff sustained injury to her person. An essential prerequisite to application of our borrowing statute, namely, that there be a state from which to borrow, is then lacking. However, it might be logically consistent with §1-3-117 to hold the action barred if, by the law of *all* the states where the action *might possibly* have arisen, the action is barred. That is not the situation here, since Nebraska and Wyoming, both of which are states where the injury could have taken place, have four-year statutes and both are discovery states. My essential disagreement with both the majority and concurring opinions is with their concept that discovery of the wrongful act and resulting injury is an essential condition to the existence of an actionable tort. I would hold that discovery is of importance only in determining when a statute of limitations begins to run. I would then hold that defendant, who bears the burden of proving facts bringing the case within an applicable statute of limitations, has failed in that burden. I would therefore not dismiss the action. . . .

[Justice McClintock stated his opinion that the wrong was committed only when the disease was "communicated" to the plaintiff, and discussed incubation periods.]

. . . Consistently with the proper holding of the majority that it is the law of the state of injury and not of the wrongful act that determines whether a tort has been committed, it is possible that the tort could have become complete in any one of 11 states in which the plaintiff, in the company of the defendant, or separately, found herself during the 18-day sojourn between the first contact and confirmation of the existence of the disease in plaintiff in Washington on April 22. . . .

Although it is the law of the place of injury that governs, the majority briefly and I think arbitrarily dismiss Wyoming as a possible place of wrong because no sexual act took place therein. If transmission of the disease through sexual intercourse is not certain and if there is an incubation period, then it is possible that transmission and planting of the infection occurred in one state and took effect in another. . . .

Defendant does not plead the statute of limitations of any particular state, and claims only that the action is barred by the provisions of our borrowing statutes, §1-3-117, W.S. 1977. In this court he relies on the District of Columbia three-year statute. I would hold that statute inapplicable on the basis already discussed, and since he has shown no other statute which governs and has not shown that the statutes of all possible places of wrong have run, he has failed in his burden. From this, it follows that the action should not be dismissed. . . .

Questions and Comments

(1) A well-known exception to the usual principle that forum statutes of limitations automatically apply in the absence of a borrowing statute is Bournias v. Atlantic Maritime Co., 220 F.2d 152 (2d Cir. 1955) (Harlan, J.—later Justice Harlan). There the question was whether the one-year limitations period of the Panamanian code or the longer period under American maritime law would apply in a case arising under the Panamanian Labor Code. The forum was the United States District Court, not an individual state, because federal maritime jurisdiction had been invoked. The United States has no borrowing statute. The court said that the Panamanian limitation would be applied if it were substantive but not if it were procedural. It then discussed the various tests for distinguishing substantive from procedural statutes of limitations, expressed a lack of satisfaction with all of them, and settled on what appeared to be the most acceptable: Statutes of limitations will be presumed to be procedural unless they are contained in the same statute that creates the substantive right. Under that test, the court said, the Panamanian statute was procedural (since it did not deem the broad Panamanian Labor Code to be a single statute). Did such a test ever make sense? Why should a United States court wish to entertain an action that arose under Panamanian law but that could not be brought in Panama?

(2) Consider also so-called "statutes of repose," which have the effect of extinguishing a cause of action after a specified period of time has elapsed from the happening of an event, such as the death of the debtor. Statutes of repose can trump the applicable statute of limitations and can even eliminate a right of action before it ever accrues. For example, a statute of repose might bar tort actions against a product manufacture for injuries that occur more than 20 years after the product was first purchased. In contrast to statutes of limitations, statutes of repose are likely to be treated as substantive, at least if they are deemed substantive by the states adopting them. *See, e.g.,* Bonti v. Ford Motor Co., 898 F. Supp. 391, 397 (S.D. Miss. 1995), *aff'd,* 85 F.3d 625 (5th Cir. 1996) (North Carolina's products liability statute of repose is substantive rather than procedural). Does consultation of the other state's characterization violate the principle embodied in section 584, reprinted at page 122 *supra*?

(3) As in *Duke*, most states have adopted some kind of borrowing statute to determine when the forum will apply its own statute of limitations to a case and when it will apply the limitations statute of another state. The Wyoming statute at issue in *Duke* is typical in borrowing the statute of limitations of the state where the cause of action "arose." Will this criterion always be appropriate, even in simple cases? What if the claim "arose" in State *A* but is to be governed by the law of State *B*?

(4) The *Duke* opinion at one point refers to the "*Schmidt* doctrine" to determine that the cause of action arose in New York, thus triggering the Wyoming borrowing statute (which applies when the cause of action "arose" in another state or country). But *Schmidt* was a New York case. Shouldn't the court have applied *Wyoming* law to determine where, for purposes of a Wyoming statute, the cause of action arose?

After the court decides that the cause of action arose in another jurisdiction, what law governs issues such as tolling and accrual? *See* Uniform Conflict of Laws—Limitations Act §3 (1982) ("If the statute of limitations of another state applies to the assertion of a claim in this State, the other state's relevant statutes and other rules of law governing tolling and accrual apply in computing the limitations period, but its statutes and other rules governing conflict of laws do not apply.").

(5) In several other places the court, in discussing the law of various states, concluded that under the law of the state being discussed, the claim accrued only when it was discovered. The court therefore ignored the laws of those states since the claim was discovered in the District of Columbia. Isn't the dissent right in saying that the majority was confusing the issue of *when* a claim arose and *where* it accrued? Specifically, could Wyoming do the following:

(a) determine that the claim had "arisen," say, in Virginia, and

(b) therefore apply the law of Virginia, under which the statute would begin to run when the claim was discovered, no matter where it was discovered?

(6) What would the *Duke* majority have done if it determined that wrongs had been committed in several states against the plaintiff and that actions were barred under the laws of some of those states but not others?

5. Public Policy

Selection from the First Restatement of Conflicts, on Public Policy
§612 (1934)

§612. Action Contrary to Public Policy

No action can be maintained upon a cause of action created in another state the enforcement of which is contrary to the strong public policy of the forum. (1948 Supp.) Likewise, a distinction has to be noted between the situation dealt with in this Section and the situation where a party sets up a defense which is contrary to the strong public policy of the forum. The latter situation involves more than a matter of denial of access to the court. The plaintiff is asking for a judgment even though there is a defense otherwise valid. It is, therefore, not within the scope of the rule of this Section.

Laboratory Corp. of America v. Hood
395 Md. 608, 911 A.2d 841 (2006)

[Parents brought suit against Laboratory Corporation, alleging that its erroneous report stating that their fetus did not have cystic fibrosis (a genetic disease that is highly likely to be fatal) contributed to their decision to have the child. The United States District Court for the District of Maryland certified questions to the Court of Appeals.]

WILNER, J.

We have before us three questions of law certified by the United States District Court for the District of Maryland pursuant to the Maryland Uniform Certification of Questions of Law Act (Maryland Code, §§12-601 through 12-613 of the Cts. & Jud. Proc. Article). The questions arise from an action by Karen and Scott Hood, Maryland residents, against two North Carolina corporations—Laboratory

Corporation of America and Laboratory Corporation of America Holdings, which we shall refer to collectively as LabCorp.

The action is one that is often, but misleadingly, denominated as "wrongful birth." The Hoods complain that the defendants were negligent in misreading a chromatograph of the DNA from an amniotic fluid specimen extracted from Ms. Hood and erroneously reporting that the fetus was not likely to be affected by cystic fibrosis (CF). Relying on the erroneous report, Ms. Hood elected to continue with the pregnancy, and that resulted in the birth of their son, Luke, who *does* have CF. The Hoods now seek to recover damages for the cost of raising and caring for Luke.

The questions certified to us are:

1. In a case where a medical laboratory receives a specimen from a Maryland physician and erroneously interprets the specimen in another State, causing injury in Maryland to Maryland residents, should this court follow the "standard of care" exception in the Restatement (First) of Conflicts of Law §380(2) and apply the substantive law of the State where the erroneous interpretation took place?

2. Does denying Maryland residents the right to bring a wrongful birth action by applying North Carolina law violate the public policy of the State of Maryland? . . .

The problem underlying the first two certified questions . . . is that, while Maryland recognizes an action of this kind by the parents, North Carolina apparently does not, and the District Court, which must apply Maryland law, including the Maryland law on conflicts of law, desires to know whether, in the situation at hand and if the action were filed in a Maryland court, we would apply the substantive law of Maryland, where the injury occurred, or of North Carolina, where the negligent acts or omissions took place. . . .

The Hoods are Maryland residents. Their first child, Zachary, was born in 1997 and was diagnosed with CF when he was two. In the present state of medical science, persons with CF are doomed to suffer from lung, gastrointestinal, pancreatic, heart, and other organ diseases, and rarely live beyond their mid-30s. In order to develop CF, a child must receive a particular gene mutation from both parents. After Zachary was diagnosed, the Hoods learned that they both carry the recessive delta F508 gene mutation that causes one of the most severe forms of CF. Because they are both carriers of that mutation, each of Karen's pregnancies carries a 25% risk of the child having CF.

In 1999, Ms. Hood became pregnant again, and she and her husband were referred by Ms. Hood's obstetrician to a genetic counselor. Genetic testing performed on the fetus revealed that it had CF, whereupon Ms. Hood terminated the pregnancy. In August, 2001, she became pregnant the third time and again decided to have the fetus tested. The Hoods had already made the decision to terminate the pregnancy if the fetus tested positive for CF. On November 27, 2001, Ms. Hood had an amniocentesis performed, in Maryland, by her obstetrician, Thomas Pinkert.

LabCorp operates a nationwide network of 35 primary testing locations and more than 1,100 patient service centers, eight of which are located in Maryland. Although it receives specimens from physicians and from its various patient service centers throughout the country, LabCorp performs all of its genetic testing on amniotic fluid at its Center for Molecular Biology and Pathology in North Carolina. The company markets genetic testing services to couples such as the

Hoods. Before the specimen taken from Ms. Hood was sent to LabCorp for testing, the Hoods' genetic counselor, Amy Kimball, who worked in Dr. Pinkert's office in Maryland, informed LabCorp that both Karen and Scott Hood carried the CF gene. The sample was sent to the LabCorp facility in North Carolina, where the DNA in it was subjected to a chromatograph that was analyzed by two LabCorp employees, Marcia Eisenberg and Nicholas Brown.

In conformance with the analysis done by Eisenberg and Brown, LabCorp reported to Dr. Pinkert that, although both parents were carriers of the delta F508 mutation, the amniotic fluid was negative for 31 common CF genetic mutations, and "[t]his fetus is not expected to be a carrier of cystic fibrosis or be affected by cystic fibrosis." Pinkert sent the report to the Hoods. Based on the LabCorp report, the Hoods elected to continue the pregnancy, resulting in the birth of Luke on May 3, 2002. Three months later, the child was found to be positive for CF. In September, 2002, LabCorp issued a corrected report which noted that the original chromatograph did, indeed, demonstrate that the fetus was positive for the delta F508 mutation that causes CF—the box containing the word "del F508" was marked with an asterisk, indicating that the fetus had CF—and stated that Eisenberg and Brown had misread the chromatograph.

The District Court issued a partial ruling on the cross-motions for summary judgment. In that ruling, the court held that, under Maryland law, the Hoods' action was for negligence, not breach of contract, and that the Maryland law of negligence therefore applied. The court observed that, in diversity cases, such as the one at hand, it was obliged to apply Maryland's choice of law rules and determined that Maryland adheres to *lex loci delicti* principles for all tort claims, *i.e.*, we apply the law of the place where the tort or wrong was committed. It concluded that, under our application of those principles, the place where the last event required to give rise to the tort occurred determines the law that should apply, that in personal injury claims the last event required to give rise to the tort is the injury, and that the injury in this action occurred in Maryland, where Luke was born. . . .

Whether Maryland or North Carolina law applies is critical to the Hoods' case. In Azzolino v. Dingfelder, 315 N.C. 103 (1985), the North Carolina Supreme Court held that the parents of a child born with even severe birth defects did not suffer any legally cognizable injury, and thus the Hoods' action could not succeed under North Carolina law. In Reed v. Campagnolo, 332 Md. 226 (1993), responding to a certified question from the U.S. District Court, we adopted a completely opposite point of view, noting that "[t]he *Azzolino* analysis does not recognize even the economic impact on the parents and, in that respect, is contrary to Maryland law." Id. at 238. That divergence forms the basis of the second certified question. If application of Restatement §380(2) would ordinarily cause North Carolina law to be applicable in this case, would Maryland nonetheless refuse to apply that law on the ground that it would be contrary to Maryland public policy to deny a Maryland resident, suing in a Maryland court for a wrong committed in Maryland, a remedy recognized in this State? . . .

Maryland Public Policy

We have not previously applied a public policy exception to the *lex loci delicti* doctrine, although our case law strongly indicates that we *would* do so in a proper case. We have long recognized, and have on occasion applied, such an exception under analogous *lex loci* principles and have implicitly recognized the exception in a tort action subject to *lex loci delicti*.

In breach of contract actions, this Court has traditionally applied the doctrine of *lex loci contractus,* under which, in deciding upon the validity and construction of a contract, we generally apply the law of the place where the contract was made. We have just as consistently held, however, that the *lex loci contractus* principle is not inflexible and that it "does not apply to a contract provision which is against Maryland public policy." Bethlehem Steel v. G.C. Zarnas & Co., 304 Md. 183, 188 (1985) and cases cited there. We cautioned in *Bethlehem Steel* that "merely because Maryland law is dissimilar to the law of another jurisdiction does not render the latter contrary to Maryland public policy" and that "for another state's law to be unenforceable, there must be a 'strong public policy against its enforcement in Maryland.'" Id. at 189, quoting in part from Texaco v. Vanden Bosche, 242 Md. 334, 340-41 (1966). *See also* National Glass v. J.C. Penney, 336 Md. 606 (1994).

In Hutzell v. Boyer, 252 Md. 227 (1969) and Hauch v. Connor, 295 Md. 120 (1983), we applied a public policy exception in the context of workers' compensation statutes, which we recognized had some affinity to contract and tort principles but were sufficiently different from both to be considered separately. The issue in those cases was whether Maryland would allow a fellow-employee action—an action implicitly permitted under the Maryland workers' compensation law but not permitted under the law where the parties were employed (*Hutzell*) or where the accident occurred (*Hauch*).

In *Hutzell,* although the parties were temporarily employed in Virginia, the employment-related accident occurred in Maryland and the parties were both residents of Maryland. In rejecting application of the Virginia law, which otherwise would have been required, the Court observed that Maryland had "a genuine interest in the welfare of a person injured within its borders, who may conceivably become a public charge due to a disabling injury" and that "[t]he social and economic problems following in the wake of a serious injury as they may affect the dependents of the person injured are properly matters of public concern." *Hutzell,* 252 Md. at 233. The *Hauch* court regarded that as a public policy exception and applied that exception to the situation in which the co-employees were residents of and employed in Maryland but where the accident occurred in Delaware.

In Harford Mutual v. Bruchey, 248 Md. 669 (1968), a Maryland couple sued a Maryland company in a Maryland court for damages arising from an automobile accident that occurred in Virginia. In addition to any direct personal injuries, the husband sued for loss of consortium, an action that, by statute, was not allowed in Virginia. We concluded that, under *lex loci delicti* principles, Virginia law would generally apply, but acknowledged "the question of whether there is extant in Maryland such a strong public policy in favor of recovery by a husband for loss of consortium as to require its courts to refuse to apply the law of a sister State which does not recognize such a right." Id. at 674. We concluded that there was "no such strong public policy." Id. We observed that a husband's right to recover for loss of consortium had been characterized as an "anachronism," a "fossil from an earlier era," an "anachronistic common law rule," and a "vestigial right," which, we said, "hardly indicates recognition of a strong public policy in Maryland in favor of recovery for deprivation of consortium." Id. at 675.

Although we did not find in *Harford Mutual* a sufficiently clear and strong public policy to disregard the *lex loci delicti* in favor of allowing a loss of consortium claim, the case cannot be read other than as recognizing that there *is* a public policy exception to the *lex loci delicti* rule and that we *would* apply it in an appropriate case. *See also* Linton v. Linton, 46 Md. App. 660 (1980); Rhee v. Combined Enterprises, Inc., 74 Md. App. 214, *cert. dismissed*, 314 Md. 123 (1988); Black v. Leatherwood, 92 Md. App. 27 (1992). We can find no principled basis upon which to recognize such an exception in contract and workers' compensation cases but to deny it in tort cases.

The question certified is thus presented: does denying Maryland residents the right to bring a wrongful birth action by applying North Carolina law violate the public policy of the State of Maryland? Should the District Court, in light of our response to the first certified question, still find this question relevant, our answer is "Yes."

This is not a case like *Harford Mutual*, which needs to be examined in context. Under long-established Maryland common law, only a husband could sue for loss of consortium in Maryland—for "the loss of society, affection, assistance, and conjugal fellowship" of his wife. The wife had no comparable right. See Coastal Tank Lines v. Canoles, 207 Md. 37 (1955). That anomaly was founded on the ancient common law premise that the husband was entitled to his wife's services and was obliged to support her but that the wife was not entitled to her husband's services and was not obliged to support him. Id. at 50-51. As the clearest basis for maintaining that unequal right in the middle of the 20th Century, the *Coastal Tank Lines* Court quoted the pronouncement from the House of Lords decision in Best v. Samuel Fox & Co., Ltd., A.C. 716 (1952), *affirming* 2. K.B. 639 (1951) that "[t]he common law is a historical development rather than a logical whole, and the fact that a particular doctrine does not logically accord with another or others is no ground for its rejection." *Coastal Tank Lines*, at 48.

In Deems v. Western Maryland Ry., 247 Md. 95, 100-101 (1967), decided a mere seven months before *Harford Mutual*, the Court, in considering a Constitutional equal protection challenge to such an unfair rule, decided, in lieu of either abolishing the action or extending it to the wife, to regard it, prospectively, as a joint action for injury to the marital relationship. Although preserving the action in its converted form, there is nothing in the *Deems* Opinion to suggest that the Court had any great attachment to the action; rather, it transformed the action into a joint one only to avoid having to resolve the Federal Constitutional attack on it, *Deems*, 247 Md. at 113, and, indeed, the Court expressly cautioned that it was not deciding the effect that any Federal statute might have in "foreclosing any claim for consortium under the Maryland law." Id. at 115. As noted, the *Harford Mutual* Court still considered the action, even in its new emanation, as vestigial, anachronistic, and a "fossil from an earlier era," and, consistently with the caution expressed in *Deems,* did not regard the existence of the action in Maryland as a reason not to apply Virginia law.

The right of parents to bring an action for wrongful birth is quite different. It is not a vestige of ancient common law illogic but, as we noted in Kassama v. Magat, 368 Md. 113, 134 (2002), is of a type that, as a practical matter, could not have been brought before the last half of the 20th Century. At its core, we said, it rests "to a large extent on the more recent advances in medical and scientific knowledge that made contraception more practical and reliable and made potential fetal injuries and defects detectable prior to birth, and even prior to conception, coupled with the loosening of the fetters on abortions triggered in 1973 by *Roe v. Wade.*" Id.

In Reed v. Campagnolo, supra, 332 Md. 226, we pointed out that "[t]he clear majority of courts that has considered the type of medical malpractice case alleged by the Reeds has concluded that there is legally cognizable injury, proximately caused by a breach of duty," id. at 235-36, and that "there is at least some economic harm to the parents in these cases—a harm that can be quantified under the general rules relating to tort damages." Id. at 236. We expressly rejected the approach of *Azzolino* as contrary to both Maryland law and the law of most States, and adopted instead the view of the Massachusetts court in Viccaro v. Milunsky, 406 Mass. 777 (1990) that the harm is not the birth itself but "the effect of the defendant's negligence on the [parents] resulting from the denial to the parents of their right, as the case may be, to decide whether to bear a child or whether to bear a child with a genetic or other defect." *Reed*, supra, 332 Md. at 237, quoting from *Viccaro.*

Reed was a carefully considered and deliberate recognition that, when prospective parents, relying on the negligent act or omission of a health care professional, elect to continue a pregnancy that they otherwise would have lawfully terminated and, as a result, are burdened with the cost and expense of raising a child with a serious genetic or other physical or mental defect, they have been injured and have a right to seek damages for that injury from the person whose negligence led to the injury. That right is a matter of important public policy in this State, flowing not only from this Court's considered view but as well from statute. *See* Maryland Code, §20-209(b), of the Health General Article, precluding the State from interfering with the decision of a woman to terminate her pregnancy at any time during the pregnancy if the fetus is affected by genetic defect or serious deformity or abnormality. We thus conclude that, if application of North Carolina law would preclude this cause of action on the ground stated in *Azzolino* that no injury has occurred, we would hold that aspect of North Carolina law to be contrary to clear, strong, and important Maryland public policy and would not apply it.

[The court commented on the difficulty of determining whether Laboratory Corporation has a duty to Scott Hood, the father of Luke Hood.]

Certified questions of law answered as set forth above; costs to be equally divided by the parties.

Holzer v. Deutsche Reichsbahn-Gesellschaft

277 N.Y. 474, 14 N.E.2d 798 (1938)

PER CURIAM.

The complaint alleges two causes of action arising out of a contract between plaintiff, a German national, and Schenker & Co. G.m.b.H., a German corporation, for services to be performed by plaintiff for three years from January 1, 1932, in Germany and in other locations outside this state. Defendants, German corporations, controlled either through stock ownership or otherwise, the transportation system known as Schenker & Co.

Both causes of action allege that the contract provides that "in the event the plaintiff should die or become unable, without fault on his part, to serve during the period of the contract the defendants would pay to him or his heirs the sum of 120,000 marks, in discharge of their obligations under the hiring aforesaid."

The first cause of action alleges that on June 21, 1933, defendants discharged plaintiff as of October 31, 1933, upon the sole ground that he is a Jew and that as the result of such discharge he was damaged in a sum upwards of $50,000.

The second cause of action alleges that in April, 1933, the German government incarcerated plaintiff in prison and in a concentration camp for about six months, that his imprisonment was not brought about by any act or fault of plaintiff but solely by reason of the policy of the government which required the elimination of all persons of Jewish blood from leading commercial, industrial, and transportation enterprises, that as a result "plaintiff became unable, without any fault on his part, to continue his services from the month of April, 1933," and has been damaged in the sum of $50,000.

The second separate defense of defendant Deutsche Reichsbahn-Gesellschaft alleges that the contract of hiring was made and was to be performed in Germany, was terminated in Germany and is governed by the laws of Germany, that subsequent to April 7, 1933, the government of Germany adopted and promulgated certain laws, decrees, and orders which required persons of non-Aryan descent, of whom plaintiff is one, to be retired.

The Special Term granted plaintiff's motion to strike out this defense, the Appellate Division affirmed and certified these questions: "(1) Is the second separate defense contained in the answer of the defendant, Deutsche Reichsbahn-Gesellschaft, sufficient in law upon the face thereof? (2) Does the complaint herein state facts sufficient to constitute a cause of action?"

The courts of this state are empowered to entertain jurisdiction of actions between citizens of foreign countries or other states of this Union based upon contracts between nonresidents to be performed outside this state. . . . Under the decisions of this court and of the Supreme Court of the United States, the law of the country or state where the contract was made and was to be performed by citizens of that country or state governs. . . . Within its own territory every government is supreme . . . and our courts are not competent to review its actions. . . . We have so held, "however objectionable" we may consider the conduct of a foreign government. Dougherty v. Equitable Life Assur. Soc. of United States. . . . "Every sovereign State is bound to respect the independence of every other sovereign State, and the courts of one country will not sit in judgment on the acts of the government of another done within its own territory." Oetjen v. Central Leather Co. . . . In the *Dougherty* Case . . . we have held: "It cannot be against the public policy of this State to hold nationals to the contracts which they have made in their own country to be performed there according to the laws of the country."

Therefore, in respect to the first cause of action, we are bound to decide, as a matter of pleading, that the complaint does not state facts sufficient to constitute a cause of action and that the second separate defense of the answer is sufficient in law upon its face. Defendants did not breach their contract with plaintiff. They were forced by operation of law to discharge him.

In respect to the second cause of action, the result is necessarily different. We are dealing merely with pleadings. Assuming, as alleged, that plaintiff became unable without any fault on his part to continue his services subsequent to April, 1933, that part of the agreement which is alleged to provide "that in the event the plaintiff should die or become unable, without fault on his part, to serve during the period of the contract the defendants would pay to him or his heirs the sum of 120,000 marks, in discharge of their obligations, under the hiring aforesaid," must be interpreted according to German law and the meaning of German words. What that law is depends upon the solution of questions of fact which must be determined on the trial. If the English words "become unable" are a correct translation of the German words employed in the contract, then they would not appear to be limited to inability caused by physical illness but might be intended to apply to any factor which might prevent his service. . . .

Questions and Comments

(1) The classic definition of "public policy" is found in Loucks v. Standard Oil Co. of New York, 120 N.E. 198, 202 (N.Y. 1918) (Cardozo, J.):

> The courts are not free to refuse to enforce a foreign right at the pleasure of the judges, to suit the individual notion of expediency or fairness. They do not close their doors unless help [to the other state] would violate some fundamental principle of justice, some prevalent conception of good morals, some deep-rooted tradition of the common weal.

With the due process clause to strike down the most serious abuses, and with a fairly uniform sense of fairness throughout the country, should there be many instances in which laws meet the criteria of the *Loucks* case?

(2) *Laboratory Corporation* rules that Maryland law should apply in that case because, at least in part, "[t]he right of parents to bring an action for wrongful birth . . . is not a vestige of ancient common law illogic [like the one upheld in *Harford Mutual*] but . . . of a type that . . . could not have been brought before the last half of the 20th Century." 395 Md. at 624. Is this distinction between *Harford Mutual* and *Laboratory Corporation* persuasive? If the common law tradition that *Harford* upheld is so "illogical" as the court suggests, why didn't the court simply reverse *Harford*? Was the court trying to reserve its power to refuse to apply Maryland law under the rule of *lex loci delicti* in the future? Or is there really a compelling value to upholding a longstanding legal tradition despite practical flaws?

(3) In another recent Maryland case, Brownlee v. Liberty Mutual Fire Insurance Co., 456 Md. 579, 175 A.3d 697 (2017), the Court of Appeals concluded that Maryland public policy did not prevent application of a Georgia law that would effectively preclude plaintiffs from recovering for damages after they suffered brain injuries as a result of exposure to lead-based paint. The contaminated property was located in Maryland and owned by Salvation Army. Salvation Army enjoyed charitable immunity, which would protect it from liability for the harm unless its liability insurance policy required the insurer to indemnify it for the harm. The insurance policy, executed and issued in Georgia, contained an exclusion clause for harm caused by certain pollutants. Under Georgia law, which was otherwise applicable as the place of the contract, the exclusion would absolve

it from having to cover the harm from lead-based paint. However, under Maryland law, the exclusion would not absolve the insurer because Maryland law requires that lead-based paint harm exclusions be stated specifically and unambiguously. Despite extensive Maryland legislative efforts designed to protect Maryland residents, particularly children, from the hazards of lead-based paint, a majority of the court declined to invoke the public policy exception without an express command from the Maryland legislature that the clause at issue was impermissible and void. Is this conclusion consistent with the same court's analysis in *Hood*, where there was no such legislative statement of Maryland public policy? How might a distinction be articulated? Does it make sense?

(4) In Mertz v. Mertz, 3 N.E.2d 597 (N.Y. 1936), Emmy sued Fred for damages resulting from his negligent use of an automobile in the state of Connecticut. Both were residents of New York, which forbade such suits between spouses. The law of Connecticut contained no such bar. The New York Court of Appeals apparently concluded that Connecticut provided the applicable law to the interspousal immunity issue but went on to refuse application of the Connecticut rule because it was against the public policy of New York. (In the alternative, the court found that questions of capacity—such as interspousal immunity—are matters for the forum.)

In light of the *Mertz* and *Holzer* cases, is it fair to say that interspousal suits are against the public policy of New York but that racial persecution is not? Or did the court in *Holzer* decline to apply the public policy exception for the reason given in the 1948 Supplement to First Restatement §612, *supra* page 146? Did the court in *Hood* overlook this limitation?

(5) Was the *Holzer* court somehow condoning racial discrimination in its opinion, or is it significant that the defendant was required by law to fire Holzer? If someone held a gun against *A*'s head and required her to commit a tort against *B*, would it be condoning the tort not to hold *A* liable?

(6) Assume that Germany had a prewar statute providing (a) that Jewish people were not allowed to hold positions in industry, (b) that it was the duty of every German citizen to report every Jewish person remaining in an industrial position after January 1, 1937, and (c) that the first person making such a report was entitled to a bounty of one tenth of the victim's wealth. If the victim owned property in New York, would the *Holzer* court have applied the principles applied in *Holzer*—that "[w]ithin its own territory every government is supreme . . . and our courts are not competent to review its actions"? Note that under the hypothetical statute, as in *Holzer*, the offending party was required to behave as it did. Would dismissal in this hypothetical case be consistent with the limitation explained in the 1948 Supplement?

(7) Should it make a difference whether public policy is invoked to defeat a foreign cause of action or invoked to defeat a defense to a foreign cause of action?

In Bradford Electric Light Co. v. Clapper, 286 U.S. 145, 160 (1932), Justice Brandeis said:

> A State may, on occasion, decline to enforce a foreign cause of action. In so doing, it merely denies a remedy, leaving unimpaired the plaintiff's substantive right, so that he is free to enforce it elsewhere. But to refuse to give effect to a substantive defense under the applicable law of another State . . . subjects the defendant to irremediable liability. This may not be done.

Is sending the parties away adequate vindication of a state's public policy, or should it try to make its judgment res judicata? In other words, is public policy merely a kind of clean-hands doctrine for the state, or does it represent the desire to see a particular result in the case no matter where it is finally decided?

(8) Brainerd Currie didn't think much of the argument made by Justice Brandeis (and termed it the "Brandeis fallacy" even though it had been voiced by others). The chief difficulty he found was that it assumes that parties can go elsewhere when the public policy doctrine is used to bar a cause of action. Often plaintiffs cannot get jurisdiction elsewhere, he said, and consequently the effect of dismissal on public policy grounds is often the equivalent of denying a defense on public policy grounds. Currie, *Selected Essays on the Conflicts of Laws* 211-212 (1963).

(9) Paulsen and Sovern, in a careful study of the public policy principle (*"Public Policy" in the Conflict of Laws*, 56 Colum. L. Rev. 969 (1956)), found that "[t]he overwhelming number of cases which have rejected foreign law on public policy grounds are cases with which the forum had some important connection." They concluded that the evil of public policy overuse was not provincialism, to which it had often been equated, but its use as a "substitute for analysis" in cases where the forum was in fact justified in applying its own law on other grounds.

How much connection with a state is sufficient to justify a state's invocation of the public policy exception? Should it depend on the purpose served by the laws at issue? And what function is that connection serving in the analysis? In Roach v. State Farm Mutual Automobile Ins. Co., 892 So. 2d 1107 (Fla. Dist. Ct. App. 2004), plaintiffs, year-round residents of Florida, were injured when the car in which they were riding as passengers collided with another car in Florida. Plaintiffs sued both drivers and the insurance company of the driver of the car in which they were passengers. Plaintiffs argued that State Farm was liable for additional sums to be paid under the underinsured motor vehicle coverage, which enabled those insured to recover additional amounts over the policy limits if the accident was caused by another driver who is underinsured. State Farm had denied payment of these additional amounts because a provision in the insurance contract limited the underinsured motorist coverage by providing for setoffs against other coverage. This limitation provision was enforceable under the laws of Indiana, where State Farm issued the policy to the driver, but was unenforceable and considered repugnant to public policy in Florida. The driver in this case was a "snowbird" who spent winters in Florida and summers in Indiana. Previous Florida case law indicated that the public policy exception was available to permanent but not temporary residents of the state, and the Florida District Court of Appeal concluded that the public policy exception could reasonably apply in the case of annual snowbirds because their insurance company is placed on notice of the regular presence of the car in the state of Florida. A majority of the Florida Supreme Court thought otherwise, however, and limited the public policy exception to cases of policies taken out by year-round, permanent residents of Florida. State Farm Mutual Auto. Ins. Co. v. Roach, 945 So. 2d 1160 (2006). According to the majority, the need to provide certainty of obligation in the case of contracts necessitates allowance of only a very narrow exception to the *lex loci contractus* rule. Which Florida court's solution seems most sensible?

(10) *Compare Laboratory Corp.* to Marchlik v. Coronet Insurance Co., 40 Ill. 2d 327 (1968), a case in which a court refused to apply foreign law, citing the public policy exception. There, a Wisconsin resident suffered an accident in Wisconsin, but the insurance policies of both drivers were issued in Illinois. The plaintiff sued the insurance companies in Illinois claiming that the court should apply Wisconsin law, which allows direct action against a tortfeasor's insurance company. In refusing to apply Wisconsin law, the *Marchlik* court stated, "Our courts and juries would be hard put to cope with the complex problems posed by other aspects of the Wisconsin law if these direct actions are permitted."

What did the court have in mind when it made this statement? Are people from Wisconsin smarter than people from Illinois? Isn't the court engaging in a great deal of speculation about the possible mischief to be posed by the Wisconsin statute? As long as Illinois would permit an action based on a Wisconsin accident against the tortfeasor and would permit an action by the tortfeasor against his insurer, why should a suit directly against the tortfeasor's insurer introduce significant complications?

On the other hand, even if the *Marchlik* court is not adept at identifying the source of its unease over the direct-action statute of Wisconsin, isn't there room for legitimate concern that juries who know that the defendant is an insurer will be more willing to find in favor of the plaintiff, even in the absence of negligence? Or do juries assume that everyone is insured? (And, of course, do they assume that the amount of coverage will be sufficient to cover whatever verdict they return?) Note the court's statement that disclosure of the fact of insurance in Illinois constitutes reversible error.

(11) Can a court still exercise the public policy exception to deny enforcement of a foreign right when the dispute involving that foreign right has been reduced to judgment? *See* Widenhouse v. Colson, 405 S.C. 55 (2013). There, the South Carolina court ruled that, even though a legal cause of action called alienation of affections (which is available in North Carolina) is contrary to South Carolina's public policy, full faith and credit cannot be denied when that cause of action has been tried and reduced to a monetary judgment. *Compare* Fauntleroy v. Lum, 210 U.S. 230 (1908).

6. Penal Laws

Selections from the First Restatement of Conflicts, on Penal Laws and Tax Claims

§§610-611 (1934)

§610. Action on Foreign Public Right

No action can be maintained on a right created by the law of a foreign state as a method of furthering its own governmental interests.

(1948 Supp.) *Caveat:* The Institute expresses no opinion whether an action can be maintained by a foreign state on a claim for taxes.

§611. Action for a Penalty

No action can be maintained to recover a penalty the right to which is given by the law of another state.

Paper Products Co. v. Doggrell
195 Tenn. 581, 261 S.W.2d 127 (1953)

TOMLINSON, J.

Appellees, Doggrell, and Konz, together with one Van E. Whitaker, Jr., were the sole stockholders in an Arkansas corporation formed by them under the name of Forrest City Wood Products, Inc. with principal office to be located in St. Francis County, Arkansas.

The Arkansas statute requires the articles of incorporation to be filed (1) with the Secretary of State and (2) thereafter in the office of the County Clerk of the County in which the corporations' principal place of business is to be located.

Doggrell and Konz, Tennessee residents, left the management of the corporation entirely to the third stockholder, Whitaker, a resident of Arkansas. The lawyer in Memphis who prepared the charter directed Whitaker to file it with the Secretary of State and then with the Clerk of the County Court of St. Francis County, Arkansas. Whitaker inadvertently failed to file it with the Clerk of the County Court of St. Francis County. It was not filed with this clerk until after the account which gave rise to this suit had been made. Neither Doggrell or Konz were [*sic*] aware of the fact that the charter had not been filed in St. Francis County as required by the Arkansas statute. Neither has received any dividends or profits or remuneration from the corporation.

Under the decisions of the Arkansas Court of last resort the stockholders of a corporation are liable as partners when the charter is not filed as required by the Arkansas statute in the county where the principal office of the corporation is to be maintained. Based on those decisions of the Arkansas Supreme Court, Whitaker, the third stockholder in the aforementioned corporation, has been adjudged by the Arkansas Court liable for a debt made by this corporation before this charter was filed in St. Francis County. . . . The Arkansas Court rendered no judgment in that case against Doggrell and Konz because no service had been had on these Tennessee residents.

Whitaker who operated and managed the business of the corporation purchased goods in the name of the corporation from Paper Products Company and issued the company's note payable in thirty days. Paper Products Company in this transaction dealt with the Forrest City Wood Products, Inc. as such and not through the personal credit of Doggrell and Konz. These two stockholders knew nothing whatever about the account in question.

Forrest City Wood Products, Inc. became bankrupt. A substantial balance of its note issued to Paper Products Company remains unpaid. Accordingly, Paper Products Company instituted this suit in Shelby County, Tennessee Circuit Court against Doggrell and Konz. It seeks a recovery against them individually because of the Arkansas law holding stockholders personally liable as partners for the accounts made by a corporation whose charter has not been filed in the County where its principal office is located.

It was the judgment of the Shelby County Circuit Court that Doggrell and Konz are not liable individually, or as partners, for this obligation of Forrest City Wood Products, because this Arkansas rule "is penal in its nature, and will not be enforced in the State Courts of Tennessee." Paper Products Company has appealed and insists that (1) the Arkansas rule is not penal in nature and (2) under the law of comity the Arkansas rule should be applied in this case.

Under Tennessee decisions, the liability of a stockholder for the debts of his corporation is determined by the law of the State in which that corporation is domiciled unless such law is contrary to the legislation or public policy of Tennessee, or is penal in nature. Under these circumstances such law of a sister State will not be enforced in Tennessee.

When a Tennessee Court is called upon to enforce the civil law of a sister jurisdiction it will determine whether such law is penal in nature or contrary to the public policy of the law of Tennessee in which it is sought to be enforced. . . . Whether the aforementioned law of Arkansas, therefore, is contrary to our public policy or penal in nature is a matter to be determined in this case by the Tennessee Court since it is in that Court that it is sought to enforce this Arkansas rule.

The Arkansas statute heretofore referred to provides that "upon the filing with the Secretary of State of articles of incorporation, *the corporate existence shall begin.*" Ark. Stats. §64-103. (Emphasis supplied.) It follows that the corporate existence of Forrest City Wood Products, Inc. had begun prior to the inadvertent failure of Whitaker to file the corporation's charter in the office of the County Court of St. Francis County, Arkansas. The Arkansas rule, therefore, is that an inadvertent failure to comply with some detail in a bona fide effort to comply with the law chartering corporations is a failure which makes the stockholders liable in Arkansas for those debts of the corporation made prior to the compliance with such required detail.

This Arkansas rule is contrary to the public policy of Tennessee, wherein the rule is that the stockholders are not liable for the debts of their corporation in a case where there has been "made a bona fide effort to comply with the provisions of law," but "have inadvertently failed in some particular, and in good faith have exercised the franchises of such corporation."

. . . It is a commonly known fact that one of the purposes of organizing a corporation for the carrying on of a business is to relieve stockholders of individual liability for the debts of the corporation. That fact is well known to those dealing with corporations. The Tennessee rule forwards the accomplishment of that purpose.

In ascertaining whether the Arkansas statute is penal in nature it is well to observe again that under the Arkansas rule the stockholders of the corporation are liable as partners for the mere failure, after the commencement of corporate existence, to file its charter in the Arkansas County of its principal office. This liability is imposed without regard to the fact that a creditor is not prejudiced by the failure to comply with this detail and was not misled thereby. There is no escape from the conclusion, therefore, that this rule prescribes a penalty in order to enforce compliance with the law of Arkansas as to the registering of a charter in the county where the principal office of the corporation is maintained. "Penalties prescribed by one state to enforce a compliance with its law will not be enforced by the courts of another state." . . .

A case directly in point is Woods v. Wicks, cited in appellees' brief. A statute of Kentucky was involved in that suit. That statute required the directors of a corporation to file and record within a specified time in a certain office a certificate stating the amount of the capital stock fixed and paid in. Stockholders were arbitrarily made liable in double the amount of their stock for failure to file such certificate. The Tennessee Court refused to hold such stockholders liable for the failure to file such certificate. In rejecting such a suit our Court said that "no court of another sovereignty can be expected to enforce such a penalty." . . .

The judgment must be affirmed with costs taxed to Paper Products Company and its surety.

On Petition to Rehear

The case of Doggrell v. Great Southern Box Company, Inc., was decided by the United States Court of Appeals for the 6th Circuit on July 9, 1953. 206 F.2d 671.* It came to that Court by appeal from the Federal District Court for the Western District of Tennessee. That case involved the identical Arkansas law and question decided by this Court in the instant case on July 17, 1953.

Preceded by well considered remarks unnecessary here to detail, the conclusion of the United States Court of Appeals in that case is that the Arkansas law in question is not penal within the meaning of the full faith and credit clause of our Federal Constitution, Article 4, §1; hence, that "the courts of Tennessee, including a United States District Court sitting in that state, are bound" to give effect to this Arkansas law in proceedings brought by a creditor of the Arkansas corporation to recover a personal money judgment against some of the stockholders of that Arkansas corporation. In the instant case this Court reached the opposite conclusion. Judge McAllister, in a dissenting opinion in the Federal case, reached the same conclusion as that reached by this Court with reference to the penal nature of this Arkansas law.

Because of the majority opinion of the United States Court of Appeals in its case, *supra*, Paper Products Company, appellant in the instant case, has filed in the instant case its petition to rehear. . . .

The expression Arkansas "law," rather than Arkansas "statute," is used by this Court because it is a decision of the Arkansas Supreme Court as to the effect which must be given a failure to comply with the Arkansas statute requiring a copy of the corporation's charter to be filed in the office of the County Clerk of the county in which the corporation's principal place of business is located. Its decision is that such failure, ipso facto, renders each stockholder of such Arkansas corporation liable for every debt incurred by that corporation prior to such filing in such county, notwithstanding the fact that such charter had been filed with the Arkansas Secretary of State, whereby, under the express language of the statute, its "corporate existence shall begin."

This Court was of the opinion that the instant case fell within the ruling of Woods v. Wicks . . . wherein this Court refused to give effect to a very similar Kentucky statute because of its penal nature. The United States Court of Appeals thought its case to be distinguishable from Woods v. Wicks because the incorporation of the Tennessee organization had been completed whereas such incorporation of the Arkansas organization lacked completion, so it is said, to the extent

---

* This decision was later set aside. 208 F.2d 310 (6th Cir. 1953)—Eds.

that a copy of its charter had not been filed in the Arkansas county of its principal office.

Apparently, in considering material such above stated distinction between the Kentucky and Arkansas organizations, the United States Court of Appeals inadvertently failed to give effect to the fact that in Tennessee the stockholders of a de facto corporation are not liable for its debts, and that corporations de facto are "those which have made a bona fide effort to comply with the provisions of law and have inadvertently failed in some particular, and in good faith have exercised the franchises of such corporation."

. . . Judge McAllister calls attention to the fact that the Arkansas organization was also a de facto corporation in Arkansas. . . .

The United States Court of Appeals felt that its case fell within Huntington v. Attrill, 146 U.S. 657. In that case it was held that the full faith and credit clause of our Federal Constitution required the Maryland Court to give effect to a New York statute said to be penal in character. Compliance with that statute, however, was clearly intended for the protection of creditors of corporations created pursuant to its provisions. The court can find no purpose of the Arkansas law other than that of better procuring compliance with a technical requirement of the Arkansas statute by inflicting a penalty merely because of a failure to so comply.

The above stated distinction between the instant case and Huntington v. Attrill, *supra*, makes it unnecessary to consider the further fact that the proceedings in the Maryland Court were to enforce a New York judgment based on a statute said to be penal in nature. In the case at bar the effort is to procure a judgment in a Tennessee Court based on an Arkansas law which the Tennessee Court regards as penal in nature and contrary to the public policy of its State.

Whether the full faith and credit clause requires the Courts of one state to enforce the law of another state penal in some respects "depends upon the question whether its purpose is to punish an offense against the public justice of the state, or to afford a private remedy to a person injured by the wrongful act." Huntington v. Attrill, *supra*. . . .

As heretofore stated, this Court thinks that there is no escape from the conclusion that the sole purpose of the Arkansas law in question is to procure a compliance with its statute as to a formal or technical requirement. But, pursuing further the immediately above stated test furnished by Huntington v. Attrill, there is particularly applicable the statement in Judge McAllister's dissenting opinion in Doggrell v. Great Southern Box Company, *supra* [206 F.2d 682], that:

> There was no wrong committed against any individual in not filing the articles with the County Clerk. To subject an innocent party, who happens to be an incorporator or original stockholder, to what may prove great financial losses or ruin, in being obliged to pay personally all the debts of the corporation merely because someone who should have complied with this technical requirement failed to do so, seems to me to subject appellant to a liability that is clearly penal in its nature.

On principle, as well as under the test pronounced by the United States Supreme Court, this Court is of the opinion that the penal nature of the Arkansas law in question is such that the Tennessee Court is not required by the full faith and credit clause of our Federal Constitution to give it effect.

The rule of comity does not apply because the Arkansas law is contrary to the law and public policy of this State. . . .

Questions and Comments

(1) Why shouldn't confessedly penal laws be enforced by other jurisdictions? If the basis for enforcing the law of other jurisdictions is some kind of comity, or respect for the sovereignty of another state, shouldn't penal laws, which obviously express some particularly strong state interest, be the *first* to be enforced?

(2) The oft-cited case defining a "penal" law is Huntington v. Attrill, 146 U.S. 657 (1892), which involved an attempt in Maryland to enforce a New York judgment based on a New York statute that imposed personal liability on directors and stockholders of a corporation for its debts when papers falsely stating the capital position of the corporation were filed. The Court determined that the law in question was not penal and that Maryland was required to enforce the judgment. The mark of a penal statute, the Court said, was that it appeared to the forum "to be, in its essential character and effect, a punishment of an offense against the public." Section 611, comment *a*, of the Restatement defines a penalty as a "sum of money exacted as punishment for a civil wrong as distinguished from compensation for the loss suffered by the injured party."

Was the Arkansas statute penal by this standard?

Note that the *Huntington* case allows a state to ignore not only the law of another jurisdiction but its judgments as well.

See generally Kutner, *Judicial Identification of "Penal Laws" in the Conflict of Laws*, 31 Okla. L. Rev. 590 (1978).

(3) Would the Paris court's remedy in the *Yahoo!* case in Chapter 1 be a penal law? This French remedy, known as astriente, was deemed compensatory rather than punitive in a case where the French court had ordered defendant to pay a fixed sum in the event that defendant further violated plaintiff's copyright. De Fontbrune v. Wofsy, 838 F.3d 992 (9th Cir. 2016). The Ninth Circuit concluded that astriente cannot be categorically deemed either punitive or compensatory; rather, it depends on how the damages are intended to function in the individual case.

(4) Finding that filing with the secretary of state was enough to cause de facto corporate existence made it easy for the court to determine that the penalty for failure to file with the local clerk was penal. But would the Tennessee courts come to a different conclusion in a case with similar facts if the Arkansas legislature, in reaction to the *Paper Products* opinion, amended its statutes to provide that de facto corporate existence was not possible in Arkansas? Note that the effect would be to impose liability on each of the partners in a partnership—not exactly a result that appears "penal."

(5) Is it fair to make the Arkansas partner (against whom an Arkansas judgment was rendered) bear the entire burden? Isn't that the effect of the *Paper Products* decision, since judgment was rendered against the third partner in Arkansas? If the Arkansas partner, after paying the Arkansas judgment, brought an action against the Tennessee partners for contribution, would the attractiveness of using the penal-law exception be as great?

(6) What would have been the result in the *Paper Products* case if Tennessee had had a law identical to that of Arkansas? Surely under those circumstances Tennessee would not have been able to find that the Arkansas law violated Tennessee public policy. But would the fact that Tennessee had an identical law make the Arkansas law any less "penal"? Do you really think that the Tennessee court would have come out the same way (refusing enforcement of the Arkansas law) if Tennessee law had been identical?

(7) In Campbell v. Mitsubishi Aircraft International, 452 F. Supp. 930 (W.D. Pa. 1978), the court, applying Pennsylvania law, found a Texas usury statute to be penal and refused to apply it. The Texas statute provided for penalties of twice the amount of interest provided for by the contract, plus attorneys' fees, when the interest rate charged exceeded that allowed in Texas. The federal district court said that under Pennsylvania law it was bound by Texas's characterization of its own statute as penal and cited several Texas cases that referred to the amount the plaintiff could recover as a "penalty."

Since Texas would obviously never refuse enforcement to its own statute on the grounds that it was penal, doesn't it follow that Texas's characterization of the statute must have been for purposes other than conflicts purposes? And doesn't it follow from that that the Texas characterization of the statute should be, at most, persuasive and not binding?

(8) Closely related to the traditional prohibition on enforcing foreign penal laws was a prohibition on enforcing foreign revenue laws. *See* First Restatement §610 comment *c* (1934) ("No action can be maintained by a foreign state to enforce its license of revenue laws, or claims for taxes."). Judge Learned Hand justified this prohibition (as well as the penal law prohibition) on the following grounds:

> While the origin of the exception in the case of penal liabilities does not appear in the books, a sound basis for it exists, in my judgment, which includes liabilities for taxes as well. Even in the case of ordinary municipal liabilities, a court will not recognize those arising in a foreign state, if they run counter to the "settled public policy" of its own. Thus a scrutiny of the liability is necessarily always in reserve, and the possibility that it will be found not to accord with the policy of the domestic state. This is not a troublesome or delicate inquiry when the question arises between private persons, but it takes on quite another face when it concerns the relations between the foreign state and its own citizens or even those who may be temporarily within its borders. To pass upon the provisions for the public order of another state is, or at any rate should be, beyond the powers of a court; it involves the relations between the states themselves, with which courts are incompetent to deal, and which are entrusted to other authorities. It may commit the domestic state to a position which would seriously embarrass its neighbor. Revenue laws fall within the same reasoning; they affect a state in matters as vital to its existence as its criminal laws. No court ought to undertake an inquiry which it cannot prosecute without determining whether those laws are consonant with its own notions of what is proper.

Moore v. Mitchell, 30 F.2d 600, 604 (2d Cir. 1929). Is this reasoning an artifact of the vested rights theory? Why is it more offensive to refuse to apply a state's tort law than to refuse to apply a state's tax law? For criticism of the tax rule, *see* Oklahoma ex rel. Oklahoma Tax Commission v. Neely, 225 Ark. 230, 282 S.W.2d 150 (1955); Leflar, *Extrastate Enforcement of Penal and Governmental Claims*, 46 Harv. L. Rev. 193

(1932). However, the Supreme Court has held that the revenue rule did not preclude an interpretation of the federal criminal wire fraud statute to apply to a scheme to evade Canadian liquor taxes. *See* Pasquantino v. United States, 544 U.S. 349 (2005).

(9) For a critique of the prohibition on enforcing foreign penal and revenue rules, *see* Dodge, *Breaking the Public Law Taboo*, 43 Harv. Intl. L.J. 161 (2002).

H. Proof of Foreign Law

Tidewater Oil Co. v. Waller

302 F.2d 638 (10th Cir. 1962)

MURRAH, C.J.

This is an appeal from a judgment of a district court in Oklahoma in a diversity suit for damages for personal injuries allegedly caused by the appellant—Tidewater Oil Company's negligence in the country of Turkey. The basic facts are that the appellee, Waller, an employee of Spartan Aircraft Company, an Oklahoma manufacturer of mobile homes, was sent to Turkey to perform repair work on behalf of his Oklahoma employer on mobile homes belonging to a pipeline company. While in Turkey, Waller undertook on behalf of his Oklahoma employer, to perform similar work on the mobile homes of Tidewater Oil Company at a remote and isolated oil well drilling site. Waller was injured when Tidewater's plane in which he was being transported crashed while attempting to land at the drilling site where the repair work was to be done.

It seems agreed that Waller was injured in the course of his employment with Spartan, his Oklahoma employer, and that he was paid $35.00 per week in lieu of Oklahoma's workmen's compensation, and all hospital and medical care. After the commencement of this suit against Tidewater, Waller filed a workmen's compensation claim with the Oklahoma Workmen's Compensation Commission, and at the same time sought and obtained an order of the Commission holding the claim in abeyance pending the outcome of this litigation.

After alleging his Oklahoma employment and his undertaking to perform work in Turkey for Tidewater on behalf of his Oklahoma employer, Waller alleged that his injuries were caused by the unsafe condition of the airstrip where Tidewater's plane was required to land and the negligent operation of it. It was specifically alleged that his right to recover was to be determined by the laws of Turkey, under which Tidewater owed Waller the duty to use ordinary care in the operation of the aircraft, and to furnish a reasonably safe place on which to land it; and that res ipsa loquitur was recognized in Turkey and applicable here.

Tidewater admitted Waller's employment in Oklahoma and his undertaking to do certain work for it in Turkey as a loaned servant of Spartan, and that the rights and liabilities of the parties were governed by the laws of the country of Turkey. It denied the allegations of negligence or that res ipsa loquitur was applicable. As a separate and primary defense, Tidewater asserted that any claim or right of action is exclusively cognizable under either the workmen's compensation law of the country of Turkey, or of the State of Oklahoma, and in either event, Tidewater was secondarily and hence exclusively liable for workmen's compensation benefits; and that the Oklahoma court was therefore without jurisdiction to entertain this suit.

In the trial of the case, neither party offered any evidence of controlling and applicable Turkish law, and the court manifestly proceeded upon the factual premise that the tort laws of Turkey permitted recovery for the asserted wrong as if in Oklahoma. . . .

[The Oklahoma statute, as interpreted by the majority, allowed Waller either to proceed under Oklahoma's workers' compensation system or, in the case of accidents occurring elsewhere, to proceed under the law of the locus.]

. . . The decisive issue, as indeed the parties ultimately seem to agree, is whether Waller, having elected to pursue his remedy under the law of Turkey, where the injury occurred, may maintain this suit under and by virtue of such laws.

It is agreed that the law of Turkey is controlling and is a matter of fact of which the Oklahoma Court cannot take judicial notice; and, having pleaded Turkish law to sustain his right of recovery, Waller is under the burden of going forward with proof of it at the risk of nonpersuasion. *See* Vol. 3 Beale, Conflict of Laws, p. 1663, §621. . . .

Tidewater takes the position that since there was no evidence of controlling Turkish law, Oklahoma law, including its workmen's compensation statutes, is applicable; and that under Section II thereof, as construed in the Mid-Continent case, it is secondarily and exclusively liable under the provisions of the Workmen's Compensation Act, as if the accident had occurred in Oklahoma. . . .

In the absence of proof of applicable foreign law, courts of the forum have rather unevenly followed three alternative courses: (1) dismissed the claim for failure to make out a prima facie case; (2) conveniently applied the law of the forum; and (3) indulged in certain presumptions as to the foreign law and applied it accordingly. . . . Courts which arbitrarily apply the law of the forum do so as a rule of convenience in disregard of the evidentiary rule of burden of proof, or going forward with the evidence at the risk of nonpersuasion. Courts which indulge in the presumption of foreign law do so by first taking judicial notice of the fundamental system of jurisprudence in the foreign country, and having noticed that its system is fundamentally the same, will indulge in the presumption that applicable law is similar and apply it accordingly. If, however, having judicially noticed that the systems of the two are fundamentally different, it will not indulge in any presumption of similarity, except the juridical principles which may be assumed to inhere in the laws of all civilized countries. . . . Oklahoma, whose conflicts rule we apply, has recognized the factual quality of applicable general law, and along with most other states has statutorily provided for the admissibility of such laws. . . . It has embraced the theory that in the absence of pleading and proof of applicable law of sister state, it will apply its own law, both general and statutory, on the convenient assumption that the law of the sister state is the same as its own. . . .

We have found no cases in which the Oklahoma courts have been confronted with application of the law of a foreign country in the absence of any proof of it, except some early cases in which they declined to take judicial notice of the laws of the Five Civilized Tribes. . . . Since the legal system prevailing in Turkey is judicially known not to be the same as Oklahoma, but is wholly different, it does not seem reasonable to presume under any circumstances that the general law of Turkey is the same or similar to Oklahoma, much less the workmen's compensation law. . . . There is a rational and, we think, admissible basis, however, for presuming that as a civilized country with a juridical system based upon civil law, Turkey recognizes the universal fundamental principle which embraces the legal duty of one to exercise due care not to injure another, and that its courts of justice will grant compensable redress for the unexcused violation of that duty. . . .

Of course if Oklahoma law is to be transplanted to Turkey and applied to a Turkish employment contract, it cannot be doubted that Waller was injured in the course of his employment under the Turkish contract; and, making application of the Oklahoma Workmen's Compensation Act as Turkish law, Tidewater would doubtlessly be primarily exclusively liable under its Turkish employment contract; for, in these circumstances, we should have no difficulty saying as a matter of law, that the maintenance of the mobile homes at the remote drilling site, was a necessary and integral part of Tidewater's hazardous business of drilling oil wells. . . . In that respect, it is important to note that Tidewater's liability is in no wise governed by Waller's Oklahoma employment contract with Spartan to which it was not a party, but rather, under the Turkey employment contract to which it was a party, and which must condition the rights of the parties.

Obviously, this suit was not tried and submitted to the jury on the theory that applicable Turkish law embraced a workmen's compensation act identical to or even similar to that of Oklahoma. Nor does the record before us indicate that either party had any such farfetched factual theory in mind at the time of trial. Rather, as we have seen, it is clear that the case was tried on the factual premise that Turkish law recognized the acts complained of as redressable wrongs. There is no suggestion that the asserted remedy is contrary to the public policy of the State of Oklahoma. Moreover, Section 4 of the Oklahoma Workmen's Compensation Act, *supra*, which grants the election to claim extra-territorial benefits, specifically provides that such right of election shall not preclude an injured employee from pursuing his remedy under the laws of the state where the injury occurred. Having accorded this right of election, we should not presume that Oklahoma would close the doors of its courts to the assertion of the remedy, even though it would have been unavailable if the injury had occurred in the State. . . . There being nothing in the public policy of the State of Oklahoma to forbid a remedy, the Oklahoma courts will enforce the right in accordance with the prevailing forms of practice and procedure. It was on this factual basis that the court formulated the law of the case and submitted it to the jury in accordance with the rules of evidence, standard of care and measure of damages prevailing in Oklahoma. . . . Inasmuch as the instructions of the court are not in issue, we will of course assume that they correctly stated the law of the case, and the judgment of the court based upon the jury verdict is sustained.

Questions and Comments

(1) Federal Rule of Civil Procedure 44.1 provides:

A party who intends to raise an issue concerning the law of a foreign country shall give notice by pleadings or other reasonable written notice. The court, in determining foreign law, may consider any relevant material or source, including testimony, whether or not submitted by a party or admissible under the Federal Rules of Evidence. The court's determination shall be treated as a ruling on a question of law.

The present form of the Rule dates from July 1, 1966. It was given exhaustive treatment (136 pages) in Miller, *Federal Rule 44.1 and the "Fact" Approach to Determining Foreign Law: Death-Knell for a Die-Hard Doctrine*, 65 Mich. L. Rev. 615 (1967).

(2) Facts similar to *Waller*'s yielded the opposite result in Walton v. Arabian American Oil Co., 233 F.2d 541 (2d Cir. 1956), a case in which the injury occurred in Saudi Arabia, the action was tried in New York, and the plaintiff refused to offer proof concerning Arabian law. The trial judge directed a verdict in favor of the defendant for failure of the plaintiff to prove his case. The Court of Appeals affirmed, rejecting plaintiff's invocation of the rule that the forum may apply its own law when the injury occurs in an uncivilized place that has no law or legal system. (Note the date of the case and the fact that knowledge about Saudi Arabia in the outside world was substantially more limited than today.)

The trial judge in the *Walton* case gave plaintiff's counsel an opportunity to prove Arabian law and indicated that he would rule against plaintiffs without such proof. Plaintiff's counsel declined. What would lead the lawyer to behave in such a way? If the lawyer had accepted the opportunity, where should he or she have turned to find out about Arabian law? Should it have made a difference that the defendant was a rich corporation with more knowledge of Arabian law and more resources, financial and otherwise, for finding out more about it?

(3) How would *Waller* and *Walton* have been handled under Fed. R. Civ. P. 44.1, set out above? The *Wofsy* court, discussed *supra* at page 161, states the following:

> Rule 44.1 . . . unshackles courts and litigants from the evidentiary and procedural requirements that apply to factual determinations. It . . . authorizes the court to "engage in its own research," eschews any requirement that the court formally take judicial notice of foreign law, and obviates the need for the court to provide "formal notice to the parties of its intention to engage in its own research on an issue of foreign law which has been raised by them, or of its intention to raise and determine independently an issue not raised by them." Fed. R. Civ. P. 44.1 advisory committee's note.

(4) *See generally* Currie, *On the Displacement of the Law of the Forum*, in *Selected Essays on the Conflict of Laws* 3-4 (1963). Currie favored a presumption in favor of the application of forum law. Other commentators, even those generally sympathetic to his assumptions, disagree. *See* Kramer, *Interest Analysis and the Presumption of Forum Law*, 56 U. Chi. L. Rev. 1301 (1989).

(5) Tidewater Oil Co. v. Waller considered using a presumption of forum law because there was insufficient evidence of what foreign law said. But there are other ways that presumptions might come in handy. Recall Linn v. Employers Reinsurance Corp., page 42 *supra*, in which the court did not know from which state the phone call of acceptance originated. A similar situation arose in Doe v. Roe, 841 F. Supp. 444 (D.D.C. 1994), where the plaintiff alleged the defendant had infected her with the herpes simplex virus after misrepresenting his health status; recovery would have been allowed under District of Columbia law, but not under Virginia law. There had been equal opportunities for infection in both

states, and it was scientifically impossible for the court to determine in which state the disease had actually been transmitted.

The court followed, in effect, the strategy advocated by Professor Kramer in the article cited in note (4), *supra*. Kramer argued that the plaintiff always has the burden of demonstrating a cause of action, so that in the absence of reason to apply the plaintiff-favoring rule, the defendant must win. The *Doe* court reasoned, analogously, that "recovery would be possible only if plaintiff could trace her injury to the District encounter. Because we conclude that no reasonable trier of fact could determine which encounter resulted in infection, we are forced to grant defendant's motion for summary judgment. We regret this unfortunate result which, if plaintiff's allegations are true, shields from liability conduct which is not only despicable, but at the least is highly irresponsible. We hope plaintiff will appeal our determination that we are unable to grant the relief she seeks." 841 F. Supp. at 449.

(6) Rule 44.1 of the Federal Rules of Civil Procedure was applied in Vishipco Line v. Chase Manhattan Bank, 660 F.2d 854 (2d Cir. 1981). Until April 24, 1975, Chase had operated a branch office in Saigon; plaintiffs had maintained demand deposit accounts in piastres at that branch. On the eve of the fall of Saigon, Chase closed the branch without permitting an opportunity to withdraw deposits. The communist regime confiscated all accounts upon taking the city, and plaintiffs sued in New York to recover the dollar value of their accounts. The district and appellate courts agreed that Vietnamese law governed; but the parties were unable to muster much evidence about the content of Vietnamese law:

> *Chase* here first contends that plaintiffs' claims were dismissible for failure to prove that under Vietnamese law they were entitled to recover. We disagree. The district court largely agreed with Chase's contention, stating:
>
> > When foreign law is an issue in a case, that law must be proved as a fact. Plaintiffs, however, presented no evidence concerning the law of Vietnam. Such failure has resulted in dismissal of a plaintiff's claims. However, since defendant has shouldered plaintiffs' burden and offered proof of Vietnamese law, there is no need to dismiss for lack of evidence on which to determine Vietnamese law.
>
> Although this statement reflects the law as it existed prior to the adoption of Rule 44.1 F.R. Civ. P. in 1966, it no longer governs the manner in which questions of foreign law are to be dealt with in the federal courts. Prior to 1966 foreign law questions were regarded as questions of fact, 9 C. Wright & A. Miller, Federal Practice and Procedure §2441 (1971), and, as the district court's citations indicate, a number of courts took the position that a failure to prove foreign law was fatal to a claim, even if the parties had not raised the issue of the applicability of foreign law on their own. Even in this state of the law, however, federal courts frequently refused to dismiss where they were sitting in a state which provided for judicial notice of foreign law.
>
> Rule 44.1 of the Federal Rules of Civil Procedure, which became effective in 1966, put to rest the idea that foreign law is a question of fact which has to be proven by the claimant in order to recover. It declared that "[t]he court's determination shall be treated as a ruling on a question of law."
>
> Chase nevertheless contends that even under the more liberal standards of Rule 44.1, plaintiffs' claims should have been dismissed for failure to provide evidence of foreign law after it became clear that under New York's choice-of-law rules the entire case would normally be governed by Vietnamese law.

This assumes that the forum's choice-of-law rules are mandatory rather than permissive. However, with the decline of the vested rights theory, *see* Currie, *On the Displacement of the Law of the Forum*, 58 Colum. L. Rev. 964, 1001 (1958), the movement has been away from a mandatory application of the forum's choice of law rules and toward the adoption of a discretionary rule. While, as the Advisory Committee's notes to Rule 44.1 make clear, a court is still permitted to apply foreign law even if not requested by a party, we believe that the law of the forum may be applied here, where the parties did not at trial take the position that plaintiffs were required to prove their claims under Vietnamese law, even though the forum's choice of law rules would have called for the application of foreign law. This reflects the view adopted by ourselves and other federal courts since 1966.

While Chase invoked foreign law under Rule 44.1 with respect to its own affirmative defenses only, neither party invoked foreign law with respect to Chase's basic obligations to its depositors and holders of certificates of deposit. Nor did Chase ever suggest that under Vietnamese law those obligations would not have formed a basis for recovery. Therefore, while Vietnamese law as invoked by Chase will be applied to those affirmative defenses which rest on Vietnamese law, the parties' failure to invoke foreign law with respect to the underlying obligations themselves would not mandate dismissal of the claims. Under New York law it is clear that, unless relieved of liability under one or more of the affirmative defenses asserted by it, Chase was obligated under its contracts with plaintiffs to pay them the amounts deposited with it.

660 F.2d 859-860. When the court wrote of "Vietnamese law," did it mean the law of the pro-American Saigon government or of the new revolutionary regime? How much law on international banking do you think the revolutionary regime had promulgated?

(7) Suppose that the parties offer proof of the content of foreign law in the form of expert affidavits and/or testimony. How reliable is an expert paid by a party to spin the law in the direction that the party prefers? Under FRCP 44.1, courts are permitted to engage in their own research on the content of foreign law. *See* Advisory Committee Notes accompanying 28 U.S.C.A. §44.1. Suppose a judge wishes to rely on an English-language description of foreign law instead of the proffered expert testimony. Are those sources more reliable? Judges Posner, Easterbrook, and Wood participated in a debate over these questions through their written opinions in Bodum U.S.A., Inc. v. La Cafetière, Inc., 621 F.3d 624 (7th Cir. 2010).

(8) What if one of the entities submitting proof of relevant foreign law is the foreign government whose law is at issue? That issue arose in Animal Science Products, Inc. v. Hebei Welcome Pharmaceutical Co., Ltd., 1385 S. Ct. 1865 (2018), where the Supreme Court directed federal courts to accord a foreign government's submission of an official statement on the meaning and interpretation of its domestic law "respectful consideration." Nevertheless, the Court held, federal courts are not bound to give these official statements conclusive effect.

(9) The approach that American courts take to the law of another state or American jurisdiction is considerably different from the approach they take to the law of other countries or their subdivisions. The full faith and credit clause of the Constitution requires some deference to the law of other states (a topic to be

discussed more fully in Chapter 4). Most states, but not all (*see, e.g.*, Retirement Credit Plan, Inc. v. Melnick, 139 Ga. Ct. App. 570 (1976)), take judicial notice of the laws of other states. But what should a State *A* court do when faced with a question about the law of State *B* and with no answer in the case law of State *B*? One solution is set out below.

(10) Through certification or some related procedure, 45 states, the District of Columbia, and Puerto Rico allow their high courts to answer questions about their law posed by a court in another jurisdiction (including another state). *See* Kaye & Weissman, *Interactive Judicial Federalism: Certified Questions in New York*, 69 Fordham L. Rev. 373, 422-423 (2000) (Appendix A). Is this a general solution to the problem of proving foreign law, at least in the interstate context? It certainly helps one court avoid errors in the interpretation of another state's law. But is this a feasible process in the run-of-the-mill choice-of-law case? Does the court to which certification is directed really want to expend its limited resources to decide a pure question of law in another court? For discussion of these issues, *see* Robbins, *Interstate Certification of Questions of Law: A Valuable Process in Need of Reform*, 76 Judicature 125 (1992); Corr & Robbins, *Interjurisdictional Certification and Choice of Law*, 41 Vand. L. Rev. 411 (1988).

And what should a court do when overseeing complex litigation and presented with uncertainties in many states' law? This topic is explored further in Chapter 10.

The full faith and credit clause provides weak limitations on one state court's (mis)interpretation of another state's law. *See* Sun Oil v. Wortman, 486 U.S. 717 (1988), reproduced *infra* page 316.

3

Modern Approaches to Choice of Law

A. Introduction

1. The "Choice-of-Law Revolution": Critical Foundations

In a remarkable series of essays beginning in the 1920s and eventually collected in book form in *The Logical and Legal Bases of the Conflict of Laws*, Professor Walter Wheeler Cook undertook an examination of the foundations of Conflicts. Much of the book attacked the position of the First Restatement. The intellectual power of Cook's work has been widely recognized. Professor Brainerd Currie, for example, said that it "discredited the vested-rights theory as thoroughly as the intellect of one man can ever discredit the intellectual product of another." Currie, *Selected Essays on the Conflict of Laws* 6 (1963). Yet Cook's efforts did not have immediate effect. The first real cracks in the theoretical monopoly of the territorialists in the courts did not occur until the early 1950s. The foundations of modern choice-of-law theory in the legal realist movement continue to engage scholars who write about choice-of-law theory. *See* Brilmayer & Seidell, *Jurisdictional Realism: Where Modern Theories of Choice of Law Went Wrong, and What Can Be Done to Fix Them*, 86 U. Chi. L. Rev. (forthcoming 2019).

Although most states have departed from the First Restatement rules, at least in the torts and contracts contexts, no alternative approach has established itself as categorically superior to the rest. To add to the confusion, some courts profess adherence to more than one approach, not recognizing the differences (and sometimes they are few in terms of actual decisions) or wishing to use the time-honored technique of covering one's derrière by invoking multiple justifications for the same conclusion.*

2.   The Choice-of-Law Revolution in the Courts: The New York Experience

The difficulty that courts have had in formulating choice-of-law theories to replace the discredited First Restatement approach is well illustrated by the experience of the New York Court of Appeals. Starting in the 1950s, the New York Court of Appeals, led by Chief Judge Fuld, set aside the First Restatement rules in search of a more satisfying approach to choice of law. *See* Reese, *Chief Judge Fuld and Choice of Law*, 71 Colum. L. Rev. 548 (1971). The New York Court of Appeals embarked upon this journey through the common-law case method, and, as a result, the court simultaneously struggled with providing just results in individual cases while developing a workable method for choosing law in future cases. As will become clearer in this chapter, the ideas expressed in the court's opinions during this journey illustrate both the goals and the tensions underlying the competing approaches to choice of law.

Auten v. Auten and Haag v. Barnes

The New York Court of Appeals signaled its move away from the First Restatement contracts rules in Auten v. Auten, 308 N.Y. 155 (1954). The case involved a couple, Margarite and Harold Auten, who married in and resided together in England for 14 years, at which point Harold left Margarite and their two children, obtained an ex parte divorce in Mexico, and resettled in New York. Margarite traveled to New York to find Harold, and they signed a separation agreement under which he promised to pay monthly support to her and she promised not to contest the divorce (or his subsequent remarriage). Later Harold failed to make the promised payments, and Margarite brought suit in England where she obtained a judgment giving her a right to alimony. When he still failed to send her money, she sued him in New York to collect the amounts promised under the support agreement. Harold argued that the English suit violated the separation agreement and thereby terminated his payment obligations. This defense would be successful under New York but not English law. The court applied English law to allow Margarite to recover. Judge Fuld noted that the application of English law was consistent with the First Restatement place-of-performance rule, because Margarite arguably failed to perform her promise in England. However, Judge Fuld stated that a better ground for decision was to

---

* This phenomenon is well (and amusingly) documented in Reppy, Eclecticism in Choice of Law: Hybrid Method or Mishmash?, 34 Mercer L. Rev. 645 (1983).

abandon the First Restatement's distinction between obligation and performance and instead to apply the "law of the place with the most significant contacts" to resolve the matter. Fuld reasoned:

> Although this 'grouping of contacts' theory may, perhaps, afford less certainty and predictability than the rigid general rules, the merit of its approach is that it gives to the place 'having the most interest in the problem' paramount control over the legal issues arising out of a particular factual context, thus allowing the forum to apply the policy of the jurisdiction 'most intimately concerned with the outcome of [the] particular litigation.' Moreover, by stressing the significant contacts, it enables the court, not only to reflect the relative interests of the several jurisdictions involved, but also to give effect to the probable intention of the parties and consideration to 'whether one rule or the other produces the best practical result.'
>
> Turning to the case before us, . . . England . . . has all the truly significant contacts, while this state's sole nexus with the matter in dispute—entirely fortuitous, at that—is that it is the place where the agreement was made and where the trustee, to whom the moneys were in the first instance to be paid, had his office. The agreement effected a separation between British subjects, who had been married in England, had children there and lived there as a family for fourteen years. It involved a husband who, according to the papers before us, had willfully deserted and abandoned his wife and children in England and was in the United States, when the agreement was signed, merely on a temporary visa. And it concerned an English wife who came to this country at that time because it was the only way she could see her husband to discuss their differences. The sole purpose of her trip to New York was to get defendant to agree to the support of his family, and she returned to England immediately after the agreement was executed. While the moneys were to be paid through the medium of a New York trustee, such payments were 'for account of' the wife and children, who, it was thoroughly understood, were to live in England. The agreement is instinct with that understanding; not only does it speak in terms of English currency in providing for payments to the wife, not only does it recite that the first payment be made to her 'immediately before sailing for England,' but it specifies that the husband may visit the children 'if he should go to England.'
>
> Nor could the parties have expected or believed that any law other than England's would govern the effect of the wife's institution of a separation action. It is most unlikely that the wife could have intended to subject her rights under English law to the law of a jurisdiction several thousand miles distant, with which she had not the slightest familiarity. On the contrary, since it was known that she was returning to England to live, both parties necessarily realized that any action which she took, whether in accordance with the agreement or in violation of it, would have to occur in England. If any thought was given to the matter at all, it was that the law of the place where she and the children would be should determine the effect of acts performed by her.

Id. at 161-163 (citations omitted).

Seven years later, Judge Fuld authored another choice-of-law opinion in Haag v. Barnes, 9 N.Y.2d 554 (1961). In 1954, Haag, a legal secretary residing in New York, was hired by Barnes, an Illinois lawyer, to perform temporary work for him while he was in New York. The two entered a romantic relationship in New York, where she became pregnant. During the pregnancy, Haag went to Chicago at Barnes's request, and the baby was born in a Chicago hospital. Barnes paid for the expenses of the birth, and, with the assistance of an attorney, Haag signed an agreement under which Barnes promised to pay specified sums for the support of the child. In return, Haag agreed to release him from further support obligations. A choice-of-law clause in the agreement stated that their agreement would be governed by Illinois law. For three years Barnes paid substantially more than he promised to pay, but Haag sued him seeking further support. Under Illinois law this subsequent suit would be barred by the previous agreement, but under New York law the suit could proceed because the prior agreement was not court approved. Judge Fuld reasoned that Illinois law should apply under a "most significant contacts" test:

> The agreement, in so many words, recites that it "shall in all respects be interpreted, construed and governed by the laws of the State of Illinois" and, since it was also drawn and signed by the complainant in Illinois, the traditional conflicts rule would, without doubt, treat these factors as conclusive and result in applying Illinois law. But, even if the parties' intention and the place of the making of the contract are not given decisive effect, they are nevertheless to be given heavy weight in determining which jurisdiction "has the most significant contacts with the matter in dispute." Auten v. Auten. . . . And, when these important factors are taken together with other of the "significant contacts" in the case, they likewise point to Illinois law. Among these other Illinois contacts are the following: (1) both parties are designated in the agreement as being "of Chicago, Illinois," and the defendant's place of business is and always has been in Illinois; (2) the child was born in Illinois; (3) the persons designated to act as agents for the principals (except for a third alternate) are Illinois residents, as are the attorneys for both parties who drew the agreement; and (4) all contributions for support always have been, and still are being, made from Chicago.
>
> Contrasted with these Illinois contacts, the New York contacts are of far less weight and significance. Chief among these is the fact that child and mother presently live in New York and that part of the "liaison" took place in New York. When these contacts are measured against the parties' clearly expressed intention to have their agreement governed by Illinois law and the more numerous and more substantial Illinois contacts, it may not be gainsaid that the "center of gravity" of this agreement is Illinois and that, absent compelling public policy to the contrary Illinois law should apply.

Id. at 559-560. One might wonder why Illinois is the state with the most significant contacts in *Haag*. First, it is not at all clear why it matters that payments were sent from Illinois or that the lawyers representing the parties were from Illinois. And one might think that when defendant goes to New York, where he hires and subsequently impregnates plaintiff, and where she and her child currently reside, that New York is the state with the most significant contacts with the matter in dispute. Further, one might think that applying New York law is more consistent with the result the court reached in *Auten*. Why does the court nevertheless conclude that Illinois law should apply?

The reception to Haag v. Barnes was not particularly warm. Professor Brainerd Currie, for example, noted one obvious point about the methodology of the "grouping of contacts" approach:

> The "grouping of contacts" theory provides no standard for determining what "contacts" are significant, or for appraising the relative significance of the

respective groups of "contacts.". . . The process of "grouping contacts" . . . deals in broad generalities about the "interest" of a state in applying its law without inquiry into how the "contacts" in question relate to the policies expressed in specific laws. One "contact" seems to be about as good as another for almost any purpose. The "contacts" are totted up and a highly subjective fiat is issued to the effect that one group of contacts or the other is more significant. The reasons for the conclusion are too elusive for objective evaluation. State interests are quite likely to be thwarted in the confusion.

Currie, *Selected Essays on the Conflict of Laws* 727-728 (1963).

The Guest Statute Cases

Two years later, Judge Fuld authored an opinion in the first of a trilogy of choice-of-law cases dealing with the applicability of guest statutes, which are laws that limit the liability of drivers who injure passengers in their vehicles. In Babcock v. Jackson, 12 N.Y.2d 473 (1963), plaintiff, defendant, and defendant's wife, all residents of Rochester, New York, went on a weekend trip to Canada in defendant's car. Defendant lost control of the car while driving in Ontario, and plaintiff was severely injured in the resulting crash. An Ontario statute in force at the time of the accident immunized drivers from liability for injuries sustained by their passengers, but under New York law drivers could be held liable for negligently injuring their passengers. The court rejected strict application of the place-of-injury rule for all issues that arise in torts cases. Instead, Judge Fuld engaged in an analysis of state interests:

> Comparison of the relative "contacts" and "interests" of New York and Ontario in this litigation, vis-à-vis the issue here presented, makes it clear that the concern of New York is unquestionably the greater and more direct and that the interest of Ontario is at best minimal. The present action involves injuries sustained by a New York guest as the result of the negligence of a New York host in the operation of an automobile, garaged, licensed and undoubtedly insured in New York, in the course of a weekend journey which began and was to end there. In sharp contrast, Ontario's sole relationship with the occurrence is the purely adventitious circumstance that the accident occurred there.
>
> New York's policy of requiring a tortfeasor to compensate his guest for injuries caused by his negligence cannot be doubted—as attested by the fact that the Legislature of this State has repeatedly refused to enact a statute denying or limiting recovery in such cases . . . and our courts have neither reason nor warrant for departing from that policy simply because the accident, solely affecting New York residents and arising out of the operation of a New York based automobile, happened beyond its borders. Per contra, Ontario has no conceivable interest in denying a remedy to a New York guest against his New York host for injuries suffered in Ontario by reason of conduct which was tortious under Ontario law. The object of Ontario's guest statute, it has been said, is "to prevent the fraudulent assertion of claims by passengers, in collusion with the drivers, against insurance companies," and, quite obviously, the fraudulent claims intended to be prevented by the statute are those asserted against Ontario defendants and their insurance carriers. Whether New York defendants are imposed upon or their insurers defrauded by a New York plaintiff is scarcely a

valid legislative concern of Ontario simply because the accident occurred there, any more so than if the accident had happened in some other jurisdiction.

. . . Ontario's interest is quite different from what it would have been had the issue related to the manner in which the defendant had been driving his car at the time of the accident. Where the defendant's exercise of due care in the operation of his automobile is in issue, the jurisdiction in which the allegedly wrongful conduct occurred will usually have a predominant, if not exclusive, concern. In such a case, it is appropriate to look to the law of the place of the tort so as to give effect to that jurisdiction's interest in regulating conduct within its borders, and it would be almost unthinkable to seek the applicable rule in the law of some other place.

. . . Although the rightness or wrongness of defendant's conduct may depend upon the law of the particular jurisdiction through which the automobile passes, the rights and liabilities of the parties which stem from their guest-host relationship should remain constant and not vary and shift as the automobile proceeds from place to place. Indeed, such a result, we note, accords with "the interests of the host in procuring liability insurance adequate under the applicable law, and the interests of his insurer in reasonable calculability of the premium.". . .

Id. at 482-484.

Judge Van Voorhis dissented; he thought more respect should be paid to the governing law at the place of injury.

In the court's second guest statute case, Tooker v. Lopez, 24 N.Y.2d 569 (1969), Catharina Tooker was killed in an accident while a passenger in a car driven by Marcia Lopez, who was also killed. Tooker, Lopez, and a second passenger, Susan Silk, were all classmates at Michigan State University, and the accident occurred while the three students were on a weekend trip from the University to Detroit, Michigan. Tooker and Lopez were both New York domiciliaries, and Silk (not a party to this action) was domiciled in Michigan. The car was owned by Lopez's father and was registered and insured in New York. In this wrongful death action, the defendant argued that suit was barred by Michigan's guest statute, which barred recovery by guests except in cases of willful misconduct or gross negligence of the driver. Judge Keating, writing for the court, decided that New York law should apply. The court didn't seem interested in any interest that Michigan might have in the outcome of this case (although a footnote surmised that Michigan's guest statute was intended to protect the owner of the vehicle). Instead, the court focused on a New York State legislative declaration accompanying the state's compulsory insurance law which stated:

The legislature determines that it is a matter of grave concern that motorists shall be financially able to respond in damages for their negligent acts, so that innocent victims of motor vehicle accidents may be recompensed for the injury and financial loss inflicted upon them.

Despite the fact that this declaration referred to insurance coverage rather than guest statute liabilities and nowhere indicated that the legislature was worried about compensation for injuries sustained outside the state, the court stated:

[I]t is clear that New York has the only real interest in whether recovery should be granted and that the application of Michigan law "would defeat a legitimate interest of the forum State without serving a legitimate interest of any other State.". . .

> New York's "grave concern" in affording recovery for the injuries suffered by Catharina Tooker, a New York domiciliary, and the loss suffered by her family as a result of her wrongful death, is evident merely in stating the policy which our law reflects. On the other hand, Michigan has no interest in whether a New York plaintiff is denied recovery against a New York defendant where the car is insured here. The fact that the deceased guest and driver were in Michigan for an extended period of time is plainly irrelevant. Indeed, the Legislature, in requiring that insurance policies cover liabilities for injuries regardless of where the accident takes place (Vehicle & Traffic Law, §311, subd. 4) has evinced commendable concern not only for residents of this State, but residents of other States who may be injured as a result of the activities of New York residents. Under these circumstances we cannot be concerned with whether Miss Tooker or Miss Lopez were [*sic*] in Michigan for a summer session or for a full college education.

Id. at 576-577. The court rejected the relevance of party expectations arguments on the grounds that (1) people don't take into account differing laws when acting, especially in the area of torts; (2) New York wishes to impose its policy preferences in favor of compensation regardless of what the parties expect; and (3) in any event, New York policyholders might well expect that their purchase of insurance guarantees that their victims would receive New York levels of compensation.

Judge Breitel dissented, arguing that the issue should be resolved according to Michigan law because Michigan was the seat of the relationship of these students. One consequence of applying New York law was that the two passengers, Silk and Tooker, would have differing rights to recovery in the same accident, a result he found unjustified. Judge Keating responded:

> [I]t is not an "implicit consequence" that the Michigan passenger injured along with Miss Lopez should be denied recovery. Under the reasoning adopted here, it is not at all clear that Michigan law would govern. We do not, however, find it necessary or desirable to conclusively resolve a question which is not now before us. It suffices to note that any anomaly resulting from the application of Michigan law to bar an action brought by Miss Silk is "the implicit consequence" of a Federal system which, at a time when we have truly become one nation, permits a citizen of one State to recover for injuries sustained in an automobile accident and denies a citizen of another State the right to recover for injuries sustained in a similar accident. The anomaly does not arise from any choice-of-law rule. . . .

Id. at 580. Are New Yorkers now equivalent to the Romans and the Englishmen, as charged by Judge Van Voorhis in his dissent in *Babcock*? Do they also turn everyone they travel with into Romans and Englishmen? The answer to this latter question came in *Neumeier*.

Before we turn to that case, note that the "center of gravity" and "most significant contacts" inquiries from *Auten* and *Haag* were replaced by a focus on "policies" and "interests" in *Babcock* and *Tooker*. Which approach makes more sense? Do the differing approaches turn at all on the fact that *Auten* and *Haag* involved contracts and family support while *Babcock* and *Tooker* involved tort actions? Which is easier for a court—determining the center of gravity of a case or determining the policy interests? Is the New York court saying that the center of gravity is the state that has a contact that triggers important policy interests? And how does a forum ascertain the policies of other states?

Neumeier v. Kuehner, 31 N.Y.2d 121 (1972), was the third case of the guest statute trilogy. Kuehner, a resident of Buffalo, New York, drove his car, which was registered and insured in New York, into Ontario to pick up Neumeier, at his home in Fort Erie, Ontario. The two were to take a trip to Long Beach, Ontario, but the car was struck by a train on the way and both were killed instantly. By this point Ontario had amended its guest statute to protect drivers from liability to their guests except when they are guilty of gross negligence, and defendant asserted that the statute applied to plaintiff's wrongful death action. Writing for the majority, Chief Judge Fuld reexamined the policy behind Ontario's guest statute:

> [A]lthough our court originally considered that the sole purpose of the Ontario statute was to protect Ontario defendants and their insurers against collusive claims . . . , "[f]urther research . . . has revealed the distinct possibility that one purpose, and perhaps the only purpose, of the statute was to protect owners and drivers against ungrateful guests.". . .

Id. at 124. In addition, these locational facts differed from those presented in *Tooker*:

> [A]lthough the host was a domiciliary of New York, the guest, for whose death recovery is sought, was domiciled in Ontario, the place of the accident and the very jurisdiction which had enacted the statute designed to protect the host from liability for ordinary negligence. It is clear that although New York has a deep interest in protecting its own residents, injured in a foreign state, against unfair or anachronistic statutes of that state, it has no legitimate interest in ignoring the public policy of a foreign jurisdiction—such as Ontario—and in protecting the plaintiff guest domiciled and injured there from legislation obviously addressed, at the very least, to a resident riding in a vehicle traveling within its borders.

Id. at 125-126.

Judge Bergen, in his dissent, argued that this distinction was "impermissible":

> There is a difference of fundamental character between justifying a departure from lex loci delictus because the court will not, as a matter of policy, permit a New York owner of a car licensed and insured in New York to escape a liability that would be imposed on him here; and a departure based on the fact a New York resident makes the claim for injury. The first ground of departure is justifiable as sound policy; the second is justifiable only if one is willing to treat the rights of a stranger permitted to sue in New York differently from the way a resident is treated. Neither because of "interest" or "contact" nor any other defensible ground is it proper to say in a court of law that the rights of one man whose suit is accepted shall be adjudged differently on the merits on the basis of where he happens to live. . . .

Id. at 132-133. Chief Judge Fuld defended the distinction:

> To distinguish *Tooker* on such a basis is not improperly discriminatory. It is quite true that, in applying the Ontario guest statute to the Ontario-domiciled passenger, we, in a sense, extend a right less generous than New York extends to a New York passenger in a New York vehicle with New York insurance. That, though, is not a consequence of invidious discrimination; it is, rather, the result of the existence of disparate rules of law in jurisdictions that have diverse and important connections with the litigants and the litigated issue.
>
> The fact that insurance policies issued in this State on New York-based vehicles cover liability, regardless of the place of the accident . . . certainly does not call for the application of internal New York law in this case. The compulsory insurance requirement is designed to *cover* a car owner's liability, not *create* it; in other words, the applicable statute was not intended to impose liability where none would otherwise exist. This being so, we may not properly look to the New York insurance requirement to dictate a choice-of-law rule which would invariably impose liability. . . . While New York may be a proper forum for actions involving its own domiciliaries, regardless of where the accident happened, it does not follow that we should apply New York law simply because some may think it is a better rule, where doing so does not advance any New York interest, nor the interest of any New York State domiciliary.

Id. at 126-127.

Looking to the future, Chief Judge Fuld advocated rules for guest statute cases:

> When in Babcock v. Jackson we rejected the mechanical place of injury rule in personal injury cases because it failed to take account of underlying policy considerations, we were willing to sacrifice the certainty provided by the old rule for the more just, fair and practical result that may best be achieved by giving controlling effect to the law of the jurisdiction which has the greatest concern with, or interest in, the specific issue raised in the litigation. . . . In consequence of the change effected—and this was to be anticipated—our decisions in multi-state highway accident cases, particularly in those involving guest-host controversies, have, it must be acknowledged, lacked consistency. This stemmed, in part, from the circumstance that it is frequently difficult to discover the purposes or policies underlying the relevant local law rules of the respective jurisdictions involved. It is even more difficult, assuming that these purposes or policies are found to conflict, to determine on some principled basis which should be given effect at the expense of the others.
>
> The single all-encompassing rule which called, inexorably, for selection of the law of the place of injury was discarded, and wisely, because it was too broad to prove satisfactory in application. There is, however, no reason why choice-of-law rules, more narrow than those previously devised, should not be successfully developed, in order to assure a greater degree of predictability and uniformity, on the basis of our present knowledge and experience. . . . *Babcock* and its progeny enable us to formulate a set of basic principles that may be profitably utilized [in guest-host conflicts], for they have helped us uncover the

underlying values and policies which are operative in this area of law. Although it was recognized that no rule may be formulated to guarantee a satisfactory result in every case, the following principles were proposed as sound for situations involving guest statutes in conflicts settings:

1. When the guest-passenger and the host-driver are domiciled in the same state, and the car is there registered, the law of the state should control and determine the standard of care which the host owes to his guest.
2. When the driver's conduct occurred in the state of his domicile and that state does not cast him in liability for that conduct, he should not be held liable by reason of the fact that liability would be imposed upon him under the tort law of the state of the victim's domicile. Conversely, when the guest was injured in the state of his own domicile and its law permits recovery, the driver who has come into that state should not—in the absence of special circumstances—be permitted to interpose the law of his state as a defense.
3. In other situations, when the passenger and the driver are domiciled in different states, the rule is necessarily less categorical. Normally, the applicable rule of decision will be that of the state where the accident occurred but not if it can be shown that displacing that normally applicable rule will advance the relevant substantive law purposes without impairing the smooth working of the multi-state system or producing great uncertainty for litigants. (*Cf.* Restatement, 2d, Conflict of Laws, P.O.D., pt. II, §§146, 159 [later adopted and promulgated May 23, 1969.])

Id. at 127-128. Rule 3 applied here, and the court concluded that New York's connection to the case provided insufficient reason to displace the law of the place of injury.

Subsequent Developments

The *Neumeier* rules continue to inform choice-of-law decisions in New York, and they have been extended beyond the guest statute context with some added nuance. Consider, for example, Schultz v. Boy Scouts of America, 65 N.Y.2d 189 (1985). Plaintiffs, domiciled in New Jersey, sued Edmund Coakeley, Boy Scouts of America, and Franciscan Brothers of the Poor, Inc., after their two sons were sexually abused by Coakeley and one committed suicide. Coakeley, a brother in the Franciscan order, was the boys' school teacher and scout leader. Coakeley apparently sexually assaulted both boys at a boy scout camp in New York, and continued to abuse at least one son after returning to New Jersey. The Boy Scouts and Franciscan Brothers were sued for negligent hiring and supervision. Plaintiffs claimed that these latter defendants had actual or constructive notice that Coakeley had previously been dismissed from another boy scout camp for similar misconduct. The Boy Scouts maintained their headquarters in New Jersey until 1979, after the abuse occurred, when they moved their headquarters to Texas. Franciscan Brothers was incorporated and headquartered in Ohio. Under New Jersey but not New York (or Texas or Ohio) law, the doctrine of charitable immunity prevents the suits against Boy Scouts and Franciscan Brothers from going forward.

After discussing the significance of *Babcock*, *Tooker*, and *Neumeier* to choice-of-law analysis in New York, the court introduced a distinction between conduct-regulating and loss-allocating rules:

These decisions also establish that the relative interests of the domicile and locus jurisdictions in having their laws apply will depend on the particular tort issue in conflict with the case. Thus, when the conflicting rules involve the appropriate standards of conduct, rules of the road, for example, the law of the place of the tort "will usually have a predominant, if not exclusive, concern" . . . because the locus jurisdiction's interests in protecting the reasonable expectations of the parties who relied on it to govern their primary conduct and in the admonitory effect that applying its law will have on similar conduct in the future assume critical importance and outweigh any interests of the common-domicile jurisdiction. . . .

. . . Conversely, when the jurisdictions' conflicting rules relate to allocating losses that result from admittedly tortious conduct, as they do here, rules such as those limiting damages in wrongful death actions, vicarious liability rules, or immunities from suit, considerations of the State's admonitory interest and party reliance are less important. Under those circumstances, the locus jurisdiction has at best a minimal interest in determining the right of recovery or the extent of the remedy in an action by a foreign domiciliary for injuries resulting from the conduct of a codomiciliary that was tortious under the laws of both jurisdictions. . . . Analysis then favors the jurisdiction of common domicile because of its interest in enforcing the decisions of both parties to accept both the benefits and the burdens of identifying with that jurisdiction and to submit themselves to its authority. . . .

As to defendant Boy Scouts, this case . . . presents . . . a "reverse" *Babcock* case because New York is the place of the tort rather than the jurisdiction of the parties' common domicile.

. . . [I]f this were a straight *Babcock* fact pattern, rather than the reverse, we would have no reason to depart from the first *Neumeier* rule and would apply the law of the parties' common domicile. Because this case presents the first case for our review in which New York is the forum-locus rather than the parties' common domicile, however, we consider the reasons most often advanced for applying the law of the forum-locus and those supporting application of the law of the common domicile.

The three reasons most often urged in support of applying the law of the forum-locus in cases such as this are: (1) to protect medical creditors who provided services to injured parties in the locus State, (2) to prevent injured tort victims from becoming public wards in the locus State, and (3) the deterrent effect application of locus law has on future tortfeasors in the locus State. . . . The first two reasons share common weaknesses. First, in the abstract, neither reason necessarily requires application of the locus jurisdiction's law, but rather invariably mandates application of the law of the jurisdiction that would either allow recovery or allow the greater recovery. . . . They are subject to criticism, therefore, as being biased in favor of recovery. Second, . . . the record contains no evidence that there are New York medical creditors or that plaintiffs are or will likely become wards of this State. Finally, although it is conceivable that application of New York's law in this case would have some deterrent effect on future tortious conduct in this State, New York's deterrent interest is considerably less because none of the parties is a resident and the rule in conflict is loss-allocating rather than conduct-regulating.

Conversely, there are persuasive reasons for consistently applying the law of the parties' common domicile. First, it significantly reduces forum-shopping opportunities, because the same law will be applied by the common-domicile and locus jurisdictions, the two most likely forums. Second, it rebuts charges that the forum-locus is biased in favor of its own laws and in favor of rules permitting recovery. Third, the concepts of mutuality and reciprocity support consistent application of the common-domicile law. In any given case, one person could be either plaintiff or defendant and one State could be either the parties' common domicile or the locus, and yet the applicable law would not change depending on their status. Finally, it produces a rule that is easy to apply and brings a modicum of predictability and certainty to an area of the law needing both.

As to defendant Franciscan Brothers, this action requires an application of the third of the rules set forth in *Neumeier* because the parties are domiciled in different jurisdictions with conflicting loss-distribution rules and the locus of the tort is New York, a separate jurisdiction. In that situation the law of the place of the tort will normally apply, unless displacing it "will advance the relevant substantive law purposes without impairing the smooth working of the multi-state system or producing great uncertainty for litigants." For the same reasons stated in our analysis of the action against defendant Boy Scouts, application of the law of New Jersey in plaintiffs' action against defendant Franciscan Brothers would further that State's interest in enforcing the decision of its domiciliaries to accept the burdens as well as the benefits of that State's loss-distribution tort rules and its interest in promoting the continuation and expansion of defendant's charitable activities in that State. Conversely, although application of New Jersey's law may not affirmatively advance the substantive law purposes of New York, it will not frustrate those interests because New York has no significant interest in applying its own law to this dispute. Finally, application of New Jersey law will enhance "the smooth working of the multistate system" by actually reducing the incentive for forum shopping and it will provide certainty for the litigants whose only reasonable expectation surely would have been that the law of the jurisdiction where plaintiffs are domiciled and defendant sends its teachers would apply, not the law of New York where the parties had only isolated and infrequent contacts as a result of Coakeley's position as Boy Scout leader. Thus, we conclude that defendant Franciscan Brothers has met its burden of demonstrating that the law of New Jersey, rather than the law of New York, should govern plaintiffs' action against it.

Id. at 198-202.

Note that the *Schultz* court lists three reasons sometimes advanced for applying the law of the forum locus. The first two—protecting local medical creditors and preventing injured parties from becoming public wards of the state—are rejected as reasons for applying New York law in part because they are "biased in favor of recovery." But aren't all underlying policies biased in this sense, either favoring recovery (if pro-plaintiff) or denying it (if pro-defendant)? What is left of the new methodology once we discard such "biased" policies? And with regard to the third reason—deterrence—why is New York's interest less where the parties are not residents? Are nonresidents supposed to be immune from local conduct-regulating rules while in New York? Regarding the Franciscan Brothers, why would New Jersey have an interest in forcing its domiciliaries to bear the costs as well as the benefits of local law? Does a state have an interest generally in applying its disadvantageous rules to locals?

The New York Court of Appeals returned to the distinction between conduct-regulating and loss-allocating rules in Padula v. Lilarn Properties Corp., 644 N.E.2d 1001 (1994). In *Padula*, plaintiff, a resident of New York, sued defendant, a New York corporation, after suffering injuries when he fell from a scaffold while working on defendant's Massachusetts property under a subcontracting agreement. Plaintiff's claim was based on alleged violations of the New York Labor Law, but the court concluded that New York's law does not apply because New York was not the situs of this accident:

> Conduct-regulating rules have the prophylactic effect of governing conduct to prevent injuries from occurring. "If conflicting conduct-regulating laws are at issue, the law of the jurisdiction where the tort occurred will generally apply because that jurisdiction has the greatest interest in regulating behavior within its borders.". . .
>
> Loss allocating rules, on the other hand, are those which prohibit, assign, or limit liability after the tort occurs, such as charitable immunity statutes, guest statutes, wrongful death statutes, vicarious liability statutes, and contribution rules. Where the conflicting rules at issue are loss allocating and the parties to the lawsuit share a common domicile, the loss allocation rule of the common domicile will apply.
>
> Thus, the fundamental question in this case, where the parties share a common domicile, is whether Labor Law §§240 and 241 are primarily conduct-regulating or loss-allocating. The relevant Labor Law provisions, sections 240 and 241, embody both conduct-regulating and loss-allocating functions requiring worksites be made safe (conduct-regulating) and failure to do so results in strict and vicarious liability of the owner of the property or the general contractor. We hold however, that sections 240 and 241 of the Labor Law are primarily conduct-regulating rules, requiring that adequate safety measures be instituted at the worksite and should not be applied to the resolution of this tort dispute arising in Massachusetts.

Id. at 1002-1003.

Is the distinction between conduct-regulating and loss-distributing rules useful? Won't most laws, as *Padula* put it, "embody both conduct-regulating and loss-allocating functions"? Are you convinced by *Padula*'s conclusion that sections 240-241 of New York's Labor Law are "primarily conduct regulating"? Doesn't the conduct-regulation/loss-allocation distinction raise a new and intractable characterization problem?

Scholars disagree about the validity and usefulness of the distinction. Professor Symeonides applauds it. Symeonides, *The Third Conflicts Restatement's First Draft on Tort Conflicts*, 92 Tul. L. Rev. 1 (2017); *see also* Borchers, *The Return of Territorialism to New York's Conflicts Law:* Padula v. Lilarn Properties Corp., 58 Alb. L. Rev. 775 (1995) (suggesting that the distinction, though not always easy to draw, is essential and serviceable). Others are critical of the distinction. O'Hara & Ribstein, *From Politics to Efficiency in Choice of Law*, 67 U. Chi. L. Rev. 1151 (2000); *see also* Perdue, *A Reexamination of the Distinction Between "Loss-Allocating" and "Conduct-Regulating Rules,"*

60 La. L. Rev. 1251, 1252 (2000) (arguing that "most tort rules are both and that the compensation and deterrence goals ascribed to the tort system cannot be separated") (citation and internal quotations removed); Hay & Ellis, *Bridging the Gap Between Rules and Approaches in Tort Choice of Law in the United States: A Survey of Current Case Law*, 27 Intl. Lawyer 369, 382 (1993) ("distinction creates more trouble than it's worth").

After reading these and other New York cases, one might conclude that New York's choice-of-law rule for torts boils down to: Apply the law of the place of injury unless the issue involves a loss-allocation dispute between common domiciliaries, in which case apply the law of the domicile. If this is correct, then the New York "revolution" amounts to nothing more than the First Restatement with a narrow exception for common domicile cases involving loss-allocation issues. Was it necessary to walk the tortured path from *Haag* to *Padula* to reach this destination? Does *Padula* suggest that the New York approach is as wooden, jurisdiction selecting, and "blind" as the traditional approach? Is there perhaps virtue in these qualities? Professor Hill has argued that the choice-of-law revolution is virtually unique in its willingness to discard the common sense of centuries and blaze new trails on a case-by-case basis. He points out that there was much more to traditional thinking than Beale's dogma and that some traditional thinking might be worth consulting. Hill, *The Judicial Function in Choice of Law*, 85 Colum. L. Rev. 1585 (1985). Does the line of cases from *Haag* to *Padula* support Hill's view? What does this line of cases suggest about the capacities of courts to view choice of law as about the pursuit of "state interests"?

B. Interest Analysis: In Theory and in Practice

With the First Restatement thoroughly discredited, and with the common law in disarray, the problem of choosing the applicable law fell mainly into the hands of academics. The most creative and influential of these was Brainerd Currie, the author of the theory known as governmental interest analysis.

1. Theoretical Foundations of Interest Analysis

Currie, Notes on Methods and Objectives in the Conflict of Laws

Selected Essays on the Conflict of Laws 177, 183-187 (1963)

We would be better off without choice-of-law rules. We would be better off if Congress were to give some attention to problems of private law, and were to legislate concerning the choice between conflicting state interests in some of the specific areas in which the need for solutions is serious. In the meantime, we would be better off if we would admit the teachings of sociological jurisprudence into the conceptualistic precincts of conflict of laws. This would imply a basic method along the following lines:

1. Normally, even in cases involving foreign elements, the court should be expected, as a matter of course, to apply the rule of decision found in the law of the forum.

2. When it is suggested that the law of a foreign state should furnish the rule of decision, the court should, first of all, determine the governmental policy expressed in the law of the forum. It should then inquire whether the relation of the forum to the case is such as to provide a legitimate basis for the assertion of an interest in the application of that policy. This process is essentially the familiar one of construction or interpretation. Just as we determine by that process how a statute applies in time, and how it applies to marginal domestic situations, so we may determine how it should be applied to cases involving foreign elements in order to effectuate the legislative purpose.

3. If necessary, the court should similarly determine the policy expressed by the foreign law, and whether the foreign state has an interest in the application of its policy.

4. If the court finds that the forum state has no interest in the application of its policy, but that the foreign state has, it should apply the foreign law.

5. If the court finds that the forum state has an interest in the application of its policy, it should apply the law of the forum, even though the foreign state also has an interest in the application of its contrary policy, and, a fortiori, it should apply the law of the forum if the foreign state has no such interest.

A probable by-product of such a method is the elimination of certain classical problems that are wholly artificial, being raised merely by the form of choice-of-law rules. The problem of characterization is ubiquitous in the law and can never be wholly avoided. Without choice-of-law rules, however, there would be no occasion for the specialized function of characterization as the mode of discriminating among the available prefabricated solutions of a problem. . . . And, though I make this suggestion with some trepidation, it seems clear that the problem of the renvoi would have no place at all in the analysis that has been suggested. Foreign law would be applied only when the court has determined that the foreign state has a legitimate interest in the application of its law and policy to the case at bar and that the forum has none. Hence, there can be no question of applying anything other than the internal law of the foreign state. . . .

It will be said that it is no great trick to dispose of the characteristic problems of a system by destroying the system itself. But my basic point is that the system itself is at fault. We have invented an apparatus for the solution of problems of conflicting interest that obscures the real problems, deals with them blindly and badly, and creates problems of its own which, in their way, are as troublesome as the ones we originally set out to solve. . . .

The suggested analysis does not imply the ruthless pursuit of self-interest by the states.

In the first place, the states of the Union are significantly restrained in the pursuit of their respective interests by the Privileges and Immunities Clause of article IV and by the Equal Protection Clause. . . .

In the second place, there is no need to exclude the possibility of rational altruism: for example, when a state has determined upon the policy of placing upon local industry all the social costs of the enterprise, it may well decide to adhere to this policy regardless of where the harm occurs and who the victim is.

In the third place, there is room for restraint and enlightenment in the determination of what state policy is and where state interests lie. . . .

I have been told that I give insufficient recognition to governmental policies other than those that are expressed in specific statutes and rules: the policy of promoting a general legal order, that of fostering amicable relations with other states, that of vindicating reasonable expectations, and so on. If this is so, it is not, I hope, because of a provincial lack of appreciation of the worth of those ideals, but because of a felt necessity to emphasize the obstacles that the present system interposes to any intelligent approach to the problem. Let us first clear away the apparatus that creates false problems and obscures the nature of the real ones. Only then can we effectively set about ameliorating the ills that arise from a diversity of laws by bringing to bear all of the resources of jurisprudence, politics, and humanism—each in its appropriate way.

Currie later restated his principles and added provisions dealing with the "disinterested forum" and objections that had been raised by others. In Currie, *Comments on* Babcock v. Jackson, 63 Colum. L. Rev. 1233, 1242-1243 (1963), he said:

If I were asked to restate the law of conflict of laws I would decline the honor. A descriptive restatement with any sort of internal consistency is impossible. Much of the existing law, or pseudo law, of the subject is irrational; profound changes destructive of the fundamental tenets of the traditional system are gathering momentum. On the assumption that the project admits of a statement of what is reasonable in existing law and what may reasonably be desired for the future, however, I volunteer the following as a substitute for all that part of the Restatement dealing with choice of law (for the purpose of finding the rule of decision):

§1. When a court is asked to apply the law of a foreign state different from the law of the forum, it should inquire into the policies expressed in the respective laws, and into the circumstances in which it is reasonable for the respective states to assert an interest in the application of those policies. In making these determinations the court should employ the ordinary processes of construction and interpretation.

§2. If the court finds that one state has an interest in the application of its policy in the circumstances of the case and the other has none, it should apply the law of the only interested state.

§3. If the court finds an apparent conflict between the interests of the two states it should reconsider. A more moderate and restrained interpretation of the policy or interest of one state or the other may avoid conflict.

§4. If, upon reconsideration, the court finds that a conflict between the legitimate interests of the two states is unavoidable, it should apply the law of the forum.

§5. If the forum is disinterested, but an unavoidable conflict exists between the laws of the two other states, and the court cannot with justice decline to adjudicate the case, it should apply the law of the forum—until someone comes along with a better idea.

§6. The conflict of interest between states will result in different dispositions of the same problem, depending on where the action is brought. If with respect to a particular problem this appears seriously to infringe a strong national interest in uniformity of decision, the court should not attempt to improvise a solution sacrificing the legitimate interest of its own state, but should leave to Congress, exercising its powers under the full faith and credit clause, the determination of which interest shall be required to yield.

The explanatory note might run a little longer. [Footnotes omitted.]

This restatement is notable for, among other things, Currie's suggestion that the forum should not automatically apply its law when it had an interest but should reconsider whether a more moderate interpretation of its law might not be feasible. Principle 3 of his "Restatement" thus represents a change from rule 5 of his earlier outline.

Currie's analysis has been enormously influential. If nothing else, it has led to a whole new terminology. Instead of determining the parties' "vested rights" under a set of specified territorial rules, the court was supposed to determine which states had "interests" through an application of the various state policies. Courts were supposed to do this by construing the statutes vying for application just as they would in a domestic case. Once they had ascertained the relevant policies or interests, the case would be seen to be either a false conflict, a true conflict, or an unprovided-for case.

Babcock and *Tooker* are generally conceded to be false conflicts because only one state had an interest. New York was interested in providing recovery for its domiciliary, while Ontario and Michigan had no interest in denying recovery simply because the accident occurred there. Currie's method requires application of the law of the only interested state.

True conflicts and unprovided-for cases involve disputes where two states and no states, respectively, have an interest in application of local law. Here, Currie's solution of applying forum law seems less than irresistible. *Neumeier* was probably an unprovided-for case because Ontario had no interest in protecting a New York defendant, while there was no reason to apply New York law to the benefit of an Ontario plaintiff. The court solved the problem through the special rules it developed. *See generally* Twerski, Neumeier v. Kuehner: *Where Are the Emperor's Clothes?*, 1 Hofstra L. Rev. 104 (1973). Currie's solution—to apply forum law—was adopted in Erwin v. Thomas, 264 Or. 454, 506 P.2d 494 (1973).

The next three cases illustrate the tribulations of courts dealing with true conflicts and unprovided-for cases.

2.   Judicial Applications

a.   *True Conflicts*

Lilienthal v. Kaufman

239 Or. 1, 395 P.2d 543 (1964)

DENECKE, J.

This is an action to collect two promissory notes. The defense is that the defendant maker has previously been declared a spendthrift by an Oregon court and placed under a guardianship and that the guardian has declared the obligations void. The plaintiff's counter is that the notes were executed and delivered in California, that the law of California does not recognize the disability of a spendthrift, and that the Oregon court is bound to apply the law of the place of the making of the contract. The trial court rejected plaintiff's argument and held for the defendant.

This same defendant spendthrift was the prevailing party in our recent decision in Olshen v. Kaufman, 235 Or. 423, 385 P.2d 161 (1963). In that case the spendthrift and the plaintiff, an Oregon resident, had gone into a joint venture to purchase binoculars for resale. For this purpose plaintiff had advanced moneys to the spendthrift. The spendthrift had repaid plaintiff by his personal check for the amount advanced and for plaintiff's share of the profits of such venture. The check had not been paid because the spendthrift had had insufficient funds in his account. The action was for the unpaid balance of the check.

The evidence in that case showed that the plaintiff had been unaware that Kaufman was under a spendthrift guardianship. The guardian testified that he knew Kaufman was engaging in some business and had bank accounts and that he had admonished him to cease these practices; but he could not control the spendthrift.

The statute applicable in that case and in this one is ORS 126.335:

> After the appointment of a guardian for the spendthrift, all contracts, except for necessaries, and all gifts, sales and transfers of real or personal estate made by such spendthrift thereafter and before the termination of the guardianship are voidable.

We held in that case that the voiding of the contract by the guardian precluded recovery by the plaintiff and that the spendthrift and the guardian were not estopped to deny the validity of plaintiff's claim. Plaintiff does not seek to overturn the principle of that decision but contends it has no application because the law of California governs, and under California law the plaintiff's claims are valid.

The facts here are identical to those in Olshen v. Kaufman, *supra*, except for the California locale for portions of the transaction. The notes were for the repayment of advances to finance another joint venture to sell binoculars. The plaintiff was unaware that defendant had been declared a spendthrift and placed under guardianship. The guardian, upon demand for payment by the plaintiff, declared the notes void. The issue is solely one involving the principles of conflict of laws.

. . .

Plaintiff contends that the substantive issue of whether or not an obligation is valid and binding is governed by the law of the place of making, California. This court has repeatedly stated that the law of the place of contract "must govern as to the validity, interpretation, and construction of the contract. . . ." Restatement 408, Conflict of Laws, §332, so announced and specifically stated that "capacity to make the contract" was to be determined by the law of the place of contract. . . .

There is no need to decide that our previous statements that the law of the place of contract governs were in error. Our purpose is to state that this portion of our decision is not founded upon that principle because of our doubt that it is correct if the *only* connection of the state whose law would govern is that it was the place of making.

In this case California has more connection with the transaction than being merely the place where the contract was executed. The defendant went to San Francisco to ask the plaintiff, a California resident, for money for the defendant's venture. The money was loaned to defendant in San Francisco, and by the terms of the note, it was to be repaid to plaintiff in San Francisco.

On these facts, apart from lex loci contractus, other accepted principles of conflict of laws lead to the conclusion that the law of California should be applied. Sterrett v. Stoddard Lumber Co. rests, at least in part, on the proposition that the validity of a note is determined by the law of the place of payment. Tentative Draft No. 6, p. 30, Restatement (Second), Conflict of Laws, §332b(a) states:

> If the place of contracting and the place of performance are in the same state, the local law of this state determines the validity of the contract. . . .

. . . The place of payment, unlike the place of making, is usually not determined fortuitously. The place is usually selected by the payee and the payee normally selects his place of business or the location of his bank. The parties at the time of contract normally do not have in mind the problem of what law should govern. If they did, it is our belief that the payee would intend the law of the place of payment to be governing.

There is another conflict principle calling for the application of California law. Ehrenzweig calls it the "Rule of Validation." Ehrenzweig, Conflict of Laws 353 (1962). . . . The "rule" is that, if the contract is valid under the law of any jurisdiction having significant connection with the contract, *i.e.*, place of making, place of performance, etc., the law of that jurisdiction validating the contract will be applied. This would also agree with the intention of the parties, if they had any intentions in this regard. They must have intended their agreement to be valid.

Thus far all signs have pointed to applying the law of California and holding the contract enforceable. There is, however, an obstacle to cross before this end can be logically reached. In Olshen v. Kaufman, *supra*, we decided that the law of Oregon, at least as applied to persons domiciled in Oregon contracting in Oregon for performance in Oregon, is that spendthrifts' contracts are voidable. Are the choice-of-law principles of conflict of laws so superior that they overcome this principle of Oregon law?

To answer this question we must determine, upon some basis, whether the interests of Oregon are so basic and important that we should not apply California law despite its several intimate connections with the transaction. The traditional method used by this court and most others is framed in the terminology of "public policy." The court decides whether or not the public policy of the forum is so strong that the law of the forum must prevail although another jurisdiction, with different laws, has more and closer contacts with the transaction. Included in "public policy" we must consider the economic and social interests of Oregon. When these factors are included in a consideration of whether the law of the forum should be applied this traditional approach is very similar to that advocated by many legal scholars. This latter theory is "that choice-of-law rules should rationally advance the policies or interests of the several states (or of the nations in the world community)."

The traditional test this court and many others have used in determining whether the public policy of the forum prevents the application of otherwise applicable conflict of laws principles is stated in the oft-quoted opinion of Mr. Justice Cardozo in Loucks v. Standard Oil Co. of New York. Foreign law will not be applied if it ". . .would violate some fundamental principle of justice, some prevalent conception of good morals, some deep-rooted tradition of the common weal.". . .

How "deep rooted [the] tradition of the common weal," particularly regarding spendthrifts, is illustrated by our decisions on foreign marriages. This court has decided that Oregon's policy voiding spendthrifts' contracts is not so strong as to void an Oregon spendthrift's marriage contract made in Washington. . . .

However, as previously stated, if we include in our search for the public policy of the forum a consideration of the various interests that the forum has in this litigation, we are guided by more definite criteria. In addition to the interests of the forum, we should consider the interests of the other jurisdictions which have some connection with the transaction.

Some of the interests of Oregon in this litigation are set forth in Olshen v. Kaufman, *supra*. The spendthrift's family which is to be protected by the establishment of the guardianship is presumably an Oregon family. The public authority which may be charged with the expense of supporting the spendthrift or his family, if he is permitted to go unrestrained upon his wasteful way, will probably be an Oregon public authority. These, obviously, are interests of some substance.

Oregon has other interests and policies regarding this matter which were not necessary to discuss in *Olshen*. As previously stated, Oregon, as well as all other states, has a strong policy favoring the validity and enforceability of contracts. This policy applies whether the contract is made and to be performed in Oregon or elsewhere.

The defendant's conduct—borrowing money with the belief that the repayment of such loan could be avoided—is a species of fraud. Oregon and all other states have a strong policy of protecting innocent persons from fraud. "The law . . . is intended as a protection to even the foolishly credulous, as against the machinations of the designedly wicked.". . .

It is in Oregon's commercial interest to encourage citizens of other states to conduct business with Oregonians. If Oregonians acquire a reputation for not honoring their agreements, commercial intercourse with Oregonians will be discouraged. If there are Oregon laws, somewhat unique to Oregon, which permit an Oregonian to escape his otherwise binding obligations, persons may well avoid commercial dealings with Oregonians.

The substance of these commercial considerations, however, is deflated by the recollection that the Oregon Legislature has determined, despite the weight of these considerations, that a spendthrift's contracts are voidable.

California's most direct interest in this transaction is having its citizen creditor paid. As previously noted, California's policy is that any creditor, in California or otherwise, should be paid even though the debtor is a spendthrift. California probably has another, although more intangible, interest involved. It is presumably to every state's benefit to have the reputation of being a jurisdiction in which contracts can be made and performance be promised with the certain knowledge that such contracts will be enforced. Both of these interests, particularly the former, are also of substance.

We have, then, two jurisdictions, each with several close connections with the transaction, and each with a substantial interest, which will be served or thwarted, depending upon which law is applied. The interests of neither jurisdiction are clearly more important than those of the other. We are of the opinion that in such a case the public policy of Oregon should prevail and the law of Oregon should be applied; we should apply that choice-of-law rule which will "advance the policies or interests of" Oregon. . . .

Courts are instruments of state policy. The Oregon legislature has adopted a policy to avoid possible hardship to an Oregon family of a spendthrift and to avoid possible expenditure of Oregon public funds which might occur if the spendthrift is required to pay his obligations. In litigation Oregon courts are the appropriate instrument to enforce this policy. The mechanical application of choice-of-law rules would be the only apparent reason for an Oregon court not advancing the interests of Oregon. The present principles of conflict of laws are not favorable to such mechanical application.

We hold that the spendthrift law of Oregon is applicable and the plaintiff cannot recover.

Judgment affirmed. [There were also a dissent and a concurring opinion.]

b. True Conflicts vs. Apparent Conflicts

When there appears to be a true conflict between the interests of two states, Currie's analysis suggests that the court reconsider whether a more restrained approach may avoid the conflict. Where a more moderate interpretation of the policy or interest of one state serves to avoid the conflict, this is referred to as an apparent conflict. The following case provides an example.

Bernkrant v. Fowler

55 Cal. 2d 588, 360 P.2d 906, 12 Cal. Rptr. 266 (1961)

TRAYNOR, J.

Plaintiffs appeal on the clerk's transcript from a judgment for defendant as executrix of the estate of John Granrud. They contend that the findings of fact do not support the judgment.

[The court begins by describing the series of events leading up to this cause of action that took place in Las Vegas. Some time before 1954, plaintiffs purchased the Granrud Garden Apartments in Las Vegas, Nevada. In July of 1954, there remained unpaid approximately $24,000 on a note payable to Granrud by the plaintiffs. At that time Granrud asked plaintiffs to pay a substantial part of their indebtedness to him. At a meeting in Las Vegas, he stated that if plaintiffs would do so, he would provide by will that any debt that remained on the purchase price at the time of his death would be canceled and forgiven. Plaintiffs then arranged for a new loan of $25,000, and executed a new note for the balance of $9,227 owing Granrud, payable in installments of $175 per month. From this new note, the plaintiffs deposited money in Granrud's bank account in Covina, California, which was subsequently used by him to buy a trailer park. After Granrud died as a resident of Los Angeles County, his will was admitted to probate, and defendant was appointed executrix of his estate. His will made no provision for cancelling the remaining balance of $6,425 due on the note at the time of his death. Plaintiffs continued to make regular payments of principal and interest to defendant under protest.]

Plaintiffs brought this action to have the note cancelled and discharged and the property reconveyed to them and to recover the amounts paid defendant after Granrud's death. The trial court concluded that the action was barred by both the Nevada and the California statute of frauds; . . .

. . . Subdivision 6 of section 1624 of the Civil Code provides that "An agreement which by its terms is not to be performed during the lifetime of the promisor, or an agreement to devise or bequeath any property, or to make any provision for any person by will" is "invalid, unless the same, or some note or memorandum thereof, is in writing, and subscribed by the party to be charged or by his agent." *See also* Code Civ. Proc. §1973, subd. 6. Plaintiffs concede that in the absence of an estoppel, the contract in this case would be invalid under this provision if it is subject thereto. They contend, however, that only the Nevada statute of frauds is applicable and point out that the Nevada statute has no counterpart to subdivision 6. Defendant contends that the California statute of frauds is applicable, and that if it is not, the Nevada statute of frauds covering real property transactions invalidates the contract.

We have found no Nevada case in point. We believe, however, that Nevada would follow the general rule in other jurisdictions, that an oral agreement providing for the discharge of an obligation to pay money secured by an interest in real property is not within the real property provision of the statute of frauds, on the ground that the termination of the security interest is merely incidental to and follows by operation of law from the discharge of the principal obligation. . . .

We are therefore confronted with a contract that is valid under the law of Nevada but invalid under the California statute of frauds if that statute is applicable. We have no doubt that California's interest in protecting estates being probated here from false claims based on alleged oral contracts to make wills is constitutionally sufficient to justify the Legislature's making our statute of frauds applicable to all such contracts sought to be enforced against such estates. . . . The Legislature, however, is ordinarily concerned with enacting laws to govern purely local transactions, and it has not spelled out the extent to which the statute of frauds is to apply to a contract having substantial contacts with another state. Accordingly, we must determine its scope in the light of applicable principles of the law of conflict of laws. . . .

In the present case plaintiffs were residents of Nevada, the contract was made in Nevada, and plaintiffs performed it there. If Granrud was a resident of Nevada at the time the contract was made, the California statute of frauds, in the absence of a plain legislative direction to the contrary, could not reasonably be interpreted as applying to the contract even though Granrud subsequently moved to California and died there. . . . The basic policy of upholding the expectations of the parties by enforcing contracts valid under the only law apparently applicable would preclude an interpretation of our statute of frauds that would make it apply to and thus invalidate the contract because Granrud moved to California and died here. Such a case would be analogous to People v. One 1953 Ford Victoria . . . where we held that a Texas mortgagee of an automobile mortgaged in Texas did not forfeit his interest when the automobile was subsequently used to transport narcotics in California although he failed to make the character investigation of the mortgagor required by California law. A mortgagee entering into a purely local transaction in another state could not reasonably be expected to take cognizance of the law of all the other jurisdictions where the property might possibly be taken, and accordingly, the California statute requiring an investigation to protect his interest could not reasonably be interpreted to apply to such out of state mortgagees. . . .

In the present case, there is no finding as to where Granrud was domiciled at the time the contract was made. Since he had a bank account in California at that time and died a resident here less than two years later it may be that he was domiciled here when the contract was made. Even if he was, the result should be the same. The contract was made in Nevada and performed by plaintiffs there, and it involved the refinancing of obligation arising from the sale of Nevada land and secured by interests therein. Nevada has a substantial interest in the contract and in protecting the rights of its residents who are parties thereto, and its policy is that the contract is valid and enforceable. California's policy is also to enforce lawful contracts. That policy, however, must be subordinated in the case of any contract that does not meet the requirements of an applicable statute of frauds. In determining whether the contract herein is subject to the California statute of frauds, we must consider both the policy to protect the reasonable expectations of the parties and the policy of the statute of frauds. . . . It is true that if Granrud was domiciled here at the time the contract was made, plaintiffs may have been alerted to the possibility that the California statute of frauds might apply. Since California, however, would have no interest in applying its own statute of frauds unless Granrud remained here until his death, plaintiffs were not bound to know that California's statute might ultimately be invoked against them. Unless they could rely on their own law, they would have to look to the laws of all the jurisdictions to which Granrud might move regardless of where he was domiciled when the contract was made. We conclude, therefore, that the contract herein does not fall within our statute of frauds. . . . Since there is thus no conflict between the law of California and the law of Nevada, we can give effect to the common policy of both states to enforce lawful contracts and sustain Nevada's interest in protecting its residents and their reasonable expectations growing out of a transaction substantially related to that state without subordinating any legitimate interest of this state.

The judgment is reversed.

Questions and Comments

(1) Is it clear that *Lilienthal* is a true conflict case? Would Currie have concurred because the Oregon court followed section 4 of his "Restatement" or would he have dissented because the court failed to follow section 3 by looking for some accommodation of the interests of Oregon and California?

(2) Is the dividing line between true and false conflict cases becoming more or less clear? Consider Gutride Safier LLP v. Reese, 2013 WL 4104462 (N.D. Cal. 2013), in which the court found a false conflict and applied the law of the forum. According to Reese, the California-based law firm recruited him as a partner in 2005, allowing the firm to "maintain a legal practice in New York, New York; file cases in New York; and triple its size by adding a number of New York lawyers to its practice." As partner, Reese was entitled to "receive an equal share with all other partners in the firm's net recovery from all cases litigated by the firm." *Id.* at *1. In February 2008, the firm received payments on two cases that Reese had worked on. Gutride and Saphier, two other partners of the firm, invited Reese to California "under the pretense that they would be celebrating the recent settlements." *Id.* Upon his arrival, Gutride and Saphier told Reese that they would not pay him what was owed under the partnership agreement and threatened him with bankruptcy if he did not leave the firm. At that same meeting, Reese signed a withdrawal agreement that, among other things, bound him "not to interfere with any of the Gutride Safier cases." *Id.* Approximately five years after Reese's resignation, Gutride Safier sued him for violating the withdrawal agreement, against which Reese counterclaimed that he signed the agreement under duress and the firm failed to pay him for his work. *Id.* Ruling that the case presented a false conflict, the court applied California law and dismissed those counterclaims as time-barred. *Id.* at *4 & *10.

Does the *Reese* case really present a "false conflict . . . within the meaning of choice-of-law analysis," *id.* at *5, as the court believes? The court contends that, even if the strength of each state's interest was a factor to consider, California would prevail over New York because "Mr. Reese does not make any allegation in his counterclaims that he exclusively performed services in New York." *Id.* at *6. Considering that, as the court acknowledges, Reese was "brought into the firm in order to establish a New York presence," *id.* at *4, are New York's interests so trivial as to justify the court's conclusion?

(3) Is there any less danger in the *Bernkrant* case than in a purely domestic California case of fraud on the estate of the deceased? If not, what justification is there for submerging the apparent California policy against enforcement of alleged oral agreements?

(4) One of the greatest points of attack on Currie's theory involved the principle contained in section 4 of his "Restatement," since it disallowed a weighing of state interests. Currie's rationale was that the judge, as an appointed or elected official of a given state, had no right to declare the policy of another state to be more important. On the other hand, yielding somewhat to his critics, Currie added section 3 of his "Restatement" to encourage judges to take a second look at the interests of the forum when an "apparent" conflict was found. But Currie was not altogether clear as to how far a court should go in being altruistic or in softening the interests of the forum when measured against the interests of other states. Is there a difference between weighing and being altruistic or avoiding "ruthlessness"?

Regardless of Currie's attitude, most others have engaged in some sort of weighing. As the late Professor Ehrenzweig put it: "As far as I can see, *all* courts and writers who have professed acceptance of Currie's interest language have transformed it by indulging in that very weighing and balancing of interests from which Currie refrained." Ehrenzweig, *A Counter-Revolution in Conflicts*

Laws? From Beale to Cavers, 80 Harv. L. Rev. 377, 389 (1966). Is this true of the *Lilienthal* case?

(5) Are you satisfied that the *Lilienthal* court did an adequate job of determining the interests of Oregon when it invoked the proposition that the legislature had already balanced the competing factors by passing the spendthrift law? Assuming, as we have since Alabama Great Southern Railroad v. Carroll, page 15 *supra*, that legislatures usually pass statutes with only domestic cases in mind, doesn't the court's reasoning in effect deny that the factors involved in a domestic spendthrift case are identical to those in an interstate conflicts case? Won't the court's approach mean that the forum will always apply its own statute if there is any basis at all for doing so?

c.   Unprovided-for Cases

Hurtado v. Superior Court

11 Cal. 3d 574, 522 P.2d 666, 114 Cal. Rptr. 106 (1974)

SULLIVAN, J.

In this proceeding, petitioner Manuel Cid Hurtado seeks a writ of mandate directing respondent superior court to vacate its ruling that the applicable measure of damages in the underlying action for wrongful death was that prescribed by California law without any maximum limitation, rather than that prescribed by the law of Mexico which limits the amount of recovery. We have concluded that the trial court correctly chose the law of California. We deny the writ.

Real parties in interest, the widow and children of Antonio Hurtado (hereinafter plaintiffs) commenced against Manuel Hurtado and Jack Rexius (hereafter defendants) the underlying action for damages for wrongful death, arising out of an automobile accident occurring in Sacramento County on January 19, 1969. Plaintiffs' decedent was riding in an automobile owned and operated by his cousin, defendant Manuel Hurtado. Defendant Hurtado's vehicle, while being driven along a two-lane paved road, collided with a pickup truck, owned and operated by defendant Rexius, which was parked partially on the side of the road and partially on the pavement on which defendant Hurtado was driving. Upon impact, the truck in turn collided with an automobile parked in front of it, owned by Rexius and occupied by his son. Decedent died as a result of the collision.

At all material times plaintiffs were, and now are residents and domiciliaries of the State of Zacatecas, Mexico. Decedent, at the time of the accident, was also a resident and domiciliary of the same place and was in California temporarily and only as a visitor. All three vehicles involved in the accident were registered in California; Manuel Hurtado, Jack Rexius and the latter's son were all residents of California. Both defendants denied liability.

Defendant Hurtado moved respondent court for a separate trial of the issue whether the measure of damages was to be applied according to the law of California or the law of Mexico. The motion was granted and at the ensuing trial of this issue the court took judicial notice (Evid. Code, §§452, 453) of the relevant Mexican law prescribing a maximum limitation of damages for wrongful death. As a result it was established that the maximum amount recoverable under

Mexican law would be 24,334 pesos or $1,946.72 at the applicable exchange rate of 12.5 pesos to the dollar. After submission of the issue on briefs, the trial court announced its intended decision and filed a memorandum opinion, ruling in substance that it would apply a measure of damages in accordance with California law and not Mexican law. Defendant Hurtado then sought a writ of mandate in the Court of Appeal to compel the trial court to vacate its ruling and to issue a ruling that Mexico's limitation of damages for wrongful death be applied. The Court of Appeal granted an alternative writ and thereafter issued a peremptory writ of mandate so directing the trial court. We granted a hearing in this court upon the petition of plaintiffs. . . .

In the landmark opinion authored by former Chief Justice Traynor for a unanimous court in Reich v. Purcell (1967) 67 Cal. 2d 551, 63 Cal. Rptr. 31, 432 P.2d 727 (*see Symposium, Comments on Reich v. Purcell (1968)* 15 U.C.L.A. L. Rev. 551-654), we renounced the prior rule, adhered to by courts for many years, that in tort actions the law of the place of the wrong was the applicable law in a California forum regardless of the issues before the court. We adopted in its place a rule requiring an analysis of the respective interests of the states involved (governmental interest approach) the objective of which is "to determine the law that most appropriately applies to the issue involved.". . .

The issue involved in the matter before us is the measure of damages in the underlying action for wrongful death. Two states or governments are implicated: (1) California—the place of the wrong, the place of defendants' domicile and residence, and the forum; and (2) Mexico—the domicile and residence of both plaintiffs and their decedent. . . .

In the case at bench, California as the forum should apply its own measure of damages for wrongful death, unless Mexico has an interest in having its measure of damages applied. Since, as we have previously explained, Mexico has no interest whatsoever in the application of its limitation of damages rule to the instant case, we conclude that the trial court correctly chose California law.

To recapitulate, we hold that whereas here in a California action both this state as the forum and a foreign state (or country) are potentially concerned in a question of choice of law with respect to an issue in tort and it appears that the foreign state (or country) has no interest whatsoever in having its own law applied, California as the forum should apply California law. Since this was done, we deny the writ.

Nevertheless, although our holding disposes of the mandamus proceeding before us, we deem it advisable to consider the argument addressed by defendant to the interest of California in applying its measure of damages for wrongful death. We do this because the argument reflects a serious misreading of *Reich* which apparently has not been confined to the parties before us.

First, defendant contends that California has no interest in applying its measure of damages in this case because Reich v. Purcell determined that the interest of a state in the law governing damages in wrongful death actions is "in determining the distribution of proceeds to the beneficiaries and that interest extends only to local decedents and beneficiaries." Decedent and plaintiffs were residents of Mexico and not "local decedents and beneficiaries" in California. Therefore, so the argument runs, California has *no* interest whatever in how plaintiff survivors, residents of Mexico, should be compensated for the wrongful death of their decedent, also a resident of Mexico, and conversely Mexico *does* have an interest.

Defendant's reading of *Reich* is inaccurate. It confuses two completely independent state interests: (1) the state interest involved in *creating* a cause of action for wrongful death so as to provide *some* recovery; and (2) the state interest involved in *limiting* the *amount* of that recovery. In *Reich* this court carefully separated these two state interests, although it referred to them in the same paragraph. The state interest in creating a cause of action for wrongful death is in "determining the distribution of proceeds to the beneficiaries"; the state interest in limiting damage is "to avoid the imposition of excessive financial burdens on them [defendants]."

In the case at bench, the entire controversy revolves about the choice of an appropriate rule of decision on the issue of the proper *measure* of damages; there is no contention that plaintiffs are not entitled under the applicable rules of decision to *some* recovery in wrongful death. The Mexican rule is a rule limiting damages. Thus, the interest of Mexico at stake is one aimed at protecting resident defendants in wrongful death actions and, as previously explained, is inapplicable to this case, because defendants are not Mexican residents. Mexico's interest in limiting damages is not concerned with providing compensation for decedent's beneficiaries. It is Mexico's interest in creating wrongful death actions which is concerned with distributing proceeds to the beneficiaries and that issue has not been raised in the case at bench.

The creation of wrongful death actions "insofar as plaintiffs are concerned" is directed toward compensating decedent's beneficiaries. California does not have this interest in applying its wrongful death statute here because plaintiffs are residents of Mexico. However, the creation of wrongful death actions is not concerned solely with plaintiffs. As to defendants the state interest in creating wrongful death actions is to deter conduct. . . .

It is manifest that one of the primary purposes of a state in creating a cause of action in the heirs for the wrongful death of the decedent is to deter the kind of conduct within its borders which wrongfully takes life. It is also abundantly clear that a cause of action for wrongful death without any limitation as to the amount of recoverable damages strengthens the deterrent aspect of the civil sanction: "the sting of unlimited recovery . . . more effectively penalize[s] the culpable defendant and deter[s] it and others similarly situated from such future conduct." Therefore when the defendant is a resident of California and the tortious conduct giving rise to the wrongful death action occurs here, California's deterrent policy of full compensation is clearly advanced by application of its own law. . . .

It is important, therefore, to recognize the three distinct aspects of a cause of action for wrongful death: (1) compensation for survivors, (2) deterrence of conduct and (3) limitation, or lack thereof, upon the damages recoverable. Reich v. Purcell recognizes that all three aspects are primarily local in character. The first aspect, insofar as *plaintiffs* are concerned, reflects the state's interest in providing for compensation and in determining the distribution of the proceeds, said interest extending only to local decedents and local beneficiaries; the second, insofar as *defendants* are concerned, reflects the state's interest in deterring conduct, said interest extending to all persons present within its border; the third, insofar as *defendants* are concerned, reflects the state's interest in protecting resident defendants from excessive financial burdens. In making a choice of law, these three aspects of wrongful death must be carefully separated. The key step in this process is delineating the issue to be decided. . . .

Defendant's final contention is that California has no interest in extending to out-of-state residents greater rights than are afforded by the state of residence, citing Ryan v. Clark Equipment Co., *supra*. Defendant urges seemingly as an absolute choice of law principle that plaintiffs in wrongful death actions are not entitled to recover more than they would have recovered under the law of the state of their residence. In effect defendant argues that the state of plaintiffs' residence has an overriding interest in denying their own residents unlimited recovery.

Limitations of damages express no such state interest. A policy of limiting recovery in wrongful death actions "does not reflect a preference that widows and orphans should be denied full recovery.". . .

Because Mexico has no interest in applying its limitation of damages in wrongful death actions to nonresident defendants or in denying full recovery to its resident plaintiffs, the trial court both as the forum, and as an interested state, correctly looked to its own law.

. . .

The alternative writ of mandate is discharged and the petition for a peremptory writ is denied.

Questions and Comments

(1) Is there any way to take seriously the court's contention that California's refusal to place a limitation on wrongful death liability represented an affirmative policy of deterrence? Is someone likely to be (a) aware of the law and (b) insufficiently aware of the dangerousness of his own behavior to be deterred by application of the law when he is not also deterred by the danger to his own life? Even if the California refusal to place a limitation on wrongful death recoveries serves some deterrent purpose, is that deterrence likely to be diminished when the rule is not applied to victims from states with limitations? That is, is the driver-to-be-deterred likely to determine the domicile of his victim before making a decision on how careful to be?

(2) The clue to "solving" both true conflicts and unprovided-for cases would seem to be to turn them into false conflicts, a food that interest analysis can easily digest. With true conflicts, this means making one of the interests go away (as in *Bernkrant*); the artificiality of some courts' ingenious efforts to turn true conflicts into false ones is dissected in Singer, *Facing Real Conflicts*, 24 Cornell Intl. L.J. 197 (1991). With unprovided-for cases this means uncovering a new interest to fill the void. Two likely sources of interests are territorially triggered conduct-regulating interests (as in *Hurtado*) and interests in burdening locals even when they are acting outside the territory. Recall, for example, the "interest," alluded to in Schultz v. Boy Scouts of America, page 182 *supra*, that New Jersey was said to have in imposing the burden of its no-recovery rule even though the New Jersey plaintiff was injured in New York.

Such interests are convenient when they turn unprovided-for cases into false conflicts. But won't recognizing them risk turning some false conflicts into true conflicts? If two Ontario residents are driving in New York when an accident occurs, is this a true conflict because New York has an interest in deterring unsafe driving by allowing recovery by a guest against a host? Doesn't the *Hurtado* analysis suggest as much?

(3) There continues to be academic writing about the problems posed by the unprovided-for case. *See* Green, *The Return of the Unprovided-For Case*, 51 Ga. L. Rev. 763 (2017). Another possible approach to unprovided-for cases is based upon Professor Robert Sedler's discussion of *Neumeier*. Sedler says that while neither state has an interest in applying its law on the issue of guest-host immunity, the two states have a common policy of compensating the victims of negligence. That makes *Neumeier* an "easy case." Whether the policy of the guest statute is to protect drivers from ungrateful guests, to protect insurance companies from fraud, or to keep insurance rates down, neither state has an interest in applying such a policy in favor of this particular defendant. Thus, the common policy of compensation should be applied. Sedler, *Interstate Accidents and the Unprovided for Case: Reflections on* Neumeier v. Kuehner, 1 Hofstra L. Rev. 125, 137-139 (1973). In *Hurtado*, one might discern a similar shared policy of allowing compensation.

Isn't Sedler getting off the hook a bit too easily? If the "ingratitude" policy is the right one, doesn't it reflect a desire not only to protect the defendant but also to keep the plaintiff from recovery on the grounds that one should not bite the hand that feeds? Dean Ely's criticism of Sedler's argument is that Ontario had no policy (shared or otherwise) for allowing a New Yorker to recover under a cause of action that it refused to recognize, while New York policy simply did not extend to Ontario plaintiffs at all. Ely, *Choice of Law and the State's Interest in Protecting Its Own*, 23 Wm. & Mary L. Rev. 173, 202-203 (1981). Does this theory of "common policies" make any sense?

3. Theoretical Criticisms of Interest Analysis

Since Currie's writings, interest analysis has garnered both strong supporters and harsh critics in the academy. Some find the whole debate of little consequence, *see* Sterk, *The Marginal Relevance of Choice of Law Theory*, 142 U. Pa. L. Rev. 949 (1994), but the debate nevertheless continues. Critics tend to attack along three lines. The first we have already seen: namely, that interest analysis has no good resolution of true conflicts. This is probably the least fundamental, because it accepts Currie's basic definition of interests and his identification of false conflicts. We have outlined his solution to true conflicts above, and our discussion below of other modern theories will describe the resolution that other authors have proposed.

The second criticism acknowledges the role that "policies" might play in choice-of-law analysis, but denies that Currie's methods for identifying interests are appropriate. In particular, a number of authors disagree with Currie's suggestion that a state has an interest in applying its law when doing so would protect a local defendant or compensate a local plaintiff. *See, e.g.,* Corr, *Interest Analysis and Choice of Law: The Dubious Dominance of Domicile*, 4 Utah L. Rev. 651

(1983). Dean Ely has been an especially forceful proponent of the idea that it is wrong to define a state's interests this way. Ely, *supra*. For one thing, this definition of "interests" seems somewhat discriminatory—a problem that we will return to in our discussion of constitutional doctrine in Chapter 4; for another, defining interests this way has certain surprising consequences. As Ely notes, this definition of interests turns all common domicile cases into false conflicts (as it does all cases where the parties are from different states with identical laws). *Id.* at 206-207. The reason is that if only domiciliary factors can trigger interests and if the parties share a domicile, there is only one state that can have an interest. False conflicts are easy to resolve because once a court decides to disregard all connecting variables other than domicile, and if all remaining variables point toward the same state, the answer is obvious.

When the parties are from states with different laws and there is no regulatory interest complicating matters, then the case is either a true conflict or an unprovided-for case, depending on whether each party prefers home-state law (as in *Lilienthal*) or each party prefers the law of the other party's home state (as in *Hurtado*). Currie's original solution was to apply forum law. Without repeatory interests, his method can therefore be summarized in a single sentence: In cases of shared domicile, apply that jurisdiction's law, but otherwise apply forum law. If one starts with a presumption that local law is designed to benefit local people, then one does not need to investigate policies at length, or even to know the content of the competing laws. One can select which jurisdiction's law to apply based on only one fact: whether the litigants come from states with the identical legal rule. Brilmayer, *Rights, Fairness, and Choice of Law*, 99 Yale L.J. 1277, 1315 (1989).

The third line of criticism of interest analysis goes beyond the argument that the definition of interests incorporates a preference for local residents. It attacks the notion that the goal of modern choice-of-law theory is, and ought to be, the effectuation of legislative policy. On the question of whether the method actually effectuates legislative policy, it has been argued that, as carried out, Currie's notion of interests did not reflect *legislative* policy but, rather, Currie's own peculiar normative vision about how far legislation ought to reach. Brilmayer, *Interest Analysis and the Myth of Legislative Intent*, 78 Mich. L. Rev. 392 (1980). *See also* Borchers, *Professor Brilmayer and the Holy Grail*, 1991 Wis. L. Rev. 465, 473. One scholar has even argued that "the movement sparked by Brainerd Currie has worked to defeat states' abilities to promote their policies." O'Hara O'Connor, *How Modern Choice of Law Helped to Kill the Private Attorney General*, 64 Mercer L. Rev. 1023, 1045 (2013). Sedler responds to the former critics by explaining the idea of legislative policy as follows:

> One reason that the critics of interest analysis have seen such difficulty in determining the policies behind the laws of the involved states is their failure to distinguish between legislative purpose and legislative motivation. Legislative purpose refers to the objectives a law is designed to accomplish, while legislative motivation may be defined as factors stimulating enactment of a law. For example, if the legislature imposes a limit on the amount recoverable for wrongful death, its purpose obviously is to limit damages awards in such cases, and the policy reflected in such a law is to protect defendants and insurers from what the legislature considers to be excessive liability. Motivation, however, may vary from one legislator to the next. Some may have feared excessive verdicts in wrongful death cases and believed that such verdicts would be unjust. Others

may have been concerned about rising insurance premiums. Others simply may have responded to the pressures of the insurance lobby.

In determining, both in the conflicts and non-conflicts situation, the policy behind a rule of substantive law, what is relevant is legislative purpose, not legislative motivation. That purpose can be determined from the provisions of the law itself, viewed functionally and in relation to other laws of the state dealing with the same subject. As the example above indicates, a collective motivation cannot be ascribed to the legislature, but a collective purpose can. That purpose must be found in the provisions of the law that the legislature has enacted. It is this collective purpose that determines the policy behind a rule of substantive law under interest analysis.

Sedler, *The Governmental Interest Approach to Choice of Law: An Analysis and Reformulation*, 25 UCLA L. Rev. 181, 197 (1977). Does this mean that any actual legislative preferences about the intended territorial scope of a statute are irrelevant in determining whether an interest exists? *See* Weintraub, *Interest Analysis in the Conflict of Laws as an Application of Sound Legal Reasoning*, 35 Mercer L. Rev. 629, 631 (1984); Posnak, *Choice of Law: Interest Analysis and Its "New Crits,"* 36 Am. J. Comp. L. 681, 687 n.42 (1988). If so, then how is the process of ascertaining "interests" simply the usual domestic process of statutory construction, as Currie asserted? Professor Brilmayer has argued that "[under interest analysis, t]he ultimate irony is that the closer one looks, the more one finds that the so-called policy analysts do not care at all about what policy making institutions, the legislatures and common law courts, would prefer the territorial reach of their substantive decisions to be." Brilmayer, *Governmental Interest Analysis: A House Without Foundations*, 46 Ohio St. L.J. 459, 461-462 (1985).

The most articulate attempt to reformulate governmental interest analysis is found in the prolific writings of Professor (and Dean) Larry Kramer. Kramer begins with one of Currie's central assumptions: that determining the proper territorial scope of a statute is not an essentially different enterprise from determining the statute's scope in domestic controversies. From this assumption follow the usual categories of false conflict, true conflict, and unprovided-for case (or, as he puts it, cases where one law provides a right, two laws provide a right, or no law provides a right). *See generally* Kramer, *Rethinking Choice of Law*, 90 Colum. L. Rev. 277 (1990). His analysis departs from Currie's in that he takes a much broader and more open-minded view about which connecting factors might give rise to a reason for applying local law. In particular, as will be discussed at page 256 *infra*, he advises the court to defer to another state's definition of its own interests, even when that state defines its interests in old-fashioned territorial terms. Kramer is therefore not bound to rigid notions about statutory application being tied to providing benefits for locals. He also rejects Currie's argument that forum law should presumptively apply, unless affirmative arguments can be given for displacing it. *Interest Analysis and the Presumption of Forum Law*, 56 U. Chi. L. Rev. 1301 (1989). His suggestions have not yet found widespread acceptance among interest analysts.

We will return to the problems of domicile and of ascertaining interests, for these problems are common to other modern choice-of-law theory as well. *See* pages 250-253 *infra*. On the jurisprudential issue of whether choice of law ought simply to address the implementation of legislative substantive policy, *see* Dane, *Vested*

Rights, Vestedness, and Choice of Law, 96 Yale L.J. 1191 (1987); Brilmayer, *Rights, Fairness, and Choice of Law*, 99 Yale L.J. 1277 (1989). For a defense that modern choice of law should, and does, concern itself with which state will experience the consequences of the judgment, *see* Weintraub, *An Approach to Choice of Law that Focuses on Consequences*, 56 Alb. L. Rev. 701 (1993).

4. A Short Note on Interest Analysis in Other Nations

In many countries, there is keen academic and judicial attention to developments in choice-of-law theory, and the events of the last few decades in the United States have provoked a fair amount of controversy.

While generalizations are made at one's peril, it is fair to say that most European countries (and many countries in other parts of the world) start with a substantial fundamental commitment to what Americans would view as traditional choice-of-law rules. However, the new methods have nonetheless provoked considerable interest around the world. A Canadian author, Professor William Maslechko, concedes that the new methods are relatively foreign to Canadian jurisprudence, but believes that Canadian courts are increasingly approaching choice-of-law problems in a functional manner, and he applauds this development. *Revolution and Counter-Revolution: An Examination of the Continuing Debate over "Interest Analysis" in the United States and Its Relevance to Canadian Conflict of Laws*, 44 U. Toronto L. Rev. 57 (1986). Another enthusiast is Professor Strikwerda of the Netherlands. "Interest analysis," he writes, "is a well-founded and rational approach to the choice-of-law problem." *Interest Analysis: No More than a "Protest Song"?* in Sumampouw, *Law and Reality: Essays on National and International Procedural Law* 301 (1992). "Clearly, the interest approach to choice of law has been the catalyst of the renovation in this field of law, even in Europe. And in my view benefits can still be reaped from interest analysis in present-day choice-of-law problems." *Id.* at 313. This is not to say that the Dutch view is uniformly positive; Professor Ted de Boer's exhaustive study of choice of law, *Beyond Lex Loci Delicti* (1987), which studied American practice in great detail, was noticeably less positive.

A French author states that the influence of American choice-of-law theory is "incontestable." Hanotiau, *The American Conflicts Revolution and European Tort Choice of Law Thinking*, 30 Am. J. Comp. L. 1, 73 (1982). He includes the Restatement of Conflicts Second and other modern theories in this assessment. Another French author concludes that the inroads modern American choice-of-law methods have made on traditional Continental thinking is "more limited than may generally be believed." Audit, *A Continental Lawyer Looks at Contemporary American Choice-of-Law Principles*, 27 Am. J. Comp. L. 589, 589 (1979).

One South African writer states flatly that the modern methods are "not for export elsewhere." Forsyth, *Private International Law* 50 (1990). Another writes,

As far as the conflict of laws of contracts is concerned, it has not been possible for me to trace any influential or significant follower in Europe of the new American theories. I have not found any writer of renown who in this field has seriously advocated replacement of the traditional structure of the conflict-of-law rule with the new structures proposed by Cavers, Currie and other Americans of the same schools. Why have these ideas had so little impact upon European thinking? Although a number of European jurists may think in grooves, they are not *all* incapable of accepting new ideas.

The explanation is probably that the new theories have been difficult to apply to the European situation. Lando, *New American Choice-of-Law Principles and the European Conflict of Laws of Contracts*, 30 Am. J. Comp. L. 19, 25 (1982). Professor Fawcett states that it is "only in tort choice of law that [governmental interest analysis] has found favour in England." *Is American Governmental Interest Analysis the Solution to English Tort Choice of Law Problems?*, 31 Intl. & Comp. L.Q. 150, 150 (1982).

Two Australian authors have, perhaps, the ultimate put-down:

> The need for [modernizing choice of law] has led to a welter of views from American writers among which are to be found emphasis on policy comparisons and evaluations, on 'governmental interests,' on the reconciliation of conflicts interests within a framework of 'conflicts justice,' on 'most significant contact,' on 'principles of preference' and so on. Many writers are fond of the word 'functional' and many seem to feel the job of solution is done once they have used this magic word and verbally discarded 'conceptual thinking' and 'mechanistic processes.' One is disposed to think that some kind of jumping on the band-wagon is involved.

Sykes & Prykes, *Australian Private International Law* 203 (3d ed. 1991).

C.   Comparative Impairment

Because Currie's concept and resolution of false conflicts is generally accepted by interest analysts, academics since Currie have concentrated on finding more satisfactory solutions to the true conflict case. Currie initially said the law of the forum should be applied in a true conflict. An element of game theory seems implicit in Currie's thinking: If someone could propose a solution to the true conflict case that would, in the long run, advance the interests of all states, that solution would be desirable. But in the absence of such a solution, the only proper thing for a judge to do is to be "true to his or her state." Normative evaluations of competing state laws must be rejected because they would elevate the judge above the local legislature. Similarly, approaches that weigh the relative importance of state laws are rejected because such decisions were political and therefore best left to the legislature.

Professor William Baxter proposed a modification of interest analysis called "comparative impairment."* It directs a court in the true conflict situation to apply

---

* Baxter, *Choice of Law and the Federal System*, 16 Stan. L. Rev. 1 (1963).

the law of the state whose policies would be most impaired (if such is determinable) by rejection of its rules. Weighing of the interests is rejected; but weighing of the harm that would be caused by refusing to carry out interests in particular cases is not. In the long run, such an approach, if engaged in by all jurisdictions, should result in benefit to each, since each will have "given in" in cases where the harm to its own interests was minimal, and "won" in cases where the harm would have been greater. In game theory terms, comparative impairment produced a positive sum game whereas, under Currie's analysis, true conflicts were treated as zero-sum games.

Several scholars have focused on the possibility that all states might be made better off if courts, through mutual cooperation, resolved true conflicts by applying the law of the state with a greater concern. *See, e.g.*, Brilmayer, *Conflict of Laws: Foundations and Future Directions*, chapter 4 (1991); Kramer, *Rethinking Choice of Law*, 90 Colum. L. Rev. 277, 315 (1990). Others doubt that the game theory analogy is appropriate; *see, e.g.*, Borchers, *Professor Brilmayer and the Holy Grail*, 1991 Wis. L. Rev. 465, 479; Weinberg, *Against Comity*, 80 Geo. L.J. 53, 55 (1991).

Bernhard v. Harrah's Club
16 Cal. 3d 313, 546 P.2d 719, 128 Cal. Rptr. 215 (1976)

SULLIVAN, J.

Plaintiff's complaint, containing only one count, alleged in substance the following: Defendant Harrah's Club, a Nevada corporation, owned and operated gambling establishments in the State of Nevada in which intoxicating liquors were sold, furnished to the public and given away for consumption on the premises. Defendant advertised for and solicited in California the business of California residents at such establishments knowing and expecting that many California residents would use the public highways in going to and from defendant's drinking and gambling establishments.

On July 24, 1971, Fern and Philip Myers, in response to defendant's advertisements and solicitations, drove from their California residence to defendant's gambling and drinking club in Nevada, where they stayed until the early morning hours of July 25, 1971. During their stay, the Myers were served numerous alcoholic beverages by defendant's employees, progressively reaching a point of intoxication rendering them incapable of safely driving a car. Nonetheless defendant continued to serve and furnish the Myers alcoholic beverages.

While still in this intoxicated state, the Myers drove their car back to California. Proceeding in a northeasterly direction on Highway 49, near Nevada City, California, the Myers' car, driven negligently by a still intoxicated Fern Myers, drifted across the center line into the lane of oncoming traffic and collided head-on with plaintiff Richard A. Bernhard, a resident of California, who was then driving his motorcycle along said highway. As a result of the collision, plaintiff suffered severe injuries. Defendant's sale and furnishing of alcoholic beverages to the Myers, who were intoxicated to the point of being unable to drive safely, was negligent and was the proximate cause of the plaintiff's injuries in the ensuing automobile accident in California for which plaintiff payed $100,000 in damages.

. . . We face a problem in the choice of law governing a tort action. As we have made clear on other occasions, we no longer adhere to the rule that the law of the place of the wrong is applicable in California forum regardless of the issues before this court. Hurtado v. Superior Court. Rather we have adopted in its place a rule requiring an analysis of the respective interests of the states involved—the objective of which is "to determine the law that most appropriately applies to the issue involved." *Hurtado*.

The issue involved in the case at bench is the civil liability of defendant tavern keeper to plaintiff, a third person, for injuries allegedly caused by the former by selling and furnishing alcoholic beverages in Nevada to intoxicated patrons who subsequently injured plaintiff in California. Two states are involved: (1) California—the place of plaintiff's residence and domicile, the place where he was injured, and the forum; and (2) Nevada—the place of defendant's residence and the place of the wrong.

We observe at the start that the laws of the two states—California and Nevada—applicable to the issue involved are not identical. California imposes liability on tavern keepers in this state for conduct such as here alleged. In Vesely v. Sager, *supra*, this court rejected the contention that

> civil liability for tavern keepers should be left to future legislative action. . . . First, liability has been denied in cases such as the one before us solely because of the judicially created rule that the furnishing of alcoholic beverages is not the proximate cause of injuries resulting from intoxication. As demonstrated, *supra*, this rule is patently unsound and totally inconsistent with the principles of proximate cause established in other areas of negligence law. . . . Second, the Legislature has expressed its intention in this area with the adoption of Evidence Code section 669, and Business and Professions Code section 25602. . . . It is clear that Business and Professions Code section 25602 [making it a misdemeanor to sell to an obviously intoxicated person] is a statute to which this presumption [of negligence, Evidence Code section 669] applies and that the policy expressed in the statute is to promote safety of the people of California. . . .

Nevada on the other hand refuses to impose such liability. In Hamm v. Carson City Nuggett, Inc., the court held it would create neither common law liability nor liability based on the criminal statute banning sale of alcoholic beverages to a person who is drunk, because "if civil liability is to be imposed, it should be accomplished by legislative act after appropriate surveys, hearings, and investigations to ascertain the need for it and the expected consequences to follow." It is noteworthy that in *Hamm* the Nevada court in relying on the common law rule denying liability cited our decision in Cole v. Rush, later overruled by us in *Vesely* to the extent that it was inconsistent with that decision.

Although California and Nevada, the two "involved states," have different laws governing the issue presented in the case at bench, we encounter a problem in selecting the applicable rule of law only if *both* states have an interest in having their respective laws applied. "[G]enerally speaking the forum will apply its own rule of decision unless a party litigant timely invokes the law of a foreign state. In such event he must demonstrate that the latter rule of decision will further the interest of the foreign state and therefore that it is an appropriate one for the forum to apply to the case before it." *Hurtado, supra*.

Defendant contends that Nevada has a definite interest in having its rule of decision applied in this case in order to protect its resident tavern keepers like defendant from being subjected to a civil liability which Nevada has not imposed either by legislative enactment or decisional law. It is urged that in *Hamm, supra,* the Supreme Court of Nevada clearly delineated the policy underlying denial of civil liability of tavern keepers who sell to obviously intoxicated patrons:

> Those opposed to extending liability point out that to hold otherwise would subject the tavern owner to ruinous exposure every time he poured a drink and would multiply litigation endlessly in a claim-conscious society. Every liquor vendor visited by the patron who became intoxicated would be a likely defendant in subsequent litigation flowing from the patron's wrongful conduct. . . . Judicial restraint is a worthwhile practice when the proposed new doctrine may have implications far beyond the perception of the court asked to declare it. They urge that if civil liability is to be imposed, it should be accomplished by legislative act after appropriate surveys, hearings, and investigations. . . . We prefer this point of view.

Accordingly defendant argues that the Nevada rule of decision is the appropriate one for the forum to apply.

Plaintiff on the other hand points out that California also has an interest in applying its own rule of decision to the case at bench. California imposes on tavern keepers civil liability to third parties injured by persons to whom the tavern keeper has sold alcoholic beverages when they are obviously intoxicated "for the purpose of protecting members of the general public from injuries to person and damage to property resulting from the excessive use of intoxicating liquor." Vesely v. Sager, *supra*. California, it is urged, has a special interest in affording this protection to all California residents injured in California.

Thus, since the case at bench involves a California resident (plaintiff) injured in this state by intoxicated drivers and a Nevada resident tavern keeper (defendant) which served alcoholic beverages to them in Nevada, it is clear that each state has an interest in the application of its respective law of liability and nonliability. It goes without saying that these interests conflict. Therefore, unlike . . . Hurtado v. Superior Court, *supra*, where we were faced with "false conflicts," in the instant case . . . we are confronted with a "true" conflicts case. We must therefore determine the appropriate rule of decision in a controversy where each of the states involved has a legitimate but conflicting interest in applying its own law in respect to the civil liability of tavern keepers.

The search for the proper resolution of a true conflicts case, while proceeding within orthodox parameters of governmental interest analysis, has generated much scholarly examination and discussion. The father of the governmental interest approach, Professor Brainerd Currie, originally took the position that in a true conflicts situation the law of the forum should always be applied. Currie, *Selected Essays on Conflicts of Laws* (1963), p. 184. However, upon further reflection, Currie suggested that when under the governmental interest approach a preliminary analysis reveals an apparent conflict of interest upon the forum's assertion of its own rule of decision, the forum should reexamine its policy to determine if a more restrained interpretation of it is more appropriate.

> To assert a conflict between the interests of the forum and the foreign state is a serious matter; the mere fact that a suggested broad conception of a local interest will conflict with that of a foreign state is a sound reason why the conception should be reexamined, with a view to a more moderate and restrained interpretation both of the policy and of the circumstances in which it must be applied to effectuate the forum's legitimate purpose. . . . An analysis of this kind . . . was brilliantly performed by Justice Traynor in Bernkrant v. Fowler.

Currie, *The Disinterested Third State (1963)* 28 Law & Contemp. Prob., pp. 754, 757; *see also* Sedler in *Symposium, Conflict of Laws Round Table, supra,* 49 Texas L. Rev. 211, at pp. 224-225. This process of reexamination requires identification of a "real interest as opposed to a hypothetical interest" on the part of the forum Sedler, *Value of Principled Preferences,* 49 Texas L. Rev. 224 and can be approached under principles of "comparative impairment." Baxter, *supra,* at 1-22.

Once this preliminary analysis has identified a true conflict of the governmental interests involved as applied to the parties under the particular circumstances of the case, the "comparative impairment" approach to the resolution of such conflict seeks to determine which state's interest would be more impaired if its policy were subordinated to the policy of the other state. This analysis proceeds on the principle that true conflicts should be resolved by applying the law of the state whose interest would be the more impaired if its law were not applied. Exponents of this process of analysis emphasize that it is very different from a weighing process. The court does not

> "weigh" the conflicting governmental interests in the sense of determining which conflicting law manifested the "better" or the "worthier" social policy on the specific issue. An attempted balancing of conflicting state policies in that sense . . . is difficult to justify in the context of a federal system in which, within constitutional limits, states are empowered to mold their polices as they wish. . . . [The process] can accurately be described as . . . accommodation of conflicting state policies, as a problem of allocating domains of lawmaking power in multi-state contexts—limitations on the reach of state policies as distinguished from evaluating wisdom of those policies. . . . [E]mphasis is placed on the appropriate scope of conflicting state policies rather than on the "quality of those policies. . . ."

Horowitz, *The Law of Choice of Law in California—A Restatement,* 21 UCLA L. Rev. 719, 753; *see also* Baxter, *supra,* at 18-19. However, the true function of this methodology can probably be appreciated only casuistically in its application to an endless variety of choice of law problems.

. . .

Mindful of the above principles governing our choice of law, we proceed to reexamine the California policy underlying the imposition of civil liability upon tavern keepers. At its broadest limits this policy would afford protection to all persons injured in California by intoxicated persons who have been sold or furnished alcoholic beverages while intoxicated regardless of where such beverages were sold or furnished. Such a broad policy would naturally embrace situations where the intoxicated actor had been provided with liquor by out-of-state tavern keepers.

Although the State of Nevada does not impose such *civil* liability on its tavern keepers, nevertheless they are subject to *criminal* penalties under a statute making it unlawful to sell or give intoxicating liquor to any person who is drunk or known to be a habitual drunkard.

We need not, and accordingly do not here determine the outer limits to which California's policy should be extended, for it appears clear to us that it must encompass defendant, who as alleged in the complaint,

> advertis[es] for and otherwise solicit[s] in California the business of California residents at defendant Harrah's Club Nevada drinking and gambling establishments, knowing and expecting said California residents, in response to said advertising and solicitation, to use the public highways of the State of California in going and coming from defendant Harrah's Club Nevada drinking and gambling establishments.

Defendant by the course of its chosen commercial practice has put itself at the heart of California's regulatory interest, namely to prevent tavern keepers from selling alcoholic beverages to obviously intoxicated persons who are likely to act in California in the intoxicated state. It seems clear that California cannot reasonably effectuate its policy if it does not extend its regulation to include out-of-state tavern keepers such as defendant who regularly and purposely sell intoxicating beverages to California residents in places and under conditions in which it is reasonably certain these residents will return to California and act therein while still in an intoxicated state. California's interest would be very significantly impaired if its policy were not applied to defendant.

Since the act of selling alcoholic beverages to obviously intoxicated persons is already proscribed in Nevada, the application of California's rule of civil liability would not impose an entirely new duty requiring the ability to distinguish between California residents and other patrons. Rather the imposition of such liability involves an increased economic exposure, which, at least for businesses which actively solicit extensive California patronage, is a foreseeable and coverable business expense. Moreover, Nevada's interest in protecting its tavern keepers from civil liability of a boundless and unrestricted nature will not be significantly impaired when as in the instant case liability is imposed only on those tavern keepers who actively solicit California business.

Therefore, upon reexamining the policy underlying California's rule of decision and giving such policy a more restrained interpretation for the purpose of this case pursuant to the principles of the law of choice of law discussed above, we conclude that California has an important and abiding interest in applying its rule of decision to the case at bench, that the policy of this state would be more significantly impaired if such rule were not applied and that the trial court erred in not applying California law.

Defendant argues, however, that even if California law is applied, the demurrer was nonetheless properly sustained because the tavern keeper's duty stated in Vesely v. Sager, *supra*, is based on Business and Professions Code section 25602, which is a criminal statute and thus without extraterritorial effect. It is quite true, as defendant argues, that in *Vesely* we determined "that civil liability results when a vendor furnishes alcoholic beverages to a customer in violation of Business and

Professions Code section 25602 and each of the conditions set forth in Evidence Code section 669, subdivision (a) is established."

It is also clear, as defendant's argument points out, that since, unlike the California vendor in *Vesely*, defendant was a Nevada resident which furnished the alcoholic beverage to the Myers in that state, the above California statute had no extraterritorial effect and that civil liability could not be posited on defendant's violation of a California criminal law. We recognize, therefore, that we cannot make the same determination as quoted above with respect to defendant that we made with respect to the defendant vendor in *Vesely*.

However, our decision in *Vesely* was much broader than defendant would have it. There, at the very outset of our opinion, we declared that the traditional common law rule denying recovery on the ground that the furnishing of alcoholic beverage is not the proximate cause of the injuries inflicted on a third person by an intoxicated individual "is patently unsound." 5 Cal. 3d at p.157. Observing that "[u]ntil fairly recently, it was uniformly held that [such] an action could not be maintained at common law," *id*. at 158, and reviewing in detail the common law rule, we concluded that "the furnishing of an alcoholic beverage to an intoxicated person may be a proximate cause of injuries inflicted by that individual upon a third person." We reasoned: "If such furnishing is a proximate cause, it is so because the consumption, resulting intoxication, and injury-producing conduct are foreseeable intervening causes, or at least the injury-producing conduct is one of the hazards which makes such furnishing negligent."

Proceeding to the question of the tavern keeper's duty in this respect and rejecting his contention that civil liability for tavern keepers should be left to future legislative action, we noted that

> liability has been denied in cases such as the one before us solely because of the judicially created rule that the furnishing of alcoholic beverages is not the proximate cause of injuries resulting from intoxication. As demonstrated, this rule is patently unsound and totally inconsistent with the principles of proximate cause established in other areas of negligence law. Other common law tort rules which were determined to be lacking in validity have been abrogated by this court and there is no sound reason for retaining the common law rule presented in this case.

In sum, our opinion in *Vesely* struck down the old common law rule of non-liability constructed on the basis that the consumption, not the sale, of alcoholic beverages was the proximate cause of injuries inflicted by the intoxicated person. Although we chose to impose liability on the *Vesely* defendant on the basis of his violating the applicable statute, the clear import of our decision was that there was no bar to civil liability under modern negligence law. Certainly, we said nothing in *Vesely* indicative of an intention to retain the former rule that an action at common law does not lie. The fact then, that in the case at bench, section 25602 of the Business and Professions Code is not applicable to this defendant in Nevada so as to warrant the imposition of civil liability on the basis of its violation, does not preclude recovery on the basis of negligence apart from the statute. Pertinent here is our observation in Rowland v. Christian. "It bears repetition that the basic policy of this state set forth by the Legislature in section 1714 of the Civil Code is that everyone is responsible for an injury caused to another by his want of ordinary care or skill in the management of his property."

Questions and Comments

(1) Is comparative impairment anything more than what Currie suggested (restraint in the interpretation of domestic policies when there is an apparent conflict) plus some of what he condemned (weighing of interests)? Professor Kanowitz thinks it sounds a lot like the latter, and adds:

> Despite the elaborate stages of the comparative impairment method revealed in *Bernhard* . . . it is hard to avoid the impression that the technique is founded essentially on an interest-counting process. This process will, in the long run, prove no more satisfactory than the contact-counting prescribed by the Second Restatement of the Conflict of Laws.

Kanowitz, *Comparative Impairment and Better Law: Grand Illusion in the Conflict of Laws*, 30 Hastings L.J. 255, 277 (1978).

(2) Even if comparative impairment is a valid theory, Professor Reppy thinks that it was misapplied to the facts of *Bernhard*:

> The court in *Bernhard* then misapplied comparative impairment to permit recovery. Nevada's interest in protecting this class of defendants, tavern keepers, from what Nevada considered to be unfair liability for injuries caused by persons becoming drunk at the tavern would have been sacrificed one hundred percent by the application of California's law imposing liability. But California's interest in seeing a California tort victim receive compensation would not have been wholly sacrificed by the application of the Nevada law, since the victim already had a cause of action against the drunk tortfeasor or could recover against his own insurer if the drunk had no liability insurance. To have deprived the California victim of a second bite at the compensation apple would not have fully defeated California's interest.

Reppy, *Eclecticism in Choice of Law: Hybrid Method or Mishmash?*, 34 Mercer L. Rev. 645.

(3) If it is California's *regulatory* interest that is at stake (and not a compensatory interest), does it make any difference that the plaintiff was a California resident? *See* Brilmayer, *Interest Analysis and the Myth of Legislative Intent*, 78 Mich. L. Rev. 392, 406 (1980).

(4) Why did the court in *Bernhard* consider it appropriate to limit the scope of its holding to those Nevada tavern owners who "actively solicit extensive California patronage"? In product-liability cases, the usual rule has become application of the law of the place of injury, rather than of the place of manufacture. Does a tavern owner anywhere within driving distance of the California border do any less to put the drunken driver into the "stream of commerce" than the manufacturer of a defective product? Doesn't the fact that the tavern owner's act was already criminal in Nevada, quite apart from his or her advertising in California, establish that Nevada's interest in protecting the tavern owner is a weak one?

(5) In 1978, the California legislature amended section 25602 of its Business and Professional Code, changing the former provision to subsection (a) and adding subsections (b) and (c). The entire statute now reads:

§25602. Sales to Drunkard or Intoxicated Person; Offense; Civil Liability

(a) Every person who sells, furnishes, gives, or causes to be sold, furnished, or given away, any alcoholic beverage to any habitual or common drunkard or to any obviously intoxicated person is guilty of a misdemeanor.

(b) No person who sells, furnishes, gives, or causes to be sold, furnished, or given away, any alcoholic beverage pursuant to subdivision (a) of this section shall be civilly liable to any injured person or the estate of such person for injuries inflicted on that person as a result of intoxication by the consumer of such alcoholic beverage.

(c) The Legislature hereby declares that this section shall be interpreted so that the holdings in cases such as Vesely v. Sager, Bernhard v. Harrah's Club and Coulter v. Superior Court be abrogated in favor of prior judicial interpretation finding the consumption of alcoholic beverages rather than the serving of alcoholic beverages as the proximate cause of injuries inflicted upon another by an intoxicated person.

Kearney v. Salomon Smith Barney, Inc.

39 Cal. 4th 95, 137 P.2d 914, 45 Cal. Rptr. 3d 730 (2006)

[California residents, clients of Salomon Smith Barney (SSB), a financial institution, brought a putative class action against SSB, alleging that SSB recorded conversations between them and SSB's brokers in its Atlanta, Georgia office, and that the recording occurred without the clients' consent in violation of California statute. A 1967 statute enacted by the California legislature created civil and criminal causes of action against any person or entity that, inter alia, records a telephone conversation without the consent, knowledge or reasonable expectation of recording, of all parties to the conversation. Any person who suffers from an unauthorized recording can sue the violator and recover the greater of $5,000 or three times the amount of actual damages sustained and can seek to enjoin and restrain any further violations of the statute. Cal. Stats. 1967, ch. 1509, §1, pp. 3584-3588, enacting Cal. Pen. Code, §§630-637.2. The clients sought injunctive relief, damages, and restitution. The Georgia legislature also enacted a privacy statute addressing the recording of telephone conversations, but it permits the recording of a conversation so long as one party to the conversation consents to that recording. Ga. Code Ann. §16-11-66. A clear majority of U.S. states permit recording with the consent of one party to the conversation (like Georgia), and about 11 states (including California) require consent by all parties to the conversation. Bast, *What's Bugging You? Inconsistencies and Irrationalities of the Law of Eavesdropping*, 47 DePaul L. Rev. 837, 870 (1998). The court concluded that both states have an interest in having their privacy statutes apply to the calls at issue, with California seeking to protect its residents from unauthorized recording and Georgia seeking to protect its residents and businesses from liability for actions taken in reasonable reliance on the protections of Georgia law.

After finding a true conflict between California and Georgia law, the court, George, C.J., continued with a comparative impairment analysis:]

A.

In considering the degree of impairment of California's interest that would result if Georgia law rather than California law were applied, we note initially that the objective of protecting individuals in California from the secret recording of confidential communications by or at the behest of another party to the communication was one of the principal purposes underlying the 1967 invasion-of-privacy enactment. . . . Assembly Speaker Unruh, the principal author of the legislation, prepared a statement that he delivered before the Senate Committee on the Judiciary in conjunction with its consideration of the bill, in which he explained the impetus for the legislation . . . : "In the first place, whereas such invasions of privacy are presently legal if one party consents to the listening in, Assembly Bill 860 would require that all parties must consent. This is a most reasonable requirement. Presently it is entirely legal for one who receives a call to be totally unaware that it is being listened to by another party. Likewise, a party may converse in person with another party who is secretly recording the conversation—he may be seriously injured by that conversation, either personally or in his business affairs—and he has no recourse at law. Assembly Bill 860 would correct this defect. It is a defect that was less meaningful before the recent development and widespread availability of eavesdropping devices, but as the advertising material which I have passed out to you indicates, it is a legal defect which is most apparent today."

In addition, it is clear that this is most certainly *not* an instance like [Offshore Rental Co. v. Continental Oil Co., 22 Cal. 3d 157, 148 Cal. Rptr. 867, 583 P.2d 721 (1978),] in which the court found that the California statute in question was "ancient" and rarely, if ever, utilized or relied upon and concluded that the state had little *current* interest in the application of its own law. On the contrary, California decisions repeatedly have invoked and vigorously enforced the provisions of section 632. [citations omitted]

Furthermore, in recent years the California Legislature has continued to add provisions to and make modifications of the invasion-of-privacy statute here at issue (see, for example, Pen. Code §§632.5-627.7 [cordless or cellular phones], 633.6 [permitting recording by victims of domestic violence upon court order]) and in addition repeatedly has enacted new legislation in related areas in an effort to increase the protection of California consumers' privacy in the face of a perceived escalation in the impingement on privacy interests caused by various business practices. (See e.g., Civ. Code §§1798.80-1798.84 [disclosure of consumer records], 1798.85-1798.86 [Social Security numbers], 1798.90.1 [driver's license information], 1798.91 [medical information], 1799-1799.2 [business records], 1799.3 [disclosure of personal information by providers of video cassette sales or rental services]). In addition, California's explicit constitutional privacy provision (Cal. Const., art. I, §1) was enacted in part specifically to protect Californians from overly intrusive business practices that were seen to pose a significant and increasing threat to personal privacy. [citations omitted]; cf. Rattray v. City of National City (9th Cir. 1994) 51 F.3d 793, 797 ["Having one's personal conversations secretly recorded may well infringe upon the right to privacy guaranteed by the California Constitution"].

Thus, we believe that California must be viewed as having a strong and continuing interest in the full and vigorous application of the provisions of section 632 prohibiting the recording of telephone conversations without the knowledge and consent of *all* parties to the conversation.

We also believe that the failure to apply section 632 in the present context would substantially undermine the protection afforded by the statute. Many companies who do business in California are national or international firms that have headquarters, administrative offices, or—in view of the recent trend toward outsourcing—at least telephone operations located outside of California. If businesses could maintain a regular practice of secretly recording all telephone conversations with their California clients or customers in which the business employee is located outside of California, that practice would represent a significant inroad into the privacy interest that the statute was intended to protect . . . an out of state company that does business in another state is required, at least as a general matter, to comply with the laws of a state and locality in which it has chosen to do business. As this court determined in *Bernhard*, . . . with regard to the need to apply California law relating to the liability of tavern owners to the out-of-state tavern owner at issue in this case, the failure to apply California law in the present context seriously would undermine the objective and purpose of the statute.

Moreover, if section 632, and, by analogy, other similar consumer-oriented privacy statutes that have been enacted in California—could not be applied effectively to out-of-state companies but only to California companies, the unequal application of the law very well might place local companies at a competitive disadvantage with their out-of-state counterparts. To the extent out-of-state companies may utilize such undisclosed recordings to further their economic interests—perhaps in selectively disclosing recordings when disclosure serves the company's interest, but not volunteering the recordings' existence (or quickly destroying them) when they would be detrimental to the company—California companies that are required to comply with California law would be disadvantaged. By contrast, application of section 632 to all companies in their dealings with California residents would treat each company equally with regard to California's concern for the privacy of the state's consumers.

In sum, we conclude that the failure to apply California law in the present context would result in a significant impairment of California's interests.

B.

By contrast, we believe that for a number of reasons, the application of California law rather than Georgia law in the context presented by the facts of this case would have a relatively less severe effect on Georgia's interests.

First, because California law, with regard to the particular matter here at issue, is more protective of privacy interests than the comparable Georgia privacy statute, the application of California law would not violate any privacy interest protected by Georgia law. In addition, there is, of course, nothing in Georgia law that *requires* any person or business to record a telephone call without providing notice to the other parties to the call, and thus persons could comply with California law without violating any provisions of the Georgia law.

Second, with respect to businesses within Georgia that record telephone calls, California law would apply only to those telephone calls that are made to or received from California, not to all telephone calls to and from such Georgia businesses. In considering the practicability of singling out California calls for distinct treatment, there would appear to be little question that it would be feasible for a business to identify those calls that its own employees *are making to* current or potential California clients. Similarly, with regard to calls *received by* a business in Georgia, it appears likely that technical tools, such as "caller ID"—are available that readily would make it possible to identify which calls received by the Georgia office are coming from California, and, even in the absence of such technological devices, there would appear to be no reason why an SSB employee, when answering a call, could not simply inquire where the client is coming from. Thus, application of California law would appear to affect only those telephone calls to or from California.

Furthermore, applying California law to a Georgia business's recordings of telephone calls between its employees and California customers will not severely impair Georgia's interests. . . . California law does not totally prohibit a party to a telephone call from recording the call, but rather prohibits only the *secret* or *undisclosed* recording of telephone conversations, that is, the recording of such calls without the knowledge of all parties to the call. Thus, if a Georgia business discloses at the outset of a call made to or received from a California customer that the call is being recorded, the parties to the call will not have a reasonable expectation that the call is not being recorded and the recording would not violate section 632. Accordingly, to the extent Georgia law is intended to protect the right of a business to record conversations when it has a legitimate business justification for doing so, the application of California law to telephone calls between a Georgia business and its California clients or customers would not defeat that interest. . . .

C.

Accordingly, because we have found that the interests of California would be severely impaired if its laws were not applied in this context, whereas Georgia's interests would not be significantly impaired if California law rather than Georgia law were applied, we conclude that . . . California law should apply in determining whether the alleged secret recording of telephone conversations at issue in this case constitutes an unlawful invasion of privacy. . . .

Questions and Comments

(1) Are you convinced that California's policies are really more impaired than are Georgia's? Why is it relevant that Georgia does not require secret

taping? Is comparative impairment systematically biased against state laws that are permissive?

(2) Note one possible consequence of *Kearney*: The policy decisions of the nearly 40 states that have chosen to enable the taping of a conversation with the consent of one party effectively will be thwarted. Companies very often adopt uniform policies and business practices in order to train employees more efficiently and effectively. Interstate businesses create uniform policies by adhering to the regulations of the most restrictive state in which the company does business. Thus, states that chose not to hinder businesses with the need to seek recording permission may nevertheless find that their businesses are forced to comply with the regulatory policy enacted in just a few states. Does it help in this context that businesses can comply with California law simply by stating at the beginning of the call that it is being recorded?

(3) Isn't there also a serious potential problem with notice to individuals and entities outside of California? Even if it were the case that caller ID can help to filter out California residents (though imperfectly so), might individuals and small businesses and other entities find themselves unknowingly ensnared in a California statutory regime that provides for criminal prosecution and punitive damages? The California Supreme Court attempted to avoid the harshness that might result from a lack of notice in three ways. First, the court limited its holding to the civil claim portion of the California statute, acknowledging that extraterritorial application of the criminal prosecution provisions might be problematic. Second, the court phrased its holding as one applying to the context of the case, which appears to be one where a sophisticated interstate company affirmatively chooses to do business in California, and it specifically stated that its holding does not address liability in the case of recording by nonbusiness entities. Third, in the final portion of the *Kearney* opinion, the court approved the issuance of an injunction against SSB but disallowed imposing monetary penalties against SSB for its past conduct on grounds that until this opinion was rendered, businesses were not on sufficient notice that California law might apply extraterritorially. This limitation was also justified on comparative impairment grounds because the compromise enables California to protect its residents while at the same time accommodating "Georgia's interest in protecting persons who acted in Georgia in reasonable reliance on Georgia law from being subject to liability on the basis of such action." *Kearney*, 39 Cal. 4th at 128. The court cautioned that future reliance by out-of-state businesses would not be reasonable, however. *Id*. at 130-131. Are these measures sufficient to protect those outside of California from unfair surprise?

(4) A federal district court followed *Kearney*'s guidance in Butler v. AdoptionMedia, LLC, 486 F. Supp. 2d 1022 (N.D. Cal. 2007). Plaintiffs, same-sex domestic partners residing in California and certified and approved to adopt in California, sought to list their profile during 2002-2003 on an adoption-related Web site operated by defendants, in Arizona. One of defendants' Web sites, ParentProfiles.com, offered a service that allowed prospective adoptive parents, for a fee, to post "profiles" containing information about themselves for review by women considering placing their babies for adoption. Defendants rejected the plaintiffs' application on grounds that the business had adopted a policy allowing

only individuals in an opposite-sex marriage to post profiles. Plaintiffs sued, alleging, inter alia, violations of California civil rights laws, and seeking damages and injunctive relief. California law prohibits marital status discrimination against registered domestic partners in California, and, although California law was not clear on that matter until January 2005, California did prohibit both sexual orientation and marital status discrimination prior to that point. In contrast, although Arizona civil rights law prohibits discrimination against certain specified categories of individuals, Arizona law does not specifically address discrimination on the basis of sexual orientation or marital status. Although Arizona law and policy on the matter seemed less clear, the district court assumed that the case presented a true conflict for choice-of-law purposes. Relying heavily on the reasoning in *Kearney*, the court concluded that the California civil rights law should apply.

Regarding California's interests, the court stated:

> If businesses with headquarters in other states could maintain a regular practice of discrimination against California residents, that practice would substantially impair the protection afforded by the statute.
>
> The court is not persuaded by defendants' argument that Arizona's interests would be seriously impaired by applying California law. In *Kearney*, the court found that because California law was more protective of privacy interests than the comparable Georgia statute, "the application of California law would not violate any interest protected by Georgia law." Moreover, the court noted, because there was "nothing in Georgia law that *requires* any person or business to record a telephone call without providing notice to the other parties to the call, . . . persons could comply with California law without violating any provision of Georgia law." [citations omitted]
>
> Similarly, in the present case, [California law] is more protective of consumers than the comparable Arizona law. Application of California law would not violate any right protected by Arizona law, and [California law] merely provides protections in addition to those specified enumerated protections in Arizona. Arizona law does not require, or even permit, discrimination by businesses against same-sex couples.

Id. at 1052-1053. Regarding defendants' argument that application of California law would place undue burden on those conducting affairs outside of California, the court stated:

> Defendants have provided no evidence that the application of California law would pose an undue and excessive burden on interstate commerce by making it impossible or infeasible for defendants to comply with the requirements of [California law] without altering their conduct with regard to ParentProfiles.com's non-California clients.
>
> In *Kearney*, the application of California law to the out-of-state defendant was "limited to the defendant's surreptitious or undisclosed recording of words spoken over the telephone by California residents while they are in California." [citation omitted] As plaintiffs point out, the same geographic limitations apply in the present case, as they are seeking to prevent defendants from discriminating against California residents while they are in California.

> The evidence shows that defendants already require all persons who wish to use the ParentProfiles service to identify their state of residence and where they are certified to adopt. Thus, defendants can easily distinguish California residents from others, and the application of California law will not require defendants to alter their policy or practice with regard to residents of other states.

Id. at 1053-1054. As in *Kearney*, this court split the issue of remedies and disallowed the plaintiffs from recovering monetary damages against defendants, thereby limiting plaintiffs' remedy to injunctive relief. The rationale the court used to limit the remedy differed from that relied upon in *Kearney*, however:

> Defendants maintain that their consistent practice of requiring all customers to agree to Arizona law and venue limits the foreseeability of being subject to liability under California law for actions that are lawful under Arizona law. They claim that Arizona's interest in protecting Arizona companies from liability for reasonable reliance on Arizona law could certainly be impaired if California law were applied in this case.
>
> The question, as the court sees it, however, is not whether defendants in this case should have reasonably relied on Arizona law. Unlike the dispute in *Kearney* regarding the application of the California statute, this case presents no conflicting decisions on point from other jurisdictions. As plaintiff points out, the relevant facts in this case are more like the facts in *Bernhard*. Defendants in this case have actively sought business connections with Californian consumers, and as of October 2002, their Internet business was more closely tied to California than to any other state (based on the profiles posted by residents of various states). California has a strong interest in regulating defendants' activities because of defendants' penetration into the California economy, and the likelihood of exposure for violating California law was a foreseeable and reasonable business expense.
>
> [T]he question of whether [California law] prohibited marital status discrimination was not completely resolved in 2002. . . . The court finds, given the status of California law in 2002, that defendants should not be subjected to damages for marital status discrimination in connection with their rejection of plaintiffs' application. However, the claim for injunctive relief can go forward.

Id. at 1055-1056. Are you convinced regarding the claimed similarities and differences between *Kearney* and *Butler*? Between *Butler* and *Bernhard*?

(5) Another recent comparative impairment case is McCann v. Foster Wheeler LLC, 225 P.3d 516 (Cal. 2010) (applying Oklahoma statute of repose to bar California plaintiff's suit based on asbestos exposure decades earlier while plaintiff was a resident of Oklahoma). Courts sometimes discuss comparative impairments in the analysis of true conflicts; in such cases, it's not always easy to determine which theory the judge is applying. *See, e.g.*, Gutride Safier LLP v. Reese, 2013 WL 4104462 (N.D. Cal. 2013).

D. The "Better Rule"

Leflar, Conflicts Law: More on Choice-Influencing Considerations
54 Cal. L. Rev. 1584, 1586-1588 (1966)

Major Choice-Influencing Considerations

A short restatement of the five summarized considerations is given here.

A. PREDICTABILITY OF RESULTS

Uniformity of results, regardless of forum, has always been a major goal in choice-of-law theory. Achievement of this goal would enable parties entering into a consensual transaction to plan it with reference to a body of law that would give them the results they desired. As a result, their transactions would normally be validated and their justified expectations thus protected. This would further the broad social policies of most forum states by sustaining legal arrangements in which parties have in good faith engaged themselves. At the same time it would discourage "forum shopping."

B. MAINTENANCE OF INTERSTATE AND INTERNATIONAL ORDER

Both nations and states within a nation are interested in facilitating the orderly legal control of transactions that in any fashion cross their boundary lines. Smooth conduct of affairs between the peoples of different nations is essential to modern civilization; the easy movement of persons and things—free social and economic commerce—between states in a federal nation is essential to the very existence of the federation. There must be a minimum of mutual interference with claims or aspirations to sovereignty. No forum whose concern with a set of facts is negligible should claim priority for its law over the law of a state which has a clearly superior concern with the facts; nor should any state's choice-of-law system be based upon deliberate across-the-board "forum preference." Encouragement of that measure of interstate and international intercourse which is in keeping with the interests of the forum state and its people has always been a prime function of conflicts law.

C. SIMPLIFICATION OF THE JUDICIAL TASK

Courts do not like to do things the hard way if an easier way serves the ends of justice substantially as well. It would be utterly impractical for a court hearing a case brought on extrastate facts to apply the whole body of procedural law of the place where the facts occurred, and not much would be gained by doing so. Courts therefore use their own procedural rules. There are, however, some outcome-determinative rules, at times classified as procedural, which are so simple that one state's rule can be used as easily as another's, so that the substance-procedure dichotomy is not sensibly applicable to them. Purely mechanical rules for choice of substantive law are also easy for courts to apply, but other considerations may outweigh simplification of the judicial task where such rules are involved. Ease in judicial performance is ordinarily not of first importance among the choice-influencing considerations, but it is important in some choices.

D. ADVANCEMENT OF THE FORUM'S GOVERNMENTAL INTERESTS

If a forum state has a genuine concern with the facts in a given case, a concern discoverable from its strongly felt social or legal policy, it is reasonable to expect the state's courts to act in accordance with that concern. This refers to legitimate concerns, not just to the local occurrence of some facts, or to the local existence of some rule of law that could constitutionally be applied to the facts. A state's governmental interests in the choice-of-law sense need not coincide with its rules of local law, especially if the local rules, whether statutory or judgemade, are old or out of tune with the times. A state's total governmental interest in a case is to be discovered from all the considerations that properly motivate the state in its law-making and law-administering tasks, viewed as of the time when the question is presented. So viewed, the circumstances may show that the forum is truly interested in applying its own law to a set of facts. If they do show this, that conclusion becomes a major choice-influencing consideration.

E. APPLICATION OF THE BETTER RULE OF LAW

The better rule of law is the most controversial of the considerations, yet a potent one. If choice of law were purely a jurisdiction-selecting process, with courts first deciding which state's law should govern and checking afterward to see what that state's law was, this consideration would not be present. Everyone knows that this is not what courts do, nor what they should do. Judges know from the beginning between which rules of law, and not just which states, they are choosing. A state's "governmental interest" in a set of facts can be analyzed only by reference to the content of the competing rules of law. Choice of law is not wholly a choice between laws as distinguished from a choice between jurisdictions, but partly it is.

A judge's natural feeling that his own state's law is better than that of other states to some extent explains forum preference. Of course the local law is sometimes not better, and most judges are perfectly capable of realizing this. The inclination of any reasonable court will be to prefer rules of law which make good socio-economic sense for the time when the court speaks, whether they be its own or another state's rules. The law's legitimate concerns with "justice in the individual case," sometimes spoken of as a choice-of-law objective, and with that "protection of justified expectations of the parties," which often corresponds with Ehrenzweig's "basic rules of validation," are furthered by deliberate preference for the better rule of law. The preference is objective, not subjective. It has to do with preferred law, not preferred parties. It is "result selective" only in the same sense that in any non-conflicts case a determination of what the law is (presumably the "better law," if there was argument about the law) controls the results of litigation. In conflict cases, just as in other cases, courts have always taken the content of competing rules into account, but they have too often used characterization, renvoi, multiple-choice rules or the like as manipulative devices to cover up what they were really doing, when there was no need at all for any cover-up.

Milkovich v. Saari

295 Minn. 155, 203 N.W.2d 408 (1973)

TODD, J.

[Plaintiff, defendant Saari, and defendant Rudd took a trip from their Ontario, Canada, homes to Duluth, Minnesota, in Ms. Saari's automobile. Plaintiff was severely injured about 40 miles south of the border when the car crashed into rock formations adjacent to the road while Ms. Rudd was driving. Plaintiff was hospitalized at Duluth for approximately 1½ months. She then returned home to Ontario. Ms. Saari's automobile was garaged, registered, and insured in Ontario.

Ontario has a guest statute, which would require plaintiff to establish gross negligence in order to recover against defendants. Minnesota does not have a guest statute. Defendants filed a motion to dismiss, arguing that Ontario's guest statute applies in this case and prevents plaintiff from establishing her cause of action for negligence. The trial court denied the motion and defendants appealed.]

The field of "conflict of laws" in tort matters has undergone dramatic change in the last decade. Prior to that time, most courts were willing to accept the doctrine of "lex loci," which proved to be easy to administer since the happening of an accident in any particular forum established that the law of the place of the accident would apply. Criticism of this entrenched doctrine mounted from all sides. The issue was met head on in Babcock v. Jackson.

While New York was experiencing its difficulties in the changing field of conflict of laws, a fact situation arose in a case appealed to the Supreme Court of New Hampshire, which allowed its learned Mr. Chief Justice Kenison to enunciate a doctrine which has been followed by many courts throughout the country, including our own Minnesota court. In Clark v. Clark, . . . a husband and wife had left their home in New Hampshire to proceed to another part of New Hampshire for a visit and were to return that evening. Part of their trip took them through Vermont, where the accident occurred. The plaintiff's wife brought action in New Hampshire against her husband and sought an order of the court that the substantive law of New Hampshire governed the rights of the parties. New Hampshire had no guest statute and Vermont did. In a carefully reasoned opinion, Mr. Chief Justice Kenison traced the history and difficulty of the lex loci rule. He then proceeded to adopt five basic "choice-influencing considerations" to be applied in these cases. The basic premises for the considerations adopted by the court were first proposed by Professor Robert Leflar in his article, "Choice-Influencing Considerations in Conflicts Law," 41 N.Y.U. L. Rev. 267, 279, and briefly stated, the tests selected by the New Hampshire court are: (a) Predictability of results; (b) maintenance of interstate and international order; (c) simplification of the judicial task; (d) advancement of the forum's governmental interests; and (e) application of the better rule of law. Predictability of results can be overlooked since basically this test relates to consensual transactions where people should know in advance what law will govern their act. Obviously, no one plans to have an accident, and, except for the remote possibility of forum shopping, this test is of little import in an automobile accident case. As to the second consideration, the court found little trouble since under this heading no more is called for than the court apply the law of no state which does not have substantial connection with the total facts and the particular issue being litigated. The third point, simplification of the judicial task, poses no problem since the courts are fully capable of administering the law of another forum if called upon to do so.

The court observed that in selecting the law of a particular case the last two considerations carry most weight. In the case before it, the court found adequate governmental interest in applying its state's law and concluded that the New Hampshire law was unquestionably the better law and should be applied. . . .

The facts of this case now complete the cycle. The choice-influencing considerations proposed by Professor Leflar and set forth by Mr. Chief Justice Kenison in Clark v. Clark were adopted by our court in Schneider v. Nichols indicating our preference for the better-law approach and our rejection of the guest statute concept of various jurisdictions. We have come to the conclusion in this case that plaintiff should be allowed to proceed with her action under our common law rules of negligence and should not be bound by the guest statute requirements of the Province of Ontario. . . .

On the consideration of governmental interest [in discussing Kell v. Henderson], Professor Leflar found adequate support for the decision rendered by the New York court. In so doing, he rejected the concept of the practical interest of the state in the supervision and safety of its state highways since the rule in question, unlike rules of the road and definitions of negligence, does not bear upon vehicle operation as such. Instead, he pointed out that the factor to be considered is the relevant effect the New York rule has on the duty of host to guest and the danger of collusion between them to defraud the host's insurer. New York's interest in applying its own law rather than Ontario law on these issues, he found to be based primarily on the status, as a justice-administering state. In that status it is strongly concerned with seeing that persons who come into New York courts to litigate controversies with substantial New York connections have these cases determined according to rules consistent with New York concepts of justice, or at least not inconsistent with them. That will be as true for nondomiciliary litigants as for domiciliaries. This interest will not manifest itself clearly if the out-of-state rule does not run contrary to some strong socio-legal policy of the forum, but it will become a major consideration if there is such a strong opposing local policy.

Professor Leflar then pointed out that this consideration leads to preference for what is regarded as the better rule of law, that New York has such a preference, and that it is a vigorous one. He concluded that the combination of the last two items, governmental interest and better rule of law, called for the application of New York law. His statements and reasoning apply equally to the facts of this case and lead to the conclusion that Minnesota should apply its better rule of law and should allow plaintiff to proceed with her action.

Strong support for the better-rule-of-law concept appears in an article by Professor Albert A. Ehrenzweig, *"False Conflicts" and the "Better Rule": Threat and Promise in Multistate Tort Laws*, 53 Va. L. Rev. 847, 853, in which he wrote:

Express recognition of the forum's right and duty to apply its own better rule as such is an ancient tradition which apparently succumbed to the 19th century's international conceptualism. We need only remember the priority given by early statutists to the statuta favorabilia of the forum against foreign statuta odiosa, or Master Aldricus' choice of the custom "potior et utilior," or Byzantium's *philanthropoteron*. The widespread disregard of foreign Sunday laws, fellow-servant rules, and married woman's incapacities, as well as statutes of frauds, and limitations on wrongful death damages, may serve as modern examples.

Now, we shall, of course, not "ask the judge simply to express a preference between two rules." This would, indeed, "abolish our centuries-old subject." But we should face the "fact of life" that judges, our best judges, often take advantage of the "looseness in the joints of the [choice-of-law] apparatus," or employ "manipulative techniques such as characterization and renvoi," and all-purpose tools such as the "most significant relationship," in order to substitute a better foreign rule for much "that is archaic and foolish" in their own law. . . .

Whether or not general express recognition of the "better-rule" approach can be justified at present, we must at least acknowledge the validity of the proposition advanced by Currie that transient ("disinterested") third states, having no incentive to follow the "stay-at-home" trend, are likely to choose what they consider the better of two foreign rules. Moreover, admiralty courts in their more forthright manner have sometimes acknowledged their bias toward a "better rule." And may we not ultimately in part explain the great willingness of American courts to permit parties to choose their own laws of a similar better-rule approach?

Although the "better-rule" principle is not generally capable of replacing conflicts rules, I see little justification within the limits set by settled law for the prevailing horror against the recognition of that principle as one of many determining the growth of conflicts law. The very growth of common-law rules is based on the judge's choice between competing principles, choices expressed in the process of overruling or distinguishing earlier judicial pronouncements. In purely domestic cases open admission of this technique is often hampered by justified respect for "certainty" and the parties' expectations, a respect which also accounts, of course, for both legislative and judicial reluctance to act with retroactive effect. In cases involving foreign elements, however, this consideration often should be, and generally is, less relevant, and the path is open for the courageous judge to prepare the ground for a domestic reform by open preference for "better" foreign solutions. . . .

[I]n Conklin v. Horner the Wisconsin court was confronted with a fact situation again exactly on all fours with our situation. There the court, speaking through Mr. Justice Heffernan, adopted the better-rule approach which we have adopted here and, in a well-reasoned opinion, arrived at the same conclusion that this court has. In the Wisconsin case, the litigants were all residents of the State of Illinois; the automobile in question was licensed and garaged in Illinois; the trip originated in Illinois with the intent and purpose to return to Illinois; and the insurance policy was issued in the State of Illinois. Illinois has a guest statute; Wisconsin does not. The court in that case first considered the problem of labeling any procedure in determining rules of law to be applied, saying:

> *We emphasized that what we adopted was not a rule, but a method of analysis that permitted dissection of the jural bundle constituting a tort and its environment to determine what elements therein were relevant to a reasonable choice of law.*
>
> When the *Wilcox* case is so viewed, it is apparent that we cannot conclude that, when one set of facts leads logically to the law of the forum, the reverse, or the apparent reverse, of these facts will lead to the opposite conclusion. [Emphasis added.]

We, too, adopt this concept that what the court is considering is a methodology and not a rule. . . .

We find then that in *Conklin* the Wisconsin court, premising its choice-of-law methodology on the factors initially propagated by Professor Leflar and Mr. Chief Justice Kenison of New Hampshire, has resolved substantially the same fact situation as now appears before us by applying the common-law liability of the forum and place of the accident rather than the guest statute of the residence of the parties. *See also* Kell v. Henderson, *supra.* Since our methodology owes a similar debt to Professor Leflar and Mr. Chief Justice Kenison we find their reasoning relevant and persuasive.

We have already noted the relative unimportance of predictability of results to tort actions. Similarly, the simplification of the judicial task need not concern us to any great extent since we have no doubt our judicial system could in the appropriate case apply the guest statute rule of gross negligence as readily as our common-law rule. Interstate and international relations are maintained without harm where, as here, the forum state has a substantial connection with the facts and issues involved. This requirement is amply met by the fact that the accident occurred in Minnesota, as well as by the fact the plaintiff was hospitalized for well over a month in the state.

The compelling factors in this case are the advancement of the forum's governmental interests and the application of the better law. While there may be more deterrent effect in our common-law rule of liability as opposed to the guest statute requirements of gross negligence, the main governmental interest involved is that of any "justice-administering state." Leflar, *supra* at 1594. In that posture, we are concerned that our courts not be called upon to determine issues under rules which, however accepted they may be in other states, are inconsistent with our own concept of fairness and equity. We might also note that persons injured in automobile accidents occurring within our borders can reasonably be expected to require treatment in our medical facilities, both public and private. In the instant case, plaintiff incurred medical bills in a Duluth hospital which have already been paid, but we are loath to place weight on the individual case for fear it might offer even minor incentives to "hospital shop" or to create litigation-directed pressures on the payment of debts to medical facilities. Suffice it to say that we recognize that medical costs are likely to be incurred with a consequent governmental interest that injured persons not be denied recovery on the basis of doctrines foreign to Minnesota.

In our search for the better rule, we are firmly convinced of the superiority of the common-law rule of liability to that of the Ontario guest statute. We can find little reason for the strict limitation of a host's liability to his guest beyond the fear of collusive suits and the vague disapproval of a guest "biting the hand that feeds him." Neither rationale is persuasive. We are convinced the judicial system can uncover collusive suits without such over-inclusive rules, and we do not find any discomfort in the prospect of a guest suing his host for injuries suffered through the host's simple negligence.

Accordingly, we hold that Minnesota law should be applied to this lawsuit.

PETERSON, J. (dissenting).

. . .

The "choice-influencing factor" in the majority opinion is simply that Minnesota law is "better law" because, unlike Ontario law, this state has no guest statute. Notwithstanding our undoubted preference for this forum's standard of liability, I am not persuaded that decision should turn on that factor alone. We may assume that these Canadian citizens have concurred in the rule of law of their own government as just, so the law of this American forum is not for them the "better" standard of justice. The litigation, indeed, was first initiated by plaintiff in the courts of Ontario and was later commenced in Minnesota as an act of forum shopping.

. . . The Wisconsin case of Conklin v. Horner is a final expression of its highest court, based upon a well-written majority opinion of Mr. Justice Heffernan. I nevertheless am more persuaded by the dissenting opinion of two justices. Mr. Chief Justice Hallows, in dissent, appropriately observed that the so-called "methodology of analysis" is really little more than a mechanical application of the law of the forum. As he wrote: "If we are going to be consistent only in applying the law of the forum, then we are merely giving lip service to the new 'significant contacts' rule."

Questions and Comments

(1) Not surprisingly, the most controversial part of Professor Leflar's approach is the "better rule" component. It is not 100 percent clear that Professor Leflar *advocated* a better-rule approach instead of simply stating that courts do in fact tend to choose what they consider to be the better rule. Professor Ehrenzweig, in the article quoted by the *Milkovich* court, seems to stand somewhere between description and advocacy, since he felt that conflicts rules should reflect what courts actually do in conflicts cases, rather than what scholars urge. In any event, it is clear that several courts have embraced explicit acceptance of the approach.

(2) Consider the posture of a lower court comparing forum law formulated by its state's supreme court to the law of another state. Presumably, if there is a supreme court decision in the forum holding that local law is "better" for a choice-of-law purposes, then this is binding. How is that any different from a state supreme court decision that the rule is "better" for substantive purposes? Why, in other words, isn't a substantive precedent also binding on choice-of-law issues—given that a choice-of-law precedent on "betterness" would be?

In Jepson v. General Casualty Co., 513 N.W.2d 467 (Minn. 1994), the Minnesota Supreme Court held that a recent legislative amendment allowing insurance contracts to prevent stacking was not evidence that Minnesota's law was "better" in a case involving a contract signed in Minnesota for an out-of-state risk involved in an out-of-state accident. Would a choice-of-law provision in a statute be given effect if it declared that this substantive law was "better" in Leflar's terms? If so, then why doesn't the simple adoption of a substantive statute declare, in effect, that this rule is better for choice-of-law purposes? Doesn't this suggest that the only sort of rule that could be declared "worse" for choice-of-law purposes is one that is not authoritative for substantive purposes? For instance, a forum's common-law rule that was outdated or eroded by subsequent decisions could be declared "worse" for choice-of-law purposes. But if such a substantive decision is not authoritative, why not simply overrule it directly for domestic purposes as well?

(3) The *Milkovich* opinion states, at page 223, that "we are concerned that our courts not be called upon to determine issues under rules which, however acceptable they may be in other states, are inconsistent with our own concept of fairness and equity." Couldn't that interest be much more rationally served in this case, and with much less disruption to the policy interests of Ontario, by a forum non conveniens dismissal? Wouldn't such an approach also have the advantage of not burdening the Minnesota courts? In light of the less drastic dismissal alternative, isn't the use of the quoted rationale to decide the issue an instance of meddling in Ontario interest?

(4) Is the determination of the "better rule" as objective as Professor Leflar tries to make it sound? In the article excerpt quoted before *Milkovich*, he says at one point that the "better rule" approach "has to do with preferred law, not preferred parties" and is therefore objective and not subjective. But isn't that just saying that it makes no nonobjective choice between parties, while leaving open the possibility that the choice between two laws is nonobjective?

In fact, if there is an objective way in a given conflicts case for a court to determine what the better rule is, why weren't the courts or the legislature of the state with the worse rule able to see that fact and change their rule?

(5) Professor Weintraub finds the use of the better-law criterion "commendable" if two limitations are observed: First, he would require that it be used only to resolve a true conflict; second, he would require that the selection of the better law be by objective standards. Such standards include rejecting the law that is an "anachronism" or is "aberrational." Weintraub, *Commentary on the Conflict of Laws* 328 (2d ed. 1980). Is that another way of saying that new laws are always better than old laws and that one should discriminate against experimentation among the states?

(6) It is a common observation that the better-rule approach for true conflict cases is little more than Currie's solution in disguise if the court determines that its own law is the better law. Moreover, as in *Milkovich*, courts routinely conclude that their own law is the better law. And yet not all courts do. *See, e.g.*, LaBounty v. American Ins. Co., 451 A.2d 161 (N.H. 1982); Bigelow v. Halloran, 313 N.W. 2d 10 (Minn. 1981); *compare* Jepson v. General Casualty Co. of Wisconsin, 513 N.W.2d 467, 473 (Minn. 1994) ("if it were true [that] forum law would always be the better law . . . this step in our choice of law analysis would be meaningless"). Moreover, an empirical study of tort conflict cases suggests that the better-law

approach does not lead to the application of forum law any more often than the other modern approaches (although the modern approaches as a group lead to the application of forum law more frequently than does the traditional approach). *See* Borchers, *The Choice-of-Law Revolution: An Empirical Study*, 49 Wash. & Lee L. Rev. 357 (1992).

(7) Consider Blamey v. Brown, 270 N.W.2d 844 (Minn. 1978), which was based on the "better law" approach, but posed a fact situation similar to the *Bernhard* case, *supra*, at 204. *Blamey* involved a one-car accident. The defendant, sole proprietor of a beer and liquor store, was in Wisconsin but within a few miles of the Minnesota border. Defendant's store sold beer to the driver of the car in which plaintiff was injured in Minnesota. The Minnesota court specifically found that "[d]efendant neither advertised in Minnesota nor attempted to attract Minnesota residents or young people [plaintiff was 15] to his establishment." The defendant did not have insurance to cover the kind of liability imposed by Minnesota since Wisconsin imposed no similar liability. The Minnesota court decided that the Minnesota statute imposing strict liability for sales of alcohol to minors was inapplicable by its own terms. But rather than apply the considerably milder Wisconsin statute (which would not have imposed liability), it applied Minnesota common-law negligence theory to hold the defendant liable while specifically holding that Wisconsin common law would not impose liability. The decision was based upon Minnesota interests and the "better law" approach.

(8) The attention that the better-rule factor has diverted from Professor Leflar's other choice-influencing considerations may be justified. Professor Reppy claims that the factors are really only two, not five. *See* Reppy, *Eclecticism in Choice of Law: Hybrid Method or Mishmash?*, 34 Mercer L. Rev. 645 (1983). Factor 3, simplification of the judicial task, is most easily satisfied by applying the law of the forum and could never influence the court away from picking what it will usually pick under factor 5, the better law—forum law. No case has ever turned on factor 2, maintenance of interstate and international order, and it is hard to imagine a conflicts case threatening that order. Predictability might sometimes be a concern, but, Reppy says, it will lose, 2 to 1, to the factors that point toward application of forum law: better law and factor 4, advancement of the forum's governmental interests.

(9) However, some courts enamored with Leflar's approach have deemphasized the controversial "better law" factor. For example, the better-rule approach was specifically limited to true conflict cases where the other considerations are in "near equipoise" in Fuerste v. Bemis, 156 N.W.2d 831 (Iowa 1968). *See also* Schumacher v. Schumacher, 676 N.W.2d 685, 691-692 (Minn. Ct. App. 2004) (noting that generally the better-rule factor "is addressed only when the other four factors are not dispositive as to which state's law should be applied"). Also, several federal courts applying Leflar's approach have refused to state which state's law was better. *See, e.g.*, Cowley v. Abbott Laboratories, Inc., 476 F. Supp. 2d 1053, 1059 (W.D. Wis. 2007) ("The Court is not in a position to determine which jurisdiction's policy better serves justice and the public interest. Such a determination is 'entrusted to the legislatures of the respective states.'"); Stupak v. Hoffman-La Roche, Inc., 287 F. Supp. 2d 968, 974 (E.D. Wis. 2003) (same, but using better-rule factor to reject use of dépecage: "it does seem clear that the better rule of law is not half of one state's law and half of the other's"); Polensky v. Continental

Casualty Co., 397 F. Supp. 2d 1164, 1171-1172 (D.N.D. 2005) ("The Court does not find that either rule of law is 'better' per se. The Court finds that this factor does not favor the application of either state's law.").

(10) In recent years Minnesota apparently has backed away from the "better law" approach. In Nodak Mutual Ins. Co. v. Am. Fam. Mut. Ins. Co., 604 N.W.2d 91, 96 (Minn. 2000), the Minnesota Supreme Court noted that "this court has not placed any emphasis on the [better-law] factor in nearly twenty years," and described its approach instead as "the significant contacts test." *See also* Montpetit v. Allina Health System, Inc., 2000 Minn. App. LEXIS 1051 (Minn. Ct. App. 2000) (better-rule approach "has been abandoned in recent years"). At least four states — Arkansas, New Hampshire, Rhode Island, and Wisconsin — still use some form of the better-law approach for torts. *See* Symeonides, *Choice of Law in the American Courts in 2010: Twenty-Fourth Annual Survey*, 59 Am. J. Comp. L. 303 (2011). For a recent intelligent defense of the better-law approach, *see* Singer, *Pay No Attention to That Man Behind the Curtain: The Place of Better Law in a Third Restatement of Conflicts*, 75 Ind. L.J. 659 (2000). For a symposium devoted to Leflar's conflicts theory, *see* 52 Ark. L. Rev. 1-232 (1999).

E. The Restatement Second and the Most Significant Relationship

The First Restatement was promulgated in 1934. Less than 20 years later, the American Law Institute called for a new Restatement because of the perceived inadequacies of the old one. The first tentative draft of the Second Restatement appeared in 1953. The final product was completed and published in 1971. Certain sections of the Second Restatement were revised in 1989 to reflect changes in legislation and case law that had occurred in the years following publication. Since then, the American Law Institute has recently begun composing the draft of a Third Restatement. However, there are those who think that it would be a mistake to change the Second Restatement too drastically at this point. Brilmayer, *What I Like Most About the Restatement (Second) of Conflicts, and Why It Should Not Be Thrown Out with the Bathwater*, 110 AJIL Unbound 144, 144 (2016). The direction that the draft Third Restatement now seems to be taking is referenced in note (1) on page 245 *infra*.

The choice-of-law process contemplated by the Second Restatement generally works as follows. The centerpiece of the Second Restatement is a "most significant relationship" test. So, for example, the general choice-of-law rules for torts and for contracts provide:

§145. The General Principle

(1) The rights and liabilities of the parties with respect to an issue in tort are determined by the local law of that state which, with respect to that issue,

has the most significant relationship to the occurrence and the parties under the principles stated in §6.

(2) Contacts to be taken into account in applying the principles of §6 to determine the law applicable to an issue include:

(a) the place where the injury occurred,

(b) the place where the conduct causing the injury occurred,

(c) the domicil, residence, nationality, place of incorporation and place of business of the parties, and

(d) the place where the relationship, if any, between the parties is centered.

These contacts are to be evaluated according to their relative importance with respect to the particular issue.

§188. Law Governing in Absence of Effective Choice by the Parties

(1) The rights and duties of the parties with respect to an issue in contract are determined by the local law of the state which, with respect to that issue, has the most significant relationship to the transaction and the parties under the principles stated in §6.

(2) In the absence of an effective choice of law by the parties (*see* §187), the contacts to be taken into account in applying the principles of §6 to determine the law applicable to an issue include:

(a) the place of contracting,

(b) the place of negotiation of the contract,

(c) the place of performance,

(d) the location of the subject matter of the contract, and

(e) the domicil, residence, nationality, place of incorporation and place of business of the parties.

These contacts are to be evaluated according to their relative importance with respect to the particular issue.

(3) If the place of negotiating the contract and the place of performance are in the same state, the local law of this state will usually be applied, except as otherwise provided in §§189-199 and 203.

The §6 referred to in Sections 145 and 188 provides:

§6. Choice-of-Law Principles

(1) A court, subject to constitutional restrictions, will follow a statutory directive of its own state on choice of law.

(2) When there is no such directive, the factors relevant to the choice of the applicable rule of law include:

the needs of the interstate and international systems,

(a) the relevant policies of the forum,

(b) the relevant policies of other interested states and the relative interests of those states in the determination of the particular issue,

(c) the protection of justified expectations,

(d) the basic policies underlying the particular field of law,

(e) certainty, predictability and uniformity of result, and

(f) ease in the determination and application of the law to be applied.

There are obvious tensions between sections 145 and 188, on the one hand, and section 6 on the other. Sections 145 and 188 look like a blind, contacts-based jurisdiction-selecting approach (i.e., an approach that picks which state's law to apply without reference to the content of state laws), while section 6 contemplates policy analysis. In addition, sections 145 and 188 state a rule, even if a highly general one, while section 6 states an approach. *See* Reese, *Choice of Law: Rules or Approach*, 57 Cornell L. Rev. 315 (1972). For these reasons, there is a certain amount of schizophrenia built into the Second Restatement. To make matters more complicated, the Second Restatement also contains more specific sections that provide presumptive rules in discrete substantive contexts. For example, section 154's presumptive choice-of-law rule for interference with marriage relationships provides:

§154. Interference with Marriage Relationship

The local law of the state where the conduct complained of principally occurred determines the liability of one who interferes with a marriage relationship, unless, with respect to the particular issue, some other state has a more significant relationship under the principles stated in §6 to the occurrence and the parties, in which event the local law of the other state will be applied.

Because of the Second Restatement's eclecticism, courts have done many different things under its banner. Sometimes they count contacts; sometimes they apply the law of the place of the injury; sometimes they perform interest analysis; often they mix several different approaches. As a result, the cases that follow cannot be said to be "typical" applications of the Second Restatement. Excellent general discussions of the methodology of the Second Restatement may be found in Reppy, *Eclecticism in Choice of Law: Hybrid Method or Mishmash?*, 34 Mercer L. Rev. 645, 655-666 (1983), and Kay, *Theory into Practice: Choice of Law in the Courts*, 34 Mercer L. Rev. 521, 552-562 (1983).

Phillips v. General Motors Corp.

995 P.2d 1002 (Mont. 2000)

REGNIER, J.

[Darrell Byrd purchased a 1985 Chevrolet pickup truck in or about February 1995 from Mike's Wholesale Cars in Newton, North Carolina, and he listed a North Carolina address in the paperwork. The truck was designed, tested, manufactured, and distributed by General Motors and originally sold by GM in North Carolina. The vehicle had fuel tanks mounted outside the frame rail.

On December 22, 1997, Darrell Byrd was driving with his wife and their two sons in the truck from their home near Fortine, Montana, where Darrell Byrd was employed and where Timothy and Samuel Byrd attended school, to North Carolina to visit family. The Byrds were domiciled in Montana before and at the time of the 1997 accident. While driving through Kansas, a semi-tractor trailer collided with the Byrds' truck, which caught on fire. Darrell, Angela, and Timothy Byrd died. Samuel Byrd, then 11 years old, was hospitalized with injuries.]

Plaintiff Alvin Phillips is the legal guardian of Samuel Byrd and the personal representative of the estates of Angela Byrd, Darrell Byrd, and Timothy Byrd. Alvin Phillips resides in Newton, North Carolina. Samuel Byrd presently resides in North Carolina. Probate proceedings for the Estates of Timothy, Angela, and Darrell Byrd are filed with and pending in the Montana Nineteenth Judicial District Court, Lincoln County, Montana.

In these product liability cases, in which Plaintiffs raise claims of negligence and strict liability, Plaintiffs seek compensatory and punitive damages related to the deaths of Darrell, Angela, and Timothy Byrd and the personal injuries sustained by Samuel Byrd. General Motors denies all liability.

[The case was filed in federal district court in Montana, which certified three questions to the Montana state court.] . . . The District Court observed that the instant case raised significant policy questions involving Montana's choice of law rules, that choice of law questions in tort cases are frequent in diversity litigation in federal court, and that it would be helpful in resolving this case and others to have a definitive determination of what the Montana choice of law rule is.

Question One

Whether, in a personal injury/product liability/wrongful death action, where there is a potential conflict of laws, Montana will follow the Restatement (Second) of Conflict of Laws, including the "most significant relationship" test set forth in §§146 and 6, in the determination of which state's substantive law to apply?

The traditional choice of law rule, known as *lex loci delicti commissi* (or the law of place where the wrong was committed), provides that the infliction of injury is actionable under the law of the state in which it was received . . . . The theoretical basis for the traditional rule was the "vested rights" theory propounded by Joseph H. Beale. The theory explained the forum's use of foreign legal rules in terms of the creation and enforcement of vested rights. According to Professor Beale's theory, the only law that can operate in a foreign territory is the law of the foreign sovereign. When an event occurred in a foreign territory (an injury caused by a defective product, for example), and under the laws of that territory that event gave rise to a right (damages), a right "vested" under that territory's law. The role of the forum court was simply to enforce the right which had vested in the foreign territory according to that territory's law. Crucial to this theory was a determination of where and when a right vested, because the law in place where the right vested would control the existence and content of the right. As evidenced by the decision in Alabama Great S. R.R. Co. v. Carroll, courts have held that for tort claims a right vested where and when an injury occurred.

Traditional practice depends on a few broad, single-contact, jurisdiction-selecting rules. Traditionalist courts find the location of the last event necessary for a right to vest and apply the law of that location. As a result, courts following the traditional approach often choose the law of a state with no interest in the resolution of the dispute, like the choice of Mississippi law in *Carroll*.

The traditional rule has largely been justified on the basis of the practical advantages that it offers: certainty, predictability, and forum neutrality. However, problems inherent in its application as well as escape devices used to avoid results perceived to be arbitrary or unfair have greatly diminished the advantages the traditional rule supposedly provides. For example, the explicit public policy exception to the *lex loci* rule allows courts to avoid the law of the place of injury by concluding that it violates the public policy of the forum. Use of the public policy escape device by *lex loci* courts continues today.

The traditional rule also no longer affords consistency and predictability across jurisdictions. While some jurisdictions still cling to the traditional rule, the vast majority of states have rejected it. . . . Professor Symeonides observes:

> As the century draws to a close, the traditional theory in tort and contract conflicts in the United States finds itself in a very precarious state. This assessment is based not simply on the relatively low number of states that still adhere to that theory, but also on the shallowness of their commitment to it. Although the degree of commitment varies from state to state, it is fair to say that very few of these states are philosophically committed to the traditional theory. . . . More often, these rules remain in place only because [a] court is able to find a way to evade them by using one of the traditional escapes, such as characterization, substance versus procedure, renvoi, or, more often, the [public policy] exception.

Symeonides, *Choice of Law in American Courts in 1998: Twelfth Annual Survey*, 47 Am. J. Comp. L. 327, 345 (1999). The Restatement (Second) of Conflict of Laws largely abandoned the traditional rule in favor of an approach which seeks to apply the law of the state with the "most significant relationship to the occurrence and the parties." Restatement (Second) of Conflict of Laws §145(1) (1971) (hereinafter "Restatement (Second)"). In adopting a policy analysis approach, the drafters noted that "experience has shown that the last event rule does not always work well. Situations arise where the state of the last event (place of injury) bears only a slight relationship to the occurrence and the parties with respect to the particular issue." Restatement (Second), Introductory Note to Ch. 7, at 412.

In abandoning the *lex loci* rule in favor of the most significant relationship test, one court observed:

> The majority of courts which have considered the question have abandoned the *lex loci* rule in favor of a more flexible approach which permits analysis of the policies and interests underlying the particular issue before the court. Additionally, the commentators are overwhelmingly opposed to its retention and, although they disagree as to a substitute approach, all advocate a method which allows Courts to focus on the policies underlying the conflicting laws . . . and the governmental interests which would be advanced by their application.

In re Air Crash Disaster at Boston, Mass. on July 31, 1973 (D. Mass. 1975), 399 F. Supp. 1106, 1110. In determining the choice of law rules for contract disputes, we adopted the approach contained in the Restatement (Second) of Conflict of Laws. We see no reason to have one choice of law approach for contracts and another for torts. For the reasons set forth above, we now hereby adopt the "most significant relationship" approach to determine the applicable substantive law for issues of tort.

Question Two

Given the facts of this case, which state's law applies to plaintiff's various tort and damages claims under Montana's choice of law rules?

The Byrds claim that under the most significant relationship test Montana law applies. General Motors contends that under this same test, the law of Kansas applies. We agree with the Byrds.

At the outset, we note that many appellate courts that have analyzed the most significant relationship test have done so in a fairly conclusory fashion. Although the analysis that follows appears somewhat tedious, our attempt is to comply with the procedures set forth in the Restatement (Second) of Conflict of Laws. We also raise an additional caveat. Any analysis under the Restatement approach is necessarily driven by the unique facts, issues, applicable law, and jurisdictions implicated in a particular case.

A.   RELEVANT RESTATEMENT PROVISIONS

Any conflict of law analysis under the Restatement must begin with §6. [The court recites section 6, reproduced *supra* pages 228-229.] Since we have no statutory directive regarding choice of law, we turn to the specific section that relates to tort and personal injury actions. [The court recites section 145, reproduced *supra* pages 227-228.] These contacts are to be evaluated according to their relative importance with respect to the particular issue.

The Restatement also has more specific sections relating to personal injury and wrongful death actions. Sections 146 and 175 provide that the rights and liabilities of the parties are to be determined in accordance with the law of the state where the injury occurred unless, with respect to a particular issue, another state has a more significant relationship. Whether another state has a more significant relationship is determined under §145(2). We further note that issues such as the tortious character of conduct, available defenses, contributory fault, and damages are all to be determined by applying the most significant relationship rule of §145. *See, e.g.*, Restatement (Second) §§156 ("Tortious Character of Conduct"), 157 ("Standard of Care"), 161 ("Defenses"), 164 ("Contributory Fault"), and 171 ("Damages").

B.   MOST SIGNIFICANT RELATIONSHIP ANALYSIS

Under the Restatement (Second) approach, the local law of the place of injury, Kansas, is presumptively applicable in a product liability and wrongful death action unless, with respect to a particular issue, a different state has a more significant relationship. *See* Restatement (Second) §§146 and 175. In order to determine whether a state other than the place of injury has a more significant relationship, the contacts listed under §145(2) "are to be taken into account in applying the principles of §6." Restatement (Second) §145(2). Accordingly, we shall address each of the factors enumerated under §6(2), taking into account, when appropriate, the contacts of §145(2).

1. NEEDS OF THE INTERSTATE AND INTERNATIONAL SYSTEM

The first factor we must consider under §6(2) is the needs of the interstate and international system. Restatement (Second) §6(2)(a). The drafters stated,

> Choice-of-law rules, among other things, should seek to further harmonious relations between states and to facilitate commercial intercourse between them. In formulating rules of choice of law, a state should have regard for the needs and policies of other states and of the community of states. Rules of choice of law formulated with regard for such needs and policies are likely to commend themselves to other states and to be adopted by these states.

Restatement §6 cmt. d.

On the facts of this case, this factor does not point toward the importance of applying any particular state's law. Rather, this factor supports the application of the Restatement approach, namely the law of the state with the most significant relationship to an issue. We believe the Restatement approach fosters harmonious relationships between states by respecting the substantive law of other states when those states have a greater interest in the determination of a particular issue litigated in a foreign jurisdiction. The Restatement approach is preferable, in our view, to the traditional *lex loci* rule which applies the law of the place of the accident which may be fortuitous in tort actions. We further conclude that there is no need to evaluate the contacts listed in §145 to this issue.

2. THE POLICIES OF INTERESTED STATES

The second and third factors we must consider are the relevant policies of the forum state and other interested states. *See* Restatement (Second) §6(2)(b) and (c). In the case *sub judice*, these are the most important factors in our analysis. The drafters stated,

> Every Rule of Law, whether embodied in a statute or in a common law rule, was designed to achieve one or more purposes. A court should have regard for these purposes in determining whether to apply its own rule or the rule of another state in the decision of a particular issue. If the purposes sought to be achieved by a local statute or common law rule would be furthered by its application to out-of-state facts, this is a weighty reason why such application should be made.

Restatement (Second) §6 cmt. e. This principle requires us to consider whether applying the law of a state with a relevant contact would further the purpose that law was designed to achieve. Upon consideration of this principle, it is clear that

Montana has the more significant relationship to the issues raised by this dispute for the reasons set forth below.

a. Place of Injury

As noted above, in product liability and wrongful death actions, the law of the place of injury is presumptively applicable unless another state has a more significant relationship. *See* Restatement (Second) §§146 and 175. The injury here occurred in Kansas. Kansas law provides for a cause of action against a manufacturer whose product causes harm as a result of its defective design. *See* Kan. Stat. Ann. §60-3302. The purpose of a state's product liability statute is to regulate the sale of products in that state and to prevent injuries incurred by that state's residents due to defective products. . . . Any conduct the state of Kansas may have been attempting to regulate through §60-3302 could not be implicated by the facts of this case as it involves neither a sale in Kansas nor an injury to a Kansas resident.

Kansas law provides for multiple defenses to a product liability claim. For example, Kansas law bars recovery for injuries occurring after "the time during which the product would be normally likely to perform or be stored in a safe manner." Kan. Stat. Ann. §60-3303(a)(1). Kansas law also allows a party defending a product liability claim to assert that the injury causing aspect of the product was in compliance with the regulatory standards relating to design or performance at the time of manufacture. *See* Kan. Stat. Ann. §60-3304(a). Once again, the overriding purpose of Kansas's product liability laws is to establish the level of safety of products sold either in Kansas or to a Kansas resident. Clearly, these rules regarding defenses were not enacted in order to grant a defense to a manufacturer when a non-Kansas resident is injured by a product not purchased in Kansas.

Under Kansas law, an award of damages for product liability may be diminished in proportion to the amount of negligence attributed to the plaintiff or decedent. General Motors asserts that the issue of comparative negligence turns upon conduct that occurred in Kansas and therefore Kansas law should apply because Kansas has an interest in regulating conduct which occurred within its borders. However, the record before us does not contain the substance of General Motors' allegations regarding the Byrds' allegedly negligent conduct. Therefore, there is no evidence that General Motors' allegations concerning the comparative negligence of the Byrds are limited to conduct occurring solely within Kansas.

Moreover, even if General Motors' allegations concerned conduct occurring solely in Kansas, the Kansas Supreme Court did not extend Kansas's comparative negligence statute to product liability causes of action in order to regulate conduct occurring in Kansas. In concluding that the comparative negligence statute applied to product liability actions, the Kansas Supreme Court stated:

> *Comparative liability provides a system for allocating responsibility* for an injury while still serving the social policy of not allowing a manufacturer or seller to escape liability for defective products merely because of slight culpability on the part of the product user in bringing about the injury.

Kennedy v. City of Sawyer, 618 P. 2d 788, 796 (Kan. 1980) (emphasis added). It is clear from the *Kennedy* decision that the Kansas Supreme Court extended Kansas's comparative negligence standard to product liability cases in order to "allocate responsibility for an injury" due to a defective product, disallowing defenses such as "assumption of the risk," "product misuse," or "unreasonable use" from completely precluding recovery under Kansas product liability law. Kansas has no interest in allocating responsibility for the injuries suffered by Montana residents and caused by a product purchased in North Carolina. Again, the purpose of a state's product liability laws is to protect and provide compensation to its residents and regulate the sale of products within its borders.

Kansas law limits the total amount recoverable for "noneconomic loss" in a personal injury action to $250,000, and limits "nonpecuniary" damages in wrongful death actions to $100,000. Kan. Stat. Ann. §§60-19a02, 1903. Section 60-1903 was enacted in an effort to alleviate a perceived crisis in the availability and affordability of liability insurance. . . . The purpose of these limitations would be furthered if any damage award issued would affect the availability or affordability of liability insurance for Kansas residents. The purpose of these limitations would not be furthered by applying them to the instant case because an award of damages against General Motors which exceeded Kansas's statutory damage limitations would not affect the availability or affordability of liability insurance for Kansas residents.

Lastly, Kansas law allows for punitive damages, but limits them to the lesser of $5 million or the defendant's highest gross annual income earned during any one of the five years immediately before the act for which such damages are awarded. The purpose of the availability and extent of punitive damage awards is to punish or deter conduct deemed wrongful when the availability of a cause of action and compensatory damages are considered an insufficient punishment or deterrence. Accordingly, the purpose of Kansas's punitive damage provisions would only be furthered on a particular set of facts if it had an interest in punishing or deterring the conduct at issue. As noted above, the purpose of Kansas's cause of action for product liability would not be furthered by its application to these facts because the pickup was not sold in Kansas nor were the Byrds Kansas residents. Correspondingly, this case does not involve conduct which Kansas was attempting to punish or deter through its punitive damage provisions.

b.   Place of Conduct

The Byrds purchased the vehicle in North Carolina. General Motors has made a general assertion that North Carolina might have an interest in having its law applied, but has not briefed us on which North Carolina laws might be applicable. Accordingly, our discussion will be somewhat general in nature. General Motors has argued that North Carolina has an interest because General Motors initially sold the truck in North Carolina, the Byrds subsequently purchased the truck in North Carolina, and the Byrds may have been North Carolina residents when they made this purchase.

The fact that the Byrds purchased the truck in North Carolina while residing there indicates that one of the purposes of North Carolina product liability law—the regulation of products sold within its borders—might be implicated by the facts of this case. However, we think it significant that a North Carolina court would not apply North Carolina law to these facts, even if the Byrds had remained in North Carolina; North Carolina still adheres to the traditional place of injury rule in tort cases. On the facts of this case, a North Carolina court would apply the law of Kansas because they still adhere to the "vested rights" theory that any right created by an injury is solely a product of the law of the territory in which that injury occurred. Accordingly, the scope of North Carolina product liability law does not include causes of action for products purchased in North Carolina by North Carolina residents which cause injury outside of North Carolina. This belies the significance of North Carolina's interest in having its law applied. We note, however, that the place of purchase may have had greater significance if North Carolina followed the Restatement's approach rather than the traditional place of injury rule.

General Motors asserts that Michigan has an interest in regulating conduct occurring in Michigan. We note that evidence of where the pickup truck was designed and manufactured is not in the record nor has General Motors briefed us on the content of the precise laws which it claims might be applicable to these facts. However, we do not believe that the purpose of any potentially applicable Michigan product liability law would be to regulate the design and manufacture of products within its borders. The purpose of product liability law is to regulate in-state sales or sales to residents and to set the level of compensation when residents are injured.

Significantly, Michigan courts have recognized that it would not further the purpose of Michigan product liability law to apply it to a similar set of facts. Michigan courts have not applied Michigan law under similar circumstances because Michigan has little interest in applying its law when its only contact with the dispute is the location of the manufacturer.

Other courts have observed that applying the law of the place of manufacture would be unfair because it would tend to leave victims under compensated as states wishing to attract and hold manufacturing companies would raise the threshold of liability and reduce compensation. We agree that stressing the importance of the place of manufacture for choice of law purposes in a product liability case would be unfair. The conclusion that the place of manufacture is a relatively unimportant factor in a product liability case is obvious when we consider a hypothetical case in which all of the relevant contacts are in the forum state except the location of the manufacturer (most likely the fact pattern for the vast majority of product liability cases). Applying the law of the place of manufacture to that case simply because the product was manufactured out-of-state would allow a state with a high concentration of industry to capture all of the benefits of a high threshold of liability and a low level of compensation. Specifically, the manufacturing state could enjoy the benefits associated with liability laws which favored manufacturers in order to attract and retain manufacturing firms and encourage business within its borders while placing the costs of its legislative decision, in the form of less tort compensation, on the shoulders of nonresidents injured by its manufacturers' products. This seems inherently unfair.

c. Residence of Parties

The Plaintiffs were residents of Montana at the time they were injured. Unlike the laws of the other states with relevant contacts under §145(2), the purposes sought to be achieved by Montana's product liability laws would be furthered by their application to this set of facts.[1] One of the central purposes of Montana's product liability scheme is to prevent injuries to Montana residents caused by defectively designed products. In contrast to Kansas, Montana has a direct interest in the application of its product liability laws because its residents were injured in this accident. Montana adopted a strict liability standard in order to afford *"maximum protection for consumers against dangerous defects in manufactured products with the focus on the condition of the product, and not on the manufacturer's conduct or knowledge." See* Sternhagen v. Dow Co. (1997), 282 Mont. 168, 176 (emphasis added).

As is clear from *Sternhagen*, the focus of Montana law is not only on the regulation of products sold in Montana, but also on providing the maximum protection and compensation to Montana residents with the focus on the condition of the product and not on the conduct of the manufacturer. Applying Montana's provisions guaranteeing strict liability and full compensation to a cause of action involving a Montana domiciliary injured by a defective product would further the purposes of Montana law by insuring that the costs to Montana residents due to injuries from defective products are fully borne by the responsible parties. It will also have the salutary effect of deterring future sales of defective products in Montana and encouraging manufacturers to warn Montana residents about defects in their products as quickly and as thoroughly as possible.

Likewise, the purposes of Montana's laws regarding the availability and extent of punitive damages in product liability actions would also be furthered by their application to these facts. This is because, as described more fully above, punitive damages serve to punish and deter conduct deemed wrongful—in this case, placing a defective product into the stream of commerce which subsequently injured a Montana resident.

Lastly, we must address whether the purpose underlying Montana's rules governing product liability would be furthered by their application in this case despite the fact that Samuel Byrd is no longer a Montana domiciliary. We believe that the application of Montana law to an injury received by a Montana domiciliary would further the purpose of that law regardless of the postaccident residency of the plaintiff. As discussed previously, the purpose of Montana product liability law is to regulate product sales in Montana and to compensate injured Montanans. Clearly, that concern arises as soon as a product is either sold in Montana or causes injury to a Montana resident. Consequently, the relevant residence of the plaintiff is the residence at the time of injury.

---

1. In analyzing the place of manufacture, we fully addressed the relative significance of General Motors' principal place of business under this principle. Neither party asserts that Delaware, General Motors' place of incorporation, has any interest in having its product liability or wrongful death statutes apply to this case.

We note that the only reason Samuel Byrd is currently residing in North Carolina is because his parents died in the accident which forms the basis of the Plaintiffs' claims. The guarantee of full compensation for Montana residents who suffer injuries due to defective products certainly will not turn on such fortuitous circumstances as a postaccident move caused by the allegedly wrongful conduct of a defendant.

d.   The Place Where the Relationship, if Any, Between the Parties Is Centered

It doesn't appear that there is a place where the relationship, if any, between General Motors and the Byrds is centered. As one court described in similar circumstances:

> Products liability arises out of the most casual "relationship" imaginable, the one-time purchase and sale of the product, and the plaintiff, as here, may have had no connection with it. The only "relationship" between the parties here is that of injured victim and alleged tortfeasor. [citation omitted]

In sum, upon an analysis of the principle requiring us to consider the policies of interested states, it appears that Montana, as the domicile of the Byrds, has a significant relationship to the issues raised by this dispute. This is because, in general, the purpose of a state's product liability law is to regulate purchases made within its borders and to protect and compensate its residents. The policies underlying Montana product liability law would be furthered on these facts because the Byrds were Montana domiciliaries at the time they were injured. The policies underlying Kansas and Michigan law would not be furthered by their application to these facts because the product was not sold in either state, nor were the Plaintiffs domiciled in either state at the time they where injured. The purposes underlying North Carolina product liability law would not be furthered on these facts because, under North Carolina's vested rights approach to conflict of laws, North Carolina would apply the law of the jurisdiction where the injury occurred, whatever that law may be.

3.   JUSTIFIED EXPECTATIONS

Although we are to consider the justified expectations of the parties, tort cases generally do not involve justified expectations. Particularly in the area of negligence, when parties act without giving thought to the legal consequences of their conduct or to the law to be applied, they have no justified expectations. *See* Restatement (Second) §6 cmt. g.

Automobile manufacturers do presumably give advance thought to the legal consequences of their conduct when designing and manufacturing their products. However, we note that the law of any state could potentially apply in a product liability action involving an automobile. For example, because North Carolina employs the traditional place of injury rule for choice of law purposes, if a North Carolina resident receives an injury from a defective vehicle while driving out-of-state, the law of the place of injury would govern that dispute.

Accordingly, any expectation General Motors had that the law of North Carolina would govern a product liability suit involving a pickup truck it sold in North Carolina would not be justified. Furthermore, . . . automobiles are moveable and frequently resold and the maintenance of a product liability action does not require privity. For example, the pickup could have been subsequently resold by the initial purchaser in a state which does not adhere to the traditional *lex loci* rule. Therefore, any expectation General Motors had that a dispute concerning this pickup truck would be governed by North Carolina's place of injury rule would not be justified.

4. BASIC POLICIES UNDERLYING PARTICULAR FIELD OF LAW

We must also consider the relevant contacts in regard to the basic policies underlying the particular field of law. *See* Restatement (Second) §6(2)(e). The drafters state that:

> This factor is of particular importance in situations where the policies of the interested states are largely the same but there are nevertheless minor differences between their relevant local law rules. In such instances, there is good reason for the court to apply the local law of the state which will best achieve the basic policy, or policies, underlying the particular field of law involved.

Restatement (Second) §6(2) cmt. h. This is not a case in which the policies of interested states are basically the same except for minor differences in their local rules. For example, although under Kansas and Montana law, manufacturers of defective products are strictly liable for injuries, North Carolina law does not permit strict liability in tort in product liability actions. Instead, it appears that the various interested states have reached different conclusions concerning the right level of compensation and deterrence for injuries caused by defective products. Therefore, we need go no further in addressing this contact.

5. CERTAINTY, PREDICTABILITY, UNIFORMITY, EASE

We are also instructed to give consideration to the certainty, predictability and uniformity of result as well as the ease in the determination and application of the law to be applied. *See* Restatement (Second) §6(2)(f) and (g). The comments state:

> Predictability and uniformity of result are of particular importance in areas where parties are likely to give advance thought to the legal consequences of their transactions. It is partly on account of these factors that the parties are permitted within broad limits to choose the law that will determine the validity and effect of their contract. . . .

Restatement (Second) §6(2) cmt. i. A consideration of this principle does not indicate that any one state has a more significant relationship than any other. Applying the law of the place of injury would not increase certainty or predictability any more than applying the law of the plaintiff's residence at the time of accident.

C. Conclusion

Under the most significant relationship approach of the Restatement (Second), the local law of the place of injury, Kansas, governs the rights and liabilities of the parties to a product liability and wrongful death action unless, with respect to a particular issue, a different state has a more significant relationship. *See* Restatement (Second) §§146 and 175. In order to determine whether a state other than the place of injury has a more significant relationship, the contacts listed under §145(2) must be analyzed in relation to the principles enumerated under §6(2). However, the principles of §6(2) need not be given equal consideration in each case. Varying weight must be given to a particular factor, or group of factors, in different areas of choice of law. *See* Restatement (Second) §6 cmt. c. On the facts before us, we give most weight to the principles requiring us to consider the relevant policies of interested states. Restatement (Second) §6(2)(b) and (c). The other principles do not indicate the significance of any one contact.

Upon an analysis of the policies of interested states, it appears that the purposes of both Montana and North Carolina product liability law would presumably be furthered by their application to these facts. The place of purchase has an interest in regulating the safety of products sold within its borders; the place of the plaintiff's residence has an interest in deterring injuries to its residents and setting the level of compensation. Significantly, however, North Carolina law would not apply its own law to these facts, even if the Byrds had been North Carolina residents at the time of injury.

The purpose behind Montana product liability laws is clearly implicated by these facts. The following factors all point toward applying Montana law: The Byrds resided in Montana at the time of the accident; General Motors does business in Montana; Montana has a direct interest in preventing defective products from causing injuries to Montana residents as well as punishing and deterring manufacturers whose products injure Montana residents; and, finally, Montana is interested in fully compensating Montana residents. All of these factors would be furthered by applying Montana product liability, defenses, damages, and wrongful death statutes to the facts of this case.

Question Three

Does Montana recognize a "public policy" exception that would require application of Montana law even where Montana's choice-of-law rules dictate application of the laws of another state, and would such an exception apply in this case?

For choice of law purposes, the public policy of a state is simply the rules, as expressed in its legislative enactments and judicial decisions, that it uses to decide controversies. The purpose of a choice of law rule is to resolve conflicts between competing policies. Considerations of public policy are expressly subsumed within the most significant relationship approach. *See* Restatement (Second) §6(2)(b) and (c) (mandating consideration of the relevant policies of the forum state and other interested states). In order to determine which state has the more significant relationship, the public policies of all interested states must be considered. A "public policy" exception to the most significant relationship test would be redundant.

Accordingly, in answer to the questions certified, we adopt the Restatement (Second) of Conflict of Laws for tort actions. Under the analysis contained in the Restatement (Second), we conclude that given the facts as presented in the District Court's Order, the laws of Montana apply. Lastly, considerations of public policy are accounted for under the analysis contained in the Restatement (Second) of Conflict of Laws.

Questions and Comments

(1) The history of the drafting of the Second Restatement helps to explain its complex methodology. The project began in 1953 as a response to the harsh criticisms of the First Restatement. The first tentative draft retained the First Restatement's jurisdiction-selecting approach but used the more flexible jurisdiction-selecting criteria of the "most significant relationship" test. Early drafts of the Second Restatement were heavily criticized by Currie and Ehrenzweig (among others) on the grounds that its rules focused too much on territorialism and ignored interest analysis. *See* Currie, *The Disinterested Third State*, 28 Law & Contemp. Probs. 754, 755 (1963); Ehrenzweig, *The "Most Significant Relationship" in the Conflicts Law of Torts: Law and Reason Versus the Restatement Second*, 28 Law & Contemp. Probs. 700, 700 (1963). Section 6 was a response to these criticisms. In the words of one writer, it was "a sop tossed . . . to members of the American Law Institute who were unhappy with a purely territorial methodology." Reppy, *Eclecticism in Choice of Law: Hybrid Method or Mishmash?*, 34 Mercer L. Rev. 645, 662 (1983).

(2) How would you characterize the Second Restatement as applied in *Phillips*? Was it a contacts-counting, center-of-gravity case? Or was it more akin to interest analysis? Does the Second Restatement allow a court to do either, or both?

(3) How far does the Second Restatement actually depart from the first? Professor Gary J. Simson appears to believe that the difference is not substantial, arguing that the "presumptive rules adopted [by the Second Restatement] frequently bear a striking and rather frightful resemblance to the territorial rules that the Second Restatement purported to lay to rest. Indeed, it is positively stunning to see the much criticized place-of-wrong rule whose illogic spurred the first overt judicial breaks with the traditional rules rise from the ashes to take on the status of a presumptive rule in section after section of the chapter on torts." Simson, *Leave Bad Enough Alone*, 75 Ind. L.J. 649, 651 (2000).

Is Professor Simson correct? More to the point, is it really a cause for concern that the *presumptive*—and hence displaceable—rules adopted by the Second Restatement have some similar features as the bright-line rules of the First Restatement, which are much harder to take exception to? One needs to look no further than *Phillips* to see that courts can remain faithful to the Second Restatement while taking exception to the presumptive rules that it provides. For more on the advantages of the multi-factor approach compared to the First Restatement's single-factor approach, *see* Brilmayer & Anglin, *Choice of Law Theory and the Metaphysics of the Stand-Alone Trigger*, 95 Iowa L. Rev. 1125 (2010).

(4) What do you think of the *Phillips* court's interest analysis? What states have an interest in the welfare of a corporation? Its state of incorporation? Headquarters? Principal place of business? Place of manufacture? Wherever it operates its business? The court says that Michigan would not have an interest in regulating the design and manufacture of products within its borders. Why not? The court's interest analysis here is faithful to Currie's proposal, but doesn't it seem at least possible that states wish to encourage safe manufacturing within their borders? The court also says that it would be unfair to apply the law of the place of manufacture because then a state could attract the manufacturing industry with lax laws "on the shoulders of nonresidents injured by the manufacturers' products." It seems reasonable that a place-of-manufacture rule could lead to a race to the bottom for product liability laws. But applying the law of the plaintiff's residence for nationally marketed products could conversely cause states to race to provide their residents with too much injury compensation, assuming that the costs of the extra liability get spread across all of the company's consumers. *See* McConnell, *A Choice-of-Law Approach to Product Liability Reform*, in *New Directions in Liability Law* 90 (Walter Olson ed., 1988).

(5) The Second Restatement is by far the most popular choice-of-law methodology in the United States. Approximately 25 states have formally embraced its approach to torts, and 24 have embraced its approach to contracts. *See* Symeonides, *Choice of Law in the American Courts in 2018: Twenty-Fourth Annual Survey*, 67 Am. J. Comp. L. __ (2019). These numbers are misleading, however. As Professor Symeonides has noted, Second Restatement courts evince wildly varying "gradations of commitment to the Second Restatement," and perform many different choice-of-law analyses in its name. *See* Symeonides, *The Judicial Acceptance of the Second Conflicts Restatement, A Mixed Blessing*, 56 Md. L. Rev. 1248, 1261-1263 (1997). Some courts use the Second Restatement's specific presumptive rules to break a true conflict, *see, e.g.*, Reichhold Chemicals, Inc. v. Hartford Accident and Indemnity Co., 703 A.2d 1132 (Conn. 1997) (applying §193 to break true conflict between New York and Washington law). Other courts ignore the Second Restatement's specific presumptive rules even when they are on point, *see, e.g.*, Allstate Insurance Co. v. Stolarz, 613 N.E.2d 936 (N.Y. 1993) (applying Second Restatement but ignoring §193 in case involving insurance stacking). Some courts use the Second Restatement to perform a "grouping-of-contacts" analysis, *see, e.g.*, Palmer v. ARCO Chem. Co., 904 P.2d 1221 (Alaska 1995), others use it to curtail but not avoid interest analysis, *see, e.g.*, Nelson v. Hix, 522 N.E.2d 1214 (Ill. 1988), and yet others use it in a manner akin to the First Restatement, *see, e.g.*, Hataway v. McKinley, 830 S.W.2d 53, 58 (Tenn. 1992). There are many other possibilities. Is the discretion that the Second Restatement obviously gives judges the key to its widespread acceptance?

(6) One author's survey of Second Restatement cases led to the following conclusions:

> Some state courts routinely list [the Restatement's] relevant sections in their opinions and try to follow them; this task is easiest when the case is controlled by one of the Restatement Second's specific narrow rules. Other state courts have not been consistent in their terminology about what approach they are following, and others have retained primary emphasis on the place of the wrong

in tort cases, even while abandoning the lex loci delicti for the Restatement Second. . . . This review of the cases suggests that, if the original Restatement was unsuccessful because of its dogmatic rigidity and its insistence on the uncritical application of a few specific rules, the Restatement Second may fail to provide enough guidance to the courts to produce even a semblance of uniformity among the states following its method. In the drafters' attempt to mollify their critics, they have created an umbrella for traditionalist and modern theorist alike: a fragile shelter that may prove itself unable to survive any but the most gentle of showers.

Kay, *Theory into Practice: Choice of Law in the Courts*, 34 Mercer L. Rev. 521, 561-562 (1983). An Oregon court was less gentle, comparing the Second Restatement to "skeet shooting with a bow and arrow: a direct hit is likely to be a rarity, if not pure luck." Fisher v. Huck, 624 P.2d 177, 178 (Or. 1981).

(7) Do the Second Restatement's specific "presumptive" rules (like §§146 and 175 at issue in *Phillips*) have any bite? Doesn't a court applying the Second Restatement with rigor always have to ensure that there is not a state with a "more significant relationship"? And doesn't this, in turn, push courts back into the conundrum of sorting out the relationship between sections 6 and 145? Isn't this what happened in *Phillips*? Why, then, have the specific provisions?

(8) One of the problems with the First Restatement that the Second Restatement retains (apparently deliberately) is characterization. Characterization is one difficulty that other modern approaches seem to have dispensed with effectively. Although section 6 sets out the general principles for all issues—substantive and procedural, tort and contract, and the like—the remainder of the Second Restatement attempts to provide more specific principles to deal with these separate categories. Resolution of the question of whether products liability or insurance indemnification (to name just two examples) should be analyzed according to sections 146 or 188 can determine the outcome of the choice-of-law process.

(9) For further analysis of the *Phillips* court's public policy analysis, *see infra* pages 268-269. For further analysis of its use of renvoi, *see infra* page 256.

America Online, Inc. v. National Health Care Discount, Inc.

121 F. Supp. 2d 1255 (D. Iowa 2000)

Zoss, Magistrate Judge.

[Plaintiff America Online, Inc. ("AOL"), a Delaware corporation, with its principal place of business in Virginia, is an Internet access provider that allows its subscribers to transmit electronic mail ("e-mail") to and from other AOL subscribers and across the Internet. Defendant National Health Care Discount, Inc. ("NHCD"), an Iowa corporation with its administrative offices in Sioux City, Iowa, and sales offices in Atlanta, Kansas City, Phoenix, Dallas, and Denver, is in the business of selling discount optical and dental service plans. Using contract e-mailers from all over the country (including, primarily, the services of Forrest Dayton of Marietta, Georgia), NHCD solicited business through large-volume, "unsolicited bulk e-mail" ("UBE"), sometimes known as "spam." Millions of these messages went to AOL users, at great expense to AOL. When AOL failed to persuade NHCD to stop sending such messages to its subscribers, it sued the company for common-law conversion, trespass, and unjust enrichment, as well as violation of various state and federal statutes.]

A federal court exercising supplemental jurisdiction over state law claims in a federal question lawsuit must follow the choice-of-law rules of the forum state. Accordingly, the court looks to Iowa's choice-of-law rules to determine which state's law applies.

As both AOL and NHCD agree, Iowa follows the "most significant relationship" test expressed in section 145, Restatement (Second) Conflict of Laws ("Restatement"). The agreement ends there, however, as the parties differ on how the Restatement factors apply in the circumstances of this case.

[The court recites sections 145 and 6 of the Second Restatement, reproduced at pages 227-228 *supra*.]

The parties only address the section 145 factors in their arguments concerning which state law applies here. As NHCD points out in its brief, none of those factors [place of injury, conduct, center of relationship, and domicile, residence, place of incorporation and of business of parties] points conclusively to Virginia—nor, however, do those factors point clearly to Iowa or to any other state. The section 145 factors provide little in the way of resolving the choice-of-law issue. The court therefore turns to the principles set forth in section 6.

The principles in section 6(2) "underlie all rules of choice of law and are used in evaluating the significance of a relationship, with respect to the particular issue, to the potentially interested states, the occurrence and the parties." Restatement §145, comment (b). Subsections 6(2)(d), (e) and (f) are less important in the field of torts than they are in other areas such as contracts, property, wills and trusts. *Id.* "Because of the relative insignificance of the above-mentioned factors in the tort area of choice of law, the remaining factors listed in §6 assume greater importance. . . ," particularly the relevant policies of "the state with the dominant interest in the determination of the particular issue." *Id.* The court finds the factors in subsections (2)(b) and (c) to be controlling; *i.e.*, the relevant policies and interests of Iowa and Virginia.

As noted previously, NHCD is an Iowa corporation, doing business in Iowa. "[A] state has an obvious interest in regulating the conduct of persons within its territory. . . ." Restatement §6, comment d. Iowa's interest in regulating the actions of corporations doing business in Iowa is embodied in the Iowa Business Corporation Act, Iowa Code chapter 490. A corporation has no rights, including the right to do business, other than the rights conferred by the state's lawmaking power, and the state retains the right to amend the conditions under which corporations may do or continue to do business, and enforce those conditions by revoking a corporation's privileges for noncompliance. The state, therefore, has a vested interest in determining the rights and liabilities of domestic corporations as to actions arising within the state.

Here, however, the only actions by NHCD that appear to have arisen within Iowa are incorporation of the entity, maintenance of an office, and issuance of checks to pay the contract e-mailers. One could add to this list the receipt of NHCD's UBE by Iowa residents. Otherwise, all the actions giving rise to this lawsuit appear to have occurred elsewhere, in a number of states. AOL is incorporated in Delaware, and likely has members who received NHCD's UBE in all fifty states. Dayton's actions originated in Georgia. The record indicates NHCD contracted with other e-mailers from, *inter alia*, New York, California, Ohio, Florida, Missouri, Michigan, Tennessee, Kansas, Ohio and Maryland. NHCD's vice president Hermann Wilms, who, among other things, was responsible for contracting with Dayton, operated out of Overland Park, Kansas.

In addition to "regulating the conduct of persons within its territory," a state also has "an obvious interest . . . in providing redress for injuries that occurred there." Restatement §6, comment e. In the instant case, because there is no clearly demonstrable place where the alleged conduct occurred, "the place where the injury occurred is a contact that, as to most issues, plays an important role in the selection of the state of the applicable law." *Id.*

The only locale in which AOL's alleged injury is clearly demonstrable is Virginia. This is the site of AOL's hardware that it alleges was overburdened by NHCD's UBE. It also is the place where AOL allegedly sustained economic loss. Although no state has a clear relationship to the events giving rise to this action, Virginia's relationship appears to be the most significant. Accordingly, the court finds Virginia law shall control the non-statutory claims raised in this lawsuit.

Questions and Comments

(1) For a 25-year retrospective symposium on the Second Restatement, *see The Silver Anniversary of the Second Conflicts Restatement*, 56 Md. L. Rev. 1193-1410 (1997). For a symposium on the need for a Third Restatement of Conflicts, with much critical analysis of the Second Restatement, *see Preparing for the Next Century — A New Restatement of Conflicts?*, 75 Ind. L.J. 399-686 (2000).

As of the publication of this edition, the drafting of a Restatement (Third) was already well underway. The Third Restatement is likely to prove radically different from the First and Second Restatements, given that current drafts explicitly favor interest analysis (now recast as "two-step theory") as the best basic approach. The black letter and reporter's notes discuss the theoretical reasons for switching to a two-step theory of interests (now termed "scope") in considerable depth, reflecting perhaps the stature of Reporter Kermit Roosevelt as an eminent scholar on choice of law. But current drafts also maintain the pattern set by the Restatement (Second) by providing a detailed set of rules specifying what should be done with particular causes of action and defense. The judge is advised to apply these rules directly, generally without recourse to the two-step analysis of statutory scope that motivated the particularized rules in the first place.

This new Restatement has already provoked at least one published exchange analyzing the already existing tentative drafts at a high theoretical level. Brilmayer and Listwa argue that the Restatement's attempt to combine the theory of interests/scope with an approach based on rules is fundamentally unworkable theoretically and may prove not to provide the sought-after advantages of predictability, avoidance of forum-shopping, and so forth. Brilmayer & Listwa, *Continuity and Change in the Draft Restatement (Third) of Conflict of Laws: One Step Forward and Two Steps Back?*, 128 Yale L.J. Forum 266 (2018). The reporter and a co-author have defended the draft Third Restatement against such criticisms. Roosevelt & Jones, *The Draft Restatement (Third) of Conflict of Laws: A Response to*

Brilmayer and Listwa, 128 Yale L.J. Forum 293, 296 (2018). Interests/scope, they argue, are supposed to reflect the policies underlying the particular statutes vying for application in the case at hand. Yet the rules that the Third Restatement asks judges to follow are not based on interpretation of particular statutes; they are based on a survey of case law and academic commentary from across the entire nation. The theory underlying Brainerd Currie's theory of interests was that a judge should not sacrifice his or her own state's interest by following rules drafted by persons lacking any authority to represent the political processes of the state. This controversy is surely not yet over.

Another source of interest in the Third Restatement is how it will treat international cases. *See* Borchers, *How "International" Should a Third Conflicts Restatement Be in Tort and Contract?*, 27 Duke J. Comp. & Intl. L. 461 (2017), and Michaels & Whytock, *Internationalizing the New Conflict of Laws Restatement*, 27 Duke J. Comp. & Intl. L. 349, 351 (2017).

For additional academic commentary on the Third Restatement, *see* Borchers, *An Essay on Predictability in Choice-of-Law Doctrine and Implications for a Third Conflicts Restatement*, 49 Creighton L. Rev. 495 (2016); Roosevelt & Jones, *What a Third Restatement of Conflict of Laws Can Do*, 110 AJIL Unbound 139, 139 (2016); Symeonides, *The Third Conflicts Restatement's First Draft on Tort Conflicts*, 92 Tul. L. Rev. 1 (2017).

(2) The Internet presents two general choice-of-law problems. The first is the problem of *complexity*. This is the problem of how to choose a single governing law for Internet activity that has multi-jurisdictional contacts. The second problem concerns *situs*. This is the problem of how to choose a governing law when the locus of relevant activity cannot easily be pinpointed in geographical space. Both problems raise similar concerns. The choice of any dispositive geographical contact or any particular law in these cases will often seem arbitrary because several jurisdictions have a legitimate claim to apply their law. Whatever law is chosen, seemingly genuine regulatory interests of the nations whose laws are not applied may be impaired.

Consider this hypothetical:

> Whose substantive legal rules apply to a defamatory message that is written by someone in Mexico, read by someone in Israel, by means of an Internet server located in the United States, injuring the reputation of a Norwegian?

Perritt, *Jurisdiction in Cyberspace*, 41 Vill. L. Rev. 1, 3 (1996). And this one:

> Which of the many plausibly applicable bodies of copyright law do we consult to determine whether a hyperlink on a World Wide Web page located on a server in France and constructed by a Filipino citizen, which points to a server in Brazil that contains materials protected by German and French (but not Brazilian) copyright law, which is downloaded to a server in the United States and reposted to a Usenet newsgroup, constitutes a remediable infringement of copyright?

Post & Johnson, *"Chaos Prevailing on Every Continent": Towards a New Theory of Decentralized Decision-Making in Complex Systems*, 73 Chi.-Kent. L. Rev. 1055, 1056 (1998).

These are genuine problems, but are they new to the Internet? Haven't we seen identical problems throughout this casebook? Indeed, aren't the problems of complexity and situs *the* problems in the conflict of laws? Are the Internet problems presented here more complex than the same issues in "real space"? Are they any more complex than similar issues presented by real-space events such as airplane crashes, mass torts, or multinational commercial transactions? Are they any more complex than a simple products liability suit arising from a two-car accident among residents of the same state? *Compare* Rutherford v. Goodyear Tire and Rubber Co., 943 F. Supp. 789, 790-791 (W.D. Ky. 1996), *aff'd*, 142 F.3d 436 (6th Cir. 1998) (two-car accident between residents of same state implicates the laws of the place of the accident, the states where the car and tire manufacturers are headquartered, the states where the car and tires were manufactured, and the state where the car was purchased). Is the real challenge of the Internet perhaps not the presence of new conflicts problems, but rather the dramatic increase in the number and percentage of intractable conflicts problems?

(3) The parties and events in *National Health Care Discount* (including the millions of UBE messages that formed the basis for the complaint) implicated contacts in every state in the union. But is every geographical contact equally significant? Why did the court discount the state of the defendant's incorporation, the states where the UBEs were received, and the states where the contract e-mailers were located? Why didn't it discuss the states where the routers and servers through which the UBEs traveled were located?

(4) Which conflicts-of-law methodology is best suited to Internet transactions? Consider:

> [C]yberspace transactions [need not] be resolved on the basis of geographical choice-of-law criteria that are sometimes difficult to apply to cyberspace, such as where events occur or where people are located at the time of the transaction. [These] are not the only choice-of-law criteria, and certainly not the best in contexts where the geographical locus of events is so unclear. Domicile (and its cognates, such as citizenship, principal place of business, habitual residence, and so on) are also valid choice-of-law criteria that have particular relevance to problems, like those in cyberspace, that involve the regulation of intangibles or of multinational transactions. [Moreover,] all choice-of-law problems [need not] be resolved by multilateral choice-of-law methodologies. A multilateral methodology asks which of several possible laws governs a transaction, and selects one of these laws on the basis of specified criteria. Multilateral methods accentuate the situs and complexity problems. But the regulatory issues that are most relevant to the cyberspace governance debate almost always involve unilateral choice-of-law methods that alleviate these problems. A unilateral method considers only whether the dispute at issue has close enough connections to the forum to justify the application of local law. If so, local law applies; if not, the case is dismissed and the potential applicability of foreign law is not considered. Unilateral choice-of-law methods make the complexity and situs problems less significant. They do not require a determination of which of a number of possible laws apply. Nor do they require a court to identify where certain events occurred. What matters is simply whether the activity has local effects that are significant enough to implicate local law.

Goldsmith, *Against Cyberanarchy*, 65 U. Chi. L. Rev. 1199, 1236-1237 (1998). Is this convincing? Did *National Health Care Discount* have any problem applying a multilateral choice-of-law method that selected a place of injury? Would interest analysis, which in many guises is a unilateral choice-of-law method, have provided a more satisfactory resolution?

(5) Because Internet communications usually cross many physical borders and thus give rise to difficult conflict-of-law problems, several commentators have suggested that Internet transactions be governed not by the law of any particular territorial government, but rather by a private law chosen by Internet users that will be uniform across particular Internet communities. Some of these commentators view the Internet as a separate "place" whose self-governance territorial governments should defer to:

> Many of the jurisdictional and substantive quandaries raised by border-crossing electronic communications could be resolved by one simple principle: conceiving of Cyberspace as a distinct "place" for purposes of legal analysis by recognizing a legally significant border between Cyberspace and the "real world." Using this new approach, we would no longer ask the unanswerable question "where" in the geographical world a Net-based transaction occurred. Instead, the more salient questions become: What rules are best suited to the often unique characteristics of this new place and the expectations of those who are engaged in various activities there? What mechanisms exist or need to be developed to determine the content of those rules and the mechanisms by which they can be enforced? Answers to these questions will permit the development of rules better suited to the new phenomena in question, more likely to be made by those who understand and participate in those phenomena, and more likely to be enforced by means that the new global communications media make available and effective. . . .
>
> If the sysops and users who collectively inhabit and control a particular area of the Net want to establish special rules to govern conduct there, and if that rule set does not fundamentally impinge upon the vital interests of others who never visit this new space, then the law of sovereigns in the physical world should defer to this new form of self-government.

Johnson & Post, *Law and Borders — The Rise of Law in Cyberspace*, 48 Stan. L. Rev. 1367, 1378-1379, 1393 (1996).

Is the Internet best thought of as a separate place? Are Internet activities self-contained? Consider this response:

> Cyberspace participants are no more self-contained than telephone users, members of the Catholic Church, corporations, and other private groups with activities that transcend jurisdictional borders. They are real people in real space transacting in a fashion that produces real-world effects on cyberspace participants and nonparticipants alike. Cyberspace users solicit and deliver kiddie porn, launder money, sexually harass, defraud, and so on. It is these and many other real-space costs — costs that cyberspace communities cannot effectively internalize — that national regulatory regimes worry about and aim to regulate.

Goldsmith, *supra*, at 1242.

F.   Wrinkles in the Theory

While modern choice-of-law theories are different from one another in many respects, they also have important similarities. The common attributes are the goal of implementing state substantive policies and the dislike of rigid rules of the First Restatement variety. Because of their substantial similarities, there are some problems that modern theories share. We have already examined some of the recent theoretical criticisms leveled against governmental interest analysis. The problems arising in the cases below are shared by modern theories generally; indeed, they are not very different from some of the issues raised by the First Restatement.

1.   Domicile

The modern theories' assumption that state policies are often triggered by domicile makes domicile a key concept to the choice-of-law process. All of the problems that we saw in Chapter 2, pages 48-63, therefore also arise in the modern theories; indeed, they arise more frequently because domicile is important to a larger percentage of cases. In addition, there are problems about how to attribute a "domicile" to corporations, because, as suggested earlier, it is not clear which states have interests in protecting a corporation. The modern treatment of this issue is somewhat unsettled. *See generally* Note, *Interest Analysis Applied to Corporations: The Unprincipled Use of a Choice of Law Method*, 98 Yale L.J. 597 (1989).

One of the problems that plagues modern choice-of-law theories is that of after-acquired domicile, an issue briefly addressed in *Phillips, supra* page 229.

Reich v. Purcell

67 Cal. 2d 551, 442 P.2d 727, 63 Cal. Rptr. 31 (1967)

TRAYNOR, C.J.

This wrongful death action arose out of a head-on collision of two automobiles in Missouri. One of the automobiles was owned and operated by defendant Joseph Purcell, a resident and domiciliary of California who was on his way to a vacation in Illinois. The other automobile was owned and operated by Mrs. Reich, the wife of plaintiff Lee Reich. The Reichs then resided in Ohio and Mrs. Reich and the Reich's two children, Jay and Jeffry, were on their way to California, where the Reichs were contemplating settling. Mrs. Reich and Jay were killed in the collision, and Jeffry was injured.

Plaintiffs, Lee Reich and Jeffry Reich, are the heirs of Mrs. Reich and Lee Reich is the heir of Jay Reich. Plaintiffs moved to California and became permanent residents here after the accident. The estates of Mrs. Reich and Jay Reich are being administered in Ohio.

The parties stipulated that judgment be entered in specified amounts for the wrongful death of Jay, for the personal injuries suffered by Jeffry, and for the damages to Mrs. Reich's automobile. For the death of Mrs. Reich they stipulated that judgment be entered for $55,000 or $25,000 depending on the court's ruling on the applicability of the Missouri limitation of damages to a maximum of $25,000. Neither Ohio nor California limit recovery in wrongful death actions. The trial court held that the Missouri limitation applied because the accident occurred there and entered judgment accordingly. Plaintiffs appealed. . . .

As the forum we must consider all of the foreign and domestic elements and interests involved in this case to determine the rule applicable. Three states are involved. Ohio is where the plaintiffs and their decedents resided before the accident and where the decedents' estates are being administered. Missouri is the place of the wrong. California is the place where defendant resides and is the forum. Although plaintiffs now reside in California, their residence and domicile at the time of the accident are the relevant residence and domicile. At the time of the accident the plans to change the family domicile were not definite and fixed, and if the choice of law were made to turn on events happening after the accident, forum shopping would be encouraged. Accordingly, plaintiffs' present domicile in California does not give this state any interest in applying its law, and since California has no limitation on damages, it also has no interest in applying its law on behalf of defendant. As a forum that is therefore disinterested in the only issue in dispute, we must decide whether to adopt the Ohio or the Missouri rule as the rule of decision for this case.

[The court concluded that Missouri, as the situs of the accident, had no interest in imposing limitations on a wrongful death recovery, while Ohio had an interest, presumably as former domiciliary state, in affording a full recovery. It therefore applied Ohio law.]

Questions and Comments

(1) Isn't the court guilty of a rather bald non-sequitur in saying, "[F]orum shopping would be encouraged. Accordingly, plaintiffs' domicile in California does not give this state any interest in applying its law . . ."? Forum-shopping *may* be evil, and it may be something to be balanced against California's desire to see a full and fair recovery for its domiciliaries (especially when injured by another domiciliary), but can it accurately be said to prevent the existence of that interest in the first place?

(2) Does the mere possibility of forum-shopping justify the court's result? Aren't courts equipped to discover (within the bounds of acceptable uncertainty) states of mind in other courts? If forum-shopping is the only concern, shouldn't the plaintiffs have been allowed to show that they would have moved to California even if they had not contemplated litigation?

(3) Even if plaintiffs moved to California precisely to take advantage of its law, does California therefore have any less of an interest in their well-being? *Compare* Shapiro v. Thomson, 394 U.S. 618 (1969), in which the Supreme Court refused to allow New York to impose a one-year residency requirement for welfare benefits as a response (in part) to fears that New York's generosity would draw prospective welfare recipients. If forum-shopping is the only worry, and if (as suggested in note (2)), we can rely on the judicial process to weed out those who move to California solely to invoke its law while suing, can we be satisfied with giving

higher judgments to those who seek out California for its sunny beaches or its lifestyle than for its law?

Might there be reasons not mentioned by the court for rejecting after-acquired domicile as providing a state with "interests"? For an argument that the real explanation for this attitude toward after-acquired domicile must be found outside the premises of modern policy analysis, *see* Brilmayer, *Rights, Fairness, and Choice of Law*, 99 Yale L.J. 1277, 1286-1287 (1989).

(4) Is the situation any different if it is the defendant who has acquired a new domicile? Is it any different if either party acquires a new domicile with law less favorable than that of the previous domicile? In Miller v. Miller, 22 N.Y.2d 12 (1968), a New York resident was killed in a car accident in Maine. Maine limited recoveries for wrongful death; New York had a policy enshrined in its constitution against wrongful death limitations. The defendant, brother of the decedent, moved to New York a few months before suit was brought. (There was no evidence of collusion.) The case was complicated by the fact that Maine repealed its limitation after the accident. The Court of Appeals said,

> Having found no considerations present here arising out of fairness to the nominal or real party defendant, we turn next to the question of whether the application of New York law here will unduly interfere with a legitimate interest of a sister State in regulating the rights of its citizens, at least with regard to conduct within its borders. Here again we perceive no reason to deny application of our own law. To the extent that the Maine limitation evinced a desire to protect its residents in wrongful death actions, that purpose cannot be defeated here since no judgment in this action will be entered against a Maine resident. Maine would have no concern with the nature of the recovery awarded against defendants who are no longer residents of that State and who are, therefore, no longer proper objects of its legislative concern. It is true that, at the time of the accident, the defendants were residents of Maine but they would have no vested right to the application of the law of their former residence unless it could be demonstrated that they had governed their conduct in reliance upon it — a reliance which is neither present nor claimed in the case at bar. Any claim that Maine has a paternalistic interest in protecting its residents against liability for acts committed while they were in Maine, should they move to another jurisdiction, is highly speculative and ignores the fact that for the very same acts committed today Maine would now impose the same liability as New York.
>
> There may be times where policy considerations such as a desire to prevent forum shopping would require us to ignore changes in domicile after the accident (Gore v. Northeast Airlines; Reich v. Purcell). In the instant case, however, the change in domicile has nothing whatever to do with a desire to achieve a more favorable legal climate, and we see no reason to ignore the facts as they are presented at the time of the litigation. The two considerations urged in the dissenting opinion — the likelihood of discouraging wrongdoers from settling in this State lest they be held to respond for their wrongdoing and the possibility that wrongdoers will settle here in a collusive attempt to fix broader liability upon the insurer — contradict each other, are speculative and are insufficient to move us to disregard the change in domicile.

In Gore v. Northeast Airlines, 373 F.2d 717 (2d Cir. 1967), a federal court applying New York conflicts law held that a widow who moved away from New York could still invoke New York's refusal to allow limitations on wrongful death recoveries, even though the state of her new domicile was less solicitous of her welfare. Does this mean a heads-I-win-tails-you-lose approach favoring forum law?

(5) In Clay v. Sun Insurance Office, Ltd., 377 U.S. 179 (1964), reproduced *infra* page 294, the Supreme Court upheld the constitutionality (though of course did not pass on the wisdom) of application of a Florida statute providing for a minimum period during which suit could be brought on an insurance contract, despite a clause in the insurance contract providing for a shorter period. The contract had been purchased and paid for in Illinois by plaintiff, who was then a resident of Illinois. He later moved to Florida where the loss occurred, and sued after the contractual period had expired but before the Florida statutory period had expired.

Professor Currie said of *Clay*:

> It is vitally important that the Florida court answer one specific question: Assuming that the policy expressed in the statute is one designed "to preserve a fair opportunity for people who have bought and paid for insurance to go to court and collect it," is the evil which that policy is designed to alleviate so acute, and is the policy so exigent, that Florida believes it necessary to apply the statute from its effective date onward for the protection of the total population of Florida, including residents who had previously entered into domestic contracts containing such "suit clauses"? In other words, is the statute construed as having retroactive effect? If the answer is no, the Court's problem is solved. If Florida has no policy of protection for residents who entered into such contracts before they were protected by the statute, it has no policy that can rationally be applied to upset vested rights under contracts made under circumstances such that Florida then had no interest in them. If the answer is yes, the Court must determine a different question—probably an easier one, since it is an ordinary question of constitutional law rather than mixed with conflict-of-laws theory. Is such retroactive legislation a reasonable exercise of the lawmaking power under the Due Process and Contracts clauses?

Currie, *The Verdict of the Quiescent Years*, in *Selected Essays on the Conflict of Laws* 584, 625-626 (1963). Currie later modified this position by noting an important difference between retroactive legislation and situations like *Clay*: A state may forgo making legislation retroactive, even though it could do so, because the evils of prior law will diminish and disappear with time—eventually, for example, all current Florida insurance contracts will have been entered or renewed after the date of the Florida statute in question. On the other hand, insured parties may continue to travel ad infinitum from Illinois to Florida. The continuing nature of the latter problem might justify application of the state's new law even when the same had not been made retroactive in domestic cases. Currie, *Conflict, Crisis and Confusion in New York*, in *Selected Essays on the Conflict of Laws* 690, 739 (1963). For criticism of Currie's revised position, *see* Hancock, *The Effect in Choice of Law Cases of the Acquisition of a New Domicile After the Commission of a Tort or Making of a Contract*, 2 Hastings Intl. & Comp. L. Rev. 215, 220-223 (1979).

The Supreme Court again allowed a postaccident change of domicile to the forum to result in the application of forum law in Allstate Insurance Co. v. Hague, page 297 *infra*.

(6) The drafters of the Restatement Second were equally perplexed by the after-acquired domicile problem. The Introductory Note to Chapter 7 (Wrongs) says:

> Mention should here be made of a problem which runs through the entire area of choice of law. This problem is whether a change in a party's relationship to a state following the occurrence should ever affect choice of the applicable law. For example, let us suppose that at the time of an automobile accident in state X the plaintiff is domiciled in state Y and the defendant is domiciled in state Z, but that the plaintiff acquires a domicil in Z before bringing suit. Should this shift of the plaintiff's domicil from Y to Z have any impact on choice of the law governing any of the issues that might arise between the plaintiff and the defendant by reason of the accident? Presumably this change of domicil should have no effect upon the law governing most of the issues involving the accident. But is this necessarily true of all issues? The problem is not dealt with in the Restatement of this Subject because existing authority is too sparse to warrant doing so.

(7) Sometimes the change in domicile occurs after some of the events leading up to the litigation but before others. In Lange v. Penn Mutual Life Insurance Co., 843 F.2d 1175 (9th Cir. 1988), a court, applying the Restatement Second, was faced with a suit to recover a life insurance policy. Plaintiff had purchased the policy while a resident of Arizona, and this was where her husband died. She then moved to Iowa and was living there at the point that her insurance claim was denied. She was still in Iowa when her complaint was filed, but moved back to Arizona before the trial began.

(8) One of the chief problems of the First Restatement was that it singled out some unique territorial connecting factor, despite the fact that the litigation involved events in a number of different states in addition. Even if one agreed that what mattered was the location of events, therefore, the choice of a single territorial event was arbitrary. On this problem, *see generally* Brilmayer & Anglin, *Choice of Law Theory and the Metaphysics of the Stand-Alone Trigger*, 95 Iowa L. Rev. 1125 (2010).

Do the modern theories have exactly the same problem with domiciliary connecting factors? First, some individuals and corporate entities have multiple connections (residence, domicile, place of incorporation, principal place of business, etc.). Second, these factors change over time. While the nemesis of the First Restatement was the case where *events* were widely scattered, the nemesis of the new learning is the case with widely scattered personal or corporate *affiliations*.

Should modern theories, just by fiat, choose a particular point in time at which to measure domicile? When should that be — the time when the cause of action "accrued" (i.e., the time when the rights "vested")? Recall the problems with "vesting" discussed in Chapter 2, especially those in determining where or when the rights "accrued" for purpose of applying the forum's borrowing statute.

(9) Plaintiff is in the process of moving from State A to State B. On the way, she becomes involved in an auto accident. Which state has an "interest" in her? Doesn't her domicile at the time of the accident depend on where the accident occurred?

2. Renvoi

Pfau v. Trent Aluminum Co.

55 N.J. 511, 263 A.2d 129 (1970)

PROCTOR, J.

This appeal presents a conflict of laws problem regarding a host's liability to his guest for negligence arising out of an automobile accident. . . .

. . . Plaintiff, Steven Pfau, a domiciliary of Connecticut, was a student at Parsons College in Iowa, and the defendant, Bruce Trent, a domiciliary of New Jersey, was a student at the same college. The boys met for the first time at Parsons.

Following the Easter vacation in 1966, the defendant, Bruce Trent, drove the automobile involved in the accident back to Iowa for his use at college. The automobile was registered in New Jersey in the name of the Trent Aluminum Company, a New Jersey corporation owned by Bruce's father. Bruce was using the car with the owner-corporation's consent. The vehicle was insured in New Jersey by a New Jersey carrier.

About a month after Bruce's return to college and several days before the accident, he agreed to drive the plaintiff to Columbia, Missouri, for a weekend visit. They never reached their destination. Shortly after leaving Parsons on April 22, 1966, and while still in Iowa, Bruce failed to negotiate a curve and the car he was operating collided with an oncoming vehicle driven by Joseph Davis. Mr. Davis and his wife and child, who were Iowa domiciliaries, were injured in the accident. Their claims have now been settled by defendants' insurance carrier. The sole question presented by this appeal is whether the Iowa guest statute [which provides that a host-driver is not liable to his passenger-guest for ordinary negligence] is applicable to this action.

[The court, following Babcock v. Jackson, discussed at pages 175-176 *supra*, inspected the purposes behind the Iowa guest statute and determined that none of them was applicable to the facts of the case. The court then discussed the interests of Connecticut, the plaintiff's domicile, and New Jersey, the forum and defendant's domicile.]

In this case, however, we are faced with a more complex situation since plaintiff is a domiciliary of Connecticut. Thus, we must consider the law of both New Jersey and Connecticut. Connecticut long ago repealed its guest statute and now permits guest-passengers to recover from their host-drivers for ordinary negligence. There is no doubt that if this plaintiff-guest had been injured in a Connecticut accident by a Connecticut host-driver, there would be no bar to recover for ordinary negligence if suit were brought in that state.

Turning to New Jersey's law, we are led to Cohen v. Kaminetsky, where we held that the strong policy of this state is to allow a guest-passenger to be compensated by his host-driver in cases of ordinary negligence. Thus, the substantive laws of Connecticut and New Jersey are in accord. . . .

It would appear that Connecticut's substantive law allowing a guest to recover for his host's ordinary negligence would give it a significant interest in having that law applied to this case. Defendants argue, however, that if we apply Connecticut's substantive law, we should apply its choice-of-law rule as well. In other words, they contend Connecticut's interest in its domiciliaries is identified not only by its substantive law, but by its choice-of-law rule. Connecticut adheres to lex loci delicti and accordingly to its decisions would most likely apply the substantive law of Iowa in this case. Defendants contend that plaintiff should not be allowed to recover when he could not do so in either Iowa where the accident occurred or in Connecticut where he is domiciled. We cannot agree for two reasons. First, it is not definite that plaintiff would be unable to recover in either of those states.[4] More importantly, however, we see no reason for applying Connecticut's choice-of-law rule. To do so would frustrate the very goals of governmental-interest analysis. Connecticut's choice-of-law rule does not identify that state's interest in the matter. Lex loci delicti was born in an effort to achieve simplicity and uniformity, and does not relate to a state's interest in having its law applied to given issues in a tort case. It is significant that in Reich v. Purcell [page 249 *supra*], the California Supreme Court applied the substantive law of Ohio to the Missouri accident. The court did not apply Ohio's choice-of-law rule which was lex loci delicti, and would have called for application of the Missouri limitation on damages. Professor Kay in her comment on Reich v. Purcell was in agreement with the above authorities that only the foreign substantive law should be applied, and she agreed with the court in *Reich* that Ohio's choice-of-law rule should be ignored. Kay, "Comment on Reich v. Purcell," 15 UCLA L. Rev., *supra* at 589 n.31. We conclude that since Iowa has no interest in this litigation, and since the substantive laws of Connecticut and New Jersey are the same, this case presents a false conflict and the Connecticut plaintiff should have the right to maintain an action for ordinary negligence in our courts. In this situation principles of comity, and perhaps the equal protection and privileges and immunities clauses of the Constitution, dictate that we should afford the Connecticut plaintiff the same protection a New Jersey plaintiff would be given.

For the reasons expressed the order of the Appellate Division is reversed and the order of the trial court striking the separate defense of the Iowa guest statute is restated.

Questions and Comments

(1) Professor Currie would probably have approved the result in *Pfau*, since he thought that interest analysis virtually did away with the problem of renvoi:

> And, though I make this suggestion with some trepidation, it seems clear that the problem of renvoi would have no place at all [under interest analysis]. Foreign law would be applied only when the court has determined that that foreign state has a legitimate interest in the application of its law and policy to

---

4. We note in this connection that contrary to defendants' contention, it is not clear what substantive law Iowa would apply to this case. That state has recently departed from the traditional lex loci delicti rule, and it cannot be assumed that Iowa would apply its guest statute to this case. Additionally, although Connecticut remains a lex loci delicti state, it has in the past employed some of the traditional escape devices to avoid the doctrine's harsh results. . . . If, as defendants urge, we should look to Connecticut's whole law, *i.e.*, both its substantive law and its choice-of-law rule, why should not Connecticut look to Iowa's whole law if suit were brought in Connecticut? If it did look to Iowa's whole law, Connecticut might well be led back to its own substantive law.

the case at bar and that the forum has none. Hence, there can be no question of applying anything other than the internal law of the foreign state. The closest approximation to the renvoi problem that will be encountered under the suggested method is the case in which neither state has an interest in the application of its law and policy; in that event, the forum would apply its own law simply on the ground that that is the more convenient disposition. Is it possible that this is, in fact, all that is involved in the typical renvoi situation?

Currie, *Selected Essays on the Conflict of Laws* 184-185 (1963) (footnotes omitted).

(2) Professor von Mehren has elaborated significantly on the idea only suggested by Currie—that a look at the conflicts rules of the other jurisdictions will shed significant light on the interests of that jurisdiction and thus be a considerable aid in applying interest analysis. That will be true, however, only when the other jurisdiction has itself adopted interest analysis, Professor von Mehren warns, since a territorial approach in the other jurisdiction is one that cannot be read as stating the other jurisdiction's interest or lack of interest in a problem. Von Mehren, *The Renvoi and Its Relation to Various Approaches to the Choice-of-Law Problem*, in *XXth Century Comparative and Conflicts Law* 380, 393-394 (1961). Recall that the court in Phillips v. General Motors, page 229 *supra*, disagreed with von Mehren because it referred to the *lex loci* attitude of North Carolina as evidence of that state's lack of interest in applying its law to an accident in Kansas. In recent years many other courts using a modern choice-of-law methodology have employed this renvoi technique to measure the foreign state's interest. *See, e.g.*, Miller v. White, 702 A.2d 392 (Vt. 1997); Sutherland v. Kennington Truck Service Ltd., 562 N.W.2d 466 (Mich. 1997); Braxton v. Anco Electric, Inc., 409 S.E.2d 914 (N.C. 1991). Egnal, *The "Essential" Role of Modern Renvoi in the Governmental Interest Analysis Approach to Choice of Law*, 54 Temple L.Q. 237 (1981).

(3) Why should it be assumed that the other state's choice-of-law decisions would matter more if they conformed to tenets of governmental interest analysis? Isn't adoption of the First (or Second) Restatement a policy decision in its own right? Can't adherence to territorial rules be taken as a commitment to the goals of predictability, territorial sovereignty, and the like? Or perhaps a state adhering to an old-fashioned approach simply believes that its substantive policies are best advanced when the substantive rule is applied on a territorial basis. Why should the forum insist on remaking the policy choices of the other state? *See generally* Brilmayer, *Conflict of Laws: Foundations and Future Directions* 94-98 (1991).

(4) What should the forum do if it determines that another potentially interested state would not apply its own law because it uses the better-law approach? If it uses the most-significant-relationship approach? If it had a statutory provision declaring its law inapplicable? Professor Larry Kramer would consult the other state's choice-of-law rules whenever the rule defines the substantive scope of its law. *Return of the Renvoi*, 66 N.Y.U. L. Rev. 979, 1012 (1991).

Richards v. United States

369 U.S. 1 (1962)

[The action arose from an airplane crash in Missouri. The airplane had been en route from Tulsa, Oklahoma, to New York City. Plaintiffs were representatives of dead passengers. The government was named as a defendant on the theory that the Federal Aviation Agency had been negligent in failing to enforce relevant statutes and regulations concerning the practices of American Airlines in the Tulsa overhaul depot. The parties were generally agreed that the alleged negligence had occurred in Oklahoma and that the harmful effects had occurred in Missouri. Under the Federal Torts Claims Act, upon which the government's liability was premised, governmental liability would arise "under circumstances where the United States, if a private person, would be liable to the claimant in accordance with the law of the place where the act or omission occurred." 28 U.S.C. §1346. Three interpretations of this section were presented to the court and supported by lower court decisions: (1) That the whole law of the place of the negligence ought to control. (2) That the internal law of the place of negligence ought to control. (3) That the internal law of the place of injury ought to control. The court rejected the last of these on the grounds that it was inconsistent with the language of the statute. It then noted that no choice could be made between the first two options solely on the basis of statutory language and that an analysis of the purpose of the act was necessary to resolve the dispute.]

We believe it fundamental that a section of a statute should not be read in isolation from the context of the whole Act, and that in fulfilling our responsibility in interpreting legislation, "we must not be guided by a single sentence or member of a sentence, but [should] look to the provisions of the whole law, and to its object and policy." We should not assume that Congress intended to set the courts completely adrift from state law with regard to questions for which it has not provided a specific and definite answer in an act such as the one before us which, as we have indicated, is so intimately related to state law. Thus, we conclude that a reading of the statute as a whole, with due regard to its purpose, requires application of the whole law of the State where the act or omission occurred.

We are led to our conclusion by other persuasive factors notwithstanding the fact that the very conflict among the lower federal courts that we must here resolve illustrates the also reasonable alternative view expressed by the petitioners. First, our interpretation enables the federal courts to treat the United States as a "private individual under like circumstances," and thus is consistent with the Act considered as a whole. The general conflict-of-laws rule, followed by a vast majority of the States, is to apply the law of the place of injury to the substantive rights of the parties. Therefore, where the forum State is the same as the one in which the act or omission occurred, our interpretation will enable the federal courts to treat the United States as an individual would be treated under like circumstances. Moreover, this interpretation of the Act provides a degree of flexibility to the law to be applied in federal courts that would not be possible under the view advanced either by the petitioners or by American. Recently there has been a tendency on the part of some States to depart from the general conflicts rule in order to take into account the interests of the State having significant contact with the parties to the litigation. We can see no compelling reason to saddle the Act with an interpretation that would prevent the federal courts from implementing this policy in choice-of-law rules where the State in which the negligence occurred has adopted it. Should the States continue this rejection of the older rule in those situations where its application might appear inappropriate or inequitable, the flexibility inherent in our interpretation will also be more in step with that judicial approach, as well as with the character of the legislation and with the purpose of the Act considered as a whole.

In the absence of persuasive evidence to the contrary, we do not believe that Congress intended to adopt the inflexible rule urged upon us by the petitioners. Despite the power of Congress to enact for litigation of this type a federal conflict-of-laws rule independent of the States' development of such rules, we should not, particularly in the type of interstitial legislation involved here, assume that it has done so. Nor are we persuaded to require such an independent federal rule by the petitioners' argument that there are other instances, specifically set forth in the Act, where the liability of the United States is not coextensive with that of a private person under state law. It seems sufficient to note that Congress has been specific in those instances where it intended the federal courts to depart completely from state law and, also, that this list of exceptions contains no direct or indirect modification of the principles controlling application of choice-of-law rules. Certainly there is nothing in the legislative history that even remotely supports the argument that Congress did not intend state conflict rules to apply to multistate tort actions brought against the Government. . . .

Our view of a State's power to adopt an appropriate conflict-of-laws doctrine in a situation touching more than one place has been indicated by our discussion in Part III of this opinion. Where more than one State has sufficiently substantial contact with the activity in question, the forum State, by analysis of the interests possessed by the States involved, could constitutionally apply to the decision of the case the law of one or another state having such an interest in the multistate activity. Thus, an Oklahoma state court would be free to apply either its own law, the law of the place where the negligence occurred, or the law of Missouri, the law of the place where the injury occurred, to an action brought in its courts and involving this factual situation. Both the Federal District Court sitting in Oklahoma, and the Court of Appeals for the Tenth Circuit, have interpreted the pertinent Oklahoma decisions, which we have held are controlling, to declare that an action for wrongful death is based on the statute of the place where the injury occurred that caused the death. Therefore, Missouri's statute controls the case at bar. It is conceded that each petitioner has received $15,000, the maximum amount recoverable under the Missouri Act, and the petitioners thus have received full compensation for their claims. Accordingly, the courts below were correct in holding that, in accordance with Oklahoma law, petitioners had failed to state claims upon which relief could be granted.

Questions and Comments

(1) Is it fair to say that *Richards* uses a kind of interest analysis since it concentrates on the policies of the Federal Tort Claims Act? If so, is the Court's decision to look to the whole law of the state where the negligence occurred inconsistent with Currie's conclusion that when foreign law was to be applied, it could only be internal law?

(2) Note that there are several differences between *Richards* and the typical renvoi case. First, there appears to be no substantive law of the deciding jurisdiction (the United States) on the tort liability issue. Thus, there must be reference

to law other than the forum's, and if the conflicts rules would refer to the law of another jurisdiction, that cannot be taken as a sign of indifference justifying use of the forum's law. Also, unlike the common renvoi case (to the extent that there is such a thing), the usual options are references to the internal law of the other jurisdiction or reference back to the forum. In the Tort Claims Act case, the reference, if any, will always be to the law of a third jurisdiction.

(3) How did Congress come to choose the conflicts rule in the Federal Tort Claims Act? Professor Leflar offers this explanation and commentary:

> Judge Goodrich learned that the draftsmen of the Act (not of course the members of Congress who enacted it) apparently thought that the quoted provision was in accord with settled conflicts law [citing Goodrich, *Yielding Place to New: Rest Versus Motion in the Conflict of Laws*, 50 Colum. L. Rev. 881, 894-895 (1950).] Even if the Act had been based on a correct understanding of the 1948 conflicts law, it would have produced a hard and fast rule contrary to the torts-conflicts law of most American states twenty-nine years later. Despite this fact, it is unlikely that Congress will correct the discrepancy between the Act and current state law. In Richards v. United States, the United States Supreme Court managed to salvage the conflicts rule of the Act by reading a kind of renvoi technique into the section so that it in effect reads "in accordance with the *conflict of laws* law of the place where the act or omission occurred." This interpretation makes the conflicts rule as up-to-date as that of the designated "place" at the time of the "act or omission" and would have been a desirable, though unlikely, interpretation if the section had been drafted more knowingly to prescribe the law of the place of harmful impact. *As interpreted*, the statute becomes almost a model for federal enactments that should leave room for future growth and improvement in locally governing law. By their innocent error, the Tort Claims Act draftsmen created an opportunity for better law than they knew.

Leflar, *Choice-of-Law Statutes*, 44 Tenn. L. Rev. 951, 958 (1977).

(4) If the Act requires that the United States be treated as a private party would be, then in cases where the United States is a party, which states have an "interest" in applying their protective laws on its behalf? The United States Court of Appeals for the Seventh Circuit considered this question:

> The plaintiff argues that since she is a nonresident of Maryland and Bethesda Naval Hospital is a federal institution rather than a private or Maryland state hospital, Maryland has no interest in enforcing its damages cap. The fact that the plaintiff is not a Maryland resident does not bear on the issue because the damages cap is for the protection of defendants rather than plaintiffs. And the fact that the defendant is a federal institution is inadmissible because the federal government has consented to have tort liability imposed on it only "to the same extent as a private individual under like circumstances." 28 U.S.C. §2674. This requires us to treat Bethesda Naval Hospital like any nonfederal hospital in Maryland.

Carter v. United States, 333 F.3d 791, 795 (7th Cir. 2003) (citations omitted).

3. Substance and Procedure

The substance-procedure dichotomy recognized even in territorialist thinking retains importance under interest analysis and related approaches. Assume that in a given case the forum has no interest but that another jurisdiction does. That situation calls for application of the other jurisdiction's substantive law. But on "truly" procedural questions, the forum *does* have an interest by virtue of the fact that its courts must involve themselves in the handling of the case. The forum state has an interest in having parties comply with rules regarding the size and color of paper on submitted briefs, for example. Similarly, the forum has an interest in requiring the parties to adhere to the forum's rules for the filing of pleadings, deadlines for filing notices of appeal, and the like. These "conflicts" between the procedures of one state and another are more often false conflicts because the fact that the litigation is in State *A* rather than State *B* removes any procedural interest that State *B* may have from the issue. Since such procedures as have been discussed also fail to affect the substantive outcome of the case if the parties comply with them (compliance being possible and imposing a minimum burden), the conflict is truly false. Thus, the traditional rule that the procedural law of the forum should apply seems quite consistent with interest analysis and its cousins.

The trouble, as usual, arises in determining what is procedural and what is substantive. Fortunately, the analysis above provides the answer to that question for the most part. Rules having to do with how the forum's courts handle cases, as opposed to how such cases come out, are procedural. Rules attempting to affect the parties' liabilities or their behavior are substantive. (This is a version of the test proposed by Justice Harlan in Hanna v. Plumer, 380 U.S. 460 (1965).) Thus, a rule of evidence requiring relevance is undoubtedly procedural since it is designed to save the time of the forum court, while a rule of privilege is substantive and more appropriately governed by the law of any of the states concerned with the reason for the privilege in the case at hand.

Occasionally, however, a procedural interest of the forum will conflict with a substantive interest of the only state interested in the substance of the case. In a variation on Cohen v. Beneficial Industrial Loan Corp., 337 U.S. 541 (1949), imagine a cause of action arising under the laws of State *A* but tried for some reason in State *B*. Imagine further that the cause of action is viewed with suspicion in State *A* and that a statute of State *A* requires the plaintiff to pay in to the clerk of the court a sum of money to be used to pay costs if the defendants prevail. The purpose of the requirement is to discourage plaintiffs with frivolous cases from bringing such suits in the hopes of getting at least minor settlements from defendants, which are viewed as particularly vulnerable to unjustified suits of the type in question. Assume further that State *B* has no general mechanism whereby money can be paid in to the clerk of the court for later purposes. A court of State *B* would be unlikely to allow its clerk to accept such money without bonding for the clerk, for which no statute of State *B* provides.

Here is a true conflict between the laws of the two states, even though State *B*'s objection to the bond is clearly procedural and State *A*'s requirement for it is clearly substantive in the sense of trying to shape people's behavior. There seems little doubt that the conflict will be resolved as Currie suggested—by applying the law of the forum.

Such cases are relatively easy to decide—cases in which the proposed procedure puts an extra burden on the forum. Much more difficult are cases in which a rule of the other state—the only one with a substantive interest in the outcome of the case—has clearly substantive effect even though its motivation seems to be more toward the procedural. Take, for example, the oft-seen justification for guest statutes—preventing fraud against insurance companies. If that is the true motivation for a given guest statute, and the state with the guest statute would otherwise impose tort liability on the driver for the usual motives, what should the forum confident of its ability to discover fraud do? Theoretically the forum could hold the trial and allow liability because the case would be a false conflict case—the antifraud interest of the other state would have been served (albeit by means different from those used by that state) and the underlying purpose of its substantive rule carried out. Similarly, there is no impairment of the procedural or substantive interests of the forum. Nonetheless, one is left with strong feelings of discomfort that a result is reached that is different from the one that the courts of the only substantively concerned jurisdiction would reach. Perhaps this is a case for application of Professor Cavers's idea that results must be comprehensible to lay people or Professor Twerski's notion that a rule developed for one purpose can give rise to expectations that deserve respect.

Professor Twerski has also pointed out the applicability of "process values" to the substance-procedure issue in conflicts law. His reference is to an idea put forward by Professor Robert Summers in *Evaluating and Improving Legal Processes—A Plea for "Process Values,"* 60 Cornell L. Rev. 1 (1974), in which Professor Summers pointed out that processes can be judged not only in terms of their efficacy in producing good results, but also in terms of certain values having to do with the process itself, such as participatory governance, fairness, rationality, and humaneness. In commenting on the implications of Summers's observations, Twerski noted:

> Professor Summers contends that we have placed inordinate emphasis on process as a means for obtaining good results, while very little emphasis has been placed on the intrinsic values to be achieved by the legal process itself. . . . He has . . . clearly identified a blind spot in our jurisprudential thinking. Its implications for the procedural-substantive dichotomy should be obvious. If we begin thinking of procedure qua procedure as implementing a broad range of social values, then we may have to reexamine the outcome-oriented approach that now dominates our thinking.

Twerski, *Book Review*, 61 Cornell L. Rev. 1045, 1061-1062 (1976).

4.   Statutes of Limitations

Ledesma v. Jack Stewart Produce, Inc.
816 F.2d 482 (9th Cir. 1987)

Before NELSON, WIGGINS and NOONAN, JJ.
NELSON, J.:
Alfonso Ledesma, Josephine Rodriguez, Rafaela Gaytan, and Jennifer Santiago seek review of the district court's dismissal of their personal injury claim

on the ground that the statute of limitations had run. They argue that under the California choice-of-law rules the district court should not have applied the one-year California statute of limitations to their claim. They further argue that, even if the California statute of limitations was properly applied, the district court should have tolled it pursuant to Cal. Civ. Proc. Code §351 (West 1982). We agree with the first contention. Accordingly, we reverse and remand to the district court for further proceedings.

On May 13, 1981, Alfonso Ledesma, Josephine Rodriguez, Rafaela Gaytan, and Jennifer Santiago ("plaintiffs"), all California residents, were injured on an Arizona highway when their van was allegedly struck by a tractor driven by defendant John Wayne Mize, an Arkansas resident, and owned by defendants Jack Stewart Produce, Inc., an Oklahoma corporation with its principal place of business in Oklahoma, and Jack Stewart, an Oklahoma resident ("defendants"). On April 7, 1983, plaintiffs filed a diversity action in the Eastern District of California, seeking damages arising out of the accident. The defendants filed a motion to dismiss under Fed. R. Civ. P. 12(b)(6), arguing that the one-year California statute of limitations applied and barred the action against them. *See* Cal. Civ. Proc. Code §340(3) (West Supp. 1987). The district court granted the defendants' motion to dismiss the action as time-barred. Plaintiffs appeal from the order of dismissal. . . .

It is well-settled that in diversity cases federal courts must apply the choice-of-law rules of the forum state. California has adopted a "governmental interest" approach to resolve choice-of-law problems. Under that approach, the court must first determine if the laws of the two jurisdictions differ. If they do differ, the court should determine whether both states have an interest in applying their respective law. If only one state has an interest, there is no "true conflict" of laws and the court should apply the law of the interested jurisdiction. If both states have an interest in having their differing laws applied, a true conflict arises; in that case the court should apply the law of the state whose interest would be more impaired if its law were not applied. . . . Nelson v. International Paint Co., 716 F.2d 640, 644 (9th Cir. 1983).

California's one-year statute of limitations clearly differs from the two-year statutes of limitations in effect in Arizona and Oklahoma and the three-year statute in Arkansas. . . . Therefore, we move to the second step of the analysis to determine whether each state has an interest in applying its law in this case. . . .

. . .

The California statute of limitations serves two purposes: it protects state residents from the burden of defending cases "in which memories have faded and evidence has been lost," and it protects the courts of the state from the need to process stale claims. *Nelson*, 716 F.2d at 644 (quoting *Ashland, supra*). The first interest does not apply here because there is no California defendant in this case. All of the defendants reside in states that do not consider twenty-three-month-old claims to be stale. Therefore, neither California, nor Oklahoma, nor Arkansas has an interest in applying its statute of limitations in order to protect the defendants. Furthermore, although California has an interest in protecting its courts from stale claims,[4] that interest is at least equally balanced by its interest in allowing its residents to recover for injuries sustained in a state that would recognize their claim as timely.

In addition, we note that the California statute of limitations is not inflexible when California plaintiffs are involved. Pursuant to Cal. Civ. Proc. Code §351, California courts will toll the statute of limitations during the time that a defendant is out of the state. That California is willing to toll its statute of limitations in order to assist resident plaintiffs in bringing claims for injury further indicates that little harm would be done to California's interest by applying the two-year statute of limitations for the benefit of the California plaintiffs. We find that, for the foregoing reasons, California's interests would not be greatly impaired by the application of Arizona's statute of limitations in this case.

We cannot say the same for Arizona. On the contrary, we find that Arizona's interest would be significantly impaired by a failure to apply its statute of limitations. The Arizona legislature has established a two-year statute of limitations for personal injury claims arising out of highway accidents. As the Supreme Court of California has recognized, "one of the primary purposes of a state in creating a cause of action . . . is to deter the kind of conduct within its borders which wrongfully [causes injury]." Hurtado v. Superior Court. Insofar as drivers tend to be more careful when their chances of incurring liability are more substantial, Arizona does have an interest in ensuring that its statute of limitations is applied in any case that arises from accidents occurring within its state borders. Were we to apply the California statute of limitations in this case, we would impede the legitimate interest of the state of Arizona in promoting highway safety by allowing a cause of action for a two-year period.

Applying the "governmental interest" analysis of California's choice-of-law rules, we conclude that Arizona's interests would be impaired by the failure to apply its statute of limitations more than California's interests would be impaired by the failure to apply its statute. California has little interest in applying its statute of limitations when no California defendant is involved and when California plaintiffs seek to recover for injuries that occurred in a state in which the claim was not time-barred. Arizona's legitimate government policy would be impaired by a failure to allow the cause of action that it has established for personal injury claims. Accordingly, we hold that the Arizona statute of limitations should apply in the present case and that the district court erred in dismissing the complaint.

We need not reach the plaintiffs' argument that the district court should have tolled the California statute of limitations during the period the defendants were out of the state.

Reversed and remanded.

---

4. While the processing of the claim in this case would affect a federal and not a California court, a federal court sitting in diversity applies the "governmental interest" analysis as would a California court. This approach ensures that "the accident of diversity of citizenship would [not] constantly disturb equal administration of justice in coordinate state and federal courts sitting side by side." *See* Klaxon Co. v. Stentor Elec. Mfg. Co., 313 U.S. 487, 496 (1941).

NOONAN, J., dissenting:

The Restatement of the Law of Conflicts states as black letter law: "An action will not be maintained if it is barred by the Statute of Limitations of the forum. . . ." Restatement (Second) of Conflicts of Law, §142(i) (1971). California has followed this rule. Hall v. Copco Pacific Ltd., 224 F.2d 884 (9th Cir. 1955). If this normal rule is applied, Ledesma cannot proceed.

. . .

Even if we should make the assumption that California would depart from the normal rule, it is difficult to see the California "interest" here. The California interest in not burdening its judicial system with stale claims is equally great whether the California resident is a defendant or a plaintiff. Consequently, even in terms of the interest of California, the California statute should apply.

Global Financial Corp. v. Triarc Corp.

93 N.Y.2d 525, 715 N.E.2d 482 (1999)

Chief Judge KAYE.

This appeal places before us a long-simmering question: where does a nonresident's contract claim accrue for purposes of the Statute of Limitations? [New York Civil Practice Law and Rules ("CPLR") section 202] requires our courts to "borrow" the Statute of Limitations of a foreign jurisdiction where a nonresident's cause of action accrued, if that limitations period is shorter than New York's. The primary issue presented by this appeal is whether, for purposes of CPLR 202, the nonresident plaintiff's contract and quantum meruit claims accrued in New York, where most of the relevant events occurred, or in plaintiff's State of residence, where it sustained the economic impact of the alleged breach.

According to the complaint, by contract dated February 1, 1988, defendant retained plaintiff to perform certain consulting services. In March 1989 plaintiff located an investment company that agreed to purchase all of defendant's outstanding shares, and between February 1988 and August 1989, plaintiff additionally advised defendant regarding corporate planning. On November 6, 1989, plaintiff demanded payment of over nine million dollars for services rendered, which defendant refused the following week.

On November 9, 1995, plaintiff commenced an action in the United States District Court for the Southern District of New York to recover its commissions and fees. Because both parties were Delaware corporations, however, on April 10, 1996, the court dismissed the complaint for lack of subject matter jurisdiction. Three months later, plaintiff brought a substantially similar suit across the street, in Supreme Court, New York County. The parties do not dispute that this action is timely if the Federal action was timely when commenced on November 9, 1995 (CPLR 205).

. . .

When a nonresident sues on a cause of action accruing outside New York, CPLR 202 requires the cause of action to be timely under the limitation periods of both New York and the jurisdiction where the cause of action accrued.[2] This prevents nonresidents from shopping in New York for a favorable Statute of Limitations.

Plaintiff argues that the New York Statute of Limitations applies because its claims accrued in New York, where the contract was negotiated, executed, substantially performed and breached. In essence, plaintiff urges that we apply a "grouping of contacts" or "center of gravity" approach—used in substantive choice-of-law questions in contract cases—to determine where contract and quantum meruit causes of action accrue for purposes of CPLR 202.

At the threshold, however, there is a significant difference between a choice-of-law question, which is a matter of common law, and this Statute of Limitations issue, which is governed by particular terms of the CPLR. In using the word "accrued" in CPLR 202 there is no indication that the Legislature intended the term "to mean anything other than the generally accepted construction applied throughout CPLR Article 2—the time when, and the place where, the plaintiff first had the right to bring the cause of action" (1 Weinstein-Korn-Miller, N.Y. Civ. Prac. P. 202.04, at 2-61).

CPLR 202 has remained substantially unchanged since 1902. While its predecessor, section 13 of the Civil Practice Act, used the word "arise" instead of "accrue," the Legislature intended no change in meaning when it adopted the present provision, in 1962, as part of the CPLR. The legislative purpose was simply to ensure that the language of CPLR 202 conformed with other CPLR provisions. Because earlier iterations of the borrowing statute predate the substantive choice-of-law "interest analysis" test used in tort cases (*see* Babcock v. Jackson, 12 N.Y.2d 473 [1963]) and the "grouping of contacts" or "center of gravity" approach used in contract cases (*see* Auten v. Auten, 308 N.Y. 155 [1954]), these choice-of-law analyses are inapplicable to the question of statutory construction presented by CPLR 202.

Indeed, while this Court has not addressed the issue in the context of a contract case, we have consistently employed the traditional definition of accrual—a cause of action accrues at the time and in the place of the injury—in tort cases involving the interpretation of CPLR 202. Martin v. Dierck Equip. Co. (43 N.Y.2d 583) is illustrative. There, the plaintiff was injured while operating a forklift at his employer's warehouse in Virginia. The forklift manufacturer and distributor were located in New York, and the forklift was sold to plaintiff's employer in New York. Plaintiff sued the manufacturer and distributor in negligence and strict products liability. The Court held that for purposes of the borrowing statute, the negligence causes of action as well as the cause of action which plaintiff labeled "breach of warranty" accrued in Virginia: "[p]laintiff possessed no cause of action, in tort or in contract, anywhere in the world until he was injured in Virginia" (*id.* at 588, 591).

When an alleged injury is purely economic, the place of injury usually is where the plaintiff resides and sustains the economic impact of the loss. Here,

---

2. CPLR 202 states: "An action based upon a cause of action accruing without the state cannot be commenced after the expiration of the time limited by the laws of either the state or the place without the state where the cause of action accrued, except that where the cause of action accrued in favor of a resident of the state the time limited by the laws of the state shall apply."

plaintiff's causes of action are time-barred whether one looks to its State of incorporation or its principal place of business. Thus, we need not determine whether it was in Delaware or Pennsylvania that plaintiff more acutely sustained the impact of its loss.

. . .

Finally, as we underscored in *ABB Power*, "CPLR 202 is designed to add clarity to the law and to provide the certainty of uniform application to litigants" (*id*. at 187). This goal is better served by a rule requiring the single determination of a plaintiff's residence than by a rule dependent on a litany of events relevant to the "center of gravity" of a contract dispute.

Accordingly, the order of the Appellate Division should be affirmed, with costs.

Questions and Comments

(1) *Ledesma* ignores the traditional assumption that statutes of limitations are procedural rules governed by forum law, and instead treats the statute of limitations choice-of-law issue like any other issue that is subject to interest analysis. Are you satisfied with the analysis? Why does California have a "weaker" interest in applying its statute of limitations to California plaintiffs than California defendants? Is the California statute of limitations designed to promote recovery for Californians? Why does it matter that "[a]ll of the defendants reside in states that do not consider the twenty-three-month-old claims to be stale"? Are statutes of limitations personal laws that travel with defendants wherever they may be sued? Why is it relevant to interest analysis that the "injuries [were] sustained in a state that would recognize their claim as timely"? Do you agree that Arizona's interest "would be significantly impaired by" a California court's failure to apply the Arizona statute of limitation in a case involving an accident in Arizona? Is it relevant that the year before *Ledesma*, the Arizona Supreme Court reaffirmed that under Arizona law, "statutes of limitation . . . are procedural and therefore governed by the law of the forum"? *See* Monroe v. Wood, 724 P.2d 30, 31 (Ariz. 1986). Doesn't this suggest that Arizona does not view its statutes of limitations to be applicable in non-Arizona courts?

Professor Symeonides reports that, as of 1999, "seventeen states have abandoned the traditional procedural characterization of statutes of limitation and have applied to conflicts involving these statutes the same choice-of-law analysis applied to substantive issues." Symeonides, *Choice of Law in the American Courts in 1999: One More Year*, 48 Am. J. Comp. L. 143, 166 (2000). In light of *Ledesma*, is this a welcome trend?

(2) Is it incongruous for the New York Court of Appeals—a leader in the development of modern choice-of-law methodologies—to employ First Restatement criteria ("a cause of action accrues at the time and in the place of the injury") in determining where a cause of action accrued for purposes of a borrowing statute? If the court really believes that the goals of clarity and uniformity for the borrowing statute are better met by the place of injury criterion than by the "center of gravity" approach, why not apply the place of injury in its common law choice-of-law decisions? Other courts that usually apply modern choice-of-law approaches but look to traditional criteria in interpreting a

borrowing statute include Combs v. International Insurance Co., 354 F.3d 568 (6th Cir. 2004) (applying Kentucky conflicts law); Rajala v. Donnelly Meiners Jordan Kline P.C., 193 F.3d 925 (8th Cir. 1999) (applying Missouri conflicts law). For cases applying a modern conflicts analysis to determine where a cause of action accrues for borrowing statute purposes, *see* Kahn v. Royal Ins. Co., 709 N.E.2d 822 (Mass. 1999) (applying most significant relationship test to determine where cause of action accrued); Celotex Corp. v. Meehan, 523 So. 2d 141 (Fla. 1988). *See also* Hall v. Summit Contractors, Inc., 158 S.W.3d 185 (Ark. 2004) (Tennessee statute of limitations applies because Arkansas borrowing statute directs court to apply foreign limitations period "if a claim is substantially based . . . upon the law of one other state.").

(3) The 1988 revisions to the Restatement of Conflicts Second set out a new approach to statutes of limitations:

§142. Statute of Limitations

Whether a claim will be maintained against the defense of the statute of limitations is determined under the principles stated in §6. In general, unless the exceptional circumstances of the case make such a result unreasonable:

    (1) The forum will apply its own statute of limitations barring the claim.

    (2) The forum will apply its own statute of limitations permitting the claim unless:

        (a) maintenance of the claim would serve no substantial interest of the forum; and

        (b) the claim would be barred under the statute of limitations of a state having a more significant relationship to the parties and the occurrence.

Applying this new approach, the Supreme Court of Massachusetts ruled that the shorter Texas limitations period should apply to a claim brought by a Massachusetts resident for injuries sustained outside a Texas hotel when she was knocked to the ground when attempting to board the hotel's transport cart. Nierman v. Hyatt Corp., 808 N.E.2d 290 (Mass. 2004). The hotel chain was incorporated in Delaware with its principal place of business in Illinois. The applicable limitation period was two years under Texas law and three years under Massachusetts law. After describing the standard articulated in the amended §142, the court stated:

The Appeals Court reasoned, essentially, that, because the Niermans are residents of this State, Massachusetts has a substantial interest in the maintenance of their claims. . . . Moreover, because Hyatt is not based in Texas, the Appeals Court assumed that Texas has no countervailing interest at stake. . . . The court's resolution of the issue is appealing for its simplicity but fails to engage the proper choice of law analysis under the principles stated in §142. . . . Specifically, we must consider (1) whether Massachusetts has a substantial interest in permitting the claims to go forward, and (2) whether Texas has a more significant relationship to the parties and the negligence claim. The two criteria are necessarily related and should be evaluated with some sensitivity to one another, . . . focusing on the statute of limitations issue, and not on the underlying tort. . . .

We begin by noting that the more significant relationship test points clearly toward the use of the Texas limitations statute. All of the events constituting the alleged negligence took place in Texas, and Texas is where the alleged injuries were suffered. Hyatt, although not a Texas corporation, operates a business there and employs Texans. The operator of the transport cart, presumably, lives in Texas. Although the Niermans are Massachusetts residents, they travelled to Texas when the alleged accident occurred. The fact that their travel reservations were booked through Massachusetts travel agents carries little weight in our analysis, because that contact has no apparent bearing on any issue in this case, let alone the limitations issue. *See* Restatement (Second), *supra* at §142 comment e (emerging trend is to bar claim if barred by "the state which, *with respect to the issue of limitations*, is the state of most significant relationship to the occurrence and to the parties stated in §6" [emphasis supplied]).

We next consider whether, regardless that Texas is the State with the closer connections to the issue, Massachusetts has any substantial interest that would be advanced by entertaining the Nierman's claims. We conclude that it does not. Massachusetts has a general interest in having its residents compensated for personal injuries suffered in another State. It cannot be said, however, that its interest in the timeliness of such an action is more compelling than that of Texas. . . . *See also* Restatement (Second), *supra* at §142 comment g (claim generally should not be maintained when some forum interest would be served, but at the expense of the State with closer connection with the case). The Texas legislature has prescribed a two-year limitations period within which the Niermans could have commenced this action. This time frame reflects its judgment as to the proper balance between the needs of its citizens to redress injuries and their right to be protected from protracted exposure to liability. Hyatt has a place of business in Texas, and all of the acts and events that gave rise to this litigation occurred there. Texas has the dominant interest in having its own statute enforced. We conclude that the Texas statute of limitations is the appropriate one to apply in this case.

Id. at 292-294. Is this analysis satisfying? Did the court ask the right questions? Should the applicable statute of limitations turn on the results of a complex legal analysis?

5. Public Policy

In Chapter 2 we considered the public policy exception to the usual conflicts rules. Does such a principle have any place in the new theories? As noted in our earlier look at the topic, Paulsen & Sovern, *"Public Policy" in the Conflict of Laws*, 56 Colum. L. Rev. 969 (1956), found that the principle was invoked in cases in which there were substantial connections between the forum and the case itself in the "overwhelming number of cases." In such cases invocation of the principle ought to be unnecessary under interest analysis.

The forum, having an interest in the subject matter of the case itself, may simply impose its own law. For similar reasons, the public policy exception seems irrelevant to the Second Restatement approach. As the *Phillips* case, reproduced *supra* page 229, noted: "In order to determine which state has the more significant relationship, the public policies of all interested states must be considered. A public policy exception to the most significant relationship test would be redundant."

The New York Court of Appeals appears to believe, to the contrary, that an interest analysis court can in certain circumstances invoke the public policy exception. In Cooney v. Osgood Machinery, Inc., 81 N.Y.2d 66 (1993), the court stated: "In view of modern choice of law doctrine, resort to the public policy exception should be reserved for those foreign laws that are truly obnoxious." Does this make any sense? Should a court that lacks an interest in its law apply its law when foreign law is "truly obnoxious"? Should it dismiss the case on forum non conveniens grounds?

What about when there are factors connecting the case to the forum, but they do not give rise to an "interest" in the usual sense? This was the situation in Schultz v. Boy Scouts of America, Inc., discussed *supra* pages 180-181, where the tort took place in New York but all other contacts pointed elsewhere, leading the New York Court of Appeals to rule that New Jersey's charitable immunity law governed. The *Schultz* court rejected a public policy argument, reasoning that although "New Jersey's statute might well run counter to our fundamental public policy," it need not decide the issue because there were in any event "insufficient contacts between the parties, transaction, and New York to warrant enforcement of New York public policy." Would the court reason the same way if it were asked to enforce a slavery contract made abroad? Does this suggest that the New Jersey statute does not in fact run afoul of New York public policy? What are the implications for the point made above about interest analysis not needing a public policy exception?

For commentary on the public policy exception under modern choice-of-law doctrines, *see* Comment, *Choice of Law: A Fond Farewell to Comity and Public Policy*, 74 Cal. L. Rev. 1447 (1986); Corr, *Modern Choice of Law and Public Policy: The Emperor Has the Same Old Clothes*, 39 U. Miami L. Rev. 647 (1985).

6. Postscript

Paul v. National Life

352 S.E.2d 550 (W. Va. 1986)

NEELY, J.:

In September of 1977 Eliza Vickers and Aloha Jane Paul, both West Virginia residents, took a weekend trip to Indiana. The two women were involved in a one-car collision on Interstate 65 in Indiana when Ms. Vickers lost control of the car. That collision took both women's lives. The administrator of Mrs. Paul's estate brought a wrongful death action against Ms. Vickers' estate and the National Life Accident Company in the Circuit Court of Kanawha County. Upon completion of discovery, the defendants below moved for summary judgment. Defendants' motion contended that: (1) the Indiana guest statute, which grants to a gratuitous host immunity from liability for the injury or death of a passenger unless that host was guilty of willful and wanton misconduct at the time of the accident, was applicable; and (2) that the record was devoid of any evidence of willful or wanton misconduct on the part of Ms. Vickers. . . .

The sole question presented in this case is whether the law of Indiana or of West Virginia shall apply. The appellees urge us to adhere to our traditional conflicts doctrine of lex loci delicti, while the appellants urge us to reject our traditional doctrine and to adopt one of the "modern" approaches to conflicts questions. Although we stand by lex loci delicti as our general conflicts rule, we nevertheless reverse the judgment of the court below.

I

Unlike other areas of the law, such as contracts, torts and property, "conflicts of law" as a body of common law is of relatively recent origin. Professor Dicey has written that he knew of no decisions in England considering conflicts of law points before the accession of James I, and it is generally acknowledged that the first authoritative work on conflicts did not appear until the publication of Joseph Story's Conflict of Laws in 1834. Accordingly, no conflicts of law doctrine has ever had any credible pretense to being "natural law" emergent from the murky mists of medieval mysticism. Indeed, the mention of conflicts of law and the jus naturale in the same breath would evoke a power guffaw in even the sternest scholar. In our post-Realist legal world, it is the received wisdom that judges, like their counterparts in the legislative branch, are political agents embodying social policy in law. Nowhere is this received wisdom more accurate than in the domain of conflict of laws.

Conflicts of law has become a veritable playpen for judicial policy-makers. The last twenty years have seen a remarkable shift from the doctrine of lex loci delicti to more "modern" doctrines, such as the more flexible, manipulable Restatement "center of gravity" test. Of the twenty-five landmark cases cited by appellants in which a state supreme court rejected lex loci delicti and adopted one of the modern approaches, the great majority of them involved the application to an automobile accident case of a foreign state's guest statute, doctrine of interspousal or intrafamily immunity, or doctrine of contributory negligence. All but one of these landmark cases was decided in the decade between 1963 and 1973, when many jurisdictions still retained guest statutes, the doctrine of interspousal immunity, and the doctrine of contributory negligence. However, in the years since 1970, these statutes and doctrines have all but disappeared from the American legal landscape. . . .

Thus nearly half of the state supreme courts of the country have wrought a radical transformation of their procedural law of conflicts in order to sidestep perceived substantive evils, only to discover later that those evils had been exorcised from American law by other means. Now these courts are saddled with a cumbersome and unwieldy body of conflicts law that creates confusion, uncertainty and inconsistency, as well as complication of the judicial task. This approach has been like that of the misguided physician who treated a case of dandruff with nitric acid, only to discover later that the malady could have been remedied with medicated shampoo. Neither the doctor nor the patient need have lost his head.

The Restatement approach has been criticized for its indeterminate language and lack of concrete guidelines.

. . .

[The court here quotes §145 of the Second Restatement, *supra* pages 227-228.]

§146. Personal Injuries

In an action for a personal injury, the local law of the state where the injury occurred determines the *rights and liabilities* of the parties, unless, with respect to the particular issue, some other state has a more significant relationship under the principles stated in §6 to the occurrence and the parties, in which event the local law of the other state will be applied.

Section 6 of the Restatement lists the following factors as important choice of law considerations in all areas of law. [The Court here quotes §6 of the Second Restatement, *supra* pages 228-229.] As Javolenus once said to Julian, *res ipsa loquitur*. The appellant cites with approval the description of the Restatement approach set forth in Conklin v. Horner, 157 N.W.2d 579, 581 (Wis. 1968):

We emphasized that what we adopted was not a rule, but a method of analysis that permitted dissection of the jural bundle constituting a tort and its environment to determine what elements therein were relevant to a reasonable choice of law.

That sounds pretty intellectual, but we still prefer a rule. The lesson of history is that methods of analysis that permit dissection of the jural bundle constituting a tort and its environment produce protracted litigation and voluminous, inscrutable appellate opinions, while rules get cases settled quickly and cheaply.

The manipulability inherent in the Restatement approach is nicely illustrated by two cases from New York, the first jurisdiction to make a clean break with lex loci delicti. The cases of Babcock v. Jackson, and Kell v. Henderson, are aptly discussed by the Supreme Court of Virginia:

In *Babcock*, an automobile guest sued her host in New York for injuries sustained in Ontario caused by the defendant's ordinary negligence. Under New York law, the guest could recover for injuries caused by the host's lack of ordinary care, but the Ontario guest statute barred such a recovery. The court abandoned its adherence to the place-of-the-wrong rule and permitted recovery. It decided that, on the guest-host issue, New York had the "dominant contacts" because the parties were domiciled in New York, were on a trip which began in New York, and were traveling in a vehicle registered and regularly garaged in New York. The court noted that Ontario had no connection with the cause of action except that the accident happened to take place there.

Kell presented the converse of *Babcock*. There, the question was also whether the New York ordinary negligence rule applied or whether the Ontario guest statute controlled. The guest was injured by the host's ordinary negligence while the parties, both residents of Ontario, were on a trip in New York which was to begin and end in Ontario. The New York court purported to follow *Babcock* but held that Ontario law would not apply.

McMillan v. McMillan, 253 S.E.2d 662, 664 (1979). It was perhaps recognition of just such gross disparities in result that prompted the Court of Appeals of New York to remark, in a towering achievement in the art of understatement, "candor requires the admission that our past decisions have lacked a precise consistency."

II

The appellant urges us in the alternative to adopt the "choice-influencing considerations approach" set forth by Professor Leflar in "Choice-Influencing Considerations and Conflicts of Law," 41 N.Y.U. L. Rev. 267 (1966). Professor Leflar has narrowed the list of considerations in conflicts cases to five:

[The court here lists Professor Leflar's choice-influencing considerations, *supra* pages 218-220.]

Professor Leflar's approach has been adopted in the guest statute context in the landmark cases of Clark v. Clark, Milkovich v. Saari, and Conklin v. Horner. In practice the cases tend to focus more on the fourth and fifth considerations that the first three, and the upshot is that the courts of New Hampshire, Minnesota and Wisconsin simply will not apply guest statutes. This seems to us a perfectly intelligible and sensible bright-line rule. However, it seems unnecessary to scrap an entire body of law and dress the rule up in a newfangled five-factor costume when the same concerns can be addressed and the same result achieved through judicious employment of the traditional public policy exception to lex loci delicti.

III

Lex loci delicti has long been the cornerstone of our conflict of laws doctrine. The consistency, predictability, and ease of application provided by the traditional doctrine are not to be discarded lightly, and we are not persuaded that we should discard them today. The appellant contends that the various exceptions that have been engrafted onto the traditional rule have made it manipulable and have undermined the predictability and uniformity that were considered its primary virtues. There is certainly some truth in this, and we generally eschew the more strained escape devices employed to avoid the sometimes harsh effects of the traditional rule. Nevertheless, we remain convinced that the traditional rule, for all of its faults, remains superior to any of its modern competitors. Moreover, if we are going to manipulate conflicts doctrine in order to achieve substantive results, we might as well manipulate something we understand. Having mastered marble, we decline an apprenticeship in bronze. We therefore reaffirm our adherence to the doctrine of lex loci delicti today.

However, we have long recognized that comity does not require the application of the substantive law of a foreign state when that law contravenes the public policy of this State. West Virginia has never had an automobile guest passenger statute. It is the strong public policy of this State that persons injured by the negligence of another should be able to recover in tort. Accordingly, we have abolished the doctrine of interspousal immunity, and we have adopted the doctrine of comparative negligence in preference to the harsh rule of contributory negligence. We abolished charitable immunity for hospitals in Adkins v. St. Francis Hospital. We held that there is no common law governmental immunity for municipal corporations in Higginbotham v. City of Charleston. And we abrogated the doctrine of parental immunity to permit an unemancipated minor child to sue for injuries received in a motor vehicle accident in Lee v. Comer. Today we declare that automobile guest passenger statutes violate the strong public policy of this State in favor of compensating persons injured by the negligence of others. Accordingly, we will no longer enforce the automobile guest passenger statutes of foreign jurisdictions in our courts.[14]

For the foregoing reasons, the order of the circuit granting summary judgment in favor of the appellees is hereby vacated, and the cause remanded for further proceedings not inconsistent with this opinion.

Reversed and remanded. . . .

Questions and Comments

(1) The court in *Paul* purported to be adhering to the traditional rules reflected in the First Restatement, but did the court correctly apply those rules? Does the First Restatement permit the use of the public policy exception to favor plaintiffs whose cases would otherwise be dismissed? *See* First Restatement §612, *supra* page 146, especially the clarification in the 1948 Supplement. Is use of the public policy exception under the First Restatement subject to a requirement that the case have some connection to the forum, as the court appeared to require in footnote 14?

(2) Is *Paul*'s indictment of modern choice-of-law doctrines fair? Is Judge Neely right to suggest that modern doctrines were an unfortunate overreaction to a few backward substantive law doctrines (such as guest statutes)? In light of his resolution of the case, is he hypocritical to criticize the manipulability of the modern approaches? Which is worse—manipulating the rigid traditional rules to reach the "just" result, or manipulating modern approaches that invite judges to reach the "just" result? Do you think a state's selection of a choice-of-law approach really affects decisional outcomes?

(3) Justice Neely is not the only judge who has decided to stick with tried-and-true methods, however imperfect. Various empirical studies have attempted to analyze the patterns of operation of the traditional as opposed to modern choice-of-law

---

14. Although we intend this to be a rule of general application, we do not intend it as an invitation to flagrant forum shopping. For example, were a resident of a guest statute jurisdiction to sue another resident of a guest statute jurisdiction over an accident occurring in a guest statute jurisdiction, the simple fact that the plaintiff was able to serve process on the defendant within our State borders would not compel us to resist application of any relevant guest statute. The State must have some connection with the controversy above and beyond mere service of process before the rule we announce today will be applied. In other words, venue must be proper under some provision *other than W. Va. Code* 56-1-1(a)(4) [1986].

methods. *See* Solimine, *An Economic and Empirical Analysis of Choice of Law*, 24 Ga. L. Rev. 49 (1989); Borchers, *The Choice-of-Law Revolution: An Empirical Study*, 49 Wash. & Lee L. Rev. 357 (1992); Thiel, *Choice of Law and the Home-Court Advantage: Evidence*, 2 Am. L. & Econ. Rev. 291 (2000). In particular, these studies asked about possible biases in the new methods (their biases in favor of recovery, toward application of forum law, and on behalf of local parties and how the traditional methods fare, by comparison).

The Borchers study, interestingly, concluded that judges applying the First Restatement act in distinctly different ways from judges applying newer methods; in particular, they display less of the three biases just mentioned. However, courts applying any of the new methods do not act substantially different from one another. Since the new methods have rather different jurisprudential underpinnings, Borchers concludes that First Restatement judges are more sincere in their commitment to apply the method honestly than judges applying any of the newer methods: "Courts do *not* take the new approaches seriously." 49 Wash. & Lee L. Rev. at 379. Of course, if one does not like what the First Restatement prescribes, the fact that judges take it seriously is not a cause for celebration.

Thiel, *supra*, using more sophisticated econometric techniques, found that the modern approaches all use forum law more often than states that use the First Restatement, and that states using interest analysis show a stronger bias toward residents in their determinations than do states using any other choice-of-law approach.

G.   Statutory Resolution of Choice-of-Law Problems

Legislatures sometimes provide us with conflicts rules, especially in cases in which the courts have not produced satisfactory results.

It is doubtful that statutory conflicts rules are a general solution to the choice-of-law problem since legislators would face the same problems as the courts, the commentators, and the Restatement drafters. The Restatements in particular illustrate a central problem: The First Restatement offered a fair amount of certainty, but at the cost of fairness. The Restatement Second offers more flexibility, and thus potentially more fairness, but at the cost of certainty. How can a legislature do better?

Salavarria v. National Car Rental System, Inc.

705 So. 2d 809 (La. App. 4th Dist. 1998)

BYRNES, J.

The relator, National Car Rental System, Inc., filed a motion for summary judgment based on the rule in Louisiana that a self-insured car rental agency has the right to restrict the use of rental vehicles to "authorized users" and, therefore, cannot be held liable for accidents caused by unauthorized users. This motion was denied because the trial court found that Florida law applied. A reversal of the denial of the motion for summary judgment would terminate the litigation as to the relator. Therefore, we have consented to grant relator's application for writs, reverse the judgment of the trial court and render judgment dismissing plaintiffs' claims against relator.

This writ presents a conflicts of law issue. The plaintiffs were the driver and passengers in a car which collided with an automobile owned by National Car Rental Systems, Inc. in 1994. The car had been rented to Mitchell Brogdon, and the driver of the National car, Heather Trempe, was not an authorized driver of the car. The plaintiffs are Louisiana residents. Brogdon and Trempe are Florida residents. National is a Delaware corporation which was doing business in Florida. The contract was entered into in Florida. The accident occurred in Louisiana. National filed a motion for summary judgment arguing that Louisiana law applies. The trial court denied the motion, finding that Florida law controls the contractual obligations arising from National's rental agreement with Brogdon.

The Louisiana Supreme Court has ruled that a self-insured rental car company has the right to limit operation of its vehicles to only those individuals to whom it gives express permission, i.e., those individuals listed as authorized drivers in the rental agreement. Hearty v. Harris, 574 So. 2d 1234 (La. 1991). Florida law apparently does not distinguish between authorized and unauthorized users of rental cars because it simply holds owners vicariously liable for mere ownership of the vehicle under a dangerous instrumentality law. Relator argues that the trial court improperly ruled that because the National Car Rental System, Inc. car rental agreement was entered into in Florida, Florida law should apply. The relator argues that because Trempe was not a party to the contract, the existence of the contract and whether Florida law applies to the obligation between Brogdon and relator is of no moment in determining the relator's obligation to Trempe. The plaintiffs do not contest the applicability of Louisiana law to the issue of the liability of Trempe, but they contest the issue of the applicability of Louisiana law to the liability of the relator, as owner of the car.

The general conflict of law statute, LSA-C.C. art. 3515 provides:

> Except as otherwise provided in this Book, an issue in a case having contacts with other states is governed by the law of the state whose policies would be most seriously impaired if its law were not applied to that issue.
>
>   That state is determined by evaluating the strength and pertinence of the relevant policies of all involved states in the light of: (1) the relationship of each state to the parties and the dispute; and (2) the policies and needs of the interstate and international systems, including the policies of upholding the justified expectations of parties and of minimizing the adverse consequences that might follow from subjecting a party to the law of more than one state.

LSA-C.C. art. 3542, the general conflict of law provision dealing specifically with delictual obligations would apply the:

> Law of the state whose policies would be most seriously impaired if its law were not applied to that issue.
>
>   That state is determined by evaluating the strength and pertinence of the relevant policies of the involved states in light of: (1) the pertinent contacts

of each state to the parties and the events giving rise to the dispute, including the place of conduct and injury, the domicile, habitual residence, or place of business of the parties, and the state in which the relationship, if any, between the parties was centered; and (2) the policies referred to in Article 3515, as well as policies of deterring wrongful conduct and of repairing the consequences of injurious acts.

Comment (b) to LSA-C.C. art. 3542 directs that the rules contained in Articles 3543 through 3546 are more specific, and where applicable, prevail over Article 3542. LSA-C.C. art 3543 provides that issues pertaining to standards of conduct and safety are governed by the law of the state in which the conduct occurred. In the instant case there is no dispute that the conduct that resulted in the plaintiffs' injuries occurred in Louisiana, and that Louisiana's standard of care must apply. Comment (a) to Article 3543 states, "by way of illustration, so-called 'rules of the road' establish or pertain to 'standards of conduct and safety,' whereas rules that impose a ceiling on the amount of compensatory damages or provide immunity from suit are 'rules of loss distribution and financial protection.'" Relator's derivative liability is a question of "loss distribution and financial protection." LSA-C.C. art. 3544 provides that issues of loss distribution and financial protections are governed, as between a person injured by an offense and the person who caused the injury, "by the law designated in the following order: . . . (2) If, at the time of the injury, the injured person and the person who caused the injury were domiciled in different states; (a) when *both the injury and the conduct that caused it occurred in one of those states, by the law of that state.*" (Emphasis added.) Since the injured persons in this case are Louisiana residents, and the person who caused the injury (Trempe) is a Florida resident, LSA-C.C. art. 3544(2)(a) is applicable. Since both the injury and the conduct that caused it occurred in Louisiana, and the plaintiffs are Louisiana domiciliaries, Louisiana law should be applied under LSA-C.C. art. 3544(2)(a).

Comment (g) under LSA-C.C. art. 3542(2)(a) reinforces the already clear language of LSA-C.C. art. 3542 in this regard:

> Domicile of either party. Subparagraph (2) deals with cases in which, at the time of the injury, the tortfeasor and the victim were not domiciled in the same state. Clause (a) of that subparagraph provides that when both the injurious conduct and the resulting injury occurred in a state where either the tortfeasor or the victim was domiciled, the law of that state shall apply, regardless of whether it provides for a higher or lower standard of financial protection than the law of the domicile of the other party. For rationale and supporting authority, see Symeonides, "Choice of Law for Torts," 453-456. When a person is injured in his home state by conduct in that state, his rights should be determined by the law of that state, even if the person who caused the injury happened to be from another state. The law of the latter state should not be interjected to the victim's detriment or benefit. By the same token, when a person acting within his home state causes injury in that state, he should be held accountable according to the law of that state, even if the injured person happened to be from another state. The law of the latter state should not be interjected to the tortfeasor's detriment or benefit.

The plaintiffs do not contend that relator, National Car Rental System, Inc., is liable to them by virtue of any provision in the rental car agreement. *If relator is liable to the plaintiffs, it is only by operation and application of Florida law, not by virtue of any contractual provision.* In fact, the terms of the rental contract specifically prohibit the use of the vehicle by any unauthorized driver. It is undisputed that Heather Trempe was not an authorized driver. In boldface uppercase type the rental agreement states:

> I UNDERSTAND THAT IF THE VEHICLE IS OBTAINED OR USED FOR ANY PROHIBITED USE OR IN VIOLATION OF THIS AGREEMENT, THEN ANY LIMITATION OF MY RESPONSIBILITY UNDER THIS AGREEMENT SHALL BE VOID AND I SHALL BE FULLY RESPONSIBLE FOR ALL LOSS AND RESULTING DAMAGES, INCLUDING LOSS OF USE, CLAIMS PROCESSING FEES, ADMINISTRATIVE CHARGES, COSTS AND ATTORNEY'S FEES. ALSO, WHERE PERMITTED BY LAW, THE LAW OPTION SHALL BE VOID AND THE LIABILITY, PAI, PEC AND SLI INSURANCE SHALL BE VOID.

We respectfully disagree with the analysis of the First Circuit in Oliver v. Davis, 679 So. 2d 462 (La. App. 1996), which involved a fact situation with much in common with the instant case. In *Oliver* the court stated that applying Florida's "dangerous instrumentality" theory of liability could be of benefit to the car rental agency:

> A rental agency would thereby be able to determine its risk of liability under the law of one state rather than having to determine the risk of liability under the laws of each state through which the vehicle travels.

Id. at 467.

The relator in this case resists having this unwanted "benefit" conferred upon it just as vigorously as did the rental agency in *Oliver*, leading this Court to conclude that it is not really a benefit to car rental agencies. The conclusion of this Court is supported by the language underlined in the boldface quoted above from the rental agreement ("**WHERE PERMITTED BY LAW**"). This language is a clear indication that the rental agency contemplated the potential application of different laws in different jurisdictions and sought to take advantage of those variations where permitted. We conclude that multi-state consistency of results for the benefit of the car rental agency is not a valid basis for preferring Florida law under the facts of this case.

The *Oliver* court suggested that we should also consider which state's policy would be most seriously impaired if its law were not applied to the issue pursuant to LSA-C.C. art. 3515. The *Oliver* court suggests that a Louisiana court might conclude that Florida's law of vicarious liability would be most seriously impaired if Louisiana law were not applied. But that is not what seriously impaired means. By that standard the state whose law is not applied would always be the most seriously impaired. "Seriously impaired" refers to the interest the state has in seeing its policies effectuated relative to the facts of the case, *i.e.*, does the state have such contacts with the cause of action that the failure to apply its laws results in a disproportionate frustration of that state's policies relative to the contacts with that state giving rise to the litigation. In the instant case, Louisiana's policies governing "loss distribution and financial protection" would be most seriously impaired by the application of Florida law because the overwhelming preponderance of the contacts out of which this litigation arises are with the state of Louisiana.

Oliver states that "the application of Florida law to the vicarious liability issue would not impair the policies promoted by Louisiana of protecting its injured citizens." *Id.* at 468. The effect of this approach would be to apply the law of greatest recovery in all conflict situations, because affording the greatest recovery would never "impair the policies promoted by Louisiana of protecting its injured citizens." But that is not the proper standard. Comment (g) to LSA-C.C. art. 3544(2)(a) quoted above makes it clear that the choice is not to be based on either the benefit or detriment to the litigants.

The *Oliver* court treats the enforcement of Florida's "dangerous instrumentality" law as an end in itself from Florida's perspective. However, it is not the enforcement of any particular law that is at issue when "impairment of policies" is referred to in conflict of law situations. It is the state policies that those laws seek to effectuate that are at issue. We must determine what Florida is trying to achieve through the mechanism of its "dangerous instrumentality-vicarious liability law." If the goal of the Florida law is to make Florida roads safer, its application to the facts of this case will not achieve that purpose. The accident occurred in Louisiana. If the goal of the Florida law is to ensure recovery for Florida residents or those injured on Florida roads, its application to the facts of this case will not achieve that purpose. The injured parties are all Louisiana residents, injured in Louisiana. Florida's policies are only impaired if those policies include a concern for the safety of Louisiana roads, or a concern for the protection and recovery of Louisiana residents injured in Louisiana. Clearly Florida has no such policies or concerns, and any attempt by Florida to enact extra-territorial laws to effectuate such policies would represent an unconstitutional overreaching, and are obviously not the policies of the state of Florida. Neither *Oliver*, nor respondents have been able to articulate any genuine interest that Florida might have in the application of its law of vicarious liability to the facts of the instant case. Nor have the respondents any legitimate expectations that if injured while driving Louisiana roads that Florida law would apply.

There are no genuine issues of material fact. . . . Therefore, we reverse the judgment of the trial court and render judgment in favor of relator, National Car Rental Systems, Inc., dismissing plaintiff's claims against relator with prejudice at plaintiffs' cost, and remand for further proceedings consistent with this opinion.

Questions and Comments

(1) Louisiana's 1992 choice-of-law statute was the first comprehensive state choice-of-law codification in the United States. The central principle of the Louisiana statute is set forth in Article 3515, which calls for application of the law of "the state whose policies would be most impaired if its laws were not applied to that issue." *See also* La. Civ. Code §3542 (comparative impairment rule for torts); La. Civ. Code §3537 (comparative impairment rule for contracts). The rest of Louisiana's choice-of-law code explains how this general principle applies in specific substantive contexts. *See* Symeonides, *Louisiana's New Law of Choice of Law for Torts: An Exegesis*, 66 Tul. L. Rev. 677 (1992) (describing these more

specific rules as "*a priori* legislative determinations of 'the state whose policies would be most impaired if not applied'"). As *Salavarria* makes clear, in the tort context these more specific rules incorporate the distinction between loss-allocation and conduct-regulating rules. *See* La. Civ. Code §§3543-3544. Finally, Article 3547 provides for escape from these more specific rules "if, from the totality of the circumstances of an exceptional case, it is clearly evident under the principles of Article 3542, that the policies of another state would be more seriously impaired if its laws were not applied to the particular issue." The Louisiana choice-of-law code's approach to torts thus seems like a mixture of comparative impairment, New York's approach, and the Second Restatement. One scholar has described this mixture as "an important effort to codify the best of modern conflicts understanding." Perdue, *A Reexamination of the Distinction Between "Loss-Allocating" and "Conduct-Regulating Rules,"* 60 La. L. Rev. 1251, 1251 (2000). Do you agree?

(2) Does codification promote predictability in governing law? Does the answer depend on the content of the codified rules? Or does a codified rule necessarily reduce judicial discretion (and thus increase predictability) when compared to the same rule applied in a common-law fashion? We have two empirical analyses of the operation of the Louisiana choice-of-law code, but they cut in two directions. Professor Borchers studied tort cases under the code. He found that trial court choice-of-law decisions under the code were affirmed on appeal 76.2 percent of the time, as compared with a 52.9 percent affirmance rate in pre-code Louisiana conflicts cases. Viewing affirmance rates as a proxy for decisional predictability, Borchers concludes that the Louisiana choice-of-law code has increased predictability. *See* Borchers, *Louisiana's Conflicts Codification: Some Empirical Observations Regarding Decisional Predictability*, 60 La. L. Rev. 1061 (2000). Professor Weintraub studied the contracts provisions of the code and obtained less happy results. Of the 32 contractual choice-of-law cases decided under the Louisiana code, 25 or so make "fundamental" errors in applying the code. *See* Weintraub, *Courts Flailing in the Waters of the Louisiana Conflicts Code: Not Waving but Drowning*, 60 La. L. Rev. 1365, 1365-1366 (2000).

Assume that Borchers is right about the code increasing choice-of-law predictability. Is this attributable to the codification itself, or the content of the rules that happen to be codified? Even if the Louisiana code increased the *predictability* of Louisiana conflicts law, would this increase conflicts *uniformity*? Doesn't uniformity require national regulation?

(3) Professor Gottesman argues that we need a federal choice-of-law statute because our current decentralized system produces enormous waste, frustrates rational planning, and is unfair. *See* Gottesman, *"Draining the Dismal Swamp": The Case for Federal Choice of Law Statutes*, 80 Geo. L.J. 1 (1991). Gottesman is largely agnostic about the content of the federal statutory rules. He argues that within fairly large bounds, many choice-of-law rules codified at the national level would address the problems with the current system. But does Congress have the power to enact such rules? Is Congress institutionally competent to craft such rules? Would such a statute make every interstate case a federal question? Gottesman addresses these and many other questions, and surveys the literature.

(4) In 2009, the Oregon legislature enacted choice-of-law statutes to govern legal disputes involving (1) contracts (ORS §§81.100-135 (2009)), and (2) torts and

other noncontractual settings (ORS §§31.850-890 (2009)). With these statutes, Oregon has become the second U.S. state and the first state with a common-law tradition to adopt a broadly applicable choice-of-law statute. For both contracts and torts, the statute provides a list of situations where Oregon law will apply, a list of presumptively applicable rules, and a set of factors to take into account in situations where the presumptive rules appear to produce inappropriate results or where presumptive rules are lacking.

For contract disputes not governed by an effective choice-of-law clause, the Oregon statute provides that Oregon law applies to certain contracts, including those involving construction to be performed in state, consumer contracts where the consumer resides and accepts the goods in state, and employment contracts where services are to be performed primarily in state. Presumptive rules are specified for particular types of contracts, including franchise, personal services, real property, and licensing contracts, among others. The presumptive rules are to apply unless "clearly inappropriate." Appropriateness is to be determined according to the statute's general rule, which also governs choice of law for contracts not otherwise addressed in the statute.

(5) One of the most litigated statutory conflicts provisions has been section 1-105(1) of the Uniform Commercial Code, which provides:

> *Except* as provided hereafter in this section, when a transaction bears a reasonable relation to this *state* and also to another *state* or nation the parties may agree that the law either of this state or of such other state or nation shall govern their rights and duties. Failing such agreement, this code [i.e., the law of this state] applies to transactions bearing an appropriate relation to this state.

Courts disagree about the meaning of the "appropriate relation" criterion. Some view it to permit application of local law on the basis of minimal contacts, regardless of whether another state has more significant contacts. *See, e.g.*, Whitaker v. Harvell-Kilgore Corp., 418 F. 2d 1010, 1016 (5th Cir. 1969). Most courts, however, equate the "appropriate relation" test with the Second Restatement's "most significant relationship" test. *See, e.g.*, In re Merritt Dredging Co., Inc., 839 F.2d 203, 206-207 (4th Cir. 1988).

In 2001, a revision of Article 1 of the UCC, which included a revision of section 1-105(1), was presented to the states for approval. The replacement provision, section 1-301(c), provided in pertinent part that "the rights and obligations of the parties are determined . . . by the law that would be selected by application of this State's conflict of laws principles." The official commentary stated that the revision was intended to remove the forum law bias present in the pre-2001 version and direct states to resolve UCC-related legal disputes by reference to the same choice-of-law principles they would use for other disputes. For a variety of reasons mostly not related to this change, section 1-301 proved unpopular with state legislatures, so in 2008 the 2001 version was again amended to essentially restore the pre-2001 language from section 1-105.

Should choice of law under the UCC be treated the same or different from other choice-of-law problems? To what extent should it matter that the UCC attempts to achieve uniformity? What choice-of-law provisions, if any, could be inserted into the UCC to promote that goal?

4

Constitutional Limitations on Choice of Law

The due process and equal protection clauses of the Fourteenth Amendment:

[N]or shall any State deprive any person of life, liberty, or property, without due process of law; nor deny to any person within its jurisdiction the equal protection of the laws. . . . [U.S. Const. amend. XIV, §1.]

The full faith and credit clause and statute:

Full Faith and Credit shall be given in each State to the public Acts, records, and judicial Proceedings of every other State. And the Congress may by general laws prescribe the Manner in which such Acts, Records and Proceedings shall be proved, and the Effect thereof. [U.S. Const. art. IV, §1.]

Such Acts, records and judicial proceedings or copies thereof, so authenticated, shall have the same full faith and credit in every court within the United States and its Territories and Possessions as they have by law or usage in the courts of such State, Territory or Possession from which they are taken. [28 U.S.C. §1738.]

The privileges and immunities clause:

The Citizens of each State shall be entitled to all Privileges and Immunities of Citizens in the several States. [U.S. Const. art. IV, §2.]

The commerce clause:

The Congress shall have power . . . To regulate Commerce with foreign Nations, and among the several States and with the Indian Tribes. . . . [U.S. Const. art. I, §8.]

The major constitutional limitations on the choice-of-law process have been the federal due process clause and the full faith and credit clause. The commerce clause places limits on state regulation as well. In addition, both the equal protection and privileges and immunities clauses are of potential relevance to modern choice-of-law theory because they arguably limit a state's right to discriminate on the basis of where activities occur or where the litigants are domiciled.

It is unclear how these five constitutional provisions fit together. Do the due process and full faith and credit clauses duplicate each other's choice-of-law functions precisely? Why does the Supreme Court sometimes rely on the commerce clause rather than on due process analysis in assessing the validity of state regulation? What is the connection between the equal protection clause and the privileges and immunities clause? And how can one tell in a particular case which constitutional provision to employ? Finding answers to these questions is further complicated by the fact that the scope and role of these clauses has changed over time.

A.   Constitutional Limitations on Choice of Law

There was a point at which traditional principles of the kind found in the First Restatement appeared to be on the way to enshrinement in the Constitution (through Supreme Court interpretation). Thus, in New York Life Insurance Co. v. Dodge, 246 U.S. 357 (1918), the Court struck down application of a Missouri nonforfeiture statute to a life insurance policy bought in Missouri and covering a Missouri domiciliary, holding that the contract and an accompanying loan agreement were not in force until accepted by the company's home office in New York. Thus, the contract was formed in New York. Missouri, the Court said, was forbidden by the due process clause from denying the company rights that had vested under New York law. The Court backed off in result, though not in rhetoric, a few years later in an almost identical case, Mutual Life Insurance Co. v. Liebing, 259 U.S. 209 (1922), by finding that the loan agreement subject to the nonforfeiture statute was a separate agreement formed in Missouri and thus subject to Missouri law.

Even if the Constitution was not to be read as implementing every detailed traditional rule, parochial choice of law continued to concern the Court. The case that follows is still cited with approval in Supreme Court decisions.

Home Insurance Co. v. Dick
281 U.S. 397 (1930)

Justice BRANDEIS delivered the opinion of the Court.

Dick, a citizen of Texas, brought this action in a court of that State against Compania General Anglo-Mexicana de Seguros S.A., a Mexican corporation, to recover on a policy of fire insurance for the total loss of a tug. Jurisdiction was asserted in rem through garnishment, by ancillary writs issued against The Home Insurance Company and Franklin Fire Insurance Company, which reinsured, by contracts with the Mexican corporation, parts of the risk which it had assumed. The garnishees are New York corporations. Upon them, service was effected by serving their local agents in Texas appointed pursuant to Texas statutes, which require the appointment of local agents by foreign corporations seeking permits to do business within the State.

The controversy here is wholly between Dick and the garnishees. The defendant has never been admitted to do business in Texas; has not done any business there; and has not authorized anyone to receive service of process or enter an appearance for it in this cause. . . .

[The insurance companies'] defense rests upon the following facts. This suit was not commenced till more than one year after the date of the loss. The policy provided: "It is understood and agreed that no judicial suit or demand shall be entered before any tribunal for the collection of any claim under this policy, unless such suits or demands are filed within one year counted as from the date on which such damage occurs." This provision was in accord with the Mexican law to which the policy was expressly made subject. It was issued by the Mexican company in Mexico to one Bonner, of Tampico, Mexico, and was there duly assigned to Dick prior to the loss. It covered the vessel only in certain Mexican waters. The premium was paid in Mexico; and the loss was "payable in the City of Mexico in current funds of the United States of Mexico, or their equivalent elsewhere." At the time the policy was issued, when it was assigned to him, and until after the loss, Dick actually resided in Mexico, although his permanent residence was in Texas. The contracts of reinsurance were effected by correspondence between the Mexican company in Mexico and the New York companies in New York. Nothing thereunder was to be done, or was in fact done, in Texas.

In the trial court, the garnishees contended that since the insurance contract was made and was to be performed in Mexico, and the one year provision was valid by its laws, Dick's failure to sue within one year after accrual of the alleged cause of action was a complete defense to the suit on the policy; that this failure also relieved the garnishees of any obligation as reinsurers, the same defense being open to them, and that they, consequently, owed no debt to the Mexican company subject to garnishment. To this defense, Dick demurred, on the ground that Article 5545 of the Texas Revised Civil Statutes (1925) provides:

> No person, firm, corporation, association or combination of whatsoever kind shall enter into any stipulation, contract, or agreement, by reason whereof the time in which to sue thereon is limited to a shorter period than two years. And no stipulation, contract, or agreement for any such shorter limitation in which to sue shall ever be valid in this State.

The trial court sustained Dick's contention and entered judgment against the garnishees. On appeal, both in the Court of Civil Appeals and in the Supreme Court of the State, the garnishees asserted that, as construed and applied, the Texas statute violated the due process clause of the Fourteenth Amendment and the contract clause. Both courts treated the policy provision as equivalent to a foreign statute of limitation; held that Article 5545 related to the remedy available in Texas courts; concluded that it was validly applicable to the case at bar; and affirmed the judgment of the trial court. The garnishees appealed to this Court on the ground that the statute, as construed and applied, violated their rights under the Federal Constitution. . . .

First. Dick contends that this Court lacks jurisdiction of the action, because the errors assigned involve only questions of local law and of conflict of laws. The argument is that while a provision requiring notice of loss within a fixed period is substantive because it is a condition precedent to the existence of the cause of action, the provision for liability only in case suit is brought within the year is not substantive because it relates only to the remedy after accrual of the cause of action; that while the validity, interpretation and performance of the substantive provisions of a contract are determined by the law of the place where it is made and is to be performed, matters which relate only to the remedy are unquestionably governed by the lex fori; and that even if the Texas court erred in holding the statute applicable to this contract, the error is one of state law or of the interpretation of the contract, and is not reviewable here.

The contention is unsound. There is no dispute as to the meaning of the provision in the policy. It is that the insurer shall not be liable unless suit is brought within one year of the loss. Whether the provision be interpreted as making the commencement of a suit within the year a condition precedent to the existence of a cause of action, or as making failure to sue within the year a breach of a condition subsequent which extinguishes the cause of action, is not of legal significance here. Nor are we concerned with the question whether the provision is properly described as relating to remedy or to substance. However characterized, it is an express term in the contract of the parties by which the right of the insured and the correlative obligation of the insurer are defined. If effect is given to the clause, Dick cannot recover from the Mexican corporation and the garnishees cannot be compelled to pay. If, on the other hand, the statute is applied to the contract, it admittedly abrogates a contractual right and imposes liability, although the parties have agreed that there should be none.

The statute is not simply one of limitation. It does not merely fix the time in which the aid of the Texas courts may be invoked. Nor does it govern only the remedies available in Texas courts. It deals with the powers and capacities of persons and corporations. It expressly prohibits the making of certain contracts. As construed, it also directs the disregard in Texas of contractual rights and obligations wherever created and assumed; and it commands the enforcement of obligations in excess of those contracted for. Therefore, the objection that, as applied to contracts made and to be performed outside of Texas, the statute violates the Federal Constitution, raises federal questions of substance; and the existence of the federal claim is not disproved by saying that the statute, or the one year provision in the policy, relates to the remedy and not to the substance.

Second. The Texas statute as here construed and applied deprives the garnishees of property without due process of law. A State may, of course, prohibit and declare invalid the making of certain contracts within its borders. Ordinarily, it may prohibit performance within its borders, even of contracts validly made elsewhere, if they are required to be performed within the State and their performance would violate its laws. But, in the case at bar, nothing in any way relating to the policy sued on, or to the contracts of reinsurance, was ever done or required to be done in Texas. All acts relating to the making of the policy were done in Mexico. All in relation to the making of the contracts of reinsurance were done there or in New York. And, likewise, all things in regard to performance were to be done outside of Texas. Neither the Texas laws nor the Texas courts were invoked for any purpose, except by Dick in the bringing of this suit. The fact that Dick's permanent residence was in Texas is without significance. At all times here material, he was physically present and acting in Mexico. Texas was, therefore, without power to affect the terms of contracts so made. Its attempt to impose a greater obligation than that agreed upon and to seize property in payment of the imposed obligation violates the guaranty against deprivation of property without due process of law.

The cases relied upon, in which it was held that a State may lengthen its statute of limitations, are not in point. In those cases, the parties had not stipulated a time limit for the enforcement of their obligations. It is true that a State may extend the time within which suit may be brought to its own courts, if, in doing so, it violates no agreement of the parties. And, in the absence of a contractual provision, the local statute of limitation may be applied to a right created in another jurisdiction even where the remedy in the latter is barred. In such cases, the rights and obligations of the parties are not varied. When, however, the parties have expressly agreed upon a time limit on their obligation, a statute which invalidates the agreement and directs enforcement of the contract after the time has expired increases their obligation and imposes a burden not contracted for.

It is true also that a State is not bound to provide remedies and procedure to suit the wishes of individual litigants. It may prescribe the kind of remedies to be available in its courts and dictate the practice and procedure to be followed in pursuing those remedies. Contractual provisions relating to these matters, even if valid where made, are often disregarded by the court of the forum, pursuant to statute or otherwise. But the Texas statute deals neither with the kind of remedy available nor with the mode in which it is to be pursued. It purports to create rights and obligations. It may not validly affect contracts which are neither made nor are to be performed in Texas.

Third. Dick urges that Article 5545 of the Texas law is a declaration of its public policy; and that a State may properly refuse to recognize foreign rights which violate its declared policy. Doubtless, a State may prohibit the enjoyment by persons within its borders of rights acquired elsewhere which violate its laws or public policy; and, under some circumstances, it may refuse to aid in the enforcement of such rights. But the Mexican corporation never was in Texas; and neither it nor the garnishees invoked the aid of the Texas courts or the Texas laws. The Mexican corporation was not before the court. The garnishees were brought in by compulsory process. Neither has asked favors. They ask only to be let alone. We need not consider how far the State may go in imposing restrictions on the conduct of its own residents, and of foreign corporations which have received permission to do business within its borders; or how far it may go in refusing to lend the aid of its courts to the enforcement of rights acquired outside its borders. It may not abrogate the rights of parties beyond its borders having no relation to anything done or to be done within them.

Fourth. Finally, it is urged that the Federal Constitution does not require the States to recognize and protect rights derived from the laws of foreign countries—that as to them, the full faith and credit clause has no application. The claims here asserted are not based upon the full faith and credit clause. They rest upon the Fourteenth Amendment. Its protection extends to aliens. Moreover, the parties in interest here are American companies. The defense asserted is based on the provision of the policy and on their contracts of reinsurance. The courts of the State confused this defense with that based on the Mexican Code. They held that even if the effort of the foreign statute was to extinguish the right, Dick's removal to Texas prior to the bar of the foreign statute, removed the cause of action from Mexico and subjected it to the Texas statute of limitation. And they applied the same rule to the provision in the policy. Whether or not that is a sufficient answer to the defense based on the foreign law, we may not consider; for, no issue under the full faith and credit clause was raised. But in Texas, as elsewhere, the contract was subject to its own limitations.

Reversed.

Questions and Comments

(1) Virtually all the contacts in this case were with Mexico. How did Dick get jurisdiction in Texas? The constitutionality of the quasi in rem jurisdiction the Court exercised was disposed of many years later in Rush v. Savchuk, 444 U.S. 320 (1980), page 461 *infra*. Should a state always be allowed to apply its own law if it has enough contacts to assert "normal" long-arm jurisdiction? *Compare* Phillips Petroleum Co. v. Shutts, page 310 *infra*.

(2) How persuasive is the Court's assertion that the statute in question is not merely one of limitation, and therefore not defensible under the exception for applying the forum's own procedural law? Is characterization a constitutional issue? What if the parties had omitted the contractual limitation in reliance on the Mexican one-year statute of limitations—the statute of the only jurisdiction with any contacts with the case? Would the result have been the same under the Court's reasoning? Would such a case be different in substance from the actual *Dick* case?

(3) Why didn't the defendants in *Dick* invoke the full faith and credit clause? Is there a good reason for state courts to pay more respect to the laws of sister states than the laws of sovereign nations?

(4) Does the Court's discussion of public policy mean that a state may never invoke its public policy when it has insufficient contacts with a case? ("[Texas] may not abrogate the rights of parties beyond its borders having no relation to anything done or to be done within them.") Does the Court's position mean, for example, that Texas would be required by the due process clause to award damages for breach of a contract for the sale of slaves if the contract was legal in the country to which it was confined? Or do the constitutional limits on application of the public policy exception apply differently when public policy is used as a door-closing device?

(5) What is the nature of the due process violation in the *Dick* case? Does due process incorporate some territorial principle per se? If so, where is that territorial principle to be found in the language of the clause or its legislative history?

If the Court relies on the notion that the Mexican insurance company had a right under the contractual clause not to be sued, and that such right was "property" protected by the due process clause, doesn't its reasoning beg the question? That is, the "right" in question can be "property" only if it really is a right, and it is a right under Mexican law but not under Texas law. Thus, one must first decide that, *as a matter of constitutional law* concerning the due process clause, Mexican law was the only applicable law. We're back where we started. These matters are discussed at great length in Martin, *Constitutional Limitations on Choice of Law*, 61 Cornell L. Rev. 185, 188-191 (1976); Kirgis, *The Roles of Due Process and Full Faith and Credit in Choice of Law*, 62 Cornell L. Rev. 94 (1976); and Martin, *A Reply to Professor Kirgis*, *id*. at 62.

(6) What if the Texas law in question had disfavored Dick—would that have made a difference? In other words, is there any difference, from a due process perspective, between a state applying its own law to aid a resident against a nonresident and a state using its own law to aid a nonresident against a resident?

(7) The Court in *Dick* states that Dick was "a citizen of Texas" and a "permanent residen[t]," and added that "[t]he fact that Dick's permanent residence was in Texas is without significance." Does this mean that Dick was domiciled in Texas? If so, does *Dick* stand for the proposition that a state's interest in applying its plaintiff-protecting law to a domiciliary is "without significance" to the validity, under the due process clause, of applying that law? What, then, are the implications of the due process clause for interest analysis? For discussion of these issues, *see* Rensberger, *Who Was Dick? Constitutional Limitations on State Choice of Law*, 1998 Utah L. Rev. 37. For an argument that considerations of fairness to the defendant should sometimes trump state interests in protecting plaintiffs, *see* Brilmayer, *Rights, Fairness, and Choice of Law*, 99 Yale L.J. 1277 (1989).

(8) Is there any pattern in the following cases, all decided within a few years after *Dick*?

(a) Delta & Pine Land Company had its principal place of business in Tennessee but did business in Mississippi. It entered an insurance contract against employee embezzlement with Hartford Accident & Indemnity Company, which was based in Connecticut but did business both in Mississippi and Tennessee. An employee of the land company embezzled some money in Mississippi. By the time of litigation, the land company had moved its chief place of business to Mississippi. The courts of Mississippi, where the action was brought, were asked to apply a Mississippi statute voiding contractual limitations on the period in which suit could be brought. The Supreme Court, in Hartford Accident & Indem. Co. v. Delta & Pine Land Co., 292 U.S. 143 (1934), held that Mississippi could not apply its own statute. "Conceding that ordinarily a state may prohibit performance within its borders even of a contract validly made elsewhere, if the performance would violate its laws . . . it may not, on grounds of policy, ignore a right which has lawfully vested elsewhere, if, as here, the interest of the forum had but slight connection with the substance of the contract obligations." *Id*. at 149-150.

(b) A New Jersey resident allowed his car to be driven by another to New York, where the driver injured the plaintiff. The plaintiff sued the owner of the car, invoking a New York statute imposing vicarious liability on owners. This time the Supreme Court upheld the application of New York law as against a due process attack. Young v. Masci, 289 U.S. 253 (1933).

(c) In Skiriotes v. Florida, 313 U.S. 69 (1941), the Supreme Court upheld against a due process attack the right of Florida to prosecute a sponge fisher for using mechanical apparatuses (diving suits, etc.) in fishing for sponges outside but adjacent to Florida's territorial waters. The Court placed considerable emphasis on the fact that the defendant was a citizen of Florida and on the state's right to regulate the conduct of its citizens even outside its borders. What if the complained-of activity had taken place within the territorial waters of an adjoining state, which encouraged the use of mechanical aids, rather than in international waters? What if the defendant had moved to another state before doing his sponge fishing? Are these cases consistent with *Dick*?

(9) As the Supreme Court continued to consider constitutional limitations on choice of law, it decided cases both under the due process clause and the full faith and credit clause. Although the distinction was not always clear, it appeared that the essence of the due process limitations was that a state had to have some minimal contacts in order to apply its own law. There was some indication that even a state with sufficient contacts to satisfy due process might be forbidden from applying its own law under full faith and credit if there were some strong reason to favor the law of another state—overwhelmingly stronger contacts, much greater interest, uniformity of treatment, or the like. In one case, Order of Commercial Travelers of Am. v. Wolfe, 331 U.S. 586 (1947), for example, the Court used the full faith and credit clause to strike down a state's application of its own law when there were clearly enough contacts to satisfy due process.

Over time, the distinctions between the two constitutional limitations began to blur. *Wolfe* was confined to its particular subject matter, fraternal benefit organizations (where, arguably, all members, even from different states, should be subject to a single law in order to avoid unequal treatment). And in a pair of workers' compensation cases that were widely viewed as stating principles of general applicability, the Court seemed to reject the notion that a state with enough contacts to satisfy due process could be prevented from applying its own law by the full faith and credit clause. The first case, Alaska Packers Assn. v. Indus. Accident Commn., 294 U.S. 532 (1935), held that the state where an employment relationship had been formed could apply its own workers' compensation law to an employee injured in another state. The second case is reproduced below.

Pacific Employers Insurance Co. v. Industrial Accident Commission

306 U.S. 493 (1939)

Justice STONE delivered the opinion of the Court.

The question is whether the full faith and credit which the Constitution requires to be given to a Massachusetts workmen's compensation statute precludes California from applying its own workmen's compensation act in the case of an injury suffered by a Massachusetts employee of a Massachusetts employer while in California in the course of his employment.

The injured employee, a resident of Massachusetts, was regularly employed there under written contract in the laboratories of the Dewey & Almy Chemical Company as a chemical engineer and research chemist. In September, 1935, in the usual course of his employment he was sent by his employer to its branch factory in California, to act temporarily as technical adviser in the effort to improve the quality of one of the employer's products manufactured there.

[The injured employee] instituted the present proceeding before the California Commission for the award of compensation under the California Act for injuries received in the course of his employment in that state, naming petitioner as insurance carrier under that Act. The California Commission directed petitioner to pay the compensation prescribed by the California Act, including the amounts of lien claims filed in the proceeding for medical, hospital and nursing services and certain further amounts necessary for such services in the future.

By the applicable Massachusetts statute, §§24, 26, c. 152, Mass. Gen. Laws (Ter. Ed. 1932), an employee of a person insured under the Act, as was the employer in this case, is deemed to waive his "right of action at common law or under the law of any other jurisdiction" to recover for personal injuries unless he shall have given appropriate notice to the employer in writing that he elects to retain such rights. Section 26 directs that without the notice his right to recover be restricted to the compensation provided by the Act for injuries received in the course of his employment, "whether within or without the commonwealth."

Section 27 (a) [of the California Workmen's Compensation statute] provides that "No contract, rule, or regulation shall exempt the employer from liability for the compensation fixed by this act." And §58 provides that the commission shall have jurisdiction over claims for compensation for injuries suffered outside the state when the employee's contract of hire was entered into within the state. Both statutes are compensation acts, substituted for the common law remedy for negligence. The California Act is compulsory. The Massachusetts Act is similarly effective unless the employee gives notice not to be bound by it, which in this case he did not do.

[Petitioner] insists that since the contract of employment was entered into in Massachusetts and the employee consented to be bound by the Massachusetts Act, that, and not the California statute, fixes the employee's right to compensation whether the injuries were received within or without the state, and that the Massachusetts statute is constitutionally entitled to full faith and credit in the courts of California.

We may assume that these provisions are controlling upon the parties in Massachusetts, and that since they are applicable to a Massachusetts contract of employment between a Massachusetts employer and employee, they do not infringe due process. Similarly the constitutionality of the provisions of the California statute awarding compensation for injuries to an employee occurring within its borders, and for injuries as well occurring elsewhere, when the contract of employment was entered into within the state, is not open to question. Alaska Packers Assn. v. Industrial Accident Commn., 294 U.S. 532 (1935).

While in the circumstances now presented, either state, if its system for administering workmen's compensation permitted, would be free to adopt and enforce the remedy provided by the statute of the other, here each has provided for itself an exclusive remedy for a liability which it was constitutionally authorized to impose. But neither is bound, apart from the compulsion of the full faith and credit clause, to enforce the laws of the other; and the law of neither can by its own force determine the choice of law to be applied in the other.

To the extent that California is required to give full faith and credit to the conflicting Massachusetts statute it must be denied the right to apply in its own courts its own statute, constitutionally enacted in pursuance of its policy to provide compensation for employees injured in their employment within the state. It must withhold the remedy given by its own statute to its residents by way of compensation for medical, hospital and nursing services rendered to the injured employee, and it must remit him to Massachusetts to secure the administrative remedy which that state has provided. We cannot say that the full faith and credit clause goes so far.

While the purpose of that provision was to preserve rights acquired or confirmed under the public acts and judicial proceedings of one state by requiring recognition of their validity in other states, the very nature of the federal union of states, to which are reserved some of the attributes of sovereignty, precludes resort to the full faith and credit clause as the means for compelling a state to substitute the statutes of other states for its own statutes dealing with a subject matter concerning which it is competent to legislate. As was pointed out in Alaska Packers Assn. v. Industrial Accident Commn.: "A rigid and literal enforcement of the full faith and credit clause, without regard to the statute of the forum, would lead to the absurd result that, wherever the conflict arises, the statute of each state must be enforced in the courts of the other, but cannot be in its own." And in cases like the present it would create an impasse which would often leave the employee remediless. Full faith and credit would deny to California the right to apply its own remedy, and its administrative machinery may well not be adapted to giving the remedy afforded by Massachusetts. Similarly, the full faith and credit demanded for the California Act would deny to Massachusetts the right to apply its own remedy, and its Department of Industrial Accidents may well be without statutory authority to afford the remedy provided by the California statute.

It has often been recognized by this Court that there are some limitations upon the extent to which a state may be required by the full faith and credit clause to enforce even the judgment of another state in contravention of its own statutes or policy. And in the case of statutes, the extrastate effect of which Congress has not prescribed, as it may under the constitutional provision, we think the conclusion is unavoidable that the full faith and credit clause does not require one state to substitute for its own statute, applicable to persons and events within it, the conflicting statute of another state, even though that statute is of controlling force in the courts of the state of its enactment with respect to the same persons and events.

This Court must determine for itself how far the full faith and credit clause compels the qualification or denial of rights asserted under the laws of one state, that of the forum, by the statute of another state. But there would seem to be little room for the exercise of that function when the statute of the forum is the expression of domestic policy, in terms declared to be exclusive in its application to persons and events within the state. Although Massachusetts has an interest in safeguarding the compensation of Massachusetts employees while temporarily abroad in the course of their employment, and may adopt that policy for itself, that could hardly be thought to support an application of the full faith and credit clause which would override the constitutional authority of another state to legislate for the bodily safety and economic protection of employees injured within it. Few matters could be deemed more appropriately the concern of the state in which the injury occurs or more completely within its power. Considerations of less weight led to the conclusion, in Alaska Packers Assn. v. Industrial Accident Commn., *supra*, that the full faith and credit clause did not require California to give effect to the Alaska Compensation Act in preference to its own. There this Court sustained the award by California of the compensation provided by its own statute for employees where the contract of employment was made within the state, although the injury occurred in Alaska, whose statute also provided compensation for the injury. Decision was rested explicitly upon the grounds that the full faith and credit exacted for the statute of one state does not necessarily preclude another state from enforcing in its own courts its own conflicting statute having no extra-territorial operation forbidden by the Fourteenth Amendment, and that no persuasive reason was shown for denying that right.

Here, California legislation not only conflicts with that of Massachusetts providing compensation for the Massachusetts employee if injured within the state of California, but it expressly provides, for the guidance of its own commission and courts, that "No contract, rule or regulation shall exempt the employer from liability for the compensation fixed by this Act." The Supreme Court of California has declared in its opinion in this case that it is the policy of the state, as expressed in its Constitution and Compensation Act, to apply its own provisions for compensation, to the exclusion of all others, and that "It would be obnoxious to that policy to deny persons who have been injured in this state the right to apply for compensation when to do so might require physicians and hospitals to go to another state to collect charges for medical care and treatment given to such persons."

Full faith and credit does not here enable one state to legislate for the other or to project its laws across state lines so as to preclude the other from prescribing for itself the legal consequences of acts within it.

Questions and Comments

(1) What type of state laws are governed by the full faith and credit clause? There is a general consensus that the framers intended the clause to apply to state statutes (which is what they meant by "public acts"), but a debate over whether they intended it to extend to common-law rules. *Compare* Laycock, *Equal Citizens of Equal and Territorial States: The Constitutional Foundations of Choice of Law*, 92 Colum. L. Rev. 249, 290-295 (1992) (common-law rules included within "judicial proceedings") *with* Whitten, *The Constitutional Limitations on State Choice of Law: Full Faith and Credit*, 12 Mem. St. U. L. Rev. 1, 56-60 (1981) (common-law rules not included). *Pacific Employers* confirmed that the clause regulates state statutes. The Court later made clear that the clause applies to clashes of common-law rules as well. *See* Carroll v. Lanza, 349 U.S. 408 (1955).

(2) What does it mean, for choice-of-law purposes, for a state to give full faith and credit to the laws of other states? Does the text of the clause suggest anything

about which state choice-of-law rules are appropriate or acceptable? Most commentators believe that, as an original matter, the clause incorporated traditional choice-of-law rules from international law, subject to Congress's implementation power under Article IV. *See* Sun Oil Co. v. Wortman, 486 U.S. 717, 723 (1988), *infra* page 316; Rheinstein, *The Constitutional Basis of Jurisdiction*, 22 U. Chi. L. Rev. 775, 788-789, 816 (1955). But the Supreme Court did not actually regulate state choice-of-law rules under the full faith and credit clause until the twentieth century. *See* Whitten, *supra* note (1).

(3) Does *Pacific Employers* stand for the proposition that any state with an interest in applying its law can do so, consistent with full faith and credit, even if other states have similar interests? How do we identify such state interests? *Pacific Employers* says that the state of injury has an interest in applying its law for full faith and credit purposes. The case that preceded it, *Alaska Packers*, discussed *supra* page 288, held that the state where an employment relationship formed has an interest (for full faith and credit purposes) in applying its workers' compensation scheme, even if the injury took place in another state. Do these decisions constitutionalize interest analysis or does the Court have a different conception of state interests in mind? Why does the full faith and credit clause focus on the interests of the state whose law is being applied instead of the interests of the state whose law is not being applied?

(4) How does the due process limitation on choice-of-law rules differ from the full faith and credit limitation? Is it correct to say that due process concerns the fairness of applying a particular state law to the defendant, while full faith and credit concerns the need to respect the sovereign prerogatives of other states? These two sets of considerations are contrasted in Kogan, *Toward a Jurisprudence of Choice of Law: The Priority of Fairness over Comity*, 62 N.Y.U. L. Rev. 651 (1987).

Watson v. Employers Liability Assurance Corp.

348 U.S. 66 (1954)

Justice BLACK delivered the opinion of the Court.

Louisiana has an insurance code which comprehensively regulates the business of insurance in all its phases. This case brings to us challenges to the constitutionality of certain provisions of that code allowing injured persons to bring direct actions against liability insurance companies that have issued policies contracting to pay liabilities imposed on persons who inflict injury. This is such a direct action brought by the appellants, Mr. and Mrs. Watson, in a Louisiana state court claiming damages against the appellee, Employers Liability Assurance Corporation, Ltd., on account of alleged personal injuries suffered by Mrs. Watson. The complaint charged that the injuries occurred in Louisiana when Mrs. Watson bought and used in that State "Toni Home Permanent" a hair-waving product alleged to have contained a highly dangerous latent ingredient put there by its manufacturer. The manufacturer is the Toni Company of Illinois, a subsidiary of the Gillette Safety Razor Company which has its headquarters in Massachusetts.

The particular problem presented with reference to enforcing the Louisiana statute in this case arises because the insurance policy sued on was negotiated and issued in Massachusetts and delivered in Massachusetts and Illinois.[1] This Massachusetts-negotiated contract contains a clause, recognized as binding and enforceable under Massachusetts and Illinois law, which prohibits direct actions against the insurance company until *after* final determination of the Toni Company's obligation to pay personal injury damages either by judgment or agreement. Contrary to this contractual "no action" clause, the challenged statutory provisions permit injured persons to sue an insurance company *before* such final determination. As to injuries occurring in Louisiana, one provision of the State's direct action statute makes it applicable, even though, as here, an insurance contract is made in another state and contains a clause forbidding such direct actions. Another Louisiana statutory provision, with which Employers long ago complied, compels foreign insurance companies to consent to such direct suits in order to get a certificate to do business in the State. The basic issue raised by the attack on both these provisions is whether the Federal Constitution forbids Louisiana to apply its own law and compels it to apply the law of Massachusetts or Illinois.

Had the policy sued on been issued in Louisiana there would be no arguable due process question. But because the policy was bought, issued and delivered outside of Louisiana, Employers invokes the due process principle that a state is without power to exercise "extraterritorial jurisdiction," that is, to regulate and control activities wholly beyond its boundaries. Such a principle was recognized and applied in Home Ins. Co. v. Dick, a case strongly relied on by Employers.

Some contracts made locally, affecting nothing but local affairs, may well justify a denial to other states of power to alter those contracts. But, as this case illustrates, a vast part of the business affairs of this Nation does not present such simple local situations. Although this insurance contract was issued in Massachusetts, it was to protect Gillette and its Illinois subsidiary against damages on account of personal injuries that might be suffered by users of Toni Home Permanents anywhere in the United States, its territories, or in Canada. As a consequence of the modern practice of conducting widespread business activities throughout the entire United States, this Court has in a series of cases held that more states than one may seize hold of local activities which are part of multistate transactions and may regulate to protect interests of its own people, even though other phases of the same transactions might justify regulatory legislation in other states.

Louisiana's direct action statute is not a mere intermeddling in affairs beyond her boundaries which are no concern of hers. Persons injured or killed in Louisiana are most likely to be Louisiana residents, and even if not, Louisiana may have to care for them. Serious injuries may require treatment in Louisiana homes or hospitals by Louisiana doctors. The injured may be destitute. They may be compelled to call upon friends, relatives, or the public for help. Louisiana has manifested its natural interest in the injured by providing remedies for recovery of damages. It has a similar interest in policies of insurance which are designed to assure ultimate payment of such damages.

---

1. The insurance policy was issued to "The Toni Company, a Division of the Gillette Safety Razor Company. . . ." Gillette is a Delaware Corporation with headquarters in Boston where the contract was negotiated with the Boston office of Employers. The Toni Company manufactures the hair-waving product in Chicago, Illinois.

Moreover, Louisiana courts in most instances provide the most convenient forum for trial of these cases. But modern transportation and business methods have made it more difficult to serve process on wrongdoers who live or do business in other states. In this case efforts to serve the Gillette Company were answered by a motion to dismiss on the ground that Gillette had no Louisiana agent on whom process could be served. If this motion is granted, Mrs. Watson, but for the direct action law, could not get her case tried without going to Massachusetts or Illinois although she lives in Louisiana and her claim is for injuries from a product bought and used there. What has been said is enough to show Louisiana's legitimate interest in safeguarding the rights of persons injured there. In view of that interest, the direct action provisions here challenged do not violate due process.

What we have said above goes far toward answering the Full Faith and Credit Clause contention. That clause does not automatically compel a state to subordinate its own contract laws to the laws of another state in which a contract happens to have been formally executed. Where, as here, a contract affects the people of several states, each may have interests that leave it free to enforce its own contract policies. We have already pointed to the vital interests of Louisiana in liability insurance that covers injuries to people in that State. Of course Massachusetts also has some interest in the policy sued on in this case. The insurance contract was formally executed in that State and Gillette has an office there. But plainly these interests cannot outweigh the interest of Louisiana in taking care of those injured in Louisiana. Since this is true, the Full Faith and Credit Clause does not compel Louisiana to subordinate its direct action provisions to Massachusetts contract rules. Pacific Employers Ins. Co. v. Commission.

Reversed.

Clay v. Sun Insurance Office, Ltd.

377 U.S. 179 (1964)

Justice DOUGLAS delivered the opinion of the Court.

This case, which invoked the diversity jurisdiction of the Federal District Court in a suit to recover damages under an insurance policy, was here before. . . . The initial question then as now is whether the 12-month-suit clause in the policy governs, in which event the claim is barred, or whether Florida's statutes nullifying such clauses if they require suit to be filed in less than five years are applicable and valid, in which event the suit is timely. The policy was purchased by petitioner in Illinois while he was a citizen and resident of that State. Respondent, a British company, is licensed to do business in Illinois, Florida, and several other States.

A few months after purchasing the policy, petitioner moved to Florida and became a citizen and resident of that State; and it was in Florida that the loss occurred two years later. When the case reached here, the majority view was that the underlying constitutional question—whether consistently with due process, Florida could apply its five-year statute to this Illinois contract—should not be reached until the Florida Supreme Court, through its certificate procedure, had construed that statute and resolved another local law question. On remand the Court of Appeals certified the two questions to the Florida Supreme Court, which answered both questions in petitioner's favor. Thereafter the Court of Appeals held that it was not compatible with due process for Florida to apply its five-year statute to this contract and that judgment should be entered for respondent. We again granted certiorari.

While there are Illinois cases indicating that parties may contract—as here—for a shorter period of limitations than is provided by the Illinois statute, we are referred to no Illinois decision extending that rule into other States whenever claims on Illinois contracts are sought to be enforced there. We see no difficulty whatever under either the Full Faith and Credit Clause or the Due Process Clause. We deal with an ambulatory contract on which suit might be brought in any one of several States. Normally, as the Court held in Pacific Employers Ins. Co. v. Industrial Accident Commn., a State having jurisdiction over a claim deriving from an out-of-state employment contract need not substitute the conflicting statute of the other State (workmen's compensation) for its own statute (workmen's compensation)—where the employee was injured in the course of his employment while temporarily in the latter State. We followed the same route in Watson v. Employers Liability Assurance Corp. where we upheld a state statute allowing direct actions against liability insurance companies in the State of the forum, even though a clause in the contract, binding in the State where it was made, prohibited direct action against the insurer until final determination of the obligation of the insured.

The Court of Appeals relied in the main on Hartford Accident & Indemnity Co. v. Delta & Pine Land Co., and Home Ins. Co. v. Dick. Those were cases where the activities in the State of the forum were thought to be too slight and too casual, as in the *Delta & Pine Land Co.* case, to make the application of local law consistent with due process, or wholly lacking, as in the *Dick* case. No deficiency of that order is present here. As Mr. Justice Black, dissenting, said when this case was here before:

> Insurance companies, like other contractors, do not confine their contractual activities and obligations within state boundaries. They sell to customers who are promised protection in States far away from the place where the contract is made. In this very case the policy was sold to Clay with knowledge that he could take his property anywhere in the world he saw fit without losing the protection of his insurance. In fact, his contract was described on its face as a "Personal Property Floater Policy (World Wide)." The contract did not even attempt to provide that the law of Illinois would govern when suits were filed anywhere else in the country. Shortly after the contract was made, Clay moved to Florida and there he lived for several years. His insured property was there all that time. The corporation knew this fact. Particularly since the company was licensed to do business in Florida, it must have known it might be sued there. . . .

. . . Florida has ample contacts with the present transaction and the parties to satisfy any conceivable requirement of full faith and credit or of due process.

Reversed.

Questions and Comments

(1) Is anything left of Home Ins. Co. v. Dick after *Watson* and *Clay*?

(2) Although in *Watson* the entire claim against Gillette arose in Louisiana, the claim against the insurance company necessarily derived in part from the contract between Gillette and the insurance company, entered into elsewhere. Is that fact irrelevant after *Pacific Employers* since that case is also one where a critical element—the employment relationship—was located outside the forum?

(3) What would the result in *Watson* have been if the insurance contract in question had not contained a clause requiring the insurance company to defend Gillette? Wouldn't allowing a suit against the insurance company in Louisiana seem more extreme—more unfair—under those circumstances?

(4) Are the factors listed by Justice Black in *Watson* in justification of the application of Louisiana law convincing? Consider:

(a) The first interest listed for Louisiana was the likelihood that persons injured in Louisiana would be Louisiana residents. However, is that a sufficient reason for applying Louisiana law, in light of the fact that Dick was a resident of Texas and his residence did not justify application of Texas law in his case?

(b) The fact that there may be medical creditors in Louisiana for someone injured there may provide a desire on Louisiana's part to provide for local trial, but should medical creditors be singled out? Isn't it equally likely that there were Texas business creditors of Dick in the *Dick* case who would have benefited from a recovery by Dick? And if the concern is for the patient, isn't the danger of discouraging medical treatment by medical creditors likely to turn on more practical questions such as whether the patient is insured?

(c) Justice Black's third Louisiana interest—that of compensation, as manifested by Louisiana tort law—is more problematical. It should first be noted that Louisiana's interest in tort compensation is being invoked to allow it to control extra-state contractual relations between the insured and the insurer. Should a state's interest in X allow it to interfere with a relationship between Y and Z? Shouldn't the state be required first to find out if there are alternative means to accomplish the same goal? And wouldn't Louisiana be able to implement its tort law by allowing a suit directly against the tortfeasor, using a long-arm statute? Should the state's failure to provide itself with a constitutionally approved method of achieving its goals justify it in interfering with the third party's rights?

(d) The same questions may be raised about Louisiana's interest in providing a convenient Louisiana trial.

(5) If *Watson* fails to make an airtight case for distinguishing *Dick*, can *Watson* nonetheless be justified on the grounds that the *effect* of the Louisiana statute is essentially no more than to change the place of trial, since the insurance company would have had to defend Gillette if Gillette had been sued in Massachusetts or Illinois?

On the other hand, even if *Watson* can be handled by this approach, what of *Clay*, in which the issue (extending a contractual limitation period) is exactly the same as in *Dick*?

(6) The Court held that "[w]e deal with an ambulatory contract on which suit might be brought in any one of several States," and "[p]articularly since the company was licensed to do business in Florida, it must have known it might be sued there." *Clay*, 377 U.S. at 181-182. How are such expectations to be measured? In Burger King Corp. v. Continental Ins. Co., 359 F. Supp. 184 (W.D. Pa. 1973), Burger King sued a New York insurance company to recover on a policy for property damage allegedly caused by an earthquake. *Id*. at 185-186. The property was located in Pennsylvania, and the policy stated that "[n]o suit . . . on this policy for the recovery of any claim shall be sustainable . . . unless commenced within twelve months next after the inception of the loss." *Id*. at 186.

However, Burger King brought the suit in Florida approximately 18 months after the Pennsylvania property was damaged. In denying the defendant's motion for summary judgment, the Court applied Florida law, which stated that any contractual provision "fixing the period of time in which suits may be instituted under any [insurance] contract . . . at a period of time less than [five years] . . . are hereby declared to be contrary to the public policy of this state, and to be illegal and void." *Id*. Could Continental Insurance have reasonably expected to be sued according to the laws of Florida when it issued an insurance policy in New York on a property in Pennsylvania?

Allstate Insurance Co. v. Hague

449 U.S. 302 (1981)

Justice BRENNAN announced the judgment of the Court and delivered an opinion, in which Justice WHITE, Justice MARSHALL, and Justice BLACKMUN joined.

This Court granted certiorari to determine whether the Due Process Clause of the Fourteenth Amendment or the Full Faith and Credit Clause of Art. IV, §1, of the United States Constitution bars the Minnesota Supreme Court's choice of substantive Minnesota law to govern the effect of a provision in an insurance policy issued to respondent's decedent. 444 U.S. 1070 (1980).

I

Respondent's late husband, Ralph Hague, died of injuries suffered when a motorcycle on which he was a passenger was struck from behind by an automobile. The accident occurred in Pierce County, Wis., which is immediately across the Minnesota border from Red Wing, Minn. The operators of both vehicles were Wisconsin residents, as was the decedent, who, at the time of the accident, resided with respondent in Hager City, Wis., which is one and one-half miles from Red Wing. Mr. Hague had been employed in Red Wing for the 15 years immediately preceding his death and had commuted daily from Wisconsin to his place of employment.

Neither the operator of the motorcycle nor the operator of the automobile carried valid insurance. However, the decedent held a policy issued by petitioner

Allstate Insurance Co. covering three automobiles owned by him and containing an uninsured motorist clause insuring him against loss incurred from accidents with uninsured motorists. The uninsured motorist coverage was limited to $15,000 for each automobile.[3]

After the accident, but prior to the initiation of this lawsuit, respondent moved to Red Wing. Subsequently, she married a Minnesota resident and established residence her new husband in Savage, Minn. At approximately the same time, a Minnesota Registrar of Probate appointed respondent personal representative of her deceased husband's estate. Following her appointment, she brought this action in Minnesota District Court seeking a declaration under Minnesota law that the $15,000 uninsured motorist coverage on each of her late husband's three automobiles could be "stacked" to provide total coverage of $45,000. Petitioner defended on the ground that whether the three uninsured motorist coverages could be stacked should be determined by Wisconsin law, since the insurance policy was delivered in Wisconsin, the accident occurred in Wisconsin, and all persons were Wisconsin residents at the time of the accident.

The Minnesota District Court disagreed. Interpreting Wisconsin law to disallow stacking, the court concluded that Minnesota's choice-of-law rules required the application of Minnesota law permitting stacking. The court refused to apply Wisconsin law as "inimical to the public policy of Minnesota" and granted summary judgment for respondent.

The Minnesota Supreme Court, sitting en banc, affirmed the District Court. The court, also interpreting Wisconsin law to prohibit stacking,[6] applied Minnesota law after analyzing the relevant Minnesota contacts and interests within the analytical framework developed by Professor Leflar. . . .[7] Although stating that the Minnesota contacts might not be, "in themselves, sufficient to mandate application of [Minnesota] law,"[8] under the first four factors, the court concluded that the fifth factor—application of the better rule of law—favored selection of Minnesota law. The court emphasized that a majority of States allow stacking and that legal decisions allowing stacking "are fairly recent and well considered in light of current uses of automobiles." In addition, the court found the Minnesota rule superior to Wisconsin's "because it requires the cost of accidents with uninsured motorists to be spread more broadly through insurance premiums than does the Wisconsin rule." Finally, after rehearing en banc, the court buttressed its initial opinion by indicating "that contracts of insurance on motor vehicles are in a class by themselves" since an insurance company "knows the automobile is a movable

---

3. Ralph Hague paid a separate premium for each automobile including an additional separate premium for each uninsured motorist coverage.

6. Respondent has suggested that this case presents a "false conflict." The court below rejected this contention and applied Minnesota law. Even though the Minnesota Supreme Court's choice of Minnesota law followed a discussion of whether this case presents a false conflict, the fact is that the court chose to apply Minnesota law. Thus, the only question before this Court is whether that choice was constitutional.

7. Minnesota had previously adopted the conceptual model developed by Professor Leflar in Milkovich v. Saari [page 220 supra].

8. The court apparently was referring to sufficiency as a matter of choice of law and not as a matter of constitutional limitation on its choice-of-law decision.

item which will be driven from state to state." From this premise the court concluded that application of Minnesota law was "not so arbitrary and unreasonable as to violate due process."

II

It is not for this Court to say whether the choice-of-law analysis suggested by Professor Leflar is to be preferred or whether we would make the same choice-of-law decision if sitting as the Minnesota Supreme Court. Our sole function is to determine whether the Minnesota Supreme Court's choice of its own substantive law in this case exceeded federal constitutional limitations. Implicit in this inquiry is the recognition, long accepted by this Court, that a set of facts giving rise to a lawsuit, or a particular issue within a lawsuit, may justify, in constitutional terms, application of the law of more than one jurisdiction. *See, e.g.,* Watson v. Employers Liability Assurance Corp. *See generally* Clay v. Sun Insurance Office, Ltd. (hereinafter cited as *Clay II*). As a result, the forum State may have to select one law from among the laws of several jurisdictions having some contact with the controversy.

In deciding constitutional choice-of-law questions, whether under the Due Process Clause or the Full Faith and Credit Clause,[10] this Court has traditionally examined the contacts of the State, whose law was applied, with the parties and with the occurrence or transaction giving rise to the litigation. *See Clay II, supra.* In order to ensure that the choice of law is neither arbitrary nor fundamentally unfair, *see* Alaska Packers Assn. v. Industrial Accident Commn., the Court has invalidated the choice of law of a State which has had no significant contact or significant aggregation of contacts, creating state interests, with the parties and the occurrence or transaction.[11]

---

10. This Court has taken a similar approach in deciding choice-of-law cases under both the Due Process Clause and the Full Faith and Credit Clause. In each instance, the Court has examined the relevant contacts and resulting interests of the State whose law was applied. *See, e.g.,* Nevada v. Hall, 440 U.S. 410, 424 (1979). Although at one time the Court required a more exacting standard under the Full Faith and Credit Clause than under the Due Process Clause for evaluating the constitutionality of choice-of-law decisions, *see* Alaska Packers Ass'n. v. Industrial Accident Commn. (interest of State whose law was applied was no less than interest of State whose law was rejected), the Court has since abandoned the weighting-of-interests requirement. Carroll v. Lanza; *see* Nevada v. Hall, *supra;* Weintraub, *Due Process and Full Faith and Credit Limitations on a State's Choice of Law,* 44 Iowa L. Rev. 449 (1959). Different considerations are of course at issue when full faith and credit is to be accorded to acts, records, and proceedings outside the choice-of-law area, such as in the case of sister state-court judgments.

11. Prior to the advent of interest analysis in the state courts as the "dominant mode of analysis in modern choice of law theory," the prevailing choice-of-law methodology focused on the jurisdiction where a particular event occurred. . . .

Hartford Accident & Indemnity Co. v. Delta & Pine Land Co. can, perhaps, best be explained as an example of that period. In that case, the Court struck down application by the Mississippi courts of Mississippi law which voided the limitations provision in a fidelity bond written in Tennessee between a Connecticut insurer and Delta, both of which were doing business in Tennessee and Mississippi. By its terms, the bond covered misapplication of funds "by an employee in any position, anywhere. . . ." After Delta discovered defalcations by one of its Mississippi-based employees, a lawsuit was commenced in Mississippi.

Two instructive examples of such invalidation are Home Ins. Co. v. Dick, and John Hancock Mutual Life Ins. Co. v. Yates. In both cases, the selection of forum law rested exclusively on the presence of one nonsignificant forum contact. [The Court described the facts and holding of *Dick*.]

The relationship of the forum State to the parties and the transaction was similarly attenuated in John Hancock Mutual Life Ins. Co. v. Yates. There, the insurer, a Massachusetts corporation, issued a contract of insurance on the life of a New York resident. The contract was applied for, issued, and delivered in New York where the insured and his spouse resided. After the insured died in New York, his spouse moved to Georgia and brought suit on the policy in Georgia. Under Georgia law, the jury was permitted to take into account oral modifications when deciding whether an insurance policy application contained material misrepresentations. Under New York law, however, such misrepresentations were to be evaluated solely on the basis of the written application. The Georgia court applied Georgia law. This Court reversed, finding application of Georgia law to be unconstitutional.

Dick and *Yates* stand for the proposition that if a State has only an insignificant contact with the parties and the occurrence or transaction, application of its law is unconstitutional. *Dick* concluded that nominal residence—standing alone—was inadequate; *Yates* held that a post-occurrence change of residence to the forum State—standing alone—was insufficient to justify application of forum law. Although instructive as extreme examples of selection of forum law, neither *Dick* or *Yates* governs this case. For in contrast to those decisions, here the Minnesota contacts with the parties and the occurrence are obviously significant. Thus, this case is like *Alaska Packers* . . . and *Clay II*—cases where this Court sustained choice-of-law decisions based on the contacts of the State, whose law was applied, with the parties and occurrence.

The lesson from *Dick* and *Yates*, which found insufficient forum contacts to apply forum law, and from *Alaska Packers* . . . and *Clay II*, which found adequate contacts to sustain the choice of forum law, is that for a State's substantive law to be selected in a constitutionally permissible manner, that State must have a significant contact or significant aggregation of contacts, creating state interests, such that choice of its law is neither arbitrary nor fundamentally unfair. Application of this principle to the facts of this case persuades us that the Minnesota Supreme Court's choice of its own law did not offend the Federal Constitution.

III

Minnesota has three contacts with the parties and the occurrence giving rise to the litigation. In the aggregate, these contacts permit selection by the Minnesota Supreme Court of Minnesota law allowing the stacking of Mr. Hague's uninsured motorist coverages.

That case, however, has scant relevance for today. It implied a choice-of-law analysis which, for all intents and purposes, gave an isolated event—the writing of the bond in Tennessee—controlling constitutional significance, even though there might have been contacts with another State (here Mississippi) which would make application of its law neither unfair nor unexpected.

First, and for our purposes a very important contact, Mr. Hague was a member of Minnesota's work force, having been employed by a Red Wing, Minn., enterprise for the 15 years preceding his death. While employment status may implicate a state interest less substantial than does resident status, that interest is nevertheless important. The State of employment has police power responsibilities towards the nonresident employee that are analogous, if somewhat less profound, than towards residents. Thus, such employees use state services and amenities and may call upon state facilities in appropriate circumstances.

In addition, Mr. Hague commuted to work in Minnesota . . . , and was presumably covered by his uninsured motorist coverage during the commute. The State's interest in its commuting nonresident employees reflects a state concern for the safety and well-being of its work force and the concomitant effect on Minnesota employers.

That Mr. Hague was not killed while commuting to work or while in Minnesota does not dictate a different result. To hold that the Minnesota Supreme Court's choice of Minnesota law violated the Constitution for that reason would require too narrow a view of Minnesota's relationship with the parties and the occurrence giving rise to the litigation. An automobile accident need not occur within a particular jurisdiction for that jurisdiction to be connected to the occurrence.

Similarly, the occurrence of a crash fatal to a Minnesota employee in another State is a Minnesota contact. If Mr. Hague had only been injured and missed work for a few weeks, the effect on the Minnesota employer would have been palpable and Minnesota's interest in having its employee made whole would be evident. Mr. Hague's death affects Minnesota's interest still more acutely, even though Mr. Hague will not return to the Minnesota work force. Minnesota's work force is surely affected by the level of protection the State extends to it, either directly or indirectly. Vindication of the rights of the estate of a Minnesota employee, therefore, is an important state concern.

Mr. Hague's residence in Wisconsin does not—as Allstate seems to argue—constitutionally mandate application of Wisconsin law to the exclusion of forum law. If, in the instant case, the accident had occurred in Minnesota between Mr. Hague and an uninsured Minnesota motorist, if the insurance contract had been executed in Minnesota covering a Minnesota registered company automobile which Mr. Hague was permitted to drive, and if a Wisconsin court sought to apply Wisconsin law, certainly Mr. Hague's residence in Wisconsin, his commute between Wisconsin and Minnesota, and the insurer's presence in Wisconsin should be adequate to apply Wisconsin's law.[22] Employment status is not a sufficiently less

---

22. Of course Allstate could not be certain that Wisconsin law would necessarily govern any accident which occurred in Wisconsin, whether brought in the Wisconsin courts or elsewhere. Such an expectation would give controlling significance to the wooden lex loci delicti doctrine. While the place of the accident is a factor to be considered in choice-of-law analysis, to apply blindly the traditional, but now largely abandoned, doctrine, would fail to distinguish between the relative importance of various legal issues involved in a lawsuit as well as the relationship of other jurisdictions to the parties and the occurrence or transaction. If, for example, Mr. Hague had been a Wisconsin resident and employee who was injured in Wisconsin and was then taken by ambulance to a hospital in Red Wing, Minn., where he languished for several weeks before dying, Minnesota's interest in ensuring that its medical creditors were paid would be obvious. Moreover, under such circumstances,

important status than residence, when combined with Mr. Hague's daily commute across state lines and the other Minnesota contacts present, to prohibit the choice-of-law result in this case on constitutional grounds.

Second, Allstate was at all times present and doing business in Minnesota. By virtue of its presence, Allstate can hardly claim unfamiliarity with the laws of the host jurisdiction and surprise that the state courts might apply forum law to litigation in which the company is involved. "Particularly since the company was licensed to do business in [the forum], it must have known it might be sued there, and that [the forum] courts would feel bound by [forum] law."[24] Clay v. Sun Insurance Offices Ltd. (Black, J., dissenting). Moreover, Allstate's presence in Minnesota gave Minnesota an interest in regulating the company's insurance obligations insofar as they affected both a Minnesota resident and court-appointed representative—respondent—and a longstanding member of Minnesota's work force—Mr. Hague.

Third, respondent became a Minnesota resident prior to institution of this litigation. The stipulated facts reveal that she first settled in Red Wing, Minn., the town in which her late husband had worked. She subsequently moved to Savage, Minn., after marrying a Minnesota resident who operated an automobile service station in Bloomington, Minn. Her move to Savage occurred "almost concurrently," with the initiation of the instant case. There is no suggestion that Mrs. Hague moved to Minnesota in anticipation of this litigation or for the purpose of finding a legal climate especially hospitable to her claim.[28] The stipulated facts, sparse as they are, negate any such inference.

While John Hancock Mutual Life Ins. Co. v. Yates held that a post-occurrence change of residence to the forum State was insufficient in and of itself to confer power on the forum State to choose its law, that case did not hold that such a change of residence was irrelevant. Here, of course, respondent's bona fide residence in Minnesota was not the sole contact Minnesota had with this litigation. And in connection with her residence in Minnesota, respondent was appointed personal representative of Mr. Hague's estate by the Registrar of Probate for the

---

the accident itself might be reasonably characterized as a bistate occurrence beginning in Wisconsin and ending in Minnesota. Thus, reliance by the insurer that Wisconsin law would necessarily govern any accident that occurred in Wisconsin, or that the law of another jurisdiction would necessarily govern any accident that did not occur in Wisconsin, would be unwarranted. *See* n.11, *supra*.

If the law of a jurisdiction other than Wisconsin did govern, there was a substantial likelihood, with respect to uninsured motorist coverage, that stacking would be allowed. Stacking was the rule in most States at the time the policy was issued. . . .

24. There is no element of unfair surprise or frustration of legitimate expectations as a result of Minnesota's choice of its law. Because Allstate was doing business in Minnesota, and was undoubtedly aware that Mr. Hague was a Minnesota employee, it had to have anticipated that Minnesota law might apply to an accident in which Mr. Hague was involved. Indeed, Allstate specifically anticipated that Mr. Hague might suffer an accident either in Minnesota or elsewhere in the United States, outside of Wisconsin, since the policy it issued offered continental coverage. At the same time, Allstate did not seek to control construction of the contract since the policy contained no choice-of-law clause dictating application of Wisconsin law.

28. The dissent suggests that considering respondent's postoccurrence change of residence as one of the Minnesota contacts will encourage forum shopping. This overlooks the fact that her change of residence was bona fide and not motivated by litigation considerations.

County of Goodhue, Minn. Respondent's residence and subsequent appointment in Minnesota as personal representative of her late husband's estate constitute a Minnesota contact which gives Minnesota an interest in respondent's recovery, an interest which the court below identified as full compensation for "resident accident victims" to keep them "off welfare rolls" and able "to meet financial obligations."

In sum, Minnesota had a significant aggregation[29] of contacts with the parties and the occurrence, creating state interests, such that application of its law was neither arbitrary nor fundamentally unfair. Accordingly, the choice of Minnesota law by the Minnesota Supreme Court did not violate the Due Process Clause or the Full Faith and Credit Clause.

Affirmed.

Justice STEWART took no part in the consideration or decision of this case.

Justice STEVENS, concurring in the judgment. As I view this unusual case— in which neither precedent nor constitutional language provides sure guidance— two separate questions must be answered. First, does the Full Faith and Credit Clause *require* Minnesota, the forum State, to apply Wisconsin law? Second, does the Due Process Clause of the Fourteenth Amendment *prevent* Minnesota from applying its own law? The first inquiry implicates the federal interest in ensuring that Minnesota respect the sovereignty of the State of Wisconsin; the second implicates the litigants' interest in a fair adjudication of their rights.[3]

I realize that both this court's analysis of choice-of-law questions and scholarly criticism of those decisions have treated these two inquiries as though they were indistinguishable. Nevertheless, I am persuaded that the two constitutional provisions protect different interests and that proper analysis requires separate consideration of each.

I

The Full Faith and Credit Clause is one of several provisions in the Federal Constitution designed to transform the several States from independent

---

29. We express no view whether the first two contacts, either together or separately, would have sufficed to sustain the choice of Minnesota law made by the Minnesota Supreme Court.

3. The two questions presented by the choice-of-law issue arise only after it is assumed or established that the defendant's contacts with the forum State are sufficient to support personal jurisdiction. Although the choice-of-law concerns—respect for another sovereign and fairness to the litigants—are similar to the two functions performed by the jurisdictional inquiry, they are not identical. In World-Wide Volkswagen Corp. v. Woodson, 444 U.S. 286, 291-292 (1980), we stated: "The concept of minimum contacts, in turn, can be seen to perform two related, but distinguishable, functions. It protects the defendant against the burdens of litigating in a distant or inconvenient forum. And it acts to ensure that the States, through their courts, do not reach out beyond the limits imposed on them by their status as coequal sovereigns in a federal system." While it has been suggested that this same minimum-contacts analysis be used to define the constitutional limitations on choice of law, the Court has made it clear over the years that the personal jurisdiction and choice-of-law inquiries are not the same. *See* Kulko v. California Superior Court; Shaffer v. Heitner; Hanson v. Denckla.

sovereignties into a single, unified Nation. The Full Faith and Credit Clause implements this design by directing that a State, when acting as the forum for litigation having multistate aspects or implications, respect the legitimate interests of other States and avoid infringement upon their sovereignty. . . .

In this case, I think the Minnesota courts' decision to apply Minnesota law was plainly unsound as a matter of normal conflicts law. Both the execution of the insurance contract and the accident giving rise to the litigation took place in Wisconsin. Moreover, when both of those events occurred, the plaintiff, the decedent, and the operators of both vehicles were all residents of Wisconsin. Nevertheless, I do not believe that any threat to national unity or Wisconsin's sovereignty ensues from allowing the substantive question presented by this case to be determined by the law of another State.

   . . .

II

It may be assumed that a choice-of-law decision would violate the Due Process Clause if it were totally arbitrary or if it were fundamentally unfair to either litigant. I question whether a judge's decision to apply the law of his own State could ever be described as wholly irrational. For judges are presumably familiar with their own state law and may find it difficult and time consuming to discover and apply correctly the law of another State. The forum State's interest in the fair and efficient administration of justice is therefore sufficient, in my judgment, to attach a presumption of validity to a forum State's decision to apply its own law to a dispute over which it has jurisdiction.

The forum State's interest in the efficient operation of its judicial system is clearly not sufficient, however, to justify the application of a rule of law that is fundamentally unfair to one of the litigants. Arguably, a litigant could demonstrate such unfairness in a variety of ways. Concern about the fairness of the forum's choice of its own rule might arise if that rule favored residents over nonresidents, if it represented a dramatic departure from the rule that obtains in most American jurisdictions, or if the rule itself was unfair on its face or as applied.[15] . . .[23]

---

15. Discrimination against nonresidents would be constitutionally suspect even if the Due Process Clause were not a check upon a State's choice-of-law decisions. Moreover, both discriminatory and substantively unfair rules of law may be detected and remedied without any special choice-of-law analysis; familiar constitutional principles are available to deal with both varieties of unfairness.

23. Comparison of this case with Home Ins. Co. v. Dick, confirms my conclusion that the application of Minnesota law in this case does not offend the Due Process Clause. In *Home Ins. Co.*, the contract expressly provided that a particular limitations period would govern claims arising under the insurance contract and that Mexican law was to be applied in interpreting the contracts; in addition, the contract was limited in effect to certain Mexican waters. The parties could hardly have made their expectations with respect to the applicable law more plain. In this case, by way of contrast, nothing in the contract suggests that Wisconsin law should be applied or that Minnesota's "stacking" rule should not be applied. In this case, unlike *Home Ins. Co.*, the court's choice of forum law results in no unfair surprise to the insurer.

In terms of fundamental fairness, it seems to me that two factors relied upon by the plurality—the plaintiff's post-accident move to Minnesota and the decedent's Minnesota employment—are either irrelevant to or possibly even tend to undermine the plurality's conclusions. When the expectations of the parties at the time of contracting are the central due process concern, as they are in this case, an unanticipated post-accident occurrence is clearly irrelevant for due process purposes. The fact that the plaintiff became a resident of the forum State after the accident surely cannot justify a ruling in her favor that would not be made if the plaintiff were a nonresident. Similarly, while the fact that the decedent regularly drove into Minnesota might be relevant to the expectations of the contracting parties,[24] the fact that he did so because he was employed in Minnesota adds nothing to the due process analysis. The choice-of-law decision of the Minnesota courts is consistent with due process because it does not result in unfairness to either litigant, not because Minnesota now has an interest in the plaintiff as resident or formerly had an interest in the decedent as employee.

III

Although I regard the Minnesota courts' decision to apply forum law as unsound as a matter of conflicts law, and there is little in this record other than the presumption in favor of the forum's own law to support that decision, I concur in the plurality's judgment. It is not this Court's function to establish and impose upon state courts a federal choice-of-law rule, nor is it our function to ensure that state courts correctly apply whatever choice-of-law rules they have themselves adopted.[25] Our authority may be exercised in the choice-of-law area only to prevent a violation of the Full Faith and Credit or the Due Process Clause. For the reasons stated above, I find no such violation in this case.

Justice POWELL, with whom THE CHIEF JUSTICE and Justice REHNQUIST join, dissenting.

My disagreement with the plurality is narrow. I accept with few reservations Part II of the plurality opinion, which sets forth the basic principles that guide us in reviewing state choice-of-law decisions under the Constitution. The Court should invalidate a forum State's decision to apply its own law only when there are

---

24. Even this factor may not be of substantial significance. At the time of contracting, the parties were aware that the insurance policy was effective throughout the United States and that the law of any State, including Minnesota, might be applicable to particular claims. The fact that the decedent regularly drove to Minnesota, for whatever purpose, is relevant only to the extent that it affected the parties' evaluation, at the time of contracting, of the likelihood that Minnesota law would actually be applied at some point in the future. However, because the applicability of Minnesota law was perceived as possible at the time of contracting, it does not seem especially significant for due process purposes that the parties may also have considered it likely that Minnesota law would be applied. This factor merely reinforces the expectation revealed by the policy's national coverage.

25. In Kryger v. Wilson, after rejecting a due process challenge to a state court's choice of law, the Court stated: "The most that the plaintiff in error can say is that the state court made a mistaken application of doctrines of the conflict of laws in deciding that the cancellation of a land contract is governed by the law of the situs instead of the place of making and performance. But that, being purely a question of local common law, is a matter with which this court is not concerned."

no significant contacts between the State and the litigation. This modest check on state power is mandated by the Due Process Clause of the Fourteenth Amendment and the Full Faith and Credit Clause of Art. IV, §1. I do not believe, however, that the plurality adequately analyzes the policies such review must serve. In consequence, it has found significant what appear to me to be trivial contacts between the forum State and the litigation.

I

. . . The significance of asserted contacts must be evaluated in light of the constitutional policies that oversight by this Court should serve. Two enduring policies emerge from our cases.

First, the contacts between the forum State and the litigation should not be so "slight and casual" that it would be fundamentally unfair to a litigant for the forum to apply its own State's law. Clay v. Sun Ins. Office, Ltd. The touchstone here is the reasonable expectation of the parties.

Second, the forum State must have a legitimate interest in the outcome of the litigation before it. Pacific Ins. Co. v. Industrial Accident Commn. The Full Faith and Credit Clause addresses the accommodation of sovereign power among the various States. Under limited circumstances, it requires one State to give effect to the statutory law of another State. To be sure, a forum State need not give effect to another State's law if that law is in "violation of its own legitimate public policy." Nonetheless, for a forum State to further its legitimate public policy by applying its own law to a controversy, there must be some connection between the facts giving rise to the litigation and the scope of the State's lawmaking jurisdiction.

Both the Due Process and Full Faith and Credit Clauses ensure that the States do not "reach out beyond the limits imposed on them by their status as coequal sovereigns in a federal system." World-Wide Volkswagen Corp. v. Woodson (addressing Fourteenth Amendment limitation on state-court jurisdiction). As the Court stated in *Pacific Ins. Co., supra:* "[T]he full faith and credit clause does not require one state to substitute for its own statute, *applicable to persons and events within it,* the conflicting statute of another state." (Emphasis added.) The State has a legitimate interest in applying a rule of decision to the litigation only if the facts to which the rule will be applied have created effects within the State, toward which the State's public policy is directed. To assess the sufficiency of asserted contacts between the forum and the litigation, the court must determine if the contacts form a reasonable link between the litigation and a state policy. In short, examination of contacts addresses whether "the state has an interest in the application of its policy in this instance." Currie, *The Constitution and the Choice of Law: Governmental Interests and the Judicial Function*, in B. Currie, *Selected Essays on the Conflict of Laws* 188, 189 (1963). If it does, the Constitution is satisfied.

In summary, the significance of the contacts between a forum State and the litigation must be assessed in light of these two important constitutional policies.[3]

---

3. The plurality today apparently recognizes that the significance of the contacts must be evaluated in light of the policies our review serves. It acknowledges that the sufficiency of the same

A contact, or a pattern of contacts, satisfies the Constitution when it protects the litigants from being unfairly surprised if the forum State applies its own law, and when the application of the forum's law reasonably can be understood to further a legitimate public policy of the forum State.

II

Recognition of the complexity of the constitutional inquiry requires that this Court apply these principles with restraint. Applying these principles to the facts of this case, I do not believe, however, that Minnesota had sufficient contacts with the "persons and events" in this litigation to apply its rule permitting stacking. I would agree that no reasonable expectations of the parties were frustrated. The risk insured by petitioner was not geographically limited. The close proximity of Hager City, Wis., to Minnesota, and the fact that Hague commuted daily to Red Wing, Minn., for many years should have led the insurer to realize that there was a reasonable probability that the risk would materialize in Minnesota. Under our precedents, it is plain that Minnesota could have applied its own law to an accident occurring within its borders. The fact that the accident did not, in fact, occur in Minnesota is not controlling because the expectations of the litigants *before* the cause of action accrues provide the pertinent perspective.

The more doubtful question in this case is whether application of Minnesota's substantive law reasonably furthers a legitimate state interest. The plurality attempts to give substance to the tenuous contacts between Minnesota and this litigation. Upon examination, however, these contacts are either trivial or irrelevant to the furthering of any public policy of Minnesota.

First, the postaccident residence of the plaintiff-beneficiary is constitutionally irrelevant to the choice-of-law question. John Hancock Mut. Life Ins. Co. v. Yates, *supra*. The plurality today insists that *Yates* only held that a postoccurrence move to the forum State could not "in and of itself" confer power on the forum to apply its own law, but did not establish that such a change of residence was irrelevant. *Ante*, at 319. What the *Yates* court held, however, was that "there was no occurrence, *nothing* done, to which the law of Georgia could apply." (Emphasis added.) Any possible ambiguity in the Court's view of the significance of a postoccurrence change of residence is dispelled by Home Ins. Co. v. Dick, *supra*, cited by the *Yates* Court, where it was held squarely that Dick's postaccident move to the forum State was "without significance."

This rule is sound. If a plaintiff could choose the substantive rules to be applied to an action by moving to a hospitable forum, the invitation to forum shopping would be irresistible. Moreover, it would permit the defendant's reasonable expectations at the time the cause of action accrues to be frustrated, because it would permit the choice-of-law question to turn on a post-accrual circumstance.

---

contacts sometimes will differ in jurisdiction and choice-of-law questions. The plurality, however, pursues the rationale for the requirement of sufficient contacts in choice-of-law cases no further than to observe that the forum's application of its own law must be "neither arbitrary nor fundamentally unfair." . . . But this general prohibition does not distinguish questions of choice of law from those of jurisdiction, or from much of the jurisprudence of the Fourteenth Amendment.

Finally, postaccrual residence has nothing to do with facts to which the forum State proposes to apply its rule; it is unrelated to the substantive legal issues presented by the litigation.

Second, the plurality finds it significant that the insurer does business in the forum State. The State does have a legitimate interest in regulating the practices of such an insurer. But this argument proves too much. The insurer here does business in all 50 States. The forum State has no interest in regulating that conduct of the insurer unrelated to property, persons, or contracts executed within the forum State. The plurality recognizes this flaw and attempts to bolster the significance of the local presence of the insurer by combining it with the other factors deemed significant: the presence of the plaintiff and the fact that the deceased worked in the forum State. This merely restates the basic question in the case.

Third, the plurality emphasizes particularly that the insured worked in the forum State.[5] The fact that the insured was a nonresident employee in the forum State provides a significant contact for the furtherance of some local policies. The insured's place of employment is not, however, significant in this case. Neither the nature of the insurance policy, the events related to the accident, nor the immediate question of stacking coverage are in any way affected or implicated by the insured's employment status. The plurality's opinion is understandably vague in explaining how trebling the benefits to be paid to the estate of a nonresident employee furthers any substantial state interest relating to employment. Minnesota does not wish its workers to die in automobile accidents, but permitting stacking will not further this interest. The substantive issue here is solely one of compensation, and whether the compensation provided by this policy is increased or not will have no relation to the State's employment policies or police power.

Neither taken separately nor in the aggregate do the contacts asserted by the plurality today indicate that Minnesota's application of its substantive rule in this case will further any legitimate state interest. The plurality focuses only on physical contacts vel non, and in doing so pays scant attention to the more fundamental reasons why our precedents require reasonable policy-related contacts in choice-of-law cases. Therefore, I dissent.

Questions and Comments

(1) How important is the fact that the decedent's connection with the state of Minnesota was an employment connection? Would frequent visits to a relative—or to a bar—be enough? How does a court determine which contacts create interests? One possibility is to ask whether there is a substantive connection between the law in question (here, the stacking rule) and the contact (here, the Minnesota employment). *See generally* Brilmayer, *Legitimate Interests in Multistate Problems: As*

---

5. The plurality exacts double service from this fact, by finding a separate contact in that the insured commuted daily to his job. . . . This is merely a repetition of the facts that the insured lived in Wisconsin and worked in Minnesota. The State does have an interest in the safety of all motorists who use its roads. This interest is not limited to employees, but extends to all nonresident motorists on its highways. This safety interest, however, cannot encompass, either in logic or in any practical sense, the determination whether a nonresident's estate can stack benefit coverage in a policy written in another State regarding an accident that occurred on another State's roads. . . .

Between State and Federal Law, 79 Mich. L. Rev. 1315 (1981); Martin, *The Constitution and Legislative Jurisdiction*, 10 Hofstra L. Rev. 133 (1981).

(2) May *Hague* at least be cited for the proposition that there is no longer any difference between due process and full faith and credit analysis of choice-of-law problems? Both the plurality and the dissenting opinions maintain that position.

(3) Both the plurality and the dissent in *Hague* concede that if the accident had taken place in Minnesota, Minnesota's stacking rule would have been applicable without difficulty. The plurality uses that point to establish (since the place of the accident could just as easily have been Minnesota) that there was no unfair surprise. Why should the fact that an accident takes place in Minnesota allow Minnesota to apply its law to the relationship between the driver and his insurance company—a relationship entered into in Wisconsin and with virtually no Minnesota contacts? Although the Court allowed an in-state incident to affect an essentially out-of-state relationship in Clay v. Sun Insurance Office, Ltd. and Watson v. Employers Liab. Assur. Corp., the issue in both of those cases was far less devastating to the insurer: the amount of time given the insured to sue in *Clay* and the place of suit in *Watson*. Do those cases apply when the effect of imposing forum law is to triple liability?

(4) In McCluney v. Jos. Schlitz Brewing Co., 649 F.2d 578 (8th Cir. 1981), the plaintiff had worked for the defendant brewing company in Missouri for many years. Eventually he was offered a promotion in the form of a transfer to North Carolina, and thereafter a promotion and transfer to corporate headquarters in Milwaukee, Wisconsin. In Milwaukee a dispute arose when the plaintiff insisted that his secretary also be transferred from North Carolina. His employment was terminated. He claimed that he had been fired; the company claimed that he had resigned. He demanded severance pay due one who has been fired, as well as a "service letter" required by Missouri statute. The company answered with a letter stating that he had resigned. He sued the company and in a trial court won (a) severance pay, (b) $1 in damages for violation of the service letter statute (for misstating the reasons for termination), and (c) $400,000 in punitive damages for violation of the Missouri service letter statute. The Court of Appeals reversed with respect to the second and third items, holding that, despite *Hague*, contacts were insufficient to allow Missouri to apply its own law to a contract of employment arising out of a promotion granted in North Carolina and implemented in Wisconsin. A dissent noted that it was not unreasonable to characterize the entire employment as arising out of a single contract, formed in Missouri, which though modified from time to time was still subject to the Missouri statute. It noted further that the contacts could be viewed as stronger than those in *Hague*: (1) not just employment in the forum (as in *Hague*) but employment by the defendant; (2) later domicile in Missouri by the defendant when he moved back to that state; and (3) substantial business transacted in Missouri by the defendant. (Ironically, the dissent argued that punitive damages were inappropriate, thereby reducing its dispute with the majority to item (b) above—actual damages of $1.)

The Supreme Court affirmed without opinion in *McCluney*, thus not explaining why the majority was right and the dissent was wrong, and not explaining in particular why the extensive contacts between the plaintiff's early employment and the state of Missouri were inadequate to support legislative jurisdiction. 454 U.S. 1071 (1981). Can any sense be made of the Court's disposition of *McCluney*?

If the real rationale for affirmance was the fact that the dollar difference between the majority and dissent was only $1, would the better course have been to dismiss "for want of a substantial federal question"?

(5) How many significant contacts is "enough" to base a choice-of-law determination on? *Allstate* provides little guidance: "for a State's substantive law to be selected in a constitutionally permissible manner, that State must have a significant contact or significant aggregation of contacts," 449 U.S. at 312-313. In AT & T Mobility v. AU Optronics Corp., the Ninth Circuit criticized the district court for making "a single contact—the location of the Plaintiff's injury—dispositive." 707 F.3d 1106, 1111-1112 (9th Cir. 2013). But isn't it characteristic of most choice-of-law theories to identify a single contact as uniquely relevant, and focus on that contact to the exclusion of other arguably relevant connecting factors? For an argument supporting the multifactor approach, *see* Brilmayer & Anglin, *Choice of Law Theory and the Metaphysics of the Stand-Alone Trigger*, 95 Iowa L. Rev. 1125 (2010).

Phillips Petroleum Co. v. Shutts

472 U.S. 797 (1985)

REHNQUIST, J., delivered the opinion of the Court, in which BURGER, C.J., and BRENNAN, WHITE, MARSHALL, BLACKMUN and O'CONNOR, JJ., joined, and in Parts I and II of which STEVENS, J., joined. STEVENS, J., filed an opinion concurring in part and dissenting in part. POWELL, J., took no part in the decision of the case.

Justice REHNQUIST delivered the opinion of the Court.

Petitioner is a Delaware corporation which has its principal place of business in Oklahoma. During the 1970's it produced or purchased natural gas from leased land located in 11 different States, and sold most of the gas in interstate commerce. Respondents are some 28,000 of the royalty owners possessing rights to the leases from which petitioner produced the gas; they reside in all 50 States, the District of Columbia, and several foreign countries. Respondents brought a class action against petitioner in the Kansas state court, seeking to recover interest on royalty payments which had been delayed by petitioner. They recovered judgment in the trial court, and the Supreme Court of Kansas affirmed the judgment over petitioner's contentions that the Due Process Clause of the Fourteenth Amendment prevented Kansas from adjudicating the claims of all the respondents, and that the Due Process Clause and the Full Faith and Credit Clause of Article IV of the Constitution prohibited the application of Kansas law to all of the transactions between petitioner and respondents. We granted certiorari to consider these claims. 469 U.S. 879 (1984). We reject petitioner's jurisdictional claim, but sustain its claim regarding the choice of law.

Because petitioner sold the gas to its customers in interstate commerce, it was required to secure approval for price increases from what was then the Federal Power Commission, and is now the Federal Energy Regulatory Commission. Under its regulations the Federal Power Commission permitted petitioner to propose and collect tentative higher gas prices, subject to final approval by the Commission. If the Commission eventually denied petitioner's proposed price increase or reduced the proposed increase, petitioner would have to refund to its customers the difference between the approved price and the higher price charged, plus interest at a rate set by statute.

Although petitioner received higher gas prices pending review by the Commission, petitioner suspended any increase in royalties paid to the royalty owners because the higher price could be subject to recoupment by petitioner's customers. Petitioner agreed to pay the higher royalty only if the royalty owners would provide petitioner with a bond or indemnity for the increase, plus interest, in case the price increase was not ultimately approved and a refund was due to the customers. Petitioner set the interest rate on the indemnity agreements at the same interest rate the Commission would have required petitioner to refund to its customers. A small percentage of the royalty owners provided this indemnity and received royalties immediately from the interim price increases; these royalty owners are unimportant to this case.

The remaining royalty owners received no royalty on the unapproved portion of the prices until the Federal Power Commission approval of those prices became final. . . .

Respondents Irl Shutts, Robert Anderson, and Betty Anderson filed suit against petitioner in Kansas state court, seeking interest payments on their suspended royalties which petitioner had possessed pending the Commission's approval of the price increases. Shutts is a resident of Kansas, and the Andersons live in Oklahoma. Shutts and the Andersons own gas leases in Oklahoma and Texas. Over petitioner's objection the Kansas trial court granted respondents' motion to certify the suit as a class action under Kansas law. Kan. Stat. Ann. §60-223 et seq. (1983). The class as certified was comprised of 33,000 royalty owners who had royalties suspended by petitioner. The average claim of each royalty owner for interest on the suspended royalties was $100.

After the class was certified respondents provided each class member with notice through first-class mail. The notice described the action and informed each class member that he could appear in person or by counsel; otherwise each member would be represented by Shutts and the Andersons, the named plaintiffs. The notices also stated that class members would be included in the class and bound by the judgment unless they "opted out" of the lawsuit by executing and returning a "request for exclusion" that was included with the notice. The final class as certified contained 28,100 members; 3,400 had "opted out" of the class by returning the request for exclusion, and notice could not be delivered to another 1,500 members, who were also excluded. Less than 1,000 of the class members resided in Kansas. Only a minuscule amount, approximately one quarter of one percent, of the gas leases involved in the lawsuit were on Kansas land.

After petitioner's mandamus petition to decertify the class was denied, the case was tried to the court. The court found petitioner liable under Kansas law for interest on the suspended royalties to all class members. The trial court relied heavily on an earlier, unrelated class action involving the same nominal plaintiff and the same defendant, *Shutts, Executor v. Phillips Petroleum Co.*, 222 Kan. 527 (1977), *cert. denied*, 434 U.S. 1068 (1978). The Kansas Supreme Court had held in *Shutts, Executor* that a gas company owed interest to royalty owners for royalties suspended pending final Commission approval of a price increase. No federal statutes touched on the liability for suspended royalties, and the court in *Shutts, Executor* held as a matter of Kansas equity law that the applicable interest rates for computation of interest on suspended royalties were the interest rates at which the gas company would have had to reimburse its customers had its interim price increase been rejected by the Commission. The court in *Shutts, Executor* viewed these as the fairest interest rates because they were also the rates that petitioner required the royalty owners to meet in their indemnity agreements in order to avoid suspended royalties.

The trial court in the present case applied the rule from *Shutts, Executor*, and held petitioner liable for prejudgment and postjudgment interest on the suspended royalties, computed at the Commission rates governing petitioner's three price increases. . . .

Petitioner raised two principal claims in its appeal to the Supreme Court of Kansas. It first asserted that the Kansas trial court did not possess personal jurisdiction over absent plaintiff class members as required by International Shoe Co. v. Washington, 326 U.S. 310 (1945), and similar cases. Related to this first claim was petitioner's contention that the "opt-out" notice to absent class members, which forced them to return the request for exclusion in order to avoid the suit, was insufficient to bind class members who were not residents of Kansas or who did not possess "minimum contacts" with Kansas. Second, petitioner claimed that Kansas courts could not apply Kansas law to every claim in the dispute. The trial court should have looked to the laws of each State where the leases were located to determine, on the basis of conflict of laws principles, whether interest on the suspended royalties was recoverable, and at what rate.

The Supreme Court of Kansas held that the entire cause of action was maintainable under the Kansas class-action statute, and the court rejected both of petitioner's claims. First, it held that the absent class members were plaintiffs, not defendants, and thus the traditional minimum contacts test of *International Shoe* did not apply. The court held that nonresident class-action plaintiffs were only entitled to adequate notice, an opportunity to be heard, an opportunity to opt out of the case, and adequate representation by the named plaintiffs. If these procedural due process minima were met, according to the court, Kansas could assert jurisdiction over the plaintiff class and bind each class member with a judgment on his claim. The court surveyed the course of the litigation and concluded that all of these minima had been met.

The court also rejected petitioner's contention that Kansas law could not be applied to plaintiffs and royalty arrangements having no connection with Kansas. The court stated that generally the law of the forum controlled all claims unless "compelling reasons" existed to apply a different law. The court found no compelling reasons, and noted that "[t]he plaintiff class members have indicated their desire to have this action determined under the laws of Kansas." . . .

[The Supreme Court's opinion as to personal jurisdiction can be found at page 364 *infra*.]

III

The Kansas courts applied Kansas contract and Kansas equity law to every claim in this case, notwithstanding that over 99 percent of the gas leases and some 97 percent of the plaintiffs in the case had no apparent connection to the State of

Kansas except for this lawsuit. Petitioner protested that the Kansas courts should apply the laws of the States where the leases were located, or at least apply Texas and Oklahoma law because so many of the leases came from those States. The Kansas courts disregarded this contention and found petitioner liable for interest on the suspended royalties as a matter of Kansas law, and set the interest rates under Kansas equity principles.

Petitioner contends that total application of Kansas substantive law violated the constitutional limitations on choice of law mandated by the Due Process Clause of the Fourteenth Amendment and the Full Faith and Credit Clause of Article IV, §1. We must first determine whether Kansas law conflicts in any material way with any other law which could apply.

[The Court next discussed the difference between Kansas law and the law of other states on the issue of interest rates.]

The conflicts on the applicable interest rates, alone—which we do not think can be labeled "false conflicts" without a more thoroughgoing treatment than was accorded them by the Supreme Court of Kansas—certainly amounted to millions of dollars in liability. We think that the Supreme Court of Kansas erred in deciding on the basis that it did that the application of its laws to all claims would be constitutional.

Four Terms ago we addressed a similar situation in Allstate Ins. Co. v. Hague [*supra* page 297].

The plurality in *Allstate* noted that a particular set of facts giving rise to litigation could justify, constitutionally, the application of more than one jurisdiction's laws. The plurality recognized, however, that the Due Process Clause and the Full Faith and Credit Clause provided modest restrictions on the application of forum law. These restrictions required "that for a State's substantive law to be selected in a constitutionally permissible manner, that State must have a significant contact or significant aggregation of contacts, creating state interests, such that choice of its law is neither arbitrary nor fundamentally unfair." *Id*. The dissenting Justices were in substantial agreement with this principle (opinion of Powell, J., joined by Burger, C.J., and Rehnquist, J.).

Petitioner owns property and conducts substantial business in the State, so Kansas certainly has an interest in regulating petitioner's conduct in Kansas. Moreover, oil and gas extraction is an important business to Kansas, and although only a few leases in issue are located in Kansas, hundreds of Kansas plaintiffs were affected by petitioner's suspension of royalties; thus the court held that the State has a real interest in protecting "the rights of these royalty owners both as individual residents of [Kansas] and as members of this particular class of plaintiffs." The Kansas Supreme Court pointed out that Kansas courts are quite familiar with this type of lawsuit, and "[t]he plaintiff class members have indicated their desire to have this action determined under the laws of Kansas." Finally, the Kansas court buttressed its use of Kansas law by stating that this lawsuit was analogous to a suit against a "common fund" located in Kansas.

We do not lightly discount this description of Kansas' contacts with this litigation and its interest in applying its law. There is, however, no "common fund" located in Kansas that would require or support the application of only Kansas law to all these claims. As the Kansas court noted, petitioner commingled the suspended royalties with its general corporate accounts. There is no specific identifiable res in Kansas, nor is there any limited amount which may be depleted before every plaintiff is compensated. Only by somehow aggregating all the separate claims in this case could a "common fund" in any sense be created, and the term becomes all but meaningless when used in such an expansive sense.

We also give little credence to the idea that Kansas law should apply to all claims because the plaintiffs, by failing to opt out, evinced their desire to be bound by Kansas law. Even if one could say that the plaintiffs "consented" to the application of Kansas law by not opting out, plaintiff's desire for forum law is rarely, if ever controlling. In most cases the plaintiff shows his obvious wish for forum law by filing there. "If a plaintiff could choose the substantive rules to be applied to an action . . . the invitation to forum shopping would be irresistible." *Allstate, supra,* at 337 (opinion of Powell, J.). Even if a plaintiff evidences his desire for forum law by moving to the forum, we have generally accorded such a move little or no significance. John Hancock Mut. Life Ins. Co. v. Yates, 299 U.S. 178, 182 (1936); Home Ins. Co. v. Dick, 281 U.S. 397, 408 (1930). In *Allstate* the plaintiff's move to the forum was only relevant because it was unrelated and prior to the litigation. Thus the plaintiffs' desire for Kansas law, manifested by their participation in this Kansas lawsuit, bears little relevance.

The Supreme Court of Kansas in its opinion in this case expressed the view that by reason of the fact that it was adjudicating a nationwide class action, it had much greater latitude in applying its own law to the transactions in question than might otherwise be the case:

> "The general rule is that the law of the forum applies unless it is expressly shown that a different law governs, and in case of doubt, the law of the forum is preferred. . . . Where a state court determines it has jurisdiction over a nationwide class action and procedural due process guarantees of notice and adequate representation are present, we believe the law of the forum should be applied unless compelling reasons exist for applying a different law. . . . Compelling reasons do not exist to require this court to look to other state laws to determine the rights of the parties involved in this lawsuit." 235 Kan., at 221-222.

We think that this is something of a "bootstrap" argument. The Kansas class-action statute, like those of most other jurisdictions, requires that there be "common issues of law or fact." But while a State may, for the reasons we have previously stated, assume jurisdiction over the claims of plaintiffs whose principal contacts are with other States, it may not use this assumption of jurisdiction as an added weight in the scale when considering the permissible constitutional limits on choice of substantive law. It may not take a transaction with little or no relationship to the forum and apply the law of the forum in order to satisfy the procedural requirement that there be a "common question of law." The issue of personal jurisdiction over plaintiffs in a class action is entirely distinct from the question of the constitutional limitations on choice of law; the latter calculus is not altered by the fact that it may be more difficult or more burdensome to comply with the constitutional limitations because of the large number of transactions which the State proposes to adjudicate and which have little connection with the forum.

Kansas must have a "significant contact or significant aggregation of contacts" to the claims asserted by each member of the plaintiff class, contacts "creating state interests," in order to ensure that the choice of Kansas law is not arbitrary or unfair. *Allstate, supra,* at 312-313. Given Kansas' lack of "interest" in claims unrelated to that State, and the substantive conflict with jurisdictions such as Texas, we conclude that application of Kansas law to every claim in this case is sufficiently arbitrary and unfair as to exceed constitutional limits.

When considering fairness in this context, an important element is the expectation of the parties. *See id.* at 333 (opinion of Powell, J.). There is no indication that when the leases involving land and royalty owners outside of Kansas were executed, the parties had any idea that Kansas law would control. Neither the Due Process Clause nor the Full Faith and Credit Clause requires Kansas "to substitute for its own [laws], applicable to persons and events within it, the conflicting statute of another state," Pacific Employees Ins. Co. v. Industrial Accident Commn., 306 U.S. 493, 502 (1939), but Kansas "may not abrogate the rights of parties beyond its borders having no relation to anything done or to be done within them." Home Ins. Co. v. Dick, *supra,* at 410.

Here the Supreme Court of Kansas took the view that in a nationwide class action where procedural due process guarantees of notice and adequate representation were met, "the law of the forum should be applied unless compelling reasons exist for applying a different law." Whatever practical reasons may have commended this rule to the Supreme Court of Kansas, for the reasons already stated we do not believe that it is consistent with the decisions of this Court. We make no effort to determine for ourselves which law must apply to the various transactions involved in this lawsuit, and we re-affirm our observation in *Allstate* that in many situations a state court may be free to apply one of several choices of law. But the constitutional limitations laid down in cases such as *Allstate* and Home Ins. Co. v. Dick must be respected even in a nationwide class action. . . .

Justice POWELL took no part in the decision of this case.

Justice STEVENS, concurring in part and dissenting in part. . . .

As the Court recognizes, there "can be no [constitutional] injury in applying Kansas law if it is not in conflict with that of any other jurisdiction connected to this suit." A fair reading of the Kansas Supreme Court's opinion in light of its earlier opinion in Shutts v. Phillips Petroleum Co. (hereinafter *Shutts I*), reveals that the Kansas court has examined the laws of connected jurisdictions and has correctly concluded that there is no "direct" or "substantive" conflict between the law applied by Kansas and the laws of those other States. Kansas has merely developed general common-law principles to accommodate the novel facts of this litigation— other state courts either agree with Kansas or have not yet addressed precisely similar claims. Consequently, I conclude that the Full Faith and Credit Clause of the Constitution did not require Kansas to apply the law of any other State, and the Fourteenth Amendment's Due Process Clause did not prevent Kansas from applying its own law in this case.

Questions and Comments

(1) The Court noted Phillips owned property and conducted substantial business in Kansas and concluded that therefore Kansas had an interest in

regulating its conduct in Kansas. Why only in Kansas? Recall that in Allstate v. Hague, the plurality relied upon Allstate's unrelated business in the forum to justify imposition of forum law to a claim arising outside the forum. Why not do the same here?

(2) Does *Shutts* say anything new about the standard for applying forum law, or does it merely say that the forum may not automatically apply its own law? What guidance has been given to the court below on remand?

(3) Whose expectations is the Court referring to? If it is the defendant's, wasn't this answered in Allstate v. Hague, where the Court said that doing unrelated business in the forum should have made Allstate Insurance familiar with forum law and able to anticipate its application? The plaintiffs, on the other hand, are unlikely to complain about unfair surprise if Kansas law is applied; they actually *prefer* Kansas law. Moreover, are they any more likely to be surprised than Lavinia Hague was in *Allstate*?

(4) Even as to those plaintiffs that might claim the benefits of Kansas law—those with a Kansas oil lease, say—it is nevertheless conceivable that some other law would be more advantageous still. Assume, for instance, that Smith owns an oil lease executed at her home in Alaska and Alaskan law is even more generous to her. If Alaska would apply its law to her, and could do so constitutionally, then it is not to her advantage to be a member of the Kansas class. Doesn't it pose formidable problems of adequacy of representation, however, to bring an absent plaintiff into a class action that is against her interest? But how can a court determine where each particular plaintiff could get the best deal, without knowing plaintiff's contacts with all 50 states and performing detailed alternative choice-of-law analyses? Should a court merely notify potential class members of this possibility and suggest that each contact a lawyer? Choice of law in class actions is explored further in Chapter 10.

(5) We still seem to know very little about what contacts would constitutionally justify application of forum law under the modern learning. Some academic writers continue to claim that the Court has adopted governmental interest analysis. Shreve, *Interest Analysis as Constitutional Law*, 48 Ohio St. L.J. 51 (1987). Does *Shutts* support this?

Sun Oil Co. v. Wortman

486 U.S. 717 (1988)

Justice SCALIA delivered the opinion of the Court. [This case is related to *Shutts*, *supra*, and the facts are similar. Respondents, owners of property in Texas, Oklahoma, and Louisiana, sued Sun Oil Company, a Delaware company with its principal place of business in Texas, in Kansas state court to recover interest on previously suspended gas royalties. The action was barred by the statute of limitations in Texas, Oklahoma, and Louisiana, but it fell within Kansas's longer five-year statute of limitations. The Kansas courts applied the Kansas statute of limitations and rejected arguments that doing so violated the full faith and credit and due process clauses. The Kansas courts also rejected the claim that it had so misconstrued the substantive laws of Texas, Oklahoma, and Louisiana as to violate the full faith and credit and due process clauses.]

II

This Court has long and repeatedly held that the Constitution does not bar application of the forum State's statute of limitations to claims that in their substance are and must be governed by the law of a different State. We granted certiorari to reexamine this issue. We conclude that our prior holdings are sound.

A

The Full Faith and Credit Clause provides:

"Full Faith and Credit shall be given in each State to the public Acts, Records, and judicial Proceedings of every other State. And the Congress may by general Laws prescribe the Manner in which such Acts, Records and Proceedings shall be proved, and the Effect thereof."

The Full Faith and Credit Clause does not compel "a state to substitute the statutes of other states for its own statutes dealing with a subject matter concerning which it is competent to legislate." Pacific Employers Ins. Co. v. Industrial Accident Commn., 306 U.S. 493, 501 (1939). Since the procedural rules of its courts are surely matters on which a State is competent to legislate, it follows that a State may apply its own procedural rules to actions litigated in its courts. The issue here, then, can be characterized as whether a statute of limitations may be considered as a procedural matter for purposes of the Full Faith and Credit Clause.

Petitioner initially argues that M'Elmoyle v. Cohen, *supra*, was wrongly decided when handed down. The holding of *M'Elmoyle*, that a statute of limitations may be treated as procedural and thus may be governed by forum law even when the substance of the claim must be governed by another State's law, rested on two premises, one express and one implicit. The express premise was that this reflected the rule in international law at the time the Constitution was adopted. This is indisputably correct, and is not challenged by petitioner. The implicit premise, which petitioner does challenge, was that this rule from international law could properly have been applied in the interstate context consistently with the Full Faith and Credit Clause.

The first sentence of the Full Faith and Credit Clause was not much discussed at either the Constitutional Convention or the state ratifying conventions. However, the most pertinent comment at the Constitutional Convention, made by James Wilson of Pennsylvania, displays an expectation that it would be interpreted against the background of principles developed in international conflicts law. *See* 2 M. Farrand, *The Records of the Federal Convention of 1787*, p.488 (rev. ed. 1966). Moreover, this expectation was practically inevitable, since there was no other developed body of conflicts law to which courts in our new Union could turn for guidance.

The reported state cases in the decades immediately following ratification of the Constitution show that courts looked without hesitation to international law for guidance in resolving the issue underlying this case: which State's law governs the statute of limitations. The state of international law on that subject being as we have described, these early decisions uniformly concluded that the forum's statute of limitations governed even when it was longer than the limitations period of the State whose substantive law governed the merits of the claim. . . . By 1820, the use of the forum statute of limitations in the interstate context was acknowledged to be "well settled." . . . Obviously, judges writing in the era when the Constitution was framed and ratified thought the use of the forum statute of limitations to be proper in the interstate context. Their implicit understanding that the Full Faith and Credit Clause did not preclude reliance on the international law rule carries great weight.

Moreover, this view of statutes of limitation as procedural for purposes of choice of law followed quite logically from the manner in which they were treated for domestic-law purposes. At the time the Constitution was adopted the rule was already well established that suit would lie upon a promise to repay a debt barred by the statute of limitations—on the theory, as expressed by many courts, that the debt constitutes consideration for the promise, since the bar of the statute does not extinguish the underlying right but merely causes the remedy to be withheld. . . . This is the same theory, of course, underlying the conflicts rule: the right subsists, and the forum may choose to allow its courts to provide a remedy, even though the jurisdiction where the right arose would not.

Unable to sustain the contention that under the original understanding of the Full Faith and Credit Clause statutes of limitations would have been considered substantive, petitioner argues that we should apply the modern understanding that they are so. It is now agreed, petitioner argues, that the primary function of a statute of limitations is to balance the competing substantive values of repose and vindication of the underlying right; and we should apply that understanding here, as we have applied it in the area of choice of law for purposes of federal diversity jurisdiction, where we have held that statutes of limitation are substantive, *see* Guaranty Trust Co. v. York, 326 U.S. 99 (1945).

To address the last point first: *Guaranty Trust* itself rejects the notion that there is an equivalence between what is substantive under the *Erie* doctrine and what is substantive for purposes of conflict of laws. *Id.*, at 108. Except at the extremes, the terms "substance" and "procedure" precisely describe very little except a dichotomy, and what they mean in a particular context is largely determined by the purposes for which the dichotomy is drawn. In the context of our *Erie* jurisprudence, *see* Erie R. Co. v. Tompkins, 304 U.S. 64 (1938), that purpose is to establish (within the limits of applicable federal law, including the prescribed Rules of Federal Procedure) substantial uniformity of predictable outcome between cases tried in a federal court and cases tried in the courts of the State in which the federal court sits. *See Guaranty Trust, supra,* at 109; Hanna v. Plumer, 380 U.S. 460, 467, 471-474 (1965). The purpose of the substance-procedure dichotomy in the context of the Full Faith and Credit Clause, by contrast, is not to establish uniformity but to delimit spheres of state legislative competence. How different the two purposes (and hence the appropriate meanings) are is suggested by this: It is never the case under *Erie* that either federal *or* state law—if the two differ—can properly be applied to a particular issue, *cf. Erie, supra,* at 72-73; but since the legislative jurisdictions of the States overlap, it is frequently the case under the Full Faith and Credit Clause that a court can lawfully apply either the law of one State or the contrary law of another, *see Shutts III*, 472 U.S., at 823 ("in many situations a state court may be free to apply one of several choices of law"). Today, for example, we do not hold that Kansas must apply its own statute of limitations to a claim governed in its substance by another State's law, but only that it may.

But to address petitioner's broader point of which the *Erie* argument is only a part—that we should update our notion of what is sufficiently "substantive" to require full faith and credit: We cannot imagine what would be the basis for such an updating. As we have just observed, the words "substantive" and "procedural" themselves (besides not appearing in the Full Faith and Credit Clause) do not have a precise content, even (indeed especially) as their usage has evolved. And if one consults the purpose of their usage in the full-faith-and-credit context, that purpose is quite simply to give both the forum State and other interested States the legislative jurisdiction to which they are entitled. If we abandon the currently applied, traditional notions of such entitlement we would embark upon the enterprise of constitutionalizing choice-of-law rules, with no compass to guide us beyond our own perceptions of what seems desirable.[2] There is no more reason to consider recharacterizing statutes of limitations as substantive under the Full Faith and Credit Clause than there is to consider recharacterizing a host of other matters generally treated as procedural under conflicts law, and hence generally regarded as within the forum State's legislative jurisdiction. *See, e.g.*, Restatement (Second) of Conflict of Laws §131 (remedies available), §133 (placement of burden of proof), §134 (burden of production), §135 (sufficiency of the evidence), §139 (privileges) (1971).

In sum, long established and still subsisting choice-of-law practices that come to be thought, by modern scholars, unwise, do not thereby become unconstitutional. If current conditions render it desirable that forum States no longer treat a particular issue as procedural for conflict of laws purposes, those States can themselves adopt a rule to that effect, or it can be proposed that Congress legislate to that effect under the second sentence of the Full Faith and Credit Clause. It is not the function of this Court, however, to make departures from established choice-of-law precedent and practice constitutionally mandatory. We hold, therefore, that Kansas did not violate the Full Faith and Credit Clause when it applied its own statute of limitations.

---

2. Contrary to Justice Brennan's concurrence, there is nothing unusual about our approach. This Court has regularly relied on traditional and subsisting practice in determining the constitutionally permissible authority of courts. . . . The concurrence's citation, of the criticism by the plurality opinion in Allstate Ins. Co. v. Hague, 449 U.S. 302 (1981), of Hartford Accident & Indemnity Co. v. Delta & Pine Land Co., 292 U.S. 143 (1934), is not to the contrary. That criticism merely rejected the view that the Constitution enshrines the rule that the law of the place of contracting governs validity of all provisions of the contract. By the time of *Allstate*, of course, such a rule could not have been characterized as a subsisting tradition, if it ever could have been, in light of escape devices such as the doctrine of public policy, characterization of an issue as procedural, and the rule that the law of the place of performance governs matters of performance.

B

Petitioner also makes a due process attack upon the Kansas court's application of its own statute of limitations.[3] Here again neither the tradition in place when the constitutional provision was adopted nor subsequent practice supports the contention. At the time the Fourteenth Amendment was adopted, this Court had not only explicitly approved (under the Full Faith and Credit Clause) forum-state application of its own statute of limitations, but the practice had gone essentially unchallenged. And it has gone essentially unchallenged since. "If a thing has been practised for two hundred years by common consent, it will need a strong case for the Fourteenth Amendment to affect it." Jackman v. Rosenbaum Co., 260 U.S. 22, 31 (1922).

A State's interest in regulating the work load of its courts and determining when a claim is too stale to be adjudicated certainly suffices to give it legislative jurisdiction to control the remedies available in its courts by imposing statutes of limitations. Moreover, petitioner could in no way have been unfairly surprised by the application to it of a rule that is as old as the Republic. There is, in short, nothing in Kansas' action here that is "arbitrary or unfair," *Shutts III*, 472 U.S., at 821-822, and the due process challenge is entirely without substance.

III

In *Shutts III*, we held that Kansas could not apply its own law to claims for interest by nonresidents concerning royalties from property located in other States. The Kansas Supreme Court has complied with that ruling, but petitioner claims that it has unconstitutionally distorted Texas, Oklahoma, and Louisiana law in its determination of that law made in *Shutts IV* and applied to this case in *Wortman III*.

To constitute a violation of the Full Faith and Credit Clause or the Due Process Clause, it is not enough that a state court misconstrue the law of another State. Rather, our cases make plain that the misconstruction must contradict law of the other State that is clearly established and that has been brought to the

---

3. Although petitioner takes up this issue after discussion of the full faith and credit claim, and devotes much less argument to it, we may note that, logically, the full faith and credit claim is entirely dependent upon it. It cannot possibly be a violation of the Full Faith and Credit Clause for a State to decline to apply another State's law in a case where that other State *itself* does not consider it applicable. Although in certain circumstances standard conflicts law considers a statute of limitations to bar the right and not just the remedy, *see* Restatement (Second) of Conflict of Laws §143 (1971), petitioner concedes that (apart from the fact that Kansas does not so regard the out-of-state statutes of limitations at issue here) Texas, Oklahoma, and Louisiana view their own statutes as procedural for choice-of-law purposes. A full faith and credit problem can therefore arise only if that disposition by those other States is invalid—that is, if they, as well as Kansas, are compelled to consider their statute of limitations substantive. The nub of the present controversy, in other words, is the scope of constitutionally permissible legislative jurisdiction, and it matters little whether that is discussed in the context of the Full Faith and Credit Clause, as the litigants have principally done, or in the context of the Due Process Clause. Since we are largely traversing ground already covered, our discussion of the due process claim can be brief.

court's attention. . . . We cannot conclude that any of the interpretations at issue here runs afoul of this standard.

[The Court then discussed the substantive laws of Texas, Oklahoma, and Louisiana.] For the reasons stated, the judgment of the Kansas Supreme Court is affirmed.

Justice KENNEDY took no part in the consideration or decision of this case.

Justice BRENNAN, with whom Justice MARSHALL and Justice BLACKMUN join, concurring in part and concurring in the judgment.

I join Parts I and III of the Court's opinion. Although I also agree with the result the Court reaches in Part II, I reach that result through a somewhat different path of analysis.

For 150 years, this Court has consistently held that a forum State may apply its own statute of limitations period to out-of-state claims even though it is longer or shorter than the limitations period that would be applied by the State out of which the claim arose. The main question presented in this case is whether this line of authority has been undermined by more recent case law concerning the constitutionality of state choice-of-law rules. *See* Phillips Petroleum Co. v. Shutts, 472 U.S. 797 (1985); Allstate Ins. Co. v. Hague, 449 U.S. 302 (1981). I conclude that it has not.

. . . The minimum requirements imposed by the Full Faith and Credit Clause[2] are that a forum State should not apply its law unless it has "a significant contact or significant aggregation of contacts, creating state interests, such that choice of its law is neither arbitrary nor fundamentally unfair," *Phillips Petroleum, supra*, at 818, quoting *Allstate, supra*, at 312-313 (plurality opinion of Brennan, J., joined by White, Marshall, and Blackmun, JJ.). The constitutional issue in this case is somewhat more complicated than usual because the question is not the typical one of whether a State can constitutionally apply its substantive law where both it and another State have certain contacts with the litigants and the facts underlying the dispute. Rather the question here is whether a forum State can constitutionally apply its limitations period, which has mixed substantive and procedural aspects, where its contacts with the dispute stem only from its status as the forum.

Were statutes of limitations purely substantive, the issue would be an easy one, for where, as here, a forum State has no contacts with the underlying dispute, it has no substantive interests and cannot apply its own law on a purely substantive matter. Nor would the issue be difficult if statutes of limitations were purely procedural, for the contacts a State has with a dispute by virtue of being the forum always create state procedural interests that make applications of the forum's law on purely procedural questions "neither arbitrary nor fundamentally unfair." *Phillips Petroleum*, 472 U.S., at 818. Statutes of limitations, however, defy characterization as either purely procedural or purely substantive. The statute of limitations a State enacts represents a balance between, on the one hand, its substantive interest in vindicating substantive claims and, on the other hand, a combination of its procedural interest in freeing its courts from adjudicating

---

2. The minimum requirements imposed by the Due Process Clause are, in this context, the same as those imposed by the Full Faith and Credit Clause. . . .

stale claims and its substantive interest in giving individuals repose from ancient breaches of law. A State that has enacted a particular limitations period has simply determined that after that period the interest in vindicating claims becomes outweighed by the combination of the interests in repose and avoiding stale claims. One cannot neatly categorize this complicated temporal balance as either procedural or substantive.

Given the complex of interests underlying statutes of limitations, I conclude that the contact a State has with a claim simply by virtue of being the forum creates a sufficient procedural interest to make the application of its limitations period to wholly out-of-state claims consistent with the Full Faith and Credit Clause. This is clearest when the forum State's limitations period is shorter than that of the claim State. A forum State's procedural interest in avoiding the adjudication of stale claims is equally applicable to in-state and out-of-state claims. That the State out of which the claim arose may have concluded that at that shorter period its substantive interests outweigh its procedural interest in avoiding stale claims would not make any difference; it would be "neither arbitrary nor fundamentally unfair," *Phillips Petroleum, supra*, at 818, for the forum State to conclude that *its* procedural interest is more weighty than that of the claim State and requires an earlier time bar, as long as the time bar applied in a nondiscriminatory manner to in-state and out-of-state claims alike.

The constitutional question is somewhat less clear where, as here, the forum State's limitations period is longer than that of the claim State. In this situation, the claim State's statute of limitations reflects its policy judgment that at the time the suit was filed the combination of the claim State's procedural interest in avoiding stale claims and its substantive interest in repose outweighs its substantive interest in vindicating the plaintiff's substantive rights. Assuming, for the moment, that each State has an equal substantive interest in the repose of defendants, then a forum State that has concluded that its procedural interest is less weighty than that of the claim State does not act unfairly or arbitrarily in applying its longer limitations period. The claim State does not, after all, have any substantive interest in *not* vindicating rights it has created. Nor will it do to argue that the forum State has no interest in vindicating the substantive rights of nonresidents: the forum State cannot discriminate against nonresidents, and if it has concluded that the substantive rights of its citizens outweigh its procedural interests at that period then it cannot be faulted for applying that determination evenhandedly.

If the different limitations periods also reflect differing assessments of the substantive interests in the repose of defendants, however, the issue is more complicated. It is, to begin with, not entirely clear whether the interest in the repose of defendants is an interest the State has as a forum or wholly as the creator of the claim at issue. Even if one assumes the latter, determining whether application of the forum State's longer limitations period would thwart the claim State's substantive interest in repose requires a complex assessment of the relative weights of both States' procedural and substantive interests. For example, a claim State may have a substantive interest in vindicating claims that, at a particular period, outweighs its substantive interest in repose standing alone but not the combination of its interests in repose and avoiding the adjudication of stale claims. Such a State would not have its substantive interest in repose thwarted by the claim's adjudication in a State that professed no procedural interest in avoiding stale claims, even if the forum State had less substantive interest in repose than the claim State, because the forum State would be according the claim State's substantive interests all the weight the claim State gives them. Such efforts to break down and weigh the procedural and substantive components and interests served by the various States' limitations period would, however, involve a difficult, unwieldy and somewhat artificial inquiry that itself implicates the strong procedural interest any forum State has in having administrable choice-of-law rules.

In light of the forum State's procedural interests and the inherent ambiguity of any more refined inquiry in this context, there is some force to the conclusion that the forum State's contacts give it sufficient procedural interests to make it "neither arbitrary nor fundamentally unfair," *Phillips Petroleum*, 472 U.S., at 818, for the State to have a per se rule of applying its own limitations period to out-of-state claims—particularly where, as here, the states out of which the claims arise view their statutes of limitations as procedural. The issue, after all, is not whether the decision to apply forum limitations law is wise as a matter of choice-of-law doctrine but whether the decision is within the range of constitutionally permissible choices, and we have already held that distinctions similar to those offered above "are too unsubstantial to form the basis for constitutional distinctions." This conclusion may not be compelled, but the arguments to the contrary are at best arguable, and any merely arguable inconsistency with our current full faith and credit jurisprudence surely does not merit deviating from 150 years of precedent holding that choosing the forum State's limitations period over that of the claim State is constitutionally permissible.

The Court's technique of avoiding close examination of the relevant interests by wrapping itself in the mantle of tradition is as troublesome as it is conclusory. It leads the Court to assert broadly (albeit in dicta) that States do not violate the Full Faith and Credit Clause by adjudicating out-of-state claims under the forum's own law on, inter alia, remedies, burdens of proof, and burdens of production. The constitutionality of refusing to apply the law of the claim State on such issues was not briefed or argued before this Court, and whether, as the Court asserts without support, there are insufficient reasons for "recharacterizing" these issues (at least in part) as substantive is a question that itself presents multiple issues of enormous difficulty and importance which deserve more than the offhand treatment the Court gives them.

Even more troublesome is the Court's sweeping dicta that *any* choice-of-law practice that is "long established and still subsisting" is constitutional. This statement on its face seems to encompass choice-of-law doctrines on purely substantive issues, and the blind reliance on tradition confuses and conflicts with the full faith and credit test we articulated just three years ago in *Phillips Petroleum. See also Allstate*, 449 U.S., at 308-309, n.11 (plurality opinion of Brennan, J., joined by White, Marshall, and Blackmun, JJ.) (stating that a 1934 case giving "controlling constitutional significance" to a traditional choice-of-law test "has scant relevance for today"). That certain choice-of-law practices have so far avoided constitutional scrutiny by this Court is in any event a poor reason for concluding their constitutional validity. Nor is it persuasive that the practice reflected the rule applied by States or in international law around the time of the adoption of the Constitution, since "[t]he very purpose of the full faith and credit clause was to alter the status of the several states as independent foreign sovereignties," Milwaukee County v. M. E. White Co., 296 U.S. 268, 276-277 (1935), not to leave matters unchanged. The Court never offers a satisfactory explanation as to why tradition should enable States to engage in practices that, under our current test, are "arbitrary" or "fundamentally unfair." The broad range of choice-of-law practices that may, in one jurisdiction or another, be traditional are not before this Court and have not been surveyed by it, and we can only guess what practices today's opinion approves sight unseen. Nor am I much comforted by the fact that the Court opines on the constitutionality of traditional choice-of-law practices only to the extent they are "still subsisting," for few cases involve challenges to practices that no longer subsist. One wonders as well how future courts will determine which practices are traditional enough (or subsist strongly enough) to be constitutional, and about the utility of requiring courts to focus on such an uncertain and formalistic inquiry rather than on the fairness and arbitrariness of the choice-of-law rule at issue. Indeed, the disarray of the Court's test is amply demonstrated by the fact that two of the Justices necessary to form the Court leave open the issue of whether a forum State could constitutionally refuse to apply a shorter limitations period regarded as substantive by the foreign State, *see post* (O'Connor, J., joined by Rehnquist, C.J., concurring in part and dissenting in part), even though in many States the subsisting tradition of applying the forum's limitations period recognizes no exception for limitations periods considered substantive by the foreign State. *See generally* Restatement (Second) of Conflict of Laws §143 and Reporter's Note (1971) (collecting cases).

In short, I fear the Court's rationale will cause considerable mischief with no corresponding benefit.

Justice O'CONNOR, with whom THE CHIEF JUSTICE joins, concurring in part and dissenting in part.

The Court properly concludes that Kansas did not violate the Full Faith and Credit Clause or the Due Process Clause when it chose to apply its own statute of limitations in this case. Different issues might have arisen if Texas, Oklahoma, or Louisiana regarded its own shorter statute of limitations as substantive. Such issues, however, are not presented in this case, and they are appropriately left unresolved. Accordingly, I join Parts I and II of the Court's opinion.

In my view, however, the Supreme Court of Kansas violated the Full Faith and Credit Clause when it concluded that the three States in question would apply the interest rates set forth in the regulations of the Federal Power Commission (FPC). The Court correctly states that misconstruing those States' laws would not by itself have violated the Constitution, for the Full Faith and Credit Clause only required the Kansas court to adhere to law that was clearly established in those States and that had been brought to the Kansas court's attention. Under the standard the Court articulates, however, the Clause was violated. Each of the three States has a statute setting an interest rate that is different from the FPC rate, and the Supreme Court of Kansas offered no valid reason whatsoever for ignoring those statutory rates. Neither has this Court suggested a colorable argument that could support the Kansas court's decision, and its affirmance of that decision effectively converts an important constitutional guarantee into a precatory admonition.

[The opinion then discussed its view of Texas, Oklahoma, and Louisiana law.]

Today's decision discards important parts of our decision in *Shutts III*, 472 U.S. 797 (1985), and of the Full Faith and Credit Clause. Faced with the constitutional obligation to apply the substantive law of another State, a court that does not like that law apparently need take only two steps in order to avoid applying it. First, invent a legal theory so novel or strange that the other State has never had an opportunity to reject it; then, on the basis of nothing but unsupported speculation, "predict" that the other State would adopt that theory if it had the chance. To call this giving full faith and credit to the law of another State ignores the language of the Constitution and leaves it without the capacity to fulfill its purpose. Rather than take such a step, I would remand this case to the Supreme Court of Kansas with instructions to give effect to the interest rates established by law in Texas, Oklahoma, and Louisiana. I therefore respectfully dissent.

Questions and Comments

(1) *Wortman* must surely make one thing even clearer: that with regard to the issue of whether an adequate nexus exists for application of local law, the due process and full faith and credit limits are identical. Justice Scalia recognized this fact in footnote 3; and the concurring opinion of Justice Brennan agreed in its footnote 2. All members of the Court who participated thus accepted the choice-of-law equivalence of the two clauses. While this result is in accord with earlier decisions, why (if they are identical) is the focus here primarily upon the interpretation of full faith and credit while earlier cases spoke in terms of due process?

What accounts for this interesting coincidence that these two rather different-sounding clauses just happen to turn out to have an identical scope in this context? Given his apparent interest in historical interpretation of constitutional provisions, why would Justice Scalia equate clauses from two different historical periods? Note that the argument that Kansas had denied other states' law full faith and credit through misinterpretation is discussed only in terms of full faith and credit and not also in due process terms. Why is this only a problem of the former, and not the latter? In the section of this chapter that follows, we will see additional problems that are amenable only to full faith and credit, and not to due process, analysis.

(2) By relying so extensively upon the understanding at the time that the Constitution was drafted, does Justice Scalia's opinion effectively give constitutional carte blanche to all First Restatement principles, or at least to all First Restatement rules adequately grounded in tradition? Has the *Wortman* majority constitutionalized the substance/procedure distinction? Did it, in footnote 3, constitutionalize renvoi? Has it constitutionalized international law, at least as it stood 200 years ago?

(3) Is Justice Brennan's decidedly non-originalist approach any better? His concurrence draws heavily on the distinction between substantive and procedural interests. Is the substance/procedure distinction any more helpful here than it was in Chapters 2 and 3? What precisely is the forum state's procedural interest in providing a longer statute of limitations than the claim state?

(4) Is Justice O'Connor's concern about opportunistic misinterpretation of foreign law a genuine one? Wouldn't it be worse for the Supreme Court to get into

the business of closely scrutinizing the accuracy of state court interpretations of foreign law?

(5) Much speculation arose just prior to the 1992 presidential elections about the likely choice-of-law implications of a possible overruling of Roe v. Wade, 410 U.S. 113 (1973). If some states were allowed to criminalize abortions, would they also be permitted to penalize local individuals traveling to obtain abortions in other states, where the abortions were legal? Recall Skiriotes v. Florida, 313 U.S. 69 (1941), page 288 *supra*, recognizing a state's right to regulate its citizens' conduct outside the state in at least certain circumstances. The topic was the subject of a symposium in 91 Mich. L. Rev. (1992); Professors Kreimer and Brilmayer both concluded, although for different reasons, that extraterritorial prohibitions on abortion would be largely impermissible. *See* Kreimer, *"But Whosoever Treasures Freedom . . .": The Right to Travel and Extraterritorial Abortions*, 91 Mich. L. Rev. 907 (1992); Brilmayer, *Interstate Preemption: The Right to Travel, the Right to Life, and the Right to Die*, 91 Mich. L. Rev. 873 (1992). *See also* Kreimer, *The Law of Choice and Choice of Law: Abortion, the Right to Travel, and Extraterritorial Regulation in American Federalism*, 67 N.Y.U. L. Rev. 451 (1992). Brilmayer argued that abortion is different from many other substantive areas, because the decision not to regulate abortion is typically a decision to afford women the affirmative freedom to make up their own minds, rather than a simple failure to regulate on the topic. *Compare* Bradford, *What Happens if* Roe *Is Overruled? Extraterritorial Regulation of Abortion by the States*, 35 Ariz. L. Rev. 87 (1993) and Van Alstyne, *Closing the Circle of Constitutional Review from* Griswold v. Connecticut *to* Roe v. Wade: *An Outline of Decision Merely Overruling* Roe, 1989 Duke L.J. 1677 (both concluding that extraterritorial regulation would be permissible).

B. The Obligation and the Right to Provide a Forum

Because the full faith and credit clause has come to require nothing more than the due process clause in the traditional choice-of-law context, its distinctive relevance to conflict of laws must be found elsewhere. One area of application is the interstate enforcement of judgments, a topic that will be addressed in Chapter 7. But there are nonjudgments contexts in which the clause has also been invoked and has provided the basis for invalidating state actions. The following cases address situations in which it is argued that the forum is according too little respect to the laws of another state. They deal with door-closing and localizing statutes pursuant to which either the forum declines to hear a foreign claim or refuses to respect the foreign state's wishes that its claim not be entertained in the forum. Why are such cases primarily a matter of full faith and credit, while choice-of-law cases can be treated equally well under either a due process or a full faith and credit analysis? *See generally* Brilmayer, *Credit Due Judgments and Credit Due Laws: The Respective Roles of Due Process and Full Faith and Credit in the Interstate Context*, 70 Iowa L. Rev. 95 (1984).

Hughes v. Fetter
341 U.S. 609 (1951)

Justice BLACK delivered the opinion of the Court.

Basing his complaint on the Illinois wrongful death statute, appellant administrator brought this action in the Wisconsin state court to recover damages for the death of Harold Hughes, who was fatally injured in an automobile accident in Illinois. The allegedly negligent driver and an insurance company were named as defendants. On their motion the trial court entered summary judgment "dismissing the complaint on the merits." It held that a Wisconsin statute, which creates a right of action only for deaths caused in that state, establishes a local public policy against Wisconsin's entertaining suits brought under the wrongful death acts of other states. The Wisconsin Supreme Court affirmed, notwithstanding the contention that the local statute so construed violated the Full Faith and Credit Clause of Art. IV, §1 of the Constitution. . . .

We are called upon to decide the narrow question whether Wisconsin, over the objection raised, can close the doors of its courts to the cause of action created by the Illinois wrongful death act.[4] Prior decisions have established that the Illinois statute is a "public act" within the provision of Art. IV, §1 that "Full Faith and Credit shall be given in each State to the public Acts . . . of every other State." It is also settled that Wisconsin cannot escape this constitutional obligation to enforce the rights and duties validly created under the laws of other states by the simple device of removing jurisdiction from courts otherwise competent. We have recognized, however, that full faith and credit does not automatically compel a forum state to subordinate its own statutory policy to a conflicting public act of another state; rather, it is for this Court to choose in each case between the competing public policies involved. The clash of interests in cases of this type has usually been described as a conflict between the public policies of two or more states. The more basic conflict involved in the present appeal, however, is as follows: On the one hand is the strong unifying principle embodied in the Full Faith and Credit Clause looking toward maximum enforcement in each state of the obligations or rights created or recognized by the statutes of sister states, on the other hand is the policy of Wisconsin, as interpreted by its highest court, against permitting Wisconsin courts to entertain this wrongful death action.

We hold that Wisconsin's policy must give way. That state has no real feeling of antagonism against wrongful death suits in general.[10] To the contrary, a forum is regularly provided for cases of this nature, the exclusionary rule extending only so far as to bar actions for death not caused locally.[11] The Wisconsin policy,

---

4. The parties concede, as they must, that if the same cause of action had previously been reduced to judgment, the Full Faith and Credit Clause would compel the courts of Wisconsin to entertain an action to enforce it. Kenney v. Supreme Lodge, 252 U.S. 411.

10. The present case is not one where Wisconsin, having entertained appellant's lawsuit, chose to apply its own instead of Illinois' statute to measure the substantive rights involved. This distinguishes the present case from those where we have said that "prima facie every state is entitled to enforce in its own courts its own statutes, lawfully enacted." Alaska Packers Assn. v. Commission.

11. It may well be that the wrongful death acts of Wisconsin and Illinois contain different provision in regard to such matters as maximum recovery and disposition of the proceeds of suit. Such differences, however, are generally considered unimportant.

moreover, cannot be considered as an application of the forum non conveniens doctrine, whatever effect that doctrine might be given if its use resulted in denying enforcement to public acts of other states. Even if we assume that Wisconsin could refuse, by reason of particular circumstances, to hear foreign controversies to which nonresidents were parties, the present case is not one lacking in close relationship with the state. For not only were appellant, the decedent, and the individual defendant all residents of Wisconsin, but also appellant was appointed administrator and the corporate defendant was created under Wisconsin laws. We also think it relevant, although not crucial here, that Wisconsin may well be the only jurisdiction in which service could be had as an original matter on the insurance company defendant. And while in the present case jurisdiction over the individual defendant apparently could be had in Illinois by substituted service, in other cases Wisconsin's exclusionary statute might amount to a deprivation of all opportunity to enforce valid death claims created by another state.

Under these circumstances, we conclude that Wisconsin's statutory policy which excludes this Illinois cause of action is forbidden by the national policy of the Full Faith and Credit Clause.[16] The judgment is reversed and the cause is remanded to the Supreme Court of Wisconsin for proceedings not inconsistent with this opinion.

Reversed and remanded.

Justice FRANKFURTER, whom Justice REED, Justice JACKSON, and Justice MINTON join, dissenting.

. . . The Full Faith and Credit Clause was derived from a similar provision in the Articles of Confederation. Art. 4, §3. The only clue to its meaning in the available records of the Constitutional Convention is a notation in Madison's Debates that "Mr. Wilson & Docr. Johnson [who became members of the committee to which the provision was referred] supposed the meaning to be that Judgments in one State should be the ground of actions in other States, & that acts of the Legislatures should be included, for the sake of Acts of insolvency &c—." II Farrand, The Records of the Federal Convention, 447. This Court has, with good reason, gone far in requiring that the courts of a State respect judgments entered by courts of other States. But the extent to which a State must recognize and enforce the rights of action created by other States is not so clear.

In the tort action before us, there is little reason to impose a "state of vassalage" on the forum. The liability here imposed does not rest on a preexisting

---

16. In certain previous cases, *e.g.*, Pacific Ins. Co. v. Commission; Alaska Packers Assn. v. Commission, this Court suggested that under the Full Faith and Credit Clause a forum state might make a distinction between statutes and judgments of sister states because of Congress' failure to prescribe the extra-state effect to be accorded public acts. Subsequent to these decisions the Judicial Code was revised so as to provide: "*Such Acts* [of the legislature of any state] . . . and judicial proceedings . . . shall have the same full faith and credit in every court within the United States . . . as they have . . . in the courts of such State . . . from which they are taken." (Italics added.) 28 U.S.C. (1946 ed., Supp. III) §1738. In deciding the present appeal, however, we have not found it necessary to rely on any changes accomplished by the Judicial Code revision.

relationship between the plaintiff and defendant. There is consequently no need for fixed rules which would enable parties, at the time they enter into a transaction, to predict its consequences. . . .

This Court should certainly not require that the forum deny its own law and follow the tort law of another State where there is a reasonable basis for the forum to close its courts to the foreign cause of action. The decision of Wisconsin to open its courts to actions for wrongful deaths within the State but close them to actions for deaths outside the State may not satisfy everyone's notion of wise policy. But it is neither novel nor without reason. Wisconsin may be willing to grant a right of action where witnesses will be available in Wisconsin and the courts are acquainted with a detailed local statute and cases construing it. It may not wish to subject residents to suit where out-of-state witnesses will be difficult to bring before the court, and where the court will be faced with the alternative of applying a complex foreign statute—perhaps inconsistent with that of Wisconsin on important issues—or fitting the statute to the Wisconsin pattern. The legislature may well feel that it is better to allow the courts of the State where the accident occurred to construe and apply its own statute, and that the exceptional case where the defendant cannot be served in the State where the accident occurred does not warrant a general statute allowing suit in the Wisconsin courts. The various wrongful death statutes are inconsistent on such issues as beneficiaries, the party who may bring suit, limitations on liability, comparative negligence, and the measure of damages. . . . The measure of damages and the relation of wrongful death actions to actions for injury surviving death have raised extremely complicated problems, even for a court applying the familiar statute of its own State. These diversities reasonably suggest application by local judges versed in them.

No claim is made that Wisconsin has discriminated against the citizens of other States and thus violated Art. IV, §2 of the Constitution. Nor is a claim made that a lack of a forum in Wisconsin deprives the plaintiff of due process. Nor is it argued that Wisconsin is flouting a federal statute. The only question before us is how far the Full Faith and Credit Clause undercuts the purpose of the Constitution, made explicit by the Tenth Amendment, to leave the conduct of domestic affairs to the States. Few interests are of more dominant local concern than matters governing the administration of law. This vital interest of the States should not be sacrificed in the interest of a merely literal reading of the Full Faith and Credit Clause.

There is no support, either in reason or in the cases, for holding that this Court is to make a de novo choice between the policies underlying the laws of Wisconsin and Illinois. I cannot believe that the Full Faith and Credit Clause provided a "writer's inkhorn" so that this Court might separate right from wrong. "Prima facie every state is entitled to enforce in its own courts its own statutes, lawfully enacted. One who challenges that right, because of the force given to a conflicting statute of another state by the full faith and credit clause, assumes the burden of showing, upon some rational basis, that of the conflicting interests involved those of the foreign state are superior to those of the forum." Mr. Justice Stone, in Alaska Packers Assn. v. Commission. In the present case, the decedent, the plaintiff, and the individual defendant were residents of Wisconsin. The corporate defendant was created under Wisconsin law. The suit was brought in the Wisconsin courts. No reason is apparent—and none is vouchsafed in the opinion of the Court—why the interest of Illinois is so great that it can force the courts of Wisconsin to grant relief in defiance of their own law.

Finally, it may be noted that there is no conflict here in the policies underlying the statute of Wisconsin and that of Illinois. The Illinois wrongful death statute has a proviso that "no action shall be brought or prosecuted in this State to recover damages for a death occurring outside of this State where a right of action for such death exists under the laws of the place where such death occurred and service of process in such suit may be had upon the defendant in such place." The opinion of the Court concedes that "jurisdiction over the individual defendant apparently could be had in Illinois by substituted service." Thus, in the converse of the case at bar—if Hughes had been killed in Wisconsin and suit had been brought in Illinois—the Illinois courts would apparently have dismissed the suit. There is no need to be "more Roman than the Romans."

Wells v. Simonds Abrasive Co.

345 U.S. 514 (1953)

Chief Justice VINSON delivered the opinion of the Court.

Cheek Wells was killed in Alabama when a grinding wheel with which he was working burst. The wheel had been manufactured by the respondent, a corporation with its principal place of business in Pennsylvania. The administratrix of the estate of Cheek Wells brought an action for damages in the federal court for the Eastern District of Pennsylvania after one year, but within two years, after the death. Jurisdiction was based upon diversity of citizenship.

The section of the Alabama Code upon which petitioner predicated her action for wrongful death provided that action ". . . must be brought within two years from and after the death. . . ." The respondent moved for summary judgment on the ground the Pennsylvania wrongful death statute required suit to be commenced within one year. In an opinion on that motion, the district judge found that the Pennsylvania statute, which was analogous to the Alabama statute, had a one-year limitation. He further found that the Pennsylvania conflict of laws rule called for the application of its own limitation rather than that of the place of the accident. Deeming himself bound by the Pennsylvania conflicts rule, he ordered summary judgment for the respondent. The Court of Appeals for the Third Circuit affirmed.

Long ago, we held that applying the statute of limitations of the forum to a foreign substantive right did not deny full faith and credit. Recently we referred to ". . . the well-established principle of conflict of laws that 'If action is barred by the statute of limitations of the forum, no action can be maintained though action is not barred in the state where the cause of action arose.' Restatement, Conflict of Laws §603 (1934)." Order of United Commercial Travelers v. Wolfe.

The rule that the limitations of the forum apply (which this Court has said meets the requirements of full faith and credit) is the usual conflicts rule of the states. However, there have been divergent views when a foreign statutory right unknown to the common law has a period of limitations included in the section creating the right. The Alabama statute here involved creates such a right and contains a built-in limitation. The view is held in some jurisdictions that such a limitation is so intimately connected with the right that it must be enforced in the forum state along with the substantive right.

We are not concerned with the reasons which have led some states for their own purposes to adopt the foreign limitation, instead of their own, in such a situation. The question here is whether the Full Faith and Credit Clause compels them to do so. Our prevailing rule is that the Full Faith and Credit Clause does not compel the forum state to use the period of limitation of a foreign state. We see no reason in the present situation to graft an exception onto it. Differences based upon whether the foreign right was known to the common law or upon the arrangement of the code of the foreign state are too unsubstantial to form the basis of constitutional distinctions under the Full Faith and Credit Clause.

We agree with the respondent that Engel v. Davenport has no application here. It presented an entirely different problem. Congress had given a statutory cause of action to seamen for certain personal injuries, placing concurrent jurisdiction in the state and federal courts. In *Engel, supra*, the two-year federal limitation rather than the one-year California limitation for similar actions was held controlling in an action brought in the California courts. Once it was decided that the intention of Congress was that the two-year limitation was meant to apply in both federal and state courts under our Federal Constitution, that was the supreme law of the land.*

Our decisions in Hughes v. Fetter and First National Bank v. United Air Lines do not call for a change in the well-established rule that the forum state is permitted to apply its own period of limitation. The crucial factor in those two cases was that the forum laid an uneven hand on causes of action arising within and without the forum state. Causes of action arising in sister states were discriminated against. Here Pennsylvania applies her one-year limitation to all wrongful death actions wherever they may arise. The judgment is affirmed.

Justice JACKSON, with whom Justice BLACK and Justice MINTON join, dissenting.

[T]he essence of the Full Faith and Credit Clause of the Constitution is that uniformities other than just those within the state are to be observed in a federal system. The whole purpose and the only need for requiring full faith and credit to foreign law is that it does differ from that of the forum. But that disparity does not cause the type of evil aimed at in Erie R. Co. v. Tompkins, *supra*, namely, that the same event may be judged by two different laws, depending upon whether a state court or a federal forum within that state is available. Application of the Full Faith and Credit Clause prevents this disparity by requiring that the law where the cause of action arose will follow the cause of action in whatever forum it is pursued.

---

* "This Constitution, and the Laws of the United States which shall be made in Pursuance thereof; and all Treaties made, or which shall be made, under the Authority of the United States, shall be the supreme Law of the Land; and the Judges in every State shall be bound thereby, any Thing in the Constitution or Laws of any State to the Contrary notwithstanding." U.S. Const. art. VI, §2.—EDS.

The Court's decision, in contrast with our position, would enable shopping for favorable forums. Suppose this plaintiff might have obtained service of process in several different states—an assumption not extravagant in the case of many national corporations. Under the Court's holding, she could choose from as many varieties of laws as of forums. Under our theory, wherever she elected to sue (if she had a choice), she would take Alabama law with her. Suppose even now she can get service in a state with no statute of limitations or a long one; can she thereby revive a cause of action that has expired under Alabama law? The Court's logic would so indicate. The life of her cause of action is then determined by the fortuitous circumstances that enable her to make service of process in a certain state or states. . . .

We think that the better view of the case before us would be that it is Alabama law which giveth and only Alabama law that taketh away.

Questions and Comments

(1) In footnote 10 of *Hughes*, the Court mentioned that the case did not involve the typical choice-of-law problem in which the forum sought to supplant the law of the alternative state by applying its own law instead. What kind of problem is this, then? Note that the claim was that Wisconsin law was invalid rather than (as in the usual choice-of-law context) that it was a valid law that could not constitutionally be applied. Does this matter?

(2) Brainerd Currie found *Hughes* paradoxical because it compelled the forum to entertain the case but did not compel it to apply Illinois law. *The Constitution and the "Transitory" Cause of Action*, in *Selected Essays on the Conflict of Laws* 282, 282-283 (1963). Whether this is in fact paradoxical has been disputed. Martin, *Constitutional Limits on Choice of Law*, 61 Cornell L. Rev. 185, 219-220 (1976); Kirgis, *The Roles of Due Process and Full Faith and Credit in Choice of Law*, 62 Cornell L. Rev. 94, 118 (1976).

(3) Can *Hughes* be squared with Gulf Oil Co. v. Gilbert, 330 U.S. 501 (1947), in which the Supreme Court approved the doctrine of forum non conveniens for the federal courts? Are the federal courts and the Wisconsin courts different enough to require one court to entertain a cause of action and not another? Or is forum non conveniens constitutional only when there are not as many contacts between the case and the forum as in *Hughes*? Or is the reason for the refusal to hear the case the critical factor? Can *Hughes* be squared with long-arm jurisdictional statutes that provide jurisdiction only where the cause of action accrued within the state?

(4) Shouldn't the recovery portions of the Illinois wrongful-death statute, to which *Hughes* said Wisconsin must give full faith and credit, be read together with that provision of the Illinois act (referred to in the last paragraph of the Frankfurter dissent and in the preceding note by Professor Currie), which would have done exactly the same thing that the Wisconsin courts attempted in *Hughes* if the facts had been reversed? In light of the no-foreign-accident provision of the Illinois statute, how can the Wisconsin courts be said to have ignored the policy of the Illinois statute?

(5) How does *Wells* compare with Sun Oil Co. v. Wortman, reprinted at page 316 *supra*? Note that *Wortman* cannot be phrased in terms of whether the forum gave

too little credit to the substantive cause of action under another state, for the forum limitations period in *Wortman* was longer, not shorter, as in *Wells*. At most, *Wortman* involves a claim of lack of respect for the foreign statute of limitations; that is, *Wortman* necessarily involves only a choice-of-law question (which limitations period to apply), while *Wells* raises arguments about respect for both the limitations period *and* the substantive cause of action. The latter is not really a choice-of-law problem because the forum has already agreed to apply the other state's substantive law.

(6) Professor Kramer provocatively argues that the public policy exception in choice of law, discussed *supra* pages 146-156, 268-269, cannot survive *Hughes* and *Wells*:

> An accurate statement of the holding in Hughes would thus seem to be that state rules that discriminate against the laws of other states are subject to some form of intermediate constitutional scrutiny; that is, they must be justified by substantial reasons, and the discrimination must bear a substantial relationship to the state's objectives. . . . This antidiscrimination principle is, in fact, how the Court explained *Hughes* in its subsequent decision in *Wells*, which said that the result turned on the fact that "the forum laid an uneven hand on causes of action arising within and without the forum state. Causes of action arising in sister states were discriminated against." But if that is the test, the public policy doctrine must be unconstitutional. For surely "offensiveness" cannot be an appropriate reason under the Full Faith and Credit Clause for refusing to entertain a claim based on another state's law. It is difficult to think of a justification more at odds with the principal mission of the Clause. . . . [The clause forbids] a state's refusal to apply another state's law, otherwise applicable under the forum's choice of law rules, on the ground that it promotes a policy the forum finds repugnant.

See Kramer, *Same-Sex Marriage, Conflict of Laws, and the Unconstitutional Public Policy Exception*, 106 Yale L.J. 1965, 1984-1987 (1997). Do you agree with this reasoning? Kramer goes on to argue that the purposes animating the full faith and credit clause—to bind states "more closely together," and to impose "mutual obligations to respect each other's laws and judgments," *id*. at 1986—are best served by elimination of the public policy exception. Couldn't one just as well argue that the public policy exception promotes interstate harmony by giving states a safety valve to avoid application of laws they deem unjust? Kramer thinks not. *See id*. at 1987-1991.

(7) *Hughes* concerns the constitutional obligation to provide a forum for a foreign cause of action. What if the state that created the cause of action does not want the action brought in another state's courts? In Tennessee Coal, Iron & R. Co. v. George, 233 U.S. 354 (1914), a plaintiff injured on the job in Alabama sued his employer in a Georgia state court under section 3910 of the 1907 Alabama Code, which provided for vicarious liability under certain circumstances. A different section of the Alabama Code stated that all actions under section 3910 must be brought "in a court of competent jurisdiction within the State of Alabama and not elsewhere." The defendant argues that the full faith and credit clause required the Georgia court to respect this provision and dismiss the case. The Supreme Court disagreed. After asserting that the right to sue was separable from the remedy, it stated that "a State cannot create a transitory cause of action and at the same time destroy the right to sue on the transitory cause of

action in any court having jurisdiction. That jurisdiction is to be determined by the law of the court's creation and cannot be defeated by the extraterritorial operation of a statute of another State, even though it created the right of action." Is *Tennessee Coal* a First Restatement relic?

Tennessee Coal was followed in Crider v. Zurich Ins. Co., 380 U.S. 39 (1965). There the forum had disregarded a provision by the state creating the cause of action, which required that the cause of action be enforced only before a local administrative tribunal. The Court agreed, relying on the fact that the forum had an interest in providing a means of recovery for the plaintiff who was a forum resident. Should such an interest be a necessary condition for entertaining the cause of action? How can the forum have an "interest" in providing recovery under another state's law?

(8) In addition to their obligation to admit certain causes of action created by other states, states also have an obligation to admit certain causes of action created by federal law. In Haywood v. Drown, 556 U.S. 729, 740 n.7 (2009), the Court explained that it "saw no reason to treat the Supremacy Clause differently" from the full faith and credit clause, citing to *Hughes*. However, the Court has also ruled in an analogous case that "[a] valid excuse to [the supremacy clause] may exist when a state court refuses jurisdiction because of a neutral state rule of judicial administration . . . unless that rule is pre-empted by federal law." Howlett v. Rose, 496 U.S. 356, 357 (1990). What would be an intelligible principle delineating permissible exceptions to the supremacy clause?

The Court has not yet elaborated on the "valid excuse" it referred to in *Howlett*. In Haywood v. Drown, 556 U.S. 729 (2009), the most recent in the line of cases arising from a state's attempted exclusion of a federal cause of action, a state prisoner brought civil rights actions in New York state court against several correction employees. The trial court dismissed the action as barred by a state jurisdictional statute requiring such causes of action to be tried in the New York Court of Claims, and the prisoner appealed. The Supreme Court held for the petitioner, ruling that "having made the decision to create courts of general jurisdiction that regularly sit to entertain analogous suits [civil rights actions against state officials other than corrections officers], New York is not at liberty to shut the doors to federal claims that it considers at odds with its local policy." *Id.* at 740. Does the Court mean that, if New York courts did not allow civil rights actions against other types of state officials, New York could have denied Haywood's suit against its correction officers? *See* Vázquez & Vladeck, *The Constitutional Right to Collateral Post-Conviction Review*, 103 Va. L. Rev. 905, 930-936 (2017). For further discussion of the supremacy clause and its constraint on states' ability to exclude unwanted federal causes of action, *see* Brilmayer & Underhill, *Congressional Obligation to Provide a Forum for Constitutional Claims: Discriminatory Jurisdictional Rules and Conflict of Laws*, 69 Va. L. Rev. 819 (1983).

Note on the Full Faith and Credit Clause in State-Court Suits Against Sister State Instrumentalities

In a series of decisions involving suits in state court against instrumentalities of sister states, the Court rendered several notable holdings regarding the states' obligations under the full faith and credit clause before ultimately holding that the federal constitutional doctrine of state sovereign immunity altogether bars suits against states in the courts of sister states. In Nevada v. Hall, 440 U.S. 410 (1979), Californians injured in a traffic accident on the California roads by an employee of the University of Nevada (a state instrumentality) sued Nevada in the California courts. The court entered judgment against Nevada, and the state sought review in the U.S. Supreme Court. After concluding that the doctrine of state sovereign immunity does not bar state-court suits against sister states, the Court considered whether, under the full faith and credit clause, the California courts were required to apply a Nevada statute placing a limit of $25,000 on any award against the state. The Court concluded that the clause did not require California courts to apply Nevada's damage cap:

> [T]his Court's decision in Pacific Insurance Co. v. Industrial Accident Commission clearly establishes that the Full Faith and Credit Clause does not require a State to apply another State's law in violation of its own legitimate public policy. . . . The interest of California afforded such respect in the *Pacific Insurance* case was in providing for "the bodily safety and economic protection of employees injured within it." In this case, California's interest is the closely related and equally substantial one of providing "full protection to those who are injured on its highways through the negligence of both residents and non-residents." To effectuate this interest, California has provided by statute for jurisdiction in its courts over residents and nonresidents alike to allow those injured on its highways through the negligence of others to secure full compensation for their injuries in the California courts.
>
> In further implementation of that policy, California has unequivocally waived its own immunity from liability for the torts committed by its own agents and authorized full recovery even against the sovereign. As the California courts have found, to require California either to surrender jurisdiction or to limit respondents' recovery to the $25,000 maximum of the Nevada statute would be obnoxious to its statutorily based policies of jurisdiction over nonresident motorists and full recovery. The Full Faith and Credit Clause does not require this result.

What goes around comes around. Franchise Tax Bd. of California v. Hyatt, 538 U.S. 488 (2003), involved a Nevada resident who moved from California to Nevada. Hyatt filed a "part-year" resident income tax return in California for 1991, claiming that he moved to Nevada in October of that year. In 1993, the California Franchise Tax Board (CFTB) conducted an audit to determine whether Hyatt had underpaid the taxes that he owed to California, concluded that Hyatt remained a resident of California until sometime in 1992, and imposed substantial assessments and penalties against Hyatt. In 1998, with the tax issues and appeals still unresolved in California, Hyatt filed a lawsuit against CFTB in Nevada state courts asserting several intentional tort claims, including invasion of privacy, outrageous conduct, abuse of process, and fraud. The Nevada Supreme Court concluded that these claims could be litigated in Nevada courts based on Nevada's sovereign immunity principles as applied to state tax authorities: Nevada state agencies are immune from suit with the exception of suits alleging intentional torts committed within the course and scope of employment. The Nevada Supreme Court declined to apply California's absolute immunity rule, reasoning that "Nevada's interest in protecting its citizens from injurious intentional torts and bad faith acts committed by sister states' governmental employees" should be accorded greater weight "than California's policy favoring complete immunity for its taxation agency." On appeal, the U.S. Supreme Court, in a unanimous opinion, rejected California's argument that the full faith and credit clause requires that Nevada courts respect California's sovereign immunity rules. Instead, it found the case to be constitutionally indistinguishable from California's actions in the *Hall* case.

The *Hyatt* case returned to the Supreme Court after the Nevada courts, on remand, declined to give the CFTB the benefit of the $50,000 limit on damages to which Nevada state entities are entitled under Nevada law. Franchise Tax Bd. of California v. Hyatt, 136 S. Ct. 1277 (2016) [hereinafter *Hyatt II*]. The Court divided 4-4 on whether Nevada v. Hall's holding on state sovereign immunity should be overruled. (Justice Scalia was widely expected to provide the fifth vote for such overruling, but he died before the case was decided.) The Court went on to consider whether Nevada had violated the full faith and credit clause by refusing to limit the CFTB's damages:

> In light of our 4-to-4 affirmance of Nevada's exercise of jurisdiction over California's state agency, we must consider the second question: Whether the Constitution permits Nevada to award damages against California agencies under Nevada law that are greater than it could award against Nevada agencies in similar circumstances. We conclude that it does not. The Nevada Supreme Court has ignored both Nevada's typical rules of immunity and California's immunity-related statutes (insofar as California's statutes would prohibit a monetary recovery that is greater in amount than the maximum recovery that Nevada law would permit in similar circumstances). Instead, it has applied a special rule of law that evinces a " 'policy of hostility' " toward California. Doing so violates the Constitution's requirement that "Full Faith and Credit shall be given in each State to the public Acts, Records and judicial Proceedings of every other State." Art. IV, § 1.
>
> The Court's precedents strongly support this conclusion. . . . [W]hen affirming a State's decision to decline to apply another State's statute on this ground, we have consistently emphasized that the State had "not adopt[ed] any policy of hostility to the public Acts" of that other State.
>
> We followed this same approach when we considered the litigation now before us for the first time. Nevada had permitted Hyatt to sue California in Nevada courts. Nevada's courts recognized that California's law of complete immunity would prevent any recovery in this case. The Nevada Supreme Court consequently did not apply California law. It applied Nevada law instead. We upheld that decision as consistent with the Full Faith and Credit Clause. But in doing so, we emphasized both that (1) the Clause does not require one State to apply another State's law that violates its "own legitimate public policy," and (2) Nevada's choice of law did not "exhibi[t] a 'policy of hostility to the public Acts' of a sister State." Rather, Nevada had evinced "a healthy regard for California's sovereign status," we said, by "relying on the contours of Nevada's own sovereign immunity from suit as a benchmark for its analysis."
>
> The Nevada decision before us embodies a critical departure from its earlier approach. Nevada has not applied the principles of Nevada law ordinarily applicable to suits against Nevada's own agencies. Rather, it has applied a special rule of law applicable only in lawsuits against its sister States, such as California. With respect to damages awards greater than $50,000, the ordinary principles of Nevada law do not "conflic[t]" with California law, for both laws

would grant immunity. Similarly, in respect to such amounts, the "polic[ies]" underlying California law and Nevada's usual approach are not "opposed"; they are consistent.

But that is not so in respect to Nevada's special rule. That rule, allowing damages awards greater than $50,000, is not only "opposed" to California law; it is also inconsistent with the general principles of Nevada immunity law. The Nevada Supreme Court explained its departure from those general principles by describing California's system of controlling its own agencies as failing to provide "adequate" recourse to Nevada's citizens. It expressed concerns about the fact that California's agencies " 'operat[e] outside' " the systems of " 'legislative control, administrative oversight, and public accountability' " that Nevada applies to its own agencies. Such an explanation, which amounts to little more than a conclusory statement disparaging California's own legislative, judicial, and administrative controls, cannot justify the application of a special and discriminatory rule. Rather, viewed through a full faith and credit lens, a State that disregards its own ordinary legal principles on this ground *is* hostile to another State. A constitutional rule that would permit this kind of discriminatory hostility is likely to cause chaotic interference by some States into the internal, legislative affairs of others. Imagine, for example, that many or all States enacted such discriminatory, special laws, and justified them on the sole basis that (in their view) a sister State's law provided inadequate protection to their citizens. Would each affected sister State have to change its own laws? Entirely? Piece-by-piece, in order to respond to the new special laws enacted by every other State? It is difficult to reconcile such a system of special and discriminatory rules with the Constitution's vision of 50 individual and equally dignified States. In light of the "constitutional equality" among the States, Nevada has not offered "sufficient policy considerations" to justify the application of a special rule of Nevada law that discriminates against its sister States. In our view, Nevada's rule lacks the "healthy regard for California's sovereign status" that was the hallmark of its earlier decision, and it reflects a constitutionally impermissible " 'policy of hostility to the public Acts' of a sister State."

In so holding we need not, and do not, intend to return to a complex "balancing-of-interests approach to conflicts of law under the Full Faith and Credit Clause." Long ago this Court's efforts to apply that kind of analysis led to results that seemed to differ depending, for example, upon whether the case involved commercial law, a shareholders' action, insurance claims, or workman's compensation statutes. We have since abandoned that approach, and we continue to recognize that a State need not " 'substitute the statutes of other states for its own statutes dealing with a subject matter concerning which it is competent to legislate.'" But here, we can safely conclude that, in devising a special—and hostile—rule for California, Nevada has not "sensitively applied principles of comity with a healthy regard for California's sovereign status." Hyatt I, 538 U.S. at 499. See Allstate v. Hague [*supra* p. 297] (Stevens, J., concurring in judgment) (Clause is properly brought to bear when a State's choice of law "threatens the federal interest in national unity by unjustifiably infringing upon the legitimate interests of another State").

Thus, although the full faith and credit clause does not require the forum state to apply its sister state's law entitling instrumentalities to immunity or to a damage cap, principles of comity having their source in the clause do (at least sometimes) prevent the forum from holding sister states liable to a greater extent than its own instrumentalities would be. Chief Justice Roberts and Justice Thomas dissented, writing that "[t]he Court's decision is contrary to our precedent holding that the Clause does not block a State from applying its own law to redress an injury within its own borders." Note that the dissenters use the word "law" to mean the forum state's whole law, including the part of its law that extends the reach of the damage cap only to the forum state's own instrumentalities. Compare Note 1, *supra* page 121.

Should the *Hyatt II* majority opinion be understood to have held that, under the Full Faith and Credit Clause, a state may apply to sister state instrumentalities its own *internal* law (that is, the law that the state applies to purely local events and parties) or the internal law of its sister state, but may not devise a special law that treats instrumentalities of sister states less favorably than the forum state's own instrumentalities? On this reading, Nevada may apply to California state instrumentalities (a) Nevada law entitling state instrumentalities to a damage cap; or (b) California law entitling state instrumentalities to immunity, but not (c) a hybrid that would entitle forum state instrumentalities but not sister state instrumentalities to a damage cap. If so, does this holding extend to suits against out-of-state parties that are not state instrumentalities? Does *Hyatt II* call into question state laws that treat out-of-state parties less favorably than local parties? Compare Section C of this Chapter, *infra*. Or is the holding limited to suits against instrumentalities of sister states?

The *Hyatt* case reached the Supreme Court a third time, and this time the Court overruled Nevada v. Hall's holding that states are not entitled to immunity from suit in the courts of sister states. 139 S. Ct. 1485 (2019). The Court in *Hyatt III* concluded (5-4) that "*Nevada v. Hall* is contrary to our constitutional design and the understanding of sovereign immunity shared by the States that ratified the Constitution" to the extent it permits states to entertain suits against sister states. *Id.* at 1492. Thus, constitutional principles quite apart from the full faith and credit clause bar suits against a state in the courts of sister states. In light of the overruling of Nevada v. Hall, does the full faith and credit holding in *Hyatt II* retain any relevance? The answer depends in part on whether that holding extends to suits that are not against state instrumentalities. Even if *Hyatt II's* holding is limited to suits involving state action, however, it may retain relevance if the doctrine of state sovereign immunity recognized in *Hyatt III* permits some such suits to proceed. For example, the parallel doctrine that protects states from suit in the federal courts does not bar suits against state *officials* sued in their personal capacity, even if based on conduct by those officials performed in their official capacities (although such officials are entitled to a different type of immunity, known as "official immunity"). *See generally* Vázquez, *What is Eleventh Amendment Immunity?*, 106 Yale L.J. 1683 (1997); Vázquez, *Eleventh Amendment Schizophrenia*, 75 Notre Dame L. Rev. 859 (2000). The Court will have to flesh out the contours of the immunity to which states are entitled under *Hyatt III*, but it is possible that it permits some suits in state court involving the conduct of sister state officials. If so, under *Hyatt II's* reading of the full faith and credit clause, states may be required to treat such officials no less favorably than they treat their own officials.

C.   Constitutional Limitations on Interstate Discrimination

Two sources of constitutional limitation on choice of law, other than due process and full faith and credit, are the equal protection clause and the privileges and immunities clause. These provisions place limits on interstate discrimination, as does the commerce clause (discussed in Section D, *infra*). In general, the First Restatement avoided equal protection and other discrimination problems by concentrating on places rather than people. The opportunity arose under interest analysis, however, to make arguments that equal protection was being denied. For example, if a driver from State *A*, with a guest statute, carries one passenger from State *A*, and one from State *B*, which has no guest statute, and is involved in an accident in State *B*, Judge Fuld's first rule would seem to dictate that the first passenger could not recover from the driver, while Judge Fuld's second rule would seem to allow the second passenger to recover. The different treatment received by the two passengers involved in the same accident strongly suggests a denial of equal protection. The cases do not yet seem to have addressed this problem, but Professors Brainerd Currie and Herma Hill Kay concluded that there are some situations in which discrimination on the basis of one's home state's law may be upheld against attack under the privileges and immunities clause. Since that clause is designed to prevent discrimination based on state citizenship, the suggestion would seem equally pertinent for equal protection. *See* Currie, *Selected Essays on the Conflict of Laws* 503-511 (1963). In response, it has been forthrightly argued that the domiciliary-based discrimination-of-interest analysis is unconstitutional. Laycock, *Equality and the Citizens of Sister States*, 15 Fla. St. L. Rev. 431 (1987) and *Equal Citizens of Equal and Territorial States: The Constitutional Foundations of Choice of Law*, 92 Colum. L. Rev. 249 (1992).

The problem is more complicated than might first appear. First, some of the old-style First Restatement rules relied upon domiciliary-connecting factors. *See, e.g.*, White v. Tennant, *supra* page 51. Arguably, these rules are different from modern choice-of-law theory in the way that they use the parties' domicile. Under the Restatement, the local person is as likely to be hurt as helped by application of local law, while under modern theory, a state may have an "interest" only if local law is of benefit to the local person.

Second, it is not always unconstitutional to give locals an advantage; different treatment is acceptable where there is an adequate justification, as the cases below demonstrate.

Third, choice of law necessarily involves the making of differentiations. The forum is not entitled simply to apply forum law to every case that comes before it. These discriminations must obviously turn on either the location of events or on the personal affiliations of individuals. Why are domiciliary connections the suspect factors? It would be possible to argue in the alternative that First Restatement rules are the ones that are unconstitutional because they treat people differently depending on "obviously irrelevant" factors, such as where an accident occurs. This view was set forth by Professors Currie and Kay in Currie, *Selected Essays in the Conflict of Laws* (1963), at 454-455 (privileges and immunities) and 575-583 (equal protection). Discrimination based on territorial factors and discrimination based on the domicile of the benefited party are therefore constitutional competitors of one another; at least one *must* be constitutional, and it is possible that *only one* is. *See generally* Gergen, *Equality and the Conflict of Laws*, 73 Iowa L. Rev. 893 (1988).

Both sides of the dispute tend to argue that the differentiation that they favor is simply a result of our having a federal system of government. Division into 50 states means a division of lawmaking power, and thus a difference in treatment. To this date, courts have not been convinced that an equal protection or privileges violation results from reliance on territorial factors. Given the Supreme Court's recent approval of traditional choice-of-law rules in Sun Oil Co. v. Wortman, *supra* page 316, one suspects that the Currie analysis of equal protection is unlikely to be adopted. Discrimination on the basis of personal affiliation, on the other hand, has long been thought problematic. The cases below survey some interstate discrimination principles and suggest that in at least certain circumstances, discrimination against nonresidents is unconstitutional.

Austin v. New Hampshire
420 U.S. 656 (1975)

Justice MARSHALL delivered the opinion of the Court.

Appellants are residents of Maine who were employed in New Hampshire during the 1970 tax year and as such were subject to the New Hampshire Commuters Income Tax. On behalf of themselves and others similarly situated, they petitioned the New Hampshire Superior Court for a declaration that the tax violates the Privileges and Immunities and Equal Protection Clauses of the Constitutions of New Hampshire and of the United States. The cause was transferred directly to the New Hampshire Supreme Court, which upheld the tax. We noted probable jurisdiction of the federal constitutional claims, and on the basis of the Privileges and Immunities Clause of Art. IV, we now reverse.

I

The New Hampshire Commuters Income Tax imposes a tax on nonresidents' New Hampshire-derived income in excess of $2,000. The tax rate is 4% except that if the nonresident taxpayer's State of residence would impose a lesser tax had the income been earned in that State, the New Hampshire tax is reduced to the amount of the tax that the State of residence would impose. Employers are required to withhold 4% of the nonresident's income, however, even if his home State would tax him at less than the full 4%. Any excess tax withheld is refunded to the nonresident upon his filing a New Hampshire tax return after the close of the tax year showing that he is entitled to be taxed at a rate less than 4%.

The Commuters Income Tax initially imposes a tax of 4% as well on the income earned by New Hampshire residents outside the State. It then exempts such income from the tax, however: (1) if it is taxed by the State from which it is derived; (2) if it is exempted from taxation by the State from which it is derived;

or (3) if the State from which it is derived does not tax such income. The effect of these imposition and exemption features is that no resident of New Hampshire is taxed on his out-of-state income. Nor is the domestic earned income of New Hampshire residents taxed. In effect, then, the State taxes only the incomes of nonresidents working in New Hampshire; it is on the basis of this disparate treatment of residents and nonresidents that appellants challenge New Hampshire's right to tax their income from employment in that State.

II

The Privileges and Immunities Clause of Art. IV, §2, cl. 1, provides: "The Citizens of each State shall be entitled to all Privileges and Immunities of Citizens in the several States." The Clause thus establishes a norm of comity without specifying the particular subjects as to which citizens of one State coming within the jurisdiction of another are guaranteed equality of treatment. The origins of the Clause do reveal, however, the concerns of central import to the Framers. During the preconstitutional period, the practice of some States denying to outlanders the treatment that its citizens demanded for themselves was widespread. The fourth of the Articles of Confederation was intended to arrest this centrifugal tendency with some particularity. It provided:

> "The better to secure and perpetuate mutual friendship and intercourse among the people of the different States in this Union, the free inhabitants of each of these States, paupers, vagabonds and fugitives from justice excepted, shall be entitled to all privileges and immunities of free citizens in the several States; and the people of each State shall have free ingress and regress to and from any other State, and shall enjoy therein all the privileges of trade and commerce, subject to the same duties, impositions and restrictions as the inhabitants thereof respectively."

The discriminations at which the Clause was aimed were by no means eradicated during the short life of the Confederation, and the provision was carried over into the comity article of the Constitution in briefer form but with no change of substance or intent, unless it was to strengthen the force of the Clause in fashioning a single nation. Thus, in the first, and long the leading, explication of the Clause, Mr. Justice Washington, sitting as Circuit Justice, deemed the fundamental privileges and immunities protected by the Clause to be essentially coextensive with those calculated to achieve the purpose of forming a more perfect Union, including "an exemption from higher taxes or impositions than are paid by the other citizens of the state."

In resolving constitutional challenges to state tax measures this Court has made it clear that "in taxation, even more than in other fields, legislatures possess the greatest freedom in classification." Our review of tax classifications has generally been concomitantly narrow, therefore, to fit the broad discretion vested in the state legislatures. When a tax measure is challenged as an undue burden on an activity granted special constitutional recognition, however, the appropriate degree of inquiry is that necessary to protect the competing constitutional value from erosion.

This consideration applies equally to the protection of individual liberties and to the maintenance of our constitutional federalism. The Privileges and Immunities Clause, by making noncitizenship or nonresidence[8] an improper basis for locating a special burden, implicates not only the individual's right to nondiscriminatory treatment but also, perhaps more so, the structural balance essential to the concept of federalism. Since nonresidents are not represented in the taxing State's legislative halls, judicial acquiescence in taxation schemes that burden them particularly would remit them to such redress as they could secure through their own State; but "to prevent [retaliation] was one of the chief ends sought to be accomplished by the adoption of the Constitution." Our prior cases, therefore, reflect an appropriately heightened concern for the integrity of the Privileges and Immunities Clause by erecting a standard of review substantially more rigorous than that applied to state tax distinctions among, say, forms of business organizations or different trades and professions.

The first such case was Ward v. Maryland, 12 Wall. 418 (1871), challenging a statute under which nonresidents were required to pay $300 per year for a license to trade in goods not manufactured in Maryland, while resident traders paid a fee varying from $12 to $150, depending upon the value of their inventory. The State attempted to justify this disparity as a response to the practice of "runners" from industrial States selling by sample in Maryland, free from local taxation and other overhead expenses incurred by resident merchants. It portrayed the fee as a "tax upon a particular business or trade, carried on in a particular mode," rather than a discrimination against traders from other States. Although the tax may not have been "palpably arbitrary," the discrimination could not be denied and the Court held that it violated the guarantee of the Privileges and Immunities Clause against "being subjected to any higher tax or excise than that exacted by law of . . . permanent residents."

In Travelers' Insurance Co. v. Connecticut, 185 U.S. 364 (1902), the Court considered a tax laid on the value of stock in local insurance corporations. The shares of nonresident stockholders were assessed at their market value, while those owned by residents were assessed at market value less the proportionate value of all real estate held by the corporation and on which it had already paid a local property tax. In analyzing the apparent discrimination thus worked against nonresidents, the Court took account of the overall distribution of the tax burden between resident and nonresident stockholders. Finding that nonresidents paid no local property taxes, while residents paid those taxes at an average rate approximating or exceeding the rate imposed by the State on nonresidents' stock, the Court upheld the scheme. While more precise equality between the two classes could have been obtained, it was "enough that the State has secured a reasonably fair distribution of burdens, and that no intentional discrimination has

---

8. For purposes of analyzing a taxing scheme under the Privileges and Immunities Clause the terms "citizen" and "resident" are essentially interchangeable. Travis v. Yale & Towne Mfg. Co., 252 U.S. 60, 79 (1920) ("a general taxing scheme . . . if it discriminates against all nonresidents, has the necessary effect of including in the discrimination those who are citizens of other States"); Smith v. Loughman, 245 N.Y. 486, 492, 157 N.E. 753, 755, *cert. denied*, 275 U.S. 560 (1927); *see* Toomer v. Witsell, 334 U.S. 385, 397 (1948).

been made against non-residents." Their contribution to state and local property tax revenues, that is, was no more than the ratable share of their property within the State.

The principles of *Ward* and *Travelers'* were applied to taxes on nonresidents' local incomes in Shaffer v. Carter, 252 U.S. 37 (1920), and Travis v. Yale & Towne Mfg. Co., *supra*. *Shaffer* upheld the Oklahoma tax on income derived from local property and business by a nonresident where the State also taxed the income—from wherever derived—of its own citizens. Putting aside "theoretical distinctions" and looking to "the practical effect and operation" of the scheme, the nonresident was not treated more onerously than the resident in any particular, and in fact was called upon to make no more than his ratable contribution to the support of the state government. The New York tax on residents' and nonresidents' income at issue in *Travis*, by contrast, could not be sustained when its actual effect was considered. The tax there granted personal exemptions to each resident taxpayer for himself and each dependent, but it made no similar provision for nonresidents. The disparity could not be "deemed to be counterbalanced" by an exemption for nonresidents' interest and dividend income because it was not likely "to benefit non-residents to a degree corresponding to the discrimination against them." Looking to "the concrete, the particular incidence" of the tax, therefore, the Court said of the many New Jersey and Connecticut residents who worked in New York:

> "They pursue their several occupations side by side with residents of the State of New York—in effect competing with them as to wages, salaries, and other terms of employment. Whether they must pay a tax upon the first $1,000 or $2,000 of income, while their associates and competitors who reside in New York do not, makes a substantial difference. . . . This is not a case of occasional or accidental inequality due to circumstances personal to the taxpayer . . . but a general rule, operating to the disadvantage of all non-residents . . . and favoring all residents. . . ."

252 U.S., at 80-81 (citations omitted).

III

Against this background establishing a rule of substantial equality of treatment for the citizens of the taxing State and nonresident taxpayers, the New Hampshire Commuters Income Tax cannot be sustained. The overwhelming fact, as the State concedes, is that the tax falls exclusively on the income of nonresidents; and it is not offset even approximately by other taxes imposed upon residents alone. Rather, the argument advanced in favor of the tax is that the ultimate burden it imposes is "not more onerous in effect," Shaffer v. Carter, *supra*, on nonresidents because their total state tax liability is unchanged once the tax credit they receive from their State of residence is taken into account. While this argument has an initial appeal, it cannot be squared with the underlying policy of comity to which the Privileges and Immunities Clause commits us.

According to the State's theory of the case, the only practical effect of the tax is to divert to New Hampshire tax revenues that would otherwise be paid to

Maine, an effect entirely within Maine's power to terminate by repeal of its credit provision for income taxes paid to another State. The Maine Legislature could do this, presumably, by amending the provision so as to deny a credit for taxes paid to New Hampshire while retaining it for the other 48 States. Putting aside the acceptability of such a scheme, and the relevance of any increase in appellants' home state taxes that the diversionary effect is said to have, we do not think the possibility that Maine could shield its residents from New Hampshire's tax cures the constitutional defect of the discrimination in that tax. In fact, it compounds it. For New Hampshire in effect invites appellants to induce their representatives, if they can, to retaliate against it.

A similar, though much less disruptive, invitation was extended by New York in support of the discriminatory personal exemption at issue in *Travis*. The statute granted the nonresident a credit for taxes paid to his State of residence on New York-derived income only if that State granted a substantially similar credit to New York residents subject to its income tax. New York contended that it thus "looked forward to the speedy adoption of an income tax by the adjoining States," which would eliminate the discrimination "by providing similar exemptions similarly conditioned." To this the Court responded in terms fully applicable to the present case. Referring to the anticipated legislative response of the neighboring States, it stated:

> "This, however, is wholly speculative; New York has no authority to legislate for the adjoining States; and we must pass upon its statute with respect to its effect and operation in the existing situation. . . . A State may not barter away the right, conferred upon its citizens by the Constitution of the United States, to enjoy the privileges and immunities of citizens when they go into other States. Nor can discrimination be corrected by retaliation; to prevent this was one of the chief ends sought to be accomplished by the adoption of the Constitution."

252 U.S., at 82.[12]

Nor, we may add, can the constitutionality of one State's statutes affecting nonresidents depend upon the present configuration of the statutes of another State.

Since we dispose of this case under Art. IV, §2, of the Constitution, we have no occasion to address the equal protection arguments directed at the disparate treatment of residents and nonresidents and at that feature of the statute that causes the rate of taxation imposed upon nonresidents to vary among them depending upon the rate established by their State of residence.

Reversed.

Justice DOUGLAS took no part in the consideration or decision of this case.

---

12. Neither *Travis* nor the present case should be taken in any way to denigrate the value of reciprocity in such matters. The evil at which they are aimed is the unilateral imposition of a disadvantage upon nonresidents, not reciprocally favorable treatment of nonresidents by States that coordinate their tax laws.

Justice BLACKMUN, dissenting. For me, this is a noncase. I would dismiss the appeal for want of a substantial federal question. We have far more urgent demands upon our limited time than this kind of litigation.

Because the New Hampshire income tax statutes operate in such a way that no New Hampshire resident is ultimately subjected to the State's income tax, the case at first glance appears to have some attraction. That attraction, however, is superficial and, upon careful analysis, promptly fades and disappears entirely. The reason these appellants, who are residents of Maine, not of New Hampshire, pay a New Hampshire tax is because the Maine Legislature—the appellant's own duly elected representatives—has given New Hampshire the option to divert this increment of tax (on a Maine resident's income earned in New Hampshire) from Maine to New Hampshire, and New Hampshire willingly has picked up that option. All that New Hampshire has done is what Maine specifically permits and, indeed, invites it to do. If Maine should become disenchanted with its bestowed bounty, its legislature may change the Maine statute. The crux is the statute of Maine, not the statute of New Hampshire. The appellants, therefore, are really complaining about their own statute. It is ironic that the State of Maine, which allows the credit, had made an appearance in this case as an amicus urging, in effect, the denial of the credit by an adjudication of unconstitutionality of New Hampshire's statute. It seems to me that Maine should be here seeking to uphold its own legislatively devised plan or turn its attention to its own legislature. . . .

One wonders whether this is just a lawyers' lawsuit. Certainly, the appellants, upon prevailing today, have no direct or apparent financial gain. Relief for them from the New Hampshire income tax results only in a corresponding, pro tanto, increase in their Maine income tax. Dollarwise, they emerge at exactly the same point. The single difference is that their State, Maine, enjoys the tax on the New Hampshire-earned income, rather than New Hampshire. Where, then, is the injury? If there is an element of injury, it is Maine-imposed.

We waste our time, therefore, theorizing and agonizing about the Privileges and Immunities Clause and equal protection in this case. But if that exercise in futility is nevertheless indicated, I see little merit in the appellants' quest for relief. It is settled that absolute equality is not a requisite under the Privileges and Immunities Clause. And I fail to perceive unconstitutional unequal protection on New Hampshire's part. If inequality exists, it is due to differences in the respective income tax rates of the States that border upon New Hampshire.

I say again that this is a noncase, made seemingly attractive by high-sounding suggestions of inequality and unfairness. The State of Maine has the cure within its grasp, and if the cure is of importance to it and to its citizens, such as appellants, it and they should be about adjusting Maine's house rather than coming here complaining of a collateral effect of its own statute.

Questions and Comments

(1) Under interest analysis it is assumed that the forum has an interest in the well-being of its own residents but not, generally, in the well-being of

nonresidents. When forum law favors a resident, it is to be applied under the Currie approach (either because the forum is the only interested jurisdiction or because forum law applies in the face of a true conflict). On the other hand, if we substitute a nonresident for the resident, the forum interest may disappear, and the analysis may yield application of a different state's law. That looks a lot like discrimination on the basis of state citizenship, forbidden by the privileges and immunities clause. That worried Currie, and he addressed the problem at length (with coauthor Herma Kay) in Chapter 10 of Currie, *Selected Essays on the Conflict of Laws* (1963). The basic answer was that such "discrimination" was acceptable if it merely resulted in subjecting the nonresident to the law of his home state.

Does *Austin* undermine the Currie solution? Professor Ely thinks so: "If *Austin* is right as written, the dominant contemporary choice-of-law theory is unconstitutional." Ely, *Choice of Law and the State's Interest in Protecting Its Own*, 23 Wm. & Mary L. Rev. 173, 186-187 (1981).

Ely notes two possible ways of avoiding that conclusion. First, *Austin* may be wrong: If the purpose of the privileges and immunities clause is to protect people from legislatures and courts of other states, with whom they have no political influence, adequate protection is afforded by treating them the way that their own legislature and courts would—that is, applying their own home state's law to them. Note, however, that under interest analysis, the nonresident is not *always* treated according to home-state law, because if the forum has an interest in applying its own law, it will do so. The nonresident, in other words, is held to his or her home-state law only in those circumstances where it is disadvantageous. Where home-state law *helps* the nonresident, its application is not guaranteed. Second, Ely says, the Court was obviously unaware of the conflicts implication of its decision in *Austin* since the plurality in *Hague*, page 297 *supra*, seemed to uphold the legitimacy of Minnesota's interest in one who had acquired a domicile in Minnesota. Such an interest should not be both a defense of applying Minnesota law against a due process attack and the basis for a privileges and immunities attack (because Minnesota would have "discriminated" against someone who had not acquired Minnesota residency by not applying its law to such a person). Ely, at 187-189.

(2) *Austin*'s implications for interest analysis might be further limited by noting: (a) In *Austin*, New Hampshire applied New Hampshire law, which itself discriminated on the basis of state residency; in a conflicts case, the forum is not applying its own law, with two different results depending on residency, but in a sense is applying two different states' laws, each of which has a legitimate claim to application; and (b) the privileges and immunities cases decided by the Supreme Court involve the state as litigant (tax cases, etc.), while conflicts cases involve the state merely as arbitrator. Are these observations enough to save interest analysis from constitutional invalidity?

(3) In Pennsylvania v. New Jersey, 426 U.S. 660 (1976), the Court turned down a suit to recover taxes "diverted" from the treasuries of the plaintiff states to the treasury of New Jersey by a New Jersey scheme virtually identical to that condemned in *Austin*.

The heart of the Court's reasoning lay in the fact that

[i]n neither of the suits at bar has the defendant State inflicted any injury upon the Plaintiff States through the imposition of the taxes held [or] alleged . . . to be unconstitutional. The injuries to the plaintiffs' fiscs were self-inflicted, resulting from decisions by their respective legislatures. . . . [N]othing prevents Pennsylvania from withdrawing that credit for taxes paid to New Jersey. No State can be heard to complain about damage inflicted by its own hand.

Id. at 664.

The Court went on to say that the equal protection and privileges and immunities clauses protect "people, not states." *Id.* at 664-665. The right of a state to maintain actions of this nature as parens patriae was rejected as carrying the potential of converting any private suit desired by the state into a case within the original jurisdiction of the Supreme Court.

(4) In Baldwin v. Montana Fish & Game Commn., 436 U.S. 371 (1978), the Supreme Court rejected a privileges and immunities attack on a Montana law that charged a substantially higher fee for nonresidents than residents for fishing and hunting licenses. Only those privileges and immunities that bear on the vitality of the nation as a whole were deemed to be within the protection of the clause. But very shortly thereafter, the Court struck down Alaska's law preferring state residents for jobs arising out of oil and gas leases or permits for oil and gas pipelines to which the state was a party. Hicklin v. Orbeck, 437 U.S. 518 (1978). Justice Brennan, who had dissented in *Baldwin*, wrote for a unanimous Court in rejecting an earlier line of cases (*see, e.g.*, Corfield v. Coryell, 6 F. Cas. 546 (C.C.E.D. Pa. 1823)) that had allowed states to discriminate with respect to benefits derived from state-owned property. Can *Baldwin* be squared with *Orbeck*?

G. D. Searle & Co. v. Cohn
455 U.S. 404 (1982)

Justice BLACKMUN delivered the opinion of the Court.

A New Jersey statute, N.J. Stat. Ann. §2A:14-22 (West) (1952), tolls the limitation period of an action against a foreign corporation that is amenable to jurisdiction in New Jersey courts but that has in New Jersey no person or officer upon whom process may be served. The United States Court of Appeals for the Third Circuit in this case held that the statute does not violate the Equal Protection and Due Process Clauses of the Fourteenth Amendment. We agree, but we vacate the Court of Appeals' Judgment and remand the case for consideration of petitioner's Commerce Clause challenge to the statute.

I

Respondents, Susan and Walter Cohn, are husband and wife. In 1963, Susan Cohn suffered a stroke. Eleven years later, in 1974, the Cohns sued petitioner, G.D. Searle & Co., in the Superior Court of New Jersey, Essex County, alleging that Susan Cohn's stroke was caused by her use of an oral contraceptive manufactured by petitioner. Petitioner was served under New Jersey's long-arm rule, N.J. Ct. Rule 4:4-4(c)(1) (1969). Petitioner removed the suit to federal court and thereafter moved for summary judgment based upon New Jersey's two-year statute of limitation, N.J. stat. Ann. §2A:14-2 (West) (1952), governing an "action at law for an injury to the person caused by . . . wrongful act." Respondents countered with §2A:14-22. That section tolls the statute of limitation for a cause of action against a foreign corporation that "is not represented" in New Jersey "by any person or officer upon whom summons or other original process may be served."

The District Court ruled that petitioner was not represented in New Jersey for the purposes of the tolling provision. Nevertheless, it held that respondents' suit was barred. According to the District Court, the tolling provision had operated to preserve only causes of action against corporate defendants that were not subject to in personam jurisdiction in New Jersey. With the enactment of New Jersey's long-arm rule, now N.J. Ct. Rule 4:4-4(c), the rationale for the pre-existing tolling provision ceased to exist. On this reasoning, the court held that the tolling provision served no logical purpose, found it invalid under the Equal Protection Clause, and ruled that the two-year statute of limitation therefore barred respondent's suit.

Respondents appealed. Before the Court of Appeals reached a decision, however, the Supreme Court of New Jersey decided Velmohos v. Maren Engineering Corp. That court ruled, as a matter of New Jersey law, that the tolling provision continued in force despite the advent of long-arm jurisdiction. In addition, the court concluded that the tolling provision did not violate the Equal Protection or Due Process Clauses of the Fourteenth Amendment, because the increased difficulty of out-of-state service provided a rational basis for tolling the statute of limitation in a suit against an unrepresented foreign corporation.

The Court of Appeals then followed the New Jersey Supreme Court's lead and reversed the District Court. Summing up what it felt to be the rational basis for the tolling provision, the Court of Appeals explained:

> "Since service of process under the long-arm statute is more difficult and time-consuming to achieve than service within the state, and since out-of-state, non-represented corporate defendants may be difficult to locate let alone serve, tolling the statute of limitations protects New Jersey plaintiffs and facilitates their lawsuits against such defendants."

Because of the novel and substantial character of the federal issue involved, we granted certiorari.

II

Like the Court of Appeals, we conclude that the New Jersey statute does not violate the Equal Protection Clause. In the absence of a classification that is inherently invidious or that impinges upon fundamental rights, a state statute is to be upheld against equal protection attack if it is rationally related to the achievement of legitimate governmental ends. The New Jersey tolling provision need satisfy only this constitutional minimum. As the Court explained in Chase Securities Corp. v. Donaldson:

"[Statutes of limitation] represent a public policy about the privilege to litigate. Their shelter has never been regarded as what now is called a "fundamental" right or what used to be called a "natural" right of the individual. He may, of course, have the protection of the policy while it exists, but the history of pleas of limitation shows them to be good only by legislative grace and to be subject to a relatively large degree of legislative control."

See also Campbell v. Holt.[6]

Petitioner insists that the tolling statute no longer is rationally related to a legitimate state objective. Repeating the argument it made below, petitioner claims that the statute's only purpose was to preserve causes of action for those New Jersey plaintiffs unable to obtain in personam jurisdiction over unrepresented foreign corporations. With the presence now of long-arm jurisdiction, petitioner contends, there is no longer a valid reason for tolling the limitation period for a suit against an amenable foreign corporation without a New Jersey representative.

We note at the outset, and in passing, that petitioner's argument fails as a matter of state law. The New Jersey Supreme Court disagreed with petitioner's interpretation of the statute. That court observed that the State's original tolling provision did not mention corporations and thus treated them like all other defendants. In 1949, the state legislature amended the statute and exempted corporations except those foreign corporations "not represented" in New Jersey. Consequently, the court reasoned, the tolling provision was not rendered meaningless by the subsequent acceptance of long-arm jurisdiction. As construed by the highest judicial authority on New Jersey law, the meaning of the tolling statute cannot be confined as narrowly as petitioner would like.

When the statute is examined under the Equal Protection Clause, it survives petitioner's constitutional challenge because rational reasons support tolling the limitation period for unrepresented foreign corporations despite the institution of long-arm jurisdiction in New Jersey. First, the unrepresented foreign corporation remains potentially difficult to locate. Long-arm jurisdiction does not alleviate this problem, since a New Jersey plaintiff must find the unrepresented foreign corporation before it can be served. It is true, of course, that respondents had little or no trouble locating this particular, well-known defendant-petitioner, but the tolling provision is premised on a reasonable assumption that unrepresented foreign corporations, as a general rule, may not be so easy to find and serve.

Second, the institution of long-arm jurisdiction in New Jersey has not made service upon an unrepresented foreign corporation the equivalent of service upon a corporation with a New Jersey representative. The long-arm rule, N.J. Ct. Rule 4:4-4(c)(1) (1969), prescribes conditions upon extraterritorial service to ensure

---

6. Before the Court of Appeals, petitioner conceded that the tolling provision does not implicate a suspect classification. Before this court, petitioner argues for a heightened level of scrutiny because it is a corporation not doing business in New Jersey and therefore is without a voice in the New Jersey legislature. Only a rational basis, however, is required to support a distinction between foreign and domestic corporations. Western & S.L.I. Co. v. Bd. of Equalization, 451 U.S. 648 (1981). The same is true here where the tolling provision treats an unrepresented foreign corporation differently from a domestic corporation and from a foreign corporation having a New Jersey representative.

that New Jersey's long-arm jurisdiction has been properly invoked. In *Velmohos*, the New Jersey Supreme Court explained:

> "Under our rules, extra-territorial service is not simply an alternative to service within the State. Plaintiffs may not resort to out-of-state service unless proper efforts to effect service in New Jersey have failed. The rule imposes a further burden on a plaintiff by requiring him to gather sufficient information to satisfy a court that service is 'consistent with due process of law.'"

Thus, there are burdens a plaintiff must bear when he sues a foreign corporation lacking a New Jersey representative that he would not bear if the defendant were a domestic corporation or a foreign corporation with a New Jersey representative.

In response to these rationales for treating unrepresented foreign corporations differently from other corporations, petitioner argues that the tolling provision is unnecessary. Petitioner cites N.J. Ct. Rule 4:2-2 and contends that a plaintiff can preserve his cause of action against a hard-to-locate corporate defendant by filing a complaint and thereby halting the running of the limitation period. But this is not an adequate substitute for the tolling provision. A court may dismiss a case if it has not been prosecuted after six months, N.J. Ct. Rule 1:13-7, or if summons is not issued within 10 days of the filing of the complaint, N.J. Ct. Rule 4:4-1. In any event, a State may provide more than one solution for a perceived problem. The Court of Appeals appropriately commented: "Nothing in law or logic prevents the New Jersey legislature from providing New Jersey plaintiffs with a mechanism for relief from the burdens of suits against nonrepresented foreign corporations which is additional to any mechanism found in the Court Rules."

Petitioner also argues that a New Jersey plaintiff's burdens do not justify leaving a defendant open to suit without any time limit. In *Velmohos*, however, the New Jersey Supreme Court expressly authorized an unrepresented foreign corporation to plead another defense in response to a tardy suit. While the tolling provision denies an unrepresented foreign corporation the benefit of the statute of limitation, the corporation, the court stated flatly, remains free to plead laches. "If a plaintiff's delay is inexcusable and has resulted in prejudice to the defendant, the latter may raise the equitable defense of laches to bar the claim." Thus, under New Jersey law, an amenable, unrepresented foreign corporation may successfully raise a bar to a plaintiff's suit if the plaintiff's delay cannot be excused and the corporation has suffered "prejudice."

In sum, because of the burdens connected with serving unrepresented foreign corporations, we agree with the Court of Appeals and the New Jersey Supreme Court that the tolling provision does not deprive an unrepresented foreign corporation of the equal protection of the laws.[7]

[The Court remanded for consideration of a commerce clause challenge to the New Jersey statute.]

---

7. Petitioner also presses a due process claim. In the Court of Appeals, petitioner argued that the tolling statute violates due process "by unfairly and irrationally denying certain foreign corporations the benefit of the Statute of Limitations without furthering any legitimate societal interest." The Court of Appeals rejected petitioner's due process challenge to the statute at the same time that it rejected petitioner's equal protection contention. Indeed, this due process argument is nothing more than a restatement of petitioner's equal protection claim.

[Justice POWELL, joined by Chief Justice BURGER, concurred in Parts I and II of the Court's opinion but dissented from Part III, feeling that it was appropriate for the Court to consider and determine the commerce clause issue. They expressed no opinion, however, on the merits of that issue.]

Justice STEVENS, dissenting.

The equal protection question in this case is novel. I agree with the Court that there is a rational basis for treating unregistered foreign corporations differently from registered corporations because they are somewhat more difficult to locate and to serve with process. Thus, a provision that merely gave plaintiffs a fair opportunity to overcome these difficulties—for example, a longer period of limitations for suits against such corporations, or a tolling provision limited to corporations that had not filed their current address with the Secretary of State—would unquestionably be permissible. But does it follow that it is also rational to deny such corporations the benefit of any statute of limitations? Because there is a rational basis for *some* differential treatment, does it automatically follow that *any* differential treatment is constitutionally permissible? I think not; in my view the Constitution requires a rational basis for the special burden imposed on the disfavored class as well as a reason for treating that class differently.

The Court avoids these troubling questions by noting that the New Jersey Supreme Court has stated that an unrepresented foreign corporation may plead the defense of laches in an appropriate case. But there are material differences between laches—which requires the defendant to prove inexcusable delay and prejudice—and the bar of limitations, which requires no such proof. Thus, the availability of this alternative defense neither eliminates the differential treatment nor provides a justification for it; the defense merely lessens its adverse consequences.

I can find no legitimate state purpose to justify the special burden imposed on unregistered foreign corporations by the challenged statute. I would reverse the judgment of the Court of Appeals.

Questions and Comments

(1) What is the difference between the privileges and immunities clause and the equal protection clauses as they bear on discrimination on the basis of state citizenship? Professor Ely implies that the rational-basis test might always be satisfied when a state treats nonresidents differently because they are nonresidents, making equal protection irrelevant, while the privileges and immunities clause is directed specifically at such discrimination. *See* Ely, *Choice of Law and the State's Interest in Protecting Its Own*, 23 Wm. & Mary L. Rev.

In this Court, petitioner has attempted to put forward a new due process argument. Petitioner notes that it can obtain the benefit of the statute of limitation by appointing an agent to accept service. Fearing that appointment of an agent might subject it to suit in New Jersey when there otherwise would not be the minimum contacts required for suit in the State under the Due Process Clause, *see* International Shoe Co. v. Washington, petitioner insists that New Jersey law violates due process by conditioning the benefit of the limitation period upon the appointment of a New Jersey agent. Because petitioner did not present this argument to the Court of Appeals, we do not address it.

173, 181 (1981). Do the opinions in *Austin* and *G. D. Searle* support this view? Another difference is that corporations cannot benefit from the privileges and immunities clause because they are not "citizens." Blake v. McClung, 172 U.S. 239 (1898).

(2) Are the distinctions between laches and a statute of limitations mentioned in Justice Stevens's dissent enough to establish his point that the discrimination against unrepresented foreign corporations is too great (even though some discrimination may be justified)? Does the majority's reference to the applicability of the laches doctrine concede the underlying point that discrimination may not be too severe, even under a rational-basis test (while denying the applicability of the point to the facts of the case)?

(3) In Burlington N. R. Co. v. Ford, 504 U.S. 648 (1992), the Supreme Court rejected an equal protection challenge to a Montana venue provision that made venue in cases brought against out-of-state corporate defendants proper in any county in the state but that restricted venue in cases brought against local corporate defendants to the county of their principal place of business. The rationale for the statute, which was upheld under a rational-basis test, was that with local defendants there was a substantial convenience justification for limiting venue to the principal place of business, but with out-of-state defendants there was very little convenience reason to favor one place of trial over another.

(4) Before this case came to the Supreme Court, the district court had dismissed an argument that the tolling provision was intended as a penalty to induce foreign corporations to obtain New Jersey licenses because it could not find any such intent in the relevant statutes. Cohn v. G. D. Searle & Co., 447 F. Supp. 903, 910-911 (D.N.J. 1978). The Supreme Court stated that "it seems to us that the District Court['s determination] was on sound ground," 455 U.S. at 413 n.8, but declined to resolve whether "New Jersey violate[d] the Commerce Clause by requiring it to register to do business in New Jersey in order to gain the benefit of the statute of limitation." *Id.* at 413. The Supreme Court addressed this question with respect to an analogous law in Ohio. *See* Bendix Autolite Corp. v. Midwesco Enterprises, Inc., 486 U.S. 888 (1988).

D.   "Extraterritorial" and "Inconsistent" Regulations

The Supreme Court has long invoked the "dormant" commerce clause as a basis for judicial preemption of state law that unduly burdens interstate commerce. The Court has devised a number of tests to serve this end. The central prohibition of the dormant commerce clause, like the prohibitions of the privileges and immunities and equal protection clauses, concerns state legislation that discriminates against out-of-staters. *See* CTS Corp. v. Dynamics Corp. of Am., 481 U.S. 69, 87 (1987). If a state law discriminates against out-of-staters, it is subject to "the strictest scrutiny of any purported legitimate local purpose and of the absence of nondiscriminatory alternatives." Hughes v. Oklahoma, 441 U.S.

322, 337 (1979). A second dormant commerce clause test applies when a state law is nondiscriminatory on its face but nonetheless significantly burdens interstate commerce. In this context the Court applies a balancing test: "Where the statute regulates evenhandedly to effectuate a legitimate local public interest, and its effects on interstate commerce are only incidental, it will be upheld unless the burden imposed on such commerce is clearly excessive in relation to the putative local benefits." Pike v. Bruce Church, Inc., 397 U.S. 137, 142 (1970).

The Supreme Court has also said that the dormant commerce clause prohibits certain state laws that regulate extraterritorially and others that lead to inconsistent regulatory burdens. These aspects of the dormant commerce clause are unsettled and poorly understood. But they are the most relevant to conflict of laws, as a state's decision to apply the law of a sister state to a case having foreign elements is generally regarded as the equivalent of a decision that forum law does not apply extraterritorially. *See Carroll*, *supra* page 17 ("Section 2590 of the Code . . . is to be interpreted in the light of universally recognized principles of private international or interstate law, as if its operation had been expressly limited to this State and as if its first line had read as follows: 'When a personal injury is received in Alabama by a servant or employee,' &c, &c."). *See generally* Vázquez, *Choice of Law as Geographic Scope Limitation*, in *Resolving Conflicts in the Law: Essays in Honour of Lea Brilmayer* (Giorgetti & Klein eds., 2019).

Brown-Forman Distillers Corp. v. New York State Liquor Auth.
476 U.S. 573 (1986)

Justice MARSHALL delivered the opinion of the Court. The State of New York requires every liquor distiller or producer that sells liquor to wholesalers within the State to sell at a price that is no higher than the lowest price the distiller charges wholesalers anywhere else in the United States. The issue in this case is whether that requirement violates the Commerce Clause of the Constitution.

I

New York extensively regulates the sale and distribution of alcoholic beverages within its borders. The State's Alcoholic Beverage Control Law (ABC Law) prohibits the manufacture and sale of alcoholic beverages within the State without the appropriate licenses, ABC Law §100(1) (McKinney 1970), and regulates the terms of all sales. . . .

This litigation concerns §101-b(3)(d) of the ABC Law, which requires any distiller or agent that files a schedule of prices to include an affirmation that "the bottle and case price of liquor to wholesalers set forth in such schedule is no higher than the lowest price at which such item of liquor will be sold by such [distiller] to any wholesaler anywhere in any other state of the United States or in the District of Columbia, or to any state (or state agency) which owns and operates retail liquor stores" during the month covered by the schedule. . . .

II

This Court has adopted what amounts to a two-tiered approach to analyzing state economic regulation under the Commerce Clause. When a state statute directly regulates or discriminates against interstate commerce, or when its effect is to favor in-state economic interests over out-of-state interests, we have generally struck down the statute without further inquiry. When, however, a statute has only indirect effects on interstate commerce and regulates evenhandedly, we have examined whether the State's interest is legitimate and whether the burden on interstate commerce clearly exceeds the local benefits. We have also recognized that there is no clear line separating the category of state regulation that is virtually per se invalid under the Commerce Clause, and the category subject to the Pike v. Bruce Church balancing approach. In either situation the critical consideration is the overall effect of the statute on both local and interstate activity.

A

Appellant does not dispute that New York's affirmation law regulates all distillers of intoxicating liquors evenhandedly, or that the State's asserted interest—to assure the lowest possible prices for its residents—is legitimate. Appellant contends that these factors are irrelevant, however, because the lowest-price affirmation provision of the ABC Law falls within that category of direct regulations of interstate commerce that the Commerce Clause wholly forbids. This is so, appellant contends, because the ABC Law effectively regulates the price at which liquor is sold in other States. By requiring distillers to affirm that they will make no sales anywhere in the United States at a price lower than the posted price in New York, appellant argues, New York makes it illegal for a distiller to reduce its price in other States during the period that the posted New York price is in effect. Appellant contends that this constitutes direct regulation of interstate commerce. The law also disadvantages consumers in other States, according to appellant, and is therefore the sort of "simple economic protectionism" that this Court has routinely forbidden. . . .

B

This Court has once before examined the extraterritorial effects of a New York affirmation statute. In Joseph E. Seagram & Sons, Inc. v. Hostetter, 384 U.S. 35 (1966), the Court considered the constitutionality, under the Commerce and Supremacy Clauses, of the predecessor to New York's current affirmation law. That law differed from the present version in that it required the distiller to affirm that its prices during a given month in New York would be no higher than the lowest price at which the item had been sold elsewhere during the *previous* month. The Court recognized in that case, as we have here, that the most important issue was whether the statute regulated out-of-state transactions. It concluded, however, that "[t]he mere fact that [the statute] is geared to appellants' pricing policies in other States is not sufficient to invalidate the statute." The Court distinguished [Baldwin v. Seelig, 294 U.S. 511 (1935)], *supra*, by concluding that any effects of New York's ABC Law on a distiller's pricing policies in other States were "largely matters of conjecture," *ibid*.

Appellant relies on United States Brewers Assn. v. Healy, 692 F.2d 275 (CA2 1982), *aff'd*, 464 U.S. 909 (1983), in seeking to distinguish the present case from *Seagram*. In *Healy*, the Court of Appeals for the Second Circuit considered a Connecticut price-affirmation statute for beer sales that is not materially different from the current New York ABC Law. The Connecticut statute, like the ABC Law, required sellers to post prices at the beginning of a month, and proscribed deviation from the posted prices during that month. The statute also required brewers to affirm that their prices in Connecticut were as low as the price at which they would sell beer in any bordering State during the effective month of the posted prices. The Court of Appeals distinguished *Seagram* based on the "prospective" nature of this affirmation requirement. It concluded that the Connecticut statute made it impossible for a brewer to lower its price in a bordering State in response to market conditions so long as it had a higher posted price in effect in Connecticut. By so doing, the statute "regulate[d] conduct occurring wholly outside the state," 692 F.2d, at 279, and thereby violated the Commerce Clause. We affirmed summarily, 464 U.S. 909 (1983).

C

We agree with appellants and with the *Healy* court that a "prospective" statute such as Connecticut's beer affirmation statute, or New York's liquor affirmation statute, regulates out-of-state transactions in violation of the Commerce Clause. Once a distiller has posted prices in New York, it is not free to change its prices elsewhere in the United States during the relevant month. Forcing a merchant to seek regulatory approval in one State before undertaking a transaction in another directly regulates interstate commerce. While New York may regulate the sale of liquor within its borders, and may seek low prices for its residents, it may not "project its legislation into [other States] by regulating the price to be paid" for liquor in those States.

That the ABC Law is addressed only to sales of liquor in New York is irrelevant if the "practical effect" of the law is to control liquor prices in other States. Southern Pacific Co. v. Arizona ex rel. Sullivan, 325 U.S. 761, 775 (1945). We cannot agree with New York that the practical effects of the affirmation law are speculative. It is undisputed that once a distiller's posted price is in effect in New York, it must seek the approval of the New York State Liquor Authority before it may lower its price for the same item in other States. It is not at all counter-intuitive, as the dissent maintains, to assume that the Liquor Authority would not permit appellant to reduce its New York price after the posted price has taken effect. . . .

Moreover, the proliferation of state affirmation laws following this Court's decision in *Seagram* has greatly multiplied the likelihood that a seller will be subjected to inconsistent obligations in different States. The ease with which

New York's lowest-price regulation can interfere with a distiller's operations in other States is aptly demonstrated by the controversy that gave rise to this lawsuit. By defining the "effective price" of liquor differently from other States, New York can effectively force appellant to abandon its promotional allowance program in States in which that program is legal, or force those other States to alter their own regulatory schemes in order to permit appellant to lower its New York prices without violating the affirmation laws of those States. Thus New York has "project[ed] its legislation" into other States, and directly regulated commerce therein, in violation of *Seelig, supra*.[6]

Questions and Comments

(1) How broadly should *Brown-Forman* be read? The opinion seems to suggest that there could be a commerce clause violation whenever a statute regulates conduct occurring wholly outside the state. *See also* Healy v. Beer Inst., Inc., 491 U.S. 324, 336 (1989) (similar case to *Brown-Forman*, asserting that "a statute that directly controls commerce occurring wholly outside the boundaries of a State exceeds the inherent limits of the enacting State's authority and is invalid regardless of whether the statute's extraterritorial reach was intended by the legislature"). Is the Court constitutionalizing territorialism? Should a commerce clause argument have been made in Allstate v. Hague, *supra* page 297? Doesn't the application of one state's law to a cross-border transaction or event always indirectly regulate conduct in another state?

(2) Note the Court's concern about potential proliferation of state laws, leading to possible inconsistent regulations. This problem is present also in garden-variety choice-of-law problems, is it not? Again, what about *Allstate*?

(3) Professors Goldsmith and Sykes note that it is commonplace in our federal system for one state's laws to have effects in another, and for multistate actors to face different regulations across states. They argue that the "extraterritoriality" and "inconsistency" prongs of the dormant commerce clause are best viewed as disguised forms of the Supreme Court's traditional dormant commerce clause "balancing" test. *See* Goldsmith & Sykes, *The Internet and the Dormant Commerce Clause*, 110 Yale L.J. 785, 803-808 (2001).

(4) California recently became the subject of a similar legal controversy, this time over California's statutes governing the production and sale of chicken eggs. In 2010, the California State Legislature passed A.B. 1437 (codified as §25996 of the California Health and Safety Code), which states that "[c]ommencing January 1, 2015, a shelled egg shall not be sold or contracted for sale for human consumption in California if the seller knows or should have known that the egg is the product of an egg-laying hen that was confined on a farm or place that is not in

---

6. While we hold that New York's prospective price affirmation statute violates the Commerce Clause, we do not necessarily attach constitutional significance to the difference between a prospective statute and the retrospective statute at issue in *Seagram*. Indeed, one could argue that the effects of the statute in *Seagram* do not differ markedly from the effects of the statute at issue in the present case. If there is a conflict between today's decision and the *Seagram* decision, however, there will be time enough to address that conflict should a case arise involving a retrospective statute. Because no such statute is before us now, we need not consider the continuing validity of *Seagram*.

compliance with animal care standards set forth in Chapter 13.8 (commencing with Section 25990)." California law would "require 116 square inches [of cage space] per [hen], compared to the industry standard 67 square inches." Stephanie Strom, *Wishing They All Could Be California Hens*, N.Y. Times, Mar. 3, 2014, available at *www.nytimes.com/2014/03/04/business/theyre-going-to-wish-they-all-could-be-california-hens.html*.

On February 3, 2014, the Attorney General of Missouri sued in the federal district court of the Eastern District of California to enjoin enforcement of A.B. 1437. Missouri ex rel. Koster v. Harris, No. 14-0067 (E.D. Cal. 2014). In the complaint, Missouri Attorney General Chris Koster argued that the California law would force Missouri farmers to "incur massive capital improvement costs to build larger habitats for some or all of Missouri's seven million egg-laying hens, or they can walk away from the state whose consumers bought *one third* of all eggs produced in Missouri last year." *Id.* The complaint alleged that the California law violates the commerce clause because it amounts to a protectionist measure against more price-competitive producers in other states. Is this case controlled by *Brown-Forman*? Why does the complaint not raise a due process objection?

The complaint alleged that the purpose of the law was protectionism; without the law, out-of-state producers would have a competitive advantage. But isn't there an argument that the real purpose was the protection of out-of-state chickens? Does that matter? Does the commerce clause prohibit all "extraterritorial legislation," or only protectionist measures? Do states have legitimate interests in the well-being of chickens residing elsewhere? The suit was eventually dismissed by the U.S. Court of Appeals for the Ninth Circuit for lack of standing. 847 F.3d 646 (9th Cir.), *cert. denied sub nom.* Missouri ex rel. Hawley v. Becerra, 137 S. Ct. 2188 (2017).

(5) In Pharmaceutical Research & Mfrs. of Am. v. Walsh, 538 U.S. 644, 669 (2003), the Court appeared to restrict the *Brown-Forman/Healy* line of cases to "price control or price affirmation statutes" that involve "tying the price of . . . in-state products to out-of-state prices." In Energy & Envt. Legal Inst. v. Epel, 793 F.3d 1169, 1170, 1173 (10th Cir. 2015), *cert. denied*, 136 S. Ct. 595 (2015), in an opinion by then-Judge Gorsuch, the court described the extraterritoriality branch of the dormant commerce clause as "the most dormant doctrine in dormant commerce clause jurisprudence," and held that this branch extended only to cases involving "(1) a price control or price affirmation regulation, (2) linking in-state prices to those charged elsewhere, with (3) the effect of raising costs for out-of-state consumers or rival businesses." These and other decisions have led scholars to pronounce the "death" of the extraterritoriality branch of the commerce clause. *See* Denning, *Extraterritoriality and the Dormant Commerce Clause: A Doctrinal Post-Mortem*, 73 La. L. Rev. 979, 990 (2013). However, in Assn. for Accessible Medicines v. Frosh, 887 F.3d 664, 670, 674 (4th Cir. 2018), *cert. denied*, 139 S. Ct. 1168 (2019), the U.S. Court of Appeals for the Fourth Circuit declared the other circuits' approaches "too narrow" and struck down a Maryland anti-gouging law that prohibited "unconscionable increase[s]" in the price of "essential" medications "made available for sale" in Maryland. The majority found the statute was invalid because it "directly regulates transactions that take place *outside Maryland*."

(6) Why are some cases perceived as choice-of-law problems, while others (like *Brown-Forman* and the chicken eggs case) are analyzed without reference to traditional choice-of-law reasoning? Would *Brown-Forman* look more like a choice-of-law problem if there were a private right of action in which some plaintiff sought to recover damages for violation of liquor pricing laws? If the defendant then claimed that its sales in other states could be regulated only under that state's laws, would this constitute a due process claim?

(7) The Supreme Court addressed the commerce clause issue left open in *G. D. Searle & Co., supra* page 347, in Bendix Autolite Corp. v. Midwesco Enterprises, Inc., 486 U.S. 888 (1988). Ohio's four-year statute of limitations was tolled for any corporation not "present" in Ohio, and to be present a foreign corporation had to appoint an agent for service of process, thereby consenting to the general jurisdiction of Ohio courts. The Court invalidated the Ohio statute on the ground that it "imposes a greater burden on out-of-state companies than it does on Ohio companies, subjecting the activities of foreign and domestic corporations to inconsistent regulations." *Id.* at 894. Acknowledging its ruling in *Searle*, the Court ruled that "it is true that serving foreign corporate defendants may be more arduous than serving domestic corporations . . . and we have held for equal protection purposes that a State rationally may make adjustments for this difference." However, the Court distinguished *G. D. Searle & Co.*, stating: "State interests that are legitimate for equal protection or due process purposes may be insufficient to withstand Commerce Clause scrutiny." *Id.* Why should commerce clause scrutiny be more demanding than equal protection and due process scrutiny?

(8) While *Brown-Forman* uses the commerce clause to invalidate state regulatory action that is "extraterritorial," the due process clause is occasionally used to similar effect. In BMW of N. Am., Inc. v. Gore, 517 U.S. 559 (1996), the Court struck down an Alabama award of punitive damages that was designed to change defendant BMW's lawful conduct in other states. Invoking the due process clause, the Court explained that "Alabama may insist that BMW adhere to a particular disclosure policy in that State," but it "does not have the power . . . to punish BMW for conduct that was lawful where it occurred and that had no impact on Alabama or its residents." *Id.* at 572-573; *see also* State Farm Mut. Auto. Ins. Co. v. Campbell, 538 U.S. 408 (2003) (applying *Gore* analysis to strike down punitive damages award rendered by jury in Utah state court). In State Bd. of Ins. v. Todd Shipyards Corp., 370 U.S. 451 (1962), the Court relied upon due process in holding that a state might not tax or regulate insurance contracts where its only connection to the contract was that the insured risk was located in the state. The Court could not have based its decision upon the commerce clause because the business of insurance has been left to state regulation under the McCarran-Ferguson Act, 15 U.S.C. §§1011-1012.

(9) The commerce clause and the due process clause both impose limits on a state's power to tax activities and property that are located primarily in another state or in a foreign nation. In Quill Corp. v. North Dakota, 504 U.S. 298 (1992), the Court invalidated on commerce clause grounds a state effort to tax out-of-state mail order businesses with no physical presence within the state. The Court applied a four-part test derived from Complete Auto Transit, Inc. v. Brady, 430 U.S. 274 (1977), upholding a tax where it "[1] is applied to an activity with a substantial nexus with the taxing State, [2] is fairly apportioned, [3] does not discriminate against interstate commerce, and [4] is fairly related to the services provided by the State." This test blends elements of antidiscrimination analysis with elements of extraterritoriality analysis. In South Dakota v. Wayfair, 138 S. Ct. 2080 (2018), the Court overruled *Quill*'s specific holding that, under this test, a state may tax a

business only if it has a physical presence in the state. Note that one consequence of invalidating the state tax under the commerce clause rather than the due process clause is that Congress has the power to overrule the Court's commerce clause decisions, a fact on which the opinion relied.

The Court's due process holdings on the states' right to tax have followed a tortuous path. In *Quill, supra,* the Court overruled earlier precedents and held that a state had a due process right to collect use taxes from mail order merchandisers with no physical presence within the state. A "use" tax is the functional equivalent of a sales tax; it is applied when the sale itself takes place outside the state, but the use occurs within. Prior to *Quill,* the Court had maintained that the state into which merchandise was sent had no right to impose a duty to collect the tax upon out-of-state sellers. The Court was unanimous in abandoning this holding, relying primarily on personal jurisdiction cases that expanded the reach of the state's long arm. The Supreme Court has recently held that the due process clause does not permit a state to tax the income from a trust that was created outside the forum by a trust instrument containing a (non-forum) choice-of-law clause; whose trustees all resided outside the forum; and the assets of which were all located outside the forum, simply because a contingent beneficiary had moved to the forum after the trust was established. N.C. Dep't of Revenue v. Kimberly Rice Kaestner 1992 Family Tr., 139 S. Ct. 2213 (2019). In Kaestner, the trustees had complete discretion to decide whether or not to distribute any of the trust assets to the beneficiary and she had received no income from the trust during her years of living in the forum. Do you think that the Supreme Court should treat this as a matter of choice of law or as a matter of personal jurisdiction?

(10) In CTS Corp. v. Dynamics Corporation of America, 481 U.S. 69 (1987), the Court considered whether an Indiana law limiting the voting rights of any entity acquiring a "control share" of a corporation incorporated in Indiana violated the commerce clause. The statute subjected the voting rights of such an entity to approval of a majority of the preexisting disinterested shareholders. The Court rejected the argument that this statute violated the commerce clause because it subjected activities to inconsistent regulations:

> The Indiana Act poses no such problem. So long as each State regulates voting rights only in the corporations it has created, each corporation will be subject to the law of only one State. No principle of corporation law and practice is more firmly established than a State's authority to regulate domestic corporations, including the authority to define the voting rights of shareholders. *See* Restatement (Second) of Conflict of Laws §304 (1971) (concluding that the law of the incorporating State generally should "determine the right of a shareholder to participate in the administration of the affairs of the corporation"). Accordingly, we conclude that the Indiana Act does not create an impermissible risk of inconsistent regulation by different States.

481 U.S. at 89.

The Court relied on similar grounds in rejecting the argument that the Indiana statute violated the commerce clause because of its potential to hinder tender offers:

> We think the Court of Appeals failed to appreciate the significance for Commerce Clause analysis of the fact that state regulation of corporate governance is regulation of entities whose very existence and attributes are a product of state law. As Chief Justice Marshall explained:

"A corporation is an artificial being, invisible, intangible, and existing only in contemplation of law. Being the mere creature of law, it possesses only those properties which the charter of its creation confers upon it, either expressly, or as incidental to its very existence. These are such as are supposed best calculated to effect the object for which it was created." Trustees of Dartmouth College v. Woodward, 4 Wheat. 518, 636 (1819).

See First National Bank of Boston v. Bellotti, 435 U.S. 765, 822-824 (1978) (Rehnquist, J., dissenting). Every State in this country has enacted laws regulating corporate governance. By prohibiting certain transactions, and regulating others, such laws necessarily affect certain aspects of interstate commerce. This necessarily is true with respect to corporations with shareholders in States other than the State of incorporation. Large corporations that are listed on national exchanges, or even regional exchanges, will have shareholders in many States and shares that are traded frequently. The markets that facilitate this national and international participation in ownership of corporations are essential for providing capital not only for new enterprises but also for established companies that need to expand their business. This beneficial free market system depends at its core upon the fact that a corporation—except in the rarest situations—is organized under, and governed by, the law of a single jurisdiction, traditionally the corporate law of the State of its incorporation.

. . .

It . . . is an accepted part of the business landscape in this country for States to create corporations, to prescribe their powers, and to define the rights that are acquired by purchasing their shares. A State has an interest in promoting stable relationships among parties involved in the corporations it charters, as well as in ensuring that investors in such corporations have an effective voice in corporate affairs.

. . .

Dynamics argues in any event that the State has "no legitimate interest in protecting the nonresident shareholders." Dynamics relies heavily on the statement by the Court [in Edgar v. MITE Corp. 457 U.S. 624 (1982),] that "[i]nsofar as the . . . law burdens out-of-state transactions, there is nothing to be weighed in the balance to sustain the law." 457 U.S., at 644. But that comment was made in reference to an Illinois law that applied as well to out-of-state corporations as to in-state corporations. We agree that Indiana has no interest in protecting nonresident shareholders of *nonresident corporations*. But this Act applies only to corporations incorporated in Indiana. We reject the contention that Indiana has no interest in providing for the shareholders of its corporations the voting autonomy granted by the Act. Indiana has a substantial interest in preventing the corporate form from becoming a shield for unfair business dealing. Moreover, unlike the Illinois statute invalidated in *MITE*, the Indiana Act applies only to corporations that have a substantial number of shareholders in Indiana. *See* Ind. Code §23-1-42-4(a)(3) (Supp. 1986). Thus, every application of the Indiana Act will affect a substantial number of Indiana residents, whom Indiana indisputably has an interest in protecting.

481 U.S. at 89-93.

CTS is in one respect a case of public regulation because the Indiana act represents a direct attempt to regulate the transfer of corporate control. From another point of view, however, the transaction in question was simply a private contract to sell shares of stock. If one focuses on the "private" characterization of the case, *CTS* resembles more nearly a typical choice-of-law dispute. The question is simply, which state's law may constitutionally be applied to the sale of stock in an Indiana corporation? The answer then seems to be, "only Indiana's." Is this correct? Does *CTS* have any relevance for private contracts for a sale of stock? Has the Court constitutionalized the internal affairs doctrine?

The commerce clause cases in the area of corporate takeovers have generated a substantial literature. In addition to discussions of the common-law internal affairs doctrine (pages 97-108 *supra*), *see* Pinto, *The Constitution and the Market for Corporate Control: State Takeover Statutes After* CTS Corp., 29 Wm. & Mary L. Rev. 699 (1988); Regan, *Siamese Essays*: (I) CTS Corp. v. General Dynamics Corp. of America *and Dormant Commerce Clause Doctrine*; (II) *Extraterritorial State Legislation*, 85 Mich. L. Rev. 1865 (1985); Langevoort, *The Supreme Court and the Politics of Corporate Takeovers: A Comment on* CTS Corp. v. General Dynamics Corp. of America, 101 Harv. L. Rev. 96 (1987); Buxbaum, *The Threatened Constitutionalization of the Internal Affairs Doctrine in Corporation Law*, 75 Cal. L. Rev. 29 (1987). For a criticism of the Regan article that is not limited to the topic of corporate takeovers, *see* Gergen, *Territoriality and the Perils of Formalism*, 86 Mich. L. Rev. 1735 (1988).

In distinguishing *MITE*, the Court expressly "agree[d] that Indiana has no interest in regulating nonresident shareholders of *nonresident corporations*" (emphasis in original). What does this reasoning suggest about whether state laws that disfavor nonresidents violate the privileges and immunities or equal protection clauses? Compare Section C of this chapter, *supra*.

(11) The "extraterritoriality" and "inconsistent regulations" prongs of the dormant commerce clause have been invoked a great deal in recent years in litigation over the validity of state regulation of the Internet. *See, e.g.*, Am. Booksellers Found. for Free Expression v. Strickland, 601 F.3d 622 (6th Cir. 2010) (Ohio statutory provision prohibiting personally directed Internet communications that disseminate material harmful to juveniles did not violate commerce clause); MaryCLE, LLC v. First Choice Internet, Inc., 890 A.2d 818 (Md. Ct. Spec. App. 2006) (Maryland spam e-mail statute did not violate commerce clause); Washington v. Heckel, 24 P.3d 404 (Wash. 2001) (application of Washington statute regulating spam e-mail to Oregon resident did not violate commerce clause); Cyberspace Communications, Inc. v. Engler, 142 F. Supp. 2d 827 (E.D. Mich. 2001) (state statute attempting to regulate dissemination of sexually explicit material to minors violates commerce clause); PSINET, Inc. v. Chapman, 167 F. Supp. 2d 878 (W.D. Va. 2001) (Virginia statute prohibiting sale, rental, or loan of indecent or obscene materials to juveniles violates commerce clause because it remains technologically impossible to restrict access by geographic origin); Am. Libraries Assn. v. Pataki, 969 F. Supp. 160 (S.D.N.Y. 1997) (New York statute prohibiting use of the Internet to communicate with minors with sexually explicit depictions violates commerce clause).

There also is a robust literature on the Internet and the dormant commerce clause. *See* Goldsmith & Sykes, *The Internet and the Dormant Commerce Clause*, 110 Yale L.J. 785 (2001); Biddle, *State Regulation of the Internet: Where Does the Balance of Federalist Power Lie?*, 37 Cal. W. L. Rev. 161, 167 (2000); Denning, *Smokey and the Bandit in Cyberspace: The Dormant Commerce Clause, the Twenty-first Amendment, and State Regulation of Internet Alcohol Sales*, 19 Const. Comment. 297 (2002); Burk, *Federalism in Cyberspace*, 28 Conn. L. Rev. 1095 (1996).

5

The Jurisdiction of Courts over Persons and Property

The right of a particular court to adjudicate a claim involves a number of different legal issues. There must be a state (or federal) long-arm statute authorizing the court to assert jurisdiction over the parties; the defendant must receive adequate notice and an opportunity to defend; venue must be appropriate; and the forum must be sufficiently convenient that the litigation avoids dismissal on the grounds of forum non conveniens. Many of these issues have been alluded to, more or less directly, in earlier chapters. And they constitute an important part of an introductory course on civil procedure.

Much of personal jurisdiction—the topic of this chapter—centers on assessments of "fairness," a notoriously spongy notion. Frequently, what seems eminently fair to one person seems outrageously unfair to the next. Some of the institutions undergirding the Supreme Court's notions of fairness, however, are oddly familiar. We will see below that one of the chief bases for jurisdictional fairness is the consent of the party objecting to forum authority. Consent arguments are commonplace in liberal political theory; philosophers from Locke to Rawls to Nozick have treated it as one of the most convincing justifications for state authority. Another argument traceable to Locke is the claim that an individual subjects him- or herself to state authority (either explicitly or implicitly) by entering into the state's territory. This theme, too, finds its way into the personal jurisdiction cases, for a defendant whose entrance into the forum and activities there give rise to the cause of action will be subject to suit. The parallels between political theory and jurisdictional theory are discussed in Brilmayer, *Jurisdictional Due Process and Political Theory*, 39 U. Fla. L. Rev. 293 (1987); *see also* Cappalli, *Locke as the Key: A Unifying and Coherent Theory of In Personam Jurisdiction*, 43 UCLA L. Rev. 99 (1992).

The discussion below is directed toward the constitutional limitations on exercising long-arm jurisdiction over a case that has attenuated connections with the forum. That is, primarily, a question of due process. At one time, due process limitations were satisfied through the expedient of serving process within the forum state's territory. Pennoyer v. Neff, 95 U.S. 714 (1877). Another alternative was to obtain jurisdiction by attaching the defendant's local property. Harris v. Balk, 198 U.S. 215 (1905). The conceptual basis for assertions of state court jurisdiction was drastically rewritten in International Shoe Co. v. Washington, 326 U.S. 310 (1945), which stated that assertions of jurisdiction are constitutional where they are based upon "minimum contacts" adequate to establish "fair play and substantial justice." This standard, as we will see, has hardly been self-explanatory.

The first basis for jurisdiction that we will examine — the defendant's consent or waiver of right to object — has not changed very substantially over the historical development of the due process clause. In other respects, however, we've come a long way since the days of *Pennoyer* and *Balk*.

A.   Consent and Waiver

1.   Consent

When parties enter into contracts with forum-selection clauses stating that the parties agree that suit either may or must be brought in the courts of a particular state, the designated state may exercise personal jurisdiction over the parties. In such cases, the parties are deemed to have explicitly consented to the court's jurisdiction. Forum-selection clauses are treated in Chapter 9. Here we discuss other consent-based rationales for the exercise of personal jurisdiction over the parties.

Phillips Petroleum Co. v. Shutts
472 U.S. 797 (1985)

[The facts of the case can be found in a portion of the opinion excerpted at page 310 *supra*.]

II

Reduced to its essentials, petitioner's argument is that unless out-of-state plaintiffs affirmatively consent, the Kansas courts may not exert jurisdiction over their claims. Petitioner claims that failure to execute and return the "request for exclusion" provided with the class notice cannot constitute consent of the out-of-state plaintiffs; thus Kansas courts may exercise jurisdiction over these plaintiffs only if the plaintiffs possess the sufficient "minimum contacts" with Kansas as that term is used in cases involving personal jurisdiction over out-of-state defendants. *E.g.*, International Shoe Co. v. Washington, 326 U.S. 310 (1945); Shaffer v. Heitner, 433 U.S. 186 (1977); World-Wide Volkswagen Corp. v. Woodson, 444 U.S. 286 (1980). Since Kansas had no prelitigation contact with many of the plaintiffs and leases involved, petitioner claims that Kansas has exceeded its jurisdictional reach and thereby violated the due process rights of the absent plaintiffs.

Although the cases like *Shaffer* and *Woodson* which petitioner relies on for a minimum contacts requirement all dealt with out-of-state defendants or parties in the procedural posture of a defendant, *cf.* New York Life Ins. Co. v. Dunlevy, 241 U.S. 518 (1916); Estin v. Estin, 334 U.S. 541 (1948), petitioner claims that the same analysis must apply to absent class-action plaintiffs. In this regard petitioner correctly points out that a chose in action is a constitutionally recognized property interest possessed by each of the plaintiffs. Mullane v. Central Hanover Bank & Trust Co., 339 U.S. 306 (1950). An adverse judgment by Kansas courts in this case may extinguish the chose in action forever through res judicata. Such an adverse judgment, petitioner claims, would be every bit as onerous to an absent plaintiff as an adverse judgment on the merits would be to a defendant. Thus, the same due process protections should apply to absent plaintiffs: Kansas should not be able to exert jurisdiction over the plaintiffs' claims unless the plaintiffs have sufficient minimum contacts with Kansas.

We think petitioner's premise is in error. The burdens placed by a State upon an absent class-action plaintiff are not of the same order or magnitude as those it places upon an absent defendant. An out-of-state defendant summoned by a plaintiff is faced with the full powers of the forum State to render judgment *against* it. The defendant must generally hire counsel and travel to the forum to defend itself from the plaintiff's claim, or suffer a default judgment. The defendant may be forced to participate in extended and often costly discovery, and will be forced to respond in damages or to comply with some other form of remedy imposed by the court should it lose the suit. The defendant may also face liability for court costs and attorney's fees. These burdens are substantial, and the minimum contacts requirement of the Due Process Clause prevents the forum State from unfairly imposing them upon the defendant.

A class-action plaintiff, however, is in quite a different posture. The Court noted this difference in Hansberry v. Lee, 311 U.S. 32, 40-41 (1940), which explained that a "class" or "representative" suit was an exception to the rule that one could not be bound by judgment in personam unless one was made fully a party in the traditional sense. *Ibid.*, citing Pennoyer v. Neff, 95 U.S. 714 (1878). As the Court pointed out in *Hansberry*, the class action was an invention of equity to enable it to proceed to a decree in suits where the number of those interested in the litigation was too great to permit joinder. The absent parties would be bound by the decree so long as the named parties adequately represented the absent class and the prosecution of the litigation was within the common interest.[1] 311 U.S., at 41.

---

1. The holding in *Hansberry*, of course, was that petitioners in that case had not a sufficient common interest with the parties to a prior lawsuit such that a decree against those parties in the

Modern plaintiff class actions follow the same goals, permitting litigation of a suit involving common questions when there are too many plaintiffs for proper joinder. Class actions also may permit the plaintiffs to pool claims which would be uneconomical to litigate individually. For example, this lawsuit involves claims averaging about $100 per plaintiff; most of the plaintiffs would have no realistic day in court if a class action were not available.

In sharp contrast to the predicament of a defendant haled into an out-of-state forum, the plaintiffs in this suit are not haled anywhere to defend themselves upon pain of a default judgment.

A plaintiff class in Kansas and numerous other jurisdictions cannot first be certified unless the judge, with the aid of the named plaintiffs and defendants, conducts an inquiry into the common nature of the named plaintiffs' and the absent plaintiffs' claims, the adequacy of representation, the jurisdiction possessed over the class, and any other matters that will bear upon proper representation of the absent plaintiffs' interest. *See, e.g.*, Kan. Stat. Ann. §60-223 (1983); Fed. Rule Civ. Proc. 23. Unlike a defendant in a civil suit, a class-action plaintiff is not required to fend for himself. *See* Kan. Stat. Ann. §60-223(d) (1983). The court and named plaintiffs protect his interests. Indeed, the class-action defendant itself has a great interest in ensuring that the absent plaintiffs' claims are properly before the forum. In this case, for example, the defendant sought to avoid class certification by alleging that the absent plaintiffs would not be adequately represented and were not amenable to jurisdiction. *See* Phillips Petroleum v. Duckworth, No. 82-54608 (Kan., June 28, 1982).

The concern of the typical class-action rules for the absent plaintiffs is manifested in other ways. Most jurisdictions, including Kansas, require that a class action, once certified, may not be dismissed or compromised without the approval of the court. In many jurisdictions such as Kansas the court may amend the pleadings to ensure that all sections of the class are represented adequately. Kan. Stat. Ann. §60-223(d) (1983); *see also, e.g.*, Fed. Rule Civ. Proc. 23(d).

Besides this continuing solicitude for their rights, absent plaintiff class members are not subject to other burdens imposed upon defendants. They need not hire counsel or appear. They are almost never subject to counter-claims or cross-claims, or liability for fees or costs.[2] Absent plaintiff class members are not subject to coercive or punitive remedies. Nor will an adverse judgment typically bind an absent plaintiff for any damages, although a valid adverse judgment may extinguish any of the plaintiff's claims which were litigated.

Unlike a defendant in a normal civil suit, an absent class-action plaintiff is not required to do anything. He may sit back and allow the litigation to run its course, content in knowing that there are safeguards provided for his

---

prior suit would bind the petitioners. But in the present case there is no question that the named plaintiffs adequately represent the class, and that all members of the class have the same interest in enforcing their claims against the defendant.

2. Petitioner places emphasis on the fact that absent class members might be subject to discovery, counterclaims, cross-claims, or court costs. Petitioner cites no cases involving any such imposition upon plaintiffs, however. We are convinced that such burdens are rarely imposed upon plaintiff class members, and that the disposition of these issues is best left to a case which presents them in a more concrete way.

protection. In most class actions an absent plaintiff is provided at least with an opportunity to "opt out" of the class, and if he takes advantage of that opportunity he is removed from the litigation entirely. This was true of the Kansas proceedings in this case. The Kansas procedure provided for the mailing of a notice to each class member by first-class mail. The notice, as we have previously indicated, described the action and informed the class member that he could appear in person or by counsel, in default of which he would be represented by the named plaintiffs and their attorneys. The notice further stated that class members would be included in the class and bound by judgment unless they "opted out" by executing and returning a "request for exclusion" that was included in the notice.

Petitioner contends, however, that the "opt out" procedure provided by Kansas is not good enough, and that an "opt in" procedure is required to satisfy the Due Process Clause of the Fourteenth Amendment. Insofar as plaintiffs who have no minimum contacts with the forum State are concerned, an "opt in" provision would require that each class member affirmatively consent to his inclusion within the class.

Because States place fewer burdens upon absent class plaintiffs than they do upon absent defendants in nonclass suits, the Due Process Clause need not and does not afford the former as much protection from state-court jurisdiction as it does the latter. The Fourteenth Amendment does protect "persons," not "defendants," however, so absent plaintiffs as well as absent defendants are entitled to some protection from the jurisdiction of a forum State which seeks to adjudicate their claims. In this case we hold that a forum State may exercise jurisdiction over the claim of an absent class-action plaintiff, even though that plaintiff may not possess the minimum contacts with the forum which would support personal jurisdiction over a defendant. If the forum State wishes to bind an absent plaintiff concerning a claim for money damages or similar relief at law,[3] it must provide minimal procedural due process protection. The plaintiff must receive notice plus an opportunity to be heard and participate in the litigation, whether in person or through counsel. The notice must be the best practicable, "reasonably calculated, under all the circumstances, to apprise interested parties of the pendency of the action and afford them an opportunity to present their objections." *Mullane*, 339 U.S., at 314-315; *cf.* Eisen v. Carlisle & Jacquelin, 417 U.S. 156, 174-175 (1974). The notice should describe the action and the plaintiffs' rights in it. Additionally, we hold that due process requires at a minimum that an absent plaintiff be provided with an opportunity to remove himself from the class by executing and returning an "opt out" or "request for exclusion" form to the court. Finally, the Due Process Clause of course requires that the named plaintiff at all times adequately represent the interests of the absent class members. *Hansberry*, 311 U.S., at 42-43, 45.

We reject petitioner's contention that the Due Process Clause of the Fourteenth Amendment requires that absent plaintiffs affirmatively "opt in" to the class, rather than be deemed members of the class if they do not "opt out."

---

3. Our holding today is limited to those class actions which seek to bind known plaintiffs concerning claims wholly or predominately for money judgments. We intimate no view concerning other types of class actions, such as those seeking equitable relief. Nor, of course, does our discussion of personal jurisdiction address class actions where the jurisdiction is asserted against a *defendant* class.

We think that such a contention is supported by little, if any precedent, and that it ignores the differences between class-action plaintiffs, on the one hand, and defendants in nonclass civil suits on the other. Any plaintiff may consent to jurisdiction. Keeton v. Hustler Magazine, Inc., 465 U.S. 770 (1984). The essential question, then, is how stringent the requirement for a showing of consent will be.

We think that the procedure followed by Kansas, where a fully descriptive notice is sent first-class mail to each class member, with an explanation of the right to "opt out," satisfies due process. Requiring a plaintiff to affirmatively request inclusion would probably impede the prosecution of those class actions involving an aggregation of small individual claims, where a large number of claims are required to make it economical to bring suit. *See, e.g., Eisen, supra*, at 161. The plaintiff's claim may be so small, or the plaintiff so unfamiliar with the law, that he would not file suit individually, nor would he affirmatively request inclusion in the class if such a request were required by the Constitution. If, on the other hand, the plaintiff's claim is sufficiently large or important that he wishes to litigate it on his own, he will likely have retained an attorney or have thought about filing suit, and should be fully capable of exercising his right to "opt out."

In this case over 3,400 members of the potential class did "opt out," which belies the contention that "opt out" procedures result in guaranteed jurisdiction by inertia. Another 1,500 were excluded because the notice and "opt out" form was undeliverable. We think that such results show that the "opt out" procedure provided by Kansas is by no means *pro forma*, and that the Constitution does not require more to protect what must be the somewhat rare species of class member who is unwilling to execute an "opt out" form, but whose claim is nonetheless so important that he cannot be presumed to consent to being a member of the class by his failure to do so. Petitioner's "opt in" requirement would require the invalidation of scores of state statutes and of the class-action provision of the Federal Rules of Civil Procedure, and for the reasons stated we do not think that the Constitution requires the State to sacrifice the obvious advantages in judicial efficiency resulting from the "opt out" approach for the protection of the *rara avis* portrayed by petitioner.

We therefore hold that the protection afforded the plaintiff class members by the Kansas statute satisfies the Due Process Clause. The interests of the absent plaintiffs are sufficiently protected by the forum State when those plaintiffs are provided with a request for exclusion that can be returned within a reasonable time to the court. *See Insurance Corp. of Ireland*, 456 U.S., at 702-703, and n.10. Both the Kansas trial court and the Supreme Court of Kansas held that the class received adequate representation, and no party disputes that conclusion here. We conclude that the Kansas court properly asserted personal jurisdiction over the absent plaintiffs and their claims against petitioner.

Questions and Comments

(1) For an authoritative account by two authors of briefs on the case, *see* Miller & Crump, *Jurisdiction and Choice of Law in Multistate Class Actions After* Phillips Petroleum Co. v. Shutts, 96 Yale L.J. 1 (1986).

(2) What is the relationship between this case and Bristol Myers Squibb v. Superior Court, reprinted at page 392 *infra*?

(3) Normally, of course, it is not necessary for the *plaintiff* to consent to jurisdiction, for the plaintiff has chosen the forum (a form of consent in and of itself). Why is plaintiff consent relevant here?

(4) Certain sorts of class actions, of course, do not guarantee class members a right to opt out. *See,* for example, Fed. R. Civ. P. 23(b)(2), involving class claims for equitable relief. In footnote 3, the Court's opinion declined to address class actions other than those wholly or predominately for money judgments. What result, then, in a 23(b)(2) action? May a multistate class action proceed even without offering a right to opt out? Or does *Shutts* suggest instead that the class action is improper because other than in money judgment actions where a right to opt out is provided, jurisdiction over absent class plaintiffs is improper? *See* Avagliano v. Sumitomo Shoji America, 107 F.R.D. 749 (1987); In Litigre Jackson Lockdown/MCO Cases, 107 F.R.D. 703 (1987); In re Asbestos School Litig., 620 F. Supp. 873 (E.D. Pa. 1985).

Brown v. Ticor Title Insurance, 982 F.2d 386 (9th Cir. 1992), dealt with a case involving both money damage and injunctive relief; earlier multidistrict litigation had been certified under Fed. R. Civ. P. 23(b)(1) and (b)(2) (as to which no "opt out" right exists) and the question was whether the current plaintiff was bound by res judicata. The court held that Brown might be bound by the earlier action insofar as he requested injunctive relief, but not as to his money damages claim. *See also* In re Real Estate and Settlement Servs. Antitrust Litig., 869 F.2d 760 (3d Cir. 1989). The Supreme Court initially agreed to hear Brown v. Ticor, but then in a per curiam opinion dismissed the case as moot on the grounds that a settlement had been reached, and because a majority felt that a nonconstitutional basis for decision would have been available but for the res judicata effect of an earlier holding on the scope of Rule 23. 511 U.S. 117 (1994).

(5) If an absent class member does not comply with discovery requests that would bear on whether he or she had minimum contacts with the forum, then may a court hold that jurisdiction exists under *Insurance Corp. of Ireland,* below?

(6) Would a better solution be to restrict multistate class actions to federal courts? Note that the Class Action Fairness Act of 2005 gave federal courts expanded diversity jurisdiction over class actions with aggregate claims in excess of $5 million dollars. *See* 28 U.S.C.A. §1332(d)(2). In addition, federal courts can exercise supplemental jurisdiction over at least some diversity class claims not falling within CAFA's ambit. Exxon Mobil Corp. v. Allapattah Services, Inc., 545 U.S. 546 (2005).

(7) Is the "consent" in *Shutts* express consent or implied consent? Is the answer that the consent at issue in *Shutts* is "real" implied consent rather than fictitious implied consent? Compare the distinction between implied-in-fact and implied-in-law contracts.

2. Waiver

Insurance Corp. of Ireland v. Compagnie des Bauxites de Guinee

456 U.S. 694 (1982)

Justice WHITE delivered the opinion of the Court.

Rule 37(b), Federal Rules of Civil Procedure, provides that a District Court may impose sanctions for failure to comply with discovery orders. Included among the available sanctions is:

> "An order that the matters regarding which the order was made or any other designated facts shall be taken to be established for the purposes of the action in accordance with the claim of the party obtaining the order."

Rule 37(b)(2)(A).

The question presented by this case is whether this rule is applicable to facts that form the basis for personal jurisdiction over a defendant. May a District Court, as a sanction for failure to comply with a discovery order directed at establishing jurisdictional facts, proceed on the basis that personal jurisdiction over the recalcitrant party has been established? Petitioners urge that such an application of the Rule would violate Due Process: If a court does not have jurisdiction over a party, then it may not create that jurisdiction by judicial fiat. They contend also that until a court has jurisdiction over a party, that party need not comply with orders of the court; failure to comply, therefore, cannot provide the ground for a sanction. In our view, petitioners are attempting to create a logical conundrum out of a fairly straightforward matter.

[Plaintiff/respondent Compagnie des Bauxites de Guinee (CBG) arranged to obtain various kinds of insurance, including "excess" insurance against business interruption. When such an interruption allegedly occurred and the insurers, including the excess insurers, refused to pay, CBG brought suit. The regular insurer did not contest jurisdiction, but the excess insurers, a group of foreign insurance companies, did. Plaintiff made certain requests for discovery in the action, which was brought in a Pennsylvania federal district court. The excess insurers refused to comply on the grounds that the requests were too burdensome. CBG sought an order to comply, which the district court granted. A series of further moves failed to produce the required material. Finally the district court warned the defendants that it would assume that there was jurisdiction, as a sanction pursuant to Rule 37, unless there was compliance. There was not, and the court entered an order finding in personam jurisdiction.]

II

The validity of an order of a federal court depends upon that court's having jurisdiction over both the subject matter and the parties. [The Court discussed the nature of subject matter jurisdiction, including its nonwaivability and the fact that it may be raised sua sponte by the court.]

None of this is true with respect to personal jurisdiction. The requirement that a court have personal jurisdiction flows not from Art. III, but from the Due Process Clause. The personal jurisdiction requirement recognizes and protects an individual liberty interest. It represents a restriction on judicial power not as a matter of sovereignty, but as a matter of individual liberty.[10] Thus, the test for

---

10. It is true that we have stated that the requirement of personal jurisdiction, as applied to state courts, reflects an element of federalism and the character of state sovereignty vis-à-vis other states. . . . Contrary to the suggestion of Justice Powell, *post*, at 5-6, our holding today does not alter the requirement that there be "minimum contacts" between the non-resident defendant and the forum state. Rather, our holding deals with how the facts needed to show those "minimum contacts" can be established when a defendant fails to comply with court-ordered discovery. The restriction on state sovereign power described in *World-Wide Volkswagen Corp.*, however, must be seen as ultimately a function of the individual liberty interest preserved by the Due Process Clause. That clause is the only source of the personal jurisdiction requirement and the clause itself makes no mention of federalism concerns. Furthermore, if the federalism concept operated as an independent restriction on the sovereign power of the court, it would not be possible to waive the personal jurisdiction requirement: Individual actions cannot change the powers of sovereignty, although the individual can subject himself to powers from which he may otherwise be protected.

personal jurisdiction requires that "the maintenance of the suit . . . not offend 'traditional notions of fair play and substantial justice.'" International Shoe v. Washington, quoting Milliken v. Meyers.

Because the requirement of personal jurisdiction represents first of all an individual right, it can, like other such rights, be waived. In McDonald v. Mabee, *supra*, the Court indicated that regardless of the power of the state to serve process, an individual may submit to the jurisdiction of the Court by appearance. A variety of legal arrangements have been taken to represent express or implied consent to the personal jurisdiction of the court. In National Rental v. Szukhent, we stated that "parties to a contract may agree in advance to submit to the jurisdiction of a given court," and in Petrowski v. Hawkeye-Security Co., the Court upheld the personal jurisdiction of a district court on the basis of a stipulation entered into by the defendant. In addition, lower federal courts have found such consent implicit in agreements to arbitrate. Furthermore, the Court has upheld state procedures which find constructive consent to the personal jurisdiction of the state court in the voluntary use of certain state procedures. Finally, unlike subject matter jurisdiction, which even an appellate court may review sua sponte, under Rule 12(h), Fed. Rules Civ. Proc., "a defense of lack of jurisdiction over the person . . . is waived" if not timely raised in the answer or a responsive pleading.

In sum, the requirement of personal jurisdiction may be intentionally waived, or for various reasons a defendant may be estopped from raising the issue. These characteristics portray it for what it is — a legal right protecting the individual. The plaintiff's demonstration of certain historical facts may make clear to the court that it has personal jurisdiction over the defendant as a matter of law — *i.e.*, certain factual showings will have legal consequences — but this is not the only way in which the personal jurisdiction of the court may arise. The actions of the defendant may amount to a legal submission to the jurisdiction of the court, whether voluntary or not.

The expression of legal rights is often subject to certain procedural rules: The failure to follow those rules may well result in a curtailment of the rights. Thus, the failure to enter a timely objection to personal jurisdiction constitutes, under Rule 12(h)(1), a waiver of the objection. A sanction under Rule 37(b)(2)(A) consisting of a finding of personal jurisdiction has precisely the same effect. As a general proposition, the Rule 37 sanction applied to a finding of personal jurisdiction creates no more of a due process problem than the Rule 12 waiver. Although "a court cannot conclude all persons interested by its mere assertion of its own power," not all rules that establish legal consequences to a party's own behavior are "mere assertions" of power.

Rule 37(b)(2)(a) itself embodies the standard established in Hammond Packing Co. v. Arkansas, 212 U.S. 322 (1909), for the Due Process limits on such rules. There the Court held that it did not violate due process for a state court to strike the answer and render a default judgment against a defendant who failed to comply with a pretrial discovery order. Such a rule was permissible as an expression of "the undoubted right of the lawmaking power to create a presumption of fact as to the bad faith and untruth of an answer begotten from the suppression of failure to produce the proof ordered. . . . [T]he preservation of due process was secured by the presumption that the refusal to produce evidence material to the administration of due process was but an admission of the want of merit in the asserted defense." Id., at 350-351.

The situation in *Hammond* was specifically distinguished from that in Hovey v. Elliot, 167 U.S. 409 (1897), in which the Court held that it did violate due process for a court to take similar action as "punishment" for failure to obey an order to pay into the registry of the court a certain sum of money. Due process is violated only if the behavior of the defendant will not support the *Hammond Packing* presumption. A proper application of Rule 37(b)(2) will, as a matter of law, support such a presumption. *See* Société Intérnationale v. Rogers, 357 U.S. 197, 209-213 (1958). If there is no abuse of discretion in the application of the Rule 37 sanction, as we find to be the case here (*see* §III), then the sanction is nothing more than the invocation of a legal presumption, or what is the same thing, the finding of a constructive waiver.

Petitioners argue that a sanction consisting of a finding of personal jurisdiction differs from all other instances in which a sanction is imposed, including the default judgment in *Hammond Packing*, because a party need not obey the orders of a court until it is established that the court has personal jurisdiction over that party. If there is no obligation to obey a judicial order, a sanction cannot be applied for the failure to comply. Until the court has established personal jurisdiction, moreover, any assertion of judicial power over the party violates due process.

This argument again assumes that there is something unique about the requirement of personal jurisdiction, which prevents it from being established or waived like other rights. A defendant is always free to ignore the judicial proceedings, risk a default judgment and then challenge that judgment on jurisdictional grounds in a collateral proceeding. By submitting to the jurisdiction of the court for a limited purpose of challenging jurisdiction, the defendant agrees to abide by that court's determination on the issue of jurisdiction: That decision will be res judicata on that issue in any further proceedings. As demonstrated above, the manner in which the court determines whether it has personal jurisdiction may include a variety of legal rules and presumptions, as well as straightforward factfinding. A particular rule may offend the due process standard of *Hammond Packing*, but the mere use of procedural rules does not in itself violate the defendant's due process rights.

[The Court concluded by finding that the sanction imposed by the district court was not an abuse of discretion under the facts of the case.]

Justice POWELL, concurring in the judgment. . . .

[I]t is possible to read the Court opinion, not as affecting the state jurisdiction, but simply as asserting that Rule 37 of the Federal Rules of Civil Procedure represents a congressionally approved basis for the exercise of personal jurisdiction by a federal district court. On this view Rule 37 vests the federal district courts with authority to take jurisdiction over persons not in compliance with discovery orders. This of course would be a more limited holding. Yet the Court does not cast its decision in these terms. And it provides no support for such an interpretation, either in the language or in the history of the Federal Rules.

In the absence of such support, I could not join the Court in embracing such a construction of the Rules of Civil Procedure. There is nothing in Rule 37 to suggest that it is intended to confer a grant of personal jurisdiction. Indeed, the clear language of Rule 82 seems to establish that Rule 37 should *not* be construed as a jurisdictional grant: "These rules shall not be construed to extend . . . the jurisdiction of the United States district courts or the venue of actions therein." Moreover, assuming that minimum contacts remain a constitutional predicate for the exercise of a State's in personam jurisdiction over an unconsenting defendant, constitutional questions would arise if Rule 37 were read to permit a plaintiff in a diversity action to subject a defendant to a "fishing expedition" in a foreign jurisdiction. A plaintiff is not entitled to discovery to establish essentially speculative allegations necessary to personal jurisdiction. Nor would the use of Rule 37 sanctions to enforce discovery orders constitute a mere abuse of discretion in such a case. For me at least, such a use of discovery would raise serious questions as to the constitutionality as well as the statutory authority of a federal court—in a diversity case—to exercise personal jurisdiction absent some showing of minimum contacts between the unconsenting defendant and the forum State.

II

In this case the facts alone—unaided by broad jurisdictional theories—more than amply demonstrate that the District Court possessed personal jurisdiction to impose sanctions under Rule 37 and otherwise to adjudicate this case. I would decide the case on this narrow basis. . . .

Questions and Comments

(1) The majority, as Justice Powell notes, does not seem to base its decision purely on a sanction rationale: Instead it invokes Hammond Packing Co. v. Arkansas for the proposition that a presumption that the facts giving rise to jurisdiction actually exist may be drawn from the defendants' silence. Is such an inference credible? What if the defendants truly thought the requests for documents were excessively burdensome?

(2) Could the result of the case be rested on a sanction rationale? Or is it improper to impose a sanction on a party over whom the court has no jurisdiction?

(3) Some exercises of authority over defendants and their cases are permitted without the trial court's determination that it can exercise personal jurisdiction over the defendant. In Sinochem International Co. Ltd. v. Malaysia International Shipping Corp., 549 U.S. 422 (2007), the Supreme Court concluded that it was permissible for a district court to dismiss the claims on grounds of forum non conveniens even though limited discovery to determine whether there was personal jurisdiction over the defendant had not yet occurred. The Court reasoned that although a federal court cannot rule on the merits of a case without first establishing that it has subject matter over the claims and personal jurisdiction over the parties, there is no mandatory sequencing of non-merits issues.

(4) If in *Insurance Corp.* the defendants had made no appearance at all, even to contest jurisdiction, the court might have entered a judgment against them, but it would have been subject to collateral attack — that is, a second court, asked to enforce the judgment, would be required to inspect the jurisdictional contacts afresh and make its own judgment. In the actual case, however, collateral attack is presumably not permitted. How can the Court justify worse treatment for the defendants who show up but don't cooperate fully as against those who don't cooperate at all by failing to show up?

(5) Waiver of the right to assert lack of jurisdiction may also occur under the Federal Rules if the defendant makes a preliminary motion and the motion does not include objection to lack of jurisdiction. Fed. R. Civ. P. 12(h). (The defendant may choose instead to include the defense in its answer.)

In some pleading systems the defense of lack of jurisdiction may not be joined with a defense on the merits; instead one must make a "special appearance" for the purpose of contesting jurisdiction. If the merits are contested, the jurisdictional issue is waived. May a court provide that *any* kind of appearance will constitute a waiver, that is, give the defendant the choice between showing up and litigating on the merits (despite a possibly meritorious jurisdictional defense) or staying away and suffering a default judgment that, if the defendant was wrong on the jurisdictional defense, will be binding and will preclude consideration of the merits? The Supreme Court said yes in York v. Texas, 137 U.S. 15 (1890), saying that the availability of collateral attack was sufficient to ensure due process.

B. Activities as a Basis for Jurisdiction

It has long been taken for granted that an individual is subject to suit in the state of his or her domicile on any cause of action whatsoever. *See, e.g.*, Milliken v. Meyer, 311 U.S. 457 (1940). By the same token, a corporation is subject to suit generally at the place of its incorporation or its principal place of business. In Perkins v. Benguet Consolidated Mining Co., 342 U.S. 437 (1952), jurisdiction over a cause of action unrelated to the defendant's forum activities was justified by the very substantial amount of business that the defendant transacted in the forum.

But the Supreme Court has repeatedly held that the forum affiliation need not be so extensive where the cause of action arises out of the defendant's forum activities. McGee v. International Life Insurance Co., 355 U.S. 220 (1957), upheld, for instance, an assertion of jurisdiction based upon the solicitation and writing of a single life insurance contract for a forum resident. Such holdings create an incentive for plaintiffs to argue that their cause of action arises out of or is related to the defendant's forum activities, for then the amount of contact shown need not be as great. Such assertions of "specific jurisdiction" are differentiated from "general jurisdiction" over all causes of action involving the particular defendant, based upon extensive contacts such as domicile or place of incorporation.

1. General and Specific Jurisdiction

Helicopteros Nacionales de Colombia, S.A. v. Hall
466 U.S. 408 (1983)

Justice BLACKMUN delivered the opinion of the Court.

We granted certiorari in this case to decide whether the Supreme Court of Texas correctly ruled that the contacts of a foreign corporation with the state of Texas were sufficient to allow a Texas state court to assert jurisdiction over the corporation in a cause of action not arising out of or related to the corporation's activities within the State.

I

Petitioner Helicopteros Nacionales de Colombia, S.A. (Helicol), is a Colombian corporation with its principal place of business in the city of Bogota in that country. It is engaged in the business of providing helicopter transportation for oil and construction companies in South America. On January 26, 1976, a helicopter owned by Helicol crashed in Peru. Four United States citizens were among those who lost their lives in the accident. Respondents are the survivors and representatives of the four decedents.

At the time of the crash, respondents' decedents were employed by Consorcio, a Peruvian consortium, and were working on a pipeline in Peru. Consorcio is the alter ego of a joint venture named Williams-Sedco-Horn (WSH). The venture had its headquarters in Houston, Tex. Consorcio had been formed to enable the venturers to enter into a contract with Petro Peru, the Peruvian state-owned oil company. Consorcio was to construct a pipeline for Petro Peru running from the interior of Peru westward to the Pacific Ocean. Peruvian law forbade construction of the pipeline by any non-Peruvian entity.

Consorcio/WSH needed helicopters to move personnel, materials, and equipment into and out of the construction area. In 1974, upon request of Consorcio/WSH, the chief executive officer of Helicol, Francisco Restrepo, flew to the United States and conferred in Houston with representatives of the three joint venturers. At that meeting, there was a discussion of prices, availability, working conditions, fuel, supplies, and housing. Restrepo represented that Helicol could have the first helicopter on the job in 15 days. The Consorcio/WSH representatives decided to accept the contract proposed by Restrepo. Helicol began performing before the agreement was formally signed in Peru on November 11, 1974.[3] The contract was written in Spanish on official government stationery and provided that the residence of all the parties would be Lima, Peru. It further stated that controversies arising out of the contract would be submitted to the jurisdiction of Peruvian courts. In addition, it provided that Consorcio/WSH would make payments to Helicol's account with the Bank of America in New York City.

---

3. Respondents acknowledge that the contract was executed in Peru and not in the United States. Tr. of Oral Arg. 22-23. *See* App. 79a; Brief for Respondents 3.

Aside from the negotiation session in Houston between Restrepo and the representatives of Consorcio/WSH, Helicol had other contacts with Texas. During the years 1970-1977, it purchased helicopters (approximately 80% of its fleet), spare parts, and accessories for more than $4 million from Bell Helicopter Company in Fort Worth. In that period, Helicol sent prospective pilots to Fort Worth for training and to ferry the aircraft to South America. It also sent management and maintenance personnel to visit Bell Helicopter in Fort Worth during the same period in order to receive "plant familiarization" and for technical consultation. Helicol received into its New York City and Panama City, Fla., bank accounts over $5 million in payments from Consorcio/WSH drawn upon First City National Bank of Houston.

Beyond the foregoing, there have been no other business contacts between Helicol and the State of Texas. Helicol never has been authorized to do business in Texas and never has had an agent for the service of process within the State. It never has performed helicopter operations in Texas or sold any product that reached Texas, never solicited business in Texas, never signed any contract in Texas, never had any employee based there, and never recruited an employee in Texas. In addition, Helicol never has owned real or personal property in Texas and never has maintained an office or establishment there. Helicol has maintained no records in Texas and has no shareholders in that State. None of the respondents or their decedents were domiciled in Texas . . . ,[5] but all of the decedents were hired in Houston by Consorcio/WSH to work on the Petro Peru pipeline project.

Respondents instituted wrongful-death actions in the District Court of Harris County, Tex., against Consorcio/WSH, Bell Helicopter Company, and Helicol. Helicol filed special appearances and moved to dismiss the actions for lack of *in personam* jurisdiction over it. The motion was denied. After a consolidated jury trial, judgment was entered against Helicol on a jury verdict of $1,141,200 in favor of respondents. . . . In ruling that the Texas courts had in personam jurisdiction, the Texas Supreme Court first held that the State's long-arm statute reaches as far as the Due Process Clause of the Fourteenth Amendment permits. Thus, the only question remaining for the court to decide was whether it was consistent with the Due Process Clause for Texas courts to assert in personam jurisdiction over Helicol.

II

The Due Process Clause of the Fourteenth Amendment operates to limit the power of a State to assert in personam jurisdiction over a nonresident defendant. Pennoyer v. Neff, 95 U.S. 714 (1878). Due process requirements are

---

5. Respondents' lack of residential or other contacts with Texas of itself does not defeat otherwise proper jurisdiction. Keeton v. Hustler Magazine, Inc., 465 U.S. 770, 780 (1984); Calder v. Jones, 465 U.S. 783, 788 (1984). We mention respondents' lack of contacts merely to show that nothing in the nature of the relationship between respondents and Helicol could possibly enhance Helicol's contacts with Texas. The harm suffered by respondents did not occur in Texas. Nor is it alleged that any negligence on the part of Helicol took place in Texas.

satisfied when in personam jurisdiction is asserted over a nonresident corporate defendant that has "certain minimum contacts with [the forum] such that the maintenance of the suit does not offend 'traditional notions of fair play and substantial justice.'" International Shoe Co. v. Washington, 326 U.S. 310, 316 (1945), quoting Milliken v. Meyer, 311 U.S. 457, 463 (1940). When a controversy is related to or "arises out of" a defendant's contacts with the forum, the Court has said that a "relationship among the defendant, the forum, and the litigation" is the essential foundation of in personam jurisdiction. Shaffer v. Heitner, 433 U.S. 186, 204 (1977).[8]

Even when the cause of action does not arise out of or relate to the foreign corporation's activities in the forum State,[9] due process is not offended by a State's subjecting the corporation to its *in personam* jurisdiction when there are sufficient contacts between the State and the foreign corporation. Perkins v. Benguet Consolidated Mining Co., 342 U.S. 437 (1952); *see* Keeton v. Hustler Magazine, Inc., 465 U.S. 770, 779-780 (1984). In *Perkins*, the Court addressed a situation in which state courts had asserted general jurisdiction over a defendant foreign corporation. During the Japanese occupation of the Philippine Islands, the president and general manager of a Philippine mining corporation maintained an office in Ohio from which he conducted activities on behalf of the company. He kept company files and held directors' meetings in the office, carried on correspondence relating to the business, distributed salary checks drawn on two active Ohio bank accounts, engaged an Ohio bank to act as transfer agent, and supervised policies dealing with the rehabilitation of the corporation's properties in the Philippines. In short, the foreign corporation, through its president, "ha[d] been carrying on in Ohio a continuous and systematic, but limited, part of its general business," and the exercise of general jurisdiction over the Philippine corporation by an Ohio court was "reasonable and just." 342 U.S., at 438, 445.

All parties to the present case concede that respondents' claims against Helicol did not "arise out of," and are not related to, Helicol's activities within Texas.[10] We thus must explore the nature of Helicol's contacts with the State of

---

8. It has been said that when a State exercises personal jurisdiction over a defendant in a suit arising out of or related to the defendant's contacts with the forum, the State is exercising "specific jurisdiction" over the defendant. *See* Von Mehren & Trautman, *Jurisdiction to Adjudicate: A Suggested Analysis*, 79 Harv. L. Rev. 1121, 1144-1164 (1966).

9. When a State exercises personal jurisdiction over a defendant in a suit not arising out of or related to the defendant's contacts with the forum, the State has been said to be exercising "general jurisdiction" over the defendant. *See* Brilmayer, *How Contacts Count: Due Process Limitations on State Court Jurisdiction*, 1980 S. Ct. Rev. 77, 80-81; Von Mehren & Trautman, 79 Harv. L. Rev., at 1136-1144; Calder v. Jones, 465 U.S., at 786.

10. Because the parties have not argued any relationship between the cause of action and Helicol's contacts with the State of Texas, we, contrary to the dissent's implication, assert no "view" with respect to that issue.

The dissent suggests that we have erred in drawing no distinction between controversies that "relate to" a defendant's contacts with a forum and those that "arise out of" such contacts. *Post*, at 420. This criticism is somewhat puzzling, for the dissent goes on to urge that, for purposes of determining the constitutional validity of an assertion of specific jurisdiction, there really should be no distinction between the two.

We do not address the validity or consequences of such a distinction because the issue has not been presented in this case. Respondents have made no argument that their cause of action either

Texas to determine whether they constitute the kind of continuous and systematic general business contacts the Court found to exist in *Perkins*. We hold that they do not.

It is undisputed that Helicol does not have a place of business in Texas and never has been licensed to do business in the State. Basically, Helicol's contacts with Texas consisted of sending its chief executive officer to Houston for a contract-negotiation session; accepting into its New York bank account checks drawn on a Houston bank; purchasing helicopters, equipment, and training services from Bell Helicopter for substantial sums; and sending personnel to Bell's facilities in Fort Worth for training.

The one trip to Houston by Helicol's chief executive officer for the purpose of negotiating the transportation-services contract with Consorcio/WSH cannot be described or regarded as a contact of a "continuous and systematic" nature, as *Perkins* described it, *see also* International Shoe Co. v. Washington, 326 U.S., at 320, and thus cannot support an assertion of in personam jurisdiction over Helicol by a Texas court. Similarly, Helicol's acceptance from Consorcio/WSH of checks drawn on a Texas bank is of negligible significance for purposes of determining whether Helicol had sufficient contacts in Texas. There is no indication that Helicol ever requested that the checks be drawn on a Texas bank or that there was any negotiation between Helicol and Consorcio/WSH with respect to the location or identity of the bank on which checks would be drawn. Common sense and everyday experience suggest that, absent unusual circumstances, the bank on which a check is drawn is generally of little consequence to the payee and is a matter left to the discretion of the drawer. Such unilateral activity of another party or a third person is not an appropriate consideration when determining whether a defendant has sufficient contacts with a forum State to justify an assertion of jurisdiction. *See* Kulko v. California Superior Court, 436 U.S. 84, 93 (1978) (arbitrary to subject one parent to suit in any State where other parent chooses to spend time while having custody of child pursuant to separation agreement); Hanson v. Denckla, 357 U.S. 235, 253 (1958) ("The unilateral activity of those who claim some relationship with a nonresident defendant cannot satisfy the requirement of contact with the forum State").

The Texas Supreme Court focused on the purchases and the related training trips in finding contacts sufficient to support an assertion of jurisdiction. We do not agree with that assessment, for the Court's opinion in Rosenberg Bros. & Co. v. Curtis Brown Co., 260 U.S. 516 (1923) (Brandeis, J., for a unanimous tribunal), makes clear that purchases and related trips, standing alone, are not a sufficient basis for a State's assertion of jurisdiction.

---

arose out of or is related to Helicol's contacts with the state of Texas. Absent any briefing on the issue, we decline to reach the questions (1) whether the terms "arising out of" and "related to" describe different connections between a cause of action and a defendant's contacts with a forum, and (2) what sort of tie between a cause of action and a defendant's contacts with a forum is necessary to a determination that either connection exists. Nor do we reach the question whether, if the two types of relationship differ, a forum's exercise of personal jurisdiction in a situation where the cause of action "relates to," but does not "arise out of," the defendant's contacts with the forum should be analyzed as an assertion of specific jurisdiction.

The defendant in *Rosenberg* was a small retailer in Tulsa, Okla., who dealt in men's clothing and furnishings. It never had applied for a license to do business in New York, nor had it at any time authorized suit to be brought against it there. It never had an established place of business in New York and never regularly carried on business in that State. Its only connection with New York was that it purchased from New York wholesalers a large portion of the merchandise sold in its Tulsa store. The purchases sometimes were made by correspondence and sometimes through visits to New York by an officer of the defendant. The Court concluded: "Visits on such business, even if occurring at regular intervals, would not warrant the inference that the corporation was present within the jurisdiction of [New York]." *Id.*, at 518.

This Court in *International Shoe* acknowledged and did not repudiate its holding in *Rosenberg. See* 326 U.S., at 318. In accordance with *Rosenberg*, we hold that mere purchases, even if occurring at regular intervals, are not enough to warrant a State's assertion of in personam jurisdiction over a non-resident corporation in a cause of action not related to those purchase transactions.[12] Nor can we conclude that the fact that Helicol sent personnel into Texas for training in connection with the purchase of helicopters and equipment in that State in any way enhanced the nature of Helicol's contacts with Texas. The training was a part of the package of goods and services purchased by Helicol from Bell Helicopter. The brief presence of Helicol employees in Texas for the purpose of attending the training sessions is no more a significant contact than were the trips to New York made by the buyer for the retail store in *Rosenberg*.

III

We hold that Helicol's contacts with the State of Texas were insufficient to satisfy the requirements of the Due Process Clause of the Fourteenth Amendment.[13] Accordingly, we reverse the judgment of the Supreme Court of Texas.

---

12. This Court in *International Shoe* cited *Rosenberg* for the proposition that "the commission of some single or occasional acts of the corporate agent in a state sufficient to impose an obligation or liability on the corporation has not been thought to confer upon the state authority to enforce it." 326 U.S., at 318. Arguably, therefore, *Rosenberg* also stands for the proposition that mere purchases are not a sufficient basis for either general or specific jurisdiction.

Because the case before us is one in which there has been an assertion of general jurisdiction over a foreign defendant, we need not decide the continuing validity of *Rosenberg* with respect to an assertion of specific jurisdiction, *i.e.*, where the cause of action arises out of or relates to the purchases by the defendant in the forum State.

13. As an alternative to traditional minimum-contacts analysis, respondents suggest that the Court hold that the State of Texas had personal jurisdiction over Helicol under a doctrine of "jurisdiction by necessity." *See* Shaffer v. Heitner, 433 U.S. 186, 211, n.37 (1977). We conclude, however, that respondents failed to carry their burden of showing that all three defendants could not be sued together in a single forum. It is not clear from the record, for example, whether suit could have been brought against all three defendants in either Colombia or Peru. We decline to consider adoption of a doctrine of jurisdiction by necessity — a potentially far-reaching modification of existing law — in the absence of a more complete record.

Justice BRENNAN, dissenting.

I

The Court expressly limits its decision in this case to "an assertion of general jurisdiction over a foreign defendant." Having framed the question in this way, the Court is obliged to address our prior holdings in Perkins v. Benguet Consolidated Mining Co., 342 U.S. 437 (1952), and Rosenberg Bros. & Co. v. Curtis Brown Co., *supra*. In *Perkins*, the Court considered a State's assertion of general jurisdiction over a foreign corporation that "ha[d] been carrying on . . . a continuous and systematic, but limited, part of its general business" in the forum. 342 U.S., at 438. Under the circumstances of that case, we held that such contacts were constitutionally sufficient "to make it reasonable and just to subject the corporation to the jurisdiction" of that State. *Id.*, at 445 (citing *International Shoe, supra*, at 317-320). Nothing in *Perkins* suggests, however, that such "continuous and systematic" contacts are a necessary minimum before a State may constitutionally assert general jurisdiction over a foreign corporation.

The Court therefore looks for guidance to our 1923 decision in *Rosenberg, supra*, which until today was of dubious validity given the subsequent expansion of personal jurisdiction that began with *International Shoe, supra*, . . .

The vast expansion of our national economy during the past several decades has provided the primary rationale for expanding the permissible reach of a State's jurisdiction under the Due Process Clause. By broadening the type and amount of business opportunities available to participants in interstate and foreign commerce, our economy has increased the frequency with which foreign corporations actively pursue commercial transactions throughout the various States. In turn, it has become both necessary and, in my view, desirable to allow the States more leeway in bringing the activities of these nonresident corporations within the scope of their respective jurisdictions. . . .

As a foreign corporation that has actively and purposefully engaged in numerous and frequent commercial transactions in the State of Texas, Helicol clearly falls within the category of nonresident defendants that may be subject to that forum's general jurisdiction. Helicol not only purchased helicopters and other equipment in the State for many years, but also sent pilots and management personnel into Texas to be trained in the use of this equipment and to consult with the seller on technical matters. Moreover, negotiations for the contract under which Helicol provided transportation services to the joint venture that employed the respondents' decedents also took place in the State of Texas. Taken together, these contacts demonstrate that Helicol obtained numerous benefits from its transaction of business in Texas. In turn, it is eminently fair and reasonable to expect Helicol to face the obligations that attach to its participation in such commercial transactions. Accordingly, on the basis of continuous commercial contacts with the forum, I would conclude that the Due Process Clause allows the State of Texas to assert general jurisdiction over petitioner Helicol.

II

. . . This is simply not a case, therefore, in which a state court has asserted jurisdiction over a nonresident defendant on the basis of wholly unrelated contacts with the forum. Rather, the contacts between Helicol and the forum are directly related to the negligence that was alleged in the respondent Hall's original complaint. Because Helicol should have expected to be amenable to suit in the Texas courts for claims directly related to these contacts, it is fair and reasonable to allow the assertion of jurisdiction in this case.

Limiting the specific jurisdiction of a forum to cases in which the cause of action formally arose out of the defendant's contacts with the State would subject constitutional standards under the Due Process Clause to the vagaries of the substantive law or pleading requirements of each State. For example, the complaint filed against Helicol in this case alleged negligence based on pilot error. Even though the pilot was trained in Texas, the Court assumes that the Texas courts may not assert jurisdiction over the suit because the cause of action "did not 'arise out of,' and [is] not related to," that training. If, however, the applicable substantive law required that negligent training of the pilot was a necessary element of a cause of action for pilot error, or if the respondents had simply added an allegation of negligence in the training provided for the Helicol pilot, then presumably the Court would concede that the specific jurisdiction of the Texas courts was applicable.

Our interpretation of the Due Process Clause has never been so dependent upon the applicable substantive law or the State's formal pleading requirements. At least since International Shoe Co. v. Washington, 326 U.S. 310 (1945), the principal focus when determining whether a forum may constitutionally assert jurisdiction over a nonresident defendant has been on fairness and reasonableness to the defendant. To this extent, a court's specific jurisdiction should be applicable whenever the cause of action arises out of *or* relates to the contacts between the defendant and the forum. It is eminently fair and reasonable, in my view, to subject a defendant to suit in a forum with which it has significant contacts directly related to the underlying cause of action. Because Helicol's contacts with the State of Texas meet this standard, I would affirm the judgment of the Supreme Court of Texas.

Questions and Comments

(1) What does it mean to say that the controversy "arises out of" or "relates to" the defendant's activities in the forum? Are these the same? In the Supreme Court Review article cited in the majority's footnote 9, the author argued that specific jurisdiction should be based upon contacts that were themselves of substantive relevance to the dispute. In rejecting this suggestion, did the dissent have an alternative conception of what "relating to" means, how it is different from "arising out of," and how both differ from total unrelatedness? Isn't this crucial if different types of contacts are to be weighted differently?

This issue has provoked considerable discussion in the courts and in the academic literature. Different definitions of the requirement that a cause of action "arise from" the local contacts can be found in: Hexacomb Corp. v. Damage Prevention Products Corp., 905 F. Supp. 557 (N.D. Ind. 1995) (defendant's contacts with the forum must be substantively related to the cause of action); Creech v. Roberts, 908 F.2d 75 (6th Cir. 1990) (contacts must be related to the "operative facts" of the controversy); Pizzaro v. Hoteles Concorde Intl., C.A., 907 F.2d 1256 (1st Cir. 1990) (in applying proximate cause test, the court examined whether the facts constituting the defendant's contacts were relevant to the proof of the elements of the plaintiff's cause of action); Nowak v. Tak How Invs., Ltd., 94 F.3d 708 (1st Cir. 1996) (court deviates from proximate cause test to exercise jurisdiction where meaningful link exists between defendant's contacts and harm suffered by plaintiff); Shopper's Food Warehouse v. Moreno, 746 A.2d 320 (D.D.C. 2000) (contacts must have a substantial connection with plaintiff's claim); Vons Companies, Inc. v. Seabest Foods, Inc., 926 P.2d 1085 (Cal. 1996) (rejecting proximate cause test as too narrow and "but for" test as too broad, and holding that there must be a substantial nexus or connection between the defendant's forum activities and the plaintiff's claim); In re Oil Spill by Amoco Cadiz Off Coast of France, 699 F.2d 909 (7th Cir. 1983) (applying "in the wake of" test to state long-arm statute).

The lower court opinion in Carnival Cruise v. Shute, reprinted at page 681 *infra*, addressed the question of whether the injury arose out of the defendant's advertising activities in the forum, answering the question in the affirmative after applying a "but for" test. Shute v. Carnival Cruise Lines, 863 F.2d 1437 (9th Cir. 1988); *see also* Ballard v. Savage, 65 F.3d 1495, 1500 (9th Cir. 1995) (reaffirming "but for" test). Many observers hoped when the Supreme Court agreed to hear the case that its decision would clarify the issue; instead, the issue was avoided by the Court's holding that jurisdiction existed on the basis of the forum-selection clause.

For academic discussion of these and other possible tests, *see* Twitchell, *The Myth of General Jurisdiction*, 101 Harv. L. Rev. 610 (1988); Brilmayer, *Related Contacts and Personal Jurisdiction*, 101 Harv. L. Rev. 1444 (1988); Twitchell, *A Rejoinder to Professor Brilmayer*, 101 Harv. L. Rev. 1465 (1988). For an analysis of the Ninth Circuit's "but for" test, *see* Comment, *Related Contacts and Personal Jurisdiction: The "But For" Test*, 82 Cal. L. Rev. 1545 (1994); Comment, *Specific Personal Jurisdiction and the "Arise From or Relate To" Requirement: What Does It Mean?*, 50 Wash. & Lee L. Rev. 1265 (1993).

(2) Why should purchases be treated qualitatively differently from other sorts of unrelated contacts? Would unrelated purchases really be constitutionally distinguishable from, for example, unrelated sales? From unrelated visits? Ought the volume of unrelated purchases be important? Does the Court really mean that no quantity of unrelated purchases could ever support general jurisdiction?

(3) Even if the majority is correct that the plaintiffs did not argue that the cause of action was related to the contacts, why does it follow that this is a problem of general jurisdiction? Why not say, in other words, that unless the defendant shows why the contacts are unrelated, it will be assumed that the problem is one of specific jurisdiction?

(4) Is it possible to have hybrid jurisdiction, where some unrelated contacts that would themselves be insufficient are combined with either some somewhat related contacts or some related contacts that would also, by themselves, be insufficient? *See* Richman, *Review Essay: Part II — A Sliding Scale to Supplement*

the Distinction Between General and Specific Jurisdiction, 72 Calif. L. Rev. 1328 (1984). *See* Camelback Ski Corp. v. Behning, 539 A.2d 1107 (Md. 1988), where the court denied jurisdiction over a Pennsylvania ski resort for injuries sustained by plaintiff while skiing.

(5) Note the *Helicopteros* majority's apparently disapproving characterization, in footnote 13, of jurisdiction by necessity as a "potentially far-reaching modification of existing law." What sort of more complete record would have encouraged the Court to address the argument? Merely a showing that the defendants could not all be sued in the same forum? That fact alone would not single out Texas as an appropriate place to litigate, would it? After all, if the three defendants could not all be sued in Peru, Colombia, or Texas, then Texas is not better situated in this regard than Peru or Colombia.

(6) At what point in time ought the defendant's contacts be measured? Should the defendant's domicile (or business contacts) be assessed as of the time that the cause of action arose or as of the time that the suit was filed? Or, are *both* relevant? *See, e.g.*, Schneider v. Linkfield, 389 Mich. 608, 209 N.W.2d 225 (1973) (defendants resided in the forum at the time of the accident; jurisdiction upheld); Greene v. Sha-Na-Na, 637 F. Supp. 591 (D. Conn. 1986) (defendant's activities subsequent to filing of complaint not counted toward personal jurisdiction).

Burnham v. Superior Court of California

495 U.S. 604 (1990)

Justice SCALIA announced the judgment of the Court and delivered an opinion in which THE CHIEF JUSTICE and Justice KENNEDY join, and in which Justice WHITE joins with respect to Parts I, II-A, II-B, and II-C.

The question presented is whether the Due Process Clause of the Fourteenth Amendment denies California courts jurisdiction over a nonresident, who was personally served with process while temporarily in that State, in a suit unrelated to his activities in the State.

I

Petitioner Dennis Burnham married Francie Burnham in 1976, in West Virginia. In 1977 the couple moved to New Jersey, where their two children were born. In July 1987 the Burnhams decided to separate. They agreed that Mrs. Burnham, who intended to move to California, would take custody of the children. Shortly before Mrs. Burnham departed for California that same month, she and petitioner agreed that she would file for divorce on grounds of "irreconcilable differences."

In October 1987, petitioner filed for divorce in New Jersey state court on grounds of "desertion." Petitioner did not, however, obtain an issuance of summons against his wife, and did not attempt to serve her with process. Mrs. Burnham, after unsuccessfully demanding that petitioner adhere to their prior agreement to submit to an "irreconcilable differences" divorce, brought suit for divorce in California state court in early January 1988.

In late January, petitioner visited southern California on business, after which he went north to visit his children in the San Francisco Bay area, where his wife resided. He took the older child to San Francisco for the weekend. Upon returning the child to Mrs. Burnham's home on January 24, 1988, petitioner was served with a California court summons and a copy of Mrs. Burnham's divorce petition. He then returned to New Jersey.

Later that year, petitioner made a special appearance in the California Superior Court, moving to quash the service of process on the ground that the court lacked personal jurisdiction over him because his only contacts with California were a few short visits to the State for the purposes of conducting business and visiting his children. The Superior Court denied the motion, and the California Court of Appeal denied mandamus relief, rejecting petitioner's contention that the Due Process Clause prohibited California courts from asserting jurisdiction over him because he lacked "minimum contacts" with the State. The court held it to be "a valid jurisdictional predicate for in personam jurisdiction" that the "defendant [was] present in the forum state and personally served with process." We granted certiorari.

II

. . .

To determine whether the assertion of personal jurisdiction is consistent with due process, we have long relied on the principles traditionally followed by American courts in marking out the territorial limits of each State's authority. That criterion was first announced in Pennoyer v. Neff, *supra*, in which we stated that due process "mean[s] a course of legal proceedings according to those rules and principles which have been established in our systems of jurisprudence for the protection and enforcement of private rights," *id.*, at 733, including the "well-established principles of public law respecting the jurisdiction of an independent State over persons and property," *id.*, at 722. In what has become the classic expression of the criterion, we said in International Shoe Co. v. Washington, 326 U.S. 310 (1945), that a State court's assertion of personal jurisdiction satisfies the Due Process Clause if it does not violate "traditional notions of fair play and substantial justice." Since *International Shoe*, we have only been called upon to decide whether these "traditional notions" permit States to exercise jurisdiction over absent defendants in a manner that deviates from the rules of jurisdiction applied in the 19th century. We have held such deviations permissible, but only with respect to suits arising out of the absent defendant's contacts with the State.[1]

---

1. We have said that "[e]ven when the cause of action does not arise out of or relate to the foreign corporation's activities in the forum State, due process is not offended by a State's subjecting the corporation to its in personam jurisdiction when there are sufficient contacts between the State and the foreign corporation." Helicopteros Nacionales de Colombia v. Hall, 466 U.S., at 414. Our only holding supporting that statement, however, involved "regular service of summons upon [the corporation's] president while he was in [the forum State] acting in that capacity." *See* Perkins v. Benguet Consolidated Mining Co., 342 U.S. 437, 440 (1952). It may be that whatever special rule exists permitting "continuous and systematic" contacts, *id.*, at 438, to support jurisdiction with respect to matters unrelated to activity in the forum, applies *only* to corporations, which have never fitted comfortably in a jurisdictional regime based primarily upon "de facto power over the defendant's person." International Shoe Co. v. Washington, 326 U.S. 310, 316 (1945). We express no

See, e.g., Helicopteros Nacionales de Colombia v. Hall, 466 U.S. 408, 414 (1984). The question we must decide today is whether due process requires a similar connection between the litigation and the defendant's contacts with the State in cases where the defendant is physically present in the State at the time process is served upon him.

B

Among the most firmly established principles of personal jurisdiction in American tradition is that the courts of a State have jurisdiction over non-residents who are physically present in the State. The view developed early that each State had the power to hale before its courts any individual who could be found within its borders, and that once having acquired jurisdiction over such a person by properly serving him with process, the State could retain jurisdiction to enter judgment against him, no matter how fleeting his visit. *See, e.g.*, Potter v. Allin, 2 Root 63, 67 (Conn. 1793); Barrell v. Benjamin, 15 Mass. 354 (1819). That view had antecedents in English common-law practice, which sometimes allowed "transitory" actions, arising out of events outside the country, to be maintained against seemingly non-resident defendants who were present in England. *See, e.g.*, Mostyn v. Fabrigas, 98 Eng. Rep. 1021 (K.B. 1774); Cartwright v. Pettus, 22 Eng. Rep. 916 (Ch. 1675). Justice Story believed the principle, which he traced to Roman origins, to be firmly grounded in English tradition: "[B]y the common law[,] personal actions, being transitory, may be brought in any place, where the party defendant may be found," for "every nation may . . . rightfully exercise jurisdiction over all persons within its domains." Story, *Commentaries on the Conflict of Laws* §§543, 554 (1846). *See also* §§530-538; Picquet v. Swan, *supra*, at 611-612 (Story, J.) ("Where a party is within a territory, he may justly be subjected to its process, and bound personally by the judgment pronounced, on such process, against him.").

Recent scholarship has suggested that English tradition was not as clear as Story thought, see Hazard, *A General Theory of State-Court Jurisdiction*, 1965 Sup. Ct. Rev. 241, 253-260; Ehrenzweig, *The Transient Rule of Personal Jurisdiction: The "Power" Myth and Forum Conveniens*, 65 Yale L.J. 289 (1956). Accurate or not, however, judging by the evidence of contemporaneous or near-contemporaneous decisions one must conclude that Story's understanding was shared by American courts at the crucial time for present purposes: 1868, when the Fourteenth Amendment was adopted. . . .

Decisions in the courts of many States in the 19th and early 20th centuries held that personal service upon a physically present defendant sufficed to confer jurisdiction, without regard to whether the defendant was only briefly in the State or whether the cause of action was related to his activities there.

Although research has not revealed a case deciding the issue in every State's courts, that appears to be because the issue was so well settled that it went unlitigated. Opinions from the courts of other States announced the rule in dictum.

---

views on these matters—and, for simplicity's sake, omit reference to this aspect of "contacts"-based jurisdiction in our discussion.

Most States, moreover, had statutes or common-law rules that exempted from service of process individuals who were brought into the forum by force or fraud, *see, e.g.,* Wanzer v. Bright, 52 Ill. 35 (1869), or who were there as a party or witness in unrelated judicial proceedings, *see, e.g.,* Burroughs v. Cocke & Willis, 56 Okla. 627, 156 P. 196 (1916); Malloy v. Brewer, 7 S.D. 587, 64 N.W. 1120 (1895). These exceptions obviously rested upon the premise that service of process conferred jurisdiction. Particularly striking is the fact that, as far as we have been able to determine, *not one* American case from the period (or, for that matter, not one American case until 1978) held, or even suggested, that in-state personal service on an individual was insufficient to confer personal jurisdiction. Commentators were also seemingly unanimous on the rule.

This American jurisdictional practice is, moreover, not merely old; it is continuing. It remains the practice of, not only a substantial number of the States, but as far as we are aware *all* the States and the federal government — if one disregards (as one must for this purpose) the few opinions since 1978 that have erroneously said, on grounds similar to those that petitioner presses here, that this Court's due-process decisions render the practice unconstitutional. We do not know of a single State or federal statute or a single judicial decision resting upon State law, that has abandoned in-state service as a basis of jurisdiction. Many recent cases reaffirm it.

C

. . . Nothing in *International Shoe* or the cases that have followed it, however, offers support for the very different proposition petitioner seeks to establish today: that a defendant's presence in the forum is not only unnecessary to validate novel, nontraditional assertions of jurisdiction, but is itself no longer sufficient to establish jurisdiction. That proposition is unfaithful to both elementary logic and the foundations of our due process jurisprudence. The distinction between what is needed to support novel procedures and what is needed to sustain traditional ones is fundamental, as we observed over a century ago:

> "[A] process of law, which is not otherwise forbidden, must be taken to be due process of law, if it can show the sanction of settled usage both in England and in this country; but it by no means followed that nothing else can be due process of law. . . . [That which], in substance, has been immemorially the actual law of the land . . . therefor[e] is due process of law. But to hold that such a characteristic is essential to due process of law, would be to deny every quality of the law but its age, and to render it incapable of progress or improvement. It would be to stamp upon our jurisprudence the unchangeableness attributed to the laws of the Medes and Persians." *Hurtado v. California*, 110 U.S. 516, 528-529 (1884).

The short of the matter is that jurisdiction based on physical presence alone constitutes due process because it is one of the continuing traditions of our legal system that define the due process standard of "traditional notions of fair play and substantial justice." That standard was developed by *analogy* to "physical presence," and it would be perverse to say it could now be turned against that touchstone of jurisdiction.

D

Petitioner's strongest argument, though we ultimately reject it, relies upon our decision in Shaffer v. Heitner, 433 U.S. 186 (1977). . . .

It goes too far to say, as petitioner contends, that *Shaffer* compels the conclusion that a State lacks jurisdiction over an individual unless the litigation arises out of his activities in the State. *Shaffer*, like *International Shoe*, involved jurisdiction over an *absent defendant*, and it stands for nothing more than the proposition that when the "minimum contact" that is a substitute for physical presence consists of property ownership it must, like other minimum contacts, be related to the litigation. Petitioner wrenches out of its context our statement in *Shaffer* that "all assertions of state-court jurisdiction must be evaluated according to the standards set forth in *International Shoe* and its progeny," 433 U.S., at 212. When read together with the two sentences that preceded it, the meaning of this statement becomes clear:

> "The fiction that an assertion of jurisdiction over property is anything but an assertion of jurisdiction over the owner of the property supports an ancient form without substantial modern justification. Its continued acceptance would serve only to allow state-court jurisdiction that is fundamentally unfair to the defendant.
>
> "We *therefore conclude* that all assertions of state-court jurisdiction must be evaluated according to the standards set forth in *International Shoe* and its progeny." *Ibid.* (emphasis added).

Shaffer was saying, in other words, not that all bases for the assertion of in personam jurisdiction (including, presumably, in-state service) must be treated alike and subjected to the "minimum contacts" analysis of *International Shoe*; but rather that quasi in rem jurisdiction, that fictional "ancient form," and in personam jurisdiction, are really one and the same and must be treated alike — leading to the conclusion that quasi in rem jurisdiction, *i.e.*, that form of in personam jurisdiction based upon a "property ownership" contact and by definition unaccompanied by personal, in-state service, must satisfy the litigation-relatedness requirement of *International Shoe*. The logic of *Shaffer*'s holding — which places all suits against absent nonresidents on the same constitutional footing, regardless of whether a separate Latin label is attached to one particular basis of contact — does not compel the conclusion that physically present defendants must be treated identically to absent ones. As we have demonstrated at length, our tradition has treated the two classes of defendants quite differently, and it is unreasonable to read *Shaffer* as casually obliterating that distinction. *International Shoe* confined its "minimum contacts" requirement to situations in which the defendant "be not present within the territory of the forum," 326 U.S., at 316, and nothing in *Shaffer* expands that requirement beyond that.

. . .

III

A few words in response to Justice Brennan's concurrence: It insists that we apply "contemporary notions of due process" to determine the constitutionality of California's assertion of jurisdiction. But our analysis today comports with that prescription, at least if we give it the only sense allowed by our precedents. The "contemporary notions of due process" applicable to personal jurisdiction are the enduring "*traditional* notions of fair play and substantial justice" established as the test by *International Shoe*. By its very language, that test is satisfied if a state court adheres to jurisdictional rules that are generally applied and have always been applied in the United States.

But the concurrence's proposed standard of "contemporary notions of due process" requires more: it measures state-court jurisdiction not only against traditional doctrines in this country, including current state-court practice, but against each Justice's subjective assessment of what is fair and just. Authority for that seductive standard is not to be found in any of our personal jurisdiction cases. It is, indeed, an outright break with the test of "traditional notions of fair play and substantial justice," which would have to be reformulated "*our* notions of fair play and substantial justice."

. . .

Because the Due Process Clause does not prohibit the California courts from exercising jurisdiction over petitioner based on the fact of in-state service of process, the judgment is

Affirmed.

Justice WHITE, concurring in part and concurring in the judgment.

I join Part I and Parts II-A, II-B, and II-C of Justice Scalia's opinion and concur in the judgment of affirmance. The rule allowing jurisdiction to be obtained over a non-resident by personal service in the forum state, without more, has been and is so widely accepted throughout this country that I could not possibly strike it down, either on its face or as applied in this case, on the ground that it denies due process of law guaranteed by the Fourteenth Amendment. Although the Court has the authority under the Amendment to examine even traditionally accepted procedures and declare them invalid, *e.g.*, Shaffer v. Heitner, 433 U.S. 186 (1977), there has been no showing here or elsewhere that as a general proposition the rule is so arbitrary and lacking in common sense in so many instances that it should be held violative of Due Process in every case. . . .

Justice BRENNAN, with whom Justice MARSHALL, Justice BLACKMUN, and Justice O'CONNOR join, concurring in the judgment.

I

I believe that the approach adopted by Justice Scalia's opinion today—reliance solely on historical pedigree—is foreclosed by our decisions in International Shoe Co. v. Washington, 326 U.S. 310 (1945), and Shaffer v. Heitner, 433 U.S. 186 (1977). In *International Shoe*, we held that a state court's assertion of personal jurisdiction does not violate the Due Process Clause if it is consistent with "traditional notions of fair play and substantial justice."[2] In *Shaffer*, we stated that "*all* assertions of state-court jurisdiction must be evaluated according to the standards set forth in *International Shoe* and its progeny." The critical insight of *Shaffer* is that all rules of jurisdiction, even ancient ones, must satisfy contemporary notions of due process. No longer were we content to limit our jurisdictional analysis to pronouncements that "[t]he foundation of jurisdiction is physical power," McDonald v. Mabee, 243 U.S. 90, 91 (1917), and that "every State possesses exclusive jurisdiction and sovereignty over persons and property within its territory." Pennoyer v. Neff, 95 U.S. 714, 722 (1878). While acknowledging that "history must be considered as supporting the proposition that jurisdiction based solely on the presence of property satisfie[d] the demands of due process," we found that this factor could not be "decisive." 433 U.S., at 211-212. We recognized that "'[t]raditional notions of fair play and substantial justice' can be as readily offended by the perpetuation of ancient forms that are no longer justified as by the adoption of new procedures that are inconsistent with the basic values of our constitutional heritage." *Id.*, at 212 (citations omitted). I agree with this approach and continue to believe that "the minimum-contacts analysis developed in *International Shoe* . . . represents a far more sensible construct for the exercise of state-court jurisdiction than the patchwork of legal and factual fictions that has been generated from the decision in Pennoyer v. Neff." *Id.*, at 219 (citation omitted) (Brennan, J., concurring in part and dissenting in part).

II

Tradition, though alone not dispositive, is of course *relevant* to the question whether the rule of transient jurisdiction is consistent with due process.[7] Tradition is salient not in the sense that practices of the past are automatically reasonable today; indeed, under such a standard, the legitimacy of transient jurisdiction would be called into question because the rule's historical "pedigree" is a matter of intense debate. The rule was a stranger to the common law and was rather weakly implanted in American jurisprudence "at the crucial time for present purposes: 1868, when the Fourteenth Amendment was adopted." *Ante*, at 2111. For

---

2. Our reference in *International Shoe* to "traditional notions of fair play and substantial justice," 326 U.S., at 316, meant simply that those concepts are indeed traditional ones, not that, as Justice Scalia's opinion suggests, *see ante*, at 2116, 2117, their specific *content* was to be determined by tradition alone. We recognized that contemporary societal norms must play a role in our analysis. *See, e.g.*, 326 U.S., at 317 (considerations of "reasonable[ness], in the context of our federal system of government").

7. I do not propose that the "contemporary notions of due process" to be applied are no more than "each Justice's subjective assessment of what is fair and just." *Ante*, at 2117. Rather, the inquiry is guided by our decisions beginning with International Shoe Co. v. Washington, 326 U.S. 310 (1945), and the specific factors that we have developed to ascertain whether a jurisdictional rule comports with "traditional notions of fair play and substantial justice." This analysis may not be "mechanical or quantitative," *International Shoe*, 326 U.S., at 319, but neither is it "freestanding," *ante*, at 2119, or dependent on personal whim. Our experience with this approach demonstrates that it is well within our competence to employ.

much of the 19th century, American courts did not uniformly recognize the concept of transient jurisdiction, and it appears that the transient rule did not receive wide currency until well after our decision in Pennoyer v. Neff, 95 U.S. 714 (1878).

Rather, I find the historical background relevant because, however murky the jurisprudential origins of transient jurisdiction, the fact that American courts have announced the rule for perhaps a century (first in dicta, more recently in holdings) provides a defendant voluntarily present in a particular state *today* "clear notice that [he] is subject to suit" in the forum. World-Wide Volkswagen Corp. v. Woodson, 444 U.S. 286, 297 (1980). Regardless of whether Justice Story's account of the rule's genesis is mythical, our common understanding *now*, fortified by a century of judicial practice, is that jurisdiction is often a function of geography. The transient rule is consistent with reasonable expectations and is entitled to a strong presumption that it comports with due process.

By visiting the forum State, a transient defendant actually "avail[s]" himself, *Burger King*, of significant benefits provided by the State. His health and safety are guaranteed by the State's police, fire, and emergency medical services; he is free to travel on the State's roads and waterways; he likely enjoys the fruits of the State's economy as well. Moreover, the Privileges and Immunities Clause of Article IV prevents a state government from discriminating against a transient defendant by denying him the protections of its law or the right of access to its courts. Subject only to the doctrine of forum non conveniens, an out-of-state plaintiff may use state courts in all circumstances in which those courts would be available to state citizens. Without transient jurisdiction, an asymmetry would arise: a transient would have the full benefit of the power of the forum State's courts as a plaintiff while retaining immunity from their authority as a defendant. *See* Maltz, *Sovereign Authority, Fairness, and Personal Jurisdiction: The Case for the Doctrine of Transient Jurisdiction*, 66 Wash. U. L.Q. 671, 698-699 (1988).

The potential burdens on a transient defendant are slight. "[M]odern transportation and communications have made it much less burdensome for a party sued to defend himself" in a State outside his place of residence. That the defendant has already journeyed at least once before to the forum—as evidenced by the fact that he was served with process there—is an indication that suit in the forum likely would not be prohibitively inconvenient. Finally, any burdens that do arise can be ameliorated by a variety of procedural devices. For these reasons, as a rule the exercise of personal jurisdiction over a defendant based on his voluntary presence in the forum will satisfy the requirements of due process.

In this case, it is undisputed that petitioner was served with process while voluntarily and knowingly in the State of California. I therefore concur in the judgment.

Justice STEVENS, concurring in the judgment.

As I explained in my separate writing, I did not join the Court's opinion in Shaffer v. Heitner, 433 U.S. 186 (1977), because I was concerned by its unnecessarily broad reach. *Id.*, at 217-219 (opinion concurring in judgment). The same concern prevents me from joining either Justice Scalia's or Justice Brennan's opinion in this case. For me, it is sufficient to note that the historical evidence and consensus identified by Justice Scalia, the considerations of fairness identified by Justice Brennan, and the common sense displayed by Justice White, all combine to demonstrate that this is, indeed, a very easy case.* Accordingly, I agree that the judgment should be affirmed.

Questions and Comments

(1) Which way do you think Justice Scalia would have voted, had he been on the Court, in Shaffer v. Heitner, page 446 *infra? Compare* his opinion for the Court in Sun Oil v. Wortman, page 316 *supra.* Is there any real reason that due process should be more tied to tradition than any other constitutional provision? Or is it simply a result of the coincidence that the Justices who penned certain important personal jurisdiction precedents happened "subjectively" to choose to phrase the test in terms of tradition?

(2) In response to Justice Scalia's charges of subjectivity, Professor Weintraub offers one objective basis for rejecting transient jurisdiction: "[T]he use of the defendant's temporary presence in the forum as grounds for personal jurisdiction is contrary to the consensus of civilized nations and, if used against foreigners, may violate international law." Weintraub, *An Objective Basis for Rejecting Transient Jurisdiction,* in *The Future of Personal Jurisdiction: A Symposium on Burnham v. Superior Court,* 22 Rutgers L.J. 611 (1991).

(3) In Grace v. MacArthur, 170 F. Supp. 442 (E.D. Ark. 1959), jurisdiction was based on service of process while in an airplane flying over the territory. Would such service meet Justice Scalia's test of tradition? Would it satisfy the test set out in the 1986 revisions to the Restatement Second, cited in the opinion?

(4) "Tag" jurisdiction is exercised regularly in human rights litigation between alien plaintiffs against alien defendants alleging human rights abuses committed abroad. For example, in Kadic v. Karadzic, 70 F.3d 232 (2d Cir. 1995), Radovan Karadzic, president of the self-proclaimed Bosnian-Serb republic of "Srpska," was served in New York while attending a conference at the United Nations. Karadzic left New York soon thereafter, and a jury returned a default judgment worth $4.5 billion. To date the judgment has not been enforced.

(5) Most courts refrain from exercising "tag jurisdiction" when the defendant is brought into the state by fraud or unlawful force for the purpose of service of process. *See, e.g.,* May Dept. Stores Co. v. Wilansky, 900 F. Supp. 1154 (E.D. Mo. 1995); Wyman v. Newhouse, 93 F.2d 313 (2d Cir. 1937); *see also* Restatement (Second) of Conflict of Laws §82 (1971); *compare* Coyne v. Grupo Industrial Trieme, S.A. de C.V., 105 F.R.D. 627, 630 n.6 (D.D.C. 1985) (extending immunity from service given defendants lured into the jurisdiction by fraud to any later attempts to serve the defendant pursuant to a long-arm statute). Courts disagree about the legal basis for this rule. Most courts hold that jurisdiction cannot be acquired when service of process is obtained fraudulently. *See, e.g., Wyman,* 93 F.2d at 315. Some courts, as well as the Restatement, conclude that jurisdiction is technically satisfied but that courts should refrain from exercising jurisdiction in favor of one who has obtained service of his summons by unlawful means. *See, e.g.,* Economy Electric Co. v. Automatic Electric Co., 118 S.E. 3 (N.C. 1923); Restatement §82 cmt. f (1971). Does anything turn on this distinction?

---

* Perhaps the adage about hard cases making bad law should be revised to cover easy cases.

Apart from its seaminess, what is objectionable about fraudulent inducement into the jurisdiction? Is basing judicial jurisdiction upon presence procured by fraud any worse than basing it on presence completely unrelated to the lawsuit? Is the difference that the defendant who enters the jurisdiction voluntarily and without fraudulent inducement knows the danger that may befall him and therefore waives the right to be free of suit by entering?

Bristol-Myers Squibb v. Superior Court

137 S. Ct. 1773 (2017)

ALITO, J., delivered the opinion of the Court.

More than 600 plaintiffs, most of whom are not California residents, filed this civil action in a California state court against Bristol-Myers Squibb Company (BMS), asserting a variety of state-law claims based on injuries allegedly caused by a BMS drug called Plavix. The California Supreme Court held that the California courts have specific jurisdiction to entertain the nonresidents' claims. We now reverse.

I

A

BMS, a large pharmaceutical company, is incorporated in Delaware and head-quartered in New York, and it maintains substantial operations in both New York and New Jersey. 1 Cal. 5th 783, 790, 377 P.3d 874, 879 (2016). Over 50 percent of BMS's work force in the United States is employed in those two States.

BMS also engages in business activities in other jurisdictions, including California. Five of the company's research and laboratory facilities, which employ a total of around 160 employees, are located there. BMS also employs about 250 sales representatives in California and maintains a small state-government advocacy office in Sacramento.

One of the pharmaceuticals that BMS manufactures and sells is Plavix, a prescription drug that thins the blood and inhibits blood clotting. BMS did not develop Plavix in California, did not create a marketing strategy for Plavix in California, and did not manufacture, label, package, or work on the regulatory approval of the product in California. BMS instead engaged in all of these activities in either New York or New Jersey. But BMS does sell Plavix in California. Between 2006 and 2012, it sold almost 187 million Plavix pills in the State and took in more than $900 million from those sales. 1 Cal. 5th, at 790-791, 377 P. 3d, at 879. This amounts to a little over one percent of the company's nationwide sales revenue.

A group of plaintiffs—consisting of 86 California residents and 592 residents from 33 other States—filed eight separate complaints in California Superior Court, alleging that Plavix had damaged their health. All the complaints asserted 13 claims under California law, including products liability, negligent misrepresentation, and misleading advertising claims. The nonresident plaintiffs did not allege that they obtained Plavix through California physicians or from any other California source; nor did they claim that they were injured by Plavix or were treated for their injuries in California.

Asserting lack of personal jurisdiction, BMS moved to quash service of summons on the nonresidents' claims, but the California Superior Court denied this motion, finding that the California courts had general jurisdiction over BMS "[b]ecause [it] engages in extensive activities in California." App. to Pet. for Cert. 150. BMS unsuccessfully petitioned the State Court of Appeal for a writ of mandate, but after our decision on general jurisdiction in Daimler AG v. Bauman, 571 U.S. 117 (2014), the California Supreme Court instructed the Court of Appeal "to vacate its order denying mandate and to issue an order to show cause why relief sought in the petition should not be granted." App. 9-10.

The Court of Appeal then changed its decision on the question of general jurisdiction. 228 Cal. App. 4th 605, 175 Cal. Rptr. 3d 412 (2014). Under *Daimler*, it held, general jurisdiction was clearly lacking, but it went on to find that the California courts had specific jurisdiction over the nonresidents' claims against BMS. 228 Cal. App. 4th 605, 175 Cal. Rptr. 3d, at 425-439.

The California Supreme Court affirmed. The court unanimously agreed with the Court of Appeal on the issue of general jurisdiction, but the court was divided on the question of specific jurisdiction. The majority applied a "sliding scale approach to specific jurisdiction." 1 Cal. 5th, at 806, 377 P. 3d, at 889. Under this approach, "the more wide ranging the defendant's forum contacts, the more readily is shown a connection between the forum contacts and the claim." *Ibid.* (internal quotation marks omitted). Applying this test, the majority concluded that "BMS's extensive contacts with California" permitted the exercise of specific jurisdiction "based on a less direct connection between BMS's forum activities and plaintiffs' claims than might otherwise be required." This attenuated requirement was met, the majority found, because the claims of the nonresidents were similar in several ways to the claims of the California residents (as to which specific jurisdiction was uncontested). The court noted that "[b]oth the resident and nonresident plaintiffs' claims are based on the same allegedly defective product and the assertedly misleading marketing and promotion of that product." And while acknowledging that "there is no claim that Plavix itself was designed and developed in [BMS's California research facilities]," the court thought it significant that other research was done in the State.

Three justices dissented. "The claims of . . . nonresidents injured by their use of Plavix they purchased and used in other states," they wrote, "in no sense arise from BMS's marketing and sales of Plavix in California," and they found that the "mere similarity" of the residents' and nonresidents' claims was not enough. The dissent accused the majority of "expand[ing] specific jurisdiction to the point that, for a large category of defendants, it becomes indistinguishable from general jurisdiction."

We granted certiorari to decide whether the California courts' exercise of jurisdiction in this case violates the Due Process Clause of the Fourteenth Amendment.[1]

---

1. California law provides that its courts may exercise jurisdiction "on any basis not inconsistent with the Constitution . . . of the United States," Cal. Civ. Proc. Code Ann. §410.10 (West 2004).

II

A

It has long been established that the Fourteenth Amendment limits the personal jurisdiction of state courts. See, *e.g.*, World-Wide Volkswagen Corp. v. Woodson, 444 U.S. 286, 291 (1980); International Shoe Co. v. Washington, 326 U.S. 310, 316-317 (1945); Pennoyer v. Neff, 95 U.S. 714, 733 (1878). Because "[a] state court's assertion of jurisdiction exposes defendants to the State's coercive power," it is "subject to review for compatibility with the Fourteenth Amendment's Due Process Clause," Goodyear Dunlop Tires Operations, S. A. v. Brown, 564 U.S. 915, 918 (2011), which "limits the power of a state court to render a valid personal judgment against a nonresident defendant," *World-Wide Volkswagen, supra*, at 291. The primary focus of our personal jurisdiction inquiry is the defendant's relationship to the forum State.

Since our seminal decision in *International Shoe*, our decisions have recognized two types of personal jurisdiction: "general" (sometimes called "all-purpose") jurisdiction and "specific" (sometimes called "case-linked") jurisdiction. *Goodyear*, 564 U.S., at 919. "For an individual, the paradigm forum for the exercise of general jurisdiction is the individual's domicile; for a corporation, it is an equivalent place, one in which the corporation is fairly regarded as at home." *Id.*, at 924. A court with general jurisdiction may hear *any* claim against that defendant, even if all the incidents underlying the claim occurred in a different State. But "only a limited set of affiliations with a forum will render a defendant amenable to" general jurisdiction in that State. *Daimler*, 571 U.S., at 137.

Specific jurisdiction is very different. In order for a state court to exercise specific jurisdiction, "the *suit*" must "aris[e] out of or relat[e] to the defendant's contacts with the *forum*." *Id.*, at 127 (internal quotation marks omitted; emphasis added). In other words, there must be "an affiliation between the forum and the underlying controversy, principally, [an] activity or an occurrence that takes place in the forum State and is therefore subject to the State's regulation." *Goodyear*, 564 U.S., at 919 (internal quotation marks and brackets omitted). For this reason, "specific jurisdiction is confined to adjudication of issues deriving from, or connected with, the very controversy that establishes jurisdiction." *Ibid.* (internal quotation marks omitted).

B

In determining whether personal jurisdiction is present, a court must consider a variety of interests. These include "the interests of the forum State and of the plaintiff in proceeding with the cause in the plaintiff's forum of choice." Kulko v. Superior Court of Cal., City and County of San Francisco, 436 U.S. 84, 92 (1978); see *Daimler, supra*, at 139, n. 20; Asahi Metal Industry Co. v. Superior Court of Cal., Solano Cty., 480 U.S. 102, 113 (1987); *World-Wide Volkswagen*, 444 U.S., at 292. But the "primary concern" is "the burden on the defendant." *Id.*, at 292. Assessing this burden obviously requires a court to consider the practical problems resulting from litigating in the forum, but it also encompasses the more abstract matter of submitting to the coercive power of a State that may have little legitimate interest in the claims in question. As we have put it, restrictions on personal jurisdiction "are more than a guarantee of immunity from inconvenient or distant litigation. They are a consequence of territorial limitations on the power of the respective States." Hanson v. Denckla, 357 U.S. 235, 251 (1958). "[T]he States retain many essential attributes of sovereignty, including, in particular, the sovereign power to try causes in their courts. The sovereignty of each State . . . implie[s] a limitation on the sovereignty of all its sister States." *World-Wide Volkswagen*, 444 U.S., at 293. And at times, this federalism interest may be decisive. As we explained in *World-Wide Volkswagen*, "[e]ven if the defendant would suffer minimal or no inconvenience from being forced to litigate before the tribunals of another State; even if the forum State has a strong interest in applying its law to the controversy; even if the forum State is the most convenient location for litigation, the Due Process Clause, acting as an instrument of interstate federalism, may sometimes act to divest the State of its power to render a valid judgment." *Id.*, at 294.

III

A

Our settled principles regarding specific jurisdiction control this case. In order for a court to exercise specific jurisdiction over a claim, there must be an "affiliation between the forum and the underlying controversy, principally, [an] activity or an occurrence that takes place in the forum State." *Goodyear*, 564 U.S., at 919 (internal quotation marks and brackets in original omitted). When there is no such connection, specific jurisdiction is lacking regardless of the extent of a defendant's unconnected activities in the State. See *id.*, at 931, n.6 ("[E]ven regularly occurring sales of a product in a State do not justify the exercise of jurisdiction over a claim unrelated to those sales").

For this reason, the California Supreme Court's "sliding scale approach" is difficult to square with our precedents. Under the California approach, the strength of the requisite connection between the forum and the specific claims at issue is relaxed if the defendant has extensive forum contacts that are unrelated to those claims. Our cases provide no support for this approach, which resembles a loose and spurious form of general jurisdiction. For specific jurisdiction, a defendant's general connections with the forum are not enough. As we have said, "[a] corporation's 'continuous activity of some sorts within a state . . . is not enough to support the demand that the corporation be amenable to suits unrelated to that activity.'" *Id.*, at 927 (quoting *International Shoe*, 326 U.S., at 318).

The present case illustrates the danger of the California approach. The State Supreme Court found that specific jurisdiction was present without identifying any adequate link between the State and the nonresidents' claims. As noted, the nonresidents were not prescribed Plavix in California, did not purchase Plavix in California, did not ingest Plavix in California, and were not injured by Plavix in California. The mere fact that *other* plaintiffs were prescribed, obtained, and ingested Plavix in California—and allegedly sustained the same injuries as did the nonresidents—does not allow the State to assert specific jurisdiction over the nonresidents' claims. As we have explained, "a defendant's relationship with a . . . third party, standing alone, is an insufficient basis for jurisdiction." *Walden*, [571 U.S. 277, 286 (2014)]. This remains true even when third parties (here, the plaintiffs who reside in California) can bring claims similar to those brought by the nonresidents. Nor is it sufficient—or even relevant—that BMS conducted research in California on matters unrelated to Plavix. What is needed—and what is missing here—is a connection between the forum and the specific claims at issue.

Our decision in *Walden*, *supra*, illustrates this requirement. In that case, Nevada plaintiffs sued an out-of-state defendant for conducting an allegedly unlawful search of the plaintiffs while they were in Georgia preparing to board a plane bound for Nevada. We held that the Nevada courts lacked specific jurisdiction even though the plaintiffs were Nevada residents and "suffered foreseeable harm in Nevada." *Id.*, at 289. Because the "*relevant* conduct occurred entirely in Georgi[a] . . . the mere fact that [this] conduct affected plaintiffs with connections to the forum State d[id] not suffice to authorize jurisdiction." *Id.*, at 291 (emphasis added).

In today's case, the connection between the nonresidents' claims and the forum is even weaker. The relevant plaintiffs are not California residents and do not claim to have suffered harm in that State. In addition, as in *Walden*, all the conduct giving rise to the nonresidents' claims occurred elsewhere. It follows that the California courts cannot claim specific jurisdiction. See *World-Wide Volkswagen*, *supra*, at 295 (finding no personal jurisdiction in Oklahoma because the defendant "carr[ied] on no activity whatsoever in Oklahoma" and dismissing "the fortuitous circumstance that a single Audi automobile, sold [by defendants] in New York to New York residents, happened to suffer an accident while passing through Oklahoma" as an "isolated occurrence").

. . .

IV

Our straightforward application in this case of settled principles of personal jurisdiction will not result in the parade of horribles that respondents conjure up. See Brief for Respondents 38-47. Our decision does not prevent the California and out-of-state plaintiffs from joining together in a consolidated action in the States that have general jurisdiction over BMS. BMS concedes that such suits could be brought in either New York or Delaware. See Brief for Petitioner 13. Alternatively, the plaintiffs who are residents of a particular State—for example, the 92 plaintiffs from Texas and the 71 from Ohio—could probably sue together in their home States. In addition, since our decision concerns the due process limits on the exercise of specific jurisdiction by a State, we leave open the question whether the Fifth Amendment imposes the same restrictions on the exercise of personal jurisdiction by a federal court. See Omni Capital Int'l, Ltd. v. Rudolf Wolff & Co., 484 U.S. 97, 102, n.5 (1987).

* * *

The judgment of the California Supreme Court is reversed, and the case is remanded for further proceedings not inconsistent with this opinion.

Justice SOTOMAYOR, dissenting.

Three years ago, the Court imposed substantial curbs on the exercise of general jurisdiction in its decision in Daimler AG v. Bauman, 571 U.S. 117 (2014). Today, the Court takes its first step toward a similar contraction of specific jurisdiction by holding that a corporation that engages in a nationwide course of conduct cannot be held accountable in a state court by a group of injured people unless all of those people were injured in the forum State.

I fear the consequences of the Court's decision today will be substantial. The majority's rule will make it difficult to aggregate the claims of plaintiffs across the country whose claims may be worth little alone. It will make it impossible to bring a nationwide mass action in state court against defendants who are "at home" in different States. And it will result in piecemeal litigation and the bifurcation of claims. None of this is necessary. A core concern in this Court's personal jurisdiction cases is fairness. And there is nothing unfair about subjecting a massive corporation to suit in a State for a nationwide course of conduct that injures both forum residents and nonresidents alike.

I

Bristol-Myers Squibb is a Fortune 500 pharmaceutical company incorporated in Delaware and headquartered in New York. It employs approximately 25,000 people worldwide and earns annual revenues of over $15 billion. In the late 1990's, Bristol-Myers began to market and sell a prescription blood thinner called Plavix. Plavix was advertised as an effective tool for reducing the risk of blood clotting for those vulnerable to heart attacks and to strokes. The ads worked: At the height of its popularity, Plavix was a blockbuster, earning Bristol-Myers billions of dollars in annual revenues.

Bristol-Myers' advertising and distribution efforts were national in scope. It conducted a single nationwide advertising campaign for Plavix, using television, magazine, and Internet ads to broadcast its message. A consumer in California heard the same advertisement as a consumer in Maine about the benefits of Plavix. Bristol-Myers' distribution of Plavix also proceeded through nationwide channels: Consistent with its usual practice, it relied on a small number of wholesalers to distribute Plavix throughout the country. One of those distributors, McKesson Corporation, was named as a defendant below; during the relevant time period, McKesson was responsible for almost a quarter of Bristol-Myers' revenue worldwide.

The 2005 publication of an article in the New England Journal of Medicine questioning the efficacy and safety of Plavix put Bristol-Myers on the defensive, as consumers around the country began to claim that they were injured by the drug. The plaintiffs in these consolidated cases are 86 people who allege they were injured by Plavix in California and several hundred others who say they were injured by the drug in other States.[2] They filed their suits in California Superior Court,

---

2. Like the parties and the majority, I refer to these people as "residents" and "nonresidents" of California as a convenient shorthand. See Brief for Petitioner 4-5, n.1; Brief for Respondents 2, n.1.

raising product-liability claims against Bristol-Myers and McKesson. Their claims are "materially identical," as Bristol-Myers concedes. See Brief for Petitioner 4, n.1. Bristol-Myers acknowledged it was subject to suit in California state court by the residents of that State. But it moved to dismiss the claims brought by the nonresident plaintiffs—respondents here—for lack of jurisdiction. The question here, accordingly, is not whether Bristol-Myers is subject to suit in California on claims that arise out of the design, development, manufacture, marketing, and distribution of Plavix—it is. The question is whether Bristol-Myers is subject to suit in California only on the residents' claims, or whether a state court may also hear the nonresidents' "identical" claims.

II

. . .

First, there is no dispute that Bristol-Myers "purposefully avail[ed] itself," *Nicastro*, 564 U.S., at 877, of California and its substantial pharmaceutical market. Bristol-Myers employs over 400 people in California and maintains half a dozen facilities in the State engaged in research, development, and policymaking. It contracts with a California-based distributor, McKesson, whose sales account for a significant portion of its revenue. And it markets and sells its drugs, including Plavix, in California, resulting in total Plavix sales in that State of nearly $1 billion during the period relevant to this suit.

Second, respondents' claims "relate to" Bristol-Myers' in-state conduct. A claim "relates to" a defendant's forum conduct if it has a "connect[ion] with" that conduct. *International Shoe*, 326 U.S., at 319. So respondents could not, for instance, hale Bristol-Myers into court in California for negligently maintaining the sidewalk outside its New York headquarters—a claim that has no connection to acts Bristol-Myers took in California. But respondents' claims against Bristol-Myers look nothing like such a claim. Respondents' claims against Bristol-Myers concern conduct materially identical to acts the company took in California: its marketing and distribution of Plavix, which it undertook on a nationwide basis in all 50 States. That respondents were allegedly injured by this nationwide course of conduct in Indiana, Oklahoma, and Texas, and not California, does not mean that their claims do not "relate to" the advertising and distribution efforts that Bristol-Myers undertook in that State. All of the plaintiffs—residents and nonresidents alike—allege that they were injured by the same essential acts. Our cases require no connection more direct than that.

Finally, and importantly, there is no serious doubt that the exercise of jurisdiction over the nonresidents' claims is reasonable. Because Bristol-Myers already faces claims that are identical to the nonresidents' claims in this suit, it will not be harmed by having to defend against respondents' claims: Indeed, the alternative approach—litigating those claims in separate suits in as many as 34 different States—would prove far more burdensome. By contrast, the plaintiffs' "interest in obtaining convenient and effective relief," *Burger King*, 471 U.S., at 477 (internal quotation marks omitted), is obviously furthered by participating in a consolidated proceeding in one State under shared counsel, which allows them to minimize costs, share discovery, and maximize recoveries on claims that may be too small to bring on their own. Cf. American Express Co. v. Italian Colors Restaurant, 570 U.S. 228, 245 (2013) (Kagan, J., dissenting) ("No rational actor would bring a claim worth tens of thousands of dollars if doing so meant incurring costs in the hundreds of thousands"). California, too, has an interest in providing a forum for mass actions like this one: Permitting the nonresidents to bring suit in California alongside the residents facilitates the efficient adjudication of the residents' claims and allows it to regulate more effectively the conduct of both nonresident corporations like Bristol-Myers and resident ones like McKesson.

Nothing in the Due Process Clause prohibits a California court from hearing respondents' claims — at least not in a case where they are joined to identical claims brought by California residents.

III

. . .

B

I fear the consequences of the majority's decision today will be substantial. Even absent a rigid requirement that a defendant's in-state conduct must actually cause a plaintiff's claim,[3] the upshot of today's opinion is that plaintiffs cannot join their claims together and sue a defendant in a State in which only some of them have been injured. That rule is likely to have consequences far beyond this case.

First, and most prominently, the Court's opinion in this case will make it profoundly difficult for plaintiffs who are injured in different States by a defendant's nationwide course of conduct to sue that defendant in a single, consolidated action. The holding of today's opinion is that such an action cannot be brought in a State in which only some plaintiffs were injured. Not to worry, says the majority: The plaintiffs here could have sued Bristol-Myers in New York or Delaware; could "probably" have subdivided their separate claims into 34 lawsuits in the States in which they were injured; and might have been able to bring a single suit in federal court (an "open . . . question"). *Ante,* at 12. Even setting aside the majority's caveats, what is the purpose of such limitations? What interests are served by preventing the consolidation of claims and limiting the forums in which they can be consolidated? The effect of the Court's opinion today is to eliminate nationwide mass actions in any State other than those in which a defendant is " 'essentially at

---

3. Bristol-Myers urges such a rule upon us, Brief for Petitioner 14-37, but its adoption would have consequences far beyond those that follow from today's factbound opinion. Among other things, it might call into question whether even a plaintiff *injured* in a State by an item identical to those sold by a defendant in that State could avail himself of that State's courts to redress his injuries — a result specifically contemplated by World-Wide Volkswagen Corp. v. Woodson, 444 U.S. 286, 297 (1980). See Brief for Civil Procedure Professors as *Amici Curiae* 14-18; see also J. McIntyre Machinery, Ltd. v. Nicastro, 564 U.S. 873, 906-907 (2011) (GINSBURG, J., dissenting). That question, and others like it, appears to await another case.

home.' "[4] See *Daimler*, 571 U.S., at 152. Such a rule hands one more tool to corporate defendants determined to prevent the aggregation of individual claims, and forces injured plaintiffs to bear the burden of bringing suit in what will often be far flung jurisdictions.

Second, the Court's opinion today may make it impossible to bring certain mass actions at all. After this case, it is difficult to imagine where it might be possible to bring a nationwide mass action against two or more defendants headquartered and incorporated in different States. There will be no State where both defendants are "at home," and so no State in which the suit can proceed. What about a nationwide mass action brought against a defendant not headquartered or incorporated in the United States? Such a defendant is not "at home" in any State. Cf. *id.*, at 152-153 (Sotomayor, J., concurring in judgment). Especially in a world in which defendants are subject to general jurisdiction in only a handful of States, see *ibid.*, the effect of today's opinion will be to curtail—and in some cases eliminate—plaintiffs' ability to hold corporations fully accountable for their nationwide conduct.

The majority chides respondents for conjuring a "parade of horribles," *ante*, at 12, but says nothing about how suits like those described here will survive its opinion in this case. The answer is simple: They will not.

* * *

It "does not offend 'traditional notions of fair play and substantial justice,'" *International Shoe*, 326 U.S., at 316, to permit plaintiffs to aggregate claims arising out of a single nationwide course of conduct in a single suit in a single State where some, but not all, were injured. But that is exactly what the Court holds today is barred by the Due Process Clause.

This is not a rule the Constitution has required before. I respectfully dissent.

BNSF Railway Co. v. Tyrrell

137 S. Ct. 1549 (2017)

GINSBURG, J., delivered the opinion of the Court.

The two cases we decide today arise under the Federal Employers' Liability Act (FELA), 35 Stat. 65, as amended, 45 U.S.C. §51 *et seq.*, which makes railroads liable in money damages to their employees for on-the-job injuries. Both suits were pursued in Montana state courts although the injured workers did not reside in Montana, nor were they injured there. The defendant railroad, BNSF Railway Company (BNSF), although "doing business" in Montana when the litigation commenced, was not incorporated in Montana, nor did it maintain its principal place of business in that State. To justify the exercise of personal jurisdiction over BNSF, the Montana Supreme Court relied on §56, which provides in relevant part:

---

4. The Court today does not confront the question whether its opinion here would also apply to a class action in which a plaintiff injured in the forum State seeks to represent a nationwide class of plaintiffs, not all of whom were injured there. Cf. Devlin v. Scardelletti, 536 U.S. 1, 9-10 (2002) ("Nonnamed class members . . . may be parties for some purposes and not for others"); see also Wood, Adjudicatory Jurisdiction and Class Actions, 62 Ind. L.J. 597, 616-617 (1987).

"Under this chapter an action may be brought in a district court of the United States, in the district of the residence of the defendant, or in which the cause of action arose, or in which the defendant shall be doing business at the time of commencing such action. The jurisdiction of the courts of the United States under this chapter shall be concurrent with that of the courts of the several States."

* * *

III

Because FELA does not authorize state courts to exercise personal jurisdiction over a railroad solely on the ground that the railroad does some business in their States, the Montana courts' assertion of personal jurisdiction over BNSF here must rest on Mont. Rule Civ. Proc. 4(b)(1), the State's provision for the exercise of personal jurisdiction over "persons found" in Montana. See *supra*, at 2-3. BNSF does not contest that it is "found within" Montana as the State's courts comprehend that rule. We therefore inquire whether the Montana courts' exercise of personal jurisdiction under Montana law comports with the Due Process Clause of the Fourteenth Amendment.

In *International Shoe*, this Court explained that a state court may exercise personal jurisdiction over an out-of-state defendant who has "certain minimum contacts with [the State] such that the maintenance of the suit does not offend 'traditional notions of fair play and substantial justice.'" 326 U.S., at 316. Elaborating on this guide, we have distinguished between specific or case-linked jurisdiction and general or all-purpose jurisdiction. See, *e.g.*, *Daimler*, 571 U.S., at 127; Goodyear Dunlop Tires Operations, S. A. v. Brown, 564 U.S. 915, 919 (2011); Helicopteros Nacionales de Colombia, S. A. v. Hall, 466 U.S. 408, 414, nn.8, 9 (1984). Because neither Nelson nor Tyrrell alleges any injury from work in or related to Montana, only the propriety of general jurisdiction is at issue here.

Goodyear and *Daimler* clarified that "[a] court may assert general jurisdiction over foreign (sister-state or foreign-country) corporations to hear any and all claims against them when their affiliations with the State are so 'continuous and systematic' as to render them essentially at home in the forum State." *Daimler*, 571 U.S., at 127 (quoting *Goodyear*, 564 U.S., at 919). The "paradigm" forums in which a corporate defendant is "at home," we explained, are the corporation's place of incorporation and its principal place of business. *Daimler*, 571 U.S., at 136-138; *Goodyear*, 564 U.S., at 924. The exercise of general jurisdiction is not limited to these forums; in an "exceptional case," a corporate defendant's operations in another forum "may be so substantial and of such a nature as to render the corporation at home in that State." *Daimler*, 571 U.S., at 139, n.19. We suggested that Perkins v. Benguet Consol. Mining Co., 342 U.S. 437 (1952), exemplified such a case. *Daimler*, 571 U.S., at 139, n.19. In *Perkins*, war had forced the defendant corporation's owner to temporarily relocate the enterprise from the Philippines to Ohio. 342 U.S., at 447-448. Because Ohio then became "the center of the corporation's wartime activities," *Daimler*, 571 U.S., at 130, n.8, suit was proper there, *Perkins*, 342 U.S., at 448.

The Montana Supreme Court distinguished *Daimler* on the ground that we did not there confront "a FELA claim or a railroad defendant." 383 Mont., at

424, 373 P.3d, at 6. The Fourteenth Amendment due process constraint described in *Daimler*, however, applies to all state-court assertions of general jurisdiction over nonresident defendants; the constraint does not vary with the type of claim asserted or business enterprise sued.[5]

BNSF, we repeat, is not incorporated in Montana and does not maintain its principal place of business there. Nor is BNSF so heavily engaged in activity in Montana "as to render [it] essentially at home" in that State. See *Daimler*, 571 U.S., at 127 (internal quotation marks omitted). As earlier noted, BNSF has over 2,000 miles of railroad track and more than 2,000 employees in Montana. But, as we observed in *Daimler*, "the general jurisdiction inquiry does not focus solely on the magnitude of the defendant's in-state contacts." *Id.*, at 139, n.20 (internal quotation marks and alterations omitted). Rather, the inquiry "calls for an appraisal of a corporation's activities in their entirety"; "[a] corporation that operates in many places can scarcely be deemed at home in all of them." *Ibid.* In short, the business BNSF does in Montana is sufficient to subject the railroad to specific personal jurisdiction in that State on claims related to the business it does in Montana. But in-state business, we clarified in *Daimler* and *Goodyear*, does not suffice to permit the assertion of general jurisdiction over claims like Nelson's and Tyrrell's that are unrelated to any activity occurring in Montana.[6]

* * *

For the reasons stated, the judgment of the Montana Supreme Court is reversed, and the cases are remanded for further proceedings not inconsistent with this opinion.

It is so ordered.

Justice SOTOMAYOR, concurring in part and dissenting in part.

The majority makes much of the fact that BNSF's contacts in Montana are only a percentage of its contacts with other jurisdictions. . . . But *International*

---

5. The Montana Supreme Court also erred in asserting that "Congress drafted the FELA to make a railroad 'at home' for jurisdictional purposes wherever it is 'doing business.'" 383 Mont. 417, 425, 373 P.3d 1, 6 (2016). As discussed, in §56's first sentence, Congress dealt with venue only, not personal jurisdiction.

6. Justice Sotomayor, dissenting in part, renews a debate comprehensively aired in Daimler AG v. Bauman. There, as again here, Justice Sotomayor treats the assertion of jurisdiction by the State of Washington courts in International Shoe Co. v. Washington, 326 U.S. 310 (1945), as an exercise of general, dispute-blind, jurisdiction, thereby overlooking the fundamental difference between *International Shoe* and these cases. In *International Shoe*, the defendant corporation's in-state activities had "not only been continuous and systematic, but also g[a]ve rise to the liabilities sued on." 326 U.S., at 317. The state courts there asserted jurisdiction not over claims that had nothing to do with the State; instead, they exercised adjudicatory authority to hold the defendant corporation accountable for activity pursued within the State of Washington. This Court, therefore, had no occasion in *International Shoe* to "engage in a comparison between International Shoe's contacts within the State of Washington and the other States in which it operated." In marked contrast to *International Shoe*, Nelson's and Tyrrell's claims have no relationship to anything that occurred or had its principal impact in Montana.

This Court's opinion is not limited to §56 because the Montana Supreme Court went on to address and decide the question: Do "Montana courts have personal jurisdiction over BNSF under Montana law?" 383 Mont., at 426, 373 P.3d, at 7. See also *id.*, at 429, 373 P.3d, at 9 ("Under Montana law, Montana courts have general personal jurisdiction over BNSF.").

Shoe, which the majority agrees is the springboard for our modern personal jurisdiction jurisprudence, applied no comparative contacts test. There the Court analyzed whether the Delaware corporation had "by its activities in the State of Washington rendered itself amenable to proceedings" in the State. 326 U.S., at 311. The Court evaluated whether the corporation had offices in the forum State, made contracts there, delivered goods there, or employed salesmen there. See *id.*, at 313. Despite acknowledging that the corporation maintained places of business in several States, *ibid.*, the Court did not engage in a comparison between International Shoe's contacts within the State of Washington and the other States in which it operated.[7] The Court noted that the corporation employed 11 to 13 salesmen in Washington but did not query how that number compared to the number of salesmen in other States. *Ibid.* As well it should not have; the relative percentage of contacts is irrelevant. The focus should be on the quality and quantity of the defendant's contacts in the forum State.[8]

. . .

2. Purposeful Availment and Foreseeability

World-Wide Volkswagen Corp. v. Woodson
444 U.S. 286 (1980)

Justice WHITE delivered the opinion of the Court.

The issue before us is whether, consistently with the Due Process Clause of the Fourteenth Amendment, an Oklahoma court may exercise in personam jurisdiction over a nonresident automobile retailer and its wholesale distributor in a products liability action, when the defendants' only connection with Oklahoma is the fact that an automobile sold in New York to New York residents became involved in an accident in Oklahoma.

I

Respondents Harry and Kay Robinson purchased a new Audi automobile from petitioner Seaway Volkswagen, Inc. (Seaway) in Massena, N.Y., in 1976. The following year the Robinson family, who resided in New York, left that State for a new home in Arizona. As they passed through the State of Oklahoma, another car

---

7. The majority responds that the language from *International Shoe* informs only a specific jurisdiction case. Ante, at 12, n.4. But the majority's view of *International Shoe* is overly restrictive. The terms "specific jurisdiction" and "general jurisdiction" are nowhere to be found in that opinion. And I continue to believe, as I noted in *Daimler*, that there is no material difference between the "continuous and systematic" terminology *International Shoe* used for what we now call specific jurisdiction and the "continuous" and "substantial" terminology it used for what we now call general jurisdiction. See *Daimler*, 571 U.S., at 128, n.6.

8. Indeed, in neither Perkins v. Benguet Consol. Mining Co., 342 U.S. 437 (1952), nor Helicopteros Nacionales de Colombia, S. A. v. Hall, 466 U.S. 408 (1984), did the Court engage in a comparative-contacts analysis.

struck their Audi in the rear, causing a fire which severely burned Kay Robinson and her two children.[1]

The Robinsons subsequently brought a products liability action in the District Court for Creek County, Okla., claiming that their injuries resulted from defective design and placement of the Audi's gas tank and fuel system. They joined as defendants the automobile's manufacturer, Audi NSU Auto Union Aktiengesellschaft (Audi); its importer, Volkswagen of America, Inc. (Volkswagen); its regional distributor, petitioner World-Wide Volkswagen Corporation (World-Wide); and its retail dealer, petitioner Seaway. Seaway and World-Wide entered special appearances,[3] claiming that Oklahoma's exercise of jurisdiction over them would offend the limitations on the State's jurisdiction imposed by the Due Process Clause of the Fourteenth Amendment.

The facts presented to the District Court showed that World-Wide is incorporated and has its business office in New York. It distributes vehicles, parts and accessories, under contract with Volkswagen, to retail dealers in New York, New Jersey, and Connecticut. Seaway, one of these retail dealers, is incorporated and has its place of business in New York. Insofar as the record reveals, Seaway and World-Wide are fully independent corporations whose relations with each other and with Volkswagen and Audi are contractual only. Respondents adduced no evidence that either World-Wide or Seaway does any business in Oklahoma, ships or sells any products to or in that State, has an agent to receive process there, or purchases advertisements in any media calculated to reach Oklahoma. In fact, as respondents' counsel conceded at oral argument, there was no showing that any automobile sold by World-Wide or Seaway has ever entered Oklahoma with the single exception of the vehicle involved in the present case.

Despite the apparent paucity of contacts between petitioners and Oklahoma, the District Court rejected their constitutional claim and reaffirmed that ruling in denying petitioners' motion for reconsideration. Petitioners then sought a writ of prohibition in the Supreme Court of Oklahoma to restrain the District Judge, respondent Charles S. Woodson, from exercising in personam jurisdiction over them. They renewed their contention that because they had no "minimal contacts," with the State of Oklahoma, the actions of the District Judge were in violation of their rights under the Due Process Clause.

The Supreme Court of Oklahoma [held] that personal jurisdiction over petitioners was authorized by Oklahoma's "Long-Arm" Statute, Okla. Stat., Tit. 12, §1701.3(a)(4) (1961) . . . [and] permitted by the United States Constitution. The Court's rationale was contained in the following paragraph:

> "In the case before us, the product being sold and distributed by the petitioners is by its very design and purpose so mobile that petitioners can foresee its possible use in Oklahoma. This is especially true of the distributor, who has the exclusive right to distribute such automobile [sic] in New York, New Jersey and

---

1. The driver of the other automobile does not figure in the present litigation.

3. Volkswagen also entered a special appearance in the District Court, but unlike World-Wide and Seaway did not seek review in the Supreme Court of Oklahoma and is not a petitioner here. Both Volkswagen and Audi remain as defendants in the litigation pending before the District Court in Oklahoma.

Connecticut. The evidence presented below demonstrated that goods sold and distributed by the petitioners were used in the State of Oklahoma, and under the facts we believe it reasonable to infer, given the retail value of the automobile, that the petitioners derive substantial income from automobiles which from time to time are used in the State of Oklahoma. This being the case, we hold that under the facts presented, the trial court was justified in concluding that the petitioners derive substantial revenue from goods used or consumed in this State."

We granted certiorari to consider an important constitutional question with respect to state-court jurisdiction and to resolve a conflict between the Supreme Court of Oklahoma and the highest courts of at least four other States. We reverse.

II

As has long been settled, and as we reaffirm today, a state court may exercise personal jurisdiction over a nonresident defendant only so long as there exist "minimum contacts" between the defendant and the forum State. International Shoe Co. v. Washington. The concept of minimum contacts, in turn, can be seen to perform two related, but distinguishable functions. It protects the defendant against the burdens of litigating in a distant or inconvenient forum. And it acts to ensure that the States, through their courts, do not reach out beyond the limits imposed on them by their status as coequal sovereigns in a federal system.

The protection against inconvenient litigations is typically described in terms of "reasonableness" or "fairness." We have said that the defendant's contacts with the forum State must be such that maintenance of the suit "does not offend 'traditional notions of fair play and substantial justice.'" International Shoe Co. v. Washington, quoting Milliken v. Meyer. The relationship between the defendant and the forum must be such that it is "reasonable . . . to require the corporation to defend the particular suit which is brought there." Implicit in this emphasis on reasonableness is the understanding that the burden on the defendant, while always a primary concern, will in an appropriate case be considered in light of other relevant factors, including the forum State's interest in adjudicating the dispute, *see* McGee v. International Life Ins. Co.; the plaintiff's interest in obtaining convenient and effective relief, *see* Kulko v. Superior Court, at least when that interest is not adequately protected by the plaintiff's power to choose the forum, *cf.* Shaffer v. Heitner; the interstate judicial system's interest in obtaining the most efficient resolution of controversies; and the shared interest of the several States in furthering fundamental substantive social policies, *see* Kulko v. Superior Court.

The limits imposed on state jurisdiction by the Due Process Clause, in its role as a guarantor against inconvenient litigation, have been substantially relaxed over the years. As we noted in McGee v. International Life Ins. Co., this trend is largely attributable to a fundamental transformation in the American economy:

"Today many commercial transactions touch two or more States and may involve parties separated by the full continent. With this increasing nationalization of commerce has come a great increase in the amount of business conducted by mail across state lines. At the same time modern transportation and communication have made it much less burdensome for a party sued to defend himself in a State where he engages in economic activity."

The historical developments noted in *McGee*, of course, have only accelerated in the generation since that case was decided.

Nevertheless, we have never accepted the proposition that state lines are irrelevant for jurisdictional purposes, nor could we and remain faithful to the principles of interstate federalism embodied in the Constitution. The economic interdependence of the States was foreseen and desired by the Framers. In the Commerce Clause, they provided that the Nation was to be a common market, a "free trade unit" in which the States are debarred from acting as separable economic entities. But the Framers also intended that the States retain many essential attributes of sovereignty, including, in particular, the sovereign power to try causes in their courts. The sovereignty of each State, in turn, implied a limitation on the sovereignty of all of its sister States — a limitation express or implicit in both the original scheme of the Constitution and the Fourteenth Amendment.

Thus, the Due Process Clause "does not contemplate that a state may make binding a judgment in personam against an individual or corporate defendant with which the state has no contacts, ties, or relations." International Shoe Co. v. Washington. Even if the defendant would suffer minimal or no inconvenience from being forced to litigate before the tribunals of another State; even if the forum State has a strong interest in applying its law to the controversy; even if the forum State is the most convenient location for litigation, the Due Process Clause, acting as an instrument of interstate federalism, may sometimes act to divest the State of its power to render a valid judgment. Hanson v. Denckla.

III

Applying these principles to the case at hand, we find in the record before us a total absence of those affiliating circumstances that are a necessary predicate to any exercise of state-court jurisdiction. Petitioners carry on no activity whatsoever in Oklahoma. They close no sales and perform no services there. They avail themselves of none of the privileges and benefits of Oklahoma law. They solicit no business there either through salespersons or through advertising reasonably calculated to reach the State. Nor does the record show that they regularly sell cars at wholesale or retail to Oklahoma customers or residents or that they indirectly, through others, serve or seek to serve the Oklahoma market. In short, respondents seek to base jurisdiction on one, isolated occurrence and whatever inferences can be drawn therefrom: the fortuitous circumstance that a single Audi automobile, sold in New York to New York residents, happened to suffer an accident while passing through Oklahoma.

It is argued, however, that because an automobile is mobile by its very definition and purpose it was "foreseeable" that the Robinsons' Audi would cause injury in Oklahoma. Yet "foreseeability" alone has never been a sufficient benchmark for personal jurisdiction under the Due Process Clause. . . . In Kulko v. Superior Court, *supra*, it was surely "foreseeable" that a divorced wife would move to California from New York, the domicile of the marriage, and that a minor daughter would live with the mother. Yet we held that California could not exercise jurisdiction in a child-support action over the former husband who had remained in New York.

If foreseeability were the criterion, a local California tire retailer could be forced to defend in Pennsylvania when a blowout occurs there: *see* Erlanger Mills, Inc. v. Cohoes Fibre Mills, Inc.; a Wisconsin seller of a defective automobile jack could be haled before a distant court for damage caused in New Jersey; or a Florida soft drink concessionaire could be summoned to Alaska to account for injuries happening there. Every seller of chattels would in effect appoint the chattel his agent for service of process. His amenability to suit would travel with the chattel. We recently abandoned the outworn rule of Harris v. Balk, that the interest of a creditor in a debt could be extinguished or otherwise affected by any State having transitory jurisdiction over the debtor. Shaffer v. Heitner. Having interred the mechanical rule that a creditor's amenability to a quasi in rem action travels with his debtor, we are unwilling to endorse an analogous principle in the present case.[11]

This is not to say, of course, that foreseeability is wholly irrelevant. But the foreseeability that is critical to due process analysis is not the mere likelihood that a product will find its way into the forum State. Rather, it is that the defendant's conduct and connection with the forum State are such that he should reasonably anticipate being haled into court there. The Due Process Clause, by ensuring the "orderly administration of the laws," gives a degree of predictability to the legal system that allows potential defendants to structure their primary conduct with some minimum assurance as to where that conduct will and will not render them liable to suit.

When a corporation "purposefully avails itself of the privilege of conducting activities within the forum State," it has clear notice that it is subject to suit there, and can act to alleviate the risk of burdensome litigation by procuring insurance, passing the expected costs on to customers, or, if the risks are too great, severing its connection with the State. Hence if the sale of a product of a manufacturer or distributor such as Audi or Volkswagen is not simply an isolated occurrence, but arises from the efforts of the manufacturer or distributor to serve, directly or indirectly, the market for its product in other States, it is not unreasonable to subject it to suit in one of those States if its allegedly defective merchandise has there been the source of injury to its owners or to others. The forum State does not exceed its powers under the Due Process Clause if it asserts personal jurisdiction over a corporation that delivers its products into the stream of commerce with the expectation that they will be purchased by consumers in the forum State. *Compare* Gray v. American Radiator & Standard Sanitary Corp.

But there is no such or similar basis for Oklahoma jurisdiction over World-Wide or Seaway in this case. Seaway's sales are made in Massena, N.Y. World-Wide's

---

11. Respondents' counsel, at oral argument, sought to limit the reach of the foreseeability standard by suggesting that there is something unique about automobiles. It is true that automobiles are uniquely mobile, that they did play a crucial role in the expansion of personal jurisdiction through the fiction of implied consent, *e.g.*, Hess v. Pawloski, and that some of the cases have treated the automobile as a "dangerous instrumentality." But today, under the regime of *International Shoe*, we see no difference for jurisdictional purposes between an automobile and any other chattel. The "dangerous instrumentality" concept apparently was never used to support personal jurisdiction; and to the extent it has relevance today it bears not on jurisdiction but on the possible desirability of imposing substantive principles of tort law such as strict liability.

market, although substantially larger, is limited to dealers in New York, New Jersey, and Connecticut. There is no evidence of record that any automobiles distributed by World-Wide are sold to retail customers outside this tri-State area. It is foreseeable that the purchasers of automobiles sold by World-Wide and Seaway may take them to Oklahoma. But the mere "unilateral activity of those who claim some relationship with a non-resident defendant cannot satisfy the requirement of contact with the forum State." Hanson v. Denckla.

In a variant on the previous argument, it is contended that jurisdiction can be supported by the fact that petitioners earn substantial revenue from goods used in Oklahoma. The Oklahoma Supreme Court so found, drawing the inference that because one automobile sold by petitioners had been used in Oklahoma, others might have been used there also. While this inference seems less than compelling on the facts of the instant case, we need not question the Court's factual findings in order to reject its reasoning.

This argument seems to make the point that the purchase of automobiles in New York, from which the petitioners earn substantial revenue, would not occur *but for* the fact that the automobiles are capable of use in distant States like Oklahoma. Respondents observe that the very purpose of an automobile is to travel, and that travel of automobiles sold by petitioners is facilitated by an extensive chain of Volkswagen service centers throughout the Country, including some in Oklahoma.[12] However, financial benefits accruing to the defendant from a collateral relation to the forum State will not support jurisdiction if they do not stem from a constitutionally cognizable contact with that State. *See* Kulko v. Superior Court. In our view, whatever marginal revenues petitioners may receive by virtue of the fact that their products are capable of use in Oklahoma is far too attenuated a contact to justify that State's exercise of in personam jurisdiction over them.

Because we find that petitioners have no "contacts, ties, or relations" with the State of Oklahoma, the judgment of the Supreme Court of Oklahoma is reversed.

Justice BRENNAN, dissenting.

The Court's opinions focus tightly on the existence of contacts between the forum and the defendant. In so doing, they accord too little weight to the strength of the forum State's interest in the case and fail to explore whether there would be any actual inconvenience to the defendant. The essential inquiry in locating the constitutional limits on state court jurisdiction over absent defendants is whether the particular exercise of jurisdiction offends "traditional notions of fair play and substantial justice." The clear focus in *International Shoe* was on fairness and reasonableness. The Court specifically declined to establish a mechanical test based on the quantum of contacts between a State and the defendant. . . . The existence of contacts, so long as there were some, was merely one way of giving content to the determination of fairness and reasonableness.

Another consideration is the actual burden a defendant must bear in defending the suit in the forum. Because lesser burdens reduce the unfairness to the defendant, jurisdiction may be justified despite less significant contacts. The burden, of course, must be of constitutional dimension. Due process limits on jurisdiction

---

12. As we have noted, petitioners earn no direct revenues from these service centers.

do not protect a defendant from all inconvenience of travel, and it would not be sensible to make the constitutional rule turn solely on the number of miles the defendant must travel to the courtroom.[1] Instead, the constitutionally significant "burden" to be analyzed relates to the mobility of the defendant's defense. For instance, if having to travel to a foreign forum would hamper the defense because witness or evidence of the defendant himself were immobile, or if there were a disproportionately large number of witnesses or amount of evidence that would have to be transported at the defendant's expense, or if being away from home for the duration of the trial would work some special hardship on the defendant, then the Constitution would require special consideration for the defendant's interests.

That considerations other than contacts between the forum and the defendant are relevant necessarily means that the Constitution does not require that trial be held in the State which has the "best contacts" with the defendant. The defendant has no constitutional entitlement to the best forum or, for that matter, to any particular forum. Under even the most restrictive view of *International Shoe*, several States could have jurisdiction over a particular cause of action. We need only determine whether the forum States in these cases satisfy the constitutional minimum. . . .

B

[T]he interest of the forum State and its connection to the litigation is strong. The automobile accident underlying the litigation occurred in Oklahoma. The plaintiffs were hospitalized in Oklahoma when they brought suit. Essential witnesses and evidence were in Oklahoma. *See* Shaffer v. Heitner. The State has a legitimate interest in enforcing its laws designed to keep its highway system safe, and the trial can proceed at least as efficiently in Oklahoma as anywhere else.

The petitioners are not unconnected with the forum. Although both sell automobiles within limited sales territories, each sold the automobile which in fact was driven to Oklahoma where it was involved in an accident.[8] It may be true, as the Court suggests, that each sincerely intended to limit its commercial impact to the limited territory, and that each intended to accept the benefits and protection of the laws only of those States within the territory. But obviously these were unrealistic hopes that cannot be treated as an automatic constitutional shield.[9]

---

1. In fact, a courtroom just across the state line from a defendant may often be far more convenient for the defendant than a courtroom in a distant corner of his own State.

8. On the basis of this fact the state court inferred that the petitioners derived substantial revenue from goods used in Oklahoma. The inference is not without support. Certainly, were use of goods accepted as a relevant contact a plaintiff would not need to have an exact count of the number of petitioners' cars that are used in Oklahoma.

9. Moreover, imposing liability in this case would not so undermine certainty as to destroy an automobile dealer's ability to do business. According jurisdiction does not expand liability except in the marginal case where a plaintiff cannot afford to bring an action except in the plaintiff's own State. In addition, these petitioners are represented by insurance companies. They not only could, but did, purchase insurance to protect them should they stand trial and lose the case. The costs of insurance no doubt are passed on to customers.

An automobile simply is not a stationary item or one designed to be used in one place. An automobile is *intended* to be moved around. Someone in the business of selling large numbers of automobiles can hardly plead ignorance of their mobility or pretend that the automobiles stay put after they are sold. It is not merely that a dealer in automobiles foresees that they will move. The dealer actually intends that the purchasers will use the automobiles to travel to distant States where the dealer does not directly "do business." The sale of an automobile does *purposefully* inject the vehicle into the stream of interstate commerce so that it can travel to distant States.

The Court accepts that a State may exercise jurisdiction over a distributor which "serves" that State "indirectly" by "deliver[ing] its products into the stream of commerce with the expectation that they will [be] purchased by consumers in other States." It is difficult to see why the Constitution should distinguish between a case involving goods which reach a distant State through a chain of distribution and a case involving goods which reach the same State because a consumer, using them as the dealer knew the customer would, took them there.[11] In each case the seller purposefully injects the goods into the stream of commerce and those goods predictably are used in the forum State.

Furthermore, an automobile seller derives substantial benefits from States other than its own. A large part of the value of automobiles is the extensive, nation-wide network of highways. Significant portions of that network have been constructed by and are maintained by the individual States, including Oklahoma. The States, through their highway programs, contribute in a very direct and important way to the value of petitioner's business. Additionally, a network of other related dealerships with their service departments operate throughout the country under the protection of the laws of the various States, including Oklahoma, and enhance the value of petitioners' businesses by facilitating their customers' traveling.

Thus, the Court errs in its conclusion (emphasis added) that "petitioners have *no* 'contacts, ties, or relations'" with Oklahoma. There obviously are contacts, and given Oklahoma's connection to the litigation, the contacts are sufficiently significant to make it fair and reasonable for the petitioners to submit to Oklahoma's jurisdiction.

III

. . .

In effect the Court is allowing defendants to assert the sovereign rights of their home States. The expressed fear is that otherwise all limits on personal jurisdiction would disappear. But the argument's premise is wrong. I would not abolish limits on jurisdiction or strip state boundaries of all significance; I would still require the plaintiff to demonstrate sufficient contacts among the parties, the forum, and the litigation to make the forum a reasonable State in which to hold the trial.

---

11. For example, I cannot understand the constitutional distinction between selling an item in New Jersey and selling an item in New York expecting it to be used in New Jersey.

Justice MARSHALL, with whom Justice BLACKMUN joins, dissenting. . . .

This is a difficult case, and reasonable minds may differ as to whether respondents have alleged a sufficient "relationship among the defendant[s], the forum, and the litigation," Shaffer v. Heitner, to satisfy the requirements of *International Shoe*. I am concerned, however, that the majority has reached its result by taking an unnecessarily narrow view of petitioners' forum-related conduct. The majority asserts that "respondents seek to base jurisdiction on one, isolated occurrence and whatever inferences can be drawn therefrom: the fortuitous circumstance that a single Audi automobile, sold in New York to New York residents, happened to suffer an accident while passing through Oklahoma." If that were the case, I would readily agree that the minimum contacts necessary to sustain jurisdiction are not present. But the basis for the assertion of jurisdiction is not the happenstance that an individual over whom petitioners had no control made a unilateral decision to take a chattel with him to a distant State. Rather, jurisdiction is premised on the deliberate and purposeful actions of the defendants themselves in choosing to become part of a nationwide, indeed a global, network for marketing and servicing automobiles.

Petitioners are sellers of a product whose utility derives from its mobility. . . .

To be sure, petitioners could not know in advance that this particular automobile would be driven to Oklahoma. They must have anticipated, however, that a substantial portion of the cars they sold would travel out of New York. . . .

[The dissenting opinion of Justice BLACKMUN is omitted.]

Questions and Comments

(1) Why did the Robinsons pursue the question of jurisdiction over the dealership and the regional distributor all the way to the Supreme Court when they knew that the court had jurisdiction over the manufacturer and the international distribution by the latter's acquiescence? Why wouldn't a judgment against them have been sufficient since, as Justice Blackmun noted (in an opinion not reproduced above), they are presumably solvent? For everything you ever wanted to know about the real story of *World-Wide Volkswagen*, *see* Adams, World-Wide Volkswagen v. Woodson — *The Rest of the Story*, 72 Neb. L. Rev. 1122 (1993).

(2) How can a Court that is so blasé about overreaching in choice of law (as in *Hague*, page 297 *supra*) be so concerned about jurisdiction? Doesn't a state do more harm when it does the former than when it does the latter? The irony was put into sharp relief when the Minnesota Supreme Court, which decided *Hague* at the state level, ruled that it had no jurisdiction in a case in which a Wisconsin border-city tavern had served alcohol to a Minnesota resident who subsequently had an accident in Minnesota. West American Insurance Co. v. Westin, Inc., 337 P.2d 676 (Minn. 1983). *Cf.* Meyers v. Kallestead, 476 N.W.2d 65 (Iowa 1991) (same, citing *World-Wide Volkswagen*). Isn't the effect of *Hague* and *World-Wide Volkswagen*, taken together, to subject defendants to marginal choices of law when and only when they have substantial *un*related contacts with the forum state? *See* Martin, *Personal Jurisdiction and Choice of Law*, 78 Mich. L. Rev. 872 (1980), and Silberman, Shaffer v. Heitner: *The End of an Era*, 53 N.Y.U. L. Rev. 33, 79-90 (1978).

(3) What would have been the outcome of the case if the Robinsons had been moving to Oklahoma and not merely passing through it on their way to Arizona? If they already lived in Oklahoma at the time of the accident? If they had lived in Oklahoma when they bought the car but the dealership did not know that fact? If they had lived in Oklahoma at the time they bought the car and the dealership did know that fact, but they were the only Oklahoma customers of the dealership? (If you find in favor of jurisdiction in the last hypothetical, would it extend to the regional distributor, which had no dealings with the Robinsons?) What if a moderate number of sales were made to Oklahoma residents and that fact was known to the dealership, but those sales had not been solicited by the dealership?

(4) What is the answer to Justice Brennan's question of why there is a difference between the case where the chain of distribution takes the car to a distant state and the case where the customer takes it there and that fact could have been predicted? Could the difference be based on the concept of *benefit*? Consider: If the state of Oklahoma were to disappear tomorrow, the effect on the defendant dealer's sales would probably be zero. (Recall that the Robinsons were New York residents when they purchased their car.) But if the product in question were one that went through a chain of distribution to Oklahoma (like the valve in Gray v. American Radiator, 22 Ill. 2d 432, 176 N.E.2d 761 (1961)), the disappearance of the state of Oklahoma would decrease sales of the product. Thus, the amount of benefit that the defendant derives from a state, in a pecuniary sense, turns very much on whether the customer or the chain of distribution takes the product into that state.

(5) In footnote 19, Justice Brennan's dissent suggests that application of an unfavorable substantive law that the defendant could not have anticipated might be a factor, under his scheme, for denying jurisdiction. But does it make sense to say that an unfair choice of law will result in a denial of jurisdiction where that choice of law itself is constitutional? Consider, for example, defendants *A* and *B*, both of whom might be subject to unfair and surprising law in State *X* if jurisdiction is asserted there. Would it be rational to deny jurisdiction and allow defendant *A* to escape the law of State *X* while subjecting defendant *B* to that same unfair and surprising law because *B*, through "substantial contacts" with State *X*, totally unrelated to the cause of action, is subject to the general in personam jurisdiction of that state?

(6) In Ohio v. Wyandotte Chemicals Corp., 401 U.S. 493 (1971), the Supreme Court refused to exercise original jurisdiction over a complaint by the state of Ohio against Michigan and Canadian corporations alleged to be polluting Lake Erie. Though it found that it had such jurisdiction, it found the exercise of the jurisdiction unnecessary because alternative forums were available, including Ohio state courts. The Court found explicitly that Ohio courts could exercise in personam jurisdiction over the out-of-state defendants for a direct intrusion of pollutants causing physical harm within the state. Is *World-Wide Volkswagen* distinguishable because the presence of the automobile in Oklahoma, unlike the presence of the pollutants in Ohio, was due to an "intervening human agency"? Or is the distinction a narrower one—that the presence of the automobile in Oklahoma was due to the activities of the plaintiff, and the plaintiff's unilateral activities should not be able to create jurisdiction? If the latter distinction is the appropriate one, does it follow that jurisdiction should exist in Oklahoma for a suit brought by the

driver of the other car if he, too, happened to have been injured by the burning of the Robinson car's gas tank (on the ground that the other driver was not instrumental in getting the Robinson vehicle into Oklahoma)?

(7) Isn't it fairer to make the Robinsons travel to New York to litigate than to require these defendants to go to Oklahoma? The Robinsons, after all, are the ones responsible for the extra interstate costs of litigation. *See* Brilmayer, *How Contacts Count: Due Process Limitations on State Court Jurisdiction*, 1980 S. Ct. Rev. 77.

(8) The Supreme Court provoked a fair amount of interest with its discussion of state sovereignty as an essential element of jurisdiction. Recall the discussion in *Insurance Co. of Ireland*, page ••• *supra. See generally* Stein, *Styles of Argument and Interstate Federalism in the Law of Personal Jurisdiction*, 65 Tex. L. Rev. 689 (1987). Isn't the dichotomy between sovereignty analysis and individual liberty analysis really a false one, though? Isn't the defendant's individual liberty claim essentially a claim that the forum has exceeded the reach of the power legitimately accorded it in a world of territorially limited states?

Kulko v. Superior Court

436 U.S. 84 (1978)

Justice MARSHALL delivered the opinion of the court.

[Appellant Ezra Kulko and appellee Sharon Kulko Horn were New York domiciliaries when they got married during a brief stay in California. They returned to New York where their two children, Darwin and Ilsa, were born. The couple and their two children resided in New York until they separated in 1972. Sharon and the children moved to California. Sharon returned briefly to New York to sign a separation agreement specifying that Ezra would pay alimony and that the children would remain with Ezra during the school year and visit Sharon on holidays. Immediately after execution of the separation agreement, Sharon flew to Haiti, where she secured a divorce decree that incorporated the terms of the separation agreement.

Subsequently, each of the children expressed their desire to live with their mother in California. Ezra acquiesced, purchased a one-way plane ticket for Ilsa, and later paid for Darwin's move. Once both children arrived, Sharon instituted a civil action in California to establish the Haitian divorce as a California judgment, to modify the judgment so as to award her full custody of the children, and to increase appellant's child support obligations. Ezra was served with process under the California long-arm statute that allows state courts to assert jurisdiction on any basis not inconsistent with the Constitution. He challenged the court's jurisdiction under the due process clause. The California Supreme Court rejected his argument and held that jurisdiction was proper because appellant had "caused an effect in [California]" by purposefully sending Ilsa into the state.]

A

In reaching its result, the California Supreme Court did not rely on appellant's glancing presence in the State some 13 years before the events that led to this controversy, nor could it have. Appellant has been in California on only two occasions, once in 1959 for a three-day military stopover on his way to Korea and again in 1960 for a 24-hour stopover on his return from Korean service. To hold such temporary visits to a State a basis for the assertion of in personam jurisdiction over unrelated actions arising in the future would make a mockery of the limitations on state jurisdiction imposed by the Fourteenth Amendment. Nor did the California court rely on the fact that appellant was actually married in California on one of his two brief visits. We agree that where two New York domiciliaries, for reasons of convenience, marry in the State of California and thereafter spend their entire married life in New York, the fact of their California marriage by itself cannot support a California court's exercise of jurisdiction over a spouse who remains a New York resident in an action relating to child support.

Finally, in holding that personal jurisdiction existed, the court below carefully disclaimed reliance on the fact that appellant had agreed at the time of separation to allow his children to live with their mother three months a year and that he had sent them to California each year pursuant to this agreement. [T]o find personal jurisdiction in a State on this basis, merely because the mother was residing there, would discourage parents from entering into reasonable visitation agreements. Moreover, it could arbitrarily subject one parent to suit in any State of the Union where the other parent chose to spend time while having custody of their offspring pursuant to a separation agreement. As we have emphasized:

> "The unilateral activity of those who claim some relationship with a nonresident defendant cannot satisfy the requirement of contact with the forum State. . . . [I]t is essential in each case that there be some act by which the defendant purposefully avails [him]self of the privilege of conducting activities within the forum State. . . ." *Hanson v. Denckla*, [357 U.S. 235, 253 (1958)].

The "purposeful act" that the California Supreme Court believed did warrant the exercise of personal jurisdiction over appellant in California was his "actively and fully consent[ing] to Ilsa living in California for the school year . . . and . . . send[ing] her to California for that purpose." We cannot accept the proposition that appellant's acquiescence in Ilsa's desire to live with her mother conferred jurisdiction over appellant in the California courts in this action. A father who agrees, in the interests of family harmony and his children's preferences, to allow them to spend more time in California than was required under a separation agreement can hardly be said to have "purposefully availed himself" of the "benefits and protection" of California's laws.[7]

Nor can we agree with the assertion of the court below that the exercise of in personam jurisdiction here was warranted by the financial benefit appellant derived from his daughter's presence in California for nine months of the year.

---

7. The court below stated that the presence in California of appellant's daughter gave appellant the benefit of California's "police and fire protection, its school system, its hospital services, its recreational facilities, its libraries and museums. . . ." But, in the circumstances presented here, these services provided by the State were essentially benefits to the child, not the father, and in any event were not benefits that appellant purposefully sought for himself.

This argument rests on the premise that, while appellant's liability for support payments remained unchanged, his yearly expenses for supporting the child in New York decreased. But this circumstance, even if true, does not support California's assertion of jurisdiction here. Any diminution in appellant's household costs resulted, not from the child's presence in California, but rather from her absence from appellant's home.

B

. . .

III

In seeking to justify the burden that would be imposed on appellant were the exercise of in personam jurisdiction in California sustained, appellee argues that California has substantial interests in protecting the welfare of its minor residents and in promoting to the fullest extent possible a healthy and supportive family environment in which the children of the State are to be raised. These interests are unquestionably important. But while the presence of the children and one parent in California arguably might favor application of California law in a lawsuit in New York, the fact that California might be the "center of gravity" for choice of law purposes does not mean that California has personal jurisdiction over the defendant. And California has not attempted to assert any particularized interest in trying such cases in its courts by, *e.g.*, enacting a special jurisdictional statute.

California's legitimate interest in ensuring the support of children resident in California without unduly disrupting the children's lives, moreover, is already being served by the State's participation in the Uniform Reciprocal Enforcement of Support Act of 1968. This statute provides a mechanism for communication between court systems in different States, in order to facilitate the procurement and enforcement of child-support decrees where the dependent children reside in a State that cannot obtain personal jurisdiction over the defendant. . . .

It cannot be disputed that California has substantial interests in protecting resident children and in facilitating child-support actions on behalf of those children. But these interests simply do not make California a "fair forum," Shaffer v. Heitner, in which to require appellant, who derives no personal or commercial benefit from his child's presence in California and who lacks any other relevant contact with the State, either to defend a child-support suit or to suffer liability by default.

IV

Accordingly, we conclude that the appellant's motion to quash service, on the ground of lack of personal jurisdiction, was erroneously denied by the California courts. The judgment of the California Supreme Court is, therefore, reversed.

Justice BRENNAN, with whom Justice WHITE and Justice POWELL join, dissenting [omitted].

Questions and Comments

(1) Why was it so clear that the marriage of the parties in California did not provide an adequate basis for jurisdiction needed for modifying child support? What if the children had been conceived during a layover in California? What if they had been born during a brief stop there? *Cf.* Poston v. Poston, 624 A.2d 853 (Vt. 1993) (no in personam jurisdiction in state of original marital domicile and birth of first child).

(2) Would it have made a difference if Kulko had urged Horn to move to California because it was a better place for the children to spend the summer? Would it have made a difference if Kulko, rather than the children, had been the instigator of their permanent move to residence with their mother?

(3) The Court emphasizes that the divorce and separation agreement were centered in New York. If Kulko had moved from New York to Florida, would New York still be an appropriate place to sue him? If not, would California then become appropriate; that is, is California jurisdiction rejected because it is altogether inappropriate, or merely because, as the facts stand, New York is a much better place to litigate (which might not be so if Kulko moved)?

(4) In McGee v. International Life Insurance Co., 355 U.S. 220 (1957), California jurisdiction over an out-of-state insurance company was upheld, despite a lack of any evidence that the company had any contacts with California apart from its solicitation of the deceased and its subsequent collection of premiums he mailed from California. In Hanson v. Denckla, 357 U.S. 235 (1958), however, the Court rejected Florida jurisdiction over a Delaware trustee of a trust established by a decedent who had moved to Florida after the trust was established, despite continued contact between the decedent and the trustee. In the latter case the trustee had not "purposefully availed itself of the privilege of conducting activities within the forum State"; *McGee* was further distinguished as a case in which the state of California had manifested strong interests in insurance by its special legislation in the area. Isn't California even more interested in the welfare of its resident children than in the insurance business? And in any event, if the standards are fair play and substantial justice and minimum contacts, what does the interest of the state have to do with either?

(5) Justice White joined the brief dissenting opinion in *Kulko*, which declares that jurisdictional cases such as *Kulko* are close calls but that the dissenters would weigh the facts slightly differently than would the *Kulko* majority. Does his majority opinion in *World-Wide Volkswagen* give any satisfactory method for resolving the ambiguities? Is it possible in such cases to do anything but produce vague verbal formulas and apply them to specific factual situations in the hope that the lower courts will get a feeling for what the Supreme Court thinks goes too far? Do *Kulko* and *World-Wide Volkswagen* represent anything more than a signal to the lower courts that they had begun to drift too far toward asserting jurisdiction since *International Shoe*, *McGee*, and Hanson v. Denckla?

(6) Is the real point of *Kulko* that the relaxations in the law of jurisdiction that bloomed in the *International Shoe* opinion were a result of the expansion of commercial transactions to a national scale, while personal relations, though they may have changed somewhat since the days of *Pennoyer*, have not changed in a similar manner? After all, the increased cost of litigation in a distant place can be passed on to the customer in the business setting, while the same cannot be said about the cost of inconvenience in litigation of personal matters.

(7) What effect ought it have on the existence of personal jurisdiction that the substantive cause of action is of one sort rather than another? If *Kulko* is in part explained by the fact that it is a domestic relations dispute, then are there other types of substantive disputes as to which special jurisdictional standards apply? In both Keeton v. Hustler Magazine, Inc., 465 U.S. 770 (1984), and Calder v. Jones, 465 U.S. 783 (1984), the Court stated in no uncertain terms that it did not matter, for purposes of personal jurisdiction, that the case was a multistate defamation action in which assertion of jurisdiction might "chill" First Amendment rights. It stated that the First Amendment had no bearing on personal jurisdiction.

Is this correct or desirable? What if a state enacted a longer long arm for cases brought against Republican defendants than for cases against Democratic defendants? What if it had a longer long arm for defamation actions than for personal injury actions? *See generally* Pielemeier, *Constitutional Limits on Choice of Law: The Special Case of Multistate Defamation*, 133 U. Pa. L. Rev. 381 (1985).

In Connolly v. Burt, 757 F.2d 242 (10th Cir. 1986), the court relied on *Keeton* and *Calder* in asserting jurisdiction over a Nebraska doctor who had written a letter of recommendation about a former student to a Colorado hospital at the hospital's request. The defendant, Connolly, had written, "In reply to your inquiry about Dr. Burt, he did spend time here as an Orthopaedic Resident from 1974-1977. His performance was well below average and he has consequently not been recommended for Board eligibility. I think he might serve adequately in some field of medicine, but not that of Orthopaedic Surgery." The Supreme Court agreed to review the case, 474 U.S. 1004 (1985), but after the defendant filed his brief on the merits the plaintiff dropped the case, and it was dismissed as moot. 475 U.S. 1063 (1986).

Walden v. Fiore

571 U.S. 277 (2014)

THOMAS, J., delivered the opinion for a unanimous Court.

This case asks us to decide whether a court in Nevada may exercise personal jurisdiction over a defendant on the basis that he knew his allegedly tortious conduct in Georgia would delay the return of funds to plaintiffs with connections to Nevada. Because the defendant had no other contacts with Nevada, and because a plaintiff's contacts with the forum State cannot be "decisive in determining whether the defendant's due process rights are violated," Rush v. Savchuk, 444 U.S. 320, 332 (1980), we hold that the court in Nevada may not exercise personal jurisdiction under these circumstances.

I

Petitioner Anthony Walden serves as a police officer for the city of Covington, Georgia. In August 2006, petitioner was working at the Atlanta Hartsfield-Jackson Airport as a deputized agent of the Drug Enforcement Administration (DEA). As part of a task force, petitioner conducted investigative stops and other law enforcement functions in support of the DEA's airport drug interdiction program.

On August 8, 2006, Transportation Security Administration agents searched respondents Gina Fiore and Keith Gipson and their carry-on bags at the San Juan airport in Puerto Rico. They found almost $97,000 in cash. Fiore explained to DEA agents in San Juan that she and Gipson had been gambling at a casino known as the El San Juan, and that they had residences in both California and Nevada (though they provided only California identification). After respondents were cleared for departure, a law enforcement official at the San Juan airport notified petitioner's task force in Atlanta that respondents had boarded a plane for Atlanta, where they planned to catch a connecting flight to Las Vegas, Nevada.

When respondents arrived in Atlanta, petitioner and another DEA agent approached them at the departure gate for their flight to Las Vegas. In response to petitioner's questioning, Fiore explained that she and Gipson were professional gamblers. Respondents maintained that the cash they were carrying was their gambling "'bank'" and winnings. App. 15, 24. After using a drug-sniffing dog to perform a sniff test, petitioner seized the cash.[9] Petitioner advised respondents that their funds would be returned if they later proved a legitimate source for the cash. Respondents then boarded their plane.

After respondents departed, petitioner moved the cash to a secure location and the matter was forwarded to DEA headquarters. The next day, petitioner received a phone call from respondents' attorney in Nevada seeking return of the funds. On two occasions over the next month, petitioner also received documentation from the attorney regarding the legitimacy of the funds.

At some point after petitioner seized the cash, he helped draft an affidavit to show probable cause for forfeiture of the funds and forwarded that affidavit to a United States Attorney's Office in Georgia.[10] According to respondents, the affidavit was false and misleading because petitioner misrepresented the encounter at the airport and omitted exculpatory information regarding the lack of drug evidence and the legitimate source of the funds. In the end, no forfeiture complaint was filed, and the DEA returned the funds to respondents in March 2007.

Respondents filed suit against petitioner in the United States District Court for the District of Nevada, seeking money damages under Bivens v. Six Unknown Fed. Narcotics Agents, 403 U.S. 388 (1971). Respondents alleged that petitioner violated their Fourth Amendment rights by (1) seizing the cash without probable cause; (2) keeping the money after concluding it did not come from drug-related activity; (3) drafting and forwarding a probable cause affidavit to support

---

9. Respondents allege that the sniff test was "at best, inconclusive," and there is no indication in the pleadings that drugs or drug residue were ever found on or with the cash. App. 21.

10. The alleged affidavit is not in the record. Because this case comes to us at the motion-to-dismiss stage, we take respondents' factual allegations as true, including their allegations regarding the existence and content of the affidavit.

a forfeiture action while knowing the affidavit contained false statements; (4) will-fully seeking forfeiture while withholding exculpatory information; and (5) with-holding that exculpatory information from the United States Attorney's Office.
. . .

II

A

This case addresses the "minimum contacts" necessary to create specific jurisdiction.[11] The inquiry whether a forum State may assert specific jurisdiction over a nonresident defendant "focuses on 'the relationship among the defendant, the forum, and the litigation.'" Keeton v. Hustler Magazine, Inc., 465 U.S. 770, 775 (1984) (quoting Shaffer v. Heitner, 433 U.S. 186, 204 (1977)). For a State to exercise jurisdiction consistent with due process, the defendant's suit-related conduct must create a substantial connection with the forum State. Two related aspects of this necessary relationship are relevant in this case.

First, the relationship must arise out of contacts that the "defendant him-self" creates with the forum State. Burger King Corp. v. Rudzewicz, 471 U.S. 462, 475 (1985). Due process limits on the State's adjudicative authority principally protect the liberty of the nonresident defendant—not the convenience of plain-tiffs or third parties. See World-Wide Volkswagen Corp., supra, at 291-292. We have consistently rejected attempts to satisfy the defendant-focused "minimum contacts" inquiry by demonstrating contacts between the plaintiff (or third par-ties) and the forum State. See Helicopteros Nacionales de Colombia, S. A. v. Hall, 466 U.S. 408, 417 (1984) ("[The] unilateral activity of another party or a third person is not an appropriate consideration when determining whether a defendant has sufficient contacts with a forum State to justify an assertion of jurisdiction"). We have thus rejected a plaintiff's argument that a Florida court could exercise personal jurisdiction over a trustee in Delaware based solely on the contacts of the trust's settlor, who was domiciled in Florida and had executed powers of appoint-ment there. Hanson v. Denckla, 357 U.S. 235, 253-254 (1958). We have likewise held that Oklahoma courts could not exercise personal jurisdiction over an auto-mobile distributor that supplies New York, New Jersey, and Connecticut dealers based only on an automobile purchaser's act of driving it on Oklahoma highways. World-Wide Volkswagen Corp., supra, at 298. Put simply, however significant the plaintiff's contacts with the forum may be, those contacts cannot be "decisive in determining whether the defendant's due process rights are violated." Rush, 444 U.S., at 332.

---

11. "Specific" or "case-linked" jurisdiction "depends on an 'affiliatio[n] between the forum and the underlying controversy'" (i.e., an "activity or an occurrence that takes place in the forum State and is therefore subject to the State's regulation"). Goodyear Dunlop Tires Operations, S. A. v. Brown, 564 U.S. 915, 919 (2011). This is in contrast to "general" or "all purpose" jurisdiction, which permits a court to assert jurisdiction over a defendant based on a forum connection unrelated to the underly-ing suit (e.g., domicile). Respondents rely on specific jurisdiction only.

Second, our "minimum contacts" analysis looks to the defendant's contacts with the forum State itself, not the defendant's contacts with persons who reside there. See, e.g., *International Shoe*, supra, at 319 (Due process "does not contemplate that a state may make binding a judgment in personam against an individual . . . with which the state has no contacts, ties, or relations"); *Hanson*, supra, at 251 ("However minimal the burden of defending in a foreign tribunal, a defendant may not be called upon to do so unless he has had the 'minimal contacts' with that State that are a prerequisite to its exercise of power over him"). Accordingly, we have upheld the assertion of jurisdiction over defendants who have purposefully "reach[ed] out beyond" their State and into another by, for example, entering a contractual relationship that "envisioned continuing and wide-reaching contacts" in the forum State, *Burger King*, supra, at 479-480, or by circulating magazines to "deliberately exploi[t]" a market in the forum State, *Keeton*, supra, at 781. And although physical presence in the forum is not a prerequisite to jurisdiction, Burger King, supra, at 476, physical entry into the State — either by the defendant in person or through an agent, goods, mail, or some other means — is certainly a relevant contact. See, e.g., *Keeton*, supra, at 773-774.

But the plaintiff cannot be the only link between the defendant and the forum. Rather, it is the defendant's conduct that must form the necessary connection with the forum State that is the basis for its jurisdiction over him. See *Burger King*, supra, at 478 ("If the question is whether an individual's contract with an out-of-state party alone can automatically establish sufficient minimum contacts in the other party's home forum, we believe the answer clearly is that it cannot"); Kulko v. Superior Court of Cal., City and County of San Francisco, 436 U.S. 84, 93 (1978) (declining to "find personal jurisdiction in a State . . . merely because [the plaintiff in a child support action] was residing there"). To be sure, a defendant's contacts with the forum State may be intertwined with his transactions or interactions with the plaintiff or other parties. But a defendant's relationship with a plaintiff or third party, standing alone, is an insufficient basis for jurisdiction. See *Rush*, supra, at 332 ("Naturally, the parties' relationships with each other may be significant in evaluating their ties to the forum. The requirements of *International Shoe*, however, must be met as to each defendant over whom a state court exercises jurisdiction"). Due process requires that a defendant be haled into court in a forum State based on his own affiliation with the State, not based on the "random, fortuitous, or attenuated" contacts he makes by interacting with other persons affiliated with the State. *Burger King*, 471 U.S., at 475 (internal quotation marks omitted).

2

These same principles apply when intentional torts are involved. In that context, it is likewise insufficient to rely on a defendant's "random, fortuitous, or attenuated contacts" or on the "unilateral activity" of a plaintiff. Ibid. (same). A forum State's exercise of jurisdiction over an out-of-state intentional tortfeasor must be based on intentional conduct by the defendant that creates the necessary contacts with the forum.

Calder v. Jones, 465 U.S. 783, illustrates the application of these principles. In *Calder*, a California actress brought a libel suit in California state court against a reporter and an editor, both of whom worked for the National Enquirer at its headquarters in Florida. The plaintiff's libel claims were based on an article written and edited by the defendants in Florida for publication in the National Enquirer, a national weekly newspaper with a California circulation of roughly 600,000.

We held that California's assertion of jurisdiction over the defendants was consistent with due process. Although we recognized that the defendants' activities "focus[ed]" on the plaintiff, our jurisdictional inquiry "focuse[d] on 'the relationship among the defendant, the forum, and the litigation.'" Id., at 788 (quoting *Shaffer*, 433 U.S., at 204). Specifically, we examined the various contacts the defendants had created with California (and not just with the plaintiff) by writing the allegedly libelous story.

We found those forum contacts to be ample: The defendants relied on phone calls to "California sources" for the information in their article; they wrote the story about the plaintiff's activities in California; they caused reputational injury in California by writing an allegedly libelous article that was widely circulated in the State; and the "brunt" of that injury was suffered by the plaintiff in that State. 465 U.S., at 788-789. "In sum, California [wa]s the focal point both of the story and of the harm suffered." Id., at 789. Jurisdiction over the defendants was "therefore proper in California based on the 'effects' of their Florida conduct in California." Ibid.

The crux of *Calder* was that the reputation-based "effects" of the alleged libel connected the defendants to California, not just to the plaintiff. The strength of that connection was largely a function of the nature of the libel tort. However scandalous a newspaper article might be, it can lead to a loss of reputation only if communicated to (and read and understood by) third persons. See Restatement (Second) of Torts §577, Comment b (1976); see also ibid. ("[R]eputation is the estimation in which one's character is held by his neighbors or associates"). Accordingly, the reputational injury caused by the defendants' story would not have occurred but for the fact that the defendants wrote an article for publication in California that was read by a large number of California citizens. Indeed, because publication to third persons is a necessary element of libel, see id., §558, the defendants' intentional tort actually occurred in California. *Keeton*, 465 U.S., at 777 ("The tort of libel is generally held to occur wherever the offending material is circulated"). In this way, the "effects" caused by the defendants' article— i.e., the injury to the plaintiff's reputation in the estimation of the California public—connected the defendants' conduct to California, not just to a plaintiff who lived there. That connection, combined with the various facts that gave the article a California focus, sufficed to authorize the California court's exercise of jurisdiction.[12]

---

12. The defendants in Calder argued that no contacts they had with California were sufficiently purposeful because their employer was responsible for circulation of the article. See Calder v. Jones, 465 U.S. 783, 789 (1984). We rejected that argument. Even though the defendants did not circulate the article themselves, they "expressly aimed" "their intentional, and allegedly tortious, actions" at California because they knew the National Enquirer "ha[d] its largest circulation" in California, and that the article would "have a potentially devastating impact" there. Id., at 789-790.

III

Applying the foregoing principles, we conclude that petitioner lacks the "minimal contacts" with Nevada that are a prerequisite to the exercise of jurisdiction over him. *Hanson*, 357 U.S., at 251. It is undisputed that no part of petitioner's course of conduct occurred in Nevada. Petitioner approached, questioned, and searched respondents, and seized the cash at issue, in the Atlanta airport. It is alleged that petitioner later helped draft a "false probable cause affidavit" in Georgia and forwarded that affidavit to a United States Attorney's Office in Georgia to support a potential action for forfeiture of the seized funds. 688 F.3d, at 563. Petitioner never traveled to, conducted activities within, contacted anyone in, or sent anything or anyone to Nevada. In short, when viewed through the proper lens—whether the defendant's actions connect him to the forum—petitioner formed no jurisdictionally relevant contacts with Nevada.

. . . As previously noted, Calder made clear that mere injury to a forum resident is not a sufficient connection to the forum. Regardless of where a plaintiff lives or works, an injury is jurisdictionally relevant only insofar as it shows that the defendant has formed a contact with the forum State. The proper question is not where the plaintiff experienced a particular injury or effect but whether the defendant's conduct connects him to the forum in a meaningful way.

Respondents' claimed injury does not evince a connection between petitioner and Nevada. Even if we consider the continuation of the seizure in Georgia to be a distinct injury, it is not the sort of effect that is tethered to Nevada in any meaningful way. Respondents (and only respondents) lacked access to their funds in Nevada not because anything independently occurred there, but because Nevada is where respondents chose to be at a time when they desired to use the funds seized by petitioner. Respondents would have experienced this same lack of access in California, Mississippi, or wherever else they might have traveled and found themselves wanting more money than they had. Unlike the broad publication of the forum-focused story in *Calder*, the effects of petitioner's conduct on respondents are not connected to the forum State in a way that makes those effects a proper basis for jurisdiction.[13]

* * *

Well-established principles of personal jurisdiction are sufficient to decide this case. The proper focus of the "minimum contacts" inquiry in intentional-tort cases is "'the relationship among the defendant, the forum, and the litigation.'" *Calder*, 465 U.S., at 788. And it is the defendant, not the plaintiff or third

---

13. Respondents warn that if we decide petitioner lacks minimum contacts in this case, it will bring about unfairness in cases where intentional torts are committed via the Internet or other electronic means (e.g., fraudulent access of financial accounts or "phishing" schemes). As an initial matter, we reiterate that the "minimum contacts" inquiry principally protects the liberty of the nonresident defendant, not the interests of the plaintiff. World-Wide Volkswagen Corp. v. Woodson, 444 U.S., 286, 291-292 (1980). In any event, this case does not present the very different questions whether and how a defendant's virtual "presence" and conduct translate into "contacts" with a particular State. To the contrary, there is no question where the conduct giving rise to this litigation took place: Petitioner seized physical cash from respondents in the Atlanta airport, and he later drafted and forwarded an affidavit in Georgia. We leave questions about virtual contacts for another day.

parties, who must create contacts with the forum State. In this case, the application of those principles is clear: Petitioner's relevant conduct occurred entirely in Georgia, and the mere fact that his conduct affected plaintiffs with connections to the forum State does not suffice to authorize jurisdiction. We therefore reverse the judgment of the Court of Appeals.

It is so ordered.

Questions and Comments

(1) In Asahi Metal Industry Co. v. Superior Court of California, the Supreme Court tackled the issue of whether a foreign business's awareness that its products will reach a forum state within the United States in the stream of commerce satisfies the minimum contacts needed for personal jurisdiction. The opinion by Justice O'Connor concluded that:

> The "substantial connection," *Burger King*, 471 U.S., at 475; *McGee*, 355 U.S., at 223, between the defendant and the forum State necessary for a finding of minimum contacts must come about by an action of the defendant purposefully directed toward the forum State. *Burger King, supra*, 471 U.S., at 476; Keeton v. Hustler Magazine, Inc., 465 U.S. 770, 774 (1984). The placement of a product into the stream of commerce, without more, is not an act of the defendant purposefully directed toward the forum State. Additional conduct of the defendant may indicate an intent or purpose to serve the market in the forum State, for example, designing the product for the market in the forum State, advertising in the forum State, establishing channels for providing regular advice to customers in the forum State, or marketing the product through a distributor who has agreed to serve as the sales agent in the forum State. But a defendant's awareness that the stream of commerce may or will sweep the product into the forum State does not convert the mere act of placing the product into the stream into an act purposefully directed toward the forum State.

While the final result was a unanimous opinion, there was a concurrence by Justice Stevens, joined by Justice White and Justice Blackmun, which argued that Justice O'Connor's opinion went too far:

> The Court seems to assume that an unwavering line can be drawn between "mere awareness" that a component will find its way into the forum State and "purposeful availment" of the forum's market. Over the course of its dealings with Cheng Shin, Asahi has arguably engaged in a higher quantum of conduct than "[t]he placement of a product into the stream of commerce, without more. . . ." Whether or not this conduct rises to the level of purposeful availment requires a constitutional determination that is affected by the volume, the value, and the hazardous character of the components. In most circumstances I would be inclined to conclude that a regular course of dealing that results in deliveries of over 100,000 units annually over a period of several years would constitute "purposeful availment" even though the item delivered to the forum State was a standard product marketed throughout the world.

(2) In *Asahi*, the majority suggests that the federal interest in foreign relations ought to be considered in the due process calculus. It has been argued that

choice of law and jurisdiction in international cases perhaps ought to reflect such federal concerns because of the exclusive federal power over international affairs. Brilmayer, *Extraterritorial Application of American Law: A Methodological and Constitutional Appraisal*, 50 Law & Contemp. Probs. 11 (1987).

(3) The first academic source arguing that the problem in *World-Wide Volkswagen* was that it was the *plaintiff* who took the car into the forum was Brilmayer, *How Contracts Counts*, 1979 S. Ct. Rev. 66. *Asahi, Burger King*, and the requirement of purposeful availment have provoked extensive critical academic scrutiny. *See, e.g.*, Sheehan, *Predicting the Future: Personal Jurisdiction for the Twenty-First Century*, 66 U. Cin. L. Rev. 385 (1998); Stewart, *A New Litany of Personal Jurisdiction*, 60 U. Colo. L. Rev. 5 (1989); *Symposium*, Asahi Metal Industry Co. v. Superior Court *and the Future of Personal Jurisdiction*, 39 S.C. L. Rev. 815 (1988); Dessem, *Personal Jurisdiction After* Asahi: *The Other (International) Shoe Drops*, 55 Tenn. L. Rev. 41 (1987); Weintraub, Asahi *Sends Personal Jurisdiction Down the Tubes*, 23 Texas Intl. L.J. 55 (1988); Cox, *The Interrelationship of Personal Jurisdiction and Choice of Law: Forging New Theory Through* Asahi Metal Industry Co. v. Superior Court, 49 U. Pitt. L. Rev. 189 (1987).

(4) "Stream of commerce" cases are common, especially in the products liability area. In addition to *World-Wide Volkswagen* and *Asahi, see* Grange Insurance Associates v. State, 110 Wash. 2d 752, 757 P.2d 933 (1988), in which it was held that there was no jurisdiction over Idaho for negligence in certifying as free of brucellosis livestock destined for immediate sale to a Washington buyer. The veterinarian's certificate specified a Washington destination for the cattle; should such conduct satisfy the *Asahi* test? *See also* Clune v. Alimak AB, 233 F.3d 538 (8th Cir. 2000); Alpine View Co. v. Atlas Copco AB, 205 F.3d 208 (5th Cir. 2000); Pennzoil Prods. Co. v. Colelli & Assocs., 149 F.3d 197 (3d Cir. 1998); Viam Corp. v. Iowa Export-Import Trading Co., 84 F.3d 424 (Fed. Cir. 1996); In re Celotex Corp. v. Rapid American Corp., 124 F.3d 619 (4th Cir. 1997); CMMC v. Salinas, 929 S.W.2d 435 (Tex. 1996).

(5) The Supreme Court recently addressed the relevance of a defendant's business structure to personal jurisdiction in the cases J. McIntyre Machinery Ltd. v. Nicastro, 564 U.S. 873 (2011), *reversing* Nicastro v. McIntyre Machinery America, Ltd., 987 A.2d 575 (N.J. 2010), and Goodyear Dunlop Tires Operations, S.A. v. Brown, 564 U.S. 915 (2011), *reversing* Brown v. Meter, 681 S.E.2d 383 (N.C. Ct. App. 2009).

In *Nicastro*, the New Jersey state courts asserted personal jurisdiction over a British manufacturer of a recycling machine that injured a scrap metal worker in New Jersey. The manufacturer commissioned another company, independent of it but carrying the same McIntyre name, to act as its exclusive U.S. distributor. The distributor sold the machine to the plaintiff's employer in New Jersey. According to the New Jersey Supreme Court, it was not necessary for the defendant to purposely avail itself of a New Jersey market or even to be aware that its product was sold in New Jersey (a fact that it denied). Instead, it was sufficient that defendant commissioned a distributor to market the product throughout the United States. Defendant either "knew or reasonably should have known that its distribution scheme would make its products available to New Jersey consumers," and, according to the New Jersey court, this availability creates a strong presumption in favor of the exercise of personal jurisdiction over defendant in the case. 987 A.2d at 593. The Supreme Court reversed, observing that McIntyre did not "engage in any activities in New Jersey that reveal an intent to invoke or benefit from the protection of its laws." 564 U.S. at 887.

In *Goodyear*, defendant Goodyear Tire. Co. subsidiaries manufactured tires that were sold in North Carolina. As in *Nicastro*, the manufacturers did not themselves handle tire distribution in the United States. Instead, they "used their Goodyear parent and affiliated companies to distribute the tires they manufactured to the United States and North Carolina." 681 S.E.2d at 386. According to the North Carolina court, personal jurisdiction could be based on defendants' purposefully injecting their product into the stream of commerce without attempting to affirmatively exclude North Carolina as a potential product market. *Id.* at 391. In *Goodyear*, however, the tire that purported to cause plaintiffs' injuries never entered the state of North Carolina. Instead, the product was manufactured in Turkey and sold in France, where the fatal injury occurred (plaintiffs were North Carolina residents). The North Carolina courts relied on the fact that some tires manufactured by defendant made their way into North Carolina in order to exercise general jurisdiction over the Turkish defendant. Justice Ginsburg, a dissenter in *Nicastro*, delivered a unanimous decision of the Supreme Court reversing the North Carolina court's decision, ruling that Goodyear's "attenuated connections to [North Carolina] fall far short of the 'continuous and systematic general business contacts.'" 564 U.S. at 929.

In both *Goodyear* and *Nicastro*, the relationship between entities in the stream of commerce turned out to be central for purposes of imputing both the activities and the mens rea of one of the entities to the defendant. In *Goodyear*, the manufacturer was using both its parent company and affiliated companies to market its products worldwide. Yet, those activities were not imputed to the manufacturer for purposes of satisfying general jurisdiction. Similarly, in *Nicastro*, a nominally independent firm's marketing efforts were not imputed to the defendant, which claimed to lack knowledge that the product was sold in New Jersey. Should it have been at all relevant that the independent marketer shared the manufacturer's name? The implications of the corporate form in the determination of general jurisdiction are further discussed in Daimler AG v. Bauman, 571 U.S. 117 (2014), *infra*.

Note on Activities-Based Personal Jurisdiction for Internet Disputes

How do personal jurisdiction concepts apply to the Internet, and in particular to a communication or activity on the World Wide Web that potentially appears in every state in the nation (not to mention every nation in the world)? Most courts agree that purely "passive" Web sites—Web sites that merely post information accessible to users in other jurisdictions—cannot be subject to personal jurisdiction in the places where they can be viewed. *See, e.g.*, Cybersell, Inc. v. Cybersell, Inc., 130 F.3d 414 (9th Cir. 1997); McGill Technology, Ltd. v. Gourmet Technologies, Inc., 300 F. Supp. 2d 501, 507 (E.D. Mich. 2004). But does it make sense to decline jurisdiction when a passive Web site viewed in other states causes harm there? Consider Bailey v. Turbine Design, Inc., 86 F. Supp. 2d 790 (W.D. Tenn. 2000), in which a Florida corporation allegedly defamed Bailey, the owner of its Tennessee competitor, when it posted unflattering information about Bailey (arrest records, a mug shot, and damning information about his company) on its Web site located in Florida. Bailey argued that personal jurisdiction in Tennessee was proper because the publication was intended to cause injury in Tennessee. The court dismissed the case for lack of personal jurisdiction simply because the Web site was "passive." Isn't the "passive" label here a poor substitute for analysis? Aren't the defendant's contacts in an important sense directed toward Tennessee? Should the defendant receive immunity from jurisdiction in Tennessee simply because the publication could be viewed anywhere?

While courts require something more than mere information on a Web page to establish that a defendant "purposefully directed" its activities to another forum, there is substantial uncertainty about what more is needed. The easiest cases involve online dealings between a Web page operator in one state and residents of another jurisdiction, especially commercial dealings such as online contracts. *See, e.g.*, CompuServe, Inc. v. Patterson, 89 F.3d 1257 (6th Cir. 1996) (personal jurisdiction in Ohio proper when Texas defendant knowingly contracts with Ohio party, transfers files to that party in Ohio, and collects revenue from related sale of software in Ohio); Zippo Mfg. Co. v. Zippo Dot Com, Inc., 952 F. Supp. 1119, 1125-1126 (W.D. Pa. 1997) (jurisdiction appropriate in Pennsylvania because defendant contracted with thousands of individuals and numerous Internet access providers in Pennsylvania). Are these cases really different from the passive Web site cases? Would it make a difference if, as is quite possible, the defendants did not know *where* the plaintiffs they were doing business with were located? Can one purposefully avail oneself of a forum without knowing the identity of the forum? Must the out-of-state Web page operator take steps to learn the geographical location of Web page users?

Some of the hardest Internet personal jurisdiction cases concern "interactive" Web sites that allow a user to exchange information with the host computer. As a general matter, courts find personal jurisdiction when such Web sites convey "something more" than passive information in a way that is aimed at the forum, but there is uncertainty about what that something more should be. The cases do give some rough guidance, however. *Compare*, for example, Illinois v. Hemi Group LLC, 622 F.3d 754 (7th Cir. 2010) (asserting personal jurisdiction in Illinois over New Mexico cigarette vendor that had an interactive Web site through which customers could purchase cigarettes, calculate their shipping charges using their ZIP codes, and create accounts, and on which the defendant stated that it would ship to any state in the country except New York), with Toys "R" Us, Inc. v. Step Two, S.A., 318 F.3d 446 (3d Cir. 2003) (declining personal jurisdiction in New Jersey over a Spanish toy company that operated an interactive online toy store that listed prices in pesetas and accepted orders only from Spanish shipping addresses, reasoning that it was not directing its activities to the United States).

Courts also sometimes use the "effects test" applied in Calder v. Jones, 465 U.S. 783 (1984), to find personal jurisdiction in intentional torts cases. *Calder* establishes jurisdiction if the defendant engages in "(1) intentional action (2) expressly aimed at the forum state (3) causing harm, the brunt of which is suffered, and the defendant knows is likely to be suffered, in the forum state." Panavision Intl. L.P. v. Toeppen, 141 F.3d 1316, 1321 (9th Cir. 1998). Not surprisingly, courts have been inconsistent in determining when Internet contacts are expressly aimed at a forum state, "where" the harm is suffered, and whether the defendant likely knew it would be suffered there.

Finally, courts sometimes use Internet contacts as a basis for asserting general jurisdiction. In Gorman v. Ameritrade Holding Corp., 293 F.3d 506 (D.C. Cir. 2002), for example, plaintiff sued Ameritrade, an online brokerage with its principal place of business in Omaha, Nebraska, in federal court in Washington, D.C., for breach of contract. There was no connection between the contract dispute and the District of Columbia, and thus no specific jurisdiction, but Ameritrade's Web site allowed residents of the District to open accounts, transfer money, and enter binding contracts over the Internet. The court held that online business can be sufficiently "continuous and systematic" to support general jurisdiction, and that "by permitting [real-time] transactions to take place 24 hours a day, the site makes it possible for Ameritrade to have contacts with the District of Columbia that are 'continuous and systematic' to a degree that traditional foreign corporations can never even approach." *See also* Gator.com Corp. v. L.L. Bean, Inc., 341 F.3d 1072, 1080 (9th Cir. 2003) (Maine firm L.L. Bean's virtual store gave the California courts general jurisdiction just as a brick-and-mortar store would, but only because it advertised extensively and performed millions of dollars of sales in California).

Goodyear Dunlop Tires Operations, S.A. v. Brown
564 U.S. 915 (2011)

[Two North Carolina residents were killed in a bus accident in France. Their estates brought suit in North Carolina state court against various foreign subsidiaries of Goodyear Dunlop Tires, which unsuccessfully moved to dismiss for lack of personal jurisdiction. On appeal, the Supreme Court unanimously held that North Carolina could not exercise general jurisdiction over the subsidiaries.]

Justice GINSBURG delivered the opinion of the Court.

This case concerns the jurisdiction of state courts over corporations organized and operating abroad. We address, in particular, this question: Are foreign subsidiaries of a United States parent corporation amenable to suit in state court on claims unrelated to any activity of the subsidiaries in the forum State?

A bus accident outside Paris that took the lives of two 13-year-old boys from North Carolina gave rise to the litigation we here consider. Attributing the accident to a defective tire manufactured in Turkey at the plant of a foreign subsidiary of The Goodyear Tire and Rubber Company (Goodyear USA), the boys' parents commenced an action for damages in a North Carolina state court; they named as defendants Goodyear USA, an Ohio corporation, and three of its subsidiaries, organized and operating, respectively, in Turkey, France, and Luxembourg. Goodyear USA, which had plants in North Carolina and regularly engaged in commercial activity there, did not contest the North Carolina court's jurisdiction over it; Goodyear USA's foreign subsidiaries, however, maintained that North Carolina lacked adjudicatory authority over them.

. . .

A court may assert general jurisdiction over foreign (sister-state or foreign-country) corporations to hear any and all claims against them when their affiliations with the State are so "continuous and systematic" as to render them essentially at home in the forum State. See *International Shoe*, 326 U.S., at 317. Specific jurisdiction, on the other hand, depends on an "affiliatio[n] between the forum and the underlying controversy," principally, activity or an occurrence that takes place in the forum State and is therefore subject to the State's regulation. von Mehren & Trautman, Jurisdiction to Adjudicate: A Suggested Analysis, 79 Harv. L. Rev. 1121, 1136 (1966) (hereinafter von Mehren & Trautman); see Brilmayer et al., A General Look at General Jurisdiction, 66 Texas L. Rev. 721, 782 (1988) (hereinafter Brilmayer). In contrast to general, all-purpose jurisdiction, specific jurisdiction is confined to adjudication of "issues deriving from, or connected with, the very controversy that establishes jurisdiction." von Mehren & Trautman 1136.

Because the episode-in-suit, the bus accident, occurred in France, and the tire alleged to have caused the accident was manufactured and sold abroad, North Carolina courts lacked specific jurisdiction to adjudicate the controversy. The North Carolina Court of Appeals so acknowledged. Brown v. Meter, 199 N.C. App. 50, 57-58 (2009). Were the foreign subsidiaries nonetheless amenable to general jurisdiction in North Carolina courts? Confusing or blending general and specific jurisdictional inquiries, the North Carolina courts answered yes. Some of the tires made abroad by Goodyear's foreign subsidiaries, the North Carolina Court of Appeals stressed, had reached North Carolina through "the stream of commerce"; that connection, the Court of Appeals believed, gave North Carolina courts the handle needed for the exercise of general jurisdiction over the foreign corporations. *Id.*, at 67-68.

A connection so limited between the forum and the foreign corporation, we hold, is an inadequate basis for the exercise of general jurisdiction. Such a connection does not establish the "continuous and systematic" affiliation necessary to empower North Carolina courts to entertain claims unrelated to the foreign corporation's contacts with the State.

. . .

II

A

The Due Process Clause of the Fourteenth Amendment sets the outer boundaries of a state tribunal's authority to proceed against a defendant. Shaffer v. Heitner, 433 U.S. 186, 207 (1977). The canonical opinion in this area remains *International Shoe*, 326 U.S. 310, in which we held that a State may authorize its courts to exercise personal jurisdiction over an out-of-state defendant if the defendant has "certain minimum contacts with [the State] such that the maintenance of the suit does not offend 'traditional notions of fair play and substantial justice.'" *Id.*, at 316 (quoting *Meyer*, 311 U.S., at 463).

Endeavoring to give specific content to the "fair play and substantial justice" concept, the Court in *International Shoe* classified cases involving out-of-state corporate defendants. First, as in *International Shoe* itself, jurisdiction unquestionably could be asserted where the corporation's in-state activity is "continuous and systematic" and *that activity gave rise to the episode-in-suit*. 326 U.S., at 317. Further, the Court observed, the commission of certain "single or occasional acts" in a State may be sufficient to render a corporation answerable in that State with respect to those acts, though not with respect to matters unrelated to the forum connections. *Id.*, at 318. The heading courts today use to encompass these two *International Shoe* categories is "specific jurisdiction." See von Mehren & Trautman 1144-1163. Adjudicatory authority is "specific" when the suit "aris[es] out of or relate[s] to the defendant's contacts with the forum." *Helicopteros*, 466 U.S., at 414, n.8.

International Shoe distinguished from cases that fit within the "specific jurisdiction" categories, "instances in which the continuous corporate operations within a state [are] so substantial and of such a nature as to justify suit against it on causes of action arising from dealings entirely distinct from those activities." 326 U.S., at 318. Adjudicatory authority so grounded is today called "general jurisdiction." *Helicopteros*, 466 U.S., at 414, n.9. For an individual, the paradigm forum for the exercise of general jurisdiction is the individual's domicile; for a corporation, it is an equivalent place, one in which the corporation is fairly regarded as at home. See Brilmayer 728 (identifying domicile, place of incorporation, and principal place of business as "paradig[m]" bases for the exercise of general jurisdiction).

[The Court outlined the history of its rulings regarding specific jurisdiction.]

. . .

The North Carolina court's stream-of-commerce analysis elided the essential difference between case-specific and all-purpose (general) jurisdiction. Flow of a manufacturer's products into the forum, we have explained, may bolster an affiliation germane to *specific* jurisdiction. See, e.g., *World-Wide Volkswagen*, 444 U.S., at 297 (where "the sale of a product . . . is not simply an isolated occurrence, but arises from the efforts of the manufacturer or distributor to serve . . . the market for its product in [several] States, it is not unreasonable to subject it to suit in one of those States if its allegedly defective merchandise *has there been the source of injury to its owner or to others*" (emphasis added)). But ties serving to bolster the exercise of specific jurisdiction do not warrant a determination that, based on those ties, the forum has *general* jurisdiction over a defendant. See, e.g., Stabilisierungsfonds Fur Wein v. Kaiser Stuhl Wine Distributors Pty. Ltd., 647 F.2d 200, 203, n.5 (C.A.D.C. 1981) (defendants' marketing arrangements, although "adequate to permit litigation of claims relating to [their] introduction of . . . wine into the United States stream of commerce, . . . would not be adequate to support general, 'all purpose' adjudicatory authority").

A corporation's "continuous activity of some sorts within a state," *International Shoe* instructed, "is not enough to support the demand that the corporation be amenable to suits unrelated to that activity." 326 U.S., at 318. Our 1952 decision in Perkins v. Benguet Consol. Mining Co. remains "[t]he textbook case of general jurisdiction appropriately exercised over a foreign corporation that has not consented to suit in the forum." Donahue v. Far Eastern Air Transport Corp., 652 F.2d 1032, 1037 (C.A.D.C. 1981).

Sued in Ohio, the defendant in *Perkins* was a Philippine mining corporation that had ceased activities in the Philippines during World War II. To the extent that the company was conducting any business during and immediately after the Japanese occupation of the Philippines, it was doing so in Ohio: the corporation's president maintained his office there, kept the company files in that office, and supervised from the Ohio office "the necessarily limited wartime activities of the company." *Perkins*, 342 U.S., at 447-448. Although the claim-in-suit did not arise in Ohio, this Court ruled that it would not violate due process for Ohio to adjudicate the controversy. *Ibid.*; see Keeton v. Hustler Magazine, Inc., 465 U.S. 770, 779-780, n.11 (1984) (Ohio's exercise of general jurisdiction was permissible in *Perkins* because "Ohio was the corporation's principal, if temporary, place of business").

. . .

North Carolina is not a forum in which it would be permissible to subject petitioners to general jurisdiction. Unlike the defendant in *Perkins*, whose sole wartime business activity was conducted in Ohio, petitioners are in no sense at home in North Carolina. Their attenuated connections to the State, see *supra*, at 2852, fall far short of the "the continuous and systematic general business contacts" necessary to empower North Carolina to entertain suit against them on claims unrelated to anything that connects them to the State. *Helicopteros*, 466 U.S., at 416.[4]

C

Respondents belatedly assert a "single enterprise" theory, asking us to consolidate petitioners' ties to North Carolina with those of Goodyear USA and other Goodyear entities. See Brief for Respondents 44-50. In effect, respondents would have us pierce Goodyear corporate veils, at least for jurisdictional purposes. See Brilmayer & Paisley, Personal Jurisdiction and Substantive Legal Relations: Corporations, Conspiracies, and Agency, 74 Cal. L. Rev. 1, 14, 29-30 (1986) (merging parent and subsidiary for jurisdictional purposes requires an inquiry "comparable to the corporate law question of piercing the corporate veil"). But see 199 N.C. App., at 64 (North Carolina Court of Appeals understood that petitioners are "separate corporate entities . . . not directly responsible for the presence in North Carolina of tires that they had manufactured"). Neither below nor in their brief in opposition to the petition for certiorari did respondents

---

4. As earlier noted, see *supra*, at 2853, the North Carolina Court of Appeals invoked the State's "well-recognized interest in providing a forum in which its citizens are able to seek redress for injuries that they have sustained." 199 N.C. App., at 68. But "[g]eneral jurisdiction to adjudicate has in [United States] practice never been based on the plaintiff's relationship to the forum. There is nothing in [our] law comparable to . . . article 14 of the Civil Code of France (1804) under which the French nationality of the plaintiff is a sufficient ground for jurisdiction." von Mehren & Trautman 1137; see Clermont & Palmer, Exorbitant Jurisdiction, 58 ME. L. REV. 474, 492-495 (2006) (French law permitting plaintiff-based jurisdiction is rarely invoked in the absence of other supporting factors). When a defendant's act outside the forum causes injury in the forum, by contrast, a plaintiff's residence in the forum may strengthen the case for the exercise of *specific jurisdiction*. See Calder v. Jones, 465 U.S. 783, 788 (1984); von Mehren & Trautman 1167-1173.

urge disregard of petitioners' discrete status as subsidiaries and treatment of all Goodyear entities as a "unitary business," so that jurisdiction over the parent would draw in the subsidiaries as well.[5] Brief for Respondents 44. Respondents have therefore forfeited this contention, and we do not address it. This Court's Rule 15.2; Granite Rock Co. v. Teamsters, 130 S. Ct. 2847, 2861 (2010).

For the reasons stated, the judgment of the North Carolina Court of Appeals is *Reversed*.

Questions and Comments

(1) The *Goodyear* Court sidesteps the question of corporate veil-piercing on the grounds that the petitioners did not raise the argument before the case came to the Supreme Court. 564 U.S. at 929. The Court's reluctance to rule for the petitioners on that issue is not surprising, given that "[l]imited liability is the rule not the exception; and on that assumption large undertakings are rested, vast enterprises are launched, and huge sums of capital attracted." Anderson v. Abbott, 321 U.S. 349, 362 (1944). However, "there are occasions when the limited liability sought to be obtained through the corporation will be qualified or denied." *Id.* What should these "exceptional occasions" include? Would an alleged human rights violation committed by a foreign subsidiary justify a U.S. court's exercise of general jurisdiction over its parent corporation? This issue was the subject of Daimler AG v. Bauman, 571 U.S. 117 (2014), *infra*. For a general analysis of this problem, *see* Brilmayer & Paisley, *Personal Jurisdiction and Substantive Legal Relations: Corporations, Conspiracies, and Agency*, 74 Cal. L. Rev. 1, 14, 29-30 (1986).

(2) *Goodyear* rules that "[a] court may assert general jurisdiction over foreign . . . corporations to hear any and all claims against them when their affiliations with the State are so 'continuous and systematic' as to render them essentially at home in the forum State." 564 U.S. at 919. What does it mean for a corporation to be "at home" in a state? The Court uses a corporation's place of incorporation and principal place of business as indicators of a corporate home. *Id.* at 924-925. According to this logic, it appears intuitive that Goodyear's Turkish, French, and Luxembourgian subsidiaries are not "at home" in the state of North Carolina. However, Goodyear USA, the parent company, was incorporated in Ohio but did not contest the North Carolina courts' general jurisdiction over it. Moreover, the Supreme Court ruled in Hertz Corp. v. Friend, 559 U.S. 77, 80 (2010), that the "principal place of business" is often the corporation's "nerve center," and that the "nerve center will typically be found at a corporation's headquarters." Don't *Goodyear* and *Hertz* indicate that Goodyear USA is not "at home" in North

---

5. In the brief they filed in the North Carolina Court of Appeals, respondents stated that petitioners were part of an "integrated world-wide efforts to design, manufacture, market and sell *their tires* in the United States, including in North Carolina." App. 485 (emphasis added). See also Brief in Opposition 18. Read in context, that assertion was offered in support of a narrower proposition: The distribution of petitioners' tires in North Carolina, respondents maintained, demonstrated petitioners' own "calculated and deliberate efforts to take advantage of the North Carolina market." App. 485. As already explained, see *supra*, at 927-930, even regularly occurring sales of a product in a State do not justify the exercise of jurisdiction over a claim unrelated to those sales.

Carolina? If neither the parent corporation nor its foreign subsidiaries are "at home" in North Carolina, what explains the affirmance of jurisdiction over the parent but not its subsidiaries?

(3) Justice Ginsburg explains the "at home" test for corporations by comparing it to the concept of domicile for natural persons: "For an individual, the paradigm forum for the exercise of general jurisdiction is the individual's domicile; for a corporation, it is an equivalent place, one in which the corporation is fairly regarded as at home." 564 U.S. at 922-925. However, given that corporations can move much more freely than people can, is it appropriate to create a test for general jurisdiction over corporations from the test for general jurisdiction over people? For example, "[a]ctual persons have no subsidiaries . . . [and] individuals cannot be and act in multiple places at the same time." Michalski, *Rights Come with Responsibilities: Personal Jurisdiction in the Age of Corporate Personhood*, 50 San Diego L. Rev. 125, 126 n.2 (2013). Professor Michalski argues that corporations can often "evade the obligations that come with personhood," and that "this discrepancy constitutes a fundamental and dangerous mismatch." *Id.*

(4) In resolving choice-of-law issues, some courts have taken into account "the relative interests of the several jurisdictions [in having their law apply]." Auten v. Auten, 308 N.Y. 155, 161 (1954). Similarly, in *Goodyear*, the state court ruled that "North Carolina has an interest in this proceeding given that Plaintiffs seek redress for injuries sustained by North Carolina citizens." Brown v. Meter, 681 S.E.2d 383, 394 (N.C. Ct. App. 2009). Should the Supreme Court have included this factor in its new test for general jurisdiction? Why or why not?

Daimler AG v. Bauman

571 U.S. 117 (2014)

[Argentine nationals sued Daimler under the Alien Tort Statute and the Torture Victims Protection Act, alleging that Daimler's wholly-owned subsidiary collaborated with Argentine security forces to kidnap, torture, and kill the plaintiffs or their family members during Argentina's "Dirty War." The District Court dismissed for lack of personal jurisdiction, but the Ninth Circuit reversed. The Supreme Court ruled that the due process clause did not permit exercise of general jurisdiction over Daimler AG.]

Justice GINSBURG delivered the opinion of the Court.

This case concerns the authority of a court in the United States to entertain a claim brought by foreign plaintiffs against a foreign defendant based on events occurring entirely outside the United States. The litigation commenced in 2004, when twenty-two Argentinian residents filed a complaint in the United States District Court for the Northern District of California against DaimlerChrysler Aktiengesellschaft (Daimler), a German public stock company, headquartered in Stuttgart, that manufactures Mercedes-Benz vehicles in Germany. The complaint alleged that during Argentina's 1976-1983 "Dirty War," Daimler's Argentinian subsidiary, Mercedes-Benz Argentina (MB Argentina) collaborated with state security forces to kidnap, detain, torture, and kill certain MB Argentina workers, among them, plaintiffs or persons closely related to plaintiffs. Damages for the alleged human-rights violations were sought from Daimler under the laws of the United States, California, and Argentina. Jurisdiction over the lawsuit was predicated on the California contacts of Mercedes-Benz USA, LLC (MBUSA), a subsidiary of Daimler incorporated in Delaware with its principal place of business in New Jersey. MBUSA distributes Daimler-manufactured vehicles to independent dealerships throughout the United States, including California.

The question presented is whether the Due Process Clause of the Fourteenth Amendment precludes the District Court from exercising jurisdiction over Daimler in this case, given the absence of any California connection to the atrocities, perpetrators, or victims described in the complaint. Plaintiffs invoked the court's general or all-purpose jurisdiction. California, they urge, is a place where Daimler may be sued on any and all claims against it, wherever in the world the claims may arise. For example, as plaintiffs' counsel affirmed, under the proffered jurisdictional theory, if a Daimler-manufactured vehicle overturned in Poland, injuring a Polish driver and passenger, the injured parties could maintain a design defect suit in California. See Tr. of Oral Arg. 28-29. Exercises of personal jurisdiction so exorbitant, we hold, are barred by due process constraints on the assertion of adjudicatory authority.

In Goodyear Dunlop Tires Operations, S.A. v. Brown, 564 U.S. 915 (2011), we addressed the distinction between general or all-purpose jurisdiction, and specific or conduct-linked jurisdiction. As to the former, we held that a court may assert jurisdiction over a foreign corporation "to hear any and all claims against [it]" only when the corporation's affiliations with the State in which suit is brought are so constant and pervasive "as to render [it] essentially at home in the forum State." *Id.*, at 919. Instructed by *Goodyear*, we conclude Daimler is not "at home" in California, and cannot be sued there for injuries plaintiffs attribute to MB Argentina's conduct in Argentina.

I

. . .

MBUSA, an indirect subsidiary of Daimler, is a Delaware limited liability corporation.[6] MBUSA serves as Daimler's exclusive importer and distributor in the United States, purchasing Mercedes-Benz automobiles from Daimler in Germany, then importing those vehicles, and ultimately distributing them to independent dealerships located throughout the Nation. Although MBUSA's principal place of business is in New Jersey, MBUSA has multiple California-based facilities, including a regional office in Costa Mesa, a Vehicle Preparation Center in Carson, and a Classic Center in Irvine. According to the record developed below, MBUSA is the largest supplier of luxury vehicles to the California market. In particular, over 10% of all sales of new vehicles in the United States take place in California, and MBUSA's California sales account for 2.4% of Daimler's worldwide sales.

---

6. At times relevant to this suit, MBUSA was wholly owned by DaimlerChrysler North America Holding Corporation, a Daimler subsidiary.

The relationship between Daimler and MBUSA is delineated in a General Distributor Agreement, which sets forth requirements for MBUSA's distribution of Mercedes-Benz vehicles in the United States. That agreement established MBUSA as an "independent contracto[r]" that "buy[s] and sell[s] [vehicles] . . . as an independent business for [its] own account." App. 179a. The agreement "does not make [MBUSA] . . . a general or special agent, partner, joint venturer or employee of DAIMLERCHRYSLER or any DaimlerChrysler Group Company"; MBUSA "ha[s] no authority to make binding obligations for or act on behalf of DAIMLERCHRYSLER or any DaimlerChrysler Group Company." *Ibid*.

. . .

Our post-*International Shoe* opinions on general jurisdiction, by comparison, are few. "[The Court's] 1952 decision in Perkins v. Benguet Consol. Mining Co. remains the textbook case of general jurisdiction appropriately exercised over a foreign corporation that has not consented to suit in the forum." *Goodyear*, 564 U.S. at 927-928 (internal quotation marks and brackets omitted). The defendant in *Perkins*, Benguet, was a company incorporated under the laws of the Philippines, where it operated gold and silver mines. Benguet ceased its mining operations during the Japanese occupation of the Philippines in World War II; its president moved to Ohio, where he kept an office, maintained the company's files, and oversaw the company's activities. Perkins v. Benguet Consol. Mining Co., 342 U.S. 437, 448 (1952). The plaintiff, an Ohio resident, sued Benguet on a claim that neither arose in Ohio nor related to the corporation's activities in that State. We held that the Ohio courts could exercise general jurisdiction over Benguet without offending due process. *Ibid*. That was so, we later noted, because "Ohio was the corporation's principal, if temporary, place of business." Keeton v. Hustler Magazine, Inc., 465 U.S. 770, 780, n.11 (1984).

The next case on point, *Helicopteros*, 466 U.S. 408, arose from a helicopter crash in Peru. Four U.S. citizens perished in that accident; their survivors and representatives brought suit in Texas state court against the helicopter's owner and operator, a Colombian corporation. That company's contacts with Texas were confined to "sending its chief executive officer to Houston for a contract-negotiation session; accepting into its New York bank account checks drawn on a Houston bank; purchasing helicopters, equipment, and training services from [a Texas-based helicopter company] for substantial sums; and sending personnel to [Texas] for training." *Id.*, at 416. Notably, those contacts bore no apparent relationship to the accident that gave rise to the suit. We held that the company's Texas connections did not resemble the "continuous and systematic general business contacts . . . found to exist in *Perkins*." *Ibid*. "[M]ere purchases, even if occurring at regular intervals," we clarified, "are not enough to warrant a State's assertion of *in personam* jurisdiction over a nonresident corporation in a cause of action not related to those purchase transactions." *Id.*, at 418.

Most recently, in *Goodyear*, we answered the question: "Are foreign subsidiaries of a United States parent corporation amenable to suit in state court on claims unrelated to any activity of the subsidiaries in the forum State?" 564 U.S. at 918-19. That case arose from a bus accident outside Paris that killed two boys from North Carolina. The boys' parents brought a wrongful-death suit in North Carolina state court alleging that the bus's tire was defectively manufactured.

The complaint named as defendants not only The Goodyear Tire and Rubber Company (Goodyear), an Ohio corporation, but also Goodyear's Turkish, French, and Luxembourgian subsidiaries. Those foreign subsidiaries, which manufactured tires for sale in Europe and Asia, lacked any affiliation with North Carolina. A small percentage of tires manufactured by the foreign subsidiaries were distributed in North Carolina, however, and on that ground, the North Carolina Court of Appeals held the subsidiaries amenable to the general jurisdiction of North Carolina courts.

We reversed, observing that the North Carolina court's analysis "elided the essential difference between case-specific and all-purpose (general) jurisdiction." *Id.*, at 926-927. Although the placement of a product into the stream of commerce "may bolster an affiliation germane to *specific* jurisdiction," we explained, such contacts "do not warrant a determination that, based on those ties, the forum has *general* jurisdiction over a defendant." *Id.*, at 927. As *International Shoe* itself teaches, a corporation's "continuous activity of some sorts within a state is not enough to support the demand that the corporation be amenable to suits unrelated to that activity." 326 U.S., at 318. Because Goodyear's foreign subsidiaries were "in no sense at home in North Carolina," we held, those subsidiaries could not be required to submit to the general jurisdiction of that State's courts. 564 U.S. at 929. See also J. McIntyre Machinery, Ltd. v. Nicastro, 564 U.S. 873, 897-900 (2011) (Ginsburg, J., dissenting) (noting unanimous agreement that a foreign manufacturer, which engaged an independent U.S.-based distributor to sell its machines throughout the United States, could not be exposed to all-purpose jurisdiction in New Jersey courts based on those contacts).

As is evident from *Perkins*, *Helicopteros*, and *Goodyear*, general and specific jurisdiction have followed markedly different trajectories post-*International Shoe*. Specific jurisdiction has been cut loose from *Pennoyer*'s sway, but we have declined to stretch general jurisdiction beyond limits traditionally recognized. As this Court has increasingly trained on the "relationship among the defendant, the forum, and the litigation," *Shaffer*, 433 U.S., at 204, *i.e.*, specific jurisdiction,[7] general jurisdiction has come to occupy a less dominant place in the contemporary scheme.[8]

---

7. Remarkably, Justice Sotomayor treats specific jurisdiction as though it were barely there. Given the many decades in which specific jurisdiction has flourished, it would be hard to conjure up an example of the "deep injustice" Justice Sotomayor predicts as a consequence of our holding that California is not an all-purpose forum for suits against Daimler. Justice Sotomayor identifies "the concept of reciprocal fairness" as the "touchstone principle of due process in this field." (citing *International Shoe*, 326 U.S., at 319). She overlooks, however, that in the very passage of *International Shoe* on which she relies, the Court left no doubt that it was addressing specific — not general — jurisdiction. See *id.*, at 319 ("The exercise of th[e] privilege [of conducting corporate activities within a State] may give rise to obligations, and, *so far as those obligations arise out of or are connected with the activities within the state*, a procedure which requires the corporation to respond to a suit brought to enforce them can, in most instances, hardly be said to be undue." (emphasis added)).

8. As the Court made plain in *Goodyear* and repeats here, general jurisdiction requires affiliations "so 'continuous and systematic' as to render [the foreign corporation] essentially at home in the forum State." 564 U.S., at 919, *i.e.*, comparable to a domestic enterprise in that State.

IV

With this background, we turn directly to the question whether Daimler's affiliations with California are sufficient to subject it to the general (all-purpose) personal jurisdiction of that State's courts. In the proceedings below, the parties agreed on, or failed to contest, certain points we now take as given. Plaintiffs have never attempted to fit this case into the *specific* jurisdiction category. Nor did plaintiffs challenge on appeal the District Court's holding that Daimler's own contacts with California were, by themselves, too sporadic to justify the exercise of general jurisdiction. While plaintiffs ultimately persuaded the Ninth Circuit to impute MBUSA's California contacts to Daimler on an agency theory, at no point have they maintained that MBUSA is an alter ego of Daimler.

Daimler, on the other hand, failed to object below to plaintiffs' assertion that the California courts could exercise all-purpose jurisdiction over MBUSA. But see Brief for Petitioner 23, n.4 (suggestion that in light of *Goodyear*, MBUSA may not be amenable to general jurisdiction in California); Brief for United States as *Amicus Curiae* 16, n.5 (hereinafter U.S. Brief) (same). We will assume then, for purposes of this decision only, that MBUSA qualifies as at home in California.

A

In sustaining the exercise of general jurisdiction over Daimler, the Ninth Circuit relied on an agency theory, determining that MBUSA acted as Daimler's agent for jurisdictional purposes and then attributing MBUSA's California contacts to Daimler. The Ninth Circuit's agency analysis derived from Circuit precedent considering principally whether the subsidiary "performs services that are sufficiently important to the foreign corporation that if it did not have a representative to perform them, the corporation's own officials would undertake to perform substantially similar services." 644 F.3d, at 920 (quoting Doe v. Unocal Corp., 248 F.3d 915, 928 (C.A.9 2001); emphasis deleted).

This Court has not yet addressed whether a foreign corporation may be subjected to a court's general jurisdiction based on the contacts of its in-state subsidiary. Daimler argues, and several Courts of Appeals have held, that a subsidiary's jurisdictional contacts can be imputed to its parent only when the former is so dominated by the latter as to be its alter ego. The Ninth Circuit adopted a less rigorous test based on what it described as an "agency" relationship. Agencies, we note, come in many sizes and shapes: "One may be an agent for some business purposes and not others so that the fact that one may be an agent for one purpose does not make him or her an agent for every purpose." 2A C. J. S., Agency §43, p. 367 (2013) (footnote omitted).[9] A subsidiary, for example, might be its parent's

---

9. Agency relationships, we have recognized, may be relevant to the existence of *specific* jurisdiction. "[T]he corporate personality," International Shoe Co. v. Washington, 326 U.S. 310 (1945), observed, "is a fiction, although a fiction intended to be acted upon as though it were a fact." *Id.*, at 316, 66 S. Ct. 154. See generally 1 W. Fletcher, Cyclopedia of the Law of Corporations §30, p. 30 (Supp. 2012-2013) ("A corporation is a distinct legal entity that can act only through its agents."). As such, a corporation can purposefully avail itself of a forum by directing its agents or distributors

agent for claims arising in the place where the subsidiary operates, yet not its agent regarding claims arising elsewhere. The Court of Appeals did not advert to that prospect. But we need not pass judgment on invocation of an agency theory in the context of general jurisdiction, for in no event can the appeals court's analysis be sustained.

The Ninth Circuit's agency finding rested primarily on its observation that MBUSA's services were "important" to Daimler, as gauged by Daimler's hypothetical readiness to perform those services itself if MBUSA did not exist. Formulated this way, the inquiry into importance stacks the deck, for it will always yield a pro-jurisdiction answer: "Anything a corporation does through an independent contractor, subsidiary, or distributor is presumably something that the corporation would do 'by other means' if the independent contractor, subsidiary, or distributor did not exist." 676 F.3d, at 777 (O'Scannlain, J., dissenting from denial of rehearing en banc).[10] The Ninth Circuit's agency theory thus appears to subject foreign corporations to general jurisdiction whenever they have an in-state subsidiary or affiliate, an outcome that would sweep beyond even the "sprawling view of general jurisdiction" we rejected in *Goodyear*. 564 U.S., at 929.[11]

B

Even if we were to assume that MBUSA is at home in California, and further to assume MBUSA's contacts are imputable to Daimler, there would still be no basis to subject Daimler to general jurisdiction in California, for Daimler's slim contacts with the State hardly render it at home there.[12]

---

to take action there. See, e.g., Asahi, 480 U.S., at 112 (opinion of O'Connor, J.) (defendant's act of "marketing [a] product through a distributor who has agreed to serve as the sales agent in the forum State" may amount to purposeful availment); *International Shoe*, 326 U.S., at 318 ("the commission of some single or occasional acts of the corporate agent in a state" may sometimes "be deemed sufficient to render the corporation liable to suit" on related claims). See also Brief for Petitioner 24 (acknowledging that "an agency relationship may be sufficient in some circumstances to give rise to *specific* jurisdiction"). It does not inevitably follow, however, that similar reasoning applies to *general* jurisdiction. Cf. *Goodyear*, 564 U.S., at 927 (faulting analysis that "elided the essential difference between case-specific and all-purpose (general) jurisdiction").

10. Indeed, plaintiffs do not defend this aspect of the Ninth Circuit's analysis. See Brief for Respondents 39, n. 18 ("We do not believe that this gloss is particularly helpful.").

11. The Ninth Circuit's agency analysis also looked to whether the parent enjoys "the right to substantially control" the subsidiary's activities. Bauman v. DaimlerChrysler Corp., 644 F.3d 909, 924 (2011). The Court of Appeals found the requisite "control" demonstrated by the General Distributor Agreement between Daimler and MBUSA, which gives Daimler the right to oversee certain of MBUSA's operations, even though that agreement expressly disavowed the creation of any agency relationship. Thus grounded, the separate inquiry into control hardly curtails the overbreadth of the Ninth Circuit's agency holding.

12. By addressing this point, Justice Sotomayor asserts, we have strayed from the question on which we granted certiorari to decide an issue not argued below. That assertion is doubly flawed. First, the question on which we granted certiorari, as stated in Daimler's petition, is "whether it violates due process for a court to exercise general personal jurisdiction over a foreign corporation based solely on the fact that an indirect corporate subsidiary performs services on behalf of the defendant in the forum State." Pet. for Cert. i. That question fairly encompasses an inquiry into whether, in light of *Goodyear*, Daimler can be considered at home in California based on MBUSA's

Goodyear made clear that only a limited set of affiliations with a forum will render a defendant amenable to all-purpose jurisdiction there. "For an individual, the paradigm forum for the exercise of general jurisdiction is the individual's domicile; for a corporation, it is an equivalent place, one in which the corporation is fairly regarded as at home." 564 U.S., at 922-926 (citing Brilmayer et al., A General Look at General Jurisdiction, 66 Texas L. Rev. 721, 728 (1988)). With respect to a corporation, the place of incorporation and principal place of business are "paradig[m] . . . bases for general jurisdiction." *Id.*, at 735. See also Twitchell, 101 Harv. L. Rev., at 633. Those affiliations have the virtue of being unique — that is, each ordinarily indicates only one place — as well as easily ascertainable. Cf. Hertz Corp. v. Friend, 559 U.S. 77, 94 (2010) ("Simple jurisdictional rules . . . promote greater predictability."). These bases afford plaintiffs recourse to at least one clear and certain forum in which a corporate defendant may be sued on any and all claims.

Goodyear did not hold that a corporation may be subject to general jurisdiction *only* in a forum where it is incorporated or has its principal place of business; it simply typed those places paradigm all-purpose forums. Plaintiffs would have us look beyond the exemplar bases *Goodyear* identified, and approve the exercise of general jurisdiction in every State in which a corporation "engages in a substantial, continuous, and systematic course of business." Brief for Respondents 16-17, and nn. 7-8. That formulation, we hold, is unacceptably grasping.

As noted, see *supra*, at 753-754, the words "continuous and systematic" were used in *International Shoe* to describe instances in which the exercise of *specific* jurisdiction would be appropriate. See 326 U.S., at 317 (jurisdiction can be asserted where a corporation's in-state activities are not only "continuous and systematic, but also give rise to the liabilities sued on"). Turning to all-purpose jurisdiction, in contrast, *International Shoe* speaks of "instances in which the continuous corporate operations within a state [are] so substantial and of such a nature as to justify suit . . . *on causes of action arising from dealings entirely distinct from those activities.*" *Id.*, at 318 (emphasis added). See also Twitchell, Why We Keep Doing Business With Doing-Business Jurisdiction, 2001 U. Chi. Legal Forum 171, 184 (*International Shoe* "is clearly not saying that dispute-blind jurisdiction exists whenever 'continuous and systematic' contacts are found.").[13] Accordingly, the

---

in-state activities. See also this Court's Rule 14.1(a) (a party's statement of the question presented "is deemed to comprise every subsidiary question fairly included therein"). Moreover, both in the Ninth Circuit, see, *e.g.*, Brief for Federation of German Industries et al. as *Amici Curiae* in No. 07-15386(CA9), p. 3, and in this Court, see, *e.g.*, U.S. Brief 13-18; Brief for Chamber of Commerce of United States of America et al. as *Amici Curiae* 6-23; Brief for Lea Brilmayer as *Amica Curiae* 10-12, *amici* in support of Daimler homed in on the insufficiency of Daimler's California contacts for general jurisdiction purposes. In short, and in light of our pathmarking opinion in *Goodyear*, we perceive no unfairness in deciding today that California is not an all-purpose forum for claims against Daimler.

13. Plaintiffs emphasize two decisions, Barrow S.S. Co. v. Kane, 170 U.S. 100 (1898), and Tauza v. Susquehanna Coal Co., 220 N.Y. 259 (1917) (Cardozo, J.), both cited in Perkins v. Benguet Consol. Mining Co., 342 U.S. 437 (1952), just after the statement that a corporation's continuous operations in-state may suffice to establish general jurisdiction. Id., at 446, and n.6. See also *International Shoe*, 326 U.S., at 318 (citing *Tauza*). *Barrow* and *Tauza* indeed upheld the exercise of general jurisdiction based on the presence of a local office, which signaled that the corporation was "doing business" in the forum. *Perkins'* unadorned citations to these cases, both decided in the era dominated by

inquiry under *Goodyear* is not whether a foreign corporation's in-forum contacts can be said to be in some sense "continuous and systematic," it is whether that corporation's "affiliations with the State are so 'continuous and systematic' as to render [it] essentially at home in the forum State." 564 U.S., at 919.[14]

Here, neither Daimler nor MBUSA is incorporated in California, nor does either entity have its principal place of business there. If Daimler's California activities sufficed to allow adjudication of this Argentina-rooted case in California, the same global reach would presumably be available in every other State in which MBUSA's sales are sizable. Such exorbitant exercises of all-purpose jurisdiction would scarcely permit out-of-state defendants "to structure their primary conduct with some minimum assurance as to where that conduct will and will not render them liable to suit." *Burger King Corp.*, 471 U.S., at 472 (internal quotation marks omitted).

It was therefore error for the Ninth Circuit to conclude that Daimler, even with MBUSA's contacts attributed to it, was at home in California, and hence subject to suit there on claims by foreign plaintiffs having nothing to do with anything that occurred or had its principal impact in California.[15]

Pennoyer's territorial thinking, see supra, at 753-754, should not attract heavy reliance today. See generally Feder, Goodyear, "Home," and the Uncertain Future of Doing Business Jurisdiction, 63 S.C. L. Rev. 671 (2012) (questioning whether "doing business" should persist as a basis for general jurisdiction).

14. We do not foreclose the possibility that in an exceptional case, see, e.g., *Perkins*, described supra, at 755-757, and n.8, a corporation's operations in a forum other than its formal place of incorporation or principal place of business may be so substantial and of such a nature as to render the corporation at home in that State. But this case presents no occasion to explore that question, because Daimler's activities in California plainly do not approach that level. It is one thing to hold a corporation answerable for operations in the forum State, see infra, at 763, quite another to expose it to suit on claims having no connection whatever to the forum State.

15. To clarify in light of Justice Sotomayor's opinion concurring in the judgment, the general jurisdiction inquiry does not "focu[s] solely on the magnitude of the defendant's in-state contacts." General jurisdiction instead calls for an appraisal of a corporation's activities in their entirety, nationwide and worldwide. A corporation that operates in many places can scarcely be deemed at home in all of them. Otherwise, "at home" would be synonymous with "doing business" tests framed before specific jurisdiction evolved in the United States. See von Mehren & Trautman 1142-1144. Nothing in *International Shoe* and its progeny suggests that "a particular quantum of local activity" should give a State authority over a "far larger quantum of . . . activity" having no connection to any in-state activity. Feder, supra, at 694.

Justice Sotomayor would reach the same result, but for a different reason. Rather than concluding that Daimler is not at home in California, Justice Sotomayor would hold that the exercise of general jurisdiction over Daimler would be unreasonable "in the unique circumstances of this case." Post, at 763. In other words, she favors a resolution fit for this day and case only. True, a multipronged reasonableness check was articulated in *Asahi*, 480 U.S., at 113-114, but not as a free-floating test. Instead, the check was to be essayed when specific jurisdiction is at issue. See also Burger King Corp. v. Rudzewicz, 471 U.S. 462, 476-478 (1985). First, a court is to determine whether the connection between the forum and the episode-in-suit could justify the exercise of specific jurisdiction. Then, in a second step, the court is to consider several additional factors to assess the reasonableness of entertaining the case. When a corporation is genuinely at home in the forum State, however, any second-step inquiry would be superfluous.

Justice Sotomayor fears that our holding will "lead to greater unpredictability by radically expanding the scope of jurisdictional discovery." But it is hard to see why much in the way of discovery would be needed to determine where a corporation is at home. Justice Sotomayor's proposal

[The Court remarked on the transnational context of this case and the significance of the Alien Tort Statute and the Torture Victims Protection Act.]

* * *

For the reasons stated, the judgment of the United States Court of Appeals for the Ninth Circuit is *Reversed*.

[A concurring opinion by Justice SOTOMAYOR is omitted.]

Questions and Comments

(1) Justice Ginsburg, the author of the unanimous opinion in *Bauman*, wrote a dissenting opinion in J. McIntyre Machinery, Ltd. v. Nicastro, 564 U.S. 873 (2011). In that dissent she criticized the majority for failing to exercise general jurisdiction over a British corporation that effectively availed itself of the U.S. market, but sold its products through a technically independent U.S. distributor in order to avoid liability litigation. 564 U.S. at 892-893. As Justice Ginsburg observes in *Bauman*, "MBUSA distributes Daimler-manufactured vehicles to independent dealerships throughout the United States, including California," Daimler AG v. Bauman, 571 U.S. 117, 122-124 (2014). How does Justice Ginsburg justify *Bauman*'s refusal to exercise general jurisdiction, in contrast to her dissent in *Nicastro*?

(2) Similar to Brown v. Meter, 681 S.E.2d 383 (N.C. Ct. App. 2009), the Ninth Circuit had ruled that California "ha[s] a significant interest in adjudicating the suit" even though "the events at issue did not take place in California and although the plaintiffs are not California residents." Bauman v. DaimlerChrysler Corp., 644 F.3d 909, 927 (9th Cir. 2011). An example of this "significant interest" may be to protect human rights and to promote responsible behavior among multinational corporations, a proposal that has some scholarly support. *See, e.g.*, Bensimon, *Corporate Liability Under the Alien Tort Statute: Can Corporations Have Their Cake and Eat It Too?*, 10 Loy. U. Chi. Intl. L. Rev. 199 (2013). When, for example, human rights violations have occurred in a state without an independent judiciary, should U.S. courts hear suits against the perpetrators on the grounds that there are no feasible alternative venues? Why or why not?

(3) An amicus brief filed by the German Institute for Human Rights and other German legal experts argued that the Supreme Court should affirm the Ninth Circuit because, among other reasons, non-U.S. venues were unavailable. Bauman v. DaimlerChrysler Corp., No. 11-965, 2013 WL 4578964, at *6. The Brief observed that Argentine law bars claims about the Dirty War and that German

---

to import *Asahi's* "reasonableness" check into the general jurisdiction determination, on the other hand, would indeed compound the jurisdictional inquiry. The reasonableness factors identified in *Asahi* include "the burden on the defendant," "the interests of the forum State," "the plaintiff's interest in obtaining relief," "the interstate judicial system's interest in obtaining the most efficient resolution of controversies," "the shared interest of the several States in furthering fundamental substantive social policies," and, in the international context, "the procedural and substantive policies of other nations whose interests are affected by the assertion of jurisdiction." 480 U.S., at 113-115 (some internal quotation marks omitted). Imposing such a checklist in cases of general jurisdiction would hardly promote the efficient disposition of an issue that should be resolved expeditiously at the outset of litigation.

courts would apply the Argentine laws that bar the plaintiffs' claims. *Id.* However, the same brief states: "Under that "Under Art. 40 EGBGB [Act Introducing the Civil Code], the substantive law applied is that of the territory where the tortfeasor committed the tortious conduct. As an alternative, the plaintiff can demand that the law of the territory where the injurious effect of the conduct is felt." *Id.* Under that alternative, couldn't the plaintiffs go to Germany and sue there, claiming that the injurious effect of Mercedez-Benz Argentina's tortious conduct is felt wherever the plaintiffs are (in the form of grief and sorrow over the loss of their loved ones)? Why do you think German law retains a provision that exposes German courts to the possibility of forum-shopping?

(4) In *Asahi*, the Court states that it has "no occasion to determine whether Congress could, consistent with the Due Process Clause of the Fifth Amendment, authorize federal court personal jurisdiction over alien defendants based on the aggregate of *national* contacts, rather than on the contacts between the defendant and the State in which the federal court sits." *See also* Omni Capital Intl. v. Rudolf Wolff & Co., 484 U.S. 97, 103 n.5 (1987) (same). Many courts have held that a national contacts test satisfies the Fifth Amendment due process clause. *See, e.g.,* Go-Video, Inc. v. Akai Elec. Co., 885 F.2d 1406 (9th Cir. 1989). Other courts have tempered this conclusion by insisting that due process requires not only minimum contacts with the nation, but also that the venue for the suit be fair and reasonable. *See, e.g.,* Peay v. Bellsouth Medical Assistance Plan, 205 F.3d 1206, 1212 (10th Cir. 2000).

A 1993 Amendment to Federal Rule of Civil Procedure 4 provides a federal long-arm statute authorization in cases arising under federal laws which themselves lack a long-arm statute. It provides: "If the exercise of jurisdiction is consistent with the Constitution and laws of the United States, serving a summons or filing a waiver of service is also *effective*, with respect to claims arising under federal law, to establish personal jurisdiction over the person of any defendant who is not subject to the jurisdiction of the courts of general jurisdiction of any state." Fed. R. Civ. P. 4(k)(2). Under Rule 4(k)(2), federal courts may exercise jurisdiction over a defendant (a) against whom a federal claim is asserted; (b) who has nationwide contacts; and (c) who is not subject to personal jurisdiction in any state. U.S.A. v. Swiss American Bank, 191 F.3d 30, 38 (7th Cir. 1999).

In addition to the question of the constitutionality of using nationwide contacts for personal jurisdiction in federal question cases, Rule 4(k)(2) raises two additional difficulties. The first is whether it exceeds the Rules Enabling Act's prohibition on Rules that "abridge, enlarge, or modify any substantive rights." 28 U.S.C. §2072(b). The Advisory Committee on the Civil Rules worried that it might. *See* H.R. Doc. No. 103-74, at 154-155 (1993). The second problem concerns the conundrum of establishing Rule 4(k)(2)'s requirement that the defendant lacks adequate contacts for personal jurisdiction in any particular state. The general rule is that the burden of proof lies with the party attempting to assert jurisdiction. But it is very hard for a plaintiff to demonstrate that the defendant lacks adequate contacts in each of the 50 states, especially since the defendant controls much of the relevant information. *See Swiss American Bank*, 191 F.3d at 40. On the other hand, shifting the burden to the defendant requires the defendant to either concede amenability to suit in either federal court (by admitting that no state court has jurisdiction) or in a state court (arguing that it has sufficient contacts with some state). *Id*. at 40-41. Courts have resolved this problem in different ways. Most courts follow the traditional rule and require the plaintiff to prove no jurisdiction in any of the 50 states. *See, e.g.*, CFMT Inc. v. Steag Microtech, Inc., 1997 WL 313161 (D. Del. 1997). The Seventh Circuit, by contrast, assigns the burden to the defendant; on this view, a defendant who wishes to defeat personal jurisdiction under Rule 4(k)(2) must name some state court in which the suit could proceed. *See* ISI Intl., Inc. v. Borden Ladner Gervais LLP, 256 F.3d 548 (7th Cir. 2001). The First Circuit, by contrast, shifts the burden to the defendant only after the plaintiff has made a prima facie for the applicability of Rule 4(k)(2). *See Swiss American Bank*, 191 F.3d at 26. For commentary on these and other aspects of Rule 4(k)(2), *see* Burbank, *The United States' Approach to International Civil Litigation: Recent Developments in Forum Selection*, 19 U. Pa. J. Intl. Econ. L. 1, 13 (1998).

Note on Personal Jurisdiction and Corporate Registration Statutes

An important issue that the Supreme Court has not yet completely settled is whether or not a foreign corporation consents to general jurisdiction in the courts of a forum state by registering to do business in that state and appointing an agent for service of process in that state. In 1988 the Delaware Supreme Court answered this question in the affirmative in Sternberg v. O'Neil, 550 A.2d 1105 (Del. 1988), but then overturned this decision in Genuine Parts Co. v. Cepec following *Daimler*. Sternberg v. O'Neil also dealt with the separate issue of jurisdiction based on property (*see infra*) and this portion of the opinion is apparently still good law.

Genuine Parts Co. v. Cepec

137 A.3d 123 (Del. 2016)

STRINE, Chief Justice, for the Majority:

I.   Introduction

Like every other state in our republic,[14] Delaware requires a foreign corporation that sells any product or service in the state to register to do business and agree to the appointment of a registered agent to receive service of process. In this case, a large Georgia corporation that properly registered to do business in Delaware has been sued in Delaware over claims having nothing to do with its

---

14. See Tanya J. Monestier, Registration Statutes, General Jurisdiction, and the Fallacy of Consent, 36 CARDOZO L. REV. 1343, 1363 (2015) ("Every state has a registration statute that requires corporations doing business in the state to register with the state and appoint an agent for service of process." (footnote omitted)); Matthew Kipp, Inferring Express Consent: The Paradox of Permitting Registration Statutes to Confer General Jurisdiction, 9 REV. LITIG. 1, 1 (1990) ("As a condition for doing business within their borders, all states require a foreign corporation to designate a local resident for service of process. This requirement is embodied in what commonly are known as registration statutes." (footnote omitted)).

activities in Delaware. Adhering to the interpretation given to our registration statutes—8 Del. C. §§371 and 376—in Sternberg v. O'Neil,[15] our Superior Court held that, notwithstanding the U.S. Supreme Court's decision in Daimler AG v. Bauman,[16] the foreign corporation consented to Delaware's general jurisdiction merely by registering to do business in Delaware. This interlocutory appeal raises the singular issue of whether Delaware may exercise general jurisdiction over a foreign corporation for claims having nothing to do with Delaware, as a price for the corporation agreeing simply to be able to do business in Delaware.

We conclude that after *Daimler*, it is not tenable to read Delaware's registration statutes as *Sternberg* did. *Sternberg*'s interpretation was heavily influenced by a prior reading given to §376 by our U.S. District Court,[17] and like that District Court decision, rested on a view of federal jurisprudence that has now been fundamentally undermined by *Daimler* and its predecessor Goodyear Dunlop Tires Operations, S.A. v. Brown.[18] Not only that, *Sternberg* was a case where the exercise of personal jurisdiction over the foreign corporation was proper under the minimum-contacts test, anyway,[19] and where the corporate governance claims at issue were closely connected to the internal affairs of a Delaware corporation.[20] Most important, *Sternberg* represented just one plausible way to read a statute that on its face does not refer explicitly to personal jurisdiction, much less to consent to personal jurisdiction.

Our duty under our law is to give as much effect as possible to a state statute, where it is constitutional to do so.[21] After *Daimler*, we hold that Delaware's

---

15. 550 A.2d 1105 (Del. 1988).

16. 134 S. Ct. 746 (2014).

17. See *Sternberg*, 550 A.2d at 1115 (" 'Section 376 does not in [its] terms limit the amenability of service of a qualified corporation to one which does business in Delaware or with respect to a cause of action arising in Delaware. By the generality of its terms, a foreign corporation qualified in Delaware is subject to service of process in Delaware on any transitory cause of action.' " (quoting D'Angelo v. Petroleos Mexicanos, 378 F. Supp. 1034, 1039 (D. Del. 1974))).

18. 131 S. Ct. 2846 (2011).

19. See *Sternberg*, 550 A.2d at 1122 ("For more than thirty years, [the foreign parent corporation] has benefited from the protections of the Delaware law in operating [its Delaware subsidiary] for commercial gain, including the benefits afforded to it directly as a shareholder of a Delaware corporation. We conclude that [the foreign corporation] intentionally established and maintained minimum contacts with Delaware by its decision to continue to operate its wholly owned subsidiary . . . as a Delaware corporation." (footnote omitted)).

20. See id. at 1107 (noting that the Ohio corporation's "alleged mismanagement" of its Delaware subsidiary is the subject of the double derivative suit).

21. See, e.g., Gonzales v. Carhart, 550 U.S. 124, 153 (2007) (" '[T]he elementary rule is that every reasonable construction must be resorted to, in order to save a statute from unconstitutionality.' " (quoting Edward J. DeBartolo Corp. v. Fla. Gulf Bldg. & Constr. Trades Council, 485 U.S. 568, 575 (1988))); I.N.S. v. St. Cyr, 533 U.S. 289, 299-300 (2001) ("[I]f an otherwise acceptable construction of a statute would raise serious constitutional problems, and where an alternative interpretation of the statute is fairly possible, [courts] are obligated to construe the statute to avoid such problems." (internal citations omitted) (internal quotation marks omitted)); Richardson v. Wile, 535 A.2d 1346, 1350 (Del. 1988) (citing Atlantis I Condo. Ass'n v. Bryson, 403 A.2d 711 (Del. 1979)) ("[W]here a possible infringement of a constitutional guarantee exists, the interpreting court should strive to construe the legislative intent so as to avoid unnecessary constitutional infirmities."); Maxwell v. Vetter, 311 A.2d 864, 867 (Del. 1973) ("The Legislature is deemed to have intended to enact a valid and constitutional statute, and the statute will be so construed whenever that construction is

registration statutes must be read as a requirement that a foreign corporation must appoint a registered agent to accept service of process, but not as a broad consent to personal jurisdiction in any cause of action, however unrelated to the foreign corporation's activities in Delaware. Rather, any use of the service of process provision for registered foreign corporations must involve an exercise of personal jurisdiction consistent with the Due Process Clause of the Fourteenth Amendment. In most situations where the foreign corporation does not have its principal place of business in Delaware, that will mean that Delaware cannot exercise general jurisdiction over the foreign corporation.[22] In that circumstance, the core statute to evaluate whether the foreign corporation is subject to specific jurisdiction is Delaware's long-arm statute, 10 Del. C. §3104. The long-arm statute operates smoothly in tandem with §376, which provides that a foreign corporation can be served via its registered agent in the state. Under the long-arm statute, a foreign corporation "submits to the jurisdiction of the Delaware courts" as to any cause of action that arises out of certain enumerated acts by the corporation in this state such as "transact[ing] any business or perform[ing] any character of work or service," or "contract[ing] to supply services or things."[23] Moreover, a plaintiff who brings a cause of action fitting under the long-arm statute against a registered foreign corporation need not use cumbersome means of service of process, but instead can serve the foreign corporation's registered agent, as contemplated in the long-arm statute.[24] We believe *Sternberg's* more far-reaching interpretation of §376 collides directly with the U.S. Supreme Court's holding in *Daimler*, and subjects §376 to invalidation. In our republic, it is critical to the efficient conduct of business, and therefore to job- and wealth-creation, that individual states not exact unreasonable tolls simply for the right to do business. Businesses select their states of incorporation and principal places of business with care, because they know that those jurisdictions are in fact "home" and places where they can be sued generally.[25] An incentive scheme where every state can claim general jurisdiction over every business that does any business within its borders for any claim would reduce the certainty of the law and subject businesses to capricious litigation

---

possible without doing violence to the legislative intent."); In re Opinion of the Justices, 177 A.2d 205, 211 (Del. 1962) ("When [] two constructions of a statute are possible and one of them is unconstitutional, the courts are bound to accept the one which is constitutional."); Fouracre v. White, 102 A. 186, 200 (Del. Super. 1917) ("It is the duty of the court to give a statute such a construction as will render it constitutional and operative if it can be done without violence to the language of the statute.").

22. See *Daimler*, 134 S. Ct. at 761 ("[A nonresident corporation will be subject to general jurisdiction where its] affiliations with the State are so 'continuous and systematic' as to render [it] essentially at home in the forum State." (quoting *Goodyear*, 131 S. Ct. at 2851)); id. at 761 n.19 (noting the "possibility that in an exceptional case, a corporation's operations in a forum other than its formal place of incorporation or principal place of business may be so substantial and of such a nature as to render the corporation at home in that State" (internal citation omitted)).

23. 10 Del. C. §3104.

24. Id. §3104(k).

25. See *Daimler*, 134 S. Ct. at 760-62. *Daimler* relied on Burger King Corp. v. Rudzewicz, 471 U.S. 462 (1985), which in turn relied on World-Wide Volkswagen Corp. v. Woodson, for the proposition that "the Due Process Clause . . . gives a degree of predictability to the legal system that allows potential defendants to structure their primary conduct with some minimum assurance as to where that conduct will and will not render them liable to suit." 444 U.S. 286, 297 (1980).

treatment as a cost of operating on a national scale or entering any state's market.[26] *Daimler* makes plain that it is inconsistent with principles of due process to exercise general jurisdiction over a foreign corporation that is not "essentially at home" in a state for claims having no rational connection to the state.[27] The foreign corporation in this case does not have its principal place of business in Delaware; nor is there any other plausible basis on which Delaware is essentially its home. Hence, Delaware cannot exercise general jurisdiction over it consistent with principles of due process. Furthermore, the plaintiffs concede that they cannot establish specific jurisdiction over the nonresident defendant under the long-arm statute or principles of due process. Therefore, the plaintiffs' claim must be dismissed for lack of personal jurisdiction. Accordingly, we reverse the Superior Court's judgment.

C. Jurisdiction Based on Property

In Harris v. Balk, 198 U.S. 215 (1905), the famous bête noir of first-year civil procedure students, Harris and Balk were from North Carolina. Harris owed Balk $180. Harris visited Maryland, where Epstein "seized" the debt owed to Balk to help satisfy a claim that Epstein had against Balk for a greater amount. The action proceeded against Harris in Maryland. He put up no defense, admitting that he owed the money to Balk and not involving himself in the merits of the dispute between Epstein and Balk. Epstein won the Maryland judgment and collected the $180. When Harris returned to North Carolina, Balk sued him for the $180. Harris claimed the Maryland judgment in bar. The Supreme Court upheld the defense. Note that two holdings were necessary to reach the result in Harris v. Balk: (1) A debt, though intangible property, is subject to seizure like tangible property; and (2) the debt is "located" where the debtor is (and not where the creditor-owner is) because that is where the debtor can be sued and the debt realized.

Perhaps the cleverest use ever made of the doctrine of Harris v. Balk occurred in Siro v. American Express Co., 99 Conn. 95, 121 A. 280 (1923). Plaintiff had a claim against American Express but either could not or did not bother to obtain personal jurisdiction over American Express in Connecticut. Instead, plaintiff's lawyers had another lawyer go to the bank and buy $620 worth of travelers' checks. He made no representation to the bank about the purpose of his purchase. As soon as he left the bank, a deputy sheriff served garnishment papers on the bank — by accepting the lawyer's money, it became indebted to American Express under the agreement by which the bank sold American Express travelers' checks. The lawyer who bought the checks had done so with money supplied by the plaintiff's attorneys, and shortly after buying them he deposited them at another bank to the account of the plaintiff's attorneys. The court upheld jurisdiction on the basis of

---

26. See id.
27. Id. at 761.

Harris v. Balk and ruled that there had been no fraudulent inducement of assets into the state because no misrepresentations had been made. The court added, "If the defendant has a good defense to the plaintiff's suit, it should rather welcome its determination by a judicial tribunal than seek to avoid or postpone the issue by a technicality."

The doctrine of Harris v. Balk survived until surprisingly recent times.

Shaffer v. Heitner
433 U.S. 186 (1977)

Justice MARSHALL delivered the opinion of the Court.

The controversy in this case concerns the constitutionality of a Delaware statute that allows a court of that State to take jurisdiction of a lawsuit by sequestering any property of the defendant that happens to be located in Delaware. Appellants contend that the sequestration statute as applied in this case violates the Due Process Clause of the Fourteenth Amendment both because it permits the state courts to exercise jurisdiction despite the absence of sufficient contacts among the defendants, the litigation, and the State of Delaware and because it authorizes the deprivation of defendants' property without providing adequate procedural safeguards. We find it necessary to consider only the first of these contentions.

I

Appellee Heitner, a nonresident of Delaware, is the owner of one share of stock in the Greyhound Corporation, a business incorporated under the laws of Delaware with its principal place of business in Phoenix, Ariz. On May 22, 1974, he filed a shareholder's derivative suit in the Court of Chancery for New Castle County, Del., in which he named as defendants Greyhound, its wholly owned subsidiary Greyhound Lines, Inc. and 28 present or former officers or directors of one or both of the corporations. In essence Heitner alleged that the individual defendants had violated their duties to Greyhound by causing it and its subsidiaries to engage in actions that resulted in the corporation's being held liable for substantial damages in a private antitrust suit and a large fine in a criminal contempt action. The activities which led to these penalties took place in Oregon.

Simultaneously with his complaint, Heitner filed a motion for an order of sequestration of the Delaware property of the individual defendants pursuant to 10 Del. C. §366. This motion was accompanied by a supporting affidavit of counsel which stated that the individual defendants were non-residents of Delaware. The affidavit identified the property to be sequestered as

> "common stock, 3% Second Cumulative Preferred Stock and stock unit credits of the Defendant Greyhound Corporation, a Delaware corporation, as well as all options and all warrants to purchase said stock issued to said individual Defendants and all contractual obligations, all rights, debts or credits due or accrued to or for the benefit of any of the said Defendants under any type of

written agreement, contract, or other legal instrument of any kind whatever between any of the individual Defendants and said corporation."

The requested sequestration order was signed the day the motion was filed. Pursuant to that order, the sequestrator "seized" approximately 82,000 shares of Greyhound common stock belonging to 19 of the defendants, and options belonging to another two defendants. These seizures are accomplished by placing "stop transfer" orders or their equivalents on the books of the Greyhound Corporation. So far as the record shows, none of the certificates representing the seized property was physically present in Delaware. The stock was considered to be in Delaware, and so subject to seizure, by virtue of a Del. C. §169, which makes Delaware the situs of ownership of all stock in Delaware corporations.

All 28 defendants were notified of the initiation of the suit by certified mail directed to their last known addresses and by publication in a New Castle County newspaper. The 21 defendants whose property was seized (hereafter referred to as appellants) responded by entering a special appearance for the purpose of moving to quash service of process and to vacate the sequestration order. They contended that the ex parte sequestration procedure did not accord them due process of law and that the property seized was not capable of attachment in Delaware. In addition, appellants asserted that under the rule of International Shoe Co. v. Washington, they did not have sufficient contacts with Delaware to sustain the jurisdiction of that State's courts.

The Court of Chancery rejected these arguments. . . .

On appeal, the Delaware Supreme Court affirmed the judgment of the court of chancery. . . .

We noted probable jurisdiction. We reverse.

II

The Delaware courts rejected appellants' jurisdictional challenge by noting that this suit was brought as a quasi in rem proceeding. Since quasi in rem jurisdiction is traditionally based on attachment or seizure of property present in the jurisdiction, not on contacts between the defendant and the State, the courts considered appellants' claimed lack of contacts with Delaware to be unimportant. This categorical analysis assumes the continuous soundness of the conceptual structure founded on the century-old case of Pennoyer v. Neff. . . .

III

The case for applying to jurisdiction in rem the same test of "fair play and substantial justice" as governs assertions of jurisdiction in personam is simple and straightforward. It is premised on recognition that "[t]he phrase, 'judicial jurisdiction over a thing,' is a customary elliptical way of referring to jurisdiction over the interests of persons in a thing." Restatement (Second) of Conflict of Laws §56, introductory note. This recognition leads to the conclusion that in order to justify an exercise of jurisdiction in rem, the basis for jurisdiction must be sufficient to justify exercising "jurisdiction over the interests of persons in a thing." The standard for determining whether an exercise of jurisdiction over the interests of persons is consistent with the Due Process Clause is the minimum contacts standard elucidated in *International Shoe.*

This argument, of course, does not ignore the fact that the presence of property in a State may bear on the existence of jurisdiction by providing contacts among the forum State, the defendant, and the litigation. For example, when claims to the property itself are the source of the underlying controversy between the plaintiff and the defendant,[24] it would be unusual for the State where the property is located not to have jurisdiction. In such cases, the defendant's claim to property located in the State would normally indicate that he expected to benefit from the State's protection of his interest. The State's strong interests in assuring the marketability of property within its borders and in providing a procedure for peaceful resolution of disputes about the possession of that property could also support jurisdiction, as would the likelihood that important records and witnesses will be found in the State.[28] The presence of property may also favor jurisdiction in cases, such as suits for injury suffered on the land of an absentee owner, where the defendant's ownership of the property is conceded but the cause of action is otherwise related to rights and duties growing out of that ownership.

It appears, therefore, that jurisdiction over many types of actions which now are or might be brought in rem would not be affected by a holding that any assertion of state court jurisdiction must satisfy the *International Shoe* standard.[30] For the type of quasi in rem action typified by Harris v. Balk and the present case, however, accepting the proposed analysis would result in significant change. These are cases where the property which now serves as the basis for state court jurisdiction is completely unrelated to the plaintiff's cause of action. Thus, although the presence of the defendant's property in a State might suggest the existence of other ties among the defendant, the State, and the litigation, the presence of the property alone would not support the State's jurisdiction. If those other ties did not exist, cases over which the State is now thought to have jurisdiction could not be brought in that forum.

---

24. This category includes true in rem actions and the first type of quasi in rem proceedings. *See* n.17 [which follows:]

[17. "A judgment in rem affects the interests of all persons in designated property. A judgment quasi in rem affects the interests of particular persons in designated property. The latter is of two types. In one the plaintiff is seeking to secure a pre-existing claim in the subject property and to extinguish or establish the nonexistence of similar interests of particular persons. In the other the plaintiff seeks to apply what he concedes to be the property of the defendant to the satisfaction of a claim against him. Restatement, Judgments, 5-9." Hanson v. Denckla, 357 U.S. 235, 246 n.12.

As did the Court in *Hanson,* we will for convenience generally use the term "in rem" in place of "in rem and quasi in rem."]

28. We do not suggest that these illustrations include all the factors that may affect the decision, nor that the factors we have mentioned are necessarily decisive.

30. *Cf.* Smit, *The Enduring Utility of In Rem Rules: A Lasting Legacy of* Pennoyer v. Neff, 48 Brook. L. Rev. 600 (1977). We do not suggest that jurisdictional doctrines other than those discussed in text, such as the particularized rules governing adjudications of status, are inconsistent with the standard of fairness.

Since acceptance of the *International Shoe* test would most affect this class of cases, we examine the arguments against adopting that standard as they relate to this category of litigation. Before doing so, however, we note that this type of case also presents the clearest illustration of the argument in favor of assessing assertions of jurisdiction by a single standard. For in cases such as *Harris* and this one, the only role played by the property is to provide the basis for bringing the defendant into court. Indeed, the express purpose of the Delaware sequestration procedure is to compel the defendant to enter a personal appearance. In such cases, if a direct assertion of personal jurisdiction over the defendant would violate the Constitution, it would seem that an indirect assertion of that jurisdiction should be equally impermissible.

The primary rationale for treating the presence of property as a sufficient basis for jurisdiction to adjudicate claims over which the State would not have jurisdiction if *International Shoe* applied is that a wrongdoer "should not be able to avoid payment of his obligations by the expedient of removing his assets to a place where he is not subject to an in personam suit." Restatement (Second) of Conflicts §66, comment *a*. This justification, however, does not explain why jurisdiction should be recognized without regard to whether the property is present in the State because of an effort to avoid the owner's obligations. Nor does it support jurisdiction to adjudicate the underlying claim. At most, it suggests that a State in which property is located should have jurisdiction to attach that property, by use of proper procedures, as security for a judgment being sought in a forum where the litigation can be maintained consistently with *International Shoe*. Moreover, we know of nothing to justify the assumption that a debtor can avoid paying his obligations by removing his property to a State in which his creditor cannot obtain personal jurisdiction over him. The Full Faith and Credit Clause, after all, makes the valid in personam judgment of one State enforceable in all other States.[36]

It might also be suggested that allowing in rem jurisdiction avoids the uncertainty inherent in the *International Shoe* standard and assures a plaintiff of a forum.[37] We believe, however, that the fairness standard of *International Shoe* can be easily applied in the vast majority of cases. Moreover, when the existence of jurisdiction in a particular forum under *International Shoe* is unclear, the cost of simplifying the litigation by avoiding the jurisdictional question may be the sacrifice of "fair play and substantial justice." That cost is too high.

We are left, then, to consider the significance of the long history of jurisdiction based solely on the presence of property in a State. Although the theory that territorial power is both essential to and sufficient for jurisdiction has been undermined, we have never held that the presence of property in a State does not automatically confer jurisdiction over the owner's interest in that property. This history must be considered as supporting the proposition that jurisdiction based

---

36. Once it has been determined by a court of competent jurisdiction that the defendant is a debtor of the plaintiff, there would seem to be no unfairness in allowing an action to realize on that debt in a State where the defendant has property, whether or not that State would have jurisdiction to determine the existence of the debt as an original matter.

37. This case does not raise, and we therefore do not consider, the question whether the presence of a defendant's property in a State is a sufficient basis for jurisdiction when no other forum is available to the plaintiff.

solely on the presence of property satisfies the demands of due process, but it is not decisive. "[T]raditional notions of fair play and substantial justice" can be as readily offended by the perpetuation of ancient forms that are no longer justified as by the adoption of new procedures that are inconsistent with the basic values of our constitutional heritage. The fiction that an assertion of jurisdiction over property is anything but an assertion of jurisdiction over the owner of the property supports an ancient form without substantial modern justification. Its continued acceptance would serve only to allow state court jurisdiction that is fundamentally unfair to the defendant.

We therefore conclude that all assertions of state court jurisdiction must be evaluated according to the standards set forth in *International Shoe* and its progeny.[39]

IV

The Delaware courts based their assertion of jurisdiction in this case solely on the statutory presence of appellants' property in Delaware. Yet that property is not the subject matter of this litigation, nor is the underlying cause of action related to the property. Appellants' holdings in Greyhound do not, therefore, provide contacts with Delaware sufficient to support the jurisdiction of that State's courts over appellants. If it exists, that jurisdiction must have some other foundation.

Appellee Heitner did not allege and does not now claim that appellants have ever set foot in Delaware. Nor does he identify any act related to his cause of action as having taken place in Delaware. Nevertheless, he contends that appellants' positions as directors and officers of a corporation chartered in Delaware provide sufficient "contacts, ties, or relations," International Shoe Co. v. Washington, with that State to give its courts jurisdiction over appellants in this stockholder's derivative action. This argument is based primarily on what Heitner asserts to be the strong interest of Delaware in supervising the management of a Delaware corporation. That interest is said to derive from the role of Delaware law in establishing the corporation and defining the obligations owed to it by its officers and directors. In order to protect this interest, appellee concludes, Delaware's courts must have jurisdiction over corporate fiduciaries such as appellants.

This argument is undercut by the failure of the Delaware Legislature to assert the state interest appellee finds so compelling. Delaware law bases jurisdiction not on appellants' status as corporate fiduciaries, but rather on the presence of their property in the State. Although the sequestration procedure used here may be most frequently used in derivative suits against officers and directors, the authorizing statute evinces no specific concern with such actions. Sequestration can be used in any suit against a non-resident, and reaches corporate fiduciaries only if they happen to own interests in a Delaware corporation,

---

39. It would not be fruitful for us to re-examine the facts of cases decided on the rationales of *Pennoyer* and *Harris* to determine whether jurisdiction might have been sustained under the standard we adopt today. To the extent that prior decisions are inconsistent with this standard, they are overruled.

or other property in the State. But as Heitner's failure to secure jurisdiction over seven of the defendants named in his complaint demonstrates, there is no necessary relationship between holding a position as a corporate fiduciary and owning stock or other interests in the corporation. If Delaware perceived its interest in securing jurisdiction over corporate fiduciaries to be as great as Heitner suggests, we would expect it to have enacted a statute more clearly designed to protect that interest.

Moreover, even if Heitner's assessment of the importance of Delaware's interest is accepted, his argument fails to demonstrate that Delaware is a fair forum for this litigation. The interest appellee has identified may support the application of Delaware law to resolve any controversy over appellants' actions in their capacities as officers and directors.[44] But we have rejected the argument that if a State's law can properly be applied to a dispute, its courts necessarily have jurisdiction over the parties to that dispute.

Appellee suggests that by accepting positions as officers or directors of a Delaware corporation, appellants performed the acts required by Hanson v. Denckla. He notes that Delaware law provides substantial benefits to corporate officers and directors, and that these benefits were at least in part the incentive for appellants to assume their positions. It is, he says, "only fair and just" to require appellants, in return for these benefits, to respond in the State of Delaware when they are accused of misusing their powers.

But like Heitner's first argument, this line of reasoning establishes only that it is appropriate for Delaware law to govern the obligations of appellants to Greyhound and its stockholders. It does not demonstrate that appellants have "purposefully avail[ed themselves] of the privilege of conducting activities within the forum State," Hanson v. Denckla, in a way that would justify bringing them before a Delaware tribunal. Appellants have simply had nothing to do with the State of Delaware. Moreover, appellants had no reason to expect to be haled before a Delaware court. Delaware, unlike some States, has not enacted a statute that treats acceptance of a directorship as consent to jurisdiction in the State. And "[i]t strains reason . . . to suggest that anyone buying securities in a corporation formed in Delaware 'impliedly consents' to subject himself to Delaware's . . . jurisdiction on any cause of action." Appellants, who were not required to acquire interests in Greyhound in order to hold their positions, did not by acquiring those interests surrender their right to be brought to judgment only in States with which they had had "minimum contacts."

The judgment of the Delaware Supreme Court must, therefore, be reversed. It is so ordered.

Justice REHNQUIST took no part in the consideration or decision of this case.

---

44. In general, the law of the State of incorporation is held to govern the liabilities of officers or directors to the corporation and its stockholders. *See* Restatement (Second) of Conflict of Laws §309. *But see* Cal. Corp. Code §2115 (West Supp. 1976). The rationale for the general rule appears to be based more on the need for a uniform and certain standard to govern the internal affairs of a corporation than on the perceived interest of the state of incorporation.

Justice POWELL, concurring.

I agree that the principles of International Shoe Co. v. Washington should be extended to govern assertions of in rem as well as in personam jurisdiction in state court. I also agree that neither the statutory presence of appellants' stock in Delaware nor their positions as directors and officers of a Delaware corporation can provide sufficient contacts to support the Delaware courts' assertion of jurisdiction in this case.

I would explicitly reserve judgment, however, on whether the ownership of some forms of property whose situs is indisputably and permanently located within a State may, without more, provide the contacts necessary to subject a defendant to jurisdiction within the State to the extent of the value of the property. In the case of real property, in particular, preservation of the common law concept of quasi in rem jurisdiction arguably would avoid the uncertainty of the general *International Shoe* standard without significant cost to "traditional notions of fair play and substantial justice."

Subject to that reservation, I join the opinion of the Court.

Justice STEVENS, concurring in the judgment.

The Due Process Clause affords protection against "judgments without notice." International Shoe Co. v. Washington (opinion of Black, J.). Throughout our history the acceptable exercise of in rem and quasi in rem jurisdiction has included a procedure giving reasonable assurance that actual notice of the particular claim will be conveyed to the defendant. Thus, publication, notice by registered mail, or extraterritorial personal service has been an essential ingredient of any procedure that serves as a substitute for personal service within the jurisdiction.

The requirement of fair notice also, I believe, includes fair warning that a particular activity may subject a person to the jurisdiction of a foreign sovereign. If I visit another state, or acquire real estate or open a bank account in it, I knowingly assume some risk that the state will exercise its power over my property or my person while there. My contact with the state, though minimal, gives rise to predictable risks.

Perhaps the same consequences should flow from the purchase of stock of a corporation organized under the laws of a foreign state, because to some limited extent one's property and affairs then become subject to the laws of the state of domicile of the corporation. As a matter of international law, that suggestion might be acceptable because a foreign investment is sufficiently unusual to make it appropriate to require the investor to study the ramifications of his decision. But a purchase of securities in the domestic market is an entirely different matter.

One who purchases shares of stock on the open market can hardly be expected to know that he has thereby become subject to suit in a forum remote from his residence and unrelated to the transaction. As a practical matter, the Delaware Sequestration Statute created an unacceptable risk of judgment without notice. Unlike the 49 other States, Delaware treats the place of incorporation as the situs of the stock, even though both the owner and the custodian of the shares are elsewhere. Moreover, Delaware denies the defendant the opportunity to defend the merits of the suit unless he subjects himself to the unlimited jurisdiction of the court. Thus, it coerces a defendant either to submit to personal jurisdiction in a forum which could not otherwise obtain such jurisdiction or to lose the securities which have been attached. If its procedure were upheld, Delaware would, in effect, impose a duty of inquiry on every purchaser of securities in the national market. For unless the purchaser ascertains both the state of incorporation of the company whose shares he is buying, and also the idiosyncrasies of its law, he may be assuming an unknown risk of litigation. I therefore agree with the Court that on the record before us no adequate basis for jurisdiction exists and that the Delaware statute is unconstitutional on its face.

How the Court's opinion may be applied in other contexts is not entirely clear to me. I agree with Mr. Justice Powell that it should not be read to invalidate in rem jurisdiction where real estate is involved. I would also not read it as invalidating other long accepted methods of acquiring jurisdiction over persons with adequate notice of both the particular controversy and also that their local activities might subject them to suit. My uncertainty as to the reach of the opinion, and my fear that it purports to decide a great deal more than is necessary to dispose of this case, persuade me merely to concur in the judgment.

Justice BRENNAN, concurring and dissenting.

I join Parts I-III of the Court's opinion. I fully agree that the minimum-contacts analysis developed in International Shoe Co. v. Washington represents a far more sensible construct for the exercise of state court jurisdiction than the patchwork of legal and factual fictions that has been generated from the decision in Pennoyer v. Neff. It is precisely because the inquiry into minimum contacts is now of such overriding importance, however, that I must respectfully dissent from Part IV of the Court's opinion. . . .

II

. . . While evidence derived through discovery might satisfy me that minimum contacts are lacking in a given case, I am convinced that as a general rule a state forum has jurisdiction to adjudicate a shareholder derivative action centering on the conduct and policies of the directors and officers of a corporation chartered by that State. Unlike the Court, I therefore would not foreclose Delaware from asserting jurisdiction over appellants were it persuaded to do so on the basis of minimum contacts.

It is well settled that a derivative lawsuit as presented here does not inure primarily to the benefit of the named plaintiff. Rather, the primary beneficiaries are the corporation and its owners, the shareholders. "The cause of action which such a plaintiff brings before the court is not his own but the corporation's. . . . Such a plaintiff may represent an important public and stockholder interest in bringing faithless managers to book."

Viewed in this light, the chartering State has an unusually powerful interest in insuring the availability of a convenient forum for litigating claims involving a possible multiplicity of defendant fiduciaries and for vindicating the State's substantive policies regarding the management of its domestic corporations. I believe that our cases fairly establish that the State's valid substantive interests are important considerations in assessing whether it constitutionally may claim jurisdiction over a given cause of action.

In this instance, Delaware can point to at least three interrelated public policies that are furthered by its assertion of jurisdiction. First, the State has a substantial interest in providing restitution for its local corporations that allegedly have been victimized by fiduciary misconduct, even if the managerial decisions occurred outside the State. . . . I, of course, am not suggesting that Delaware's varied interests would justify its acceptance of jurisdiction over any transaction touching upon the affairs of its domestic corporations. But a derivative action which raises allegations of abuses of the basic management of an institution whose existence is created by the State and whose powers and duties are defined by state law fundamentally implicates the public policies of that forum.

To be sure, the Court is not blind to these considerations. It notes that the State's interests "may support the application of Delaware law to resolve any controversy over appellants' actions in their capacities as officers and directors." But this, the Court argues, pertains to choice of law, not jurisdiction. I recognize that the jurisdictional and choice-of-law inquiries are not identical. Hanson v. Denckla. But I would not compartmentalize thinking in this area quite so rigidly as it seems to me the Court does today, for both inquiries "are often closely related and to a substantial degree depend upon similar considerations." *Id*. (Black, J. dissenting). In either case an important linchpin is the extent of contacts between the controversy, the parties, and the forum state. While constitutional limitations on the choice of law are by no means settled, *see, e.g.*, Home Ins. Co. v. Dick, important considerations certainly include the expectancies of the parties and the fairness of governing the defendants' acts and behavior by rules of conduct created by a given jurisdiction. *See, e.g.*, Restatement (Second) Choice of Law §6. These same factors bear upon the propriety of a State's exercising jurisdiction over a legal dispute. At the minimum, the decision that it is fair to bind a defendant by a State's laws and rules should prove to be highly relevant to the fairness of permitting that same State to accept jurisdiction for adjudicating the controversy. . . .

I, therefore, would approach the minimum contacts analysis differently than does the Court. Crucial to me is the fact that appellants voluntarily associated themselves with the State of Delaware, "invoking the benefits and protections of its laws," Hanson v. Denckla; International Shoe Co. v. Washington, by entering into a long term and fragile relationship with one of its domestic corporations. They thereby elected to assume powers and to undertake responsibilities wholly derived from that State's rules and regulations, and to become eligible for those benefits that Delaware law makes available to its corporations' officials. *E.g.*, 8 Del. C. §§143 (interest-free loans); 145 (indemnification). While it is possible that countervailing issues of judicial efficiency and the like might clearly favor a different forum, they do not appear on the meager record before us; and, of course, we are concerned solely with "minimum" contacts, not the "best" contacts. I thus do not believe that it is unfair to insist that appellants make themselves available to suit in a competent forum that Delaware might create for vindication of its important public policies directly pertaining to appellants' fiduciary associations with the State.

Sternberg v. O'Neil

550 A.2d 1105 (Del. 1988)

HOLLAND, J.:

The appellant, Richard Sternberg ("Sternberg"), brought a double derivative suit[1] against GenCorp Inc. ("GenCorp"), its wholly owned subsidiary, RKO General, Inc. ("RKO General"), and certain past and present officers and directors of both corporations. GenCorp is an Ohio corporation qualified to do business in Delaware under 8 Del. C. §371. RKO General is a Delaware corporation. The Court of Chancery found "that the complaint does not allege a constitutionally permissible basis for the assertion of personal jurisdiction over either GenCorp or those individual defendants who are not directors of RKO General." The Court of Chancery also found that GenCorp was an indispensable party. It, therefore, held that "the complaint must be dismissed as to all defendants."

On appeal, we conclude on two bases, that the Court of Chancery erred, as a matter of law, when it determined that it lacked personal jurisdiction over GenCorp. First, when GenCorp registered to do business in Delaware and appointed an agent in Delaware to receive service of process, it consented to the general jurisdiction of Delaware courts. Second, we hold alternatively, that GenCorp's ownership of a Delaware corporation, whose alleged mismanagement is the subject of the double derivative suit, constitutes a "minimum contact" with Delaware which satisfies due process and enables Delaware courts to exercise specific personal jurisdiction over GenCorp in this matter. Therefore, we reverse the Court of Chancery's decision to dismiss the complaint as to GenCorp. However, we affirm the dismissal of the complaint as to the individual nonresident defendants, who are not directors of RKO General.

Facts

GenCorp, an Ohio corporation, has its principal place of business in Akron, Ohio, and was known as The General Tire & Rubber Company until 1984 when it changed its name. GenCorp is qualified to conduct business in Delaware as a foreign corporation. RKO General, a Delaware corporation, has its principal place of business in New York, New York. All of RKO General's common stock has been owned by GenCorp since it was acquired in 1955. Sternberg is a shareholder of GenCorp.

Sternberg's complaint in the Court of Chancery alleged, *inter alia*, that the directors and officers of RKO General and GenCorp breached their fiduciary duties to the GenCorp shareholders when they made numerous false and misleading statements and omissions to the Federal Communications Commission

---

1. A "double derivative" action is a derivative action maintained by the shareholders of a parent corporation or holding company on behalf of a subsidiary company. *See* 13 W. Fletcher, *Cyclopedia of the Law of Private Corporations* §5977 (rev. perm. ed. Supp. 1988). The wrongs addressed include wrongs directly incurred by the parent corporation as well as those indirectly incurred, because of wrongs suffered by the subsidiary company. *Id.*

("FCC") about an investigation of GenCorp by the Securities and Exchange Commission ("SEC"). . . . Sternberg's double derivative claim is premised upon his allegation that the individual defendants, officers and directors of GenCorp and RKO General, failed to manage the affairs of GenCorp and RKO General in a "fair, careful and prudent manner" and that such failure constitutes a breach of their fiduciary duties.

[Discussion of general jurisdiction and consent omitted.]

. . . The question which we will address is whether a foreign corporation's ownership of a Delaware corporate subsidiary, constitutes a due process minimum contact which permits Delaware courts to assert specific jurisdiction over the foreign parent corporation in a double derivative action.

GenCorp is an Ohio corporation. For more than thirty years, GenCorp has owned 100% of the issued and outstanding shares of RKO General, a Delaware corporation. Sternberg's action is a double derivative suit. One aspect of the suit alleges mismanagement and breaches of fiduciary duty on the part of the directors of RKO General, the Delaware corporation, resulting in detriment to that corporation and therefore to GenCorp, the sole stockholder of that Delaware corporation. The other aspect of the Sternberg suit alleges mismanagement and breaches of fiduciary duty on the part of the GenCorp directors. Sternberg's complaint alleges that as a result of the breaches of fiduciary duty by the directors and officers of each of the corporations, RKO General has lost its radio and television broadcast licenses or the value thereof, to the detriment of both GenCorp and RKO General.

We must decide whether or not Delaware has specific jurisdiction to hear this controversy. The Court of Chancery concluded that GenCorp's ownership of a Delaware subsidiary was an insufficient contact with this State to establish a basis for personal jurisdiction. . . . The Court of Chancery ruled that Delaware had no authority to exercise in personam jurisdiction over GenCorp and that since GenCorp was an indispensable party, the entire case must be dismissed. On appeal, GenCorp argues that this conclusion was correct and is mandated by the holding in *Shaffer*.

[The court discusses the facts and holding of *Shaffer*.]

. . . As one legal scholar has observed "whatever its nuances, the obvious impact of *Shaffer* is to limit jurisdiction where the property of a non-resident is seized in order to provide a basis for prosecuting an unrelated claim." Lilly, *Jurisdiction over Domestic and Alien Defendants*, 69 Va. L. Rev. 85, 98 (1983).

. . . Jurisdiction over a wholly owned Delaware subsidiary does not automatically establish jurisdiction over the parent corporation in *any* forum. *Cf.* Cannon Mfg. Co. v. Cudahy Packing Co., 267 U.S. 333 (1925).[28] Therefore, both the parent and the subsidiary corporation's contacts with the forum state must be assessed individually.

---

28. For a discussion of the "*Cannon* Doctrine," see Brilmayer & Paisley, *Personal Jurisdiction and Substantive Legal Relations: Corporations, Conspiracies and Agency*, 74 Calif. L. Rev. 1, 2-8 (1986). For a case distinguishing *Cannon*, see Waters v. Deutz Corp., Del. Supr., 479 A.2d 273, 275 (1984).

GenCorp and Delaware

Although GenCorp did not *form* RKO General as a Delaware subsidiary, it knew at the time of its acquisition that RKO General was incorporated under the laws of the State of Delaware. The record reflects that GenCorp has owned and operated RKO General as a Delaware subsidiary since 1955 — more than 30 years. We find that the difference between creating a wholly owned subsidiary in Delaware and purchasing a Delaware subsidiary is a distinction without significance, when the subsidiary is not thereafter reincorporated in another state.

The decision to reincorporate or not to reincorporate in a particular jurisdiction is a deliberate one. The majority stockholders in a parent corporation can vote to change the state of incorporation of the parent, or of a subsidiary, anytime there is a preference to be governed by the laws of another jurisdiction. In fact, after the United States Supreme Court decision in *Shaffer*, the Delaware corporation involved in that litigation, Greyhound, reincorporated in Arizona. Conversely, it is well known that many corporations have chosen to incorporate or reincorporate in the State of Delaware, although the reasons for the decision have been debated. These competing positions are discussed at length in Macey & Miller, *Toward an Interest-Group Theory of Delaware Corporate Law*, 65 Tex. L. Rev. 469 (1987).

. . . Although scholars may debate its motivation, the fact remains that for more than thirty years, GenCorp has made the conscious decision to operate RKO General, its subsidiary, as a *Delaware* corporation. For more than thirty years, GenCorp has benefited from the protections of the Delaware law in operating RKO General for commercial gain, including the benefits afforded to it directly as a shareholder of a Delaware corporation. We conclude that GenCorp intentionally established and maintained minimum contacts with Delaware by its decision to continue to operate its wholly owned subsidiary, RKO General, as a Delaware corporation.

. . . Delaware has a legitimate interest in Sternberg's double derivative claim. . . . In this case, GenCorp used the benefits and protections of the State of Delaware to maintain a corporate subsidiary. Sternberg's double derivative suit alleges that the operation of RKO General, the wholly owned Delaware subsidiary, has caused damage to RKO General, GenCorp and the GenCorp stockholders. Delaware has an interest in holding accountable those responsible for the operation of a Delaware corporation. Moreover, just as the internal affairs doctrine mandates the application of Ohio law to the internal operations of GenCorp, that same doctrine mandates the application of Delaware law to the internal operation of RKO General. It is a basic principle of Delaware corporation law that the directors of Delaware corporations are subject to fiduciary duties. Specifically, the Delaware law provides that "in a parent and wholly owned subsidiary context, the directors of the subsidiary are obligated only to manage the affairs of the subsidiary in the best interests of the parent and its shareholders."

The United States Supreme Court has recognized that "[a] State has an interest in promoting stable relationships among parties involved in the corporation it charters." CTS Corp. v. Dynamics Corp. of America, 481 U.S. 69 (1987). In particular, the Supreme Court noted that states have "a substantial interest in preventing the corporate form from becoming a shield for unfair business dealing." *Id*. 107.

In this case, Delaware has a legitimate interest in providing a forum for hearing and applying Delaware law to a double derivative claim related to the internal operation of a wholly owned Delaware subsidiary. . . . In this case, Delaware also has an interest in providing a forum for efficiently litigating, in a single proceeding, all issues and damages arising out of a double derivative claim alleging harm based upon the foreign parent corporation's maintenance of a Delaware subsidiary.

In a shareholder's derivative suit, the shareholder sues on behalf of the corporation for harm done to the corporation. Therefore, the damages recovered in the suit are paid to the corporation. R. Clark, *Corporate Law*, 639-640 (1986).[41] In a single derivative suit the corporation is an indispensable party. The presence of the corporation is required so that it can receive the monetary award in the event of recovery. The same logic has been held to apply in a double derivative suit. The parent corporation is an indispensable party in a double derivative suit against a subsidiary because any recovery for losses suffered by the subsidiary that were being sued upon would go to the parent. Thus, the Court of Chancery was correct in concluding that if it did not have jurisdiction over the parent corporation, the entire double derivative suit must be dismissed.

Delaware has more than an interest in providing a sure forum for shareholder derivative litigation involving the internal affairs of its domestic corporations. Delaware has an obligation to provide such a forum. All "traditional notions of fair play and substantial justice" would be offended if Delaware permitted GenCorp to use its laws to maintain a Delaware subsidiary and then declined to exercise jurisdiction over GenCorp in a double derivative suit, where GenCorp was an indispensable party.

We conclude that fairness and justice permit jurisdiction to be asserted by Delaware under the totality of the circumstances of this case. We find that the exercise of specific jurisdiction in this case is consistent with the requirements of due process. We hold that GenCorp's ownership of RKO General is a minimum contact with Delaware which is sufficient to support an exercise of specific jurisdiction by the Delaware Courts over GenCorp to hear and decide Sternberg's double derivative complaint.[45]

---

41. The normal derivative suit was "two suits in one: (1) The plaintiff brought a suit in equity against the corporation seeking an order against it; (2) to bring a suit for damages or other legal injury for damages or other relief against some third person who had caused legal injury to the corporation." R. Clark, *Corporate Law*, 639-640 (1986).

45. We note that legal scholars have suggested two ways of establishing jurisdiction over the parent *based on jurisdiction over the subsidiary:*

> These two methods for establishing jurisdiction involve showing either that the absent parent instigated the subsidiary's local activities or that the absent parent and the subsidiary are in fact a single legal entity. The first method we call *attribution*, the second *merger*. They are obviously similar in that both involve disregarding separate entity status and shifting responsibility for the subsidiary's actions onto the parent. The difference between attribution and merger lies in the extent of this shifting of responsibility. Under the attribution theory, only the precise conduct shown to be instigated by the parent is attributed to the parent; the rest of the subsidiary's actions still pertain only to the subsidiary. The two corporations remain distinct entities. If merger is shown, however, all of the activities of the subsidiary are by definition activities of the parent. Merger requires a greater showing of interconnectedness than attribution, but once

This holding is an independent and alternative basis for reversing the Court of Chancery's decision not to exercise specific jurisdiction over GenCorp.

[The court then decided that the individual directors of RKO were subject to jurisdiction, while the officers and directors of GenCorp were not.]

Questions and Comments

(1) *Shaffer* purports to lay down the same standards for in personam and quasi in rem jurisdiction, citing *International Shoe* as the source for the former standards. But *International Shoe* required minimum contacts between the defendant and the forum state, while *Shaffer* requires minimum contacts among the forum state, the litigation, and the defendant. Can the apparent distinction be eliminated?

(2) If, as suggested in note (1) *supra*, the standards are now the same for in personam and quasi in rem jurisdiction, doesn't it follow that whenever a long-arm statute, if it existed, would be constitutional, quasi in rem jurisdiction would also be constitutional, and conversely, that if quasi in rem jurisdiction is not constitutional, a long-arm statute would not be either? If that proposition is true, was the Delaware statute that it discussed unconstitutional? On the other hand, if a long-arm statute would not be constitutional under the facts of *Shaffer*, why did the majority opinion say, "If Delaware perceived its interest in securing jurisdiction over corporate fiduciaries to be as great as Heitner suggests, we would expect it to have enacted a statute more clearly designed to protect that interest"? And why did it say, "Delaware, unlike some States, has not enacted a statute that treats

---

shown, its scope is broader. Under both theories, the parent is declared responsible for in-state activities of the subsidiary, but in attribution the responsibility results from causing a separate legal entity to act while in merger there is no separate legal entity at all.

Brilmayer & Paisley, *Personal Jurisdiction and Substantive Legal Relations: Corporations, Conspiracies and Agency*, 74 Cal. L. Rev. 1, 12 (1986) (emphasis in original). The allegations in Sternberg's double derivative law suit appear to fit into the attribution method for establishing jurisdiction. In this double derivative action, Sternberg alleges that the parent-subsidiary relationship was simply the vehicle by which GenCorp caused RKO General to carry out its own wishes, which then ultimately led to the injury to GenCorp. The attribution principle is mentioned in a footnote in *Burger King Corp.*, where the United States Supreme Court said,

[W]e have previously noted that when commercial activities are "carried on on behalf of" an out-of-state party, those activities may sometimes be ascribed to the party, . . . at least where he is a "primary participant[t]" in the enterprise and has acted purposefully in directing those activities.

Burger King Corp. v. Rudzewicz, 471 U.S. at 479 n.22, (citing International Shoe Co. v. Washington, 326 U.S. 310, 320 (1945)); Calder v. Jones, 465 U.S. 783, 790 (1984).

Sternberg also argues that the corporate existence of GenCorp and RKO General should be ignored. In essence, Sternberg argues for the merger method of establishing jurisdiction based upon the findings of the FCC. *Cf.* Lucas v. Gulf & Western Industries, Inc., 666 F.2d 800, 806 (1981). Our analysis makes it unnecessary to base a finding of specific jurisdiction upon either one of these theories. However, we recognize the merit of both approaches if the facts in a given case support their applicability. *See* Waters v. Deutz Corp., Del. Supr., 479 A.2d 273 (1984); Japan Petroleum Co. (Nigeria) Ltd. v. Ashland Oil, Inc., 456 F. Supp. 831, 839 (D. Del. 1978); *Cf.* Akzona, Inc. v. E. I. Du Pont De Nemours & Co., 607 F. Supp. 227, 237-240 (D. Del. 1984).

acceptance of a directorship as consent to jurisdiction in the State"? Of what relevance are these observations unless such a statute would be constitutional?

Has Delaware solved these problems with the statute and analysis in *Sternberg*?

(3) As *Sternberg* suggests, there has been considerable litigation over the effect on jurisdictional analysis of corporate ties. *See, e.g.*, Miller v. Honda Motor Co. Ltd., 779 F.2d 769 (1st Cir. 1985). In Keeton v. Hustler, 465 U.S. 770 n.13 (1984), the Supreme Court made clear that jurisdiction could not be predicated merely upon the fact of corporate ownership. The defendants were *Hustler* magazine, which was subject to jurisdiction in New Hampshire, and its parent corporation and sole owner, LFP Inc. and Larry Flynt. The fact that the magazine was subject to jurisdiction did not automatically subject the others; as to each party, jurisdiction had to be established. This is sometimes known as the *Cannon* doctrine from Cannon Manufacturing Co. v. Cudahy Packing Co., 267 U.S. 333 (1925). Where the parent controls the subsidiary's forum activities, however, jurisdiction over the parent may be appropriate. *See, e.g.*, Hill by Hill v. Showa Denko, K.K., 425 S.E.2d 609 (W. Va. 1992). *See generally* Blumberg, *The Increasing Recognition of Enterprise Principles in Determining Parent and Subsidiary Corporation Liabilities*, 28 Conn. L. Rev. 295 (1996); Alexander, *Unlimited Shareholder Liability Through a Procedural Lens*, 106 Harv. L. Rev. 387 (1992); Brilmayer & Paisley, *Personal Jurisdiction and Substantive Legal Relations: Corporations, Conspiracy, and Agency*, 74 Cal. L. Rev. 1 (1986).

(4) In Daimler AG v. Bauman, 571 U.S. at 117 (2014), the Supreme Court had a chance to address the issue of whether courts could base general jurisdiction over a parent corporation on the parent's control over a subsidiary's foreign activities. However, the Court ruled upon the dispute without reaching the issue.

(5) Is *Sternberg* consistent with *Shaffer*? Can it be explained as consistent on the ground that the defendant, GenCorp, owned property in Delaware that was "related to" the controversy? Is the test for "related" or specific jurisdiction the same for assets as it is for activities, as discussed in Section B, *supra*? Was the property in *Shaffer* any less closely related to the controversy than the property in *Sternberg*? Is there any more of a Delaware interest in one case than in the other?

In Anderson v. Heartland Oil and Gas, Inc., 819 P.2d 1192 (Kan. 1991), the court upheld jurisdiction over two Colorado defendants whose only connection with the forum was that they were corporate directors and officers of a Kansas corporation. "Jurisdiction over individual officers, directors, and employees of a domestic corporation, for claims that may result in personal liability, is predicated merely upon jurisdiction over the corporation itself." *Id*. at 1200. Note that the rationale—that there is jurisdiction over the corporation—seems potentially quite expansive. Wouldn't it extend even to directors of a *nonresident* corporation that happened to be subject to forum jurisdiction for some other reason (e.g., because it had committed a tort or breached a contract there, or because it carried on substantial unrelated business)? Is the rationale consistent with Shaffer v. Heitner?

(6) Footnote 37 of the *Shaffer* opinion suggests that quasi in rem jurisdiction might yet be available when "no other forum is available to the plaintiff." When might such circumstances occur? When the defendant is domiciled outside the country? Would that be discriminating against foreign defendants? Should the fact

that a claim is barred by the statutes of limitations of other states bring it within the rationale of footnote 37 and allow a forum with otherwise inadequate contacts to assert jurisdiction? Compare footnote 13 in *Helicopteros, supra*, where the Court declined to adopt the theory of jurisdiction by necessity, which it apparently deemed rather novel.

(7) In Grand Bahama Petroleum Co. v. Canadian Transportation Agencies, 450 F. Supp. 447 (W.D. Wash. 1978), the court upheld garnishment of a bank account in a district having no contacts with the defendant other than the bank account. The case involved a claim for services to a ship, and the court distinguished *Shaffer* on those grounds. It noted that attachment jurisdiction has traditionally been the keystone of admiralty litigation, that such litigation usually involves people in commerce who are away from home for long periods of time, that admiralty has always been treated separately, as indicated by the separate listing of admiralty in Article III of the Constitution as a basis for federal jurisdiction, and the fact that maritime attachment jurisdiction does not trace back to Pennoyer v. Neff but has its own long history recognizing such attachment.

(8) Some states authorize quasi in rem jurisdiction after *Shaffer*. In these states, attachment plus notice authorize the court to exercise jurisdiction over a foreign defendant and limit the extent of the judgment to the value of the property attached. This exercise of jurisdiction is limited by the constitutional "minimum contacts" test and largely operates in states that have not extended their long arm to the limits of the Constitution. *See, e.g.*, Cargill Inc. v. Sabine Trading & Shipping Co., 756 F.2d 224 (2d Cir. 1984) (New York's limited appearance statutes apply in diversity action where the sole basis of jurisdiction was quasi in rem); Campbell v. Landmark First National Bank of Fort Lauderdale, 421 So. 2d 813 (Fla. 1982) (denying motion to quash constructive service in quasi in rem claim seeking imposition of a constructive trust and on accounting); Britton v. Howard Savings Bank, 727 F.2d 315 (1984) (upholding writ of attachment under amended New Jersey statute allowing prejudgment jurisdictional attachment where it conforms with due process).

(9) Traditionally, judgments of courts lacking jurisdiction over either person or property are considered void and thus not entitled to full faith and credit or res judicata effect. After *Shaffer*, what would be the remedy for a person who suffered a quasi in rem judgment *before Shaffer* was decided? Would a default judgment based on quasi in rem jurisdiction give rise to actions to recover the property?

(10) In Rush v. Savchuk, 444 U.S. 320 (1980), the Supreme Court applied the logic of *Shaffer* to invalidate quasi in rem jurisdiction over a defendant on the basis of attachment of the contractual obligation of his insurer to defend and indemnify him in the suit. This so-called *Seider* jurisdiction (the doctrine was derived from Seider v. Roth, 17 N.Y.2d 111 (N.Y. 1966)) allowed plaintiffs to attach the defendant's insurance policy, and thus sue, in any state in which the insurance company did business. In *Rush*, the Court reasoned that because *International Shoe*'s minimum contacts analysis applied to each defendant separately, and because the contacts of the insurer could not be attributed to the insured, *Seider* jurisdiction is unconstitutional unless the insured had minimum contacts with the forum.

Rush insinuated that direct action statutes—which allow an injured party to sue the tortfeasor's insurance company directly instead of proceeding first against the tortfeasor—are constitutional. *See* 444 U.S. at 331-332. The Court distinguished direct action statutes from *Seider* jurisdiction on the basis of the fact that the former requires that the nominal defendant (the insured) have minimum contacts with the forum as a prerequisite to bringing suit against the insurer. *See id.*; *compare* Watson v. Employers Liability Assurance Corp., 348 U.S. 66 (1954), reproduced *supra* page 292, which upheld the constitutionality of applying a direct action statute to an out-of-state insurance company.

(11) The Internet creates new forms of intangible property that implicate many difficult jurisdictional issues. This is especially true of Internet domain names, which are the unique verbal names—such as aol.com, mcdonalds.com, and disney.com—that correlate with Web pages and Internet addresses. From 1992 to 1998, during the early years of Internet growth, Network Solutions, Inc. ("NSI"), a private company in Virginia, held a contractual monopoly from the U.S. government to register and maintain domain name information. As a general matter, NSI doled out domain names on a first-come, first-served basis. This led many to engage in "cybersquatting," a term that refers to the registration of domain names similar or identical to protected trademarks with the intent of intercepting Internet traffic intended for the mark owner or selling the domain name to mark owners for hefty fees. In 1999, Congress enacted the Anticybersquatting Consumer Protection Act ("ACPA"), 15 U.S.C. §1125 (d), which establishes civil liability for registering a domain name that is identical or confusingly similar to a trademark with the "bad faith intent to profit from that mark." The ACPA provides that a trademark holder may proceed against the cybersquatter not only in an in personam action, but also, in certain circumstances, against the domain name itself in an in rem action. This raises the questions (a) where is the property located? and (b) is the assertion of in rem jurisdiction over domain names consistent with Shaffer v. Heitner?

Caesars World Inc. v. Caesars-Palace.com, 112 F. Supp. 2d 502 (E.D. Va. 2000), a domain name dispute in Virginia federal court against an out-of-state defendant, addresses these questions in a typical way:

> [D]efendant Casares.com argues that under Shaffer v. Heitner, in rem jurisdiction is only constitutional in those circumstances where the res provides minimum contacts sufficient for in personam jurisdiction. The court rejects this argument, and concludes that under *Shaffer*, there must be minimum contacts to support personal jurisdiction only in those in rem proceedings where the underlying cause of action is unrelated to the property which is located in the forum state. Here the property, that is, the domain name, is not only related to the cause of action but is its entire subject matter. Accordingly, it is unnecessary for minimum contacts to meet personal jurisdiction standards.
>
> To the extent that minimum contacts are required for in rem jurisdiction under *Shaffer*, moreover, the fact of domain name registration with Network Solutions, Inc., in Virginia supplies that. Given the limited relief afforded by the Act, namely "the forfeiture or cancellation of the domain name or the transfer of the domain name to the owner of the mark," no due process violation occurs here as to defendants personally. The court considers the enactment of the Anticybersquatting Consumer Protection Act a classic case of the distinction

between in rem jurisdiction and in personam jurisdiction and a proper and constitutional use of in rem jurisdiction.

In further support of its constitutional challenge, defendant Casares.com
argues that a domain name registration is not a proper kind of thing to serve as
a res. In this regard, defendant contends, among other things, a domain name
is merely data that forms part of an Internet addressing computer protocol
and therefore, is not property. Defendant Casares.com contends further that
even if it were property, it has no situs in Virginia. The court finds this line of
argument unpersuasive. There is no prohibition on a legislative body making
something property. Even if a domain name is no more than data, Congress can
make data property and assign its place of registration as its situs.

Is *Caesar's World* correct to say that "under *Shaffer*, there must be minimum contacts to support personal jurisdiction only in those in rem proceedings
where the underlying cause of action is unrelated to the property which is located
in the forum state"? Does the court correct any possible error when it says that
"[t]o the extent that minimum contacts are required for in rem jurisdiction under
Shaffer, . . . the fact of domain name registration with Network Solutions, Inc.,
in Virginia supplies that"? Did the owner of caesarcasino.com purposefully avail
itself of the benefits of Virginia when it registered its name on NSI's Web site?
Does it matter whether it knew where NSI's headquarters were?

6

Conflict of Laws in the Federal System

To this point, our discussion has implicitly assumed, by and large, that conflict of laws involves only problems of relations between the states that are resolved in state courts. This chapter considers how conflicts analysis might change when a conflicts issue arises in litigation in federal, rather than state, court. In particular, this chapter considers how the *Erie* doctrine is used to determine when federal rather than state law applies and, when state law continues to apply, how federal courts resolve the question of which state's substantive law controls. Section A covers the *Erie* doctrine as it applies to choice of law and judgment recognition. Section B covers federal common law, considering circumstances where, notwithstanding the *Erie* doctrine, federal law works to preempt state law that impinges on the harmonious relations between the states.

A. The *Erie* Doctrine

Erie Railroad v. Tompkins

304 U.S. 64 (1938)

Justice BRANDEIS delivered the opinion of the Court.

The question for decision is whether the oft-challenged doctrine of Swift v. Tyson shall now be disapproved. Tompkins, a citizen of Pennsylvania, was injured on a dark night by a passing freight train of the Erie Railroad Company while walking along its right of way at Hughes town in that State. He claimed that the accident occurred through negligence in the operation, or maintenance, of the train; that he was rightfully on the premises as licensee because he was on a commonly used beaten footpath which ran for a short distance alongside the tracks: and that he was struck by something which looked like a door projecting from one of the moving cars. To enforce that claim he brought an action in the federal court for southern New York, which had jurisdiction because the company is a corporation of that State. It denied liability; and the case was tried by a jury.

The Erie insisted that its duty to Tompkins was no greater than that owed to a trespasser. It contended, among other things, that its duty to Tompkins, and hence its liability, should be determined in accordance with the Pennsylvania law; that under the law of Pennsylvania, as declared by its highest court, persons who use pathways along the railroad right of way—that is a longitudinal pathway as distinguished from a crossing—are to be deemed trespassers; and that the railroad is not liable for injuries to undiscovered trespassers resulting from its negligence, unless it be wanton or willful. Tompkins denied that any such rule had been established by the decisions of the Pennsylvania courts; and contended that, since there was no statute of the State on the subject, the railroad's duty and liability is to be determined in federal courts as a matter of general law.

The trial judge refused to rule that the applicable law precluded recovery. The jury brought in a verdict of $30,000; and the judgment entered thereon was affirmed by the Circuit Court of Appeals, which held that it was unnecessary to consider whether the law of Pennsylvania was as contended, because the question was one not of local, but of general law and that

> upon questions of general law the federal courts are free, in the absence of a local statute, to exercise their independent judgment as to what the law is; and it is well settled that the question of the responsibility of a railroad for injuries caused by its servants is one of general law. Where the public has made open and notorious use of a railroad right of way for a long period of time and without objection, the company owes to persons on such permissive pathway a duty of care in the operation of its trains. It is likewise generally recognized law that a jury may find that negligence exists toward a pedestrian using a permissive path on the railroad right of way if he is hit by some object projecting from the side of the train.

The Erie had contended that application of the Pennsylvania rule was required, among other things, by §34 of the Federal Judiciary Act of September 24, 1789, c.20, 28 U.S.C. §725, which provides:

> The laws of the several States, except where the Constitution, treaties, or statutes of the United States otherwise require or provide, shall be regarded as rules of decision in trials at common law, in the courts of the United States, in cases where they apply.

Because of the importance of the question whether the federal court was free to disregard the alleged rule of the Pennsylvania common law, we granted certiorari.

First. Swift v. Tyson held that federal courts exercising jurisdiction on the ground of diversity of citizenship need not, in matters of general jurisprudence, apply the unwritten law of the State as declared by its highest court; that they are free to exercise an independent judgment as to what the common law of the State is—or should be; and that, as there stated by Mr. Justice Story:

> [T]he true interpretation of the thirty-fourth section limited its application to state laws strictly local, that is to say, to the positive statutes of the state, and the construction thereof adopted by the local tribunals, and to rights and titles to things having a permanent locality, such as the rights and titles to real estate, and other matters immovable and intraterritorial in their nature and character. It never has been supposed by us, that the section did apply, or was intended to apply, to questions of a more general nature, not at all dependent upon local statutes or local usages of a fixed and permanent operation, as, for example, to the construction of ordinary contracts or other written instruments, and especially to questions of general commercial law, where the state tribunals are called upon to perform the like functions as ourselves, that is, to ascertain upon general reasoning and legal analogies, what is the true exposition of the contract of instrument, or what is the just rule furnished by the principles of commercial law to govern the case.

The Court in applying the rule of §34 to equity cases, in Mason v. United States said: "The statute, however, is merely declarative of the rule which would exist in the absence of the statute." The federal courts assumed, in the broad field of "general law," the power to declare rules of decision which Congress was confessedly without power to enact as statutes. Doubt was repeatedly expressed as to the correctness of the construction given §34 and as to the soundness of the rule which it introduced. But it was the more recent research of a competent scholar, who examined the original document, which established that the construction given to it by the Court was erroneous; and that the purpose of the section was merely to make certain that, in all matters except those in which some federal law is controlling, the federal courts exercising jurisdiction in diversity of citizenship cases would apply as their rules of decision the law of the State, unwritten as well as written.

Criticism of the doctrine became widespread after the decision of Black & White Taxicab Co. v. Brown & Yellow Taxicab Co. There, Brown and Yellow, a Kentucky corporation owned by Kentuckians, and the Louisville and Nashville Railroad, also a Kentucky corporation, wished that the former should have the exclusive privilege of soliciting passenger and baggage transportation at the Bowling Green, Kentucky, railroad station; and that the Black and White, a competing Kentucky corporation, should be prevented from interfering with that privilege. Knowing that such a contract would be void under the common law of Kentucky, it was arranged that the Brown and Yellow reincorporate under the law of Tennessee, and that the contract with the railroad should be executed there. The suit was then brought by the Tennessee corporation in the federal court for Western Kentucky to enjoin competition by the Black and White; an injunction issued by the District Court was sustained by the Court of Appeals; and this Court, citing many decisions in which the doctrine of Swift v. Tyson had been applied, affirmed the decree.

Second. Experience in applying the doctrine of Swift v. Tyson had revealed its defects, political and social; and the benefits expected to flow from the rule did not accrue. Persistence of state courts in their own opinions on questions of common law prevented uniformity; and the impossibility of discovering a satisfactory line of demarcation between the province of general law and that of local law developed a new well of uncertainties.

On the other hand, the mischievous results of the doctrine had become apparent. Diversity of citizenship jurisdiction was conferred in order to prevent apprehended discrimination in state courts against those not citizens of the State. Swift v. Tyson introduced grave discrimination by non-citizens against citizens. It made rights enjoyed under the unwritten "general law" vary according to whether enforcement was sought in the state or in the federal court; and the privilege of selecting the court in which the right should be determined was conferred upon the non-citizen. Thus, the doctrine rendered impossible equal protection of the law. In attempting to promote uniformity of law throughout the United States, the doctrine had prevented uniformity in the administration of the law of the State.

The discrimination resulting became in practice far-reaching. This resulted in part from the broad province accorded to the so-called "general law" as to which federal courts exercised an independent judgment. In addition to questions of purely commercial law, "general law" was held to include the obligations under contracts entered into and to be performed within the State, the extent to which a carrier operating within a State may stipulate for exemption from liability for his own negligence or that of his employee; the liability for torts committed within the State upon persons resident or property located there, even where the question of liability depended upon the scope of a property right conferred by the State; and the right to exemplary or punitive damages. Furthermore, state decisions construing local deeds, mineral conveyances, and even devises of real estate were disregarded.

In part the discrimination resulted from the wide range of persons held entitled to avail themselves of the federal rule by resort to the diversity of citizenship jurisdiction. Through this jurisdiction individual citizens willing to remove from their own State and become citizens of another might avail themselves of the federal rule. And, without even change of residence, a corporate citizen of the State could avail itself of the federal rule by reincorporating under the laws of another State, as was done in the Taxicab case.

The injustice and confusion incident to the doctrine of Swift v. Tyson have been repeatedly urged as reasons for abolishing or limiting diversity of citizenship jurisdiction. Other legislative relief has been proposed. If only a question of statutory construction were involved, we should not be prepared to abandon a doctrine so widely applied throughout nearly a century. But the unconstitutionality of the course pursued has now been made clear and compels us to do so.

Third. Except in matters governed by the Federal Constitution or by Acts of Congress, the law to be applied in any case is the law of the State. And whether the law of the State shall be declared by its Legislature in a statute or by its highest court in a decision is not a matter of federal concern. There is no federal general common law. Congress has no power to declare substantive rules of common law applicable in a State whether they be local in their nature or "general," be they commercial law or a part of the law of torts. And no clause in the Constitution purports to confer such a power upon the federal courts. As stated by Mr. Justice Field when protesting in Baltimore & Ohio R. Co. v. Baugh, against ignoring the Ohio common law of fellow servant liability:

> I am aware that what has been termed the general law of the country—which is often little less than what the judge advancing the doctrine thinks at the time should be the general law on a particular subject—has been often advanced in judicial opinions of this court to control a conflicting law of a State. I admit that learned judges have fallen into the habit of repeating this doctrine as a convenient mode of brushing aside the law of a State in conflict with their views. And I confess that, moved and governed by the authority of the great names of those judges, I have, myself, in many instances, unhesitatingly and confidently, but I think now erroneously, repeated the same doctrine. But, notwithstanding the great names which may be cited in favor of the doctrine, and notwithstanding the frequency with which the doctrine has been reiterated, there stands, as a perpetual protest against its repetition, the Constitution of the United States, which recognizes and preserves the autonomy and independence of the States—independence in their legislative and independence in their judicial departments. Supervision over either the legislative or the judicial action of the States is in no case permissible except as to matters by the Constitution specifically authorized or delegated to the United States. Any interference with either, except as thus permitted, is an invasion of the authority of the State and, to that extent, a denial of its independence.

The fallacy underlying the rule declared in Swift v. Tyson is made clear by Mr. Justice Holmes. The doctrine rests upon the assumption that there is "a transcendental body of law outside of any particular State but obligatory within it unless and until changed by statute," that federal courts have the power to use their judgment as to what the rules of common law are; and that in the federal courts "the parties are entitled to an independent judgment on matters of general law":

> [B]ut law in the sense in which courts speak of it today does not exist without some definite authority behind it. The common law so far as it is enforced in a State, whether called common law or not, is not the common law generally but the law of that State existing by the authority of that State without regard to what it may have been in England or anywhere else. [T]he authority and only authority is the State, and if that be so, the voice adopted by the State as its own [whether it be of its Legislature or of its Supreme Court] should utter the last word.

Thus the doctrine of Swift v. Tyson is, as Mr. Justice Holmes said, "an unconstitutional assumption of powers by courts of the United States which no lapse of time or respectable array of opinion should make us hesitate to correct." In disapproving that doctrine we do not hold unconstitutional §34 of the Federal Judiciary Act of 1789 or any other Act of Congress. We merely declare that in applying the doctrine this Court and the lower courts have invaded rights which in our opinion are reserved by the Constitution to the several States.

Fourth. The defendant contended that by the common law of Pennsylvania as declared by its highest court in Falchetti v. Pennsylvania R. Co., 307 Pa. 203, the only duty owed to the plaintiff was to refrain from wilful or wanton injury. The plaintiff denied that such is the Pennsylvania law. In support of their respective contentions the parties discussed and cited many decisions of the Supreme Court of the State. The Circuit Court of Appeals ruled that the question of liability is one of general law; and on that ground declined to decide the issue of state law. As we hold this was error, the judgment is reversed and the case remanded to it for further proceedings in conformity with our opinion.

Reversed.

[A concurring opinion of Justice REED and a dissenting opinion of Justice BUTLER are omitted.]

Questions and Comments

(1) The Court makes it clear in *Erie* that it is handing down a constitutional decision. But what clause of the Constitution does the Court interpret in its opinion?

(2) Justice Brandeis's opinion says at one point: "Congress has no power to declare substantive rules of common law applicable in a State whether they be local in their nature or 'general,' be they commercial law or a part of the law of torts." Much has happened since the *Erie* decision. Is it likely that today's Supreme Court would strike down a federal statute purporting to establish rules for liability for injury along the right-of-way of a railroad engaged in interstate commerce? If not, should *Erie* be overruled because its underlying assumptions have been eroded? Or can *Erie* be upheld even if one assumes that Congress has authority to declare substantive law in the case of Tompkins's injury? On what theory?

(3) Assuming that Congress has the constitutional authority to legislate the rules of liability involved in Tompkins's accident, can it delegate to the Court the task of making up such substantive rules? In Textile Workers Union of America v. Lincoln Mills, 353 U.S. 448 (1957), the Supreme Court faced a challenge to the constitutionality of §301 of the Taft-Hartley Act, 29 U.S.C. §85 (1976). The statute conferred jurisdiction on the federal courts for disputes arising between employers and labor unions, even though no substantive rules to govern these disputes were suggested by the legislation. The problem was that there was no obvious federal-question jurisdiction, and diversity of citizenship was absent. The Court rejected a "protective jurisdiction" theory that would have allowed Congress to give the federal courts jurisdiction in areas of federal concern even though diversity was absent and no specific substantive federal rules of decision were involved. But the Court did not conclude that the statute was unconstitutional under Article III. It instead concluded that Congress intended by the grant of jurisdiction in §301 to give the federal courts substantive rulemaking power in the area—in other words, the courts could develop a federal common law under the Taft-Hartley Act (often by borrowing from state contract law and the like).

In light of *Lincoln Mills, supra*, could Congress amend the Rules of Decision Act (discussed in *Erie* as §34 of the Judiciary Act of 1789) to provide that the federal courts can form their own common law? Or is a narrower grant, limited to a single field like labor law, a necessary condition for such a delegation?

(4) If Congress's failure to legislate concerning Tompkins's injury is taken as indicating a lack of federal policy in the area, can *Erie* be seen as a false conflict case? If so, would the result in *Erie* be required by the Court's reasoning in

Home Insurance Co. v. Dick? Or is the fact that the accident took place within the geographical borders of the United States enough to take *Erie* out of the scope of Dick? Does *Dick* forbid a state to apply its own law when it has no interest or when it has no contact, or when it has neither? Can analogies to the constitutionality of interstate conflicts resolution help to sort out the *Erie* problem?

(5) The earlier draft of the Rules of Decision Act discovered by Professor Charles Warren provided: "[T]he Statute law of the several States in force for the time being and their unwritten or common law now in use, whether by adoption from the common law of England, the ancient statutes of the same or otherwise" should be rules of decision in the federal courts. In the legislative process, the quoted phrase was shortened to "laws of the several states." Warren, *New Light on the History of the Federal Judiciary Act of 1789*, 37 Harv. L. Rev. 49 (1923). Is it clear that this new phrase is simply a substitute for the earlier language?

Note: *Erie* and Substance vs. Procedure

As all veterans of Civil Procedure know, the "real" *Erie* problem is in distinguishing substance vs. procedure. The problem first reared its ugly head in Guaranty Trust Co. v. York, 326 U.S. 99 (1945), where the question was whether to apply a state statute of limitations or federal laches doctrine to a diversity action brought in federal court. The Court assumed that the *Erie* principle would not apply to issues that are "procedural" rather than "substantive," presumably for the same reason that that distinction is made in ordinary conflicts cases where the substantive, but not the procedural, law of State *B* may be applied in the courts of State *A*. (Recall the double play on this issue in Sampson v. Channell, page 124 *supra*, where a federal court decided that the burden of proof was "substantive" for *Erie* purposes and therefore applied the law of the state in which it was sitting—whose law declared the issue "procedural" for conflicts purposes.)

To determine whether an issue is substantive or procedural, Justice Frankfurter produced his well-known outcome-determination test:

> [D]oes it significantly affect the result of a litigation for a federal court to disregard a law of a State that would be controlling in an action upon the same claim by the same parties in a State court? [T]he outcome of the litigation in federal court should be substantially the same, so far as legal rules determine the outcome of a litigation, as it would be if tried in a State court.

326 U.S. at 109.

Several subsequent Supreme Court cases have wrestled with *Erie* and the substance/procedure dichotomy. Perhaps most noteworthy is Hanna v. Plumer, 380 U.S. 460 (1965), in which a federal court sitting in diversity confronted the question of whether state or federal rules on personal service applied to the case. The relevant state rule required personal in-hand service on an executor or administrator of an estate, while Federal Rule 4(d)(1) required only one of several options, including leaving service with a person of suitable age and discretion at the defendant's dwelling place. The federal rule was held to prevail, in part because it did not interfere with the twin aims of *Erie*: "discouragement of forum-shopping and avoidance of inequitable administration of the laws." *Id*. at 468. More fundamentally, however, the Court noted that *Erie* had never been successfully invoked to void a federal rule. Validity of the federal rules were typically determined under the Rules Enabling Act, 28 U.S.C. §2072 (1958), which empowered the Supreme Court to promulgate rules of procedure for the federal district courts, so long as the rules do "not abridge, enlarge, or modify any substantive right. Under the Enabling Act, the Court asks "whether the rule really regulates procedure—the judicial process for enforcing rights and duties recognized by substantive law and for justly administering remedy and redress for disregard or infraction of them." *Id.* at 464 (quoting Sibbach v. Wilson & Co., 312 U.S. 1, 14 (1941)). Although that test also turns on a distinction between substance and procedure, "[t]he line between 'substance' and 'procedure' shifts as the legal context shifts." *Id.* at 471. In the context of the federal rules, Congress, the Advisory Committee, and the Supreme Court have all determined that the rules are valid, and that judgment is entitled to significant deference. Thus, a federal rule will be deemed valid, even when it occupies "the uncertain area between substance and procedure," so long as it is "rationally capable of classification as either." *Id.* at 472.

Gasperini v. Center for Humanities, Inc., 518 U.S. 415 (1996), involved the compatibility of (a) a New York state statute that empowered appellate courts to review jury verdicts and to order new trials when the jury's award "deviates materially from what would be reasonable compensation," and (b) the federal court's more lenient practice of reviewing excessive jury verdicts under a "shocks the conscience" standard. The Court first noted that the state statute was motivated by the "'substantive" purpose of limiting excessive awards and was "outcome-effective" in the sense that it led to different results than the federal standard. The Court noted that although *Hanna* modified the mechanical outcome-determination test from *Guaranty-Trust* by directing that the inquiry should be guided by the twin aims of *Erie*, under that test too New York's statute should be deemed substantive.

Because the federal practice stemmed from the Seventh Amendment of the US Constitution, however, the majority took steps to accommodate federal as well as state interests. Specifically, the Court noted that deferential appellate review of a trial court's denial of a motion to set aside a jury verdict was an "essential characteristic" of the federal court system that was informed by the Seventh Amendment's reexamination clause, which states that "no fact, tried by a jury, shall be otherwise reexamined in any Court of the United States, than according to the rules of the common law." To accommodate federal interests, the Court held that federal district courts should apply the state "deviates materially" standard, subject to appellate review under the federal abuse of discretion standard, which was deemed consistent with the reexamination clause. For criticism of *Gasperini,* see Floyd, Erie *Awry: A Comment on Gasperini v. Center for Humanities, Inc.,* 1997 BYU L. Rev. 267.

Shady Grove Orthopedic Assocs. v. Allstate Ins. Co., 559 U.S. 393 (2010), involved state and federal rules on class actions. Medical providers filed a putative class action in federal district court against Allstate after the insurer failed to compensate the provider for interest due on overdue claims under New York law. Although that class action was permissible under Federal Rule of Civil Procedure 23, which sets out the prerequisites for bringing a class action in federal courts, a majority of Justices concluded that it conflicted with New York law, which prohibits class actions in suits for penalties or statutory minimum damages. A majority of Justices also concluded that the federal rather than the state rule should apply in the diversity action. Justice Scalia, writing for four of the Justices, reasoned that the Rules Enabling Act, rather than *Erie,* controls the validity of a federal rule of procedure, and under the Act the rule is valid so long as it "really regulates procedure." Under this looser standard set forth in *Hanna* and other cases, a rule is valid even if it incidentally affects a party's rights, so long as it regulates only the process for enforcing those rights, and not the rights themselves, the available remedies, or the rules of decision for adjudicating either.

Allstate argued that the New York law was substantive, but the plurality concluded that the nature of the state rule was irrelevant to the inquiry. What mattered was whether the federal rule was substantive or procedural. In a concurring opinion, Justice Stevens thought that the nature of state law could matter. In particular, he thought that a federal procedural rule would have to give way to substantive state law if it is "so intertwined with a state right or remedy that it functions to define the scope of the state created right." *Id.* at 423.

Justice Ginsburg authored a dissenting opinion joined by three of her colleagues. She reasoned that the Court's *Erie* cases involving federal rules all reflect its efforts to remain within the bounds of both the Rules Enabling Act and the Rules of Decision Act, and the most common way that the Court has steered this course is to read the federal rules narrowly, leaving room for the operation of state law. Consistent with that line of reasoning, Justice Ginsberg argued that Rule 23 should be interpreted as providing considerations that are necessary to class certification but not commanding that a class action remedy is always available. In contrast, the New York statute defines when the remedy is available, and in that sense, it defines the dimensions of the claim itself. By this reasoning, Rule 23 is valid and applies in diversity cases, but New York law also applies, and it works to defeat plaintiff's ability to maintain a class action.

Questions and Comments

(1) Professor Sedler has noted a relationship between the substance/procedure dichotomy in *Erie* and conflicts cases:

> It is submitted that the *Erie* outcome test can furnish [a conflicts] guide, for *the underlying rationale for the application of the state law in an* Erie *situation is substantially the same as the rationale for the application of the lex loci in a conflicts situation.* The sole purpose of a federal court in a diversity case is to furnish an impartial forum. The only purpose of a court in a conflicts case, once it has decided that it will look to the law of another state, is to serve as a forum of convenience. In each situation the court should use as a model as much of the law of the reference point as will materially affect the outcome. [Emphasis in original.]

Sedler, *The* Erie *Outcome Test as a Guide to Substance and Procedure in the Conflicts of Laws,* 37 N.Y.U. L. Rev. 813, 821-822 (1962).

(2) Conflicts learning can be used on *Erie* cases as well. In Leathers, Erie *and Its Progeny as Choice of Law Cases,* 11 Hous. L. Rev. 791 (1974), the author

suggests that the *post-Erie* cases can best be analyzed under interest analysis, and that for the most part they turn out to be false conflict cases. The substance-procedure dichotomy as such is rejected because the distinction between the two shifts as the use to which the distinction is being put changes. For other arguments on behalf of cross-fertilization between *Erie* and interstate conflicts, *see* Bauer, *The* Erie *Doctrine Revisited: How a Conflicts Perspective Can Aid the Analysis*, 74 Notre Dame L. Rev. 1235 (1999); and Weinberg, *The Federal-State Conflict of Laws: "Actual" Conflicts*, 70 Tex. L. Rev. 1743 (1992).

(3) In an important article, Professor John Ely has cast considerable light on the "*Erie* problem." Ely, *The Irrepressible Myth of* Erie, 87 Harv. L. Rev. 693 (1974). Ely's thesis is that there are three separate but related questions raised in the various cases that have been identified with the *Erie* label: First is the *Erie* principle itself, considered as a constitutional issue. Second is the Rules of Decision Act of 1789, which provides:

> The laws of the several states, except where the Constitution or treaties of the United States or Acts of Congress otherwise require or provide, shall be regarded as rules of decision in civil actions in the courts of the United States, in cases where they apply.

The third is the Rules Enabling Act of 1934, which provides in part:

> The Supreme Court shall have the power to prescribe by general rules ... the practice and procedure of the district courts.... Such rules shall not abridge, enlarge, or modify any substantive right....

Disputing what he calls the "enclave" theory of states' rights—that there are rights reserved to the states other than those which remain after enumerated federal rights—Ely starts with the proposition that the Constitution, by providing for federal jurisdiction, justifies the federal courts in following any rules that are in fact procedural at least in part, even if they have substantive effect. A constitutional limitation in the *Erie* case was applied there because the rule in question—the standard of care owed by the railroad—was in no sense a procedural matter. The Constitution, however, should stay in the background until Congress prescribes a rule of decision in diversity cases by statute, since the Rules of Decision Act (as interpreted in *Erie* and *York*) protects state law as much as the Constitution does. When a federal rule is involved, however, the Rules Enabling Act is the relevant legislation.

The difference between the two acts is this: Outcome determination, properly defined, is the standard for the Rules of Decision Act. (The proper test, Ely says, is whether the litigant will get a different result in state court, playing by state court rules, than he will get in federal court, playing by the federal rules in question.) Whether a rule affects "substantive" rights, properly defined, is the standard for the Rules Enabling Act. Thus, for example, a federal practice (not embodied in a federal rule) that allowed extensive pretrial discovery where the same was not allowed in state court would have to be viewed as outcome-determinative and thus forbidden by the Rules of Decision Act (as interpreted by *Erie* and *York*). But if the federal practice is made a federal rule, the Rules Enabling Act takes over and allows the rule if it (a) is procedural (it is), and (b) does not abridge substantive rights (it doesn't, even though it may affect the outcome, since the *reason* for the state's failure to have discovery almost undoubtedly represents a judgment about proper procedure, and not how people's lives should be governed). The Constitution would be satisfied merely by showing that the rule was in part procedural, even if it does affect substantive rights.

Although agreeing with much of Professor Ely's general analysis, Professor Chayes disagreed with many of his applications in an article entitled *The Bead Game*, 87 Harv. L. Rev. 741 (1974); followed by Ely, *The Necklace*, 87 Harv. L. Rev. 753 (1974); followed by Mishkin, *The Thread*, 87 Harv. L. Rev. 1682 (1974).

1. *Erie* and Choice of Law

Klaxon Co. v. Stentor Electric Manufacturing Co.

313 U.S. 487 (1941)

Justice REED delivered the opinion of the Court.

The principal question in this case is whether in diversity cases the federal courts must follow conflict of laws rules prevailing in the states in which they sit. . . .

In 1918, respondent, a New York corporation, transferred its entire business to petitioner, a Delaware corporation. Petitioner contracted to use its best efforts to further the manufacture and sale of certain patented devices covered by the agreement, and respondent was to have a share of petitioner's profits. The agreement was executed in New York, the assets were transferred there, and petitioner began performance there although later moved its operations to other states. Respondent was voluntarily dissolved under New York law in 1919. Ten years later it instituted this action in the United States District Court for the District of Delaware, alleging that petitioner had failed to perform its agreement to use its best efforts. Jurisdiction rested on diversity of citizenship. In 1939 respondent recovered a jury verdict of $100,000, upon which judgment was entered. Respondent then moved to correct the judgment by adding interest at the rate of six percent from June 1, 1929, the date the action had been brought. The basis of the motion was the provision in §480 of the New York Civil Practice Act directing that in contract actions interest be added to the principal sum "whether theretofore liquidated or unliquidated." The District Court granted the motion, taking the view that the rights of the parties were governed by New York law and that under New York law the addition of such interest was mandatory. The Circuit Court of Appeals affirmed and we granted certiorari, limited to the question whether §480 of the New York Civil Practice Act is applicable to an action in the federal court in Delaware.

The Circuit Court of Appeals was of the view that under New York law the right to interest before verdict under §480 went to the substance of the obligation, and that proper construction of the contract in suit fixed New York as the place of performance. It then concluded that §480 was applicable to the case because it is clear by what we think is undoubtedly the better view of the law that the rules for ascertaining the measure of damages are not a matter of procedure at all, but are matters of substance which should be settled by reference to the law of the appropriate state according to the type of case being tried in the forum. The measure of damages for breach of contract is determined by the law of the place of performance; Restatement, Conflict of Laws §413. The court referred also to §418 of the Restatement, which makes interest part of the damages to be determined by the law of the place of performance. Application of the New York statute apparently followed from the court's independent determination of the "better view" without regard to Delaware law, for no Delaware decision or statute was cited or discussed.

We are of opinion that the prohibition declared in [*Erie*] against such independent determinations by the federal courts, extends to the field of conflict of laws. The conflict of laws rules to be applied by the federal court in Delaware must conform to those prevailing in Delaware's state courts.[2] Otherwise, the accident of diversity of citizenship would constantly disturb equal administration of justice in coordinate state and federal courts sitting side by side. See [*Erie*]. Any other ruling would do violence to the principle of uniformity within a state, upon which the [*Erie*] decision is based. Whatever lack of uniformity this may produce between federal courts in different states is attributable to our federal system, which leaves to a state, within the limits permitted by the Constitution, the right to pursue local policies diverging from those of its neighbors. It is not for the federal courts to thwart such local policies by enforcing an independent "general law" of conflict of laws. Subject only to review by this Court on any federal question that may arise, Delaware is free to determine whether a given matter is to be governed by the law of the forum or some other law.... This Court's views are not the decisive factor in determining the applicable conflicts rule.... And the proper function of the Delaware federal court is to ascertain what the state law is, not what it ought to be.

Respondent makes the further argument that the judgment must be affirmed because, under the full faith and credit clause of the Constitution, the state courts of Delaware would be obliged to give effect to the New York statute. The argument rests mainly on the decision of this Court in John Hancock Mutual Life Ins. Co. v. Yates, where a New York statute was held such an integral part of a contract of insurance, that Georgia was compelled to sustain the contract under the full faith and credit clause. Here, however, §480 of the New York Civil Practice Act is in no way related to the validity of the contract in suit, but merely to an incidental item of damages, interest, with respect to which courts at the forum have commonly been free to apply their own or some other law as they see fit. Nothing in the Constitution ensures unlimited extraterritorial recognition of all statutes or of any statute under all circumstances. Pacific Employers Insurance Co. v. Industrial Accident Comm'n. The full faith and credit clause does not go so far as to compel Delaware to apply §480 if such application would interfere with its local policy.

Accordingly, the judgment is reversed and the case remanded to the Circuit Court of Appeals for decision in conformity with the law of Delaware.

---

2. An opinion in Sampson v. Channell [page 124 *supra*] reaches the same conclusion....

Questions and Comments

(1) *Compare* Judge Friendly in Nolan v. Transocean Airlines, 276 F.2d 280, 281 (2d Cir. 1960): "Our principal task . . . is to determine what New York courts would think California courts would think on an issue about which neither has thought."

(2) In *Klaxon*, Justice Reed's opinion says, at the very end, "The full faith and credit clause does not go so far as to compel Delaware to apply §480 if such application would interfere with its local policy." What local policy? If the Delaware courts applied New York substantive law to the merits, what is the *Delaware* policy concerning the assessment of interest after the case has been brought but before judgment has been entered? Traditionally, of course, the interest issue could be called "procedural," but what is the procedural interest in this interest? A rule granting interest, like New York's, might discourage delaying tactics by the defendant, but what procedural policy could lie behind a rule denying interest during the suit? Surely it is not too hard to calculate. And is it fair to say, as Justice Reed does, that the question is only one of "incidental" damages, when the amount of interest is 6 percent of $100,000 for ten years?

(3) If the Court's upholding of the possibility of applying Delaware law means that Delaware has some kind of interest in the issue, doesn't that make *Klaxon* a true conflict case with respect to the interest issue? If so, doesn't that fact put it outside the rationale for *Erie* developed in note (4) at page 470 *supra*? In other words, isn't there a fundamental difference between diversity cases raising issues of internal law and diversity cases raising conflicts issues, because in the former there is only one interested jurisdiction (the state) and a disinterested forum, while in the latter there are two interested jurisdictions (two states) and a disinterested forum? Granting that a federal court may not impose a nonexistent federal interest over an actual state interest, does it follow that a federal court may not choose between two state interests? As a neutral, isn't the federal court in a better position to choose than are the courts of either state?

(4) If the lack of federal interest or constitutional power is the basis for *Erie* and you aren't convinced by the arguments in the previous note, does the full faith and credit clause remain as a basis for a contrary conclusion in *Klaxon*?

(5) The desire for uniformity and to avoid forum-shopping remain as policies promoted by *Erie* whether or not its decision is constitutionally mandated. But does *Klaxon* promote uniformity? At least in the case of a true conflict, isn't it almost assured that there will be another jurisdiction where suit could have been brought? In other words, don't recent developments in long-arm jurisdiction make interstate forum-shopping as likely as intrastate forum-shopping? Is one worse than the other? And given the result in Van Dusen v. Barrack (discussed in *Ferens*, *infra*), which rules that a case transferred under §1404 will take the transferor state's law with it, will it be possible to avoid the evils of forum-shopping, whatever they are, with enough regularity to make the quest worthwhile?

(6) Academics have continued to argue that choice of law is an appropriate subject for federal regulation either by statute, *see* Gottesman, *Draining the Dismal Swamp: The Case for Federal Choice of Law Statutes*, 80 Geo. L.J. 1 (1991), or by incremental federal common law, *see* Trautman, *Toward*

Federalizing Choice of Law, 70 Tex. L. Rev. 1715 (1992). One area particularly ripe for federal regulation might be choice of law in complex litigation. In 1993, the American Law Institute proposed to federalize many choice-of-law and choice-of-forum issues that arise in complex litigation in federal court. The introductory notes to Chapter 6 of the 1993 Proposed Final Draft of its Complex Litigation Project recognized the disuniformity between state and federal courts that federalization would create, but suggested the solution of consolidation of state and federal court cases. As to the disuniformity that would then still persist between large complex cases (which would fall under the new federal standard) and smaller litigation (that would fall under *Klaxon*), "the need to achieve justice among the litigants by assuring the uniform and economical treatment of their dispute justifies this difference." This choice-of-law proposal was never adopted, and the ALI abandoned it in its *Principles of the Law of Aggregate Litigation* (2010). The topic is further explored in Chapter 10, *infra*.

(7) If *Klaxon* were abandoned, what would replace it? In his article promoting comparative impairment, Professor Baxter contemplated that the approach could be developed by federal rather than state courts:

> Baseball's place as the favorite American pastime would not long survive if the responsibilities of the umpire were transferred to the first team member who managed to rule on a disputed event. Responsibility for allocating spheres of legal control among member states of a federal system cannot sensibly be placed elsewhere than with the federal government. . . . Governmental interests can be identified in choice cases, and the unavoidable allocation of spheres of control ought to be made as those interests dictate by applying the principle of comparative impairment. The process of allocation ought to be committed to the federal government; for the alternative is to place that responsibility, not in the hands of the states, but ad hoc in the hands now of this state, now of that, as determined by promptitude of private party action and the expanding limits of service of process. . . .

Baxter, *Choice of Law and the Federal System*, 16 Stan. L. Rev. 1, 23, 33 (1963).

Assuming that eventual federal control over choice-of-law questions is appropriate, is the time yet ripe? How about a less drastic (though perhaps sweeping) approach, in which federal courts would apply state conflicts rules only in cases of true conflicts? *See, e.g.*, Lester v. Aetna Life Ins. Co., 433 F.2d 844 (5th Cir. 1970), *cert. denied*, 402 U.S. 909 (1971); Day & Zimmerman, Inc. v. Challoner, 423 U.S. 3, 4 (1975).

Ferens v. John Deere Co.

494 U.S. 516 (1989)

Justice KENNEDY delivered the opinion of the Court.

Section 1404(a) of Title 28 states: "For the convenience of parties and witnesses, in the interest of justice, a district court may transfer any civil action to any other district or division where it might have been brought." 28 U.S.C. §1404(a) (1982 ed.). In Van Dusen v. Barrack, 376 U.S. 612 (1964), we held that, following a transfer under §1404(a) initiated by a defendant, the transferee court must follow the choice-of-law rules that prevailed in the transferor court. We now decide that, when a plaintiff moves for the transfer, the same rule applies.

I

Albert Ferens lost his right hand when, the allegation is, it became caught in his combine harvester, manufactured by Deere & Company. The accident occurred while Ferens was working with the combine on his farm in Pennsylvania. For reasons not explained in the record, Ferens delayed filing a tort suit, and Pennsylvania's 2-year limitations period expired. In the third year, he and his wife sued Deere in the United States District Court for the Western District of Pennsylvania, raising contract and warranty claims as to which the Pennsylvania limitations period had not yet run. The District Court had diversity jurisdiction, as Ferens and his wife are Pennsylvania residents, and Deere is incorporated in Delaware with its principal place of business in Illinois.

Not to be deprived of a tort action, the Ferenses in the same year filed a second diversity suit against Deere in the United States District Court for the Southern District of Mississippi, alleging negligence and products liability. Diversity jurisdiction and venue were proper. The Ferenses sued Deere in the District Court in Mississippi because they knew that, under [*Klaxon*], the federal court in the exercise of diversity jurisdiction must apply the same choice-of-law rules that Mississippi state courts would apply if they were deciding the case. A Mississippi court would rule that Pennsylvania substantive law controls the personal injury claim but that Mississippi's own law governs the limitation period.

Although Mississippi has a borrowing statute which, on its face, would seem to enable its courts to apply statutes of limitations from other jurisdictions, the State Supreme Court has said that the borrowing statute "only applies where a nonresident [defendant] in whose favor the statute has accrued afterwards moves into this state." Louisiana & Mississippi R. Transfer Co. v. Long, 159 Miss. 654, 667 (1930). The borrowing statute would not apply to the Ferenses' action because, as the parties agree, Deere was a corporate resident of Mississippi before the cause of action accrued. The Mississippi courts, as a result, would apply Mississippi's 6-year statute of limitations to the tort claim arising under Pennsylvania law and the tort action would not be time barred under the Mississippi statute. *See* Miss. Code Ann. §15-1-49 (1972).

The issue now before us arose when the Ferenses took their forum shopping a step further: having chosen the federal court in Mississippi to take advantage of the State's limitations period, they next moved, under §1404(a), to transfer the action to the federal court in Pennsylvania on the ground that Pennsylvania was a more convenient forum. The Ferenses acted on the assumption that, after the transfer, the choice-of-law rules in the Mississippi forum, including a rule requiring application of the Mississippi statute of limitations, would continue to govern the suit.

Deere put up no opposition, and the District Court in Mississippi granted the §1404(a) motion. The court accepted the Ferenses' arguments that they resided in Pennsylvania; that the accident occurred there; that the claim had no connection to Mississippi; that a substantial number of witnesses resided in the Western

District of Pennsylvania but none resided in Mississippi; that most of the documentary evidence was located in the Western District of Pennsylvania but none was located in Mississippi; and that the warranty action pending in the Western District of Pennsylvania presented common questions of law and fact.

The District Court in Pennsylvania consolidated the transferred tort action with the Ferenses' pending warranty action but declined to honor the Mississippi statute of limitations as the District Court in Mississippi would have done. It ruled instead that, because the Ferenses had moved for transfer as plaintiffs, the rule in *Van Dusen* did not apply. Invoking the 2-year limitations period set by Pennsylvania law, the District Court dismissed their tort action.

The Court of Appeals for the Third Circuit affirmed. . . .

II

Section 1404(a) states only that a district court may transfer venue for the convenience of the parties and witnesses when in the interest of justice. It says nothing about choice of law and nothing about affording plaintiffs different treatment from defendants. We touched upon these issues in *Van Dusen*, but left open the question presented in this case. In *Van Dusen*, an airplane flying from Boston to Philadelphia crashed into Boston Harbor soon after takeoff. The personal representatives of the accident victims brought more than 100 actions in the District Court for the District of Massachusetts and more than 40 actions in the District Court for the Eastern District of Pennsylvania. When the defendants moved to transfer the actions brought in Pennsylvania to the federal court in Massachusetts, a number of the Pennsylvania plaintiffs objected because they lacked capacity under Massachusetts law to sue as representatives of the decedents. The plaintiffs also averred that the transfer would deprive them of the benefits of Pennsylvania's choice-of-law rules because the transferee forum would apply to their wrongful-death claims a different substantive rule. The plaintiffs obtained from the Court of Appeals a writ of mandamus ordering the District Court to vacate the transfer.

We reversed. . . . [W]e held that the Court of Appeals erred in its assumption that Massachusetts law would govern the action following transfer. The legislative history of §1404(a) showed that Congress had enacted the statute because broad venue provisions in federal Acts often resulted in inconvenient forums and that Congress had decided to respond to this problem by permitting transfer to a convenient federal court under §1404(a). We said:

> "This legislative background supports the view that §1404(a) was not designed to narrow the plaintiff's venue privilege or to defeat the state-law advantages that might accrue from the exercise of this venue privilege but rather the provision was simply to counteract the inconveniences that flowed from the venue statutes by permitting transfer to a convenient federal court. The legislative history of §1404(a) certainly does not justify the rather startling conclusion that one might 'get a change of a law as a bonus for a change of venue.' Indeed, an interpretation accepting such a rule would go far to frustrate the remedial purposes of §1404(a). If a change in the law were in the offing, the parties might

well regard the section primarily as a forum-shopping instrument. And, more importantly, courts would at least be reluctant to grant transfers, despite considerations of convenience, if to do so might conceivably prejudice the claim of a plaintiff who initially selected a permissible forum. We believe, therefore, that both the history and purposes of §1404(a) indicate that it should be regarded as a federal judicial housekeeping measure, dealing with the placement of litigation in the federal courts and generally intended, on the basis of convenience and fairness, simply to authorize a change of courtrooms." Id., at 635-637 (footnotes omitted).

We thus held that the law applicable to a diversity case does not change upon a transfer initiated by a defendant.

III

The quoted part of *Van Dusen* reveals three independent reasons for our decision. First, §1404(a) should not deprive parties of state-law advantages that exist absent diversity jurisdiction. Second, §1404(a) should not create or multiply opportunities for forum shopping. Third, the decision to transfer venue under §1404(a) should turn on considerations of convenience and the interest of justice rather than on the possible prejudice resulting from a change of law. Although commentators have questioned whether the scant legislative history of §1404(a) compels reliance on these three policies, *see* Note, Choice of Law after Transfer of Venue, 75 Yale L.J. 90, 123 (1965), we find it prudent to consider them in deciding whether the rule in *Van Dusen* applies to transfers initiated by plaintiffs. We decide that, in addition to other considerations, these policies require a transferee forum to apply the law of the transferor court, regardless of who initiates the transfer. A transfer under §1404(a), in other words, does not change the law applicable to a diversity case.

A

The policy that §1404(a) should not deprive parties of state-law advantages, although perhaps discernible in the legislative history, has its real foundation in *Erie* [*supra* page 465]. See *Van Dusen*, 376 U.S., at 637. The *Erie* rule remains a vital expression of the federal system and the concomitant integrity of the separate States. We explained *Erie* in Guaranty Trust Co. v. York [*supra* page 471], as follows:

> In essence, the intent of [the *Erie*] decision was to insure that, in all cases where a federal court is exercising jurisdiction solely because of the diversity of citizenship of the parties, the outcome of the litigation in the federal court should be substantially the same, so far as legal rules determine the outcome of a litigation, as it would be if tried in a State court. The nub of the policy that underlies *Erie* is that for the same transaction the accident of a suit by a nonresident litigant in a federal court instead of in a State court a block away should not lead to a substantially different result.

In Hanna v. Plumer [*supra* page 471], we held that Congress has the power to prescribe procedural rules that differ from state-law rules even at the expense of altering the outcome of litigation. This case does not involve a conflict. As in *Van Dusen*, our interpretation of §1404(a) is in full accord with the *Erie* rule.

The *Erie* policy had a clear implication for *Van Dusen*. The existence of diversity jurisdiction gave the defendants the opportunity to make a motion to transfer venue under §1404(a), and if the applicable law were to change after transfer, the plaintiff's venue privilege and resulting state-law advantages could be defeated at the defendant's option. To allow the transfer and at the same time preserve the plaintiff's state-law advantages, we held that the choice-of-law rules should not change following a transfer initiated by a defendant. Transfers initiated by a plaintiff involve some different considerations, but lead to the same result. Applying the transferor law, of course, will not deprive the plaintiff of any state-law advantages. A defendant, in one sense, also will lose no legal advantage if the transferor law controls after a transfer initiated by the plaintiff; the same law, after all, would have applied if the plaintiff had not made the motion. In another sense, however, a defendant may lose a nonlegal advantage. Deere, for example, would lose whatever advantage inheres in not having to litigate in Pennsylvania, or, put another way, in forcing the Ferenses to litigate in Mississippi or not at all.

We, nonetheless, find the advantage that the defendant loses slight. A plaintiff always can sue in the favorable state court or sue in diversity and not seek a transfer. By asking for application of the Mississippi statute of limitations following a transfer to Pennsylvania on grounds of convenience, the Ferenses are seeking to deprive Deere only of the advantage of using against them the inconvenience of litigating in Mississippi. The text of §1404(a) may not say anything about choice of law, but we think it not the purpose of the section to protect a party's ability to use inconvenience as a shield to discourage or hinder litigation otherwise proper. The section exists to eliminate inconvenience without altering permissible choices under the venue statutes. This interpretation should come as little surprise. As in our previous cases, we think that "[t]o construe §1404(a) this way merely carries out its design to protect litigants, witnesses and the public against unnecessary inconvenience and expense, not to provide a shelter for . . . proceedings in costly and inconvenient forums." Continental Grain Co. v. Barge FBL-585, 364 U.S. 19, 27 (1960). By creating an opportunity to have venue transferred between courts in different States on the basis of convenience, an option that does not exist absent federal jurisdiction, Congress, with respect to diversity, retained the *Erie* policy while diminishing the incidents of inconvenience.

Applying the transferee law, by contrast, would undermine the *Erie* rule in a serious way. It would mean that initiating a transfer under §1404(a) changes the state law applicable to a diversity case. We have held, in an isolated circumstance, that §1404(a) may pre-empt state law. *See* Stewart Organization, Inc. v. Ricoh Corp., 487 U.S. 22 (1988) (holding that federal law determines the validity of a forum selection clause). In general, however, we have seen §1404(a) as a housekeeping measure that should not alter the state law governing a case under *Erie. See Van Dusen, supra; see also Stewart Organization, supra*, at 37 (Scalia, J., dissenting) (finding the language of §1404(a) "plainly insufficient" to work a change in the applicable state law through preemption). The Mississippi statute of limitations, which everyone agrees would have applied if the Ferenses had not moved for a transfer, should continue to apply in this case.

In any event, defendants in the position of Deere would not fare much better if we required application of the transferee law instead of the transferor law. True, if the transferee law were to apply, some plaintiffs would not sue these defendants for fear that they would have no choice but to litigate in an inconvenient forum. But applying the transferee law would not discourage all plaintiffs from suing. Some plaintiffs would prefer to litigate in an inconvenient forum with favorable law than to litigate in a convenient forum with unfavorable law or not to litigate at all. The Ferenses, no doubt, would have abided by their initial choice of the District Court in Mississippi had they known that the District Court in Pennsylvania would dismiss their action. If we were to rule for Deere in this case, we would accomplish little more than discouraging the occasional motions by plaintiffs to transfer inconvenient cases. Other plaintiffs would sue in an inconvenient forum with the expectation that the defendants themselves would seek transfer to a convenient forum, resulting in application of the transferor law under *Van Dusen*. In this case, for example, Deere might have moved for a transfer if the Ferenses had not.

B

Van Dusen also sought to fashion a rule that would not create opportunities for forum shopping. Some commentators have seen this policy as the most important rationale of *Van Dusen*, but few attempt to explain the harm of forum shopping when the plaintiff initiates a transfer. An opportunity for forum shopping exists whenever a party has a choice of forums that will apply different laws. The *Van Dusen* policy against forum shopping simply requires us to interpret §1404(a) in a way that does not create an opportunity for obtaining a more favorable law by selecting a forum through a transfer of venue. In the *Van Dusen* case itself, this meant that we could not allow defendants to use a transfer to change the law.

No interpretation of §1404(a), however, will create comparable opportunities for forum shopping by a plaintiff because, even without §1404(a), a plaintiff already has the option of shopping for a forum with the most favorable law. The Ferenses, for example, had an opportunity for forum shopping in the state courts because both the Mississippi and Pennsylvania courts had jurisdiction and because they each would have applied a different statute of limitations. Diversity jurisdiction did not eliminate these forum shopping opportunities; instead, under *Erie*, the federal courts had to replicate them. *See Klaxon*, 313 U.S., at 496 ("Whatever lack of uniformity [*Erie*] may produce between federal courts in different states is attributable to our federal system, which leaves to a state, within the limits permitted by the Constitution, the right to pursue local policies diverging from those of its neighbors"). Applying the transferor law would not give a plaintiff an opportunity to use a transfer to obtain a law that he could not obtain through his initial forum selection. If it does make selection of the most favorable law more convenient, it does no more than recognize a forum shopping choice that already exists. This fact does not require us to apply the transferee law. Section 1404(a), to reiterate, exists to make venue convenient and should not allow the defendant to use inconvenience to discourage plaintiffs from exercising the opportunities that they already have.

Applying the transferee law, by contrast, might create opportunities for forum shopping in an indirect way. The advantage to Mississippi's personal injury lawyers that resulted from the State's then applicable 6-year statute of limitations has not escaped us; Mississippi's long limitation period no doubt drew plaintiffs to the State. Although *Sun Oil* held that the federal courts have little interest in a State's decision to create a long statute of limitations or to apply its statute of limitations to claims governed by foreign law, we should recognize the consequences of our interpretation of §1404(a). Applying the transferee law, to the extent that it discourages plaintiff-initiated transfers, might give States incentives to enact similar laws to bring in out-of-state business that would not be moved at the instance of the plaintiff.

C

Van Dusen also made clear that the decision to transfer venue under §1404(a) should turn on considerations of convenience rather than on the possibility of prejudice resulting from a change in the applicable law. We reasoned in *Van Dusen* that, if the law changed following a transfer initiated by the defendant, a district court "would at least be reluctant to grant transfers, despite considerations of convenience, if to do so might conceivably prejudice the claim of a plaintiff." 376 U.S., at 636. The court, to determine the prejudice, might have to make an elaborate survey of the law, including statutes of limitations, burdens of proof, presumptions, and the like. This would turn what is supposed to be a statute for convenience of the courts into one expending extensive judicial time and resources. Because this difficult task is contrary to the purpose of the statute, in *Van Dusen* we made it unnecessary by ruling that a transfer of venue by the defendant does not result in a change of law. This same policy requires application of the transferor law when a plaintiff initiates a transfer.

If the law were to change following a transfer initiated by a plaintiff, a district court in a similar fashion would be at least reluctant to grant a transfer that would prejudice the defendant. Hardship might occur because plaintiffs may find as many opportunities to exploit application of the transferee law as they would find opportunities for exploiting application of the transferor law. If the transferee law were to apply, moreover, the plaintiff simply would not move to transfer unless the benefits of convenience outweighed the loss of favorable law.

Some might think that a plaintiff should pay the price for choosing an inconvenient forum by being put to a choice of law versus forum. But this assumes that §1404(a) is for the benefit only of the moving party. By the statute's own terms, it is not. Section 1404(a) also exists for the benefit of the witnesses and the interest of justice, which must include the convenience of the court. Litigation in an inconvenient forum does not harm the plaintiff alone. As Justice Jackson said:

> Administrative difficulties follow for courts when litigation is piled up in congested centers instead of being handled at its origin. Jury duty is a burden that ought not to be imposed upon the people of a community which has no relation

to the litigation. In cases which touch the affairs of many persons, there is reason for holding the trial in their view and reach rather than in remote parts of the country where they can learn of it by report only. There is a local interest in having localized controversies decided at home. There is an appropriateness too, in having the trial of a diversity case in a forum that is at home with the state law that must govern the case, rather than having a court in some other forum untangle problems in conflicts of laws, and in law foreign to itself.

Gulf Oil Corp. v. Gilbert, 330 U.S. 501, 508-509 (1947). The desire to take a punitive view of the plaintiff's actions should not obscure the systemic costs of litigating in an inconvenient place.

D

This case involves some considerations to which we perhaps did not give sufficient attention in *Van Dusen*. Foresight and judicial economy now seem to favor the simple rule that the law does not change following a transfer of venue under §1404(a). Affording transfers initiated by plaintiffs different treatment from transfers initiated by defendants may seem quite workable in this case, but the simplicity is an illusion. If we were to hold that the transferee law applies following a §1404(a) motion by a plaintiff, cases such as this would not arise in the future. Although applying the transferee law, no doubt, would catch the Ferenses by surprise, in the future no plaintiffs in their position would move for a change of venue.

Other cases, however, would produce undesirable complications. The rule would leave unclear which law should apply when both a defendant and a plaintiff move for a transfer of venue or when the court transfers venue on its own motion. The rule also might require variation in certain situations, such as when the plaintiff moves for a transfer following a removal from state court by the defendant, or when only one of several plaintiffs requests the transfer, or when circumstances change through no fault of the plaintiff making a once convenient forum inconvenient. True, we could reserve any consideration of these questions for a later day. But we have a duty, in deciding this case, to consider whether our decision will create litigation and uncertainty. On the basis of these considerations, we again conclude that the transferor law should apply regardless of who makes the §1404(a) motion.

IV

Some may object that a district court in Pennsylvania should not have to apply a Mississippi statute of limitations to a Pennsylvania cause of action. This point, although understandable, should have little to do with the outcome of this case. Congress gave the Ferenses the power to seek a transfer in §1404(a), and our decision in *Van Dusen* already could require a district court in Pennsylvania to apply the Mississippi statute of limitations to Pennsylvania claims. Our rule may seem too generous because it allows the Ferenses to have both their choice of law and their choice of forum, or even to reward the Ferenses for conduct that seems manipulative. We nonetheless see no alternative rule that would produce a more acceptable result. Deciding that the transferee law should apply, in effect, would tell the Ferenses that they should have continued to litigate their warranty action in Pennsylvania and their tort action in Mississippi. Some might find this preferable, but we do not. We have made quite clear that "[t]o permit a situation in which two cases involving precisely the same issues are simultaneously pending in different District Courts leads to the wastefulness of time, energy and money that §1404(a) was designed to prevent." *Continental Grain*, 364 U.S., at 26.

From a substantive standpoint, two further objections give us pause but do not persuade us to change our rule. First, one might ask why we require the Ferenses to file in the District Court in Mississippi at all. Efficiency might seem to dictate a rule allowing plaintiffs in the Ferenses' position not to file in an inconvenient forum and then to return to a convenient forum though a transfer of venue, but instead simply to file in the convenient forum and ask for the law of the inconvenient forum to apply. Although our rule may invoke certain formality, one must remember that §1404(a) does not provide for an automatic transfer of venue. The section, instead, permits a transfer only when convenient and "in the interest of justice." Plaintiffs in the position of the Ferenses must go to the distant forum because they have no guarantee, until the court there examines the facts, that they may obtain a transfer. No one has contested the justice of transferring this particular case, but the option remains open to defendants in future cases. Although a court cannot ignore the systemic costs of inconvenience, it may consider the course that the litigation already has taken in determining the interest of justice.

Second, one might contend that, because no per se rule requiring a court to apply either the transferor law or the transferee law will seem appropriate in all circumstances, we should develop more sophisticated federal choice-of-law rules for diversity actions involving transfers. To a large extent, however, state conflicts-of-law rules already ensure that appropriate laws will apply to diversity cases. Federal law, as a general matter, does not interfere with these rules. See *Sun Oil*, 486 U.S., at 727-729. In addition, even if more elaborate federal choice-of-law rules would not run afoul of *Klaxon* and *Erie*, we believe that applying the law of the transferor forum effects the appropriate balance between fairness and simplicity.

For the foregoing reasons, we conclude that Mississippi's statute of limitations should govern the Ferenses' action. We reverse and remand for proceedings consistent with this opinion.

Justice SCALIA, with whom Justice BRENNAN, Justice MARSHALL, and Justice BLACKMUN join, dissenting.

The question we must answer today is whether 28 U.S.C. §1404(a) (1982 ed.) and the policies underlying *Klaxon*—namely, uniformity within a State and the avoidance of forum shopping—produce a result different from *Klaxon* when the suit in question was not filed in the federal court initially, but was transferred there under §1404(a) on plaintiff's motion. In *Van Dusen*, we held that a result different from *Klaxon* is produced when a suit has been transferred under §1404(a) on defendant's motion. Our reasons were two. First, we thought it highly unlikely that Congress, in enacting §1404(a), meant to provide defendants with a device by which to manipulate the substantive rules that would be applied. That conclusion rested upon the fact that the law grants the plaintiff the advantage of choosing the venue in which his action will be tried, with whatever state-law advantages accompany that choice. A defensive use of §1404(a) in order to deprive the plaintiff of this "venue privilege," *id.*, at 634, would allow the defendant to "'get a change of law as a bonus for a change of venue,'" *id.*, at 636 (citation omitted), and would permit the defendant to engage in forum shopping among States, a privilege that the *Klaxon* regime reserved for plaintiffs. Second, we concluded that the policies of *Erie* and *Klaxon* would be undermined by application of the transferee court's choice-of-law principles in the case of a defendant-initiated transfer, because then "the 'accident' of federal diversity jurisdiction" would enable the defendant "to utilize a transfer to achieve a result in federal court which could not have been achieved in the courts of the State where the action was filed," *id.*, at 638. The goal *of Erie* and *Klaxon*, we reasoned, was to prevent "forum shopping" as between state and federal systems; the plaintiff makes a choice of forum law by filing the complaint, and that choice must be honored in federal court, just as it would have been honored in state court, where the defendant would not have been able to transfer the case to another State.

We left open in *Van Dusen* the question presented today, viz., whether "the same considerations would govern" if a plaintiff sought a §1404(a) transfer. 376 U.S., at 640. In my view, neither of those considerations is served—and indeed both are positively defeated—by a departure from *Klaxon* in that context. First, just as it is unlikely that Congress, in enacting §1404(a), meant to provide the defendant with a vehicle by which to manipulate in his favor the substantive law to be applied in a diversity case, so too is it unlikely that Congress meant to provide the *plaintiff* with a vehicle by which to appropriate the law of a distant and inconvenient forum in which he does not intend to litigate, and to carry that prize back to the State in which he wishes to try the case. Second, application of the transferor court's law in this context would encourage forum shopping between federal and state courts in the same jurisdiction on the basis of differential substantive law. It is true, of course, that the plaintiffs here did not select the *Mississippi* federal court in preference to the Mississippi state courts because of any differential substantive law; the former, like the latter, would have applied Mississippi choice-of-law rules and thus the Mississippi statute of limitations. But one must be blind to reality to say that it is the *Mississippi* federal court in which these plaintiffs have chosen to sue. That was merely a way station en route to suit in the *Pennsylvania* federal court. The plaintiffs were seeking to achieve exactly what *Klaxon* was designed to prevent: the use of a Pennsylvania federal court instead of a Pennsylvania state court in order to obtain application of a different substantive law. Our decision in *Van Dusen* compromised "the principle of uniformity within a state," *Klaxon*, *supra*, at 496, only in the abstract, but today's decision compromises it precisely in the respect that matters—*i.e.*, insofar as it bears upon the plaintiff's choice between a state and a federal forum. The significant federal judicial policy expressed in *Erie* arid *Klaxon* is reduced to a laughingstock if it can so readily be evaded through filing-and-transfer.

The Court is undoubtedly correct that applying the *Klaxon* rule after a plaintiff-initiated transfer would deter a plaintiff in a situation such as exists here from seeking a transfer, since that would deprive him of the favorable substantive law. But that proves only that this disposition achieves what *Erie* and *Klaxon* are designed to achieve: preventing the plaintiff from using "the accident of diversity of citizenship," *Klaxon*, 313 U.S., at 496, to obtain the application of a different law within the State where he wishes to litigate. In the context of the present case, he must either litigate in the State of Mississippi under Mississippi law, or in the Commonwealth of Pennsylvania under Pennsylvania law.

[I]t seems to me that a proper calculation of systemic costs [of the Court's decision] would go as follows: Saved by the Court's rule will be the incremental cost of trying in forums that are inconvenient (but not so inconvenient as to prompt the court's sua sponte transfer) those suits that are now filed in such forums for choice-of-law purposes. But incurred by the Court's rule will be the costs of considering and effecting transfer, not only in those suits but in the indeterminate number of additional suits that will be filed in inconvenient forums now that filing-and-transfer is an approved form of shopping for law; plus the costs attending the necessity for transferee courts to figure out the choice-of-law rules (and probably the substantive law) of distant States much more often than our *Van Dusen* decision would require. It should be noted that the file-and-transfer ploy sanctioned by the Court today will be available not merely to achieve the relatively rare (and generally un-needed) benefit of a longer statute of limitations, but also to bring home to the desired state of litigation all sorts of favorable choice-of-law rules regarding substantive liability—in an era when the diversity among the States in choice-of-law principles has become kaleidoscopic.

Thus, even as an exercise in giving the most extensive possible scope to the policies of §1404(a), the Court's opinion seems to me unsuccessful. But as I indicated by beginning this opinion with the Rules of Decision Act, that should not be the object of the exercise at all. The Court and I reach different results largely because we approach the question from different directions. For the Court, this case involves an "interpretation of §1404(a)," *ante*, at 524, and the central issue is whether *Klaxon* stands in the way of the policies of that statute. For me, the case involves an interpretation of the Rules of Decision Act, and the central issue is whether §1404(a) alters the "principle of uniformity within a state" which *Klaxon* says that Act embodies. I think my approach preferable, not only because the Rules of Decision Act does, and §1404(a) does not, address the specific subject of which law to apply, but also because, as the Court acknowledges, our jurisprudence under that statute is "a vital expression of the federal system and the concomitant integrity of the separate States," *ante*, at 523. To ask, as in effect the Court does, whether *Erie* gets in the way of §1404(a), rather than whether §1404(a) requires adjustment *of Erie*, seems to me the expression of a mistaken sense of priorities.

For the foregoing reasons, I respectfully dissent.

Questions and Comments

(1) The *Van Dusen* Court justified its result that transfers retain transferor court choice-of-law principles by observing that 28 U.S.C. §1404 was intended only to change the courthouse, and nothing else. But what if such a desire is impossible to accomplish? Doesn't §1404 plus the decision in *Van Dusen* give plaintiffs a right they never had before—the right to choose an inconvenient forum with favorable law, secure in the knowledge that §1404 will allow transfer to a convenient forum?

Did Congress intend to give plaintiffs this advantage in passing §1404? Thus interpreted, won't §1404 *encourage* federal-state forum-shopping by plaintiffs (by removing the limitation of convenience), thus countering the only justification for *Klaxon*?

(2) Even if *Van Dusen* correctly determined that plaintiffs properly possess this advantage, does the *Ferens* holding go too far by turning litigation into even more of an artificial game than it would otherwise be?

(3) If the *Ferens* dissent is correct that the issue is easily resolved by reference to the Rules of Decision Act, then wouldn't *Van Dusen* have to be overruled? How can the Act itself require a federal court to apply the same law as the state court across the street, when all it says is that "the laws of the several states . . . shall be regarded as rules of decisions," without saying which states? The notion that the relevant state is the one in which the federal court sits stems from *Erie*, not from the text of the Act, and *Erie* did not purport to be addressing matters such as choice of law after change of venue; indeed, if it had addressed such issues, its opinions could have been dismissed as dicta.

If *Klaxon* rests on constitutional principles, then why shouldn't it take precedence over the Rules of Decision Act, even assuming that the dissent is correct about what the Act requires? If section 1404(a) has equal standing to the Rules of Decision Act (both being statutes) then which one should govern in case of conflict?

(4) How should a similar case be treated if transfer were sought under 28 U.S.C. §1406, which allows transfer when venue in the original forum is improperly laid? In Martin v. Stokes, 623 F.2d 469 (6th Cir. 1980), the court held that the law of the transferee forum would apply in cases transferred under §1406. This rule has gathered a consensus across the circuits, *see, e.g.*, Eggleton v. Plasser & Theurer, 495 F.3d 582, 588 (8th Cir. 2007) (citing Doering ex rel. Barrett v. Cooper Mountain, Inc., 259 F.3d 1202, 1209 (10th Cir. 2001) and Schaeffer v. Village of Ossining, 58 F.3d 48, 50 (2d Cir. 1995)), but the Supreme Court has not yet weighed in. Is the consensus correct? What should be the result under a §1404 transfer if the courts of the state in which suit was originally brought would have dismissed the case on forum non conveniens grounds? Would *Erie* principles then dictate a change in law accompanying the transfer? If so and if there were *two* possible transferee forums with different choice-of-law rules, how should the transferor court choose between them?

(5) Should the *Van Dusen* principle be applied to a §1404 or §1407 transfer in a federal question case when the transfer is to a different circuit with a different interpretation of federal law controlling an issue in the case? Writing for the D.C. Circuit, Judge (now Justice) Ruth Bader Ginsburg concluded that in a §1407 transfer, the transferee court should use its own best judgment on matters of federal law and *can*, accordingly, apply the law of the transferee court. This seems to be the general rule for both §1404 and §1407 transfers. *See* Rensberger, *The Metasplit: The Law Applied After Transfer in Federal Question Cases*, 2018 Wis. L. Rev. 847, 858-877. But some courts have created statute-specific exceptions that have complicated the doctrine. *E.g.*, Eckstein v. Balcor Film Investors, 8 F.3d 1121, 1126 (7th Cir. 1993) (Easterbrook, J.) ("We agree with Korean Air Lines that a transferee court normally should use its own best judgment about the meaning of

federal law when evaluating a federal claim, but §27A [of the Securities Exchange Act] instructs us to act differently.").

(6) A perceptive discussion of the general *Ferens/Van Dusen* problem may be found in Note, *Choice of Law in Federal Court After Transfer of Venue*, 63 Cornell L. Rev. 149 (1977), which was cited several times in the *Ferens* majority opinion. The piece asserts that "[i]n the few reported cases where plaintiffs moved for transfer from proper forums, however, the defendants argued for the law of the transferor. This suggests that plaintiff-transferors often blunder in selecting an initial forum." *Id.* at 156 (footnote omitted). Should the blundering plaintiff have the right to the law of the transferee forum if it favors him, on the ground that he could have filed there in the first place? Does *Ferens* clearly preclude that result?

(7) Both the majority and the dissent in *Ferens* attempted to make it appear that their conclusions were compelled by the existing statutory scheme. If you were in charge of writing the statutes to govern federal venue, how would you draft them to avoid the *Ferens* problem?

Note: *Erie* and Choice of Forum

Sometimes defendant files a motion to transfer venue on grounds that the parties entered into a contract that includes an exclusive choice-of-court clause. Such clauses state that the parties agree to resolve some or all of their disputes exclusively in the courts located in a particular county, state, or country. In these cases, the transfer turns on the enforceability of the choice-of-court clause. As discussed more fully in Chapter 9, *infra*, enforcement of choice-of-court clauses is typically a question of state law when the claims at issue are state law claims litigated in state court and a question of federal law when the claims at issue are federal law claims. Under the federal law of enforcement, choice-of-court clauses carry with them a strong presumption of enforceability. Not all states adopt this strong presumption.

What happens when a federal court sitting in diversity is presented with a challenge to the enforceability of choice-of-court clauses? In Stewart Organization, Inc. v. Ricoh Corp., 487 U.S. 22 (1988), the Court concluded that federal law governed the question of the enforceability of the clauses, but the majority stopped short of concluding that the strong presumption of validity applied to federal law claims should also be applied in diversity cases. Writing for the majority, Justice Marshall reasoned that §1404(a) is sufficiently broad that it controls transfers that involve choice-of-court clauses. Because §1404(a) is constitutional under *Hanna*'s test that federal statutes need only be capable of rational classification as procedural, it controls in diversity actions notwithstanding contrary state law.

Under §1404(a) the district court is instructed to consider both convenience and fairness, and the presence of the forum-selection clause, as well as the relative bargaining power of the parties, would both be relevant to both considerations. The clause would not control the outcome of the §1404(a) inquiry, however, because the court must also take into account the convenience of third parties as well as public interest concerns. In some cases, the clause would be enforced in federal court even though it would not be considered valid in state court, and in other cases the opposite inconsistency could result. Even so, Congress intended that a "flexible and multifaceted analysis" be applied. *Id.* at 31.

Justices Kennedy and O'Connor concurred, writing separately to state that they believed that the strong presumption of validity applied to federal law claims should also apply in the §1404(a) analysis because the presumption furthers important private and public interests.

Justice Scalia dissented, arguing that §1404(a) does not clearly extend to the issue of enforcement of choice-of-court clauses, because enforcement necessarily involves contract law principles, and nothing in §1404(a) indicates that Congress intended that state contract law principles be preempted. Moreover, judge-made principles for use in the federal courts would be inconsistent with the twin aims of *Erie*. Specifically, a federal rule for enforcement would create forum-shopping and would result in different treatment of diverse and local contracting parties. Instead, Justice Scalia thought that state law should be used to determine whether a forum-selection clause is enforceable. If so, the court should either transfer the case (assuming that transfer is warranted under §1404(a)) or dismiss it (if a §1404(a) transfer is not warranted). If the clause is not enforceable under state law, then the district court should consider whether the case should nevertheless be transferred under §1404(a) for independent reasons.

Which view of the role of §1404(a) seems to make most sense? For a critical account of *Ricoh*, *see* Mullenix, *Another Choice of Forum, Another Choice of Law: Consensual Adjudicatory Procedure in Federal Court*, 57 Fordham L. Rev. 291 (1988). If contract law principles are to be considered as part of a consideration of convenience or fairness, must the principle derive from state law, using the principles derived from *Erie* and *Klaxon*? And, under the *Ricoh* majority's view, how much weight should a forum-selection clause be given under §1404(a)? *See* Clermont, *Governing Law on Forum-Selection Agreements*, 66 Hastings L.J. 643 (2015).

In Atlantic Marine Const. Co. v. U.S. District Court for the Western Dist. of Texas, 134 S. Ct. 568 (2013), a unanimous Court concluded that a district court should transfer a case to the contractually chosen forum unless extraordinary circumstances unrelated to the convenience of the parties clearly disfavored the transfer. The Court further concluded that the presence of a valid choice-of-court clause alters the usual §1404(a) analysis in three ways. First, plaintiff's choice of forum is given no deference; indeed, plaintiff bears the burden of establishing the presence of extraordinary circumstances necessary to defeat the transfer. Second, only public interest factors will be relevant; the clause conclusively determines the private interests. Third, *Van Dusen/Ferens* does not apply to these transfers. In other words, the choice-of-law principles of the contractually chosen rather than the transferor court will apply. The Court did not consider how a district court should determine whether the choice-of-court clause is valid. Most courts of appeals have concluded that federal common law should govern this issue, *see, e.g.*, Albemarle Corp. v. AstraZeneca UK Ltd., 628 F.3d 643, 650 (4th Cir. 2010), but one held that state law controls, *see* Jackson v. Payday Fin., LLC, 764 F.3d 765, 774-775 (7th Cir. 2014). For academic treatments, *compare* Steinman, Atlantic Marine *Through the Lens of* Erie, 66 Hastings L.J. 795, 804-819 (2015) (state law should govern), *with* Sachs, *The Forum Selection Defense*, 10 Duke J. Const. L. & Pub. Poly. 1, 14-26 (2014) (federal common law should govern).

Forum non conveniens is a doctrine that gives courts discretion to dismiss a case within their jurisdiction if there is a more convenient forum elsewhere.

28 U.S.C. §1404 replaced the common law forum non conveniens doctrine with respect to federal court dismissals to other federal courts. But the doctrine of forum non conveniens retains validity in state court (because there is no general provision for transfer between state courts). It also applies in federal court if the preferred forum is a non-U.S. court. For example, in Piper Aircraft Co. v. Reyno, 454 U.S. 235 (1981), the Supreme Court ruled that a forum non conveniens dismissal to a Scottish court was appropriate in a case involving an airplane crash in Scotland. In *Atlantic Marine,* the Court stated that forum non conveniens also was the proper procedural mechanism for district courts to use when a contract chooses a state or foreign forum.

Piper held that under the forum non conveniens doctrine, federal district courts have discretion to dismiss a case if they determine that there is an adequate alternate forum and various private and public interest factors weigh in favor of adjudicating the case in that forum. *See id.* at 257-261. The Court further held that in determining whether an alternate forum is "adequate," it was generally irrelevant that the laws or procedures in the alternate forum were less favorable to the plaintiff than those available in the United States. *Id.* at 247-255.

A number of states have adopted forum non conveniens standards different from the federal standard set out in *Piper. See* Davies, *Time to Change the Federal* Forum Non Conveniens *Analysis,* 77 Tul. L. Rev. 309, 315 (2002) (finding at least seven states differ from the federal standard). What happens then when a federal court, sitting in diversity, has to choose what standard to apply? *Piper* expressly left open "whether under [*Erie*], state or federal law of *forum non coveniens* applies in a diversity case," 454 U.S. at 249 n.13, because the state and federal standards in that case were identical. And the Court has subsequently avoided the question. But an "overwhelming majority" of lower federal courts have held that federal law governs forum non conveniens decisions in diversity cases. 14D Wright et al., *Federal Practice and Procedure* §3828.5, at 727 n.10 (4th ed. 2013) (collecting cases).

Is this apparent consensus consistent with *Erie*? Are state courts bound to follow the federal standard too, or are they free to apply state law? The Supreme Court has avoided this question too but suggested in American Dredging Co. v. Miller, 510 U.S. 443 (1994), that state courts *would* be free to apply state forum non conveniens law. *See* Born & Rutledge, *International Civil Litigation in United States Courts* 440 (6th ed. 2018) (making this point). The Court noted that, at least in the admiralty context, the federal forum non conveniens doctrine is a procedural rule and not one that trumps state law. It reasoned in part:

> At bottom, the doctrine of forum non conveniens is nothing more or less than a supervening venue provision, permitting displacement of the ordinary rules of venue when, in light of certain conditions, the trial court thinks that jurisdiction ought to be declined. But venue is a matter that goes to process rather than substantive rights—determining which among various competent courts will decide the case. *Id.* at 453.

Should this reasoning extend to non-admiralty cases?

Relatedly, should state courts be bound by the federal forum non conveniens standards when they adjudicate international cases? The question only comes up in forum non conveniens cases involving dismissals to foreign fora. Scholars disagree about the answer. For the view that forum non conveniens should be treated as federal common-law rule binding on the states, *see, e.g.,* Greenberg, *The Appropriate Source of Law for Forum Non Conveniens Decisions in International Cases: A Proposal for the Development of Federal Common Law,* 4 Intl. Tax & Bus. Law. 155, 156 (1986); Lowenfeld, *Nationalizing International Law: Essay in Honor of Louis Henkin,* 36 Colum. J. Transnatl. L. 121, 136-138 (1997). For two very different views about why the *Piper* standards do not trump state forum non conveniens law, *see* Goldsmith, *Federal Courts, Foreign Affairs, and Federalism,* 83 Va. L. Rev. 1617 (1997); Stein, Erie *and Court Access,* 100 Yale L.J. 1935 (1991).

2. *Erie* and Judgments

Semtek Intl. Inc. v. Lockheed Martin Corp.

531 U.S. 497 (2001)

Justice SCALIA delivered the opinion of the Court.

This case presents the question whether the claim-preclusive effect of a federal judgment dismissing a diversity action on statute-of-limitations grounds is determined by the law of the State in which the federal court sits.

I

Petitioner filed a complaint against respondent in California state court, alleging breach of contract and various business torts. Respondent removed the case to the United States District Court for the Central District of California on the basis of diversity of citizenship, *see* 28 U.S.C. §§1332, 1441, and successfully moved to dismiss petitioner's claims as barred by California's 2-year statute of limitations. In its order of dismissal, the District Court, adopting language suggested by respondent, dismissed petitioner's claims "in [their] entirety on the merits and with prejudice." Without contesting the District Court's designation of its dismissal as "on the merits," petitioner appealed to the Court of Appeals for the Ninth Circuit, which affirmed the District Court's order. 168 F.3d 501 (1999) (table). Petitioner also brought suit against respondent in the State Circuit Court for Baltimore City, Maryland, alleging the same causes of action, which were not time barred under Maryland's 3-year statute of limitations. Respondent sought injunctive relief against this action from the California federal court under the All Writs Act, 28 U.S.C. §1651, and removed the action to the United States District Court for the District of Maryland on federal-question grounds (diversity grounds were not available because Lockheed "is a Maryland citizen," 988 F. Supp. 913, 914 (1997)). The California federal court denied the relief requested, and the Maryland federal court remanded the case to state court because the federal question arose only by way of defense. Following a hearing, the Maryland state court granted respondent's motion to dismiss on the ground of res judicata. Petitioner then returned to the California federal court and the Ninth Circuit, unsuccessfully moving both courts to amend the former's earlier order so as to indicate that the dismissal was not "on the merits." Petitioner also appealed the Maryland trial court's order of dismissal to the Maryland Court of Special Appeals. The Court of Special Appeals affirmed, holding that, regardless of whether California would have accorded claim-preclusive effect to a statute-of-limitations dismissal by one of its own courts, the dismissal by the California federal court barred the complaint filed in Maryland, since the res judicata effect of federal diversity judgments is prescribed by federal law, under which the earlier dismissal was on the merits and claim preclusive. After the Maryland Court of Appeals declined to review the case, we granted certiorari.

II

Petitioner contends that the outcome of this case is controlled by Dupasseur v. Rochereau, 21 Wall. 130, 135 (1875), which held that the res judicata effect of a federal diversity judgment "is such as would belong to judgments of the State courts rendered under similar circumstances," and may not be accorded any "higher sanctity or effect." Since, petitioner argues, the dismissal of an action on statute-of-limitations grounds by a California state court would not be claim preclusive, it follows that the similar dismissal of this diversity action by the California federal court cannot be claim preclusive. While we agree that this would be the result demanded by *Dupasseur*, the case is not dispositive because it was decided under the Conformity Act of 1872, 17 Stat. 196, which required federal courts to apply the procedural law of the forum State in nonequity cases. That arguably affected the outcome of the case. *See Dupasseur, supra*, at 135. *See also* Restatement (Second) of Judgments §87, Comment a, p.315 (1980) (*hereinafter* Restatement) ("Since procedural law largely determines the matters that may be adjudicated in an action, state law had to be considered in ascertaining the effect of a federal judgment").

Respondent, for its part, contends that the outcome of this case is controlled by Federal Rule of Civil Procedure 41(b), which provides as follows:

> Involuntary Dismissal: Effect Thereof. For failure of the plaintiff to prosecute or to comply with these rules or any order of court, a defendant may move for dismissal of an action or of any claim against the defendant. Unless the court in its order for dismissal otherwise specifies, a dismissal under this subdivision and any dismissal not provided for in this rule, other than a dismissal for lack of jurisdiction, for improper venue, or for failure to join a party under Rule 19, operates as an adjudication upon the merits.

Since the dismissal here did not "otherwise specify" (indeed, it specifically stated that it *was* "on the merits"), and did not pertain to the excepted subjects of jurisdiction, venue, or joinder, it follows, respondent contends, that the dismissal "is entitled to claim preclusive effect."

Implicit in this reasoning is the unstated minor premise that all judgments denominated "on the merits" are entitled to claim-preclusive effect. That premise is not necessarily valid. The original connotation of an "on the merits" adjudication is one that actually "passes directly on the substance of [a particular] claim" before the court. Restatement §19, Comment _a_, at 161. That connotation remains common to every jurisdiction of which we are aware. See _ibid_. ("The prototypical [judgment on the merits is] one in which the merits of [a party's] claim are in fact adjudicated [for or] against the [party] after trial of the substantive issues"). And it is, we think, the meaning intended in those many statements to the effect that a judgment "on the merits" triggers the doctrine of res judicata or claim preclusion.

But over the years the meaning of the term "judgment on the merits" "has gradually undergone change," R. Marcus, M. Redish, & E. Sherman, Civil Procedure: A Modern Approach 1140-1141 (3d ed. 2000), and it has come to be applied to some judgments (such as the one involved here) that do _not_ pass upon the substantive merits of a claim and hence do _not_ (in many jurisdictions) entail claim-preclusive effect. That is why the Restatement of Judgments has abandoned the use of the term—"because of its possibly misleading connotations," Restatement §19, Comment a, at 161.

In short, it is no longer true that a judgment "on the merits" is necessarily a judgment entitled to claim-preclusive effect; and there are a number of reasons for believing that the phrase "adjudication upon the merits" does not bear that meaning in Rule 41(b). To begin with, Rule 41(b) sets forth nothing more than a default rule for determining the import of a dismissal (a dismissal is "upon the merits," with the three stated exceptions, unless the court "otherwise specifies"). This would be a highly peculiar context in which to announce a federally prescribed rule on the complex question of claim preclusion, saying in effect, "All federal dismissals (with three specified exceptions) preclude suit elsewhere, unless the court otherwise specifies."

And even apart from the purely default character of Rule 41(b), it would be peculiar to find a rule governing the effect that must be accorded federal judgments by other courts ensconced in rules governing the internal procedures of the rendering court itself. Indeed, such a rule would arguably violate the jurisdictional limitation of the Rules Enabling Act: that the Rules "shall not abridge, enlarge or modify any substantive right," 28 U.S.C. §2072(b). In the present case, for example, if California law left petitioner free to sue on this claim in Maryland even after the California statute of limitations had expired, the federal court's extinguishment of that right (through Rule 41(b)'s mandated claim-preclusive effect of its judgment) would seem to violate this limitation.

Moreover, as so interpreted, the Rule would in many cases violate the federalism principle of _Erie_, by engendering "'substantial' variations [in outcomes] between state and federal litigation" which would "likely . . . influence the choice of a forum," _Hanna_, 380 U.S. at 467-468. With regard to the claim-preclusion issue involved in the present case, for example, the traditional rule is that expiration of the applicable statute of limitations merely bars the remedy and does not extinguish the substantive right, so that dismissal on that ground does not have claim-preclusive effect in other jurisdictions with longer, unexpired limitation periods. See Restatement (Second) of Conflict of Laws §§142(2), 143 (1969); Restatement of Judgments §49, Comment _a_ (1942). Out-of-state defendants sued on state claims in California and in other States adhering to this traditional rule would systematically remove state-law suits brought against them to federal court—where, unless otherwise specified, a statute-of-limitations dismissal would bar suit everywhere.

Finally, if Rule 41(b) did mean what respondent suggests, we would surely have relied upon it in our cases recognizing the claim-preclusive effect of federal judgments in federal-question cases. Yet for over half a century since the promulgation of Rule 41(b), we have not once done so.

We think the key to a more reasonable interpretation of the meaning of "operates as an adjudication upon the merits" in Rule 41(b) is to be found in Rule 41(a), which, in discussing the effect of voluntary dismissal by the plaintiff, makes clear that an "adjudication upon the merits" is the opposite of a "dismissal without prejudice":

> "Unless otherwise stated in the notice of dismissal or stipulation, the dismissal is without prejudice, except that a notice of dismissal operates as an adjudication upon the merits when filed by a plaintiff who has once dismissed in any court of the United States or of any state an action based on or including the same claim."

See also 18 Wright & Miller, §4435, at 329, n.4 ("Both parts of Rule 41 . . . use the phrase 'without prejudice' as a contrast to adjudication on the merits"); 9 *id.*, §2373, at 396, n.4 ("'With prejudice' is an acceptable form of shorthand for 'an adjudication upon the merits'"). The primary meaning of "dismissal without prejudice," we think, is dismissal without barring the defendant from returning later, to the same court, with the same underlying claim. That will also ordinarily (though not always) have the consequence of not barring the claim from *other* courts, but its primary meaning relates to the dismissing court itself. Thus, Black's Law Dictionary (7th ed. 1999) defines "dismissed without prejudice" as "removed from the court's docket in such a way that the plaintiff may refile the same suit on the same claim," *id.*, at 482, and defines "dismissal without prejudice" as "[a] dismissal that does not bar the plaintiff from refiling the lawsuit within the applicable limitations period," *ibid*.

We think, then, that the effect of the "adjudication upon the merits" default provision of Rule 41(b)—and, presumably, of the explicit order in the present case that used the language of that default provision—is simply that, unlike a dismissal "without prejudice," the dismissal in the present case barred refiling of the same claim in the United States District Court for the Central District of California. That is undoubtedly a necessary condition, but it is not a sufficient one, for claim-preclusive effect in other courts.[2]

_____

2. We do not decide whether, in a diversity case, a federal court's "dismissal upon the merits" (in the sense we have described), under circumstances where a state court would decree only a "dismissal without prejudice," abridges a "substantive right" and thus exceeds the authorization of the Rules Enabling Act. We think the situation will present itself more rarely than would the arguable violation of the Act that would ensue from interpreting Rule 41(b) as a rule of claim preclusion; and if it is a violation, can be more easily dealt with on direct appeal.

III

Having concluded that the claim-preclusive effect, in Maryland, of this California federal diversity judgment is dictated neither by Dupasseur v. Rochereau, as petitioner contends, nor by Rule 41(b), as respondent contends, we turn to consideration of what determines the issue. Neither the Full Faith and Credit Clause, U.S. Const., Art. IV, §1, nor the full faith and credit statute, 28 U.S.C. §1738, addresses the question. By their terms they govern the effects to be given only to state-court judgments (and, in the case of the statute, to judgments by courts of territories and possessions). And no other federal textual provision, neither of the Constitution nor of any statute, addresses the claim-preclusive effect of a judgment in a federal diversity action.

It is also true, however, that no federal textual provision addresses the claim-preclusive effect of a federal-court judgment in a federal-question case, yet we have long held that States cannot give those judgments merely whatever effect they would give their own judgments, but must accord them the effect that this Court prescribes. The reasoning of that line of cases suggests, moreover, that even when States are allowed to give federal judgments (notably, judgments in diversity cases) no more than the effect accorded to state judgments, that disposition is by direction of *this* Court, which has the last word on the claim-preclusive effect of *all* federal judgments:

> It is true that for some purposes and within certain limits it is only required that the judgments of the courts of the United States shall be given the same force and effect as are given the judgments of the courts of the States wherein they are rendered; but it is equally true that whether a Federal judgment has been given due force and effect in the state court is a Federal question reviewable by this court, which will determine for itself whether such judgment has been given due weight or otherwise. . . .
>
> When is the state court obliged to give to Federal judgments only the force and effect it gives to state court judgments within its own jurisdiction? Such cases are distinctly pointed out in the opinion of Mr. Justice Bradley in Dupasseur v. Rochereau [which stated that the case was a diversity case, applying state law under state procedure]. *Deposit Bank*, 191 U.S., at 514-515.

In other words, in *Dupasseur* the State was allowed (indeed, required) to give a federal diversity judgment no more effect than it would accord one of its own judgments only because reference to state law was *the federal rule that this Court deemed appropriate*. In short, federal common law governs the claim-preclusive effect of a dismissal by a federal court sitting in diversity. See *generally* R. Fallen, D. Meltzer, & D. Shapiro, Hart and Wechsler's The Federal Courts and the Federal System 1473 (4th ed. 1996); Degnan, Federalized Res Judicata, 85 Yale L.J. 741 (1976).

It is left to us, then, to determine the appropriate federal rule. And despite the sea change that has occurred in the background law since *Dupasseur* was decided—not only repeal of the Conformity Act but also the watershed decision of this Court in *Erie*—we think the result decreed by *Dupasseur* continues to be correct for diversity cases. Since state, rather than federal, substantive law is at issue there is no need for a uniform federal rule. And indeed, nationwide uniformity in the substance of the matter is better served by having the same claim-preclusive rule (the state rule) apply whether the dismissal has been ordered by a state or a federal court. This is, it seems to us, a classic case for adopting, as the federally prescribed rule of decision, the law that would be applied by state courts in the State in which the federal diversity court sits. [Citations omitted.] As we have alluded to above, any other rule would produce the sort of "forum-shopping . . . and . . . inequitable administration of the laws" that *Erie* seeks to avoid, *Hanna*, 380 U.S., at 468, since filing in, or removing to, federal court would be encouraged by the divergent effects that the litigants would anticipate from likely grounds of dismissal. *See* Guaranty Trust Co. v. York, 326 U.S. at 109-110.

This federal reference to state law will not obtain, of course, in situations in which the state law is incompatible with federal interests. If, for example, state law did not accord claim-preclusive effect to dismissals for willful violation of discovery orders, federal courts' interest in the integrity of their own processes might justify a contrary federal rule. No such conflict with potential federal interests exists in the present case. Dismissal of this state cause of action was decreed by the California federal court only because the California statute of limitations so required; and there is no conceivable federal interest in giving that time bar more effect in other courts than the California courts themselves would impose.

Because the claim-preclusive effect of the California federal court's dismissal "upon the merits" of petitioner's action on statute-of-limitations grounds is governed by a federal rule that in turn incorporates California's law of claim preclusion (the content of which we do not pass upon today), the Maryland Court of Special Appeals erred in holding that the dismissal necessarily precluded the bringing of this action in the Maryland courts. The judgment is reversed, and the case remanded for further proceedings not inconsistent with this opinion.

Questions and Comments

(1) *Semtek* rejects defendant's interpretation of Rule 41 in part because it "would in many cases violate the federalism principle of [*Erie*] by engendering 'substantial variations [in outcomes] between state and federal litigation which would likely . . . influence the choice of a forum.'" *See Semtek, supra* at page 495 (internal quotations removed). Is this the right test? Contrast *Semtek* with *Hanna*, 380 U.S. at 469-470, which stated that it is "incorrect [to assume] that the rule of [*Erie*] constitutes the appropriate test of the validity and therefore the applicability of a Federal Rule of Civil Procedure." *Compare also* Professor Ely's analysis, *supra* pages 474-475. Does *Semtek* portend closer judicial scrutiny under *Erie* of the Federal Rules of Civil Procedure? Or does this passage from *Semtek* simply state a canon of interpretation for federal rules of civil procedure that might clash with state law? Even if it is "merely" a canon, won't it lead to systemic underenforcement of the federal rules?

(2) *Semtek* holds that the federal common-law rule for the claim-preclusive effects of dismissals by federal courts in diversity should incorporate the state-law preclusion rule unless "the state law is incompatible with federal interests." Does the Court ever offer a *reason* why judge-made federal common law should govern? Why doesn't the Court apply the "twin-aims" test to decide whether state law

governs? Is *Semtek*'s rule of usually applying state law unless there is an important federal interest consistent with *Klaxon*, *supra* page 475, which holds that federal courts must (not may) apply state choice-of-law rules in diversity?

(3) How does the preclusion rule announced in *Semtek* comport with related preclusion rules under the full faith and credit clause and statute, discussed *infra* Chapter 7?

7

Recognition of Judgments

"It is just as important that there be a place to end as there should be a place to begin litigation."* That is the principle underlying the concept of finality for judgments. And yet numerous considerations may militate against the finality of certain judgments. Most jurisdictions have a fairly elaborate system of law designed to give sufficient but not undue respect to judgments. Questions concerning this body of law generally arise in attacks on judgments. An attack may be either *direct* or *collateral*. A direct attack is an attempt to reopen or set aside the judgment itself. Rule 59 of the Federal Rules of Civil Procedure, for example, provides for the granting of a new trial for limited reasons and for a limited period of time (motions must be made within ten days after entry of judgment), and Rule 60 provides more limited grounds (such as fraud, newly discovered evidence, and the like) and a somewhat less limited time period for relieving a party of a final judgment. Such attacks on the original judgment are generally entertained only (or at least preferentially) in the court that rendered the original judgment.†

A more common concern is the collateral attack on a judgment, or, viewed from the opposite side, the binding effect of a judgment on subsequent litigation. Sometimes the entire question is labeled the problem of *res judicata*, but usually that term is reserved to describe the effect of a judgment itself on a subsequent case raising the same cause of action, while *collateral estoppel* refers to the effects of findings of fact actually contested in one lawsuit upon a subsequent piece of litigation that may involve a different cause of action but some of the same facts.

---

* Stoll v. Gottlieb, 305 U.S. 165, 172 (1938).

† *See, e.g.*, Lapin v. Shulton, Inc., 333 F.2d 169 (9th Cir. 1964).

Thus, for example, a default judgment may be given res judicata effect in a subsequent suit involving the same cause of action, but can be given no collateral estoppel effect because there is no actual contest over facts in a case terminated by a default judgment.

Res judicata, as narrowly defined, may further be broken down into two categories: *bar* and *merger*. "Bar" refers to the effect of the original judgment in preventing relitigation of the cause of action that was actually litigated. "Merger," on the other hand, refers to the effect of the original judgment in preventing litigation of matters that are considered so closely related to what was actually litigated that they should have been litigated all at once. The entire dispute, in other words, is said to have merged in the original judgment whether or not all parts of the dispute were actually litigated. To the extent that it is justified, bar is based on the idea that there is usually no good reason to litigate a matter twice, and that the chance that a second piece of litigation is likely to produce a better result is outweighed by the costs of relitigation. Merger, on the other hand, cannot be justified by a desire to avoid *re*litigation of matters, since it deals with matters that should have been but were not litigated originally. Instead it finds its justification in the concept of waiver and in a desire to protect the courts and the parties from needless fractionalization of disputes—from having to become involved in two lawsuits where one would do.

Collateral estoppel is limited to establishing, for purposes of the second piece of litigation, facts determined in previous litigation that were "(1) litigated by the parties; (2) determined by the tribunal; and (3) necessarily so determined."[*] It is somewhat more difficult to defend the role of collateral estoppel than that of res judicata. Although some time may be saved by refusal to reinquire into facts, the very complexity of the rules concerning collateral estoppel tends to consume a great deal of court time, and, since the cause of action is likely to be different if collateral estoppel rather than res judicata is at stake, it is probable that the parties will have to litigate at least some issues whether or not the doctrine is applied. On the other hand, the doctrine does preserve a certain seemliness about the law: It tends to guarantee that courts will not reach inconsistent conclusions, based on inconsistent factual findings, at least between identical parties.

Both res judicata and collateral estoppel require some identity of parties. Res judicata requires either absolute identity or *privity*—a legal connection with a party to the first action sufficient to make it fair that the nonparty be bound by or be able to take advantage of the former judgment. Collateral estoppel classically had the same requirements, but more recently there has been a relaxation of what is called the *mutuality* requirement. Mutuality requires that for *A* to take advantage of a factual finding in previous litigation against *B*, *B* must have been able to take advantage of the factual finding if it had gone the other way. A relaxation of the mutuality rule (which is also a relaxation of the identity-of-parties requirement) is seen in those jurisdictions that allow *A* to take advantage of a finding of fact against *B* in a previous suit pitting *C* against *B*. In other words, relaxation of the mutuality requirement allows a fact to be used against someone who *was* a party to previous litigation even though it is being so used by a person who was *not*

---

[*] James, Hazard & Leubsdorf, *Civil Procedure* 704 (5th ed. 2001).

a party to previous litigation. (A requirement that has not been relaxed is that the person against whom the finding is used must have been a party to the previous suit or in privity with one.)

None of the intricacies of the discussion above requires more than a single jurisdiction. Res judicata and collateral estoppel are common-law rules applicable within an individual court system. For present purposes, however, the chief interest in these two doctrines arises when the effect of a judgment or finding of fact from a court in State X is considered in a court in State Y. The broad outlines of State Y's obligation to honor State X's judgment are contained in the full faith and credit clause of the Constitution, and 28 U.S.C. §1738:

> [U.S. Const. art. IV, §1:] Full Faith and Credit shall be given in each State to the public Acts, Records, and judicial Proceedings of every other State. And the Congress may by general Laws prescribe the Manner in which such Acts, Records and Proceedings shall be proved, and the Effect thereof.

> [28 U.S.C. §1738:] State and Territorial statutes and judicial proceedings; full faith and credit.

> The Acts of legislature of any State, Territory, or Possession of the United States, or copies thereof, shall be authenticated by affixing the seal of such State, Territory or Possession thereto.

> The records and judicial proceedings of any court of any such State, Territory or Possession, or copies thereof, shall be proved or admitted in other courts within the United States and its Territories and Possessions by the attestation of the clerk and seal of the court annexed, if a seal exists, together with a certificate of a judge of the court that the said attestation is in proper form.

> Such Acts, records and judicial proceedings or copies thereof, so authenticated, shall have the same full faith and credit in every court within the United States and its Territories and Possessions as they have by law or usage in the courts of such State, Territory or Possession from which they are taken.

Commonly, full faith and credit questions arise in the United States when judgments from the courts of one state are presented for enforcement in the courts of another.* The statutory texts above, however, do little to answer many difficult problems in these cases, such as: What jurisdictional defects in the first judgment, if any, relieve the second court of the obligation to enforce a judgment; need the enforcing state respect a judgment contrary to its own deeply held substantive interests; and which state's laws apply as to mechanical or procedural issues of judgments enforcement? After examining these questions, this chapter takes a look at a special problem in the area of judgments enforcement, namely, domestic relations law.

---

* Is there any basis in the full faith and credit clause or the implementing statute for requiring the states to give full faith and credit to the judgments of federal courts? If the full faith and credit clause does not authorize such a rule, is there any other basis in the Constitution for requiring such recognition by the states? In fact, the Supreme Court has always required recognition of federal court judgments. *See, e.g.*, Metcalf v. Watertown, 153 U.S. 671 (1894). Would any other result be acceptable? *See generally* Burbank, *Federal Judgments Law: Sources of Authority and Sources of Rules*, 70 Tex. L. Rev. 1551 (1992).

A.   Jurisdictional Requirements

Durfee v. Duke
375 U.S. 106 (1963)

Justice STEWART delivered the opinion of the Court.

The United States Constitution requires that "Full Faith and Credit shall be given in each State to the . . . judicial Proceedings of every other State." The case before us presents questions arising under this constitutional provision and under the federal statute enacted to implement it.

In 1956 the petitioners brought an action against the respondent in a Nebraska court to quiet title to certain bottom land situated on the Missouri River. The main channel of that river forms the boundary between the States of Nebraska and Missouri. The Nebraska court had jurisdiction over the subject matter of the controversy only if the land in question was in Nebraska. Whether the land was Nebraska land depended entirely upon a factual question—whether a shift in the river's course had been caused by avulsion or accretion. The respondent appeared in the Nebraska court and through counsel fully litigated the issues, explicitly contesting the court's jurisdiction over the subject matter of the controversy.[1] After a hearing the court found the issues in favor of the petitioners and ordered that title to the land be quieted in them. The respondent appealed, and the Supreme Court of Nebraska affirmed the judgment after a trial de novo on the record made in the lower court. The State Supreme Court specifically found that the rule of avulsion was applicable, that the land in question was in Nebraska, that the Nebraska courts therefore had jurisdiction of the subject matter of the litigation, and that title to the land was in the petitioners. Durfee v. Keiffer, 168 Neb. 272. The respondent did not petition this Court for a writ of certiorari to review that judgment.

Two months later the respondent filed a suit against the petitioners in a Missouri court to quiet title to the same land. Her complaint alleged that the land was in Missouri. The suit was removed to a Federal District Court by reason of diversity of citizenship. The District Court after hearing evidence expressed the view that the land was in Missouri but held that all the issues had been adjudicated and determined in the Nebraska litigation, and that the judgment of the Nebraska Supreme Court was res judicata and "is now binding upon this court." The Court of Appeals reversed, holding that the District Court was not required to give full faith and credit to the Nebraska judgment, and that normal res judicata principles were not applicable because the controversy involved land and a court in Missouri was therefore free to retry the question of the Nebraska court's jurisdiction over the subject matter. We granted certiorari to consider a question important to the administration of justice in our federal system. For the reasons that follow, we reverse the judgment before us.

---

1. This is, therefore, not a case in which a party, although afforded an opportunity to contest subject-matter jurisdiction, did not litigate the issue. *Cf.* Chicot County Drainage Dist. v. Baxter State Bank, 308 U.S. 371.

The constitutional command of full faith and credit, as implemented by Congress, requires that "judicial proceedings . . . shall have the same full faith and credit in every court within the United States . . . as they have by law or usage in the courts of such State . . . from which they are taken." Full faith and credit thus generally requires every State to give to a judgment at least the res judicata effect which the judgment would be accorded in the State which rendered it. "By the Constitutional provision for full faith and credit, the local doctrines of res judicata, speaking generally, become part of national jurisprudence, and therefore federal questions cognizable here." Riley v. New York Trust Co.

It is not questioned that the Nebraska courts would give full res judicata effect to the Nebraska judgment quieting title in the petitioners. It is the respondent's position, however, that whatever effect the Nebraska courts might give to the Nebraska judgment, the federal court in Missouri was free independently to determine whether the Nebraska court in fact had jurisdiction over the subject matter, *i.e.*, whether the land in question was actually in Nebraska.

In support of this position the respondent relies upon the many decisions of this Court which have held that a judgment of a court in one State is conclusive upon the merits in a court in another State only if the court in the first State had power to pass on the merits—had jurisdiction, that is, to render the judgment. As Mr. Justice Bradley stated the doctrine in the leading case of Thompson v. Whitman, 18 Wall. 457, "we think it clear that the jurisdiction of the court by which a judgment is rendered in any State may be questioned in a collateral proceeding in another State, notwithstanding the provision of the fourth article of the Constitution and the law of 1790, and notwithstanding the averments contained in the record of the judgment itself." The principle has been restated and applied in a variety of contexts.

However, while it is established that a court in one State, when asked to give effect to the judgment of a court in another State, may constitutionally inquire into the foreign court's jurisdiction to render that judgment, the modern decisions of this Court have carefully delineated the permissible scope of such an inquiry. From these decisions there emerges the general rule that a judgment is entitled to full faith and credit—even as to questions of jurisdiction—when the second court's inquiry disclosed that those questions have been fully and fairly litigated and finally decided in the court which rendered the original judgment.

With respect to questions of jurisdiction over the person,[2] this principle was unambiguously established in Baldwin v. Iowa State Traveling Men's Assn. There it was held that a federal court in Iowa must give binding effect to the judgment of a federal court in Missouri despite the claim that the original court did not have jurisdiction over the defendant's person, once it was shown to the court in Iowa that the question had been fully litigated in the Missouri forum. "Public policy," said the Court, "dictates that there be an end of litigation; that those who have contested an issue shall be bound by the result of the contest, and that matters once tried shall be considered forever settled as between the parties. We see

---

2. It is not disputed in the present case that the Nebraska courts had jurisdiction over the respondent's person. She entered a general appearance in the trial court, and initiated the appeal to the Nebraska Supreme Court.

no reason why this doctrine should not apply in every case where one voluntarily appears, presents his case and is fully heard, and why he should not, in the absence of fraud, be thereafter concluded by the judgment of the tribunal to which he has submitted his cause."

Following the *Baldwin* case, this Court soon made clear in a series of decisions that the general rule is no different when the claim is made that the original forum did not have jurisdiction over the subject matter. In each of these cases the claim was made that a court, when asked to enforce the judgment of another forum, was free to retry the question of that forum's jurisdiction over the subject matter. In each case this Court held that since the question of subject-matter jurisdiction had been fully litigated in the original forum, the issue could not be retried in a subsequent action between the parties.

The reasons for such a rule are apparent. In the words of the Court's opinion in Stoll v. Gottlieb, *supra,*

> We see no reason why a court, in the absence of an allegation of fraud in obtaining the judgment, should examine again the question whether the court making the earlier determination on an actual contest over jurisdiction between the parties, did have jurisdiction of the subject matter of the litigation. . . . Courts to determine the rights of parties are an integral part of our system of government. It is just as important that there should be a place to end as that there should be a place to begin litigation. After a party has his day in court, with opportunity to present his evidence and his view of the law, a collateral attack upon the decision as to jurisdiction there rendered merely retries the issue previously determined. There is no reason to expect that the second decision will be more satisfactory than the first.

To be sure, the general rule of finality of jurisdictional determinations is not without exceptions. Doctrines of federal pre-emption or sovereign immunity may in some contexts be controlling. Kalb v. Feuerstein [page 512 *infra*]; U.S. v. U.S. Fid. Co., 309 U.S. 506.[3]

---

3. It is to be noted, however, that in neither of these cases had the jurisdictional issues actually been litigated in the first forum.

The Restatement of Conflict of Laws recognizes the possibility of such exceptions:

> Where a court has jurisdiction over the parties and determines that it has jurisdiction over the subject matter, the parties cannot collaterally attack the judgment on the ground that the court did not have jurisdiction over the subject matter, unless the policy underlying the doctrine of res judicata is outweighed by the policy against permitting the court to act beyond its jurisdiction. Among the factors appropriate to be considered in determining that collateral attack should be permitted are that
>
>   (a) the lack of jurisdiction over the subject matter was clear;
>   (b) the determination as to jurisdiction depended upon a question of law rather than of fact;
>   (c) the court was one of limited and not of general jurisdiction;
>   (d) the question of jurisdiction was not actually litigated;
>   (e) the policy against the court's acting beyond its jurisdiction is strong.

Restatement, Conflict of Laws §451(2) (Supp. 1948). *See* Restatement, Judgments §10 (1942).

But no such overriding considerations are present here.

It is argued that an exception to this rule of jurisdictional finality should be made with respect to cases involving real property because of this Court's emphatic expression of the doctrine that courts of one State are completely without jurisdiction directly to affect title to land in other States. This argument is wide of the mark. Courts of one State are equally without jurisdiction to dissolve the marriages of those domiciled in other States. But the location of land, like the domicile of a party to a divorce action, is a matter "to be resolved by judicial determination." Sherrer v. Sherrer. The question remains whether, once the matter has been fully litigated and judicially determined, it can be retried in another State in litigation between the same parties. Upon the reason and authority of the cases we have discussed, it is clear that the answer must be in the negative.

It is to be emphasized that all that was ultimately determined in the Nebraska litigation was title to the land in question as between the parties to the litigation there. Nothing there decided, and nothing that could be decided in litigation between the same parties or their privies in Missouri, could bind either Missouri or Nebraska with respect to any controversy they might have, now or in the future, as to the location of the boundary between them, or as to their respective sovereignty over the land in question. Either State may at any time protect its interest by initiating independent judicial proceedings here.

For the reasons stated, we hold in this case that the federal court in Missouri had the power and, upon proper averments, the duty to inquire into the jurisdiction of the Nebraska courts to render the decree quieting title to the land in the petitioners. We further hold that when that inquiry disclosed, as it did, that the jurisdictional issues had been fully and fairly litigated by the parties and finally determined in the Nebraska courts, the federal court in Missouri was correct in ruling that further inquiry was precluded. Accordingly the judgment of the Court of Appeals is reversed, and that of the District Court is affirmed.

Justice BLACK, concurring.

Petitioners and respondent dispute the ownership of a tract of land adjacent to the Missouri River, which is the boundary between Nebraska and Missouri. Resolution of this question turns on whether the land is in Nebraska or Missouri. Neither State, of course, has power to make a determination binding on the other as to which State the land is in. U.S. Const., Art. III, §2; 28 U.S.C. §1251(a). However, in a private action brought by these Nebraska petitioners, the Nebraska Supreme Court has held that the disputed tract is in Nebraska. In the present suit, brought by this Missouri respondent in Missouri, the United States Court of Appeals has refused to be bound by the Nebraska court's judgment. I concur in today's reversal of the Court of Appeals' judgment, but with the understanding that we are not deciding the question whether the respondent would continue to be bound by the Nebraska judgment should it later be authoritatively decided, either in an original proceeding between the States in this Court or by a compact between the two States under Art. I, §10, that the disputed tract is in Missouri.

Fall v. Eastin
215 U.S. 1 (1909)

Justice McKENNA delivered the opinion of the court.

The question in this case is whether a deed to land situated in Nebraska, made by a commissioner under the decree of a court of the State of Washington in an action for divorce, must be recognized in Nebraska under the due faith and credit clause of the Constitution of the United States.

[Plaintiff filed suit in Nebraska state court, seeking to quiet title to Nebraska land and to cancel a deed and mortgage that interfered with her property rights. The land was acquired by plaintiff and her then husband, E.W. Fall, during the marriage. The couple eventually moved to Washington State, and separated in January 1895. In February 1895, her husband brought suit against her for divorce in Washington State court. He sought both a decree of divorce and title to the Nebraska property. Plaintiff contested the divorce action, and, in the alternative, sought a decree awarding her the Nebraska property, subject to an existing mortgage of $1,000. The Washington State court granted the divorce, and, pursuant to a state statute directing divorce courts to divide the marital property in a just and equitable fashion, ordered E.W. Fall to "convey all his right, title and interest in and to the land within five days from the date of the decree." Instead, E.W. Fall conveyed his deed to defendant Elizabeth Eastin and executed and recorded the mortgage. The Washington State commissioner executed a separate deed to plaintiff. Plaintiff sought from the Nebraska court a decree that she owns the property and a declaration that the original deed and mortgage are null and void.]

The question is in narrow compass. The full faith and credit clause of the Constitution of the United States is invoked by plaintiff to sustain the deed executed under the decree of the court of the State of Washington. The argument in support of this is that the Washington court, having had jurisdiction of the parties and the subject-matter, in determination of the equities between the parties to the lands in controversy, decreed a conveyance to be made to her. This conveyance, it is contended, was decreed upon equities, and was as effectual as though her "husband and she had been strangers and she had bought the land from him and paid for it and he had then refused to convey it to her." In other words, that the decree of divorce in the State of Washington, which was made in consummation of equities which arose between the parties under the law of Washington, was "evidence of her right to the legal title of at least as much weight and value as a contract in writing, reciting the payment of the consideration for the land, would be."

The defendant, on the other hand, contends . . . that "the Washington court had neither power nor jurisdiction to affect in the least, either legally or equitably," lands situated in Nebraska . . . .

In considering these propositions we must start with a concession of jurisdiction in the Washington court over both the parties and the subject-matter. Jurisdiction in that court is the first essential, but the ultimate question is, What is the effect of the decree upon the land and of the deed executed under it? . . .

The territorial limitation of the jurisdiction of courts of a State over property in another State has a limited exception in the jurisdiction of a court of equity, but it is an exception well defined. A court of equity having authority to act upon the person may indirectly act upon real estate in another State, through the instrumentality of this authority over the person. Whatever it may do through the party it may do to give effect to its decree respecting property, whether it goes to the entire disposition of it or only to affect it with liens or burdens. Story on *Conflict of Laws* §544 . . . .

But, however plausibly the contrary view may be sustained, we think that the doctrine that the court, not having jurisdiction of the res, cannot affect it by its decree, nor by a deed made by a master in accordance with the decree, is firmly established. [W]hen the subject-matter of a suit in a court of equity is within another State or country, but the parties within the jurisdiction of the court, the suit may be maintained and remedies granted which may directly affect and operate upon the person of the defendant and not upon the subject-matter, although the subject-matter is referred to in the decree, and the defendant is ordered to do or refrain from certain acts toward it, and it is thus ultimately but *indirectly* affected by the relief granted. In such case the decree is not of itself legal title, nor does it transfer the legal title. It must be executed by the party, and obedience is compelled by proceedings in the nature of contempt, attachment or sequestration. On the other hand, where the suit is strictly local, the subject-matter is specific property, and the relief when granted is such that it *must* act directly upon the subject-matter, and not upon the person of the defendant, the jurisdiction must be exercised in the State where the subject matter is situated. 3 *Pomeroy's Equity*, §§1317, 1318, and notes.

This doctrine is entirely consistent with the provision of the Constitution of the United States, which requires a judgment in any State to be given full faith and credit in the courts of every other State. This provision does not extend the jurisdiction of the courts of one State to property situated in another, but only makes the judgment rendered conclusive on the merits of the claim or subject-matter of the suit. "It does not carry with it into another State the efficacy of a judgment upon property or persons, to be enforced by execution. To give it the force of a judgment in another State it must become a judgment there; and can only be executed in the latter as its laws permit." M'Elmoyle v. Cohen, 13 Pet. 312.

Plaintiff seems to contend for a greater efficacy for a decree in equity affecting real property than is given to a judgment at law for the recovery of money simply . . . .

. . . There is, however, much temptation in the facts of this case to [grant effect to the Washington decree and conveyance]. As we have seen, the husband of the plaintiff brought suit against her in Washington for divorce, and, attempting to avail himself of the laws of Washington, prayed also that the land now in controversy be awarded to him. She appeared in the action, and, submitting to the jurisdiction which he had invoked, made counter-charges and prayers for relief. She established her charges, she was granted a divorce, and the land decreed to her. He, then, to defeat the decree and in fraud of her rights, conveyed the land to the defendant in this suit. This is the finding of the trial court. It is not questioned by the Supreme Court, but, as the ruling of the latter court, that the decree in Washington gave no such equities as could be recognized in Nebraska as justifying an action to quiet title, does not offend the Constitution of the United States, we are constrained to affirm its judgment.

Justice HARLAN and Justice BREWER dissent.

Justice HOLMES, concurring specially. I am not prepared to dissent from the judgment of the court, but my reasons are different from those that have been stated.

The real question concerns the effect of the Washington decree. As between the parties to it, that decree established in Washington a personal obligation of the husband to convey to his former wife. A personal obligation goes with the person. If the husband had made a contract, valid by the law of Washington, to do the same thing, I think there is no doubt that the contract would have been binding in Nebraska. So I conceive that a Washington decree for the specific performance of such a contract would be entitled to full faith and credit as between the parties in Nebraska. But it does not matter to its constitutional effect what the ground of the decree may be, whether a contract or something else. Fauntleroy v. Lum. (In this case it may have been that the wife contributed equally to the accumulation of the property, and so had an equitable claim.) A personal decree is equally within the jurisdiction of a court having the person within its power, whatever its ground and whatever it orders the defendant to do. Therefore I think that this decree was entitled to full faith and credit in Nebraska.

But the Nebraska court carefully avoids saying that the decree would not be binding between the original parties had the husband been before the court. The ground on which it goes is that to allow the judgment to affect the conscience of purchasers would be giving it an effect in rem. It treats the case as standing on the same footing as that of an innocent purchaser. Now if the court saw fit to deny the effect of a judgment upon privies in title, or if it considered the defendant an innocent purchaser, I do not see what we have to do with its decision, however wrong. I do not see why it is not within the power of the State to do away with equity or with the equitable doctrine as to purchasers with notice if it sees fit. Still less do I see how a mistake as to notice could give us jurisdiction. If the judgment binds the defendant it is not by its own operation, even with the Constitution behind it, but by the obligation imposed by equity upon a purchaser with notice. The ground of decision below was that there was no such obligation. The decision, even if wrong, did not deny to the Washington decree its full effect.

Questions and Comments

(1) The Court in *Durfee* stated that the court in which recognition or enforcement is sought has the power to inquire into the subject matter jurisdiction of the court that rendered the judgment. Note the importance of distinguishing whether the law denies the court jurisdiction from whether the law requires the court to deny relief on the merits. For a recent discussion of this distinction, *see* V.L. v. E.L., 136 S. Ct. 1017 (2016) (per curiam): "[I]n general, subject-matter jurisdiction addresses 'whether a court has jurisdiction to decide a particular class of cases,' not whether a court should grant relief in any given case. . . . [Section] 19-8-5(a) does not speak to whether a court has the power to decide a general class of cases. It only provides a rule of decision to apply in determining if a particular adoption should be allowed. Section 19-8-5(a) does not become jurisdictional just because it is 'mandatory' and 'must be strictly construed.' This Court 'has long

rejected the notion that all mandatory prescriptions, however emphatic, are properly typed jurisdictional.' . . . As Justice Holmes observed more than a century ago, 'it sometimes may be difficult to decide whether certain words in a statute are directed to jurisdiction or to merits.' *Fauntleroy v. Lum* [*infra* page 516]. In such cases, especially where the Full Faith and Credit Clause is concerned, a court must be 'slow to read ambiguous words, as meaning to leave the judgment open to dispute, or as intended to do more than fix the rule by which the court should decide.' *Id.* That time-honored rule controls here."

(2) Is Fall v. Eastin consistent with Durfee v. Duke? Does *Durfee* overrule *Fall*? Or is the difference that in *Fall* it was agreed that the land at issue was outside the forum, whereas in *Durfee* that was precisely the subject of the dispute?

(3) Several different interpretations of *Fall* are possible. The most immediately obvious is simply that a judgment rendered without jurisdiction is void and can be collaterally attacked elsewhere. In the alternative, *Fall* might mean that states have such a strong substantive interest in land within their borders that no other state can interfere. Or, possibly *Fall* hinges on the special nature of the system for recording interests in land—that although the rendering state might transfer a legal right to the property, this right would not become effective against third parties until properly recorded at the situs.

Which of these rationales best explains *Fall*? Which makes it the most consistent with *Durfee*? Note that if the judgment were a judgment for money or personal property, the prevailing party would still have to seek execution in the place where the property was located. Which state's laws would apply on the issue of the proper method of execution? Does the rendering state exceed its authority if it tries to execute the judgment directly? Does it infringe on the substantive interests of the state where the property was located? Does it infringe on the situs's interests in controlling the procedures by which judgments are enforced?

(4) Reception of the "land taboo" has not been warm among the commentators. *See, e.g.*, Baxter, *Choice of Law and the Federal System*, 16 Stan. L. Rev. 1, 15-17 (1963); Hancock, *Equitable Conversion and the Land Taboo in the Conflict of Laws*, 17 Stan. L. Rev. 1095 (1965), also *Full Faith and Credit to Foreign Laws and Judgments in Real Property Litigation*, 18 Stan. L. Rev. 1299 (1966), and *Conceptual Devices for Avoiding the Land Taboo in Conflict of Laws*, 20 Stan. L. Rev. 1 (1967); and Currie, *Full Faith and Credit to Foreign Land Decrees*, 21 U. Chi. L. Rev. 620 (1954). Currie suggests a number of end runs, including a careful arranging of the relief requested in the original action, with a request in the second court for a decree awarding title, the first decree to act as res judicata or to provide collateral estoppel effect.

(5) What was the nature of the action brought by the Nebraska plaintiff in *Durfee*? If you were the Nebraska plaintiff, would you be satisfied that you had completely "won" your case in light of Justice Black's concurring opinion? Is there any justification for suggesting, as Justice Black does, that a subsequent decision that the land was not in Nebraska should undercut the authority of the Nebraska judgment? Doesn't *Durfee* stand for the proposition that the land *was* in Nebraska, for purposes of this litigation, and that that fact can't be reexamined?

If the two states had previously litigated the question of sovereignty over the land in the Supreme Court, would the Court's determination of the issue be binding by way of res judicata, or merely by way of stare decisis? Would it matter?

What if the states had agreed that one of them owned the land, without litigating the issue, before the private litigation in *Durfee* (but after the dispute had arisen). Should such an agreement affect the private litigation? Would it make any difference if it appeared that the agreement had been a compromise, with several parcels of land involved?

(6) What would have happened if the Court in *Durfee* had come out the other way—that is, if it had granted the Missouri federal district court the right to determine, on its own, whether the Nebraska court correctly concluded that the land was in Nebraska? The federal marshal from Missouri and the sheriff from Nebraska could end up with inconsistent marching orders. Didn't the Supreme Court *have* to decide *Durfee* the way it did?

(7) Does *Durfee* guarantee that there won't be any shoot-outs between the sheriff and the marshal? What if the Missouri party had not appeared in the Nebraska proceedings, but the Nebraska court had claimed subject-matter jurisdiction over the dispute by virtue of the land's presence within the state, and in rem jurisdiction for the same reason, thus binding all parties? Isn't that consistent with *Shaffer*, page 446 *supra*? Would *Durfee* make the Nebraska judgment binding under such circumstances? If not, and if the Nebraska party refuses to appear in a Missouri proceeding with jurisdiction based on the presence of the land in Missouri, who will keep the peace when sheriffs from the respective states show up to enforce the orders of their courts?

Kalb v. Feuerstein

308 U.S. 433 (1940)

Justice BLACK delivered the opinion of the Court.

Appellants are farmers. Two of appellees, as mortgagees, began foreclosure on appellants' farm March 7, 1933, in the Walworth (Wisconsin) County Court: judgment of foreclosure was entered April 21, 1933; July 20, 1935, the sheriff sold the property under the judgment; September 16, 1935, while appellant Ernest Newton Kalb had duly pending in the bankruptcy court a petition for composition and extension of time to pay his debts under §75 of the Bankruptcy Act (Frazier-Lemke Act), the Walworth County Court granted the mortgagees' motion for confirmation of the sheriff's sale; no stay of the foreclosure or of the subsequent action to enforce it was ever sought or granted in the state or bankruptcy court; December 16, 1935, the mortgagees, who had purchased at the sheriff's sale, obtained a writ of assistance from the state court; and March 12, 1936, the sheriff executed the writ by ejecting appellants and their family from the mortgaged farm.

The questions in both No. 120 and No. 121 are whether the Wisconsin County Court had jurisdiction, while the petition under the Frazier-Lemke Act was pending in the bankruptcy court, to confirm the sheriff's sale and to order appellants dispossessed, and, if it did not, whether its action in the absence of direct appeal is subject to collateral attack.

No. 120. After ejection from their farm, appellants brought an action in equity in the Circuit Court of Walworth County, Wisconsin, against the mortgagees who had purchased at the sheriff's sale, for restoration of possession, for cancellation of the sheriff's deed and for removal of the mortgagees from the farm.

Demurrer was sustained for failure to state a cause of action and the complaint was dismissed. The Supreme Court of Wisconsin affirmed.

No. 121 is a suit in the state court by appellant Ernest Newton Kalb against the mortgagees, the sheriff and the County Court judge who confirmed the foreclosure sale and issued the writ of assistance. Damages are sought for conspiracy to deprive appellant of possession, for assault and battery, and for false imprisonment. As in No. 120, demurrer was sustained, and the Supreme Court of Wisconsin affirmed.

In its first opinion the Supreme Court of Wisconsin said: "It is the contention of the plaintiff [mortgagor] that this statute is self-executing—that is, that it requires no application to the state or federal court in which foreclosure proceedings are pending for a stay; in other words, that it provides for a statutory and not for a judicial stay. Plaintiff's claims under the Bankruptcy Act present a question which clearly arises under the laws of the United States and therefore present a federal question upon which determination of the federal courts is controlling." Addressing itself solely to this federal question of construing the Frazier-Lemke Act, the Wisconsin court decided that the federal Act did not itself as an automatic statutory stay terminate the state court's jurisdiction when the farmer filed his petition in the bankruptcy court. Since there had been no judicial stay, it held that the confirmation of sale and writ of assistance were not in violation of the Act. . . .

[I]f appellants are right in their contention that the federal Act of itself, from the moment the petition was filed and so long as it remained pending, operated, in the absence of the bankruptcy court's consent, to oust the jurisdiction of the state court so as to stay its power to proceed with foreclosure, to confirm a sale, and to issue an order ejecting appellants from their farm, the action of the Walworth County Court was not merely erroneous but was beyond its power, void, and subject to collateral attack.

It is generally true that a judgment by a court of competent jurisdiction bears a presumption of regularity and is not thereafter subject to collateral attack. But Congress, because its power over the subject of bankruptcy is plenary, may by specific bankruptcy legislation create an exception to that principle and render judicial acts taken with respect to the person or property of a debtor whom the bankruptcy law protects nullities and vulnerable collaterally. Although the Walworth County Court had general jurisdiction over foreclosures under the law of Wisconsin, a peremptory prohibition by Congress in the exercise of its supreme power over bankruptcy that no state court have jurisdiction over a petitioning farmer-debtor or his property, would have rendered the confirmation of sale and its enforcement beyond the County Court's power and nullities subject to collateral attack. The State cannot, in the exercise of control over local laws and practice, vest state courts with power to violate the supreme law of the land. The Constitution grants Congress exclusive power to regulate bankruptcy and under this power Congress can limit the jurisdiction which courts, state or federal, can exercise over the person and property of a debtor who duly invokes the bankruptcy law. If Congress has vested in the bankruptcy courts exclusive jurisdiction over farmer-debtors and their property, and has by its Act withdrawn from all other courts all power under any circumstances to maintain and enforce foreclosure proceedings against them, its Act is the supreme law of the land which all courts—state and federal—must observe. The wisdom and desirability of an automatic statutory ouster of jurisdiction of all except bankruptcy courts over farmer-debtors and their property were considerations for Congress alone.

We think the language and broad policy of the Frazier-Lemke Act conclusively demonstrate that Congress intended to, and did deprive the Wisconsin County Court of the power and jurisdiction to continue or maintain in any manner the foreclosure proceedings against appellants without the consent after hearing of the bankruptcy court in which the farmer's petition was then pending. . . .

Thus Congress repeatedly stated its unequivocal purpose to prohibit—in the absence of consent by the bankruptcy court in which a distressed farmer has a pending petition—a mortgagee or any court from instituting, or maintaining if already instituted, any proceeding against the farmer to sell under mortgage foreclosure, to confirm such a sale, or to dispossess under it. . . .

The mortgagees who sought to enforce the mortgage after the petition was duly filed in the bankruptcy court, the Walworth County Court that attempted to grant the mortgagees relief, and the sheriff who enforced the court's judgment, were all acting in violation of the controlling Act of Congress. Because that state court had been deprived of all jurisdiction or power to proceed with the foreclosure, the confirmation of the sale, the execution of the sheriff's deed, the writ of assistance, and the ejection of appellants from their property—to the extent based upon the court's actions—were all without authority of law. Individual responsibility for such unlawful acts must be decided according to the law of the State. We therefore express no opinion as to other contentions based upon state law and raised by appellees in support of the judgments of the Supreme Court of Wisconsin.

Congress manifested its intention that the issue of jurisdiction in the foreclosing court need not be contested or even raised by the distressed farmer-debtor. The protection of the farmers was left to the farmers themselves or to the Commissioners who might be laymen, and considerations as to whether the issue of jurisdiction was actually contested in the County Court,[18] or whether it could have been contested,[19] are not applicable where the plenary power of Congress over bankruptcy has been exercised as in this Act.

The judgments in both cases are reversed and the causes are remanded to the Supreme Court of Wisconsin for further proceedings not inconsistent with this opinion.

Questions and Comments

(1) It is clear, isn't it, that Congress had the *right* to do what the Court claimed it did in *Kalb*, since the federal courts are not bound by the full faith and credit clause, and in any event, the full faith and credit clause provides for congressional implementation?

(2) But that leaves the question whether Congress actually had the intent attributed to it by the Court. The legislation in question was the result of the

---

18. Stoll v. Gottlieb [305 U.S. 165 (1938)].
19. *Chicot County* [308 U.S. 371 (1940)].

Depression. Congress may have been especially solicitous of farmers. But where is the affirmative indication that it wished to go so far? Isn't the Court's verbiage about voidness and nullities a smoke screen to avoid discussion of the central issue; that is, what was the intent of Congress on this particular issue? Why would Congress want to give someone the protection of a statutory defense he didn't even raise if, as in *Chicot* (*infra* note 7), a defense of unconstitutionality cannot be so used even when raising it would have seemed futile (because the statute had not yet been declared unconstitutional)?

(3) More recently, the Supreme Court has been reluctant to infer congressional intent not to abide by res judicata or collateral estoppel. Thus, in Allen v. McCurry, 449 U.S. 90 (1980), the Court held that a civil rights claim brought under 28 U.S.C. §1983, alleging an illegal search and seizure, was barred by an earlier state court ruling in a criminal prosecution that the search and seizure had been legal. And in Kremer v. Chem. Const. Corp., 456 U.S. 461 (1982), the Court ruled that full faith and credit was due to findings of nondiscrimination made by a state administrative agency and reviewed by state courts, thus barring a subsequent Title VII action in the federal courts.

(4) How true is it, as a general matter, that a jurisdictional defect renders a judgment subject to collateral attack? In Thompson v. Whitman, 85 U.S. 457 (1873), the Supreme Court held that lack of subject matter jurisdiction in one proceeding could allow a collateral attack in a later proceeding. There a ship had been seized in New Jersey waters under a statute that provided for seizure of ships operated by nonresidents raking clams in New Jersey waters. The statute provided for proceedings in the county of seizure to sell the ship. After Whitman's ship had been seized and he had been given notice of the pending forfeiture proceedings, his ship was sold. He then sued the sheriff in a New York state court. The action was removed to federal court by the sheriff, who interposed the defense of the previous adjudication. The jury found that the seizure had not occurred in the county in which the New Jersey proceedings took place, and that the ship operators had not been raking clams. The Supreme Court denied the sheriff's demand that the New Jersey proceedings be taken as conclusive on those two issues because they went to the jurisdiction of the New Jersey tribunal.

(5) Does a lack of Article III "case or controversy" jurisdiction render a judgment subject to collateral attack? Swift & Co. v. United States, 276 U.S. 311 (1928) (no). What about lack of diversity of citizenship? McCormick v. Sullivant, 23 U.S. 192 (1825) (no).

(6) What if the party seeking to attack the jurisdiction of the first tribunal appeared in the original proceedings but failed to argue the jurisdictional issue, and the court consequently did not decide it? In Chicot Cty. Drainage Dist. v. Baxter State Bank, 308 U.S. 371 (1940), the opportunity to raise a jurisdictional issue was held sufficient to foreclose it later, even though the issue was *in fact* not raised.

(7) If the defendant objects to personal jurisdiction and fails to persuade the court, then this determination is binding even if some later court believes that there was in fact no personal jurisdiction. Baldwin v. Iowa State Traveling Men's Assn. 283 U.S. 522 (1931). Most jurisdictions offer the device of the *special appearance* or its equivalent, to raise jurisdictional issues. One who appears *generally* is said to have acceded to the court's jurisdiction; one who appears *specially* raises only the jurisdictional issue as a preliminary matter. If she wins on that

issue, the case is dismissed; if she loses, she has the option of arguing the merits or appealing on the basis of the court's jurisdictional decision. There are dangers, of course, in relying too strongly on the jurisdictional appeal—if it fails, one will have waived the defense on the merits. In the federal courts and states with similar rules, special appearances are unnecessary—the equivalent is provided for by the opportunity to make motions based on jurisdictional questions and provisions that jurisdictional issues are not waived by pleading to the merits if jurisdictional objections are also timely raised. *See* Federal Rules of Civil Procedure 12 and 13.

Should a state be required to offer the equivalent of the special appearance? In other words, should a state be allowed to give a litigant the choice between appearing and thereby waiving jurisdictional defenses, or staying away, with the danger that a later court will disagree with the jurisdiction defense and give effect to the default judgment rendered by the first court? In York v. Texas, 137 U.S. 15 (1890), the Supreme Court said Texas could pose that hard choice to litigants who believed that the Texas courts had no personal jurisdiction over them. The availability of collateral attack was said to be enough to satisfy due process. Texas amended its court rules in 1962 to allow special appearances. Texas Rule of Civil Procedure 120a.

B. Substantive Interests of the Enforcing State

Fauntleroy v. Lum
210 U.S. 230 (1908)

Justice HOLMES delivered the opinion of the court.

This is an action upon a Missouri judgment brought in a court of Mississippi. . . . The defendant pleaded that the original cause of action arose in Mississippi out of a gambling transaction in cotton futures; that he declined to pay the loss; that the controversy was submitted to arbitration, the question as to the illegality of the transaction, however, not being included in the submission; that an award was rendered against the defendant; that thereafter, finding the defendant temporarily in Missouri, the plaintiff brought suit there upon the award; that the trial court refused to allow the defendant to show the nature of the transaction, and that by the laws of Mississippi the same was illegal and void, but directed a verdict if the jury should find that the submission and award were made, and remained unpaid; and that a verdict was rendered and the judgment in suit entered upon the same. (The plaintiff in error is an assignee of the judgment, but nothing turns upon that.) The plea was demurred to on constitutional grounds, and the demurrer was overruled subject to exception. Thereupon replications were filed, again setting up the Constitution of the United States (Art. IV, §1), and were demurred to. The Supreme Court of Mississippi held the plea good and the replications bad, and judgment was entered for the defendant. Thereupon the case was brought here.

The main argument urged by the defendant to sustain the judgment below is addressed to the jurisdiction of the Mississippi courts.

The laws of Mississippi make dealing in futures a misdemeanor, and provide that contracts of that sort, made without intent to deliver the commodity or to pay the price, "shall not be enforced by any court." The defendant contends that this language deprives the Mississippi courts of jurisdiction, and that the case is like Anglo-American Provision Co. v. Davis Provision Co. No. 1. There the New York statutes refused to provide a court into which a foreign corporation could come, except upon causes of action arising within the State, etc., and it was held that the State of New York was under no constitutional obligation to give jurisdiction to its Supreme Court against its will. One question is whether that decision is in point.

No doubt it sometimes may be difficult to decide whether certain words in a statute are directed to jurisdiction or to merits, but the distinction between the two is plain. One goes to the power, the other only to the duty of the court. Under the common law it is the duty of a court of general jurisdiction not to enter a judgment upon a parol promise made without consideration; but it has power to do it, and, if it does, the judgment is unimpeachable, unless reversed. Yet a statute could be framed that would make the power, that is, the jurisdiction of the court dependent upon whether there was a consideration or not. Whether a given statute is intended simply to establish a rule of substantive law, and thus to define the duty of the court, or is meant to limit its power, is a question of construction and common sense. When it affects a court of general jurisdiction and deals with a matter upon which that court must pass, we naturally are slow to read ambiguous words, as meaning to leave the judgment open to dispute, or as intended to do more than to fix the rule by which the court should decide.

The case quoted concerned a statute plainly dealing with the authority and jurisdiction of the New York court. The statute now before us seems to us only to lay down a rule of decision. The Mississippi court in which this action was brought is a court of general jurisdiction and would have to decide upon the validity of the bar, if the suit upon the award or upon the original cause of action had been brought there. The words "shall not be enforced by any court" are simply another, possibly less emphatic, way of saying that an action shall not be brought to enforce such contracts. As suggested by the counsel for the plaintiff in error, no one would say that the words of the Mississippi statute of frauds, "An action shall not be brought whereby to charge a defendant," go to the jurisdiction of the court. Of course it could be argued that logically they had that scope, but common sense would revolt. . . . We regard this question as open under the decisions below, and we have expressed our opinion upon it independent of the effect of the judgment, although it might be that, even if jurisdiction of the original cause of action was withdrawn, it remained with regard to a suit upon a judgment based upon an award, whether the judgment or award was conclusive or not. But it might be held that the law as to jurisdiction in one case followed the law in the other, and therefore we proceed at once to the further question, whether the illegality of the original cause of action in Mississippi can be relied upon there as a ground for denying a recovery upon a judgment of another State.

The doctrine laid down by Chief Justice Marshall was "that the judgment of a state court should have the same credit, validity, and effect in every other court in the United States, which it had in the State where it was pronounced, and that whatever pleas would be good to a suit thereon in such State, and none others, could be pleaded in any other court of the United States." There is no doubt that this quotation was supposed to be an accurate statement of the law as late as Christmas v. Russell, where an attempt of Mississippi, by statute, to go behind judgments recovered in other States was declared void, and it was held that such judgments could not be impeached even for fraud. . . .

We assume that the statement of Chief Justice Marshall is correct. It is confirmed by the Act of May 26, 1790, c. 11, 1 Stat. 122 (Rev. Stat. §905), providing that the said records and judicial proceedings "shall have such faith and credit given to them in every court within the United States, as they have by law or usage in the courts of the State from whence the said records are or shall be taken." Whether the award would or would not have been conclusive, and whether the ruling of the Missouri court upon that matter was right or wrong, there can be no question that the judgment was conclusive in Missouri on the validity of the cause of action. A judgment is conclusive as to all the media concludendi, and it needs no authority to show that it cannot be impeached either in or out of the State by showing that it was based upon a mistake of law. Of course a want of jurisdiction over either the person or the subject-matter might be shown. But as the jurisdiction of the Missouri court is not open to dispute the judgment cannot be impeached in Mississippi even if it went upon a misapprehension of the Mississippi law.

We feel no apprehensions that painful or humiliating consequences will follow upon our decision. No court would give judgment for a plaintiff unless it believed that the facts were a cause of action by the law determining their effect. Mistakes will be rare. In this case the Missouri court no doubt supposed that the award was binding by the law of Mississippi. If it was mistaken it made a natural mistake. The validity of its judgment, even in Mississippi, is, as we believe, the result of the Constitution as it always has been understood, and is not a matter to arouse the susceptibilities of the States, all of which are equally concerned in the question and equally on both sides.

Judgment reversed.

Justice WHITE, with whom concurred Justice HARLAN, Justice McKENNA and Justice DAY, dissenting.

. . . This court now reverses on the ground that the due faith and credit clause obliged the courts of Mississippi, in consequence of the action of the Missouri court, to give efficacy to transactions in Mississippi which were criminal, and which were against the public policy of that State. Although not wishing in the slightest degree to weaken the operation of the due faith and credit clause as interpreted and applied from the beginning, it to me seems that this ruling so enlarges that clause as to cause it to obliterate all state lines, since the effect will be to endow each State with authority to overthrow the public policy and criminal statutes of the others, thereby depriving all of their lawful authority. Moreover, the ruling now made, in my opinion, is contrary to the conceptions which caused the due faith and credit clause to be placed in the Constitution, and substantially overrules the previous decisions of this court interpreting that clause. My purpose is to briefly state the reasons which lead me to these conclusions. . . .

When the Constitution was adopted the principles of comity by which the decrees of the courts of one State were entitled to be enforced in another were generally known, but the enforcement of those principles by the several States had no absolute sanction, since they rested but in comity. Now it cannot be denied that under the rules of comity recognized at the time of the adoption of the Constitution, and which at this time universally prevail, no sovereignty was or is under the slightest moral obligation to give effect to a judgment of a court of another sovereignty, when to do so would compel the State in which the judgment was sought to be executed to enforce an illegal and prohibited contract, when both the contract and all the acts done in connection with its performance had taken place in the latter State. This seems to me conclusive of this case, since both in treatises of authoritative writers (Story, *Conflict of Law* §609), and by repeated adjudications of this court it has been settled that the purpose of the due faith and credit clause was not to confer any new power, but simply to make obligatory that duty which, when the Constitution was adopted rested, as has been said, in comity alone. . . .

No special reference has been made by me to the arbitration, because that is assumed by me to be negligible. If the cause of action was open for inquiry for the purpose of deciding whether the Missouri court had jurisdiction to render a judgment entitled to be enforced in another State, the arbitration is of no consequence. The violation of law in Mississippi could not be cured by seeking to arbitrate in that State in order to fix the sum of the fruits of the illegal acts. The ancient maxims that something cannot be made out of nothing, and that which is void for reasons of public policy cannot be made valid by confirmation or acquiescence, seem to my mind decisive.

I therefore dissent.

Questions and Comments

(1) Would there be any harm in limiting full faith and credit to judgments that themselves were not based on unconstitutional denial of full faith and credit to the laws of another state? That is what Missouri did, isn't it, when it failed to apply Mississippi law on the illegality of these contracts, with no apparent connection between the case and Missouri? How about refusing full faith and credit whenever both of two factors are present: (a) denial of full faith and credit in arriving at the first judgment, and (b) violation of the criminal laws of the interested jurisdiction? Would that disrupt any rational scheme of federalism?

(2) Section 103 of the Restatement Second says:

> A judgment rendered in one State of the United States need not be recognized or enforced in a sister State if such recognition or enforcement is not required by the national policy of full faith and credit because it would involve an improper interference with important interests of the sister State.

The comment warns that the section has "an extremely narrow scope of application." It concedes, almost as an afterthought, that "[t]he Supreme Court of the United States has the final voice in determining what exceptions there are to full faith and credit, and the nature of these exceptions." The only case cited in the comment that failed to recognize a sister-state judgment is Williams v. North Carolina, 325 U.S. 226 (1945). *Williams* concluded that a state could reexamine the supposed domicile of one party to ex parte divorce proceedings to see if the rendering court actually had jurisdiction (which is based upon domicile in divorce proceedings). Does that sound like an application of the principle set out above? The reporter's note cites a few other cases offering borderline support, including several concurring or dissenting opinions. Professor Ehrenzweig, in *The Second Conflicts Restatement: A Last Appeal for Its Withdrawal*, 113 U. Pa. L. Rev. 1230, 1240 (1965), stated that there was "no authority whatsoever" for §103.

(3) The *penal exception*: In Huntington v. Attrill, 146 U.S. 657 (1892), the Supreme Court stated that one state need not enforce the "penal" claims of another, even if they were embodied in a judgment. Recall the discussion of that case in Paper Products Co. v. Doggrell, page 157 *supra*. Whether a law is penal "depends upon the question whether its purpose is to punish an offense against the public justice of the state, or to afford a private remedy to a person injured by a wrongful act." 146 U.S. at 657. *Compare* Heath v. Alabama, 474 U.S. 82 (1985), holding that the double jeopardy clause does not preclude a second prosecution in a second state. Does *Heath* suggest that the second state need not respect the criminal judgments of the first?

(4) Can a court order be penal? In Settle v. Settle, 550 P.2d 445 (Or. Ct. App. 1976), the court, in dictum, indicated that a foreign decree would be considered punitive "only if it is clear that the court awarded or changed [child] custody because it was insulted by one parent disregarding its authority." 550 P.2d at 447. The mother had argued that an Indiana court had taken custody from her because she had left the state with the children, contrary to court order. The Oregon court found, however, that the basis for the Indiana action was her lack of fitness.

In Holbein v. Rigot, 245 So. 2d 57 (Fla. 1971), the Florida Supreme Court ruled that the punitive-damages portion of a Texas judgment was not exempt from full faith and credit enforcement in Florida on the grounds that it was a penal claim. "[O]ur holding is that plaintiff's Texas suit insofar as it sought to recover punitive damages was based on common law liability arising from fraud to redress a private wrong inflicted on plaintiffs and did not purport to redress a public wrong predicated on a statute that is penal in the international sense which may not be enforced in the courts of other states." *Id*. at 61. "*[M]ay* not be enforced"? Is it more important that a private wrong is being redressed, or that no statute is involved? And isn't one purpose of punitive damages to discourage future activity of the same kind directed against others? Isn't that an offense against the public justice?

(5) Milwaukee Cty. v. M.E. White Co., 296 U.S. 268 (1935), laid to rest the old rule that one state does not have to enforce the tax judgments of another state. In light of that case, and *International Shoe*, might it make sense to deny enforcement to another state's tax *law*, but honor its judgment, so that the dirty work of correctly interpreting state tax laws would fall on local courts?

Thomas v. Washington Gas Light Co.

448 U.S. 261 (1980)

Justice STEVENS announced the judgment of the Court and delivered an opinion in which Justice BRENNAN, Justice STEWART, and Justice BLACKMUN join.

Petitioner received an award of disability benefits under the Virginia Workmen's Compensation Act. The question presented is whether the obligation of the District of Columbia to give full faith and credit to that award bars a supplemental award under the District's Workmen's Compensation Act.

[Petitioner, a District of Columbia resident, was hired by respondent in the District to perform work primarily in the District but also in Virginia and Maryland. In January 1971, he sustained a back injury while at work in Arlington, Virginia. Several weeks later the Virginia Industrial Commission approved the parties' "Industrial Commission of Virginia Memorandum of Agreement as to Payment of Compensation" providing for benefits of $62 per week. The Commission issued an award directing that payments continue "during incapacity," subject to various contingencies and changes set forth in the Virginia statute.]

In 1974, petitioner notified the Department of Labor of his intention to seek compensation under the District of Columbia Act. Respondent opposed the claim primarily on the ground that since, as a matter of Virginia law, the Virginia award excluded any other recovery "at common law or otherwise" on account of the injury in Virginia, the District of Columbia's obligation to give that award full faith and credit precluded a second, supplemental award in the District.

The administrative law judge agreed with respondent that the Virginia award must be given res judicata effect in the District to the extent that it was res judicata in Virginia. He held, however, that the Virginia award, by its terms, did not preclude a further award of compensation in Virginia. Moreover, he construed the statutory prohibition against additional recovery "at common law or otherwise" as merely covering "common law and other remedies under Virginia law." After the taking of medical evidence, petitioner was awarded permanent total disability benefits payable from the date of his injury with a credit for the amounts previously paid under the Virginia award.

The Benefits Review Board upheld the award. Its order, however, was reversed by the United States Court of Appeals for the Fourth Circuit, which squarely held that a "second and separate proceeding in another jurisdiction upon the same injury after a prior recovery in another State [is] precluded by the Full Faith and Credit Clause." We granted certiorari and now reverse.

I

Respondent contends that the District of Columbia was without power to award petitioner additional compensation because of the Full Faith and Credit Clause of the Constitution or, more precisely, because of the federal statute implementing that Clause. An analysis of this contention must begin with two decisions from the 1940's that are almost directly on point: Magnolia Petroleum Co. v. Hunt, 320 U.S. 430, and Industrial Commission of Wisconsin v. McCartin, 330 U.S. 622.

In *Magnolia*, a case relied on heavily both by respondent and the Court of Appeals, the employee hired a Louisiana worker in Louisiana. The employee was later injured during the course of his employment in Texas. A tenuous majority held that Louisiana was not permitted to award the injured worker supplementary compensation under the Louisiana Act after he had already obtained a recovery from the Texas Industrial Accident Board: "Respondent was free to pursue his remedy in either state but, having chosen to seek it in Texas, where the award was res judicata, the full faith and credit clause precludes him from again seeking a remedy in Louisiana upon the same grounds."

Little more than three years later, the Court severely curtailed the impact of *Magnolia*. In *McCartin*, the employer and the worker both resided in Illinois and entered into an employment contract there for work to be performed in Wisconsin. The employee was injured in the course of that employment. He initially filed a claim with the Industrial Commission of Wisconsin. Prior to this Court's decision in *Magnolia*, the Wisconsin Commission informed him that under Wisconsin law, he could proceed under the Illinois Workmen's Compensation Act, and then claim compensation under the Wisconsin Act, with credit to be given for any payments made under the Illinois Act. Thereafter, the employer and the employee executed a contract for payment of a specific sum in full settlement of the employee's right under Illinois law. The contract expressly provided, however, that it would "not affect any rights that applicant may have under the Workmen's Compensation Act of the State of Wisconsin." The employee then obtained a supplemental award from the Wisconsin Industrial Commission; but the Wisconsin state courts vacated it under felt compulsion of the intervening decision in *Magnolia*.

This Court reversed, holding without dissent that *Magnolia* was not controlling. Although the Court could have relied exclusively on the contract provision reserving the employee's rights under Wisconsin law to distinguish the case from *Magnolia*, Justice Murphy's opinion provided a significantly different ground for the Court's holding when it said

> the reservation spells out what we believe to be implicit in [the Illinois Workmen's Compensation] Act—namely, that an award of the type here involved does not foreclose an additional award under the laws of another state. And in the setting of this case, that fact is of decisive significance.

Earlier in the opinion, the Court had stated that "[o]nly some unmistakable language by a state legislature or judiciary would warrant our accepting . . . a construction" that a workmen's compensation statute "is designed to preclude any recovery by proceedings brought in another state." The Illinois statute, which the Court held not to contain the "unmistakable language" required to preclude a supplemental award in Wisconsin, broadly provided:

> No common law or statutory right to recover damages for injury or death sustained by any employee while engaged in the line of his duty as such employee, other than the compensation herein provided, shall be available to any employee who is covered by the provisions of this act. . . .

The Virginia Workmen's Compensation Act's exclusive remedy provision is not exactly the same as Illinois'; but it contains no "unmistakable language" directed at precluding a supplemental compensation award in another State that was not also in the Illinois Act. Consequently, *McCartin* by its terms, rather than the earlier *Magnolia* decision, is controlling as between the two precedents. Nevertheless, the fact that we find ourselves comparing the language of two state statutes, neither of which has been construed by the highest court of either State, in an attempt to resolve an issue arising under the Full Faith and Credit Clause makes us pause to inquire whether there is a fundamental flaw in our analysis of this federal question.

II

We cannot fail to observe that, in the Court's haste to retreat from *Magnolia*, it fashioned a rule that clashes with normally accepted full faith and credit principles. It has long been the law that "the judgment of a state court should have the same credit, validity, and effect, in every other court in the United States, which it had in the state where it was pronounced." Hampton v. McConnel, 3 Wheat. 234, 235 (Marshall, C.J.). This rule, if not compelled by the Full Faith and Credit Clause itself, is surely required by 28 U.S.C. §1738, which provides that the

> Acts, records and judicial proceedings . . . [of any State] shall have the same full faith and credit in every court within the United States . . . as they have by law or usage in the courts of [the] State . . . from which they are taken.

Thus, in effect, by virtue of the full faith and credit obligations of the several States, a State is permitted to determine the extraterritorial effect of its judgment; but it may only do so indirectly, by prescribing the effect of its judgments within the State.

The *McCartin* rule, however, focusing as it does on the extraterritorial intent of the rendering State, is fundamentally different. It authorizes a State, by drafting or construing its legislation in "unmistakable language," directly to determine the extraterritorial effect of its workmen's compensation awards. An authorization to a state legislature of this character is inconsistent with the rule established in Pacific Employers Ins. Co. v. Industrial Accident Commission [discussed at page 288 *supra*]: "This Court must determine for itself how far the full faith and credit clause compels the qualification or denial of rights asserted under the laws of one state, that of the forum, by the statute of another state." It follows inescapably that the *McCartin* "unmistakable language" rule represents an unwarranted delegation to the States of this Court's responsibility for the final arbitration of full faith and credit questions. The Full Faith and Credit Clause "is one of the provisions incorporated into the Constitution by its framers for the purpose of transforming an aggregation of independent, sovereign States into a nation." Sherrer v. Sherrer, 334 U.S. 343, 355. To vest the power of determining the extraterritorial effect of a State's own laws and judgments in the State itself risks the very kind of parochial entrenchment on the interests of other States that it was the purpose of the Full Faith and Credit Clause and other provisions of Art. IV of the Constitution to prevent. *See* Nevada v. Hall [*supra* page 335].

Thus, a re-examination of *McCartin*'s unmistakable language test reinforces our tentative conclusion that it does not provide an acceptable basis on which to distinguish *Magnolia*. But if we reject that test, we must decide whether to overrule either *Magnolia* or *McCartin*. In making this kind of decision, we must take into account both the practical values served by the doctrine of stare decisis and the principles that inform the Full Faith and Credit Clause.

III

The doctrine of stare decisis imposes a severe burden on the litigant who asks us to disavow one of our precedents. For that doctrine not only plays an important role in orderly adjudication; it also serves the broader societal interests in even-handed, consistent, and predictable application of legal rules. When rights have been created or modified in reliance on established rules of law, the arguments against their change have special force.[18]

It is therefore appropriate to begin the inquiry by considering whether a rule that permits, or a rule that forecloses, successive workmen's compensation awards is more consistent with settled practice. The answer to this question is pellucidly clear.

It should first be noted that *Magnolia*, by only the slimmest majority, effected a dramatic change in the law that had previously prevailed throughout the United States. Of greater importance is the fact that as a practical matter the "unmistakable language" rule of construction announced in *McCartin* left only the narrowest area in which *Magnolia* could have any further precedential value. For the exclusivity language in the Illinois Act construed in *McCartin* was typical of most state workmen's compensation laws. Consequently, it was immediately recognized that *Magnolia* no longer had any significant practical impact. Moreover, since a state legislature seldom focuses on the extraterritorial effect of its enactments, and since a state court has even less occasion to consider whether an award under its State's law is intended to preclude a supplemental award under another State's workmen's compensation act, the probability that any State would thereafter announce a new rule against supplemental awards in other States was extremely remote. As a matter of fact, subsequent cases in the state courts have overwhelmingly followed *McCartin* and permitted successive state workmen's compensation awards. Thus, all that really remained of *Magnolia* after *McCartin* was a largely theoretical difference between what the Court described as "unmistakable language" and the broad language of the exclusive remedy provision in the Illinois Workmen's Compensation Act involved in *McCartin*.

This history indicates that the principal values underlying the doctrine of stare decisis would not be served either by attempting to revive *Magnolia* or by attempting to preserve the uneasy coexistence of *Magnolia* and *McCartin*. The latter attempt could only breed uncertainty and unpredictability, since the application of the "unmistakable language" rule of *McCartin* necessarily depends on a determination by one state tribunal of the effect to be given to statutory language

---

18. The doctrine of stare decisis has a more limited application when the precedent rests on constitutional grounds. . . .

The full faith and credit area presents special problems because the Constitution expressly delegates to Congress the authority "by general Laws [to] prescribe the Manner in which [the States'] Acts, Records and Proceedings shall be proved, *and the effect thereof.*" (Emphasis added.) Yet it is quite clear that Congress' power in this area is not exclusive, for this Court has given effect to the Clause beyond that required by implementing legislation. *See* Bradford Electric Co. v. Clapper. [T]he *Clapper* case rested on the constitutional Clause alone. *Carroll*, which for all intents and purposes buried whatever was left of *Clapper* after *Pacific Employers* . . . cast no doubt on *Clapper*'s reliance on the Full Faith and Credit Clause itself.

enacted by the legislature of a different State. And the former would represent a rather dramatic change that surely would not promote stability in the law. Moreover, since *Magnolia* has been so rarely followed, there appears to be little danger that there has been any significant reliance on its rule. We conclude that a fresh examination of the full faith and credit issue is therefore entirely appropriate.

IV

Three different state interests are affected by the potential conflict between Virginia and the District of Columbia. Virginia has a valid interest in placing a limit on the potential liability of companies that transact business within its borders. Both jurisdictions have a valid interest in the welfare of the injured employee— Virginia because the injury occurred within that State, and the District because the injured party was employed and resided there. And finally, Virginia has an interest in having the integrity of its formal determinations of contested issues respected by other sovereigns.

The conflict between the first two interests was resolved in Alaska Packers Association v. Industrial Accident Commission [discussed at page 288 *supra*], and a series of later cases. [The Court then discussed *Alaska Packers, Pacific Employers*, *supra* page 288, and *Nevada v. Hall, supra* page 335, which establish the principle that states need not subordinate their interests to those of other states when choosing governing laws.]

It is thus perfectly clear that petitioner could have sought a compensation award in the first instance either in Virginia, the State in which the injury occurred, *Pacific Employers, supra*, or in the District of Columbia, where petitioner resided, his employer was principally located and the employment relation was formed, *Alaska Packers, supra*. And as those cases underscore, compensation could have been sought under either compensation scheme even if one statute or the other purported to confer an exclusive remedy on petitioner. Thus, for all practical purposes, respondent and its insurer would have had to measure their potential liability exposure by the more generous of the two workmen's compensation schemes in any event. It follows that a State's interest in limiting the potential liability of businesses within the State is not of controlling importance.

It is also manifest that the interest in providing adequate compensation to the injured worker would be fully served by the allowance of successive awards. In this respect the two jurisdictions share a common interest and there is no danger of significant conflict.

The ultimate issue, therefore, is whether Virginia's interest in the integrity of its tribunal's determinations forecloses a second proceeding to obtain a supplemental award in the District of Columbia. We return to the Court's prior resolution of this question in *Magnolia*.

The majority opinion in *Magnolia* took the position that the case called for a straightforward application of full faith and credit law: the worker's injury gave rise to a cause of action; relief was granted by the Texas Industrial Accident Board; that award precluded any further relief in Texas; and further relief was therefore precluded elsewhere as well. The majority relied heavily on Chicago, R.I. & P.R. Co. v. Schendel, 270 U.S. 611, for the propositions that a workmen's compensation award stands on the same footing as a court judgment, and that a compensation award under one State's law is a bar to a second award under another State's law.

But *Schendel* did not compel the result in *Magnolia*. In *Schendel*, the Court held that an Iowa state compensation award, which was grounded in a contested factual finding that the deceased railroad employee was engaged in intrastate commerce, precluded a subsequent claim under the Federal Employers' Liability Act brought in the Minnesota state courts, which would have required a finding that the employee was engaged in interstate commerce. *Schendel* therefore involved the unexceptionable full faith and credit principle that resolutions of factual matters underlying a judgment must be given the same res judicata effect in the forum State as they have in the rendering State. *See* Durfee v. Duke [*supra* page 504]. The Minnesota courts could not have granted relief under the FELA and also respected the factual finding made in Iowa.

In contrast, neither *Magnolia* nor this case concerns a second State's contrary resolution of a factual matter determined in the first State's proceedings. Unlike the situation in *Schendel*, which involved two mutually exclusive remedies, compensation could be obtained under either Virginia's or the District's workmen's compensation statutes on the basis of the same set of facts. A supplemental award gives full effect to the facts determined by the first award and also allows full credit for payments pursuant to the earlier award. There is neither inconsistency nor double recovery.

We are also persuaded that *Magnolia*'s reliance on *Schendel* for the proposition that workmen's compensation awards stand on the same footing as court judgments was unwarranted. To be sure, as we held in *Schendel*, the factfindings of state administrative tribunals are entitled to the same res judicata effect in the second State as findings by a court. But the critical differences between a court of general jurisdiction and an administrative agency with limited statutory authority forecloses the conclusion that constitutional rules applicable to court judgments are necessarily applicable to workmen's compensation awards.

A final judgment entered by a court of general jurisdiction normally establishes not only the measure of the plaintiff's rights but also limits of the defendant's liability. A traditional application of res judicata principles enables either party to claim the benefit of the judgment insofar as it resolved issues the court has jurisdiction to decide. Although a Virginia court is free to recognize the perhaps paramount interests of another State by choosing to apply that State's law in a particular case, the Industrial Commission of Virginia does not have that power. Its jurisdiction is limited to questions arising under the Virginia Workmen's Compensation Act. Typically, a workmen's compensation tribunal may only apply its own State's law. In this case, the Virginia Commission could and did establish the full measure of petitioner's rights under Virginia law, but it neither could nor purported to determine his rights under the law of the District of Columbia. Full faith and credit must be given to the determination that the Virginia Commission had the authority to make; but by a parity of reasoning, full faith and credit need not be given to determinations that it had no power to make. Since it was not requested, and had no authority, to pass on petitioner's rights under District of Columbia law, there can be no constitutional objection to a fresh adjudication of those rights.

It is true, of course, that after Virginia entered its award, that State had an interest in preserving the integrity of what it had done. And it is squarely within the purpose of the Full Faith and Credit Clause, as explained in *Pacific Employers*, "to preserve rights acquired or confirmed under the public acts" of Virginia by requiring other States to recognize their validity. Thus, Virginia had an interest in having respondent pay petitioner the amounts specified in its award. Allowing a supplementary recovery in the District does not conflict with that interest.

As we have already noted, Virginia also has a separate interest in placing a ceiling on the potential liability of companies that transact business within the State. But past cases have established that that interest is not strong enough to prevent other States with overlapping jurisdiction over particular injuries from giving effect to their more generous compensation policies when the employee selects the most favorable forum in the first instance. Thus, the only situations in which the *Magnolia* rule would tend to serve that interest are those in which an injured workman has either been constrained by circumstances to seek relief in the less generous forum or has simply made an ill-advised choice of his first forum.

But in neither of those cases is there any reason to give extra weight to the first State's interest in placing a ceiling on the employer's liability than it otherwise would have had. For neither the first nor the second State has any overriding interest in requiring an injured employee to proceed with special caution when first asserting his claim. Compensation proceedings are often initiated informally, without the advice of counsel, and without special attention to the choice of the most appropriate forum. Often the worker is still hospitalized when benefits are sought as was true in this case. And indeed, it is not always the injured worker who institutes the claim. This informality is consistent with the interests of both States. A rule forbidding supplemental recoveries under more favorable workmen's compensation schemes would require a far more formal and careful choice on the part of the injured worker than may be possible or desirable when immediate commencement of benefits may be essential.

Thus, whether or not the worker has sought an award from the less generous jurisdiction in the first instance, the vindication of that State's interest in placing a ceiling on employers' liability would inevitably impinge upon the substantial interests of the second jurisdiction in the welfare and subsistence of disabled workers—interests that a court of general jurisdiction might consider, but which must be ignored by the Virginia Industrial Commission. The reasons why the statutory policy of exclusivity of the other jurisdictions involved in *Alaska Packers* and *Pacific Employers, supra*, could not defeat California's implementation of its own compensation policies therefore continue to apply even after the entry of a workmen's compensation award.

Of course, it is for each State to formulate its own policy whether to grant supplemental awards according to its perception of its own interests. We simply conclude that the substantial interests of the second State in these circumstances should not be overridden by another State through an unnecessarily aggressive application of the Full Faith and Credit Clause, as was implicitly recognized at the time of *McCartin*.

We therefore would hold that a State has no legitimate interest within the context of our federal system in preventing another State from granting a supplemental compensation award when that second State would have had the power to apply its workmen's compensation law in the first instance. The Full Faith and Credit Clause should not be construed to preclude successive workmen's compensation awards. Accordingly, Magnolia Petroleum Co. v. Hunt should be overruled.

The judgment of the Court of Appeals is reversed.

Justice WHITE, with whom THE CHIEF JUSTICE and Justice POWELL join, concurring in the judgment.

I agree that the judgment of the Court of Appeals should be reversed, but I am unable to join in the reasoning by which the plurality reaches that result. Although the plurality argues strenuously that the rule of today's decision is limited to awards by state workmen's compensation boards, it seems to me that the underlying rationale goes much further. If the employer had exercised its statutory right of appeal to the Supreme Court of Virginia and that Court upheld the award, I presume that the plurality's rationale would nevertheless permit a subsequent award in the District of Columbia. Otherwise, employers interested in cutting off the possibility of a subsequent award in another jurisdiction need only seek judicial review of the award in the first forum. But if such a judicial decision is not preclusive in the second forum, then it appears that the plurality's rationale is not limited in its effect to judgments of administrative tribunals.

The plurality contends that unlike courts of general jurisdiction, workmen's compensation tribunals generally have no power to apply the law of another State and thus cannot determine the rights of the parties thereunder. Yet I see no reason why a judgment should not be entitled to full res judicata effect under the Full Faith and Credit Clause merely because the rendering tribunal was obligated to apply the law of the forum—provided, of course, as was certainly the case here, that the forum could constitutionally apply its law. The plurality's analysis seems to grant state legislatures the power to delimit the scope of a cause of action for federal full faith and credit purposes merely by enacting choice of law rules binding on the State's workmen's compensation tribunals. The plurality criticizes the *McCartin* case for vesting in the State the power to determine the extraterritorial effect of its own laws and judgments; yet it seems that its opinion is subject to the same objection. In any event, I am not convinced that Virginia, by instructing its industrial commission to apply Virginia law, could be said to have intended that the cause of action which merges in the Virginia judgment would not include claims under the laws of other States which arise out of precisely the same operative facts.

As a matter of logic, the plurality's analysis would seemingly apply to many everyday tort actions. I see no difference for full faith and credit purposes between a statute which lays down a forum-favoring choice of law rule and a common-law doctrine stating the same principle. Hence when a court, having power in the abstract to apply the law of another State, determines by application of the forum's choice of law rules to apply the substantive law of the forum, I would think that under the plurality's analysis the judgment would not determine rights arising under the law of some other State. Suppose, for example, that in a wrongful death action the court enters judgment on liability against the defendant, and determines to apply the law of the forum which sets a limit on the recovery allowed. The plurality's analysis would seem to permit the plaintiff to obtain a subsequent judgment in a second forum for damages exceeding the first forum's liability limit.

The plurality does say that factual determinations by a workmen's compensation board will be entitled to collateral estoppel effect in a second forum. While this rule does, to an extent, circumscribe the broadest possible implications of the plurality's reasoning, there would remain many cases, such as the wrongful death example discussed above, in which the second forum could provide additional recovery as a matter of substantive law while remaining true to the first forum's factual determinations. Moreover, the dispositive issues in tort actions are frequently mixed questions of law and fact as to which the second forum might apply its own rule of decision without obvious violation of the principles articulated by four Members of the Court. Actions by the defendant which satisfy the relevant standard of care in the first forum might nevertheless be considered "negligent" under the law of the second forum.

Hence the plurality's rationale would portend a wide-ranging reassessment of the principles of full faith and credit in many areas. Such a reassessment is not necessarily undesirable if the results are likely to be healthy for the judicial system and consistent with the underlying purposes of the Full Faith and Credit Clause. But at least without the benefit of briefs and arguments directed to the issue, I cannot conclude that the rule advocated by the plurality would have had such a beneficial impact.

One purpose of the Full Faith and Credit Clause is to bring an end to litigation. As the Court noted in Riley v. New York Trust Co., 315 U.S. 343, 348-349 (1941): "Were it not for this full faith and credit provision, so far as the Constitution controls the matter, adversaries could wage again their legal battles whenever they meet in other jurisdictions. Each state could control its own courts but itself could not project the effect of its decisions beyond its own boundaries." The plurality's opinion is at odds with this principle of finality. Plaintiffs dissatisfied with a judgment would have every incentive to seek additional recovery elsewhere, so long as the first forum applied its own law and there was a colorable argument that as a matter of law the second forum would permit a greater recovery. It seems to me grossly unfair that the plaintiff, having the initial choice of the forum, should be given the additional advantage of a second adjudication should his choice prove disappointing. Defendants, on the other hand, would no longer be assured that the judgment of the first forum is conclusive as to their obligations, and would face the prospect of burdensome and multiple litigation based on the same operative facts. Such litigation would also impose added strain on an already overworked judicial system.

Perhaps the major purpose of the Full Faith and Credit Clause is to act as a nationally unifying force. Sherrer v. Sherrer, 334 U.S. 343, 355 (1948). The plurality's rationale would substantially undercut that function. When a former judgment is set up as a defense under the Full Faith and Credit Clause, the court would be obliged to balance the various state interests involved. But the State of the second forum is not a neutral party to this balance. There seems to be a substantial danger—not presented by the firmer rule of res judicata—that the court in evaluating a full faith and credit defense would give controlling weight to its own parochial interests in concluding that the judgment of the first forum is not res judicata in the subsequent suit.

I would not overrule either *Magnolia* or *McCartin*. To my mind, Chief Justice Stone's opinion in *Magnolia* states the sounder doctrine; as noted. I do not see any overriding differences between workmen's compensation awards and court judgments that justify different treatment for the two. However, *McCartin* has been on the books for over 30 years and has been widely interpreted by state and federal courts as substantially limiting *Magnolia*. Unlike the plurality's opinion, *McCartin* is not subject to the objection that its principles are applicable outside the workmen's compensation area. Although I find *McCartin* to rest on questionable foundations, I am not now prepared to overrule it. And I agree with the plurality that *McCartin*, rather than *Magnolia*, is controlling as between the two precedents since the Virginia Workmen's Compensation Act lacks the "unmistakable language" which *McCartin* requires if a workmen's compensation award is to preclude a subsequent award in another State. I therefore concur in the judgment.

Justice REHNQUIST, with whom Justice MARSHALL joins, dissenting.

This is clearly a case where the whole is less than the sum of its parts. In choosing between two admittedly inconsistent precedents, [*Magnolia* and *McCartin*], six of us agree that . . . *McCartin*, is analytically indefensible. The remaining three Members of the Court concede that it "rest[s] on questionable foundations." Nevertheless, when the smoke clears, it is *Magnolia* rather than *McCartin* that the plurality suggests should be overruled. Because I believe that *Magnolia* was correctly decided, and because I fear that the rule proposed by the plurality is both ill-considered and ill-defined, I dissent. . . .

One might support that, having destroyed *McCartin*'s ratio decidendi, the plurality would return to the eminently defensible position adopted in *Magnolia*. But such is not the case. The plurality instead raises the banner of "stare decisis" and sets out in search of a new rationale to support the result reached in *McCartin*, significantly failing to even attempt to do the same thing for *Magnolia*.

If such post hoc rationalization seems a bit odd, the theory ultimately chosen by the plurality is even odder. It would seem that, contrary to the assumption of this Court for at least the past 40 years, a judgment awarding workmen's compensation benefits is no longer entitled to full faith and credit unless, and only to the extent that, such a judgment resolves a disputed issue of fact. I believe that the plurality's justification for such a theory, which apparently first surfaced in a cluster of articles written in the wake of *Magnolia*, does not withstand close scrutiny.

The plurality identified three different "state interests" at stake in the present case: Virginia's interest in placing a limit on the potential liability of companies doing business in that State, Virginia's interest in the "integrity of its formal determinations of contested issues," and a shared interest of Virginia and the District of Columbia in the welfare of the injured employee. The plurality then undertakes to balance these interests and concludes that none of Virginia's concerns outweighs the concern of the District of Columbia for the welfare of petitioner.

Whenever this Court, or any court, attempts to balance competing interests it risks undervaluing or even overlooking important concerns. I believe that the plurality's analysis incorporates both errors. First, it asserts that Virginia's interest in limiting the liability of businesses operating within its borders can never outweigh the District of Columbia's interest in protecting its residents. In support of this proposition it cites [*Alaska Packers* and *Pacific Employers*]. Both of those cases, however, involved the degree of faith and credit to be afforded *statutes* of one State by the courts of another State. The present case involves an enforceable *judgment* entered by Virginia after adjudicatory proceedings. In *Magnolia* Mr. Chief Justice Stone, who authored *both Alaska Packers and Pacific Employers*, distinguished those two decisions for precisely this reason, chastising the lower court in that case for overlooking "the distinction, long recognized and applied by this Court . . . between the full faith and credit required to be given to judgments and that to which local common and statutory law is entitled under the Constitution and laws of the United States." This distinction, which has also been overlooked by the plurality here, makes perfect sense, since Virginia surely has a stronger interest in limiting an employer's liability to a fixed amount when that employer has already been haled before a Virginia tribunal and adjudged liable than when the employer simply claims the benefit of a Virginia statute in a proceeding brought in another State.

In a similar vein, the plurality completely ignores any interest that Virginia might assert in the finality of its adjudications. While workmen's compensation awards may be "nonfinal" in the sense that they are subject to continuing supervision and modification, Virginia nevertheless has a cognizable interest in requiring persons who avail themselves of its statutory remedy to eschew other alternative remedies that might be available to them. Otherwise, as apparently is the result here, Virginia's efforts and expense on an applicant's behalf are wasted when that applicant obtains a duplicative remedy in another State.

At base, the plurality's balancing analysis is incorrect because it recognizes no significant difference between the events that transpired in this case and those that *would* have transpired had petitioner initially sought his remedy in the District of Columbia. But there are differences. The Commonwealth of Virginia has expended its resources, at petitioner's behest, to provide petitioner with a remedy for his injury and a resolution of his "dispute" with his employer. That employer similarly has expended its resources, again at petitioner's behest, in complying with the judgment entered by Virginia. These efforts, and the corresponding interests in seeing that those efforts are not wasted, lie at the very heart of the divergent constitutional treatment of judgments and statutes. In this case, of course, Virginia and respondent expended very few resources in the administrative process. But that observation lends no assistance to the plurality, which would flatly hold that Virginia has absolutely no power to guarantee that a workmen's compensation award will be treated as a final judgment by other States.

In further support of its novel rule, the plurality attempts to distinguish the judgment entered in this case from one entered by a "court of general jurisdiction." Specifically, the plurality points out that the Industrial Commission of Virginia, unlike a state court of general jurisdiction, was limited by statute to consideration of Virginia law. According to the plurality, because the Commission "was not requested, and had no authority, to pass on petitioner's rights under District of Columbia law, there can be no constitutional objection to a fresh adjudication of those rights."

This argument might have some force if petitioner had somehow had Virginia law thrust upon him against his will. In this case, however, petitioner was free to choose the applicable law simply by choosing the forum in which he filed his initial claim. Unless the District of Columbia has an interest in forcing its residents to accept its law regardless of their wishes, I fail to see how the Virginia Commission's inability to look to District of Columbia law impinged upon that latter jurisdiction's interests. I thus fail to see why petitioner's election, as consummated in his Virginia award, should not be given the same full faith and credit as would be afforded a judgment entered by a court of general jurisdiction.

I suspect that my Brethren's insistence on ratifying *McCartin*'s result despite condemnation of its rationale is grounded in no small part upon their concern that injured workers are often coerced or maneuvered into filing their claims in jurisdictions amenable to their employers. There is, however, absolutely no evidence of such overreaching in the present case. Indeed, had there been "fraud, imposition, [or] mistake" in the filing of petitioner's claim, he would have been permitted, upon timely motion, to vacate the award. *See* Harris v. Diamond Construction Co., 184 Va. 711, 720 (1946). In this regard, the award received by petitioner is treated no differently than any other judicial award, nor should it be. . . .

I fear that the plurality, in its zeal to remedy a perceived imbalance in bargaining power, would badly distort an important constitutional tenet. Its "interest analysis," once removed from the statutory choice-of-law context considered by the Court in *Alaska Packers* and *Pacific Employers*, knows no metes or bounds. Given the modern proliferation of quasi-judicial methods for resolving disputes and of various tribunals of limited jurisdiction, such a rule could only lead to confusion. I find such uncertainty unacceptable, and prefer the rule originally announced in [*Magnolia*], a rule whose analytical validity is, even yet, unchallenged.

The Full Faith and Credit Clause did not allot to this Court the task of "balancing" interests where the "public Acts, Records, and judicial Proceedings" of a State were involved. It simply directed that they be given the "Full Faith and Credit" that the Court today denies to those of Virginia. I would affirm the judgment of the court below.

Questions and Comments

(1) Does the plurality answer satisfactorily *any* of the objections expressed in the concurring and dissenting opinions? In particular, isn't Justice Rehnquist right that the majority's rationale would operate at any time, in any kind of case, when a second forum would offer more (or different) damages on the same facts?

(2) What if State *A* offers a lump sum for the loss of a limb, with no compensation for pain and suffering and no punitive damages; State *B* gives no lump-sum compensation, instead requires proof of lost potential income, but does grant compensation for pain and suffering (but no punitive damages); and State *C* offers compensation for actual losses plus punitive damages? Is the injured worker with appropriate contacts with the three states entitled to the lump sum in State *A*, compensation for pain and suffering in State *B*, and punitive damages in State *C*? In other words, isn't it likely that the decision to grant one kind of damages is made at least in part because of the decision not to grant another? Wouldn't the total award collected above violate the policy of *each* state?

(3) What is the connection between *Thomas* and *Fauntleroy*? Doesn't the *Thomas* plurality allow the enforcing state to override the rendering state's finality interests with its own substantive interests? Isn't that contrary to *Fauntleroy*— or was there more "inconsistency" between the first and second resolutions in *Fauntleroy* than in *Thomas*?

(4) Why was the plurality so concerned that the *Magnolia/McCartin* rule rested interpretation of the federal statute upon state law—isn't that what the wording of the statute requires? *Compare* Marrese v. Am. Acad. of Orthopaedic Surgeons, 470 U.S. 373 (1984), in which the Court instructed the federal district courts to conduct a close reading of the preclusion rules of the rendering state to determine how much preclusive effect was due. For an excellent discussion of *Washington Gas Light, see* Sterk, *Full Faith and Credit, More or Less, to Judgments: Doubts About* Thomas v. Washington Gas Light Co., 69 Geo. L.J. 1329 (1981).

(5) In Univ. of Tennessee v. Elliot, 478 U.S. 788 (1986), the Supreme Court held that 28 U.S.C. §1738 is not applicable to unreviewed state administrative fact-finding because section 1738 antedates the development of administrative agencies. It further held that application of a common-law preclusion rule would not be appropriate. Would it have been better in *Thomas* to rest the decision on the administrative nature of workers' compensation boards?

Baker v. General Motors Corp.

522 U.S. 222 (1998)

Justice GINSBURG delivered the opinion of the Court.

[Ronald Elwell worked for the Engineering Analysis Group of General Motors Corporation from 1959 until 1989. During this time he often aided GM lawyers defending GM against product liability actions. Between 1987 and 1991, the Elwell-GM employment relationship soured, resulting in failed negotiations over the terms of Elwell's retirement. In May 1991, Elwell appeared as a witness for the plaintiffs in a product liability action against GM in Georgia and testified that the GM pickup truck fuel system was inferior to competing products. The next month Elwell sued GM in a Michigan state court, alleging wrongful discharge and other tort and contract claims. GM counterclaimed, contending that Elwell had breached his fiduciary duty to GM by disclosing privileged and confidential information and misappropriating documents. In August 1992, the parties entered into a settlement. Elwell received an undisclosed sum of money and agreed to the Michigan court's entry of a permanent injunction preventing him from disclosing GM's trade secrets and other confidential information, or from "testifying, without the prior written consent of General Motors Corporation, either upon deposition or at trial, as an expert witness, or as a witness of any kind, and from consulting with attorneys or their agents in any litigation already filed, or to be filed in the future, involving General Motors Corporation as an owner, seller, manufacturer and/or designer of the product(s) in issue." The injunction contained an exception that stated: "[This provision] shall not operate to interfere with the jurisdiction of the Court in . . . Georgia [where the litigation involving the fuel tank was still pending]." The injunction contained no other limitation, but a separate settlement agreement between the parties provided: "It is agreed that [Elwell's] appearance and testimony, if any, at hearings on Motions to quash subpoena or at deposition or trial or other official proceeding, if the Court or other tribunal so orders, will in no way form a basis for an action in violation of the Permanent Injunction or this Agreement." In the six years since the Elwell-GM settlement, Elwell testified against GM both in Georgia and in several other jurisdictions in which Elwell had been subpoenaed to testify.

[Meanwhile, in September 1991, Kenneth and Steven Baker sued GM in Missouri state court to recover for the death of their mother in a highway accident in Missouri in a Chevrolet S-10 Blazer. After GM removed the case to federal court, the Bakers subpoenaed Elwell. GM objected to Elwell's appearance as a deponent or trial witness on the ground that the Michigan injunction barred his testimony. The district court allowed the Bakers to depose Elwell and to call him as a witness at trial on the grounds that (1) blocking Elwell's testimony pursuant to the Michigan injunction would violate Missouri's "public policy"; and (2) because a Michigan court could modify the Michigan injunction, so too could a Missouri federal court. Following GM's appeal from an $11.3 million jury award, the U.S. Court of Appeals for the Eighth Circuit reversed on the ground that Elwell's testimony should not have been admitted. The court reasoned that the trial court erroneously relied on Missouri's policy favoring disclosure of relevant, nonprivileged information because of Missouri's "equally strong public policy in favor of full faith and credit." The Eighth Circuit also noted that the Michigan court "has been asked on several occasions to modify the injunction, [but] has yet to do so," and noted that, if the Michigan court did not intend to block Elwell's testimony in cases like the Bakers', "the injunction would . . . have been unnecessary." The Supreme Court granted certiorari "to decide whether the full faith and credit requirement stops the Bakers, who were not parties to the Michigan proceeding, from obtaining Elwell's testimony in their Missouri wrongful death action."]

II

A

Our [Full Faith and Credit Clause] precedent differentiates the credit owed to laws (legislative measures and common law) and to judgments. "In numerous cases this Court has held that credit must be given to the judgment of another state although the forum would not be required to entertain the suit on which the judgment was founded." Milwaukee County v. M. E. White Co., 296 U.S. 268, 277 (1935). The Full Faith and Credit Clause does not compel "a state to substitute the statutes of other states for its own statutes dealing with a subject matter concerning which it is competent to legislate." Pacific Employers Ins. Co. v. Industrial Accident Commn. [*supra* page 288] at 501; *see* Phillips Petroleum Co. v. Shutts [*supra* page 310] at 818-819. Regarding judgments, however, the full faith and credit obligation is exacting. A final judgment in one State, if rendered by a court with adjudicatory authority over the subject matter and persons governed by the judgment, qualifies for recognition throughout the land. For claim and issue preclusion (res judicata) purposes, in other words, the judgment of the rendering State gains nationwide force.

A court may be guided by the forum State's "public policy" in determining the *law* applicable to a controversy. *See* Nevada v. Hall [*supra* page 335]. But our decisions support no roving "public policy exception" to the full faith and credit due *judgments*. *See* Fauntleroy v. Lum [*supra* page 516] (judgment of Missouri court entitled to full faith and credit in Mississippi even if Missouri judgment rested on a misapprehension of Mississippi law). In assuming the existence of a ubiquitous "public policy exception" permitting one State to resist recognition of another State's judgment, the District Court in the Bakers' wrongful-death action misread our precedent. "The full faith and credit clause is one of the provisions incorporated into the Constitution by its framers for the purpose of transforming an aggregation of independent, sovereign States into a nation." Sherrer v. Sherrer, 334 U.S. 343, 355 (1948). We are "aware of [no] considerations of local policy or law which could rightly be deemed to impair the force and effect which the full faith and credit clause and the Act of Congress require to be given to [a money] judgment outside the state of its rendition." Magnolia Petroleum Co. v. Hunt, 320 U.S. 430, 438 (1943).

The Court has never placed equity decrees outside the full faith and credit domain. Equity decrees for the payment of money have long been considered equivalent to judgments at law entitled to nationwide recognition. *See, e.g.,* Barber v. Barber, 323 U.S. 77 (1944) (unconditional adjudication of petitioner's right to recover a sum of money is entitled to full faith and credit); *see also* A. Ehrenzweig, *Conflict of Laws* §51, p.182 (rev. ed. 1962) (describing as "indefensible" the old doctrine that an equity decree, because it does not "merge" the claim into the judgment, does not qualify for recognition). We see no reason why the preclusive effects of an adjudication on parties and those "in privity" with them, *i.e.,* claim preclusion and issue preclusion (res judicata and collateral estoppel), should differ depending solely upon the type of relief sought in a civil action. *Cf. Barber*, 323 U.S. at 87 (Jackson, J., concurring) (Full Faith and Credit Clause and its implementing statute speak not of "judgments" but of " 'judicial proceedings' without limitation"); Fed. Rule Civ. Proc. 2 (providing for "one form of action to be known as 'civil action,' " in lieu of discretely labeled actions at law and suits in equity).

Full faith and credit, however, does not mean that States must adopt the practices of other States regarding the time, manner, and mechanisms for enforcing judgments. Enforcement measures do not travel with the sister state judgment as preclusive effects do; such measures remain subject to the evenhanded control of forum law. *See* McElmoyle ex rel. Bailey v. Cohen, 13 Peters 312, 325 (1839) (judgment may be enforced only as "laws [of enforcing forum] may permit"); *see also* Restatement (Second) of Conflict of Laws §99 (1969) ("The local law of the forum determines the methods by which a judgment of another state is enforced.").

Orders commanding action or inaction have been denied enforcement in a sister State when they purported to accomplish an official act within the exclusive province of that other State or interfered with litigation over which the ordering State had no authority. Thus, a sister State's decree concerning land ownership in another State has been held ineffective to transfer title, *see* Fall v. Eastin, 215 U.S. 1, although such a decree may indeed preclusively adjudicate the rights and obligations running between the *parties* to the foreign litigation, *see, e.g.,* Robertson v. Howard, 229 U.S. 254, 261 (1913) ("It may not be doubted that a court of equity in one State in a proper case could compel a defendant before it to convey property situated in another State."). And antisuit injunctions regarding litigation elsewhere, even if compatible with due process as a direction constraining parties to the decree, *see* Cole v. Cunningham, 133 U.S. 107 (1890), in fact have not controlled the second court's actions regarding litigation in that court. *See, e.g.*, James v. Grand Trunk Western R. Co., 14 Ill. 2d 356, 372, 152 N.E.2d 858, 867 (1958); *see also* E. Scoles & P. Hay, *Conflict of Laws* §24.21, p.981 (2d ed. 1992) (observing that antisuit injunction "does not address, and thus has no preclusive effect on, the merits of the litigation [in the second forum]").[9] Sanctions for violations of an injunction, in any event, are generally administered by the court that issued the injunction. *See, e.g.*, Stiller v. Hardman, 324 F.2d 626, 628 (CA2 1963) (nonrendition forum enforces monetary relief portion of a judgment but leaves enforcement of injunctive portion to rendition forum).

B

With these background principles in view, we turn to the dimensions of the order GM relies upon to stop Elwell's testimony. Specifically, we take up the question: What matters did the Michigan injunction legitimately conclude?

As earlier recounted, the parties before the Michigan County Court, Elwell and GM, submitted an agreed-upon injunction, which the presiding judge signed. While no issue was joined, expressly litigated, and determined in the Michigan proceeding,[11] that order is *claim* preclusive between Elwell and GM. Elwell's claim for wrongful discharge and his related contract and tort claims have "merged in the judgment," and he cannot sue again to recover more. Similarly, GM cannot sue Elwell elsewhere on the counterclaim GM asserted in Michigan.

Michigan's judgment, however, cannot reach beyond the Elwell-GM controversy to control proceedings against GM brought in other States, by other parties, asserting claims the merits of which Michigan has not considered. Michigan has no power over those parties, and no basis for commanding them to become

---

9. This Court has held it impermissible for a state court to enjoin a party from proceeding in a federal court, see Donovan v. Dallas, 377 U.S. 408 (1964), but has not yet ruled on the credit due to a state court injunction barring a party from maintaining litigation in another State, see Ginsburg, *Judgments in Search of Full Faith and Credit: The Last-in-Time Rule for Conflicting Judgments*, 82 Harv. L. Rev. 798, 823 (1969); see also Reese, *Full Faith and Credit to Foreign Equity Decrees*, 42 Iowa L. Rev. 183, 198 (1957) (urging that, although this Court "has not yet had occasion to determine [the issue], . . . full faith and credit does not require dismissal of an action whose prosecution has been enjoined," for to hold otherwise "would mean in effect that the courts of one state can control what goes on in the courts of another"). State courts that have dealt with the question have, in the main, regarded antisuit injunctions as outside the full faith and credit ambit.

11. In no event, we have observed, can issue preclusion be invoked against one who did not participate in the prior adjudication. Thus, Justice Kennedy emphasizes the obvious in noting that the Michigan judgment has no preclusive effect on the Bakers, for they were not parties to the Michigan litigation. Such an observation misses the thrust of GM's argument. GM readily acknowledges "the commonplace rule that a person may not be bound by a judgment *in personam* in a case to which he was not made a party." But, GM adds, the Michigan decree does not bind the Bakers; it binds *Elwell* only. Most forcibly, GM insists that the Bakers cannot object to the binding effect GM seeks for the Michigan judgment because the Bakers have no constitutionally protected interest in obtaining the testimony of a particular witness. Given this argument, it is clear that issue preclusion principles, standing alone, cannot resolve the controversy GM presents.

intervenors in the Elwell-GM dispute. *See* Martin v. Wilks, 490 U.S. 755, 761-763 (1989). Most essentially, Michigan lacks authority to control courts elsewhere by precluding them, in actions brought by strangers to the Michigan litigation, from determining for themselves what witnesses are competent to testify and what evidence is relevant and admissible in their search for the truth. *See* Restatement (Second) of Conflict of Laws §§137-139 (1969 and rev. 1988) (forum's own law governs witness competence and grounds for excluding evidence).

As the District Court recognized, Michigan's decree could operate against Elwell to preclude him from *volunteering* his testimony. But a Michigan court cannot, by entering the injunction to which Elwell and GM stipulated, dictate to a court in another jurisdiction that evidence relevant in the Bakers' case—a controversy to which Michigan is foreign—shall be inadmissible. This conclusion creates no general exception to the full faith and credit command, and surely does not permit a State to refuse to honor a sister state judgment based on the forum's choice of law or policy preferences. Rather, we simply recognize that, just as the mechanisms for enforcing a judgment do not travel with the judgment itself for purposes of Full Faith and Credit [*McElmoyle, supra*], and just as one State's judgment cannot automatically transfer title to land in another State [*Fall, supra*], similarly the Michigan decree cannot determine evidentiary issues in a lawsuit brought by parties who were not subject to the jurisdiction of the Michigan court.[12]

The language of the consent decree is informative in this regard. Excluding the then-pending Georgia action from the ban on testimony by Elwell without GM's permission, the decree provides that it "shall not operate to *interfere with the jurisdiction* of the Court in . . . Georgia." But if the Michigan order, extended to the Georgia case, would have "interfered with the jurisdiction" of the Georgia court, Michigan's ban would, in the same way, "interfere with the jurisdiction" of courts in other States in cases similar to the one pending in Georgia.

In line with its recognition of the interference potential of the consent decree, GM provided in the settlement agreement that, if another court ordered Elwell to testify, his testimony would "in no way" render him vulnerable to suit in Michigan for violation of the injunction or agreement. The Eighth Circuit regarded this settlement agreement provision as merely a concession by GM that "some courts might fail to extend full faith and credit to the [Michigan] injunction." As we have explained, however, Michigan's power does not reach into a Missouri courtroom to displace the forum's own determination whether to admit or exclude evidence relevant in the Bakers' wrongful-death case before it. In that light, we see no altruism in GM's agreement not to institute contempt or breach-of-contract proceedings against Elwell in Michigan for giving subpoenaed testimony elsewhere. Rather, we find it telling that GM ruled out resort to the court that entered the injunction,

---

12. Justice Kennedy inexplicably reads into our decision a sweeping exception to full faith and credit based solely on "the integrity of Missouri's judicial processes." The Michigan judgment is not entitled to full faith and credit, we have endeavored to make plain, because it impermissibly interferes with Missouri's control of litigation *brought by parties who were not before the Michigan court*. Thus, Justice Kennedy's hypothetical misses the mark. If the Bakers had been parties to the Michigan proceedings and had actually litigated the privileged character of Elwell's testimony, the Bakers would of course be precluded from relitigating that issue in Missouri.

for injunctions are ordinarily enforced by the enjoining court, not by a surrogate tribunal.

In sum, Michigan has no authority to shield a witness from another jurisdiction's subpoena power in a case involving persons and causes outside Michigan's governance. Recognition, under full faith and credit, is owed to dispositions Michigan has authority to order. But a Michigan decree cannot command obedience elsewhere on a matter the Michigan court lacks authority to resolve. *See* [*Thomas, supra* page 520] at 282-283 (plurality opinion) ("Full faith and credit must be given to [a] determination that [a State's tribunal] had the authority to make; but by a parity of reasoning, full faith and credit need not be given to determinations that it had no power to make.").

Justice SCALIA, concurring in the judgment.

I agree with the Court that enforcement measures do not travel with sister-state judgments as preclusive effects do. It has long been established that "the judgment of a state Court cannot be enforced out of the state by an execution issued within it." *McElmoyle supra* at 325. To recite that principle is to decide this case.

General Motors asked a District Court in Missouri to *enforce* a Michigan injunction. The Missouri court was no more obliged to enforce the Michigan injunction by preventing Elwell from presenting his testimony than it was obliged to enforce it by holding Elwell in contempt. The Full Faith and Credit Clause "did not make the judgments of other States domestic judgments to all intents and purposes, but only gave a general validity, faith, and credit to them, *as evidence.* No execution can issue upon such judgments without a new suit in the tribunals of other States." Thompson v. Whitman, 85 U.S. 457 (1874) (emphasis added) (quoting J. Story, *Conflict of Laws* §609). A judgment or decree of one State, to be sure, may be grounds for an action (or a defense to one) in another. But the Clause and its implementing statute

> "establish a rule of evidence, rather than of jurisdiction. While they make the record of a judgment, rendered after due notice in one State, conclusive evidence in the courts of another State, or of the United States, of the matter adjudged, they do not affect the jurisdiction, either of the court in which the judgment is rendered, or of the court in which it is offered in evidence. Judgments recovered in one State of the Union, when proved in the courts of another government, whether state or national, within the United States, differ from judgments recovered in a foreign country in no other respect than in not being reexaminable on their merits, nor impeachable for fraud in obtaining them, if rendered by a court having jurisdiction of the cause and of the parties." Wisconsin v. Pelican Ins. Co., 127 U.S. 265, 291-292 (1888) (citation omitted).

The judgment that General Motors obtained in Michigan "does not carry with it, into another State, the efficacy of a judgment upon property or persons, to be enforced by execution. To give it the force of a judgment in another State, it must be made a judgment there; and can only be executed in the latter as its laws may permit." Lynde v. Lynde, 181 U.S. 183, 187 (1901) (quoting *McElmoyle, supra*, at 325). *See, e.g.,* Watts v. Waddle, 6 Peters 389, 392 (1832), a case involving a suit to obtain an equity decree ordering the conveyance of land, duplicating such a decree already issued in another State.

Because neither the Full Faith and Credit Clause nor its implementing statute requires Missouri to execute the injunction issued by the courts of Michigan, I concur in the judgment.

Justice KENNEDY, with whom Justices O'CONNOR and THOMAS join, concurring in the judgment.

I concur in the judgment. In my view the case is controlled by well-settled full faith and credit principles which render the majority's extended analysis unnecessary and, with all due respect, problematic in some degree. This separate opinion explains my approach.

I

The majority, of course, is correct to hold that when a judgment is presented to the courts of a second State it may not be denied enforcement based upon some disagreement with the laws of the State of rendition. Full faith and credit forbids the second State from questioning a judgment on these grounds. There can be little doubt of this proposition. We have often recognized the second State's obligation to give effect to another State's judgments even when the law underlying those judgments contravenes the public policy of the second State.

My concern is that the majority, having stated the principle, proceeds to disregard it by announcing two broad exceptions. First, the majority would allow courts outside the issuing State to decline to enforce those judgments "purporting to accomplish an official act within the exclusive province of [a sister] State." Second, the basic rule of full faith and credit is said not to cover injunctions "interfering with litigation over which the ordering State had no authority." The exceptions the majority recognizes are neither consistent with its rejection of a public policy exception to full faith and credit nor in accord with established rules implementing the Full Faith and Credit Clause. As employed to resolve this case, furthermore, the exceptions to full faith and credit have a potential for disrupting judgments, and this ought to give us considerable pause. Our decisions have been careful not to foreclose all effect for the types of injunctions the majority would place outside the ambit of full faith and credit. These authorities seem to be disregarded by today's holding. For example, the majority chooses to discuss the extent to which courts may compel the conveyance of property in other jurisdictions. That subject has proven to be quite difficult. Some of our cases uphold actions by state courts affecting land outside their territorial reach. *E.g.*, Robertson v. Howard, 229 U.S. 254, 261 (1913) ("It may not be doubted that a court of equity in one State in a proper case could compel a defendant before it to convey property situated in another State"). Nor have we undertaken before today to announce an exception which denies full faith and credit based on the principle that the prior judgment interferes with litigation pending in another jurisdiction. As a general matter, there is disagreement among the state courts as to their duty to recognize decrees enjoining proceedings in other courts.

Subjects which are at once so fundamental and so delicate as these ought to be addressed only in a case necessarily requiring their discussion, and even then with caution lest we announce rules which will not be sound in later application. We might be required to hold, if some future case raises the issue, that an otherwise valid judgment cannot intrude upon essential processes of courts outside the issuing State in certain narrow circumstances, but we need not announce or define that principle here. Even if some qualification of full faith and credit were required where the judicial processes of a second State are sought to be controlled in their procedural and institutional aspects, the Court's discussion does not provide sufficient guidance on how this exception should be construed in light of our precedents. The majority's broad review of these matters does not articulate the rationale underlying its conclusions. In the absence of more elaboration, it is unclear what it is about the particular injunction here that renders it undeserving of full faith and credit. The Court's reliance upon unidentified principles to justify omitting certain types of injunctions from the doctrine's application leaves its decision in uneasy tension with its own rejection of a broad public policy exception to full faith and credit.

The following example illustrates the uncertainty surrounding the majority's approach. Suppose the Bakers had anticipated the need for Elwell's testimony in Missouri and had appeared in a Michigan court to litigate the privileged character of the testimony it sought to elicit. Assume further the law on privilege were the same in both jurisdictions. If Elwell, GM, and the Bakers were before the Michigan court and Michigan law gave its own injunction preclusive effect, the Bakers could not relitigate the point, if general principles of issue preclusion control. Perhaps the argument can be made, as the majority appears to say, that the integrity of Missouri's judicial processes demands a rule allowing relitigation of the issue; but, for the reasons given below, we need not confront this interesting question.

In any event, the rule would be an exception. Full faith and credit requires courts to do more than provide for direct enforcement of the judgments issued by other States. It also "requires federal courts to give the same preclusive effect to state court judgments that those judgments would be given in the courts of the State from which the judgments emerged." Kremer v. Chemical Constr. Corp., 456 U.S. 461, 466 (1982). Through full faith and credit, "the local doctrines of *res judicata*, speaking generally, become a part of national jurisprudence. . . ." Riley v. New York Trust Co., 315 U.S. 343, 349 (1942). And whether or not an injunction is enforceable in another State on its own terms, the courts of a second State are required to honor its issue preclusive effects.

II

In the case before us, of course, the Bakers were neither parties to the earlier litigation nor subject to the jurisdiction of the Michigan courts. The majority pays scant attention to this circumstance, which becomes critical. The beginning point of full faith and credit analysis requires a determination of the effect the judgment has in the courts of the issuing State. In our most recent full faith and credit cases, we have said that determining the force and effect of a judgment should be the first step in our analysis. "If the state courts would not give preclusive effect to the prior judgment, 'the courts of the United States can accord it no greater efficacy' under §1738." Haring v. Prosise, 462 U.S. 306, 313, n.6 (1983) (quoting

Union & Planters' Bank v. Memphis, 189 U.S. 71, 75 (1903)). A conclusion that the issuing State would not give the prior judgment preclusive effect ends the inquiry, making it unnecessary to determine the existence of any exceptions to full faith and credit. We cannot decline to inquire into these state-law questions when the inquiry will obviate new extensions or exceptions to full faith and credit.

If we honor the undoubted principle that courts need give a prior judgment no more force or effect [than] the issuing State gives it, the case before us is resolved. Here the Court of Appeals and both parties in their arguments before our Court seemed to embrace the assumption that Michigan would apply the full force of its judgment to the Bakers. Michigan law does not appear to support the assumption.

The simple fact is that the Bakers were not parties to the Michigan proceedings, and nothing indicates Michigan would make the novel assertion that its earlier injunction binds the Bakers or any other party not then before it or subject to its jurisdiction. For collateral estoppel to apply under Michigan law, "the same parties must have had a full opportunity to litigate the issue, and there must be mutuality of estoppel." Nummer v. Treasury Dept., 448 Mich. 534, 542. Since the Bakers were not parties to the Michigan proceedings and had no opportunity to litigate any of the issues presented, it appears that Michigan law would not treat them as bound by the judgment. The majority cites no authority to the contrary.

It makes no difference that the judgment in question is an injunction. The Michigan Supreme Court has twice rejected arguments that injunctions have preclusive effect in later litigation, relying in no small part on the fact that the persons against whom preclusion is asserted were not parties to the earlier litigation.

. . . [D]etermining as a threshold matter the extent to which Michigan law gives preclusive effect to the injunction eliminates the need to decide whether full faith and credit applies to equitable decrees as a general matter or the extent to which the general rules of full faith and credit are subject to exceptions. Michigan law would not seek to bind the Bakers to the injunction and that suffices to resolve the case. For these reasons, I concur in the judgment.

Questions and Comments

(1) The thrust of *Baker* is that a judgment from one state that purports to require an official to act within the exclusive province of another state need not be given full faith and credit. Does the Court provide guidance about where the legitimate effect of the rendering court's judgment ends and the exclusive province of the other state begins? Is Justice Kennedy correct to claim that the majority in *Baker* creates a new exception to the bar on invoking local public policy to resist a foreign judgment?

(2) The *Baker* Court says that the Michigan judgment "cannot reach beyond the Elwell-GM controversy," but it also confirms that the judgment is preclusive as between Elwell and GM. What if GM had brought a separate suit against Elwell in Missouri to enforce the injunction against him? Would the injunction be entitled to full faith and credit in this context? If so, what would happen if Elwell were nonetheless called to testify in the Bakers' case in federal court?

(3) The Restatement stated in 1971 that "the Supreme Court has not had occasion to determine whether full faith and credit *requires* a State of the United

States to enforce a valid judgment of a sister State that orders the doing of an act other than the payment of money or that enjoins the doing of an act." Restatement (Second) of Conflict of Laws §102 comment *c* (1971) (emphasis added). Does *Baker* resolve this issue? On the one hand, it holds that the Michigan injunction need not be enforced in Missouri. On the other hand, the Court makes clear that, as a general matter, the full faith and credit clause applies to equity decrees. For an excellent analysis of *Baker* and its implications for how the full faith and credit clause applies to equity decrees, *see* Price, *Full Faith and Credit and the Equity Conflict*, 84 Va. L. Rev. 747 (1998).

(4) What about antisuit injunctions that order parties not to litigate a case elsewhere? In Cole v. Cunningham, 133 U.S. 107, 134 (1890), the Court held that antisuit injunctions did not violate the full faith and credit clause. But the Supreme Court has never resolved whether antisuit injunctions must be given full faith and credit. Prior to *Baker*, most lower courts held that the full faith and credit clause does not compel recognition of an antisuit injunction. *See, e.g.,* Laker Airways Ltd. v. Sabena, Belgian World Airlines, 731 F.2d 909, 934 (D.C. Cir. 1984) (dicta); James v. Grand Trunk W. R. Co., 152 N.E.2d 858 (Ill. 1958); *but see* Bard v. Charles R. Myers Ins. Agency, Inc., 839 S.W.2d 791 (Tex. 1992) (liquidation order issued by Vermont receivership court, prohibiting prosecution of any action against company in receivership that would interfere with receiver's conduct of company's affairs, given full faith and credit by Texas court). *James* reasoned that the antisuit injunction need not be respected because it operated upon the parties and not the court. What are *Baker*'s implications for antisuit injunctions?

(5) *Baker* may have opened the door for courts to avoid recognizing sister-state judgments in the context of simultaneous litigation occurring in multiple states. In Wamsley v. Nodak Mut. Ins. Co., 178 P.3d 102 (Mont. 2008), insureds, residents of North Dakota, were killed in Montana, and their surviving children, as representatives of the estate, sued the insurer, a North Dakota company, to recover stacked uninsured motorist benefits. The estate demanded stacked benefits from Nodak and threatened to file suit in Montana, where a state statute prohibiting stacking had just been struck down as unconstitutional. Nodak repeatedly asked the estate for more time to investigate the matter before responding, and, after nearly six weeks of stalling, Nodak filed a declaratory judgment action in North Dakota seeking a determination that stacking was not permitted under the policy. The estate filed suit against Nodak in Montana state court a few days later, and the Montana court denied Nodak's request to stay the Montana proceedings in deference to the North Dakota court proceedings. The North Dakota court first determined that North Dakota law would apply to the action. Shortly thereafter, the Montana court ruled that stacking would be permitted but had not yet issued a judgment when the North Dakota court granted summary judgment to Nodak on grounds that stacking was not permitted. The Montana court refused to recognize the North Dakota court judgment, and that determination was upheld by the Montana Supreme Court. Citing *Baker*, the state supreme court concluded that the North Dakota rulings were not due full faith and credit because they impermissibly interfered with the Montana litigation. That court also cited section 103 of the Second Restatement, *supra* page 519, which states that it is permissible to refuse recognition of a sister-state judgment if "it would involve

an improper interference with important interests of the sister State." According to the Montana court, Nodak filed the North Dakota declaratory judgment action in an attempt to obtain North Dakota law through the back door in Montana and thereby avoid an adverse judgment. Furthermore, Nodak misled the estate to buy time in order to file suit first in an attempt to thwart Montana's judicial process. Citing *Baker* again, the Montana court stated that the declaratory judgment mechanism in one state should not be used to assert control over litigation occurring in another state. The court concluded:

> We also recognize that this case presents a unique set of circumstances for which no clear rule in the full faith and credit jurisprudence has been established. *See Baker*, 522 U.S. at 245 (Kennedy, J., concurring) (noting that the United States Supreme Court has never exactly determined at what point "an otherwise valid judgment cannot intrude upon essential process of courts outside of the issuing State. . . ."). Nonetheless, we conclude it would defeat the purpose of forging national unity to use full faith and credit to needlessly expand a single cause of action into multi-state litigation. If anything, such a use of the full faith and credit clause simply balkanizes the legal process, brings state courts into greater conflict, and diminishes respect for the type of state sovereignty the first Congress envisioned. For these reasons, we conclude the District Court did not err in declining to accord full faith and credit to the competing rulings issued by the North Dakota courts. *Id.* at 115.

Judge Warner authored a separate opinion concurring in part and dissenting in part. Judge Warner agreed that the full faith and credit clause did not require the Montana court to recognize the North Dakota judgment but believed that North Dakota law should have applied to resolve the dispute in any event:

> The insurance contract at issue here was between residents of North Dakota who conduct their business there. It was entered in North Dakota and the vehicles were principally garaged in North Dakota. Nodak set its rates and the insured's paid their premiums in North Dakota. The parties and the insurance contract have virtually no connection to Montana other than the "fortuity that the accident occurred [h]ere." Considering that the tort claims the Estate makes against Stanton only peripherally involve the contract claims against Nodak, the place where the insurance contract was negotiated, the place where it was made, the place of performance, the principal location of the insured autos, and considering the domicile, residence, and place of business of the parties, it becomes obvious that North Dakota law should apply to the Estate's claims against Nodak. See Restatement (Second) of Conflict of Laws §188(2).
>
> Further, in my view, this Court should grant comity to North Dakota in this instance for a reason which the Court does not mention. The Montana Supreme Court has the right and the duty to correctly interpret Montana law for the benefit of Montana citizens. Still, Montana is a part of the United States and the judgments of our sister states are important—especially to the citizens of those other states. The only Montanans affected by the Court's decision today are the local lawyers. The refusal to grant comity in this case, where only North Dakota policy is directly affected, impinges unnecessarily upon the harmonious interstate relations which are part and parcel of the spirit of cooperative federalism.

> There are now two diametrically opposed judgments, one in North Dakota and the other in Montana. It remains to be seen if Montana's decision today aids the Estate's pursuit of an insurance payment the Wamsleys did not bargain for, or only necessitates further litigation between North Dakota citizens. I would defer to the North Dakota judgment and dissent from the Court's decision not to do so. *Id*. at 120.

Does *Wamsley* seem like an appropriate application of the *Baker* principles? Is it correctly decided?

(6) Later in the same year as the *Wamsley* decision, the Supreme Court of Nevada determined that it was permissible for a Nevada court to refuse to recognize a Montana court judgment also involving the stacking of uninsured motorist benefits. Tenas v. Progressive Preferred Ins. Co., 238 P.3d 860 (Nev. 2008). The insured, a resident of Nevada, sought to stack the benefits of her two automobile insurance policies after her daughter was injured in an accident in Montana. Progressive's policy included a choice-of-law clause stating that it was governed by Nevada law. In these cases, Progressive filed its declaratory judgment action in Nevada first, and Tenas filed her suit in Montana state court a few days later. The Montana court resolved its action first. It granted summary judgment to Tenas and applied Montana law because Nevada's anti-stacking rule violated Montana public policy. The Nevada state court thereafter granted summary judgment in favor of Progressive, finding that Nevada law applied and that Tenas was not entitled to stacked benefits. The Nevada Supreme Court concluded that the Montana court should have honored the first-to-file rule:

> As recognized by the Supreme Court of Montana, the "first to file" rule is "a generally recognized doctrine of . . . comity which permits a district court to decline jurisdiction over an action when a complaint involving the same parties and issues has already been filed in another district." *Wamsley* at 109-110. We conclude that despite Montana's interests in resolving the issue as to stacking of the uninsured motorist coverage in Barnes's insurance policy, the Montana district court should have declined jurisdiction because Progressive already had an identical pending action in Nevada that had been commenced before the Montana action. *See id*. While the "first to file" rule "is not a rigid or inflexible rule to be mechanically applied," we agree with Progressive that Montana should not have adjudicated this matter because Nevada was the best forum to dispute the underlying issue; the insurance policy had been issued in Nevada to Tenas and Barnes, who were Nevada residents. *See id*. Even though "Montana has a well-established practice of applying Montana law to automobile accidents occurring within its borders," the insurance policy in this case was governed by Nevada law, as provided in the insurance policy's choice of law provision. *See id*. Therefore, we conclude that the Nevada district court did not err in adjudicating this matter, as Montana law had compelled the Montana district court to abate or stay Tenas's subsequently filed action in Montana. *See id*.

It seems pretty clear with its repeated citation to *Wamsley* that the Nevada Supreme Court is announcing a rule of reciprocity here, is it not? *Wamsley* simply does not lend support to the court's statements except for the fact that it too justified ignoring a sister-state's judgment. Is the Nevada court's determination here more or less justified than the Montana court's determination in *Wamsley*? Does *Tenas* logically follow from *Baker*?

Note: Foreign Judgments

The full faith and credit clause applies to the "public acts, records, and judicial proceedings" of *states* and thus does not apply to judgments by courts of foreign states. Nor does any federal statute or treaty govern the recognition and enforcement of foreign judgments. In 1895, the Supreme Court held that foreign judgments are generally enforceable as a matter of common law "comity," as long as the foreign government from which the judgment issued, as a matter of "reciprocity," would enforce a similar U.S. judgment. *See* Hilton v. Guyot, 159 U.S. 113 (1895).

Hilton was a diversity case applying the general common law. Today, the recognition and enforcement of foreign judgments is thought to be primarily a matter of state law. Most states—39 in all, plus the District of Columbia—have adopted some version of the Uniform Foreign Money Judgments Recognition Act, 13 U.L.A. 261 (1986 & Supp.) ("UFMJRA"), or the updated version, the Uniform Foreign-Country Money Judgments Recognition Act ("UFCMJRA"). The UFMJRA provides that a foreign judgment that is "final and conclusive and enforceable where rendered" is "conclusive between the parties to the extent that it grants or denies recovery of a sum of money," and is "enforceable in the same manner as the judgment of a sister state which is entitled to full faith and credit." *Id.* §§2-3. It further provides that a "foreign judgment *is not conclusive*" if it was "rendered under a system which does not provide impartial tribunals or procedures compatible with the requirements of due process of law," or if it was rendered by a court that lacked personal and subject matter jurisdiction. *Id.* §4(a) (emphasis added). It also provides that a foreign judgment "*need not be recognized*" if (a) the defendant did not receive notice in the original proceeding; (b) the judgment was obtained by fraud; (c) the cause of action "on which the judgment is based is repugnant to the public policy of this state"; (d) there is a conflict with another final and conclusive judgment; (e) there is inconsistency between the initial proceeding and a forum selection clause; or (f) in cases based on personal service, "the foreign court was a seriously inconvenient forum for the trial of the action." *Id.* §4(b) (emphasis added).

The result of these state laws is that foreign judgments are often recognized and enforced in the United States, but they receive much more scrutiny in U.S. courts than the judgments of sister states, especially on public policy and procedural adequacy grounds. *See, e.g.,* Matusevitch v. Telnikoff, 877 F. Supp. 1 (D.D.C. 1995) (declining to enforce libel judgment from England because doing so would, in light of the lower speech protections in England, violate public policy); Maxwell Schuman & Co. v. Edwards, 663 S.E.2d 329 (N.C. Ct. App. 2008) (declining to enforce, on public policy grounds, Canadian court's award of contingency legal fees in child custody case); Aguerre v. Schering-Plough Corp., 924 A.2d 571 (N.J. Super. Ct. App. Div. 2007) (declining to enforce, on public policy grounds, Argentine court's judgment memorializing whistleblower settlement agreement); Osorio v. Dole Food Co., 665 F. Supp. 2d 1307 (S.D. Fla. 2009) (declining to enforce Nicaraguan court's $97 million judgment for workers exposed to pesticides because

Nicaraguan judicial system failed to comport with requirements of due process); Najas Cortés v. Orion Sec., Inc., 842 N.E.2d 162 (Ill. App. Ct. 2005) (declining to enforce default judgment from Ecuador because service of process was insufficient to put defendant on notice of lawsuit); Bridgeway Corp. v. Citibank, 45 F. Supp. 2d 276 (S.D.N.Y. 1999), *aff'd*, Bridgeway Corp. v. Citibank, 201 F.3d 134 (2d Cir. 2000) (declining to enforce banking dispute judgment from Liberia because Liberian judicial system was not impartial and failed to comport with requirements of due process).

Is there a good reason to give foreign judgments less respect than the judgments of sister states? Professors von Mehren and Trautman argue that there is, since (a) in the case of sister-state judgments there are federal policies present that are absent in the international context, (b) the legal systems of the states are more similar and founded on like principles, and (c) the judgments of sister states are subject to Supreme Court review if they show some serious excess. Von Mehren & Trautman, *Recognition of Foreign Adjudications: A Survey and Suggested Approach*, 81 Harv. L. Rev. 1601, 1607 (1968). Do you agree? Do these same reasons suggest that non-forum law should be given less respect in an international choice-of-law case than in a domestic one?

Should the enforcement of foreign country judgments be regarded as a matter of state law? Note that the uniform laws mentioned above require the courts to engage in potentially sensitive inquiries about the legal systems and practices of foreign countries. For example, a judgment is not conclusive if it was "rendered under a system which does not provide impartial tribunals or procedures compatible with the requirements of due process of law." *Cf.* Zschernig v. Miller, 389 U.S. 429 (1968) (striking down Oregon probate law because it called for "minute inquiries concerning the actual administration of foreign law" and "make[s] unavoidable judicial criticism of nations established on a more authoritarian basis than our own"). *See generally* Vázquez, *W[h]ither* Zschernig?, 46 Vill. L. Rev. 1259 (2001); Goldsmith, *Federal Courts, Foreign Affairs, and Federalism*, 83 Va. L. Rev. 1617 (1997).

The non-uniform treatment of foreign judgments across U.S. states has led to a movement to federalize foreign judgment recognition law in order to promote international trade. *See, e.g.*, Silberman & Lowenfeld, *A Different Challenge for the ALI; Herein of Foreign Country Judgments, an International Treaty, and an American Statute*, 75 Ind. L. Rev. 635 (2000). The non-uniform treatment also creates a strategic incentive for judgment creditors to bring their foreign judgments to more lenient state courts for recognition and then use the domesticated judgment to obtain enforcement in the stricter state courts. One scholar has argued that rather than federalize foreign judgment recognition law, Congress should remove state obligations to recognize sister-state judgments that do no more than domesticate foreign judgments. Then states would be left free to experiment with the best rules for foreign judgment recognition. Shill, *Ending Judgment Arbitrage: Jurisdictional Competition and the Enforcement of Foreign Money Judgments in the United States*, 54 Harv. Intl. L. Rev. 459 (2013).

For years nations have tried and failed to develop a treaty to regulate the recognition and enforcement of foreign judgments under the auspices of the Hague Conference on Private International Law ("the Conference"). The Conference's first attempt, in 1971, produced a treaty that has only been ratified or acceded to by five states. *See* Convention on the Recognition and Enforcement of Foreign Judgments in Civil and Commercial Matters, Feb. 1, 1971, 1144 U.N.T.S. 249. In 1992, the United States proposed that the Conference draft a new convention on the topic, but this too failed on the ground, among others, that it would require one state to enforce judgments made in another state under potentially widely divergent judicial rules and processes. *See* Woodward, Jr., *Saving the Hague Choice of Court Convention*, 29 U. Pa. J. Intl. L. 657, 660-661 (2008); Murphy, *Negotiation of Convention on Jurisdiction and Enforcement of Judgments*, 95 Am. J. Intl. L. 418 (2001). The Conference instead pursued the more modest goal of developing a treaty that imposed obligations to recognize and enforce both choice-of-court (forum-selection) agreements and the judgments rendered in cases adjudicated pursuant to such agreements. *See* Convention on Choice of Court Agreements, June 30, 2005, 44 I.L.M. 1294. This treaty, however, has been slow to gather support. The European Union, Mexico, Singapore, Montenegro, and Denmark have ratified the treaty. The United States, China, and the Ukraine have signed but not ratified it. Another attempt at a convention on the recognition and enforcement of judgments is once again being pursued by the Conference, with final negotiations scheduled for June 2019. Why do you think nations have been unable to agree on a treaty for recognizing and enforcing foreign judgments?

C.   The Enforcing State's Law of Judgments

Union National Bank v. Lamb

337 U.S. 38 (1949)

Justice DOUGLAS delivered the opinion of the Court.

Missouri has a statute which limits the life of a judgment to ten years after its original rendition or ten years after its revival. Missouri also provides that no judgment can be revived after ten years from its rendition. These provisions are applicable to all judgments whether rendered by a Missouri court or by any other court.

Petitioner has a Colorado judgment against respondent. It was obtained in 1927 and revived in Colorado in 1945 on personal service upon respondent in Missouri. Suit was then brought in Missouri on the revived Colorado judgment. The Supreme Court of Missouri, though assuming that the judgment was valid in Colorado, refused to enforce it because the original judgment under Missouri's law could not have been revived in 1945. It held that the lex fori governs the limitations of actions and that the Full Faith and Credit Clause of the Constitution, Art. IV, §1, did not require Missouri to recognize Colorado's more lenient policy as respects revival of judgments.

Roche v. McDonald is dispositive of the merits. Roche had a Washington judgment against McDonald. He brought suit on that judgment in Oregon. He obtained a judgment in Oregon at a time when the original judgment had by Washington law expired and could not be revived. Roche then sued in Washington on the Oregon judgment. The Court reversed the Supreme Court of Washington which had held that full faith and credit need not be given the Oregon judgment since it would have been void and of no effect if rendered in Washington. The Court held that once the court of the sister State had jurisdiction over the parties and of the subject matter its judgment was valid and could not be impeached in the State of the forum, even though it could not have been obtained there. . . . For in those cases the Court had held that the State of the forum could not defeat the foreign judgment because it was obtained by a procedure hostile to or inconsistent with that of the forum or because it was based on a cause of action which the forum itself would not have recognized.

Any other result would defeat the aim of the Full Faith and Credit Clause and the statute enacted pursuant to it. It is when a clash of policies between two states emerges that the need of the Clause is the greatest. It and the statute which implements it are indeed designed to resolve such controversies. There is no room for an exception, as Roche v. McDonald makes plain, where the clash of policies relates to revived judgments rather than to the nature of the underlying claims as in Fauntleroy v. Lum, *supra*. It is the judgment that must be given full faith and credit. In neither case can its integrity be impaired, save for attacks on the jurisdiction of the court that rendered it.

Cases of statute of limitations against a cause of action on a judgment (M'Elmoyle v. Cohen) involve different considerations. . . . They do not undermine the integrity of the judgment on which suit is brought. In this case it is the 1945 Colorado judgment that claims full faith and credit in Missouri. No Missouri statute of limitations is tendered to cut off a cause of action based on judgments of that vintage.

It is argued, however, that under Colorado law the 1945 Colorado judgment is not a new judgment and that the revivor did no more than extend the statutory period in which to enforce the old judgment. It is said that those were the assumptions on which the Missouri court proceeded. But we would have to add to and subtract from its opinion to give it that meaning. For when it placed revived judgments on the same basis as original judgments, it did so because of Missouri not Colorado law.

This is not a situation where Colorado law also makes that conclusion plain. The Colorado authorities which have been cited to us indeed seem to hold just the opposite. Thus La Fitte v. Salisbury holds that a revived judgment has the effect of a new one. We are referred to no Colorado authorities to the contrary.

But since the status of the 1945 judgment under Colorado law was not passed upon by the Missouri court, we do not determine the question. For the same reason we do not consider whether the service on which the Colorado judgment was revived satisfied due process. Both of those questions will be open on remand of the cause.

The suggestion that we follow the course taken in Minnesota v. National Tea Co. and vacate the judgment and remand the cause to the Missouri court so that it may first pass on these questions would be appropriate only if it were uncertain whether that court adjudicated a federal question. That course is singularly inappropriate here since it is plain that the Missouri court held that, whatever the effect of revivor under Colorado law, the Colorado judgment was not entitled to full faith and credit in Missouri. That holding is a ruling on a federal question and it cannot stand if, as assumed, the Colorado judgment had the force and effect of a new one.

Reversed. [Dissenting opinion is omitted.]

Watkins v. Conway
385 U.S. 188 (1966)

PER CURIAM.

This litigation began when appellant Watkins brought a tort action against Conway in a circuit court of Florida. On October 5, 1955, that court rendered a $25,000 judgment for appellant. Five years and one day later, appellant sued upon this judgment in a superior court of Georgia. Appellee raised §3-701 of the Georgia Code as a bar to the proceeding: "Suits upon foreign judgments.—All suits upon judgments obtained out of this State shall be brought within five years after such judgments shall have been obtained." The Georgia trial court gave summary judgment for appellee. In so doing, it rejected appellant's contention that §3-701 when read against the longer limitation period of domestic judgments set forth in Ga. Code §§110-1001, 110-1002 (1935), was inconsistent with the Full Faith and Credit and Equal Protection Clauses of the Federal Constitution. The Georgia Supreme Court affirmed, also rejecting appellant's constitutional challenge to §3-701. . . .

Although appellant lays his claim under two constitutional provisions, in reality his complaint is simply that Georgia has drawn an impermissible distinction between foreign and domestic judgments. He argues that the statute is understandable solely as a reflection of Georgia's desire to handicap out-of-state judgment creditors. If appellant's analysis of the purpose and effect of the statute were correct, we might well agree that it violates the Federal Constitution. For the decisions of this Court which appellee relies upon do not justify the discriminatory application of a statute of limitations to foreign actions.[1]

But the interpretation which the Georgia courts have given §3-701 convinces us that appellant has misconstrued it. The statute bars suits on foreign judgments only if the plaintiff cannot revive his judgment in the State where it was originally obtained. For the relevant date in applying §3-701 is not the date of the original judgment, but rather it is the date of the latest revival of the judgment. In the case at bar, for example, all appellant need do is return to Florida and revive his judgment. He can then come back to Georgia within five years and file suit free of the limitations of §3-701.

It can be seen, therefore, that the Georgia statute has not discriminated against the judgment from Florida. Instead, it has focused on the law of that State. If Florida had a statute of limitations of five years or less on its own judgments, the appellant would not be able to recover here. But this disability would flow from the conclusion of the Florida Legislature that suits on Florida judgments should be barred after that period. Georgia's construction of §3-701 would merely honor

---

1. The case most directly in point, M'Elmoyle v. Cohen, 13 Pet. 312, upheld the Georgia statute with which we deal today. But the parties in that case did not argue the statute's shorter limitation for foreign judgments as the ground of its invalidity. Instead, the issue presented to this Court concerned the power of the States to impose any statute of limitations upon foreign judgments. The language of Mr. Justice Wayne's opinion—"may not the law of a state fix different times for barring the remedy in a suit upon a judgment of another state, and for those of its own tribunals," 13 Pet., at 328—must be read against this argument. And, of course, that opinion cannot stand against an equal-protection claim, since it was written nearly 30 years before the Fourteenth Amendment was adopted.. . .

and give effect to that conclusion. Thus, full faith and credit is insured, rather than denied, the law of the judgment State. Similarly, there is no denial of equal protection in a scheme that relies upon the judgment State's view of the validity of its own judgments. Such a scheme hardly reflects invidious discrimination.

Affirmed. Justice DOUGLAS dissents.

Questions and Comments

(1) Does the rule of M'Elmoyle v. Cohen, cited by the majority in *Union National Bank*, make sense? It allowed the forum state to apply its own statute of limitations to foreign judgments, viewing such an application as other than an attack on the merits of the foreign judgment. Is this because statutes of limitations are "procedural" and the enforcing state is the forum? Compare the discussion of *M'Elmoyle* in Sun Oil Co. v. Wortman, page 317 *supra*. But if the purpose of the statute of limitations is to protect either the parties or the courts (or both), isn't the domestic statute inappropriate on a foreign judgment because (a) the foreign judgment is supposed to be conclusive on the rights of the parties, including how much delay will be allowed, and (b) there is no intelligible forum procedural interest in limiting an action brought on a foreign judgment—an action that may be one of the simplest of all actions, since virtually no evidence need be taken?

(2) What other "procedural" rule might the enforcing state apply? What about its rules of jurisdiction? In Kenney v. Supreme Lodge of the World, 252 U.S. 411 (1920), the Court stated that phrasing a failure to enforce another state's judgments in terms of a lack of jurisdiction in the enforcing court is not an adequate explanation. The Illinois Supreme Court had held that since the original action could not have been brought in Illinois, there was no jurisdiction to enforce a judgment either. Justice Holmes responded:

> It is plain that a State cannot escape its constitutional obligations by the simple device of denying jurisdiction in such cases to courts otherwise competent. Whether the Illinois statute should be construed [to deny jurisdiction, rather than to forbid the claim on substantive grounds] was for the Supreme Court of the State to decide, but read as that court read it, it attempted to achieve a result that the Constitution of the United States forbade.

Might there not be other, more traditionally "jurisdictional" rules as to which the enforcing state might apply its own law?

(3) The majority (and the omitted dissent) seem to assume in *Union National Bank* that it is critical whether the 1945 Colorado proceedings merely extended the statute of limitations on the original Colorado judgment or actually created a new judgment. The disagreement is in what to do about the uncertainty concerning that question. The distinction is significant because one may ignore a foreign statute of limitations, but not a foreign judgment. But is the dichotomy helpful? Why would Colorado ever find itself in a position to distinguish between the two views? Since Colorado will either enforce the new judgment if it is one, or enforce its own statute of limitations, if that is what the 1945 proceedings affected, there is no need to answer the question. If it makes little difference to Colorado, why should such

great emphasis be placed on it in Missouri? Moreover, is it clear that there should be such a clear line between the effect given to the statute of limitation on the judgment (it may be ignored) and the effect given to a finding that there is a new judgment (it must be implemented)? What is a rule concerning mandatory counterclaims—a law that can be ignored, or an effect of a judgment that must be honored? (*See* note (5) *infra*.) What is the proper category for a Virginia statute saying that once a workers' compensation award has been made, no other action may be brought—a statute of limitations, which can be ignored, or a rule prescribing the effect of a judgment, which must be obeyed?

(4) Is the Court's reasoning in *Watkins* credible? The Court purports to find, in the Georgia statute considered there, a kind of super full faith and credit because it makes the ability to enforce one's judgment in Georgia turn on whether it is still good where it was rendered. But why make the party with the judgment go back home to Florida? Why not simply refer to Florida law? And what if Florida requires new service of process, the defendant is absent, and the Florida courts don't have a continuing-jurisdiction theory that would allow them to consider that the jurisdiction from the first action continued for the second? What if the judgment is still good in Florida but cannot be revived? Is it likely that Georgia really intended such extreme deference to the limitations of other states with statutes longer than five years (but shorter than the plaintiff waited) and not to those states with statutes of less than five years (which would get ignored by Georgia, applying its own five-year statute)? In any event, does *Watkins* have implications for the question whether a state's apparent discrimination against out-of-state parties in choice of law is valid when such parties are merely relegated to the law of their home state? *Cf.* discussion of *Austin*, *supra* page 340.

(5) May an enforcing court apply its own compulsory counterclaim rules? If a counterclaim that was not raised in the original proceedings would have been compulsory in the rendering court but is not treated as compulsory in the enforcing court (or vice versa), which court's counterclaim rules apply?

In Chapman v. Aetna Finance, 615 F.2d 361 (5th Cir. 1980), it was held that section 1738 did not require the federal court to apply the rendering court's compulsory counterclaim rules (although the rules were ultimately applied, anyway, under a comity theory):

> The "intended function" of the full faith and credit clause, as applied to judicial proceedings, is to avoid "relitigation in other states of adjudicated issues." Fulfillment of that function plainly does not depend on extraterritorial application of essentially procedural res judicata rules. The Georgia compulsory counterclaim rule tracks Fed. R. Civ. P. 13(a), whose purpose is "to prevent multiplicity of actions.". . . Operating as it does to forfeit an unlitigated claim, Georgia's compulsory counterclaim rule is not unlike a statute of limitations, which . . . would not ordinarily be entitled to full faith and credit in foreign jurisdictions.

Chapman is commonly thought to have been overruled by Migra v. Warren City School Dist. Bd. of Ed., 465 U.S. 75 (1984), holding federal courts to a more literal interpretation of section 1738, which states that the enforcing state must give the judgment "the same" effect as it would have in the rendering state. *See, e.g.,* Dubroff v. Dubroff, 833 F.2d 557 (5th Cir. 1987); McDougald v. Jenson, 786 F.2d 1465 (11th Cir. 1986). Does *Migra* dispense with the argument that the enforcing state may apply its own judgments law on "procedural" issues?

Because *Migra* dealt with federal deference to a state court judgment in the same state, and because it dealt with a civil rights action (the plaintiff raised constitutional challenges to official actions), it might be thought that it is limited to that context, with its special federalism concerns. The argument would be that the Supreme Court was particularly interested in restricting relitigation in federal courts of politically sensitive issues that the local state courts had already addressed. However, the more literal interpretation of section 1738, requiring reference to the rendering state's compulsory counterclaim rules, has also been followed by state courts; *see, e.g.,* Nottingham v. Weld, 377 S.E.2d 621 (Va. 1989) (involving a garden-variety automobile accident). The increasing attention to the literal language of section 1738 (the "same effect" as in the rendering state) has also been manifested in the context of a subsequent antitrust action brought in federal court. *See* Marrese v. Am. Acad. of Orthopaedic Surgeons, 470 U.S. 373 (1985).

(6) What happens when the enforcement court wants to give a judgment greater effect than the rendering court? Consider Hart v. American Airlines, 304 N.Y.S.2d 810 (N.Y. Sup. Ct. 1969). Of various actions instituted following a plane crash in Kentucky, the first to be tried to conclusion was the one brought in Texas federal court that resulted in a jury verdict for plaintiffs based on a finding of defendant American Airlines' negligence. *Hart* was a later action against American Airlines arising from the same accident but brought by different plaintiffs. The plaintiffs in *Hart* argued that the Texas judgment collaterally estopped the defendant from contesting liability. The defendant argued that the full faith and credit clause precluded the application of collateral estoppel in the New York action because Texas law required mutuality. The New York court disagreed:

> The State of Texas has no legitimate interest in imposing its rules on collateral estoppel upon these New York residents. . . . The fact that the plaintiffs herein involved are New York domiciliaries, as were their decedents, sufficiently establishes this State's superior interest in the issue of collateral estoppel. It may be observed that these plaintiffs occupy much the same relationship to the State of Texas as the nonresident *Hart* plaintiffs do to New York, and the unavailability of the New York rule on collateral estoppel to the *Hart* plaintiffs is equally relevant in holding the instant resident plaintiffs outside the scope of the Texas rule on that issue.
>
> Defendant's reliance on "full faith and credit" to defeat the application of collateral estoppel herein is misplaced. This is not a situation where the judgment, as such, of the Texas court is sought to be enforced. What is here involved is a policy determination by our courts that "One who has had his day in court should not be permitted to litigate the question anew," and, further, refusal "to tolerate a condition where, on relatively the same set of facts, one fact-finder, be it court or jury" may find a party liable while another exonerates him leading to the "inconsistent results which are always a blemish on a judicial system." It is in order to carry out these policy determinations in the disposition of cases

in this jurisdiction that an evidentiary use is being made of a particular issue determination made in the Texas action.

Id. at 813-814. Is there any full faith and credit issue in this case at all; that is, is there anything in the principle of full faith and credit that would suggest that a state may not give *more* effect to a judgment than the rendering state would? Is it being too literal to reach a result under the full faith and credit clause's requirement that the second state give the "same" effect that the first state would give? *Compare* Columbia Casualty Co. v. Playtex FP Inc., 584 A.2d 1214 (Del. 1991) (application of local collateral estoppel law in circumstance similar to *Hart* "is clearly at variance with the purpose and spirit of the full faith and credit clause"). On the general issue of which state's preclusion law to apply, *see* Shreve, *Judgments from a Choice-of-Law Perspective*, 40 Am J. Comp. L. 985 (1992).

(7) The Supreme Court has specifically held that a federal court may not give a judgment greater effect than would the state where it was rendered. Migra v. Warren City Sch. Dist. Bd. of Educ., 465 U.S. 75 (1984); Marrese v. Am. Acad. of Orthopaedic Surgeons, 470 U.S. 373, 384 (1984). Would it result in forum-shopping or *Erie* problems if a state court, in contrast, were allowed to give another state's judgment greater effect than would the rendering state?

Treinies v. Sunshine Mining Co.

308 U.S. 66 (1939)

Justice REED delivered the opinion of the Court.

[In this action, the Sunshine Mining Company, a Washington corporation, filed a bill of interpleader against (1) Evelyn H. Treinies and other citizens of the state of Washington; and (2) Katherine Mason and other citizens of the state of Idaho, who are adverse claimants to certain stock and dividends of the corporation. The bill was filed after two courts rendered inconsistent judgments as to ownership of the stock.] The Superior Court of Spokane County, Washington, in administering the estate of Amelia Pelkes, adjudged that it was the property of John Pelkes, assignor of petitioner, Evelyn H. Treinies; and the District Court of Shoshone County, Idaho, adjudged that the same property belonged to respondent, Katherine Mason. . . .

The alleged rights of the respective claimants arose as follows: Amelia Pelkes, the wife of John Pelkes, died testate in Spokane, Washington, in 1922, leaving her husband and one child, Katherine Mason, the offspring of a former marriage, as the beneficiaries of her will. As a part of her community estate, there were 30,598 shares of Sunshine Mining stock. It was considered valueless and was not inventoried or appraised. The order of distribution assigned a three-fourths undivided interest in these shares to Pelkes and a one-fourth to Mrs. Mason, an omnibus clause covering unknown property. The estate of Mrs. Pelkes was not distributed according to the order of distribution. Instead Pelkes and his stepdaughter, Mrs. Mason, divided the inventoried property between themselves in accordance with their wishes.

It is the contention of Pelkes and his assignee that this partition of the property was in consideration of the release by Mrs. Mason to Pelkes of all of her interest in the shares of the stock of the Sunshine Mining Company. On the other hand, Mrs. Mason asserts that Pelkes was to hold one-half of the amount owned, 15,299 shares, in trust for her.

In August, 1934, Mrs. Mason instituted a suit in the District Court of Idaho for Shoshone County against Pelkes, Evelyn H. Treinies, the Sunshine Mining Company, and others not important here, alleging that she was the owner of 15,299 shares of the stock, that these had been acquired by Miss Treinies from Pelkes with knowledge of Mrs. Mason's rights, and praying that the trust be established and the stock and dividends be awarded to her, Mrs. Mason. It was finally decreed by the District Court on August 18, 1936, after an appeal to the Supreme Court of Idaho, that the stock and dividends belonged to Mrs. Mason. Certiorari to the Supreme Court of Idaho was refused by this Court.

Before the entry of the first decree of the District Court of Idaho, Katherine Mason filed a petition in the Superior Court of Spokane County, Washington, in the probate proceedings involving Amelia Pelkes' will, to remove the executor, John Pelkes, for failure to file his report of distribution and for dissipation of the Sunshine stock. Pelkes by cross-petition claimed the stock. Thereupon Mrs. Mason applied to the Supreme Court of Washington for a writ of prohibition against further proceedings in the Superior Court on the ground of lack of jurisdiction in that court to determine the controversy over the stock. The writ was refused. On May 31, 1935, a judgment was entered in the Superior Court upholding in full the ownership of Pelkes.

After the Supreme Court of Idaho had decided the Idaho suit against Pelkes and Miss Treinies, they filed in August, 1936, a suit in the Superior Court of Washington against Katherine Mason and others alleging that they were the owners of the stock, further alleging that the Idaho decree was invalid for lack of jurisdiction, and asking that their title to the stock be quieted and the Sunshine Mining Company, a party to this and the Idaho suit, be compelled to recognize their ownership. It was at this point in the litigation that the Sunshine Mining Co. filed the bill of interpleader now under consideration. Further proceedings in the suit to quiet title were enjoined by the District Court in this action. [The Court first considered, sua sponte, its own jurisdiction in the case since there was no diversity between the interpleader plaintiff, Sunshine Mining Company, and the Washington defendants. The Court noted that the Interpleader Statute, 28 U.S.C. §1335, requires only minimal diversity—that at least one claimant be diverse in citizenship from at least one adverse claimant. The Court determined that the minimal diversity satisfied the requirement of §2, Article III of the Constitution granting jurisdiction to the federal courts over "Controversies . . . between Citizens of different States."]

Res Judicata of the Idaho Decree.—On the merits, petitioner's objection to the decree below is that it fails to consider and give effect to the Washington judgment of May 31, 1935, awarding the property in question to Pelkes, petitioner's assignor. It is petitioner's claim that the Washington judgment must be considered as effective in this litigation because the question of the jurisdiction of the Washington court was actually litigated before the Supreme Court of Washington and determined favorably to petitioner by the refusal to grant a writ of prohibition against the exercise of jurisdiction by the Washington Superior Court in probate.

This failure to give effect to the judgment is said to infringe the full faith and credit clause of the Constitution. . . .[1]

The Court of Appeals correctly determined that the issue of jurisdiction vel non of the Washington court could not be relitigated in this interpleader. As the Idaho District Court was a court of general jurisdiction, its conclusions are unassailable collaterally except for fraud or lack of jurisdiction. The holding by the Idaho court of no jurisdiction in Washington necessarily determined the question raised here as to the Idaho jurisdiction against Miss Treinies' contention. She is bound by that judgment.

The power of the Idaho court to examine into the jurisdiction of the Washington court is beyond question. Even where the decision against the validity of the original judgment is erroneous, it is a valid exercise of judicial power by the second court.

One trial of an issue is enough. "The principles of res judicata apply to questions of jurisdiction as well as to other issues," as well to jurisdiction of the subject matter as of the parties.

Decree affirmed.

Questions and Comments

(1) Presumably the enforcing state must address any arguments raised against the validity of a judgment it is called on to enforce, including whether there was personal jurisdiction in a default judgment, whether under prevailing law of collateral estoppel the first judgment involved sufficiently similar issues to be entitled to preclusive effect, whether there was adequate notice in the first suit, and the like. On occasion, the enforcing court will decide that the prior judgment is unenforceable. What if it decides wrongly? Doesn't the very authority to address such issues include the authority to make an occasional mistake? Why should such a mistake be entitled to less preclusive effect than a substantive error? If litigating a jurisdictional issue can foreclose later collateral attack (as we saw in Section A of this chapter), then why shouldn't we give the same effect to full and fair litigation of an issue of judgments law? Is anything more than this involved in *Treinies*? On

---

1. It is unnecessary to consider whether the Idaho determination as to the jurisdiction of the Washington court was properly made. As the procedure by which a state court examines into the question of the jurisdiction of the court of a sister state is a matter within the control of the respective states (Adam v. Saenger, 303 U.S. 59, 63), it need only be added that such procedure is subject to question only on direct appeal.

It was stipulated by all parties to the Idaho cause that the Idaho courts might take judicial notice of the statutes and decisions of Washington. Some constitutional and statutory provisions relating to the jurisdiction of the Superior Court were pleaded and admitted. It has long been the rule in Idaho that its courts do not take judicial notice of the laws of another state and that without allegation and evidence it will be assumed the laws are the same as those of Idaho. While none of these cases involved a stipulation, the decision of the Supreme Court of Idaho declares the law of that jurisdiction. It follows from the Idaho court's refusal to look into the statutes of Washington that the jurisdiction of the Washington court was presumed to be governed by Idaho law. Under proper proof, the Idaho court would have been compelled to examine the jurisdiction of the Washington court under Washington law.

the other hand, won't the Court's decision encourage parties to attempt to have valid judgments undercut by the courts of other states because the last-in-time rule will make binding the ruling of the second state? Which concern seems more significant?

(2) If review had been sought from the final order of the Idaho district court, and it had been upheld by the Idaho Supreme Court with certiorari denied by the U.S. Supreme Court, would the result of this case have been any different? Should the Supreme Court be required to take cases that allege that the courts of one state have denied full faith and credit to the judgments of another?

(3) In Parsons Steel v. First Alabama Bank, 474 U.S. 518 (1986), a state court had (arguably, erroneously) refused to give sufficient res judicata effect to an earlier federal court judgment. After losing the res judicata argument in state court, the bank waited until the entire case was resolved and, on entry of judgment, returned to the federal court to request an injunction. The Supreme Court held that this avenue was foreclosed by the Anti-Injunction Act, 28 U.S.C. §2283, even though that Act allowed a federal court to issue injunctions "to protect or effectuate its judgments." The Court of Appeals had upheld the District Court's right to issue the injunction, but the Supreme Court disagreed:

> In reaching this holding, the majority explicitly declined to consider the possible preclusive effect, pursuant to the Full Faith and Credit Act, 28 U.S.C. §1738, of the state's determination after full litigation by the parties that the earlier federal-court judgment did not bar the state action. According to the majority, "while a federal court is generally bound by other state court determinations, the relitigation exception empowers a federal court to be the final adjudicator as to the res judicata effects of its prior judgments on a subsequent state action.". . .
>
> In our view, the majority of the Court of Appeals gave unwarrantedly short shrift to the important values of federalism and comity embodied in the Full Faith and Credit Act. As recently as last March, in Marrese v. American Academy of Orthopaedic Surgeons, 470 U.S. 373 (1985), we reaffirmed our holding in Migra v. Warren City School Dist. Bd. of Education, 465 U.S. 75 (1984), that under the Full Faith and Credit Act a federal court must give the same preclusive effect to a state-court judgment as another court of that State would give. . . . The Full Faith and Credit Act thus "[allows] the States to determine, subject to the requirements of the statute and the Due Process Clause, the preclusive effect of judgments in their own courts."
>
> In the instant case, however, the Court of Appeals did not consider the possible preclusive effect under Alabama law of the state-court judgment, and particularly of the state court's resolution of the res judicata issue, concluding instead that the relitigation exception to the Anti-Injunction Act limits the Full Faith and Credit Act. We do not agree. . . .
>
> We believe that the Anti-Injunction Act and the Full Faith and Credit Act can be construed consistently, simply by limiting the relitigation exception of the Anti-Injunction Act to those situations in which the state court has not yet ruled on the merits of the res judicata issue. Once the state court has finally rejected a claim of res judicata, then the Full Faith and Credit Act becomes

applicable and federal courts must turn to state law to determine the preclusive effect of the state court's decision. . . .

We hold, therefore, that the Court of Appeals erred by refusing to consider the possible preclusive effect, under Alabama law, of the state-court judgment. Even if the state court mistakenly rejected respondents' claim of res judicata, this does not justify the highly intrusive remedy of a federal-court injunction against the enforcement of the state-court judgment. Rather, the Full Faith and Credit Act requires that federal courts give the state-court judgment, and particularly the state court's resolution of the res judicata issue, the same preclusive effect it would have had in another court of the same State. Challenges to the correctness of a state court's determination as to the conclusive effect of a federal judgment must be pursued by way of appeal through the state-court system and certiorari from this Court.

We think the District Court is best situated to determine and apply Alabama preclusion law in the first instance. Should the District Court conclude that the state-court judgment is not entitled to preclusive effect under Alabama law and the Full Faith and Credit Act, it would then be in the best position to decide the propriety of a federal-court injunction under the general principles of equity, comity, and federalism discussed in Mitchum v. Foster, 407 U.S. 225, 243 (1972).

(4) The *Treinies* last-in-time rule addresses courts' obligations under the full faith and credit clause. Consequently, a U.S. court faced with inconsistent foreign judgments need not recognize and enforce the more recent judgment. A case on point is Byblos Bank Europe, S.A. v. Sekerbank Turk Anonym Syrketi, 885 N.E.2d 191 (N.Y. 2008). Byblos, a Belgian bank, had lent $2.5 million to Sekerbank, a Turkish bank, but one of Sekerbank's employees embezzled the loan proceeds and Sekerbank chose not to pay back the loan. Byblos filed lawsuits for breach of the loan agreement seeking to attach Sekerbank's assets in Belgium, Turkey, and Germany. The Turkish court dismissed the action on the merits, and Sekerbank attempted to get the other two courts to recognize the Turkish judgment. The German court recognized the Turkish judgment, but the Belgian courts ultimately refused to recognize it, relying on a now-repealed Belgian statute that requires merits review of foreign judgments as a prerequisite to enforcement. The Belgian court found that the Turkish court judgment was affected by substantial error and entered a contrary judgment in favor of Byblos for $5 million. Byblos then brought the Belgian judgment to a New York state court seeking enforcement of it, and the Court of Appeals of New York decided that the Belgian court judgment should not be recognized. In New York, recognition of judgments rendered outside of the United States is governed by the Uniform Foreign Country Money-Judgments Recognition Act rather than by the full faith and credit clause, and the Act is silent regarding how a court should treat inconsistent judgments. The court may, at its discretion, choose to enforce the earlier, the later, or neither judgment. In this case, the court concluded that enforcement of the Belgian judgment was not appropriate because the Belgian court, as the last-in-time court, departed from normal res judicata principles in rendering its decision. Does this resolution seem sensible?

D.   Domestic Relations: A Special Problem of Judgments

Domestic relations law presents some unique legal problems because of the interplay between the rules of full faith and credit to judgments and the peculiar theoretical basis for jurisdiction in a divorce action. The theory says that a divorce action is an action in rem, the marriage relationship being the res. As with Harris v. Balk (discussed at pages 445-446, *supra*), the problem lies in part in locating the res. Here, the theory indicates that the res is located where either party is domiciled. Thus, there are two states that can grant a divorce to a separated couple domiciled separately. But no more than two states should be available, since domicile, and not mere in personam jurisdiction, is a requisite for full faith and credit to the divorce decree.

This peculiar set of jurisdictional rules raises problems in the context of collateral attacks on judgments of divorce. In Williams v. North Carolina I, 317 U.S. 287 (1942), the state of North Carolina had prosecuted for bigamous cohabitation two North Carolinians who had run off to Nevada to get divorced from their stay-at-home spouses in ex parte Nevada proceedings, and had returned "married" to each other to live in the same small town. The Supreme Court reversed the conviction because it had not been established conclusively that the parties were not domiciled in Nevada. On retrial and conviction, the Supreme Court affirmed in Williams v. North Carolina II, 325 U.S. 226 (1945), because in the second trial the jury had been properly instructed that the Nevada divorce judgments could be found to be void only if the parties did not obtain bona fide domicile in Nevada. Justice Frankfurter's opinion stressed that North Carolina could not be bound by the ex parte conclusions of the Nevada court concerning the parties' domicile.

1.   Ex Parte "Divisible Divorce"

Estin v. Estin
334 U.S. 541 (1948)

Opinion of the Court by Justice DOUGLAS, announced by Justice REED.

This case, here on certiorari to the Court of Appeals of New York, presents an important question under the Full Faith and Credit Clause of the Constitution. Article IV, §1. It is whether a New York decree awarding respondent $180 per month for her maintenance and support in a separation proceeding survived a Nevada divorce decree which subsequently was granted petitioner.

The parties were married in 1937 and lived together in New York until 1942 when the husband left the wife. There was no issue of the marriage. In 1943 she brought an action against him for a separation. He entered a general appearance. The court, finding that he had abandoned her, granted her a decree of separation and awarded her $180 per month as permanent alimony. In January 1944 he went to Nevada where in 1945 he instituted an action for divorce. She was notified of the action by constructive service but entered no appearance in it. In May, 1945, the Nevada court, finding that petitioner had been a bona fide resident of Nevada since January 30, 1944, granted him an absolute divorce "on the ground of three years continual separation, without cohabitation." The Nevada decree made no provision for alimony, though the Nevada court had been advised of the New York decree.

Prior to that time petitioner had made payments of alimony under the New York decree. After entry of the Nevada decree he ceased paying. Thereupon respondent sued in New York for a supplementary judgment for the amount of the arrears. Petitioner appeared in the action and moved to eliminate the alimony provisions of the separation decree by reason of the Nevada decree. The Supreme Court denied the motion and granted respondent judgment for the arrears. The judgment was affirmed by the Appellate Division, and then by the Court of Appeals.

We held in Williams v. North Carolina, *supra*, (1) that a divorce decree granted by a State to one of its domiciliaries is entitled to full faith and credit in a bigamy prosecution brought in another State, even though the other spouse was given notice of the divorce proceeding only through constructive service; and (2) that while the finding of domicile by the court that granted the decree is entitled to prima facie weight, it is not conclusive in a sister State but might be relitigated there. The latter course was followed in this case, as a consequence of which the Supreme Court of New York found, in accord with the Nevada court, that petitioner "is now and since January, 1944, has been a bona fide resident of the State of Nevada."

Petitioner's argument therefore is that the tail must go with the hide—that since by the Nevada decree, recognized in New York, he and respondent are no longer husband and wife, no legal incidence of the marriage remains. We are given a detailed analysis of New York law to show that the New York courts have no power either by statute or by common law to compel a man to support his ex-wife, that alimony is payable only so long as the relation of husband and wife exists, and that in New York, as in some other states, a support order does not survive divorce.

The difficulty with that argument is that the highest court in New York has held in this case that a support order can survive divorce and that this one has survived petitioner's divorce. That conclusion is binding on us, except as it conflicts with the Full Faith and Credit Clause. It is not for us to say whether that ruling squares with what the New York courts said on earlier occasions. It is enough that New York today says that such is her policy. The only question for us is whether New York is powerless to make such a ruling in view of the Nevada decree.

We can put to one side the case where the wife was personally served or where she appeared in the divorce proceedings. The only service on her in this case was by publication and she made no appearance in the Nevada proceeding. The requirements of procedural due process were satisfied and the domicile of the husband in Nevada was foundation for a decree effecting a change in the marital capacity of both parties in all the other States of the Union, as well as in Nevada. But the fact that marital capacity was changed does not mean that every other legal incidence of the marriage was necessarily affected.

Although the point was not adjudicated in Barber v. Barber, the Court in that case recognized that while a divorce decree obtained in Wisconsin by a husband from his absent wife might dissolve the vinculum of the marriage, it did not mean that he was freed from payment of alimony under an earlier separation decree granted by New York. An absolutist might quarrel with the result and demand a rule that once a divorce is granted, the whole of the marriage relation is dissolved, leaving no roots or tendrils of any kind. But there are few areas of the law in black and white. The greys are dominant and even among them the shades are innumerable. For the eternal problem of the law is one of making accommodations between conflicting interests. This is why most legal problems end as questions of degree. That is true of the present problem under the Full Faith and Credit Clause. The question involves important considerations both of law and policy which it is essential to state.

The situations where a judgment of one State has been denied full faith and credit in another State, because its enforcement would contravene the latter's policy, have been few and far between. The Full Faith and Credit Clause is not to be applied, accordion-like, to accommodate our personal predilections. It substituted a command for the earlier principles of comity and thus basically altered the status of the States as independent sovereigns. Williams v. North Carolina. It ordered submission by one State even to hostile policies reflected in the judgment of another State, because the practical operation of the federal system, which the Constitution designed, demanded it. The fact that the requirements of full faith and credit, so far as judgments are concerned, are exacting, if not inexorable, does not mean, however, that the State of the domicile of one spouse may, through the use of constructive service, enter a decree that changes every legal incidence of the marriage relationship.

Marital status involves the regularity and integrity of the marriage relation. It affects the legitimacy of the offspring of marriage. It is the basis of criminal laws, as the bigamy prosecution in Williams v. North Carolina dramatically illustrates. The State has a considerable interest in preventing bigamous marriages and in protecting the offspring of marriages from being bastardized. The interest of the State extends to its domiciliaries. The State should have the power to guard its interest in them by changing or altering their marital status and by protecting them in that changed status throughout the farthest reaches of the nation. For a person domiciled in one State should not be allowed to suffer the penalties of bigamy for living outside the State with the only one which the State of his domicile recognizes as his lawful wife. And children born of the only marriage which is lawful in the State of his domicile should not carry the stigma of bastardy when they move elsewhere. These are matters of legitimate concern to the State of the domicile. They entitle the State of the domicile to bring in the absent spouse through constructive service. In no other way could the State of the domicile have and maintain effective control of the marital status of its domiciliaries.

Those are the considerations that have long permitted the State of the matrimonial domicile to change the marital status of the parties by an ex parte divorce proceeding, Thompson v. Thompson, considerations which in the *Williams* cases we thought were equally applicable to any State in which one spouse had established a bona fide domicile. But those considerations have little relevancy here. In this case New York evinced a concern with this broken marriage when both parties were domiciled in New York and before Nevada had any concern with it. New York was rightly concerned lest the abandoned spouse be left impoverished and perhaps become a public charge. The problem of her livelihood and support is plainly a matter in which her community had a legitimate interest. The New York court, having jurisdiction over both parties, undertook to protect her by granting her a judgment of permanent alimony. Nevada, however, apparently follows the rule that dissolution of the marriage puts an end to a support order. But the question is whether Nevada could under any circumstances adjudicate rights of respondent under the New York judgment when she was not personally served or did not appear in the proceeding.

Bassett v. Bassett, 141 F.2d 954, held that Nevada could not. We agree with that view.

The New York judgment is a property interest of respondent, created by New York in a proceeding in which both parties were present. It imposed obligations on petitioner and granted rights to respondent. The property interest which it created was an intangible, jurisdiction over which cannot be exerted through control over a physical thing. Jurisdiction over an intangible can indeed only arise from control or power over the persons whose relationships are the source of the rights and obligations.

Jurisdiction over a debtor is sufficient to give the State of his domicile some control over the debt which he owes. It can, for example, levy a tax on its transfer by will, appropriate it through garnishment or attachment (*see* Harris v. Balk, 198 U.S. 215), collect it and administer it for the benefit of creditors. But we are aware of no power which the State of domicile of the debtor has to determine the personal rights of the creditor in the intangible unless the creditor has been personally served or appears in the proceeding. The existence of any such power has been repeatedly denied. Pennoyer v. Neff, New York Life Ins. Co. v. Dunlevy.

We know of no source of power which would take the present case out of that category. The Nevada decree that is said to wipe out respondent's claim for alimony under the New York judgment is nothing less than an attempt by Nevada to restrain respondent from asserting her claim under that judgment. That is an attempt to exercise an in personam jurisdiction over a person not before the court. That may not be done. Since Nevada had no power to adjudicate respondent's rights in the New York judgment, New York need not give full faith and credit to that phase of Nevada's judgment. A judgment of a court having no jurisdiction to render it is not entitled to the full faith and credit which the Constitution and statute of the United States demand. Williams v. North Carolina.

The result in this situation is to make the divorce divisible—to give effect to the Nevada decree insofar as it affects marital status and to make it ineffective on the issue of alimony. It accommodates the interests of both Nevada and New York in this broken marriage by restricting each State to the matters of her dominant concern.

Since Nevada had no jurisdiction to alter respondent's rights in the New York judgment, we do not reach the further question whether in any event that judgment would be entitled to full faith and credit in Nevada. And it will be time enough to consider the effect of any discrimination shown to out-of-state ex parte divorces when a State makes that its policy.

Affirmed.

Justice JACKSON, dissenting.

If there is one thing that the people are entitled to expect from their law-makers, it is rules of law that will enable individuals to tell whether they are married and, if so, to whom. Today many people who have simply lived in more than one state do not know, and the most learned lawyer cannot advise them with any confidence. The uncertainties that result are not merely technical, nor are they trivial; they affect fundamental rights and relations such as the lawfulness of their cohabitation, their children's legitimacy, their title to property, and even whether they are law-abiding persons or criminals. In a society as mobile and nomadic as ours, such uncertainties affect large numbers of people and create a social problem of some magnitude. It is therefore important that, whatever we do, we shall not add to the confusion. I think that this decision does just that.

The Court reaches the Solomon-like conclusion that the Nevada decree is half good and half bad under the full faith and credit clause. It is good to free the husband from the marriage; it is not good to free him from its incidental obligations. Assuming the judgment to be one which the Constitution requires to be recognized at all, I do not see how we can square this decision with the command that it be given *full* faith and credit. For reasons which I stated in dissenting in Williams v. North Carolina, I would not give standing under the clause to constructive service divorces obtained on short residence. But if we are to hold this divorce good, I do not see how it can be less good than a divorce would be if rendered by the courts of New York.

May v. Anderson
345 U.S. 528 (1953)

Justice BURTON delivered the opinion of the Court.

The question presented is whether, in a habeas corpus proceeding attacking the right of a mother to retain possession of her minor children, an Ohio court must give full faith and credit to a Wisconsin decree awarding custody of the children to their father when that decree is obtained by the father in an ex parte divorce action in a Wisconsin court which had no personal jurisdiction over the mother. For the reasons hereafter stated, our answer is no.

[The parties, Leona Anderson May and Owen Anderson, were formerly married in Wisconsin, where they resided together until December 1946. At that time, the couple agreed that Leona should take their three children to Ohio so that she could "think over her future course." In January 1947, Leona decided to stay in Ohio, and, when she informed Owen of her decision, he filed suit in Wisconsin, seeking a decree of divorce and an award of custody of the children. Leona received a copy of the summons and petition but she did not participate in the proceedings. In February 1947, the Wisconsin court granted the divorce and awarded custody of the children to Owen subject to a right by Leona to reasonable visitation. Owen then took the decree to Ohio where he demanded and obtained the children, with the assistance of a local police officer.

In July 1951 the children visited their mother in Ohio and she refused to surrender them. Owen filed a petition for a writ of habeas corpus in a probate court in Ohio. Under Ohio procedure, that writ tests only the immediate right to possession of the children and does not permit either the modification of a past custody award or a settling of rights to future custody. The probate court decided that it was obliged by the full faith and credit clause to accept the Wisconsin decree as binding upon the mother. Accordingly, it ordered the children discharged from further restraint by her, but the order has been held in abeyance pending appeal.]

Separated as our issue is from that of the future interests of the children, we have before us the elemental question whether a court of a state, where a mother is neither domiciled, resident nor present, may cut off her immediate right to the care, custody, management and companionship of her minor children without having jurisdiction over her in personam. Rights far more precious to appellant than property rights will be cut off if she is to be bound by the Wisconsin award of custody. "[I]t is now too well settled to be open to further dispute that the 'full faith and credit' clause and the act of Congress passed pursuant to it, do not entitle a judgment in personam to extra-territorial effect if it be made to appear that it was rendered without jurisdiction over the person sought to be bound."

In Estin v. Estin and Kreiger v. Kreiger this Court upheld the validity of a Nevada divorce obtained ex parte by a husband, resident in Nevada, insofar as it dissolved the bonds of matrimony. At the same time, we held Nevada powerless to cut off, in that proceeding, a spouse's right to financial support under the prior decree of another state. In the instant case, we recognize that a mother's right to custody of her children is a personal right entitled to at least as much protection as her right to alimony.

In the instant case, the Ohio courts gave weight to appellee's contention that the Wisconsin award of custody binds appellant because, at the time it was issued, her children had a technical domicile in Wisconsin, although they were neither resident nor present there. We find it unnecessary to determine the children's legal domicile because, even if it be with their father, that does not give Wisconsin, certainly as against Ohio, the personal jurisdiction that it must have in order to deprive their mother of her personal right to their immediate possession.[8]

The judgment of the Supreme Court of Ohio, accordingly, is reversed and the cause is remanded to it for further proceedings not inconsistent with this opinion. . . .

Justice JACKSON, whom Justice REED joins, dissenting.

The Court apparently is holding that the Federal Constitution prohibits Ohio from recognizing the validity of this Wisconsin divorce decree insofar as it settles custody of the couple's children. In the light of settled and unchallenged precedents of this Court, such a decision can only rest upon the proposition that Wisconsin's courts had no jurisdiction to make such a decree binding upon appellant.

A conclusion that a state must not recognize a judgment of a sister commonwealth involves very different considerations than a conclusion that it must do so.

---

8. . . . The instant case does not present the special considerations that arise where a parent, with or without minor children, leaves a jurisdiction for the purpose of escaping process or otherwise evading jurisdiction, and we do not have here the considerations that arise when children are unlawfully or surreptitiously taken by one parent from the other.

If Wisconsin has rendered a valid judgment, the Constitution not only requires every state to give it full faith and credit, but 28 U.S.C. §1738, referring to such judicial proceedings, commands that they "shall have the same full faith and credit in every court within the United States and its Territories and Possessions as they have by law or usage in the courts of such State, Territory or Possession from which they are taken." The only escape from obedience lies in a holding that the judgment rendered in Wisconsin, at least as to custody, is void and entitled to no standing even in Wisconsin. It is void only if it denies due process of law.

The Ohio courts reasoned that although personal jurisdiction over the wife was lacking, domicile of the children in Wisconsin was a sufficient jurisdictional basis to enable Wisconsin to bind all parties interested in their custody. This determination that the children were domiciled in Wisconsin has not been contested either at our bar or below. Therefore, under our precedents, it is conclusive. The husband, plaintiff in the case, was at all times domiciled in Wisconsin; the defendant-wife was a Wisconsin native, was married there and both were domiciled in that State until her move in December 1946, when the parties stipulate that she acquired an Ohio domicile. The children were born in Wisconsin, were always domiciled there, and were physically resident in Wisconsin at all times until December 1946, when their mother took them to Ohio with her. But the Ohio court specifically found that she brought the children to Ohio with the understanding that if she decided not to go back to Wisconsin the children were to be returned to that State. In spite of the fact that she did decide not to return, she kept the children in Ohio. It was under these circumstances that the Wisconsin decree was rendered in February 1947, less than two months after the wife had given up her physical residence in Wisconsin and held the children out of the State in breach of her agreement.

The difference between a proceeding involving the status, custody and support of children and one involving adjudication of property rights is too apparent to require elaboration. In the former, courts are no longer concerned primarily with the proprietary claims of the contestants for the "res" before the court, but with the welfare of the "res" itself. Custody is viewed not with the idea of adjudicating rights *in* the children, as if they were chattels, but rather with the idea of making the best disposition possible for the welfare of the children. To speak of a court's "cutting off" a mother's right to custody of her children, as if it raised problems similar to those involved in "cutting off" her rights in a plot of ground, is to obliterate these obvious distinctions. Personal jurisdiction of all parties to be affected by a proceeding is highly desirable, to make certain that they have had valid notice and opportunity to be heard. But the assumption that it overrides all other considerations and in its absence a state is constitutionally impotent to resolve questions of custody flies in the face of our own cases.

Questions and Comments

(1) It is clear, isn't it, that domicile should provide enough of an interest for the state to grant the divorce? Think of the situation of the defendant spouse who cannot be found—should the other remain perpetually married? And if the state of domicile may grant a divorce, wouldn't it be intolerable for it not to be given full faith and credit, so that a person might be married in one place and not

another? If this reasoning holds, is there any sensible alternative to the holding in Estin v. Estin that Nevada could terminate the marriage of the parties but not the husband's obligation to support his former wife?

(2) The conceptual framework for the doctrine of divisible divorce—that the basic divorce action is in rem, with the marriage relationship the res, located where either spouse lives, while other aspects of the action are in personam—received an interesting test in Carr v. Carr, 46 N.Y.2d 270 (1978). There, decedent Paul Carr had obtained an ex parte Honduran divorce from his wife Ann in 1967. At the time, Ann was living in New York. Later, Paul married Barbara, who at all relevant times lived in California. When Paul died and Ann learned that Barbara had applied for survivor benefits under the Foreign Service Retirement and Disability System (Paul had been with the Foreign Service), Ann brought an action in New York to invalidate the Honduran divorce and declare herself Paul's lawful surviving spouse. The New York court decided that it had no jurisdiction, despite the possibility of saying that the marital "res" was in New York. It pointed out that the real defendant was Barbara, and that she had never had any contacts with New York.

Along similar lines, California refused jurisdiction in a case brought by a Californian to have defendant declared his father. Hartford v. Superior Court, 47 Cal. 2d 447 (1956). Defendant was not domiciled in California, but plaintiff sought to analogize the father-son relationship to the marriage relationship and thus avoid the need for in personam jurisdiction. Justice Traynor said that the difference between divorce and establishing paternity was the difference "between the state's power to insulate its domiciliary from a relationship with one not within its jurisdiction and its lack of power to reach out and fasten a relationship upon a person over whom it has no jurisdiction." Is the distinction significant?

(3) Wasn't the result in May v. Anderson clearly wrong for the reasons stated by Justice Jackson? If the presence of real property within the state gives the state enough interest to determine the rights in it of those over whom it has no in personam jurisdiction, why can't the same be said when the "property" is a child—in whom the state presumably has a stronger interest? Wouldn't such reasoning work under *Shaffer*, page 446 *supra*? And even if it is considered necessary to obtain in personam jurisdiction over the wife in *May*, didn't Wisconsin have "minimal contacts" with her under the *International Shoe* standard? Isn't it strange that after *May* there is *no state* where either of the spouses can stay at home and sue? (Of course either can go to the domicile of the other, but at the risk of less favorable law.)

Is there anything in *Kulko*, *supra* page 413, that suggests a different result?

(4) Is the rule that a state can grant a divorce if one of its spouses is a domiciliary a constitutional rule? If so, does this mean that a non-domicile state has no constitutional authority to grant a divorce? If a non-domicile state issues a judgment of divorce, may other states recognize it?

Note: Full Faith and Credit and Bilateral Divorce

Under *Williams II*, *supra* page 558, a sister state is entitled to ignore a divorce decree issued in an ex parte proceeding if the recognizing court determines that the spouse seeking the divorce was not a bona fide domiciliary of the state issuing the judgment. Can a decree be similarly challenged when the divorce proceedings were bilateral?

In Johnson v. Muelberger, 340 U.S. 581 (1951), a daughter seeking to defeat her step-mother's spousal claim to a statutory one-third right to her father's estate argued that the step-mother was not validly married to her father. Specifically, the daughter argued that her father's divorce from his second wife was invalid, thereby defeating his subsequent attempt to marry her step-mother. Although decedent and his second wife resided in New York, in 1942, she filed for and obtained a divorce in Florida without satisfying Florida's 90-day residency jurisdictional requirement. Decedent had appeared in the Florida proceedings and contested the merits. In 1944 decedent married the step-mother, and in 1945 he died, leaving his entire estate to his daughter by will. New York's Surrogate's Court determined that the daughter could not attack the validity of the Florida decree because the divorce was contested and was not subject to collateral attack in Florida, but the New York Court of Appeals reversed. The U.S. Supreme Court concluded that the Florida court decree was entitled to full faith and credit. Under full faith and credit principles, a party who is personally served or who appears personally in divorce proceedings would not be permitted to challenge the decree, and third parties would be permitted to challenge the decree only if the challenge was permitted under the laws of the rendering state. According to Florida law, if the divorcing parties are unable to collaterally attack the decree, third parties are similarly barred. As a result, the third-party challenge is impermissible throughout the United States.

Presumably ex parte proceedings are special for full faith and credit purposes because domicile determinations lack the reliability produced by adversarial proceedings. But are bilateral divorces any more adversarial regarding jurisdictional questions, at least when couples have a joint interest in thwarting domicile divorce constraints? Could these incentives be dampened with a choice-of-law rule requiring divorce courts to apply the law of the marital domicile? If both spouses were willing to lie about a change of domicile of one spouse in order to obtain the divorce, should third parties be permitted to contest its validity?

Should third parties ever be permitted to contest the validity of others' divorces? If not, can you comfortably distinguish the situation in Matter of Ranftle, 81 A.D.3d 566, 917 N.Y.S.2d 195 (2011), where third parties are entitled to challenge the validity of a marriage? Should the state be permitted to prosecute colluding spouses for bigamy if they remarry?

Should the IRS be permitted to mount a collateral attack on a bilateral divorce? The principle of *Muelberger* presumably does not apply in the case of a bilateral divorce granted by another country, since the full faith and credit clause applies only to state judgments. In Boyter v. Commissioner of Internal Revenue, 668 F.2d 1382 (4th Cir. 1982), the Boyters had twice obtained year-end divorces, once in Haiti and once in the Dominican Republic. After filing separate tax returns (to avoid the "marital penalty"), they remarried. The Fourth Circuit ruled that under the Internal Revenue Code the IRS was bound by state law on the question of whether the Boyters were married. Without answering that question, the court remanded the case for a determination of whether the divorce was a "sham transaction" not deserving recognition under the Internal Revenue Code. Is it consistent to say that state law will be followed to determine whether the Boyters were validly divorced but that, even if they were, their divorce may be considered a "sham transaction"? Foreign country divorces will routinely be given comity if they appear regular and if the parties were actually domiciled in the foreign country at the time.

2.   Modifications: Child Custody and Support

Yarborough v. Yarborough

290 U.S. 202 (1933)

Justice BRANDEIS delivered the opinion of the Court.

On August 10, 1930, Sadie Yarborough, then sixteen years of age, was living with her maternal grandfather, R. D. Blowers, at Spartanburg, South Carolina. Suing by him as guardian ad litem, she brought this action in a court of that State to require her father, W. A. Yarborough, a resident of Atlanta, Georgia, to make provision for her education and maintenance. She alleged "that she is now ready for college and is without funds and, unless the defendant makes provision for her, will be denied the necessities of life and an education, and will be dependent upon the charity of others."[1] Jurisdiction was obtained by attachment of defendant's property. Later he was served personally within South Carolina.

In bar of the action, W. A. Yarborough set up, among other defenses, a judgment entered in 1929 by the Superior Court of Fulton County, Georgia, in a suit for divorce brought by him against Sadie's mother. He alleged that by the judgment the amount thereafter to be paid by him for Sadie's education and maintenance had been determined; that the sum so fixed had been paid; and that the judgment had been fully satisfied by him. He claimed that in Georgia the judgment was conclusive of the matter here in controversy; that having been satisfied, it relieved him, under the Georgia law, of all obligation to provide for the education and maintenance of their minor child; and that the full faith and credit clause of the Federal Constitution (Art. IV, §1) required the South Carolina court to give to that judgment the same effect in this proceeding which it has, and would have, in Georgia. The trial court denied the claim; ordered W. A. Yarborough to pay to the grandfather, as trustee, fifty dollars monthly for Sadie's education and support; and to pay $300 as fees of her counsel.

For sometime prior to June, 1927, W. A. Yarborough, his wife and their daughter Sadie had lived together at Atlanta, Georgia, where he then was, and ever since has been, domiciled. In that month, Sadie's mother left Atlanta for Hendersonville, N.C., where she remained during the summer. Sadie joined her there, after a short stay at a camp. In September, 1927, while they were at Hendersonville, W. A. Yarborough brought, in the Superior Court for Fulton County, at Atlanta, suit against his wife for a total divorce on the ground of mental

---

1. There was no suggestion that plaintiff would be destitute or become a public charge. Indeed, her grandfather testified that he was able and willing to provide $125 a month for her education and maintenance (the amount sought by plaintiff), if her father was unable to do so.

and physical cruelty. Mrs. Yarborough filed an answer and also a cross-suit in which she prayed a total divorce, the custody of the child and "that provision for permanent alimony be made for the support of the respondent and the minor child above mentioned [Sadie], and for the education of said minor child." An order, several times modified, awarded to the wife the custody of Sadie and, as temporary alimony, sums "for the support and maintenance of herself and her minor daughter Sadie." Hearings were held from time to time at Atlanta. At some of these, Sadie (and also her grandfather) was personally present. But she was not formally made a party to the litigation; she was not served with process; and no guardian ad litem was appointed for her therein.

[A] decree of total divorce, with the right in each to remarry, was entered on June 7, 1929; the wife was ordered to pay the costs; and jurisdiction of the case "was retained for the purpose of further enforcement of the orders of the court theretofore passed."[3] Among such orders, was the provision for the maintenance and education of Sadie here relied upon as res judicata. It was entered on January 17, 1929 (after the rendition of the first verdict). . . . It was contended below in the trial court, and there held, that the provision of the decree of the Georgia court directing the payment to R. D. Blowers, trustee, of $1,750 to be "expended by him in his discretion for the benefit of the minor child, including her education, support, maintenance, medical attention and other necessary items of expenditure" was not intended to relieve the father from all further liability to support Sadie. This contention appears to have been abandoned. It is clear that Mrs. Yarborough, her husband and the court intended that this provision should absolve Sadie's father from further obligation to support her. That the term "permanent alimony" as used in the decree of the Georgia court, means a final provision for the minor child is shown by both the legislation of the State and the decisions of its highest court. The refusal of the South Carolina court to give the judgment effect as against Sadie is now sought to be justified on other grounds.

The fact that Sadie has become a resident of South Carolina does not impair the finality of the judgment. South Carolina thereby acquired the jurisdiction to determine her status and the incidents of that status. Upon residents of that State it could impose duties for her benefit. Doubtless, it might have imposed upon her grandfather who was resident there a duty to support Sadie. But the mere fact of Sadie's residence in South Carolina does not give that State the power to impose such a duty upon the father who is not a resident and who long has been domiciled in Georgia. He has fulfilled the duty which he owes her by the law of his domicile and the judgment of its court. Upon that judgment he is entitled to rely. It was settled by Sistare v. Sistare, 218 U.S. 1, that the full faith and credit clause applies to an unalterable decree of alimony for a divorced wife. The clause applies, likewise, to an unalterable decree of alimony for a minor child. We need not consider whether South Carolina would have power to require the father, if he were domiciled there, to make further provision for the support, maintenance, or education of his daughter.

Reversed.

---

3. Custody of Sadie had been awarded to the mother; and it had been ordered that the father be allowed the privilege of visiting his said minor daughter [at regular intervals]. . . .

Justice STONE, dissenting.

I think the judgment should be affirmed.

The divorce decree of the Georgia court purported to adjudicate finally, both for the present and for the future, the right of a minor child of the marriage to support and maintenance, by directing her father to make a lump sum payment for that purpose. More than two years later, after the minor had become a domiciled resident of South Carolina, and after the sum paid had been exhausted, a court of that State, on the basis of her need as then shown, has rendered a judgment directing further payments for her support out the property of the father in South Carolina, in addition to that already commanded by the Georgia judgment.

For present purposes we may take it that the Georgia decree, as the statutes and decisions of the State declare, is unalterable and, as pronounced, is effective to govern the rights of the parties in Georgia. But there is nothing in the decree itself, or in the history of the proceedings which led to it, to suggest that it was rendered with any purpose or intent to regulate or control the relationship of parent and child, or the duties which flow from it, in places outside the State of Georgia where they might later come to reside. It would hardly be thought that Georgia, by judgment of its courts more than by its statutes, would attempt to regulate the relationship of parents and child domiciled outside of the State at the very time the decree was rendered; and, in the face of constitutional doubts that arise here, it is far from clear that its decree is to be interpreted as attempting to do more than to regulate that relationship while the infant continued to be domiciled within the State. But if we are to read the decree as though it contained a clause, in terms, restricting the power of any other state, in which the minor might come to reside, to make provision for her support, then, in the absence of some law of Congress requiring it, I am not persuaded that the full faith and credit clause gives sanction to such control by one state of the internal affairs of another.

Congress has said that the public records and the judicial proceedings of each state are to be given such faith and credit in other states as is accorded to them in the state "from which they are taken." But this broad language has never been applied without limitations. *See* McElmoyle v. Cohen, 13 Pet. 312. Between the prohibition of the due process clause, acting upon the courts of the state from which such proceedings may be taken, and the mandate of the full faith and credit clause, acting upon the state to which they may be taken, there is an area which federal authority has not occupied. As this Court has often recognized, there are many judgments which need not be given the same force and effect abroad which they have at home, and there are some, though valid in the state where rendered, to which the full faith and credit clause gives no force elsewhere. In the assertion of rights, defined by a judgment of one state, within the territory of another, there is often an inescapable conflict of interest of the two states, and there comes a point beyond which the imposition of the will of one state beyond its own borders involves a forbidden infringement of some legitimate domestic interest of the other. That point may vary with the circumstances of the case; and in the absence of provisions more specific than the general terms of the congressional enactment this Court must determine for itself the extent to which one state may qualify or deny rights claimed under proceedings or records of other states.

The question presented here is whether the support and maintenance of a minor child, domiciled in South Carolina, is so peculiarly a subject of domestic concern that Georgia law can not impair South Carolina's authority. The subject matter of the judgment in each state is the duty which government may impose on a parent to support a minor child. The maintenance and support of children domiciled within a state, like their education and custody, is a subject in which government itself is deemed to have a peculiar interest and concern. Their tender years, their inability to provide for themselves, the importance to the state that its future citizens should be clothed, nourished and suitably educated, are considerations which lead all civilized countries to assume some control over the maintenance of minors.[12] The states very generally make some provision from their own resources for the maintenance and support of orphans or destitute children, but in order that children may not become public charges the duty of maintenance is one imposed primarily upon the parents, according to the needs of the child and their ability to meet those needs. This is usually accomplished by suit brought directly by some public officer, by the child by guardian or next friend, or by the mother, against the father for maintenance and support. The measure of the duty is the needs of the child and the ability of the parent to meet those needs at the very time when performance of the duty is invoked. Hence, it is no answer in such a suit that at some earlier time provision was made for the child, which is no longer available or suitable because of his greater needs, or because of the increased financial ability of the parent to provide for them, or that the child may be maintained from other sources.

In view of the universality of these principles it comes as a surprise that any state, merely because it has made some provision for the support of a child, should, either by statute or judicial decree, so tie its own hands as to foreclose all future inquiry into the duty of maintenance however affected by changed conditions.

Even though the Constitution does not deny to Georgia the power to indulge in such a policy for itself, it by no means follows that it gives to Georgia the privilege of prescribing that policy for other states in which the child comes to live. South Carolina has adopted a different policy. It imposes on the father or his property located within the state the duty to support his minor child domiciled there. . . .

The decision in Sistare v. Sistare lends no support to the contention that South Carolina can be precluded by a judgment of another state from providing for the future maintenance and support of a destitute child domiciled within its own borders, out of the property of her father, also located there. Here the Georgia decree did not end the relationship of parent and child, as a decree of divorce may end the marriage relationship. Had the infant continued to reside in Georgia, and had she sought in the courts of South Carolina to compel the application of property of her father, found there, to her further maintenance and support, full faith and credit to the Georgia decree applied to its own domiciled resident might have required the denial of any relief. *Cf.* Bates v. Bodie, 245 U.S.

---

12. This control is particularly important in the case of the children of divorced couples. They are usually young; in Maryland over 60% are under ten years of age when divorce occurs. Divorces are often not contested and the intervention of a disinterested judge is frequently nominal. Allowances for children in the divorce court are typically small. Marshall & May, *The Divorce Court*, 31, 79-80, 82, 226-321, 323.

520; Thompson v. Thompson, 226 U.S. 551. But when she became a domiciled resident of South Carolina, a new interest came into being,—the interest of the State of South Carolina as a measure of self-preservation to secure the adequate protection and maintenance of helpless members of its own community and its prospective citizens. That interest was distinct from any which Georgia could conclusively regulate or control by its judgment, even though rendered while the child was domiciled in Georgia. The present decision extends the operation of the full faith and credit clause beyond its proper function of affording protection to the domestic interests of Georgia and makes it an instrument for encroachment by Georgia upon the domestic concerns of South Carolina.

Justice CARDOZO concurs in this opinion.

Questions and Comments

(1) Isn't there a striking resemblance between the dissenting opinion in *Yarborough* and the plurality opinion in Thomas v. Washington Gas Light, page 520 *supra*? Both suggest that the rendering state is overreaching if it attempts to define the continuing effect of its judgments in another state. Does that suggest that the *Thomas* plurality is inconsistent with the majority holding in *Yarborough*?

(2) *Yarborough* dealt with an unusual state law, which made awards of child support unmodifiable. If one takes seriously the text of the full faith and credit statute, then it seems clear that other states must treat the award as unmodifiable also. But conversely, the language of the full faith and credit statute offers enormous freedom to modify judgments from states with res judicata rules making such awards modifiable as a domestic matter.

(3) One related area in which this reasoning caused great problems was the modification of child custody awards. A disgruntled parent might simply take the child to another state and attempt to get a modification before some more sympathetic judicial forum. The problem of interstate child kidnapping grew to such serious proportions that 28 U.S.C. §1738 was amended, adding a new section in the effort to limit a state's power to modify awards rendered in other states. The current version of the statute, known as the Parental Kidnapping Prevention Act (or PKPA), provides:

§1738A. Full Faith and Credit Given to Child Custody Determinations

(a) The appropriate authorities of every State shall enforce according to its terms, and shall not modify except as provided in subsections (f), (g), and (h) of this section, any custody determination or visitation determination made consistently with the provisions of this section by a court of another State.

(b) As used in this section, the term—

. . .

(3) "custody determination" means a judgment, decree, or other order of a court providing for the custody of a child, and includes permanent and temporary orders, and initial orders and modifications;

. . .

(9) "visitation determination" means a judgment, decree, or other order of a court providing for the visitation of a child and includes permanent and temporary orders and initial orders and modifications.

(c) A child custody or visitation determination made by a court of a State is consistent with the provisions of this section only if—

(1) such court has jurisdiction under the law of such State; and

(2) one of the following conditions is met:

(A) such State (i) is the home State of the child on the date of the commencement of the proceeding, or (ii) had been the child's home State within six months before the date of the commencement of the proceeding and the child is absent from such State because of his removal or retention by a contestant or for other reasons, and a contestant continues to live in such State;

(B) (i) it appears that no other State would have jurisdiction under subparagraph (A), and (ii) it is in the best interest of the child that a court of such State assume jurisdiction because (I) the child and his parents, or the child and at least one contestant, have a significant connection with such State other than mere physical presence in such State, and (II) there is available in such State substantial evidence concerning the child's present or future care, protection, training, and personal relationships;

(C) the child is physically present in such State and (i) the child has been abandoned, or (ii) it is necessary in an emergency to protect the child because the child, a sibling, or parent of the child has been subjected to or threatened with mistreatment or abuse;

(D) (i) it appears that no other State would have jurisdiction under subparagraph (A), (B), (C), or (E), or another State has declined to exercise jurisdiction on the ground that the State whose jurisdiction is in issue is the more appropriate forum to determine the custody or visitation of the child, and (ii) it is in the best interest of the child that such court assume jurisdiction; or

(E) the court has continuing jurisdiction pursuant to subsection (d) of this section.

(d) The jurisdiction of a court of a State which has made a child custody or visitation determination consistently with the provisions of this section continues as long as the requirement of subsection (c)(1) of this section continues to be met and such State remains the residence of the child or of any contestant.

(e) Before a child custody or visitation determination is made, reasonable notice and opportunity to be heard shall be given to the contestants, any parent whose parental rights have not been previously terminated and any person who has physical custody of a child.

(f) A court of a State may modify a determination of the custody of the same child made by a court of another State, if—

(1) it has jurisdiction to make such a child custody determination; and

(2) the court of the other State no longer has jurisdiction, or it has declined to exercise such jurisdiction to modify such determination.

(g) A court of a State shall not exercise jurisdiction in any proceeding for a custody or visitation determination commenced during the pendency of a proceeding in a court of another State where such court of that other State is exercising jurisdiction consistently with the provisions of this section to make a custody determination.

(h) A court of a State may not modify a visitation determination made by a court of another State unless the court of the other State no longer has jurisdiction to modify such determination or has declined to exercise jurisdiction to modify such determination.

(4) The PKPA was in part a response to the perceived inadequacies in the Uniform Child Custody Jurisdiction Act ("UCCJA"), 9 U.L.A. §116, which has been adopted in every state. For a valuable discussion of the history of the two laws, the way they fit together, and the many difficulties in their application, *see* Goldstein, *The Tragedy of the Interstate Child: A Critical Reexamination of the Uniform Child Custody Jurisdiction Act and the Parental Kidnapping Prevention Act*, 25 U.C. Davis L. Rev. 845 (1992). In 1997, the Commissioners on Uniform State Laws promulgated the Uniform Child Custody Jurisdiction and Enforcement Act ("UCCJEA"), a revision of the UCCJA designed to bring it into conformity with the PKPA and to further clarify the jurisdictional and substantive law of interstate child custody. For analysis of the UCCJEA, *see* Spector, *Uniform Child-Custody Jurisdiction and Enforcement Act*, 32 Fam. L.Q. 301, 305 (1998); Hoff, *The ABC's of the UCCJEA: Interstate Child-Custody Practice Under the New Act*, 32 Fam. L.Q. 267, 278 (1998). For cases applying both the PKPA and UCCJEA, *see* Jorgensen v. Vargas, 627 N.W.2d 550 (Iowa 2001); Seamans v. Seamans, 73 Ark. App. 27 (2001); In re Marriage of Newsome, 68 Cal. App. 4th 949 (1998).

(5) The Supreme Court has held that the PKPA does not create a federal cause of action. Thompson v. Thompson, 484 U.S. 174 (1988). Primary responsibility for enforcement of the Act therefore rests with state courts, with appellate review to the United States Supreme Court.

(6) Is an Indian tribe a "State" within the meaning of the PKPA? *See* In re Larch, 872 F.2d 66 (1988), holding that tribal courts are bound by the Act.

(7) International child custody cases are subject to a web of overlapping conventions, the primary one of which is the Hague Convention on the Civil Aspects of International Child Abduction (1980). For commentary, *see* Symposium, *Symposium Issue Celebrating Twenty Years: The Past and Promise of the 1980 Hague Convention on the Civil Aspects of International Child Abduction*, 33 N.Y.U. J. Intl. L. & Pol. 1 (2000); Harper, *The Limitations of the Hague Convention and Alternative Remedies for a Parent Including Re-Abduction*, 9 Emory Intl. L. Rev. 257 (1995); Finan, *Convention on the Rights of the Child: A Potentially Effective Remedy in Cases of International Child Abduction*, 34 Santa Clara L. Rev. 1007 (1994). A federal statute does provide a cause of action for wrongful removal or retention under the Convention, and the Supreme Court has stated that U.S. courts should act in accordance with a broad interpretation of Convention obligations. *See* Abbott v. Abbott, 560 U.S. 1 (2010).

8

Extraterritoriality of Federal Law

This chapter focuses on the extraterritorial scope of federal law. The issues confronted in the cases below have close parallels to those in the state law choice-of-law cases we analyzed in Chapters 2 and 3, some of which involved conflicts between state law and foreign law. Recall that, in some of the cases discussed above, the court understood choice-of-law rules to function as implicit limitations on the extraterritorial scope of forum law. *See, e.g., Carroll, supra* page 15 ("Section 2590 of the Code . . . is to be interpreted in the light of universally recognized principles of private international or interstate law, as if its operation had been expressly limited to this State and as if its first line had read as follows: 'When a personal injury is received in Alabama by a servant or employee,' &c, &c."). If so, then the doctrines that the Court has articulated to address the extraterritorial scope of federal statutes might be understood as a federal choice-of-law doctrine for conflicts between federal law and foreign law. *See* Vázquez, *Choice of Law as Geographic Scope Limitation*, in *Resolving Conflicts in the Law: Essays in Honour of Lea Brilmayer* (Giorgetti & Klein eds., 2019).

The cases below show that federal extraterritoriality doctrine has traversed much the same path as state choice-of-law doctrine—but has recently taken a sharp turn back to a more territorialist approach. As you read these cases, consider whether, in the context of federal law, the question of extraterritoriality implicates special concerns, including concerns grounded in separation of powers, U.S. foreign policy, and international law, that justify a sharply different approach than for state choice of law. We begin by looking at the federal courts' shifting approaches to determining the extraterritorial scope of the federal antitrust laws. We then focus on the Court's current approach to federal extraterritoriality: the presumption against extraterritoriality.

A. The Extraterritorial Scope of the Antitrust Laws

This section traces the federal courts' evolving approaches to determining the extraterritorial scope of the federal antitrust laws, which parallel in some respects the shifting choice-of-law approaches employed by the state courts, discussed in Chapters 2 and 3, *supra*. The principal statutes are the Sherman Act, enacted in 1890, and the Clayton Act, enacted in 1914. Section 1 of the Sherman Act declares illegal "[e]very contract, combination in the form of trust or otherwise, or conspiracy, in restraint of trade or commerce among the several States, or with foreign nations." Section 2 provides that "[e]very person who shall monopolize, or attempt to monopolize, or combine or conspire with any other person or persons, to monopolize any part of the trade or commerce among the several States, or with foreign nations, shall be deemed guilty of a felony." Section 4 of the Clayton Act provides that "any person who shall be injured in his business or property by reason of anything forbidden in the antitrust laws may sue therefor in any district court of the United States in the district in which the defendant resides or is found or has an agent, without respect to the amount in controversy, and shall recover threefold the damages by him sustained, and the cost of suit, including a reasonable attorney's fee."

1. Unilateral Approaches

a. *The Place of the Conduct*

American Banana Co. v. United Fruit Co.

213 U.S. 347 (1909)

Mr. Justice HOLMES delivered the opinion of the court:

This is an action brought to recover threefold damages under the act to protect trade against monopolies. The circuit court dismissed the complaint upon motion, as not setting forth a cause of action. This judgment was affirmed by the circuit court of appeals, and the case then was brought to this court by writ of error.

The allegations of the complaint may be summed up as follows: The plaintiff is an Alabama corporation, organized in 1904. The defendant is a New Jersey corporation, organized in 1899. Long before the plaintiff was formed, the defendant, with intent to prevent competition and to control and monopolize the banana trade, bought the property and business of several of its previous competitors, with provision against their resuming the trade, made contracts with others, including a majority of the most important, regulating the quantity to be purchased and the price to be paid, and acquired a controlling amount of stock in still others. For the same purpose it organized a selling company, of which it held the stock, that by agreement sold at fixed prices all the bananas of the combining parties. By this and other means it did monopolize and restrain the trade and maintained unreasonable prices. The defendant being in this ominous attitude, one McConnell, in 1903, started a banana plantation in Panama, then part of the United States of Columbia, and began to build a railway (which would afford his only means of export), both in accordance with the laws of the United States of Columbia. He was notified by the defendant that he must either combine or stop. Two months later, it is believed at the defendant's instigation, the governor of Panama recommended to his national government that Costa Rica be allowed to administer the territory through which the railroad was to run, and this although that territory had been awarded to Colombia under an arbitration agreed to by treaty. The defendant, and afterwards, in September, the government of Costa Rica, it is believed by the inducement of the defendant, interfered with McConnell. In November, 1903, Panama revolted and became an independent republic, declaring its boundary to be that settled by the award. In June, 1904, the plaintiff bought out McConnell and went on with the work, as it had a right to do under the laws of Panama. But in July, Costa Rican soldiers and officials, instigated by the defendant, seized a part of the plantation and a cargo of supplies and have held them ever since, and stopped the construction and operation of the plantation and railway. In August one Astua, by *ex parte* proceedings, got a judgment from a Costa Rican court, declaring the plantation to be his, although, it is alleged, the proceedings were not within the jurisdiction of Costa Rica, and were contrary to its laws and void. Agents of the defendant then bought the lands from Astua. The plaintiff has tried to induce the government of Costa Rica to withdraw its soldiers, and also has tried to persuade the United States to interfere, but has been thwarted in both by the defendant and has failed. The government of Costa Rica remained in possession down to the bringing of the suit.

As a result of the defendant's acts the plaintiff has been deprived of the use of the plantation, and the railway, the plantation, and supplies have been injured. The defendant also, by outbidding, has driven purchasers out of the market and has compelled producers to come to its terms, and it has prevented the plaintiff from buying for export and sale. This is the substantial damage alleged. . . .

It is obvious that, however stated, the plaintiff's case depends on several rather startling propositions. In the first place, the acts causing the damage were done, so far as appears, outside the jurisdiction of the United States, and within that of other states. It is surprising to hear it argued that they were governed by the act of Congress.

No doubt in regions subject to no sovereign, like the high seas, or to no law that civilized countries would recognize as adequate, such countries may treat some relations between their citizens as governed by their own law, and keep, to some extent, the old notion of personal sovereignty alive. See The Hamilton (Old Dominion S. S. Co. v. Gilmore) 207 U.S. 398, 403, 52 L. ed. 264, 269, 28 Sup. Ct. Rep. 133; Hart v. Gumpach, L. R. 4 P. C. 439, 463, 464; British South Africa Co. v. Companhia de Mocambique, [1893] A. C. 602. They go further, at times, and declare that they will punish anyone, subject or not, who shall do certain things, if they can catch him, as in the case of pirates on the high seas. In cases immediately affecting national interests they may go further still and may make, and, if they get the chance, execute, similar threats as to acts done within another recognized jurisdiction. An illustration from our statutes is found with regard to criminal correspondence with foreign governments. . . . But the general and almost universal rule is that the character of an act as lawful or unlawful must be determined wholly by the law of the country where the act is done. Slater v. Mexican Nat. R. Co. 194 U.S. 120, 126. This principle was carried to an extreme in Milliken v. Pratt [*supra* page 44]. For another jurisdiction, if it should happen to lay hold of the actor, to treat him according to its own notions rather than those of the place where he did the acts, not only would be unjust, but would be an interference with the authority of another sovereign, contrary to the comity of nations, which the other state concerned justly might resent. Phillips v. Eyre, L. R. 4 Q. B. 225, 239, L. R. 6 Q. B. 1, 28; Dicey, Confl. L. 2d ed. 647. . . .

The foregoing considerations would lead, in case of doubt, to a construction of any statute as intended to be confined in its operation and effect to the territorial limits over which the lawmaker has general and legitimate power. 'All legislation is prima facie territorial.' Ex parte Blain, L. R. 12 Ch. Div. 522, 528; State v. Carter, 27 N. J. L. 499; People v. Merrill, 2 Park. Crim. Rep. 590, 596. Words having universal scope, such as 'every contract in restraint of trade,' 'every person who shall monopolize,' etc., will be taken, as a matter of course, to mean only everyone subject to such legislation, not all that the legislator subsequently may be able to catch. In the case of the present statute, the improbability of the United States attempting to make acts done in Panama or Costa Rica criminal is obvious, yet the law begins by making criminal the acts for which it gives a right to sue. We think it entirely plain that what the defendant did in Panama or Costa Rica is not within the scope of the statute so far as the present suit is concerned. Other objections of a serious nature are urged, but need not be discussed.

For again, not only were the acts of the defendant in Panama or Costa Rica not within the Sherman act, but they were not torts by the law of the place, and therefore were not . . . torts at all, however contrary to the ethical and economic postulates of that statute. . . .

Questions and Comments

(1) *American Banana* was decided during the heyday of the territorialist approach to choice of law reflected in the First Restatement. Like the court in *Carroll*, *supra* page 17, the Court understood the question before it as involving the "construction of [the] statute," and it presumed that "[w]ords having universal scope" were not intended to be read literally, but were instead meant by the legislature to be "confined in [their] operation and effect to the territorial limits over which the lawmaker has general and legitimate power."

(2) In applying the principle that "[a]ll legislation is prima facie territorial," why did the Court focus on the place where "the acts causing the damage were done" rather than, as in the *Carroll* case, the place of the injury? What was the place of the plaintiff's injury in *American Banana*?

(3) The Court soon departed from *American Banana*'s construction of the Sherman Act as applicable only to acts performed within the territory of the United States. The "place of the conduct" test was replaced by the "effects" test, which received its canonical expression in the *Alcoa* case, excerpted below. (The Second Circuit decided the appeal in *Alcoa* in lieu of the Supreme Court because the Supreme Court lacked a quorum.)

b.   The Effects Test

United States v. Aluminum Co. of America
148 F.2d 416 (2d Cir. 1945)

L. HAND, Circuit Judge.

. . . [This] action was brought under [the Sherman Antitrust Act], praying the district court to adjudge that the defendant, Aluminum Company of America, was monopolizing interstate and foreign commerce, particularly in the manufacture and sale of 'virgin' aluminum ingot, and that it be dissolved; and further to adjudge that that company and the defendant, Aluminum Limited, had entered into a conspiracy in restraint of such commerce. . . . On June 12, 1944, the Supreme Court, declaring that a quorum of six justices qualified to hear the case was wanting, referred the appeal to this court under §29 of Title 15. . . . For convenience we have divided our discussion into four parts: (1) whether 'Alcoa' monopolized the market in 'virgin' aluminum ingot; (2) whether 'Alcoa' was guilty of various unlawful practices, ancillary to the establishment of its monopoly; (3) whether 'Limited' and 'Alcoa' were in an unlawful conspiracy; and whether, if not, 'Limited' was guilty of a conspiracy with foreign producers; (4) what remedies are appropriate in the case of each defendant who may be found to have violated the Act.

[Parts I-II omitted.]

III.

'Limited.'

. . .

'Limited' was incorporated in Canada on May 31, 1928, to take over those properties of 'Alcoa' which were outside the United States.

[W]e are concerned [here] only with whether Congress chose to attach liability to the conduct outside the United States of persons not in allegiance to it. That being so, the only question open is whether Congress intended to impose the liability, and whether our own Constitution permitted it to do so: as a court of the United States, we cannot look beyond our own law. Nevertheless, it is quite true that we are not to read general words, such as those in this Act, without regard to the limitations customarily observed by nations upon the exercise of their powers; limitations which generally correspond to those fixed by the 'Conflict of Laws.' We should not impute to Congress an intent to punish all whom its courts can catch, for conduct which has no consequences within the United States. American

Banana Co. v. United Fruit Co., 213 U.S. 347, 357; United States v. Bowman, 260 U.S. 94, 98; Blackmer v. United States, 284 U.S. 421, 437. On the other hand, it is settled law—as 'Limited' itself agrees—that any state may impose liabilities, even upon persons not within its allegiance, for conduct outside its borders that has consequences within its borders which the state reprehends; and these liabilities other states will ordinarily recognize. Strassheim v. Daily, 221 U.S. 280, 284, 285; Lamar v. United States, 240 U.S. 60, 65, 66, Ford v. United States, 273 U.S. 593, 620, 621; Restatement of Conflict of Laws Sec. 65. It may be argued that this Act extends further. Two situations are possible. There may be agreements made beyond our borders not intended to affect imports, which do affect them, or which affect exports. Almost any limitation of the supply of goods in Europe, for example, or in South America, may have repercussions in the United States if there is trade between the two. Yet when one considers the international complications likely to arise from an effort in this country to treat such agreements as unlawful, it is safe to assume that Congress certainly did not intend the Act to cover them. Such agreements may on the other hand intend to include imports into the United States, and yet it may appear that they had no effect upon them. That situation might be thought to fall within the doctrine that intent may be a substitute for performance in the case of a contract made within the United States; or it might be thought to fall within the doctrine that a statute should not be interpreted to cover acts abroad which have no consequence here. We shall not choose between these alternatives; but for argument we shall assume that the Act does not cover agreements, even though intended to affect imports or exports, unless its performance is shown actually to have had some effect upon them. Where both conditions are satisfied, the situation certainly falls within such decisions as United States v. Pacific & Artic R. & Navigation Co., 228 U.S. 87; Thomsen v. Cayser, 243 U.S. 66, and United States v. Sisal Sales Corporation, 274 U.S. 268. It is true that in those cases the persons held liable had sent agents into the United States to perform part of the agreement; but an agent is merely an animate means of executing his principal's purposes, and, for the purposes of this case, he does not differ from an inanimate means; besides, only human agents can import and sell ingot.

Both agreements would clearly have been unlawful, had they been made within the United States; and it follows from what we have just said that both were unlawful, though made abroad, if they were intended to affect imports and did affect them. . . .

Questions and Comments

(1) As Justice Holmes did in *American Banana*, Judge Hand in *Alcoa* understood the question before the Court to involve the construction of forum law to determine its territorial reach, and once again the Court noted that "general words" in a statute were not to be read literally. Instead, the statute was to be read in light of "the limitations customarily observed by nations upon the exercise of their powers; limitations which generally correspond to those fixed by the 'Conflict of Laws.'" As in *Carroll, supra* page 17, choice-of-law rules functioned as implicit limitations on the geographic scope of forum law.

(2) Rather than apply a strict presumption that the statute applies only to conduct that occurred on U.S. soil, the Court read the statute to apply if the conduct was intended to, and did, cause effects on U.S. territory. If it was "settled law . . . that any state may impose liabilities, even upon persons not within its allegiance, for conduct outside its borders that has consequences within its borders which the state reprehend," why did the Court limit the reach of the statute to conduct that not only had such effects, but also was *intended* to have such effects?

(3) *Alcoa*'s effects test was interpreted broadly by subsequent courts. Rather than require both actual and intended effects, some courts concluded that the Sherman Act applied to conduct having actual *or* intended effects on U.S. commerce. As recounted in *Timberlane*, excerpted below, the broad extraterritorial application of U.S. antitrust laws caused significant international friction, leading other countries to take retaliatory action. The *Timberlane* court sought to alleviate these tensions by articulating a multilateral analysis for determining the geographic scope of the antitrust laws.

2. Multilateral Approaches

Timberlane Lumber Co. v. Bank of America, N.T. and S.A.

549 F.2d 597 (9th Cir. 1976)

CHOY, Circuit Judge:

. . .

This action raises important questions concerning the application of American antitrust laws to activities in another country, including actions of foreign government officials. The district court dismissed the Timberlane action under the act of state doctrine and for lack of subject matter jurisdiction. . . . We vacate . . . and remand.

I. The Timberlane Action

The basic allegation of the Timberlane plaintiffs is that officials of the Bank of America and others located in both the United States and Honduras conspired to prevent Timberlane, through its Honduras subsidiaries, from milling lumber in Honduras and exporting it to the United States, thus maintaining control of the Honduran lumber export business in the hands of a few select individuals financed and controlled by the Bank. The intent and result of the conspiracy, they contend, was to interfere with the exportation to the United States, including Puerto Rico, of Honduran lumber for sale or use there by the plaintiffs, thus directly and substantially affecting the foreign commerce of the United States.

. . .

Cast of Characters

There are three affiliated plaintiffs in the Timberlane action. Timberlane Lumber Company is an Oregon partnership principally involved in the purchase and distribution of lumber at wholesale in the United States and the importation of lumber into the United States for sale and use. . . . ([The plaintiffs] will be collectively referred to as "Timberlane.")

The primary defendants are Bank of America Corporation (Bank), a California corporation, and its wholly-owned subsidiary, Bank of America National Trust and Savings Association, which operates a branch in Tegucigalpa, Honduras. Several employees of the Bank [and numerous Honduran individuals] have also been named and served as defendants. . . .

Facts as Alleged

. . .

Timberlane, with a long history in the lumber business, [was] in search of alternative sources of lumber for delivery to its distribution system on the East Coast of the United States. After study, it decided to try Honduras. In 1971, [a subsidiary] was formed, tracts of forest land were acquired, plans for a modern log-processing plant were prepared, and equipment was purchased and assembled for shipment from the United States to . . . [the subsidiary] in Honduras.

Realizing that they were faced with better-financed and more vigorous competition from Timberlane and its Honduran subsidiaries, the defendants and others. . . . [engaged in a] conspiracy to disrupt Timberlane's efforts. [Numerous acts in furtherance of the conspiracy, most performed in Honduras, were alleged.] . . .

As a result of the conspiracy, Timberlane's complaint claimed damages then estimated in excess of $5,000,000. Plaintiffs also allege that there has been a direct and substantial effect on United States foreign commerce, and that defendants intended the results of the conspiracy, including the impact on United States commerce. . . .

Extraterritorial Reach of the United States Antitrust Laws

There is no doubt that American antitrust laws extend over some conduct in other nations. There was language in the first Supreme Court case in point, American Banana Co. v. United Fruit Co. [*supra* page 576], casting doubt on the extension of the Sherman Act to acts outside United States territory. But subsequent cases have limited American Banana to its particular facts, and the Sherman Act—and with it other antitrust laws—has been applied to extraterritorial conduct. See, e.g., Continental Ore Co. v. Union Carbide & Carbon Corp., 370 U.S. 690 (1962); United States v. Sisal Sales Corp., 274 U.S. 268 (1927); United States v. Aluminum Co. of America, 148 F.2d 416, (2d Cir. 1945) (the "Alcoa" case). The act may encompass the foreign activities of aliens as well as American citizens. *Alcoa, supra.*

That American law covers some conduct beyond this nation's borders does not mean that it embraces all, however. Extraterritorial application is understandably a matter of concern for the other countries involved. Those nations have sometimes resented and protested, as excessive intrusions into their own spheres, broad assertions of authority by American courts. Our courts have recognized this concern and have, at times, responded to it, even if not always enough to satisfy all the foreign critics. See *Alcoa*, 148 F.2d at 443. In any event, it is evident that

at some point the interests of the United States are too weak and the foreign harmony incentive for restraint too strong to justify an extraterritorial assertion of
jurisdiction.

What that point is or how it is determined is not defined by international law.
Nor does the Sherman Act limit itself.[14] In the domestic field the Sherman Act
extends to the full reach of the commerce power. To define it somewhat more mod-
estly in the foreign commerce area courts have generally, and logically, fallen back
on a narrower construction of congressional intent, such as expressed in Judge
Learned Hand's oft-cited opinion in *Alcoa*, 148 F.2d at 443:

> (T)he only question open is whether Congress intended to impose the liabil-
> ity and whether our own Constitution permitted it to do so: as a court of the
> United States we cannot look beyond our own law. Nevertheless, it is quite
> true that we are not to read general words, such as those in this Act, without
> regard to the limitations customarily observed by nations upon the exercise
> of their powers; limitations which generally correspond to those fixed by the
> "Conflict of Laws." We should not impute to Congress an intent to punish all
> whom its courts can catch, for conduct which has no consequences within the
> United States.

It is the effect on American foreign commerce which is usually cited to
support extraterritorial jurisdiction. *Alcoa* set the course, when Judge Hand
declared, id.:

> (I)t is settled law . . . that any state may impose liabilities, even upon persons
> not within its allegiance, for conduct outside its borders that has consequences
> within its borders which the state reprehends; and these liabilities other states
> will ordinarily recognize.[15]

Despite its description as "settled law," *Alcoa*'s assertion has been roundly
disputed by many foreign commentators as being in conflict with international
law, comity, and good judgment. Nonetheless, American courts have firmly concluded that there is some extraterritorial jurisdiction under the Sherman Act.

Even among American courts and commentators, however, there is no consensus on how far the jurisdiction should extend. The district court here concluded
that a "direct and substantial effect" on United States foreign commerce was a prerequisite, without stating whether other factors were relevant or considered. The
same formula was employed, to some extent, by . . . [other] district courts [and]

---

14. The tendency seems to be for federal regulatory statutes to contain sweeping jurisdictional
language. Sections 1 and 2 of the Sherman Act, 15 U.S.C. §§1, 2, reach, respectively, "(e)very contract . . . in restraint of . . ." and "(e)very person who shall monopolize, or attempt to monopolize . . .
any part of" "the trade or commerce among the several States, or with foreign nations." Although
it may be "evident from the text of the antitrust statutes" that "some (actual or intended) effect on
our foreign commerce is a prerequisite to jurisdiction," *Occidental Petroleum*, 331 F. Supp. at 102
(emphasis in original), the statutory terms themselves are not precise or limited enough to provide
additional guidance to the courts.

15. Such an assertion of authority based on internal consequences is generally described as the
"objective territorial" principle of jurisdiction. See W. Fugate, *supra*, at 35-39.

has been identified and advocated by several commentators. See, e.g., Restatement (Second) of Foreign Relations Law of the United States §18. . . .[18]

Other courts have used different expressions, however. See, e.g., Thomsen v. Cayser, 243 U.S. 66, 88 (1917) ("the combination affected the foreign commerce of this country"); *Alcoa*, 148 F.2d at 444 ("intended to affect imports and exports (and) . . . is shown actually to have had some effect on them");[19] United States v. Imperial Chemical Industries, Ltd., 100 F. Supp. 504, 592 (S.D.N.Y. 1951) ("a conspiracy . . . which affects American commerce"); United States v. Timken Roller Bearing Co., 83 F. Supp. 284, 309 (N.D. Ohio 1949), modified and affirmed, 341 U.S. 593 (1951) ("a direct and influencing effect on trade").

Few cases have discussed the nature of the effect required for jurisdiction, perhaps because most of the litigated cases have involved relatively obvious offenses and rather significant and apparent effects on competition within the United States. It is probably in part because the standard has not often been put to a real test that it seems so poorly defined. William Fugate, who has identified the "direct and substantial" standard as the rule, has described the meaning of that phrase as being "quite broad." What the threshold of significance is, however, has not been identified. Nor is it quite clear what the "direct-indirect" distinction is supposed to mean. It might well be, as was said in the context of transnational securities regulation:

> Although courts have spoken in terms of the Restatement and of congressional policy, findings that an American effect was direct, substantial, and foreseeable, or within the scope of congressional intent, have little independent analytic significance. Instead, cases appear to turn on a reconciliation of American and foreign interests in regulating their respective economies and business affairs . . . .

Implicit in that observation, as it is in several of the cases and commentaries employing the "effects" test, is the suggestion that factors other than simply the effect on the United States are weighed, and rightly so. As former Attorney General

---

18. Restatement §18 reads:

> A state has jurisdiction to prescribe a rule of law attaching legal consequences to conduct that occurs outside its territory and causes an effect within its territory, if either
>
> (a) the conduct and its effect are generally recognized as constituent elements of a crime or tort under the law of states that have reasonably developed legal systems, or
>
> (b)(i) the conduct and its effect are constituent elements of activity to which the rule applies; (ii) the effect within the territory is substantial; (iii) it occurs as a direct and foreseeable result of the conduct outside the territory; and (iv) the rule is not inconsistent with the principles of justice generally recognized by states that have reasonably developed legal systems.

The "direct" and "substantial" requirements come from (b)(ii) and (iii). Comment a to this section specifically indicates, however, that this rule applies only to aliens, since United States citizens may be bound by nationality, and governs only where there has been no significant conduct within the United States, since otherwise territorial jurisdiction could be asserted.

19. This portion of *Alcoa* referred only to a combination of foreigners, specifically for whom the intent requirement may have been imposed, not American citizens or corporations. Further, Judge Hand's opinion noted that either intent or effect individually might suffice, but that both were present in that case, so that the question did not have to be faced.

(then Professor) Katzenbach observed, the effect on American commerce is not, by itself, sufficient information on which to base a decision that the United States is the nation primarily interested in the activity causing the effect. "[A]nything that affects the external trade and commerce of the United States also affects the trade and commerce of other nations, and may have far greater consequences for others than for the United States." Katzenbach, Conflicts on an Unruly Horse, 65 Yale L.J. 1087, 1150 (1956).

The effects test by itself is incomplete because it fails to consider other nations' interests. Nor does it expressly take into account the full nature of the relationship between the actors and this country. Whether the alleged offender is an American citizen, for instance, may make a big difference; applying American laws to American citizens raises fewer problems than application to foreigners. . . .

American courts have, in fact, often displayed a regard for comity and the prerogatives of other nations and considered their interests as well as other parts of the factual circumstances, even when professing to apply an effects test. To some degree, the requirement for a "substantial" effect may silently incorporate these additional considerations, with "substantial" as a flexible standard that varies with other factors. The intent requirement suggested by *Alcoa* is one example of an attempt to broaden the court's perspective, as is drawing a distinction between American citizens and non-citizens.

The failure to articulate these other elements in addition to the standard effects analysis is costly, however, for it is more likely that they will be overlooked or slighted in interpreting past decisions and reaching new ones. Placing emphasis on the qualification that effects be "substantial" is also risky, for the term has a meaning in the interstate antitrust context which does not encompass all the factors relevant to the foreign trade case. . . .

A tripartite analysis seems to be indicated. As acknowledged above, the antitrust laws require in the first instance that there be *some* effect — actual or intended — on American foreign commerce before the federal courts may legitimately exercise subject matter jurisdiction under those statutes. Second, a greater showing of burden or restraint may be necessary to demonstrate that the effect is sufficiently large to present a cognizable injury to the plaintiffs and, therefore, a civil violation of the antitrust laws. Third, there is the additional question which is unique to the international setting of whether the interests of, and links to, the United States — including the magnitude of the effect on American foreign commerce — are sufficiently strong, vis-à-vis those of other nations, to justify an assertion of extraterritorial authority.

It is this final issue which is both obscured by undue reliance on the "substantiality" test and complicated to resolve. An effect on United States commerce, although necessary to the exercise of jurisdiction under the antitrust laws, is alone not a sufficient basis on which to determine whether American authority should be asserted in a given case as a matter of international comity and fairness. In some cases, the application of the direct and substantial test in the international context might open the door too widely by sanctioning jurisdiction over an action when these considerations would indicate dismissal. At other times, it may fail in the other direction, dismissing a case for which comity and fairness do not require forebearance, thus closing the jurisdictional door too tightly — for the Sherman Act does reach some restraints which do not have both a direct and substantial effect on the foreign commerce of the United States. A more comprehensive inquiry is necessary. We believe that the field of conflict of laws presents the proper approach, as was suggested, if not specifically employed, in *Alcoa* in expressing the basic limitation on application of American laws:

> [W]e are not to read general words, such as those in this Act, without regard to the limitations customarily observed by nations upon the exercise of their powers; limitations which generally correspond to those fixed by the "Conflict of Laws."

148 F.2d at 443. The same idea is reflected in Restatement (Second) of Foreign Relations Law of the United States §40:

> Where two states have jurisdiction to prescribe and enforce rules of law and the rules they may prescribe require inconsistent conduct upon the part of a person, each state is required by international law to consider, in good faith, moderating the exercise of its enforcement jurisdiction . . . .[27]

. . .

What we prefer is an evaluation and balancing of the relevant considerations in each case—in the words of Kingman Brewster, a "jurisdictional rule of reason."[29] Balancing of the foreign interests involved was the approach taken by the Supreme Court in Continental Ore Co. v. Union Carbide & Carbon Corp., 370 U.S. 690 (1962), where the involvement of the Canadian government in the alleged monopolization was held not to require dismissal. The Court stressed that there was no indication that the Canadian authorities approved or would have approved of the monopolization, meaning that the Canadian interest, if any, was slight and was outweighed by the American interest in condemning the restraint. Similarly, in Lauritzen v. Larsen, 345 U.S. 571 (1953), the Court used a like approach in declining to apply the Jones Act to a Danish seaman, injured in Havana on a Danish ship, although he had signed on to the ship in New York.

The elements to be weighed include the degree of conflict with foreign law or policy, the nationality or allegiance of the parties and the locations or principal places of business of corporations, the extent to which enforcement by either state can be expected to achieve compliance, the relative significance of effects on the United States as compared with those elsewhere, the extent to which there is explicit purpose to harm or affect American commerce, the foreseeability of such effect, and the relative importance to the violations charged of conduct within the United States as compared with conduct abroad.[31] A court evaluating these

---

27. This section was obviously fashioned with trade regulation problems in mind, for all five illustrations presented in the comment to this section involve such regulation. It also indicates that "jurisdictional" forebearance in the international setting is more a question of comity and fairness than one of national power.

29. K. Brewster, *supra*, at 446. See also Restatement, Second, Conflict of Laws §§6, 10, 42, 50.

31. Restatement (Second) of Foreign Relations Law of the United States s 40 states that a court should act in the light of such factors as

(a) vital national interests of each of the states,

(b) the extent and the nature of the hardship that inconsistent enforcement actions would impose upon the person,

factors should identify the potential degree of conflict if American authority is asserted. A difference in law or policy is one likely sore spot, though one which may not always be present.[32] Nationality is another; though foreign governments may have some concern for the treatment of American citizens and business residing there, they primarily care about their own nationals.[33] Having assessed the conflict, the court should then determine whether in the face of it the contacts and interests of the United States are sufficient to support the exercise of extraterritorial jurisdiction.

We conclude, then, that the problem should be approached in three parts: Does the alleged restraint affect, or was it intended to affect, the foreign commerce of the United States? Is it of such a type and magnitude so as to be cognizable as a violation of the Sherman Act? As a matter of international comity and fairness, should the extraterritorial jurisdiction of the United States be asserted to cover it? The district court's judgment found only that the restraint involved in the instant suit did not produce a direct and substantial effect on American foreign commerce. That holding does not satisfy any of these inquiries. . . .

From Timberlane's complaint it is evident that there are grounds for concern as to at least a few of the defendants, for some are identified as foreign citizens. Moreover, it is clear that most of the activity took place in Honduras, though the conspiracy may have been directed from San Francisco, and that the most direct economic effect was probably on Honduras. However, there has been no indication of any conflict with the law or policy of the Honduran government, nor any comprehensive analysis of the relative connections and interests of Honduras and the United States. Under these circumstances, the dismissal by the district court cannot be sustained on jurisdictional grounds.

We, therefore, vacate the dismissal and remand the Timberlane action. . . .

(c) the extent to which the required conduct is to take place in the territory of the other state,

(d) the nationality of the person, and

(e) the extent to which enforcement by action of either state can reasonably be expected to achieve compliance with the rule prescribed by that state.

President (then Professor) Brewster lists these variables:

(a) the relative significance to the violations charged of conduct within the United States as compared with conduct abroad; (b) the extent to which there is explicit purpose to harm or affect American consumers or Americans' business opportunities; (c) the relative seriousness of effects on the United States compared with those abroad; (d) the nationality or allegiance of the parties or in the case of business associations, their corporate location, and the fairness of applying our law to them; (e) the degree of conflict with foreign laws and policies, and (f) the extent to which conflict can be avoided without serious impairment of the interests of the United States or the foreign country.

K. Brewster, *supra* at 446.

32. Particularly in the field of trade regulation, American laws may not be duplicated by the other nation. That does not necessarily indicate a "conflict," however, since non-prohibition does not always mean affirmative approval. See P. Areeda, *supra* at 127.

33. Some argue that a defendant's American citizenship might be enough by itself to support jurisdiction. See Restatement (Second) of Foreign Relations Law of the United States §30.

Questions and Comments

(1) Like the courts before it, the Ninth Circuit in *Timberlane* understood the question before it to concern the "extraterritorial reach" of the U.S. antitrust laws. Previous cases had sought to answer that question by looking only to the conduct's links to the United States. The tests adopted in these cases were unilateral in this sense. *Timberlane* broke new ground by holding that the extraterritorial reach of the antitrust laws depended not only on the conduct's links to the United States, but also required a "balancing" of the U.S. interest in applying the law against the countervailing interests of other states. In assessing the statute's applicability to the dispute, the court should ask "whether the interests of, and links to, the United States—including the magnitude of the effect on American foreign commerce—are sufficiently strong, vis-à-vis those of other nations, to justify an assertion of extraterritorial authority." *Timberlane* thus departed from the previous courts' unilateral approach to the extraterritoriality issue, adopting a decidedly multilateral approach to determining the extraterritorial reach of the statute.

(2) In articulating this test, the court in *Timberlane* was influenced by developments in domestic choice-of-law doctrine. (Note that the court's citation of the Second Restatement of Conflicts in footnote 29.) Is the *Timberlane* approach the federal counterpart to the Second Restatement?

(3) The district court had dismissed the Timberlane action for lack of subject matter jurisdiction. The Ninth Circuit, too, treated the issue before it as one of jurisdiction, calling the approach it adopted the "jurisdictional rule of reason." In what respect is the extraterritoriality issue one of jurisdiction? For clarification of this question, *see* Justice Scalia's opinions in *Hartford Fire*, *infra* page 590, and *Morrison*, *infra* page 615.

(4) Although *Timberlane*'s multilateral approach broke new ground in the antitrust context, the Supreme Court had previously adopted a multilateral approach to determining the extraterritorial reach of other statutes. The *Timberlane* court relied in part on the Supreme Court's celebrated decision in Lauritzen v. Larsen. The question in *Lauritzen* was whether the Jones Act gave a cause of action to a Danish seaman injured on board a Danish flag vessel while the ship was temporarily docked in New York. Justice Jackson's opinion first responded to the seaman's argument that the Jones Act gave him a cause of action because of the "literal catholicity" of the statute's language:

> If read literally, Congress has conferred an American right of action which requires nothing more than that plaintiff be "any seaman who shall suffer personal injury in the course of his employment." It makes no explicit requirement that either the seaman, the employment or the injury have the slightest connection with the United States. Unless some relationship of one or more of these to our national interest is implied, Congress has extended our law and opened our courts to all alien seafaring men injured anywhere in the world in service of watercraft of every foreign nation—a hand on a Chinese junk, never outside Chinese waters, would not be beyond its literal wording. . . . [W]e are simply dealing with a problem of statutory construction rather commonplace in a federal system by which courts often have to decide whether "any" or "every" reaches to the limits of the enacting authority's usual scope or is to be applied to foreign events or transactions.

In deciding that question, the Court invoked "the long-heeded admonition of Mr. Chief Justice Marshall that 'an act of congress ought never to be construed to violate the law of nations if any other possible construction remains. . . .'" The *Charming Betsy*, 2 Cranch 64, 118. The Court noted that "Congress in 1920 wrote these all-comprehending words, not on a clean slate, but [against the background of] a seasoned body of maritime law developed by the experience of American courts long accustomed to dealing with admiralty problems in reconciling our own with foreign interests and in accommodating the reach of our own laws to those of other maritime nations." The Court proceeded to "review the several factors which, alone or in combination, are generally conceded to influence choice of law to govern a tort claim, particularly a maritime tort claim, and the weight and significance accorded them," including (1) the place of the wrong, (2) the law of the flag, (3) allegiance or domicile of the injured, (4) allegiance of the defendant shipowner, (5) place of contract, (6) inaccessibility of foreign forum, and (7) law of the forum. As described by Justice Frankfurter in Romero v. International Terminal Operating Co., 358 U.S. 354, 383-384 (1958), the *Lauritzen* approach is based on "due recognition of our self-regarding respect for the relevant interests of foreign nations," with "the controlling consideration [being] the interacting interests of the United States and foreign countries."

(5) The *Timberlane* court also relied on the Restatement Second of Foreign Relations Law. *See* n.31. The *Timberlane* decision, in turn, influenced the Third Restatement of Foreign Relations Law, adopted in 1987. According to §402 of the Third Restatement, a state's "jurisdiction to prescribe" under international law — that is, its power to make its laws applicable to persons or events — extends to:

> (1) (a) conduct that, wholly or in substantial part, takes place within its territory; (b) the status of persons, or interests in things, present within its territory; (c) conduct outside its territory that has or is intended to have substantial effect within its territory;
>
> (2) the activities, interests, status, or relations of its nationals outside as well as within its territory; and
>
> (3) certain conduct outside its territory by persons not its nationals that is directed against the security of the state or against a limited class of other state interests.

According to §403, international law additionally imposes a "reasonableness" requirement:

> (1) Even when one of the bases for jurisdiction under §402 is present, a state may not exercise jurisdiction to prescribe law with respect to a person or activity having connections with another state when the exercise of such jurisdiction is unreasonable.
>
> (2) Whether exercise of jurisdiction over a person or activity is unreasonable is determined by evaluating all relevant factors, including, where appropriate:
>
> (a) the link of the activity to the territory of the regulating state, *i.e.*, the extent to which the activity takes place within the territory, or has substantial, direct, and foreseeable effect upon or in the territory;
>
> (b) the connections, such as nationality, residence, or economic activity, between the regulating state and the person principally responsible

for the activity to be regulated, or between that state and those whom the regulation is designed to protect;

(c) the character of the activity to be regulated, the importance of regulation to the regulating state, the extent to which other states regulate such activities, and the degree to which the desirability of such regulation is generally accepted.

(d) the existence of justified expectations that might be protected or hurt by the regulation;

(e) the importance of the regulation to the international political, legal, or economic system;

(f) the extent to which the regulation is consistent with the traditions of the international system;

(g) the extent to which another state may have an interest in regulating the activity; and

(h) the likelihood of conflict with regulation by another state.

(3) When it would not be unreasonable for each of two states to exercise jurisdiction over a person or activity, but the prescriptions by the two states are in conflict, each state has an obligation to evaluate its own as well as the other state's interest in exercising jurisdiction, in light of all the relevant factors, including those set out in Subsection (2); a state should defer to the other state if that state's interest is clearly greater.

Restatement (Third) of Foreign Relations Law §403 (1987). Section 403 was applied (or, according to Justice Scalia, misapplied) in the *Hartford Fire* case, excerpted below.

Hartford Fire Ins. Co. v. California

509 U.S. 764 (1993)

Justice SOUTER announced the judgment of the Court and delivered the opinion of the Court with respect to Parts I, II-A, III, and IV, and an opinion concurring in the judgment with respect to Part II-B.

The Sherman Act makes every contract, combination, or conspiracy in unreasonable restraint of interstate or foreign commerce illegal. 26 Stat. 209, as amended, 15 U.S.C. §1. These consolidated cases present questions about the application of that Act to the insurance industry, both here and abroad. The plaintiffs (respondents here) allege that both domestic and foreign defendants (petitioners here) violated the Sherman Act by engaging in various conspiracies to affect the American insurance market. A group of domestic defendants argues that the McCarran-Ferguson Act, 59 Stat. 33, as amended, 15 U.S.C. §1011 *et seq.*, precludes application of the Sherman Act to the conduct alleged; a group of foreign defendants argues that the principle of international comity requires the District Court to refrain from exercising jurisdiction over certain claims against it. We hold that most of the domestic defendants' alleged conduct is not immunized from antitrust liability by the McCarran-Ferguson Act, and that, even assuming it applies, the principle of international comity does not preclude District Court jurisdiction over the foreign conduct alleged.

I

The two petitions before us stem from consolidated litigation comprising the complaints of 19 States and many private plaintiffs alleging that the defendants, members of the insurance industry, conspired in violation of §1 of the Sherman Act to restrict the terms of coverage of commercial general liability (CGL) insurance available in the United States. Because the cases come to us on motions to dismiss, we take the allegations of the complaints as true.

A

According to the complaints, the object of the conspiracies was to force certain primary insurers (insurers who sell insurance directly to consumers) to change the terms of their standard CGL insurance policies to conform with the policies the defendant insurers wanted to sell. The District Court . . . dismissed the three claims that named only certain London-based defendants, invoking international comity and applying the Ninth Circuit's decision in Timberlane Lumber Co. v. Bank of America, N.T. & S.A., 549 F.2d 597 (1976). . . . The Court of Appeals reversed. . . . [A]s to the three claims brought solely against foreign defendants, the court applied its *Timberlane* analysis, but concluded that the principle of international comity was no bar to exercising Sherman Act jurisdiction.

We granted certiorari in No. 91-1111 to address two narrow questions about the scope of McCarran-Ferguson Act antitrust immunity, and in No. 91-1128 to address the application of the Sherman Act to the foreign conduct at issue.[9] We now affirm in part, reverse in part, and remand.

[The Court first discussed the liability of the domestic insurance companies.]

III

Finally, we take up the question presented by No. 91-1128, whether certain claims against the London reinsurers should have been dismissed as improper applications of the Sherman Act to foreign conduct. The Fifth Claim for Relief in the California Complaint alleges a violation of §1 of the Sherman Act by certain London reinsurers who conspired to coerce primary insurers in the United States to offer CGL coverage on a claims-made basis, thereby making "occurrence CGL coverage . . . unavailable in the State of California for many risks." The Sixth Claim for Relief in the California Complaint alleges that the London reinsurers violated §1 by a conspiracy to limit coverage of pollution risks in North America, thereby rendering "pollution liability coverage . . . almost entirely unavailable for the vast majority of casualty insurance purchasers in the State of California." The Eighth Claim for Relief in the California Complaint alleges a further §1 violation

---

9. The question presented in No. 91-1128 is: "Did the court of appeals properly assess the extraterritorial reach of the U.S. antitrust laws in light of this Court's teachings and contemporary understanding of international law when it held that a U.S. district court may apply U.S. law to the conduct of a foreign insurance market regulated abroad?" Pet. for Cert. in No. 91-1128, p. i.

by the London reinsurers who, along with domestic retrocessional reinsurers, conspired to limit coverage of seepage, pollution, and property contamination risks in North America, thereby eliminating such coverage in the State of California.

At the outset, we note that the District Court undoubtedly had jurisdiction of these Sherman Act claims, as the London reinsurers apparently concede. See Tr. of Oral Arg. 37 ("Our position is not that the Sherman Act does not apply in the sense that a minimal basis for the exercise of jurisdiction doesn't exist here. Our position is that there are certain circumstances, and that this is one of them, in which the interests of another State are sufficient that the exercise of that jurisdiction should be restrained").[21] Although the proposition was perhaps not always free from doubt, see American Banana Co. v. United Fruit Co., 213 U.S. 347 (1909), it is well established by now that the Sherman Act applies to foreign conduct that was meant to produce and did in fact produce some substantial effect in the United States. See Matsushita Elec. Industrial Co. v. Zenith Radio Corp., 475 U.S. 574, 582, n.6 (1986); United States v. Aluminum Co. of America, 148 F.2d 416, 444 (CA2 1945) (L. Hand, J.); Restatement (Third) of Foreign Relations Law of the United States §415, and Reporters' Note 3 (1987) (hereinafter Restatement (Third) Foreign Relations Law); 1 P. Areeda & D. Turner, Antitrust Law ¶236 (1978); cf. Continental Ore Co. v. Union Carbide & Carbon Corp., 370 U.S. 690, 704 (1962); Steele v. Bulova Watch Co., 344 U.S. 280, 288 (1952); United States v. Sisal Sales Corp., 274 U.S. 268, 275-276, (1927).[22] Such is the conduct alleged here: that the London reinsurers engaged in unlawful conspiracies to affect the market for insurance in the United States and that their conduct in fact produced substantial effect.[23] See 938 F.2d, at 933.

---

21. One of the London reinsurers, Sturge Reinsurance Syndicate Management Limited, argues that the Sherman Act does not apply to its conduct in attending a single meeting at which it allegedly agreed to exclude all pollution coverage from its reinsurance contracts. Brief for Petitioner Sturge Reinsurance Syndicate Management Ltd. in No. 91-1128, p. 22. Sturge may have attended only one meeting, but the allegations, which we are bound to credit, remain that it participated in conduct that was intended to and did in fact produce a substantial effect on the American insurance market.

22. Justice Scalia believes that what is at issue in this litigation is prescriptive, as opposed to subject-matter, jurisdiction. *Post*, at 2918. The parties do not question prescriptive jurisdiction, however, and for good reason: it is well established that Congress has exercised such jurisdiction under the Sherman Act. See G. Born & D. Westin, International Civil Litigation in United States Courts 542, n.5 (2d ed. 1992) (Sherman Act is a "prime exampl[e] of the simultaneous exercise of prescriptive jurisdiction and grant of subject matter jurisdiction").

23. Under §402 of the Foreign Trade Antitrust Improvements Act of 1982 (FTAIA), 96 Stat. 1246, 15 U.S.C. §6a, the Sherman Act does not apply to conduct involving foreign trade or commerce, other than import trade or import commerce, unless "such conduct has a direct, substantial, and reasonably foreseeable effect" on domestic or import commerce. §6a(1)(A). The FTAIA was intended to exempt from the Sherman Act export transactions that did not injure the United States economy, see H.R.Rep. No. 97-686, pp. 2-3, 9-10 (1982); P. Areeda & H. Hovenkamp, Antitrust Law ¶ 236'a, pp. 296-297 (Supp. 1992), and it is unclear how it might apply to the conduct alleged here. Also unclear is whether the Act's "direct, substantial, and reasonably foreseeable effect" standard amends existing law or merely codifies it. See *id.*, ¶236'a, p. 297. We need not address these questions here. Assuming that the FTAIA's standard affects this litigation, and assuming further that that standard differs from the prior law, the conduct alleged plainly meets its requirements.

According to the London reinsurers, the District Court should have declined to exercise such jurisdiction under the principle of international comity.[24] The Court of Appeals agreed that courts should look to that principle in deciding whether to exercise jurisdiction under the Sherman Act. *Id.*, at 932. This availed the London reinsurers nothing, however. To be sure, the Court of Appeals believed that "application of [American] antitrust laws to the London reinsurance market 'would lead to significant conflict with English law and policy,'" and that "[s]uch a conflict, unless outweighed by other factors, would by itself be reason to decline exercise of jurisdiction." *Id.*, at 933 (citation omitted). But other factors, in the court's view, including the London reinsurers' express purpose to affect United States commerce and the substantial nature of the effect produced, outweighed the supposed conflict and required the exercise of jurisdiction in this litigation. *Id.*, at 934.

When it enacted the FTAIA, 96 Stat. 1246, 15 U.S.C. §6a, Congress expressed no view on the question whether a court with Sherman Act jurisdiction should ever decline to exercise such jurisdiction on grounds of international comity. See H.R.Rep. No. 97-686, p. 13 (1982) ("If a court determines that the requirements for subject matter jurisdiction are met, [the FTAIA] would have no effect on the court['s] ability to employ notions of comity . . . or otherwise to take account of the international character of the transaction") (citing *Timberlane*). We need not decide that question here, however, for even assuming that in a proper case a court may decline to exercise Sherman Act jurisdiction over foreign conduct (or, as Justice Scalia would put it, may conclude by the employment of comity analysis in the first instance that there is no jurisdiction), international comity would not counsel against exercising jurisdiction in the circumstances alleged here.

The only substantial question in this litigation is whether "there is in fact a true conflict between domestic and foreign law." Société Nationale Industrielle Aérospatiale v. United States Dist. Court for Southern Dist. of Iowa, 482 U.S. 522, 555 (1987) (Blackmun, J., concurring in part and dissenting in part). The London reinsurers contend that applying the Act to their conduct would conflict significantly with British law, and the British Government, appearing before us as *amicus curiae*, concurs. See Brief for Petitioners Merrett Underwriting Agency Management Ltd. et al. in No. 91-1128, pp. 22-27; Brief for Government of United Kingdom of Great Britain and Northern Ireland as *Amicus Curiae* 10-14. They

---

24. Justice Scalia contends that comity concerns figure into the prior analysis whether jurisdiction exists under the Sherman Act. *Post*, at 19-20. This contention is inconsistent with the general understanding that the Sherman Act covers foreign conduct producing a substantial intended effect in the United States, and that concerns of comity come into play, if at all, only after a court has determined that the acts complained of are subject to Sherman Act jurisdiction. See United States v. Aluminum Co. of America, 148 F.2d 416, 444 (CA2 1945) ("[I]t follows from what we have . . . said that [the agreements at issue] were unlawful [under the Sherman Act], though made abroad, if they were intended to affect imports and did affect them"); Mannington Mills, Inc. v. Congoleum Corp., 595 F.2d 1287, 1294 (CA3 1979) (once court determines that jurisdiction exists under the Sherman Act, question remains whether comity precludes its exercise); H.R.Rep. No. 97-686, supra, at 13. But cf. Timberlane Lumber Co. v. Bank of America, N.T. & S.A., 549 F.2d 597, 613 (CA9 1976); 1 J. Atwood & K. Brewster, Antitrust and American Business Abroad 166 (1981). In any event, the parties conceded jurisdiction at oral argument, see *supra*, at 2908-2909, and we see no need to address this contention here.

assert that Parliament has established a comprehensive regulatory regime over the London reinsurance market and that the conduct alleged here was perfectly consistent with British law and policy. But this is not to state a conflict. "[T]he fact that conduct is lawful in the state in which it took place will not, of itself, bar application of the United States antitrust laws," even where the foreign state has a strong policy to permit or encourage such conduct. Restatement (Third) Foreign Relations Law §415, Comment *j*; see *Continental Ore Co., supra*, 370 U.S., at 706-707. No conflict exists, for these purposes, "where a person subject to regulation by two states can comply with the laws of both." Restatement (Third) Foreign Relations Law §403, Comment *e*.[25] Since the London reinsurers do not argue that British law requires them to act in some fashion prohibited by the law of the United States, see Reply Brief for Petitioners Merrett Underwriting Agency Management Ltd. et al. in No. 91-1128, pp. 7-8, or claim that their compliance with the laws of both countries is otherwise impossible, we see no conflict with British law. See Restatement (Third) Foreign Relations Law §403, Comment *e*, §415, Comment *j*. We have no need in this litigation to address other considerations that might inform a decision to refrain from the exercise of jurisdiction on grounds of international comity.

IV

The judgment of the Court of Appeals is affirmed in part and reversed in part, and the cases are remanded for further proceedings consistent with this opinion.

It is so ordered.

Justice SCALIA delivered a dissenting opinion with respect to Part II, in which Justice O'CONNOR, Justice KENNEDY, and Justice THOMAS have joined. . . .

. . . With respect to the petition in No. 91-1128, I dissent from the Court's ruling concerning the extraterritorial application of the Sherman Act. . . .

II

Petitioners in No. 91-1128, various British corporations and other British subjects, argue that certain of the claims against them constitute an inappropriate extraterritorial application of the Sherman Act. It is important to distinguish two distinct questions raised by this petition: whether the District Court had jurisdiction, and whether the Sherman Act reaches the extraterritorial conduct alleged here. On the first question, I believe that the District Court had subject-matter jurisdiction over the Sherman Act claims against all the defendants (personal jurisdiction is not contested). Respondents asserted nonfrivolous claims under the Sherman Act, and 28 U.S.C. §1331 vests district courts with subject-matter jurisdiction over cases "arising under" federal statutes. As precedents such as

---

25. Justice Scalia says that we put the cart before the horse in citing this authority, for he argues it may be apposite only after a determination that jurisdiction over the foreign acts is reasonable. But whatever the order of cart and horse, conflict in this sense is the only substantial issue before the Court.

Lauritzen v. Larsen, 345 U.S. 571 (1953), make clear, that is sufficient to establish the District Court's jurisdiction over these claims. *Lauritzen* involved a Jones Act claim brought by a foreign sailor against a foreign shipowner. The shipowner contested the District Court's jurisdiction, see *id.*, at 573, apparently on the grounds that the Jones Act did not govern the dispute between the foreign parties to the action. Though ultimately agreeing with the shipowner that the Jones Act did not apply, the Court held that the District Court had jurisdiction.

> "As frequently happens, a contention that there is some barrier to granting plaintiff's claim is cast in terms of an exception to jurisdiction of subject matter. A cause of action under our law was asserted here, and the court had power to determine whether it was or was not well founded in law and in fact." 345 U.S., at 575.

See also Romero v. International Terminal Operating Co., 358 U.S. 354, 359 (1959).

The second question—the extraterritorial reach of the Sherman Act—has nothing to do with the jurisdiction of the courts. It is a question of substantive law turning on whether, in enacting the Sherman Act, Congress asserted regulatory power over the challenged conduct. See EEOC v. Arabian American Oil Co. [*infra* page 606] (*Aramco*) ("It is our task to determine whether Congress intended the protections of Title VII to apply to United States citizens employed by American employers outside of the United States"). If a plaintiff fails to prevail on this issue, the court does not dismiss the claim for want of subject-matter jurisdiction—want of power to adjudicate; rather, it decides the claim, ruling on the merits that the plaintiff has failed to state a cause of action under the relevant statute. See *Romero, supra*, 358 U.S., at 384 (holding no claim available under the Jones Act); American Banana Co. v. United Fruit Co., 213 U.S. 347, 359 (1909) (holding that complaint based upon foreign conduct "alleges no case under the [Sherman Act]").

There is, however, a type of "jurisdiction" relevant to determining the extraterritorial reach of a statute; it is known as "legislative jurisdiction," *Aramco, supra*, 499 U.S., at 253; Restatement (First) Conflict of Laws §60 (1934), or "jurisdiction to prescribe," 1 Restatement (Third) of Foreign Relations Law of the United States 235 (1987) (hereinafter Restatement (Third)). This refers to "the authority of a state to make its law applicable to persons or activities," and is quite a separate matter from "jurisdiction to adjudicate," see *id.*, at 231. There is no doubt, of course, that Congress possesses legislative jurisdiction over the acts alleged in this complaint: Congress has broad power under Article I, §8, cl. 3, "[t]o regulate Commerce with foreign Nations," and this Court has repeatedly upheld its power to make laws applicable to persons or activities beyond our territorial boundaries where United States interests are affected. See Ford v. United States, 273 U.S. 593, 621-623 (1927); United States v. Bowman, 260 U.S. 94, 98-99 (1922); *American Banana, supra*, 213 U.S. at 356. But the question in this litigation is whether, and to what extent, Congress *has* exercised that undoubted legislative jurisdiction in enacting the Sherman Act.

Two canons of statutory construction are relevant in this inquiry. The first is the "longstanding principle of American law 'that legislation of Congress, unless a contrary intent appears, is meant to apply only within the territorial jurisdiction of the United States.'" *Aramco, supra*, 499 U.S., at 248 (quoting Foley Bros., Inc.

v. Filardo, 336 U.S. 281, 285 (1949)). Applying that canon in *Aramco*, we held that the version of Title VII of the Civil Rights Act of 1964 then in force, 42 U.S.C. §§2000e to 2000e-17 (1988 ed.), did not extend outside the territory of the United States even though the statute contained broad provisions extending its prohibitions to, for example, "'any activity, business, or industry in commerce.'" *Id.*, 499 U.S., at 249 (quoting 42 U.S.C. §2000e(h)). We held such "boilerplate language" to be an insufficient indication to override the presumption against extraterritoriality. *Id.*, at 251; see also *id.*, at 251-253. The Sherman Act contains similar "boilerplate language," and if the question were not governed by precedent, it would be worth considering whether that presumption controls the outcome here. We have, however, found the presumption to be overcome with respect to our antitrust laws; it is now well established that the Sherman Act applies extraterritorially. See Matsushita Elec. Industrial Co. v. Zenith Radio Corp., 475 U.S. 574, 582, n.6 (1986); Continental Ore Co. v. Union Carbide & Carbon Corp., 370 U.S. 690, 704 (1962); see also United States v. Aluminum Co. of America, 148 F.2d 416 (CA2 1945).

But if the presumption against extraterritoriality has been overcome or is otherwise inapplicable, a second canon of statutory construction becomes relevant: "[A]n act of congress ought never to be construed to violate the law of nations if any other possible construction remains." Murray v. Schooner Charming Betsy, 2 Cranch 64, 118, 2 L.Ed. 208 (1804) (Marshall, C.J.). This canon is "wholly independent" of the presumption against extraterritoriality. *Aramco*, 499 U.S., at 264. It is relevant to determining the substantive reach of a statute because "the law of nations," or customary international law, includes limitations on a nation's exercise of its jurisdiction to prescribe. See Restatement (Third) §§401-416. Though it clearly has constitutional authority to do so, Congress is generally presumed not to have exceeded those customary international-law limits on jurisdiction to prescribe.

Consistent with that presumption, this and other courts have frequently recognized that, even where the presumption against extraterritoriality does not apply, statutes should not be interpreted to regulate foreign persons or conduct if that regulation would conflict with principles of international law. For example, in Romero v. International Terminal Operating Co., 358 U.S. 354 (1959), the plaintiff, a Spanish sailor who had been injured while working aboard a Spanish-flag and Spanish-owned vessel, filed a Jones Act claim against his Spanish employer. The presumption against extraterritorial application of federal statutes was inapplicable to the case, as the actionable tort had occurred in American waters. See *id.*, at 383. The Court nonetheless stated that, "in the absence of a contrary congressional direction," it would apply "principles of choice of law that are consonant with the needs of a general federal maritime law and with due recognition of our self-regarding respect for the relevant interests of foreign nations in the regulation of maritime commerce as part of the legitimate concern of the international community." *Id.*, at 382-383. "The controlling considerations" in this choice-of-law analysis were "the interacting interests of the United States and of foreign countries." *Id.*, at 383.

Romero referred to, and followed, the choice-of-law analysis set forth in Lauritzen v. Larsen, 345 U.S. 571 (1953). As previously mentioned, *Lauritzen* also involved a Jones Act claim brought by a foreign sailor against a foreign employer. The *Lauritzen* Court recognized the basic problem: "If [the Jones Act were] read literally, Congress has conferred an American right of action which requires nothing more than that plaintiff be 'any seaman who shall suffer personal injury in the course of his employment.'" *Id.*, at 576. The solution it adopted was to construe the statute "to apply only to areas and transactions in which *American law would be considered operative under prevalent doctrines of international law.*" *Id.*, at 577 (emphasis added). To support application of international law to limit the facial breadth of the statute, the Court relied upon—of course—Chief Justice Marshall's statement in *Schooner Charming Betsy*, quoted *supra*. It then set forth "several factors which, alone or in combination, are generally conceded to influence choice of law to govern a tort claim." 345 U.S., at 583 (discussing factors). See also McCulloch v. Sociedad Nacional de Marineros de Honduras, 372 U.S. 10, 21-22 (1963) (applying *Schooner Charming Betsy* principle to restrict application of National Labor Relations Act to foreign-flag vessels).

Lauritzen, Romero, and *McCulloch* were maritime cases, but we have recognized the principle that the scope of generally worded statutes must be construed in light of international law in other areas as well. [T]he principle was expressed in United States v. Aluminum Co. of America, 148 F.2d 416 (CA2 1945), the decision that established the extraterritorial reach of the Sherman Act. In his opinion for the court, Judge Learned Hand cautioned "we are not to read general words, such as those in [the Sherman] Act, without regard to the limitations customarily observed by nations upon the exercise of their powers; limitations which generally correspond to those fixed by the 'Conflict of Laws.'" *Id.*, at 443.

More recent lower court precedent has also tempered the extraterritorial application of the Sherman Act with considerations of "international comity." See, [e.g.,] Timberlane Lumber Co. v. Bank of America, N.T. & S.A., 549 F.2d 597, 608-615 (CA9 1976). The "comity" they refer to is not the comity of courts, whereby judges decline to exercise jurisdiction over matters more appropriately adjudged elsewhere, but rather what might be termed "prescriptive comity": the respect sovereign nations afford each other by limiting the reach of their laws. That comity is exercised by legislatures when they enact laws, and courts assume it has been exercised when they come to interpreting the scope of laws their legislatures have enacted. It is a traditional component of choice-of-law theory. See J. Story, Commentaries on the Conflict of Laws §38 (1834) (distinguishing between the "comity of the courts" and the "comity of nations," and defining the latter as "the true foundation and extent of the obligation of the laws of one nation within the territories of another"). Comity in this sense includes the choice-of-law principles that, "in the absence of contrary congressional direction," are assumed to be incorporated into our substantive laws having extraterritorial reach. *Romero, supra*, 358 U.S., at 382-383; see also *Lauritzen, supra*, 345 U.S., at 578-579; Hilton v. Guyot, 159 U.S. 113, 162-166 (1895). Considering comity in this way is just part of determining whether the Sherman Act prohibits the conduct at issue.[9]

In sum, the practice of using international law to limit the extraterritorial reach of statutes is firmly established in our jurisprudence. In proceeding to apply that practice to the present cases, I shall rely on the Restatement (Third) for the

---

9. Some antitrust courts, including the Court of Appeals in the present cases, have mistaken the comity at issue for the "comity of courts," which has led them to characterize the question presented as one of "abstention," that is, whether they should "exercise or decline jurisdiction." Mannington Mills, Inc. v. Congoleum Corp., 595 F.2d 1287, 1294, 1296 (CA3 1979); see also In re Insurance Antitrust Litigation, 938 F.2d 919, 932 (CA9 1991). As I shall discuss, that seems to be the error the Court has fallen into today. Because courts are generally reluctant to refuse the exercise of conferred jurisdiction, confusion on this seemingly theoretical point can have the very practical consequence of greatly expanding the extraterritorial reach of the Sherman Act.

relevant principles of international law. Its standards appear fairly supported in the decisions of this Court construing international choice-of-law principles (*Lauritzen, Romero,* and *McCulloch*) and in the decisions of other federal courts, especially *Timberlane*. Whether the Restatement precisely reflects international law in every detail matters little here, as I believe this litigation would be resolved the same way under virtually any conceivable test that takes account of foreign regulatory interests.

Under the Restatement, a nation having some "basis" for jurisdiction to prescribe law should nonetheless refrain from exercising that jurisdiction "with respect to a person or activity having connections with another state when the exercise of such jurisdiction is unreasonable." Restatement (Third) §403(1). The "reasonableness" inquiry turns on a number of factors including, but not limited to: "the extent to which the activity takes place within the territory [of the regulating state]," *id.*, §403(2)(a); "the connections, such as nationality, residence, or economic activity, between the regulating state and the person principally responsible for the activity to be regulated," *id.*, §403(2)(b); "the character of the activity to be regulated, the importance of regulation to the regulating state, the extent to which other states regulate such activities, and the degree to which the desirability of such regulation is generally accepted," *id.*, §403(2)(c); "the extent to which another state may have an interest in regulating the activity," *id.*, §403(2)(g); and "the likelihood of conflict with regulation by another state," *id.*, §403(2)(h). Rarely would these factors point more clearly against application of United States law. The activity relevant to the counts at issue here took place primarily in the United Kingdom, and the defendants in these counts are British corporations and British subjects having their principal place of business or residence outside the United States.[10] Great Britain has established a comprehensive regulatory scheme governing the London reinsurance markets, and clearly has a heavy "interest in regulating the activity," *id.*, §403(2)(g). See 938 F.2d, at 932-933; *In re Insurance Antitrust Litigation*, 723 F. Supp. 464, 487-488 (N.D. Cal. 1989); see also J. Butler & R. Merkin, Reinsurance Law A.1.1-02 (1992). Finally, §2(b) of the McCarran-Ferguson Act allows state regulatory statutes to override the Sherman Act in the insurance field, subject only to the narrow "boycott" exception set forth in §3(b) — suggesting that "the importance of regulation to the [United States]," Restatement (Third) §403(2)(c), is slight. Considering these factors, I think it unimaginable that an assertion of legislative jurisdiction by the United States would be considered reasonable, and therefore it is inappropriate to assume, in the absence of statutory indication to the contrary, that Congress has made such an assertion.

It is evident from what I have said that the Court's comity analysis, which proceeds as though the issue is whether the courts should "decline to exercise . . . jurisdiction," rather than whether the Sherman Act covers this conduct, is simply misdirected. I do not at all agree, moreover, with the Court's conclusion that the issue of the substantive scope of the Sherman Act is not in the cases. See *ante*, at n.22; *ante*, at n.24. To be sure, the parties did not make a clear distinction between

---

10. Some of the British corporations are subsidiaries of American corporations, and the Court of Appeals held that "[t]he interests of Britain are at least diminished where the parties are subsidiaries of American corporations." *Id.*, at 933. In effect, the Court of Appeals pierced the corporate veil in weighing the interests at stake. I do not think that was proper.

adjudicative jurisdiction and the scope of the statute. Parties often do not, as we have observed (and have declined to punish with procedural default) before. See the excerpt from *Lauritzen* quoted *supra*, at 14; see also *Romero*, 358 U.S., at 359. It is not realistic, and also not helpful, to pretend that the only really relevant issue in this litigation is not before us. In any event, if one erroneously chooses, as the Court does, to make adjudicative jurisdiction (or, more precisely, abstention) the vehicle for taking account of the needs of prescriptive comity, the Court still gets it wrong. It concludes that no "true conflict" counseling nonapplication of United States law (or rather, as it thinks, United States judicial jurisdiction) exists unless compliance with United States law would constitute a *violation* of another country's law. That breathtakingly broad proposition, which contradicts the many cases discussed earlier, will bring the Sherman Act and other laws into sharp and unnecessary conflict with the legitimate interests of other countries — particularly our closest trading partners.

In the sense in which the term "conflic[t]" was used in *Lauritzen*, 345 U.S., at 582, 592, and is generally understood in the field of conflicts of laws, there is clearly a conflict in this litigation. The petitioners here, like the defendant in *Lauritzen*, were not compelled by any foreign law to take their allegedly wrongful actions, but that no more precludes a conflict-of-laws analysis here than it did there. See *id.*, at 575-576 (detailing the differences between foreign and United States law). Where applicable foreign and domestic law provide different substantive rules of decision to govern the parties' dispute, a conflict-of-laws analysis is necessary. See generally R. Weintraub, Commentary on Conflict of Laws 2-3 (1980); Restatement (First) of Conflict of Laws §1, Comment *c* and Illustrations (1934).

Literally the *only* support that the Court adduces for its position is §403 of the Restatement (Third) — or more precisely Comment *e* to that provision, which states:

> "Subsection (3) [which says that a State should defer to another state if that State's interest is clearly greater] applies only when one state requires what another prohibits, or where compliance with the regulations of two states exercising jurisdiction consistently with this section is otherwise impossible. It does not apply where a person subject to regulation by two states can comply with the laws of both. . . ."

The Court has completely misinterpreted this provision. Subsection (3) of §403 (requiring one State to defer to another in the limited circumstances just described) comes into play only after subsection (1) of §403 has been complied with — *i.e.*, after it has been determined that the exercise of jurisdiction by *both* of the two States is not "unreasonable." That prior question is answered by applying the factors (*inter alia*) set forth in subsection (2) of §403, that is, precisely the factors that I have discussed in text and that the Court rejects. . . .[11]

---

11. The Court skips directly to subsection (3) of §403, apparently on the authority of Comment *j* to §415 of the Restatement (Third). See *ante*, at 2911. But the preceding commentary to §415 makes clear that "[a]ny exercise of [legislative] jurisdiction under this section is subject to the requirement of reasonableness" set forth in §403(2). Restatement (Third) §415, Comment *a*. Comment *j* refers back to the conflict analysis set forth in §403(3), which, as noted above, comes after the reasonableness analysis of §403(2).

Questions and Comments

(1) The *Timberlane* approach had been widely adopted by the Courts of Appeals, and was the prevailing approach to antitrust extraterritoriality until the *Hartford Fire* decision in 1993. The District of Columbia Circuit in Laker Airways Ltd. v. Sabena, 731 F.2d 909 (D.C. Cir. 1984), had expressed some skepticism about the approach, noting that "[t]hose contacts which do purport to provide a basis for distinguishing between competing bases of jurisdiction, and which are thus crucial to the balancing process, generally incorporate purely political factors which the court is neither qualified to evaluate comparatively nor capable of properly balancing." In the end, however, the court in *Laker* merely concluded that the balancing approach was not suitable for the specific sort of a case before it — a case presenting a conflict between U.S. antitrust laws and a foreign law specifically designed to thwart enforcement of the U.S. antitrust laws.

(2) What was left of the *Timberlane* approach after *Hartford Fire*? The majority held that a "comity" analysis is applicable, at best, when the case presents a "true conflict." How does the Court understand the concept of a true conflict? Does the Court understand it in the same way as Professor Currie? How many of the cases that you have read so far in this casebook have involved a true conflict as understood by the majority?

(3) Before *Hartford Fire*, the courts had developed the "foreign sovereign compulsion" doctrine to address the sort of conflict the majority believed should (at best) trigger a comity analysis. This doctrine "provides, in broad terms, that State A generally may not require an individual or company to do an act on the territory of State B that would violate the laws of State B." Born & Rutledge, *International Civil Litigation in United States Courts* 853 (6th ed. 2018). This doctrine applies beyond the antitrust context, yet the courts have had very few occasions to apply it. Did *Hartford Fire*, for all practical purposes, inter *Timberlane*'s jurisdictional rule of reason?

(4) The majority appeared to believe that its holding followed from a straightforward reading of §403 of the Third Restatement of Foreign Relations Law, *supra* pages 589-590. The dissenters claimed that the majority simply misread the Restatement. Who is right?

(5) Did the majority in *Hartford Fire* limit the scope of the jurisdictional rule of reason because of concerns similar to those expressed in *Laker*? Or did *Timberlane* suffer an ignominious death as a result of a mistake?

(6) The majority noted that the defendants had conceded the existence of subject matter jurisdiction, and understood the issue before it to be about whether the courts should "decline[] to exercise such jurisdiction under the principle of international comity." The dissenters insisted that the comity analysis is relevant to whether the antitrust laws reach the defendant's conduct, not whether the court has subject matter jurisdiction or whether the court should decline to exercise jurisdiction if it exists. Based on the preceding antitrust decisions, who has the better argument? The Court's opinion in *Morrison* (*infra* page 615), authored by Justice Scalia writing for a unanimous Court on this point, later clarified that the extraterritoriality issue does not concern the subject matter jurisdiction of the court, but is rather a "merits issue" — that is, it addresses whether the relevant federal law reaches the conduct on which the suit is based.

(7) *Hartford Fire* was decided after the Supreme Court had reinvigorated the presumption against extraterritoriality as the generally applicable approach to the question of federal extraterritoriality. The dissenting opinion asserts that the presumption against extraterritoriality is inapplicable to the Sherman Act because prior case law had already "well established that the Sherman Act applies extraterritorially." but, in such circumstances, "a second canon of statutory construction becomes relevant: '[A]n act of congress ought never to be construed to violate the law of nations if any other possible construction remains.' Murray v. Schooner Charming Betsy." The relevant rules of international law, according to the dissenters, are those set forth in section 403 of the Third Restatement of Foreign Relations Law (*supra* pages 589-590), which codified a version of the *Timberlane* jurisdictional rule of reason. As you read the cases in Section B, consider when, if ever, the courts will have occasion to apply the *Charming Betsy* principle today. For an argument that the *Charming Betsy* presumption should replace rather than supplement the presumption against extraterritoriality, *see* Knox, *A Presumption Against Extrajurisdictionality*, 104 Am. J. Intl. L. 351 (2010).

Hoffman-La Roche Ltd. v. Empagran S.A.
542 U.S. 155 (2004)

[Purchasers of vitamins filed a class action suit alleging that various vitamin manufacturers and distributors had engaged in a conspiracy to raise vitamin prices in the United States and foreign countries, in violation of U.S. antitrust law. The issue in this appeal was whether foreign purchasers of the vitamins could maintain an action under the Sherman Act for their foreign harm, in light of the Foreign Trade Antitrust Improvements Act of 1982 (FTAIA). The FTAIA provides that the Sherman Act "shall not apply to conduct involving trade or commerce . . . with foreign nations (other than import trade or import commerce)" unless the conduct has "a direct, substantial and reasonably foreseeable effect" on domestic commerce, U.S. imports, or U.S. exports, and "such effect gives rise to a claim" under the Sherman Act.]

Justice BREYER delivered the opinion of the Court.

. . .

The price-fixing conduct significantly and adversely affects both customers outside the United States and customers within the United States, but the adverse foreign effect is independent of any adverse domestic effect. In these circumstances, we find that the FTAIA exception does not apply (and thus the Sherman Act does not apply) for two main reasons.

First, this Court ordinarily construes ambiguous statutes to avoid unreasonable interference with the sovereign authority of other nations. This rule of construction reflects principles of customary international law—law that (we must assume) Congress ordinarily seeks to follow. *See* Restatement (Third) of Foreign Relations Law of the United States §§403(1), 403(2) (1986) (hereinafter Restatement) (limiting the unreasonable exercise of prescriptive jurisdiction with respect to a person or activity having connections with another State); Murray v. Schooner Charming Betsy, 6 U.S. 64 (1804) ("[A]n act of Congress ought never to be construed to violate the law of nations if any other possible construction remains"); Hartford Fire Insurance Co. v. California, 509 U.S. 764 (1993) (Scalia, J., dissenting) (identifying rule of construction as derived from the principle of "prescriptive comity").

This rule of statutory construction cautions courts to assume that legislators take account of the legitimate sovereign interests of other nations when they write American laws. It thereby helps the potentially conflicting laws of different nations work together in harmony — a harmony particularly needed in today's highly interdependent commercial world.

No one denies that America's antitrust laws, when applied to foreign conduct, can interfere with a foreign nation's ability independently to regulate its own commercial affairs. But our courts have long held that application of our antitrust laws to foreign anticompetitive conduct is nonetheless reasonable, and hence consistent with principles of prescriptive comity, insofar as they reflect a legislative effort to redress domestic antitrust injury that foreign anticompetitive conduct has caused. *See* United States v. Aluminum Co. of America, 148 F.2d 416, 443-444 (CA2 1945) (L. Hand, J.)

But why is it reasonable to apply those laws to foreign conduct insofar as that conduct causes independent foreign harm and that foreign harm alone gives rise to the plaintiff's claim? Like the former case, application of those laws creates a serious risk of interference with a foreign nation's ability independently to regulate its own commercial affairs. But, unlike the former case, the justification for that interference seems insubstantial. . . . Why should American law supplant, for example, Canada's or Great Britain's or Japan's own determination about how best to protect Canadian or British or Japanese customers from anticompetitive conduct engaged in significant part by Canadian or British or Japanese or other foreign companies?

We recognize that principles of comity provide Congress greater leeway when it seeks to control through legislation the actions of American companies; and some of the anticompetitive price-fixing conduct alleged here took place in America. But the higher foreign prices of which the foreign plaintiffs here complain are not the consequence of any domestic anticompetitive conduct that Congress sought to forbid, for Congress did not seek to forbid any such conduct insofar as it is here relevant, i.e., insofar as it is intertwined with foreign conduct that causes independent foreign harm. Rather Congress sought to release domestic (and foreign) anticompetitive conduct from Sherman Act constraints when that conduct causes foreign harm. Congress, of course, did make an exception where that conduct also causes domestic harm. . . .

We thus repeat the basic question: Why is it reasonable to apply this law to conduct that is significantly foreign insofar as that conduct causes independent foreign harm and that foreign harm alone gives rise to the plaintiff's claim? We can find no good answer to the question. . . .

[E]ven where nations agree about primary conduct, say price fixing, they disagree dramatically about appropriate remedies. The application, for example, of American private treble-damages remedies to anticompetitive conduct taking place abroad has generated considerable controversy. And several foreign nations have filed briefs here arguing that to apply our remedies would unjustifiably permit their citizens to bypass their own less generous remedial schemes, thereby upsetting a balance of competing considerations that their own domestic antitrust laws embody. . . .

Respondents alternatively argue that comity does not demand an interpretation of the FTAIA that would exclude independent foreign injury cases across the board. Rather, courts can take (and sometimes have taken) account of comity considerations case by case, abstaining where comity considerations so dictate.

In our view, however, this approach is too complex to prove workable. The Sherman Act covers many different kinds of anticompetitive agreements. Courts would have to examine how foreign law, compared with American law, treats not only price fixing but also, say, information-sharing agreements, patent-licensing price conditions, territorial product resale limitations, and various forms of joint venture, in respect to both primary conduct and remedy. The legally and economically technical nature of that enterprise means lengthier proceedings, appeals, and more proceedings—to the point where procedural costs and delays could themselves threaten interference with a foreign nation's ability to maintain the integrity of its own antitrust enforcement system. Even in this relatively simple price-fixing case, for example, competing briefs tell us (1) that potential treble-damage liability would help enforce widespread anti-price-fixing norms (through added deterrence) and (2) the opposite, namely that such liability would hinder antitrust enforcement (by reducing incentives to enter amnesty programs). How could a court seriously interested in resolving so empirical a matter—a matter potentially related to impact on foreign interests—do so simply and expeditiously?

. . . Where foreign anticompetitive conduct plays a significant role and where foreign injury is independent of domestic effects, Congress might have hoped that America's antitrust laws, so fundamental a component of our own economic system, would commend themselves to other nations as well. But, if America's antitrust policies could not win their own way in the international marketplace for such ideas, Congress, we must assume, would not have tried to impose them, in an act of legal imperialism, through legislative fiat.

Second, the FTAIA's language and history suggest that Congress designed the FTAIA to clarify, perhaps to limit, but not to expand in any significant way, the Sherman Act's scope as applied to foreign commerce. And we have found no significant indication that at the time Congress wrote this statute courts would have thought the Sherman Act applicable in these circumstances. . . .

Taken together, these two sets of considerations, the one derived from comity and the other reflecting history, convince us that Congress would not have intended the FTAIA's exception to bring independently caused foreign injury within the Sherman Act's reach.

Respondents point to several considerations that point the other way. For one thing, the FTAIA's language speaks in terms of the Sherman Act's applicability to certain kinds of conduct. The FTAIA says that the Sherman Act applies to foreign "conduct" with a certain kind of harmful domestic effect. Why isn't that the end of the matter? How can the Sherman Act both apply to the conduct when one person sues but not apply to the same conduct when another person sues?

Moreover, the exception says that it applies if the conduct's domestic effect gives rise to "*a* claim," not to "*the plaintiff's* claim" or "*the claim at issue*" (emphasis added). The alleged conduct here did have domestic effects, and those effects were harmful enough to give rise to "a" claim. Respondents concede that this claim is not their own claim; it is someone else's claim. But, linguistically speaking, they say, that is beside the point. Nor did Congress place the relevant words "gives rise to a claim" in the FTAIA to suggest any geographical limitation; rather it did so for a here neutral reason, namely, in order to make clear that the domestic effect must be an adverse (as opposed to a beneficial) effect.

Despite their linguistic logic, these arguments are not convincing. Linguistically speaking, a statute can apply and not apply to the same conduct, depending upon other circumstances; and those other circumstances may include the nature of the lawsuit (or of the related underlying harm). It also makes linguistic sense to read the words "a claim" as if they refer to the "plaintiff's claim" or "the claim at issue."

At most, respondents' linguistic arguments might show that respondents' reading is the more natural reading of the statutory language. But those arguments do not show that we must accept that reading. And that is the critical point. The considerations previously mentioned—those of comity and history—make clear that the respondents' reading is not consistent with the FTAIA's basic intent. If the statute's language reasonably permits an interpretation consistent with that intent, we should adopt it. And, for the reasons stated, we believe that the statute's language permits the reading that we give it.

Finally, respondents point to policy considerations that we have previously discussed, namely, that application of the Sherman Act in present circumstances will (through increased deterrence) help protect Americans against foreign-caused anticompetitive injury. As we have explained, however, the plaintiffs and supporting enforcement-agency amici have made important experience-backed arguments (based upon amnesty-seeking incentives) to the contrary. We cannot say whether, on balance, respondents' side of this empirically based argument or the enforcement agencies' side is correct. But we can say that the answer to the dispute is neither clear enough, nor of such likely empirical significance, that it could overcome the considerations we have previously discussed and change our conclusion.

For these reasons, we conclude that petitioners' reading of the statute's language is correct. That reading furthers the statute's basic purposes, it properly reflects considerations of comity, and it is consistent with Sherman Act history. . . .

Questions and Comments

(1) Congress enacted the Foreign Trade Antitrust Improvements Act (FTAIA) in 1982 to clarify the application of U.S. antitrust laws to foreign conduct. In pertinent part, the FTAIA states that the antitrust laws will not apply to nonimport commerce with foreign nations unless the conduct at issue has a "direct, substantial, and reasonably foreseeable effect" on domestic commerce and "such effect gives rise to a claim under" the antitrust laws. In *Empagran*, the Court held that U.S. antitrust law, as modified by the FTAIA, does not apply to the foreign effects of foreign anticompetitive conduct, where the foreign effects are independent of any domestic effects.

(2) Does the opinion in *Empagran* more closely resemble the approach of the majority in *Hartford Fire* or that of the dissent? Note that the Court relies on

the *Charming Betsy* presumption, citing the *Hartford Fire* dissent for the point. And, it clearly rejects the idea that "comity" is relevant only in cases presenting "true conflicts," as the majority in *Hartford Fire* understood the concept. The Court also found in international law a "reasonableness" principle (specifically, the principle that nations should avoid "unreasonable interference with the sovereign authority of other nations").

(3) On the other hand, the Court rejected the case-by-case *Timberlane*-style analysis that the *Hartford Fire* dissenters said was contemplated by international law (specifically, §403 of the Third Restatement). The Court (with the *Hartford Fire* dissenters now on board) noted that "[the case-by-case] approach is too complex to prove workable." *Compare* this reasoning with the *Laker* critique of *Timberlane, supra* page 600. What role, exactly, does "comity" play in extraterritoriality analysis, as contemplated by the *Empagran* Court?

(4) If *American Banana* represents the traditional territorial approach, and *Timberlane* adopts a more modern approach, is the "comity" analysis in *Empagran* analogous to Currie's vision of a "restrained and moderate interpretation" for true conflicts, or Baxter's theory of "comparative impairment"? In rejecting as "unworkable" a case-by-case multilateral approach to the extraterritoriality issue, does *Empagran* reflect the same desire for certainty and predictability that led the New York Court of Appeals in Neumeier v. Kuehner, *supra* page 178, to seek more determinate choice-of-law rules? Or was *Empagran*'s rejection of case-by-case balancing of interests driven more by administrability concerns?

(5) Just as the Third Restatement was influenced by *Timberlane* when it adopted the reasonableness analysis of §403, the Fourth Restatement of Foreign Relations Law, adopted in 2018, relied heavily on *Empagran*. According to §211 of the Fourth Restatement, "[c]ustomary international law permits exercises of prescriptive jurisdiction if there is a genuine connection between the subject of the regulation and the state seeking to regulate." Usually, prescriptive jurisdiction "rests on a specific connection between the state and the subject being regulated, such as territory, effects, active personality, passive personality, or protection." But, expressly departing from the Third Restatement, the Fourth Restatement asserts that "state practice does not support a requirement of case-by-case balancing to establish reasonableness as a matter of international law." Fourth Restatement, §211, reporter's note 3. In describing U.S. practice, the Fourth Restatement recognizes that the Court in *Empagran* said that ambiguous statutes should "ordinarily [be] construe[d] to avoid unreasonable interference with the sovereign authority of other nations." Fourth Restatement §204, reporter's note 1. According to the new Restatement, this "reasonableness" principle is an example of "prescriptive comity," which the courts apply to supplement other principles of statutory interpretation, such as the presumption against extraterritoriality, discussed in Section B, *infra*. These "comity limitations" may take different forms under different statutes. For example, the Restatement notes that, "[c]ourts considering application of certain provisions of the Bankruptcy Code have tended to apply a choice-of-law analysis that frequently looks to the 'center of gravity' of a transaction. See, e.g., In re French, 440 F.3d 145, 151-152 (4th Cir. 2006); In re Florsheim Group Inc., 336 B.R. 126, 130 (N.D. Ill. 2005); In re Maxwell Commc'n Corp. plc, 170 B.R. 800, 809 (Bankr. S.D.N.Y. 1994)." *Id.*, reporter's note 5. Thus, according to the Fourth Restatement, a multilateral approach to extraterritoriality remains possible

for particular statutes, as a supplementary means of interpretation, "if consistent with the text, history, and purpose of the statutory provision in question." *Id.*, reporter's note 4. If these "comity limitations" supplement the presumption against extraterritoriality, however, in what contexts will the courts have occasion to apply them? If such limitations are not required by international law, on what basis do the courts read them into statutes? *Compare Empagran, supra* pages 601-602, linking the "reasonableness" requirement to customary international law and citing the Third Restatement and the *Charming Betsy* case.

B. The Court's Current Approach: The Presumption Against Extraterritoriality

EEOC v. Arabian American Oil Co.

499 U.S. 244 (1991)

Chief Justice REHNQUIST delivered the opinion of the Court.

These cases present the issue whether Title VII applies extraterritorially to regulate the employment practices of United States employers who employ United States citizens abroad. The United States Court of Appeals for the Fifth Circuit held that it does not, and we agree with that conclusion. Petitioner Boureslan is a naturalized United States citizen who was born in Lebanon. The respondents are two Delaware corporations, Arabian American Oil Company (Aramco), and its subsidiary, Aramco Service Company (ASC). Aramco's principal place of business is Dhahran, Saudi Arabia, and it is licensed to do business in Texas. ASC's principal place of business is Houston, Texas.

In 1979, Boureslan was hired by ASC as a cost engineer in Houston. A year later he was transferred, at his request, to work for Aramco in Saudi Arabia. Boureslan remained with Aramco in Saudi Arabia until he was discharged in 1984. After filing a charge of discrimination with the Equal Employment Opportunity Commission (EEOC or Commission), he instituted this suit in the United States District Court for the Southern District of Texas against Aramco and ASC. He sought relief under both state law and Title VII of the Civil Rights Act of 1964, 42 U.S.C. §§2000e-2000e-17, on the ground that he was harassed and ultimately discharged by respondents on account of his race, religion, and national origin.

Respondents filed a motion for summary judgment on the ground that the District Court lacked subject-matter jurisdiction over Boureslan's claim because the protections of Title VII do not extend to United States citizens employed abroad by American employers. The District Court agreed and dismissed Boureslan's Title VII claim; it also dismissed his state-law claims for lack of pendent jurisdiction and entered final judgment in favor of respondents. A panel for the Fifth Circuit affirmed. After vacating the panel's decision and rehearing the case en banc, the court affirmed the District Court's dismissal of Boureslan's complaint. . . .

Both parties concede, as they must, that Congress has the authority to enforce its laws beyond the territorial boundaries of the United States. Whether Congress has in fact exercised that authority in this case is a matter of statutory construction. It is our task to determine whether Congress intended the protections of Title VII to apply to United States citizens employed by American employers outside of the United States.

It is a longstanding principle of American law "that legislation of Congress, unless a contrary intent appears, is meant to apply only within the territorial jurisdiction of the United States." Foley Bros., Inc. v. Filardo, 336 U.S. 281, 285 (1949). This "canon of construction . . . is a valid approach whereby unexpressed congressional intent may be ascertained." *Ibid.* It serves to protect against unintended clashes between our laws and those of other nations which could result in international discord. *See* McCulloch v. Sociedad Nacional de Marineros de Honduras, 372 U.S. 10, 20-22 (1963).

In applying this rule of construction, we look to see whether "language in the [relevant Act] gives any indication of a congressional purpose to extend its coverage beyond places over which the United States has sovereignty or has some measure of legislative control." *Foley Bros., supra,* at 285. We assume that Congress legislates against the backdrop of the presumption against extraterritoriality. Therefore, unless there is "the affirmative intention of the Congress clearly expressed," *Benz, supra,* at 147, we must presume it "is primarily concerned with domestic conditions." *Foley Bros., supra,* at 285.

Boureslan and the EEOC contend that the language of Title VII evinces a clearly expressed intent on behalf of Congress to legislate extraterritorially. They rely principally on two provisions of the statute. First, petitioners argue that the statute's definitions of the jurisdictional terms "employer" and "commerce" are sufficiently broad to include United States firms that employ American citizens overseas. Second, they maintain that the statute's "alien exemption" clause, 42 U.S.C. §2000e-1, necessarily implies that Congress intended to protect American citizens from employment discrimination abroad. Petitioners also contend that we should defer to the EEOC's consistently held position that Title VII applies abroad. We conclude that petitioners' evidence, while not totally lacking in probative value, falls short of demonstrating the affirmative congressional intent required to extend the protections of Title VII beyond our territorial borders.

Title VII prohibits various discriminatory employment practices based on an individual's race, color, religion, sex, or national origin. *See* §§2000e-2, 2000e-3. An employer is subject to Title VII if it has employed 15 or more employees for a specified period and is "engaged in an industry affecting commerce." An industry affecting commerce is "any activity, business, or industry in commerce or in which a labor dispute would hinder or obstruct commerce or the free flow of commerce and includes any activity or industry 'affecting commerce' within the meaning of the Labor-Management Reporting and Disclosure Act of 1959 [(LMRDA)] [29 U.S.C. §401 et seq.]." §2000e(h). "Commerce," in turn, is defined as "trade, traffic, commerce, transportation, transmission, or communication among the several States; or between a State and any place outside thereof; or within the District of Columbia, or a possession of the United States; or between points in the same State but through a point outside thereof." §2000e(g).

Petitioners argue that by its plain language, Title VII's "broad jurisdictional language" reveals Congress's intent to extend the statute's protections to employment discrimination anywhere in the world by a United States employer who affects trade "between a State and any place outside thereof." More precisely, they assert that since Title VII defines "States" to include States, the District of Columbia, and specified territories, the clause "between a State and any place outside thereof" must be referring to areas beyond the territorial limit of the United States.

Respondents offer several alternative explanations for the statute's expansive language. They contend that the "or between a State and any place outside thereof" clause "provides the jurisdictional nexus required to regulate commerce that is not wholly within a single state, presumably as it affects both interstate and foreign commerce" but not to "regulate conduct exclusively *within* a foreign country." They also argue that since the definitions of the terms "employer," "commerce," and "industry affecting commerce" make no mention of "commerce with foreign nations," Congress cannot be said to have intended that the statute apply overseas. In support of this argument, petitioners point to Title II of the Civil Rights Act of 1964, governing public accommodation, which specifically defines commerce as it applies to foreign nations. Finally, respondents argue that while language present in the first bill considered by the House of Representatives contained the terms "foreign commerce" and "foreign nations," those terms were deleted by the Senate before the Civil Rights Act of 1964 was passed. They conclude that these deletions "[are] inconsistent with the notion of a clearly expressed congressional intent to apply Title VII extraterritorially."

We need not choose between these competing interpretations as we would be required to do in the absence of the presumption against extraterritorial application discussed above. Each is plausible, but no more persuasive than that. The language relied upon by petitioners—and it is they who must make the affirmative showing—is ambiguous, and does not speak directly to the question presented here. The intent of Congress as to the extraterritorial application of this statute must be deduced by inference from boilerplate language which can be found in any number of congressional Acts, none of which have ever been held to apply overseas.

Petitioners' reliance on Title VII's jurisdictional provisions also finds no support in our case law; we have repeatedly held that even statutes that contain broad language in their definitions of "commerce" that expressly refer to "*foreign* commerce" do not apply abroad. . . .

The EEOC places great weight on an assertedly similar "broad jurisdictional grant in the Lanham Act" that this Court held applied extraterritorially in Steele v. Bulova Watch Co., 344 U.S. 280, 286 (1952). In *Steele*, we addressed whether the Lanham Act, designed to prevent deceptive and misleading use of trademarks, applied to acts of a United States citizen consummated in Mexico. The Act defined commerce as "all commerce which may lawfully be regulated by Congress." 15 U.S.C. §1127. The stated intent of the statute was "to regulate commerce within the control of Congress by making actionable the deceptive and misleading use of marks in such commerce." *Ibid*. While recognizing that "the legislation of Congress will not extend beyond the boundaries of the United States unless a contrary legislative intent appears," the Court concluded that in light of the fact that the allegedly unlawful conduct had some effects within the United States, coupled with the Act's "broad jurisdictional grant" and its "sweeping reach into 'all commerce which may lawfully be regulated by Congress,'" the statute was properly interpreted as applying abroad. *Steele, supra*, at 285, 287.

The EEOC's attempt to analogize these cases to *Steele* is unpersuasive. The Lanham Act by its terms applies to "all commerce which may lawfully be regulated by Congress." The Constitution gives Congress the power "to regulate Commerce with foreign Nations, and among the several States, and with the Indian Tribes." U.S. Const., Art. I, §8, cl. 3. Since the Act expressly stated that it applied to the extent of Congress' power over commerce, the Court in *Steele* concluded that Congress intended that the statute apply abroad. By contrast, Title VII's more limited, boilerplate "commerce" language does not support such an expansive construction of congressional intent. Moreover, unlike the language in the Lanham Act, Title VII's definition of "commerce" was derived expressly from the LMRDA, a statute that this Court had held, prior to the enactment of Title VII, did not apply abroad. *McCulloch, supra,* at 15.

Thus petitioner's argument based on the jurisdictional language of Title VII fails both as a matter of statutory language and of our previous case law. Many Acts of Congress are based on the authority of that body to regulate commerce among the several States, and the parts of these Acts setting forth the basis for legislative jurisdiction will obviously refer to such commerce in one way or another. If we were to permit possible, or even plausible, interpretations of language such as that involved here to override the presumption against extraterritorial application, there would be little left of the presumption.

Petitioners argue that Title VII's "alien exemption provision," 42 U.S.C. §2000e-1, "clearly manifests an intention" by Congress to protect United States citizens with respect to their employment outside of the United States. The alien-exemption provision says that the statute "shall not apply to an employer with respect to the employment of aliens outside any State." Petitioners contend that from this language a negative inference should be drawn that Congress intended Title VII to cover United States *citizens* working abroad for United States employers. There is "no other plausible explanation that the alien exemption exists," they argue, because "if Congress believed that the statute did not apply extraterritorially, it would have had no reason to include an exemption for a certain category of individuals employed outside the United States." Since "the statute's jurisdictional provisions cannot possibly be read to confer coverage only upon aliens employed outside the United States," petitioners conclude that "Congress could not rationally have enacted an exemption for the employment of aliens abroad if it intended to foreclose *all* potential extraterritorial applications of the statute."

Respondents resist petitioners' interpretation of the alien-exemption provision and assert two alternative *raisons d'etre* for that language. First, they contend that since aliens are included in the statute's definition of employee[1] and the definition of commerce includes possessions as well as "States," the purpose of the exemption is to provide that employers of aliens in the possessions of the

---

1. Title VII defines "employee" as: "an individual employed by an employer, except that the term 'employee' shall not include any person elected to public office in any State or political subdivision of any State by the qualified voters thereof, or any person chosen by such officer to be on such officer's personal staff, or an appointee on the policy making level or an immediate adviser with respect to the exercise of the constitutional or legal powers of the office. The exemption set forth in the preceding sentence shall not include employees subject to the civil service laws of a State government, governmental agency or political subdivision." 42 U.S.C. §2000e(f).

United States are not covered by the statute. Thus, the "outside any State" clause means outside any State, but within the control of the United States. Respondents argue that "this reading of the alien exemption provision is consistent with and supported by the historical development of the provision.". . . Second, respondents assert that by negative implication, the exemption "confirms the coverage of aliens in the United States.". . .

If petitioners are correct that the alien-exemption clause means that the statute applies to employers overseas, we see no way of distinguishing in its application between United States employers and foreign employers. Thus, a French employer of a United States citizen in France would be subject to Title VII—a result at which even petitioners balk. The EEOC assures us that in its view the term "employer" means only "American employer," but there is no such distinction in this statute and no indication that the EEOC in the normal course of its administration had produced a reasoned basis for such a distinction. Without clearer evidence of congressional intent to do so than is contained in the alien-exemption clause, we are unwilling to ascribe to that body a policy which would raise difficult issues of international law by imposing this country's employment-discrimination regime upon foreign corporations operating in foreign commerce.

This conclusion is fortified by the other elements in the statute suggesting a purely domestic focus. The statute as a whole indicates a concern that it not unduly interfere with the sovereignty and laws of the States. *See, e.g.*, 42 U.S.C. §2000h-4 (stating that the Act should not be construed to exclude the operation of state law or invalidate any state law unless inconsistent with the purposes of the Act); §2000e-5 (requiring the EEOC to accord substantial weight to findings of state or local authorities in proceedings under state or local law); §2000e-7 (providing that nothing in Title VII shall affect the application of state or local law unless such law requires or permits practices that would be unlawful under Title VII); §§2000e-5(c), (d), and (e) (provisions addressing deferral to state discrimination proceedings). While Title VII consistently speaks in terms of "States" and state proceedings, it fails even to mention foreign nations or foreign proceedings.

Similarly, Congress failed to provide any mechanisms for overseas enforcement of Title VII. . . .

It is also reasonable to conclude that had Congress intended Title VII to apply overseas, it would have addressed the subject of conflicts with foreign laws and procedures. In amending the Age Discrimination in Employment Act of 1967 (ADEA), 29 U.S.C. §621 et seq., to apply abroad, Congress specifically addressed potential conflicts with foreign law by providing that it is not unlawful for an employer to take any action prohibited by the ADEA "where such practices involve an employee in a workplace in a foreign country, and compliance with [the ADEA] would cause such employer . . . to violate the laws of the country in which such workplace is located." §623(f)(1). Title VII, by contrast, fails to address conflicts with the laws of other nations. . . .

Our conclusion today is buttressed by the fact that "when it desires to do so, Congress knows how to place the high seas within the jurisdictional reach of a statute." Argentine Republic v. Amerada Hess Shipping Corp., 488 U.S. 428, 440 (1989). Congress' awareness of the need to make a clear statement that a statute applies overseas is amply demonstrated by the numerous occasions on which it has expressly legislated the extraterritorial application of a statute. . . . Indeed, after several courts had held that the ADEA did not apply overseas, Congress amended §11(f) to provide: "The term 'employee' includes any individual who is a citizen of the United States employed by an employer in a workplace in a foreign country." 29 U.S.C. §630(f). . . . The expressed purpose of these changes was to "make provisions of the Act apply to citizens of the United States employed in foreign countries by U.S. corporations or their subsidiaries." S. Rep. No. 98-467, p.2 (1984). Congress, should it wish to do so, may similarly amend Title VII and in doing so will be able to calibrate its provisions in a way that we cannot.

Petitioners have failed to present sufficient affirmative evidence that Congress intended Title VII to apply abroad. Accordingly, the judgment of the Court of Appeals is

Affirmed.

Justice MARSHALL, with whom Justice BLACKMUN and Justice STEVENS join, dissenting.

. . .

Because it supplies the driving force of the majority's analysis, I start with "[t]he canon . . . that legislation of Congress, unless a contrary intent appears, is meant to apply only within the territorial jurisdiction of the United States." [Foley Bros., Inc. v. Filardo, 336 U.S. 281, 285 (1949).] The majority recasts this principle as "the need to make *a clear statement* that a statute applies overseas." So conceived, the presumption against extraterritoriality allows the majority to derive meaning from various instances of statutory silence—from Congress' failure, for instance, "to mention foreign nations or foreign proceedings," "to provide any mechanisms for overseas enforcement," or to "addres[s] the subject of conflicts with foreign laws and procedures." At other points, the majority relies on its reformulation of the presumption to avoid the "need [to] choose between . . . competing interpretations" of affirmative statutory language that the majority concludes "does not speak *directly* to the question" of extraterritoriality. In my view, the majority grossly distorts the effect of this rule of construction upon conventional techniques of statutory interpretation. . . .

[T]he presumption against extraterritoriality is *not* a "clear statement" rule. Clear-statement rules operate less to reveal *actual* congressional intent than to shield important values from an *insufficiently strong* legislative intent to displace them. When they apply, such rules foreclose inquiry into extrinsic guides to interpretation, and even compel courts to select less plausible candidates from within the range of permissible constructions. The Court's analysis in *Foley Brothers* was by no means so narrowly constrained. Indeed, the Court considered the entire range of conventional sources "whereby *unexpressed* congressional intent may be ascertained," 336 U.S., at 285 (emphasis added), including legislative history, statutory structure, and administrative interpretations. Subsequent applications of the presumption against extraterritoriality confirm that we have not imposed the drastic clear-statement burden upon Congress before giving effect to its intention that a particular enactment apply beyond the national boundaries. *See, e.g.*, Steele v. Bulova Watch Co., 344 U.S. 280, 286-287 (1952) (relying on "broad jurisdictional grant" to find intention that Lanham Act applies abroad). . . .

Confirmation that Congress did *in fact* expect Title VII's central prohibition to have an extraterritorial reach is supplied by the so-called "alien exemption" provision. The alien-exemption provision states that Title VII "shall not apply to an employer with respect to the employment of aliens *outside any State.*" ([E]mphasis added). Absent an intention that Title VII *apply* "outside any State," Congress would have had no reason to craft this extraterritorial exemption. And because only discrimination against aliens is exempted, employers remain accountable for discrimination against United States citizens abroad.

The inference arising from the alien-exemption provision is more than sufficient to rebut the presumption against extraterritoriality. . . .

The history of the alien-exemption provision confirms the inference that Congress expected Title VII to have extraterritorial application. As I have explained, the Court in *Foley Brothers* declined to construe the Eight Hour Law to apply extraterritorially in large part because of "[t]he absence of any distinction between citizen and alien labor" under the Law:

> "Unless we were to read such a distinction into the statute we should be forced to conclude . . . that Congress intended to regulate the working hours of a citizen of Iran who chanced to be employed on a public work of the United States in that foreign land. . . . An intention so to regulate labor conditions which are the primary concern of a foreign country should not be attributed to Congress in the absence of a clearly expressed purpose." 336 U.S., at 286.

The language comprising the alien-exemption provision first appeared in an employment-discrimination bill introduced only seven weeks after the Court decided *Foley Brothers,* see H.R. 4453, 81st Cong., 1st Sess. (1949), and was clearly aimed at insulating that legislation from the concern that prevented the Court from adopting an extraterritorial construction of the Eight Hour Law. The legislative history surrounding Title VII leaves no doubt that Congress had extraterritorial application in mind when it revived the alien-exemption provision from the earlier antidiscrimination bill:

> "In section 4 of the Act, a limited exception is provided for employers with respect to employment of aliens outside of any State. . . . *The intent of [this] exemption is to remove conflicts of law which might otherwise exist between the United States and a foreign nation in the employment of aliens outside the United States by an American enterprise.*" H.R.Rep. No. 570, 88th Cong., 1st Sess. 4 (1963) (emphasis added), reprinted in Civil Rights, Hearings on H.R. 7152, as amended, before Subcommittee No. 5 of the Committee on the Judiciary, 88th Cong., 1st Sess. 2303 (Civil Rights Hearings).[4]

---

4. The alien-exemption provision was originally part of H.R. 405, 88th Cong., 1st Sess. (1963), reprinted in Civil Rights Hearings, at 2330. This bill, along with others, was incorporated (with amendments immaterial to the alien-exemption provision) into H.R. 7152, the bill that became the Civil Rights Act of 1964. See H.R. Rep. No. 914, 88th Cong. 1st Sess., 57 (1963), U.S. Code Cong. & Admin. News 1964, p. 2355 (additional views of Rep. Meader). The Committee Report accompanying H.R. 405 was likewise incorporated into the record of committee hearings held on the various bills from which H.R. 7152 derived. See Civil Rights Hearings, at 2300.

See also S. Rep. No. 867, 88th Cong., 2d Sess., 11 (1964) ("Exempted from the bill are . . . U.S. employers employing citizens of foreign countries *in foreign lands*" (emphasis added)).

Notwithstanding the basic rule of construction requiring courts to give effect to all of the statutory language, the majority never advances an alternative explanation of the alien-exemption provision that is consistent with the majority's own conclusion that Congress intended Title VII to have a purely domestic focus. The closest that the majority comes to attempting to give meaning to the alien-exemption provision is to identify without endorsement "two alternative raisons d'etre for that language" offered by respondents. Neither of these explanations is even minimally persuasive. . . .

Questions and Comments

(1) Note that the Court in *Aramco* considers only whether or not U.S. law applies. It never considers the potential application of Saudi Arabian law. This *unilateral* conflicts methodology contrasts with the *multilateral* approaches we saw in most of the choice-of-law cases in Chapters 2 and 3, and in some of the federal extraterritoriality cases discussed in Section A of this chapter, in which courts consider the interests of the forum and of other states. Why might the current Court prefer a unilateral methodology in cases involving federal-law conflicts with foreign law? Is this phenomenon related to the penal law taboo discussed *supra* pages 156-162? Does it have something to do with not wanting to offend a foreign sovereign by misapplying its law? Does the Court not consider Saudi Arabian law out of deference to the U.S. political branches? Is it better to resolve the applicability of American law unilaterally, or with reference to the laws and interests of other states? For analysis of these issues, *see* McConnaughay, *Reviving the "Public Law Taboo" in International Conflict of Laws*, 35 Stan. J. Intl. L. 255 (1999); Dodge, *Extraterritoriality and Conflict-of-Laws Theory: An Argument for Judicial Unilateralism*, 39 Harv. Intl. L.J. 101 (1998); Weintraub, *The Extraterritorial Application of Antitrust and Securities Laws: An Inquiry into the Utility of a "Choice-of-Law" Approach*, 70 Tex. L. Rev. 1799 (1992); Brilmayer, *The Extraterritorial Application of American Law: A Methodological and Constitutional Appraisal*, 50 Law & Contemp. Probs. 11 (1987).

(2) *Aramco* seems to rely on reasoning similar to the *Carroll* case, which stated at page 17 *supra* that "universally recognized principles of private international or interstate law" hold that legislation applies only to local events. Indeed, in the years between *American Banana* and *Aramco*, the Court had departed from a strict presumption against extraterritoriality, invoking the presumption infrequently, especially in the decades preceding *Aramco*. For this reason, some scholars view *Aramco* as a regression to outmoded territorialist thinking. *See, e.g.,* Born, *A Reappraisal of the Extraterritorial Reach of U.S. Law*, 24 Law & Poly. Intl. Bus. 1 (1992); Kramer, *Vestiges of Beale: Extraterritorial Application of American Law*, 1991 S. Ct. Rev. 179. Professor Bradley disagrees. He maintains that the presumption against extraterritoriality applied in cases like *Aramco* is grounded less in old territorial assumptions than in separation of powers principles such as a judicial desire not to impinge on political branch prerogatives by violating international law or causing foreign relations controversy. *See* Bradley,

Territorial Intellectual Property Rights in an Age of Globalism, 37 Va. J. Intl. L. 505, 550-561 (1997). Which is the right view? Which finds more support in *Aramco*? The Court in *Aramco* explains that the presumption "protect[s] against unintended clashes between our laws and those of other nations which could result in international discord." Is it possible to give effect to such concerns by means of a less rigid presumption? Do separation of powers and international relations concerns have more salience in the federal extraterritoriality context than in the context of state choice of law?

(3) In addition to attempting to avoid unintended clashes with foreign law and avoiding international discord, the presumption also "reflects the more prosaic 'commonsense notion that Congress generally legislates with domestic concerns in mind.' *Smith v. United States*, 507 U.S. 197, 204, n.5 (1993)." *RJR Nabisco*, *infra* page 629. Does the fact that the legislature had only domestic concerns in mind support the conclusion that the statute should apply only to domestic conduct? Isn't this is the same assumption that underlies state choice of law? For state courts, however, the assumption that the legislature had only domestic cases in mind serves as a springboard to a more conventional effort to construe the statute with respect to its geographic scope, including by reference to the statute's purposes. Does the Supreme Court's preference for a more rigid canon of construction for federal statutes reflect an aversion to purposive approaches to statutory interpretation?

(4) In *Aramco*, why wasn't the presumption against extraterritoriality overcome by indications in the statute that suggested an extraterritorial scope? Why does the Court insist that Congress's intent be "clearly expressed" in the statute? The dissent notes that the statute's legislative history clearly indicated that the the alien exemption was inserted to make clear that the statute would not apply to aliens employed by U.S. enterprises abroad. What was the majority's response to the argument based on legislative history? Did the majority hold that, in determining whether the presumption against extraterritoriality has been rebutted, legislative history cannot be consulted?

(5) The plaintiffs in *Aramco* also brought claims under state law, which were dismissed for lack of pendent jurisdiction. Should state law also be subject to a presumption against extraterritoriality? Should such a rule be required by federal law? Does it make sense to limit the reach of federal law for the purpose of avoiding international friction, but not to impose a similar restriction of the reach of state law? But, if the presumption against extraterritoriality is merely a rule for construing federal statutes, what would be the basis for imposing it on the states? *See* Fourth Restatement of Foreign Relations Law §203, reporter's note 5 (asserting that the federal presumption against extraterritoriality does not apply to state statutes, but noting that some states have adopted their own presumptions against extraterritoriality).

(6) Congress quickly overturned the specific holding of *Aramco* concerning the scope of Title VII. In the Civil Rights Act of 1991, Congress amended the definition of "employee" in Title VII to provide that, "[w]ith respect to employment in a foreign country, [the term employee] includes an individual who is a citizen of the United States." Congress also added the following provisions:

> (b) It shall not be unlawful under [this statute] . . . for an employer (or a corporation controlled by an employer), labor organization, employment agency, or

joint labor-management committee controlling apprenticeship or other training or retraining (including on-the-job training programs) to take any action otherwise prohibited by such section, with respect to an employee in a workplace in a foreign country if compliance with such section would cause such employer (or such corporation), such organization, such agency, or such committee to violate the law of the foreign country in which such workplace is located.

(c) (1) If an employer controls a corporation whose place of incorporation is a foreign country, any practice prohibited by [this statute] engaged in by such corporation shall be presumed to be engaged in by such employer.

(2) [This statute] shall not apply with respect to the foreign operations of an employer that is a foreign person not controlled by an American employer.

Does this statute show that the Court in *Aramco* erred in its original interpretation of Title VII? Or does it show the system of separation of powers working well, because Congress specified Title VI's extraterritorial scope with a precision that the Court never could have achieved?

Morrison v. National Australia Bank Ltd.

561 U.S. 247 (2010)

Justice SCALIA delivered the opinion of the Court.

We decide whether §10(b) of the Securities Exchange Act of 1934 provides a cause of action to foreign plaintiffs suing foreign and American defendants for misconduct in connection with securities traded on foreign exchanges.

I

Respondent National Australia Bank Limited (National) was, during the relevant time, the largest bank in Australia. Its Ordinary Shares — what in America would be called "common stock" — are traded on the Australian Stock Exchange Limited and on other foreign securities exchanges, but not on any exchange in the United States. There are listed on the New York Stock Exchange, however, National's American Depositary Receipts (ADRs), which represent the right to receive a specified number of National's Ordinary Shares.

The complaint alleges the following facts, which we accept as true. In February 1998, National bought respondent HomeSide Lending, Inc., a mortgage-servicing company headquartered in Florida. HomeSide's business was to receive fees for servicing mortgages. The rights to receive those fees, so-called mortgage-servicing rights, can provide a valuable income stream. . . . From 1998 until 2001, National's annual reports and other public documents touted the success of HomeSide's business. . . . But on July 5, 2001, National announced that it was writing down the value of HomeSide's assets by $450 million; and then again on September 3, by another $1.75 billion. The prices of both Ordinary Shares and ADRs slumped. After downplaying the July writedown, National explained the September writedown as the result of a failure to anticipate the lowering of prevailing interest rates (lower interest rates lead to more refinancings, *i.e.*, more early repayments of mortgages), other mistaken assumptions in the financial models, and the loss of goodwill. According to the complaint, however, HomeSide, Race, Harris, and another HomeSide senior executive who is also a respondent here had manipulated HomeSide's financial models to make the rates of early repayment unrealistically low in order to cause the mortgage-servicing rights to appear more valuable than they really were. . . .

As relevant here, petitioners Russell Leslie Owen and Brian and Geraldine Silverlock, all Australians, purchased National's Ordinary Shares in 2000 and 2001, before the writedowns. They sued National, HomeSide, Cicutto, and the three HomeSide executives in the United States District Court for the Southern District of New York for alleged violations of §§10(b) . . . of the Securities Exchange Act of 1934, and SEC Rule 10b-5, 17 CFR §240.10b-5 (2009), promulgated pursuant to §10(b). They sought to represent a class of foreign purchasers of National's Ordinary Shares during a specified period up to the September writedown.

Respondents moved to dismiss for lack of subject-matter jurisdiction under Federal Rule of Civil Procedure 12(b)(1) and for failure to state a claim under Rule 12(b)(6). The District Court granted the motion on the former ground, finding no jurisdiction because the acts in this country were, "at most, a link in the chain of an alleged overall securities fraud scheme that culminated abroad." The Court of Appeals for the Second Circuit affirmed on similar grounds. The acts performed in the United States did not "compris[e] the heart of the alleged fraud."

II

[The Court here clarifies that the question before it was "the extraterritorial reach of §10(b)," which is *not* a question of subject-matter jurisdiction. "[T]o ask what conduct §10(b) reaches is to ask what conduct §10(b) prohibits, which is a merits question. Subject-matter jurisdiction, by contrast, refers to a tribunal's 'power to hear a case.'" (Citations omitted.) Notwithstanding the lower court's procedural error, the Court concluded that it was appropriate to reach the merits.]

III

A

It is a "longstanding principle of American law 'that legislation of Congress, unless a contrary intent appears, is meant to apply only within the territorial jurisdiction of the United States.'" EEOC v. Arabian American Oil Co., 499 U.S. 244, 248, (1991) (*Aramco*) (quoting Foley Bros., Inc. v. Filardo, 336 U.S. 281, 285 (1949)). This principle represents a canon of construction, or a presumption about a statute's meaning, rather than a limit upon Congress's power to legislate, see Blackmer v. United States, 284 U.S. 421, 437 (1932). It rests on the perception that Congress ordinarily legislates with respect to domestic, not foreign, matters. Smith v. United States, 507 U.S. 197, 204, n.5 (1993). Thus, "unless there is the affirmative intention of the Congress clearly expressed" to give a statute extraterritorial effect, "we must presume it is primarily concerned with domestic conditions." *Aramco, supra,* at 248 (internal quotation marks omitted). The canon or presumption applies regardless of whether there is a risk of conflict between the

American statute and a foreign law, see Sale v. Haitian Centers Council, Inc., 509 U.S. 155, 173-174 (1993). When a statute gives no clear indication of an extraterritorial application, it has none.

Despite this principle of interpretation, long and often recited in our opinions, the Second Circuit believed that, because the Exchange Act is silent as to the extraterritorial application of §10(b), it was left to the court to "discern" whether Congress would have wanted the statute to apply. See 547 F.3d, at 170 (internal quotation marks omitted). This disregard of the presumption against extraterritoriality did not originate with the Court of Appeals panel in this case. It has been repeated over many decades by various courts of appeals in determining the application of the Exchange Act, and §10(b) in particular, to fraudulent schemes that involve conduct and effects abroad. That has produced a collection of tests for divining what Congress would have wanted, complex in formulation and unpredictable in application. . . .

Commentators have criticized the unpredictable and inconsistent application of §10(b) to transnational cases. . . . The criticisms seem to us justified. The results of judicial-speculation-made-law—divining what Congress would have wanted if it had thought of the situation before the court—demonstrate the wisdom of the presumption against extraterritoriality. Rather than guess anew in each case, we apply the presumption in all cases, preserving a stable background against which Congress can legislate with predictable effects.[5]

B

Rule 10b-5, the regulation under which petitioners have brought suit,[6] was promulgated under §10(b), and "does not extend beyond conduct encompassed

---

5. The concurrence urges us to cast aside our inhibitions and join in the judicial lawmaking, because "[t]his entire area of law is replete with judge-made rules." It is doubtless true that, because the implied private cause of action under §10(b) and Rule 10b-5 is a thing of our own creation, we have also defined its contours. But when it comes to "the scope of [the] conduct prohibited by [Rule 10b-5 and] §10(b), the text of the statute controls our decision." It is only with respect to the additional "elements of the 10b-5 private liability scheme" that we "have had 'to infer how the 1934 Congress would have addressed the issue[s] had the 10b-5 action been included as an express provision in the 1934 Act.'" [Citations omitted.]

6. Rule 10b-5 makes it unlawful:

"for any person, directly or indirectly, by the use of any means or instrumentality of interstate commerce, or of the mails or of any facility of any national securities exchange,

"(a) To employ any device, scheme, or artifice to defraud,

"(b) To make any untrue statement of a material fact or to omit to state a material fact necessary in order to make the statements made, in the light of the circumstances under which they were made, not misleading, or

"(c) To engage in any act, practice, or course of business which operates or would operate as a fraud or deceit upon any person, in connection with the purchase or sale of any security." 17 CFR §240.10b-5 (2009).

The Second Circuit considered petitioners' appeal to raise only a claim under Rule 10b-5(b), since it found their claims under subsections (a) and (c) to be forfeited. 547 F.3d, at 176, n.7. We do likewise.

by §10(b)'s prohibition." United States v. O'Hagan, 521 U.S. 642, 651 (1997). Therefore, if §10(b) is not extraterritorial, neither is Rule 10b-5.

On its face, §10(b) contains nothing to suggest it applies abroad:

> "It shall be unlawful for any person, directly or indirectly, by the use of any means or instrumentality of interstate commerce or of the mails, or of any facility of any national securities exchange — . . . '[t]o use or employ, in connection with the purchase or sale of any security registered on a national securities exchange or any security not so registered, . . . any manipulative or deceptive device or contrivance in contravention of such rules and regulations as the [Securities and Exchange] Commission may prescribe . . . .' " 15 U.S.C. 78j(b).

Petitioners and the Solicitor General contend, however, that three things indicate that §10(b) or the Exchange Act in general has at least some extraterritorial application.

First, they point to the definition of "interstate commerce," a term used in §10(b), which includes "trade, commerce, transportation, or communication . . . between any foreign country and any State." 15 U.S.C. §78c(a)(17). But "we have repeatedly held that even statutes that contain broad language in their definitions of 'commerce' that expressly refer to '*foreign* commerce' do not apply abroad." *Aramco*, 499 U.S., at 251; see *id.*, at 251-252 (discussing cases). The general reference to foreign commerce in the definition of "interstate commerce" does not defeat the presumption against extraterritoriality.

Petitioners and the Solicitor General next point out that Congress, in describing the purposes of the Exchange Act, observed that the "prices established and offered in such transactions are generally disseminated and quoted throughout the United States and foreign countries." 15 U.S.C. §78b(2). The antecedent of "such transactions," however, is found in the first sentence of the section, which declares that "transactions in securities as commonly conducted upon securities exchanges and over-the-counter markets are affected with a national public interest." §78b. Nothing suggests that this *national* public interest pertains to transactions conducted upon *foreign* exchanges and markets. The fleeting reference to the dissemination and quotation abroad of the prices of securities traded in domestic exchanges and markets cannot overcome the presumption against extraterritoriality.

Finally, there is §30(b) of the Exchange Act, 15 U.S.C. §78dd(b), which *does* mention the Act's extraterritorial application: "The provisions of [the Exchange Act] or of any rule or regulation thereunder shall not apply to any person insofar as he transacts a business in securities without the jurisdiction of the United States," unless he does so in violation of regulations promulgated by the Securities and Exchange Commission "to prevent . . . evasion of [the Act]." (The parties have pointed us to no regulation promulgated pursuant to §30(b).) The Solicitor General argues that "[this] exemption would have no function if the Act did not apply in the first instance to securities transactions that occur abroad." Brief for United States as *Amicus Curiae* 14.

We are not convinced. In the first place, it would be odd for Congress to indicate the extraterritorial application of the whole Exchange Act by means of a provision imposing a condition precedent to its application abroad. And if the whole

Act applied abroad, why would the Commission's enabling regulations be limited to those preventing "evasion" of the Act, rather than all those preventing "violation"? The provision seems to us directed at actions abroad that might conceal a domestic violation, or might cause what would otherwise be a domestic violation to escape on a technicality. At most, the Solicitor General's proposed inference is possible; but possible interpretations of statutory language do not override the presumption against extraterritoriality. See *Aramco, supra*, at 253.

The Solicitor General also fails to account for §30(a), which reads in relevant part as follows:

> "It shall be unlawful for any broker or dealer . . . to make use of the mails or of any means or instrumentality of interstate commerce for the purpose of effecting on an exchange not within or subject to the jurisdiction of the United States, any transaction in any security the issuer of which is a resident of, or is organized under the laws of, or has its principal place of business in, a place within or subject to the jurisdiction of the United States, in contravention of such rules and regulations as the Commission may prescribe. . . ." 15 U.S.C. §78dd(a).

Subsection 30(a) contains what §10(b) lacks: a clear statement of extraterritorial effect. Its explicit provision for a specific extraterritorial application would be quite superfluous if the rest of the Exchange Act already applied to transactions on foreign exchanges—and its limitation of that application to securities of domestic issuers would be inoperative. Even if that were not true, when a statute provides for some extraterritorial application, the presumption against extraterritoriality operates to limit that provision to its terms. See Microsoft Corp. v. AT & T Corp., 550 U.S. 437, 455-456 (2007). No one claims that §30(a) applies here.

The concurrence claims we have impermissibly narrowed the inquiry in evaluating whether a statute applies abroad, citing for that point the dissent in *Aramco,* see *post,* at 2891. But we do not say, as the concurrence seems to think, that the presumption against extraterritoriality is a "clear statement rule," *ibid.,* if by that is meant a requirement that a statute say "this law applies abroad." Assuredly context can be consulted as well. But whatever sources of statutory meaning one consults to give "the most faithful reading" of the text, there is no clear indication of extraterritoriality here. The concurrence does not even try to refute that conclusion, but merely puts forward the same (at best) uncertain indications relied upon by petitioners and the Solicitor General. As the opinion *for the Court* in *Aramco* (which we prefer to the dissent) shows, those uncertain indications do not suffice.[8]

In short, there is no affirmative indication in the Exchange Act that §10(b) applies extraterritorially, and we therefore conclude that it does not.

---

8. The concurrence notes that, post-*Aramco*, Congress provided explicitly for extraterritorial application of Title VII, the statute at issue in *Aramco*. All this shows is that Congress knows how to give a statute explicit extraterritorial effect—and how to limit that effect to particular applications, which is what the cited amendment did. See Civil Rights Act of 1991, §109, 105 Stat. 1077.

IV

A

Petitioners argue that the conclusion that §10(b) does not apply extraterritorially does not resolve this case. They contend that they seek no more than domestic application anyway, since Florida is where HomeSide and its senior executives engaged in the deceptive conduct of manipulating HomeSide's financial models; their complaint also alleged that Race and Hughes made misleading public statements there. This is less an answer to the presumption against extraterritorial application than it is an assertion—a quite valid assertion—that that presumption here (as often) is not self-evidently dispositive, but its application requires further analysis. For it is a rare case of prohibited extraterritorial application that lacks *all* contact with the territory of the United States. But the presumption against extraterritorial application would be a craven watchdog indeed if it retreated to its kennel whenever *some* domestic activity is involved in the case. The concurrence seems to imagine just such a timid sentinel, but our cases are to the contrary. In *Aramco*, for example, the Title VII plaintiff had been hired in Houston, and was an American citizen. See 499 U.S., at 247. The Court concluded, however, that neither that territorial event nor that relationship was the "focus" of congressional concern, *id.*, at 255, but rather domestic employment. See also *Foley Bros.*, 336 U.S., at 283, 285-286.

Applying the same mode of analysis here, we think that the focus of the Exchange Act is not upon the place where the deception originated, but upon purchases and sales of securities in the United States. Section 10(b) does not punish deceptive conduct, but only deceptive conduct "in connection with the purchase or sale of any security registered on a national securities exchange or any security not so registered." 15 U.S.C. §78j(b). Those purchase-and-sale transactions are the objects of the statute's solicitude. It is those transactions that the statute seeks to "regulate," see Superintendent of Ins. of N.Y. v. Bankers Life & Casualty Co., 404 U.S. 6, 12 (1971); it is parties or prospective parties to those transactions that the statute seeks to "protec[t]," *id.*, at 10. And it is in our view only transactions in securities listed on domestic exchanges, and domestic transactions in other securities, to which §10(b) applies.[9]

The primacy of the domestic exchange is suggested by the very prologue of the Exchange Act, which sets forth as its object "[t]o provide for the regulation of securities exchanges . . . operating in interstate and foreign commerce and through the mails, to prevent inequitable and unfair practices on such exchanges . . . ." 48 Stat. 881. We know of no one who thought that the Act was intended to "regulat[e]" *foreign* securities exchanges—or indeed who even believed that under established principles of international law Congress had the power to do so. The

---

9. The concurrence seems to think this test has little to do with our conclusion in Part III, *supra*, that §10(b) does not apply extraterritorially. That is not so. If §10(b) did apply abroad, we would not need to determine which transnational frauds it applied to; it would apply to all of them (barring some other limitation). Thus, although it is true, as we have said, that our threshold conclusion that §10(b) has no extraterritorial effect does not resolve this case, it is a necessary first step in the analysis.

Act's registration requirements apply only to securities listed on national securities exchanges. 15 U.S.C. §78*l* (a).

With regard to securities *not* registered on domestic exchanges, the exclusive focus on *domestic* purchases and sales[10] is strongly confirmed by §30(a) and (b), discussed earlier. The former extends the normal scope of the Exchange Act's prohibitions to acts effecting, in violation of rules prescribed by the Commission, a "transaction" in a United States security "on an exchange not within or subject to the jurisdiction of the United States." §78dd(a). And the latter specifies that the Act does not apply to "any person insofar as he transacts a business in securities without the jurisdiction of the United States," unless he does so in violation of regulations promulgated by the Commission "to prevent the evasion [of the Act]." §78dd(b). Under both provisions it is the foreign location of the *transaction* that establishes (or reflects the presumption of) the Act's inapplicability, absent regulations by the Commission.

The same focus on domestic transactions is evident in the Securities Act of 1933, 48 Stat. 74, enacted by the same Congress as the Exchange Act, and forming part of the same comprehensive regulation of securities trading. See Central Bank of Denver, N.A. v. First Interstate Bank of Denver, N. A., 511 U.S. 164, 170-171 (1994). That legislation makes it unlawful to sell a security, through a prospectus or otherwise, making use of "any means or instruments of transportation or communication in interstate commerce or of the mails," unless a registration statement is in effect. 15 U.S.C. §77e(a)(1). The Commission has interpreted that requirement "not to include . . . sales that occur outside the United States." 17 CFR §230.901 (2009).

Finally, we reject the notion that the Exchange Act reaches conduct in this country affecting exchanges or transactions abroad for the same reason that *Aramco* rejected overseas application of Title VII to all domestically concluded employment contracts or all employment contracts with American employers: The probability of incompatibility with the applicable laws of other countries is so obvious that if Congress intended such foreign application "it would have addressed the subject of conflicts with foreign laws and procedures." 499 U.S., at 256. Like the United States, foreign countries regulate their domestic securities exchanges and securities transactions occurring within their territorial jurisdiction. And the regulation of other countries often differs from ours as to what constitutes fraud, what disclosures must be made, what damages are recoverable, what discovery is available in litigation, what individual actions may be joined in a single suit, what attorney's fees are recoverable, and many other matters. See, *e.g.*, Brief for United Kingdom of Great Britain and Northern Ireland as *Amicus Curiae* 16-21. The Commonwealth of Australia, the United Kingdom of Great Britain and Northern Ireland, and the Republic of France

---

10. That is in our view the meaning which the presumption against extraterritorial application requires for the words "purchase or sale of . . . any security not so registered" in §10(b)'s phrase "in connection with the purchase or sale of any security registered on a national securities exchange *or any security not so registered.*" (Emphasis added.) Even without the presumption against extraterritorial application, the only alternative to that reading makes nonsense of the phrase, causing it to cover all purchases and sales of registered securities, and all purchases and sales of nonregistered securities—a thought which, if intended, would surely have been expressed by the simpler phrase "all purchases and sales of securities."

have filed *amicus* briefs in this case. So have (separately or jointly) such international and foreign organizations as the International Chamber of Commerce, the Swiss Bankers Association, the Federation of German Industries, the French Business Confederation, the Institute of International Bankers, the European Banking Federation, the Australian Bankers' Association, and the Association Francaise des Entreprises Privées. They all complain of the interference with foreign securities regulation that application of §10(b) abroad would produce, and urge the adoption of a clear test that will avoid that consequence. The transactional test we have adopted—whether the purchase or sale is made in the United States, or involves a security listed on a domestic exchange—meets that requirement.

B

The Solicitor General suggests a different test, which petitioners also endorse: "[A] transnational securities fraud violates [§]10(b) when the fraud involves significant conduct in the United States that is material to the fraud's success." Neither the Solicitor General nor petitioners provide any textual support for this test. The Solicitor General sets forth a number of purposes such a test would serve: achieving a high standard of business ethics in the securities industry, ensuring honest securities markets and thereby promoting investor confidence, and preventing the United States from becoming a "Barbary Coast" for malefactors perpetrating frauds in foreign markets. But it provides no textual support for the last of these purposes, or for the first two as applied to the foreign securities industry and securities markets abroad. It is our function to give the statute the effect its language suggests, however modest that may be; not to extend it to admirable purposes it might be used to achieve. . . .

As case support for the "significant and material conduct" test, the Solicitor General relies primarily on Pasquantino v. United States, 544 U.S. 349 (2005).[11] In that case we concluded that the wire-fraud statute, 18 U.S.C. §1343 (2000 ed., Supp. II), was violated by defendants who ordered liquor over the phone from a store in Maryland with the intent to smuggle it into Canada and deprive the Canadian

---

11. Discussed in Brief for United States as *Amicus Curiae* 22-23. The Solicitor General also cites, without description, a number of antitrust cases to support the proposition that domestic conduct with consequences abroad can be covered even by a statute that does not apply extraterritorially: Continental Ore Co. v. Union Carbide & Carbon Corp., 370 U.S. 690 (1962); United States v. Sisal Sales Corp., 274 U.S. 268 (1927); Thomsen v. Cayser, 243 U.S. 66 (1917); United States v. Pacific & Arctic R. & Nav. Co., 228 U.S. 87 (1913). These are no longer of relevance to the point (if they ever were), since *Continental Ore* overruled the holding of American Banana Co. v. United Fruit Co., 213 U.S. 347, 357 (1909), that the antitrust laws do not apply extraterritorially. See W.S. Kirkpatrick & Co. v. Environmental Tectonics Corp., Int'l, 493 U.S. 400, 407-408 (1990). Moreover, the pre-*Continental Ore* cases all involved conspiracies to restrain trade in the United States, see *Sisal Sales, supra*, at 274-276; *Thomsen, supra*, at 88; *Pacific & Arctic, supra*, at 105–106. And although a final case cited by the Solicitor General, Steele v. Bulova Watch Co., 344 U.S. 280, 287–288 (1952), might be read to permit application of a nonextraterritorial statute whenever conduct in the United States contributes to a violation abroad, we have since read it as interpreting the statute at issue—the Lanham Act—to have extraterritorial effect, *Aramco*, 499 U.S. 244, 252 (1991) (quoting 15 U.S.C. §1127).

Government of revenue. 544 U.S., at 353, 371. Section 1343 prohibits "any scheme or artifice to defraud," — fraud *simpliciter*, without any requirement that it be "in connection with" any particular transaction or event. The *Pasquantino* Court said that the petitioners' "offense was complete the moment they executed the scheme inside the United States," and that it was "[t]his domestic element of petitioners' conduct [that] the Government is punishing." *Id.*, at 371. Section 10(b), by contrast, punishes not all acts of deception, but only such acts "in connection with the purchase or sale of any security registered on a national securities exchange or any security not so registered." Not deception alone, but deception with respect to certain purchases or sales is necessary for a violation of the statute.

The Solicitor General points out that the "significant and material conduct" test is in accord with prevailing notions of international comity. If so, that proves that *if* the United States asserted prescriptive jurisdiction pursuant to the "significant and material conduct" test it would not violate customary international law; but it in no way tends to prove that that is what Congress has done. . . .

* * *

Section 10(b) reaches the use of a manipulative or deceptive device or contrivance only in connection with the purchase or sale of a security listed on an American stock exchange, and the purchase or sale of any other security in the United States. This case involves no securities listed on a domestic exchange, and all aspects of the purchases complained of by those petitioners who still have live claims occurred outside the United States. Petitioners have therefore failed to state a claim on which relief can be granted. We affirm the dismissal of petitioners' complaint on this ground.

It is so ordered.

Justice SOTOMAYOR took no part in the consideration or decision of this case.

Justice BREYER, concurring in part and concurring in the judgment. [Omitted.]

Justice STEVENS, with whom Justice GINSBURG joins, concurring in the judgment.

While I agree that petitioners have failed to state a claim on which relief can be granted, my reasoning differs from the Court's. I would adhere to the general approach that has been the law in the Second Circuit, and most of the rest of the country, for nearly four decades.

I

Today the Court announces a new "transactional test," for defining the reach of §10(b) of the Securities Exchange Act of 1934 (Exchange Act), 15 U.S.C. §78j(b), and SEC Rule 10b-5, 17 CFR §240.10b-5(b) (2009): Henceforth, those provisions will extend only to "transactions in securities listed on domestic exchange[s] and domestic transactions in other securities." If one confines one's gaze to the statutory text, the Court's conclusion is a plausible one. But the federal courts have been construing §10(b) in a different manner for a long time, and the

Court's textual analysis is not nearly so compelling, in my view, as to warrant the abandonment of their doctrine. . . .

Repudiating the Second Circuit's approach in its entirety, the Court establishes a novel rule that will foreclose private parties from bringing §10(b) actions whenever the relevant securities were purchased or sold abroad and are not listed on a domestic exchange.[12] The real motor of the Court's opinion, it seems, is not the presumption against extraterritoriality but rather the Court's belief that transactions on domestic exchanges are "the focus of the Exchange Act" and "the objects of [its] solicitude." In reality, however, it is the "public interest" and "the interests of investors" that are the objects of the statute's solicitude. And while the clarity and simplicity of the Court's test may have some salutary consequences, like all bright-line rules it also has drawbacks.

Imagine, for example, an American investor who buys shares in a company listed only on an overseas exchange. That company has a major American subsidiary with executives based in New York City; and it was in New York City that the executives masterminded and implemented a massive deception which artificially inflated the stock price—and which will, upon its disclosure, cause the price to plummet. Or, imagine that those same executives go knocking on doors in Manhattan and convince an unsophisticated retiree, on the basis of material misrepresentations, to invest her life savings in the company's doomed securities. Both of these investors would, under the Court's new test, be barred from seeking relief under § 10(b).

The oddity of that result should give pause. For in walling off such individuals from §10(b), the Court narrows the provision's reach to a degree that would surprise and alarm generations of American investors—and, I am convinced, the Congress that passed the Exchange Act. Indeed, the Court's rule turns §10(b) jurisprudence (and the presumption against extraterritoriality) on its head, by withdrawing the statute's application from cases in which there is *both* substantial wrongful conduct that occurred in the United States *and* a substantial injurious effect on United States markets and citizens.

III

In my judgment, if petitioners' allegations of fraudulent misconduct that took place in Florida are true, then respondents may have violated §10(b), and could potentially be held accountable in an enforcement proceeding brought by the Commission. But it does not follow that shareholders who have failed to allege

---

12. The Court's opinion does not, however, foreclose the Commission from bringing enforcement actions in additional circumstances, as no issue concerning the Commission's authority is presented by this case. The Commission's enforcement proceedings not only differ from private §10(b) actions in numerous potentially relevant respects, see Brief for United States as *Amicus Curiae* 12-13, but they also pose a lesser threat to international comity, *id.*, at 26-27; cf. *Empagran*, 542 U.S., at 171 (" '[P]rivate plaintiffs often are unwilling to exercise the degree of self-restraint and consideration of foreign governmental sensibilities generally exercised by the U.S. Government' " (quoting Griffin, Extraterritoriality in U.S. and EU Antitrust Enforcement, 67 Antitrust L.J. 159, 194 (1999); alteration in original)).

that the bulk or the heart of the fraud occurred in the United States, or that the fraud had an adverse impact on American investors or markets, may maintain a private action to recover damages they suffered abroad. Some cases involving foreign securities transactions have extensive links to, and ramifications for, this country; this case has Australia written all over it. Accordingly, for essentially the reasons stated in the Court of Appeals' opinion, I would affirm its judgment. . . .

Questions and Comments

(1) The Court in *Morrison* clarified that extraterritoriality is a merits question concerning the reach of federal statutes, not a question of subject matter jurisdiction.

(2) The Court also rejected the argument that the presumption was inapplicable to the statute before it because the Second Circuit had long applied a different approach to determining the extraterritorial reach of the securities laws. The Court stated: "Rather than guess anew in each case, *we apply the presumption in all cases*, preserving a stable background against which Congress can legislate with predictable effects." (Emphasis added.) Recall that *Morrison*'s author had previously concluded that the presumption did not apply to U.S. antitrust laws because precedent had established that U.S. antitrust laws applied extraterrorially. *Hartford Fire*, *supra* at page 596 (Scalia, J., dissenting). Does *Morrison* establish that the presumption now applies even to statutes, such as the Sherman Act and the Jones Act, that had previously been found by the courts to apply extraterritorially? Or, does *Morrison* hold that federal statutes are "grandfathered out" of the presumption only if *the Supreme Court* has previously found them to apply extraterritorially.

(3) *Morrison* also clarifies that the presumption is not a clear statement rule. It says that "context" can be considered as well, but apparently only as a "source[] of statutory meaning [that] give[s] 'the most faithful reading' of the text." Can legislative history be consulted? *Compare Aramco*, *supra* page 606 and note 4, page 614.

(4) *Morrison*'s principal contribution to federal extraterritoriality doctrine is to identify extactly *what* has to have occurred on U.S. territory for a case to be covered by a statute that the Court has found not to apply extraterritorially. In other words, how does one determine whether a non-extraterritorial statute reaches a case in which some of the underlying conduct occurred in the United States and some did not? To answer that question, the Court tells us, we must ascertain the " 'focus' of congressional concern." Apparently, the statute is being applied domestically — not extraterritorially — if, in any given case, the conduct or event that was the "focus" of Congress's concern in enacting the statute occurred in the United States. If other conduct or events occurred in the United States, but the conduct or event that was the "focus" of Congress's concern occurred outside the United States, then the statute is being applied extraterritorially.

(5) How does one determine what conduct or events were the "focus of congressional concern"? Does the inquiry into Congress's focus bring Congress's purposes into the analysis through the back door?

(6) The Court in *Morrison* concluded that, in enacting §10(b), Congress was focused on "purchases and sales of securities." Therefore, if the purchase or sale

of the security occurred outside the United States, the statute does not apply, even if the underlying fraud occurred in the United States. Does it follow that the statute does extend to cases in which the purchase or sale of the security occurred in the United States, even if the fraud occurred outside the United States? In Parkcentral Global Hub Ltd. v. Porsche Auto. Holdings SE, 763 F.3d 198, 215 (2d Cir. 2014) (per curiam), the Second Circuit held that the domestic-transaction requirement was a "necessary" but not "sufficient" condition of the statute's applicability. It held that, if the defendants were not parties to the domestic transactions, §10(b) would not apply if the claims were "predominantly foreign." Id. at 216. Is that holding consistent with Morrison's reasoning? Did the court in Parkcentral hold that the Securities Act does not extend to some "domestic" cases? See Fourth Restatement of Foreign Relations Law §204, reporter's note 4.

(7) In explaining why Congress's focus was the purchase or sale of the security rather than the fraud, the Court wrote: "Section 10(b) does not punish deceptive conduct, but only deceptive conduct 'in connection with the purchase or sale of any security registered on a national securities exchange or any security not so registered.'" But, isn't it equally true that §10(b) doesn't punish the sale of a security, but only the sale of a security through deceptive conduct? Does that mean that Congress's focus was both the sale of the security and the deceptive conduct? If so, would it follow that the statute applies if either one took place in the United States? Or would it apply only if both took place in the United States?

(8) For a discussion of the presumption against extraterritoriality after Morrison, see Brilmayer, The New Extraterritoriality: Morrison v. National Australia Bank, Legislative Supremacy, and the Presumption Against Extraterritorial Application of American Law, 40 Sw. L. Rev. 655 (2011); Colangelo, A Unified Approach to Extraterritoriality, 97 Va. L. Rev. 1019 (2011); Dodge, Morrison's Effects Test, 40 Sw. L. Rev. 687 (2011).

(9) Morrison was followed by Kiobel v. Royal Dutch Petroleum Co., 569 U.S. 108 (2013), which concerned the extraterritorial scope of a federal common-law cause of action inferred from the Alien Tort Statute ("ATS"), 28 U.S.C. §1350. The ATS provides that "[t]he district courts shall have original jurisdiction of any civil action by an alien for a tort only, committed in violation of the law of nations or a treaty of the United States." In Sosa v. Alvarez-Machain, 542 U.S. 692, 732 (2004), the Supreme Court held that the ATS, though a mere jurisdictional statute, permits federal courts to recognize private causes of action for a modest number of international law violations as a matter of federal common law. The plaintiffs in Kiobel were Nigerian nationals, residing in the United States, who sued Dutch, British, and Nigerian corporations under the ATS for allegedly aiding and abetting the Nigerian government in committing violations of international law in Nigeria. The Court held that the presumption against extraterritoriality applied to ATS causes of action, and dismissed the case. It reasoned that the presumption applied with special force in the ATS context because the danger of unwarranted judicial interference in the conduct of foreign policy normally present in the extraterritorial application of a federal statute was "magnified" when the issue was the extraterritorial application of judge-made ATS causes of action. And, it determined that the presumption was not overcome either by the original understanding of the statute, or by the term "any" in the phrase "any civil action," or by the fact that jurisdiction under the statute extended to torts "in violation of the law of nations." But the Court was

somewhat vague about when local conduct connected to the cause of action suffices to satisfy the presumption or render it inapplicable. "[E]ven where the claims touch and concern the territory of the United States, they must do so with sufficient force to displace the presumption against extraterritorial application," the Court explained, adding that "[c]orporations are often present in many countries, and it would reach too far to say that mere corporate presence suffices." For critical reactions to the Court's application of the presumption against extraterritoriality in *Kiobel, see* Vázquez, *Things We Do with Presumptions: Reflections on Kiobel v. Royal Dutch Petroleum*, 89 Notre Dame L. Rev. 1719 (2014); Cleveland, *The* Kiobel *Presumption and Extraterritoriality*, 52 Colum. J. Transnatl. L. 8 (2013); Hafetz, *Human Rights Litigation and the National Interest:* Kiobel's *Application of the Presumption Against Extraterritoriality to the Alien Tort Statute*, 28 Md. J. Intl. L. 107 (2013).

RJR Nabisco, Inc. v. European Community
136 S. Ct. 2090 (2016)

Justice ALITO delivered the opinion of the Court.

The Racketeer Influenced and Corrupt Organizations Act (RICO), 18 U.S.C. §§1961-1968, created four new criminal offenses involving the activities of organized criminal groups in relation to an enterprise. §§1962(a)-(d). RICO also created a new civil cause of action for "[a]ny person injured in his business or property by reason of a violation" of those prohibitions. §1964(c). We are asked to decide whether RICO applies extraterritorially—that is, to events occurring and injuries suffered outside the United States.

I

A

RICO is founded on the concept of racketeering activity. The statute defines "racketeering activity" to encompass dozens of state and federal offenses, known in RICO parlance as predicates. These predicates include any act "indictable" under specified federal statutes, §§1961(1)(B)-(C), (E)-(G), as well as certain crimes "chargeable" under state law, §1961(1)(A), and any offense involving bankruptcy or securities fraud or drug-related activity that is "punishable" under federal law, §1961(1)(D). A predicate offense implicates RICO when it is part of a "pattern of racketeering activity"—a series of related predicates that together demonstrate the existence or threat of continued criminal activity. H.J. Inc. v. Northwestern Bell Telephone Co., 492 U.S. 229, 239 (1989); see §1961(5) (specifying that a "pattern of racketeering activity" requires at least two predicates committed within 10 years of each other).

RICO's §1962 sets forth four specific prohibitions aimed at different ways in which a pattern of racketeering activity may be used to infiltrate, control, or operate "a[n] enterprise which is engaged in, or the activities of which affect, interstate or foreign commerce." These prohibitions can be summarized as follows. Section

1962(a) makes it unlawful to invest income derived from a pattern of racketeering activity in an enterprise. Section 1962(b) makes it unlawful to acquire or maintain an interest in an enterprise through a pattern of racketeering activity. Section 1962(c) makes it unlawful for a person employed by or associated with an enterprise to conduct the enterprise's affairs through a pattern of racketeering activity. Finally, §1962(d) makes it unlawful to conspire to violate any of the other three prohibitions.

Violations of §1962 are subject to criminal penalties, §1963(a), and civil proceedings to enforce those prohibitions may be brought by the Attorney General, §§1964(a)-(b). Separately, RICO creates a private civil cause of action that allows "[a]ny person injured in his business or property by reason of a violation of section 1962" to sue in federal district court and recover treble damages, costs, and attorney's fees. §1964(c).

B

This case arises from allegations that petitioners—RJR Nabisco and numerous related entities (collectively RJR)—participated in a global money-laundering scheme in association with various organized crime groups. Respondents—the European Community and 26 of its member states—first sued RJR in the Eastern District of New York in 2000, alleging that RJR had violated RICO. . . .

[T]he complaint alleges that RJR violated each of RICO's prohibitions. RJR allegedly used income derived from the pattern of racketeering to invest in, acquire an interest in, and operate the RJR Money-Laundering Enterprise in violation of §1962(a); acquired and maintained control of the enterprise through the pattern of racketeering in violation of §1962(b); operated the enterprise through the pattern of racketeering in violation of §1962(c); and conspired with other participants in the scheme in violation of §1962(d).[3] These violations allegedly harmed respondents in various ways, including through competitive harm to their state-owned cigarette businesses, lost tax revenue from black-market cigarette sales, harm to European financial institutions, currency instability, and increased law enforcement costs.

RJR moved to dismiss the complaint, arguing that RICO does not apply to racketeering activity occurring outside U.S. territory or to foreign enterprises. The District Court agreed and dismissed the RICO claims as impermissibly extraterritorial.

The Second Circuit reinstated the RICO claims. It concluded that, "with respect to a number of offenses that constitute predicates for RICO liability and are alleged in this case, Congress has clearly manifested an intent that they apply extraterritorially." 764 F.3d 129, 133 (2014). "By incorporating these statutes into RICO as predicate racketeering acts," the court reasoned, "Congress has clearly communicated its intention that RICO apply to extraterritorial conduct to the

---

3. The complaint also alleges that RJR committed a variety of state-law torts. Those claims are not before us.

extent that extraterritorial violations of these statutes serve as the basis for RICO liability." *Id.*, at 137. Turning to the predicates alleged in the complaint, the Second Circuit found that they passed muster. The court concluded that the money laundering and material support of terrorism statutes expressly apply extraterritorially in the circumstances alleged in the complaint. *Id.*, at 139-140. The court held that the mail fraud, wire fraud, and Travel Act statutes do *not* apply extraterritorially. *Id.*, at 141. But it concluded that the complaint states *domestic* violations of those predicates because it "allege[s] conduct in the United States that satisfies every essential element" of those offenses. *Id.*, at 142.

RJR sought rehearing, arguing (among other things) that RICO's civil cause of action requires a plaintiff to allege a domestic *injury*, even if a domestic pattern of racketeering or a domestic enterprise is not necessary to make out a violation of RICO's substantive prohibitions. The panel denied rehearing and issued a supplemental opinion holding that RICO does not require a domestic injury. 764 F.3d 149 (C.A.2 2014) (*per curiam*). If a foreign injury was caused by the violation of a predicate statute that applies extraterritorially, the court concluded, then the plaintiff may seek recovery for that injury under RICO. *Id.*, at 151. The Second Circuit later denied rehearing en banc, with five judges dissenting. 783 F.3d 123 (2015). . . .

II

The question of RICO's extraterritorial application really involves two questions. First, do RICO's substantive prohibitions, contained in §1962, apply to conduct that occurs in foreign countries? Second, does RICO's private right of action, contained in §1964(c), apply to injuries that are suffered in foreign countries? We consider each of these questions in turn. To guide our inquiry, we begin by reviewing the law of extraterritoriality.

It is a basic premise of our legal system that, in general, "United States law governs domestically but does not rule the world." Microsoft Corp. v. AT&T Corp., 550 U.S. 437, 454, (2007). This principle finds expression in a canon of statutory construction known as the presumption against extraterritoriality: Absent clearly expressed congressional intent to the contrary, federal laws will be construed to have only domestic application. Morrison v. National Australia Bank Ltd., 561 U.S. 247, 255 (2010). The question is not whether we think "Congress would have wanted" a statute to apply to foreign conduct "if it had thought of the situation before the court," but whether Congress has affirmatively and unmistakably instructed that the statute will do so. *Id.*, at 261. "When a statute gives no clear indication of an extraterritorial application, it has none." *Id.*, at 255.

There are several reasons for this presumption. Most notably, it serves to avoid the international discord that can result when U.S. law is applied to conduct in foreign countries. See, *e.g.*, *Kiobel* [*supra* page 626]; *Aramco* [*supra* page 606]. But it also reflects the more prosaic "commonsense notion that Congress generally legislates with domestic concerns in mind." Smith v. United States, 507 U.S. 197, 204, n.5 (1993). We therefore apply the presumption across the board, "regardless of whether there is a risk of conflict between the American statute and a foreign law." *Morrison, supra,* at 255.

Twice in the past six years we have considered whether a federal statute applies extraterritorially. In *Morrison,* we addressed the question whether §10(b) of the Securities Exchange Act of 1934 applies to misrepresentations made in connection with the purchase or sale of securities traded only on foreign exchanges. We first examined whether §10(b) gives any clear indication of extraterritorial effect, and found that it does not. 561 U.S., at 262-265. We then engaged in a separate inquiry to determine whether the complaint before us involved a permissible *domestic* application of §10(b) because it alleged that some of the relevant misrepresentations were made in the United States. At this second step, we considered the "'focus' of congressional concern," asking whether §10(b)'s focus is "the place where the deception originated" or rather "purchases and sale of securities in the United States." *Id.,* at 266. We concluded that the statute's focus is on domestic securities transactions, and we therefore held that the statute does not apply to frauds in connection with foreign securities transactions, even if those frauds involve domestic misrepresentations.

In *Kiobel,* we considered whether the Alien Tort Statute (ATS) confers federal-court jurisdiction over causes of action alleging international-law violations committed overseas. We acknowledged that the presumption against extraterritoriality is "typically" applied to statutes "regulating conduct," but we concluded that the principles supporting the presumption should "similarly constrain courts considering causes of action that may be brought under the ATS." 133 S. Ct., at 1664. We applied the presumption and held that the ATS lacks any clear indication that it extended to the foreign violations alleged in that case. *Id.,* at 1665-1669. Because "all the relevant conduct" regarding those violations "took place outside the United States," *id.,* at 1670, we did not need to determine, as we did in *Morrison,* the statute's "focus."

Morrison and *Kiobel* reflect a two-step framework for analyzing extraterritoriality issues. At the first step, we ask whether the presumption against extraterritoriality has been rebutted—that is, whether the statute gives a clear, affirmative indication that it applies extraterritorially. We must ask this question regardless of whether the statute in question regulates conduct, affords relief, or merely confers jurisdiction. If the statute is not extraterritorial, then at the second step we determine whether the case involves a domestic application of the statute, and we do this by looking to the statute's "focus." If the conduct relevant to the statute's focus occurred in the United States, then the case involves a permissible domestic application even if other conduct occurred abroad; but if the conduct relevant to the focus occurred in a foreign country, then the case involves an impermissible extraterritorial application regardless of any other conduct that occurred in U.S. territory.

What if we find at step one that a statute clearly *does* have extraterritorial effect? Neither *Morrison* nor *Kiobel* involved such a finding. But we addressed this issue in *Morrison,* explaining that it was necessary to consider §10(b)'s "focus" only because we found that the statute does not apply extraterritorially: "If §10(b) did apply abroad, we would not need to determine which transnational frauds it applied to; it would apply to all of them (barring some other limitation)." 561 U.S., at 267, n.9. The scope of an extraterritorial statute thus turns on the limits

Congress has (or has not) imposed on the statute's foreign application, and not on the statute's "focus."[5]

III

With these guiding principles in mind, we first consider whether RICO's substantive prohibitions in §1962 may apply to foreign conduct. Unlike in *Morrison* and *Kiobel,* we find that the presumption against extraterritoriality has been rebutted—but only with respect to certain applications of the statute.

A

The most obvious textual clue is that RICO defines racketeering activity to include a number of predicates that plainly apply to at least some foreign conduct. These predicates include the prohibition against engaging in monetary transactions in criminally derived property, which expressly applies, when "the defendant is a United States person," to offenses that "tak[e] place outside the United States." 18 U.S.C. §1957(d)(2). Other examples include the prohibitions against the assassination of Government officials, §351(i) ("There is extraterritorial jurisdiction over the conduct prohibited by this section"); §1751(k) (same), and the prohibition against hostage taking, which applies to conduct that "occurred outside the United States" if either the hostage or the offender is a U.S. national, if the offender is found in the United States, or if the hostage taking is done to compel action by the U.S. Government, §1203(b). At least one predicate—the prohibition against "kill[ing] a national of the United States, while such national is outside the United States"—applies *only* to conduct occurring outside the United States. §2332(a).

We agree with the Second Circuit that Congress's incorporation of these (and other) extraterritorial predicates into RICO gives a clear, affirmative indication that §1962 applies to foreign racketeering activity—but only to the extent that the predicates alleged in a particular case themselves apply extraterritorially. Put another way, a pattern of racketeering activity may include or consist of offenses committed abroad in violation of a predicate statute for which the presumption against extraterritoriality has been overcome. To give a simple (albeit grim) example, a violation of §1962 could be premised on a pattern of killings of Americans abroad in violation of §2332(a)—a predicate that all agree applies extraterritorially—whether or not any domestic predicates are also alleged.

We emphasize the important limitation that foreign conduct must violate "a predicate statute that manifests an unmistakable congressional intent to apply extraterritorially." 764 F.3d, at 136. Although a number of RICO predicates have extraterritorial effect, many do not. The inclusion of *some* extraterritorial predicates does not mean that *all* RICO predicates extend to foreign conduct. This is

---

5. Because a finding of extraterritoriality at step one will obviate step two's "focus" inquiry, it will usually be preferable for courts to proceed in the sequence that we have set forth. But we do not mean to preclude courts from starting at step two in appropriate cases. Cf. Pearson v. Callahan, 555 U.S. 223, 236-243 (2009).

apparent for two reasons. First, "when a statute provides for some extraterritorial application, the presumption against extraterritoriality operates to limit that provision to its terms." *Morrison*, 561 U.S., at 265. Second, RICO defines as racketeering activity only acts that are "indictable" (or, what amounts to the same thing, "chargeable" or "punishable") under one of the statutes identified in §1961(1). If a particular statute does not apply extraterritorially, then conduct committed abroad is not "indictable" under that statute and so cannot qualify as a predicate under RICO's plain terms.

RJR resists the conclusion that RICO's incorporation of extraterritorial predicates gives RICO commensurate extraterritorial effect. It points out that "RICO itself" does not refer to extraterritorial application; only the underlying predicate statutes do. Brief for Petitioners 42. RJR thus argues that Congress could have intended to capture only *domestic* applications of extraterritorial predicates, and that any predicates that apply only abroad could have been "incorporated . . . solely for when such offenses are part of a broader pattern whose overall locus is domestic." *Id.*, at 43.

The presumption against extraterritoriality does not require us to adopt such a constricted interpretation. While the presumption can be overcome only by a clear indication of extraterritorial effect, an express statement of extraterritoriality is not essential. "Assuredly context can be consulted as well." *Morrison, supra*, at 265. Context is dispositive here. Congress has not expressly said that §1962(c) applies to patterns of racketeering activity in foreign countries, but it has defined "racketeering activity"—and by extension a "pattern of racketeering activity"—to encompass violations of predicate statutes that *do* expressly apply extraterritorially. Short of an explicit declaration, it is hard to imagine how Congress could have more clearly indicated that it intended RICO to have (some) extraterritorial effect. This unique structure makes RICO the rare statute that clearly evidences extraterritorial effect despite lacking an express statement of extraterritoriality.

We therefore conclude that RICO applies to some foreign racketeering activity. A violation of §1962 may be based on a pattern of racketeering that includes predicate offenses committed abroad, provided that each of those offenses violates a predicate statute that is itself extraterritorial. . . .

B

RJR contends that, even if RICO may apply to foreign patterns of racketeering, the statute does not apply to foreign *enterprises*. Invoking *Morrison*'s discussion of the Exchange Act's "focus," RJR says that the "focus" of RICO is the enterprise being corrupted—not the pattern of racketeering—and that RICO's enterprise element gives no clear indication of extraterritorial effect. Accordingly, RJR reasons, RICO requires a domestic enterprise.

This argument misunderstands *Morrison*. As explained above, *supra*, only at the second step of the inquiry do we consider a statute's "focus." Here, however, there is a clear indication at step one that RICO applies extraterritorially. We therefore do not proceed to the "focus" step. The *Morrison* Court's discussion of the statutory "focus" made this clear, stating that "[i]f §10(b) did apply abroad, we would not need to determine which transnational frauds it applied to; it would apply to all of them (barring some other limitation)." 561 U.S., at 267, n.9. The same is true here. RICO — or at least §§1962(b) and (c) — applies abroad, and so we do not need to determine which transnational (or wholly foreign) patterns of racketeering it applies to; it applies to all of them, regardless of whether they are connected to a "foreign" or "domestic" enterprise. This rule is, of course, subject to the important limitation that RICO covers foreign predicate offenses only to the extent that the underlying predicate statutes are extraterritorial. But within those bounds, the location of the affected enterprise does not impose an independent constraint. . . .

C

Applying these principles, we agree with the Second Circuit that the complaint does not allege impermissibly extraterritorial violations of §§1962(b) and (c).

The alleged pattern of racketeering activity consists of five basic predicates: (1) money laundering, (2) material support of foreign terrorist organizations, (3) mail fraud, (4) wire fraud, and (5) violations of the Travel Act. The Second Circuit observed that the relevant provisions of the money laundering and material support of terrorism statutes expressly provide for extraterritorial application in certain circumstances, and it concluded that those circumstances are alleged to be present here. 764 F.3d, at 139-140. The court found that the fraud statutes and the Travel Act do not contain the clear indication needed to overcome the presumption against extraterritoriality. But it held that the complaint alleges *domestic* violations of those statutes because it "allege[s] conduct in the United States that satisfies every essential element of the mail fraud, wire fraud, and Travel Act claims." *Id.*, at 142. . . .

IV

We now turn to RICO's private right of action, on which respondents' lawsuit rests. Section 1964(c) allows "[a]ny person injured in his business or property by reason of a violation of section 1962" to sue for treble damages, costs, and attorney's fees. Irrespective of any extraterritorial application of §1962, we conclude that §1964(c) does not overcome the presumption against extraterritoriality. A private RICO plaintiff therefore must allege and prove a *domestic* injury to its business or property.

A

The Second Circuit thought that the presumption against extraterritoriality did not apply to §1964(c) independently of its application to §1962, reasoning that the presumption "is primarily concerned with the question of what *conduct* falls within a statute's purview." 764 F.3d, at 151. We rejected that view in *Kiobel*, holding that the presumption "constrain[s] courts considering causes of action" under the ATS, a "'strictly jurisdictional'" statute that "does not directly regulate conduct or afford relief." We reached this conclusion even though the underlying substantive law consisted of well-established norms of international law, which by definition apply beyond this country's borders.

The same logic requires that we separately apply the presumption against extraterritoriality to RICO's cause of action despite our conclusion that the presumption has been overcome with respect to RICO's substantive prohibitions. "The creation of a private right of action raises issues beyond the mere consideration whether underlying primary conduct should be allowed or not, entailing, for example, a decision to permit enforcement without the check imposed by prosecutorial discretion." Sosa v. Alvarez-Machain, 542 U.S. 692, 727 (2004). Thus, as we have observed in other contexts, providing a private civil remedy for foreign conduct creates a potential for international friction beyond that presented by merely applying U.S. substantive law to that foreign conduct. See, *e.g.*, *Kiobel*, *supra* ("Each of th[e] decisions" involved in defining a cause of action based on "conduct within the territory of another sovereign" "carries with it significant foreign policy implications").

Consider antitrust. In that context, we have observed that "[t]he application . . . of American private treble-damages remedies to anticompetitive conduct taking place abroad has generated considerable controversy" in other nations, even when those nations agree with U.S. substantive law on such things as banning price fixing. F. Hoffmann-La Roche Ltd. v. Empagran S.A., 542 U.S. 155, 167 (2004). Numerous foreign countries—including some respondents in this case—advised us in *Empagran* that "to apply [U.S.] remedies would unjustifiably permit their citizens to bypass their own less generous remedial schemes, thereby upsetting a balance of competing considerations that their own domestic antitrust laws embody." *Ibid.*[9]

We received similar warnings in *Morrison*, where France, a respondent here, informed us that "most foreign countries proscribe securities fraud" but "have made very different choices with respect to the best way to implement that proscription," such as "prefer[ring] 'state actions, not private ones'" for the enforcement of law." Brief for Republic of France as *Amicus Curiae*, O.T. 2009, No. 08-1191, p. 20; see *id.*, at 23 ("Even when foreign countries permit private rights of action for securities fraud, they often have different schemes" for litigating them and "may approve of different measures of damages"). Allowing foreign investors to pursue private suits in the United States, we were told, "would upset that delicate balance and offend the sovereign interests of foreign nations." *Id.*, at 26.

Allowing recovery for foreign injuries in a civil RICO action, including treble damages, presents the same danger of international friction. See Brief for United

---

9. *Empagran* concerned not the presumption against extraterritoriality *per se*, but the related rule that we construe statutes to avoid unreasonable interference with other nations' sovereign authority where possible. See F. Hoffmann–La Roche Ltd. v. Empagran S.A., 542 U.S. 155, 164 (2004); see also Hartford Fire Ins. Co. v. California, 509 U.S. 764, 814-815 (1993) (Scalia, J., dissenting) (discussing the two canons). As the foregoing discussion makes clear, considerations relevant to one rule are often relevant to the other.

States as *Amicus Curiae* 31-34. This is not to say that friction would necessarily result in every case, or that Congress would violate international law by permitting such suits. It is to say only that there is a potential for international controversy that militates against recognizing foreign-injury claims without clear direction from Congress. Although "a risk of conflict between the American statute and a foreign law" is not a prerequisite for applying the presumption against extraterritoriality, *Morrison*, 561 U.S., at 255, where such a risk is evident, the need to enforce the presumption is at its apex.

Respondents urge that concerns about international friction are inapplicable in this case because here the plaintiffs are not foreign citizens seeking to bypass their home countries' less generous remedies but rather the foreign countries themselves. Respondents assure us that they "are satisfied that the[ir] complaint . . . comports with limitations on prescriptive jurisdiction under international law and respects the dignity of foreign sovereigns." Even assuming that this is true, however, our interpretation of §1964(c)'s injury requirement will necessarily govern suits by nongovernmental plaintiffs that are not so sensitive to foreign sovereigns' dignity. We reject the notion that we should forgo the presumption against extraterritoriality and instead permit extraterritorial suits based on a case-by-case inquiry that turns on or looks to the consent of the affected sovereign. See *Morrison*, *supra*, at 261 ("Rather than guess anew in each case, we apply the presumption in all cases"); cf. *Empagran*, 542 U.S., at 168. Respondents suggest that we should be reluctant to permit a foreign corporation to be sued in the courts of this country for events occurring abroad if the nation of incorporation objects, but that we should discard those reservations when a foreign state sues a U.S. entity in this country under U.S. law—instead of in its own courts and under its own laws—for conduct committed on its own soil. We refuse to adopt this double standard. "After all, in the law, what is sauce for the goose is normally sauce for the gander." Heffernan v. City of Paterson, 136 S. Ct. 1412, 1418 (2016).

B

Nothing in §1964(c) provides a clear indication that Congress intended to create a private right of action for injuries suffered outside of the United States. The statute provides a cause of action to "[a]ny person injured in his business or property" by a violation of §1962. §1964(c). The word "any" ordinarily connotes breadth, but it is insufficient to displace the presumption against extraterritoriality. See *Kiobel*. The statute's reference to injury to "business or property" also does not indicate extraterritorial application. If anything, by cabining RICO's private cause of action to particular kinds of injury—excluding, for example, personal injuries—Congress signaled that the civil remedy is not coextensive with §1962's substantive prohibitions. The rest of §1964(c) places a limit on RICO plaintiffs' ability to rely on securities fraud to make out a claim. This too suggests that §1964(c) is narrower in its application than §1962, and in any event does not support extraterritoriality.

The Second Circuit did not identify anything in §1964(c) that shows that the statute reaches foreign injuries. Instead, the court reasoned that §1964(c)'s extraterritorial effect flows directly from that of §1962. Citing our holding in

Sedima, S.P.R.L. v. Imrex Co., 473 U.S. 479 (1985), that the "compensable injury" addressed by §1964(c) "necessarily is the harm caused by predicate acts sufficiently related to constitute a pattern," *id.*, at 497, the Court of Appeals held that a RICO plaintiff may sue for foreign injury that was caused by the violation of a predicate statute that applies extraterritorially, just as a substantive RICO violation may be based on extraterritorial predicates. 764 F.3d, at 151. Justice Ginsburg advances the same theory. See *post*, at 2113-2114 (opinion concurring in part and dissenting in part). This reasoning has surface appeal, but it fails to appreciate that the presumption against extraterritoriality must be applied separately to both RICO's substantive prohibitions and its private right of action. It is not enough to say that a private right of action must reach abroad because the underlying law governs conduct in foreign countries. Something more is needed, and here it is absent.

Respondents contend that background legal principles allow them to sue for foreign injuries, invoking what they call the "'traditional rule' that 'a plaintiff injured in a foreign country' could bring suit 'in American courts.'" Brief for Respondents 41 (quoting *Sosa*, 542 U.S., at 706-707). But the rule respondents invoke actually provides that a court will ordinarily "apply *foreign* law to determine the tortfeasor's liability" to "a plaintiff injured in a foreign country." *Id.*, at 706 (emphasis added). Respondents' argument might have force if they sought to sue RJR for violations of *their own laws* and to invoke federal diversity jurisdiction as a basis for proceeding in U.S. courts. The question here, however, is not "whether a federal court has jurisdiction to entertain a cause of action provided by foreign or even international law. The question is instead whether the court has authority to recognize a cause of action *under U.S. law*" for injury suffered overseas. *Kiobel, supra* (emphasis added). As to that question, the relevant background principle is the presumption against extraterritoriality, not the "traditional rule" respondents cite.

Respondents and Justice Ginsburg point out that RICO's private right of action was modeled after §4 of the Clayton Act, 15 U.S.C. §15; see Holmes v. Securities Investor Protection Corporation, 503 U.S. 258, 267-268 (1992), which we have held allows recovery for injuries suffered abroad as a result of antitrust violations, see Pfizer Inc. v. Government of India, 434 U.S. 308, 314-315, (1978). It follows, respondents and Justice Ginsburg contend, that §1964(c) likewise allows plaintiffs to sue for injuries suffered in foreign countries. We disagree. Although we have often looked to the Clayton Act for guidance in construing §1964(c), we have not treated the two statutes as interchangeable. We have declined to transplant features of the Clayton Act's cause of action into the RICO context where doing so would be inappropriate. For example, in *Sedima* we held that a RICO plaintiff need not allege a special "racketeering injury," rejecting a requirement that some lower courts had adopted by "[a]nalog[y]" to the "antitrust injury" required under the Clayton Act. 473 U.S., at 485, 495.

There is good reason not to interpret §1964(c) to cover foreign injuries just because the Clayton Act does so. When we held in *Pfizer* that the Clayton Act allows recovery for foreign injuries, we relied first and foremost on the fact that the Clayton Act's definition of "person"—which in turn defines who may sue under that Act—"explicitly includes 'corporations and associations existing under or authorized by . . . the laws of any foreign country.' " 434 U.S., at 313.[11] RICO lacks the language that the *Pfizer* Court found critical. See 18 U.S.C. §1961(3).[12]

To the extent that the *Pfizer* Court cited other factors that might apply to §1964(c), they were not sufficient in themselves to show that the provision has extraterritorial effect. For example, the *Pfizer* Court, writing before we honed our extraterritoriality jurisprudence in *Morrison* and *Kiobel*, reasoned that Congress "[c]learly . . . did not intend to make the [Clayton Act's] treble-damages remedy available only to consumers in our own country" because "the antitrust laws extend to trade 'with foreign nations' as well as among the several States of the Union." 434 U.S., at 313-314. But we have emphatically rejected reliance on such language, holding that " 'even statutes . . . that expressly refer to "*foreign* commerce" do not apply abroad.' " *Morrison*, 561 U.S., at 262-263. This reasoning also fails to distinguish between extending *substantive antitrust law* to foreign conduct and extending a *private right of action* to foreign injuries, two separate issues that, as we have explained, raise distinct extraterritoriality problems. See *supra*, at 2105-2108. Finally, the *Pfizer* Court expressed concern that it would "defeat th[e] purposes" of the antitrust laws if a defendant could "escape full liability for his illegal actions." 434 U.S., at 314. But this justification was merely an attempt to "divin[e] what Congress would have wanted" had it considered the question of extraterritoriality—an approach we eschewed in *Morrison*, 561 U.S., at 261. Given all this, and in particular the fact that RICO lacks the language that *Pfizer* found integral to its decision, we decline to extend this aspect of our Clayton Act jurisprudence to RICO's cause of action.

Underscoring our reluctance to read §1964(c) as broadly as we have read the Clayton Act is Congress's more recent decision to define precisely the antitrust laws' extraterritorial effect and to exclude from their reach most conduct that "causes only foreign injury." *Empagran*, 542 U.S., at 158 (describing Foreign Trade Antitrust Improvements Act of 1982); see also *id*., at 169-171, 173-174 (discussing how the applicability of the antitrust laws to foreign injuries may depend on whether suit is brought by the Government or by private plaintiffs). Although this later enactment obviously does not limit §1964(c)'s scope by its own force, it does counsel against importing into RICO those Clayton Act principles that are at odds with our current extraterritoriality doctrine.

---

11. *Pfizer* most directly concerned whether a foreign government is a "person" that may be a Clayton Act plaintiff. But it is clear that the Court's decision more broadly concerned recovery for foreign injuries, see 434 U.S. at 315 (expressing concern that "persons doing business both in this country and abroad might be tempted to enter into anticompetitive conspiracies affecting American consumers in the expectation that the illegal profits they could safely extort abroad would offset any liability to plaintiffs at home"), as respondents themselves contend, see Brief for Respondents 44 ("[T]his Court clearly recognized in *Pfizer* that Section 4 extends to foreign injuries").

12. This does not mean that foreign plaintiffs may not sue under RICO. The point is that RICO does not include the explicit foreign-oriented language that the *Pfizer* Court found to support foreign-injury suits under the Clayton Act.

C

Section 1964(c) requires a civil RICO plaintiff to allege and prove a domestic injury to business or property and does not allow recovery for foreign injuries. The application of this rule in any given case will not always be self-evident, as disputes may arise as to whether a particular alleged injury is "foreign" or "domestic." But we need not concern ourselves with that question in this case. As this case was being briefed before this Court, respondents filed a stipulation in the District Court waiving their damages claims for domestic injuries. The District Court accepted this waiver and dismissed those claims with prejudice. Respondents' remaining RICO damages claims therefore rest entirely on injury suffered abroad and must be dismissed.[13]

The judgment of the United States Court of Appeals for the Second Circuit is reversed, and the case is remanded for further proceedings consistent with this opinion.

So ordered.

Justice SOTOMAYOR took no part in the consideration or decision of this case.

Justice GINSBURG, with whom Justice BREYER and Justice KAGAN join, concurring in Parts I, II, and III and dissenting from Part IV and from the judgment.

In enacting the Racketeer Influenced and Corrupt Organizations Act (RICO), 18 U.S.C. §1961 *et seq.*, Congress sought to provide a new tool to combat "organized crime and its economic roots." Russello v. United States, 464 U.S. 16, 26, (1983). RICO accordingly proscribes various ways in which an "enterprise," §1961(4), might be controlled, operated, or funded by a "pattern of racketeering activity," §1961(1), (5). See §1962. RICO builds on predicate statutes, many of them applicable extraterritorially. Congress not only armed the United States with authority to initiate criminal and civil proceedings to enforce RICO, §§1963, 1964(b), Congress also created in §1964(c) a private right of action for "[a]ny person injured in his business or property by reason of a violation of [RICO's substantive provision]."

Invoking this right, respondents, the European Community and 26 member states, filed suit against petitioners, RJR Nabisco, Inc., and related entities.

---

13. In respondents' letter notifying this Court of the waiver of their domestic-injury damages claims, respondents state that "[n]othing in the stipulation will affect respondents' claims for equitable relief, including claims for equitable relief under state common law that are not at issue in this case before this Court." Letter from David C. Frederick, Counsel for Respondents, to Scott S. Harris, Clerk of Court (Feb. 29, 2016). Although the letter mentions only state-law claims for equitable relief, Count 5 of respondents' complaint seeks equitable relief under RICO. App. to Pet. for Cert. 260a-262a, Complaint ¶¶181-188. This Court has never decided whether equitable relief is available to private RICO plaintiffs, the parties have not litigated that question here, and we express no opinion on the issue today. We note, however, that any claim for equitable relief under RICO based on foreign injuries is necessarily foreclosed by our holding that §1964(c)'s cause of action requires a domestic injury to business or property. It is unclear whether respondents intend to seek equitable relief under RICO based on domestic injuries, and it may prove unnecessary to decide whether §1964(c) (or respondents' stipulation) permits such relief in light of respondents' state-law claims. We leave it to the lower courts to determine, if necessary, the status and availability of any such claims.

Alleging that petitioners orchestrated from their U.S. headquarters a complex money-laundering scheme in violation of RICO, respondents sought to recover for various injuries, including losses sustained by financial institutions and lost opportunities to collect duties. Denying respondents a remedy under RICO, the Court today reads into §1964(c) a domestic-injury requirement for suits by private plaintiffs nowhere indicated in the statute's text. Correctly, the Court imposes no such restriction on the United States when it initiates a civil suit under §1964(b). Unsupported by RICO's text, inconsistent with its purposes, and unnecessary to protect the comity interests the Court emphasizes, the domestic-injury requirement for private suits replaces Congress' prescription with one of the Court's own invention. Because the Court has no authority so to amend RICO, I dissent.

I

As the Court recounts, "Congress ordinarily legislates with respect to domestic, not foreign, matters." Morrison v. National Australia Bank Ltd., 561 U.S. 247, 255, (2010). So recognizing, the Court employs a presumption that "'legislation . . . is meant to apply only within the territorial jurisdiction of the United States.'" Ibid. (quoting EEOC v. Arabian American Oil Co., 499 U.S. 244, 248 (1991) (Aramco)). But when a statute demonstrates Congress' "affirmative inten[t]" that the law should apply beyond the borders of the United States, as numerous RICO predicate statutes do, the presumption is rebutted, and the law applies extraterritorially to the extent Congress prescribed. See Morrison, 561 U.S., at 255 (quoting Aramco, 499 U.S., at 248). The presumption, in short, aims to distinguish instances in which Congress consciously designed a statute to reach beyond U.S. borders, from those in which nothing plainly signals that Congress directed extraterritorial application.

In this case, the Court properly holds that Congress signaled its "affirmative inten[t]," Morrison, 561 U.S., at 255, that RICO, in many instances, should apply extraterritorially. As the Court relates, Congress deliberately included within RICO's compass predicate federal offenses that manifestly reach conduct occurring abroad. See, e.g., §§1956-1957 (money laundering); §2339B (material support to foreign terrorist organizations). Accordingly, the Court concludes, when the predicate crimes underlying invocation of §1962 thrust extraterritorially, so too does §1962. I agree with that conclusion.

I disagree, however, that the private right of action authorized by §1964(c) requires a domestic injury to a person's business or property and does not allow recovery for foreign injuries. One cannot extract such a limitation from the text of §1964(c), which affords a right of action to "[a]ny person injured in his business or property by reason of a violation of section 1962." Section 1962, at least subsections (b) and (c), all agree, encompasses foreign injuries. How can §1964(c) exclude them when, by its express terms, §1964(c) is triggered by "a violation of section 1962"? To the extent RICO reaches injury abroad when the Government is the suitor pursuant to §1962 (specifying prohibited activities) and §1963 (criminal penalties) or §1964(b) (civil remedies), to that same extent, I would hold, RICO reaches extraterritorial injury when, pursuant to §1964(c), the suitor is a private plaintiff.

II

A

I would not distinguish, as the Court does, between the extraterritorial compass of a private right of action and that of the underlying proscribed conduct. Instead, I would adhere to precedent addressing RICO, linking, not separating, prohibited activities and authorized remedies. See Sedima, S.P.R.L. v. Imrex Co., 473 U.S. 479, 495 (1985) ("If the defendant engages in a pattern of racketeering activity in a manner forbidden by [§1962], and the racketeering activities injure the plaintiff in his business or property, the plaintiff has a claim under §1964(c)."); *ibid.* (refusing to require a "distinct 'racketeering injury'" for private RICO actions under §1964(c) where §1962 imposes no such requirement).[2]

To reiterate, a §1964(c) right of action may be maintained by "[a]ny person injured in his business or property by reason of a violation of *section 1962*" (emphasis added). "[I]ncorporating one statute . . . into another," the Court has long understood, "serves to bring into the latter all that is fairly covered by the reference." Panama R. Co. v. Johnson, 264 U.S. 375, 392 (1924). RICO's private right of action, it cannot be gainsaid, expressly incorporates §1962, whose extraterritoriality, the Court recognizes, is coextensive with the underlying predicate offenses charged. See *ante,* at 2101-2106. See also *ante,* at 2102 ("[I]t is hard to imagine how Congress could have more clearly indicated that it intended RICO to have (some) extraterritorial effect."). The sole additional condition §1964(c) imposes on access to relief is an injury to one's "business or property." Nothing in that condition should change the extraterritoriality assessment. In agreement with the Second Circuit, I would hold that "[i]f an injury abroad was proximately caused by the violation of a statute which Congress intended should apply to injurious conduct performed abroad, [there is] no reason to import a domestic injury requirement simply because the victim sought redress through the RICO statute." 764 F.3d 149, 151 (2014).

What §1964(c)'s text conveys is confirmed by its history. As this Court has repeatedly observed, Congress modeled §1964(c) on §4 of the Clayton Act, 15 U.S.C. §15, the private civil-action provision of the federal antitrust laws, which employs nearly identical language: "[A]ny person who shall be injured in his business or property by reason of anything forbidden in the antitrust laws may sue therefor." Clayton Act §4, the Court has held, provides a remedy for injuries both foreign and domestic. Pfizer Inc. v. Government of India, 434 U.S. 308, 313-314 (1978) ("Congress did not intend to make the [Clayton Act's] treble-damages

---

2. Insisting that the presumption against extraterritoriality should "apply to §1964(c) independently of its application to §1962," the Court cites Kiobel v. Royal Dutch Petroleum Co. That decision will not bear the weight the Court would place on it. As the Court comprehends, the statute there at issue, the Alien Tort Statute, 28 U.S.C. §1350, is a spare jurisdictional grant that itself does not "regulate conduct or afford relief." *Kiobel.* With no grounding for extraterritorial application in the statute, *Kiobel* held, courts have no warrant to fashion, on their own initiative, claims for relief that operate extraterritorially. See *ibid.* ("[T]he question is not what Congress has done but instead what courts may do.").

remedy available only to consumers in our own country."); Continental Ore Co. v. Union Carbide & Carbon Corp., 370 U.S. 690, 707-708 (1962) (allowing recovery in Clayton Act §4 suit for injuries in Canada).

"The similarity of language in [the two statutes] is, of course, a strong indication that [they] should be interpreted *pari passu*," Northcross v. Board of Ed. of Memphis City Schools, 412 U.S. 427, 428, (1973) (*per curiam*), and I see no contradictory indication here.[3] Indeed, when the Court has addressed gaps in §1964(c), it has aligned the RICO private right of action with the private right afforded by Clayton Act §4. See, *e.g.*, [Klehr v. A.O. Smith Corp.,], 521 U.S. [179], at 188-189 (1997) (adopting for private RICO actions Clayton Act §4's accrual rule—that a claim accrues when a defendant commits an act that injures a plaintiff's business—rather than criminal RICO's "most recent, predicate act" rule); [Holmes v. Securities Investor Protection Corp.,], 503 U.S. [258], at 268 (1992) (requiring private plaintiffs under §1964(c), like private plaintiffs under Clayton Act §4, to show proximate cause); Agency Holding Corp. v. Malley-Duff & Associates, Inc., 483 U.S. 143, 155-156 (1987) (applying to §1964(c) actions Clayton Act §4's shorter statute of limitations instead of "catchall" federal statute of limitations applicable to RICO criminal prosecutions).

This very case illustrates why pinning a domestic-injury requirement onto §1964(c) makes little sense. All defendants are U.S. corporations, headquartered in the United States, charged with a pattern of racketeering activity directed and managed from the United States, involving conduct occurring in the United States. In particular, according to the complaint, defendants received in the United States funds known to them to have been generated by illegal narcotics trafficking and terrorist activity, conduct violative of §1956(a)(2); traveled using the facilities of interstate commerce in furtherance of unlawful activity, in violation of §1952; provided material support to foreign terrorist organizations "in the United States and elsewhere," in violation of §2339B; and used U.S. mails and wires in furtherance of a "scheme or artifice to defraud," in violation of §§1341 and 1343. In short, this case has the United States written all over it.

B

The Court nevertheless deems a domestic-injury requirement for private RICO plaintiffs necessary to avoid international friction. When the United States considers whether to initiate a prosecution or civil suit, the Court observes, it will

---

3. The Court asserts that "[t]here is good reason not to interpret §1964(c) to cover foreign injuries just because the Clayton Act does." The Clayton Act's definition of "person," 15 U.S.C. §12, the Court observes, "explicitly includes 'corporations and associations existing under or authorized by . . . the laws of any foreign country.'" RICO, the Court stresses, lacks this "critical" language. *Ibid*. The Court's point is underwhelming. RICO's definition of "persons" is hardly confining: "any individual or entity capable of holding a legal or beneficial interest in property." 18 U.S.C. §1961(3). Moreover, there is little doubt that Congress anticipated §1964(c) plaintiffs like the suitors here. See 147 Cong. Rec. 20676, 20710 (2001) (remarks of Sen. Kerry) ("Since some of the money-laundering conducted in the world today also defrauds foreign governments, it would be hostile to the intent of [the USA PATRIOT Act, which added as RICO predicates additional money laundering offenses,] for us to interject into the statute any rule of construction of legislative language which would in any way limit our foreign allies access to our courts to battle against money laundering.").

take foreign-policy considerations into account, but private parties will not. It is far from clear, however, that the Court's blanket rule would ordinarily work to ward off international discord. Invoking the presumption against extraterritoriality as a bar to *any* private suit for injuries to business or property abroad, this case suggests, might spark, rather than quell, international strife. Making such litigation available to domestic but not foreign plaintiffs is hardly solicitous of international comity or respectful of foreign interests. Cf. *Pfizer*, 434 U.S., at 318-319 ("[A] foreign nation is generally entitled to prosecute any civil claim in the courts of the United States upon the same basis as a domestic corporation or individual might do. To deny him this privilege would manifest a want of comity and friendly feeling." (internal quotation marks omitted)).

RICO's definitional provisions exclude "[e]ntirely foreign activity." 783 F.3d 123, 143 (Lynch, J., dissenting from denial of rehearing en banc). Thus no suit under RICO would lie for injuries resulting from "[a] pattern of murders of Italian citizens committed by members of an Italian organized crime group in Italy." *Ibid*. That is so because "murder is a RICO predicate only when it is 'chargeable under state law' or indictable under specific federal statutes." *Ibid*. (citing §1961(1)(A), (G)).

To the extent extraterritorial application of RICO could give rise to comity concerns not present in this case, those concerns can be met through doctrines that serve to block litigation in U.S. courts of cases more appropriately brought elsewhere. Where an alternative, more appropriate forum is available, the doctrine of *forum non conveniens* enables U.S. courts to refuse jurisdiction. See Piper Aircraft Co. v. Reyno, 454 U.S. 235 (1981) (dismissing wrongful-death action arising out of air crash in Scotland involving only Scottish victims); Restatement (Second) of Conflict of Laws §84 (1969). Due process constraints on the exercise of general personal jurisdiction shelter foreign corporations from suit in the United States based on conduct abroad unless the corporation's "affiliations with the [forum] in which suit is brought are so constant and pervasive 'as to render it essentially at home [there].'" Daimler AG v. Bauman, [supra page 432] (quoting Goodyear Dunlop Tires Operations, S.A. v. Brown, 564 U.S. 915, 919 (2011); alterations omitted). These controls provide a check against civil RICO litigation with little or no connection to the United States.

* * *

The Court hems in RICO out of concern about establishing a "double standard." *Ante*, at 2108. But today's decision does exactly that. U.S. defendants commercially engaged here and abroad would be answerable civilly to U.S. victims of their criminal activities, but foreign parties similarly injured would have no RICO remedy. "'Sauce for the goose'" should indeed serve the gander as well. See *ibid*. (quoting Heffernan v. City of Paterson). I would resist reading into §1964(c) a domestic-injury requirement Congress did not prescribe. Instead, I would affirm the Second Circuit's sound judgment:

> "To establish a compensable injury under §1964(c), a private plaintiff must show that (1) the defendant 'engage[d] in a pattern of racketeering activity in a manner forbidden by' §1962, and (2) that these 'racketeering activities' were the proximate cause of some injury to the plaintiff's business or property." 764 F.3d, at 151 (quoting *Sedima*, 473 U.S., at 495; *Holmes*, 503 U.S., at 268.

Because the Court overturns that judgment, I dissent.

Justice BREYER, concurring in part, dissenting in part, and dissenting from the judgment.

I join Parts I through III of the Court's opinion. But I do not join Part IV. The Court there holds that the private right of action provision in the Racketeer Influenced and Corrupt Organizations Act (RICO), 18 U.S.C. §1964(c), has no extraterritorial application. Like Justice Ginsburg, I believe that it does.

In saying this, I note that this case does not involve the kind of purely foreign facts that create what we have sometimes called "foreign-cubed" litigation (*i.e.*, cases where the plaintiffs are foreign, the defendants are foreign, and all the relevant conduct occurred abroad). See, *e.g.*, Morrison v. National Australia Bank Ltd., 561 U.S. 247, 283, n.11 (2010) (Stevens, J., concurring in judgment). Rather, it has been argued that the statute at issue does not extend to such a case. See 18 U.S.C. §1961(1) (limiting qualifying RICO predicates to those that are, *e.g.*, "chargeable" under state law, or "indictable" or "punishable" under federal law); Tr. of Oral Arg. 32, 33-34 (respondents conceding that all of the relevant RICO predicates require some kind of connection to the United States). And, as Justice Ginsburg points out, "this case has the United States written all over it."

Unlike the Court, I cannot accept as controlling the Government's argument as *amicus curiae* that "[a]llowing recovery for foreign injuries in a civil RICO action . . . presents the . . . danger of international friction." The Government does not provide examples, nor apparently has it consulted with foreign governments on the matter. See Tr. of Oral Arg. 26 ("[T]o my knowledge, [the Government] didn't have those consultations" with foreign states concerning this case). By way of contrast, the European Community and 26 of its member states tell us "that the complaint in this case, which alleges that American corporations engaged in a pattern of racketeering activity that caused injury to respondents' businesses and property, comports with limitations on prescriptive jurisdiction under international law and respects the dignity of foreign sovereigns." Brief for Respondents 52-53; see also Tr. of Oral Arg. 31 (calling the European Union's "vett[ing] exercise" concerning this case "comprehensiv[e]"). In these circumstances, and for the reasons given by Justice Ginsburg, I would not place controlling weight on the Government's contrary view.

Consequently, I join Justice Ginsburg's opinion.

Questions and Comments

(1) The Court in *RJR Nabisco* stated that the presumption against extraterritoriality applies "regardless of whether the statute in question regulates conduct, affords relief, or merely confers jurisdiction." Can that possibly be right? A statute conferring jurisdiction on federal courts serves to allocate judicial power as between the federal courts and the state courts. If such a statute does not confer jurisdiction over cases because the events occurred abroad, the consequence would be to relegate such cases to the state courts. If the purpose of the presumption against extraterritoriality is to avoid international friction, does it make sense to assign cases based on conduct or events occurring abroad to the *state* courts? Does *Kiobel* establish that the presumption applies to statutes conferring federal

jurisdiction? The Fourth Restatement of Foreign Relations Law asserts in §203, comment *a*, that "[t]he presumption against extraterritoriality . . . does not apply to provisions granting subject-matter jurisdiction to federal courts." Reporter's note 3 explains: "In *RJR Nabisco*, the Supreme Court stated in dictum that the presumption against extraterritoriality applies 'regardless of whether the statute in question regulates conduct, affords relief, or merely confers jurisdiction.' But the Court did not apply the presumption against extraterritoriality to the provisions upon which subject-matter jurisdiction rested in that case. The Court also suggested that the plaintiffs could have brought suit under their own laws relying on diversity jurisdiction, despite the fact that the federal diversity jurisdiction statute lacks the clear indication of extraterritoriality required to rebut the presumption."

(2) The Court also clarified that *Morrison* established a two-step analysis. The first question for any given statute is whether the presumption against extraterritoriality has been rebutted, so that the statute does apply to conduct or events that occurred outside the United States. In the second step — which must be reached if the statute is not extraterritorial — the court has to ascertain the "focus" of congressional concern, in order to determine whether the case before it involves a domestic or extraterritorial application of the statute.

(3) The Court also held that the presumption must be applied separately to a statute's provisions creating a private right of action. Thus, even if the presumption has been rebutted for the statute's substantive provisions, there is no private right of action unless the presumption is rebutted for the latter provisions or the case involves a domestic application of the latter provisions. The Court concluded that the presumption was not rebutted for the RICO right of action. The next step, under the two-step approach, should have been to ascertain the "focus" of Congress's concern in enacting the private right of action. Instead, the Court jumped from the premise that the provision conferring the private right of action did not apply extraterritorially to the conclusion that the case could proceed only if the plaintiff alleged "domestic injury." Is it self-evident that Congress's focus in enacting a private right of action is to compensate for injuries rather than to give efficacy to the underlying prohibition? Should the issue turn on that question?

(4) Is the requirement of domestic injury a throwback to the the First Restatement's "place of injury" rule for torts?

(5) If, for federal statutes conferring a private right of action, the substantive and remedial provisions must independently satisfy the presumption against extraterritoriality, does that mean that, if the presumption is not rebutted, such a statute confers a remedy only if *both* the underlying conduct *and* the injury occurred in the United States? If so, then is the rule actually more restrictive than Professor Beale's? Under Beale's rule, forum law applies as long as the injury occurred in the forum state, even if the acts causing the injury occurred elsewhere. For the claim that the approach of *RJR Nabisco* takes a far narrower approach to extraterritoriality than the First Restatement, *see* Vázquez, *Out-Beale-ing Beale*, 110 AJIL Unbound 68 (2016).

(6) For further analysis of *RJR Nabisco*, *see* Stephan, *Private Litigation as a Foreign Relations Problem*, 110 AJIL Unbound 40 (2016); Colangelo, *The Frankenstein's Monster of Extraterritoriality Law*, 110 AJIL Unbound 51 (2016);

Bookman, *Doubling Down on Litigation Isolationism*, 110 AJIL Unbound 57 (2016); Buxbaum, T*he Scope and Limitations of the Presumotion Against Territoriality*, 110 AJIL Unbound 62 (2016); Francq, *A European Story*, 110 AJIL Unbound 74 (2016): Dodge, *The Presumption Against Extraterritoriality in Two Steps*, 110 AJIL Unbound 45 (2016).

9

Choosing Legal Regimes

When states adopt differing legal rules, opportunities are created for private parties to choose their preferred set of rules to govern their activities. With increasing frequency, interstate and internationally mobile parties strategically locate their assets and activities and/or place clauses into their contracts designed to help them avoid the courts and law of undesired jurisdictions. In some cases, parties are also able to affirmatively opt into preferred legal regimes. In the United States, for example, incorporating businesses typically can choose the law that will apply to the internal affairs of the corporation simply by choosing the state of incorporation. Ship owners can choose much of the law that applies to onboard activities by choosing the nation in which to register the ship (known as "the law of the flag"). And, within the United States, credit card companies are permitted to charge any interest rates or fees that are permissible in the state where the company locates its lending operations.

In contracts, companies regularly incorporate clauses specifying the law that will govern the transaction and/or the forum (court or arbitration) where any future disputes between the parties will be resolved. These contract choices help provide the parties with predictability and notice regarding the rules that they are expected to follow, and it allows a company operating in many places to adopt a single set of company policies (which inevitably take into account governing laws). Choice also enables parties to choose the legal regime that best suits the particular needs of the transaction. Choice reduces the costs of outdated and poorly crafted rules by making it easy for parties to avoid them. Finally, choice can generate competition among governments to generate more efficient laws in order to attract transactional and litigation business.

647

Party choice can prove problematic, however. A knowledgeable party might choose a law or forum that benefits it at the expense of a less knowledgeable party. In addition, state efforts to regulate harmful conduct are thwarted when parties can easily circumvent those rules. Moreover, jurisdictional competition can lead to states adopting rules that attract transactional or litigation business at the expense of others, including less mobile state residents.

This chapter considers the extent to which party choice is permitted, and provokes thought regarding the boundaries of private choices. Section A explores contractual choice of law, Section B treats choice-of-court clauses, and Section C covers the legal treatment of arbitration clauses.

A.   Contractual Choice of Law

Recall from Chapter 2, *supra* page 45, that the First Restatement made no provision for the enforcement of choice-of-law clauses, and Beale (as well as some courts) was hostile to them on the ground that they created "private legislation." In contrast, the Second Restatement explicitly endorses party autonomy to choose the applicable law in a wide range of circumstances. Its treatment is enormously popular among courts—including (as the first case below demonstrates) courts that do not otherwise follow the Second Restatement. The Contracts portion of the Second Restatement begins with section 186, which states:

§186. Applicable Law

Issues in contract are determined by the law chosen by the parties in accordance with the rule of §187 and otherwise by the law selected in accordance with the rule of §188.

If the parties have chosen a governing law in their agreement, that choice is given significant weight:

§187. Law of the State Chosen by the Parties

(1) The law of the state chosen by the parties to govern their contractual rights and duties will be applied if the particular issue is one which the parties could have resolved by an explicit provision in their agreement directed to that issue.

(2) The law of the state chosen by the parties to govern their contractual rights and duties will be applied, even if the particular issue is one which the parties could not have resolved by an explicit provision in their agreement directed to that issue, unless either

(a) the chosen state has no substantial relationship to the parties or the transaction and there is no other reasonable basis for the parties' choice, or

   (b) application of the law of the chosen state would be contrary to a fundamental policy of a state which has a materially greater interest than the chosen state in the determination of the particular issue and which, under the rule of §188, would be the state of the applicable law in the absence of an effective choice of law by the parties.
   (3) In the absence of a contrary indication of intention, the reference is to the local law of the state of the chosen law.

Note the strong presumption in favor of enforcing the parties' choice of governing law. Why are parties permitted, under subsection (2)(b), to violate the "fundamental policy" of a state that has half, but not a "materially greater," interest in the issue at stake? If the issue is one that the parties could not have resolved by an explicit provision of their contract, why should a state with a "materially greater" interest in the case not get to apply its law, in the face of a contrary contractual provision, simply because the policy is merely important, and not fundamental? And as long as the forum is willing to allow parties to choose law other than its own, even when it has policies on point, why is the choice limited to the law of a state with "substantial connection"?

Nedlloyd Lines B.V. v. Superior Court of San Mateo County Seawinds Ltd.

834 P.2d 1148, 3 Cal. 4th 459, 11 Cal. Rptr. 2d 330 (1992)

BAXTER, J.

We granted review to consider the effect of a choice-of-law clause in a contract between commercial entities to finance and operate an international shipping business. In our order granting review, we limited our consideration to the question whether and to what extent the law of Hong Kong, chosen in the parties' agreement, should be applied in ruling on defendant's demurrer to plaintiff's complaint.

We conclude the choice-of-law clause, which requires that the contract be "governed by" the law of Hong Kong, a jurisdiction having a substantial connection with the parties, is fully enforceable and applicable to claims for breach of the implied covenant of good faith and fair dealing and for breach of fiduciary duties allegedly arising out of the contract. Our conclusion rests on the choice-of-law rules derived from California decisions and the Restatement Second of Conflict of Laws, which reflect strong policy considerations favoring the enforcement of freely negotiated choice-of-law clauses. Based on our conclusion, we will reverse the judgments of the Court of Appeal and remand for further proceedings.

Plaintiff and real party in interest Seawinds Limited (Seawinds) is a shipping company, currently undergoing reorganization under chapter 11 of the United States Bankruptcy Code, whose business consists of the operation of three container ships. Seawinds was incorporated in Hong Kong in late 1982 and has its principal place of business in Redwood City, California. Defendants and petitioners Nedlloyd Lines B.V., Royal Nedlloyd Group N.V., and KNSM Lines B.V. (collectively referred to as Nedlloyd) are interrelated shipping companies incorporated in the Netherlands with their principal place of business in Rotterdam.

In March 1983, Nedlloyd and other parties (including an Oregon corporation, a Hong Kong corporation, a British corporation, three individual residents of California, and a resident of Singapore) entered into a contract to purchase shares of Seawinds' stock. The contract, which was entitled "Shareholders' Agreement in Respect of Seawinds Limited," stated that its purpose was "to establish [Seawinds] as a joint venture company to carry on a transportation operation." The agreement also provided that Seawinds would carry on the business of the transportation company and that the parties to the agreement would use "means reasonably available" to ensure the business was a success.

The shareholders' agreement between the parties contained the following choice-of-law and forum selection provision: "This agreement shall be governed by and construed in accordance with Hong Kong law and each party hereby irrevocably submits to the nonexclusive jurisdiction and service of process of the Hong Kong courts."

In January 1989, Seawinds sued Nedlloyd, alleging in essence that Nedlloyd breached express and implied obligations under the shareholders' agreement by: "(1) engaging in activities that led to the cancellation of charter hires that were essential to Seawinds' business; (2) attempting to interfere with a proposed joint service agreement between Seawinds and the East Asiatic Company, and delaying its implementation; (3) making and then reneging on commitments to contribute additional capital, thereby dissuading others from dealing with Seawinds; and (4) making false and disparaging statements about Seawinds' business operations and financial condition." Seawinds' original and first amended complaint included causes of action for breach of contract, breach of the implied covenant of good faith and fair dealing (in both contract and tort), and breach of fiduciary duty. This matter comes before us after trial court rulings on demurrers to Seawinds' complaints.

Nedlloyd demurred to Seawinds' original complaint on the grounds that it failed to state causes of action for breach of the implied covenant of good faith and fair dealing (either in contract or in tort) and breach of fiduciary duty. In support of its demurrer, Nedlloyd contended the shareholders' agreement required the application of Hong Kong law to Seawinds' claims. In opposition to the demurrer, Seawinds argued that California law should be applied to its causes of action. . . .

I

We have not previously considered the enforceability of a contractual choice-of-law provision. We have, however, addressed the closely related issue of the enforceability of a contractual choice-of-forum provision, and we have made clear that, "No satisfying reason of public policy has been suggested why enforcement should be denied a forum selection clause appearing in a contract entered into freely and voluntarily by parties who have negotiated at arm's length." Smith, Valentino & Smith, Inc. v. Superior Court (1976) 551 P.2d 1206. The forum selection provision in *Smith* was contained within a choice-of-law clause, and we observed that, "Such choice of law provisions are usually respected by California courts." We noted this result was consistent with the modern approach of section 187 of the Restatement Second of Conflict of Laws (Restatement). Prior Court of Appeal decisions, although not always explicitly referring to the Restatement, also overwhelmingly reflect the modern, mainstream approach adopted in the Restatement.[1] We affirm this approach. In determining the enforceability of the arm's-length contractual choice-of-law provisions, California courts shall apply the principles set forth in Restatement section 187, which reflect a strong policy favoring enforcement of such provisions.

. . . [T]he proper approach under Restatement section 187, subdivision (2) is for the court first to determine either: (1) whether the chosen state has a substantial relationship to the parties or their transaction, or (2) whether there is any other reasonable basis for the parties' choice of law. If neither of these tests is met, that is the end of the inquiry, and the court need not enforce the parties' choice of law.[4] If, however, either test is met, the court must next determine whether the chosen state's law is contrary to a *fundamental* policy of California.[5] If there is no such conflict, the court shall enforce the parties' choice of law. If, however, there is a fundamental conflict with California law, the court must then determine whether California has a "materially greater interest than the chosen state in the determination of the particular issue. . . ." (Rest., §187, subd. (2).) If California has a materially greater interest than the chosen state, the choice of law shall not be enforced, for the obvious reason that in such circumstance we will decline to enforce a law contrary to this state's fundamental policy.[6] We now apply the Restatement test to the facts of this case.

---

1. Federal courts applying California's conflicts law have also adhered to this approach. The mainstream nature of this approach is further reflected by a recent study indicating that 15 states other than California follow the general approach of the Restatement Second.

4. As noted above, a different result might obtain under Restatement section 187, subdivision (1), which appears to allow the parties *in some circumstances* to specify the law of a state that has no relation to the parties or their transaction. The Restatement gives these two illustrations: "4. In State *X*, *A* establishes a trust and provides that *B*, the trustee, shall be paid commissions at the highest rate permissible under the local law of state *Y*. *A and B are both domiciled in X, and the trust has no relation to any state but X.* In *X*, the highest permissible rate of commissions for trustees is 5 per cent. In *Y*, the highest permissible rate is 4 per cent. The choice-of-law provision will be given effect, and *B* will be held entitled to commissions at the rate of 4 per cent. 5. Same facts as in Illustration 4 except that the highest permissible rate of commissions in *X* is 4 per cent and in *Y* is 5 per cent. Effect will not be given to the choice-of-law provision since under *X* local law the parties lacked power to provide for a rate of commissions in excess of 4 per cent and *Y*, the state of the chosen law, has no relation to the parties or the trust." (Rest., §187, subd. (1), com. c., illus. 4 & 5, p. 564; italics added.)

5. To be more precise, we note that Restatement section 187, subdivision (2) refers not merely to the forum state—for example, California in the present case—but rather to the state ". . . which, under the rule of §188, would be the state of the applicable law in the absence of an effective choice of law by the parties." For example, there may be an occasional case in which California is the forum, and the parties have chosen the law of another state, but the law of yet a third state, rather than California's, would apply absent the parties' choice. In that situation, a California court will look to the fundamental policy of the third state in determining whether to enforce the parties' choice of law. The present case is not such a situation.

6. There may also be instances when the chosen state has a materially greater interest in the matter than does California, but enforcement of the law of the chosen state would lead to a result contrary to a fundamental policy of California. In some such cases, enforcement of the law of the chosen state may be appropriate despite California's policy to the contrary. Careful consideration, however, of California's policy and the other state's interest would be required. No such question is present in this case, and we thus need not and do not decide how Restatement section 187 would apply in such circumstances.

II

B

1

As to the first required determination, Hong Kong—"the chosen state"—clearly has a "substantial relationship to the parties." (Rest. §187, subd. (2)(a).) The shareholders' agreement, which is incorporated by reference in Seawinds' first amended complaint, shows that Seawinds is incorporated under the laws of Hong Kong and has a registered office there. The same is true of one of the shareholder parties to the agreement—Red Coconut Trading Co. The incorporation of these parties in Hong Kong provides the required "substantial relationship" (*Id.*, com. f [substantial relationship present when "one of the parties is domiciled" in the chosen state]).

Moreover, the presence of two Hong Kong corporations as parties also provides a "reasonable basis" for a contractual provision requiring application of Hong Kong law. "If one of the parties resides in the chosen state, the parties have a reasonable basis for their choice." The reasonableness of choosing Hong Kong becomes manifest when the nature of the agreement before us is considered. A state of incorporation is certainly at least one government entity with a keen and intimate interest in internal corporate affairs, including the purchase and sale of its shares, as well as corporate management and operations. (*See* Corp. Code, §102 [applying California's general corporation law to domestic corporations].)

2

We next consider whether application of the law chosen by the parties would be contrary to "a fundamental policy" of California. We perceive no fundamental policy of California requiring the application of California law to Seawinds' claims based on the implied covenant of good faith and fair dealing. The covenant is not a government regulatory policy designed to restrict freedom of contract, but an implied promise inserted in an agreement to carry out the presumed intentions of contracting parties.

Seawinds directs us to no authority exalting the *implied* covenant of good faith and fair dealing over the *express* covenant of these parties that Hong Kong law shall govern their agreement. We have located none. Because Seawinds has identified no fundamental policy of our state at issue in its essentially contractual dispute with Nedlloyd, the second exception to the rule of section 187 of the Restatement does not apply.

C

1

Seawinds contends that, whether or not the choice-of-law clause governs Seawinds' implied covenant claim, Seawinds' fiduciary duty claim is somehow independent of the shareholders' agreement and therefore outside the intended scope of the clause. Seawinds thus concludes California law must be applied to this claim. We disagree.

When two sophisticated, commercial entities agree to a choice-of-law clause like the one in this case, the most reasonable interpretation of their actions is that they intended for the clause to apply to all causes of action arising from or related to their contract. Initially, such an interpretation is supported by the plain meaning of the language used by the parties. The choice-of-law clause in the shareholders' agreement provides: "This agreement shall be *governed by* and construed in accordance with Hong Kong law and each party hereby irrevocably submits to the non-exclusive jurisdiction and service of process of the Hong Kong courts." (Italics added.)[7]

The phrase "governed by" is a broad one signifying a relationship of absolute direction, control, and restraint. Thus, the clause reflects the parties' clear contemplation that "the agreement" is to be completely and absolutely controlled by Hong Kong law. No exceptions are provided. In the context of this case, the agreement to be controlled by Hong Kong law is a shareholders' agreement that expressly provides for the purchase of shares in Seawinds by Nedlloyd and creates the relationship between shareholder and corporation that gives rise to Seawinds' cause of action. Nedlloyd's fiduciary duties, if any, arise from—and can exist only because of—the shareholders' agreement pursuant to which Seawinds' stock was purchased by Nedlloyd.

In order to control completely the agreement of the parties, Hong Kong law must also govern the stock purchase portion of that agreement and the legal duties created by or emanating from the stock purchase, including any fiduciary duties. If Hong Kong law were not applied to these duties, it would effectively control only part of the agreement, not all of it. Such an interpretation would be inconsistent with the unrestricted character of the choice-of-law clause.

Our conclusion in this regard comports with common sense and commercial reality. When a rational businessperson enters into an agreement establishing a transaction or relationship and provides that disputes arising from the agreement shall be governed by the law of an identified jurisdiction, the logical conclusion is that he or she intended that law to apply to *all* disputes arising out of the transaction or relationship. We seriously doubt that any rational businessperson, attempting to provide by contract for an efficient and businesslike resolution of possible future disputes, would intend that the laws of multiple jurisdictions would apply to a single controversy having its origin in a single, contract-based relationship. Nor do we believe such a person would reasonably desire a protracted litigation battle concerning only the threshold question of what law was to be applied to

---

7. As we have noted, the choice-of-law clause states: "This agreement shall be governed by and *construed in accordance with Hong Kong law. . . .*" (Italics added.) The agreement, of course, includes the choice-of-law clause itself. Thus the question of whether that clause is ambiguous as to its scope (i.e., whether it includes the fiduciary duty claim) is a question of contract interpretation that in the normal course should be determined pursuant to Hong Kong law. The parties in this case, however, did not request judicial notice of Hong Kong law on this question of interpretation (Evid. Code, §452, subd. (f)) or supply us with evidence of the relevant aspects of that law (Evid. Code, §453, subd. (b)). The question therefore becomes one of California law.

which asserted claims or issues. Indeed, the manifest purpose of a choice-of-law clause is precisely to avoid such a battle.

Seawinds' view of the problem—which would require extensive litigation of the parties' supposed intentions regarding the choice-of-law clause to the end that the laws of multiple states might be applied to their dispute—is more likely the product of postdispute litigation strategy, not predispute contractual intent. If commercially sophisticated parties (such as those now before us) truly intend the result advocated by Seawinds, they should, in fairness to one another and in the interest of economy in dispute resolution, negotiate and obtain the assent of their fellow parties to explicit contract language specifying what jurisdiction's law applies to what issues.

For the reasons stated above, we hold a valid choice-of-law clause, which provides that a specified body of law "governs" the "agreement" between the parties, encompasses all causes of action arising from or related to that agreement, regardless of how they are characterized, including tortious breaches of duties emanating from the agreement or the legal relationships it creates.

2

Applying the test we have adopted we find no reason not to apply the parties' choice of law to Seawinds' cause of action for breach of fiduciary duty. As we have explained, Hong Kong, the chosen state, has a "substantial relationship to the parties" because two of those parties are incorporated there. Moreover, their incorporation in that state affords a "reasonable basis" for choosing Hong Kong law.

Seawinds identifies no fundamental public policy of this state that would be offended by application of Hong Kong law to a claim by a Hong Kong corporation against its allegedly controlling shareholder. We are directed to no California statute or constitutional provision designed to preclude freedom of contract in this context. Indeed, even in the absence of a choice-of-law clause, Hong Kong's overriding interest in the internal affairs of corporations domiciled there would in most cases require application of its law. *See* Rest. §306 [obligations owed by majority shareholder to corporation determined by the law of the state of incorporation except in unusual circumstances not present here].

For strategic reasons related to its current dispute with Nedlloyd, Seawinds seeks to create a fiduciary relationship by disregarding the law Seawinds voluntarily agreed to accept as binding—the law of a state that also happens to be Seawinds' own corporate domicile. To allow Seawinds to use California law in this fashion would further no ascertainable fundamental policy of California; indeed, it would undermine California's policy of respecting the choices made by parties to voluntarily negotiated agreements.

LUCAS, C.J., and ARABIAN and GEORGE, JJ., concur.

PANELLI, J., concurring and dissenting.

I generally concur in the majority opinion's explanation of the standards controlling when a contractual choice-of-law provision will be honored by the courts of this state and with the majority's application of these standards to Seawinds' cause of action for breach of the covenant of good faith and fair dealing. I write separately to express my disagreement with the majority's conclusion, based on the record before us, that the choice-of-law clause in this case governs Seawinds' cause of action for breach of fiduciary duty. In my view, the majority's analysis of the scope of the choice-of-law clause is unsound.

The choice-of-law clause in this case reads in pertinent part: "This agreement shall be governed by and construed in accordance with Hong Kong law. . . ."[1] The majority determines that the scope of the choice-of-law clause, which was incorporated into the first amended complaint by attachment, extends to related, *noncontractual* causes of action, such as Seawinds' breach of fiduciary duty claim. In so doing, the majority opinion adopts the rule that "[w]hen two sophisticated, commercial entities agree to a choice-of-law clause like the one in this case, the most reasonable interpretation of their actions is that they intended for the clause to apply to all causes of action arising from or related to their contract." Without citing any authority, the majority opinion announces a binding rule of contractual interpretation, based solely upon "common sense and commercial reality."

. . . In this case, the language of the incorporated contract easily can be read to apply only to contractual causes of action: "*This agreement* shall be governed . . . by Hong Kong law."

In my view, the majority's mistaken construction of the choice-of-law clause is clear when the language used in the present contract is compared, as Nedlloyd urges us to do, with the language construed by this court in Smith, Valentino & Smith, Inc. v. Superior Court (1976) 551 P.2d 1206. In that case, this court determined that claims for unfair competition and intentional interference with advantageous business relationships were governed by a choice-of-forum clause as "actions or proceedings instituted by . . . [Smith] under this Agreement with respect to any matters arising under *or growing out of this agreement. . . .*" In contrast to the language used by Nedlloyd and Seawinds in their agreement, the contractual language, "arising under or growing out of this agreement," which was used in *Smith*, explicitly shows an intent to embrace related noncontractual claims, as well as contractual claims. Although similar language was readily available to them, the sophisticated parties in the present case did not draft their choice-of-law clause to clearly encompass related noncontractual causes of action.[2] . . .

Finally, the majority's rule effectively subordinates the intent of the contracting parties to the need for predictability in commercial transactions. The majority strikes this balance despite the fact that our Legislature has commanded otherwise. Under California law, "[a] contract must be so interpreted as to give effect to the mutual intention of the parties as it existed at the time of contracting, so far as the same is ascertainable and lawful." (Civ. Code, §1636.) In contrast to this legislative command, the majority conclusively presumes that choice-of-law

---

1. I agree with the majority that the scope of the choice-of-law clause in this contract is a question that would ordinarily be determined under Hong Kong law. I further agree with the majority that, since the parties neither produced any evidence of Hong Kong law relating to this subject nor requested judicial notice of any such law, we may apply California law to ascertain the scope of the clause.

2. Despite the majority's artfully crafted argument, the words "governed by" do not assist in defining what causes of action the choice-of-law clause was intended to address. Rather, the parties defined the scope of their choice-of-law clause by choosing the phrase "[t]his agreement."

clauses entered into between or among commercial entities apply to related non-contractual causes of action regardless of whether the intent of the parties or the contract language (as in this case) shows otherwise. I believe that the departure by the majority from established California law is unwarranted and is unnecessary to further the goals of predictability in the enforcement of contracts and protection of the justified expectations of contracting parties. These goals can be adequately protected within the framework of the current law governing contractual interpretation by enforcing choice-of-law clauses in a manner consistent with the language of the contract and the intent of the parties.

I am keenly aware of the need for predictability in the enforcement of commercial contracts. Nevertheless, although courts and litigants may wish the law were otherwise, not every issue can be conclusively determined at the pleading stage. On the present record, the scope of the choice-of-law clause must be construed in favor of Seawinds.

Questions and Comments

(1) Choice-of-law clauses are routinely incorporated into large commercial contracts and are also increasingly common in smaller-scale consumer contracts. Sometimes they are included because the law of one specific state is thought particularly desirable by one or both parties. But surprisingly often, the parties do not even bother to research the chosen law before they include a clause selecting it. This suggests that the parties may be as attracted by the avoidance of uncertainty and litigation expenses over choice-of-law matters, per se, as by the perceived benefits of any particular law. Note that the beneficiary of the increased certainty might well be the defendant, for it is typically the plaintiff who benefits from the chance to forum-shop for a more desirable substantive law.

(2) Despite their obvious advantages in reducing uncertainty, choice-of-law clauses can be, themselves, a source of litigation, as the *Nedlloyd* case suggests. Under the Restatement Second test, there are two main sources of controversy, both illustrated by *Nedlloyd*.

At the outset, courts must determine whether (1) or (2) is the applicable subsection; the former is unqualifiedly permissive, while the latter imposes conditions on enforcement of the clause. Subsection (1) applies to issues on which the parties had the freedom to contract explicitly for the substantive terms and simply chose to do so in a shorthand manner, namely by selecting a law that so provides. Many rules of contract law are default rules, which the parties can override by specific contract terms; as to these, they may select any state's law, even if it has no connection to the controversy. Subsection (2), in contrast, deals with what are sometimes called "mandatory" rules, which the parties could not defeat by more detailed drafting of the substantive terms of the contract; this category would include, for example, rules prohibiting punitive damages or outlawing certain kinds of disclaimers. As to these, a reasonable basis for selecting the chosen state must be shown, and the chosen law must not offend a "materially greater interest" of the state whose law must otherwise apply. These requirements are vague, which compromises the certainty advantage to choosing law. Note also that application of section 187(2) requires a prior determination of the law that would otherwise apply, which seems to be precisely the issue that a choice-of-law clause should help avoid.

(3) The second potential controversy under section 187 is determining the scope of the choice-of-law clause. As *Nedlloyd* suggests, the parties' dispute may include claims that are not, strictly speaking, contractual; in addition to the sort of claim at issue there (breach of fiduciary duty), other examples include claims based on fraud or misrepresentation. Does the selected law govern these issues as well? The *Nedlloyd* court states (in footnote 7) that the scope of the choice-of-law clause must be determined by consulting the chosen state's law. Given that section 187(3) states that the reference is to the chosen state's local law, and not its choice-of-law rules, this result is not compelled. What reasons could be given for the court's result? The court also decided that under California law the clause should be read broadly, to include a claim for breach of fiduciary duty; some courts have concluded otherwise. *See, e.g.*, Klock v. Lehman Bros. Kuhn Loeb, Inc., 584 F. Supp. 210 (S.D.N.Y. 1984); Carlock v. Pillsbury Co., 719 F. Supp. 791 (D. Minn. 1989).

(4) Another issue concerning the scope of choice-of-law clauses is whether selection of a state's laws requires application of that state's "procedural" rules, including statutes of limitation. Should the fact that such issues are ordinarily resolved under forum law mean that the choice-of-law clause has no relevance to resolving them? Note that the parties might, if they so chose, specify in the contract a time period for bringing suit; does this cast doubt on the "procedural" characterization? Consider also whether forum law or the law specified in the contract should be used to determine whether a prevailing party can recover attorneys' fees. *See* Midwest Medical Supply Co. v. Wingert, 317 S.W.3d 530 (Tex. Ct. App. 2010) (recovery of attorneys' fees deemed substantive and therefore determined according to the law chosen by the parties).

(5) An interesting California case involved the contractual intersection of choice-of-law clauses and jury waivers. In Rincon EV Realty LLC v. CP III Rincon Towers, Inc., 213 Cal. Rptr. 3d 410 (Cal. Ct. App. 2017), the parties had signed agreements designating New York law for any disputes, and providing that the parties waive all rights to a jury trial. Although both parties' principal place of business was New York and the loan at issue originated and was dispersed in New York, the commercial property at issue was located in California. The California court concluded that California's rule preventing parties from waiving their rights to a jury trial applied notwithstanding the parties' choice of New York law, under which parties are permitted to waive their jury trial rights. Applying the *Nedlloyd* court's Second Restatement reasoning, the *Rincon* court concluded that enabling the parties to waive their jury trial rights to legal claims would violate a "fundamental" and "sacred" California policy. Moreover, California had a materially greater interest in the resolution of the issue because the litigation was occurring in California. For all litigants in California courts, the jury trial right is deemed essential to California's balanced and fair justice system. What is New York's interest in this case? Is California's interest really materially greater than New York's?

(6) A few states have adopted legislation providing for virtually automatic enforcement of clauses choosing that state's law. For example, New York law provides:

§5-1401. Choice of Law

1. The parties to any contract, agreement or undertaking, contingent or otherwise, in consideration of, or relating to any obligation arising out of a transaction covering in the aggregate not less than two hundred fifty thousand dollars, including a transaction otherwise covered by subsection one of section 1-105 of the uniform commercial code, may agree that the law of this state shall govern their rights and duties in whole or in part, whether or not such contract, agreement or undertaking bears a reasonable relation to this state. This section shall not apply to any contract, agreement or undertaking (a) for labor or personal services, (b) relating to any transaction for personal, family or household services, or (c) to the extent provided to the contrary in subsection two of section 1-105 of the uniform commercial code.

2. Nothing contained in this section shall be construed to limit or deny the enforcement of any provision respecting choice of law in any other contract, agreement or undertaking.

(Section 5-1402 of the General Obligations Law, analogously, provides for enforcement of clauses choosing New York as the forum.) California, Delaware, Florida, Illinois, and Texas have all passed similar statutes, though the minimum transaction dollar amount necessary to trigger automatic enforcement varies from $100,000 to $1,000,000. Does the fact that each of these statutes provides for enforcement of clauses choosing forum law, but not clauses choosing the law of other states, discriminate against sister states' laws? Is there any good reason for distinguishing between the two? Consult Hughes v. Fetter, page 327 *supra*.

Banek, Inc. v. Yogurt Ventures U.S.A., Inc.

6 F.3d 357 (6th Cir. 1993)

GUY, Circuit Judge.

In this interlocutory appeal, plaintiff, Banek, Inc., appeals the district court's ruling that a choice of law provision contained in the parties' franchise agreement was valid and enforceable. Upon review of the record and consideration of the arguments of the parties, we conclude that the district court's decision was correct and affirm.

I

Plaintiff, Banek, Inc., owned by Mr. and Mrs. Banek, entered into negotiations with defendant Yogurt Ventures U.S.A., Inc., a Georgia corporation owned by defendants John and Richard Stern, for the purchase of a Freshens Yogurt franchise to be located in Monroe, Michigan. After negotiating several changes in the agreement, the parties signed a "Franchise and Development Agreement" in February 1990. Sales at the Monroe location were not as expected, and Banek closed its Freshens franchise in March 1992. In October 1991, prior to shutting down, Banek filed suit in state court against Yogurt Ventures. The suit alleged breach of contract, various violations of the Michigan Franchise Investment Law (MFIL), violations of the Federal Trade Commission Franchise Rules, common law fraud and misrepresentation, and negligence. In May 1992, after closing the Monroe site, Banek filed a separate action against John and Richard Stern. These two cases were then consolidated. Following removal to federal court based on diversity jurisdiction, defendants moved for dismissal of all counts on various theories.

The district court granted defendants' motion in part and denied it in part. The court ruled that the choice of law provision in the parties' agreement, providing that Georgia law is to govern the rights and obligations of the parties, was valid and enforceable under Michigan law and thus dismissed plaintiff's claim alleging violations of the MFIL. . . . Only the ruling concerning the choice of law provision is before this court on interlocutory appeal.

II

The franchise agreement between these parties provides:

This Agreement was made and entered into in the State [of] Georgia and all rights and obligations of the parties hereto shall be governed by and construed in accordance with the laws of the State of Georgia.

We see the issue in this appeal as involving three separate, sequential questions. First, is this a valid choice of law clause or is it a waiver of rights which is prohibited under the MFIL? Second, if the clause is valid, is this choice of law provision enforceable under Michigan choice of law rules? Third, if this provision is valid and enforceable, does Georgia law govern all claims between the parties or only contract claims?

We begin with answering the first question in the affirmative. Plaintiff . . . argue[s] that the choice of law provision in the agreement operates as a waiver of the rights and protections under the MFIL and thus is void under Mich. Comp. Laws Ann. §445.1527. That section provides:

Each of the following provisions is void and unenforceable if contained in any documents relating to a franchise:
. . . (b) A requirement that a franchisee assent to a release, assignment, novation, waiver, or estoppel which deprives a franchisee of rights and protections provided in this act. This shall not preclude a franchisee, after entering into a franchise agreement, from settling any and all claims.
. . . (f) A provision requiring that arbitration or litigation be conducted outside this state. This shall not preclude the franchisee from entering into an agreement, at the time of arbitration, to conduct arbitration at a location outside this state.

Plaintiff argues that the choice of law provision making Georgia law applicable acts as a waiver of "rights and protections" provided under the MFIL. We disagree.

The Michigan legislature was specific enough to include forum selection provisions in the list of void provisions, but did not specify choice of law provisions. Seemingly, the Michigan legislature understood that the burdens of being forced to arbitrate a claim in a foreign forum are significant, as subsection (f) makes arbitration or litigation of forum selection clauses void. However, litigating in Michigan does not require that Michigan law must govern the dispute. The statute does not expressly void choice of law provisions, and we decline to imply such a prohibition. The Michigan legislature may have purposefully omitted choice of law provisions from those clauses prohibited because it may have realized that other states' laws might provide more protection to franchisees; thus, if a franchisee and franchisor want to choose a different state's law to govern any disputes, the parties may so contract. Providing that waivers and releases are void is not equivalent to voiding choice of law provisions. *See* Tele-Save Merchandising Co. v. Consumers Distrib. Co., 814 F.2d 1120, 1122-1123 (6th Cir. 1987) (Ohio law voiding any waiver of the Ohio Business Opportunity Plans Act did not void choice of law provision).

The cases cited by plaintiff . . . are inapposite. As noted in Wright-Moore Corp. v. Ricoh Corp., 908 F.2d 128, 134 (7th Cir. 1990), "the strength of non-waiver provisions among states varies." In *Wright-Moore*, the Indiana statute made it unlawful to enter into an agreement "limiting litigation brought for breach of the agreement in any manner whatsoever," Ind. Code §23-2-2.7-1(10), and thus the court held that the choice of law provision in the contract at issue was void. Other states expressly include choice of law provisions in the list of void and unenforceable provisions. *See, e.g.*, Minn. Stat. §80C.21. The Michigan statute is not so strongly worded, perhaps for the reason expressed above. Alternatively or additionally, the Michigan legislature may have recognized that requiring all franchises located in Michigan be governed by Michigan law, regardless of any agreement to the contrary, would make Michigan a less desirable target state for franchisors, making franchises in Michigan more expensive to own. This would be largely because of a national franchisor's need for uniformity in its business affairs. Having to comply with differing laws for each of the states in which it does business increases expenses. In any event, Michigan has not indicated a desire to bar choice of law provisions either expressly or implicitly.

That brings us to the second question: Should the valid choice of law provision be enforced under Michigan's choice of law rules? It is a well-accepted principle that a federal court in a diversity case must apply the conflict of law rules of the state in which it sits. Klaxon Co. v. Stentor Elec. Mfg. Co., 313 U.S. 487, 490 (1941). Therefore, this court must look to Michigan conflict of law principles to determine whether Michigan or Georgia law governs this dispute.

Michigan has adopted the approach articulated in Restatement (Second) of Conflict of Laws §187 (1971). Under section 187, a contractual choice of law provision will govern unless either:

> (a) the chosen state has no substantial relationship to the parties or the transaction and there is no other reasonable basis for the parties' choice, or
> (b) application of the law of the chosen state would be contrary to a fundamental policy of a state which has a materially greater interest than the chosen state in the determination of the particular issue and which, under

the rule of §188, would be the state of the applicable law in the absence of an effective choice of law by the parties.

In the present case, the parties do not dispute that there is a substantial relationship with the State of Georgia. Assuming without deciding that under section 188 Michigan law would apply, plaintiff argues that to enforce the choice of law provision and apply Georgia law would violate Michigan's public policy, as expressed in the MFIL, to protect franchisees from over-reaching by franchisors and from the superior bargaining power franchisors possess. Initially, we note that this is not a case of a take-it-or-leave-it adhesion contract. Banek successfully negotiated multiple changes in Yogurt Ventures' standard franchise agreement, dispelling the claim of unfair bargaining power.[2]

As we have stated previously, we "move cautiously when asked to hold contract clauses unenforceable on public policy grounds. . . . " Moses v. Business Card Express, Inc., 929 F.2d 1131, 1139 (6th Cir.) (1991). While we agree with plaintiff that the comprehensive and paternalistic franchise investment law represents Michigan public policy,[3] that does not end the inquiry. The more central question in this case is whether the parties have selected, through their choice of law provision, a jurisdiction in which there is a substantial erosion of the quality of protection that the MFIL would otherwise provide. A court may not assume that, merely because Michigan has adopted a franchise statute, the application of Georgia's laws would be contrary to Michigan's public policy. Tele-Save, 814 F.2d at 1123.

"In order for the chosen state's law to violate the fundamental policy of [the forum state], it must be shown that there are significant differences in the application of the law of the two states." Id. Banek has failed to show any specific significant differences between the application of Georgia law and Michigan law to their claims. [The court concluded that the rights, obligations, and remedies provided under Georgia statute and common law were all comparable to Michigan law, or at least provided adequate redress]. . . .

[P]laintiff has failed to demonstrate how application of Georgia law would violate a specific fundamental policy of Michigan. . . .

Finally, because the choice of law provision in the contract is valid and enforceable, we must determine its scope. Plaintiff contends that Georgia law should only govern contract claims, while defendant argues that all claims arising out of the parties' franchise dealings should be governed under Georgia law. This court faced a similar question in Moses where the choice of law provision

---

2. Banek was not forced into this investment decision, but chose to negotiate an agreement with the defendant. Having negotiated that agreement, including several changes beneficial to Banek's position, it is now attempting to escape one of the contract's provisions.

The price that Banek paid for its franchise reflected the terms of the agreement. We are hesitant to void the choice of law provision because that would mean Banek would be getting more than it bargained for.

3. Various aspects of the MFIL evidence that it represents public policy of Michigan: provisions for enforcement by both public and private actions, Mich. Comp. Laws Ann. §§445.1531, 445.1535; the imposition of joint and several liability of owners, directors, officers, and employees of the franchisor, [Id.] §445.1532; recovery of attorney fees in private actions, [Id.] §445.1531; and the imposition of penalties and fines, including up to seven years imprisonment and up to $10,000 in fines, [Id.] §445.1538. Enforcement of the act's provisions by the attorney general would not be affected by a choice of law provision in a franchise contract.

read: "This Franchise and License Agreement and the construction thereof shall be governed by the laws of the state of Michigan." We held that the clause clearly referred to more than just the construction of the agreement and extended to plaintiff's claims of fraud and misrepresentation. In the present case, the contract provides "this Agreement was made and entered into in the State [of] Georgia and all rights and obligations of the parties hereto shall be governed by and construed in accordance with the laws of the State of Georgia." As in *Moses*, we find that the choice of law provision is sufficiently broad so as to cover plaintiff's claims of fraud and misrepresentation. Had these claims only been tangentially related to the franchise relationship, we would be much more inclined to find the choice of law provision not applicable. The claims of fraud and misrepresentation that plaintiff has asserted here are directly related to the franchise agreement.

The order of the district court is affirmed.

Questions and Comments

(1) Why does the *Banek* court ask whether the choice-of-law clause is valid under the Michigan franchise law *before* performing a choice-of-law analysis? Why does it assume the Michigan law governs this issue? Would the Michigan franchise law apply to a franchise agreement in Georgia between Georgia domiciliaries? What is the difference between the court's first and second "sequential questions"?

(2) Would the *Banek* court have enforced the choice-of-law clause if the parties had not negotiated the contract and changed some of its terms? If the Michigan franchise law expressly prohibited choice-of-law clauses? If there were "significant differences" between the Michigan and Georgia franchise regimes? Which of these factors is most important under section 187(2)(b)? More generally, how do courts determine when a state policy is "fundamental" within the meaning of section 187(2)(b)? Is this the same inquiry as the traditional public policy exception to choice of law?

(3) What are the extraterritorial limits on a state's application of its franchise laws? In Instructional Systems, Inc. v. Computer Curriculum Corp., 614 A.2d 124 (N.J. 1992), a New Jersey firm (ISI) was the exclusive distributor in 11 Northeast states from 1974 to 1989 of an educational computer product made by a California firm (CCC). When their contract, which contained a California choice-of-law clause, expired in 1989, CCC offered ICI a new contract that reduced its marketing territory to three states. ISI sued CCC in New Jersey, alleging that the new contract imposed unreasonable performance standards in violation of the New Jersey Franchise Act. The court held that the New Jersey Franchise Act governed not only distribution activities in New Jersey, but also in other states included in the original contract. The court reasoned: "To the extent that it is applicable, the New Jersey Act regulates instate conduct that has out-of-state effects. . . . [T]he State regulation is applicable . . . to specific transactions affecting New Jersey, *i.e.*, franchises that have a 'place of business' in New Jersey." *Id*. at 368-389. The Third Circuit subsequently ruled that this holding did not violate constitutional limitations on interstate discrimination and extraterritorial regulation. *See* Instructional Sys. v. Computer Curriculum Corp., 35 F.3d 813 (3d Cir. 1994). Do you agree?

(4) In another case a Washington choice-of-law clause was enforced in a contract between a Canadian franchisor and a California franchisee. 1-800-Got Junk LLC v. Superior Court, 116 Cal. Rptr. 3d 923 (Cal. Ct. App. 2010). Despite the lack of substantial relationship between Washington and the parties and transaction, the clause could be enforced because there was a reasonable basis for the choice of Washington law: A multistate franchisor would want to conduct business according to a single law and Washington was closest to the company's Vancouver, Canada, headquarters. As with the Michigan franchise law in *Banek*, the California franchise law expressly prohibited the use of choice-of-forum clauses when the forum chosen was outside of California but did not expressly prohibit the use of choice-of-law clauses. A provision of the California law did state that "any condition, stipulation or provision purporting to bind any person to waive compliance with any provision of this law is contrary to public policy and void," but the court found this provision inapplicable because Washington law actually provided stronger protections to franchisees than did California law.

(5) What should a court do when a choice-of-law clause specifies a law that, if applied, will invalidate the contract? Should it be enforced? Restatement (Second) §187 comment *e*, n.4 provides:

> On occasion, the parties may choose a law that would declare the contract invalid. In such situations, the chosen law will not be applied by reason of the parties' choice. To do so would defeat the expectations of the parties which it is the purpose of the present rule to protect. The parties can be assumed to have intended that the provisions of the contract would be binding upon them. . . . If the parties have chosen a law that would invalidate the contract, it can be assumed that they did so by mistake. If, however, the chosen law is that of the state of the otherwise applicable law under the rule of §188, this law will be applied even when it invalidates the contract.

Why should parties be relieved of the unfortunate and perhaps unforeseen consequences of a choice-of-law clause in this context and not in others? Shouldn't the parties be held to their bargain? What is different about a choice-of-law clause that invalidates the contract itself?

(6) Sometimes a court encounters a choice-of-law clause that, if applicable, would invalidate a clause or term of the contract rather than the contract as a whole. Courts are split regarding whether the choice-of-law clause should be considered a mistake as applied to the invalidated contract provision. Consider, for example, Kipin Industries, Inc. v. Van Deilen International, Inc., 182 F.3d 490 (6th Cir. 1999). In *Kipin*, plaintiff, a Pennsylvania corporation with its principal place of business in Pennsylvania, contracted with defendant, a Michigan corporation with its principal place of business in Michigan, to perform work at a site owned by a third party in Kentucky. The contract provided that it "shall be deemed to be executed in the State of Michigan, and should be construed according to Michigan Law," and that disputes "shall be adjudicated by a court of competent jurisdiction sitting in the State of Michigan." The contract also included an explicit prohibition against the placement of liens by plaintiff on the property of the third party. The lien waiver prohibition was invalid under Michigan law, which provided that "[a] person shall not require, as part of any contract for an improvement, that the

right to a construction lien be waived in advance of work performed. A waiver obtained as part of a contract for an improvement is contrary to public policy, and shall be invalid. . . . " Mich. Comp. Laws Ann. §570.1115(1). Kentucky law, the law the court determined would apply in the absence of a choice-of-law clause, permitted parties to enter into pre-work lien waivers. After defendant failed to pay plaintiff for work that was performed, plaintiff filed suit against defendant and placed a lien on the third party's property, an action that defendant challenged in the lawsuit against it. Citing the Restatement comment above, the Sixth Circuit determined that, although Michigan law would apply to the contract more generally, the choice of Michigan law would be deemed a "mistake" as applied to the lien waiver provision. Does this determination seem sensible to you? Isn't a choice of law that invalidates a term of the contract different from a choice of law that invalidates the entire contract? Isn't the inference of mistake more powerful in the latter context? And is it problematic to apply Michigan law to parts of the contract and Kansas law to others? Would a court have allowed the parties to do that directly?

Regarding the scope of the choice-of-law clause, do you agree with the *Kipin* court's conclusion that the choice-of-law clause—providing that the contract should be "construed" according to Michigan law—was meant to include not only Michigan rules of contract interpretation, but rather all of Michigan substantive law? Under what law should the court interpret the choice-of-law clause to reach this conclusion? For a different view of a similar clause, see Heating & Air Specialists Inc. v. Jones, 180 F.3d 923, 930 (8th Cir. 1999) (concluding that clause providing that "laws of the State of Texas shall govern [the contract's] interpretation" referred to Texas contract interpretation rules and did not preclude application of otherwise applicable Arkansas law); Arnon v. Aetna Life Ins. Co., 860 F.3d 97 (2d Cir. 2017) (choice-of-law clause that provided insurance contract was to be "construed in line with" the laws of the jurisdiction where the plan was delivered held to "set forth only which jurisdiction's law of contract interpretation and contract construction will be applied," not the full breadth of the law of the chosen state).

(7) Professors O'Hara and Ribstein have argued that the expansion of party autonomy in choice of law both promotes individual welfare and pressures legislatures to enact efficient laws. *See* O'Hara & Ribstein, *The Law Market* (2009); O'Hara & Ribstein, *From Politics to Efficient in Choice of Law*, 67 U. Chi. L. Rev. 1151 (2000); Kobayashi & Ribstein, *Choosing Law by Contract*, in *The Fall and Rise of Freedom of Contract* 325 (1999).

Cook Sign Co. v. Combs

2008 WL 3898267

Court of Appeals of Minnesota
UNPUBLISHED OPINION
CONNOLLY, J.

Appellant challenges the district court's grant of a temporary injunction prohibiting him from violating his noncompete agreement with respondent. Because we conclude that the noncompete agreement was supported by consideration, Minnesota law was the proper choice of law, and the district court did not abuse its discretion in granting the temporary injunction, we affirm.

[Cook Sign Company, a North Dakota corporation, is in the business of designing, fabricating, installing, and servicing custom-manufactured signs. Cook purchased much of the assets of Art-N-Sign, a Minnesota sign-manufacturing company, in January 2007, and, in the process, it offered employment to Daniel Combs, an Art-N-Sign employee for more than ten years. On January 20, 2007, Combs met with Cook's CEO, Dave Walstad, to discuss Combs's coming to work for respondent. Walstad stated in an affidavit that, after that meeting, "[appellant] knew that he would be required to sign the noncompete agreement as a condition of working at Cook." The specific terms of the noncompete were not discussed, however. Combs signed the employment offer when he arrived for work the next day. The employment offer contained a clause referring to (but not actually containing) the noncompete agreement:

> A signing bonus of $2,500 will be paid during the first check run of your term of employment. In addition, if your annual income for 2007 is not greater than $55,000, a second half payment of $2,500 will be paid in January 2008.
>   In return for this income guarantee and signing bonus, we ask that you sign a 1 year [noncompete] agreement.

The employment agreement stated that disputes would be resolved according to North Dakota law. Combs signed the noncompete agreement early the following month. This agreement identifies Minnesota as the choice of law for resolution of disputes.

In June 2007, Combs resigned his position at Cook and accepted a sales position with Indigo SignWorks, a North Dakota company. Cook initiated litigation, obtained a temporary restraining order, and then obtained a temporary injunction enjoining Combs from working for Indigo. Combs appealed.]

I. The district court did not err in concluding that the choice-of-law analysis required application of Minnesota law.

Appellant argues that North Dakota law should be applied because it is the law that governs the employment agreement. Respondent asserts that the applicable law is that of Minnesota as explicitly stated by the noncompete agreement. After a careful and thorough analysis, the district court determined that Minnesota was the proper choice of law.

When confronted with a choice-of-law question, it must first be established that there is an actual conflict between the laws of the two states. *Medtronic, Inc. v. Advanced Bionics Corp.*, 630 N.W.2d 438, 454 (Minn. App. 2001). There is a clear conflict in this case because North Dakota does not recognize noncompete agreements,[4] whereas Minnesota looks upon noncompete agreements with disfavor, but nonetheless, deems them "enforceable if they serve a legitimate

---

4. North Dakota Century Code §9-08-06 (2006) states that "[e]very contract by which anyone is restrained from exercising a lawful profession, trade, or business of any kind is to that extent void" except selling the goodwill of a business and partnership relations.

employer interest and are not broader than necessary to protect this interest." Kallok v. Medtronic, Inc., 573 N.W.2d 356, 361 (Minn. 1998).

The next step is to balance guiding factors established by the Minnesota Supreme Court. These factors are: (1) predictability of result; (2) maintenance of interstate and international order; (3) simplification of the judicial task; (4) advancement of the forum's governmental interest; and (5) application of the better rule of law.

A. PREDICTABILITY OF RESULT

The factor applies primarily to consensual transactions where the parties desire advance notice of which state law will govern in future disputes. It is intended to protect the justified expectations of the parties to the transaction. There is a clear choice-of-law provision in the noncompete agreement. It states: "Construction and interpretation of this Agreement shall at all times and in all respects be governed by the laws of the State of Minnesota." The plain language of the agreement provides for the application of Minnesota law. This is what the parties bargained for, and their choice should not be altered without good reason.

Appellant argues that the employment agreement is governed by North Dakota law, but because respondent knew that North Dakota would not enforce a noncompete agreement, respondent chose Minnesota law for the noncompete agreement. Appellant argues that this type of forum shopping is disfavored. The district court dispatched this argument succinctly:

> Even though the Employment Offer elects the laws of the State of North Dakota, the Agreement, not the Employment Offer, is the focus of this litigation. As such, in carefully construing the terms of the Agreement, the Court concludes that the language contained therein provides that the laws of the State of Minnesota shall govern and the Agreement itself provided the parties with notice of such.

This factor favors applying Minnesota law.

B. MAINTENANCE OF INTERSTATE AND INTERNATIONAL ORDER

The primary issue under this factor is whether applying Minnesota law would manifest disrespect for North Dakota's sovereignty or impede interstate commerce. "Evidence of forum shopping, or that application of Minnesota's law would promote forum shopping, would indicate such disrespect." Id.

Appellant claims that respondent was forum shopping because, as a North Dakota company, it knew that North Dakota would not enforce the noncompete agreement. Therefore, it chose Minnesota law to govern the noncompete agreement. Appellant argues that this conduct manifests a lack of respect for the law and sovereignty of North Dakota. Respondent asserts that North Dakota has no interest in this case because appellant is a Minnesota resident who lives and works in Minnesota.

Once again, the district court correctly addressed this issue:

> While [appellant] argues that [respondent] is forum shopping in its selection of Minnesota law, the Court again finds that the plain language of the agreement dictates that it is governed by the laws of the State of Minnesota. As such, applying Minnesota law is not evidence of forum shopping, nor would its application promote forum shopping—the application of Minnesota law was considered and agreed to by the parties.

Because the parties explicitly agreed to apply Minnesota law in the noncompete agreement, it is not disrespectful to North Dakota to apply Minnesota law to this dispute. This factor favors applying Minnesota law.

C.   SIMPLIFICATION OF THE JUDICIAL TASK

This third factor is often considered insignificant because courts can as easily apply another state's laws as their own. Although Minnesota courts are fully capable of applying the law of another state, the judicial task is obviously simplified when a Minnesota court applies Minnesota law.

Although this is generally the case, it would have been equally, if not more, simple to apply North Dakota law to this case. This is true because North Dakota will not enforce a noncompete agreement. Therefore, had the district court applied North Dakota law, it would have been unnecessary to analyze the temporary-injunction issue because the case would have been dismissed. Therefore, this factor does not seem to significantly favor application of either state's law, although North Dakota law might be slightly favored.

D.   ADVANCEMENT OF THE FORUM'S GOVERNMENTAL INTEREST

The fourth factor involves inquiry into the choice of law that would most effectively advance a "significant interest of the forum state." "Minnesota's governmental interests will most clearly be advanced by application of Minnesota law." Hague v. Allstate Ins. Co., 289 N.W.2d 43, 49 (Minn. 1978).

Appellant admits that "[m]ost typically, Minnesota's interests would be advanced by application of its law." But he goes on to argue that because respondent engaged in forum shopping in its choice of Minnesota, this factor actually favors North Dakota. As previously discussed, both parties acknowledged the application of Minnesota law when they signed the agreement. Applying North Dakota law "would not advance Minnesota's interests and would reduce the protection afforded under Minnesota law to employers who enter into legal noncompete contracts." *Advanced Bionics*, 630 N.W.2d at 455. This factor favors applying Minnesota law.

E. APPLICATION OF THE BETTER RULE OF LAW

This factor "should be applied only when the choice-of-law question remains unresolved after the other factors are considered." *Id*. Because three factors clearly favor Minnesota, and only one is neutral or slightly favors North Dakota, this factor is insignificant. The district court properly applied Minnesota law to this case.

. . .

Questions and Comments

(1) Because *Cook Sign* is an unpublished opinion, it is technically nonprecedential in Minnesota. Nevertheless, it has been favorably cited by a U.S. District Court in Minnesota and an Ohio state appellate court and relied upon by several litigants in their briefs. The opinion presents a unique combination of currently relevant choice-of-law issues. Note first that this court relied on the state's default approach to choice of law, Leflar's choice-influencing considerations, to determine whether the contractual choice of Minnesota law would be honored. Can you think of a reason why this court would not have proceeded with the now standard Second Restatement analysis? Does the court's approach seem conceptually coherent?

(2) The *Cook Sign* court rejected Combs's argument that Cook Sign was shopping for Minnesota law with its choice-of-law clause. Does that conclusion seem sound? Company attorneys drafting the employment agreement and the noncompete agreement were careful to produce two separate documents with two separate choices of law: North Dakota for the employment agreement and Minnesota for the noncompete clause. Should employers be permitted to engage in this type of *dépeçage* with a hybrid of laws governing different aspects of the employment relationship? Suppose that states engage in policy tradeoffs by bundling together compensation protections for employees and competition protections for employers. Does the use of two separate clauses enable a company to get its competition protections while avoiding the employee's compensation protections? The court seems to think that forum-shopping is not an issue because the parties chose Minnesota law, but there is no evidence in the record that Combs actually agreed to the choice of Minnesota law. Indeed, there is no evidence that he paid any attention to the clause, let alone understood the consequence of it. Is the court perhaps influenced by the fact that Combs was given a signing bonus in return for agreeing to the noncompete clause? Should that fact make a difference?

(3) States with generous enforcement of noncompete clauses enable employers to protect their investments in employee skills training and confidential information. States with less generous or no enforcement of noncompete clauses give priority to the employee's ability to earn a livelihood. Given that Combs was based in Minnesota and Cook Sign in North Dakota, is the court correct that Minnesota has a governmental interest in enforcing its law here? If so, does the choice-of-law clause add to that interest in any way?

(4) Because state laws differ on the enforcement of noncompete clauses in employment contracts, the parties sometimes strategically file claims. When an employee leaves the firm to work for a competitor located in a state with no or poor enforcement of noncompete clauses, the first employer typically files suit in a court located in the state designated in the choice-of-law clause and that court typically enforces the choice-of-law clause. *See, e.g.*, Medtronic, Inc. v. Gibbons, 684 F.2d 565 (8th Cir. 1982); Shipley Co. v. Kozlowski, 926 F. Supp. 28 (D. Mass. 1996). New employers often know before first employers that the employee is about to switch jobs, however, so sometimes the employee, with the assistance of the new employer, files a declaratory judgment action in a court located in the state of new employment. If that state is less generous regarding the enforcement of noncompete clauses, then the court is much less likely to enforce the choice-of-law clause. These latter courts typically rely on the public policy language of the Second Restatement to strike down the choice-of-law provision. *See, e.g.*, Barnes Group, Inc. v. C & C Prods., Inc., 716 F.2d 1023 (4th Cir. 1983); Enron Capital & Trade Resources Corp. v. Pokalsky, 490 S.E.2d 136 (Ga. Ct. App. 1997); DeSantis v. Wackenhut Corp., 793 S.W.2d 670 (Tex. 1990). The ultimate result from this strategic litigation turns on the parties' race to judgment, which the court might or might not assist. Although the full faith and credit clause requires all the other states to give effect to a final judgment, there is no constitutional requirement that courts stay their hands in response to a sister state's issuance of a preliminary injunction. In these situations, courts can differ regarding the permissible actions of the parties and the merits of the enforceability of the covenant not to compete. *See* Ethicon Endo-Surgery, Inc. v. Pemberton, 2010 WL 5071848 (Mass. Super. 2010).

Hall v. Sprint Spectrum L.P.

376 Ill. App. 3d 822, 876 N.E.2d 1036, 315 Ill. Dec. 446 (2007)

STEWART, J.

The defendants, Sprint Spectrum L.P. and SprintCom, Inc., both doing business as Sprint PCS Group (collectively referred to as Sprint), appeal . . . from an order of the circuit court of Madison County certifying a 48-state class in a putative class action lawsuit filed by the plaintiff, Jessica Hall. We affirm.

Background

Sprint provides wireless communications services to millions of customers throughout the United States. Sprint is headquartered in Overland Park, Kansas, but operates and conducts its business throughout the United States, including within the State of Illinois.

In June 2003, Hall, a resident of Madison County, Illinois, entered into a cell phone service contract with Sprint at a Radio Shack store in Granite City, Illinois. In doing so, she agreed to be bound to a one-year contract and to pay a $150 early termination fee if she did not remain a customer for a full year. Hall's account included two cell phone numbers.

[Later that year, Hall attempted to cancel her contract, but Sprint refused to assent to the cancellation unless Hall paid the early termination fee. In addition, Sprint insisted that she pay the fee twice, once for each of her cell phone numbers.

Hall filed a class action complaint and a motion for class action certification in the trial court. She alleged five causes of action: (1) breach of contract; (2) violation of the Kansas Consumer Protection Act (Kan. Stat. Ann. §50-623 et seq. (West 2005)); (3) statutory fraud under the Illinois Consumer Fraud Act and the consumer protection statutes of the other states where Sprint does business; (4) unjust enrichment; and (5) relief from unlawful penalties. Each cause of action rested on the theory that early termination fees are unlawful penalties. The complaint sought damages for all early termination fees Sprint had collected from U.S. consumers.]

In her first amended complaint, Hall alleged that Sprint placed the following express choice-of-law provision in all of its contracts: "This Agreement is governed by and must be construed under federal law and the laws of the State of Kansas, without regard to choice of law principles." Accordingly, . . . the first amended complaint alleged that Kansas common law should be applied nationally (counts 1, 4, and 5) and the Kansas Consumer Protection Act should be applied nationally (count 2) or that the Illinois Consumer Fraud Act should be applied to Illinois residents and the consumer fraud acts of the other 47 states should be applied to residents of those states (count 3).

[Following a hearing and motion to reconsider, the trial court entered a formal, written order, certifying the following 48-state class: "All persons who were charged a Sprint Early Termination Fee because they canceled their cellular or wireless agreement before the end of its term." The order contemplates the application of Kansas law based on the express choice-of-law provision contained in Sprint's form contract.]

This court granted Sprint's petition for leave to appeal.

Analysis

[The court first determined that the trial court's class certification was predicated upon the application of Kansas law to all of plaintiffs' claims based on the choice-of-law provision contained in Sprint's form contract.]

Sprint next argues that if the 48-state class certification was predicated upon the application of the Kansas Consumer Protection Act, the order must be reversed for two reasons: (1) based on the language of the statute, the Kansas Consumer Protection Act, like the Illinois Consumer Fraud Act, cannot be applied extraterritorially; and (2) the Kansas Consumer Protection Act cannot be applied to all class members because the choice-of-law provision does not govern noncontractual claims, such as statutory fraud. We disagree.

This is not a case like Avery v. State Farm Mutual Automobile Insurance Co., 216 Ill. 2d 100 (2005), where the plaintiff sought extraterritorial application of a statute based on the terms of the statute. Instead, in this case, the trial court enforced a voluntary and broadly worded choice-of-law provision in an adhesion contract drafted by Sprint to determine the validity and legality of a provision within the same contract—the early termination fee provision.

Sprint's choice-of-law provision states that the agreement should be governed by the law of Kansas. The only issue in this case is the validity of the early termination fee, and by the parties' own choice, that issue is governed by Kansas law. The fact that Kansas law might not otherwise apply is irrelevant, because the parties chose to apply Kansas law.

Ordinarily, Illinois follows the Restatement (Second) of Conflict of Laws (1971) in making choice-of-law decisions. Section 187 of the Restatement applies when the parties, as here, have made an express choice of law in their contract. Section 187(2) of the Restatement (Second) of Conflict of Laws provides, in pertinent part:

> (2) The law of the state chosen by the parties to govern their contractual rights and duties will be applied . . . unless either
>> (a) the chosen state has no substantial relationship to the parties or the transaction and there is no other reasonable basis for the parties' choice, or
>> (b) application of the law of the chosen state would be contrary to a fundamental policy of a state which has a materially greater interest than the chosen state in the determination of the particular issue and which, under the rule of §188, would be the state of the applicable law in the absence of an effective choice of law by the parties.

The public policy of a State must be sought in its constitution, legislative enactments[,] and judicial decisions.

In the present case, there is no question that Kansas and Missouri have a "substantial relationship to the parties or the transaction," because defendant SprintCom, Inc., is a Kansas corporation with its principal place of business in Kansas and defendant Sprint Spectrum L.P. is a Missouri limited partnership. In addition, there is no argument here that the Illinois constitution or legislative enactments articulate a public policy against applying a foreign state's consumer protection laws or that Illinois has a "materially greater interest" in the litigation than Kansas or Missouri. Therefore, the trial court properly found that the express choice-of-law provision contained in Sprint's form contract governs the contract.

These principles apply with equal force to the interpretation of the contract at issue and to the validity of its provisions. *See* Restatement (Second) §187(2), Comment *e*, at 565 ("Prime objectives of contract law are to protect the justified expectations of the parties and to make it possible for them to foretell with accuracy what will be their rights and liabilities under the contract. These objectives may best be attained in multistate transactions by letting the parties choose the law to govern the validity of the contract and the rights created thereby. In this way, certainty and predictability of result are most likely to be secured. Giving parties this power of choice is also consistent with the fact that, in contrast to other areas of the law, persons are free within broad limits to determine the nature of their contractual obligations").

Sprint argues that because the Kansas Consumer Protection Act does not purport to have any extraterritorial application, it cannot be applied to any transaction that occurred outside Kansas, notwithstanding the parties' express choice-of-law provision stating that Kansas law would apply. Sprint argues that the Kansas Consumer Protection Act applies only to a "consumer transaction" (see Kan. Stat. Ann. §§50-626(a), 50-627(a) (West 2005)), which is defined as "a sale, lease, assignment[,] or other disposition for value of property or services *within this state*" (emphasis added) (Kan. Stat. Ann. §50-624(c) (West 2005)).

However, the issue is not the territorial application of the Kansas Consumer Protection Act but whether the parties chose to apply Kansas law to govern the validity of the provisions in their contract. The fact that Kansas law might not otherwise apply is irrelevant because the parties expressly agreed that Kansas law would apply. *See* Davis v. Miller, 269 Kan. 732, 739 (2000) ("Despite the legislative intent and the clear language of the [act], parties can bind themselves to the provisions of an otherwise inapplicable act by incorporating choice of law provisions in an enforceable contract. As long as application of a statute or act is not contrary to public policy, a court will uphold application of an otherwise inapplicable statute or act"); Bartlett Bank & Trust Co. v. McJunkins, 147 Ill. App. 3d 52, 59 (1986) ("Even where the [Uniform Commercial] Code is otherwise inapplicable, the parties may incorporate the Code into their agreement and that agreement will be given effect"). Therefore, the trial court properly found that the parties bound themselves to the provisions of the Kansas Consumer Protection Act by incorporating the express choice-of-law provision in their enforceable contract.

Sprint also argues that Hall's claims are "noncontractual" and, therefore, that the choice-of-law provision should not apply to them. Hall has alleged a variety of claims, including breach of contract and statutory fraud. Each of these claims is based on the theory that the early termination fee is an unlawful penalty. The principle that a *contract penalty is illegal and unenforceable is, itself, fundamentally a creature of contract law. See* Restatement (Second) of Contracts §356, Comment *a*, at 157 (1981) ("[T]he parties to a contract are not free to provide a penalty for its breach. The central objective behind the system of contract remedies is compensatory, not punitive. Punishment of a promisor for having broken his promise has no justification on either economic or other grounds and a term providing such a penalty is unenforceable on grounds of public policy"). Hall's various claims do not reflect differing sources of the law so much as alternative theories whereby she and the other class members can bring an action to enforce the same underlying legal principle that comes from contract law, not tort law.

Before *Avery*, Illinois courts traditionally held that where a contract contained an express choice-of-law provision, the consumer protection law of the designated state would apply.

In *Avery*, the Illinois Supreme Court held, "[A] plaintiff may pursue a private cause of action under the Consumer Fraud Act if the circumstances that relate to the disputed transaction occur primarily and substantially in Illinois." *Avery*, 216 Ill. 2d at 187. The court in *Avery* discussed Martin v. Heinold Commodities, Inc., 117 Ill. 2d 67 (1987), wherein the Illinois Supreme Court allowed the certification of the claims of the plaintiff class under the Illinois Consumer Fraud Act even with respect to the non-Illinois plaintiffs. Although the court in *Martin* held that the application of Illinois law to a multistate class was consistent with principles of due process, the court in *Avery* noted that the *Martin* court did not address the scope of the Illinois Consumer Fraud Act as a matter of statutory interpretation. The Avery court did not overrule *Martin* but, instead, distinguished it as follows:

> In *Martin* . . . , this court specifically based its decision on the following facts: (1) the contracts containing the deceptive statements were all executed in Illinois; (2) the defendant's principal place of business was in Illinois; (3) *the contract contained express choice-of-law and forum-selection clauses specifying that any litigation would be conducted in Illinois under Illinois law*; (4) complaints regarding the defendant's performance were to be directed to its Chicago office; and (5) payments for the defendant's services were to be sent to its Chicago office. Given these circumstances, this court concluded that the [Illinois Consumer Fraud] Act could apply to the whole class. (Emphasis added.) Avery, 216 Ill. 2d at 189.

The *Avery* court found that, unlike *Martin*, virtually no circumstances relating to the disputed claims and practices at issue occurred or existed in Illinois for those plaintiffs who were not Illinois residents. Therefore, the *Avery* court concluded, "[T]he circuit court erred in certifying a nationwide class that included class members whose claims proceedings took place outside Illinois." *Avery*, 216 Ill. 2d at 190. Because the court decided the propriety of the certification order on statutory interpretation grounds, it declined to consider whether the certification of the nationwide class was unconstitutional or violated express choice-of-law rules.

In the present case, as in *Martin* and unlike in *Avery*, the parties' contract contained an express choice-of-law provision. Moreover, as this court recently stated in Barbara's Sales, Inc. v. Intel Corp., 367 Ill. App. 3d 1013 (2006), "*Avery* in no way breaks with choice-of-law precedent and does not change the choice-of-law analysis to be applied." Therefore, under the express choice-of-law provision contained in the parties' contract, Kansas law, including the Kansas Consumer Protection Act, is applicable.

Sprint next argues that applying the Kansas Consumer Protection Act to non-Kansas class members would violate their due process rights under Phillips Petroleum Co. v. Shutts [page 364 *supra*]. We disagree.

In *Phillips Petroleum Co.*, the United States Supreme Court stated:

> Kansas must have a 'significant contact or significant aggregation of contacts' to the claims asserted by each member of the plaintiff class, contacts 'creating state interests,' in order to ensure that the choice of Kansas law is not arbitrary or unfair. . . .
>
> When considering fairness in this context, an important element is the expectation of the parties.

Because Sprint's form contract contained an express choice-of-law provision, the class members had reason to anticipate that Kansas law would govern their consumer fraud claim. Accordingly, enforcing the express choice-of-law provision is consistent with fulfilling the expectations of the parties and is not arbitrary or unfair. As long as the law chosen in the contract satisfies the "substantial relationship to the parties or the transaction" test, as it does in this case, enforcing it will not violate due process. *See* [Restatement (Second) §187(2)(a)].

[The court then rejected Sprint's argument that Illinois does not have a sufficient interest in this case to proceed with a 48-state class action under the law of Kansas.]

. . .

Questions and Comments

(1) Sprint placed a choice-of-law clause in its contracts and, as a result, all consumer rights will be determined according to the law of Kansas despite the fact that consumers play no material role in the choice of Kansas law. As a general matter, should companies be permitted to use a choice-of-law clause to circumvent the consumer protection laws of the state where the consumer resides? At least in part, state consumer protection laws are intended to protect consumers from the fact that they pay attention to only a very few terms in the contracts that they sign. Why then hold the consumer to a choice-of-law clause, the import of which the consumer almost assuredly largely or completely ignored?

(2) For the most part, the Uniform Commercial Code allows contracts to specify the governing law so long as the transaction bears a reasonable relation to the state whose law is chosen. A recent UCC amendment would have replaced the reasonable relationship test with a bifurcated treatment of choice-of-law clauses. The amendment would have expanded permissible choices for commercial parties by enabling parties to nonconsumer contracts to choose even unrelated law for their contracts. At the same time, it would have shrunk permissible choices in consumer contracts by disenabling companies from using choice-of-law clauses to circumvent mandatory consumer rules in the state of the consumer's residence (or place of ordering and delivery). That amendment was abandoned in 2008 after widespread rejection by state legislatures. *See* UCC §1-301 (2008 Amendments).

(3) The European Union has recently adopted choice-of-law rules to be applied throughout the EU. Rome I Regulation on the law applicable to contractual obligations, Regulation (EC) No. 593/2008, provides in Article 6 that choice-of-law clauses are enforceable in consumer contracts but in general they are not permitted to be used to circumvent mandatory consumer protection rules in the consumer's habitual country of residence (with a limited exception if the counterparty conducts no business there). This consumer protection does not apply to financial instruments or to contracts in furtherance of the customer's profession. A similar approach is taken for individual employment contracts. There too choice-of-law clauses are permitted, but Article 8 states that they cannot be used to deprive employees of protections afforded by the mandatory laws of the place where the employee habitually carries out her work.

(4) Note that even when effective, choice-of-law clauses take away only the consumer's private right of action under her home state consumer protection laws. State attorneys general are typically empowered to bring enforcement actions against offending firms under the consumer protection statutes. Is that avenue

sufficient? At least one court thought not. In a case striking down a New York choice-of-law clause as applied to Kentucky consumers who sued their Internet service provider for uncompensated service failures, the Kentucky Supreme Court stated:

> We acknowledge that customers could pursue a remedy through the Attorney General, who is vested with authority under the Kentucky Consumer Protection Act to pursue litigation against companies who would improperly overcharge its customers. However, as noted by the Attorney General, "with the limited resources of the Commonwealth the Attorney General is simply unable to pursue each and every violator and must limit its case selection to those matters involving the greatest public interest." Brief of the Attorney General of Kentucky, pg. 4. Accordingly, the theoretical availability of this remedy does not alter our conclusions.

Schnuerle v. Insight Communications Co, L.P., 2010 WL 5129850 at *5, n.5 (Ky. 2010). Wouldn't a state with a fundamental policy and a materially greater interest allocate sufficient resources to its AG's office to pursue public actions against those who violate the fundamental policy? What is the difference between "the greatest public interest" mentioned in *Schnuerle* and "fundamental policy" from the Second Restatement?

(5) Choice-of-law clauses provide companies with other significant benefits mentioned earlier in this chapter, including uniformity, predictability, and fit. Given these benefits, company disputes with a consumer often include a fight over the choice-of-law clause, with the company seeking enforcement of its clause and the consumer seeking to have it stricken from the contract. In today's consumer class action environment, however, the arguments are sometimes reversed, as they were in *Hall*. The topic of choice of law in class actions will be explored in greater depth in Chapter 10. For now, note that Sprint's choice of Kansas law helped to establish that the plaintiffs' claims involved "common issues of law and fact" as required for class certification. Sprint hoped to defeat the class action certification so that it could force consumers to bring their claims against Sprint individually. For this reason, it actually argued that the court should strike down its own clause.

(6) The *Hall* court found irrelevant the fact that the Kansas legislature did not intend for its law to apply extraterritorially. Can parties decide that a law applies even if the legislature states otherwise? Should the answer depend on whether the state intended a narrow territorial application out of deference to other states or due to a conviction that broader application would constitute poor policy? Courts are split on the question whether parties can choose a law in circumstances where the enacting legislature indicated, explicitly or implicitly, that the law should not apply. Indeed, even the Illinois courts don't agree on this question as it relates to the Consumer Fraud Act. *See* International Profit Assocs., Inc. v. Linus Alarm Corp., 971 N.E.2d 1183 (Ill. App. 2d 2012) (rejecting *Hall* court's reasoning and concluding that the parties cannot contract into the Act with choice-of-law and choice-of-forum clauses). *Compare* 1-800-Got Junk? LLC v. Superior Court, *supra* page 663 (permissible for franchise contract between Canadian franchisor and California franchisee to designate Washington law even

though Washington franchise protection statute does not, by its terms, apply to out-of-state franchises) *with* Taylor v. 1-800-Got Junk? LLC, 387 Fed. Appx. 727 (9th Cir. 2010) (Washington franchise law does not apply to dispute between Canadian franchisor and Oregon franchisee by its terms despite Washington choice-of-law clause).

(7) Is the court's conclusion in *Hall* that the parties' choice of Kansas law refers to Kansas's internal law but not Kansas's limitations on the geographic scope of Kansas law, the result contemplated by §187(3) of the Second Restatement, which provides that "[i]n the absence of a contrary indication of intention, the reference is to the local law of the state of the chosen law"? Why did the court not discuss that section?

(8) Would it be constitutionally permissible for a state to attempt to prevent parties from choosing its law if it would not otherwise apply? Put differently, if in Tennessee Coal, Iron & Railroad Co. v. George, *supra* page 333-334, Alabama was not permitted to create a law and restrict its enforcement to its own courts, may a state create a law but limit the locational facts to which it applies? Would the problem be one of privileges and immunities? If a state cannot effectively limit private parties from choosing its law, does that have a chilling effect on law creation? Might party choice actually encourage legal innovation?

(9) The *Hall* court concluded that it was constitutionally permissible for Kansas law to apply to all of the contracts because the express choice-of-law provision ensures that the application of Kansas law is neither arbitrary nor fundamentally unfair under the due process and full faith and credit clauses. Surely the presence of a choice-of-law clause in a contract helps to prevent unfair surprise, and, in this case, Kansas had a significant connection to the transaction and claims because Sprint is headquartered there. Consider a different case, however, one where the parties choose a law that has no direct connection to the parties or their transaction. Under the Second Restatement, even if the chosen state has no substantial relationship to the parties or the transaction, the choice of law can be valid if there is another reasonable basis for the parties' choice. Restatement (Second) §187(2)(a). Might that choice nevertheless fail constitutional scrutiny if there is no "significant contact or significant aggregation of contacts" "creating state interests" in the application of the chosen law? The Supreme Court of Mississippi apparently thought so. In Sentinel Industrial Contracting Corp. v. Kimmins Industrial Service Corp., 743 So. 2d 954 (Miss. 1999), a subcontractor sued a general contractor for failure to pay for extra costs associated with the subcontractor's performance under the contract. The general contractor had contracted with Exxon Chemical Fertilizer Company to dismantle an ammonia plant located in Mississippi and reassemble it in Pakistan, and that contract provided that it was to be governed by the law of Texas. When the subcontractor argued that the choice-of-law clause in the main contract should apply to the subcontract because the main contract was incorporated into the subcontract by reference, the Mississippi court disagreed, stating that because Texas has little contact with or interest in the outcome of a contract dispute involving parties from elsewhere and work to be performed in Mississippi, applying Texas law in the case would be unconstitutional.

B. Choice-of-Court Clauses

The Bremen v. Zapata Off-Shore Co.

407 U.S. 1 (1972)

Chief Justice BURGER delivered the opinion of the Court.

We granted certiorari to review a judgment of the United States Court of Appeals for the Fifth Circuit declining to enforce a forum-selection clause governing disputes arising under an international towage contract between petitioners and respondent. The circuits have differed in their approach to such clauses. For the reasons stated hereafter, we vacate the judgment of the Court of Appeals.

In November 1967, respondent Zapata, a Houston-based American corporation, contracted with petitioner Unterweser, a German corporation, to tow Zapata's ocean-going, self-elevating drilling rig *Chaparral* from Louisiana to a point off Ravenna, Italy, in the Adriatic Sea, where Zapata had agreed to drill certain wells.

Zapata had solicited bids for the towage, and several companies including Unterweser had responded. Unterweser was the low bidder and Zapata requested it to submit a contract, which it did. The contract submitted by Unterweser contained the following provision, which is at issue in this case:

Any dispute arising must be treated before the London Court of Justice.

In addition the contract contained two clauses purporting to exculpate Unterweser from liability for damages to the towed barge.

After reviewing the contract and making several changes, but without any alteration in the forum-selection or exculpatory clauses, a Zapata vice president executed the contract and forwarded it to Unterweser in Germany, where Unterweser accepted the changes, and the contract became effective.

On January 5, 1968, Unterweser's deep sea tug *Bremen* departed Venice, Louisiana, with the *Chaparral* in tow bound for Italy. On January 9, while the flotilla was in international waters in the middle of the Gulf of Mexico, a severe storm arose. The sharp roll of the *Chaparral* in Gulf waters caused its elevator legs, which had been raised for the voyage, to break off and fall into the sea, seriously damaging the *Chaparral*. In this emergency situation Zapata instructed the *Bremen* to tow its damaged rig to Tampa, Florida, the nearest port of refuge.

On January 12, Zapata, ignoring its contract promise to litigate "any dispute arising" in the English courts, commenced a suit in admiralty in the United States District Court at Tampa, seeking $3,500,000 damages against Unterweser in personam and the *Bremen* in rem, alleging negligent towage and breach of contract. . . .

We hold, with the six dissenting members of the Court of Appeals, that far too little weight and effect were given to the forum clause in resolving this controversy. For at least two decades we have witnessed an expansion of overseas commercial activities by business enterprises based in the United States. The barrier of distance that once tended to confine a business concern to a modest territory no longer does so. Here we see an American company with special expertise contracting with a foreign company to tow a complex machine thousands of miles across seas and oceans. The expansion of American business and industry will hardly be encouraged if, notwithstanding solemn contracts, we insist on a parochial concept that all disputes must be resolved under our laws and in our courts. Absent a contract forum, the considerations relied on by the Court of Appeals would be persuasive reasons for holding an American forum convenient in the traditional sense, but in an era of expanding world trade and commerce, the absolute aspects of [this] doctrine . . . have little place and would be a heavy hand indeed on the future development of international commercial dealings by Americans. We cannot have trade and commerce in world markets and international waters exclusively on our terms, governed by our laws, and resolved in our courts.

Forum-selection clauses have historically not been favored by American courts. Many courts, federal and state, have declined to enforce such clauses on the ground that they were "contrary to public policy," or that their effect was to "oust the jurisdiction" of the court. Although this view apparently still has considerable acceptance, other courts are tending to adopt a more hospitable attitude toward forum-selection causes. This view, advanced in the well-reasoned dissenting opinion in the instant case, is that such clauses are prima facie valid and should be enforced unless enforcement is shown by the resisting party to be "unreasonable" under the circumstances. We believe this is the correct doctrine to be followed by federal district courts sitting in admiralty. It is merely the other side of the proposition recognized by this Court in National Equipment Rental, Ltd. v. Szukhent, holding that in federal courts a party may validly consent to be sued in a jurisdiction where he cannot be found for service of process through contractual designation of an "agent" for receipt of process in that jurisdiction. In so holding, the Court stated: "[I]t is settled . . . that parties to a contract may agree in advance to submit to the jurisdiction of a given court, to permit notice to be served by the opposing party, or even to waive notice altogether." This approach is substantially that followed in other common-law countries including England. It is the view advanced by noted scholars and that adopted by the Restatement [Second] of the Conflict of Laws. It accords with ancient concepts of freedom of contract and reflects an appreciation of the expanding horizons of American contractors who seek business in all parts of the world. Not surprisingly, foreign businessmen prefer, as we do, to have disputes resolved in their own courts, but if that choice is not available, then in a neutral forum with expertise in the subject matter. Plainly, the courts of England meet the standards of neutrality and long experience in admiralty litigation. The choice of that forum was made in an arm's-length negotiation by experienced and sophisticated businessmen, and absent some compelling and countervailing reason it should be honored by the parties and enforced by the courts.

The argument that such clauses are improper because they tend to "oust" a court of jurisdiction is hardly more than a vestigial legal fiction. It appears to rest at core on historical judicial resistance to any attempt to reduce the power and business of a particular court and has little place in an era when all courts are overloaded and when businesses once essentially local now operate in world markets. It reflects something of a provincial attitude regarding the fairness of other tribunals. No one seriously contends in this case that the forum-selection clause "ousted" the District Court of jurisdiction over Zapata's action. The threshold question is whether that court should have exercised its jurisdiction to do more than give effect to the legitimate expectations of the parties, manifested in their freely negotiated agreement, by specifically enforcing the forum clause.

There are compelling reasons why a freely negotiated private international agreement, unaffected by fraud, undue influence, or overweening bargaining power, such as that involved here, should be given full effect. In this case, for example, we are concerned with a far from routine transaction between companies of two different nations contemplating the tow of an extremely costly piece of equipment from Louisiana across the Gulf of Mexico and the Atlantic Ocean, through the Mediterranean Sea to its final destination in the Adriatic Sea. In the course of the voyage, it was to traverse the waters of many jurisdictions. The *Chaparral* could have been damaged at any point along the route, and there were countless possible ports of refuge. That the accident occurred in the Gulf of Mexico and the barge was towed to Tampa in an emergency were mere fortuities. It cannot be doubted for a moment that the parties sought to provide for a neutral forum for the resolution of any disputes arising during the tow. Manifestly much uncertainty and possibly great inconvenience to both parties could arise if a suit could be maintained in any jurisdiction in which an accident might occur or if jurisdiction were left to any place where the *Bremen* or Unterweser might happen to be found.[15] The elimination of all such uncertainties by agreeing in advance on a forum acceptable to both parties is an indispensable element in international trade, commerce, and contracting. There is strong evidence that the forum clause was a vital part of the agreement, and it would be unrealistic to think that the parties did not conduct their negotiations, including fixing the monetary terms, with the consequences of the forum clause figuring prominently in their calculations. Under these circumstances, as Justice Karminski reasoned in sustaining jurisdiction over Zapata in the High Court of Justice, "[t]he force of an agreement for litigation in this country, freely entered into between two competent parties, seems to me to be very powerful."

Thus, in the light of present-day commercial realities and expanding international trade we conclude that the forum clause should control absent a strong showing that it should be set aside. Although their opinions are not altogether explicit, it seems reasonably clear that the District Court and the Court of Appeals placed the burden on Unterweser to show that London would be a more convenient forum than Tampa, although the contract expressly resolved that issue. The correct approach would have been to enforce the forum clause specifically unless Zapata could clearly show that enforcement would be unreasonable and unjust, or that the clause was invalid for such reasons as fraud or overreaching. Accordingly, the case must be remanded for reconsideration.

---

15. At the very least, the clause was an effort to eliminate all uncertainty as to the nature, location, and outlook of the forum in which these companies of differing nationalities might find themselves. Moreover, while the contract here did not specifically provide that the substantive law of England should be applied, it is the general rule in English courts that the parties are assumed, absent contrary indication, to have designated the forum with the view that it should apply its own law. It is therefore reasonable to conclude that the forum clause was also an effort to obtain certainty as to the applicable substantive law.

We note, however, that there is nothing in the record presently before us that would support a refusal to enforce the forum clause. The Court of Appeals suggested that enforcement would be contrary to the public policy of the forum under Bisso v. Inland Waterways Corp., because of the prospect that the English courts would enforce the clauses of the towage contract purporting to exculpate Unterweser from liability for damages to the *Chaparral*. A contractual choice-of-forum clause should be held unenforceable if enforcement would contravene a strong public policy of the forum in which suit is brought, whether declared by statute or by judicial decision. It is clear, however, that whatever the proper scope of the policy expressed in *Bisso*, it does not reach this case. *Bisso* rested on considerations with respect to the towage business strictly in American waters, and those considerations are not controlling in an international commercial agreement. . . .

Courts have also suggested that a forum clause, even though it is freely bargained for and contravenes no important public policy of the forum, may nevertheless be "unreasonable" and unenforceable if the chosen forum is *seriously* inconvenient for the trial of the action. Of course, where it can be said with reasonable assurance that at the time they entered the contract, the parties to a freely negotiated private international commercial agreement contemplated the claimed inconvenience, it is difficult to see why any such claim of inconvenience should be heard to render the forum clause unenforceable. We are not here dealing with an agreement between two Americans to resolve their essentially local disputes in a remote alien forum. In such a case, the serious inconvenience of the contractual forum to one or both of the parties might carry greater weight in determining the reasonableness of the forum clause. The remoteness of the forum might suggest that the agreement was an adhesive one, or that the parties did not have the particular controversy in mind when they made their agreement; yet even there the party claiming should bear a heavy burden of proof. Similarly, selection of a remote forum to apply differing foreign law to an essentially American controversy might contravene an important public policy of the forum. For example, so long as *Bisso* governs American courts with respect to the towage business in American waters, it would quite arguably be improper to permit an American tower to avoid that policy by providing a foreign forum for resolution of his disputes with an American towee.

This case, however, involves a freely negotiated international commercial transaction between a German and an American corporation for towage of a vessel from the Gulf of Mexico to the Adriatic Sea. As noted, selection of a London forum was clearly a reasonable effort to bring vital certainty to this international transaction and to provide a neutral forum experienced and capable in the resolution of admiralty litigation. Whatever "inconvenience" Zapata would suffer by being forced to litigate in the contractual forum as it agreed to do was clearly foreseeable at the time of contracting. In such circumstances it should be incumbent on the party seeking to escape his contract to show that trial in the contractual forum will be so gravely difficult and inconvenient that he will for all practical purposes be deprived of his day in court. Absent that, there is no basis for concluding that it would be unfair, unjust, or unreasonable to hold that party to his bargain. . . .

Zapata's remaining contentions do not require extended treatment. It is clear that Unterweser's action in filing its limitation complaint in the District Court in Tampa was, so far as Zapata was concerned, solely as a defensive measure made necessary as a response to Zapata's breach of the forum clause of the contract. . . .

Justice DOUGLAS, dissenting. . . .

Respondent is a citizen of this country. Moreover, if it were remitted to the English court, its substantive rights would be adversely affected. Exculpatory provisions in the towage control provide (1) that petitioners, the masters and the crews "are not responsible for defaults and/or errors in the navigation of the tow" and (2) that "[d]amages suffered by the towed object are in any case for account of its Owners."

Under our decision in Dixilyn Drilling Corp. v. Crescent Towing & Salvage Co., "a contract which exempts the tower from liability for its own negligence" is not enforceable, though there is evidence in the present record that it is enforceable in England. That policy was first announced in Bisso v. Inland Waterways Corp. Although the casualty occurred on the high seas, the *Bisso* doctrine is nonetheless applicable.

Moreover, the casualty occurred close to the District Court, a number of potential witnesses, including respondent's crewmen, reside in that area, and the inspection and repair work were done there. The testimony of the tower's crewmen, residing in Germany, is already available by way of depositions taken in the proceedings.

All in all, the District Court judge exercised his discretion wisely in enjoining petitioners from pursuing the litigation in England.

I would affirm the judgment below.

Carnival Cruise Lines, Inc. v. Shute

499 U.S 585 (1991)

Justice BLACKMUN delivered the opinion of the Court.

In this admiralty case we primarily consider whether the United States Court of Appeals for the Ninth Circuit correctly refused to enforce a forum-selection clause contained in tickets issued by petitioner Carnival Cruise Lines, Inc., to respondents Eulala and Russel Shute.

I

The Shutes, through an Arlington, Wash., travel agent, purchased passage for a 7-day cruise on petitioner's ship, the *Tropicale*. Respondents paid the fare to the agent who forwarded the payment to petitioner's headquarters in Miami, Fla. Petitioner then prepared the tickets and sent them to respondents in the State of Washington. The face of each ticket, at its left-hand lower corner, contained this admonition:

"SUBJECT TO CONDITIONS OF
CONTRACT ON LAST PAGES
IMPORTANT! PLEASE READ CONTRACT—
ON LAST PAGES 1, 2, 3" App. 15.

The following appeared on "contract page 1" of each ticket:

TERMS AND CONDITIONS OF PASSAGE
CONTRACT TICKET

3. (a) The acceptance of this ticket by the person or persons named hereon as passengers shall be deemed to be an acceptance and agreement by each of them of all of the terms and conditions of this Passage Contract Ticket.

8. It is agreed by and between the passenger and the Carrier that all disputes and matters whatsoever arising under, in connection with or incident to this Contract shall be litigated, if at all, in and before a Court located in the State of Florida, U.S.A., to the exclusion of the Courts of any other state or country."

The last quoted paragraph is the forum-selection clause at issue.

II

Respondents boarded the *Tropicale* in Los Angeles, Cal. The ship sailed to Puerto Vallarta, Mexico, and then returned to Los Angeles. While the ship was in international waters off the Mexican coast, respondent Eulala Shute was injured when she slipped on a deck mat during a guided tour of the ship's galley. Respondents filed suit against petitioner in the United States District Court for the Western District of Washington, claiming that Mrs. Shute's injuries had been caused by the negligence of Carnival Cruise Lines and its employees.

Petitioner moved for summary judgment, contending that the forum clause in respondents' tickets required the Shutes to bring their suit against petitioner in a court in the State of Florida. Petitioner contended, alternatively, that the District Court lacked personal jurisdiction over petitioner because petitioner's contacts with the State of Washington were insubstantial. The District Court granted the motion, holding that petitioner's contacts with Washington were constitutionally insufficient to support the exercise of personal jurisdiction.

The Court of Appeals reversed. Reasoning that "but for" petitioner's solicitation of business in Washington, respondents would not have taken the cruise and Mrs. Shute would not have been injured, the court concluded that petitioner had sufficient contacts with Washington to justify the District Court's exercise of personal jurisdiction.

Turning to the forum-selection clause, the Court of Appeals acknowledged that a court concerned with the enforceability of such a clause must begin its analysis with *The Bremen*, where this Court held that forum-selection clauses, although not "historically . . . favored," are "prima facie valid." *Id.* The appellate court concluded that the forum clause should not be enforced because it "was not freely bargained for." As an "independent justification" for refusing to enforce the clause, the Court of Appeals noted that there was evidence in the record to indicate that "the Shutes are physically and financially incapable of pursuing this litigation in Florida" and that the enforcement of the clause would operate to deprive them of their day in court and thereby contravene this Court's holding in *The Bremen*. We granted certiorari to address the question whether the Court of Appeals was correct in holding that the District Court should hear respondents' tort claim against petitioner. Because we find the forum-selection clause to be dispositive of this question, we need not consider petitioner's constitutional argument as to personal jurisdiction. . . .

III

We begin by noting the boundaries of our inquiry. First, this is a case in admiralty, and federal law governs the enforceability of the forum-selection clause we scrutinize. Second, we do not address the question whether respondents had sufficient notice of the forum clause before entering the contract for passage. Respondents essentially have conceded that they had notice of the forum-selection provision. Additionally, the Court of Appeals evaluated the enforceability of the forum clause under the assumption, although "doubtful," that respondents could be deemed to have had knowledge of the clause.

Within this context, respondents urge that the forum clause should not be enforced because, contrary to this Court's teachings in *The Bremen*, the clause was not the product of negotiation, and enforcement effectively would deprive respondents of their day in court. Additionally, respondents contend that the clause violates the Limitation of Vessel Owner's Liability Act, 46 U.S.C. App. §183c. We consider these arguments in turn.

IV

A

Both petitioner and respondents argue vigorously that the Court's opinion in *The Bremen* governs this case, and each side purports to find ample support for its position in that opinion's broad-ranging language. This seeming paradox derives in large part from key factual differences between this case and *The Bremen*, differences that preclude an automatic and simple application of *The Bremen*'s general principles to the facts here.

[The Court discusses the facts and holding of *The Bremen*, reproduced *supra* page 677.]

In applying *The Bremen*, the Court of Appeals in the present litigation took note of the foregoing "reasonableness" factors and rather automatically decided that the forum-selection clause was unenforceable because, unlike the parties in *The Bremen*, respondents are not business persons and did not negotiate the terms of the clause with petitioner. Alternatively, the Court of Appeals ruled that the clause should not be enforced because enforcement effectively would deprive respondents of an opportunity to litigate their claim against petitioner.

The Bremen concerned a "far from routine transaction between companies of two different nations contemplating the tow of an extremely costly piece of equipment from Louisiana across the Gulf of Mexico and the Atlantic Ocean, through the Mediterranean Sea to its final destination in the Adriatic Sea." These facts suggest that, even apart from the evidence of negotiation regarding the forum clause, it was entirely reasonable for the Court in *The Bremen* to have expected Unterweser and Zapata to have negotiated with care in selecting a forum for the resolution of disputes arising from their special towing contract.

In contrast, respondents' passage contract was purely routine and doubtless nearly identical to every commercial passage contract issued by petitioner and most other cruise lines. In this context, it would be entirely unreasonable for us to assume that respondents—or any other cruise passenger—would negotiate with petitioner the terms of a forum-selection clause in an ordinary commercial cruise ticket. Common sense dictates that a ticket of this kind will be a form contract the terms of which are not subject to negotiation, and that an individual purchasing the ticket will not have bargaining parity with the cruise line. But by ignoring the crucial differences in the business contexts in which the respective contracts were executed, the Court of Appeals' analysis seems to us to have distorted somewhat this Court's holding in *The Bremen*.

In evaluating the reasonableness of the forum clause at issue in this case, we must refine the analysis of *The Bremen* to account for the realities of form passage contracts. As an initial matter, we do not adopt the Court of Appeals' determination that a nonnegotiated forum-selection clause in a form ticket contract is never enforceable simply because it is not the subject of bargaining. Including a reasonable forum clause in a form contract of this kind well may be permissible for several reasons: First, a cruise line has a special interest in limiting the fora in which it potentially could be subject to suit. Because a cruise ship typically carries passengers from many locales, it is not unlikely that a mishap on a cruise could subject the cruise line to litigation in several different fora. *See The Bremen*, 407 U.S., at 13. Additionally, a clause establishing ex ante the forum for dispute resolution has the salutary effect of dispelling any confusion about where suits arising from the contract must be brought and defended, sparing litigants the time and expense of pretrial motions to determine the correct forum and conserving judicial resources that otherwise would be devoted to deciding those motions. *See* Stewart Organization, Inc. v. Ricoh Corp., 487 U.S. 22, 33 (1988). (concurring opinion). Finally, it stands to reason that passengers who purchase tickets containing a forum clause like that at issue in this case benefit in the form of reduced fares reflecting the savings that the cruise line enjoys by limiting the fora in which it may be sued.

We also do not accept the Court of Appeals' "independent justification" for its conclusion that *The Bremen* dictates that the clause should not be enforced because "[t]here is evidence in the record to indicate that the Shutes are physically and financially incapable of pursuing this litigation in Florida." We do not defer to the Court of Appeals' findings of fact. In dismissing the case for lack of personal jurisdiction over petitioner, the District Court made no finding regarding the physical and financial impediments to the Shutes' pursuing their case in Florida. The Court of Appeals' conclusory reference to the record provides no basis for this Court to validate the finding of inconvenience. Furthermore, the Court of Appeals did not place in proper context this Court's statement in *The Bremen* that "the serious inconvenience of the contractual forum to one or both of the parties might carry greater weight in determining the reasonableness of the forum clause." 407 U.S. at 17. The Court made this statement in evaluating a hypothetical "agreement between two Americans to resolve their essentially local disputes in a remote alien forum." *Ibid.* In the present case, Florida is not a "remote alien forum," nor—given the fact that Mrs. Shute's accident occurred off the coast of Mexico—is this dispute an essentially local one inherently more suited to resolution in the State of Washington than in Florida. In light of these distinctions, and because respondents do not claim lack of notice of the forum clause, we conclude that they have not satisfied the "heavy burden of proof," *ibid.*, required to set aside the clause on grounds of inconvenience.

It bears emphasis that forum-selection clauses contained in form passage contracts are subject to judicial scrutiny for fundamental fairness. In this case, there is no indication that petitioner set Florida as the forum in which disputes were to be resolved as a means of discouraging cruise passengers from pursuing legitimate claims. Any suggestion of such a bad-faith motive is belied by two facts: Petitioner has its principal place of business in Florida, and many of its cruises depart from and return to Florida ports. Similarly, there is no evidence that petitioner obtained respondents' accession to the forum clause by fraud or overreaching. Finally, respondents have conceded that they were given notice of the forum provision and, therefore, presumably retained the option of rejecting the contract with impunity. In the case before us, therefore, we conclude that the Court of Appeals erred in refusing to enforce the forum-selection clause.

[The Court then rejected the respondents' argument based on the Limitation of Vessel Owner's Liability Act.]

The judgment of the Court of Appeals is reversed.

Justice STEVENS, with whom Justice MARSHALL joins, dissenting.

The court prefaces its legal analysis with a factual statement that implies that a purchaser of a Carnival Cruise Lines passenger ticket is fully and fairly notified about the existence of the choice of forum clause in the fine print on the back of the ticket. Even if this implication were accurate, I would disagree with the Court's analysis. But, given the Court's preface, I begin my dissent by noting that only the most meticulous passenger is likely to become aware of the forum-selection provision. I have therefore appended to this opinion a facsimile of the relevant text, using the type size that actually appears in the ticket itself. A careful reader will find the forum-selection clause in the 8th of the 25 numbered paragraphs.

Of course, many passengers, like the respondents in this case, will not have an opportunity to read paragraph 8 until they have actually purchased their tickets. By this point, the passengers will already have accepted the condition set forth in paragraph 16(a), which provides that "[t]he Carrier shall not be liable to make any refund to passengers in respect of . . . tickets wholly or partly not used by a passenger." Not knowing whether or not that provision is legally enforceable, I assume that the average passenger would accept the risk of having to file suit in Florida in the event of an injury, rather than canceling—without a refund—a planned vacation at the last minute. The fact that the cruise line can reduce its litigation costs, and therefore its liability insurance premiums, by forcing this choice on its passengers does not, in my opinion, suffice to render the provision reasonable. *Cf.* Steven v. Fidelity & Casualty Co. of New York, 58 Cal. 2d 862, 883 (1962) (refusing to enforce limitation on liability in insurance policy because insured "must purchase the policy before he even knows its provisions").

Forum-selection clauses in passenger tickets involve the intersection of two strands of traditional contract law that qualify the general rule that courts will enforce the terms of a contract as written. Pursuant to the first strand, courts traditionally have reviewed with heightened scrutiny the terms of contracts of adhesion, form contracts offered on a take-or-leave basis by a party with stronger bargaining power to a party with weaker power. Some commentators have questioned whether contracts of adhesion can justifiably be enforced at all under traditional contract theory because the adhering party generally enters into them without manifesting knowing and voluntary consent to all their terms. *See, e.g.,* Rakoff, *Contracts of Adhesion: An Essay in Reconstruction,* 96 Harv. L. Rev. 1173, 1179-1180 (1983); Slawson, *Mass Contracts: Lawful Fraud in California,* 48 S. Cal. L. Rev. 1, 12-13 (1974); K. Llewellyn, *The Common Law Tradition* 370-371 (1960).

The common law, recognizing that standardized form contracts account for a significant portion of all commercial agreements, has taken a less extreme position and instead subjects terms in contracts of adhesion to scrutiny for reasonableness. Judge J. Skelly Wright set out the state of the law succinctly in Williams v. Walker-Thomas Furniture Co., 350 F.2d 445, 449-450 (1965) (footnotes omitted):

> Ordinarily, one who signs an agreement without full knowledge of its terms might be held to assume the risk that he has entered a one-sided bargain. But when a party of little bargaining power, and hence little real choice, signs a commercially unreasonable contract with little or no knowledge of its terms, it is hardly likely that his consent, or even an objective manifestation of his consent, was ever given to all of the terms. In such a case the usual rule that the terms of the agreement are not to be questioned should be abandoned and the court should consider whether the terms of the contract are so unfair that enforcement should be withheld.

See also Steven, 58 Cal. 2d, at 879-883; Henningsen v. Bloomfield Motors, Inc., 32 N.J. 358 (1960).

The second doctrinal principle implicated by forum-selection clauses is the traditional rule that "contractual provisions, which seek to limit the place or court in which an action may . . . be brought, are invalid as contrary to public policy." *See* Dougherty, *Validity of Contractual Provision Limiting Place or Court in Which Action May Be Brought,* 31 A.L.R. 4th 404, 409, §3 (1984). *See also* Home Insurance Co. v. Morse, 20 Wall. 445, 451 (1874). Although adherence to this general rule has declined in recent years, particularly following our decision in *The Bremen,* the prevailing rule is still that forum-selection clauses are not enforceable if they were not freely bargained for, create additional expense for one party, or deny one party a remedy. *See* 31 A.L.R. 4th, at 409-438 (citing cases). A forum-selection clause in a standardized passenger ticket would clearly have been unenforceable under the common law before our decision in *The Bremen*, *see* 407 U.S., at 9, and n.10, and, in my opinion, remains unenforceable under the prevailing rule today.

The Bremen, which the Court effectively treats as controlling this case, had nothing to say about stipulations printed on the back of passenger tickets. That case involved the enforceability of a forum-selection clause in a freely negotiated international agreement between two large corporations providing for the towage of a vessel from the Gulf of Mexico to the Adriatic Sea. The Court recognized that such towage agreements had generally been held unenforceable in American courts but held that the doctrine of those cases did not extend to commercial arrangements between parties with equal bargaining power.

Questions and Comments

(1) Isn't what's really at stake in *The Bremen* the enforceability of the contractual clauses exculpating Unterweser from liability for damages? What does this suggest about the relationship between choice-of-forum clauses and choice of law? What about Justice Douglas's argument that if a contractual term would be unenforceable in a U.S. court but enforceable in a London court, the parties should not be allowed to evade the application of U.S. law by litigating in London? Note that in all federal circuits that have considered the issue, English forum-selection and choice-of-law clauses in contracts between Lloyd's of London and American names were deemed enforceable despite explicit provisions in the U.S. securities laws forbidding parties from contractually waiving their rights under the Acts. *See* Lipcon v. Underwriters at Lloyd's, London, 148 F.3d 1285 (11th Cir. 1998) (discussing cases).

(2) In the context of interstate and international commerce, it can be very useful for parties to designate the place where their disputes will be resolved. As will be seen in the next section, contracting parties have very broad ability to contract for the arbitration of their disputes. Once parties can circumvent courts altogether, it seems less troublesome to allow them to stay in court but choose the forum. Perhaps this helps explain why the Supreme Court has so strongly endorsed the enforcement of choice-of-court clauses. Many of the states have followed suit.

(3) In addition, the Hague Convention on Choice of Court Agreements, adopted in 2005, calls for worldwide enforcement of choice-of-forum clauses as well as of the judgments rendered by courts selected in the parties' contracts, subject to public policy exceptions. The Convention would not apply to consumer or employment contracts, and other subject matters are similarly excluded. But for international commercial entities, it would facilitate both court choice and judgment enforcement. As of publication of this edition, Mexico, the European Union, Denmark, the United Kingdom, Singapore, and Montenegro have ratified the Convention, and both the United States and China have signed but not yet ratified the Convention. For analyses of how the Hague Convention might affect or be affected by litigation in U.S. courts, *see* Woodward, *Saving the Hague Choice of Court Convention*, 29 U. Pa. J. Intl. L. 657 (2008); Heiser, *The Hague Convention on Choice of Court Agreements*, 31 U. Pa. J. Intl. L. 1013 (2010).

(4) In support of its holding, *The Bremen* makes much of the fact that the choice-of-forum clause was negotiated at arm's length. *Carnival Cruise*, by

contrast, suggests that this factor is not particularly important. Which view is right? The dissent in *Carnival Cruise* is suspicious of contract clauses that are not individually bargained for. But isn't the price term of this sort of contract often presented on a "take it or leave it" basis? The buyer can shop around for a better price, as he or she can shop for a cruise line without forum-selection clauses, but in many cases does not bargain with a particular seller for either a price reduction or for omitting the clause. Is there a meaningful distinction between these two types of contract provisions?

(5) The majority in *Carnival Cruise* suggests that it need not consider the claim that the Shutes did not have adequate notice of the provision because the notice issue had been conceded by the Shute's brief. What would the majority do in cases in which the consumer did not see the fine print in time? *Compare* Oxman v. Amoroso, 659 N.Y.S.2d 963, 967 (City Ct. 1997) (forum-selection and choice-of-law clauses unenforceable because written in small and undistinguishable print unfit for consumer transactions) *with* Cross v. Kloster Cruise Lines, 897 F. Supp. 1304 (D. Or. 1995) (forum-selection clause on ticket enforceable despite being in very fine print with smudged pages since the plaintiff admitted that she noticed provision and demonstrated her ability to do so on the record).

Does a party even need to view a forum-selection clause for it to be binding? The Seventh Circuit thought not in Hill v. Gateway 2000, 105 F.3d 1147 (7th Cir. 1997), a case involving the enforceability of an arbitration agreement contained in the Statement of Terms that accompanied a computer ordered by telephone. The plaintiffs saw the Statement of Terms but never read them closely and never laid eyes on the arbitration agreement. Writing for the court, Judge Easterbrook reasoned:

> A contract need not be read to be effective; people who accept [the computer] take the risk that the unread terms may in retrospect prove unwelcome. Terms inside Gateway's box stand or fall together. If they constitute the parties' contract because the Hills had an opportunity to return the computer after reading them, then all must be enforced. . . . Payment preceding the revelation of full terms is common for air transportation, insurance, and many other endeavors. Practical considerations support allowing vendors to enclose the full legal terms with their products. Cashiers cannot be expected to read legal documents to customers before ringing up sales. If the staff at the other end of the phone for direct-sales operations such as Gateway's had to read the four-page statement of terms before taking the buyer's credit card number, the droning voice would anesthetize rather than enlighten many potential buyers. Others would hang up in a rage over the waste of their time. And oral recitation would not avoid customers' assertions (whether true or feigned) that the clerk did not read term X to them, or that they did not remember or understand it. Writing provides benefits for both sides of commercial transactions. Customers as a group are better off when vendors skip costly and ineffectual steps such as telephonic recitation, and use instead a simple approve-or-return device. Competent adults are bound by such documents, read or unread.

Id. at 1148-1149. Is this reasoning persuasive? Does it apply to court choice-of-forum clauses in addition to arbitration agreements? Is it consistent with *Carnival Cruise*? Does the answer depend on whether the parties bound by the clause had the opportunity to cancel the contract without penalty? *Compare* Johnson v. Holland America Line-Westours, Inc., 206 Wis. 2d 562, 572 (Ct. App. 1996) (forum-selection clause not enforceable since plaintiffs received cruise tickets less than 45 days before departure and would have forfeited half of purchase price if they had thereafter canceled their trip); Corna v. American Hawaii Cruises, Inc., 794 F. Supp. 1005, 1012 (D. Haw. 1992) (refusing to enforce forum-selection clause where plaintiffs had no opportunity to reject the forum-selection clause without forfeiture of purchase price and additional penalties).

(6) *Carnival Cruise* also declined to consider the claim that the Shutes were unable to sue in Florida because the claim was supported by an inadequate factual record. What if it is prohibitively expensive or otherwise very inconvenient for parties to travel to the selected forum? Consider Sudduth v. Occidental Peruana, Inc., 70 F. Supp. 2d 691 (E.D. Tex. as 1999), a lawsuit in the United States between U.S. employees and their U.S. employer for unpaid benefits under a contract for work in the Peruvian jungle. The court declined to enforce the Peruvian forum-selection clause in the contract, reasoning:

> The Defendants provided transportation to and from the foreign country and were fully aware that the only contact the Plaintiffs had with the forum was the completion of the project. All material facts and witnesses are located in the United States. The contracts were mailed from California to Texas and Louisiana, a majority of the documents were signed in Texas, and the breach of contract occurred when the correct salary due was not placed in the Plaintiffs' bank accounts. In addition: the Plaintiffs' employment was initially sought within the United States; Plaintiffs worked in Peru for a limited time period; salaries were paid by United States banks; transportation to and from South America was paid by the Defendants; and an inconvenient forum was surreptitiously chosen by the Defendant. This Court holds the Plaintiffs will be "deprived of their day in court" because of the grave inconvenience and unfairness in the enforcement of the forum selection clause. The inconvenience of trying this case extends past the difficulties in travel. Plaintiffs' financial status and failing health require that the case should be tried in the Eastern District of Texas. . . . In addition, there is evidence that six of the eight Plaintiffs cannot afford the cost of travel to Peru, the expense of a trial in Peru, and the heavy burden of requiring a translator to translate communications between the Peruvian attorney and at the trial proceedings. The enforcement of the forum selection clause would be unfair because it would require every American party to travel to a foreign country to litigate an essentially local dispute.

Id. at 696-697. Is this reasoning consistent with *Carnival Cruise*? Should physical or financial inability to travel to the selected forum be a defense to the forum-selection clause's enforcement? Does the court here mistakenly view its inquiry as whether the selected forum is the most convenient? Or is it performing a "fundamental fairness" analysis? For a different view of the relevance of convenience and expense to the enforcement of forum-selection clauses, *see* Design Strategy Corp. v. Nghiem, 14 F. Supp. 2d 298 (S.D.N.Y. 1998).

(7) Much of the commentary on *Carnival Cruise* has been critical. *See, e.g.*, Borchers, *Forum Selection Agreements in the Federal Courts After Carnival Cruise: A Proposal for Congressional Reform*, 67 Wash. L. Rev. 55

(1992); Mullenix, *Another Easy Case, Some More Bad Law: Carnival Cruise Lines and Contractual Personal Jurisdiction*, 27 Tex. Intl. L.J. 323 (1992); Purcell, *Geography as a Litigation Weapon: Consumers, Forum-Selection Clauses and the Rehnquist Court*, 40 UCLA L. Rev. 423 (1992). This commentary focuses on the unfairness to the Shutes of being required to litigate in a distant forum against a wealthy corporation. Scholars have also attacked the Court's economic analysis: "The [forum-selection clause] is not negotiated, the specific market is noncompetitive, the issue of forum choice is of trivial importance to an individual passenger ex ante, and the unadvised passenger cannot be expected to assign a suitable value to the clause; hence, the savings resulting from the enforcement of the clause went straight to the bottom line of Carnival Lines." Carrington & Haagen, *Contract and Jurisdiction*, 1996 Sup. Ct. Rev. 331, 356.

A more sympathetic view of *Carnival Cruise* can be found in Solimine, *Forum-Selection Clauses and the Privatization of Procedure*, 25 Cornell Intl. L.J. 51 (1992). Solimine downplays the lack of bargaining power of purchasers, points out that form contracts reduce transaction costs, and notes that some studies show that Americans do not like bargaining; he additionally notes that the Shutes likely can retain Florida counsel without much difficulty. *Id.* at 83-84 & n.201.

Judge Posner takes an intermediate position:

> Why might a court be more suspicious of a forum selection clause contained in a contract than of the contract itself? There are two reasons, one bad, one good. The bad reason is that courts used to look askance at agreements to "oust" their jurisdiction. . . . All this nonsense was swept away by *Bremen*.
>
> Yet there really is something special about forum selection clauses after all. They could interfere with the orderly allocation of judicial business and injure other third-party interests (that is, interests of persons other than the parties to the contract containing the clause) as well. Suppose, to take an extreme but illustrative example, that the state and federal courts in Alaska became immensely popular forums for litigating contract disputes and as a result thousands of contracts were signed designating Alaska as the forum in the event of suit. Not only would these clauses impose great burdens on the courts in Alaska; they would impose great burdens on witnesses who were not employees of the parties (the inconvenience to employees would have been taken into account when the clause was drafted). The burdens on the Alaska courts would include not only the obvious ones but also the difficulty of having always to be applying other states' laws, one of the considerations that has been thought to justify limiting parties' power to specify by contract the law to be applied to their dispute if one arises. Restatement (Second) of Conflict of Laws §187(2)(a).
>
> [T]he only good reason for treating a forum-selection clause differently from any other contract (specifically, from the contract in which the clause appears) is the possibility of adverse effects on third parties. Where that possibility is slight, the clause should be treated like any other contract. What is more, if any inconvenience to third parties can be cured by a change of venue under section 1404(a), that is the route to follow, rather than striking down the clause. This approach enables a clean separation between issues of general contract validity and the third-party consequences which alone justify treating the validity of a forum-selection clause differently from that of the contract that contains it.

Northwestern Natl. Ins. Co. v. Donovan, 916 F.2d 372, 376 (7th Cir 1990); *see also id*. ("If ever there was a case for stretching the concept of fraud in the name of unconscionability, it was *Shute*; and perhaps no stretch was necessary.").

(8) In Smith, Valentino, & Smith, Inc. v. Superior Court, 17 Cal. 3d 491 (1976), the parties had agreed to a more interesting version of a forum-selecting and forum-ousting provision. The contract between a Pennsylvania corporation and a California corporation appointed as its agent for various purposes provided that if the California party brought suit it must be in Philadelphia, and if the Pennsylvania party brought suit it had to be in Los Angeles. The California party brought suit in California, and the Supreme Court of California refused to set aside an order of the lower court staying the proceedings. The court found nothing against public policy in such an agreement.

(9) The Supreme Court has held that denials of dismissal motions based on contractual forum-selection clauses are not immediately appealable in federal court. Lauro Lines s.r.l. v. Chasser, 490 U.S. 495 (1989) (no immediate appeal). The case involved a suit arising out of the hijacking of the Achille Lauro, and the District Court had refused to enforce the clause because the ticket gave insufficient notice to passengers that they were waiving their opportunity to sue in a domestic forum. State courts often do permit appeals when the trial court refuses to enforce a choice-of-court clause. *See, e.g.*, In re Autonation, Inc., 228 S.W.3d 663 (Tex. 2007) (permitting appeal by writ of mandamus); Ex parte Textron, Inc., 2011 WL 118255 (Ala. 2011); Bernstein v. Wysoki, 77 A.D.3d 241 (N.Y. App. Div. 2010) (permitting immediate appeal).

America Online, Inc. v. Superior Court of Alameda County

90 Cal. App. 4th 1, 108 Cal. Rptr. 2d 699 (1st App. Cal. 2001)

RUVOLO, J.

[This is a class action filed by former subscribers to America Online, Inc. ("AOL"), a Virginia Internet access provider, alleging that AOL continued to debit the class plaintiffs' credit cards for monthly service fees after termination of plaintiffs' AOL subscription. The complaint alleged violations of California's Unfair Business Practices Act, Bus. & Prof. Code, §§17200 et seq., California's CLRA, common law conversion/trespass, and common law fraud. AOL filed a motion to dismiss based on a forum-selection clause contained in AOL's online "Terms of Service" (TOS) agreement. Paragraph 8 of the TOS, entitled "LAW AND LEGAL NOTICES," states:

> You expressly agree that exclusive jurisdiction for any claim or dispute with AOL or relating in any way to your membership or your use of AOL resides in the courts of Virginia and you further agree and expressly consent to the exercise of personal jurisdiction in the courts of Virginia in connection with any such dispute including any claim involving AOL or its affiliates, subsidiaries, employees, contractors, officers, directors, telecommunications providers and content providers. . . .

Additionally, paragraph 8 contained a choice-of-law provision designating Virginia law as being applicable to any dispute between the parties: "The laws of the Commonwealth of Virginia, excluding its conflicts-of-law rules, govern this Agreement and your membership." The lead plaintiff described the TOS provision on his home computer as a "densely worded, small-size text that was hard to read on the computer screen." The district court rejected AOL's motion to dismiss, and AOL filed this petition for writ of mandamus. After holding that AOL had the burden of proof on the enforceability of the forum-selection clause, the court turned to consider the enforcement issue.]

III. . . .

B.   OVERVIEW OF FORUM SELECTION CLAUSE ENFORCEMENT

AOL correctly posits that California favors contractual forum selection clauses so long as they are entered into freely and voluntarily, and their enforcement would not be unreasonable. This favorable treatment is attributed to our law's devotion to the concept of one's free right to contract, and flows from the important practical effect such contractual rights have on commerce generally.

We agree with these sentiments, and view such clauses as likely to become even more ubiquitous as this state and nation become acculturated to electronic commerce. Moreover, there are strong economic arguments in support of these agreements, favoring both merchants and consumers, including reduction in the costs of goods and services and the stimulation of e-commerce.

But this encomium is not boundless. Our law favors forum selection agreements only so long as they are procured freely and voluntarily, with the place chosen having some logical nexus to one of the parties or the dispute, and so long as California consumers will not find their substantial legal rights significantly impaired by their enforcement. Therefore, to be enforceable, the selected jurisdiction must be "suitable," "available," and able to "accomplish substantial justice." [*The Bremen, supra* page 677.] The trial court determined that the circumstances of contract formation did not reflect Mendoza's exercised free will, and that the effect of enforcing the forum selection clause here would violate California public policy by eviscerating important legal rights afforded to this state's consumers.

C.   ENFORCEMENT OF THE FORUM SELECTION CLAUSE VIOLATES STRONG CALIFORNIA PUBLIC POLICY

California courts will refuse to defer to the selected forum if to do so would substantially diminish the rights of California residents in a way that violates our state's public policy. . . .

In Hall v. Superior Court, 150 Cal. App. 3d 411 (1983) (*Hall*), two California investors exchanged their interests in an oil and gas limited partnership in return for stock in one of their co-investors, Imperial Petroleum, Inc., a Utah corporation. Closer to the facts of this case, the contract embodying their exchange agreement contained *both* forum selection and choice of law provisions identifying Nevada as the selected forum and governing law. A dispute arose, and the two investors sued

Imperial in California. Imperial asserted the forum selection clause, and the trial court found the forum selection clause was enforceable.

In reversing the lower court's decision, the appellate court undertook an examination of both the choice of law clause as well as the forum selection clause noting that the enforceability of these clauses were "inextricably bound up" in one another. The reason for considering them together was that absent a choice of law clause, the selected forum could apply California law to the dispute under the selected forum's conflict of laws principles. If so, there would be no risk that substantive law might be employed which would materially diminish rights of California residents in violation of California public policy. However, where the effect of the transfer would be otherwise, the forum selection clause would not be enforced: "While California does not have any public policy against a choice of law provision, . . . an agreement designating [a foreign] law will not be given effect if it would violate a strong California public policy . . . [or] result in an evasion of . . . a statute of the forum protecting its citizens." *Id.* at 416-417.[6]

The *Hall* court determined that if the pending securities litigation were transferred to Nevada where Nevada law would be applied, the plaintiffs would lose the benefit of California's Corporate Securities Law of 1968 which would otherwise govern the transaction in question. This California law was designed to protect the public from fraud and deception in securities matters, by providing statutory remedies for violations of the California Corporations Code. For this reason, the remedial scheme, like the CRLA involved in this case, contains an anti-waiver provision. Corp. Code, §25701. The court concluded: "We believe the right of a buyer of securities in California to have California law and its concomitant nuances apply to any future dispute arising out of the transaction is a 'provision' within the meaning of [Corporations Code] section 25701 which cannot be waived or evaded by stipulation of the parties to a securities transaction. Consequently, we hold the choice of Nevada law provision in this agreement violates section 25701 and the public policy of this state [citation] and for that reason deny enforcement of the forum selection clause as unreasonable." Hall, *supra* at p.418.

The CLRA parallels the Corporate Securities Law of 1968, at issue in *Hall*, insofar as the CRLA is a legislative embodiment of a desire to protect California consumers and furthers a strong public policy of this state. . . . Certainly, the CLRA provides remedial protections *at least* as important as those under the Corporate Securities Law of 1968. Therefore, by parity of reasoning, enforcement of AOL's forum selection clause, which is also accompanied by a choice of law provision favoring Virginia, would necessitate a waiver of the statutory remedies of the CLRA, in violation of that law's anti-waiver provision, Civ. Code, §1751, and California public policy. For this reason alone, we affirm the trial court's ruling.

This conclusion is reinforced by a statutory comparison of California and Virginia consumer protection laws, which reveals Virginia's law provides

---

6. At oral argument, counsel for AOL suggested for the first time that a Virginia court might apply California's consumer protection law to resolve this dispute. Not only was this suggestion legally unsupported, but we find it counter-intuitive to believe that a Virginia court would invoke California law to resolve a contract-based consumer dispute against a Virginia domiciliary where the parties agreed to have Virginia law applied, and where Virginia has a statutory consumer protection law of its own.

significantly less consumer protection to its citizens than California law provides for our own. [The court notes that remedies under the Virginia law are less favorable to consumers than under California law, and that the Virginia law is hostile to class actions while class actions are an important consumer right under California law.] The unavailability of class action relief in this context is sufficient in and by itself to preclude enforcement of the TOS forum selection clause.

In addition to the unavailability of class actions and the apparent limitation in injunctive relief, neither punitive damages, nor enhanced remedies for disabled and senior citizens are recoverable under Virginia's law. More nuanced differences are the reduced recovery under the VCPA for "unintentional" acts, a shorter period of limitations, and Virginia's use of a Lodestar formula alone to calculate attorney fees recovery. Quite apart from the remedial limitations under Virginia law relating to injunctive and class action relief, the cumulative importance of even these less significant differences is substantial. Enforcement of a forum selection clause, which would impair these aggregate rights, would itself violate important California public policy. For this additional reason the trial court was correct in denying AOL's motion to stay or to dismiss.

In so holding we reject Mendoza's contention that the clause should not be enforced simply because it would be patently unreasonable to require him or other AOL customers who form the putative class to travel to Virginia to litigate the relatively nominal individual sums at issue. He points out that in 1998 and 1999, not a single suit by a non-Virginia resident appears to have been filed in AOL's Virginia home county, a development Mendoza suggests is directly related to the fact that the cost of prosecuting a claim in Virginia vastly exceeds the amounts normally at issue in individual claims against AOL.

But the additional cost or inconvenience necessitated by litigation in the selected forum is not part of the calculus when considering whether a forum selection clause should be enforced. . . . Yet Mendoza contends that [the California Supreme Court's] admonition not to consider convenience and cost in evaluating the validity of forum selection clauses applies only where there remains a "practical option [of travel to the selected forum] in terms of the expense and value of the controversy." As we understand it, Mendoza is arguing that expense in litigating in the selected forum can be considered if it exceeds the amount in controversy or at least renders the choice to litigate "impractical."

We disagree. . . . No case of which we are aware has interpreted this language as Mendoza suggests we should. Moreover, it is not at all clear what monetary amount was in dispute in that case, or whether it was "practical" to bring the litigation in the selected forum. Although the current dispute between Mendoza and AOL might make it impractical for Mendoza to pursue an individual claim in Virginia, there may be other potential disputes between Mendoza and AOL arising from their relationship which would have significantly greater value. Are we to parse the enforceability of the forum selection clause, then, based on the economic value of the particular claim in issue, so that the clause can be enforced some of the time (depending on the value of the claim), but not all of the time? If so, should trial courts use an objective standard, or consider the proclivities of the individual claimant who may not feel litigation in the selected forum is worth it? How should trial judges calculate the costs of litigation? Should they consider the extent to which the selected forum allows for the recovery of costs, including travel-related expenses? Should courts compute the extent to which extraordinary costs in enforcing contractual rights are included in the consideration paid for the goods or services purchased? . . . It was perhaps just such [concerns] that, in part, moved the Supreme Court to pronounce costs and convenience "[are] not the test of reasonableness [of forum selection clauses]."

Questions and Comments

(1) Because Internet communications and services can appear in literally every state and nation in the world, and because of the potential jurisdictional and choice-of-law confusion arising from these ubiquitous contacts, it is easy to understand why the companies providing such services insist on forum-selection clauses. But the ubiquity of contacts related to these services also raises the question whether consumers should have to litigate claims arising around the world from their use of the services in a single forum, especially when the value of the claims are often much less than the cost of travel to the distant forum. How should courts resolve this tension? Does the framework from *Carnival Cruise*, reproduced *supra* page 681, apply straightforwardly to the Internet context? What are the relevant differences between the forum-selection clauses at issue in *Carnival Cruise* and the one at issue in *America Online*?

(2) In *America Online*, it is unclear whether plaintiffs affirmatively consented to the AOL clause, or merely ran their eyes over the paragraph containing the clause as they clicked through pages of legal notices. Does affirmative consent to the clause matter to its enforcement? When you visit Internet portals and Web sites, the sponsoring entity routinely places choice-of-law and/or choice-of-forum clauses in the "terms of service" provisions accessible via a link at the bottom of the site's main page. Most users never actually view those terms. Should that matter for enforceability?

Recall the analysis in Hill v. Gateway 2000, 105 F.3d 1147 (7th Cir. 1997), discussed *supra* pages 688-689. A somewhat different view was expressed in Specht v. Netscape Communication Corp., 2001 U.S. Dist. LEXIS 2073 (2001), where the court held that an arbitration agreement contained in the unread License Agreement that accompanied downloaded Internet software was unenforceable. *Compare* Pollstar v. Gigmania Ltd., No. CIV-F-00-5671, 2000 WL 33266437 (E.D. Cal. 2000) (expressing concern about the enforceability of online "browse-wrap" license agreements).

What would happen to Internet activity if every user had to read and affirmatively consent to forum-selection clauses on every Web page visited?

(3) The real concern in *America Online* seems to be not forum selection, but rather governing law. Would the *America Online* court have enforced the forum-selection clause if AOL's Terms of Service chose a Virginia forum but California governing law? In fact, such choices are relatively rare. A study of merger agreements showed that, depending on the state, somewhere between 70 and 95 percent of agreements that chose both a governing law and a jurisdiction for resolving disputes chose the same state for both. Eisenberg & Miller, *Ex Ante Choices of Law and Forum: An Empirical Analysis of Corporate Merger Agreements*, 59 Vand.

L. Rev. 1975, 2007 (2006). What does this suggest about the relationship between forum-selection clauses and choice-of-law clauses?

(4) *America Online* says the forum-selection clause must have "some logical connection to one of the parties or the dispute." *Compare* Restatement (Second) Conflict of Laws §187(2)(a) (1971) (*law* chosen by parties governs unless "the chosen state has no substantial relationship to the parties or the transaction and there is no other reasonable basis for the parties' choice"). Virginia is presumably such a logical choice because it is the headquarters of AOL and the location of most of AOL's computer servers. In cases involving portals and related services that can be accessed on a worldwide basis, is every forum a logical choice? Is the defendant's headquarters the only logical choice? Do criteria of "logical choice" and "substantial relationship" make sense as applied to the Internet?

(5) Many have proposed that the controversies that arise out of the Internet are best resolved not by courts, but by a variety of private dispute resolution mechanisms due to the worldwide nature of the activity and its common use by individuals and small entities. For a nice summary of this viewpoint, *see* Perritt, *Dispute Resolution in Cyberspace: Demand for New Forms of ADR*, 15 Ohio St. J. on Disp. Resol. 675, 676 (2000). We consider the enforceability of private arbitration clauses in the next section.

Wong v. PartyGaming Ltd.

589 F.3d 821 (6th Cir. 2009)

Before: MERRITT, GIBBONS, and MCKEAGUE, Circuit Judges.

MCKEAGUE, J., delivered the opinion of the court.

Rose Wong and Patrick Gibson (together "plaintiffs") filed a lawsuit on behalf of themselves and similarly situated Ohio residents against PartyGaming Ltd., a Gibraltar-based company which hosts online poker games. In the suit, plaintiffs alleged breach of contract, misrepresentation, and violation of Ohio consumer protection laws. PartyGaming moved to dismiss the suit pursuant to a forum selection clause in its terms and conditions, which plaintiffs had agreed to when they registered on the site. The forum selection clause specified that all disputes would be subject to the exclusive jurisdiction of the courts of Gibraltar. Plaintiffs appeal the district court's dismissal of the suit sua sponte for forum non conveniens. For the following reasons, we affirm the decision of the district court.

I

PartyGaming runs an online poker business, which plaintiffs actively participated in as players. It is a publicly owned Gibraltar company, with its shares traded on the London Stock Exchange. To participate in online poker games, customers must register on PartyGaming's website and agree to its "Terms and Conditions of Use." Two such terms and conditions are relevant to this suit. The first relevant term contains PartyGaming's anti-collusion policy, which states that customers are prohibited from holding more than one account and that PartyGaming is committed to preventing collusion and cheating. As part of its anti-collusion policy,

PartyGaming also provides information on its website regarding a "Collusion Prevention System" used to identify and ban colluding players and detect multi-account players. The Terms and Conditions also provide that the agreement shall be governed by the laws of Gibraltar and any disputes shall be subject to the exclusive jurisdiction of the courts of Gibraltar. The first paragraph of the Terms and Conditions of Use contains the following warning: "IMPORTANT—PLEASE READ THESE TERMS AND CONDITIONS CAREFULLY BEFORE ACCEPTING THIS AGREEMENT, THEN PRINT THESE TERMS AND CONDITIONS AND STORE THEM."

Plaintiffs . . . filed a diversity suit against PartyGaming in September 2006 in the Northern District of Ohio. The suit alleged that PartyGaming, through its anti-collusion policy, affirmatively represented that collusion and multi-account players did not occur on its website. The suit also claimed that PartyGaming affirmatively represented that it did not encourage gambling by minors or gambling addicts. Plaintiffs contended that these representations were false and, as such, violated Ohio consumer protection laws, breached the agreement, and negligently, recklessly, or intentionally induced plaintiffs to join the website. Plaintiffs sought certification of a class of all similarly situated individuals, which the district court provisionally certified, consisting of all persons in the state of Ohio who paid a registration fee on PartyGaming's website.[1]

. . . PartyGaming . . . filed a motion to dismiss plaintiffs' . . . complaint. The motion claimed improper venue under Federal Rules of Civil Procedure ("FRCP") 12(b)(3), due to the Gibraltar forum selection clause. . . . [T]he district court found the Gibraltar forum selection clause valid . . . and dismissed the action sua sponte for forum non conveniens.

II

To support its dismissal for forum non conveniens, the district court cited to the Gibraltar forum selection clause. Thus, as a threshold matter, we must determine whether the clause should be enforced. We review the enforceability of a forum selection clause de novo. In deciding this matter, we confront a choice-of-law issue of whether Ohio or federal law governs the inquiry into the enforceability of a forum selection clause when a federal court exercises diversity jurisdiction.

1. APPLICABLE LAW

To resolve this issue, we first look to the binding law of the Supreme Court and the law of this Circuit. In the context of admiralty cases, the Supreme Court has announced a federal policy favoring enforcement of forum selection clauses and has held that such clauses "should control absent a strong showing that [they] should be set aside." [*Shute, supra* page 681; *The Bremen, supra* page 677.] The

---

1. A motion to certify a class of citizens of twenty-three other states was pending before the district court when the dismissal was ordered.

Court has also stated that federal law governs the inquiry when a federal court, sitting in diversity, evaluates a forum selection clause in the context of a 28 U.S.C. §1404(a) motion to transfer venue or in the context of any federal statute. Stewart Org., Inc. v. Ricoh Corp., 487 U.S. 22 (1988). The Court has provided guidance in these two contexts, but it has declined to decide the *Erie* issue of which law governs when a federal court, sitting in diversity, evaluates a forum selection clause in the absence of a controlling federal statute. *Id.* The Sixth Circuit has also declined to answer this question. In the past, we have noted that we did not need to decide the issue because both federal and state law treat forum selection clauses similarly. While our past decisions have maintained harmony between federal and state courts on the issue, a review of recent state cases reveals the possible emergence of differences in how state and federal law treat the enforcement of forum selection clauses. Ohio state courts have also noted the differences between federal and state law on the enforceability of forum selection clauses.

Because this Circuit has not affirmatively decided which law governs when a federal court sits in diversity, we look to the law of other Circuits for guidance. In deciding this issue, six Circuits have held that the enforceability of a forum selection clause implicates federal procedure and should therefore be governed by federal law.[5] Both the Seventh and Tenth Circuits have held that the law which governs the contract as a whole also governs the enforceability of the forum selection clause. *See,* Abbott Labs. v. Takeda Pharms. Co., 476 F.3d 421, 423 (7th Cir. 2007) ("Simplicity argues for determining the validity . . . of a forum selection clause . . . by reference to the law of the jurisdiction whose law governs the rest of the contract. . . . "); Yavuz v. 61 MM, Ltd., 465 F.3d 418, 428 (10th Cir. 2006) ("We see no particular reason . . . why a forum-selection clause . . . should be singled out as a provision not to be interpreted in accordance with the law chosen by the contracting parties."). The First Circuit has not affirmatively decided the issue. Finally, different panels in the Fourth Circuit have reached different results on the issue.

Given the possibility of diverging state and federal law on an issue of great economic consequence, the risk of inconsistent decisions in diversity cases, and the strong federal interest in procedural matters in federal court, we find persuasive the law used in the majority of circuits and now adopt it. . . . [F]orum selection clauses significantly implicate federal procedural issues. Further, while we recognize that we are not bound by the law of other Circuits, this court has also routinely looked to the majority position of other Circuits in resolving undecided

---

5. *See, e.g.,* Fru-Con Constr. Corp. v. Controlled Air, Inc., 574 F.3d 527, 538 (8th Cir. 2009) ("[E]nforcement . . . of the contractual forum selection clause was a federal court procedural matter governed by federal law."); Doe 1 v. AOL LLC, 552 F.3d 1077, 1083 (9th Cir. 2009) ("We apply federal law to the interpretation of the forum selection clause."); Ginter ex rel. Ballard v. Belcher, Prendergast & Laporte, 536 F.3d 439, 441 (5th Cir. 2008) ("We begin with federal law, not state law, to determine the enforceability of a forum-selection clause."); Phillips v. Audio Active Ltd., 494 F.3d 378, 384 (2d Cir. 2007) ("[T]he rule set out in *M/S Bremen* applies to the question of enforceability of an apparently governing forum selection clause, irrespective of whether a claim arises under federal or state law."); P & S Bus. Machs. v. Canon USA, Inc., 331 F.3d 804, 807 (11th Cir. 2003) ("Consideration of whether to enforce a forum selection clause in diversity suit is governed by federal law. . . . "); Jumara v. State Farm Ins. Co., 55 F.3d 873, 877 (3d Cir. 1995) ("[T]he effect to be given a contractual forum selection clause in diversity cases is determined by federal not state law.").

issues of law. We therefore hold that in this diversity suit, the enforceability of the forum selection clause is governed by federal law. We now turn to the merits of the enforceability of the forum selection clause.

2. ENFORCEABILITY OF THE FORUM SELECTION CLAUSE

A forum selection clause should be upheld absent a strong showing that it should be set aside. *Shute*. When evaluating the enforceability of a forum selection clause, this court looks to the following factors: (1) whether the clause was obtained by fraud, duress, or other unconscionable means; (2) whether the designated forum would ineffectively or unfairly handle the suit; and (3) whether the designated forum would be so seriously inconvenient such that requiring the plaintiff to bring suit there would be unjust. The party opposing the forum selection clause bears the burden of showing that the clause should not be enforced.

Under the first factor, the party opposing the clause must show fraud in the inclusion of the clause itself. "General claims of fraud do not suffice to invalidate the forum selection clause." [citation omitted.] . . . [P]laintiffs argue that the Gibraltar forum selection clause was obtained by fraud because PartyGaming falsely represented that collusion and multi-account players did not occur on its website. In advancing this claim, plaintiffs argue general fraud only, rather than fraud in the inclusion of the clause itself. Plaintiffs do not allege that PartyGaming falsely represented the chosen forum. . . . Nor do they contend that their agreement to the forum selection clause was obtained unknowingly or unwillingly. Thus, plaintiffs have not shown the clause to be unenforceable under the first prong.

Under the second factor, plaintiffs must show that a Gibraltar court would ineffectively or unfairly handle the suit. Different or less favorable foreign law or procedure alone does not satisfy this prong. Rather, the foreign law must be such that a risk exists that the litigants will be denied any remedy or will be treated unfairly. Under this prong, we have previously enforced forum selection clauses that specified an English forum, a German forum, and a Brazilian forum. . . .

In the present case, both parties agree that Gibraltar, as a British territory, is governed by English law. Plaintiffs contend that Gibraltar would not be an adequate forum because (1) Gibraltar does not allow jury trials and (2) Gibraltar does not allow class-action suits for damages. As to plaintiffs' first claim, this argument ignores our precedent upholding an alternative forum even when jury trials were unavailable. Further, almost all non-U.S. forums would be inadequate under plaintiffs' argument because few countries outside of the United States offer jury trials in civil cases. Finally, other Circuits have held that lack of jury trials does not render a forum inadequate. *See, e.g.*, Rivera v. Centro Medico de Turabo, Inc., 575 F.3d 10, 23-24 (1st Cir. 2009); Lockman Found. v. Evangelical Alliance Mission, 930 F.2d 764, 768 (9th Cir. 1991). Thus, plaintiffs' first argument lacks merit.

Turning to the second argument, plaintiffs offer a statement from an English lawyer and cite English case law to support their claim that Gibraltar does not allow class-action suits for damages. PartyGaming counters with its own expert statement and case citation, claiming that the suit could be maintained in class-action form. Fortunately, we need not decide whether a suit could be maintained in class form in Gibraltar because, even assuming that plaintiffs are correct, the unavailability of representative litigation would not render the forum ineffective. "The fact that parties will have to structure their case differently than if they were litigating in federal court is not a sufficient reason to defeat a forum selection clause." Plaintiffs have not alleged that they *could not* bring the suit in Gibraltar, but only that they could not bring it in class form. Thus, they have not shown that Gibraltar would be an ineffective or unfair forum.

To meet the third prong of our test, the plaintiff must show that enforcement of the clause would be so inconvenient such that its enforcement would be unjust or unreasonable. This finding must be based on more than mere inconvenience of the party seeking to avoid the clause. We have previously held that enforcement of a forum selection clause would not be unreasonable where the opposing party failed to produce any evidence that it was exploited or unfairly treated. Further, the Supreme Court has held that a forum selection clause is not unreasonable simply because it appears in a non-negotiated consumer contract. *Shute.* In this case, plaintiffs are not sophisticated business entities with the ability to negotiate the forum, and continuing the suit in Gibraltar would no doubt be an inconvenience. Yet even with these considerations, plaintiffs have not carried their "heavy burden" of showing that enforcing this forum selection clause would be unjust or unreasonable. *See id.* Aside from their claims that a Gibraltar forum forecloses the possibility of a jury trial or class-action suit, plaintiffs have failed to show how litigating in Gibraltar would be such an inconvenient forum to yield it unjust or unreasonable. We therefore affirm the district court's conclusion that the forum selection clause is enforceable. We now turn to the district court's dismissal for forum non conveniens.

III

This court reviews a district court's dismissal for forum non conveniens for an abuse of discretion. Forum non conveniens is a flexible doctrine. When a district court weighs the relevant factors, its decision deserves substantial deference. In weighing these factors, the district court must first establish an adequate alternative forum. Then, the court must weigh the relevant public and private factors. The court should also give deference to the plaintiff's choice of home forum.

At the outset, we address the district court's sua sponte dismissal for forum non conveniens. Plaintiffs argue that the dismissal amounted to an abuse of discretion because the district court raised forum non conveniens sua sponte. Plaintiffs claim that the district court was not properly briefed on the relevant forum non conveniens factors because the court was evaluating a motion to dismiss for improper venue under FRCP 12(b)(3), rather than a motion to dismiss for forum non conveniens. . . . The doctrine falls within the court's inherent authority. So long as the district court has "facts relevant to the issue of forum non conveniens," it can raise the doctrine on its own accord. In this case, the court had pending before it PartyGaming's motion to dismiss for improper venue. Given that forum non conveniens is simply "a supervening venue provision," facts relevant to the motion to dismiss for improper venue would also be relevant to the forum non conveniens analysis. . . . We now turn to the district court's forum non conveniens analysis.

1. Adequate Alternative Forum

Under the first part of the analysis, an adequate alternative forum must be identified. This requirement will be satisfied if the defendant is "amenable to process" in the foreign jurisdiction. Piper Aircraft Co. v. Reyno, 454 U.S. 235, 255 n.22 (1981). An alternative forum is inadequate if "the remedy provided by [it] is so clearly inadequate or unsatisfactory that it is no remedy at all." *Id*. Less favorable law in the alternative forum will not, on its own, make the forum inadequate. In this case, the district court determined that Gibraltar was an appropriate alternative forum. Plaintiffs argue that this finding was an abuse of discretion because (1) the district court did not determine whether PartyGaming was amenable to process in Gibraltar, and (2) the district court did not consider their claim that they could not maintain their suit in class form. . . .

. . . Plaintiffs . . . correctly note that the district court in this case did not make a specific finding on whether PartyGaming is amenable to process in Gibraltar. However, their argument fails to show an abuse of discretion because this case presents no real question of whether PartyGaming is amenable to process in Gibraltar. PartyGaming consented to submit itself to the jurisdiction of Gibraltar with the forum selection clause and, thus, is amenable to process there. Further, the district court found that PartyGaming is a Gibraltar corporation, with its principal place of business in Gibraltar. This finding also indicates that PartyGaming is amenable to process there. Thus, plaintiffs have failed to show an abuse of discretion on this issue.

In their second claim, plaintiffs argue that the district court abused its discretion by failing to consider their expert's opinion that they could not maintain a class-action suit in Gibraltar. While the district court did not make a specific finding on plaintiffs' expert, it did acknowledge, and ultimately rejected, plaintiffs' claim that they could not bring the suit in class form. Further, even assuming that plaintiffs correctly characterize Gibraltar law, the inability to bring a class suit would not render Gibraltar an inadequate alternative forum. In *Piper Aircraft*, the Supreme Court noted that the alternative forum had to be so inadequate such that "no remedy at all" was available. "[D]ismissal on the grounds of forum non conveniens may be granted even though the law applicable in the alternative forum is less favorable to the plaintiff's chance of recovery." *Id*. Thus, the district court did not abuse its discretion in finding Gibraltar to be an adequate alternative forum.

2. Public Factors

After the district court determines that an adequate alternative forum exists, it must weigh the relevant public and private factors in favor of a different forum. The public factors include court congestion, local interest in the matter, interest in having the trial at home with the law that governs, avoidance of conflict-of-law problems or application of foreign law, and unfairness in burdening local citizens with jury duty. In this case, the district court found that public factors weighed in favor of a Gibraltar trial because PartyGaming is a Gibraltar company, whose operations might be greatly affected by the suit, and other Gibraltar gaming companies might be affected by the suit. The district court further found that Gibraltar law would govern the suit, due to the choice-of-law clause, and Gibraltar had an interest in hearing "a case involving a substantial player in [its] comparatively small economy."

In claiming an abuse of discretion, plaintiffs cite Ohio's interest in having its consumer protection laws enforced and claim that the district court did not separately analyze the choice-of-law provision to determine its enforceability. While Ohio might have an interest in this matter, this court has held, and the district court noted, that when state law conflicts with a forum selection clause, the court should not categorically uphold the state policy over the clause. . . . Further, Ohio has no interest in the laws of the twenty-three other states over which plaintiffs seek class certification. But Gibraltar would have an interest over the entire suit.

In their second argument, plaintiffs claim that the district court abused its discretion by finding that Gibraltar law governs without separately evaluating the enforceability of the choice-of-law clause under Ohio law. Plaintiffs argued in the district court that the Gibraltar choice-of-law provision was not enforceable because Ohio has significantly greater interest in the case. In response, the district court simply stated "it is clear from the governing law clause that Gibraltar law should be applied." To begin with, it is not clear from our case law whether the district court was required to separately conduct a choice-of-law analysis for forum non conveniens purposes.

Further, the choice-of-law clause was only one public factor advanced by the district court for its decision. The court's decision is also supported by its finding that Gibraltar has an interest in the litigation. *See Piper Aircraft* (noting that other public interest factors weighed in favor of a Scotland trial even if the district court improperly found Scottish law applied). Finally, plaintiff's argument that Ohio has a significantly greater interest in the matter would not, on its own, render the choice-of-law provision unenforceable. Thus, we conclude that the district court did not abuse its discretion in finding that public factors weigh in favor of a Gibraltar forum.

3.   PRIVATE FACTORS

In weighing private factors, the district court should consider the ease of access to evidence, ability to obtain witness attendance, and practical problems such as ease, expeditiousness, and expense. In this case, the district court found that private factors weighed in favor of a Gibraltar forum because relevant evidence and witnesses would be located there. The court further found that plaintiffs would not encounter many obstacles litigating in Gibraltar. Finally, the district court advanced the forum selection clause as a private factor weighing in favor of a Gibraltar forum. Plaintiffs claim that this was an abuse of discretion because nothing in the record indicates that relevant witnesses and documents are located in Gibraltar and modern technology makes close proximity to evidence unnecessary. We agree with plaintiffs that the district court was not fully briefed on the location of possible evidence and witnesses. However, this represented only one factor used by the district court in its determination that private factors weighed in favor of a Gibraltar forum. Even if the district court erred in this finding, the Gibraltar forum selection clause weighs strongly as a private factor given our policy favoring enforcement of these clauses.

See The Bremen. Thus, we conclude that the district court did not abuse its discretion in finding that private factors weigh in favor of Gibraltar.

4. DEFERENCE TO PLAINTIFFS' CHOICE OF FORUM

Finally, plaintiffs argue that the district court abused its discretion because it did not give proper deference to their choice of a home forum. . . . While deference should be afforded to a U.S. plaintiff's choice of home forum, choice of home forum is not a dispositive issue. . . . When dismissing for forum non conveniens pursuant to a forum selection clause, federal courts have generally given less deference to a plaintiff's choice of home forum. *See, e.g.,* Evolution Online Sys., Inc. v. Koninklijke PTT Nederland N.V., 145 F.3d 505, 511 (2d Cir. 1998) ("[T]he district court would begin its forum non conveniens assessment of *Gulf Oil* factors with a level set of balances, rather than one weighted heavily in favor of plaintiff's choice of forum."); Jumara v. State Farm Ins. Co., 55 F.3d 873, 880 (3d Cir. 1995) ("[W]hile courts normally defer to a plaintiff's choice of forum, such deference is inappropriate where the plaintiff has already freely contractually chosen an appropriate venue."); In re Ricoh Corp., 870 F.2d 570, 573 (11th Cir. 1989) ("[W]e see no reason why a court should accord deference to the forum in which the plaintiff filed its action."). Thus, the district court did not abuse its discretion by not giving deference to plaintiffs' choice of home forum.

IV

For the foregoing reasons, we affirm the decision of the district court.

MERRITT, J., concurring.

I concur in much of the reasoning of the court, if we look at the problem in a purely legalistic way. But for me the most important considerations are not the splits in the circuits or the ambiguities inherit in the existing law on forum selection clauses, but rather the fact that the gambling contract entered into between the parties here is likely illegal in Ohio but completely legal in Gibraltar. If we read Ohio law as controlling the contract in question, the parties probably are guilty of a crime under Ohio law, the contract is void, and both parties could be extradited and prosecuted together in an Ohio criminal court.[1]

Surely the parties assumed that if the plaintiff won at gambling, the plaintiff would get some money and if the plaintiff lost, the winner and the house would split the winnings. So when the plaintiff comes into court and says he wants money in an Ohio court under what he regards as an Ohio contract, but does not want

---

1. *See* Ohio Rev. Code Ann. §2915.02(A) (2003) (prohibiting any person from engaging in "conduct that facilitates any game of chance conducted for profit" or "engag[ing] in betting or in playing any scheme or game of chance as a substantial source of income or livelihood"); Ohio Rev. Code Ann. §2915.01(D) (2003) (defining poker as a game of chance); Ohio Rev. Code Ann. §3763.01 (2003) (gaming contracts void).

the Ohio court to say that under the governing Ohio law the gambling contract is illegal, the plaintiff is a bit inconsistent in his logic, to say the least.

This illegality factor is particularly salient because the defendant now reports that it has completely stopped carrying on its online gambling business in Ohio and in the United States because Congress recently passed a criminal statute outlawing this kind of internet gambling. *See* Unlawful Internet Gambling Enforcement Act (UIGEA) of 2006, 31 U.S.C. §§5361-5367 (effective October 13, 2006).

Obviously, neither the plaintiff nor the defendant's employees want to go to jail in Ohio. On a principle analogous to the rule of lenity I would interpret the forum selection clause as controlled by English law which, so far as I can tell, is the only way to keep the contract from being void and subject to criminal penalties. It also reduces the risk that the plaintiff and others will go to jail under Ohio law or even under the Federal Wire Act or RICO.[3]

Now, of course, the parties have not raised this point. Neither wants to admit the existence of any criminal law problem with their activities. But sometimes courts have to raise embarrassing questions that both parties to litigation had rather we overlooked.

Questions and Comments

(1) The *America Online* and *Wong* courts come to very different conclusions regarding the reasonableness of the forum-selection clauses in consumer contracts entered into online. What accounts for these different attitudes? Does Judge Merritt's concurrence help provide an answer?

(2) How much difference must there be between forum law and procedure and the chosen law and procedure before a court justifiably refuses to enforce a forum-selection clause? Must it be impossible for the plaintiff to bring a viable claim in the chosen forum before the court strikes the clause? The *America Online* and *Wong* courts appear to answer this question differently. Should this analysis turn on whether the contract involves consumers or two sophisticated contracting parties? On the likelihood that the complaining party actually saw the forum-selection clause? On something else?

(3) Might the difference in court attitude toward the forum-selection clauses have anything to do with the fact that *America Online* involved an interstate case where most states permit class actions and Virginia is an outlier, whereas *Wong* involved an international case and most other nations do not provide plaintiffs with such a device? The same can be said for jury availability. Within the United States, jury trials are possible virtually everywhere, but outside the United States

---

3. *See* 18 U.S.C. §1084 (2000) (unlawful to "use a wire communication facility for the transmission in interstate and foreign commerce of bets and wagers on sporting events and contests, and for the transmission of a wire communication which entitled the recipient to receive money and credit as a result of bets and wagers"); 18 U.S.C. §1962(c) (2000) ("It shall be unlawful for any person employed by or associated with any enterprise engaged in, or the activities of which affect, interstate or foreign commerce, to conduct or participate, directly or indirectly, in the conduct of such enterprise's affairs through a pattern of racketeering activity or collection of unlawful debt.")

they are much less common. Punitive damages are also more readily available within the United States than without.

(4) Should state or federal law apply to the enforcement of forum-selection clauses in diversity cases? As the *Wong* court notes, there is near consensus across the federal circuits that forum-selection clauses are procedural and therefore federal law applies to their enforcement. The conclusion seems to fly in the face of *Erie*, however, because very often the outcome of the case is significantly affected by where the litigation occurs. Moreover, at least one of the parties cared about the issue enough to attempt to resolve it in the contract, which suggests that they thought the matter substantial (is this the same thing?). Finally, the disparate treatment between state and federal courts generates strong motivation for defendants seeking forum-selection clause enforcement to remove cases to federal court because disparities virtually always take the form of lesser enforcement in the state courts. On the other hand, federal court enforcement helps to enhance the U.S. position in international commerce, a concern the Supreme Court expressed in *The Bremen*. The Supreme Court's role in promoting international trade opportunities is further discussed in the next section.

In Atlantic Marine Const. Co. v. U.S. Dist. Ct. for the Western Dist. of Texas, 134 S. Ct. 568 (2013), the Supreme Court confirmed that forum non conveniens was the correct vehicle for the district courts when considering whether to dismiss an action in deference to a forum-selection clause choosing a state or foreign court. This conclusion helped justify the use of §1404(a) as the vehicle for considering whether to transfer a case to another federal court in deference to a forum-selection clause. Specifically, because §1404(a) codifies the forum non conveniens factors to be used when considering transfers, it would enable a substantially similar analysis across cases involving forum-selection clauses. *Id*. at 580. The Court did not specifically state whether state or federal forum non conveniens principles would apply, but its analysis seemed to assume the application of the federal doctrine.

(5) Also in *Atlantic Marine*, a unanimous Court concluded that a federal district court should transfer a case to the contractually chosen forum unless extraordinary circumstances unrelated to the convenience of the parties clearly disfavored the transfer. The Court further concluded that the presence of a valid choice-of-court clause alters the usual §1404(a) analysis in three ways. First, plaintiff's choice of forum is given no deference; indeed, plaintiff bears the burden of establishing the presence of extraordinary circumstances necessary to defeat the transfer. Second, only public interest factors will be relevant; the clause conclusively determines the private interests. Third, *Van Dusen/Ferens* does not apply to these transfers. In other words, the choice-of-law principles of the contractually chosen rather than the transferor court will apply. The Court did not consider how a district court should determine whether the choice-of-court clause is valid.

(6) Note that by treating choice-of-forum clause enforcement through a forum non conveniens analysis, the federal courts can treat the enforcement question as essentially procedural, justifying displacement of state law principles. The enforcement analysis used in state courts, by contrast, tends to focus on contract law principles, which are clearly substantive. Is the forum non conveniens analysis an equally effective tool for the job?

(7) Sometimes plaintiff files suit in the forum exclusively chosen in the contract and the defendant argues that the court should nevertheless dismiss the case on grounds of forum non conveniens. Should an otherwise enforceable clause preclude forum non conveniens dismissal from the chosen forum? Several courts have held to the contrary, deciding that the public interest and third-party private interest factors cannot be waived by the contracting parties. *See* Heiser, *The Hague Convention on Choice of Court Agreements: The Impact on Forum Non Conveniens, Transfer of Venue, Removal, and Recognition of Judgments in United States Courts*, 31 U. Pa. J. Intl. L. 1013, nn.31-34 and accompanying text (2010) (discussing cases).

(8) We saw in the choice-of-law clause section a willingness on the part of some courts to enforce choice-of-law clauses even in the face of state statutes prohibiting evasion of local law with a forum-selection clause. The converse can be true too: Sometimes courts enforce forum-selection clauses even though state statutes forbid evasion of local law with choice-of-law clauses. Consider, for example, Rafael Rodriguez Barril v. Conbraco Industries, Inc., 619 F.3d 90 (1st Cir. 2010), a case in which a Puerto Rican sales representative of a North Carolina company brought suit in Puerto Rico Superior Court for wrongful termination. The defendant company removed the case to federal court and then obtained enforcement of a forum-selection clause that provided for resolution of disputes exclusively in North Carolina state or federal courts. Plaintiff opposed enforcement of the clause on grounds that a state law protecting sales representatives from termination stated explicitly that sales representative contracts are governed by Puerto Rico law and that contrary contract provisions are "null." The court concluded that this was a prohibition on the use of contrary choice-of-law provisions only and that the use of forum-selection clauses could have been but was not addressed by the legislature. The court advised plaintiff to bring his public policy argument to the attention of the North Carolina court.

Similarly, a forum-selection clause designating Florida courts for dispute resolution was enforced by the Texas courts in a case brought by an employer against a former Texas employee based on a noncompete clause in the employment contract. In re Autonation, Inc., 228 S.W.3d 663 (Tex. 2007). Plaintiff argued against enforcement of the forum-selection clause by pointing out that the Texas courts had previously refused to enforce choice-of-law clauses in noncompete agreements, reasoning that such provisions violated Texas public policy. The court distinguished the two situations, stating that while it was permissible for Texas courts to insist on applying Texas law to cases litigated in its courts, demanding that all litigation occur in local courts was more problematic. A concurring judge reasoned that enforcing the forum-selection clause was justified only because it left open the possibility that Florida courts might uphold Texas public policy.

Is it credible that when a court or legislature closes off one means of escaping from local laws it intends to leave the door open for escape through other means? If courts are to engage in this reasoning, does it make more sense to uphold choice-of-court clauses on the theory that other courts might uphold local public policy than to uphold choice-of-law clauses, where circumvention of local policy is certain? In fact, courts do seem more willing to enforce choice-of-court clauses than choice-of-law clauses. O'Hara & Ribstein, *The Law Market* 71-73 (2009) (discussing state incentives).

C. Arbitration Clauses

1. The Federal Arbitration Act and Arbitrability

Arbitration clauses provide a third mechanism for influencing governing laws and dispute resolution procedures. In most cases, parties may contract to have their disputes resolved by arbitrators rather than by courts, and chosen arbitration can take multiple forms. Parties can opt for binding or nonbinding arbitration; the former type effectively precludes the parties from resorting to courts for a determination of the merits of the claim(s). Sometimes the parties enter into predispute arbitration agreements, where they contract to arbitrate as part of a larger transaction. Alternatively, agreements to arbitrate can be made after a dispute arises. The discussion that follows focuses on predispute agreements to resolve claims with binding arbitration.

Arbitration can provide a number of benefits to contracting parties. First, parties can tailor dispute resolution to their particular needs by choosing the arbitration association, location, and/or applicable rules of procedure. Relatedly, parties can opt for expedited resolution of their claims, making arbitration, at least in theory, more cost effective and less time-consuming than court litigation. Second, the parties choose the arbitrator and can provide in the arbitration clause that the arbitrator must possess particular qualifications. This tailoring enables the parties to opt for industry experts and/or arbitrators with expertise in particular fields of law, which carries the potential of improving the accuracy of decisions. Third, arbitration is less public than are most court proceedings, so parties are better able to keep commercial information confidential. Fourth, as discussed below, arbitration awards are more reliably enforced across national borders than are court awards.

Fifth, party ability to choose governing law can be enhanced through arbitration. In many arbitral contexts, arbitration associations require their arbitrators to apply the law chosen in a contract. For example, the International Center for Dispute Resolution, the international division of the American Arbitration Association, states in Article 28(1) of its arbitration rules that "[t]he tribunal shall apply the substantive law(s) or rules of law designated by the parties as applicable to the dispute." *http://www.internationalarbitrationlaw.com/ icdr-arbitration-rules/* (last visited 7/15/14). And JAMS states in its employment arbitration rules that "[i]n determining the merits of the dispute the arbitrator shall be guided by the rules of law agreed upon by the parties." *JAMS Employment Arbitration Rules and Procedures*, Rule 24(c) (2014), available at *http://www.jamsadr.com/rules-employment-arbitration/* (last visited 7/15/ 14). Where these rules exist, parties may have greater assurance that their choice-of-law clause will be enforced.

Indeed, arbitration can enable parties to opt out of government-created laws altogether. Some industry arbitration forums use private law to resolve disputes, and parties opting for arbitration often can designate private law not in force in any country. Private law can come from private lawmaking bodies who propose rules that aren't enacted, and some industries create their own trade rules for resolving disputes. For examples of the use of private law to resolve intra-industry disputes, see Bernstein, *Opting Out of the Legal System: Extralegal Contractual Relations in the Diamond Industry*, 21 J. Legal Stud. 115 (1992); Bernstein, *Merchant Law in a Merchant Court: Rethinking the Code's Search for Immanent Business Norms*, 144 U. Pa. L. Rev. 1765 (1996); Bernstein, *Private Commercial Law in the Cotton Industry: Creating Cooperation Through Rules, Norms and Institutions*, 99 Mich. L. Rev. 1724 (2001). For a good discussion of the use of arbitration to get out from under law, *see* Ware, *Default Rules from Mandatory Rules: Privatizing Law Through Arbitration*, 83 Minn. L. Rev. 703 (1999). Finally, parties opting for arbitration often can alter specific rules that would otherwise apply under governing law by, for example, more effectively specifying cost allocations or limiting recoverable remedies.

These benefits (and others) explain party preference for arbitration clauses, but sometimes the clauses can prove controversial. As with both choice-of-law and choice-of-court clauses, a party with superior bargaining power can push one-sided arbitration clauses onto unsuspecting trade partners, and interested third parties would be excluded from arbitration. Courts wishing to strike arbitration clauses are somewhat limited by federal law, however.

Over the last century, the United States has experienced substantially increased enforcement of both agreements to arbitrate and arbitral awards. Traditionally, courts were fairly uniformly hostile to predispute agreements to arbitrate. Carbonneau, *Cases and Materials on the Law and Practice of Arbitration* 47 (3d ed. 2002). Both American and English courts refused to enforce irrevocable arbitration agreements, castigating them as "ousting" the courts of jurisdiction. Sturges & Murphy, *Some Confusing Matters Relating to Arbitration Under the United States Arbitration Act*, 17 Law & Contemp. Probs. 580 (1952). Congress stepped in to change this treatment in 1925 with the passage of a law now known as the Federal Arbitration Act ("FAA"), 9 U.S.C. §§1-16. As part of the FAA, arbitration agreements were deemed enforceable and courts were instructed to refer cases to arbitration, with limited exceptions:

§2.   Validity, irrevocability, and enforcement of agreements to arbitrate

. . . [A] contract evidencing a transaction involving commerce to settle by arbitration a controversy thereafter arising out of such contract or transaction, or the refusal to perform the whole or any part thereof, or an agreement in writing to submit to arbitration an existing controversy arising out of such a contract, transaction, or refusal, shall be valid, irrevocable, and enforceable, save upon such grounds as exist at law or in equity for the revocation of any contract.

§3.   Stay of proceedings where issue therein referable to arbitration

If any suit or proceeding be brought in any of the courts of the United States upon any issue referable to arbitration under an agreement in writing for such arbitration, the court in which such suit is pending, upon being satisfied that the issue involved in such suit or proceeding is referable to arbitration under such an agreement, shall on application of one of the parties stay the trial of the action until such arbitration has been had in accordance with the terms of the agreement, provided the applicant for the stay is not in default in proceeding with such arbitration.

§4.   Failure to arbitrate under agreement; petition to United States court having jurisdiction for order to compel arbitration; . . .

A party aggrieved by the alleged failure, neglect, or refusal of another to arbitrate under a written agreement for arbitration may petition any United States district court which, save for such agreement, would have jurisdiction under Title 28, in a civil action or in admiralty of the subject matter of a suit arising out of the controversy between the parties, for an order directing that such arbitration proceed in the manner provided for in such agreement. . . . The court shall hear the parties, and upon being satisfied that the making of the agreement for arbitration or the failure to comply therewith is not in issue, the court shall make an order directing the parties to proceed to arbitration in accordance with the terms of the agreement.

In addition, the FAA mandates enforcement of arbitral awards. When requested, courts are with limited exception instructed to issue a court judgment confirming the arbitrator's award, 9 U.S.C. §9, and that judgment carries the same force under the full faith and credit clause as does other judgments. *Id.* §13. Courts are permitted to vacate an award only when (1) "the award was procured by corruption, fraud, or undue means"; (2) "there was evident partiality or corruption in one or more of the arbitrators"; (3) "the arbitrators were guilty of misconduct" that prejudiced the rights of any party; or (4) "the arbitrators exceeded their powers, or so imperfectly executed them that a mutual, final, and definite award upon the subject matter submitted was not made." *Id.* §10. According to Supreme Court precedent, courts also can set aside arbitral awards in cases where the arbitrator manifestly disregarded clearly applicable law called to the arbitrator's attention, although more recent cases have questioned whether this is an independent ground for review. *See* Hall Street Assocs. v. Mattel, Inc., 552 U.S. 576, 585 (2008) (tentative statement in dicta); Stolt-Nielsen, S.A. v. AnimalFeeds Intl. Corp., 559 U.S. 662, 672 n.3 (2010) (declining to decide question). Court ability to modify or correct arbitral awards is also significantly limited. FAA §11.

Finally, parties can appeal court orders that fail to enforce or to otherwise give effect to the arbitration clause or award, but federal courts may not hear appeals from interlocutory orders that aid the enforcement of the arbitration clause. 9 U.S.C. §16.

Over time, U.S. Supreme Court decisions have reinforced the importance of arbitration as a dispute resolution tool. For example, the Court's decisions have interpreted the scope of the FAA quite broadly. Although not technically mandated by its language, the FAA now constrains both state and federal courts. Moses H. Cone Memorial Hospital v. Mercury Construction Co., 460 U.S. 1 (1983); Southland Corp. v. Keating, 465 U.S. 1 (1984). Furthermore, agreements subject to FAA enforcement are "transactions involving commerce, which include all transactions that Congress could regulate under its Commerce Clause authority, including consumer contracts. Allied-Bruce Terminix Companies, Inc. v. Dobson, 513 U.S. 265 (1995). Despite language in the FAA that could have been interpreted to exclude employment disputes from arbitration,* arbitration clauses in almost all employment contracts are enforceable. Gilmer v. Interstate/Johnson Lane Corp., 500 U.S. 20 (1991).

According to the Supreme Court, the FAA also prevents state lawmakers from singling out arbitration agreements for special rules that do not apply to other types of contract provisions. *See* Perry v. Thomas, 482 U.S. 483 (1987) (FAA pre-empts California Labor Law provision stating that employees could bring wage collection actions to court notwithstanding having entered into private agreements to arbitrate); *Southland Corp., supra* (to extent that California Franchise Investment Law prohibits the use of arbitration to resolve claims brought under it, the statute is preempted by the FAA); Doctor's Associates, Inc. v. Casarotto, 517 U.S. 681 (1996) (Montana law prohibiting the enforcement of arbitration clauses unless the first page of the contract provided conspicuous notice preempted by the FAA).

Note: Arbitrability

What types of claims are subject to resolution in arbitration rather than in the courts? Under section 3 of the FAA, a court is required to enforce an arbitration clause only to the extent that the parties' dispute involves an "issue referable to arbitration." At first, courts took the position that although private law claims were referable to arbitration, statutory claims creating a private right of action that invoked the public interest were not so referable. Over time, however, the Supreme Court seems to have eroded this defense. First, as noted above, the FAA preempts states from holding particular state claims off bounds from arbitration. Federal claims can be nonarbitrable if a federal statute indicates a congressional intent to withhold them from arbitration. However, the Supreme Court has not held a federal claim off bounds from arbitration for several decades. In the meantime, the Court has held that federal RICO, antitrust, employment discrimination, securities law, and Credit Repair Organization Act claims are all subject to arbitration. Indeed, the Court has recently suggested that federal claims are subject to arbitration unless Congress expressly states otherwise. CompuCredit Corp. v. Greenwood, 132 S. Ct. 665 (2012). More recently still, the Court has stated that congressional intent to displace the FAA with another federal statute must be "clear and manifest." Epic Systems Corp. v. Lewis, 138 S. Ct. 1612, 1624 (2018).

Prior to this shift in treatment, arbitration of public law claims was viewed with suspicion because arbitrators need not be expert in federal (or any) legal principles and plaintiffs might have difficulty proving their claims with the limited discovery sometimes afforded in arbitration. *See, e.g.,* Wilko v. Swan, 346 U.S. 427 (1953). A congressional intent to prevent the arbitration of public law claims was sometimes found in the nonwaiver language of federal statutes; where present, these provisions state that contractual efforts to modify or abridge rights or protections afforded under the statute are void. In *Wilko*, for example, the Court

---

* Section 1 of the FAA, provides in part, ". . . but nothing herein contained shall apply to contracts of employment of seamen, railroad employees, or any other class of workers engaged in foreign or interstate commerce." 9 U.S.C. §1.

concluded that similar nonwaiver language in federal securities statutes extended to plaintiffs' right to file suit in state or federal court. *Id*. at 432-437.

By the 1970s, however, international trade pressures and the need for allowing parties to cross-border contracts to provide for resolution of their disputes in a neutral forum caused a shift in the Court's reasoning. In Scherk v. Alberto-Culver Co, 417 U.S. 506 (1974), for example, the Court exempted international securities disputes from the restrictions of *Wilko*, and relied heavily on its reasoning in *The Bremen* for allowing international parties to choose to arbitrate their disputes:

> An agreement to arbitrate before a specified tribunal is, in effect, a specialized kind of forum-selection clause that posits not only the situs of suit but also the procedure to be used in resolving the dispute. The invalidation of such an agreement in the case before us would not only allow the respondent to repudiate its solemn promise but would, as well, reflect a "parochial concept that all disputes must be resolved under our laws and in our courts. . . . We cannot have trade and commerce in world markets and international waters exclusively on our terms, governed by our laws, and resolved in our courts.

Id. at 519. Similar statements were used by the Court in Mitsubishi Motors Corp. v. Soler Chrysler-Plymouth, Inc., 473 U.S. 614 (1985), to support its conclusion that antitrust claims arising under international commercial agreements could be arbitrated.

Moreover, as the *Scherk* Court noted in a footnote, 417 U.S. at 520 n.15, in 1970 the United States acceded to the United Nations Convention on the Recognition and Enforcement of Foreign Arbitral Awards, also known as the New York Convention, which obligates member nations to enforce international arbitration agreements. The Court's conclusion was not dictated by the Convention, because the Convention allows member nations to decide what claims are arbitrable. For example, Article II(1) of the Convention states that a court is obligated to enforce a written agreement to arbitrate if the dispute is one "concerning a subject matter capable of settlement by arbitration." And Article V(2) permits a court to refuse to enforce an arbitral award if it determines either that "(*a*) The subject matter of the difference is not capable of settlement by arbitration under the law of that country; or (*b*) The recognition or enforcement of the award would be contrary to the public policy of that country." Nevertheless, the Convention does reflect a worldwide movement toward enabling international commercial parties the freedom to choose private dispute resolution mechanisms. Today the Convention boasts approximately 150 member nations, and the member list includes virtually all of the developed and much of the developing world. *See http://www.uncitral .org/uncitral/en/uncitral_texts/arbitration/NYConvention_status.html* (last visited 7/15/14).

Eventually the Court abandoned its distinction between domestic and international commerce, and it overturned *Wilko*, enabling all securities claims to be arbitrated. Rodriguez de Quijas v. Shearson/American Express, Inc., 490 U.S. 477 (1989). Part of the problem with the domestic/international distinction is that nothing in the FAA or the public law statutes justified it. Moreover, private parties committed to arbitration often can turn a domestic into an international transaction without difficulty, thus depriving the distinction of force. In addition, once the benefit of arbitration is conferred on international companies, it makes little sense to continue to hinder domestic competitors. This reasoning is developed more fully in O'Hara & Ribstein, *The Law Market* (2009).

In *Rodriguez de Quijas*, the Court acknowledged that its reading of Congress's antiwaiver provision was clouded by an unwarranted hostility to arbitration:

> The shift in the Court's views on arbitration away from those adopted in *Wilko* is shown by the flat statement in *Mitsubishi*: "By agreeing to arbitrate a statutory claim, a party does not forgo the substantive rights afforded by the statute; it only submits to their resolution in an arbitral, rather than a judicial, forum." To the extent that *Wilko* rested on suspicion of arbitration as a method of weakening the protections afforded in the substantive law to would-be complainants, it has fallen far out of step with our current strong endorsement of the federal statutes favoring this method of resolving disputes.

Id. at 481. Today, a majority of Justices consistently conclude that there is no a priori reason to believe that substantive rights will be treated any differently in arbitration than in litigation. As a result, the arbitration clause is merely a choice of forum that is entitled to enforcement under the FAA.

This reasoning is somewhat suspect, however. For one, if choice-of-law clauses are more readily enforced in arbitration than in court, then it is altogether possible that arbitration will alter the substantive rights of the parties. The possibility arose in *Mitsubishi*, when the United States government filed an amicus brief expressing concern that the arbitrators, located outside of the United States, would ignore federal antitrust laws and instead apply the law of the Swiss Confederation, as designated in the parties' sales contract. In a footnote, the Court declined to speculate on what law the arbitrators might apply, in part because the parties stipulated that the dispute had been referred to arbitration under U.S. antitrust law. However, the Court did state that failure to apply U.S. laws might justify judicial interference: "[I]n the event the choice-of-forum and choice-of-law clauses operated in tandem as a prospective waiver of a party's right to pursue statutory remedies for antitrust violations, we would have little hesitation in condemning the agreement as against public policy." 473 U.S. at 637 n.19. In *Mitsubishi* itself, the Court indicated that the question should be reserved for the award enforcement stage. In practice, arbitral awards are rarely challenged on grounds that the arbitrator failed to apply U.S. laws. For a general discussion, *see* Drahozal, *Is Arbitration Lawless?*, 40 Loy. L.A. L. Rev. 187 (2006).

Arbitration can also alter substantive rights in the context of adhesion contracts. In consumer and employment contracts, for example, the company chooses the arbitration forum and rules, and, for most claims, the company is the defendant. In these circumstances, companies might have incentives to choose unfair dispute resolution in order to defeat potential claims against it. In *Wilko*, the fact that investors do not enter into arm's length transactions contributed to the Court's conclusion that securities claims should be resolved in courts. Since overturning *Wilko*, however, the Court has been reluctant to distinguish between contract settings when deciding questions of arbitrability.

At least three factors can justify this reluctance. First, Congress can always enact laws preventing contracting parties from having to arbitrate their claims.

For example, in the Dodd-Frank Wall Street Reform and Consumer Protection Act (2010), Congress declared that arbitration clauses in mortgage agreements were not enforceable. Under the Military Lending Act (2007), mandatory arbitration clauses are unenforceable in loan contracts entered into by active-duty military service personnel. Broader legislation that would deem unenforceable arbitration clauses in all consumer and employment contracts has been introduced but not enacted for several years. Should these questions be left to Congress?

Second, statutory offenses can be separately enforced by government agencies, so the voluntary submission of the private dispute to arbitration does not necessarily leave companies unregulated by laws expressing public interests. In Gilmer v. Interstate/Johnson Lane Corp., 500 U.S. 20 (1991), for example, the Court noted that although the employee must have his ADEA claim resolved in arbitration, the EEOC has independent authority to investigate violations of the Act. Convincing? Recall a similar discussion in Section A above with regard to enforcement of choice-of-law clauses.

Third, the fairness of chosen arbitration procedures can be scrutinized in individual cases, making a blanket nonarbitrability determination unnecessary. Recall that section 2 of the FAA, *supra* page 708, provides that agreements to arbitrate "shall be valid, irrevocable, and enforceable, save upon such grounds as exist at law or in equity for the revocation of any contract." Stated differently, courts are entitled to subject arbitration clauses to the same scrutiny that is given to other contracts under contract law. A court could refuse to enforce an arbitration agreement that was procured by fraud, for example. One common argument raised by consumers and employees to avoid enforcement of the arbitration clause is that it, or some portion of it, is unconscionable. If the forum or the procedures chosen are unlikely to lead to a fair resolution of the parties' dispute, a court can decline to refer the parties to arbitration. This topic is explored in the following section.

2. Policing the Clauses

States are permitted to decline to enforce arbitration agreements using general common law contract principles—agreement, consideration, fraud, duress, mistake, etc. The most common doctrine used by courts to ensure the fairness of arbitration clauses in recent decades is unconscionability. The specific contours of the unconscionability doctrine vary across the states, but in general the defense requires a showing of both procedural and substantive unconscionability. Procedural unconscionability exhibits an absence of meaningful choice, with a focus on the relative bargaining power of the parties and the circumstances surrounding the formation of the contract. A list of factors that courts commonly consider include:

(1) whether each party had a reasonable opportunity to understand the terms and conditions of the agreement; (2) whether there was a lack of opportunity for meaningful negotiation; (3) whether the agreement was printed on a duplicate or boilerplate form drafted solely by the party in the strongest bargaining

position; (4) whether the terms of the agreement were explained to the weaker party; (5) whether the aggrieved party had a meaningful choice or instead felt compelled to accept the terms of the agreement; and (6) whether the stronger party employed deceptive practices to obscure key contractual provisions.

Spann v. American Express Travel Related Services Co., 224 S.W.3d 698, 715 (Tenn. Ct. App. 2006). Substantive unconscionability is present when a contract is infected by terms that are fundamentally unfair or unreasonably unfavorable to the weaker party.

Because states vary in how easily procedural and substantive unconscionability can be demonstrated, a court's conclusion on unconscionability can turn on the applicable substantive law. For example, in some states an adhesion contract is per se procedurally unconscionable, whereas in other states more than just take-it-or-leave-it terms is necessary. In some states the weaker party has a fair opportunity to read and understand the terms of a contract so long as the terms are not affirmatively hidden, whereas in other states the stronger party might have a positive duty to explain terms, use simple language and conspicuous presentation, etc. And, of course, the degree of unfairness necessary before a court will strike a contract or term can also vary. Farnsworth, *Contracts* §4.28 (4th ed. 2004), provides a general description of the unconscionability doctrine as developed in U.S. courts.

Using unconscionability, courts have refused to enforce arbitration clauses that (1) force the weaker party to incur prohibitive costs in order to pursue claims, Mendez v. Palm Harbor Homes, 45 P.3d 594 (Wash. Ct. App. 2002); (2) force a party to arbitrate using rules that unfairly favor the other party, Samaniego v. Empire Today, LLC, 140 Cal. Rptr. 3d 492 (Cal. Ct. App. 2012); and (3) require only one of the parties to resort to arbitration while enabling the other party to bring its claims in court, Armendariz v. Foundation Health Psychcare Services, 6 P.3d 669 (Cal. 2000).

In addition, prior to 2011, some courts refused to enforce arbitration clauses that prohibited consumers or employees from bringing claims against the company as a class. The concern with these class waivers was that companies would be able to use arbitration in order to avoid class actions and thereby defeat liability altogether. In the case that follows, however, the Supreme Court concluded that this use of the unconscionability doctrine was not permitted under the FAA.

AT&T Mobility LLC v. Concepcion

563 U.S. 333 (2011)

Justice SCALIA delivered the opinion of the Court.

Section 2 of the Federal Arbitration Act (FAA) makes agreements to arbitrate "valid, irrevocable, and enforceable, save upon such grounds as exist at law or in equity for the revocation of any contract." 9 U.S.C. §2. We consider whether the FAA prohibits States from conditioning the enforceability of certain arbitration agreements on the availability of classwide arbitration procedures.

I

In February 2002, Vincent and Liza Concepcion entered into an agreement for the sale and servicing of cellular telephones with AT&T Mobility LCC (AT&T). The contract provided for arbitration of all disputes between the parties, but required that claims be brought in the parties' "individual capacity, and not as a plaintiff or class member in any purported class or representative proceeding.". . .

The . . . agreement provides that customers may initiate dispute proceedings by completing a one-page Notice of Dispute form available on AT&T's Web site. AT&T may then offer to settle the claim; if it does not, or if the dispute is not resolved within 30 days, the customer may invoke arbitration by filing a separate Demand for Arbitration, also available on AT&T's Web site. In the event the parties proceed to arbitration, the agreement specifies that AT&T must pay all costs for nonfrivolous claims; that arbitration must take place in the county in which the customer is billed; that, for claims of $10,000 or less, the customer may choose whether the arbitration proceeds in person, by telephone, or based only on submissions; that either party may bring a claim in small claims court in lieu of arbitration; and that the arbitrator may award any form of individual relief, including injunctions and presumably punitive damages. The agreement, moreover, denies AT&T any ability to seek reimbursement of its attorney's fees, and, in the event that a customer receives an arbitration award greater than AT&T's last written settlement offer, requires AT&T to pay a $7,500 minimum recovery and twice the amount of the claimant's attorney's fees.[3]

The Concepcions purchased AT&T service, which was advertised as including the provision of free phones; they were not charged for the phones, but they were charged $30.22 in sales tax based on the phones' retail value. In March 2006, the Concepcions filed a complaint against AT&T in the United States District Court for the Southern District of California. The complaint was later consolidated with a putative class action alleging, among other things, that AT&T had engaged in false advertising and fraud by charging sales tax on phones it advertised as free.

In March 2008, AT&T moved to compel arbitration under the terms of its contract with the Concepcions. The Concepcions opposed the motion, contending that the arbitration agreement was unconscionable and unlawfully exculpatory under California law because it disallowed classwide procedures. The District Court denied AT&T's motion. It described AT&T's arbitration agreement favorably, noting, for example, that the informal dispute-resolution process was "quick, easy to use" and likely to "promp[t] full or . . . even excess payment to the customer *without* the need to arbitrate or litigate"; that the $7,500 premium functioned as "a substantial inducement for the consumer to pursue the claim in arbitration" if a dispute was not resolved informally; and that consumers who were members of a class would likely be worse off. Nevertheless, relying on the California Supreme Court's decision in Discover Bank v. Superior Court, 36 Cal. 4th 148 (2005), the court found that the arbitration provision was unconscionable because AT&T had not shown that bilateral arbitration adequately substituted for the deterrent effects of class actions.

---

3. The guaranteed minimum recovery was increased in 2009 to $10,000.

The Ninth Circuit affirmed, also finding the provision unconscionable under California law as announced in *Discover Bank*. It also held that the *Discover Bank* rule was not preempted by the FAA because that rule was simply "a refinement of the unconscionability analysis applicable to contracts generally in California.". . .

II

. . . Under California law, courts may refuse to enforce any contract found "to have been unconscionable at the time it was made," or may "limit the application of any unconscionable clause." Cal. Civ. Code Ann. §1670.5(a) (West 1985). A finding of unconscionability requires "a 'procedural' and a 'substantive' element, the former focusing on 'oppression' or 'surprise' due to unequal bargaining power, the latter on 'overly harsh' or 'one-sided' results." *Armendariz v. Foundation Health Pyschcare Servs., Inc.*, 24 Cal. 4th 83 (2000).

In *Discover Bank*, the California Supreme Court applied this framework to class-action waivers in arbitration agreements and held as follows:

> "[W]hen the waiver is found in a consumer contract of adhesion in a setting in which disputes between the contracting parties predictably involve small amounts of damages, and when it is alleged that the party with the superior bargaining power has carried out a scheme to deliberately cheat large numbers of consumers out of individually small sums of money, then . . . the waiver becomes in practice the exemption of the party 'from responsibility for [its] own fraud, or willful injury to the person or property of another.' Under these circumstances, such waivers are unconscionable under California law and should not be enforced." 36 Cal. 4th, at 162 (quoting Cal. Civ. Code Ann. §1668).

California courts have frequently applied this rule to find arbitration agreements unconscionable. [citations omitted]

III

A

The Concepcions argue that the *Discover Bank* rule, given its origins in California's unconscionability doctrine and California's policy against exculpation, is a ground that "exist[s] at law or in equity for the revocation of any contract" under FAA §2. Moreover, they argue that even if we construe the *Discover Bank* rule as a prohibition on collective-action waivers rather than simply an application of unconscionability, the rule would still be applicable to all dispute-resolution contracts, since California prohibits waivers of class litigation as well.

When state law prohibits outright the arbitration of a particular type of claim, the analysis is straightforward: The conflicting rule is displaced by the FAA. But the inquiry becomes more complex when a doctrine normally thought to be generally applicable, such as duress or, as relevant here, unconscionability, is alleged to have been applied in a fashion that disfavors arbitration. In *Perry v. Thomas*, 482 U.S. 483 (1987), for example, we noted that the FAA's preemptive effect might extend even to grounds traditionally thought to exist "'at law or in equity for the revocation of any contract.'" *Id.*, at 492, n. 9 (emphasis deleted). We said that a court may not "rely on the uniqueness of an agreement to arbitrate as a basis for a state-law holding that enforcement would be unconscionable, for this would enable the court to effect what . . . the state legislature cannot." *Id.*, at 493.

An obvious illustration of this point would be a case finding unconscionable or unenforceable as against public policy consumer arbitration agreements that fail to provide for judicially monitored discovery. The rationalizations for such a holding are neither difficult to imagine nor different in kind from those articulated in *Discover Bank*. A court might reason that no consumer would knowingly waive his right to full discovery, as this would enable companies to hide their wrongdoing. Or the court might simply say that such agreements are exculpatory—restricting discovery would be of greater benefit to the company than the consumer, since the former is more likely to be sued than to sue. See *Discover Bank, supra,* at 161 (arguing that class waivers are similarly one-sided). And, the reasoning would continue, because such a rule applies the general principle of unconscionability or public-policy disapproval of exculpatory agreements, it is applicable to "any" contract and thus preserved by §2 of the FAA. In practice, of course, the rule would have a disproportionate impact on arbitration agreements; but it would presumably apply to contracts purporting to restrict discovery in litigation as well.

Other examples are easy to imagine. The same argument might apply to a rule classifying as unconscionable arbitration agreements that fail to abide by the Federal Rules of Evidence, or that disallow an ultimate disposition by a jury (perhaps termed "a panel of twelve lay arbitrators" to help avoid preemption). Such examples are not fanciful, since the judicial hostility towards arbitration that prompted the FAA had manifested itself in "a great variety" of "devices and formulas" declaring arbitration against public policy. And although these statistics are not definitive, it is worth noting that California's courts have been more likely to hold contracts to arbitrate unconscionable than other contracts. [citations omitted]

The Concepcions suggest that all this is just a parade of horribles, and no genuine worry. "Rules aimed at destroying arbitration" or "demanding procedures incompatible with arbitration," they concede, "would be preempted by the FAA because they cannot sensibly be reconciled with Section 2." The "grounds" available under §2's saving clause, they admit, "should not be construed to include a State's mere preference for procedures that are incompatible with arbitration and 'would wholly eviscerate arbitration agreements.'"

We largely agree. Although §2's saving clause preserves generally applicable contract defenses, nothing in it suggests an intent to preserve state-law rules that stand as an obstacle to the accomplishment of the FAA's objectives. . . .

We differ with the Concepcions only in the application of this analysis to the matter before us. We do not agree that rules requiring judicially monitored discovery or adherence to the Federal Rules of Evidence are "a far cry from this case." The overarching purpose of the FAA, evident in the text of §§2, 3, and 4, is to ensure the enforcement of arbitration agreements according to their terms so as to facilitate streamlined proceedings. Requiring the availability of classwide arbitration interferes with fundamental attributes of arbitration and thus creates a scheme inconsistent with the FAA.

B

The "principal purpose" of the FAA is to "ensur[e] that private arbitration agreements are enforced according to their terms." *Volt*, 489 U.S., at 478. This purpose is readily apparent from the FAA's text. Section 2 makes arbitration agreements "valid, irrevocable, and enforceable" as written (subject, of course, to the saving clause); §3 requires courts to stay litigation of arbitral claims pending arbitration of those claims "in accordance with the terms of the agreement"; and §4 requires courts to compel arbitration "in accordance with the terms of the agreement" upon the motion of either party to the agreement (assuming that the "making of the arbitration agreement or the failure . . . to perform the same" is not at issue). In light of these provisions, we have held that parties may agree to limit the issues subject to arbitration, to arbitrate according to specific rules, and to limit *with whom* a party will arbitrate its disputes. [citations omitted]

The point of affording parties discretion in designing arbitration processes is to allow for efficient, streamlined procedures tailored to the type of dispute. It can be specified, for example, that the decisionmaker be a specialist in the relevant field, or that proceedings be kept confidential to protect trade secrets. And the informality of arbitral proceedings is itself desirable, reducing the cost and increasing the speed of dispute resolution.

. . . Contrary to the dissent's view, our cases place it beyond dispute that the FAA was designed to promote arbitration. They have repeatedly described the Act as "embod[ying] [a] national policy favoring arbitration," *Buckeye Check Cashing*, 546 U.S., at 443, and "a liberal federal policy favoring arbitration agreements, notwithstanding any state substantive or procedural policies to the contrary," *Moses H. Cone*, 460 U.S., at 24. Thus, in *Preston v. Ferrer*, holding preempted a state-law rule requiring exhaustion of administrative remedies before arbitration, we said: "A prime objective of an agreement to arbitrate is to achieve 'streamlined proceedings and expeditious results,'" which objective would be "frustrated" by requiring a dispute to be heard by an agency first. 552 U.S., at 357-358. That rule, we said, would "at the least, hinder speedy resolution of the controversy." *Id.*, at 358.

California's *Discover Bank* rule similarly interferes with arbitration. Although the rule does not *require* classwide arbitration, it allows any party to a consumer contract to demand it *ex post*. The rule is limited to adhesion contracts, but the times in which consumer contracts were anything other than adhesive are long past.[6] [citations omitted] The rule also requires that damages be predictably small, and that the consumer allege a scheme to cheat consumers. The former

---

6. Of course, States remain free to take steps addressing the concerns that attend contracts of adhesion—for example, requiring class-action-waiver provisions in adhesive arbitration agreements to be highlighted. Such steps cannot, however, conflict with the FAA or frustrate its purpose to ensure that private arbitration agreements are enforced according to their terms.

requirement, however, is toothless and malleable (the Ninth Circuit has held that damages of $4,000 are sufficiently small, see *Oestreicher v. Alienware Corp.*, 322 Fed. Appx. 489, 492 (2009) (unpublished)), and the latter has no limiting effect, as all that is required is an allegation. Consumers remain free to bring and resolve their disputes on a bilateral basis under *Discover Bank*, and some may well do so; but there is little incentive for lawyers to arbitrate on behalf of individuals when they may do so for a class and reap far higher fees in the process. And faced with inevitable class arbitration, companies would have less incentive to continue resolving potentially duplicative claims on an individual basis.

Although we have had little occasion to examine classwide arbitration, our decision in *Stolt-Nielsen* is instructive. In that case we held that an arbitration panel exceeded its power under §10(a)(4) of the FAA by imposing class procedures based on policy judgments rather than the arbitration agreement itself or some background principle of contract law that would affect its interpretation. We then held that the agreement at issue, which was silent on the question of class procedures, could not be interpreted to allow them because the "changes brought about by the shift from bilateral arbitration to class-action arbitration" are "fundamental." 130 S. Ct. at 1776. This is obvious as a structural matter: Classwide arbitration includes absent parties, necessitating additional and different procedures and involving higher stakes. Confidentiality becomes more difficult. And while it is theoretically possible to select an arbitrator with some expertise relevant to the class-certification question, arbitrators are not generally knowledgeable in the often-dominant procedural aspects of certification, such as the protection of absent parties. The conclusion follows that class arbitration, to the extent it is manufactured by *Discover Bank* rather than consensual, is inconsistent with the FAA.

First, the switch from bilateral to class arbitration sacrifices the principal advantage of arbitration—its informality—and makes the process slower, more costly, and more likely to generate procedural morass than final judgment. . . . [B]efore an arbitrator may decide the merits of a claim in classwide procedures, he must first decide, for example, whether the class itself may be certified, whether the named parties are sufficiently representative and typical, and how discovery for the class should be conducted. A cursory comparison of bilateral and class arbitration illustrates the difference. According to the American Arbitration Association (AAA), the average consumer arbitration between January and August 2007 resulted in a disposition on the merits in six months, four months if the arbitration was conducted by documents only. As of September 2009, the AAA had opened 283 class arbitrations. Of those, 121 remained active, and 162 had been settled, withdrawn, or dismissed. Not a single one, however, had resulted in a final award on the merits. For those cases that were no longer active, the median time from filing to settlement, withdrawal, or dismissal—not judgment on the merits—was 583 days, and the mean was 630 days.[7]

---

7. The dissent claims that class arbitration should be compared to class litigation, not bilateral arbitration. Whether arbitrating a class is more desirable than litigating one, however, is not relevant. A State cannot defend a rule requiring arbitration-by-jury by saying that parties will still prefer it to trial-by-jury.

Second, class arbitration *requires* procedural formality. The AAA's rules governing class arbitrations mimic the Federal Rules of Civil Procedure for class litigation. And while parties can alter those procedures by contract, an alternative is not obvious. If procedures are too informal, absent class members would not be bound by the arbitration. For a class-action money judgment to bind absentees in litigation, class representatives must at all times adequately represent absent class members, and absent members must be afforded notice, an opportunity to be heard, and a right to opt out of the class. At least this amount of process would presumably be required for absent parties to be bound by the results of arbitration.

We find it unlikely that in passing the FAA Congress meant to leave the disposition of these procedural requirements to an arbitrator. Indeed, class arbitration was not even envisioned by Congress when it passed the FAA in 1925; as the California Supreme Court admitted in *Discover Bank*, class arbitration is a "relatively recent development." 36 Cal. 4th, at 163. And it is at the very least odd to think that an arbitrator would be entrusted with ensuring that third parties' due process rights are satisfied.

Third, class arbitration greatly increases risks to defendants. Informal procedures do of course have a cost: The absence of multilayered review makes it more likely that errors will go uncorrected. Defendants are willing to accept the costs of these errors in arbitration, since their impact is limited to the size of individual disputes, and presumably outweighed by savings from avoiding the courts. But when damages allegedly owed to tens of thousands of potential claimants are aggregated and decided at once, the risk of an error will often become unacceptable. Faced with even a small chance of a devastating loss, defendants will be pressured into settling questionable claims. Other courts have noted the risk of "in terrorem" settlements that class actions entail [citation omitted], and class arbitration would be no different.

Arbitration is poorly suited to the higher stakes of class litigation. In litigation, a defendant may appeal a certification decision on an interlocutory basis and, if unsuccessful, may appeal from a final judgment as well. Questions of law are reviewed *de novo* and questions of fact for clear error. In contrast, 9 U.S.C. §10 allows a court to vacate an arbitral award *only* where the award "was procured by corruption, fraud, or undue means"; "there was evident partiality or corruption in the arbitrators"; "the arbitrators were guilty of misconduct in refusing to postpone the hearing . . . or in refusing to hear evidence pertinent and material to the controversy[,] or of any other misbehavior by which the rights of any party have been prejudiced"; or if the "arbitrators exceeded their powers, or so imperfectly executed them that a mutual, final, and definite award . . . was not made." The AAA rules do authorize judicial review of certification decisions, but this review is unlikely to have much effect given these limitations; review under §10 focuses on misconduct rather than mistake. And parties may not contractually expand the grounds or nature of judicial review. We find it hard to believe that defendants would bet the company with no effective means of review, and even harder to believe that Congress would have intended to allow state courts to force such a decision.

. . . The dissent claims that class proceedings are necessary to prosecute small-dollar claims that might otherwise slip through the legal system. But States cannot require a procedure that is inconsistent with the FAA, even if it is desirable for unrelated reasons. Moreover, the claim here was most unlikely to go unresolved. As noted earlier, the arbitration agreement provides that AT&T will pay claimants a minimum of $7,500 and twice their attorney's fees if they obtain an arbitration award greater than AT&T's last settlement offer. The District Court found this scheme sufficient to provide incentive for the individual prosecution of meritorious claims that are not immediately settled, and the Ninth Circuit admitted that aggrieved customers who filed claims would be "essentially guarantee[d]" to be made whole. Indeed, the District Court concluded that the Concepcions were *better off* under their arbitration agreement with AT&T than they would have been as participants in a class action, which "could take months, if not years, and which may merely yield an opportunity to submit a claim for recovery of a small percentage of a few dollars."

* * *

Because it "stands as an obstacle to the accomplishment and execution of the full purposes and objectives of Congress," California's *Discover Bank* rule is preempted by the FAA. The judgment of the Ninth Circuit is reversed, and the case is remanded for further proceedings consistent with this opinion.

[Justice THOMAS concurred. Although joining Justice Scalia's opinion in full, he wrote separately to state his belief that the FAA section 2 exception for enforcing arbitration clauses should be interpreted to include only those grounds in law and equity that address the making of a contract.]

. . . This would require enforcement of an agreement to arbitrate unless a party successfully asserts a defense concerning the formation of the agreement to arbitrate, such as fraud, duress, or mutual mistake. Contract defenses unrelated to the making of the agreement — such as public policy — could not be the basis for declining to enforce an arbitration clause. . . .

The court's analysis and conclusion [in *Discover Bank*] that the arbitration agreement was exculpatory reveals that the *Discover Bank* rule does not concern the making of the arbitration agreement. Exculpatory contracts are a paradigmatic example of contracts that will not be enforced because of public policy. . . . Refusal to enforce a contract for public-policy reasons does not concern whether the contract was properly made.

Justice BREYER, with whom Justice GINSBURG, Justice SOTOMAYOR, and Justice KAGAN join, dissenting.

The Federal Arbitration Act says that an arbitration agreement "shall be valid, irrevocable, and enforceable, *save upon such grounds as exist at law or in equity for the revocation of any contract.*" 9 U.S.C. §2 (emphasis added). California law sets forth certain circumstances in which "class action waivers" in *any* contract are unenforceable. In my view, this rule of state law is consistent with the federal Act's language and primary objective. . . .

I

The California law in question consists of an authoritative state-court interpretation of two provisions of the California Civil Code. The first provision makes unlawful all contracts "which have for their object, directly or indirectly, to exempt anyone from responsibility for his own . . . violation of law." Cal. Civ. Code Ann. §1668 (West 1985). The second provision authorizes courts to "limit the application of any unconscionable clause" in a contract so "as to avoid any unconscionable result." §1670.5(a).

. . . The *Discover Bank* rule does not create a "blanket policy in California against class action waivers in the consumer context." *Provencher v. Dell, Inc.*, 409 F. Supp. 2d 1196, 1201 (C.D. Cal. 2006). Instead, it represents the "application of a more general [unconscionability] principle." *Gentry v. Superior Ct.*, 42 Cal. 4th 443, 457 (2007). Courts applying California law have enforced class-action waivers where they satisfy general unconscionability standards. [citations omitted] And even when they fail, the parties remain free to devise other dispute mechanisms, including informal mechanisms, that, in context, will not prove unconscionable.

II

A

The *Discover Bank* rule is consistent with the federal Act's language. It "applies equally to class action litigation waivers in contracts without arbitration agreements as it does to class arbitration waivers in contracts with such agreements." 36 Cal. 4th, at 165-166. Linguistically speaking, it falls directly within the scope of the Act's exception permitting courts to refuse to enforce arbitration agreements on grounds that exist "for the revocation of *any* contract." 9 U.S.C. §2 (emphasis added). The majority agrees. . . .

III

The majority's . . . view (that *Discover Bank* stands as an "obstacle" to the accomplishment of the federal law's objective) rests primarily upon its claims that the *Discover Bank* rule increases the complexity of arbitration procedures, thereby discouraging parties from entering into arbitration agreements, and to that extent discriminating in practice against arbitration. These claims are not well founded.

For one thing, a state rule of law that would sometimes set aside as unconscionable a contract term that forbids class arbitration is not (as the majority claims) like a rule that would require "ultimate disposition by a jury" or "judicially monitored discovery" or use of "the Federal Rules of Evidence." Unlike the majority's examples, class arbitration is consistent with the use of arbitration. It is a form of arbitration that is well known in California and followed elsewhere. Indeed, the AAA has told us that it has found class arbitration to be "a fair, balanced, and efficient means of resolving class disputes." And unlike the majority's examples, the *Discover Bank* rule imposes equivalent limitations on litigation; hence it cannot fairly be characterized as a targeted attack on arbitration.

. . . For another thing, the majority's argument that the *Discover Bank* rule will discourage arbitration rests critically upon the wrong comparison. The majority compares the complexity of class arbitration with that of bilateral arbitration.

And it finds the former more complex. But, if incentives are at issue, the *relevant* comparison is not "arbitration with arbitration" but a comparison between class arbitration and judicial class actions. After all, in respect to the relevant set of contracts, the *Discover Bank* rule similarly and equally sets aside clauses that forbid class procedures — whether arbitration procedures or ordinary judicial procedures are at issue.

Why would a typical defendant (say, a business) prefer a judicial class action to class arbitration? AAA statistics "suggest that class arbitration proceedings take more time than the average commercial arbitration, but may take *less time* than the average class action in court." Data from California courts confirm that class arbitrations can take considerably less time than in-court proceedings in which class certification is sought. And a single class proceeding is surely more efficient than thousands of separate proceedings for identical claims. Thus, if speedy resolution of disputes were all that mattered, then the *Discover Bank* rule would reinforce, not obstruct, that objective of the Act.

The majority's related claim that the *Discover Bank* rule will discourage the use of arbitration because "[a]rbitration is poorly suited to . . . higher stakes" lacks empirical support. Indeed, the majority provides no convincing reason to believe that parties are unwilling to submit high-stake disputes to arbitration. And there are numerous counterexamples. [citations omitted]

Further, even though contract defenses, *e.g.*, duress and unconscionability, slow down the dispute resolution process, federal arbitration law normally leaves such matters to the States. A provision in a contract of adhesion (for example, requiring a consumer to decide very quickly whether to pursue a claim) might increase the speed and efficiency of arbitrating a dispute, but the State can forbid it. [state court case citations omitted] The *Discover Bank* rule amounts to a variation on this theme. California is free to define unconscionability as it sees fit, and its common law is of no federal concern so long as the State does not adopt a special rule that disfavors arbitration.

Because California applies the same legal principles to address the unconscionability of class arbitration waivers as it does to address the unconscionability of any other contractual provision, the merits of class proceedings should not factor into our decision. If California had applied its law of duress to void an arbitration agreement, would it matter if the procedures in the coerced agreement were efficient?

Regardless, the majority highlights the disadvantages of class arbitrations, as it sees them. But class proceedings have countervailing advantages. In general agreements that forbid the consolidation of claims can lead small-dollar claimants to abandon their claims rather than to litigate. I suspect that it is true even here, for as the Court of Appeals recognized, AT&T can avoid the $7,500 payout (the payout that supposedly makes the Concepcions' arbitration worthwhile) simply by paying the claim's face value, such that "the maximum gain to a customer for the hassle of arbitrating a $30.22 dispute is still just $30.22."

What rational lawyer would have signed on to represent the Concepcions in litigation for the possibility of fees stemming from a $30.22 claim? In California's perfectly rational view, nonclass arbitration over such sums will also sometimes have the effect of depriving claimants of their claims (say, for example, where claiming the $30.22 were to involve filling out many forms that require technical legal knowledge or waiting at great length while a call is placed on hold). *Discover Bank* sets forth circumstances in which the California courts believe that the terms of consumer contracts can be manipulated to insulate an agreement's author from liability for its own frauds by "deliberately cheat[ing] large numbers of consumers out of individually small sums of money." 36 Cal. 4th, at 162-163. Why is this kind of decision—weighing the pros and cons of all class proceedings alike—not California's to make?

Brewer v. Missouri Title Loans

364 S.W.3d 486 (Mo. 2012) (en banc)

TEITELMAN, C.J.

Missouri Title Loans, Inc. appeals a judgment finding that a class arbitration waiver contained in its loan agreement, promissory note and security agreement (agreement) is unenforceable. In Brewer v. Missouri Title Loans, Inc., 323 S.W.3d 18 (Mo. banc 2010), this Court affirmed the judgment insofar as it held that the class arbitration waiver is unconscionable and reversed that part of the judgment ordering that the claim be submitted to an arbitrator to determine suitability for class arbitration. This Court held that the appropriate remedy was to strike the entire arbitration agreement.

The United States Supreme Court vacated *Brewer* in Missouri Title Loans, Inc. v. Brewer, 131 S. Ct. 2875 (2011), and remanded the case to this Court for further consideration in light of AT & T Mobility, LLC v. Concepcion [*supra* page 714]. Applying *Concepcion,* this Court finds that the presence and enforcement of the class arbitration waiver does not make the arbitration clause unconscionable. This Court instead applies traditional Missouri contract law in looking at the agreement as a whole to determine the conscionability of the arbitration provision. This Court holds that Brewer has demonstrated unconscionability in the formation of the agreement. The appropriate remedy is revocation of the arbitration clause contained within the agreement. Consequently, the judgment is affirmed in part and reversed in part, and the case is remanded.

Facts

Beverly Brewer borrowed $2,215 from the title company. The loan was secured by the title to Brewer's automobile. The annual percentage rate on the loan was 300 percent. The agreement provided that Brewer must resolve any claim against the title company in binding, individual arbitration governed by the Federal Arbitration Act (the act). No customer ever successfully has renegotiated the terms of the contract, including the arbitration provisions. Although the agreement provided that Brewer waived her right to litigate a dispute in court, the title company specifically retained its "right to seek possession of the Collateral in the event of default by judicial or other process including self-help repossession." In other words, the title company may utilize the courts to repossess the customer's vehicle, but the customer must go to arbitration to complain about violations of its rights under the contract.

In addition, the agreement stated that "[t]he parties agree to be responsible for their own expenses, including fees for attorneys, experts and witnesses." Unlike some arbitration contracts, such as the contract at issue in *Concepcion*, the agreement did not provide an attorney fee multiplier or guaranteed minimum recovery if the consumer is awarded more than the title company's last offer. The arbitration contract in *Concepcion* provided that a consumer who is awarded more than AT & T's last offer is entitled to a minimum recovery of $7,500 and to double his or her attorney's fees. The cumulative real-world effect of the arbitration provisions in this case is that a consumer's minimum and maximum recovery from the title company are identical — $0.00 — for no consumer ever has filed an individual claim for arbitration against the title company.

Brewer made two payments to the title company of more than $1,000, but the payment only reduced her loan principal by 6 cents. Brewer filed a class action petition against the title company alleging violations of numerous statutes, including the state merchandising practices act. The title company filed a motion to dismiss or to stay the claims and to compel Brewer to arbitrate her claims individually. [At issue on remand is whether the arbitration clause and/or class waiver are unenforceable because unconscionable.]

On remand, the title company asserts that the [FAA] wholly preempts Missouri's common law of unconscionability. Alternatively, the title company asserts that the availability of statutory attorney's fees negates Brewer's unconscionability defense because the fee provisions make it possible for consumers with small dollar claims to obtain counsel. Before addressing the title company's arguments, this Court must first address the law established in *Concepcion*.

Analysis

I. AT&T v. CONCEPCION

Determining the law established in *Concepcion* is complicated. . . . *Concepcion* is best understood by considering Justice Scalia's majority opinion as further informed by Justice Thomas' concurrence. Both opinions, for slightly different reasons, stand for the proposition that the act generally does not permit a state to bar class action waivers by finding an arbitration agreement unconscionable on the basis of a class action waiver alone. The Scalia opinion does not state, however, that the federal act otherwise preempts traditional state law defenses to contract formation such as unconscionability, duress or fraud, and Justice Thomas is clear that he would apply those defenses. But *Concepcion* teaches these defenses cannot be used in a way that would hold otherwise valid arbitration agreements unenforceable for the sole reason that they bar class relief. . . .

In *Concepcion*, the . . . plaintiffs [filed] a class action [lawsuit] alleging in part that AT&T had engaged in false advertising and fraud by charging sales tax on the phones it had advertised as free. AT&T filed a motion to compel individual arbitration pursuant to its contract with the plaintiffs. The district court specifically found that the arbitration agreement "was 'quick, easy to use' and likely to 'promp[t] full or . . . even excess payment to the customer without the need to arbitrate or litigate.'" The district court also found that the provision of a

$7,500 premium in the event the consumer was awarded more than AT&T's final written settlement offer served as "substantial inducement" for the consumer to pursue individual arbitration as opposed to class arbitration. Although individual arbitration was more beneficial to a consumer than class arbitration, the district court held that the arbitration provision was unconscionable under the California Supreme Court's decision in *Discover Bank*.

Given this factual context, the question framed by the Scalia opinion is "whether §2 [of the FAA] preempts California's [*Discover Bank*] rule classifying most collective-arbitration waivers in consumer contracts as unconscionable." *Discover Bank* held that a class action waiver in a consumer contract of adhesion is unconscionable when consumer claims against the defendant are predictably small and the plaintiff alleges a scheme to cheat consumers. Notably absent from the formulation of the *Discover Bank* rule is any finding that the consumer is worse off under individual arbitration as opposed to class arbitration or that the individual terms of the arbitration agreement are otherwise onerous or unfair. The practical effect of the *Discover Bank* rule, therefore, is to invalidate class arbitration waivers in most consumer contracts even if traditional factors of unconscionability are absent.

The lack of any requirement of showing actual unconscionability meant that *Discover Bank* created an essentially categorical requirement of class arbitration, which resulted in class arbitration being "manufactured by Discover Bank, rather than consensual. . . . " Requiring class arbitration under these circumstances sacrifices the federal act's goals of facilitating the prompt, informal resolution of disputes while also substantially disadvantaging defendants who did not consent to class arbitration in the first instance. . . . The net result of applying *Discover Bank* is that class arbitration waivers are rarely enforced. Instead, defendants are required to submit to procedures to which they did not consent, and consumers may be required to participate in class arbitration even if individual arbitration is more favorable to their interests. Consequently, the majority opinion held that the act preempted California's *Discover Bank* rule "[b]ecause it 'stands as an obstacle to the accomplishment and execution of the full purposes and objectives of Congress. . . . '"

Although the majority held that the *Discover Bank* rule was preempted by the federal act, it does not follow, as the title company contends, that all state law unconscionability defenses are preempted by the federal act in all cases. First, the expressly stated issue in *Concepcion* was whether California's *Discover Bank* rule was preempted, not whether all state law unconscionability defenses are preempted. . . . [C]onsistent with the stated issue in *Concepcion*, the Supreme Court's holding was expressly limited to finding that "California's *Discover Bank* rule is preempted by the act."

Second, the majority specifically acknowledged that the §2 saving clause "permits agreements to arbitrate to be invalidated by 'generally applicable contract defenses, such as fraud, duress, or unconscionability,' but not by defenses that apply only to arbitration or that derive their meaning from the fact that an agreement to arbitrate is at issue." . . .

Finally, the majority opinion discusses in detail the many ways in which the arbitration provisions at issue in *Concepcion* are fair and reasonable and do not lead to an unconscionable result. This discussion would be superfluous if the majority intended to establish a rule completely preempting all state law unconscionability defenses. Therefore, the *Concepcion* majority recognizes that a case-by-case approach provides the appropriate analytical framework for assessing the applicability of state law contract defenses pursuant to the §2 saving clause. . . . [A]nalysis of whether a particular state contract defense is preempted because it "stand[s] as an obstacle to the accomplishment of the act's objectives" depends on the factual posture of individual cases.

In his concurring opinion, Justice Thomas agrees that the federal act preempts state law contract defenses rooted in public policy concerns regarding arbitration, even if the policy nominally applies to contracts generally. Like the majority opinion, Justice Thomas notes that state law contract defenses including "fraud, duress, and unconscionability 'may be applied to invalidate arbitration agreements without contravening §2.'" But Justice Thomas focuses his analysis on the text of the §2 saving clause. The saving clause refers only to defenses that result in "revocation" of a contract and omits any reference to the "invalidation" or "nonenforcement" of a contract[; thus, he reasons that] the federal act requires "enforcement of an agreement to arbitrate unless a party successfully asserts a defense concerning the formation of the agreement. . . . " Id. at 1755 (emphasis added). "Contract defenses that are unrelated to the making of the agreement — such as public policy — are not valid grounds for declining to enforce an arbitration agreement." Because the *Discover Bank* rule relies on a public policy rationale and does not concern the making of the arbitration agreement, Justice Thomas concludes that the act requires preemption of the *Discover Bank* rule and enforcement of the arbitration provision in AT&T's agreement.

After setting out this discussion, Justice Thomas nonetheless concurs in Justice Scalia's opinion because the twin foundations of both analyses are the same. First, the federal act does not preempt state law contract defenses pertaining to the formation of a contract. Justice Thomas recognizes this point explicitly, while the majority does so inferentially. The majority holds that the federal act preempts *Discover Bank* because it "stand[s] as an obstacle to the accomplishment and execution the full purposes and objectives of Congress. . . . " Application of the *Discover Bank* rule has nothing to do with contract formation. Consequently, the Supreme Court's preemption of Discover Bank does not preempt all state law defenses to contract formation.

The second and related proposition supported by both opinions is that the federal act preemption analysis requires a case-specific assessment of the arbitration contract at issue. The majority opinion holds that state law contract defenses, including unconscionability, are preempted only if the defense "stand[s] as an obstacle to the accomplishment of the act's objectives." The question of whether a state law unconscionability defense stands as "an obstacle to the accomplishment of the act's objectives" requires analysis of the particular facts of the case. Likewise, Justice Thomas' focus on contract formation defenses such as fraud, duress, and unconscionability necessarily requires an analysis of the facts leading to the alleged formation of the contract at issue. Therefore, at a minimum, the rationales of both the majority opinion and Justice Thomas' concurrence permit state courts to apply state law defenses to the formation of the particular contract at issue.

This interpretation is confirmed by the Supreme Court's holding in Marmet Health Care Center, Inc. v. Brown, 132 S. Ct. 1201 (2012). In *Marmet*, a state court held that the federal act does not preempt state public policy against pre-dispute arbitration agreements that apply to personal injury and wrongful death claims against nursing homes. Alternatively, the state court held that the arbitration agreements were unconscionable. The Supreme Court reversed the judgment because the state court's public policy rationale is the type of "categorical rule" prohibiting arbitration of a particular type of claim identified in *Concepcion* as "contrary to the terms and coverage of the FAA." The Supreme Court remanded the case for consideration of whether, absent the public policy rationale, the arbitration clauses at issue "are unenforceable under state common law principles that are not specific to arbitration and pre-empted by the FAA." 132 S. Ct. at 1204. The Supreme Court's remand for consideration of generally applicable state law contract defenses, such as unconscionability, confirms that *Concepcion* permits state courts to apply state law defenses to the formation of the particular contract at issue. . . .

III.   DEFENSES TO CONTRACT FORMATION

Unlike *Concepcion*, which concerned the enforceability of a class waiver, the issue in this case is whether the arbitration agreement as a whole is unconscionable.[3] The purpose of the unconscionability doctrine is to guard against one-sided contracts, oppression and unfair surprise. Oppression and unfair surprise can occur during the bargaining process or may become evident later, when a dispute or other circumstances invoke the objectively unreasonable terms. In either case, the unconscionability is linked inextricably with the process of contract formation because it is at formation that a party is required to agree to the objectively unreasonable terms.

The evidence in this case supports a determination that the agreement's arbitration clause is unconscionable. There was evidence that the entire agreement—including the arbitration clause—was non-negotiable and was difficult for the average consumer to understand and that the title company was in a superior bargaining position. Brewer could not negotiate the terms of the agreement, including the terms of the arbitration clause. Indeed, the evidence further demonstrated that no consumer ever successfully had renegotiated the terms of the title company's arbitration contract.

----

3. While Missouri courts traditionally have discussed unconscionability under the lens of procedural unconscionability, and substantive unconscionability, *Concepcion* instead dictates a review that limits the discussion to whether state law defenses such as unconscionability impact the formation of a contract. In fact, in his concurring opinion, Justice Thomas specifically delineated past precedent of the Supreme Court applying defenses relevant to the formation of a contract. [citations omitted] Accordingly, the analysis in this Court's ruling today—as well as this Court's ruling in Robinson v. Title Lenders, Inc.,—no longer focuses on a discussion of procedural unconscionability or substantive unconscionability, but instead is limited to a discussion of facts relating to unconscionability impacting the formation of the contract. Future decisions by Missouri's courts addressing unconscionability likewise shall limit review of the defense of unconscionability to the context of its relevance to contract formation.

The evidence also demonstrated that the terms of the agreement are extremely one-sided. Unlike in *Concepcion*, in which AT&T shouldered the costs of arbitration and would pay double the customer's attorney's fees if the customer recovered more than AT&T had offered prior to arbitration, the agreement here provides that the parties are to bear their own costs. In *Concepcion*, the arbitration clause waived AT&T's right to seek reimbursement for attorney's fees incurred in defending against a consumer's claim. In contrast, the title company did not waive its right to seek attorney's fees. . . . The fact that no consumer ever has arbitrated a claim against the title company under these terms makes it clear that the agreement stands as a substantial obstacle not just to arbitration but also to the resolution of any consumer disputes against the title company.

The evidence in this case is also fundamentally different from that in *Concepcion* because Brewer presented expert testimony from three consumer lawyers who testified it was unlikely that a consumer could retain counsel to pursue individual claims. There was no such record in *Concepcion*. A claim such as Brewer's would require significant expertise and discovery, and it would not be financially viable for an attorney because of the complicated nature of the case and the small damages at issue. The title company presented no contrary evidence from attorneys who said they were willing to take such cases other than on a pro bono or rare voluntary basis.

While the majority opinion in *Concepcion* makes it clear that the unavailability of counsel is not alone sufficient to invalidate the requirement of individual arbitration, it remains one of the relevant considerations in assessing the overall conscionability of an arbitration contract. The *Discover Bank* rule was not preempted because it conditioned the enforceability of an arbitration contract on the availability of an attorney. Instead, the critical flaw leading to the preemption of the *Discover Bank* rule was that it required class arbitration even if class arbitration disadvantaged consumers and was unnecessary for the consumer to obtain a remedy. *Discover Bank*, therefore, was inconsistent with the core purpose of the federal act, which is to ensure enforcement of private arbitration agreements to promote informal, efficient dispute resolution. Because the purpose of the act is to ensure efficient dispute resolution, the analysis in *Concepcion* assumes the availability of a practical, viable means of individualized dispute resolution through arbitration. In some cases, the availability of counsel is a relevant consideration for determining whether the act's interest in dispute resolution will be satisfied. As noted above, the totality of Brewer's evidence, including the lack of available counsel, demonstrates that there is no practical, viable means of individualized dispute resolution.

The title company asserts that the availability of attorney's fees and punitive damages under the state merchandising practices act negates Brewer's argument that attorneys are unwilling to handle claims such as hers. The title company notes that reported cases indicate that some lawyers are willing to handle cases brought under the federal truth in lending and fair debt collection practices acts and that this proves that statutory damages provide sufficient financial incentive for attorneys to assist consumers in individual, small dollar claims. The deficiency in the title company's argument is that it presents a totally theoretical position that attorneys should want to take such cases. Speculation is not a substitute for evidence. In this case, there was specific and uncontradicted evidence before the trial court demonstrating that attorneys were unlikely to take claims such as Brewer's on an individual basis. Even if some attorneys may take some cases because of the potential availability of fees under the merchandising practices act, this does not prove that Brewer would have the benefit of counsel in attempting to obtain a remedy on an individual basis.

Finally, . . . the title company drafted the agreement to bind the consumer to individual arbitration for all claims against the title company, but it specifically reserved its right to forego arbitration "to seek possession of the Collateral in the event of default by judicial or other process including self-help repossession." In the context of a title loan transaction, this is a particularly onerous provision because among the lender's chief remedies in the event of default is either judicial or self-help repossession. The title company reserves its right to obtain its primary remedies through the court system while requiring Brewer to obtain her only meaningful remedy — monetary compensation for the alleged violation of consumer protection laws — through individual arbitration.[4]

The disparity in bargaining power, in addition to the disparity between Brewer's remedial options and the title company's remedial options, constitutes strong evidence that the agreement is unconscionable. The title company requires Brewer to arbitrate all of her claims in the interests of efficient, streamlined dispute resolution. However, when the title company's interests are at stake, the title company is free to discard the efficiencies of arbitration in favor of litigating a claim against Brewer. It is unlikely that the ramifications of such provisions are comprehended by the average consumer or comport with the reasonable expectations of an average member of the public. . . .

Conclusion

The judgment finding the class arbitration waiver unconscionable is affirmed because the entire arbitration agreement is unconscionable and unenforceable. The judgment is reversed, however, to the extent that it severs the class arbitration waiver and requires an arbitrator to determine the propriety of class arbitration. The case is remanded.

STITH, J., PFEIFFER, Sp. J., and WOLFF, Sr. J., concur.

FISCHER, J., dissents in separate opinion [omitted], in which BRECKENRIDGE, J., concurs.

RUSSELL and DRAPER, JJ., not participating.

---

4. Not only does the title company retain the right to seek judicial remedies, the title company further protects its interests by charging an extremely high interest rate to compensate for the risks inherent in its lending practices. While there is no allegation that the 300-percent annual interest rate that the title company charges is illegal, it plainly illustrates the fact that the agreement is drafted to limit substantially the remedial options of often financially distressed consumers while allowing the title company substantial latitude in protecting its financial interests.

PRICE, J., dissenting.

. . . [T]he majority here, just as in *Brewer I*, strikes down an arbitration clause in an attempt to balance the scales between poor consumers and businesses. Regardless of whether this is a laudable goal,[1] it is forbidden by the FAA, *Concepcion* and the law of Missouri because the rule the majority establishes is directed solely at invalidating arbitration agreements.

I dissent. I would enforce the contract as written. . . .

III. Analysis

Despite the majority's claims to the contrary, *Concepcion* is not difficult to understand or apply. It provides that an agreement to arbitrate may be invalidated by "generally applicable contract defenses, such as fraud, duress, or unconscionability, but not by defenses that apply only to arbitration or that derive their meaning from the fact that an agreement to arbitrate is at issue." . . . Missouri state law principles of unconscionability apply, unless those principles apply only to agreements to arbitrate or they derive meaning just because an agreement to arbitrate is at issue.

While Justice Thomas wrote separately in *Concepcion*, he expressly concurred in the majority opinion and made it the controlling statement of law. Justice Thomas, however, individually advocated that only issues related to the "making of the agreement" should be grounds for revocation of an agreement to arbitrate. Id. at 1754 (Thomas, J., concurring) (reasoning that an agreement to arbitrate should be enforced unless a defense concerning the formation of the agreement applies, such as fraud, duress or mutual mistake).

The majority of this Court uses Justice Thomas' concurrence to combine the issues of substantive and procedural unconscionability and do away with the requirement that the contract be procedurally unconscionable. The majority's reliance on the concurrence is misplaced, though, as Justice Thomas argued that a deficiency in the "formation of the contract" must exist to find the agreement unconscionable. Traditional procedural unconscionability issues are those that reflect problems in the formation of the contract. The majority fails to establish that Brewer has proven a defense regarding the formation of the agreement, thereby failing to meet Justice Thomas' suggested test, the *Concepcion* majority's test, and the requirements of unconscionability under Missouri law. [The dissent then argues that Missouri law requires both procedural and substantive unconscionability, and that the arbitration clause at issue is neither procedurally nor substantively unconscionable.] . . .

. . . Courts simply may not apply state public policy concerns to invalidate an arbitration agreement, even if the public policy at issue aims to prevent undesirable results to consumers. Concepcion, *supra* (rejecting the argument that small-dollar claims require class proceedings because states "cannot require a procedure that is inconsistent with the FAA."). The Supreme Court has made it clear that a

---

1. I do not contest that some of the terms in the title loan agreement are harsh.

state public policy against enforcing arbitration agreements shall not influence a state court's unconscionability finding. *Marmet, supra.*

. . . The rewards and attorneys' fees in the *Concepcion* contract . . . were never stated as requirements for finding the contract conscionable. Moreover, Missouri law already provides effective alternative remedies. The Missouri merchandising practices act allows a court to award a consumer attorneys' fees and punitive damages if appropriate.[10] While it may be generous for a company to contract as the company did in *Concepcion*, such a contract would create duplicate remedies in Missouri.

No evidence was presented showing that Brewer could not get an attorney to handle her case. In fact, the suit itself, with Brewer's counsel of record, proves the contrary. More importantly, such provisions in a contract provide no evidence as to the procedural conscionability of the contract at formation.

IV.   Conclusion

The majority's newly created right to an attorney for consumer claims morphs into a right to class arbitration proceedings, and then morphs into a right to void individual arbitration agreements altogether. While this is certainly clever lawyering, it is not the law and it openly flaunts the FAA and *Concepcion*. In this case, Brewer admits she did not read the contract and, although she knew of other lenders, she did not shop around for better terms and provisions. Despite the harsh terms of the contract she signed, it was her agreement. She was not cheated in its formation, and she should not be allowed to escape the contract's substantive provisions, including a provision to arbitrate, after receiving the benefits of the contract.

This case is nothing more than evidence of the majority's refusal to abide by controlling federal law because it disfavors the use of individual arbitration clauses in consumer contracts and prefers class action litigation that dramatically increases the cost and risk to the business community. These types of value decisions are more appropriately left to the legislative arena. In fact, those decisions were made by the United States Congress in the FAA and interpreted by the United States Supreme Court in *Concepcion*. It is our role to follow and apply the controlling law, not to engage in intellectual gymnastics to create "life after *Concepcion*."

Questions and Comments

(1) Which opinion in *Concepcion* seems most sound? Note that the enacting Congress clearly had no intent whatsoever regarding class waivers because the class mechanism did not exist in 1925, and the legislative history indicates that Congress was focused on providing merchants rather than consumers and employees with an alternative forum for dispute resolution. *See generally* Moses,

---

10. "The court may, in its discretion, award punitive damages and may award to the prevailing party attorney's fees, based on the amount of time reasonably expended, and may provide such equitable relief as it deems necessary or proper." Section 407.025, RSMo Supp.2009.

Arbitration Law: Who's in Charge, 40 Seton Hall L. Rev. 147 (2010). What, then, justifies the majority's conclusion that state regulation of class arbitration waivers should be preempted? As a matter of policy, should states have been left to experiment with enforcement of these clauses? Does promotion of a national market somehow justify a single rule that favors individual rather than class arbitration?

(2) AT&T's arbitration clause was uncommonly generous to customers who wished to pursue individual claims against the company. To what extent might this factor have influenced the Court's conclusion? If a clause is less generous to the consumer, would a state court be permitted to strike the arbitration clause? Could it strike a class waiver? Note that the majority and dissent in *Brewer* disagree on the answer to these questions.

(3) The upshot of *Concepcion* is that in most contexts companies can use arbitration clauses to defeat class proceedings altogether. Is this a good result? Some have suggested that companies place arbitration clauses in their standard form agreements primarily as a device to circumvent class proceedings. *See* Eisenberg, Miller & Sherwin, *Arbitration's Summer Soldiers: An Empirical Study of Arbitration Clauses in Consumer and Nonconsumer Contracts*, 41 U. Mich. J.L. Reform 871, 894 (2008). Since *Concepcion*, the Supreme Court has been consistent in protecting parties' contractual choice of individualized arbitration. *See* DirectTV, Inc. v. Imburgia, 136 S. Ct. 463 (2015); Epic Systems Corp. v. Lewis, 138 S. Ct. 1612 (2018).

(4) Is the *Concepcion* majority correct that forcing parties to arbitrate through class proceedings will discourage them from choosing arbitration? Presumably companies derive multiple benefits from arbitration, but it does seem clear that many companies steer far clear of class action arbitration (as opposed to class action litigation). For example, *Discover Card* provided in its agreement for court litigation rather than arbitration in the event that its no-class-arbitration provision was struck down. Issacharoff & Delaney, *Credit Card Accountability*, 73 U. Chi. L. Rev. 157 (2006). *But see* Skirchak v. Dynamics Research Corp., 508 F.3d 49, 63 (1st Cir. 2007) ("At oral argument we asked the parties whether each would prefer to be in arbitration even if the class action waiver clause was stricken. The company said it would prefer to be in arbitration; the plaintiffs agreed.").

(5) After *Concepcion*, would it be permissible for a state to refuse to enforce a class arbitration waiver unless the waiver is conspicuously presented in the arbitration agreement with bold type or capital letters? In footnote 6, the *Concepcion* majority opinion suggests that this regulation of class waivers would be permissible. Prior to *Concepcion*, the Utah legislature enacted such a rule for application to arbitration clauses found in credit card agreements. Utah Code Ann. §704C-4-105(2)(c)(i)-(ii) (2006). Is this an effective substitute form of regulation? Is it even permissible under the FAA? In Doctor's Associates, Inc. v. Casarotto, 517 U.S. 681 (1996), the Supreme Court held that a Montana statute that required notice of an arbitration clause to be provided in conspicuous type on the first page of a contract was preempted by the FAA. As with California's treatment of class waivers in *Concepcion*, Montana's statute impermissibly treated arbitration agreements differently than other contracts. How then can Utah's statute be upheld? Does *Concepcion* limit the reach of *Casarotto*, and if so, how? Does it matter that the Montana statute applied to all contracts but the Utah statute just applies to consumer credit card agreements? If so, why?

(6) More generally, consider the *Brewer* dissent's position that after *Concepcion* states cannot employ unconscionability principles that apply only to agreements to arbitrate or that "derive meaning just because an agreement to arbitrate is at issue." The statement seems like a reasonable interpretation of the *Concepcion* majority opinion, but does it effectively eliminate states' ability to use contract doctrines to ensure the fairness of arbitration clauses? Presumably the fairness of a contract clause turns on the substance of a clause and the context in which it is used — isn't that always an individualized rather than a general treatment? And if *Concepcion* really does merely reinforce the general proposition that states cannot treat arbitration clauses differently from the way they treat other clauses, what was wrong with the *Discover Bank* rule? It appeared to treat class waivers the same, whether applied in arbitration or litigation.

(7) It is clear from *Concepcion* that the FAA functions to limit or alter the unconscionability defense as applied to arbitration. But exactly how is the defense limited or altered? The majority and dissent in *Brewer* disagree on the answer to this question. Is one conclusion more convincing than the other? How would you answer this question?

(8) Note that the Supreme Court's interpretation of the FAA forces states to treat the enforcement of arbitration clauses differently than they typically treat choice-of-court clauses. Recall from Section B that state courts are permitted to regulate the enforcement of choice-of-court clauses as they see fit, with most willing to enforce them unless they are somehow unreasonable or unfair. In contrast, arbitration clauses can only be scrutinized using generally applicable contract doctrines, and those doctrines apparently cannot be modified to take into account the peculiar circumstances of arbitration. Specifically, recall the California court's conclusion in *America Online*, that the Virginia choice-of-court clause was not enforceable. If the company had opted for the same laws and procedures in arbitration (to be held in Virginia) rather than in the Virginia courts, could the California courts refuse to enforce the arbitration clause?

(9) Should the parties (or the contract drafter) be permitted to choose the applicable law for providing the content of the general contract law defenses? Courts vary in their views on this question. *See, e.g.,* Bridge Fund Capital Corp. v. Fastbucks Franchise Corp., 622 F.3d 996 (9th Cir. 2010) (California forum law applied instead of Texas law designated in the contract); Schnuerle v. Insight Communications Co., 2010 WL 5129850 (Ky. 2010) (Kentucky forum law applied instead of New York law designated in the contract); Coady v. Cross Country Bank, 729 S.W.2d 732 (Wis. Ct. App. 2007) (Wisconsin forum law rather than Delaware law chosen by the parties applies); Bragel v. General Steel Corp., 2006 WL 2623931 (Mass. Super. 2006) (unpublished opinion) (Colorado law selected by the parties applies); Spann v. American Express Travel Related Services Co., 224 S.W.3d 698 (Tenn. Ct. App. 2006) (Utah law chosen by the parties applies); Hubbert v. Dell Corp., 359 Ill. App. 3d 976 (2005) (applying Texas law designated in the contract).

(10) Some of the major arbitration associations have adopted standards designed to ensure that individuals subject to arbitration as a consequence of terms found in a business's standard form agreement are not deprived of fundamental rights. The AAA, for example, posts a Consumer Due Process Protocol, *see*

https://www.adr.org/sites/default/files/document_repository/Consumer%20 Due%20Process%20Protocol%20(1).pdf, which must be substantially satisfied as a prerequisite to AAA administration of the claim. The Protocol requires that the consumer be given fair notice of both the arbitration provision and its import. The Protocol also states that fees must be reasonable to the consumer, even if that means that the company must subsidize those fees. The consumer must be given the option to proceed in small claims court instead of arbitration. Furthermore, the arbitrator should retain the ability to grant any remedy that would be available in court.

JAMS posts Minimum Standards of Procedural Fairness, *http://www .jamsadr.com/rules-consumer-minimum-standards/*, its own Protocol to be applied to similar contracts. JAMS minimum standards are even more onerous. In addition to requirements similar to those found in the AAA Protocol, the arbitration agreement must be reciprocally binding (if the consumer must arbitrate, so too must the company). Furthermore, consumers must be entitled to: (1) participate in the selection of the arbitrator; (2) make reasonable discovery requests; and (3) obtain a hearing in their hometown area. Does the evolution of such protocols suggest that court oversight of arbitration clauses is unnecessary? Or might the arbitration association actions be attributable to court disapproval of the former state of arbitration for standard form contracts? Do you predict that arbitration associations will engage in more or less self-regulation in the aftermath of *Concepcion*? How does the *Brewer* opinion inform your analysis?

10

Choice of Law in Complex Litigation

A. Introduction

In many of the cases reproduced in previous chapters, the choice-of-law problem involved a choice between two jurisdictions' laws and the dispute involved a single defendant and a single plaintiff. This chapter considers a much more difficult question that currently plagues many U.S. courts: how to determine the applicable law when a large number of plaintiffs each bring one or more claims, at times against multiple defendants, which are treated as a single case in at least some respects. The following materials consider two complex litigation contexts: (1) putative class action proceedings in state and federal courts ("class action cases"); and (2) pretrial proceedings in Multidistrict Litigation cases ("MDL cases"). MDL cases are multiple related actions filed in different federal district courts but transferred to a single federal district court for consolidated pretrial proceedings.

The class action device enables multiple plaintiffs to consolidate their individual claims into a single lawsuit. The class action is particularly helpful in situations where a number of individuals all suffer relatively small harms from the same basic cause, because in these circumstances many of the individual harms might

737

go unaddressed or the cases ineffectively prosecuted without a device that enables plaintiffs to pool the value of their claims. Class actions are not available anytime plaintiffs wish to aggregate their claims, however. Rules governing the certification of class actions in state and federal courts are designed to ensure that the proposed class action would further the aims of efficiency and fair adjudication. Federal Rule of Civil Procedure 23 governs class action certification in federal courts, and several states have adopted rules that mirror Rule 23. Rule 23(a) describes the attributes of an action that are necessary for class action certification. It provides:

> (a) Prerequisites. One or more members of a class may sue or be sued as representative parties on behalf of all members only if:
>
> (1) the class is so numerous that joinder of all members is impracticable;
>
> (2) there are questions of law or fact common to the class;
>
> (3) the claims or defenses of the representative parties are typical of the claims or defenses of the class; and
>
> (4) the representative parties will fairly and adequately protect the interests of the class.

These prerequisites are commonly referred to as numerosity, commonality, typicality, and adequacy, respectively. Numerosity, commonality, and typicality all help to ensure that the claims are appropriate for class treatment rather than individual prosecution. Typicality and adequacy help to address fairness problems that can arise with the reality that very few class plaintiffs will be actively involved in the prosecution of the claims and yet the ultimate resolution will bind all plaintiffs.

In addition to satisfying these four prerequisites, certification requires that the proposed class action falls into one of the types of class actions described in Rule 23(b):

> (b) Types of Class Actions. A class action may be maintained if Rule 23(a) is satisfied and if:
>
> (1) prosecuting separate actions by or against individual class members would create a risk of:
>
> (A) inconsistent or varying adjudications with respect to individual class members that would establish incompatible standards of conduct for the party opposing the class; or
>
> (B) adjudications with respect to individual class members that, as a practical matter, would be dispositive of the interests of the other members not parties to the individual adjudications or would substantially impair or impede their ability to protect their interests;
>
> (2) the party opposing the class has acted or refused to act on grounds that apply generally to the class, so that final injunctive relief or corresponding declaratory relief is appropriate respecting the class as a whole; or
>
> (3) the court finds that the questions of law or fact common to class members predominate over any questions affecting only individual members, and that a class action is superior to other available methods for fairly and efficiently adjudicating the controversy. The matters pertinent to these findings include:
>
> (A) the class members' interests in individually controlling the prosecution or defense of separate actions;

(B) the extent and nature of any litigation concerning the controversy already begun by or against class members;

(C) the desirability or undesirability of concentrating the litigation of the claims in the particular forum; and

(D) the likely difficulties in managing a class action.

Subsection (b)(1) is designed to cover situations where the remedy ordered by a court in an earlier action might effectively limit or preclude the remedies that are available to plaintiffs and courts in later actions. For example, this subsection is occasionally applied to limited fund cases, where all plaintiffs seeking money damages must recover from a fixed and limited fund with a value that is likely not large enough to satisfy all of the claims. Subsection (b)(2) covers situations where plaintiffs seek primarily declaratory or injunctive relief and that relief would be appropriately administered to the class as a whole. Subsection (b)(3) covers the typical actions where plaintiffs seek primarily money damages but there is no limited fund problem. Cases can fall into more than one of these categories. Note that the certification requirements are more onerous for cases that fall under subsection (b)(3). What might justify the differing certification standards here?

Choice of law is relevant to class certification under Rule 23 in a number of ways. For example, the governing laws applied to each claim can influence whether "the claims or defenses of the representative parties are typical of the claims or defenses of the class" under Rule 23(a). More importantly, if the individual claims will be resolved pursuant to differing jurisdictions' governing laws, and the class is seeking certification under Rule 23(b)(3), then the "questions of law or fact common to class members" might fail to "predominate over" "questions affecting only individual members." In addition, multiple governing laws might render the class action inferior to other methods of adjudicating the controversy. In these situations, courts might determine that under Rule 23(b)(3)(D) "the likely difficulties in managing a class action" are too large to justify certification.

As with all actions, the choice-of-law determination here can significantly affect the likely success of the plaintiffs' claims and, once the governing law is known, the case is more likely to settle. However, choice of law appears to be even more significant in putative class actions than in other actions for two reasons: (1) Class actions almost never go to trial or appeal thereafter, so the choice-of-law determinations are more likely to have controlling significance in these cases; and (2) the certifiability of a class action based on state law often turns on the governing law. As the cases in this chapter illustrate, the viability of dozens, hundreds, or even thousands of claims can thus turn on the choice-of-law determination, even when the laws of every connected state provide remedy to plaintiffs.

Because the choice-of-law determination is so important to the viability of the class action, plaintiffs' attorneys often attempt to file class claims in courts that use choice-of-law methods that increase the likelihood that the certification prerequisites will be deemed satisfied. Strategic class action filings in state courts have been somewhat limited with Congress's passage of the Class Action Fairness Act of 2005 ("CAFA"). CAFA was designed to discipline some of the state courts that were notorious for certifying nationwide class actions. It facilitated defendants' removal of class actions to federal court by relaxing the diversity of citizenship requirement for class claims with more than $5,000,000 in controversy. *See* 28 U.S.C.A. §1332(d)(2). However, CAFA did not directly address choice of law for class actions. Under *Klaxon*, federal courts sitting in diversity must continue to apply state choice-of-law rules, so it appears that strategic filings continue, with choice-of-law arguments sometimes made in federal rather than state court. Given the flexibility of state choice-of-law rules, however, federal courts are far from fully constrained in their determinations.

MDL cases also are significantly influenced by choice-of-law determinations, although the effects in these cases are more subtle. Under 28 U.S.C. §1407, the Judicial Panel on Multidistrict Litigation, which consists of seven federal district and circuit court judges, may transfer "civil actions involving one or more common questions of fact" that "are pending in different districts" "to any district for coordinated or consolidated pretrial proceedings." These pretrial consolidations are authorized in circumstances where the Judicial Panel determines "that transfers for such proceedings will be for the convenience of parties and witnesses and will promote the just and efficient conduct of such actions." *Id.* §1407(a). Among other pretrial determinations, the transferee judge is empowered to issue determinations regarding the governing law(s) for the consolidated actions. When a case that involves state law claims is transferred from one federal district court to another, the transferee court must apply the choice-of-law principles of the state where the transferor court is located. Van Dusen v. Barrack, 376 U.S. 612 (1964). When state law claims are consolidated under §1407, the transferee court is required to apply the choice-of-law principles of the states where the individual claims were each originally filed. *See Manual for Complex Litigation* §31.132 at 254 (3d ed. 1995). In practice, however, the transferee court, faced with a bundle of claims involving the same or similar events, may view the choice-of-law inquiry differently than would a court faced with a single claim. Given the flexibility in state choice-of-law doctrine, the transferee court is often able to adjust the governing law in order to "promote the just and efficient conduct of such actions." Cases consolidated for pretrial purposes typically settle prior to being sent back for trial. *See Annual Report of the Director of the Administrative Office of the U.S. Courts* 21 (1990) (nearly 96 percent of cases consolidated under §1407 between 1968 and 1990 were terminated by the transferee courts). Thus, choice-of-law determinations made by the transferee court are unlikely to be reviewed by the transferor court and are quite capable of significantly influencing the outcome of nationwide litigation.

This chapter explores some of the approaches that courts have taken to resolve choice-of-law issues in complex litigation. Class action plaintiffs' attorneys sometimes seek to remove state choice-of-law impediments to certification by casting claims under federal law — securities, antitrust, RICO, or other federal private rights of action. When such efforts fail or are unavailable, plaintiffs pursue other strategies, including arguments that (1) state law is sufficiently uniform or can be melded together so that no choice-of-law problem impedes class certification; (2) although state laws differ, the relevant choice-of-law analysis points to a single state's governing law; or (3) although multiple state laws apply to the claims, the class action can manageably be broken into subclasses to take into account the varying governing laws. Some of these strategies also are present in consolidated MDL proceedings.

B.   Approaches to Choice of Law

Recall that in Phillips Petroleum Co. v. Shutts, *supra* page 310, the U.S. Supreme Court rejected the Kansas Supreme Court's position that it had more latitude in applying its own law to the claims due to the fact that it was adjudicating a nationwide class action:

> [W]hile a state may . . . assume jurisdiction over the claims of plaintiffs whose principal contacts are with other States, it may not use this assumption of jurisdiction as an added weight in the scale when considering the permissible constitutional limits on choice of substantive law. . . . The issue of personal jurisdiction over plaintiffs in a class action is entirely distinct from the question of the constitutional limitations on choice of law; the latter calculus is not altered by the fact that it may be more difficult or more burdensome to comply with the constitutional limitations because of the large number of transactions which the State proposes to adjudicate and which have little connection with the forum. . . .
>
> . . . [T]he constitutional limitations laid down in cases such as *Allstate* and Home Ins. Co. v. Dick must be respected even in a nationwide class action.

Within this constitutional constraint, what can and should courts do to resolve the choice-of-law issues?

1.   No Choice Necessary

Ferrell v. Allstate Insurance Co.

144 N.M. 405 (2008)

Bosson, J.

This appeal arises as a result of the district court's decision to certify a multi-state class in New Mexico for the purposes of litigating a class action lawsuit against Allstate Insurance Company (Allstate). Plaintiffs are Allstate insureds who contend that Allstate is liable for breach of contract for failing to include installment fees that are charged when an insured opts to pay the premium in monthly installments in the total premium calculation. Allstate counters that the installment fees are not part of the premium; instead, the fees are imposed when an insured chooses to pay the policy in installments rather than in one lump sum.[1]

---

1. Plaintiffs acknowledge that the underlying issue in this case may, in fact, be moot based on the Court of Appeals' recent decision in Nakashima v. State Farm Mutual Automobile Insurance Co., 141 N.M. 239, *cert. denied*, 141 N.M. 401. Despite the similarities between *Nakashima* and this appeal, Plaintiffs believe that their facts are distinguishable from *Nakashima*. Class certification, however, is not the appropriate time to decide the merits of a case. Because the validity of class certification is the only issue on appeal, we do not reach the question of mootness.

Plaintiffs originally requested that the district court certify a nationwide class, but eventually narrowed the class to fifteen states, including New Mexico. The district court . . . certified a class of thirteen states and found that there was no conflict among the laws of the thirteen states such that application of New Mexico law to the plaintiffs from those states was appropriate. The district court declined to certify the plaintiffs from either Hawaii or Washington because, unlike the policies from the other thirteen states, the insurance policies issued in those states contained specific information about installment fees. The district court "retain[ed] jurisdiction to create subclasses or otherwise alter or amend [the certification order] before a decision on the merits." Allstate appealed the class certification to the Court of Appeals. . . .

The Court of Appeals first reviewed the laws of the states connected to the dispute and determined that the laws of the thirteen states potentially conflicted with one another, due to unresolved ambiguities in each state's law. Based upon this conclusion, the Court determined it would be inappropriate to apply New Mexico law to the entire multi-state class. . . . [T]he Court undertook a conflict-of-laws analysis and determined that the laws of the state where each insurance contract was entered into would separately apply to the plaintiffs from that state. In other words, if the multi-state class action were to proceed, the district court would have to apply the laws of each of the thirteen states connected to the dispute. Because the "need to apply the ambiguous laws of the other class states would render [the] case unmanageable and not superior as a matter of law," the Court of Appeals decertified the class with respect to all out-of-state class members. The Court of Appeals affirmed the certification with respect to New Mexico class members only, . . . subject to the district court's discretion. We granted certiorari to review significant, novel issues relevant to New Mexico class action jurisprudence. . . .

Discussion

The district court's certification was appropriate if the court properly considered the requirements of our class action rule, portions of which can only be satisfied in a multi-state class action by considering conflict-of-laws principles. We begin our discussion with an overview of our class action rule, which forms the backdrop of this appeal. We then discuss the Court of Appeals' determination that the laws of the thirteen states connected to this dispute conflicted. In so doing, we consider as a vital threshold inquiry whether the class proponent has the burden of affirmatively disproving a hypothetical conflict between the laws of the relevant states, as the Court of Appeals held, or whether the party opposing certification has the burden of affirmatively proving that the laws of the relevant states actually conflict.

CLASS ACTIONS IN GENERAL

[The court set out the text of Rule 1-023(A) and (B), and noted that its language mirrors that of FRCP 23.] Thus, we may seek guidance from federal law applying the rule. . . .

RULE 1-023(B): CLASS ACTIONS MAINTAINABLE

In addition to meeting all of the threshold requirements of Rule 1-023(A), a district court may only certify a class if the class meets the requirements of one of the categories contained in Rule 1-023(B). Of the three categories of Rule 1-023(B), only subsection (B)(3) is relevant to this appeal because it is the category that generally applies when class members seek monetary damages. Rule 1-023(B)(3) provides that a class action is maintainable only if "the court finds that the questions of law or fact common to the members of the class predominate over any questions affecting only individual members, and that a class action is superior to other available methods for the fair and efficient adjudication of the controversy." "Subdivision (b)(3) encompasses those cases in which a class action would achieve economies of time, effort, and expense, and promote uniformity of decision as to persons similarly situated, without sacrificing procedural fairness or bringing about other undesirable results." 1 Conte & Newberg, *supra*, §3:1, at 214 (quoting Rules Advisory Committee to 1966 Amendments to Rule 23).

The requirements contained in subsection (B)(3) are commonly referred to as predominance and superiority. Our class action rule does not define predominance and superiority, but [Rule 1-023(B)(3)] contains several factors to consider when making a determination about whether predominance and superiority have been met. Those relevant factors include:

(a) the interest of members of the class in individually controlling the prosecution or defense of separate actions; (b) the extent and nature of any litigation concerning the controversy already commenced by or against members of the class; (c) the desirability or undesirability of concentrating the litigation of the claims in the particular forum; (d) the difficulties likely to be encountered in the management of a class action.

Class actions involving plaintiffs from multiple states present particular challenges for district courts, and may "implicate the predominance and superiority requirements . . . because of the combination of individual legal and factual issues that need to be determined." 7AA Charles Alan Wright et al., *Federal Practice and Procedure* §1780.1, at 202 (3d ed. 2005). If too many separate state laws must be applied, then the class proponent may have a difficult time persuading the district court that common questions of law predominate and that a class action is the superior method of litigation. A determination that the district court will have to apply the laws of multiple states also impacts the court's ability to manage the proposed class. *See* Rule 1-023(B)(3)(d); 7AA Wright et al., *supra*, §1780.1, at 211 ("[C]ourts also have found that the class device is not a superior method to adjudicate the claims [of a multi-state class] because differences in state law make the action unmanageable.").

A decision to apply the laws of several states does not, however, necessarily foreclose class certification. A court may be able to manage a class through the use of subclasses or by grouping certain issues together that can be resolved by applying one state's law. *See* In re Sch. Asbestos Litig., 789 F.2d 996, 1011 (3d Cir. 1986) (affirming class certification under Rule 23(b)(3) because, even though "manageability [was] a serious concern, . . . [m]anageability is a practical problem, one with which the district court generally has a greater degree of expertise and familiarity than does an appellate court").

Thus, a certifying court must first determine which law will apply to the class so that it can then assess the predominance and superiority of the proposed class action. Plaintiffs bear the initial burden of producing evidence of the various states' laws and demonstrating "'that class certification does not present insuperable obstacles.' If the defendant wishes to contest the plaintiff's characterization of the laws of the relevant states, the defendant must "inform the district court of any errors they perceive." If the defendant fails to bring any "'clearly established' contradictory law" to the court's attention, the district court cannot be faulted if it concludes that the laws of the jurisdictions connected to the dispute do not conflict such that a single state's law may be applied to the entire class. [Berry v. Fed. Kemper Life Assurance Co., 2004-NMCA-116] [quoting Sun Oil Co. v. Wortman, *supra* page 316].

In this case, the district court's decision to certify the class was proper if the district court correctly determined that New Mexico law applied to the entire class. A district court's choice to apply forum law is appropriate if (1) the choice to apply forum law is constitutional or (2) an application of the forum's choice-of-law rules leads to the selection of forum law. A forum's choice to apply its own law is constitutional if the law of the forum does not actually conflict with the law of any other jurisdiction connected to the dispute. *See Shutts* [*supra* page 310] ("There can be no injury in applying [forum] law if it is not in conflict with that of any other jurisdiction connected to this suit."). Additionally, a forum's choice to apply its own law is constitutional, even if the laws of the states connected to the dispute actually conflict, if the forum state has "a significant contact or significant aggregation of contacts, creating state interests, such that choice of its law is neither arbitrary nor fundamentally unfair." *Id*. [quoting Allstate Ins. Co. v. Hague, *supra* page 297]. The parties to this appeal have focused their arguments on whether the Court of Appeals correctly found an actual conflict between New Mexico law and the laws of the other twelve states. We will concentrate our analysis in a similar fashion.

CONFLICT-OF-LAWS

. . . [W]hen the laws of the relevant states do not actually conflict, the court may avoid a conflict-of-law analysis and may apply forum law to the entire class. *See Shutts* ("We must first determine whether [forum] law conflicts in any material way with any other law which could apply. There can be no injury in applying [forum] law if it is not in conflict with that of any other jurisdiction connected to this suit."). If, however, the laws of the relevant states actually conflict, or if the laws of certain of the relevant states conflict, then the forum court must resolve that conflict using the choice-of-law rules contained in the forum state's conflict-of-laws doctrine.

A district court's conclusion that the laws of the various states do not actually conflict is particularly important in multi-state class actions. If the law of a single state can be applied to the entire class, it is more likely that the class will meet the predominance and superiority requirements of our class action rule. The converse is true as well. If the laws of the states connected to the dispute actually conflict, and if the court's choice-of-law analysis provides that the laws of several states must apply to the class, then it is less likely that the class will meet the certification requirements.

WHEN CAN THE LAWS OF THE INTERESTED STATES BE SAID TO ACTUALLY CONFLICT SUCH THAT APPLICATION OF FORUM LAW IS INAPPROPRIATE?

In the instant appeal, the Court of Appeals concluded that a district court may only apply forum law to class members from other states if the laws of the states connected to the dispute "are identical, or different, but produce *identical* results" (emphasis added). While acknowledging the apparent similarities among the states' laws, the Court of Appeals was nevertheless troubled because "[n]one of the class states [had] appellate court opinions interpreting the statutory definition of premium or otherwise deciding whether fees constitute premium in the context of a breach of contract issue." Despite the lack of evidence that the difference in state law would actually influence the outcome of a trial on the merits, the Court of Appeals concluded that where the laws of the relevant states "*could* produce different results," (emphasis added), it would be inappropriate to apply New Mexico law to the entire class.

The Court limited its analysis to a comparison of the statutory definition of premium, and to the issue of whether fees constitute premiums. The Court noted that six states "have a statutory definition of 'premium' that is materially the same as the definition found in New Mexico's Section 59A-18-3." The Court further stated that three states "have statutes that essentially define premium as 'the consideration for insurance' but do not provide the list of examples that New Mexico's statute does." And, while three states did not have a statutory definition of premium, the Court acknowledged that two of those states had appellate opinions "holding that fees charged by insurance companies for the privilege of paying in monthly installments constitute 'gross premium' for purposes of statutory or constitutional provisions that require insurance companies to pay taxes on the 'gross premiums' collected.". . .

The question before us . . . is whether an actual conflict exists when the laws of the other states *could* hypothetically produce different results or whether an actual conflict requires a showing of something more. In answering that question, we examine whether the uncertainty created by the lack of appellate precedent necessarily creates an actual conflict. We also consider who must demonstrate the existence of an actual conflict and who carries the burden of failing to prove that an actual conflict exists.

We begin our discussion with [*Shutts*] and *Sun Oil*, two U.S. Supreme Court cases . . . before turning our attention to . . . *Berry*, a case similar to *Ferrell*, involving appellate review of a district court's decision to certify a multi-state class. In [*Shutts*], the U.S. Supreme Court reviewed the constitutionality of the Kansas court's decision to apply principles of Kansas law to the claims of a multi-state class. . . . [T]he Court held that a court may apply forum law when that law does not "conflict[] in *any material way* with any other law which could apply." (emphasis added). Alternatively, the forum court may apply its own state law, even if forum law conflicts with the laws of the other states connected to the dispute, as long as the forum has "a significant contact or significant aggregation of contacts, creating state interests, such that choice of its law is neither arbitrary nor fundamentally unfair." *Id.* [quoting *Hague, supra*]. "Given Kansas' lack of 'interest' in claims unrelated to that State, and the substantive conflict with jurisdictions such as Texas, we conclude that application of Kansas law to every claim in this case is sufficiently arbitrary and unfair as to exceed constitutional limits." *Id.* Having so concluded, the Supreme Court reversed the Kansas court's decision to apply Kansas law and remanded the case for the Kansas court to apply the laws of the other states connected to the dispute.

In *Sun Oil*, the U.S. Supreme Court had the opportunity to review how the Kansas court complied with the constitutional mandates set forth in [*Shutts*]. The Kansas court in *Sun Oil* again chose to apply principles of Kansas law to the entire class to determine the prejudgment interest rate with respect to the plaintiffs' claim for royalties. On appeal, to the U.S. Supreme Court, the defendant-oil company argued that the Kansas trial court had "unconstitutionally distorted" the laws of the other states when it concluded that the laws of those states did not materially conflict with the law of Kansas.

The U.S. Supreme Court acknowledged that the statutes of the relevant states were facially different, yet upheld the Kansas court's decision to apply Kansas law to determine the prejudgment interest rate for the entire class. The oil company had failed to present the court with any clearly established case law demonstrating that, under similar circumstances, the other states would apply their state's statutory rate, rather than the rate chosen by the Kansas court. The U.S. Supreme Court held that the Kansas court's interpretation of unsettled law was valid, even though the highest court of a sister state had yet to rule on the issue. *See id.* at n.4 (relying on a previous opinion where the Court had stated that "[t]here was neither allegation nor proof that the court of last resort in Louisiana had considered the question or made any ruling upon it, and so it became the duty of the Texas courts . . . to decide the question according to their independent judgment" (quoted authority omitted)); *see also Berry*, (relying on [*Shutts*] and *Sun Oil* for the proposition that "the forum court [is not] required to try to match or divine the result of the case as if it were being decided in the other states"). Additionally, the Supreme Court noted that simply because a forum court must interpret the laws of a sister state does not necessarily mean that the forum court is foreclosed from applying forum law, if the court interprets that law to be similar to the forum law. *See Sun Oil* (noting that the Kansas court was called upon to interpret a Texas appellate court decision and, in so doing, distinguished that case from the case at bar based on the "eminently reasonable ground" that the disputes did not involve the same legal claim).

. . . In *Berry*, the district court certified a nationwide class seeking damages against a life insurance company based on breach of contract and breach of the duty of good faith. In its conflict-of-laws analysis, the *Berry* court relied on [*Shutts*] and *Sun Oil* as a framework for determining whether the district court appropriately considered the differences between the laws of the various states when it decided to apply New Mexico law to the claims of the entire multi-state class. From those cases, the *Berry* Court distilled several overarching principles that a court should consider when making a determination about whether a conflict exists.

The Court noted that, as an initial step, "courts dealing with multistate class actions must consider and evaluate how the laws of other states apply to the class claims." While "[t]he forum state cannot simply assume that its law will govern[,] . . . the forum court [is not] required to try to match or divine the result of the case as if it were being decided in the other states. The forum court is only bound by 'clearly established' law brought to its attention." After setting forth these general principles, the Court then utilized them to analyze the plaintiffs' claims arising under both breach of contract, and breach of good faith and fair dealing.

With respect to the breach of contract claim, the *Berry* court focused on the significance of the demonstrated conflicts, not on potential conflicts. Rather than requiring an affirmative showing that the laws would produce identical results, the court noted that "the law in this area [was] *uniform enough*," there was "*no significant variation* in the cases from the standard approach to interpretation of insurance contracts," and there were "no *fatal* contradictions of law," (emphases added). Significantly, the *Berry* court rejected the defendant's argument that it would be improper to apply New Mexico law to the entire class because a determination of "whether the policy would be deemed ambiguous 'could' vary from state to state."

The *Berry* court rejected this argument for two reasons, which we find persuasive. First, the court noted that the district court had yet to decide that an ambiguity existed. Second, the court stated that it saw "no significant variation among the states concerning how [the] decision [about ambiguity] is made." Thus, the court rejected the defendant's argument—that the laws could potentially produce different results—because "there is no need to forecast how the inquiry would actually be resolved in any other court because the case is here, and the decision is to be made here in accordance with reasonably uniform rules." Because the laws of the relevant states were sufficiently uniform to allow the application of New Mexico law, the Court affirmed the district court's certification decision with respect to the breach of contract claim. *Id.*

The *Berry* court's discussion of the breach of good faith and fair dealing claim is illustrative of the level of proof required by a defendant to establish that an actual conflict exists. In its analysis, the court relied on actual variations among the laws of certain states in making the determination that the laws of the various states were not sufficiently uniform to apply New Mexico law. Significantly, the defendant cited established cases from the class states with holdings that were contrary to New Mexico law. Because the laws of the states were not sufficiently uniform, the court decertified the class with respect to the breach of good faith and fair dealing claim.

Having reviewed both *Ferrell* and *Berry*, it is clear that the two New Mexico Court of Appeals' opinions set forth conflicting standards for what constitutes an actual conflict. Plaintiffs argue that *Berry* and *Sun Oil* set forth rules that a court should follow when determining whether the laws of the states connected to the dispute can be said to conflict. The *Ferrell* court disagreed and did not rely on *Sun Oil* for what constitutes an actual conflict, because that court concluded that *Sun Oil* "does not say anything about when the laws of two jurisdictions can be said to 'conflict.'"

. . .

In addition to reading *Sun Oil* differently, *Berry* and *Ferrell* diverge on the issue of who bears the risk of ambiguity in the law. Both opinions appropriately place the initial burden of persuasion on the class proponent by requiring the plaintiffs to persuade the district court that there are no significant variations among the laws of the states connected to the dispute. However, the opinions apportion the risk of ambiguity differently. The *Berry* court places the risk of ambiguity on *the party opposing certification* by requiring that party to demonstrate that the laws of the various states actually conflict. The *Ferrell* court, on the other hand, places the risk of ambiguity *on the party seeking certification* by requiring that party to disprove all hypothetical conflicts before a court can conclude that forum law applies.

By placing the risk of ambiguity on the party seeking certification, the Court of Appeals' opinion in *Ferrell* can be read as holding that the party seeking certification cannot meet its burden if the laws of the other states are unclear or unsettled, despite significant facial similarities between the statutes at issue. Such a holding places an intolerable burden on the party seeking certification. Multistate class actions might never be possible if courts must await final appellate court decisions in each state resolving all hypothetical conflicts.

We agree with Plaintiffs that *Berry* sets forth the preferable analysis. The party opposing certification must establish that the laws of the relevant states actually conflict. *Sun Oil*. If the class proponents have met their burden and the party opposing certification fails to show that the laws of the relevant states actually conflict through clearly established, plainly contradictory law, then the district court cannot be faulted if it concludes that there is *no material* conflict between the laws of the relevant states.

The *Berry* court's approach is consistent with the principles underlying our class action rule—judicial economy and fairness to the parties. *See* Brooks v. Norwest Corp., 2004-NMCA-134, ¶9 ("The core policy behind the Rule is to provide a forum for plaintiffs with small claims who otherwise would be without any practical remedy. At the same time, the district court must ensure that a class action is not only efficient, but that it is a fair method to all parties, including absent class members and defendants."). This approach, while not necessarily favoring certification in all situations, does not act as an undue impediment to certification. Similarly, it ensures that the class certification is fair to all parties. Defendants cannot complain about the application of forum law if they have not presented law from another state to the contrary demonstrating a real, irreconcilable, and material conflict. Further, the plaintiffs will not face the unduly burdensome task of having to disprove all hypothetical conflicts.

WAS AN ACTUAL CONFLICT PROVEN SUCH THAT IT WAS INAPPROPRIATE FOR THE DISTRICT COURT TO DETERMINE THAT NEW MEXICO LAW COULD APPLY TO THE ENTIRE CLASS?

. . . In this case, the district court found that the class met the requirements of Rule 1-023(B). The district court made its determination based on its understanding of the various states' laws as presented by the parties. Plaintiffs presented the court with surveys detailing the laws from the various states involved in an attempt to meet their burden of showing that the predominance and superiority requirements of Rule 1-023 were met. These surveys consisted of: (1) excerpts from the relevant statutory provisions, (2) statutory definitions of "premium," and (3) case citations for various legal propositions relating to breach of contract. Allstate submitted a memorandum in opposition, which included a discussion regarding variations among the states' laws. In its memorandum, Allstate specifically argued that the relevant states differed with respect to certain affirmative defenses as well as contract interpretation, including the use of extrinsic evidence to resolve an ambiguity in the contract. Allstate also argued that the definition of premium varied from state-to-state. . . .

Plaintiffs suggested that the variations among the laws of the states connected to the dispute were either irrelevant or did not rise to the level of constitutional significance. For example, in its briefing, Allstate contended that the states differed with respect to authorizing or implying a private right of action for violations of the state insurance code. Plaintiffs countered that they were not seeking a private right of action under any state insurance code, but rather were suing under a common-law theory of breach of contract. Further, Plaintiffs noted that many of the conflicts discussed by Allstate arose in states other than those implicated in the proposed class. More to the point, Plaintiffs insisted that the definition of premium did not vary materially from state to state, and this went to the heart of Plaintiffs' class-wide claims for breach of contract. Additionally, Plaintiffs noted that the affirmative defenses that Allstate argued defeated class certification were simply "hypothetical."

After [an extensive] hearing, the district court concluded that "a class action is a superior method of litigation instead of individual lawsuits in each member's respective state." The court also concluded that the case was manageable because "there [was] no *debilitating* conflict of law among the thirteen (13) states on the issues of contract interpretation, right to jury trial, and the definition and specification of insurance policy premiums, the issues to be adjudicated under the breach of contract claim." (Emphasis added.) Significantly, the district court excluded the plaintiffs from Hawaii and Washington, which demonstrates that the court considered the differences between the policies, and the breach of contract claims premised on those policies, in the relevant states.

And, while Allstate argues that certain states may take a different approach with respect to the "four corners" rule for resolving an ambiguity in the contract, the district court's decision about whether an ambiguity exists would again be made using relatively uniform rules. If the district court determines that an ambiguity exists in some contracts, and that the states where those contracts were entered into vary significantly in their approach to the "four corners" doctrine, the district court may revisit its certification decision. Until that time, "there is no need to forecast how the inquiry would actually be resolved in any other court because the case is here, and the decision is to be made here in accordance with reasonably uniform rules." *Berry*.

Thus, Plaintiffs met their burden of showing that the laws of the class states were similar enough to support certification. The statutes at issue do not present "fatal contradictions of law." *Berry*. And while Allstate presented evidence of some differences between the laws of the class states, the district court was not persuaded that the differences rose to the level of constitutional significance. In a case such as this one, where the statutes of the other states have yet to be definitively construed by a state appellate court, any conflict will likely be hypothetical. A hypothetical conflict should not preclude the district court from deciding, on balance, that forum law may be applied to the entire class. Instead, under *Berry* and *Sun Oil*, the party opposing class certification must provide the district court with evidence that an actual conflict exists before a court will be faulted for concluding that forum law may apply to the entire class. In this case, the Court of Appeals implicitly acknowledged that Allstate had not met this burden when it stated "that if a New Mexico court were to apply New Mexico's statutory definition of premium to plaintiffs from other states, doing so would not run afoul of [*Sun Oil*]. [T]he court would not be ruling in contravention of the clearly established laws of other jurisdictions because . . . there is no clearly established law from any of the jurisdictions on the issue of whether fees constitute premium."

Thus, we conclude that the district court's decision to apply New Mexico law, in the absence of a demonstrated, material conflict, was proper. Because the district court's decision to apply New Mexico law to the entire class was appropriate, we conclude that the court did not abuse its discretion when it certified the class, and we remand to the district court for further proceedings consistent with this Opinion.

On remand the district court retains jurisdiction over the class and may revisit its certification decision. *See* Rule 1-023(C)(1). Thus, the court may need to consider changes in the laws of the class states that may have occurred while this appeal has been pending to ensure that class certification is still appropriate. *See Ferrell* ("If the court has second thoughts on any issue, it can reconsider and either decertify or modify certification if the manageability of damages adjudication or distribution proves to be an intolerable burden on the judicial system or otherwise proves to create a situation that is less fair and efficient than other available techniques.").

CONTINUED VIABILITY OF THE RESTATEMENT (FIRST) OF CONFLICT OF LAWS FOR MULTI-STATE CLASS ACTION LAWSUITS

After determining that an actual conflict existed in this case, the Court of Appeals correctly relied on the Restatement (First) of Conflict of Laws and the place of contracting rule contained within the Restatement (First) to determine what law ought apply to the class members from states other than New Mexico. However, we note that the Court of Appeals' adoption of the actual conflict doctrine represents a divergence from the analysis traditionally undertaken under the Restatement (First) because, as discussed below, the Restatement (First) does not contemplate a comparison of the laws of the states involved.

Despite being contrary to a traditional choice-of-law analysis, the Court's decision to adopt the actual conflict doctrine is consistent with the procedures required by our class action rule. As discussed above, a district court must undertake an analysis of the laws of the relevant states to ensure that the predominance and superiority requirements of the class action rule are met. If a court finds that the laws of the relevant states are similar enough to meet the predominance requirement, but then has to apply the laws of the state where the insured entered into the contract, the district court's analysis regarding predominance would have been in vain. Thus, a strict adherence to the traditional principles espoused by the Restatement (First) may render multi-state class actions a virtual nullity. Because we reverse the Court of Appeals' determination that an actual conflict exists in this case, we could stop at this point. However, because the doctrine we currently follow may no longer be appropriate for multi-state class action litigation, we resolve this potential problem in this Opinion for the benefit of our class action jurisprudence.

New Mexico has traditionally followed the Restatement (First). The Restatement (First) consists of rules for each substantive area of the law, which are based on a particular pre-determined contact. Thus, under the Restatement (First), a court does not choose between competing laws, but simply chooses between competing jurisdictions. If a party argues that the laws of the state where the right vested conflict with a fundamental public policy of New Mexico, a New Mexico court may refuse to apply that state's law.

As the Court of Appeals correctly noted, if an actual conflict exists, a court presiding over a multi-state class action lawsuit in a Restatement (First) jurisdiction must make an initial determination of which state or states' law applies to the controversy, based upon the traditional principles of the Restatement (First). Following this traditional approach literally, when faced with a multi-state class action, a court could not consider the laws of the other states connected to the dispute; instead the court would be required to apply the rule from the Restatement (First) that pertains to the claim alleged. *See* Leflar et al., *supra*, §86, at 256 (noting that a court in a state that has adopted the Restatement (First) "ha[s] only to determine . . . the nature of the issue before it . . . , look up the choice-of-law rule conceptually appropriate to that type of case, then apply the rule to the facts").

Thus, with respect to the instant appeal, the district court would have simply applied the Restatement (First) §311, "the [law of] 'the place of contracting.'" Assuming that the place of making the contract was the state where the insured entered into the contract, the district court would have been required to apply the separate law of each of the thirteen states involved in the class action, without considering the competing laws and policies of the other states connected to the suit. This leads to problems and could conflict with the policy behind class actions, i.e., the district court would have no choice but to apply the thirteen states' laws, which may make the class action unmanageable.

Because of the mechanical nature of its application, the Restatement (First) has been widely criticized as being inflexible, rigid, and leading to unjust results. Another criticism levied against the Restatement (First) is that it does not recognize choice-of-law provisions. Currently only eleven states, including New Mexico, continue to follow the choice-of-law rules set forth in the Restatement (First) with respect to contract claims.

Twenty-four states have rejected the Restatement (First) in favor of the Restatement (Second) of Conflict of Laws (1971) with respect to contract conflicts. The Restatement (Second) eschews a rigid, mechanical selection of a particular jurisdiction and, instead, focuses on the content of the laws of the states connected to the dispute. As such, a court does not choose between two competing jurisdictions, but between competing bodies of law, and competing public policies. *See* Leflar et al., *supra*, §100, at 282-284. Additionally, the Restatement (Second) proceeds issue by issue, rather than by an entire claim, so one issue may be resolved under the law of one jurisdiction, while another issue may be resolved under the law of a different jurisdiction. Further, the Restatement (Second), unlike the Restatement (First), acknowledges the realities of modern contracts and respects party autonomy by allowing the parties to choose the law that will govern the dispute. Restatement (Second) §187. If the contract has a valid choice-of-law provision, that law presumptively applies.

In the absence of an enforceable choice-of-law provision, and if the rules regarding specific types of contracts or specific issues in contract do not supply the law to be applied, the Restatement (Second) relies on the "most significant relationship" test which is used to determine which state has the most significant relationship to the transaction and to the parties. *Id.* §188(1), at 575. A court considers a variety of contacts when making a determination about which state's law applies to the dispute. *See id.* (listing the following relevant contacts "(a) the place of contracting, (b) the place of negotiation of the contract, (c) the place of performance, (d) the location of the subject matter of the contract, and (e) the domicil, residence, nationality, place of incorporation and place of business of the parties"). Significantly, a court must consider both the number of contacts in a given jurisdiction, and even more importantly, the quality of those contacts. *See id.* ("These contacts are to be evaluated according to their relative importance with respect to the particular issue."). The qualitative nature of a particular contact is determined by reference to the "Choice-of-Law Principles" set forth in Section 6, which include: (a) the needs of the interstate and international systems, (b) the relevant policies of the forum, (c) the relevant policies of other interested states and the relative interests of those states in the determination of the particular issue, (d) the protection of justified expectations, (e) the basic policies underlying the particular field of law, (f) certainty, predictability and uniformity of result, and (g) ease in the determination and application of the law to be applied.

After comparing the Restatement (First) and the Restatement (Second), it is apparent that the rigidity of the Restatement (First) is particularly ill-suited for the complexities present in multi-state class actions. It does not allow a court to consider the competing policies of the states implicated by the suit.[3] We conclude

---

3. Our courts have been willing to consider the Restatement (Second) approach in other circumstances. *See* Fed. Deposit Ins. Corp. v. Hiatt, 117 N.M. 461, 470 (1994) (Montgomery, C.J., dissenting) ("I wish to register my continuing objection to this Court's rigid adherence to the lex loci contractus choice-of-law rule for deciding which state's law will govern a dispute over a contract." (footnote omitted)); *id.* at 470 n.3 (noting that "[i]n State Farm Mutual Insurance Co. v. Conyers . . . [the New Mexico Supreme] Court displayed a willingness to consider an approach, such as that embodied in Section 6 of the [Second Restatement], other than the strict lex loci contractus rule." (citation omitted)); State Farm Mut. Ins. Co. v. Conyers, 109 N.M. 243, 247 (1989) ("In any event, in this case it is not necessary for us either to reaffirm a lex loci contractus rule categorically or to adopt or reject for all cases the Restatement (Second) 'significant relationship' tests. Even were we to apply a Restatement (Second) analysis, New Mexico law would still govern the outcome of this particular dispute."); In Re Gilmore, 124 N.M. 119 ("The approach, if not the result, [taken by the New Mexico Supreme Court] in *Torres* is consistent with the Restatement Second. . . . Although our Supreme Court has followed the Restatement Second in some respects—principally, with regard to forum non conveniens, and jurisdiction—we are well aware that it has not embraced the Restatement Second with respect to choice-of-law issues in either tort or contract."); Scoles et al., *supra*, §2.21, at 90 ("New Mexico's highest court has recently acknowledged its past adherence to the *lex loci delicti* rule but did not in fact apply it." (citing Torres v. State, 119 N.M. 609 (1995))).

that the Restatement (Second) is a more appropriate approach for multi-state contract class actions.

Thus, if a district court determines that the laws of the states implicated in a multi-state contract class action actually conflict, the court should then apply the principles of the Restatement (Second) to determine which law applies to the disputed issue. Once the court determines which law applies, the court must then determine whether the application of that chosen law is constitutional. Only then may a district court determine whether the class meets the requirements of our class action rule.

. . .

Questions and Comments

(1) As footnote 1 of the *Ferrell* court's opinion indicates, another New Mexico court (*Nakashima*) had already ruled on the merits of the same basic claim brought against State Farm Insurance Company. That court determined that the monthly payment fee did not constitute premium for purposes of state insurance law and therefore that the fee did not need to be included in the premium calculation. If *Nakashima* represents New Mexico law, does it now govern the outcome for *Ferrell* plaintiffs in all 13 states? Put differently, did the New Mexico court determine that defendant failed to prove dissimilarities between New Mexico law and the law of the other 12 states and that therefore they all were deemed to be the same in content? Or was the New Mexico Supreme Court instead saying that the district court could treat the laws as similar until dissimilarities appeared on the jurisprudential landscape? If the latter interpretation is correct, can the plaintiffs move to decertify the class with respect to the New Mexico plaintiffs? Would the New Mexico court retain jurisdiction over the case under those circumstances?

(2) The *Ferrell* opinion suggests that application of forum law is not only constitutionally permissible but also correct as a matter of choice-of-law policy when the laws of other states is unknown. Does that seem correct? The *Sun Oil* court's constitutional treatment of choice of law may have resulted from its frustration with monitoring state court choice-of-law decisions rather than from any conclusion that its test constituted sound choice-of-law policy. On the other hand, the court's strategy of proceeding with forum law unless a conflict is clearly established is commonly used for choice-of-law problems outside the class action context. Is there anything different about class actions that suggests a different approach should be followed?

(3) Does *Shutts* require the court to conduct a detailed choice-of-law inquiry for class actions? The Eighth Circuit reversed a district court's determination that Minnesota law applied to a nationwide consumer class action brought by plaintiffs with synthetic heart valves even though the valves were produced in Minnesota by defendant firm whose principal place of business was Minnesota. In re St. Jude Medical, Inc., 425 F.3d 1116 (8th Cir. 2005). The court stated:

> The district court's class certification was in error because the district court did not conduct a thorough conflicts-of-law analysis with respect to each plaintiff class member before applying Minnesota law. The Supreme Court has held an individualized choice-of-law analysis must be applied to each plaintiff's claim in

a class action. *Shutts*. . . . Therefore we must first decide whether any conflicts actually exist.

Id. at 1120. Does this seem correct? Isn't it sufficient that each claim involves a connection with Minnesota significant enough to satisfy the constitutional test set forth in *Hague*? Does this passage suggest that *Shutts* might require more from choice of law in class actions than is required in other litigation contexts? In re LILCO Securities Litigation, 111 F.R.D. 663 (E.D.N.Y. 1986), suggests otherwise. In *LILCO*, a district court initially certified a class action brought by investors against the Long Island Lighting Company alleging securities law violations as well as fraud, breach of fiduciary duty, and waste of corporate assets. The court reasoned:

> Without doubt, *Shutts* does not require us to apply the law of each state on which the plaintiffs reside nor does it prohibit the application of one state's law to all plaintiffs, regardless of residence. Defendants, therefore, misread *Shutts* when they argue that this Court may be forced to consider the law of all fifty states. In any event, the spectre of having to apply different substantive law does not warrant refusing to certify a class on the common law claims. . . . At this juncture, it is not necessary for the Court to decide the choice of law issue.

Id. at 670.

(4) Whether or not required by *Shutts*, at what point should the choice-of-law inquiry occur? Some courts have taken the position that a detailed choice-of-law analysis must be conducted prior to certification. Compaq Computer Corp. v. Lapray, 135 S.W.3d 657 (Tex. 2004). In contrast, the Supreme Court of Arkansas, like the Eastern District of New York in *LILCO*, determined that choice-of-law inquiries were not necessary at the certification stage. General Motors Corp. v. Bryant, 285 S.W.3d 634 (Ark. 2008). The *Bryant* court was unconcerned that multiple laws might end up being applied to the case. Furthermore, the court noted that if choice-of-law difficulties rendered the class action unmanageable, the "class can always be decertified at a later date if necessary." *Id*. at 641. Which view seems more reasonable?

(5) Relatedly, from what vantage point should a court measure similarities and differences across state laws? Some state laws are generally uniform when stated as a general concept even though there are fine gradations in how those laws have been applied to individual factual scenarios. Consider, for example, Cole v. General Motors Corp., 484 F.3d 717 (5th Cir. 2007). In *Cole*, the district court certified a nationwide class action involving breach of contract and warranty claims against GM for problems associated with the side-impact airbag system in some Cadillac De Ville models. On appeal, the Fifth Circuit ordered the class action decertified for failure to satisfy the predominance standard of Rule 23(b)(3). Its opinion suggested that the choice-of-law inquiry needs to take into account fine gradations in the law:

> The party seeking certification of a nationwide class must . . . provide an "extensive analysis" of state law variations to reveal whether these pose "insuperable obstacles." And the district court must then consider how these variations

affect predominance. Failure to engage in an analysis of state law variations is grounds for decertification. . . .

Plaintiffs assert that they have analyzed the applicable laws of the fifty-one jurisdictions and that they are "virtually the same." They conclude that predominance is unfettered in this case because any variations in the substantive law applicable to this case are "not significant and would not affect the result." They further conclude that "neither complex jury instructions nor multiple separate trials would be required to try the common issues in this proceeding under the laws of the 51 jurisdictions."

As support for their arguments, plaintiffs provided the district court with an extensive catalog of the statutory text of the warranty and redhibition laws of the fifty-one jurisdictions implicated in this suit; included in this catalog is the text of the relevant provisions of the Louisiana Civil Code and the UCC provisions of the forty-nine states and the District of Columbia. Plaintiffs additionally provided an overview of textual variations in the relevant UCC provisions as adopted by the fifty jurisdictions. Finally, plaintiffs submitted a report from an expert on contract law who opined, after analyzing some variations, that "the few variations in the provisions of UCC Article 2 relevant to this case are such that they do not affect the result" and that Louisiana law "does not differ from Article 2 in a manner that would affect the result."

. . .

We conclude that plaintiffs did not sufficiently demonstrate the predominance requirement because they failed both to undertake the required "extensive analysis" of variations in state law concerning their claims and to consider how these variations affect predominance. Plaintiffs' assertion of predominance relied primarily on the textual similarities of each jurisdiction's applicable law and on the general availability of legal protection in each jurisdiction for express and implied warranties. Plaintiffs' largely textual presentation of legal authority oversimplified the required analysis and glossed over the glaring substantive legal conflicts among the applicable laws of each jurisdiction.

As we explain below, there are numerous variations in the substantive laws of express and implied warranty among the fifty-one jurisdictions that the plaintiffs failed to "extensively analyze" for their impact on predominance. . . .

Id. at 725-726. Is there a principled way of determining the appropriate vantage point for determining whether laws differ?

(6) Note the *Ferrell* plaintiffs' strategy for maintaining a multistate class action in the face of competing state laws: Plaintiffs included in the requested class insureds from states where the legal definition of premium could possibly include the monthly installment fee. From that vantage point, the disagreement between the Court of Appeals and the state supreme court becomes one of the appropriate number of states in the class action. Both courts seem to agree that the class could include plaintiffs from states whose laws were clearly the same as New Mexico's and could not include plaintiffs from states whose laws clearly differed from New Mexico's, but what of the plaintiffs from states that had not yet addressed the question?

(7) The court in *Ferrell* distinguishes the burden of persuasion regarding governing law and the risk of ambiguity when the governing law is unclear. Plaintiffs bear the initial burden of persuading the court that the laws of the states connected to the dispute do not vary significantly. But the party opposing certification

bears the risk of ambiguity in that that party must demonstrate that the laws of the states actually conflict. Does this distinction make sense?

(8) In *Ferrell*, the New Mexico Supreme Court announced that in future cases the Second Restatement approach would apply in class actions even though the state uses the First Restatement approach to make choice-of-law decisions in other contexts. The court stated that retaining the First Restatement approach for class actions might "render multistate class actions a virtual nullity." Does that seem correct? The court justified its switch in approach by claiming that the First Restatement approach does not permit a comparison of laws as is required for class action certification. Is this rationale convincing? In practice, regardless of approach, choice-of-law issues tend not to arise unless the parties note a difference in laws worth fighting over.

Is it appropriate for a court to use a different choice-of-law approach for class actions given the complexity of the choice-of-law problem in this context as well as its import beyond simply setting governing legal standards? Is it legitimate for a court to apply a different substantive legal standard to claims brought in the aggregate from those that would apply when the same claims are brought individually? Several scholars think not:

> When one posits that the claims of individuals in a class action, would, in the absence of the class context, be decided under different laws, it is not clear why aggregation should alter that result. Certainly as conceived by the 1996 amendments to Rule 23, the class action was not designed, nor could it have purported, to change the substantive rights of the parties. The reason for the class device is that a coherence of rights and claims *already exists* among potential class members, and it is the existence of those elements that makes the representative suit appropriate. To use the class action as the justification for altering choice of law rules would be to put the cart before the horse and to misunderstand the role of both class actions and choice of law.

Silberman, *The Role of Choice of Law in National Class Actions*, 156 U. Pa. L. Rev. 2001, 2022 (2007-2008). *See also* Kramer, *Choice of Law in Complex Litigation*, 71 N.Y.U. L. Rev. 547, 549 (1996); Nagareda, *Aggregation and Its Discontents; Class Settlement Pressure, Class-Wide Arbitration, and CAFA*, 106 Colum. L. Rev. 1872, 1911 (2006). That view is far from uniform, however:

> There is a strong claim that large-scale aggregations of parties justify choices of law that would not be made if each element in the aggregation were the subject of a separate action. The justifications run in both directions—the choice facilitates the procedural advantages of aggregation, and aggregation facilitates a choice of law that yields overall more satisfactory results than those that would be achieved by separate actions. . . .
>
> . . . Events that entangle two or more law-giving jurisdictions invoke additional interests often referred to in the choice-of-law process. There are shared interests in uniformity of outcome, interests that are associated with equal treatment of actors caught up in indistinguishable events. The interest in uniformity and quality is bolstered by the interest in mutual accommodation, the recognition that subordination of event-specific interests of any particular

jurisdiction for that set of events will be repaid by subordination of others' interests when another set of events comes to be litigated. In addition, there is an interest in the efficient and consistent application of whatever set of rules is chosen. This interest is better served by aggregation than by repeated litigation in multiple forums.

Cooper, *Aggregation and Choice of Law*, 14 Roger Williams U. L. Rev. 12, 13-14 (2009). *See also* Cabraser, *The Manageable Nationwide Class: A Choice-of-Law Legacy of* Phillips Petroleum Co. v. Shutts, 74 UMKC L. Rev. 543, 567 (2006). Which viewpoint seems correct?

(9) Relatedly, in 1994 the American Law Institute's project on Complex Litigation proposed a uniform choice-of-law code to govern cases consolidated in the federal courts. ALI, *Complex Litigation: Statutory Recommendations and Analysis* §§6.01-6.03 (1994). The drafters acknowledged that their proposal would result in disparate treatment between parties involved in smaller actions not involving consolidation and those involved in cases that have been transferred for consolidation. However, the disparate treatment was justified by "the need to achieve justice among the litigants by assuring the uniform and economical treatment of their dispute." *Id*. at Choice of Law, Introductory Note, p. 308. The drafters' solution was to advocate the careful cabining of those cases deemed appropriate for consolidated treatment. *Id*. at 309. The proposed code was never enacted.

(10) If crafting a separate choice-of-law approach for complex litigation seems legitimate and appropriate, what approach makes most sense?

2. Single Governing Law

Courts sympathetic to the value of class actions sometimes seek the application of a single state's law to plaintiffs' claims. To be consistent with *Shutts*, however, the choice must be one that is constitutionally permissible as applied to each individual claim. When multiple plaintiffs sue a single defendant for the same basic conduct, a defendant-based connection, such as defendant's principal place of business or place of conduct (manufacture, contracts processing, training, etc.) can provide the basis for a single, constitutionally permissible choice of law.

Ysbrand v. DaimlerChrysler Corp.

81 P.3d 618 (Okla. 2003)

HODGES, J.

This opinion reviews the trial court's determination that this dispute meets the requirements for a class action found at Title 12, §2023, of the Oklahoma Statutes. The class certification order is affirmed as to the warranty claims asserted but is reversed as to the claim for fraud and deceit.

Defendant, DaimlerChrysler, is a Delaware corporation with its principal place of business in Michigan. It manufactured over one million 1996 and 1997 model "minivans" equipped with front passenger seat air bags. Plaintiffs, each an owner of one of the minivans, have asserted Uniform Commercial Code claims for "breach of express warranty," "breach of implied warranty of merchantability," and "breach of implied warranty of fitness." In addition, they assert a claim for "fraud and deceit."

Plaintiffs' claims are based on their assertion that the front passenger seat air bags are defective due to "1) their propensity to deploy with overly aggressive force and 2) their propensity to deploy during a low speed collision." Plaintiffs further assert that DaimlerChrysler failed to warn purchasers that this defect has the potential to kill or seriously injure a child or small adult seated in the front passenger seat. According to Plaintiffs, there are air bags available which deploy with less force and at higher collision speeds. They claim that these bags are currently used as replacements when a bag has been deployed. Plaintiffs seek damages in an amount sufficient to allow owners to install the "safer" air bags or, in the alternative, replacement of the "defective" air bags by DaimlerChrysler.

Following initial discovery and a hearing, the trial court issued a twenty-one page order certifying a class consisting of [current owners of the minivans at issue but excluding both owners who have suffered personal injury from air-bag deployment and owners who have had their airbags deactivated or replaced.][2] DaimlerChrysler now appeals the class certification order. . . .

Class action is a procedural device provided by Title 12, §2023, of the Oklahoma Statutes. It permits plaintiffs to "vindicat[e] the rights of individuals who otherwise might not consider it worth the candle to embark on litigation in which the optimum result might be more than consumed by the cost." Section 2023 requires, as does its federal counterpart numerosity, commonality, typicality, and adequacy of representation. In addition, the court must find that "questions of law or fact common to the members of the class predominate over any questions affecting only individual members, and that a class action is superior to other available methods for the fair and efficient adjudication of the controversy." *Id.* at §2023(B)(3).

DaimlerChrysler challenges the trial court's determination that each of these requirements was demonstrated by Plaintiffs. Its challenge is focused primarily on whether common questions of law and fact predominate and whether a class action is superior to other available methods of adjudicating the controversy. . . .

---

2. The trial court's class certification followed the litigation of similar issues in Louisiana and unsuccessful attempts to remove this case to federal court. The decision in In re Air Bag Products Liability Litigation, 7 F. Supp. 2d 792 (E.D. La. 1998), involved allegations of air bag defects against several automobile manufacturers and dealers. All claims were dismissed or summarily adjudicated in favor of defendants under Louisiana and Texas law. No class certification was involved. Thus, nothing about that decision impacts the issue of class certification presented in this litigation.

The class certification also followed the refusal of the National Highway Traffic Safety Administration (NHTSA) to further investigate following its determination that vehicles, including 1996 Chrysler minivans, "had rates of air bag deployments per 100 collision claims that are similar to that of many other vehicles." In doing so, NHTSA noted its "need to allocate and prioritize [its] limited resources."

I.   Common Issues of Law or Fact

A.   ISSUES OF LAW

DaimlerChrysler argues that common issues of law or fact do not predominate because varying state laws will apply to the asserted claims and defenses. It cites KMC Leasing, Inc. v. Rockwell-Standard Corp., 2000 OK 51, 9 P.3d 683, in which this Court found no abuse of discretion in the trial court's refusal to certify a class for lack of predominating issues. The proposed class consisted of private aircraft owners who alleged four different product defects against multiple defendants in different states. The matter required application of differing terms in hundreds of nonuniform aircraft purchase contracts. Because the substantive law of numerous states applied to issues which were not common to the entire class, there was no predominance and the trial court did not err in refusing to certify the class.

In this matter the trial court determined that "the alleged choice of law problems identified by [DaimlerChrysler did] not bar certification." It relied upon In re Bridgestone/Firestone, Inc. Tires Liability Litigation, 155 F. Supp. 2d 1069 (S.D. Ind. 2001), which granted class certification upon a finding of predominance.

In *Firestone*, a federal district court sitting in Indiana determined which state's substantive law applied to a nationwide state law class action. Buyers had asserted tort and contract claims against Ford Motor Co. and Bridgestone/Firestone, Inc. for alleged tire defects on Ford's Explorer model sport utility vehicle. The court reasoned that because "the relationship between the parties [was] simply that of buyer and seller," the place where the products were purchased was not significant to the claims for product defect. Rather, it was "the conduct of Defendants as manufacturers" which was the focus of the litigation. Therefore, the law of Michigan and Tennessee, the principal places of business of the manufactures, controlled.[4]

The trial court's application of *Firestone* to this matter evidences its intent to apply the substantive law of Michigan, DaimlerChrysler's principal place of business, to the claims and defenses asserted. Application of Oklahoma's choice of law rules supports that conclusion.

1.   CHOICE OF LAW — UCC CLAIMS

The "most significant relationship" test applies to an action for breach of warranty in a sale of goods under Article 2 of the UCC. [citations omitted] This test

---

4. The Court of Appeals for the Seventh Circuit reversed the decision. *See* In re Bridgestone/Firestone Inc., 288 F.3d 1012 (7th Cir. 2002), *cert. den.* 537 U.S. 1105 (2003). It did so based on its determination that "Indiana is a lex loci delicti state: in all but exceptional cases it applies the law of the place where harm occurred." As a result, "Indiana's choice-of-law rule selects the 50 states and multiple territories where the buyers live, and not the place of the sellers' headquarters, for these suits." Thus, "[b]ecause these claims must be adjudicated under the law of so many jurisdictions, a single nationwide class is not manageable." Although the Seventh Circuit rejected the lower court's conclusion as to which choice of law rule Indiana utilizes, the lower court's analysis under a most significant relationship test remains persuasive.

is guided by principles and contacts from the Restatement (Second) of Conflicts (1971). It determines which state's law is most directly connected to the parties and the transaction.

Under section 6 of the Restatement, the factors relevant to any choice of law decision include: (a) the needs of the interstate and international systems, (b) the relevant policies of the forum, (c) the relevant policies of other interested states and the relative interests of those states in the determination of the particular issue, (d) the protection of justified expectations, (e) the basic policies underlying the particular field of law, (f) certainty, predictability and uniformity of result, and (g) ease in the determination and application of the law to be applied.

The contacts to be considered in applying these principles to an issue in contract include: (a) the place of contracting, (b) the place of negotiation of the contract, (c) the place of performance, (d) the location of the subject matter of the contract, and (e) the domicil, residence, nationality, place of incorporation and place of business of the parties. *The contacts are to be evaluated according to their relative importance with respect to the particular issue. Id.* at §188(2) (emphasis added).

However, a third provision, section 191, applies to a sale of interests in chattel. "So in a contract for the sale of goods the most significant contact is the place of delivery unless another state has a more significant relationship." As comment f to section 191 explains: "On occasion, a state which is not the place of delivery will nevertheless, with respect to the particular issue, be the state of most significant relationship to the transaction, the parties and the chattel and hence the state of the applicable law." The particular dispute in this matter presents such an occasion in which "the local law of some state other than that of delivery should be applied in any event because of the intensity of the interest of that state in the determination of the particular issue." *Id.*

All 50 states and the District of Columbia bear some relationship to the parties and transactions in this dispute by virtue of the nationwide sales of the minivans. The question becomes whether the relationship of each state where the vehicles were purchased is more significant to the parties and this litigation than that of Michigan, the principal place of business of DaimlerChrysler.

The Restatement's section 188(2) contacts of the place of contracting, the place of negotiation and performance, and the location of the subject matter are of diminished significance to the sales of the minivans. The UCC warranties are not something which is negotiated in the purchase of a new car. Thus, the relative interest of each buyer's home state in applying its version of the UCC is more or less equal. By contrast, Michigan's interest in having its regulatory scheme applied to the conduct of a Michigan manufacturer is most significant. Michigan is where the decisions concerning the design, manufacture, and distribution of the minivans were made. Michigan is the only state where conduct relevant to all class members occurred. The principal place of DaimlerChrysler's business is the most important contact with respect to the UCC warranty claims.

The selection of Michigan law furthers the relevant factors stated in section 6 of the *Restatement*. The needs of the interstate system and the basic policies of predictability and uniformity of result require that the issue of product defect be determined in one forum with one result rather than in 51 jurisdictions with the very real possibility of conflicting decisions. While the interest of each home state in applying its local law is significant, Michigan's interest in the conduct of its manufacturer, and thus its connection to the warranty issues, is greater. Michigan law applies. It should be noted that this conclusion is consistent with the constitutional imperative that "for a state's substantive law to be selected in a constitutionally permissible manner, that state must have a significant aggregation of contacts, creating state interests, such that choice of its law is neither arbitrary nor fundamentally unfair." [*Shutts, supra* page 310 (quoting *Hague, supra* page 297).]

2. CHOICE OF LAW — FRAUD AND MISREPRESENTATION

Section 148 of the *Restatement*[6] applies to actions to recover pecuniary damages for false representations whether fraudulent, negligent, or innocent. Subsection (2) applies to this dispute because the nationwide representations in DaimlerChrysler's advertising were made in states outside each class member's home state. The home state is where each class member acted in reliance on those representations by purchasing a minivan. Thus, this Court is directed to consider:

(a) the place, or places, where the plaintiff acted in reliance upon the defendant's representations,

(b) the place where the plaintiff received the representations,

(c) the place where the defendant made the representations,

(d) the domicil, residence, nationality, place of incorporation and place of business of the parties,

(e) the place where a tangible thing which is the subject of the transaction between the parties was situated at the time, and

(f) the place where the plaintiff is to render performance under a contract which he has been induced to enter by the false representations of the defendant.

The comments to subsection (2) describe (a), (b), (c), and (d) as the "more important of these contacts." Comment j articulates the general approach:

> If any two of the above-mentioned contacts, apart from the defendant's . . . place of business, are located wholly in a single state, this will usually be the state of the applicable law with respect to most issues. So when the plaintiff acted in reliance upon the defendant's representations in a single state, this state

---

6. §148. Fraud and Misrepresentation

(1) When the plaintiff has suffered pecuniary harm on account of his reliance on the defendant's false representations and when the plaintiff's action in reliance took place in the state where the false representations were made and received, the local law of this state determines the rights and liabilities of the parties unless, with respect to the particular issue, some other state has a more significant relationship under the principles stated in §6 to the occurrence and the parties, in which event the local law of the other state will be applied.

(2) When the plaintiff's action in reliance took place in whole or in part in a state other than that where the false representations were made, the forum will consider such of the following contacts, among others, as may be present in the particular case in determining the state which, with respect to the particular issue, has the most significant relationship to the occurrence and the parties: [contacts provided in the text].

will usually be the state of the applicable law, with respect to most issues, if (a) the defendant's representations were received by the plaintiff in this state, or (b) this state is the state of plaintiff's domicil. . . .

In this matter, each class member presumably received the representation in their home state, their place of domicile. Therefore, the contacts point to each class member's home state for the applicable law. Applying the law of 51 jurisdictions to the fraud claim presents an overwhelming burden which would make the class unmanageable and a class action determination of that claim inappropriate. The class action certified by the trial court will go forward only on the warranty claims asserted.

B.   Issues of Fact

[The court concluded that individualized issues of fact were minimal and did not appear to defeat a finding of predominance.]

II.   Superiority

A.   Class Action versus Administrative Remedy.

DaimlerChrysler argues that a class action is not superior because the National Traffic and Motor Vehicle Safety Act impliedly preempts this warranty and common law tort action. Thus, it urges, the National Highway Traffic Safety Administration (NHTSA) must adjudicate this controversy. The Act, however, expressly provides that compliance with its provisions does not immunize a manufacturer from liability under common law or for warranty claims. 49 U.S.C. §30103.

DaimlerChrysler also argues that, without regard to implied administrative preemption, the administrative remedy of a NHTSA complaint is superior to a class action. The argument must fail.

A class action may be maintained only when it is "superior to other *available* methods for the fair and efficient adjudication of the controversy." Okla. Stat. tit. 12, §2023(B)(3) (2001) (emphasis added). There is no administrative method of adjudication available to Plaintiffs. The NHTSA has declined to investigate further. *See supra* n.2. An alternate method for adjudication must be *available* in order for it to be superior.

The question then becomes whether class action is superior to individual litigation. As the trial court found, the individual claims are not substantial enough to support individual litigation. In addition, the prosecution of separate individual actions would inevitably result in inconsistent results.

B.   Logistics of Class Management

. . . There will be logistical problems in any nationwide class action. The fact that travel for counsel, parties, and witnesses will be necessary would be true no matter where the action was pursued. Plaintiffs have chosen Sequoyah County. None of the logistical problems, however, prevent the trial court from resolving this dispute as a class action. As the trial court observed, the advantage of adjudicating the common issues in a single proceeding far outweighs the logistic demands of class treatment. . . .[8]

AFFIRMED IN PART; REVERSED IN PART.

OPALA, V.C.J., LAVENDER, KAUGER, SUMMERS, BOUDREAU, JJ., concur.

WATT, C.J., HARGRAVE, J., concur in part; dissent in part.

WINCHESTER, J., dissents.

Questions and Comments

(1) Do you agree that the court's analysis regarding the UCC claims is consistent with the Second Restatement approach? The court identified a Second Restatement default rule (place of delivery) and then proceeded to replace that default rule on grounds that DaimlerChrysler's principal place of business had a more significant relationship to the dispute. Note that under the court's analysis the "dispute" appears to be the litigation as a whole, not the individual claims. Regarding the claims for fraud and misrepresentation, the court identified the relevant default rule and then applied it without asking whether another state might have a more significant relationship to the dispute. If one were to view the issue from the perspective of the litigation as a whole, then DaimlerChrysler's principal place of business might well prove more significant. But here the court's analysis never moved beyond the perspective of the individual claims. Why did the court shift perspectives when considering the different claims? Which perspective should a court take when treating choice of law under the Second Restatement?

(2) The Oklahoma legislature apparently takes a less charitable view of using its state courts as a locus for nationwide class actions. In 2009, it enacted Title 12, §2023(D)(3), which provides:

> For actions filed after November 1, 2009, class membership shall be limited, unless otherwise agreed to by the defendant, only to individuals or entities who are:
>
> > a. residents of this state, or
> > b. nonresidents of this state who:
> > > (1) own an interest in property located in this state where the property is relevant to the class action, or
> > > (2) have a significant portion of the nonresident's cause of action arising from conduct occurring within the state.

Is it constitutionally permissible for a state court to close its doors to outsiders seeking class action relief? *See* Chapter 4 *supra*.

---

8. The class certification remains subject to modification and "may be altered or amended before the decision on the merits." Okla. Stat. tit. 12, §2023(C)(1) (2001). If necessary the class "may be divided into subclasses and each subclass treated as a class." *Id*. at §2023(C)(4).

(3) Other cases have considered defendant-based contacts as a mechanism for determining that a single law applies to all claims. *See, e.g.*, Garza v. Gama, 240 Ariz. 373 (Ariz. Ct. App. 2016) (using defendant's headquarters as governing law in case brought on behalf of 80,000 transient employee truck drivers residing in several states).

(4) The *Ysbrand* court discusses In re Bridgestone/Firestone, Inc. Tires Product Liability Litigation. As indicated in footnote 4 of the *Ysbrand* court's opinion, the Seventh Circuit in *Bridgestone* reversed the district court's certification of a nationwide class of plaintiffs asserting breach of warranty and consumer fraud claims against both Ford Motor Company and Bridgestone/Firestone for reduced value of their automobiles resulting from the vehicles' defective tires. The district court, applying Indiana choice-of-law rules, concluded that the law of defendant's headquarters should apply to claims against each defendant. The Seventh Circuit disagreed that Indiana courts would apply the law of defendant's headquarters. Judge Easterbrook, writing for the court, pointed out that Indiana was a First Restatement state and that "in all but exceptional cases it applies the law of the place where the harm occurred." 288 F.3d at 1016. The harm in this case was financial, and "was suffered in the places where the vehicles and tires were purchased at excessive prices or resold at depressed prices. Those injuries occurred in all 50 states, the District of Columbia, Puerto Rico, and U.S. territories such as Guam. The *lex loci delicti* points to the places of these injuries, not the defendant's corporate headquarters, as the source of law." *Id*. In response to plaintiffs' claim that in 1987 the Indiana courts signaled a more flexible approach to the choice-of-law question, Judge Easterbrook wrote:

> Has Indiana since 1987 applied the law of a state where a product was designed, or promotional materials drafted, to a suit arising out of an injury in Indiana? As far as we can tell, the answer is no—not even once, and the state has had plenty of opportunities. Yet since 1987 both Indiana and this court have routinely applied Indiana law when injury caused by a defective product occurred in Indiana to Indiana residents. Neither Indiana nor any other state has applied a uniform place-of-defendant's headquarters rule to products-liability cases. It is not hard to devise an argument that such a uniform rule would be good on many dimensions, but that argument has not carried the day with state judges, and it is state law rather than a quest for efficiency in litigation (or in product design decisions) that controls.

Id. Why might courts be reluctant to adopt a general choice-of-law rule that the law of defendant's manufacture or principal place of business applies to product liability or warranty claims? Would not such a rule create perverse incentives for firms to locate themselves in places where consumer protections are relatively weak? If such a rule also enabled the certification of class actions brought by consumers against defendants, however, both companies and their consumers might be better off. Does that argument justify a new choice-of-law rule?

(5) In the class action context, it is not uncommon to see plaintiffs making choice-of-law arguments typically made by defendants outside of class actions, and vice versa. For example, in *Bridgestone/Firestone*, plaintiffs argued for application of the law of defendants' headquarters. Advocacy positions are similarly turned around in the context of choice-of-law clause enforcement. Consumers who bring

actions against companies traditionally attempted to circumvent the choice-of-law clause while defendant companies sought broad enforcement of those clauses. By contrast, in the class action context, defendants sometimes attempt to undo their own choice-of-law clauses while consumers rely on them to argue that all claims are subject to a single law — that chosen in the contract. *See* Schnall v. AT&T Wireless Services, *infra* page 773 for an example.

(6) Courts handling pretrial proceedings in MDL cases also sometimes focus on defendant-based contacts to arrive at the application of a single governing law for all of the consolidated cases. In In re Air Crash Disaster near Chicago, Illinois on May 25, 1979, 644 F.2d 594 (7th Cir. 1981), the Seventh Circuit used this approach to conclude that none of the plaintiffs were entitled to recover punitive damages in their cases against defendants American Airlines and McDonnell Douglas Corp. Shortly after takeoff on an American flight scheduled to fly from Chicago, Illinois, to Los Angeles, California, all 271 people on the plane plus two on the ground were killed when the plane lost its engine and crashed. The MDL included 181 wrongful death actions filed in Illinois, California, New York, Michigan, Hawaii, and Puerto Rico. Plaintiffs and their decedents resided in 11 states and territories, plus 3 foreign countries. McDonnell Douglas Corp. ("MDC"), the aircraft's manufacturer, was incorporated in Maryland and had its principal place of business in Missouri. Plaintiffs sought punitive damages on the ground that MDC had acted egregiously in the design and manufacture of the plane, both of which occurred in California. American was incorporated in Delaware, and its principal place of business moved from New York to Texas in 1979. Plaintiffs sought punitive damages against American based on egregious maintenance of the aircraft, and American's maintenance center was located in Oklahoma. The court noted that U.S. states were fairly evenly split on the question whether punitive damages were recoverable in wrongful death actions. Missouri, Oklahoma, and Texas permitted the recovery of punitive damages, but Illinois, California, and New York did not permit them.

The Seventh Circuit separately conducted a choice-of-law analysis for (1) cases filed in Illinois and New York, which the court concluded were states that would apply the Second Restatement; (2) actions filed in California, a comparative impairment state; (3) actions filed in Michigan and Puerto Rico, which the court concluded would apply the *lex loci delicti* rule; and (4) the case filed in Hawaii, where the governing choice-of-law principles were unknown. For each approach, the court separately considered the choice-of-law results for claims against MDC and American.

For claims against MDC under the Second Restatement, the court concluded that punitive damages were not recoverable. The court determined that the states of plaintiffs' residences could be ignored under the Second Restatement because plaintiffs' states could have a legitimate interest in full compensation for their residences but not the actual recovery of punitive damages. Defendants' states and the state of the place of injury could have an interest in the recovery of punitive damages. In this action, Missouri, MDC's principal place of business, was deemed to have an interest in holding its company accountable and in deterring its egregious conduct, and California, the place of design and manufacture of the plane, was deemed to have an interest in protecting its corporate activities from financial liabilities. Thus, there was a true conflict. To resolve the conflict, the court took into account Illinois's interests. Although the place of injury is largely fortuitous for plane crashes, the state's interests were still relevant. Because Illinois was the site of a very busy airport, the court thought Illinois had interests both in not being the site of crashes and in protecting companies who do business in the state. Thus, Illinois law represented a balance of interests and, with the interests of other states equally divergent, could appropriately apply. Thus, recovery of punitive damages was not permitted.

For claims against American under the Second Restatement, the court utilized a similar analysis. First, the court concluded that American's principal place of business was New York on the date of the crash (an issue hotly contested by the parties). A true conflict existed between the laws and interests of New York and Oklahoma, the place of American's conduct, so here too Illinois law was used to break the tie, and the recovery of punitive damages was not permitted.

Under the comparative impairment approach as applied to MDC, both Missouri and California had strong current interests in applying their punitive damages laws, and neither law was archaic or isolated. Missouri could effectuate its interests somewhat by using its criminal law to discipline its corporations, and California's protections could be achieved somewhat with corporate liability insurance. The court concluded that the two states' laws would be equally impaired if not applied. Here too Illinois law tipped the scales. A similar reasoning was applied to claims against American under comparative impairment: New York and Oklahoma laws would be equally impaired, and Illinois's laws and policies became the deciding factor.

Under the *lex loci delicti* rule, for claims against both American and MDC, the law of the place of injury, Illinois, applied. Here too that meant plaintiffs could not recover punitive damages.

Finally, the Seventh Circuit turned to the claim filed in Hawaii. Unable to glean Hawaii's choice-of-law approach, the court thought it appropriate to presume that Hawaii courts would apply forum law. Unfortunately, Hawaii's punitive damages rule was also unclear. The court concluded that Hawaii courts would not permit the recovery of punitive damages in wrongful death cases, and stated that this result would not be unjust, given the result of the other cases.

Judge Cudahy concurred in the result, but wrote separately to comment:

> Some questions remain for me whether Missouri would, in fact, have a strong interest in imposing financial sanctions on its own corporate domiciliary, employing Missouri citizens and paying Missouri taxes, as punishment for that corporation's *extraterritorial* torts affecting non-residents of Missouri. The finding of such a Missouri interest may impute an unusual level or [sic] altruism to Missouri policy and may overstate the commitment to Missouri (or any other state) to "corporate accountability" in circumstances where both the misconduct and the injuries took place outside the borders of the domiciliary state.

Id. at 633. Both the majority and the concurring opinions lamented the failure of Congress to federalize the governing tort law for air disasters.

Evaluate the Seventh Circuit's analysis. *See also* In re Air Crash Disaster at Sioux City, Iowa, on July 19, 1989, 734 F. Supp. 1425 (N.D. Ill. 1990) (utilizing similar defendant-based contacts to determine a single applicable law for each defendant applied to all claims against it).

(7) Although the temptation of some courts to apply a single defendant-based law to all claims is controversial among scholars for the now familiar reason that it threatens to alter the parties' substantive rights as a result of aggregation, others have advocated for the approach. *See* Issacharoff, *Settled Expectations in a World of Unsettled Law: Choice of Law After the Class Action Fairness Act*, 106 Colum. L. Rev. 1839 (2006); Cabraser, *Just Choose: The Jurisprudential Necessity to Select a Single Governing Law for Mass Claims Arising from Nationally Marketed Consumer Goods and Services*, 14 Roger Williams U. L. Rev. 29 (2009).

(8) In Barbara's Sales, Inc. v. Intel Corporation, 879 N.E.2d 910 (Ill. 2007), the Illinois Supreme Court rejected class certification for personal computer purchasers suing the chip manufacturer. Plaintiffs had argued that California law could apply to all of plaintiffs' claims because that state was the principal place of business for defendant. The state appellate court concluded that this result was consistent with the Restatement (Second) of Conflict of Laws, in part because under section 6, "[t]he needs of the interstate system . . . require one forum with one result rather than results in 51 jurisdictions with the distinct possibility of conflicting decisions." *Id.* at 921. The state supreme court strongly disagreed:

> This declaration completely ignores the distinct interests of the differing states embodied in our federalist system and constitutional precedent. . . .
>
> Moreover, an examination of the reasoning behind this factor shows that it is not fit for the appellate court's purpose to obtain "one forum with one result." The goals of the "needs of the interstate system" principle are "to make the interstate and international systems work well," to promote "harmonious relations," and "to facilitate commercial intercourse between them." Restatement Second §6, Comment d. The Restatement also directs courts to strive to adopt "the same choice of law" rules reflected in other states' precedent. *Id.* The application of California law or Illinois law, as plaintiffs urge in this nationwide class, to a citizen of Washington state who purchased his computer in Washington state does nothing to improve the harmonious relations between the states. Thus, we are not persuaded that section 6 of the Restatement compels us to apply California law.

Id. at 921-922. Do you agree? This is clearly a different conclusion from that of the *Ysbrand* court. If Restatement drafters were to compose a list of factors that courts should and do take into account when determining the applicable law for class actions, what factors would you recommend be on that list?

Note on General Consensus Law

Is it ever appropriate in complex litigation for a court to choose to apply a single set of legal principles that are not rooted in any one jurisdiction?

Consider In re Agent Orange Product Liability Litigation, 580 F. Supp. 690 (E.D.N.Y. 1984). The case involved a class product liability action brought by Vietnam War veterans for injuries that they suffered as a result of their exposure to herbicides manufactured by defendants and purchased by the U.S. government for use in aiding the Vietnam War efforts. Cases were filed across the country, transferred to the Eastern District of New York (Judge Weinstein) for pretrial consolidation, and then certified as a nationwide class action based in part on Judge Weinstein's conclusion that all claims involved a question of federal law. The Second Circuit reversed the district court's ruling that the claims presented federal questions and remanded the action for consideration under state law.

Judge Weinstein thought that all of the claims should be decided according to a single governing law because the veterans were all in the service of the U.S. government working toward the same goals when they were exposed to Agent Orange. Plaintiffs lived in all or nearly all of the U.S. states and territories as well as in some foreign countries, and defendants and their relevant activities were similarly scattered. Because the cases were initially filed in other district courts and the claims were based in state law, the district court felt constrained to apply the choice-of-law rules of the states from which the individual cases were originally transferred. Because transferor courts were located across the country, the district court conducted a survey of choice-of-law results under all of the existing approaches to choice of law. It concluded that whether using the First Restatement, Second Restatement, interest analysis, Leflar, or forum law approaches to choice of law, the state courts across the country would apply "national consensus law" to the claims. Judge Weinstein reasoned:

> It is entirely reasonable to assume that the state courts would recognize the strong national interest in a uniform national rule. A considerable number of states have already recognized the unique nature of the Agent Orange litigation problem. Given the strong state-federal interest in uniformity, the lack of a federal statute or of a uniform state statute, and the Second Circuit opinion denying that the federal common law controls of its own force all substantive issues in Agent Orange, what would state courts do? Would they not look to the first court that dealt with the issue or to a neutral body to formulate the uniform rules they could all accept for this unique litigation? And is not a federal court charged with adjudicating all or nearly all the Agent Orange cases such a body? . . .
>
> Once it is conceded, as we think it must be, that each of the jurisdictions involved would appreciate the overwhelming need for uniformity, to what single state's law could any state look to as controlling? Given the plethora of states and nations with contacts and the impossibility without a full trial of even knowing where the allegedly offending dioxin was produced, it becomes apparent that no acceptable test can point to any single state. Thus, the law is driven in this most unusual case to either federal or national consensus substantive law as the only workable approach.

Id. at 710-711.

Does it make sense for a court to apply general consensus law in this circumstance? The content of that national consensus law was left for later articulation, but the case settled soon thereafter. What would be the best way to determine the content of national consensus law, assuming that the approach was legitimate? Would it be a good idea for a court to apply substantive rules that were routinely applied across the states and throw out outlier rules that exist in only one or a few states? Is there any important distinction between choosing a choice-of-law approach used solely in class actions (i.e., *Ferrell*) and choosing a governing law used solely in class actions (i.e., *Agent Orange*)? Is Judge Weinstein's national consensus law approach constitutionally permissible under *Shutts*? Does your answer depend at all on the method for determining national consensus law? For an argument that applying law that reflects the "average law" in the United States to all claims would be permissible, *see* McCloud & Rosenberg, *A Solution to the Choice of Law Problem of Differing State Laws in Class Actions: Average Law*, 79 Geo. Wash. L. Rev. 374 (2011). Is the approach consistent with the mandates of *Erie*?

The case for uniform treatment of plaintiffs is particularly compelling in *Agent Orange*, but concerns for uniformity and manageability are present in many class action cases, and was specifically mentioned by the *Ysbrand* court in its Second Restatement analysis. Could general consensus law serve as a choice-of-law approach in other class action contexts? In practice, this approach is almost never used by courts, and has been heavily criticized where attempted.

In In re Rhone-Polenc Rorer, Inc., 51 F.3d 1293 (7th Cir. 1995), for example, the Seventh Circuit reversed a district court's decision to certify a nationwide class for purposes of resolving some but not all issues involved in the claims. Plaintiffs were hemophiliacs infected by the HIV/AIDS virus and defendants were drug companies who manufactured blood solids. Prior to knowing about the disease, its transmission through blood, and methods available for killing the virus contained in blood, the defendants manufactured contaminated solids that led to a large number of infections and deaths. Plaintiffs alleged that defendants were negligent in failing to protect them from infection, and they proffered two theories for negligence. Under the first, the plaintiffs argued that the manufacturers should have done more to protect blood solid recipients from contracting Hepatitis B, a transmission problem that was known when plaintiffs were infected. If the defendants had taken more care to prevent Hepatitis B transmission, then "serendipitously," the preventative actions also would have prevented the transmission of HIV. Second, plaintiffs argued that the manufacturers should have known of the risk of HIV transmission sooner and should have taken preventative steps earlier than they did. Federal Rule of Civil Procedure 23(c)(4) permits a district court to certify a class action with respect to particular issues only. In this case, the district court certified a class for purposes of trial on the question whether the defendants were negligent. If defendants were found negligent, then individual cases would be litigated to determine whether individual plaintiffs were entitled to relief. The Seventh Circuit reversed the district court's certification. Writing for the panel, Judge Posner stated:

> We believe that [the district court judge] was responding imaginatively and in the best of faith to the challenge that mass torts, graphically illustrated by the avalanche of asbestos litigation, pose for the federal courts. But the plan that he has devised for the HIV-hemophilia litigation exceeds the bounds of allowable judicial discretion. Three concerns, none of them

necessarily sufficient in itself but cumulatively compelling, persuade us to this conclusion.

The first is a concern with forcing these defendants to stake their companies on the outcome of a single jury trial, or be forced by fear of the risk of bankruptcy to settle even if they have no legal liability, when it is entirely feasible to allow a final, authoritative determination of their liability for the colossal misfortune that has befallen the hemophiliac population to emerge from a decentralized process of multiple trials, involving different juries, and different standards of liability, in different jurisdictions; and when, in addition, the preliminary indications are that the defendants are not liable for the grievous harm that has befallen the members of the class. These qualifications are important. In most class actions—and those the ones in which the rationale for the procedure is most compelling—individual suits are infeasible because the claim of each class member is tiny relative to the expense of litigation. That plainly is not the situation here. A notable feature of this case, and one that has not been remarked upon or encountered, so far as we are aware, in previous cases, is the demonstrated great likelihood that the plaintiffs' claims, despite their human appeal, lack legal merit. This is the inference from the defendants' having won 92.3 percent (12/13) of the cases to have gone to judgment. Granted, thirteen is a small sample and further trials, if they are held, may alter the pattern that the sample reveals. But whether they do or not, the result will be robust if these further trials are permitted to go forward, because the pattern that results will reflect a consensus, or at least a pooling of judgment, of many different tribunals.

For this consensus or maturing of judgment the district judge proposes to substitute a single trial before a single jury instructed in accordance with no actual law of any jurisdiction—a jury that will receive a kind of Esperanto instruction, merging the negligence standards of the 50 states and the District of Columbia. One jury, consisting of six persons (the standard federal civil jury nowadays consists of six regular jurors and two alternates), will hold the fate of an industry in the palm of its hand. This jury, jury number fourteen, may disagree with twelve of the previous thirteen juries—and hurl the industry into bankruptcy. That kind of thing can happen in our system of civil justice (it is not likely to happen, because the industry is likely to settle—whether or not it really is liable) without violating anyone's legal rights. But it need not be tolerated when the alternative exists of submitting an issue to multiple juries constituting in the aggregate a much larger and more diverse sample of decision-makers. That would not be a feasible option if the stakes to each class member were too slight to repay the cost of suit, even though the aggregate stakes were very large and would repay the costs of a consolidated proceeding. But this is not the case with regard to the HIV-hemophilia litigation. Each plaintiff if successful is apt to receive a judgment in the millions. With the aggregate stakes in the tens or hundreds of millions of dollars, or even in the billions, it is not a waste of judicial resources to conduct more than one trial, before more than six jurors, to determine whether a major segment of the international pharmaceutical industry is to follow the asbestos manufacturers into Chapter 11.

We have hinted at the second reason for concern that the district judge exceeded the bounds of permissible judicial discretion. He proposes to have a jury determine the negligence of the defendants under a legal standard that does not actually exist anywhere in the world. One is put in mind of the concept of "general" common law that prevailed in the era of Swift v. Tyson.

The assumption is that the common law of the 50 states and the District of Columbia, at least so far as bears on a claim of negligence against drug companies, is basically uniform and can be abstracted in a single instruction. It is no doubt true that at some level of generality the law of negligence is one, not only nationwide but worldwide. Negligence is a failure to take due care, and due care a function of the probability and magnitude of an accident and the costs of avoiding it. A jury can be asked whether the defendants took due care. And in many cases such differences as there are among the tort rules of the different states would not affect the outcome. The Second Circuit was willing to assume *dubitante* that this was true of the issues certified for class determination in the Agent Orange litigation. In re Diamond Shamrock Chemicals Co., 725 F.2d 858, 861 (2d Cir. 1984).

We doubt that it is true in general, and we greatly doubt that it is true in a case such as this in which one of the theories pressed by the plaintiffs, the "serendipity" theory, is novel. If one instruction on negligence will serve to instruct the jury on the legal standard of every state of the United States applicable to a novel claim, implying that the claim despite its controversiality would be decided identically in all 50 states and the District of Columbia, one wonders what the Supreme Court thought it was doing in the *Erie* case when it held that it was *unconstitutional* for federal courts in diversity cases to apply general common law rather than the common law of the state whose law would apply if the case were being tried in state rather than federal court. Erie R.R. v. Tompkins, 304 U.S. 64 (1938). The law of negligence, including subsidiary concepts such as duty of care, foreseeability, and proximate cause, may as the plaintiffs have argued forcefully to us differ among the states only in nuance, though we think not, for a reason discussed later. But nuance can be important, and its significance is suggested by a comparison of differing state pattern instructions on negligence and differing judicial formulations of the meaning of negligence and the subordinate concepts. "The common law is not a brooding omnipresence in the sky, but the articulate voice of some sovereign or quasi sovereign that can be identified." Southern Pacific Co. v. Jensen, 244 U.S. 205, 222 (1917) (Holmes, J., dissenting). The voices of the quasi-sovereigns that are the states of the United States sing negligence with a different pitch.

The "serendipity" theory advanced by the plaintiffs in *Wadleigh* is that if the defendants did not do enough to protect hemophiliacs from the risk of Hepatitis B, they are liable to hemophiliacs for any consequences — including infection by the more dangerous and at the time completely unknown AIDS virus — that proper measures against Hepatitis B would, all unexpectedly, have averted. This theory of liability, which draws support from Judge Friendly's opinion in Petition of Kinsman Transit Co., 338 F.2d 708, 725 (2d Cir. 1964), dispenses, rightly or wrongly from the standpoint of the Platonic Form of negligence, with proof of foreseeability, even though a number of states, in formulating their tests for negligence, incorporate the foreseeability of the risk into the test. These states follow Judge Cardozo's famous opinion in Palsgraf v. Long Island R.R., 248 N.Y. 339 (1928), under which the HIV plaintiffs might (we do not say would — we express no view on the substantive issues in this litigation) be barred from recovery on the ground that they were unforeseeable victims of the alleged failure of the defendants to take adequate precautions against infecting hemophiliacs with Hepatitis B and that therefore the drug companies had not violated any duty of care to them.

The plaintiffs' second theory focuses on the questions when the defendants should have learned about the danger of HIV in the blood supply and when, having learned about it, they should have taken steps to eliminate the danger or at least warn hemophiliacs or their physicians of it. These questions also may be sensitive to the precise way in which a state formulates its standard of negligence. If not, one begins to wonder why this country bothers with different state legal systems.

Both theories, incidentally, may be affected by differing state views on the role of industry practice or custom in determining the existence of negligence. In some states, the standard of care for a physician, hospital, or other provider of medical services, including blood banks, is a professional standard, that is, the standard fixed by the relevant profession. In others, it is the standard of ordinary care, which may, depending on judge or jury, exceed the professional standard. Which approach a state follows, and whether in those states that follow the professional-standard approach manufacturers of blood solids would be assimilated to blood banks as providers of medical services entitled to shelter under the professional standard, could make a big difference in the liability of these manufacturers. We note that persons infected by HIV through blood transfusions appear to have had little better luck suing blood banks than HIV-positive hemophiliacs have had suing the manufacturers of blood solids.

The diversity jurisdiction of the federal courts is, after *Erie*, designed merely to provide an alternative forum for the litigation of state-law claims, not an alternative system of substantive law for diversity cases. But under the district judge's plan the thousands of members of the plaintiff class will have their rights determined, and the four defendant manufacturers will have their duties determined, under a law that is merely an amalgam, an averaging, of the nonidentical negligence laws of 51 jurisdictions. No one doubts that Congress could constitutionally prescribe a uniform standard of liability for manufacturers of blood solids. It might we suppose promulgate pertinent provisions of the Restatement (Second) of Torts. The point of *Erie* is that Article III of the Constitution does not empower the federal courts to create such a regime for diversity cases.

If in the course of individual litigations by HIV-positive hemophiliacs juries render special verdicts that contain findings which do not depend on the differing state standards of negligence — for example a finding concerning the date at which one or more of the defendants learned of the danger of HIV contamination of the blood supply — these findings may be given collateral estoppel effect in other lawsuits, at least in states that allow "offensive" use of collateral estoppel. In that way the essential purpose of the class action crafted by Judge Grady will be accomplished. If there are relevant differences in state law, findings in one suit will not be given collateral estoppel effect in others, and that is as it should be. . . .

Id. at 1299-1302. Should the certification decision turn on the likely legal merits of the case? On the viability of individually litigated cases? Do these factors inevitably become relevant as a way of prioritizing the fairness claims of plaintiffs and defendants in class action litigation? Are there other ways to balance these concerns? Judge Posner mentions collateral estoppel as a more just alternative to class action certification. Is his argument convincing? What do you think of the notion that decentralized litigation has benefits that should not be discounted in the certification decision?

3.   Multiple Governing Laws

Schnall v. AT&T Wireless Services, Inc.

225 P.3d 929 (Wash. 2010) (en banc)

MADSEN, C.J. [with four Justices joining]

This case asks our court to decide whether Washington will become a locus of nationwide class action litigation. In the context of this case, we believe the trial court did not abuse its discretion by declining to certify such a class. To the extent a class action is feasible here, the only appropriately certified class for plaintiffs' contract claims is a *state* wide class. We reverse, in part, and remand for proceedings consistent with this opinion.

Facts

Customers of AT&T Wireless Services, Inc. (AT&T) filed a nationwide class action alleging the company misled consumers when it billed them for a charge that was not included in advertised monthly rates and was not described clearly in billing statements. The Federal Communications Commission (FCC) requires telecommunications companies like AT&T to contribute to the Universal Service Fund (USF), a fund created by the Telecommunications Act of 1996 that subsidizes phone and Internet service to low-income and rural areas. The FCC expressly permits companies to recover USF contributions from customers. AT&T recovered its contributions from customers by charging a Universal Connectivity Charge (UCC), listed in customer agreements as either "Other Charges & Credits" or "Taxes, Surcharges & Regulatory Fees." Named plaintiff Martin Schnall claims this categorization of the UCC violates the Washington Consumer Protection Act (CPA) and further, that AT&T violated the terms of its contract by failing to disclose the charge at the time he signed his agreement for wireless service. Schnall further claims AT&T violated the terms of its user contracts by increasing the UCC charge without notice. Schnall sought certification of a nationwide class of all AT&T customers "who have been improperly billed and paid a universal connectivity charge that they did not owe."

The trial court determined that "individual questions predominated over common questions" and denied class certification on all of Schnall's claims. Schnall appealed that decision to Division One of the Court of Appeals which reversed the trial court and certified the class. . . .

Enforceability of Choice of Law Clauses

The parties initially dispute whether the choice of law clauses in the customers' contracts are enforceable. The choice of law clauses in this case require customers to litigate asserted violations of their contract in the respective jurisdiction where they signed the contract. This jurisdiction is often based on the customer's area code.

We interpret contract provisions to render them enforceable whenever possible. Further, "[w]e generally enforce contract choice of law provisions.". . . [The court quoted from §187(2) of the Restatement (Second) of Conflict of Laws, which treats the enforceability of choice-of-law clauses as applied to matters that parties could not have resolved with an explicit provision in their agreement. *See supra* pages 648-649.]

The choice of law provisions in this case were mostly based on customers' area codes, not on forums having no substantial relationship to the parties or location of the transaction between them. While it is true that AT&T is headquartered in Washington State, the customer's area code is left to the discretion of the customer, and this area code often corresponds with the customer's place of residence: in effect the *customer* selected which forum's law would apply when he requested phone service from AT&T. AT&T should not now be forced to face the enormous cost and complexity presented by a nationwide class action when they conscionably included choice of law provisions in their customers' contracts and the choice of forum is dictated by the consumer.

Schnall presents no valid reason why we should now invalidate the choice of law clause each customer signed when he or she purchased wireless service from AT&T. The trial court did not abuse its discretion when it held

> [t]here does not seem to be any public policy reason not to enforce the choice of law provision of the agreements in this case. The law of the state associated with the area code will generally be the law of the customer's home state, thereby applying to that customer the law with which he or she is most familiar.

Upholding the trial court's decision to deny certification of a *nation* wide class does nothing to prevent persons outside of Washington from filing statewide class actions in each of their respective home states. Indeed, the citizens of California have already filed such a statewide class action.

Class Certification of Contract Claims

Schnall brings two types of claims before the court: one based in contract, the other based on the CPA. The differences between these two types of claims have important implications for analysis of their suitability as class action claims. AT&T argues the trial court was correct in deciding that the choice of law clauses in each customer's contract caused individual issues to predominate over common ones. . . . The trial court held: "[a]pplying the law of the customer's home state to the contract claims in this case makes the contract claims unmanageable."

To validly certify a nationwide class for the contract claims, Schnall must meet the requirements of CR 23(a): numerosity, commonality, typicality, and adequacy of representation. Once those have been met, he must further satisfy the tougher standard of CR 23(b)(3) and prove that common legal and factual issues *predominate* over individual issues and that a class action is an otherwise superior form of adjudication. Factors to be considered by the court when assessing predominance and superiority include

> (A) the interest of members of the class in individually controlling the prosecution or defense of separate actions; (B) the extent and nature of any litigation concerning the controversy already commenced by or against members of the

class; (C) the desirability or undesirability of concentrating the litigation of the claims in the particular forum; (D) the difficulties likely to be encountered in the management of a class action.

CR 23(b)(3). It is "incumbent upon class counsel to prove to the court . . . that there are no significant differences in the various state laws, or if there are variations, that they can be managed by the trial court."

The Court of Appeals held that a "common nucleus of operative facts" predominated, but failed to substantially analyze the issue of predominance, especially in consideration of the potential application of 50 different states' laws. The Court of Appeals' predominance analysis reads more like a CR 23(a) commonality test: "The common nucleus of facts among all class members on this breach of contract claims *is*. . . . The common legal theory *is*. . ." (emphasis added). Simply stating the existence of commonalities does not prove predominance. The trial court's analysis on this point is more thorough and is clearly supportable under our abuse of discretion standard.

As the Court of Appeals noted, the trial court "made several findings about the individual issues the contract claim raised." The trial court found that the choice of law clauses, the interpretation of the contract terms, the differences in the materials and information each potential class member received, and the availability of differing affirmative defenses created a predominance of individual issues over common ones.

Because CR 23 is identical to its federal counterpart, "cases interpreting the analogous federal provision are highly persuasive." The Court of Appeals reached a conclusion that flies in the face of this "highly persuasive" federal law regarding nationwide class action certification: "[b]ased primarily on the burden of applying multiple states' laws, an *overwhelming number* of federal courts have denied certification of nationwide state-law class actions." [extensive case citations omitted]

Even where courts find that a nationwide, state-law governed class otherwise meets Rule 23(a) and 23(b)(3) criteria, "the choice-of-law inquiry will ordinarily make or break certification." This is because if the laws of 50 jurisdictions apply to plaintiffs' claims, "the variations in the laws of the states . . . 'may swamp any common issues and defeat predominance.'" [citations omitted]

The choice of law provisions in this case will do more than cause variations in damages. The availability of the voluntary payment doctrine alone could abrogate AT&T's liability for all customers who voluntarily paid the UCC after receiving the informational flyer detailing their responsibility for its payment and reside in states employing the doctrine. This is only one example.

The Court of Appeals dismissed the trial court's concerns in part because it determined that "extrinsic evidence" "will not be necessary here because these consumers entered into a standardized contract." However, there is no support cited for this conclusion. Indeed, some Washington courts have held just the opposite: "When material extrinsic evidence shows that outside agreements were relied upon, those parol agreements should be given effect rather than allowing boilerplate 'to vitiate the manifest understanding of the parties.'" [citation omitted] Further, simply because the Court of Appeals finds extrinsic evidence would be unnecessary under Washington law does not mean that the law of all other 49 states would exclude such evidence as well.

An additional concern is the availability of affirmative defenses. As the trial court noted, "[s]ome states, such as Illinois, . . . allow as a contract claim defense, the voluntary payment doctrine which prohibits a contract claim for refund of a sum voluntarily paid." The Court of Appeals suggested the trial court employ subclasses and master's hearings to sort out the morass. However, the availability of these mechanisms for efficient management of large class actions cannot change the predominance of the individualized issues in this case. *See* 2 Alba Conte & Herbert B. Newberg, *Newberg on Class Actions* §4:32, at 286-287 (4th ed. 2002) (noting courts have found "subclasses would not cure the problems" of diverse factual issues and that "when a court determines that a multitude of mini-trials will be necessary to dispose of individual claims, the court will likely find that common questions do not predominate."). As the trial court noted, "[w]hile Washington would be only one of fifty jurisdictions' law[s] which would have to be addressed in resolving the contract claims, it is illustrative of the issues that would arise."

SUPERIORITY ANALYSIS

Even if individualized issues did not predominate, CR 23(b)(3) also requires "that a class action [be] *superior* to other available methods for the fair and efficient adjudication of the controversy." *See* 4 Conte & Newberg, *supra*, §13:11, at 406 ("It must be emphasized that, under the rule, a class action *must be superior, not just as good as*, other available methods." (emphasis added)). The superiority requirement "focuses upon a comparison of available alternatives."

In more traditional statewide class actions, these alternatives include joinder, intervention, or consolidation. The most obvious alternative to the proposed nationwide class action in this case is numerous statewide class actions brought by the citizens of each state against AT&T. This is not a case where the choice is either a nationwide class action or no action at all. Given the sheer number of AT&T customers in each of the 50 states, no one state's citizens will be left out in the class action cold without the possibility of amassing enough individual claims within their state to cover litigation costs.

Although it is true that small amounts of money are at issue and the decision will have broad impact, there is simply no efficiency in asking a trial judge to manage the laws of 50 different states as they apply to plaintiffs' contract claims and the varied factual scenarios inherent therein. *See* Miller & Crump, *Jurisdiction and Choice of Law in Multistate Class Actions After Phillips Petroleum Co. v. Shutts*, 96 Yale L.J. 1, 64 (1986) ("Beyond the difficult task of correctly determining foreign law, the nationwide class action may present an even greater problem because of the sheer burden of organizing and following fifty or more different bodies of complex substantive principles. Although the comparison obviously is inexact, one can appreciate the magnitude of the trial judge's task by imagining a first-year law student who, instead of a course in contracts, is required simultaneously to enroll in fifty courses, each covering the contract law of a single state, and to apply each body of law correctly on the final examination.").

Further, Washington has no interest in seeing contracts executed by AT&T representatives in other states with citizens of those states examined and adjudicated in Washington courts. Certified as a nationwide class action, this case would present an unwarranted and unnecessary burden on the state judicial system, all at a large cost to taxpayers. *See* R.J. Reynolds Tobacco Co. v. Engle, 672 So. 2d 39, 41 (Fla. Dist. Ct. App. 1996) ("No doubt a tremendous number of retired judges, special masters, and general masters would have to be appointed by the court in order to complete this herculean task within a reasonable period of time — all at a staggering cost to the taxpayers."). There is no sound reason in this case for this court to force Washington trial courts to entertain the contract claims of citizens from around the nation. Their state courts are equally as prepared, if not better situated to apply the contract laws of their states. . . . This court does not dispute, however that if the contract class were constructed as a statewide class, it would meet the requirements of both CR 23(a) and (b)(3).

EXTRATERRITORIAL APPLICATION OF WASHINGTON'S CONSUMER PROTECTION ACT

The trial court and the Court of Appeals both noted that the CPA was applicable to all plaintiffs' claims because they arose from statute instead of contract. However, nothing in our law indicates that CPA claims by nonresidents for acts occurring outside of Washington can be entertained under the statute. "Because the laws of each state are designed to regulate and protect the interest of that state's own residents and citizens, each state has a measurable, and usually predominant, interest in having its own substantive laws apply." While it is true that "Washington has a strong interest in regulating any behavior by Washington businesses which contravenes the CPA," the CPA indicates the legislature's intent to limit its application to deceptive acts that affect the citizens and residents of Washington. The CPA states: "[u]nfair methods of competition and unfair or deceptive acts or practices in the conduct of any trade or commerce are hereby declared unlawful." RCW 19.86.020. "Trade" or "commerce" is defined as "the sale of assets or services, and any commerce directly or indirectly *affecting the people of the state of Washington*." RCW 19.86.010(2) (emphasis added). To state a CPA claim a person must show that the unfair or deceptive act affected the people of the state of Washington. This geographic and jurisdictional limitation originates in the CPA's history as a tool used by the State attorney general to protect the citizens of Washington. The attorney general of the state of Washington has no power outside the geographic boundary of this state. It is understood that her actions will be brought on "behalf of persons residing in the state." RCW 19.86.080(1).

This statutory and jurisdictional limitation cannot be obviated simply because the claimants are private citizens. Indeed, our courts retained this limitation for private attorneys general through the requirement that the private claimants prove a defendant's practices affect "the public interest." Hangman Ridge Training Stables, Inc. v. Safeco Title Ins. Co., 105 Wash. 2d 778, 784 (1986). Because of the statute's jurisdictional limitation, applicable to both the attorney general and private claimants, a private claimant cannot state a CPA claim by proving the defendant's practices affected the public interest or the citizens of *another* state. *See Lyon*, 194 F.R.D. at 215 ("State consumer fraud acts are designed to either protect state residents or protect consumers engaged in transactions within the state.").

RCW 19.86.920 does not indicate otherwise. This portion of the CPA empowers courts analyzing unfair competition claims to consider "whether conduct restrains or monopolizes trade or commerce" even when those market effects are felt outside of Washington. RCW 19.86.920. This provision merely closes a potential loophole in the CPA that would allow companies to escape liability by claiming their methods of competition are within Washington's boundaries even though those methods effectively monopolize trade *outside* the state. This portion of the statute does not give Washington the power to enforce its laws outside its territorial borders.

Even the general extraterritorial flavor of RCW 19.86.920 cannot change the clear standing limitations in the statute: a claimant must allege injury in trade or commerce that "directly or indirectly affect[s] the people of the state of Washington." RCW 19.86.010(2); Panag v. Farmers Ins. Co. of Wash., 166 Wash. 2d 27, 38 (2009) ("[T]he *Hangman Ridge*-test incorporates the issue of standing, particularly the elements of public interest impact and injury."). In the context of this case, the CPA only applies to claims brought by persons residing in Washington.

REMAINING WASHINGTON PLAINTIFFS' CPA CLAIMS

The question then remains, can a class of Washington only CPA plaintiffs be certified? The trial court correctly found that "proof of causation is an essential element of a CPA action." *Hangman Ridge* requires CPA plaintiffs to establish a causal link "between the unfair or deceptive act complained of and the injury suffered." We have more recently held that this causal link must establish that the "injury complained of . . . would not have happened" if not for defendant's violative acts. *Indoor Billboard*, 162 Wash. 2d at 82. The quantum of proof necessary to establish the proximate, "but for" causation required by the CPA is not fully developed in our case law. However, *Indoor Billboard* clearly establishes that proximate cause in a class action cannot be established by "mere payment" of an allegedly injurious charge, though that payment can be "considered with all other relevant evidence on the issue of proximate cause." *Id.* at 83. *Indoor Billboard* did not reject individual reliance as a method of proving causation under the CPA, but merely held that plaintiffs cannot be required to show reliance where other evidence is sufficient to establish "but for" causation. . . .

As the trial court recognized, this court does not *require* proof of individual reliance from CPA claimants as a separate element. But, where knowledge of the truth would defeat a claim of misrepresentation, that alleged misrepresentation has been eliminated as the "but for" cause of the claimant's injury. In misrepresentation and deception or fraud cases, the claimant may be called upon to offer more individualized proof that she had no knowledge of the truth because the remaining evidence is simply insufficient to establish "but for" causation. In the case at hand, for example, some plaintiffs received materials that "specifically list the 'universal connectivity charge' as one of the fees, taxes, and surcharges which the customer is responsible for paying." Under plaintiffs' misrepresentation theory of causation the trial court will need to decide . . . whether "individual class members were actually deceived and whether they would have" purchased their cellular service, or paid the UCC but for AT&T's marketing of the cost of the cellular plan or their explanations regarding the genesis of the UCC.

The trial judge found that "[i]n the context of" a nationwide CPA action, proof of causality for each plaintiff "must necessarily be individual for each potential class member," resulting in an uncertifiable class in which "individual issues would predominate over class issues and a class action would be unmanageable." However, the trial court provided no specific analysis of whether proof of causality would be so individualized among a class comprised only of Washington customers. For example, if Washington customers all had received no information regarding the UCC, proof of causality could be more common than if they all had received different and allegedly fraudulent representations: proving a plaintiff relied on an affirmative misrepresentation is necessarily individualized, but proving the lack of information was the common cause of each plaintiffs' decision to sign up for wireless service could be more generalized.

Because the trial court did not analyze the causality element of plaintiffs' CPA claims as it would apply only to the facts and evidence pertaining to Washington customers, we remand for further consideration of this issue in accordance with our opinion.

In sum, we agree with the trial court that this action should not be certified as a *nation* wide class action. Washington need not apply its Consumer Protection Act, or its contract laws, to the citizens of other states in order to protect the interests of the citizens of Washington. A nationwide class would be unmanageable and unduly burdensome on the trial court and the state judicial system and serve no real benefit to plaintiffs who are free to bring statewide class actions in their home states.

SANDERS, J. (dissenting). [with three Justices joining]

Because the trial court abused its discretion when it denied nationwide class certification absent a sufficient analysis of the feasibility of such a class, I dissent . . . .

. . . As recognized by the Court of Appeals, subclasses and master's hearings could be used to address differing state contract laws. Not every state contract law is materially different for purposes here, and the trial court abused its discretion by failing to consider whether the laws of the states could be grouped together in a manageable number of subclasses. I agree with the trial court and Court of Appeals that the Washington CPA can be applied nationwide; the majority all but ignores that AT&T, a party to every transaction at issue, is headquartered in Redmond, Washington, and the decisions, representations, and communications were made, formulated, and/or approved there. I disagree with the majority's view of causation under the CPA. The CPA and CR 23 (governing class certification), are intended to be liberally construed and should provide the class with a forum to litigate these claims. The majority creates impossible evidentiary burdens for the class that preclude it and future classes from challenging conduct as alleged here—a corporation nickel and diming consumers wholesale, escaping litigation by only taking small amounts of money from each customer.

ENFORCEABILITY OF CHOICE OF LAW PROVISIONS

The majority concludes that the choice of law clauses in the individual customers' contracts should be enforced. The majority's analysis appears to address only the contract claims and not the CPA ones. I concur with the application of the choice of law clauses to the contract claims. As explained more fully below, however, this application of different state contract laws does not necessarily defeat class certification because subclasses and other mechanisms could likely be used to address any variances.

The choice of law clauses do not apply to the CPA claims.[3] The CPA claims are based upon statute, not contract, and many of the claims arose *before* the class members even entered into their contracts with AT&T pertaining to choice of law. The first element of a CPA action — an unfair or deceptive act — can arise prior to a contract; a litigant need only show an act "had the capacity to deceive a substantial portion of the public." *Hangman Ridge, supra*.[4] That is the case here where the CPA claims relate to the use of allegedly deceptive language, advertising, and promotional materials.

CLASS CERTIFICATION OF CONTRACT CLAIMS

The majority endorses the trial court's view that individual issues predominate over the common legal and factual issues due to the "interpretation of the contract terms" and "the availability of differing affirmative defenses" under the laws of 50 different states. The trial court listed potential differences in contract interpretation, the voluntary payment doctrine, and the interpretation of arbitration agreements as examples of where the claims would need to be analyzed under 50 different state laws. However, not *every* law of the 50 states has a different approach to contract interpretation and affirmative defenses. Where state laws materially differ, subclasses could be established to address those differences. [citations omitted][5]

The trial court abused its discretion by failing to determine whether the laws of the states could be separated into a few, manageable subclasses. The trial court only referenced speculative differences in the law of every state without

---

3. I can only assume that the majority, silent on this issue, does not find the choice of law clauses applicable to the CPA claims. If it did, its further analysis of the "extraterritorial" application of and causation issues under the CPA would be rendered dictum since the multistate-law issue the majority finds so damning to class certification with regard to the contract claims would also apply to the CPA claims.

4. A litigant can make such a showing even prior to suffering an injury, because the CPA not only vindicates individual rights but protects the public interest. This protection of the public interest extends to misrepresentations made to one person, where those misrepresentations have the capacity to deceive a substantial portion of the public — for example, if they are made in a standard form contract. [citations omitted]

5. The majority cites over 50 cases in which federal courts declined to certify a class based on Fed. R. Civ. P. 23 where multiple state laws applied. But this list of cases, devoid of detail or discussion, merely supports the obvious proposition that under some facts, application of numerous state laws can defeat class certification. There is no need to counter in kind to cite to the equally obvious corollary — that under some facts the potential application of multiple state laws can be managed, and class certification *is* warranted.

determining whether material differences actually existed in each. I would therefore remand this issue to provide the parties an opportunity to further brief, and the trial court to fully consider, whether subclasses could be created to address materially different state laws within a nationwide class.

SUPERIORITY ANALYSIS

CR 23(b)(3) requires a court to find that "a class action is superior to other available methods for the fair and efficient adjudication of the controversy." The majority concludes that a nationwide class action is not superior to other available methods—namely, that individual state class actions are better suited to resolve the controversy. However, the majority's reasoning does not support this conclusion.

First, the majority asserts that, although class actions permit claims involving small amounts of money to be brought to court, this does not weigh in favor of a nationwide class because there are enough AT&T customers to bring 50 individual statewide class action suits.[6] This ignores the significant advantages of a nationwide suit. The claims in every state involve the nature of the universal connectivity charge (UCC), an apparent nationwide approach to charging fees in relation to the UCC, omissions or the same or similar misrepresentations to further that approach, and the same defendant corporation. A nationwide suit avoids a 50-fold redundancy of litigation, which will substantially increase the costs of the litigation to both parties, particularly attorney fees; result in redundant discovery, including repetitive document production and depositions; result in redundant relitigation of the same issues; and saddle the judiciary of all 50 states with significant costs to redundantly try statewide class action suits based on the actions of a single Washington corporation.

Next, the majority claims it would be inefficient to have a trial judge manage a claim litigated under 50 different state laws.[7] As more fully discussed *infra*, the law of all 50 states will not conflict and, as recognized by the Court of Appeals, subclasses and master's hearings can be used to address subsets of class members. The trial court abused its discretion, asserting a nationwide class would be unmanageable without analyzing the extent to which the state laws are materially similar and can be grouped into multistate subclasses.

Finally, the majority asserts Washington has no interest in having claims against a Washington corporation litigated in this state if they involve customers from other states. But as later discussed in more detail, Washington has a substantial interest in assuring Washington corporations conduct business in a fair and honest manner. Washington also has a substantial interest to provide a forum to resolve the legal issues of Washington businesses.

---

6. The majority provides no basis for its insinuation that a class is waiting in every state to file a statewide class action suit now that the majority is dissolving the nationwide class action here. A nationwide class provides no risk that the consumers of any states will be left behind.

7. The majority opines that granting class certification here would force Washington to "become a locus for nationwide class action litigation." But perhaps it should, where the litigation involves the conduct of a Washington corporation stemming from corporate decision making occurring in this state.

Pending a determination that the contract laws of the 50 states do not materially differ from one another so as to preclude a manageable number of subclasses to address those differences, a nationwide class is the most efficient, economical, and reliable way to assure that every class member is provided a forum in which to bring his or her claim.

"EXTRATERRITORIAL" APPLICATION OF WASHINGTON'S CONSUMER PROTECTION ACT

The trial court and the Court of Appeals agreed that the Washington CPA was applicable to the nationwide class because AT&T is headquartered in Redmond, Washington. Washington regulates the behavior of Washington businesses; the purpose of the CPA is not only to protect the public *from* unfair and deceptive acts, but also to "foster fair and honest competition" among businesses. *See* RCW 19.86.920. If a Washington business is acting in an unfair or dishonest way nationwide, Washington has a strong interest to address the full, nationwide effects of that behavior; Washington should not become a harbor for businesses engaging in unscrupulous practices out of state.

The majority instead ignores this interest, mischaracterizing transactions between a Washington corporation and an out-of-state citizen as wholly extraterritorial, and then misreading the statutory language of the CPA to exclude "claims by nonresidents for acts occurring outside of Washington." First, these transactions are not wholly extraterritorial. At least one party—AT&T—is native to Washington in every transaction here. The transactions involve AT&T's formulation of its representations, the approval and distribution of those representations, and the offer and acceptance of the agreements.[9] Significant portions of each transaction occurred in Washington.[10]

Second, the statutory language of the CPA applies to transactions between a Washington party and an out-of-state party in two ways here. RCW 19.86.020 requires that the "[u]nfair methods of competition and unfair or deceptive acts or practices" must be "in the conduct of any trade or *commerce*." (Emphasis added.) "Commerce" under the CPA is described as "any commerce directly or indirectly affecting the *people* of the state of Washington." RCW 19.86.010(2) (emphasis added). "Person" is defined to include "natural persons, *corporations*, trusts, unincorporated associations and partnerships." RCW 19.86.010(1) (emphasis added). Thus, the transaction here is "commerce" that "directly . . . affect[s]" AT&T, a corporation headquartered in Washington and thus a "person" under the CPA. The CPA therefore applies.

Furthermore, RCW 19.86.010(2) also encompasses commerce that *indirectly* affects the people of the state of Washington. Ignoring, as the majority does, that

---

9. To the extent AT&T branch offices in other states offered and accepted the contracts with customers, the AT&T headquarters would have provided them the authority to do so under the representations and omissions challenged here.

10. The CPA claims also include allegations of omissions. To the extent AT&T decided to omit information or failed to provide information it should have to consumers, those decisions or oversights would be attributable to decisions made at AT&T's headquarters in Washington.

the statutory definition of "person" includes corporations, AT&T's exchange of goods and services with individuals outside the state of Washington is still commerce that indirectly affects Washingtonians. First, the Washington employees of AT&T are "natural persons," and AT&T's commerce with the claimants indirectly affects the nature and availability of their employment. Second, to the extent "the people of the state of Washington," is read as a broader appeal to the public interest, the commerce and trade AT&T brings into Washington, and the alleged unfair and dishonest method by which it does so, affects the state economy and thus affects the Washington public at large.

The transactions here, between a Washington resident and out-of-state customers, originating at least in part in this state, fall well within the jurisdictional boundaries of the CPA.[11] The CPA encompasses the nationwide class action proposed here.

REMAINING WASHINGTON PLAINTIFFS' CPA CLAIMS (CAUSATION)

To prevail on a private CPA claim, a plaintiff must show the defendant (1) engaged in an unfair or deceptive act or practice, (2) in trade or commerce, (3) that affects the public interest, (4) and injured the plaintiff's business or property, and (5) there is a causal link between the unfair or deceptive act and the injury suffered. The fifth requirement, causation, is at issue here.

. . . The class members agreed to pay AT&T a certain amount for services; AT&T charged more than that amount; AT&T misrepresented that the excess charges were imposed by the federal government on the consumer; those charges were not imposed by the federal government on the consumer; and the class members paid the excess charges. A trier of fact could make the common sense inference that people do not willingly pay more money for commercial services than they must and, in particular, more than they originally agreed. People do, however, expect to be taxed; AT&T's misrepresentation of the fee as a mandatory federal tax on consumers causes class members to pay the "tax." Payment of the UCC in light of the nature of the misrepresentation and reasonable inferences drawn from common sense provides a sufficient basis for a trier of fact to find causation, as envisioned in *Indoor Billboard*. Therefore the causation requirement does not preclude class certification here.

Despite our decision in *Indoor Billboard* the majority elevates the bar to prove causation far beyond any evidentiary standard that could be met by a class action seeking redress for a misrepresentation under the CPA. . . .[13]

The majority's holding is nothing short of a disaster for plaintiffs, the CPA and CR 23, and the jurisprudence of this court. The majority's requirement of

---

11. Although the statutory language here is clear, ambiguity would be liberally resolved with a construction that effectuates the CPA's purposes, including the fostering of fair and honest competition. *See* RCW 19.86.920.

13. The majority requires satisfaction of a difficult evidentiary burden since class members are forced to prove a negative—that they did not know the true nature of the UCC. The majority does not explain why it is not sufficient that the plaintiffs allege ignorance—a factual allegation that must be taken as true for the purposes of class certification. After class certification AT&T could still put forth evidence that some plaintiffs had additional information concerning the UCC through

a showing of individualized reliance for misrepresentation claims under the CPA creates an individual issue that will predominate over the class issues here, *and in every CPA misrepresentation class action in the future.* Under the majority's reasoning there is no longer any legal recourse for individuals who fall victim to the misrepresentations of corporations when those misrepresentations do not cause sufficient loss to make an individual lawsuit economically feasible. Yet assuring such access to the courts, even when the economic stakes are too small individually, is precisely the purpose of CR 23, which the majority so effectively eviscerates.

The majority's holding also flies in the face of this court's history of liberally construing CR 23 and the CPA to effectuate their purposes. [citations omitted] The CPA, which permits private citizens to act as private attorneys general to protect the public interest against unfair and deceptive practices, no longer provides any ability to protect the public now if a corporation misrepresents its charges or services to the public. The majority's requirement of proof that *each* class member did not know the truth of the lie will destroy any class action. . . .

Here, the surrounding facts provide a basis for a causal connection. Class members, after entering into a contract with AT&T at a certain price, would not have rationally intended to pay more without a valid justification for the additional charge. A trier of fact could draw the inference that individuals were motivated by the most obvious source—a belief that the charge was a mandatory federal tax on consumers.

The majority's view of causation is excessive and contrary to this court's previous holdings. Rather than render the CPA and CR 23 ineffectual in addressing the wholesale bilking of consumers, I would certify the class. . . .

. . . The majority . . . errs when it neuters the Washington Consumer Protection Act, rendering its protection lean and lank, by providing a safe haven for businesses in Washington to engage in unfair or dishonest practices outside the state of Washington. I would remand the nationwide class certification issue to the trial court for reconsideration in light of the discussion here.

NOTE: On motion for reconsideration, the Washington Supreme Court withdrew the above opinion. In a very similar replacement opinion, the still-divided court came to the same basic conclusion, that the trial court had properly declined to certify a nationwide class, although a remand for possible certification of a statewide class of Washington plaintiffs was appropriate. Schnall v. AT&T Wireless Service, Inc., 259 P.3d 129 (Wash. 2011). In the new opinion, however, the majority toned down its rhetoric about not wanting to be the locus of a national suit and instead emphasized the importance of giving deference to trial court certification decisions. Moreover, the majority no longer rested any of its analysis on a conclusion that the Washington CPA was not intended to apply to plaintiffs outside of Washington when the defendant is a Washington company. In a footnote, the majority stated that it did not need to address that question once it concluded

---

materials it circulated. The trial court could utilize subclasses or master's hearings to permit a trier of fact to determine whether those materials conveyed the true nature of the charge to its recipients. This method does not wholesale extinguish individuals' ability to bring a class action under the CPA for misrepresentation, as does the majority.

that a nationwide class was inappropriate for other reasons. The same footnote acknowledged that the state attorney general had submitted a brief providing "credible reasons" why the CPA might well apply extraterritorially. *Id*. at 136, n.4.

In re Telectronics Pacing Systems, Inc.
172 F.R.D. 271 (S.D. Ohio 1997)

SPIEGEL, Senior D.J.

For the fourth time in little more than a year, this Court addresses the question whether class certification is appropriate in this case. . . .

I.   Background

A.   THE PARTIES

This is a products liability action concerning pacemakers containing the Accufix Atrial "J" Lead. Plaintiffs in this action are recipients of the Accufix Atrial "J" Lead Pacemaker Model 330-801 and Model 329-701 ("J Lead").

Defendant, TPLC, Incorporated ("TPLC"), is a Delaware corporation engaged in the business of designing, manufacturing, and marketing medical devices including the Accufix Atrial "J" Lead pacemakers at issue in this case. They manufactured the "J" Lead pacemakers Models 330-801 and 329-701 from 1988 until 1994. Defendant, Telectronics Pacing Systems, Incorporated ("TPSI"), is also a Delaware corporation. TPSI's sole business is to hold certain industrial property rights, real estate and the equity interest in TPLC. [Two Australian companies acting as holding company and parent company were originally named in the suit but Plaintiffs do not seek class certification against them.]

B.   THE "J" LEAD CONTROVERSY

A pacemaker is a device that uses electrical impulses to reproduce or regulate the rhythms of the heart. It is driven by a battery and connected to the heart by leads and electrodes. [The pacemaker models at issue in this case] utilize a retention wire to hold the atrial lead in the shape of a "J". . . .

The retention wire is encased in polyurethane insulation and bends back and forth within the system. The bending has caused the retention wire to break in some instances and poke through the polyurethane. The retention wire is not electrically active in the pacing circuit. Consequently, it has nothing to do with the conduction of the electrical signal or the operation of the pacing system. A fracture, however, can cause serious injury to the heart or blood vessels if it pokes through the polyurethane.

Approximately 25,000 pacemakers with "J" Leads were implanted in hearts of United States residents. Between December 1988 and February 1993, TPLC received reports of at least seven fractures of "J" Lead retention wires. On October 21, 1994, TPLC notified the Food and Drug Administration ("FDA") that it was recalling all unsold leads. Telectronics' President, James W. Dennis, then sent a letter to all doctors on November 3, 1994, notifying them that TPLC was voluntarily recalling all unimplanted Accufix Atrial "J" Lead pacemakers. . . .

By August 1996, TPLC had received notice of at least thirty-two injuries due to fractures, including six deaths. Additionally, eight others have died while having their lead extracted. [Company documents indicate that the fracture rate is somewhere between 12 and 20 percent.]

In response to the fracture problem, TPLC has done three things to control the situation. First, TPLC has established the Accufix Research Institute ("ARI") to manage the lead recall. The ARI communicates with doctors and patients concerning patient management recommendations. ARI is conducting a Multi-Center study ("MCS") involving twelve hospitals to monitor a subset of leads over time. ARI analyzes the data from the MCS to assess the risk of injury from the "J" wire fracture as well as the risk of injury from lead extraction.

Secondly, TPLC formed a Physicians Advisory Committee ("PAC") to provide advice concerning clinical management of lead patients. The PAC reviews information from the MCS and other sources. The PAC then makes recommendations to the ARI concerning patient care.

Upon the PAC's recommendation, Telectronics sent a letter to doctors [notifying them of the fracture problem and advising them that implantees should receive fluoroscopic screening every six months to detect early signs of fracture.]

Finally, TPLC has agreed to "reimburse reasonable unreimbursed medical expenses for screening and Lead extraction that are consistent with patient management guidelines."

C. Procedural History

Plaintiffs, Elise and Eugene Owens, filed the lead action in this case on February 13, 1995, alleging injury due to a defective "J" lead. Plaintiffs allege that it was TPLC's negligent manufacture or design of the "J" Lead that causes the retention wire to fracture. The Panel on Multi-District Litigation ("MDL Panel") selected this Court as the transferee court for all claims involving the Accufix "J" Lead. Presently, over 400 cases are pending before this Court for pretrial proceedings.

The Court appointed a Plaintiffs' Steering Committee ("PSC") to coordinate discovery and other pretrial proceedings on behalf of Plaintiffs in the cases transferred to this Court. The Court ordered the PSC to file a Master Complaint. . . .

The Court initially certified a worldwide class of all "J" Lead implantees for the common issues of medical monitoring, negligence, strict liability, fraud, misrepresentation, and breach of warranty. On February 23, 1996, the Court decertified the international class. TPLC moved to have the Court reconsider the class certification in light of the Sixth Circuit's decision in In re American Medical Systems, 75 F.3d 1069 (6th Cir. 1996). On July 16, 1996, the Court granted the motion to reconsider and decertified this case as a class action (hereinafter Decertification Order).

D.   CLASS STRUCTURE

Plaintiffs have now filed a Renewed Motion for Class Certification. . . .

Plaintiffs seek to certify a nationwide class on claims of medical monitoring, negligence, strict liability and punitive damages. State products liability law encompasses several different causes of action.

"That branch of the law commonly called 'products liability' is often spoken of as a unitary, coherent body of statute and precedent when in fact there are at least three common theories of recovery for damages sustained as a result of a defective product. In a 'products liability' case, a plaintiff may seek recovery, as did this plaintiff, upon (1) a theory of negligence; (2) a theory of 'strict liability'; or (3) a theory of breach of warranty, either express or implied." Ragland Mills, Inc. v. General Motors Corp., 763 S.W.2d 357, 359 (Mo. App. 1989) (citations omitted). However, not all states permit all three causes of action in products liability actions. *See e.g.*, O.R.C. §2307.71 et seq. (establishing strict liability as the exclusive remedy in all products liability actions); Washington Water Power Co. v. Graybar Elcc. Co., 112 Wash. 2d 847 (1989) (finding that Washington Product Liability Act, RCWA 7.72.010(4), preempts common-law causes of action for harms caused by product defects).

In our Decertification Order, we found that Plaintiffs must demonstrate how this case can be managed as a class action in light of the variations in state law. Furthermore, we required Plaintiffs to come forward with exact definitions of subclasses, its representatives, and the reasons each subclass meets the requirements of Rule 23. Consequently, Plaintiffs have proposed ten subclasses (Subclass 6 contains three sub-subclasses) which take into account the variations of state law.

First, Plaintiffs propose one nationwide subclass for all medical monitoring claims. It is defined as follows:

> SUBCLASS ONE: all persons who have had the Accufix atrial "J" pacemaker leads . . . placed in their bodies whose leads have not been explanted and who seek the establishment of a medical monitoring and research program.

The medical monitoring program which Plaintiffs seek would provide diagnostic testing for each class member, as well as conduct research on better methods of detecting fractured leads and determine safer methods for removing the fractured leads.

Plaintiffs seek to certify two negligence subclasses. Subclass Two would represent "J" Lead implantees who reside in states whose law permits a cause of action for negligence in a product liability action and allows the introduction of the state-of-the-art evidence.[2] Subclass Three would be made up of "J" Lead implantees residing in states whose law does not allow introduction of state-of-the-art evidence in negligence actions.

---

2. State-of-the-art evidence is "evidence that a product's danger was scientifically undiscoverable at the time the defendant distributed the product." "[T]he effect of the 'state-of-the-art' defense is to permit a defendant to rebut the presumption of knowledge of its product's harmful propensities . . . by proving the impossibility of knowledge, even by experts in the field." [citations omitted]

Plaintiffs have proposed four strict liability subclasses. Subclass Four consists of implantees from states which follow Restatement (Second) of Torts Section 402A[3] and which allow the introduction of state-of-the-art evidence. Subclass Five consists of implantees from states which follow Restatement (Second) of Torts Section 402A and which do not allow the introduction of state-of-the-art evidence. Subclass Six consists of implantees from states which follow a modified version of Restatement (Second) of Torts Section 402A and which allow the introduction of state-of-the-art evidence.[4] Subclass Six is further divided into three sub-subclasses based upon whether the state requires a showing that the product is defective, unreasonably dangerous or both. Subclass Seven consists of three states which follow the Greenman v. Yuba Power Products, formulation of strict liability.[5]

Plaintiffs propose three subclasses covering claims for punitive damages. Plaintiffs have divided the classes based upon level of culpability which must be shown in order to justify punitive damages.

Finally, Plaintiffs have chosen not to seek certification of the remaining causes of action: fraud, loss of consortium, breach of warranty, misrepresentation and infliction of emotional distress.

II.   Elements of Rule 23(a)

[The court found that the proposed class meets the requirements of Rule 23(a)—numerosity, commonality, typicality, and adequacy.]

III.   Elements of Rule 23(b) and Medical Monitoring Class

. . . In order for a class action to be maintainable, the putative class must also satisfy one of the three subsections of Rule 23(b), in addition to the requirements of Rule 23(a). Rule 23(b) states as follows:

(1) the prosecution of separate actions by or against individual members of the class would create a risk of

(A) inconsistent or varying adjudications with respect to individual members of the class which would establish incompatible standards of conduct for the party opposing the class, or

(B) adjudications with respect to individual members of the class which would as a practical matter be dispositive of the interests of the other members not parties to the adjudications or substantially impair or impede their ability to protect their interests; or

---

3. Restatement (Second) of Torts §402A states that "[o]ne who sells any product in a defective condition unreasonably dangerous to the user . . . is subject to liability for physical harm thereby caused to the ultimate user. . . ."

4. States which apply a modified version of Restatement (Second) Torts §402A incorporate negligence elements into the strict liability formulation.

5. Under *Greenman*, plaintiff need not show that the product was unreasonably dangerous but merely that the product was defective.

(2) the party opposing the class has acted or refused to act on grounds generally applicable to the class, thereby making appropriate final injunctive relief or
corresponding declaratory relief with respect to the class as a whole; or

(3) the court finds that the questions of law or fact common to the members
of the class predominate over any questions affecting only individual members,
and that a class action is superior to other available methods for the fair and efficient adjudication of the controversy.

Fed. R. Civ. P. 23(b). The elements of Rule 23(b) overlap, and often a class may
satisfy more than one of the subsections of Rule 23(b).

Turning to the requirements of Rule 23(b) as applied to the specific subclasses, we find that certifying a medical monitoring class is justified under both
Rule 23(b)(1)(A) and 23(b)(3). . . .

A. CLASS CERTIFICATION OF MEDICAL MONITORING PURSUANT TO RULE 23(B)(1)(A).

Rule 23(b)(1)(A) states that class certification is proper if separate actions
"would create a risk of inconsistent or varying adjudications with respect to
individual members of the class which would establish incompatible standards
of conduct for the party opposing the class. . . ." Fed. R. Civ. P. 23(b)(1)(A).
"The phrase 'incompatible standards of conduct' is thought to refer to the situation where different results in separate actions would impair the opposing party's ability to pursue a uniform continuing course of conduct." "[S]ubdivision
(b)(1)(A) is applicable when practical necessity forces the opposing party to act
in the same manner toward the individual class members and thereby makes
inconsistent adjudications in separate actions unworkable or intolerable."

The medical monitoring claim here is an ideal candidate for class certification pursuant to Rule 23(b)(1)(A) because separate adjudications would impair
TPLC's ability to pursue a single uniform medical monitoring program. Presently,
TPLC is conducting a research program which is investigating the cause of the
fractures, looking for better ways to detect the fractures and seeking safer methods
of extracting the damaged leads. Plaintiffs seek the establishment of a medical
monitoring program which would include diagnostic testing and research. TPLC
asserts that medical monitoring beyond that recommended by TPLC's Physicians'
Advisory Committee is not warranted. TPLC's research program is a uniform benefit to the class of "J" lead implantees as a whole. Any judicially-imposed modification of this program would then, by necessity, affect all of the "J" lead implantees. Furthermore, separate judicial orders pertaining to medical monitoring could
require TPLC to institute differing types of monitoring programs which TPLC
would have to reconcile.

TPLC argues that the recommendations of the Physicians' Advisory
Committee are subject to approval by the FDA. TPLC insists that "the Court [will]
have to reconcile its involvement in a medical monitoring program with FDA's
statutorily mandated oversight function. . . . The potential for unnecessary conflict
and expense with no patient benefit is readily apparent, with TPLC caught in an
impossible position between the judicial and executive branches of government."

Whether FDA regulations preempt or otherwise limit state law tort claims for medical monitoring goes to the merits of the class claims and must be determined at a later date.

However, individual adjudication of implantees' claims for medical monitoring would not alleviate TPLC's fear of conflicting standards of medical monitoring imposed by the judicial branch and executive branch. In fact, the danger of courts imposing conflicting duties upon Telectronics would only be compounded if the question of medical monitoring is not certified as a class action pursuant to Rule 23(b)(1)(A). Presently, there are over 400 individual actions consolidated before this Court by the Judicial Panel for Multidistrict Litigation. Certainly, a large number of similar cases are pending in state courts across the country. Thus, TPLC could still face multiple and conflicting orders rendered from different courts regarding the scope and necessity of a medical monitoring program which may also conflict with FDA imposed requirements. Accordingly, the Court certifies the medical monitoring subclass under Rule 23(b)(1)(A).

. . . [T]here are also significant policy reasons for requiring one medical monitoring class. Any research component should be coordinated in order to maximize resources and avoid duplication. To promote consistency in treatment, doctors should also be given one set of advice in terms of treatment options for their "J" lead patients.

B. Class Certification of Medical Monitoring Pursuant to Rule 23(b)(1)(B).

The argument for certification of a medical monitoring subclass is bolstered by the fact that separate adjudications may adversely affect other implantees' ability to recover anything. Under Rule 23(b)(1)(B), certification is justified if adjudications by individual class members might "as a practical matter be dispositive of the interests of the other members not parties to the adjudications or substantially impair or impede their ability to protect their interests." Fed. R. Civ. P. 23(b)(1)(B). The most common use of subsection (b)(1)(B) is in limited fund cases. "A limited fund exists when a fixed asset or piece of property exists in which all class members have a preexisting interest, and an apportionment or determination of the interests of one class member cannot be made without affecting the proportionate interests of other class members similarly situated." In the same limited circumstances, the potential or probable insolvency of the defendant due to a large number of pending tort actions can create a limited fund appropriate for adjudication under Rule 23(b)(1)(B). *See e.g.*, In re Asbestos Litigation, 90 F.3d 963, 983 (5th Cir. 1996) (citing cases).

[The court noted that this could be a limited fund case given that TPLC has recently sold all of its assets to another corporation. However, it lacked the information necessary to confidently make that conclusion.] . . . The possibility of the existence of a limited fund, however, lends further support to a conclusion that medical monitoring class should be certified under Rule 23(b)(1).

C. Class Certification of Medical Monitoring Pursuant to Rule 23(b)(3).

In addition, we note that a medical monitoring subclass also satisfies Rule 23(b)(3). Rule 23(b)(3) has two primary requirements: (1) that common issues predominate over individual issues, and (2) class treatment is superior to other methods of adjudication.

First, TPLC's defense to Plaintiffs' medical monitoring claim clearly predominates over any individual issues raised by the medical monitoring claims. TPLC acknowledges that all "J" lead implantees require medical monitoring to prevent injury due to fracture. Telectronics' primary defense to Plaintiffs' claims for additional or different medical monitoring than that offered by TPLC is that its medical monitoring program has been approved by the FDA and is the best program available under present research and technology. This defense is common to all implantees and is the predominant issue regarding the appropriateness of a court ordered medical monitoring program.

Second, class certification of a medical monitoring class is also the superior method of dealing with the medical monitoring claims. As pointed out in our discussion of Rule 23(b)(1), there is risk that TPLC could be ordered to conduct conflicting medical monitoring programs if individual implantees pursue medical monitoring claims in separate actions. In addition, practically speaking, for many of the "J" Lead recipients their only realistic claim may be for medical monitoring. This is not the type of claim that is likely to lead to large damage awards. While TPLC has to its credit instituted a significant medical monitoring program, Plaintiffs have every right to challenge the adequacy of this program. Thus, it appears that many of the proposed class members have small monetary claims that would be difficult to pursue in individual actions. The superiority prong of Rule 23(b)(3) is satisfied if aggregation of small monetary claims is required to ensure vindication of legal rights. *See* Scholes v. Stone, McGuire & Benjamin, 143 F.R.D. 181, 185 (N.D. Ill. 1992) (finding plaintiffs had satisfied superiority prong in part because many class members had claims which would be uneconomical to pursue individually); Wehner v. Syntex Corp., 117 F.R.D. 641, 645 (N.D. Cal. 1987) (finding class action superior where "[i]n practical terms, plaintiffs . . . may be economically precluded from bringing separate lawsuits and thus be barred access to the judicial system.").

Defendants counter that class certification of a medical monitoring subclass is unmanageable in light of the variations in state law of medical monitoring. We disagree. TPLC acknowledges that all implantees require medical monitoring. The critical questions are whether the present monitoring program is adequate and whether Telectronics will be required to continue it. Thus, most variations in state law regarding medical monitoring are immaterial.

One major distinction in the law of medical monitoring is relevant in this situation. In some states, medical monitoring is only recoverable if the plaintiff shows physical injury. Without a fracture of the "J" Lead, class members in those states may be unable to pursue claims for monitoring even though TPLC concedes that monitoring is required. Thus, pursuant to Rule 23(c)(4), the Court will divide the medical monitoring class into two subclasses: (1) implantees from states that do not require present physical injury to recover for medical monitoring, and

(2) implantees from state that require present physical injury in order to recover for medical monitoring.

IV.

A. NEGLIGENCE AND STRICT LIABILITY SUBCLASSES AND RULE 23(B).

. . . Both the negligence and strict liability claims are primarily actions for damages which are generally certified pursuant to Rule 23(b)(3). . . . Rule 23(b)(3) has two primary requirements: (1) that common issues predominate over individual issues, and (2) class treatment is superior to other methods of adjudication. Rule 23(b)(3) parallels Rule 23(a)(2) in that both subdivisions require that common issues exist, but 23(b)(3)'s predominance test goes further by insuring that the common issues predominate over individual issues. The inquiry is mainly a pragmatic one: do the common issues justify a common adjudication?

B. DO COMMON ISSUES PREDOMINATE?

That common issues predominate over individual issues does not require that the class members' claims be proven by identical evidence or that individualized proof cannot be introduced on some issues.

> No matter how individualized the issue of damages may be, these issues may be reserved for individual treatment with the question of liability tried as a class action. Consequently, the mere fact that questions peculiar to each individual member of the class remain after the common questions of the defendant's liability have been resolved does not dictate the conclusion that a class action is impermissible.

Sterling v. Velsicol Chem. Corp., 855 F.2d 1188, 1196-1197 (6th Cir. 1988); *see also* In re American Medical Systems, 75 F.3d at 1084 (quoting *Sterling* with approval). Generally, mass tort accidents are appropriate for resolution on a class-wide basis because the cause of the accident is a single course of conduct. . . . Numerous courts have found that common issues predominate when a large number of lawsuits arise from a single disaster or single course of conduct. [citations omitted]

The Sixth Circuit in *American Medical Systems*, however, found that products liability actions differed from mass tort cases because products liability cases usually involve factual and legal issues that vary dramatically from individual to individual. Nevertheless, the Sixth Circuit did not close the door on product liability class actions but instead held that district courts must exercise great care before certifying such a class. [75 F.3d] at 1089 ("This is not to say that a class action in [medical product liability/personal injury cases] will never be appropriate, but it is to say that strict adherence to Rule 23 in products liability cases involving . . . medical products which require FDA approval is especially important.").

The issues common for all of the negligence and strict liability claims are whether TPLC negligently designed or manufactured the "J" Leads or whether TPLC's "J" Leads are defective. Both issues seek to resolve whether TPLC is legally responsible for the "J" Lead fractures.

The "J" Lead controversy appears to be the exception to the general rule that medical products liability actions require extensive proof of individualized issues. This case does not involve many of the factual and legal complications which prevented certification in other medical products liability actions. First, this case involves two nearly identical pacemaker leads manufactured by one company. Compare In re Copley Pharmaceutical, Inc., 158 F.R.D. 485 (D. Wyo. 1994) (certifying class involving one product manufactured by one defendant), with In re American Medical Systems, 75 F.3d at 1085 (finding class action involving ten different penile implant models did not satisfy predominance prong); Georgine v. Amchem Prods., 83 F.3d 610, 626 (3d Cir. 1996) cert. granted, 519 U.S. 957 (1996) (decertifying in part because "[t]he class members' claims vary widely in character. Class members were exposed to different asbestos-containing products for different amounts of time, in different ways, over different periods of time."), and Castano v. American Tobacco Co., 84 F.3d 734, 742-743 n.15 (5th Cir. 1996) (". . . The class members were exposed to nicotine through different products, for different amounts of time, and over different time periods."). Second, Plaintiffs all allege one defect—a potential for or actual fracture of the retention wire. Cf. In re American Medical Systems, 75 F.3d at 1085 (finding common issues did not predominate in product liability action where class members alleged multiple defects with their product). Third, in traditional medical product liability situations, causation is often the overarching issue that requires extensive individualized proof; the same is not true in this situation. . . .

The other individual issues—whether an individual implantee's retention wire has fractured and what are the individual's damages—do not preclude class certification. Whether a particular individual's lead has fractured is easily resolved because a fracture is detectable by a fluoroscope. The damage issue, although requiring individualized proof, does not preclude class certification. Therefore, we find common issues predominate.

C. IS CLASS TREATMENT SUPERIOR?

"That common question predominate is not itself sufficient to justify a class action under subdivision (b)(3) for another method of handling the litigious situation may be available which has greater practical advantages." Fed. R. Civ. Pro. 23, Advisory Committee Note. Plaintiffs must also demonstrate that this litigation would be superior to all other methods of litigation. Fed. R. Civ. P. 23(b)(3). "[T]he purpose of the superiority requirement is to assure that the class action is the most efficient and effective means of settling the controversy. . . ." "The rule asks us to balance, in terms of fairness and efficiency, the merits of a class action against those of 'alternative available methods' of adjudication."

Rule 23(b)(3) identifies four factors which should be examined by the court to determine whether class treatment would be fair and efficient.

(A) the interest of members of the class in individually controlling the prosecution or defense of separate actions;

(B) the extent and nature of any litigation concerning the controversy already commenced by or against members of the class;

(C) the desirability or undesirability of concentrating the litigation of the claims in the particular forum;

(D) the difficulties likely to be encountered in the management of a class action.

Efficiency and economy are factors in favor of certification under the superiority prong. Here, because it appears likely that there is a single cause of the "J" Lead fracture, a single determination of causation would efficiently resolve a large issue in this case for all class members. This conclusion, however, is not enough to find class treatment the superior method of dealing with the "J" Lead cases.

Several recent circuit court decisions have focused upon the fourth factor as a possible roadblock to class certification in diversity actions. *See e.g.*, In re American Medical Systems Inc., 75 F.3d at 1085 (noting that district judge failed to consider how state law variations would affect the appropriateness of class treatment). Thus, in order to demonstrate that a class action is superior to other forms of litigation in the context of diversity based actions, Plaintiffs must show that such an action is manageable in light of state law variations.[13]

In our Decertification Order, we found that Plaintiffs had failed to make such a showing. We held that Plaintiffs must come forward with the exact definition of subclasses, their representatives, and the reasons each subclass meets the prerequisites of Rule 23(a) and (b). Furthermore, the variations in state law must guide Plaintiffs' creation of subclasses.

1.   NEGLIGENCE SUBCLASSES

Taking into account the state law variations regarding negligence, Plaintiffs have divided the subclasses to reflect the forty-six jurisdictions that permit the introduction of state-of-the-art evidence and the two jurisdictions which do not.

Plaintiffs state that forty-seven jurisdictions permit plaintiffs in product liability actions to bring negligence claims. Plaintiffs assert that all states that recognize negligence as a cause of action in a products liability action apply the same

---

13. Plaintiffs argue that this Court could apply one state's law to all of the class members' claims under Ohio choice-of-law rules. There is some support for Plaintiffs' conclusion. *See* In re Bendectin Litigation, 857 F.2d 290, 303-305 (6th Cir. 1988) (approving district court's choice of the law from the state of manufacture, under Ohio choice-of-law rules, in products liability actions consolidated for trial from across the country). We, however, question the correctness of that ruling and further question the continuing validity of that holding in light of the Sixth Circuit's later ruling in In re American Medical Systems. Accordingly, in an abundance of caution, we will presume the law of the state of residence of individual class members would apply to those claims. If at some later point, the Court finds that one state's law will apply to all class members' claims, the appropriateness of class certification will be more readily apparent.

elements to determine liability: duty, breach, causation, injury and damage. Not only do all states use the same elements to define a cause of action for negligence, many of those states look to the same source for a standard in products liability cases. *See* Restatement (Second) of Torts §395 and Appendix (cited with approval by courts in thirty-six states); [case citations omitted].

As discussed earlier, the predominant issue to be decided in this case is whether TPLC is legally responsible for the "J" Lead fractures. A major element of that question is whether state law provides a defense because the product was designed, inspected, tested, labeled or produced with the best knowledge and technology reasonably available at the time.

TPLC counters that just because those jurisdictions all recognize a cause of action in negligence in a products liability case does not mean that the law of negligence is universal. TPLC insists that the law of negligence is too diverse to certify a nationwide products liability class action. TPLC argues that Plaintiffs have failed to properly consider all of the nuances of state law in defining its proposed subclasses. Finally, TPLC argues that the Court cannot decide for itself that any differences are insignificant. Presumably, this means that the Court may not, in essence, overlook these differences, no matter how slight, and certify a class which contains implantees from states whose pattern jury instructions are not identical.

We disagree. . . . First, state law does not need to be universal in order to justify nationwide class certification.

Secondly, while it is certainly true that state tort law varies, the question under the superiority prong of Rule 23(b)(3) is can the relevant variations be dealt with in a simple and efficient manner. It seems certain though that only particular nuances should be relevant to the question of class certification. The Court must make a careful inquiry to determine which variations might impede class certification. Obviously, the Court will have to determine whether the variations are significant and whether they are material to the issues contested in the case. In other words, are there nuances in the state law at issue in the case which must be addressed in order to satisfy Erie R.R. v. Tompkins. It seems that the Court has three options in making this inquiry: (1) find that state law is sufficiently similar that a single class is appropriate, (2) find that the state law varies so much that class certification is inappropriate, or (3) find that state law variations can be categorized and then divided into subclasses.

Thus, if the elements of the cause of action are the same and the legal standards on "important/meaningful/significant/pivotal" issues are substantial similar the state laws can be grouped for purposes of class certification. In looking at the nuances of state law, it is important to distinguish between nuances that are pertinent to the issues being certified and those which are unimportant to these questions.

Specifically, TPLC argues that the use of the term "proximate cause" varies from state to state. For example, California and Oklahoma no longer use the term "proximate cause" in jury instructions in negligence cases. On the other hand, TPLC asserts that Georgia and Nebraska require the trial court to instruct the jury on proximate cause.

While we might agree that these variations in language are technically "nuances" in state law, minute and insignificant differences cannot preclude class certification or else no class could ever be certified in this context. Upon review of the case law and pattern jury instructions from the various states, we find this a distinction without a difference. Some states may have done away with the use of the term "proximate cause," but those states still instruct juries on the concept of legal causation. While we agree that some states, for example Georgia, mandate that trial courts instruct juries on the meaning of proximate cause, the real point to these cases is not the term "proximate" but the concept of legal causation. As the Georgia Supreme Court later explained . . . , the need for an instruction on proximate cause is because causation is a necessary element of any decision on liability. Dietz v. Becker, 434 S.E.2d 103, 106 (1993). . . .

Likewise, states that have eliminated use of the term "proximate cause" still retain causation as an essential element of a negligence action. Often, the deletion of the term "proximate cause" is merely a cosmetic change in the state's law or jury instructions. . . .

We find that the differences in state law regarding "proximate cause" instructions are insignificant, and therefore, they present no hurdle to class certification on negligence classes proposed by Plaintiffs.

2.   SUPERIORITY AND STRICT LIABILITY SUBCLASSES

Plaintiffs divide the strict liability issue into subclasses in order to take into account the variations in state law. Plaintiffs assert that forty-six jurisdictions recognize some form of strict liability in products liability actions. Plaintiffs contend that thirty-two jurisdictions follow the version of strict liability outlined in the Restatement (Second) of Torts §402A. Plaintiffs assert that eleven states apply a modified version of §402A which incorporates some elements of negligence into the strict liability formulation. Finally, three states follow the California Supreme Court decision in Greenman v. Yuba Power Products, 59 Cal. 2d 57 (1963), which held that the plaintiff need only show that the product was defective.

In addition to the various formulations of strict liability, as with the negligence subclasses, Plaintiffs subdivide the strict liability claims under §402A on the basis of whether the state allows introduction of state of the art evidence. Plaintiffs further subdivide the modified §402A jurisdictions on the basis of whether the jurisdiction requires proof that the product was either defective, unreasonably dangerous or both.

The Court has reviewed the subclass distinctions and finds that they adequately account for variations in the state law of strict liability. Plaintiffs have created subclasses which sufficiently take into account state law variations in the law of strict liability. . . . Accordingly, we find that the strict liability subclasses satisfy the requirements of Rule 23(b)(3).

V.   Punitive Damages

We previously denied certification of a punitive damages class because we found that punitive damages, like compensatory damages, must be measured individually based upon the facts and local law. We find here that the proposed punitive damages subclasses fail to satisfy Rule 23(b). Plaintiffs have failed to take into account adequately the multiple variations in the law of punitive damages. The law of punitive damages has undergone significant change in the last couple of years. In many instances, state legislatures have stepped in and imposed varying procedures for the imposition of punitive damages. State law also evidences substantial variances in standards of conduct and proof. A further complication arises because some states that apply a similar standard of conduct sometimes require different standards of proof. For example, both Arkansas and Alabama require a showing of willful or wanton conduct in order to award punitive damages. Consequently, Plaintiffs group Alabama and Arkansas in Subclass Eight. These two states, however, require different standards of proof. In Alabama, Plaintiff must prove punitive damages are recoverable clear and convincing evidence. In Arkansas, punitive damages are recoverable upon by preponderance of the evidence. Plaintiffs' proposed Subclass Eight includes both states.

It is not appropriate to group together in one subclass implantees from states whose laws provide for different standards of proof. Any attempt to do so would make it nearly impossible to properly instruct a jury and would be hopelessly confusing to the jury. This is merely one example of the complications in attempting to accommodate state law variations on punitive damages.

Thus, we are not convinced that Plaintiffs have shown that class certification is the superior method of dealing with the punitive damages claim. Accordingly, the Court denies certification of any punitive damages subclasses at this time.

However, the Court contemplates conducting a summary jury trial before the trial on the merits in hopes of encouraging the Parties to settle this litigation. . . . We may submit the question of punitive damages to the summary jury through a series of interrogatories reflecting the different standards and burdens of proof. Following the summary jury trial we may revisit the question whether punitive damages should be certified for class action treatment.

VI. Conclusion

. . . The Court hereby Certifies subclasses for Medical Monitoring, Negligence and Strict Liability as outlined in the Appendix to this Order. The Court, however, does not certify any punitive damage subclasses.

Questions and Comments

(1) Both the *Schnall* and *Telectronics* courts focused on choice of law tied to the states of the plaintiffs' residences. Are there types of claims or approaches to choice of law that are more likely to lead to plaintiff-based choices of law? Would the *Schnall* court have focused on plaintiffs' residences even in the absence of the choice-of-law clause?

(2) The application of multiple governing laws can work to defeat class certification, but some courts are willing to divide claims into subclasses depending on the applicable law and factual divergence of the claims. Rule 23(c)(5) states: "When appropriate, a class may be divided into subclasses that are each treated as a class under this rule." Obviously, the greater the number of differing state laws and the greater the factual variances, the less likely any court is to certify the class. But other factors come into play as well. In *Telectronics*, for example, the court was

willing to certify the class action for many of the claims, despite the fact that ten or more subclasses plus some special jury instructions would be necessary in order for the class to proceed. The *Schnall* majority was unwilling to certify the class action even though, given the small number of relevant legal differences, a much smaller number of subclasses would be needed to resolve the case. What might account for the differences in the courts' willingness to certify a nationwide class?

One relevant difference is that *Schnall* is a state court decision while *Telectronics* is a federal court decision. Federal courts often have more generous resources available to oversee complex litigation involving subclassing. In federal courts there is also less mismatch between the tax base used to finance the court's class action and the geographic residence of plaintiffs seeking class relief. If this distinction actually matters, then there may be some irony in Congress's efforts in CAFA to rein in certification of nationwide class actions by removing decisions to the federal courts.

Another difference between the two cases is that in *Telectronics*, part of the plaintiffs' claims—the seeking of medical monitoring remedies—was certifiable as a nationwide class under Rule 23(b)(1) without regard to satisfaction of the predominance and superiority prongs of Rule 23(b)(3). Because the medical monitoring claims were closely tied to the negligence and strict liability claims, the court might have been more willing to stretch to certify the latter claims than might a court faced with a request to certify a nationwide class under Rule 23(b)(3) alone.

A third difference between the two cases is the fact that while there are 300 plaintiffs in *Telectronics*, there are thousands in *Schnall*. The difference in number of plaintiffs can affect the likely viability of single-state class actions (though the dissenting judges in *Schnall* disagreed with the majority over both the viability and the relevance of the possibility of single-state actions). In some other cases, such as *Rhone-Poulenc Rorer* (*supra* page 769), courts take into account whether the claims are individually viable when rendering the certification decision. In what sense do these considerations matter to the certification decision? How large a factor should they be? Should we be concerned about the potentially wasteful duplication of litigation efforts present with multiple litigation?

(3) Of course, to some extent the varying decisions turn on judicial attitudes toward the class action mechanism. Class actions can enable redress for plaintiffs who each suffer small harms, but they also can be used to force companies to pay large sums of money simply out of fear of even larger jury verdicts. Judge Posner explained the problem in *Rhone-Poulenc Rorer*:

> Three hundred is not a trivial number of lawsuits. The potential damages in each one are great. But the defendants have won twelve of the first thirteen, and, if this is a representative sample, they are likely to win most of the remaining ones as well. Perhaps in the end, if class-action treatment is denied (it has been denied in all the other hemophiliac HIV suits in which class certification has been sought), they will be compelled to pay damages in only 25 cases, involving a potential liability of perhaps no more than $125 million altogether. These are guesses, of course, but they are at once conservative and usable for the limited purpose of comparing the situation that will face the defendants if the class certification stands. All of a sudden they will face thousands of plaintiffs. Many may already be barred by the statute of limitations, as we have

suggested, though its further running was tolled by the filing of [this case] as a class action.

Suppose that 5,000 of the potential class members are not yet barred by the statute of limitations. And suppose the named plaintiffs in *Wadleigh* win the class portion of this case to the extent of establishing the defendants' liability under either of the two negligence theories. It is true that this would only be prima facie liability, that the defendants would have various defenses. But they could not be confident that the defenses would prevail. They might, therefore, easily be facing $25 billion in potential liability (conceivably more), and with it bankruptcy. They may not wish to roll these dice. That is putting it mildly. They will be under intense pressure to settle. If they settle, the class certification — the ruling that will have forced them to settle — will never be reviewed. Judge Friendly, who was not given to hyperbole, called settlements induced by a small probability of an immense judgment in a class action "blackmail settlements." Henry J. Friendly, *Federal Jurisdiction: A General View* 120 (1973). Judicial concern about them is legitimate, not "sociological," as it was derisively termed in In re Sugar Antitrust Litigation, 559 F.2d 481, 483 n.1 (9th Cir. 1977). . . .

51 F.3d at 1298-1299. Other judges, however, question whether it is appropriate to use certification as a means to protect defendants. In a portion of the *Telectronics* opinion not reproduced above, the district court noted:

There has been much discussion regarding the need to reform or improve how federal courts deal with mass tort litigation. While we agree changes might be appropriate, the district courts are left to fight the battles and resolve the Parties disputes' with the tools provided by Congress and our appellate courts. Thus, we must grant or deny certification on the basis of the federal rules as written today and interpreted by the Sixth Circuit and the Supreme Court.

In deciding this question, the Court is mindful of the applicable law and rules, the procedural and substantive legal rights of the Parties and the ethical concerns raised by adjudication of mass tort claims. Recently, several Circuit Courts have been highly critical of the use of class actions in mass tort and product liability cases. While we recognize the difficulties inherent in diversity based-class actions as outlined by the Circuit Courts, we continue to believe that class action provides the fairest, most efficient and economical means of dealing with these types of cases. We believe courts must play an important role in the efficient resolution of mass tort action. This is especially so where, as here, there is a danger that the expense of litigation and potential for large damage awards threaten to bankrupt the defendant and leave some class members without a remedy.

We also strongly disagree with those Circuit Courts which have allowed their apparent economic biases to influence their interpretation of the requirements of Rule 23. For example, in Castano v. American Tobacco Co., 84 F.3d 734, 746 (5th Cir. 1996), the Fifth Circuit found that class certification of all nicotine dependent individuals was not superior under Rule 23(b)(3) because of the strategic effect class certification has upon the defendants' chances.

> In the context of mass tort class actions, certification dramatically affects the stakes for defendants. Class certification magnifies and strengthens the number of unmeritorious claims. Aggregation of claims also makes it more likely that a defendant will be found liable and results in significantly higher damage awards.

> *See also* Matter of Rhone-Poulenc Rorer Inc., 51 F.3d 1293 (7th Cir. 1995). To credit the Fifth Circuit's statement is to also state that its converse—denying class certification makes it less likely defendants will be found liable or responsible for lower damage awards—is true. Plaintiffs in individual actions will have to bear a greater share of the cost and risk for maintaining their action as compared to plaintiffs in a class action. Often an individual action pits a single plaintiff relying on his or her own resources to fund the litigation against the vast resources of a large manufacturer and the large law firms which represents [sic] it.
>
> Obviously, the procedural rules affect the outcome of litigation. These Circuit Courts seemed to ignore the essence of Rule 23 because of their philosophical disagreement with the effects of Rule 23.

172 F.R.D. at 275-276. Is it legitimate for a court to take into account its own normative views on class actions as part of its "superiority" analysis under Rule 23(b)(3)? Is it inevitable?

(4) Is it appropriate for a court to consider the likely merits of a case when deciding whether to certify? Most courts think not. Indirectly, however, the strength of plaintiffs' claims inevitably matters. For example, if defendant's behavior is so egregious that it is wrongful under all laws, then the differences will matter little to recovery and may also matter little to the certification decision. As one court noted, "[a] breach is a breach is a breach, whether you are on the sunny shores of California or enjoying a sweet afternoon breeze in New Jersey." Klay v. Humana, Inc., 382 F.3d 1241, 1263 (11th Cir. 2004). If plaintiffs instead must stretch to find viable theories for recovery, recognition of those theories might well vary across jurisdictions, making at least nationwide class certification less likely.

(5) In *Klay*, the Eleventh Circuit ultimately determined that class certification was inappropriate because, although there were no significant differences in the legal standard that applied to each breach of contract claim, factual differences in plaintiffs' situations precluded class treatment. Recall that Rule 23(b)(3) requires that "questions of law or fact common to class members predominate over any questions affecting only individual members." A case that would involve some subclassing given minor variations in governing law might be certified if the factual makeup of the claims is quite similar but not be certified if factual differences exist across claims.

(6) The majority and dissent in the first *Schnall* opinion disagreed about whether the Washington CPA applies extraterritorially. Which appears to have the better argument? Is the majority's recasting of the grounds for its decision a concession that it was wrong? The majority and dissent apparently both agree that the choice-of-law clause in the customer agreement does not cover causes of action under consumer protection acts. Does that conclusion seem sound?

(7) Note the relationship between choice-of-law clauses and class actions. Some companies place choice-of-law clauses into their standard form contracts choosing a single governing law that is friendly to the company's interests. The chosen law might be company-friendly relative to other applicable laws, but the fact of a single chosen law enhances the likelihood that proposed class actions will be certified. AT&T chose a different strategy by pegging the governing law to the location of the customer. That strategy disenables the company from choosing the law best suited to its interests, and it disenabled the company from conducting its business according to a single governing law. However, the clause as written basically ensured enforcement (who can complain if the customer effectively chooses the governing law and court?), enabled certainty regarding the governing

law that applied to each individual contract, and helped to defeat certification of a nationwide class. Should we expect to see many more companies choosing the law associated with plaintiffs' residence? Note that one upshot of the *Concepcion* case, *supra* page 714, which also involved AT&T's cell phone service agreements, is that companies may be able to avoid class proceedings with an arbitration clause coupled with a class ban. If so, then the company could choose a single governing law and still avoid class actions. Does that seem appropriate?

(8) The dissenting judges in *Schnall* and the *Air Crash Disaster Near Chicago* (*supra* page 765) cases both invoke an interest on the part of the state of the principal place of business of defendant to foster corporate accountability. Does this interest seem reasonable? Is this a more enlightened application of interest analysis? Or something else?

(9) Plaintiffs can sometimes circumvent the problem of the application of multiple state laws under Rule 23(b)(3)'s predominance and superiority tests by seeking certification as a limited fund or as a claim for injunctive relief under Rules 23(b)(1) or (2). These provisions enable class action certification where:

> (1) prosecuting separate actions by or against individual class members would create a risk of:
>> (A) inconsistent or varying adjudications with respect to individual class members that would establish incompatible standards of conduct for the party opposing the class; or
>> (B) adjudications with respect to individual class members that, as a practical matter, would be dispositive of the interests of the other members not parties to the individual adjudications or would substantially impair or impede their ability to protect their interests;
> (2) the party opposing the class has acted or refused to act on grounds that apply generally to the class, so that final injunctive relief or corresponding declaratory relief is appropriate respecting the class as a whole.

Why should these situations be treated differently? Is the court supposed to apply multiple governing laws in these cases, if applicable? Or is the court to choose a single governing law? Might your answer turn on the specific basis for class certification?

(10) When the claims in a proposed class action present difficulties with respect to predominance and/or superiority, a federal court can instead certify a class to resolve individual issues. Rule 23(c)(4) provides: "When appropriate, an action may be brought or maintained as a class action with respect to particular issues." In Hohider v. United Parcel Service, Inc., 574 F.3d 169, 201 n.25 (3d Cir. 2009), the Third Circuit noted that "[t]he interaction between the requirements for class certification under Rule 23(a) and (b) and the authorization of issues classes under Rule 23(c)(4) is a difficult matter that has generated divergent interpretations among the courts." In addition to discussing some of the cases that had grappled with this form of certification, the court provided some guidance:

> [We] believe several considerations are relevant to determining "[w]hen [it is] appropriate" for a court to certify a class only "with respect to particular issues": the type of claim(s) and issue(s) in question; the overall complexity of the case and the efficiencies to be gained by granting partial certification; the substantive law underlying the claim(s), including any choice-of-law questions it may present; the impact partial certification will have on the constitutional

and statutory rights of both the class members and the defendant(s); the potential preclusive effect that resolution of the proposed issues class will have; and so forth. *See, e.g., Principles of the Law of Aggregate Litigation* ch. 2 (A.L.I. Proposed Final Draft Apr. 1, 2009).

Id. at 201. How often and under what circumstances should issue classes be certified?

(11) Sometimes counsel for both plaintiffs and defendant seek certification of a class action for purposes of settlement only. Although many class action cases, including those presented in this chapter, pit plaintiffs seeking certification against defendants opposing certification, the parties' interests can align. In particular, a defendant facing multiple suits with likely liabilities in many different courts might want all actions settled in a single case, if the defendant can negotiate a satisfactory deal. When settlement classes are certified, the certification occurs simultaneously with the termination of the action. If a case no longer requires judicial management, the court might be tempted to circumvent analysis under Rule 23(a) and (b) and simply ask whether the proposed settlement seems fair and reasonable. The U.S. Supreme Court has held that federal courts are required to conduct the same basic certification inquiry for settlement class certification that it conducts for other certifications. Amchem Products, Inc. v. Windsor, 521 U.S. 591 (1997). In addition to satisfying the requirements of Rule 23(a), class settlement certifications under Rule 23(b)(3) must satisfy both predominance and superiority. However, the manageability prong of the inquiry can be ignored, given that no trial is contemplated. *Id.*

In practice, however, a court faced with a proposed settlement class is also more likely to find that the predominance requirement is satisfied because the litigation difficulties associated with a lack of predominance need not be addressed by the court. Consider, for example, In re Prudential Insurance Co. America Sales Practices Litigation, 148 F.3d 283 (3d Cir. 1998), a case in which a proposed nationwide settlement class was certified despite multiple state and federal law claims, including federal securities law violations, common law fraud, breach of contract, bad faith, negligent misrepresentation, negligence, unjust enrichment, and breach of state consumer fraud statutes. Despite multiple potential differences in state laws as well as factual differences pertinent to issues of causation and reliance, the district court and the Third Circuit concluded that the common issues of law and fact predominated. Some of the potential problems associated with a failure to take into account differentially situated plaintiffs were resolved with the parties' proposed claim resolution mechanism, and the differences in governing laws fell into "a limited number of predictable patterns." *Id.* at 315. For a contrary example, *see* In re Hyundai and Kia Fuel Economy Litigation, 881 F.3d 679 (9th Cir. 2018) (reversing and remanding district court's certification of settlement class for failing to perform a rigorous choice-of-law analysis prior to certifying the class).

(12) Note that in MDL cases, it is common for the transferee court to apply multiple governing legal rules as well as multiple conflict-of-laws principles to the various claims before it. As noted at page 740 *supra*, when federal court jurisdiction is based on diversity, the transferee court must apply the choice-of-law principles of the state where the individual action was filed. After cases are transferred for consolidation, however, new cases often are filed directly in the transferee court.

Which state's choice-of-law rules should apply to those new direct-file claims? Most transferee courts apply forum choice-of-law principles to these cases. *See, e.g.,* In re Trasylol Prods. Liab. Litig., No. 1:08-MD-01928, 2011 WL 1033650, at *3 (S.D. Fla. Jan. 18, 2011); In re Vioxx Prods. Liab. Litig., 522 F. Supp. 2d 799, 806 (E.D. La. 2007). Does that make sense, if the only connection between the forum and the claims, and perhaps the only justification for locating venue in the transferee court, is the fact of consolidation? For a discussion of relevant cases and proposed solutions, *see* Bradt, *The Shortest Distance: Direct Filing and Choice of Law in Multidistrict Litigation*, 88 Notre Dame L. Rev. 759 (2012). And what law applies when a case that was directly filed is later transferred to the district where it would have been filed without the MDL? *See* Wahl v. General Electric Co., 786 F.3d 491 (6th Cir. 2015) (concluding that law of state where case transferred to applies).

Table of Cases

Principal cases are indicated by italics.

Abbott v. Abbott, 573
Abbott Labs. v. Takeda Pharms. Co., 698
Adam v. Saenger, 555
Adkins v. St. Francis Hosp., 273
Agency Holding Corp. v. Malley-Duff &
    Assocs., Inc., 641
Agent Orange Prod. Liability Litig., In re,
    767–769
Aguerre v. Schering-Plough Corp., 545
Air Bag Prods. Liability Litig., In re, 758
Air Crash Disaster at Boston, Mass. on July 31,
    1973, In re, 231
Air Crash Disaster at Sioux City, Iowa, on July
    19, 1989, In re, 766
Air Crash Disaster near Chi., Ill. on May 25,
    1979, In re, 765, 801
Akzona, Inc. v. E. I. Du Pont De Nemours &
    Co., 459
Alabama Great S. R.R. v. Carroll, *15*, 24,
    28, 47, 108, 112, 195, 230–231, 353, 524,
    575, 580
Alaska Packers Assn. v. Industrial Accident
    Comm'n, 288, 289–292, 299, 300, 327, 328,
    329, 525, 527, 531, 532
Albemarle Corp. v. AstraZeneca UK Ltd., 491
Allen v. McCurry, 515
Allied-Bruce Terminix Cos. v. Dobson, 709
Allstate Ins. Co. v. Hague, 252, *297*, 309–310,
    313–315, 316, 319, 321, 323, 337, 346, 356,
    411, 744, 746, 754, 761
Allstate Ins. Co. v. Stolarz, 242
Alpine View Co. v. Atlas Copco AB, 424
Aluminum Co. of Am.; United States v.,
    579, 580–581, 582–584, 586, 592, 593, 596,
    597, 602
Amchem Prods., Inc. v. Windsor, 802
American Banana Co. v. United Fruit Co., *576*,
    578–579, 580, 582, 592, 595, 605, 613, 622
American Booksellers Found. for Free
    Expression v. Strickland, 361
American Dredging Co. v. Miller, 492

American Express Co. v. Italian Colors
    Rest., 399
American Libraries Assn. v. Pataki, 361
American Med. Sys., In re, 786, 792, 793–794
America Online, Inc. v. National Health Care
    Discount, Inc., *243*, 247–248
America Online, Inc. v. Superior Court of
    Alameda Cnty., *691*, 695–696, 704, 734
Anderson v. Abbott, 431
Anderson v. Heartland Oil and Gas, Inc., 460
Anglo-Am. Provision Co. v. Davis Provision Co.
    No. 1, 517
Animal Sci. Prods., Inc. v. Hebei Welcome
    Pharm. Co., 168
AOL LLC; Doe 1 v., 698
Application of. *See name of party*
Arabian Am. Oil Co.; EEOC v., 595–596,
    606, 613–615, 616, 618–621, 622, 625,
    629, 639
Argentine Republic v. Amerada Hess Shipping
    Corp., 610
Armendariz v. Foundation Health Pyschcare
    Servs., Inc., 714, 716
Arnon v. Aetna Life Ins. Co., 664
Asahi Metal Indus. Co. v. Superior Court of
    Cal., 394, 423–424, 437, 439, 440, 441
Asbestos Litig., In re, 790
Asbestos Sch. Litig., In re, 369
Association for Accessible Meds. v. Frosh, 357
AT&T Mobility LLC v. AU Optronics
    Corp., 310
AT&T Mobility LLC v. Concepcion, 714,
    724–729, 731, 732–734, 735, 801
Atlantic Marine Const. Co. v. U.S. Dist. Ct. for
    the W. Dist. of Tex., 491, 492, 705
Atlantis I Condo. Assn. v. Bryson, 443
Austin v. New Hampshire, *340*, 346–347,
    352, 551
Auten v. Auten, 172–174, 177, 265, 431
Autonation, Inc., In re, 691, 706
Avagliano v. Sumitomo Shoji Am., 369

Avery v. State Farm Mut. Auto. Ins. Co., 670, 672–673
Azzolino v. Dingfelder, 148, 151

Babcock v. Jackson, 175–177, 179, 181, 186–187, 220, 254, 265, 271–272
Bailey v. Turbine Design, Inc., 425
Bakalar v. Vavra, 14
Baker v. General Motors Corp., *533*, 541–545
Baldwin v. Iowa State Traveling Men's Assn., 505–506, 515
Baldwin v. Montana Fish & Game Comm'n, 347
Baldwin v. Seelig, 355, 356
Ballard v. Savage, 382
Baltimore & Ohio R.R. Co. v. Baugh, 469
Banek, Inc. v. Yogurt Ventures U.S.A., Inc., *658*, 662–663
Barbara's Sales, Inc. v. Intel Corp., 673, 767
Barber v. Barber, 535, 559
Bard v. Charles R. Myers Ins. Agency, Inc., 542
Barker v. St. Louis Cnty., 130
Barnes Group, Inc. v. C & C Prods., Inc., 669
Barrell v. Benjamin, 385
Barrow S.S. Co. v. Kane, 438
Bartlett Bank & Trust Co. v. McJunkins, 672
Bassett v. Bassett, 561
Bates v. Bodie, 570
Bauman v. DaimlerChrysler Corp., 436, 437
Bell; State v., 74
Bendectin Litig., In re, 794
Bendix Autolite Corp. v. Midwesco Enters., Inc., 352, 358
Bergner & Engel Brewing Co. v. Dreyfus, 61
Bernhard v. Harrah's Club, *204*, 210–211, 213
Bernkrant v. Fowler, *191*, 194, 207
Bernstein v. Wysoki, 691
Berry v. Federal Kemper Life Assurance Co., 744, 746–748, 749–750
Best v. Samuel Fox & Co., Ltd., 150
Bethlehem Steel v. G.C. Zarnas & Co., 149
Bisso v. Inland Waterways Corp., 680, 681
Bivens v. Six Unknown Fed. Narcotics Agents, 418
Bjornquist v. Boston & A. R. Co., 59
Black v. Leatherwood, 150
Black & White Taxi Co. v. Brown & Yellow Taxi Co., 128, 467
Blackmer v. United States, 580, 616
Blackwell v. Lurie, *89*
Blaine v. Murphy, 62
Blake v. McClung, 352
Blamey v. Brown, 226
BMW of N. Am., Inc. v. Gore, 358
BNSF Ry. Co. v. Tyrrell, *400*
Bodum U.S.A., Inc. v. La Cafetière, Inc., 168
Bonti v. Ford Motor Co., 145

Bournias v. Atlantic Mar. Co., 145
Bowman; United States v., 580, 595
Boyter v. Commissioner of Internal Revenue, 566
Bradford Elec. Light Co. v. Clapper, 154, 524
Bragel v. General Steel Corp., 734
Braxton v. Anco Elec., Inc., 256
The Bremen v. Zapata Off-Shore Co., 677, 682–685, 687, 692, 697, 703, 705
Brewer v. Missouri Title Loans, 724, 731, 733–734, 735
Bridge Fund Capital Corp. v. Fastbucks Franchise Corp., 734
Bridgestone/ Firestone, Inc. Tires Prod. Liability Litig., In re, 759, 764
Bridgeway Corp. v. Citibank, 546
Bristol-Myers Squibb v. Superior Court, 368, *392*
British S. Africa Co. v. Companhia de Mocambique, 577
Britton v. Howard Sav. Bank, 461
Bronislawa K. v. Tadeusz K., Matter of, 77
Brooks v. Norwest Corp., 748
Brown v. Meter, 424, 425, 428, 430, 432, 440
Brown v. Ticor Title Ins., 369
Brown-Forman Distillers Corp. v. New York State Liquor Auth., *353*, 356–358
Brownlee v. Liberty Mut. Fire Ins. Co., 153
Buckeye v. Buckeye, 109–111
Bullard v. MRA Holding, 28, *29*, 31–32
Burger King Corp. v. Continental Ins. Co., 297, 390, 398, 420, 423–424, 439
Burger King Corp. v. Rudzewicz, 419, 439, 444, 459
Burlington N. R.R. Co. v. Ford, 352
Burnham v. Superior Court of Cal., *383*
Burr v. Beckler, *82*, 86, 108, 118, 120
Burroughs v. Cocke & Willis, 386
Burwell v. Whitmoyer, 142
Butler v. AdoptionMedia, LLC, 215–217
Byblos Bank Europe, S.A. v. Sekerbank Turk Anonym Syrketi, 557

Caesars World Inc. v. Caesars-Palace.com, 462–463
Calder v. Jones, 376, 377, 417, 420, 421, 422, 426, 430, 459
Camelback Ski Corp. v. Behning, 383
Campbell v. Crampton, 40
Campbell v. Holt, 349
Campbell v. Landmark First Nat'l Bank of Fort Lauderdale, 461
Campbell v. Mitsubishi Aircraft Int'l, 162
Cannon Mfg. Co. v. Cudahy Packing Co., 456, 460
Cargill Inc. v. Sabine Trading & Shipping Co., 461

Carlock v. Pillsbury Co., 657
Carnival Cruise Lines, Inc. v. Shute, 382, *681*, 687–689, 691, 695, 697, 699, 700
Carr v. Carr, 565
Carroll v. Lanza, 291, 299
Carter, State v., 578
Carter v. United States, 259
Cartwright v. Pettus, 385
Cassirer v. Thyssen-Bornemisza Collection Found., 13
Castano v. American Tobacco Co., 793, 799
Celotex Corp. v. Meehan, 267
Celotex Corp. v. Rapid Am. Corp., In re, 424
Central Bank of Denver, N.A. v. First Interstate Bank of Denver, N.A., 621
Centros Ltd. v. Erhvervs-og Selskabsstyrelsen, 108
CFMT Inc. v. Steag Microtech, Inc., 442
Chapman v. Aetna Fin., 551
Chase Secs. Corp. v. Donaldson, 348
Chicago, R.I. & P.R. Co. v. Schendel, 525–526
Chicot Cnty. Drainage Dist. v. Baxter State Bank, 504, 514–515
Christmas v. Russell, 518
Clark v. Clark, 220–221, 272
Clay v. Sun Ins. Office, Ltd., 252, *294*, 296–297, 299, 300, 302, 306, 309
Clune v. Alimak AB, 424
CMMC v. Salinas, 424
Coady v. Cross Country Bank, 734
Coastal Tank Lines v. Canoles, 150
Cohen v. Beneficial Indus. Loan Corp., 260
Cohn v. G. D. Searle & Co., 352
Cole v. Cunningham, 536, 542
Cole v. General Motors Corp., 754–755
Cole v. Rush, 205
Colonial Life & Accident Ins. Co. v. Hartford Fire Ins. Co., 114
Columbia Cas. Co. v. Playtex FP Inc., 553
Combs v. International Ins. Co., 267
Compaq Computer Corp. v. Lapray, 754
Complete Auto Transit, Inc. v. Brady, 358
CompuCredit Corp. v. Greenwood, 710
CompuServe, Inc. v. Patterson, 426
Conklin v. Horner, 222–223, 271, 272
Connolly v. Burt, 417
Conry v. Maloney, 115–116
Continental Grain Co. v. Barge FBL-585, 482, 486
Continental Ore Co. v. Union Carbide & Carbon Corp., 582, 586, 592, 594, 596, 622, 641
Cook Sign Co. v. Combs, *664*, 668
Cooney v. Osgood Mach., Inc., 269
Cope v. Anderson, 140
Copley Pharm., Inc., In re, 793
Corfield v. Coryell, 347
Corna v. American Haw. Cruises, Inc., 689

Coulter v. Superior Court, 211
Cowley v. Abbott Labs., Inc., 226
Coyne v. Grupo Indus. Trieme, 391
Creech v. Roberts, 382
Crider v. Zurich Ins. Co., 334
Cross v. Kloster Cruise Lines, 688
Cruikshank v. Cruikshank, 77
CTS Corp. v. Dynamics Corp. of Am., 352, 359, 360–361, 457
Cutts v. Najdrowski, 115–116
Cybersell, Inc. v. Cybersell, Inc., 425
Cyberspace Commc'ns, Inc. v. Engler, 361

Daimler AG v. Bauman, 393–394, 397, 400–402, 403, 425, 431, *432*, 440, 442, 443, 444, 460, 642
Damato, Estate of, In re, *114*, 121
D'Angelo v. Petroleos Mexicanos, 443
Davis v. Miller, 672
Day & Zimmerman, Inc. v. Challoner, 478
Deems v. Western Maryland Ry., 150
De Fontbrune v. Wofsy, 161, 166
DeSantis v. Wackenhut Corp., 669
Design Strategy Corp. v. Nghiem, 689
Devine v. Rook, 140
Devlin v. Scardelletti, 400
Diamond Shamrock Chems. Co., In re, 771
Dietz v. Becker, 796
DirectTV, Inc. v. Imburgia, 733
Discover Bank v. Superior Court, 715–724, 726–727, 729, 734
Dixilyn Drilling Corp. v. Crescent Towing & Salvage Co., 681
Doctor's Assocs., Inc. v. Casarotto, 710, 733
Doe v. *See name of opposing party*
Doering ex rel. Barrett v. Cooper Mountain, Inc., 489
Doggrell v. Great S. Box Co., 159, 160
Donahue v. Far E. Air Transp. Corp., 429
Donovan v. Dallas, 536
Dougherty v. Equitable Life Assurance Soc. of United States, 152
Dowis v. Mud Slingers, Inc., 30
Dubroff v. Dubroff, 552
Duke v. Housen, *136*, 145–146
Dunbar v. Seger-Thomschitz, 14
Dupasseur v. Rochereau, 494, 497
Durfee v. Duke, 87, *504*, 510–512, 526
Durfee v. Keiffer, 504

Earle v. Earle, 77
Easterling Lumber Co. v. Pierce, 125
Eckstein v. Balcor Film Investors, 489
Economy Elec. Co. v. Automatic Elec. Co., 391
Edgar v. MITE Corp, 360

Edward J. DeBartolo Corp. v. Florida Gulf
    Bldg. & Constr. Trades Council, 443
EEOC v. *See name of opposing party*
Eggleton v. Plasser & Theurer, 489
Eisen v. Carlisle & Jacquelin, 367, 368
Emery v. Emery, 109
Energy & Envt. Legal Inst. v. Epel, 357
Engel v. Davenport, 331
English v. Sanchez, 90
Enron Capital & Trade Res. Corp.
    v. Pokalsky, 669
Epic Sys. Corp. v. Lewis, 710, 733
Erie R.R. Co. v. Tompkins, 13, 31, 125–128,
    318, 331, *465*, 470–474, 476, 477, 481, 482,
    483, 486–487, 488, 489, 490–491, 492, 495,
    497–498, 553, 698, 705, 771, 772, 795
Erlanger Mills, Inc. v. Cohoes Fibre Mills,
    Inc., 407
Erwin v. Thomas, 187
Estate of. *See name of party*
Estin v. Estin, 365, *558*, 563
Ethicon Endo-Surgery, Inc. v. Pemberton, 669
Evolution Online Sys., Inc. v. Koninklijke PTT
    Nederland N.V., 703
Ex parte. *See name of party*
Exxon Mobil Corp. v. Allapattah Servs.,
    Inc., 369
Ezeonu; People v., 74, 76, 79

Falchetti v. Pennsylvania R.R. Co., 469
Fall v. Eastin, *508*, 511, 535, 537
Fauntleroy v. Lum, 156, 510, 511, *516*, 533,
    535, 548
Federal Deposit Ins. Corp. v. Hiatt, 752
Ferens v. John Deere Co., 477, *478*, 489–490,
    491, 705
Ferrell v. Allstate Ins. Co., 741, 745, 747–748,
    750, 753, 755–756, 769
First Nat'l Bank v. United Air Lines, 331
First Nat'l Bank of Boston v. Bellotti, 360
Fisher v. Huck, 243
Fitts v. Minnesota Mining & Mfg. Co., 31
Florsheim Group Inc., In re, 605
Foley Bros., Inc. v. Filardo, 595–596, 607, 611–
    612, 616, 620
Ford v. United States, 580, 595
Forsyth v. Barnes, 83
Fouracre v. White, 444
Franchise Tax Bd. of Cal. v. Hyatt, 538 U.S. 488
    (2003), 335, 336, 338
Franchise Tax Bd. of Cal. v. Hyatt, 136 S. Ct.
    1277 (2016), 336, 338
Franchise Tax Bd. of Cal. v. Hyatt, 139 S. Ct.
    1485 (2019), 338
Francis v. Humphrey, 126
French, In re, 605

Friese v. Superior Court, 107
Fru-Con Constr. Corp. v. Controlled Air,
    Inc., 698
Fuerste v. Bemis, 226

Garner, In re, 92
Garza v. Gama, 764
Gasperini v. Center for Humanities, Inc., 472
Gator.com Corp. v. L.L. Bean, Inc., 427
G. D. Searle & Co. v. Cohn, *347*, 352
General Motors Corp. v. Bryant, 754
Gentry v. Superior Court, 722
Genuine Parts Co. v. Cepec, 442
Georgine v. Amchem Prods., 793
Ghassemi v. Ghassemi, *65*, 74–75, 79
Gilmer v. Interstate/Johnson Lane Corp.,
    710, 713
Gilmore, In re, 752
Ginter ex rel. Ballard v. Belcher, Prendergast &
    Laporte, 698
Global Fin. Corp. v. Triarc Corp., *264*
Gonzales v. Carhart, 443
*Goodyear Dunlop Tires Operations, S.A. v.
    Brown*, 394–395, 401–402, 419, 424–425,
    427, 431–432, 433, 434, 435, 436, 437, 438,
    439, 440, 443, 444, 642
Gore v. Northeast Airlines, 251
Gorman v. Ameritrade Holding Corp., 427
Go-Video, Inc. v. Akai Elec. Co., 441
Grace v. MacArthur, 391
Grand Bahama Petroleum Co. v. Canadian
    Transp. Agencies, 461
Grange Ins. Assocs. v. State, 424
Granite Rock Co. v. Teamsters, 431
Grant v. McAuliffe, *132*, 135
Gray v. American Radiator & Standard Sanitary
    Corp., 407, 412
Greene v. Sha-Na-Na, 383
Greenman v. Yuba Power Prods., 788, 796
Guaranty Trust Co. v. York, 318, 471, 472, 474,
    481, 498
Guinness v. Miller, 133
Gulf Oil Co. v. Gilbert, 332, 485
Gutride Safier LLP v. Reese, 194, 217

Haag v. Barnes, 173–174, 177, 184
Hague v. Allstate Ins. Co., 667
Hall v. Sprint Spectrum L.P., *669*, 675–676
Hall v. Summit Contractors, Inc., 267
Hall v. Superior Court, 692–693
Hall St. Assocs. v. Mattel, Inc., 709, 718
The Hamilton (Old Dominion S.S. Co.
    v. Gilmore), 577
Hamm v. Carson, 205, 206

Hammond Packing Co. v. Arkansas, 371–372, 373

Hampton v. McConnel, 523

Hangman Ridge Training Stables, Inc. v. Safeco Title Ins. Co., 777, 778, 780

Hanna v. Plumer, 260, 471–473, 482, 490, 495, 498

Hansberry v. Lee, 365, 367

Hanson v. Denckla, 115–116, 303, 378, 395, 406, 408, 414, 416, 419, 420, 422, 448, 451, 454

Harford Mut. v. Bruchey, 149–150, 153

Haring v. Prosise, 540

Harris v. Balk, 364, 407, 445, 446, 448, 449, 450, 558, 561

Harris v. Diamond Constr. Co, 532

Hart v. American Airlines, 552–553

Hart v. Gumpach, 577

Hartford v. Superior Court, 565

Hartford Accident & Indem. Co. v. Delta & Pine Land Co., 286–287, 295, 299, 319

Hartford Fire Ins. Co. v. California, 588, *590*, 600, 601, 602, 604–605, 625, 634

Hataway v. McKinley, 242

Hauch v. Connor, 149

Haumschild v. Continental Cas. Co., *109*, 112–113

Haywood v. Drown, 334

Healy v. Beer Inst., Inc., 356

Hearty v. Harris, 275

Heath v. Alabama, 520

Heating & Air Specialists Inc. v. Jones, 664

Heffernan v. City of Paterson, 635, 642

HelicopterosNacionales de Colombia, S.A. v. Hall, *375*, 383, 384–385, 401, 403, 419, 429, 430, 434, 461

Henningsen v. Bloomfield Motors, Inc., 686

Hertz Corp. v. Friend, 431, 438

Hess v. Pawloski, 407

Hexacomb Corp. v. Damage Prevention Prods. Corp., 382

Hicklin v. Orbeck, 347

Higginbotham v. City of Charleston, 273

Hill by Hill v. Showa Denko, K.K., 460

Hill v. Gateway 2000, 688, 695

Hilton v. Guyot, 545, 597

H.J. Inc. v. Northwestern Bell Tel. Co., 627

Hoffman-La Roche Ltd. v. Empagran S.A., *601*, 604–606, 634, 635, 637

Hohider v. United Parcel Serv., Inc., 801

Holbein v. Rigot, 520

Holmes v. Securities Investor Protection Corp., 636, 641, 642

Holzer v. Deutsche Reichsbahn-Gesellschaft, *151*, 154

Home Ins. Co. v. Dick, *282*, 286–287, 288, 293, 295, 296, 300, 304, 307, 314, 315, 454, 471

Home Ins. Co. v. Morse, 686

Hovey v. Elliot, 372

Howlett v. Rose, 334

Hubbert v. Dell Corp., 734

Hughes v. Fetter, *327*, 331, 332–334, 658

Hughes v. Oklahoma, 352–353

Huntington v. Attrill, 160, 161, 520

Hurtado v. California, 386

Hurtado v. Superior Court, *195*, 199–200, 205, 206, 263

Hutchison v. Ross, 96

Hutzell v. Boyer, 149

Hyundai and Kia Fuel Econ. Litig., In re, 802

Illinois v. Hemi Group LLC, 426

Imperial Chem. Indus., Ltd.; United States v., 584

Incuria v. Incuria, Matter of, 77

Indoor Billboard/Wash., Inc. v. Integra Telecom of Wash., Inc., 778, 783

Industrial Comm'n of Wis. v. McCartin, 521–524, 527–528, 530, 532, 533

In re. *See name of party*

INS v. *See name of opposing party*

Instructional Sys., Inc. v. Computer Curriculum Corp., 662

Insurance Antitrust Litig., In re, 592, 597, 598

Insurance Corp. of Ireland v. Compagnie des Bauxites de Guinee, 368, *369*, 374, 413

International Profit Assocs., Inc., v. Linus Alarm Corp., 675

International Shoe Co. v. Washington, 312, 364, 365, 371, 377, 378–381, 384, 386–389, 394–395, 398, 400–403, 405, 407, 408–409, 411, 417, 420, 428–429, 435, 436, 438, 447, 448, 449, 450, 452–454, 459, 461, 520, 565

Irving Trust Co. v. Maryland Cas. Co., *103*

ISI Int'l, Inc. v. Borden Ladner Gervais LLP, 442

Jackman v. Rosenbaum Co., 320

Jackson v. Payday Fin., LLC, 491, 628–629, 631, 633, 635, 640, 642

Jackson Lockdown/MCO Cases, In re, 369

James v. Grand Trunk W. R.R. Co., 536, 542

Japan Petroleum Co. (Nigeria) Ltd. v. Ashland Oil, Inc., 262, 459

Jefferson Indus. Bank v. First Golden Bancorp., 107

Jefferson Pilot Broad. Co. v. Hilary & Hogan, Inc., 107

Jepson v. General Cas. Co., 225

J. McIntyre Mach., Ltd. v. Nicastro, 398, 399, 424–425, 431–432, 435, 440

John A. Tolman Co. v. Reed, 119

John Hancock Mut. Life Ins. Co. v. Yates, 300, 302, 307, 314, 476
Johnson v. Holland Am. Line-Westours, Inc., 689
Johnson v. Muelberger, 566
Jones v. Erie R.R. Co., 130
Jorgensen v. Vargas, 573
Joseph E. Seagram & Sons, Inc. v. Hostetter, 354, 355, 356
Jumara v. State Farm Ins. Co., 698, 703

Kadic v. Karadzic, 391
Kaestner Family Trust v. Department of Revenue, 359
Kahn v. Royal Ins. Co., 267
Kalb v. Feuerstein, 506, *512*, 514
Kallok v. Medtronic, Inc., 665
Kamer van Koophandel en Fabrieken voor Amsterdam v. Inspire Art Ltd., 108
Kassama v. Magat, 150
Kearney v. Salomon Smith Barney, Inc., 211, 215–217
Keeton v. Hustler Magazine, Inc., 368, 376, 377, 417, 419, 420, 421, 423, 430, 434, 460
Kell v. Henderson, 221, 223, 271
Kennedy v. City of Sawyer, 235
Kenney v. Supreme Lodge of the World, 327, 550
Kinsman Transit Co., Petition of, 771
Kiobel v. Royal Dutch Petroleum Co., 626–627, 629–631, 633, 634, 635, 637, 640, 643
Kipin Indus., Inc. v. Van Deilen Int'l, Inc., 663–664
Klaxon Co. v. Stentor Elec. Mfg. Co., 13, 30, 263, *475*, 477–478, 479, 483, 486–488, 489, 491, 499, 660, 740
Klay v. Humana, Inc, 800
Klock v. Lehman Bros. Kuhn Loeb, Inc., 657
KMC Leasing, Inc. v. Rockwell-Standard Corp., 759
Kreiger v. Kreiger, 563
Kremer v. Chemical Constr. Corp., 515, 540
Kryger v. Wilson, 305
Kulko v. Superior Court, 303, 378, 394, 405, 406, 408, *413*, 416–417, 420, 565

Laboratory Corp. of Am. v. Hood, 146, 153–154, 156
LaBounty v. American Ins. Co., 225
La Fitte v. Salisbury, 548
Laker Airways Ltd. v. Sabena, Belgian World Airlines, 542, 600, 605
Lamar v. United States, 580
Lange v. Penn Mut. Life Ins. Co., 253
Lapin v. Shulton, Inc., 501

Larch, In re, 573
Lauritzen v. Larsen, 21, 586, 588, 589, 595, 596–599
Lauro Lines s.r.l. v. Chasser, 691
Ledesma v. Jack Stewart Produce, Inc., 261, 266
Lester v. Aetna Life Ins. Co., 478
Levy v. Daniels' U-Drive Auto Renting Co., 23–24, 108
Levy v. Steiger, 127–128
LICRA & UEJF v. Yahoo! Inc., 5, 7
LILCO Secs. Litig., In re, 754
Lilienthal v. Kaufman, 187, 193, 195, 200
Linn v. Employers Reinsurance Corp., 42, 46, 166
Linton v. Linton, 150
Lipcon v. Underwriters at Lloyd's, London, 687
Lockman Found. v. Evangelical Alliance Mission, 699
Loucks v. Standard Oil Co. of N.Y., 21, 153, 190
Louisiana & Miss. R.R. Transfer Co. v. Long, 479
Lucas v. Gulf & W. Indus., Inc., 459
Lynde v. Lynde, 538

Magnolia Petroleum Co. v. Hunt, 521–528, 530–531, 533, 535
Malloy v. Brewer, 386
Mannington Mills, Inc. v. Congoleum Corp., 593, 597
Mansfield Hardwood Lumber Co. v. Johnson, 106
Marchlik v. Coronet Ins. Co., 156
Marmet Health Care Ctr., Inc. v. Brown, 728, 731
Marra v. Bushee, 32
Marrese v. American Acad. of Orthopaedic Surgeons, 533, 552, 553, 556
Marriage of. *See name of party*
Martin v. Dierck Equip. Co., 265
Martin v. Heinold Commodities, Inc., 672–673
Martin v. Stokes, 489
Martin v. Wilks, 537
Martin Luther King, Jr., Ctr. For Soc. Change, Inc. v. American Heritage Prods., Inc., 30
MaryCLE, LLC v. First Choice Internet, Inc., 361
Mason v. United States, 467
Matsushita Elec. Indus. Co. v. Zenith Radio Corp., 592, 596
Matter of. *See name of party*
Matusevitch v. Telnikoff, 545
Maxwell v. Vetter, 443
Maxwell Commc'n Corp. plc, In re, 605
Maxwell Schuman & Co. v. Edwards, 545
May, Matter of, 77
May v. Anderson, 562, 565

May Dept. Stores Co. v. Wilansky, 391
May's Estate, In re, 75
McCann v. Foster Wheeler LLC, 217
McCluney v. Jos. Schlitz Brewing Co., 309
McCormick v. Sullivant, 515
McCulloch v. Sociedad Nacional de Marineros de Honduras, 597–598, 607, 608
McDermott Inc. v. Lewis, *99*, 105, 122
McDonald v. Mabee, 371, 389
McDougald v. Jenson, 552
McElmoyle ex rel. Bailey v. Cohen, 535, 537, 538, 569
McGee v. International Life Ins. Co., 374, 405–406, 416, 423
McGill Tech., Ltd. v. Gourmet Techs., Inc., 425
McMillan v. McMillan, 272
Medtronic, Inc. v. Advanced Bionics Corp., 665, 668
Medtronic, Inc. v. Gibbons, 669
M'Elmoyle v. Cohen, 317, 509, 548, 549, 550
Mendez v. Palm Harbor Homes, 714
Menzel v. List, 10
Merrill; People v., 578
Merrill Lynch, Pierce, Fenner & Smith, Inc. v. Shackelford, 90
Merritt Dredging Co., In re, 280
Mertz v. Mertz, 154
Metcalf v. Watertown, 503
Metropolitan Life Ins. Co. v. Holding, 74–75
Microsoft Corp. v. AT&T Corp., 619, 629
Midwest Med. Supply Co. v. Wingert, 657
Migra v. Warren City Sch. Dist. Bd. of Educ., 551–552, 553, 556
Milkovich v. Saari, *220*, 224–225, 272, 298
Miller v. Honda Motor Co., 460
Miller v. Miller, 251
Miller v. White, 256
Milliken v. Meyer, 371, 374, 377, 405
Milliken v. Pratt, 44, 46, 578
Milwaukee Cnty. v. M.E. White Co., 324, 520, 534
Minnesota v. National Tea Co., 548
Missouri ex rel. Hawley v. Becerra, 357
Missouri ex rel. Koster v. Harris, 357
Mitchum v. Foster, 557
Mitsubishi Motors Corp. v. Soler Chrysler-Plymouth, Inc., 711–712
Modianos v. Tuttle, United States ex rel., 70
Monroe v. Wood, 266
Montpetit v. Allina Health Sys., Inc., 227
Moore v. Mitchell, 162
Morrison v. National Australia Bank Ltd., 588, 600, *615*, 625–626, 629–631, 632, 634–635, 637, 639, 643, 644
Morson v. Second Nat'l Bank of Boston, *93*, 95
Moses v. Business Card Express, Inc., 661, 662

Moses H. Cone Mem'l Hosp. v. Mercury Constr. Co., 709, 718
Mostyn v. Fabrigas, 385
Mullane v. Central Hanover Bank & Trust Co., 365, 367
Murray v. Schooner Charming Betsy, 589, 596, 597, 601, 605, 606
Mutual Life Ins. Co. v. Liebing, 282

Najas Cortés v. Orion Sec., Inc., 546
Nakashima v. State Farm Mut. Auto. Ins. Co., 741, 753
National Glass v. J.C. Penney, 149
National Rental v. Szukhent, 371
Nedlloyd Lines B.V. v. Superior Court of San Mateo Cnty. Seawinds Ltd., *649*, 656–657
Nelson v. Hix, 242
Nelson v. International Paint Co., 262
Neumeier v. Kuehner, 177–182, 187, 199, 605
Nevada v. Hall, 299, 335, 336, 338, 523, 525, 535
Newsome, Marriage of, In re, 573
New York Life Ins. Co. v. Dodge, 282
New York Life Ins. Co. v. Dunlevy, 365, 561
Nicastro v. McIntyre Mach. Am., Ltd., 424, 425
Nierman v. Hyatt Corp., 267–268
Nodak Mut. Ins. Co. v. American Family Mut. Ins. Co., 227
Nolan v. Transocean Airlines, 477
Norlin Corp. v. Rooney, Pace Inc., 99–100, 106
Northcross v. Board of Ed. of Memphis City Schs., 641
Northwestern Nat'l Ins. Co. v. Donovan, 691
Nottingham v. Weld, 552
Nowak v. Tak How Invs., Ltd., 382
Nummer v. Treasury Dept., 541

Oestreicher v. Alienware Corp., 719
Oetjen v. Central Leather Co., 152
Offshore Rental Co. v. Continental Oil Co., 212
O'Hagan; United States v., 618
Ohio v. Purse, 121
Ohio v. Wyandotte Chems. Corp., 412
Oil Spill by Amoco Cadiz Off Coast of France, In re, 382
Oklahoma ex rel. Oklahoma Tax Comm'n v. Neely, 162
Old Dominion S.S. Co. v. Gilmore, 577
O'Leary v. Illinois Terminal R.R., *129*
Oliver v. Davis, 277
Olshen v. Kaufman, 188–190
Omni Capital Int'l, Ltd. v. Rudolf Wolff & Co., 396, 441
1-800-Got Junk? LLC v. Superior Court, 663, 675

Opinion of the Justices, In re, 444
Order of Commercial Travelers of Am.
  v. Wolfe, 288
Orkin v. Taylor, 12
Osorio v. Dole Food Co., 545
Oxman v. Amoroso, 688

Pacific & Arctic R.R. & Navigation Co.; United
  States v., 580, 622
*Pacific Emp'rs Ins. Co. v. Industrial Accident
  Comm'n, 288,* 291–292, 296, 306, 315, 317,
  328, 335, 523–527, 531, 532, 534
Padula v. Lilarn Properties Corp., 183, 184
Palmer v. ARCO Chem. Co., 242
Palmer Nat'l Bank v. Van Doren, 120
Palsgraf v. Long Island R.R., 771
Panag v. Farmers Ins. Co. of Wash., 778
Panama R.R. Co. v. Johnson, 640
Panavision Int'l L.P. v. Toeppen, 426
P & S Bus. Machs. v. Canon USA, Inc., 698
Paper Prods. Co. v. Doggrell, 157, 161–162, 520
Parkcentral Global Hub Ltd. v. Porsche Auto.
  Holdings SE, 626
Parsons Steel v. First Alabama Bank, 556
Pasquantino v. United States, 163, 622, 623
Paul v. National Life, 31, *269,* 273
Pearson v. Callahan, 631
Peay v. Bellsouth Med. Assistance Plan, 441
Pennoyer v. Neff, 364, 365, 376, 384, 389–390,
  394, 417, 435, 448, 450, 561
Pennsylvania v. New Jersey, 346
Pennzoil Prods. Co. v. Colelli & Assocs., 424
People v. *See name of opposing party*
Perkins v. Benguet Consol. Mining Co., 374,
  377, 378, 380, 384, 401, 403, 429–430, 434,
  435, 438
Perry v. Lewis, 85
Perry v. Thomas, 710, 716–717
Petition of. *See name of party*
Petrowski v. Hawkeye-Sec. Co., 371
Pfau v. Trent Aluminum Co., 254, 255
Pfizer Inc. v. Government of India, 636–637,
  640, 642
Pharmaceutical Research & Mfrs. of Am.
  v. Walsh, 357
Phillips v. Audio Active Ltd., 698
Phillips v. Eyre, 578
Phillips v. General Motors Corp., 229, 241–242,
  243, 256, 268
Phillips Petroleum Co. v. Duckworth, 366
Phillips Petroleum Co. v. Shutts, 286, *310,*
  316, 319, 320, 321–323, 325, *364,* 368–369,
  534, 673, 741, 744, 745, 746, 753–754, 757,
  761, 769
Picquet v. Swan, 385
Pike v. Bruce Church, Inc., 353

Pinney v. Nelson, 107
Piper Aircraft Co. v. Reyno, 492, 642, 701, 702
Pizzaro v. Hoteles Concorde Int'l, C.A., 382
Polensky v. Continental Cas. Co., 226–227
Pollstar v. Gigmania Ltd., 695
Poole v. Perkins, 38, 44–46, 119
Popkin & Stern, In re, 92
Poston v. Poston, 416
Potter v. Allin, 385
Preston v. Ferrer, 718
Pritchard v. Norton, 45
Provencher v. Dell, Inc., 722
Prudential Ins. Co. Am. Sales Practices Litig.,
  In re, 802
PSINET, Inc. v. Chapman, 361

Quill Corp. v. North Dakota, 358, 359

Rafael Rodriguez Barril v. Conbraco Indus.,
  Inc., 706
Ragland Mills, Inc. v. General Motors
  Corp., 787
Rajala v. Donnelly Meiners Jordan Kline
  P.C., 267
Ranftle, Matter of, 566
Rattray v. City of National City, 213
Real Estate and Settlement Servs. Antitrust
  Litig., In re, 369
Reed v. Campagnolo, 148, 151
Reichhold Chems., Inc. v. Hartford Accident
  and Indem. Co., 242
Reich v. Purcell, 196–197, *249,* 251, 255
Retirement Credit Plan, Inc. v. Melnick, 169
Reynolds v. United States, 78
Rhee v. Combined Enters., Inc., 150
Rhone-Poulenc Rorer, Inc., In re, 769, 798, 800
Richards v. United States, 256, 258
Richardson v. Wile, 443
Ricoh Corp., In re, 703
Riley v. New York Trust Co., 505, 529, 540
Rincon EV Realty LLC v. CP III Rincon
  Towers, Inc., 657
Risdon Enter., Inc. v. Colemill Enter., Inc., 30
Rivera v. Centro Medico de Turabo, Inc., 699
RJR Nabisco, Inc. v. European Cmty., 614,
  643–644
R.J. Reynolds Tobacco Co. v. Engle, 777
Roach v. State Farm Mut. Auto. Ins. Co., 155
Robertson v. Howard, 535, 539
Robinson v. Title Lenders, Inc., 728
Roche v. McDonald, 547
Rodriguez de Quijas v. Shearson/Am. Express,
  Inc., 711–712
Rodriguez Diaz v. Sierra Martinez, 53, 62
Roe; Doe v., 166–167

Roe v. Wade, 151, 326
Rogers v. Guaranty Trust Co. of New York, 102
Romero v. International Terminal Operating Co., 589, 595, 596–599
Rosenberg Bros. & Co. v. Curtis Brown Co., 378–380
Rubman v. Rubman, 77
Rush v. Savchuk, 286, 417, 420, 461–462
Russello v. United States, 638
Rutherford v. Goodyear Tire and Rubber Co., 247
Ryan v. Clark Equip. Co., 198

Sadler v. NCR Corp., 107
St. Cyr; INS v., 443
St. Jude Med., Inc., In re, 753
Salavarria v. National Car Rental Sys., Inc., 274, 279
Sale v. Haitian Cntrs. Council, Inc., 617
Samaniego v. Empire Today, LLC, 714
Sampson v. Channell, 124, 132, 471, 476
Schaeffer v. Village of Ossining, 489
Scherk v. Alberto-Culver Co., 711
Schnall v. AT&T Wireless Servs., Inc., 765, 773, 784–785, 797–798, 800–801
Schneider v. Linkfield, 383
Schneider v. Nichols, 221
Schnuerle v. Insight Commc'ns Co., 675, 734
Scholes v. Stone, McGuire & Benjamin, 791
School Asbestos Litig., In re, 743
Schultz v. Boy Scouts of Am., 180–182, 198, 269
Schumacher v. Schumacher, 226
Schwartz v. Heyden Newport Chem. Corp., 141
Seamans v. Seamans, 573
Sedima, S.P.R.L. v. Imrex Co., 636, 640, 642
Seider v. Roth, 461–462
Semtek Int'l Inc. v. Lockheed Martin Corp., 493, 498–499
Sentinel Indus. Contracting Corp. v. Kimmins Indus. Serv. Corp., 676
Settle v. Settle, 520
Seymour v. Seymour, 115
Shady Grove Orthopedic Assocs. v. Allstate Ins. Co., 472
Shaffer v. Carter, 343
Shaffer v. Heitner, 303, 365, 377, 379, 387–390, 391, 405, 407, 409, 411, 419, 421, 428, 435, 446, 456, 457, 459, 460, 461, 462–463, 512, 565
Shapiro v. Thomson, 250
Sherrer v. Sherrer, 507, 523, 525, 535
Shipley Co. v. Kozlowski, 669
Shopper's Food Warehouse v. Moreno, 382
Shute v. Carnival Cruise Lines, 382

Shutts, Executor v. Phillips Petroleum Co., 311–312, 315
Sibbach v. Wilson & Co., 472
Simmons v. Simmons, 77
Simon v. United States, 113
Sinochem Int'l Co. v. Malaysia Int'l Shipping Corp., 373
Siro v. American Express Co., 445
Sisal Sales Corp.; United States v., 580, 582, 592, 622
Sistare v. Sistare, 570
Skirchak v. Dynamics Research Corp., 733
Skiriotes v. Florida, 288, 326
Slater v. Mexican Nat'l R.R., 21, 578
Smith, Valentino & Smith, Inc. v. Superior Court, 650, 655, 691
Smith v. Loughman, 342
Smith v. United States, 614, 616, 629
Société Intérnationale v. Rogers, 372
Société Nationale Industrielle Aérospatiale v. United States Dist. Court for S. Dist. of Iowa, 593
Sood, Application of, 77
Sosa v. Alvarez-Machain, 626, 634, 636
South Dakota v. Wayfair, 359
Southern Pac. Co. v. Arizona ex rel. Sullivan, 355
Southern Pac. Co. v. Jensen, 771
Southland Corp. v. Keating, 709, 710
Spann v. American Express Travel Related Servs. Co., 714, 734
Specht v. Netscape Comm'n Corp., 695
Spinozzi v. ITT Sheraton Corp., 31
Stabilisierungsfonds Fur Wein v. Kaiser Stuhl Wine Distribs. Pty. Ltd., 429
State v. See name of opposing party
State Bd. of Ins. v. Todd Shipyards Corp., 358
State Farm Mut. Auto. Ins. Co. v. Campbell, 358
State Farm Mut. Auto. Ins. Co. v. Roach, 155
State Farm Mut. Ins. Co. v. Conyers, 752
Steele v. Bulova Watch Co., 592, 608–609, 611, 622
Stephens v. Stephens, 90
Sterling v. Velsicol Chem. Corp., 792
Sternberg v. O'Neil, 442, 443, 455, 460
Sternhagen v. Dow Co., 237
Steven v. Fidelity & Cas. Co. of New York, 686
Stewart Org., Inc. v. Ricoh Corp., 482, 490–491, 684, 698
Stifel v. Hopkins, 56, 59, 62
Stiller v. Hardman, 536
Stoll v. Gottlieb, 501, 506, 514
Stolt-Nielsen, S.A. v. AnimalFeeds Int'l Corp., 709, 719
Strassheim v. Daily, 580
Stupak v. Hoffman-La Roche, Inc., 226
Sudduth v. Occidental Peruana, Inc., 689

Sugar Antitrust Litig., In re, 799

Sun Oil Co. v. Wortman, 169, 292, *316*, 325, 326, 332, 339, 391, 484, 486, 550, 744, 745–746, 747–748, 750, 753

Superintendent of Ins. of N.Y. v. Bankers Life & Cas. Co., 620

Sutherland v. Kennington Truck Serv. Ltd., 256

Swift v. Tyson, 124, 126, 128, 465, 467–469, 770

Swift & Co. v. United States, 515

Swiss Am. Bank; United States v., 441–442

Tallmadge, In re, 116

Tauza v. Susquehanna Coal Co., 438

Taylor v. 1-800-Got Junk? LLC, 676

Telectronics Pacing Sys., Inc., In re, *785*, 797–799, 800

Tele-Save Merch. Co. v. Consumers Distrib. Co., 660, 661

Tenas v. Progressive Preferred Ins. Co., 544

Tennessee Coal, Iron & R.R. Co. v. George, 334, 676

Texaco v. Vanden Bosche, 149

Textile Workers Union of Am. v. Lincoln Mills, 470

Textron, Inc., Ex parte, 691

Thomas v. Washington Gas Light Co., *520*, 533, 538

Thompson v. Thompson, 560, 571, 573

Thompson v. Whitman, 505, 515, 538

Thomsen v. Cayser, 580, 584, 622

Thomson v. Kyle, *83*, 86

Tidewater Oil Co. v. Waller, *163*, 166

Timberlane Lumber Co. v. Bank of Am., N.T. & S.A., *581*, 588–589, 591, 593, 597, 600, 605

Timken Roller Bearing Co.; United States v., 584

Toll v. Moreno, 62

Tolman v. Stryker Corp., 25

Tooker v. Lopez, 176–179, 181, 187

Toomer v. Witsell, 342

Torres v. State, 752

Totten, In re, 115

Toys "R" Us, Inc. v. Step Two, S.A., 426

Trasylol Prods. Liab. Litig., In re, 803

Travelers' Ins. Co. v. Connecticut, 342

Travis v. Yale & Towne Mfg. Co., 342, 343–344

Treinies v. Sunshine Mining Co., *553*, 557

Trustees of Dartmouth Coll. v. Woodward, 360

Überseering BV v. Nordic Constr. Co. Baumanagement GmbH (NCC), 108

Uboh-Abiola v. Abiola, 77, 78

Union & Planters' Bank v. Memphis, 541

Union Nat'l Bank v. Chapman, 41

Union Nat'l Bank v. Lamb, 547, 550

United States v. *See name of opposing party*

United States ex rel. *See name of party*

United States Brewers Assn. v. Healy, 355

University of Chi. v. Dater, *117*, 121–122

University of Tenn. v. Elliot, 533

Unocal Corp.; Doe v., 436

U.S. Fid. Co.; United States v., 506

Valtz v. Penta Inv. Corp., 106

Vanderpoel v. Gorman, 104, 105

Van Dusen v. Barrack, 477, 478, 480–485, 487, 488–490, 491, 705, 740

VantagePoint Venture Partners 1996 v. Examen, Inc., 105

Van Voorhis v. Brintnall, 77

Velmohos v. Maren Eng'g Corp., 348, 350

Vesely v. Sager, 205, 206, 208–209, 211

Viam Corp. v. Iowa Export-Import Trading Co., 424

Viccaro v. Milunsky, 151

Vioxx Prods. Liab. Litig., In re, 803

Vishipco Line v. Chase Manhattan Bank, 167–168

V.L. v. E.L., 510

Vons Cos. v. Seabest Foods, Inc., 382

Wahl v. General Elec. Co., 803

Walden v. Fiore, 396, *417*

Walton v. Arabian Am. Oil Co., 166

Wamsley v. Nodak Mut. Ins. Co., 542, 544–545

Wanzer v. Bright, 386

Ward v. Maryland, 342

Washington v. Heckel, 361

Washington Water Power Co. v. Graybar Elec. Co., 787

Waters v. Deutz Corp., 456, 459

Watkins v. Conway, *549*, 551

Watson v. Employers Liab. Assurance Corp., *292*, 295, 296–297, 299, 309, 462

Watts v. Waddle, 538

Weede v. Iowa S. Utils. Co. of Del., 106

Wehner v. Syntex Corp., 791

Wells v. Simonds Abrasive Co., *330*, 332–333

West Am. Ins. Co. v. Westin, Inc., 411

Western Air Lines, Inc. v. Sobieski, 102

Western & S.L.I. Co. v. Board of Equalization, 349

Whitaker v. Harvell-Kilgore Corp., 280

White v. Tennant, *51*, 339

Widenhouse v. Colson, 156

Wilko v. Swan, 710–712

Williams v. North Carolina, 519, 558, 559–562, 565

Williams v. Walker-Thomas Furniture Co., 686

Wilmington Trust Co. v. Wilmington Trust Co., 96
Wilson v. Louisiana-Pac. Res., Inc., 106
Winters v. Maxey, 31
Wisconsin v. Pelican Ins. Co., 538
Wong v. PartyGaming Ltd., *696*, 704–705
Woods v. Wicks, 158, 159
World Interactive Gaming Corp.; People v., 8
World-Wide Volkswagen Corp. v. Woodson, 303, 306, 365, 370, 390, 394–396, 399, *403*, 411, 412, 416, 419, 422, 424, 429, 444
Wright-Moore Corp. v. Ricoh Corp., 660
W.S. Kirkpatrick & Co. v. Environmental Tectonics Corp., Int'l, 622

Wyman v. Newhouse, 391

Yarborough v. Yarborough, *567*, 571
Yavuz v. 61 MM, Ltd., 698
York v. Texas, 374, 516
Young v. Masci, 288
Ysbrand v. DaimlerChrysler Corp., *757*, 764, 769

Ziady v. Curley, 57, 59
Zippo Mfg. Co. v. Zippo Dot Com, Inc., 426
Zschernig v. Miller, 546

Table of Secondary Authorities

Adams, *World-Wide Volkswagen v. Woodson*—the Rest of the Story, 72 Neb. L. Rev. 1122 (1993), 411

Alexander, Unlimited Shareholder Liability Through a Procedural Lens, 106 Harv. L. Rev. 387 (1992), 108, 460

ALI, Complex Litigation: Statutory Recommendations and Analysis (1994), 757

_____, Principles of the Law of Aggregate Litigation (2010), 478, 802

Allen & O'Hara, Second Generation Law and Economics of Conflict of Laws: Baxter's Comparative Impairment and Beyond, 51 Stan. L. Rev. 1011 (1999), 113

Annual Report of the Director of the Administrative Office of the U.S. Courts (1990), 740

Areeda & Hovenkamp, Antitrust Law (Supp. 1992), 592

Areeda & Turner, Antitrust Law (1978), 592

Atwood & Brewster, Antitrust and American Business Abroad (1981), 593

Audit, A Continental Lawyer Looks at Contemporary American Choice-of-Law Principles, 27 Am. J. Comp. L. 589 (1979), 202

Bast, What's Bugging You? Inconsistencies and Irrationalities of the Law of Eavesdropping, 47 DePaul L. Rev. 837 (1998), 211

Bauer, The *Erie* Doctrine Revisited: How a Conflicts Perspective Can Aid the Analysis, 74 Notre Dame L. Rev. 1235 (1999), 474

Baxter, Choice of Law and the Federal System, 16 Stan. L. Rev. 1 (1963), 203, 207, 478, 511

Beale, The Conflict of Laws (1935), 21, 45, 61, 120, 164

Bensimon, Corporate Liability Under the Alien Tort Statute: Can Corporations Have Their Cake and Eat It Too?, 10 Loy. U. Chi. Int'l L. Rev. 199 (2013), 440

Bernstein, Merchant Law in a Merchant Court: Rethinking the Code's Search for Immanent Business Norms, 144 U. Pa. L. Rev. 1765 (1996), 708

_____, Opting Out of the Legal System: Extralegal Contractual Relations in the Diamond Industry, 21 J. Legal Stud. 115 (1992), 708

_____, Private Commercial Law in the Cotton Industry: Creating Cooperation Through Rules, Norms and Institutions, 99 Mich. L. Rev. 1724 (2001), 708

Biddle, State Regulation of the Internet: Where Does the Balance of Federalist Power Lie?, 37 Cal. W. L. Rev. 161 (2000), 361

Black's Law Dictionary (7th ed. 1999), 496

Blumberg, The Increasing Recognition of Enterprise Principles in Determining Parent and Subsidiary Corporate Liabilities, 28 Conn. L. Rev. 295 (1996), 460

Bookman, Doubling Down on Litigation Isolationism, 110 AJIL Unbound 57 (2016), 645

Borchers, The Choice-of-Law Revolution: An Empirical Study, 49 Wash. & Lee L. Rev. 357 (1992), 226

_____, An Essay on Predictability in Choice-of-Law Doctrine and Implications for a Third Conflicts Restatement, 49 Creighton L. Rev. 495 (2016), 246

_____, Forum Selection Agreements in the Federal Courts After *Carnival Cruise*: A Proposal for Congressional Reform, 67 Wash. L. Rev. 55 (1992), 689–690

_____, How "International" Should a Third Conflicts Restatement Be in Tort and Contract?, 27 Duke J. Comp. & Int'l L. 461 (2017), 246

_____, Louisiana's Conflicts Codification: Some Empirical Observations Regarding Decisional Predictability, 60 La. L. Rev. 1061 (2000), 279

_____, Professor Brilmayer and the Holy Grail, 1991 Wis. L. Rev. 465 (1991), 200, 204

_____, The Return of Territorialism to N.Y.'s Conflicts Law: *Padula v. Lilarn Properties Corp.*, 58 Alb. L. Rev. 775 (1995), 183

Born, A Reappraisal of the Extraterritorial Reach of U.S. Law, 24 Law & Poly. Int'l Bus. 1 (1992), 613

Born & Rutledge, International Civil Litigation in United States Courts (6th ed. 2018), 492, 600

Born & Westin, International Civil Litigation in United States Courts (2d ed. 1992) , 592

Bradford, What Happens if *Roe* is Overruled? Extraterritorial Regulation of Abortion by the States, 35 Ariz. L. Rev. 87 (1993), 326

Bradley, Territorial Intellectual Property Rights in an Age of Globalism, 37 Va. J. Int'l L. 505 (1997), 613–614

Bradt, The Shortest Distance: Direct Filing and Choice of Law in Multidistrict Litigation, 88 Notre Dame L. Rev. 759 (2012), 803

Brilmayer, Conflict of Laws: Foundations and Future Directions (1991), 204, 256

_____, Credit Due Judgments and Credit Due Laws: The Respective Roles of Due Process and Full Faith and Credit in the Interstate Context, 70 Iowa L. Rev. 95 (1984), 326

_____, The Extraterritorial Application of American Law: A Methodological and Constitutional Appraisal, 50 Law & Contemp. Probs. 11 (1987), 424, 613

_____, Governmental Interest Analysis: A House Without Foundations, 46 Ohio St. L.J. 459 (1985), 201

_____, How Contacts Count, 1979 S. Ct. Rev. 66, 424

_____, How Contacts Count: Due Process Limitations on State Court Jurisdiction, 1980 S. Ct. Rev. 77, 377, 413

_____, Interest Analysis and the Myth of Legislative Intent, 78 Mich. L. Rev. 392 (1980), 200, 210

_____, Interstate Preemption: The Right to Travel, the Right to Life, and the Right to Die, 91 Mich. L. Rev. 873 (1992), 326

_____, Jurisdictional Due Process and Political Theory, 39 U. Fla. L. Rev. 293 (1987), 363–364

_____, Legitimate Interests in Multistate Problems: As Between State and Federal Law, 79 Mich. L. Rev. 1315 (1981), 308–309

_____, The New Extraterritoriality: *Morrison v. National Australia Bank*, Legislative Supremacy, and the Presumption Against Extraterritorial Application of American Law, 40 Sw. L. Rev. 655 (2011), 626

_____, Related Contacts and Personal Jurisdiction, 101 Harv. L. Rev. 1444 (1988), 382

_____, Rights, Fairness, and Choice of Law, 99 Yale L.J. 1277 (1989), 32, 200, 202, 251, 287

_____, What I Like Most About the Restatement (Second) of Conflicts, and Why It Should Not Be Thrown Out with the Bathwater, 110 AJIL Unbound 144 (2016), 227

Brilmayer & Anglin, Choice of Law Theory and the Metaphysics of the Stand-Alone Trigger, 95 Iowa L. Rev. 1125 (2010), 241, 253, 310

Brilmayer & Listwa, Continuity and Change in the Draft Restatement (Third) of Conflict of Laws: One Step Forward and Two Steps Back?, 128 Yale L.J. Forum 266 (2018), 245

Brilmayer & Paisley, Personal Jurisdiction and Substantive Legal Relations: Corporations, Conspiracy, and Agency, 74 Cal. L. Rev. 1 (1986), 430, 431, 456, 459, 460

Brilmayer & Seidell, Jurisdictional Realism: Where Modern Theories of Choice of Law Went Wrong, and What Can Be Done to Fix Them, 86 U. Chi. L. Rev. (2019), 171–172

Brilmayer & Underhill, Congressional Obligation to Provide a Forum for Constitutional Claims: Discriminatory Jurisdictional Rules and Conflict of Laws, 69 Va. L. Rev. 819 (1983), 334

Brilmayer et al., A General Look at General Jurisdiction, 66 Tex. L. Rev. 721 (1988), 428, 429, 438

Burbank, Federal Judgments Law: Sources of Authority and Sources of Rules, 70 Tex. L. Rev. 1551 (1992), 503

_____, The United States' Approach to International Civil Litigation: Recent Developments in Forum Selection, 19 U. Pa. J. Int'l Econ. L. 1 (1998), 442

Burk, Federalism in Cyberspace, 28 Conn. L. Rev. 1095 (1996), 361

Butler & Merkin, Reinsurance Law (1992), 598

Buxbaum, The Scope and Limitations of the Presumotion Against Territoriality, 110 AJIL Unbound 62 (2016), 645

———, The Threatened Constitutionalization of the Internal Affairs Doctrine in Corporation Law, 75 Cal. L. Rev. 29 (1987), 361

Cabraser, Just Choose: The Jurisprudential Necessity to Select a Single Governing Law for Mass Claims Arising from Nationally Marketed Consumer Goods and Services, 14 Roger Williams U. L. Rev. 29 (2009), 767

———, The Manageable Nationwide Class: A Choice-of-Law Legacy of *Phillips Petroleum Co. v. Shutts*, 74 U.M.K.C. L. Rev. 543 (2006), 757

Cappalli, Locke as the Key: A Unifying and Coherent Theory of In Personam Jurisdiction, 43 UCLA L. Rev. 99 (1992), 364

Carbonneau, Cases and Materials on the Law and Practice of Arbitration (3d ed. 2002), 708

Carrington & Haagen, Contract and Jurisdiction, 1996 Sup. Ct. Rev. 331, 690

Cavers, The Choice-of-Law Process (1965), 31

Chayes, The Bead Game, 87 Harv. L. Rev. 741 (1974), 475

Clark, Corporate Law (1986), 458

Clermont, Governing Law on Forum-Selection Agreements, 66 Hastings L.J. 643 (2015), 491

Clermont & Palmer, Exorbitant Jurisdiction, 58 Me. L. Rev. 474 (2006), 430

Cleveland, The *Kiobel* Presumption and Extraterritoriality, 52 Colum. J. Transnat'l L. 8 (2013), 627

Cohan, Honor Killings and the Cultural Defense, 40 Cal. W. Int'l L.J. 177 (2010), 78

Colangelo, The Frankenstein's Monster of Extraterritoriality Law, 110 AJIL Unbound 51 (2016), 644

———, A Unified Approach to Extraterritoriality, 97 Va. L. Rev. 1019 (2011), 626

Comment, Choice of Law: A Fond Farewell to Comity and Public Policy, 74 Cal. L. Rev. 1447 (1986), 269

———, Related Contacts and Personal Jurisdiction: The "But For" Test, 82 Cal. L. Rev. 1545 (1994), 382

———, Specific Personal Jurisdiction and the "Arise From Or Relate To" Requirement: What Does It Mean?, 50 Wash. & Lee L. Rev. 1265 (1993), 382

Conte & Newberg, Newberg on Class Actions (4th ed. 2002), 776

Cook, The Logical and Legal Bases of the Conflict of Laws (1942), 21, 177

Cooper, Aggregation and Choice of Law, 14 Roger Williams U. L. Rev. 12 (2009), 757

Corr, Interest Analysis and Choice of Law: The Dubious Dominance of Domicile, 4 Utah L. Rev. 651 (1983), 199–200

———, Modern Choice of Law and Public Policy: The Emperor Has the Same Old Clothes, 39 U. Miami L. Rev. 647 (1985), 269

Corr & Robbins, Interjurisdictional Certification and Choice of Law, 41 Vand. L. Rev. 411 (1988), 169

Cox, The Interrelationship of Personal Jurisdiction and Choice of Law: Forging New Theory Through *Asahi Metal Indus. Co. v. Superior Court*, 49 U. Pitt. L. Rev. 189 (1987), 424

Cramton, Currie & Kay, Conflict of Laws 25 (3d ed. 1981), 46, 57

Currie, Comments on *Babcock v. Jackson*, 63 Colum. L. Rev. 1233 (1963), 186

———, Conflict, Crisis and Confusion in N.Y., in Selected Essays on the Conflict of Laws (1963), 252

———, The Constitution and the Choice of Law: Governmental Interests and the Judicial Function, in Selected Essays on the Conflict of Laws (1963), 306

———, The Constitution and the "Transitory" Cause of Action in Selected Essays on the Conflict of Laws (1963), 332

———, The Disinterested Third State, 28 Law & Contemp. Probs. 754 (1963), 207, 241

———, Full Faith and Credit to Foreign Land Decrees, 21 U. Chi. L. Rev. 620 (1954), 511

———, Notes on Methods and Objectives in the Conflict of Laws, in Selected Essays on the Conflict of Laws (1963), 184

———, On the Displacement of the Law of the Forum, 58 Colum. L. Rev. 964 (1958), 168

_____, On the Displacement of the Law of the Forum, in Selected Essays on the Conflict of Laws (1963), 166

_____, Selected Essays on the Conflict of Laws (1963), 21, 135, 155, 171, 175, 206, 256, 339, 346

_____, The Verdict of the Quiescent Years, in Selected Essays on the Conflict of Laws (1963), 252

Dane, Conflict of Laws, in A Companion to the Philosophy of Law and Legal Theory (Patterson ed., 1996), 62

_____, Vested Rights, Vestedness, and Choice of Law, 96 Yale L.J. 1191 (1987), 32, 132, 201–202

_____, Whereof One Cannot Speak: Legal Diversity and the Limits of a Restatement of Conflict of Laws, 75 Ind. L.J. 511 (2000), 75

Davies, Time to Change the Federal *Forum Non Conveniens* Analysis, 77 Tul. L. Rev. 309 (2002), 492

de Boer, Beyond Lex Loci Delicti (1987), 202

Degnan, Federalized Res Judicata, 85 Yale L.J. 741 (1976), 497

Denning, Extraterritoriality and the Dormant Commerce Clause: A Doctrinal Post-Mortem, 73 La. L. Rev. 979 (2013), 357

_____, Smokey and the Bandit in Cyberspace: The Dormant Commerce Clause, the Twenty-first Amendment, and State Regulation of Internet Alcohol Sales, 19 Const. Comment. 297 (2002), 361

Dessem, Personal Jurisdiction after *Asahi*: The Other (International) Shoe Drops, 55 Tenn. L. Rev. 41 (1987), 424

Dodge, Breaking the Public Law Taboo, 43 Harv. Int'l L.J. 161 (2002), 163

_____, Extraterritoriality and Conflict-of-Laws Theory: An Argument for Judicial Unilateralism, 39 Harv. Int'l L.J. 101 (1998), 613

_____, *Morrison*'s Effects Test, 40 Sw. L. Rev. 687 (2011), 626

_____, The Presumption Against Extraterritoriality in Two Steps, 110 AJIL Unbound 45 (2016), 645

Dougherty, Validity of Contractual Provision Limiting Place or Court in Which Action May Be Brought, 31 A.L.R. 4th 404 (1984), 686

Drahozal, Is Arbitration Lawless?, 40 Loy. L.A. L. Rev. 187 (2006), 712

Egnal, The "Essential" Role of Modern Renvoi in the Governmental Interest Analysis Approach to Choice of Law, 54 Temple L.Q. 237 (1981), 256

Ehrenzweig, Conflict of Laws (1962), 139, 189, 535

_____, A Counter-Revolution in Conflicts Laws? From Beale to Cavers, 80 Harv. L. Rev. 377 (1966), 194–195

_____, "False Conflicts" and the "Better Rule": Threat and Promise in Multistate Tort Laws, 53 Va. L. Rev. 847 (1967), 222

_____, The "Most Significant Relationship," in the Conflicts Law of Torts: Law and Reason Versus the Restatement Second, 28 Law & Contemp. Probs. 700 (1963), 241

_____, The Second Conflicts Restatement: A Last Appeal for Its Withdrawal, 113 U. Pa. L. Rev. 1230 (1965), 520

_____, The Transient Rule of Personal Jurisdiction: The "Power" Myth and Forum Conveniens, 65 Yale L.J. 289 (1956), 385

Eisenberg & Miller, Ex Ante Choices of Law and Forum: An Empirical Analysis of Corporate Merger Agreements, 59 Vand. L. Rev. 1975 (2006), 695–696

Eisenberg, Miller & Sherwin, Arbitration's Summer Soldiers: An Empirical Study of Arbitration Clauses in Consumer and Nonconsumer Contracts, 41 U. Mich. J.L. Reform 871 (2008), 733

Ely, Choice of Law and the State's Interest in Protecting Its Own, 23 Wm. & Mary L. Rev. 173 (1981), 199, 200, 346, 351–352

_____, The Irrepressible Myth of *Erie*, 87 Harv. L. Rev. 693 (1974), 474

_____, The Necklace, 87 Harv. L. Rev. 753 (1974), 475

Fallen, Meltzer, & Shapiro, Hart and Wechsler's The Federal Courts and the Federal System (4th ed. 1996), 497

Farnsworth, Contracts (4th ed. 2004), 714

Farrand, The Records of the Federal Convention of 1787 (rev. ed. 1966), 317

Fawcett, Is American Governmental Interest Analysis the Solution to English Tort Choice of Law Problems?, 31 Int'l & Comp. L.Q. 150 (1982), 203

Feder & Goodyear, "Home," and the Uncertain Future of Doing Business Jurisdiction, 63 S.C. L. Rev. 671 (2012), 439

Federal Judicial Center, Manual for Complex Litig. (3d ed. 1995), 740

Finan, Convention on the Rights of the Child: A Potentially Effective Remedy in Cases of International Child Abduction, 34 Santa Clara L. Rev. 1007 (1994), 573

Fletcher, Cyclopedia of the Law of Corporations (Supp. 2012–2013), 436

_____, Cyclopedia of the Law of Private Corporations (rev. perm. ed. Supp. 1988), 455

Floyd, *Erie* Awry: A Comment on *Gasperini v. Center for Humanities, Inc.*, 1997 B.Y.U. L. Rev. 267 (1997), 472

Forsyth, Private International Law (1990), 202

Francq, A European Story, 110 AJIL Unbound 74 (2016), 645

Gergen, Equality and the Conflict of Laws, 73 Iowa L. Rev. 893 (1988), 340

_____, Territoriality and the Perils of Formalism, 86 Mich. L. Rev. 1735 (1988), 361

Ginsburg, Judgments in Search of Full Faith and Credit: The Last-in-Time Rule for Conflicting Judgments, 82 Harv. L. Rev. 798 (1969), 536

Goldsmith, Against Cyberanarchy, 65 U. Chi. L. Rev. 1199 (1998), 8, 248

_____, Federal Courts, Foreign Affairs, and Federalism, 83 Va. L. Rev. 1617 (1997), 493, 546

Goldsmith & Sykes, The Internet and the Dormant Commerce Clause, 110 Yale L.J. 785 (2001), 356, 361

Goldstein, The Tragedy of the Interstate Child: A Critical Reexamination of the Uniform Child Custody Jurisdiction Act and the Parental Kidnapping Prevention Act, 25 U.C. Davis L. Rev. 845 (1992), 573

Goodrich, Yielding Place to New: Rest Versus Motion in the Conflict of Laws, 50 Colum. L. Rev. 881 (1950), 259

Goodrich & Scoles, Handbook of the Conflict of Laws (1964), 21

Gottesman, "Draining the Dismal Swamp": The Case for Federal Choice of Law Statutes, 80 Geo. L.J. 1 (1991), 279, 477

Green, The Return of the Unprovided-For Case, 51 Ga. L. Rev. 763 (2017), 199

Greenberg, The Appropriate Source of Law for Forum Non Conveniens Decisions in International Cases: A Proposal for the Development of Federal Common Law, 4 Int'l Tax & Bus. Law. 155 (1986), 493

Griffin, Extraterritoriality in U.S. and EU Antitrust Enforcement, 67 Antitrust L.J. 159 (1999), 624

Hafetz, Human Rights Litigation and the National Interest: *Kiobel's* Application of the Presumption Against Extraterritoriality to the Alien Tort Statute, 28 Md. J. Int'l L. 107 (2013), 627

Hancock, Conceptual Devices for Avoiding the Land Taboo in Conflict of Laws, 20 Stan. L. Rev. 1 (1967), 511

_____, The Effect in Choice of Law Cases of the Acquisition of a New Domicile after the Commission of a Tort or Making of a Contract, 2 Hast. Int'l & Comp. L. Rev. 215 (1979), 252

_____, Equitable Conversion and the Land Taboo in the Conflict of Laws, 17 Stan. L. Rev. 1095 (1965), 511

_____, Full Faith and Credit to Foreign Laws and Judgments in Real Property Litigation, 18 Stan. L. Rev. 1299 (1966), 511

Hanotiau, The American Conflicts Revolution and European Tort Choice of Law Thinking, 30 Am. J. Comp. L. 1 (1982), 202

Hansmann & Kraakman, A Procedural Focus on Unlimited Shareholder Liability, 106 Harv. L. Rev. 446 (1992), 108

_____, Toward Unlimited Shareholder Liability for Corporate Torts, 100 Yale L.J. 1879 (1991), 107–108

Harper, The Limitations of the Hague Convention and Alternative Remedies for a Parent Including Re-Abduction, 9 Emory Int'l L. Rev. 257 (1995), 573

Hay, Flexibility Versus Predictability and Uniformity in Choice of Law, 226 Recueil des Cours 285 (1991), 22

Hay & Ellis, Bridging the Gap Between Rules and Approaches in Tort Choice of Law in the United States: A Survey of Current Case Law, 27 Int'l Law 369 (1993), 184

Hazard, A General Theory of State-Court Jurisdiction, 1965 Sup. Ct. Rev. 241 (1965), 385

Heiser, The Hague Convention on Choice of Court Agreements: The Impact on Forum Non Conveniens, Transfer of Venue, Removal, and Recognition of Judgments in United States Courts, 31 U. Pa. J. Int'l L. 1013 (2010), 687, 706

Hill, The Judicial Function in Choice of Law, 85 Colum. L. Rev. 1585 (1985), 184

Hirsch, Fear Not the Asset Protection Trust, 27 Cardozo L. Rev. 2685 (2006), 97

Hoff, The ABC's of the UCCJEA: Interstate Child-Custody Practice Under the New Act, 32 Fam. L.Q. 267 (1998), 573

Horowitz, The Law of Choice of Law in California—A Restatement, 21 UCLA L. Rev. 719 (1974), 207

Issacharoff, Settled Expectations in a World of Unsettled Law: Choice of Law After the Class Action Fairness Act, 106 Colum. L. Rev. 1839 (2006), 767

Issacharoff & Delaney, Credit Card Accountability, 73 U. Chi. L. Rev. 157 (2006), 733

James, Hazard, & Leubsdorf, Civil Procedure (5th ed. 2001), 502

Johnson & Post, Law and Borders—The Rise of Law in Cyberspace, 48 Stan. L. Rev. 1367 (1996), 8, 248

Juenger, How Do You Rate a Century?, 37 Willamette L. Rev. 89 (2001), 113

Kanowitz, Comparative Impairment and Better Law: Grand Illusion in the Conflict of Laws, 30 Hastings L.J. 255 (1978), 210

Kaplan, Foreign Corporations and Local Corporate Policy, 21 Vand. L. Rev. 433 (1968), 102, 103

Katzenbach, Conflicts on an Unruly Horse, 65 Yale L.J. 1087 (1956), 585

Kay, Theory into Practice: Choice of Law in the Courts, 34 Mercer L. Rev. 521 (1983), 229, 243

Kaye & Weissman, Interactive Judicial Federalism: Certified Questions in New York, 69 Fordham L. Rev. 373 (2000), 169

Kipp, Inferring Express Consent: The Paradox of Permitting Registration Statutes to Confer General Jurisdiction, 9 Rev. Litig. 1 (1990), 442

Kirgis, The Roles of Due Process and Full Faith and Credit in Choice of Law, 62 Cornell L. Rev. 94 (1976), 287, 332

Knox, A Presumption Against Extrajurisdictionality, 104 Am. J. Int'l L. 351 (2010), 601

Kobayashi & Ribstein, Choosing Law by Contract, in The Fall and Rise of Freedom of Contract (1999), 664

Kogan, Toward a Jurisprudence of Choice of Law: The Priority of Fairness over Comity, 62 N.Y.U. L. Rev. 651 (1987), 292

Kozyris, Corporate Wars and Choice of Law, 1985 Duke L.J. 1, 102, 103

Kramer, Choice of Law in Complex Litigation, 71 N.Y.U. L. Rev. 547 (1996), 756

_____, Interest Analysis and the Presumption of Forum Law, 56 U. Chi. L. Rev. 1301 (1989), 166, 167, 201

_____, Rethinking Choice of Law, 90 Colum. L. Rev. 277 (1990), 201, 204

_____, Return of the Renvoi, 66 N.Y.U. L. Rev. 979 (1991), 256

_____, Same-Sex Marriage, Conflict of Laws, and the Unconstitutional Public Policy Exception, 106 Yale L.J. 1965 (1997), 333

_____, Vestiges of Beale: Extraterritorial Application of American Law, 1991 S. Ct. Rev. 179 (1991), 613

Kreimer, "But Whosoever Treasures Freedom . . .": The Right to Travel and Extraterritorial Abortions, 91 Mich. L. Rev. 907 (1992), 326

_____, The Law of Choice and Choice of Law: Abortion, the Right to Travel, and Extraterritorial Regulation in American Federalism, 67 N.Y.U. L. Rev. 451 (1992), 326

Kutner, Judicial Identification of "Penal Laws" in the Conflict of Laws, 31 Okla. L. Rev. 590 (1978), 161

Lando, New American Choice-of-Law Principles and the European Conflict of Laws of Contracts, 30 Am. J. Comp. L. 19 (1982), 203

Langevoort, The Supreme Court and the Politics of Corporate Takeovers: A Comment on *CTS Corp. v. General Dynamics Corp. of America*, 101 Harv. L. Rev. 96 (1987), 361

Laycock, Equal Citizens of Equal and Territorial States: The Constitutional Foundations of Choice of Law, 92 Colum. L. Rev. 249 (1992), 291, 339

_____, Equality and the Citizens of Sister States, 15 Fla. St. L. Rev. 431 (1987), 339

Leathers, *Erie* and Its Progeny as Choice of Law Cases, 11 Hous. L. Rev. 791 (1974), 473

Leebron, Limited Liability, Tort Victims, and Creditors, 91 Colum. L. Rev. 1565 (1991), 108

Leflar, American Conflicts Law (1968), 86

_____, Choice-Influencing Considerations and Conflicts of Law, 41 N.Y.U. L. Rev. 267 (1966), 220, 272

_____, Choice-of-Law Statutes, 44 Tenn. L. Rev. 951 (1977), 259

_____, Conflicts Law: More on Choice-Influencing Considerations, 54 Cal. L. Rev. 1584 (1966), 218

_____, Extrastate Enforcement of Penal and Governmental Claims, 46 Harv. L. Rev. 193 (1932), 162

Lilly, Jurisdiction over Domestic and Alien Defendants, 69 Va. L. Rev. 85 (1983), 456

Llewellyn, The Common Law Tradition (1960), 686

LoPucki, The Essential Structure of Judgment Proofing, 51 Stan. L. Rev. 147 (1998), 97

Lorenzen, Selected Articles on the Conflict of Laws (1947), 21

_____, The Theory of Qualifications and Conflict of Laws, 20 Colum. L. Rev. 247 (1920), 120

Lowenfeld, Nationalizing International Law: Essay in Honor of Louis Henkin, 36 Colum. J. Transnat'l L. 121 (1997), 493

Macey & Miller, Toward an Interest-Group Theory of Delaware Corporate Law, 65 Tex. L. Rev. 469 (1987), 102, 457

Maltz, Sovereign Authority, Fairness, and Personal Jurisdiction: The Case for the Doctrine of Transient Jurisdiction, 66 Wash. U. L.Q. 671 (1988), 390

Marcus, Redish, & Sherman, Civil Procedure: A Modern Approach (3d ed. 2000), 495

Marshall & May, The Divorce Court (1932), 570

Martin, All Men Are (or Should Be) Created Equal: An Argument Against the Use of the Cultural Defense in a Post-Booker World, 15 Wm. & Mary Bill Rts. J. 1305 (2007), 78

_____, Constitutional Limitations on Choice of Law, 61 Cornell L. Rev. 185 (1976), 287, 332

_____, The Constitution and Legislative Jurisdiction, 10 Hofstra L. Rev. 133 (1981), 309

_____, Personal Jurisdiction and Choice of Law, 78 Mich. L. Rev. 872 (1980), 411

Maslechko, Revolution and Counter-Revolution: An Examination of the Continuing Debate over "Interest Analysis" in the U.S. and its Relevance to Canadian Conflict of Laws, 44 U. Toronto L. Rev. 57 (1986), 202

McCloud & Rosenberg, A Solution to the Choice of Law Problem of Differing State Laws in Class Actions: Average Law, 79 Geo. Wash. L. Rev. 374 (2011), 769

McConnaughay, Reviving the "Public Law Taboo" in International Conflict of Laws, 35 Stan. J Int'l L. 255 (1999), 613

McConnell, A Choice-of-Law Approach to Product Liability Reform, in New Directions in Liability Law (Olson ed., 1988), 242

Michaels & Whytock, Internationalizing the New Conflict of Laws Restatement, 27 Duke J. Comp. & Int'l L. 349, 351 (2017), 246

Michalski, Rights Come with Responsibilities: Personal Jurisdiction in the Age of Corporate Personhood, 50 San Diego L. Rev. 125 (2013), 432

Miller, Federal Rule 44.1 and the "Fact" Approach to Determining Foreign Law: Death-Knell for a Die-Hard Doctrine, 65 Mich. L. Rev. 615 (1967), 166

Miller & Crump, Jurisdiction and Choice of Law in Multistate Class Actions after *Phillips Petroleum Co. v. Shutts*, 96 Yale L.J. 1 (1986), 368, 776

Mishkin, The Thread, 87 Harv. L. Rev. 1682 (1974), 475

Monestier, Registration Statutes, General Jurisdiction, and the Fallacy of Consent, 36 Cardozo L. Rev. 1343 (2015), 442

Moses, Arbitration Law: Who's In Charge, 40 Seton Hall L. Rev. 147 (2010), 732–733

Mullenix, Another Choice of Forum, Another Choice of Law: Consensual Adjudicatory Procedure in Federal Court, 57 Fordham L. Rev. 291 (1988), 491

_____, Another Easy Case, Some More Bad Law: *Carnival Cruise Lines* and Contractual Personal Jurisdiction, 27 Tex. Int'l L.J. 323 (1992), 690

Murphy, Negotiation of Convention on Jurisdiction and Enforcement of Judgments, 95 Am. J. Int'l L. 418 (2001), 547

Nagareda, Aggregation and its Discontents; Class Settlement Pressure, Class-Wide Arbitration, and CAFA, 106 Colum. L. Rev. 1872 (2006), 756

Note, Choice of Law after Transfer of Venue, 75 Yale L.J. 90 (1965), 481

_____, Choice of Law in Federal Court after Transfer of Venue, 63 Cornell L. Rev. 149 (1977), 490

_____, The Cultural Defense in the Criminal Law, 99 Harv. L. Rev. 1293 (1986), 78

_____, Interest Analysis Applied to Corporations: The Unprincipled Use of a Choice of Law Method, 98 Yale L.J. 597 (1989), 249

Nussbaum, Conflict Theories of Contracts: Cases Versus Restatement, 51 Yale L. Rev. 893 (1942), 45

O'Hara & Ribstein, From Politics to Efficiency in Choice of Law, 67 U. Chi. L. Rev. 1151 (2000), 113, 183, 664

_____, The Law Market (2009), 664, 706, 712

O'Hara O'Connor, How Modern Choice of Law Helped to Kill the Private Attorney General, 64 Mercer L. Rev. 1023 (2013), 200

Paulsen & Sovern, "Public Policy" in the Conflict of Laws, 56 Colum. L. Rev. 969 (1956), 155, 268

Perdue, A Reexamination of the Distinction Between "Loss-Allocating" and "Conduct-Regulating Rules," 60 La. L. Rev. 1251 (2000), 183–184, 279

Perritt, Dispute Resolution in Cyberspace: Demand for New Forms of ADR, 15 Ohio St. J. on Disp. Resol. 675 (2000), 696

_____, Jurisdiction in Cyberspace, 41 Villanova L. Rev. 1 (1996), 246

_____, Will the Judgment-Proof Own Cyberspace?, 32 Int'l Lawyer 1121 (1998), 9

Pielemeier, Constitutional Limits on Choice of Law: The Special Case of Multistate Defamation, 133 U. Pa. L. Rev. 381 (1985), 417

Pinto, The Constitution and the Market for Corporate Control: State Takeover Statutes After *CTS Corp.*, 29 Wm. & Mary L. Rev. 699 (1988), 361

Posnak, Choice of Law: Interest Analysis and Its "New Crits," 36 Am. J. Comp. L. 681 (1988), 201

Post & Johnson, "Chaos Prevailing on Every Continent": Towards a New Theory of Decentralized Decision-Making in Complex System, 73 Chi.-Kent. L. Rev. 1055 (1998), 246

Price, Full Faith and Credit and the Equity Conflict, 84 Va. L. Rev. 747 (1998), 542

Prosser, Law of Torts, 135

Purcell, Geography as a Litigation Weapon: Consumers, Forum-Selection Clauses and the Rehnquist Court, 40 U.C.L.A. L. Rev. 423 (1992), 690

Rakoff, Contracts of Adhesion: An Essay in Reconstruction, 96 Harv. L. Rev. 1173 (1983), 686

Reese, Chief Judge Fuld and Choice of Law, 71 Colum. L. Rev. 548 (1971), 172

_____, Choice of Law: Rules or Approach, 57 Cornell L. Rev. 315 (1972), 229

_____, Full Faith and Credit to Foreign Equity Decrees, 42 Iowa L. Rev. 183 (1957), 536

Reese & Kaufman, The Law Governing Corporate Affairs: Choice of Law and the Impact of Full Faith and Credit, 58 Colum. L. Rev. 1118 (1958), 101

Regan, Siamese Essays: (I) *CTS Corp. v. General Dynamics Corp. of America* and Dormant Commerce Clause Doctrine; (II) Extraterritorial State Legislation, 85 Mich. L. Rev. 1865 (1985), 361

Rensberger, The Metasplit: The Law Applied After Transfer in Federal Question Cases, 2018 Wis. L. Rev. 847, 489

_____, Who Was Dick? Constitutional Limitations on State Choice of Law, 1998 Utah L. Rev. 37 (1998), 287

Reppy, Eclecticism in Choice of Law: Hybrid Method or Mishmash?, 34 Mercer L. Rev. 645 (1983), 172, 210, 226, 229, 241

Rheinstein, The Constitutional Basis of Jurisdiction, 22 U. Chi. L. Rev. 775 (1955), 292

Ribstein & O'Hara, Corporations and the Market for Law, 2008 U. Ill. L. Rev. 661, 107

Richman, Review Essay: Part II—A Sliding Scale to Supplement the Distinction Between General and Specific Jurisdiction, 72 Cal. L. Rev. 1328 (1984), 382–383

Risinger, "Substance" and "Procedure" Revisited, 30 UCLA L. Rev. 189 (1982), 132

Robbins, Interstate Certification of Questions of Law: A Valuable Process in Need of Reform, 76 Judicature 125 (1992), 169

Roosevelt & Jones, The Draft Restatement (Third) of Conflict of Laws: A Response to Brilmayer and Listwa, 128 Yale L.J. Forum 293, 296 (2018), 245–246

_____, What a Third Restatement of Conflict of Laws Can Do, 110 AJIL Unbound 139 (2016), 246

Sachs, The Forum Selection Defense, 10 Duke J. Const. L. & Pub. Pol'y 1 (2014), 491

Schumacher, Rights of Action Under Death and Survival Statutes, 23 Mich. L. Rev. 114 (1924), 133

Scoles & Hay, Conflict of Laws (2d ed. 1992), 536

Scoles et al., Conflict of Laws (3d ed. 2000), 2

_____, Conflict of Laws (4th ed. 2004), 752

Sedler, The *Erie* Outcome Test as a Guide to Substance and Procedure in the Conflicts of Laws, 37 N.Y.U. L. Rev. 813 (1962), 473

_____, The Governmental Interest Approach to Choice of Law: An Analysis and Reformulation, 25 UCLA L. Rev. 181 (1977), 201

_____, Interstate Accidents and the Unprovided for Case: Reflections on *Neumeier v. Kuehner*, 1 Hofstra L. Rev. 125 (1973), 199

_____, Value of Principled Preferences, 49 Texas L. Rev. 224, 207

Sheehan, Predicting the Future: Personal Jurisdiction for the Twenty-First Century, 66 U. Cin. L. Rev. 385 (1998), 424

Shill, Ending Judgment Arbitrage: Jurisdictional Competition and the Enforcement of Foreign Money Judgments in the United States, 54 Harv. Int'l L. Rev. 459 (2013), 546

Shreve, Interest Analysis as Constitutional Law, 48 Ohio St. L.J. 51 (1987), 316

_____, Judgments from a Choice-of-Law Perspective, 40 Am J. Comp. L. 985 (1992), 553

Silberman, The Role of Choice of Law in National Class Actions, 156 U. Pa. L. Rev. 2001 (2007–2008), 756

_____, *Shaffer v. Heitner*: The End of an Era, 53 N.Y.U. L. Rev. 33 (1978), 411

Silberman & Lowenfeld, A Different Challenge for the ALI; Herein of Foreign Country Judgments, an International Treaty, and an American Statute, 75 Ind. L. Rev. 635 (2000), 546

Simson, Leave Bad Enough Alone, 75 Ind. L.J. 649, 651 (2000), 241

Singer, Facing Real Conflicts, 24 Cornell Int'l L.J. 197 (1991), 198

_____, Pay No Attention to That Man Behind the Curtain: The Place of Better Law in a Third Restatement of Conflicts, 75 Ind. L. J. 659 (2000), 227

Slawson, Mass Contracts: Lawful Fraud in California, 48 S. Cal. L. Rev. 1 (1974), 686

Smit, The Enduring Utility of In Rem Rules: A Lasting Legacy of *Pennoyer v. Neff*, 48 Brook. L. Rev. 600 (1977), 448

Solimine, An Economic and Empirical Analysis of Choice of Law, 24 Ga. L. Rev. 49 (1989), 274

_____, Forum-Selection Clauses and the Privatization of Procedure, 25 Cornell Int'l L.J. 51 (1992), 690

Spector, Uniform Child-Custody Jurisdiction and Enforcement Act, 32 Fam. L.Q. 301 (1998), 573

Stein, *Erie* and Court Access, 100 Yale L.J. 1935 (1991), 493

_____, Styles of Argument and Interstate Federalism in the Law of Personal Jurisdiction, 65 Tex. L. Rev. 689 (1987), 413

Steinman, *Atlantic Marine* Through the Lens of *Erie*, 66 Hastings L.J. 795 (2015), 491

Stephan, Private Litigation as a Foreign Relations Problem, 110 AJIL Unbound 40 (2016), 644

Sterk, Asset Protection Trusts: Trust Law's Race to the Bottom?, 85 Cornell L. Rev. 1035 (2000), 97

_____, Full Faith and Credit, More or Less, to Judgments: Doubts about *Thomas v. Washington Gas Light Co.*, 69 Geo. L.J. 1329 (1981), 533

_____, The Marginal Relevance of Choice of Law Theory, 142 U. Pa. L. Rev. 949 (1994), 199

Stevenson, Breaching the Great Firewall: China's Internet Censorship and the Quest for Freedom of Expression in a Connected World, 30 B.C. Int'l & Comp. L. Rev. 531 (2007), 8

_____, Depecage: Embracing Complexity to Solve Choice-of-Law Issues, 37 Ind. L. Rev. 303 (2003), 113

Stewart, A New Litany of Personal Jurisdiction, 60 U. Colo. L. Rev. 5 (1989), 424

Story, Commentaries on the Conflict of Laws, 51, 270, 385, 509, 519, 538, 597

Strikwerda, Interest Analysis: No More than a "Protest Song"?, in Law and Reality: Essays on National and International Procedural Law (1992), 202

Sturges & Murphy, Some Confusing Matters Relating to Arbitration under the United States Arbitration Act, 17 Law & Contemp. Prob. 580 (1952), 708

Sumampouw, Law and Reality: Essays on National and International Procedural Law (1992), 202

Summers, Evaluating and Improving Legal Processes—A Plea for "Process Values," 60 Cornell L. Rev. 1 (1974), 261

Sykes & Prykes, Australian Private International Law (3d ed. 1991), 203

Symeonides, Choice of Law in the American Courts in 1998: Twelfth Annual Survey, 47 Am. J. Comp. L. 327 (1999), 231

_____, Choice of Law in the American Courts in 1999: One More Year, 48 Am. J. Comp. L. 143 (2000), 266

_____, Choice of Law in the American Courts in 2010: Twenty-Fourth Annual Survey, 59 Am. J. Comp. L. 303 (2011), 227

_____, Choice of Law in the American Courts in 2018: Thirty-Second Annual Survey, 67 Am. J. Comp. L. (2019), 31, 242

_____, A Choice-of-Law Rule for Conflicts Involving Stolen Cultural Property, 38 Vand. J. Transnatl. L. 1177 (2005), 14

_____, The Judicial Acceptance of the Second Conflicts Restatement, A Mixed Blessing, 56 Md. L. Rev. 1248 (1997), 242

_____, Louisiana's New Law of Choice of Law for Torts: An Exegesis, 66 Tul. L. Rev. 677 (1992), 278

_____, The Third Conflicts Restatement's First Draft on Tort Conflicts, 92 Tul. L. Rev. 1 (2017), 183, 246

Symposium, *Asahi Metal Indus. Co. v. Superior Court* and the Future of Personal Jurisdiction, 39 S.C. L. Rev. 815 (1988), 424

_____, Comments on *Reich v. Purcell*, 15 U.C.L.A. L. Rev. 551 (1968), 196

_____, Preparing for the Next Century—a New Restatement of Conflicts?, 75 Ind. L.J. 399 (2000), 245

_____, The Silver Anniversary of the Second Conflicts Restatement, 56 Md. L. Rev. 1193 (1997), 245

_____, Symposium Issue Celebrating Twenty Years: The Past and Promise of the 1980 Hague Convention on the Civil Aspects of International Child Abduction, 33 N.Y.U. J. Int'l L. & Pol. 1 (2000), 573

Thiel, Choice of Law and the Home-Court Advantage: Evidence, 2 Am. L. & Econ. Rev. 291 (2000), 274
Trautman, Toward Federalizing Choice of Law, 70 Tex. L. Rev. 1715 (1992), 477–478
Traynor, Is This Conflict Really Necessary?, 37 Tex. L. Rev. 657 (1959), 136
Trimble, The Future of Cybertravel: Legal Implications of the Evasion of Geolocation, 22 Fordham Intell. Prop. Media & Ent. L.J. 567 (2012), 7–8
Turner, The Innocent Buyer of Art Looted During World War II, 32 Vand. J. Transnatl. L. 1511 (1999), 10
Twerski, Book Review, 61 Cornell L. Rev. 1045 (1976), 261
_____, *Neumeier v. Kuehner:* Where Are the Emperor's Clothes?, 1 Hofstra L. Rev. 104 (1973), 187
Twitchell, The Myth of General Jurisdiction, 101 Harv. L. Rev. 610 (1988), 382, 438
_____, A Rejoinder to Professor Brilmayer, 101 Harv. L. Rev. 1465 (1988), 382
_____, Why We Keep Doing Business With Doing-Business Jurisdiction, 2001 U. Chi. Legal Forum 171, 438

Van Alstyne, Closing the Circle of Constitutional Review from *Griswold v. Connecticut* to *Roe v. Wade*: An Outline of a Decision Merely Overruling *Roe*, 1989 Duke L.J. 1677, 326
Vázquez, Choice of Law as Geographic Scope Limitation, in Resolving Conflicts in the Law: Essays in Honour of Lea Brilmayer (2019), 353, 575
_____, Eleventh Amendment Schizophrenia, 75 Notre Dame L. Rev. 859 (2000), 338
_____, Out-Beale-ing Beale, 110 AJIL Unbound 68 (2016), 644
_____, What is Eleventh Amendment Immunity?, 106 Yale L.J. 1683 (1997), 338
_____, W[h]ither Zschernig?, 46 Vill. L. Rev. 1259 (2001), 546
_____, Things We Do with Presumptions: Reflections on *Kiobel v. Royal Dutch Petroleum*, 89 Notre Dame L. Rev. 1719 (2014), 627
Vázquez & Vladeck, The Constitutional Right to Collateral Post-Conviction Review, 103 Va. L. Rev. 905 (2017), 334
Vernon, Statutes of Limitation in the Conflict of Laws: Borrowing Statutes, 32 Rocky Mtn. L. Rev. 287 (1960), 139
Von Mehren, The Renvoi and Its Relation to Various Approaches to the Choice-of-Law Problem, in XXth Century Comparative and Conflicts Law (1961), 256
Von Mehren & Trautman, Jurisdiction to Adjudicate: A Suggested Analysis, 79 Harv. L. Rev. 1121 (1966), 377, 428, 429, 430, 439
_____, Recognition of Foreign Adjudications: A Survey and Suggested Approach, 81 Harv. L. Rev. 1601 (1968), 546

Ware, Default Rules from Mandatory Rules: Privatizing Law Through Arbitration, 83 Minn. L. Rev. 703 (1999), 708
Warren, New Light on the History of the Federal Judiciary Act of 1789, 37 Harv. L. Rev. 49 (1923), 471
Weinberg, Against Comity, 80 Geo. L.J. 53 (1991), 204
_____, The Federal-State Conflict of Laws: "Actual" Conflicts, 70 Tex. L. Rev. 1743 (1992), 474
Weintraub, An Approach to Choice of Law that Focuses on Consequences, 56 Alb. L. Rev. 701 (1993), 202
_____, *Asahi* Sends Personal Jurisdiction Down the Tubes, 23 Texas Int'l L.J. 55 (1988), 424
_____, Commentary on the Conflict of Laws (1980), 21, 57, 225, 599
_____, Courts Flailing in the Waters of the Louisiana Conflicts Code: Not Waving But Drowning, 60 La. L. Rev. 1365 (2000), 279

_____, Due Process and Full Faith and Credit Limitations on a State's Choice of Law, 44 Iowa L. Rev. 449 (1959), 299

_____, The Extraterritorial Application of Antitrust and Securities Laws: An Inquiry Into the Utility of a "Choice-of-Law" Approach, 70 Tex. L. Rev. 1799 (1992), 613

_____, Interest Analysis in the Conflict of Laws as an Application of Sound Legal Reasoning, 35 Mercer L. Rev. 629 (1984), 201

_____, An Objective Basis for Rejecting Transient Jurisdiction, in The Future of Personal Jurisdiction: a Symposium on *Burnham v. Superior Court*, 22 Rutgers L.J. 611 (1991), 391

_____, Obstacles to Sensible Choice of Law for Determining Marital Property Rights on Divorce or in Probate: *Hanau* and the Situs Rule, 25 Hous. L. Rev. 1113 (1988), 86

Whitten, The Constitutional Limitations on State Choice of Law: Full Faith and Credit, 12 Mem. St. U. L. Rev. 1 (1981), 291, 292

Williston on Contracts (3d ed. 1961), 23

Wood, Adjudicatory Jurisdiction and Class Actions, 62 Ind. L. J. 597 (1987), 400

Woodward, Saving the Hague Choice of Court Convention, 29 U. Pa. J. Int'l L. 657 (2008), 547, 687

Wright et al., Federal Practice and Procedure (3d ed. 2005), 743

_____, Federal Practice and Procedure (4th ed. 2013), 492

Table of Restatement Sections

Restatement (First) of Conflicts, on Contracts

§311	33, 751
§312	33
§314	34
§315	34
§323	34
§325	34
§326	34–35, 43
§332	35
§333	35–36, 45, 80, 109, 120
§334	36
§335	36
§336	37
§340	37
§355	37
§358	37–38, 109
§360	38
§361	38

Restatement (First) of Conflicts, on Corporations

§154	97
§155	97
§165	97
§166	98
§182	98
§183	98
§187	98
§188	98
§190	98
§191	98–99
§192	99
§205	99

Restatement (First) of Conflicts, on Domicile

§7	114, 116
§8	114

§9	48
§10	48
§11	49
§12	49
§13	49
§14	49
§15	49
§16	50
§18	50
§19	50
§20	50
§21	50
§23	50
§25	50
§27	50
§41	51

Restatement (First) of Conflicts, on Judicial Jurisdiction

§60	595
§65	580

Restatement (First) of Conflicts, on Marriage and Legitimacy

§121	63, 75
§122	63
§123	63
§128	63–64
§129	64
§130	64
§132	64, 75
§133	64
§134	64
§136	65
§137	65
§138	65
§139	65
§140	65
§141	65

**Restatement (First) of Conflicts,
on Penal Laws and Tax Claims**

§610	156, 162
§611	156

**Restatement (First) of Conflicts,
on Personal Property**

§255	87
§256	87, 94
§257	87, 94
§258	87, 94
§260	87
§261	87–88
§289	88
§290	88
§291	88
§300	88
§301	88
§302	88
§306	89
§307	89

**Restatement (First) of Conflicts,
on Procedure**

§584	122
§585	122
§588	122
§591	123
§594	123
§595	123, 130
§596	123
§597	123
§599	123
§600	123
§601	123–124
§606	124

**Restatement (First) of Conflicts,
on Public Policy**

§612	146, 154, 273

**Restatement (First) of Conflicts,
on Real Property**

§211	79
§214	79
§216	79
§217	79
§218	80

§219	80
§220	80
§221	80
§222	80
§223	80
§225	80
§226	80
§227	81
§237	81
§238	81
§244	81
§245	81
§246	81
§248	81
§249	82
§250	82
§251	82

**Restatement (First) of Conflicts,
on Statutes of Limitations**

§603	136, 330
§604	136
§605	136

**Restatement (First) of Conflicts,
on Trusts of Personal Property**

§294	95
§295	95
§296	95
§297	95
§298	95

**Restatement (First) of Conflicts,
on Wrongs**

§377	25, 32, 132, 133, 139
§378	25, 109
§379	26
§380	147, 148
§382	26–27
§384	27, 105, 109
§385	27
§386	27
§387	27
§390	27, 133
§391	27–28
§398	28
§399	28
§412	28
§413	476
§418	476
§421	28
§451	506

Restatement (Second) of Conflicts

§6	228–229, 230, 232, 233, 238–240, 243, 244, 245, 268, 271, 454, 586, 752, 760, 767
§10	586
§13	58
§15	58
§17	62
§42	586
§50	586
§56	447
§66	449
§82	391
§84	642
§99	535
§102	542
§103	519, 542
§131	319
§133	319
§134	319
§135	319
§137	537
§138	537
§139	319, 537
§142	264, 267, 268, 495
§143	320, 324, 495
§145	227–228, 229, 231, 232, 233, 240, 243, 271
§146	180, 230, 232, 233, 234, 240, 243, 271
§148	761
§154	229
§156	232
§157	232
§159	180
§161	232
§164	232
§171	232
§175	232, 233, 234, 240
§186	648
§187	648–649, 650–651, 652, 656–657, 660–661, 662, 663, 671, 674, 676, 690, 696, 752, 774
§188	228, 229, 243, 543, 661, 752, 760
§214, Introductory Note (Tentative Draft No. 5)	86–87
§304	359
§309	451
§332	188
§332 (Tentative Draft No. 6)	189

Restatement (Second) of Contracts

§356	672

Restatement (Second) of Foreign Relations

§18	584
§30	587
§40	586

Restatement (Third) of Foreign Relations

§401	596
§402	589, 596
§403	589–590, 594, 596, 598, 599, 600, 601, 605
§404	596
§405	596
§406	596
§407	596
§408	596
§409	596
§410	596
§411	596
§412	596
§413	596
§414	596
§415	592, 594, 596, 599
§416	596

Restatement (Fourth) of Foreign Relations

§203	614, 644
§204	605, 626
§211	605

Restatement (First) of Judgments

§10	506
§49	495

Restatement (Second) of Judgments

§19	495
§87	494, 495

Restatement (Second) of Torts

§395	795
§402A	788, 796
§558	421
§577	421

Index

Abortion, constitutional limitations on choice-of-law and, 326
Administrative proceedings, recognition of judgments and, 533
Adoption
  comparative impairment, 215–217
  by same-sex couples, 215–217
After-acquired domicile, 252–253
Alien Tort Statute, 626
American Arbitration Association (AAA), 719–720, 722, 723, 734–735
American Law Institute, Complex Litigation project, 757
Anticybersquatting Consumer Protection Act (ACPA), 462
Anti-Injunction Act of 1793, 556
Antisuit injunctions, 542
Antitrust law
  arbitration, 710–712
  effects test, 579–581
  extraterritoriality of federal statutes, 576–606
  foreign sovereign compulsion doctrine, 600
  insurance law, 590–601
  jurisdictional rule of reason, 581–606
  multilateral approaches, 581–606
  place of conduct, 576–579
  unilateral approaches, 576–581
Apparent conflicts, interest analysis and, 191–195
Arbitration, 707–735
  arbitrability, 710–713
  benefits of, 707–708
  class waivers, 714, 732–734
  Commerce Clause, 709
  contractual choice of, 733
  employment law and, 710
  enforceability of clauses and awards, 707–710
  historical background, 710–712
  international contracts, 711
  judicial scrutiny, 713–735
  preemption, 733
  unconscionability, 713–735

Attachment, jurisdiction over, 461
Australia, reception to interest analysis, 203

"Better Rule," 218–227
  considerations, 218–220
  insurance law, 225
  limitations of, 226–227
  objective vs. subjective nature, 225
  in tort law, 225–226
  true conflicts, 225
Bilateral divorce, recognition of judgments and, 565–567
Borrowing statutes, 139–145, 264–267
"Brandeis fallacy," 154–155
Burden of persuasion in class actions, 747–748, 755–756
Burden of proof
  applicable law, 44
  procedure vs. substance, 124–132
  proof of foreign law, 164

CAFA (Class Action Fairness Act of 2005), 369, 739–740, 798
California
  contractual choice-of-law in, 657–658
  divorce jurisdiction statute, 565
  dramshop laws, 211
Canada, interest analysis in, 202
"Case or controversy" requirement, 515
Characterization, 108–114
  renvoi, and, 114
  Restatement (First) of Conflicts, 108–114
  Restatement (Second) of Conflicts, 243
Chattels, and choice of law, 87–88, 95
Child custody. *See* Custody of children
Child support
  full faith and credit, 567–573
  jurisdiction, 413–417
  recognition of judgments, 567–573
  res judicata, 568

Choice-of-court clauses, 677–706
    appealability, 691
    choice-of-law compared, 687–688, 695, 702,
        705–706
    enforceability of, 677–691
    forum non conveniens, 706
    Internet, 691–696
    jury trials, 704
    negotiation of, 687
    noncompete agreements, 706
    state vs. federal law, 705
Choice-of-law clauses. *See* Contractual
        choice-of-law
Civil rights, recognition of judgments and,
        515, 552
Civil Rights Act of 1991, extraterritorial reach,
        614–615
Clarifying Lawful Overseas Use of Data Act
        (2018, CLOUD Act), 9
Class Action Fairness Act of 2005. *See* CAFA
Class actions, 737–803
    generally, 737–740
    burden of persuasion for certification,
        755–756
    certification, 738–740, 754–759, 763–764,
        767, 772, 797–802
    choice-of-law clauses, 674–675, 764–765
    choice-of-law issues, 699–700, 732–734,
        741–803
    commonality, 738
    consent to jurisdiction, 364–369
    constitutional limitations on choice-of-law,
        310–316
    contracts as basis for single governing
        law, 723
    FRCP, 369, 738–739, 769, 797–802
    general consensus law, 767–772
    individual issues, certification for, 801–802
    injunctive relief, 801
    judicial attitudes toward, 798–800
    mass tort litigation, 769, 792, 799
    merits of case, consideration of, 800
    multiple governing laws, 773–803
    no choice-of-law necessary, 741–757
    nonresident claims, jurisdiction over,
        392–400
    in Oklahoma, 763
    predominance standard, 739, 754–755,
        801–802
    settlement, certification for, 802
    single governing law, 757–772
    state vs. federal courts, 798
    subclasses, 790–792, 794–798
    superiority standard, 800–802
    time of choice-of-law determination, 754
CLOUD Act (Clarifying Lawful Overseas Use
        of Data Act of 2018), 9

Collateral attack on judgments
    generally, 501–503, 506, 515–516
    divorce, 558, 566
    jurisdictional defects, 374
Collateral estoppel, 501–503, 515, 552–553
Comity
    extraterritoriality of federal statutes,
        544, 578
    marriage recognition, 65–79
    penal laws, 157, 161
Commerce Clause
    "dormant" commerce clause, 352–353,
        356–357, 361
    extraterritorial injunctions, 361
    extraterritorial regulations, 352–361
    inconsistent regulations, 352–353, 356, 361
    Internet regulations, 361
    as limitation on choice of law, 352–361
    statutes of limitations, 358
    taxation, 358–359
    text of, 282
Comparative impairment, 203–217
    adoption, 215–217
    dramshop laws, 204–211
    product liability, 210
    state interests, 210, 214–217
    true conflicts, 203–204
    wiretapping, 211–217
Complex litigation. *See* Class actions;
        Multidistrict Litigation (MDL)
Conduct regulation vs. loss allocation, 181–184
Conflict of laws
    arbitration, 707–735. *See also* Arbitration
    choice-of-court clauses, 677–706
    class actions, 737–803. *See also* Class actions
    constitutional limitations on choice-of-
        law, 281–361. *See also* Constitutional
        limitations on choice-of-law
    contractual choice-of-law, 648–677. *See also*
        Contractual choice-of-law
    Erie principles, 465–499. *See also* Erie
        doctrine
    extraterritoriality of federal law, 575–645.
        See also Extraterritoriality of federal
        statutes
    federal common law, 497–498
    jurisdiction, 363–463. *See also* Jurisdiction
    modern approaches, 171–280. *See also*
        Modern approaches
    Multidistrict Litigation (MDL), 737, 740,
        765–766, 802–803
    recognition of judgments, 501–573. *See also*
        Recognition of judgments
    *Restatements. See Restatement (First) of
        Conflicts; Restatement (Second) of
        Conflicts*
    scope, 1–2

traditional approaches, 15–169. *See also*
    Traditional approaches
Consent to jurisdiction, 364–369
    class actions, 364–369
    corporations, 442–445
    implied consent, 369, 451
    registration as, 442–445
Constitution, U.S. *See also* specific Clause or
    Amendment
    extraterritoriality of provisions, 609
    limitations on choice-of-law, 281–361. *See
        also* Constitutional limitations on
        choice-of-law
Constitutional limitations on choice-of-law,
    281–361
    abortion, 326
    characterization, 286
    class actions, 310–316
    Commerce Clause. *See* Commerce Clause
    contract law, 296–297
    discrimination, 339–352
    domicile, 287
    door-closing statutes, 326–334
    "dormant" commerce clause, 352–353,
        356–357, 361
    due process. *See* Due process
    equal protection. *See* Equal protection
    extraterritorial regulations, 352–361. *See
        also* Extraterritorial regulations
    forum non conveniens, 332
    full faith and credit. *See* Full faith and credit
    historical background, 282
    inconsistent regulations, 352–361
    insurance law, 296–297, 309
    interstate discrimination, 339–352. *See also*
        Interstate discrimination
    localizing statutes, 326
    obligation to provide forum, 326–338
    Privileges and Immunities Clause. *See*
        Privileges and Immunities Clause
    procedure vs. substance, 325
    public policy, 286, 333
    quasi in rem jurisdiction, 286
    renvoi, 325
    Restatement (First) of Conflicts, 325
    right to provide forum, 326–338
    state interests, 315–316
    statutes of limitations, 316–326
    taxation, 335–336
    territoriality, 286–287
    tort law, 296
Consumer protection, contractual choice-of-law
    and, 674–675
Contract law, choice of law, 35–48, 227,
    648–649
    acceptance, 33–35
    capacity, 35–36

constitutional limitations on choice-of-law,
    296–297
contractual choice-of-law, 648–677. *See also*
    Contractual choice-of-law
corporations compared, 107
incorporation of substantive law
    through, 23–24
intent of parties as relevant
    consideration, 44–45
negotiable instruments, 37
performance, 37–38
place of contracting, 33–38, 45–47
place of performance, 37–38, 45–47
promissory notes, 45
Restatement (First) of Conflicts, 35–48
rule of validation, or *lex validitatis*, 45
sealed instruments, 36
statutes of frauds, 36, 46–47
UCC. *See* Uniform Commercial Code
Contractual choice-of-law, 648–677
    in California, 657–658
    class actions, 674–675
    constitutional limitations, 676
    consumer protection, 674–675
    in Delaware, 658
    efficient laws, 664
    in employment law, 664–669
    enforceability, 648–677
    in European Union, 674
    extraterritorial intent of legislature, 675
    in Florida, 658
    forum-shopping, 666–668
    franchises, 658–664
    in Illinois, 658
    jury waivers, 657
    mandatory substantive rules, 656, 674
    in New York, 657–658
    noncompete agreements, 664–669
    procedural rules, application of, 657
    Restatement (Second) of Conflicts, 648–649,
        656–657, 663, 669, 676
    scope of clause, 657, 664
    statutes of limitations, 657
    in Texas, 658
    UCC, 674
    validity of contract under law chosen, 663
Convention on Choice of Court Agreements,
    547, 687
Convention on the Recognition and
    Enforcement of Foreign Judgments in
    Civil and Commercial Matters, 547
Corporations, 97–108
    Commerce Clause limitations on regulation,
        352–361
    consent to jurisdiction, 442–445
    contract law compared, 107
    internal affairs doctrine, 99–108

jurisdiction over, 374–383, 424–425, 427–445,
      455–463
   Restatement (First) of Conflicts, 97–99
   tort law compared, 107
Counterclaims, recognition of judgments
      and, 552
Coverture rule, 86
Criticisms
   of interest analysis, 199–202
   of modern approaches generally, 269–274
Custody of children
   domicile, 567–573
   full faith and credit, 567–573
   modification of custody determination,
      567–573
   recognition of judgments, 567–573
Customary international law, 596, 601, 606
Cyberspace. *See* Internet
"Cybersquatting," and jurisdiction, 462

Debts, as basis for jurisdiction, 445–446
Dépeçage, 113
Direct action statutes, 156, 462
Discrimination
   interstate, constitutional limitations on,
      339–352
   public policy and, 151–155
Dispute resolution, role of conflict of laws in, 2
Diversity jurisdiction
   CAFA, 369
   domicile, 53–63
   Erie doctrine, 465–499
   forum state rules, 262
   state vs. federal law, 13, 124–128, 697–699,
      705, 740, 771–772, 802
"Divisible divorce," recognition of judgments
      and, 558–567
Divorce
   bilateral divorce and judgment recognition,
      565–567
   child custody. *See* Custody of children
   child support. *See* Child support
   collateral attack on judgments, 558, 566
   "divisible divorce," 558–567
   domicile, as basis for jurisdiction, 558–561
   full faith and credit, 558–566
   recognition of judgments, 558–567
   state interests, 571–573
   taxation issues, 566
Dodd-Frank Wall Street Reform and Consumer
      Protection Act, 108
Domain names, jurisdiction over, 462–463
Domestic relations law. *See* Child support;
      Custody of children; Divorce; Marriage
Domicile, 48–63
   after-acquired, 252–253

citizenship compared, 62
constitutional limitations on use for
      choice-of-law, 287
custody of children, 567–573
divorce jurisdiction, 558–561
forum-shopping issues, 250–252
insurance law, 252–253
intent element, 50–53, 62
military personnel, 62
in modern approaches, 249–253
new domicile, relevance of, 251–253
presence element, 50, 62–63
Restatement (First) of Conflicts, 48–51, 62
Door-closing statutes, 326–334
"Dormant" commerce clause, 352–353,
      356–357, 361
Dramshop laws, comparative impairment and,
      204–211
Due process
   choice of law constraint, 282–288, 402
   contractual choice-of-law, 676
   extraterritorial regulations, 358, 361
   full faith and credit compared, 291–295,
      297–310, 325, 335–336
   jurisdiction, 363–463
   taxation, 335–336, 359
   text of clause, 281

Employment law
   and arbitration, 710
   constitutional limitations on choice-of-law,
      288–292, 296, 309–310
   contractual choice-of-law in, 664–669
   extraterritoriality of federal statutes, 606–615
   noncompete agreements, 664–669, 706
Enforcement of judgments. *See* Recognition of
      judgments
Equal protection
   interstate discrimination, 339–340, 347–352
   Privileges and Immunities Clause compared,
      351–352
   statutes of limitations, 347–352
   text of clause, 281
   venue provisions, application to, 352
Erie doctrine, 465–499
   choice of law, 475–493
   forum selection clauses, 490–493, 698,
      704–706
   forum shopping, 471, 477–489, 491, 498
   judgments, 493–499
   Rules Enabling Act, 472–474, 495
   Rules of Decision Act, 470–471, 473–474,
      488–489
   substance versus procedure, 471–475
   transfer under 28 U.S.C. §1404 or §1407,
      477–493, 698, 705

European Union
   contractual choice-of-law in, 674
   interest analysis in, 202–203
   internal affairs doctrine in, 108
Ex parte "divisible divorce," recognition of
      judgments and, 558–567
Expert witness, proof of foreign law and, 168
Extraterritoriality of constitutional
      provisions, 609
Extraterritoriality of federal
      statutes, 575–645
   Alien Tort Statute, 626
   antitrust law, 576–606
   comity, 578
   domestic injury, 644
   due process clause limits, 642
   employment law, 606–615
   foreign citizens, 577, 585, 587, 626
   maritime law, 589
   prescriptive jurisdiction, 605. *See also*
      Prescriptive jurisdiction
   presumption against extraterritoriality, 601,
      606–645
   Restatement (Second) of Conflicts, 642
   Restatement (Third) of Foreign Relations
      Law, 589–590, 592–599, 600–601
   RICO, 627–645
   securities law, 615–627
   true conflicts, 593, 599–600, 605
   unilateral methodology, 613
   U.S. citizens, 585, 606–615
Extraterritorial regulations, 352–361
   Commerce Clause, 352–361
   due process, 358

False conflicts, interest analysis and, 187,
      194, 198
Federal Arbitration Act (FAA)
   generally, 708–710
   arbitrability, 710–713
   preemption, 710, 716–718, 725, 733
   replacement of, 710
Federal common law, 497–498
Federal Employers' Liability Act (FELA),
      400–403
Federal question jurisdiction, 13, 470, 489, 493,
      496–497, 768
Federal Rules of Civil Procedure (FRCP)
   class actions, 369, 738–739, 769, 797–802
   direct attack on judgments, 501
   and *Erie*, 474, 493–499
   jurisdiction, 369–374
   long-arm jurisdiction, 441
   proof of foreign law, 165–168
   special appearance, 515–516
Federal Tort Claims Act, 256–259

FELA (Federal Employers' Liability Act),
      400–403
Fellow servant doctrine, 22–23
First Amendment
   on Internet regulation, 8
   jurisdiction, relevance to, 417
Foreign judgments, recognition of, 545–547,
      557, 567, 573
Foreign sovereign compulsion doctrine, 600
Foreign Trade Antitrust Improvements Act of
      1982, extraterritoriality of, 601–606
Foreseeability, jurisdiction and, 403–445
Forum non conveniens
   "Better Rule," 225
   choice-of-court clauses, 696–706
   constitutional limitations of, 332, 345–346
   federal vs. state, 492
   jurisdiction, relation to, 373
   public policy exception, as alternative,
      268–269
   transfer motions, 489, 491–493
Forum-shopping
   contractual choice-of-law, 656, 666–668
   domicile issues, 250–252
   Erie doctrine, 471, 477–489, 491, 498
   governing law, and, 31–32
Fourteenth Amendment. *See* Due process;
      Equal protection
France, interest analysis in, 202
Franchises
   contractual choice-of-law, 658–664
   extraterritoriality of state law, 662
   jurisdiction over, 662–663
Fraud, jurisdiction obtained by, 391–392
FRCP. *See* Federal Rules of Civil Procedure
Full faith and credit
   generally, 4
   bilateral divorce, 565–567
   child support, 567–573
   contractual choice-of-law, 676
   custody of children, 567–573
   divorce, 558–566
   door-closing statutes, 326–334
   due process compared, 291–295, 297–310,
      325, 335–336
   ex parte "divisible divorce," 558–567
   proof of foreign law, and, 168
   recognition of judgments, 501–573
   state interests, 291–292, 296, 315, 325, 333–338
   state laws applicable to, 291–292
   text of clause, 281
   text of statute, 281
   wrongful death actions, 327–334

Garnishment, jurisdiction over, 461
General consensus law, 767–772

General jurisdiction, 374–403, 425, 427–445
Good faith purchasers of stolen property, 9–14
Guest statute cases (New York), 175–180

Hague Conference on Private International
     Law, 546–547
Hague Convention on Choice of Court
     Agreements, 547, 687
Hague Convention on the Civil Aspects of
     International Child Abduction, 573
Holocaust Victims Redress Act, 11–12
Hybrid jurisdiction, 382–383

Incestuous marriage, recognition of, 73
Inconsistent regulations, constitutionality of,
     352–361
Inconvenient forum. *See* Forum non conveniens
Injunctive relief
     Anti-Injunction Act of 1793, 556
     antisuit injunctions, 542
     class actions, 801
In personam jurisdiction, 363–373
Insurance law
     "Better Rule," 225
     class actions, 741–753
     constitutional limitations on choice-of-law,
          282–287, 292–310
     domicile, 252–253
     jurisdiction, 416, 461–462
     recognition of judgments, 543–544
Intentional torts, choice of law, 28–32
Interactive web sites, personal jurisdiction over,
     425–427
Interest analysis, 184–203
     apparent conflicts, 191–195
     criticisms of, 199–202
     "disinterested forum," 186–187
     in European Union, 202–203
     false conflicts, 187, 194, 198
     in foreign countries, 202–203
     judicial application of, 187–199
     problems defining interests, 199–202
     public policy, 268–269
     renvoi, 255–256, 258–259
     in *Restatement (Second) of
          Conflicts*, 242
     state interests. *See* State interests
     statutes of limitations, choice of
          law, 266
     theoretical foundations, 184–187
     true conflicts, 187–195, 198–201
     unprovided-for cases, 195–199
Internal affairs doctrine, 99–108
International Center for Dispute Resolution,
     choice-of-law rule, 707

Internet
     choice-of-court clauses, 691–696
     choice-of-law method suitability, 246–248
     Commerce Clause limitations on state
          regulation, 361
     comparative impairment, 215–217
     First Amendment rights, 8
     interactive versus passive web sites, 426
     jurisdiction over, 4–9, 425–427, 462–463
     most significant relationship test, 243–248
     private law, 248
     recognition of judgments, 4–9
Interspousal immunity, choice-of-law treatment,
     109–113, 154
Interstate commerce. *See* Commerce Clause
Interstate discrimination
     constitutional limitations on choice-of-law,
          339–352
     domicile as connecting factor, 340
     equal protection, 339–340, 347–352
     licenses and permits, 347
     Privileges and Immunities Clause, 339–347,
          351–352
     residence requirements, 346
     Restatement (First) of Conflicts, 339
     state interests, 345–346
     taxation, 346–347
     venue provisions, 352

JAMS, arbitration services and rules, 707, 735
Jones Act, 588, 595–596
Judicial notice, content of foreign law and, 129,
     141, 164, 167
Judicial Panel on Multidistrict Litigation, 740, 790
Jurisdiction, 363–463
     generally, 363–364
     activities in forum as basis for, 374–445
     agency relationships, 420, 436
     antitrust law and jurisdictional rule of
          reason, 581–606
     attachment, 445–446, 461
     business/corporate structure, 424–425,
          427–445
     chain of distribution, 412
     child support, 413–417
     commercial transactions vs. personal
          relations, 417
     consent to, 364–369. *See also* Consent to
          jurisdiction
     corporations, 374–383, 424–425, 427–445,
          455–463
     debts, 445–446
     direct action statutes, 462
     diversity jurisdiction, 13, 53–63, 124–128,
          369, 465–499, 697–699, 705, 740,
          771–772, 802

domain names, 462–463
due process, 363–463
federal question jurisdiction, 13, 470, 489,
        493, 496–497, 768
FELA, 400–403
First Amendment rights, 417
foreign citizens, 432
foreign parties and events, 432–442
foreseeability, 403–445
franchises, 662–663
fraud, obtained by, 391–392
FRCP, 369–374
garnishment, 461
general jurisdiction, 374–403, 425, 427–445
hybrid jurisdiction, 382–383
in insurance law, 416, 461–462
interactive vs. passive web sites, 426
Internet, 4–9, 425–427, 462–463
long-arm jurisdiction, 4–9, 363–364, 391,
        417, 441, 459, 461
minimum contacts test, 364–365, 367, 369,
        373, 387, 416, 420, 423, 446–454
by necessity, 383, 461
nonresident claims in class actions, 392–400
in personam jurisdiction, 363–373
prescriptive jurisdiction, 605. *See also*
        Prescriptive jurisdiction
property, as basis for, 445–463
purchases as basis for, 382, 407
purposeful availment, 403–445
quasi in rem jurisdiction, 286, 447–448,
        459–461
recognition of judgments, jurisdictional
        requirements, 504–516
registration as basis for, 442–445
res judicata, 461
Restatement (Second) of Conflicts, 391
sovereignty, relationship to, 413
specific jurisdiction, 374–403, 428–429,
        455–456, 460
state interests, 427–432
stream of commerce cases, 407, 423–425,
        428–429
"tag" jurisdiction, 383–391
time of measuring contacts, 383
transient jurisdiction, 383–391
waiver of, 369–374. *See also* Waiver of
        jurisdiction
Jury trials
    choice-of-court clauses, 699–700, 704
    public policy, 156
    waivers, 657

Laches and statutes of limitations
        compared, 352
"Land taboo," 511

"Last act" doctrine, 23, 47
Last-in-time rule, 556–557
Legislative resolution of choice-of-law
        problems. *See* Statutory resolution of
        choice-of-law problems
Lex loci delicti, 30–32, 148–150, 153, 155
Licenses and permits, interstate discrimination
        in, 347
Limitations of actions. *See* Statutes of
        limitations
Long-arm jurisdiction
    generally, 4–9
    constitutional limitations, 363–364
    FRCP, 441
    immunity from service, 391
    minimum contacts vs., 461
    quasi in rem vs., 459
    type of action, 417
Louisiana
    acquisitive prescription, 1
    statutory resolution of choice-of-law
        problems in, 274–279

Maritime law, extraterritorial reach, 589
Marriage, 63–79
    bigamy and polygamy, 76–78, 559–560, 566
    characterization of interspousal immunity,
        109–113
    divorce. *See* Divorce
    first cousins, 72–74
    foreign, recognition of, 65–79
    incestuous, 73
    place of celebration, 63–64, 67–69
    renvoi, 121
    Restatement (First) of Conflicts, 63–65, 74
    uniformity principle, 74–75
    validity of, 63–64, 65–79, 565
Mass tort litigation, 769, 792, 799
MDL. *See* Multidistrict Litigation
Military personnel, domicile of, 62
Modern approaches
    "Better Rule," 218–227. *See also* "Better Rule"
    comparative impairment, 203–217. *See also*
        Comparative impairment
    domicile, 249–253
    interest analysis, 184–203. *See also* Interest
        analysis
    most significant relationship test,
        227–248. *See also* Most significant
        relationship test
    in New York, 172–184
    procedure vs. substance, 260–261
    public policy, 268–269
    renvoi, 254–259
    Restatement Second, 227–248
    statutes of limitations, 261–268

Most significant relationship test, 227–248
  certainty and predictability, 228, 239
  Internet transactions and, 243–248
  justified expectations, 228, 238–239
  in New York, 172–175
  policies of interested states, 228,
      233–238, 240
  popularity of, 242
  Restatement (Second) of Conflicts, 227–
      229, 240–241, 245
Multidistrict Litigation (MDL)
  generally, 737, 740
  choice-of-law issues, 740, 765–766, 802–803

Nationality, prescriptive jurisdiction and, 598
Nazi-confiscated art, 9–14
Necessity, jurisdiction by, 383, 461
Negligence, choice of law, 15–28
Negotiable instruments, 37
Netherlands, reception of interest analysis
    in, 202
New York
  conduct regulation vs. loss allocation,
      181–184
  contractual choice-of-law in, 657–658
  evolution of choice-of-law, 172–184
  good faith purchasers of stolen property in,
      10–11, 13
  guest statute cases, 175–180
  most significant relationship test in, 172–175
  Restatement (First) of Conflicts, moving
      away from, 172–175
New York Convention, 711
Noncompete agreements, 664–669, 706
Nonintentional torts, choice of law, 15–28

Obligation to provide forum, 326–338
Oklahoma, class actions in, 763
Oregon, statutory resolution of choice-of-law
    problems in, 279–280

Parental kidnapping, 571–573
Parental Kidnapping Prevention Act of 1980
    (PKPA), 571–573
Passive personality, prescriptive jurisdiction
    and, 605
Passive web sites, personal jurisdiction over,
    425–427
Penal laws, 156–163
  comity, 157, 161
  defined, 161
  public policy, relationship to, 162
  recognition of judgments, 162, 520
  Restatement (First) of Conflicts, 156, 162

revenue laws compared, 162–163
  usury, 162
Personal property, choice of law, 87–97
Preemption
  arbitration, 733
  FAA, 710, 716–718, 725, 733
Prenuptial agreements, 2–4
Prescriptive jurisdiction, 605
  nationality, 598
  passive personality, 605
Presumptions
  extraterritoriality, against, 601, 606–645
  forum law, in favor of, 166
Privileges and Immunities Clause
  equal protection compared, 351–352
  interstate discrimination, 339–347, 351–352
  sovereign immunity, 334–338
  text of, 281
Procedure vs. substance
  burden of proof, 124–132
  constitutional limitations on
      choice-of-law, 325
  ease of application, 131
  modern approach, 260–261
  outcome determination, 131
  "process values," 261
  Restatement (First) of Conflicts, 122–124
  state interests, relevance, 260–261
  statutes of frauds, 132
  statutes of limitations, 132, 136–146,
      261–268
  survival of actions, 132–136
  traditional approach, 122–136
Product liability, comparative impairment, 217
Promissory notes, choice of law, 38–42, 44–45
Proof of foreign law, 163–169
  burden of proof, 164
  expert witness, 168
  FRCP, 165–168
  judicial notice, 129, 141, 164, 167
Property law, choice of law, 79–97
  chattels, 87–88, 95
  coverture, 86
  personal property, 87–97
  real property, 79–87
  renvoi, 114, 121–122
  Restatement (First) of Conflicts, 79–82, 87–
      89, 94–95, 114, 121–122
  Rule Against Perpetuities, 96–97
  situs rule, 79–82, 86, 94
  stock, 93–95
  trusts, 96–97
  UCC, 95
Public Company Accounting Reform and
    Investor Protection Act, 108
Public policy
  "Brandeis fallacy," 154–155

connection with state, 154–155
constitutional limitations on choice-of-law, 286, 333
defined, 153
discrimination, 151–155
insurance exclusions, 153–154
interest analysis, 268–269
interspousal immunity, 154
judgments, 156, 518–519
jury trials, 156
modern approach, 268–269
penal laws, relationship, 162
Restatement (First) of Conflicts, 146
Restatement (Second) of Conflicts, 268–269
traditional approach, 146–156
wrongful birth, 146–151
Purchases as basis for jurisdiction, 382, 407
Purposeful availment as basis for jurisdiction, 403–445

Quasi in rem jurisdiction, 286, 447–448, 459–461

Racketeer Influenced and Corrupt Organizations Act of 1970 (RICO), 627–645, 710
Real property, choice of law, 79–87
Recognition of judgments, 501–573
    administrative proceedings, 533
    antisuit injunctions, 542
    bilateral divorce, 565–567
    "case or controversy," jurisdictional defect, 515
    child support, 567–573
    civil rights actions, 515, 552
    counterclaims, 552
    custody of children, 567–573
    damages, 532
    disability benefits awards, 520–533
    divorce, 558–567
    ex parte "divisible divorce," 558–567
    foreign judgments, 545–547, 557, 567, 573
    full faith and credit, 501–573
    greater effect of judgment, 553
    insurance law, 543–544
    interests of enforcing state, 516–547
    Internet, 4–9
    jurisdictional requirements, 504–516
    "land taboo," 511
    last-in-time rule, 556–557
    law of judgments of enforcing state, 547–557
    official act required by judgment, 533–541
    penal laws, 162, 520
    procedural rules, application of, 550

Restatement (Second) of Conflicts, 519, 535, 541–542
    simultaneous litigation, 542–544
    special appearance, and jurisdictional defect, 515–516
    statutes of limitations, 547–551
    tax judgments, 520
    validity of previous judgment, effect of determination, 555–556
Renvoi
    constitutional limitations on choice-of-law, 325
    Federal Tort Claims Act, 256–259
    intent of parties, as resolution, 121
    interest analysis, 255–256, 258–259
    marriage, 121
    modern approach, 254–259
    property law, 114, 121–122
    Restatement (First) of Conflicts, 114
    state interests, 258–259
    traditional approach, 114–122
Res judicata
    generally, 501–505, 511, 515–516, 556–557
    child support, 568
    Erie implications, 493–495
    jurisdiction, when lacking, 461, 515
Residence requirements, interstate discrimination, 346
Restatement (First) of Conflicts
    characterization, 108–114
    in class actions, 756, 764
    constitutional limitations on choice-of-law, 325
    contract law, 35–48
    corporations, 97–99
    criticism of, historical background, 171–172
    dépeçage, 113
    domicile, 48–51, 62
    interstate discrimination, 339
    marriage, 63–65, 74
    New York moving away from, 172–175
    penal laws, 156, 162
    procedure vs. substance, 122–124
    property law, 79–82, 87–89, 94–95, 114, 121–122
    public policy, 146
    renvoi, 114
    revenue laws, 162–163
    statutes of limitations, 136, 266
    tort law, 25–28, 31–32
Restatement (Second) of Conflicts
    characterization, 243
    in class actions, 756, 760–761, 763, 765–767, 769, 774
    contractual choice-of-law, 648–649, 656–657, 663, 669, 676
    extraterritoriality of federal statutes, 642

historical background, 241
interest analysis, use in, 242
jurisdiction, 391
in MDL, 765–766
most significant relationship test, 227–229, 240–241, 245
popularity of, 242
presumptive rules, 229, 242–243
public policy, 268–269
recognition of judgments, 519, 535, 541–542
statutes of limitations, 267–268
Restatement (Third) of Conflicts, 245–246
Restatement (Third) of the Foreign Relations Law of the United States, 589–590, 592–599, 600–601
Restatement (Fourth) of the Foreign Relations Law of the United States, 605
Revenue laws, compared to penal laws, 162–163
RICO (Racketeer Influenced and Corrupt Organizations Act of 1970), 627–645, 710
Right to provide forum, 326–338
Rule Against Perpetuities, choice of law, 96–97

Same-sex couples, adoption by, 215–217
Sarbanes-Oxley Act, 108
Securities law
    arbitrability, 710–712
    choice-of-court clause enforcement, 687, 693
    extraterritoriality of federal statutes, 615–627
Settlement, class action certification for, 802
Sherman Act of 1890, extraterritorial reach, 576, 578–579, 581–583, 590–604
Situs rule, for property, 79–82, 86, 94
South Africa, reception to interest analysis, 202–203
Sovereign immunity
    Privileges and Immunities Clause, 334–338
    waiver of, 335
Sovereignty, jurisdiction and, 413
Special appearance
    recognition of judgments, 515–516
    waiver of jurisdiction, 374
Specific jurisdiction, 374–403, 428–429, 455–456, 460
Spousal support, 2–4
Stare decisis, relation to res judicata, 511
State interests
    as choice-of-law goal, 200–201
    comparative impairment, 210, 214–217
    constitutional limitations on choice-of-law, 315–316
    defining interests, 199–200
    divorce, 571–573

full faith and credit, 291–292, 296, 315, 325, 333–338
interstate discrimination, 345–346
jurisdiction, 427–432
procedure vs. substance, 260–261
renvoi, 258–259
theoretical foundation of interest analysis, 184–187
Statutes of frauds
    in contract law, 36, 46–47
    procedure vs. substance, 132
Statutes of limitations
    accrual of cause, 145–146
    borrowing statutes, 139–145, 264–267
    Commerce Clause, 358
    constitutional limitations on choice-of-law, 316–326
    contractual choice-of-law, 657
    equal protection, 347–352
    interest analysis, 266
    laches compared, 352
    modern approach, 261–268
    procedure vs. substance, 132, 136–146, 261–268
    recognition of judgments, 547–551
    Restatement (First) of Conflicts, 136, 266
    Restatement (Second) of Conflicts, 267–268
    Schmidt doctrine, 145
    statutes of repose compared, 145
    traditional approach, 136–146
Statutes of repose, 145
Statutory resolution of choice-of-law problems, 274–280
    federal, 279
    in Louisiana, 274–279
    in Oregon, 279–280
    predictability, 279
    UCC, 280
Stock, choice of law, 93–95
Stolen property, good faith purchasers of, 9–14
Stream of commerce cases, jurisdiction in, 407, 423–425, 428–429
Substance vs. procedure. *See* Procedure vs. substance
Survival of actions, 132–136

"Tag" jurisdiction, 383–391
Taxation
    Commerce Clause, 358–359
    constitutional limitations on choice-of-law, 335–336
    divorce issues, 566
    due process, 335–336, 359
    interstate discrimination, 346–347
    recognition of judgments, 520
Terezin Declaration, 12–13

Territoriality
    as choice-of-law principle, 22
    constitutional limitations on choice-of-law,
        286–287
Tort law, choice of law, 15–32
    "Better Rule," 225–226
    characterization, 112–113
    constitutional limitations on
        choice-of-law, 296
    corporations compared, 107
    duty or privilege to act, 26
    Federal Tort Claims Act, and renvoi,
        256–259
    fellow servant doctrine, 22–23
    intentional torts, 28–32
    jurisdiction in, 417–425
    "last act" doctrine, 23, 47
    lex loci delicti, 30–32, 148–150, 153, 155
    mass tort litigation, 769, 792, 799
    nonintentional torts, 15–28
    privilege, 26–27
    Restatement (First) of Conflicts,
        25–28, 31–32
Traditional approaches to choice of
    law, 15–169
    characterization, 108–114
    contract law, 33–48
    corporations, 97–108
    domicile, 48–63
    marriage, 63–79
    penal laws, 156–163
    procedure vs. substance, 122–136
    property law, 79–97
    public policy, 146–156
    renvoi, 114–122
    statutes of limitations, 136–146
    tort law, 15–32
Transient jurisdiction, 383–391
True conflicts
    "Better Rule," 225
    comparative impairment, 203–204
    extraterritoriality of federal statutes, 593,
        599–600, 605
    interest analysis, 187–195, 198–201,
        202–203
Trusts, choice of law, 96–97, 651

Unconscionability of arbitration clauses,
    713–735
Uniform Child Custody Jurisdiction Act (1997,
    UCCJA), 573
Uniform Child Custody Jurisdiction and
    Enforcement Act (2002, UCCJEA), 573
Uniform Commercial Code (UCC)
    contractual choice-of-law, 674
    property law, 95
    statutory resolution of choice-of-law
        problems, 280
Uniform Foreign-Country Money Judgments
    Recognition Act (1986, UFCMJRA), 545
Uniform Foreign Money Judgments
    Recognition Act (2005, UFMJRA),
    545, 557
Uniformity principle
    in choice of law, 21–22
    in marriage, 74–75
United Nations Convention on the Recognition
    and Enforcement of Foreign Arbitral
    Awards, 711
Unlawful Internet Gambling Enforcement Act
    of 2006, 9
Unprovided-for cases, interest analysis and,
    195–199
Usury, as penal law, 162

Venue, equal protection and, 352
Vested rights theory, 20–21
Vicarious liability, full faith and credit and,
    333–334

Waiver of jurisdiction, 369–374
    collateral attack on judgments, 374
    sanction rationale, 373
    special appearance, 374
Waiver of sovereign immunity, 335
Web sites. *See* Internet
Wiretapping, comparative impairment and,
    211–217
Wrongful birth, and public policy, 146–151
Wrongful death actions, full faith and credit
    and, 327–334